WOOLLCOTT'S
SECOND READER

WOOLLCOTT'S SECOND READER

NEW YORK

THE VIKING PRESS

MCMXXXVII

PUBLISHED IN NOVEMBER 1937
SECOND PRINTING DECEMBER 1937

CONTENTS

v

CONTENTS

FOREWORD

At a time when Helen Hayes was a new-risen star, she was escorted through Italy by a paternalistic cicerone who tacitly, at every point from the baptistry-doors in Florence to the gaudy façade of the cathedral at Orvieto, exacted, as his fee, an expression of rapture. Finally he promised to show her, from an exceeding high mountain, the most beautiful view in all that storied countryside. Wherefore, when her already sated eyes had drunk their fill, she knew what was expected of her. Being an obliging creature and even then unique in her talent for expressing any emotion an occasion might call for, she gave a really superb performance of a woman entranced. But he turned away dissatisfied. "When I showed that to Eleanor Robson," he said, "she burst into tears."

Now while this *Reader* is another tour of certain bypaths in the realms of gold—for some it will often be a return visit—at least it is conducted by a guide less exigent. Indeed, the editor of any such anthology would do well to avoid an injudicious mannerism which in our time is threatening to become a national habit. With increasing frequency, the editor of this one is approached by some neighbor whose conversation has this alienating gambit. "Well, Mr. W," he will say, "I heard a story yesterday which you're sure to like." Or: "Here's something that'll make you laugh your head off." Every now and again I am agile enough to cut in with some such comment as: "Perhaps you'd better let me be the judge of that." But when I do, the insensate raconteur only stares at me uncomprehendingly or gives a nervous laugh, and in either event then goes on with his story, which as often as not proves to be one I can hear all the way through without once rolling on the floor in uncontrollable merriment. Wherefore, in the matter of liking the works in this anthology, let me begin by saying merely that I do and you may.

The editor's task would be simplified if, in his relation to the potential reader, it could be thought of in terms of a colloquy familiar enough to us all—certainly a commonplace in any home I have ever known. For some years my only base was a small riverside flat in which there was not room to hang so much as a miniature, what with all the wall-space squandered either on windows or shelves. Even so, there seemed never to be any place to put the spate of new books as they came along, so that these would accumulate in leaning towers on every table and chair-arm and I could see visitors only by peering at them over ramparts of beautiful letters. Wherefore, to the literal, there might have seemed something more than a little idiotic in a question so often put to me on his way to bed by anyone whom I happened to be sheltering for the night. "Old man," he would say, "have you anything to read?"

Yet the meaning was always clear enough. What such a one sought from me at the moment was certainly no list of the fifty best books wherewith to be wrecked on that desert island. After all, he was only going to bed. Then he would already have encountered (or, if that was his temperament, successfully avoided) the current best-seller and he would not need to be told by the likes of me or anyone else that *Moby Dick* and *Urn Burial* were pretty good, too. No, he would want me to point him off the beaten track to something he might more readily have missed or —the world is so full of a number of things—had once enjoyed and then basely forgotten.

In this spirit and "after much debate internal" (to say nothing of search parties in the second-hand bookstores) the foregoing table of contents was finally arrived at. Even in the midst of some suitable misgivings about it, I am consoled by the memory of my experiences with its predecessor. Quite typical were two letters which, some months after its publication, actually arrived in one morning's mail. A professor at Chicago University wrote to thank me for reviving that incomparable period piece of the early nineties, *The Dolly Dialogues*. My, my, how it took him back to a time when all the world was young. "But, my dear man," he added, "whatever possessed you to include such weak and ugly violence as *A Handful of Dust?*" The other letter was from an artist living angrily on a Connecticut farm, who wrote to tell me that she hoped I'd ladle out no more such insipid stuff as *The Dolly Dialogues*. "But," she said, "I shall always be grateful to you as the man who put me in the way of reading *A Handful of Dust.*" To a hasty scorekeeper, it might seem that the returns from these two counties rather tended to cancel each other. Nonsense. To my own way of figuring, they left me two up.

Now let us turn to an old Chinese novel called *Shui Hu Chuan,* a title so defiant of any translator that, when Pearl Buck made a version for English readers a few years ago, she arbitrarily called it *All Men Are Brothers*. That dictum, besides having been a saying of Confucius, has all the advantage of being God's own truth —especially indisputable, one would think, by those who note how, more and more as the years go by, men are taking as their model, in the matter of fraternity, the relation between Cain and Abel. In the landscape of Chinese literature, this adventure story of the Sung dynasty looms as large as does *Don Quixote* in the literature of the Western world. Like the *Iliad* or the legends of Robin Hood, it is assumed to have been a slow growth of multiple and unidentified authorship. The form now available in China is a version which must have been written in the fourteenth or fifteenth century. At that time it acquired a plaintive and propitiatory foreword, usually attributed to Shih Nai-an of

Tung-tu. That foreword, set down on rice paper long ago on the other side of the world, might serve as a preamble to any book in any land at any time and shall so serve, without more ado, for this one.

ALEXANDER WOOLLCOTT

Bomoseen, Vermont
September 1937.

PREFACE TO

ALL MEN ARE BROTHERS

by

SHIH NAI-AN

PREFACE TO
"All Men Are Brothers"

A MAN who lives until he is thirty years of age without marrying should not then marry. A man who has not been governor before the age of forty should not then seek for a governorship. At fifty years he should not found a home, nor at sixty set out upon travels. Why is this said? Because the time for such things is passed and he will, if he undertake them, have little space left to him in which to enjoy them.

When the morning sun has just risen, palely bright, we wash head and face, wrap the kerchief about our heads, take food, chew a bit of this or that, and when the work of this is done we stand and ask: "Is it yet noon?" Noon has already long come. This is as it is in the hours before noon. From it may be known how pass the hours after noon. So one day is over. How do a hundred years differ from it? There is only sadness when we think of it. Where can joy be found? I ever marvel that people say: "How old is that one this year? How many are his heaped years?" What is this "How many?"? They are the heaped years. Can anyone bring them back and count them? Can anyone see that which is passed and gone? It is gone. Even as I finish this very sentence the time which has passed before it is gone. Sorrow is this to the heart!

Of all joys nothing brings more joy than friendship, and the most joyful part of friendship is quiet talk together among friends. Who can deny this? Yet it has not always been easy for me to gain this companionship. Sometimes the wind blows and it is cold; sometimes rain falls and the road is muddy; sometimes I am ill; sometimes when I go to seek my friends they are away and I miss them. At such times I feel I am in prison.

3

I have only a little poor land. I plant for the most part grain for wine. I cannot drink much wine myself, but when my friends come they like to drink it. My door is near a river and on its banks lie the deep shadows of beautiful trees. There my friends gather and stand about and sit down and walk as they please. I have only four old women servants to cook rice and vegetables and such dishes. The others are but children; large and small, there are ten odd of us, although the young ones can at their best but run about for us and greet guests and escort them when they go or bring in the cards of those who come. When they are idle, men- and maid-servants, I teach them to make brooms and to weave mats—brooms to sweep the floors and mats for my friends to sit upon.

When my friends are all come there should be sixteen of us, but there are not many days when all can come. Yet except on days of great winds or of mighty rains, there are few days when none come. Usually six or seven gather together each day. When my friends are come they do not necessarily drink wine; if they like to do so, they may, but they need not if it is not their wish—each man to his own heart. We do not depend on wine for our happiness. Conversation is our delight. What we talk of is not the affairs of the nation. This is because not only do I feel it right to keep my humble position, but also because our place is far distant from affairs of state, and political news is only hearsay, and hearsay is never true and it is a waste of saliva to talk of it. Neither do we talk of people's sins. Men under Heaven have no sins originally and we ought not to malign them. What we speak of ought not to be such as to frighten persons. What I speak of I want people to understand easily; although after all they cannot understand, because I speak of that of which they had never heard and moreover every man is intent on his own affairs.

My friends are all contemptuous of high places. They are wide of heart and they understand everything, and so what they discourse upon has its influence on all, and therefore when our day's talk is over, a matter is ended. Yet there is no one to write out our words, although sometimes I think I will put down what we have said in a book to leave to those who come after us. But until now I have not put it down thus. Why? When the desire for fame is over, the heart grows languid. We discourse for pleasure and the making of books is tiresome. Moreover, when we are gone no one will read what we have said. Or if perhaps this year we make the book, the next year we will surely regret it.

In this book there are seventy chapters. When my friends were gone and I sat alone under the lamp, I wrote in idleness. At times when the wind blew and the rains fell and no one came, then also did I write. Turning the book over and over in my mind it became at last such a habit to me that it was not necessary even to open my book and take up my brush and prepare something to write and read for my own diversion. For when at times I walked along my garden wall, or at night covered by my quilt I lay awake, or when I picked up the end of my girdle and twisted it in my fingers, or when I stared unseeing at some object, at such times the stuff of which my book is made came crowding into my mind.

Some may ask thus: "You have said already that you did not make a book from your discourse with friends; why then have you now made this book alone?" But if this book is made it is without fame, and if it be not made no harm is done. When the heart is idle and there is nothing to force its will, whether the reader is good and learned or evil and unlearned, anyone can read this book. Whether the book is well done or not, it is not important enough to worry over.

Alas, I was born to die! How can I know what those who come after me and read my book will think of it? I cannot even know what I myself, born into another incarnation, will think of it. I do not even know if I myself afterwards can even read this book. Why therefore should I care?

THE
LADY'S MAID'S
BELL

by

EDITH WHARTON

THE LADY'S MAID'S BELL

I⊤ was the autumn after I had the typhoid. I'd been three months in hospital, and when I came out I looked so weak and tottery that the two or three ladies I applied to were afraid to engage me. Most of my money was gone, and after I'd boarded for two months, hanging about the employment-agencies, and answering any advertisement that looked any way respectable, I pretty nearly lost heart, for fretting hadn't made me fatter, and I didn't see why my luck should ever turn. It did though—or I thought so at the time. A Mrs. Railton, a friend of the lady that first brought me out to the States, met me one day and stopped to speak to me: she was one that had always a friendly way with her. She asked me what ailed me to look so white, and when I told her, "Why, Hartley," says she, "I believe I've got the very place for you. Come in tomorrow and we'll talk about it."

The next day, when I called, she told me the lady she'd in mind was a niece of hers, a Mrs. Brympton, a youngish lady, but something of an invalid, who lived all the year round at her country-place on the Hudson, owing to not being able to stand the fatigue of town life.

"Now, Hartley," Mrs. Railton said, in that cheery way that always made me feel things must be going to take a turn for the better, "now understand me; it's not a cheerful place I'm sending you to. The house is big and gloomy; my niece is nervous, vapourish; her husband—well, he's generally away; and the two children are dead. A year ago I would as soon have thought of shutting a rosy active girl like you into a vault; but you're not particularly brisk yourself just now, are you? and a quiet place, with country air and wholesome food and early hours, ought to be the very thing for you. Don't mistake me," she added, for I suppose I looked a trifle downcast; "you may find it dull but you won't be unhappy. My niece is an angel. Her former maid, who died last spring, had been with her twenty years and worshipped the ground she walked on. She's a kind mistress to all, and where the mistress is kind, as you know, the servants are generally good-humoured, so you'll probably get on well enough with the rest of the household. And you're the very woman I want for my niece; quiet, well mannered, and educated above your station. You read aloud well, I think? That's a good thing; my niece likes to be read to. She wants a maid that can be something of a companion: her last was, and I can't say how she misses her. It's a lonely life . . . Well, have you decided?"

"Why, ma'am," I said, "I'm not afraid of solitude."

"Well, then, go; my niece will take you on my recommendation. I'll telegraph her at once and you can take the afternoon train. She has no one to wait on her at present, and I don't want you to lose any time."

I was ready enough to start, yet something in me hung back; and to gain time I asked, "And the gentleman, ma'am?"

"The gentleman's almost always away, I tell you," said Mrs. Railton, quick-like, "and when he's there," says she suddenly, "you've only to keep out of his way."

I took the afternoon train and got out at D—— station at about four o'clock. A groom in a dog-cart was waiting, and we drove off at a smart pace. It was a dull October day, with rain hanging close overhead, and by the time we turned into Brympton Place woods the daylight was almost gone. The drive wound through the woods for a mile or two, and came out on a gravel court shut in with thickets of tall black-looking shrubs. There were no lights in the windows, and the house *did* look a bit gloomy.

I had asked no questions of the groom, for I never was one to get my notion of new masters from their other servants: I prefer to wait and see for myself. But I could tell by the look of everything that I had got into the right kind of house, and that things were done handsomely. A pleasant-faced cook met me at the back door and called the house-maid to show me up to my room. "You'll see madam later," she said. "Mrs. Brympton has a visitor."

I hadn't fancied Mrs. Brympton was a lady to have many visitors, and somehow the words cheered me. I followed the house-maid upstairs, and saw, through a door on the upper landing, that the main part of the house seemed well furnished, with dark panelling and a number of old portraits. Another flight of stairs led us up to the servants' wing. It was almost dark now, and the house-maid excused herself for not having brought a light. "But there's matches in your room," she said, "and if you go careful you'll be all right. Mind the step at the end of the passage. Your room is just beyond."

I looked ahead as she spoke, and half-way down the passage I saw a woman standing. She drew back into a doorway as we passed and the house-maid didn't appear to notice her. She was a thin woman with a white face, and a darkish stuff gown and apron. I took her for the housekeeper and thought it odd that she didn't speak, but just gave me a long look as she went by. My room opened into a square hall at the end of the passage. Facing my door was another which stood open; the house-maid exclaimed when she saw it:

"There—Mrs. Blinder's left that door open again!" said she, closing it.

"Is Mrs. Blinder the housekeeper?"

"There's no housekeeper: Mrs. Blinder's the cook."

"And is that her room?"

"Laws, no," said the house-maid, cross-like. "That's nobody's room. It's empty, I mean, and the door hadn't ought to be open. Mrs. Brympton wants it kept locked."

She opened my door and led me into a neat room, nicely furnished, with a picture or two on the walls; and having lit a candle she took leave, telling me that the servants'-hall tea was at six, and that Mrs. Brympton would see me afterward.

I found them a pleasant-spoken set in the servants' hall, and by what they let fall I gathered that, as Mrs. Railton had said, Mrs. Brympton was the kindest of ladies; but I didn't take much notice of their talk, for I was watching to see the pale woman in the dark gown come in. She didn't show herself, however, and I wondered if she ate apart; but if she wasn't the housekeeper, why should she? Suddenly it struck me that she might be a trained nurse, and in that case her meals would of course be served in her room. If Mrs. Brympton was an invalid it was likely enough she had a nurse. The idea annoyed me, I own, for they're not always the easiest to get on with, and if I'd known I shouldn't have taken the place. But there I was and there was no use pulling a long face over it; and not being one to ask questions I waited to see what would turn up.

When tea was over the house-maid said to the footman: "Has Mr. Ranford gone?" and when he said yes, she told me to come up with her to Mrs. Brympton.

Mrs. Brympton was lying down in her bedroom. Her lounge stood near the fire and beside it was a shaded lamp. She was a delicate-looking lady, but when she smiled I felt there was nothing I wouldn't do for her. She spoke very pleasantly, in a low voice, asking me my name and age and so on, and if I had everything I wanted, and if I wasn't afraid of feeling lonely in the country.

"Not with you I wouldn't be, madam," I said, and the words surprised me when I'd spoken them for I'm not an impulsive person, but it was just as if I'd thought aloud.

She seemed pleased at that, and said she hoped I'd continue in the same mind; then she gave me a few directions about her toilet, and said Agnes the house-maid would show me next morning where things were kept.

"I am tired tonight, and shall dine upstairs," she said. "Agnes will bring me my tray, that you may have time to unpack and settle yourself; and later you may come and undress me."

"Very well, ma'am," I said. "You'll ring, I suppose?"

I thought she looked odd.

"No—Agnes will fetch you," says she quickly, and took up her book again.

Well—that was certainly strange: a lady's maid having to be fetched by the house-maid whenever her lady wanted her! I wondered if there were no bells in the house; but the next day I satisfied myself that there was one in every room, and a special one ringing from my mistress's room to mine; and after that it did strike me as queer that, whenever Mrs. Brympton wanted anything, she rang for Agnes, who had to walk the whole length of the servants' wing to call me.

But that wasn't the only queer thing in the house. The very next day I found out that Mrs. Brympton had no nurse; and then I asked Agnes about the woman I had seen in the passage the afternoon before. Agnes said she had seen no one, and I saw that she thought I was dreaming. To be sure, it was dusk when we went down the passage, and she had excused herself for not bringing a light; but I had seen the woman plain enough to know her again if we should meet. I decided that she must have been a friend of the cook's, or of one of the other women-servants; perhaps she had come down from town for a night's visit, and the servants wanted it kept secret. Some ladies are very stiff about having their servants' friends in the house overnight. At any rate, I made up my mind to ask no more questions.

In a day or two another odd thing happened. I was chatting one afternoon with Mrs. Blinder, who was a friendly disposed woman, and had been longer in the house than the other servants, and she asked me if I was quite comfortable and had everything I needed. I said I had no fault to find with my place or with my mistress, but I thought it odd that in so large a house there was no sewing-room for the lady's maid.

"Why," says she, "there *is* one: the room you're in is the old sewing-room."

"Oh," said I; "and where did the other lady's maid sleep?"

At that she grew confused, and said hurriedly that the servants' rooms had all been changed about last year, and she didn't rightly remember.

That struck me as peculiar, but I went on as if I hadn't noticed: "Well, there's a vacant room opposite mine, and I mean to ask Mrs. Brympton if I mayn't use that as a sewing-room."

To my astonishment, Mrs. Blinder went white, and gave my hand a kind of squeeze. "Don't do that, my dear," said she trembling-like. "To tell you the truth, that was Emma Saxon's room, and my mistress has kept it closed ever since her death."

"And who was Emma Saxon?"

"Mrs. Brympton's former maid."

"The one that was with her for so many years?" said I, remembering what Mrs. Railton had told me.

Mrs. Blinder nodded.

"What sort of woman was she?"

"No better walked the earth," said Mrs. Blinder. "My mistress loved her like a sister."

"But I mean—what did she look like?"

Mrs. Blinder got up and gave me a kind of angry stare. "I'm no great hand at describing," she said; "and I believe my pastry's rising." And she walked off into the kitchen and shut the door after her.

II

I had been near a week at Brympton before I saw my master. Word came that he was arriving one afternoon, and a change passed over the whole household. It was plain that nobody loved him below stairs. Mrs. Blinder took uncommon care with the dinner that night, but she snapped at the kitchen-maid in a way quite unusual with her; and Mr. Wace, the butler, a serious, slow-spoken man, went about his duties as if he'd been getting ready for a funeral. He was a great Bible-reader, Mr. Wace was, and had a beautiful assortment of texts at his command; but that day he used such dreadful language, that I was about to leave the table, when he assured me it was all out of Isaiah; and I noticed that whenever the master came Mr. Wace took to the prophets.

About seven, Agnes called me to my mistress's room; and there I found Mr. Brympton. He was standing on the hearth; a big fair bull-necked man, with a red face and little bad-tempered blue eyes: the kind of man a young simpleton might have thought handsome, and would have been like to pay dear for thinking it.

He swung about when I came in, and looked me over in a trice. I knew what the look meant, from having experienced it once or twice in my former places. Then he turned his back on me, and went on talking to his wife; and I knew what *that* meant, too. I was not the kind of morsel he was after. The typhoid had served me well enough in one way: it kept that kind of gentleman at arm's-length.

"This is my new maid, Hartley," says Mrs. Brympton in her kind voice; and he nodded and went on with what he was saying.

In a minute or two he went off, and left my mistress to dress for dinner, and I noticed as I waited on her that she was white, and chill to the touch.

Mr. Brympton took himself off the next morning, and the whole house drew a long breath when he drove away. As for my mistress, she put on her hat and furs (for it was a fine winter morning) and went out for a walk in the gardens, coming back quite fresh and rosy, so that for a minute, before her colour faded, I could guess what a pretty young lady she must have been, and not so long ago, either.

She had met Mr. Ranford in the grounds, and the two came back together, I remember, smiling and talking as they walked along the terrace under my window. That was the first time I saw Mr. Ranford, though I had often heard his name mentioned in the hall. He was a neighbour, it appeared, living a mile or two beyond Brympton, at the end of the village; and as he was in the habit of spending his winters in the country he was almost the only company my mistress had at that season. He was a slight tall gentleman of about thirty, and I thought him rather melancholy-looking till I saw his smile, which had a kind of surprise in it, like the first warm day in spring. He was a great reader, I heard, like my mistress, and the two were for ever borrowing books of one another, and sometimes (Mr. Wace told me) he would read aloud to Mrs. Brympton by the hour, in the big dark library where she sat in the winter afternoons. The servants all liked him, and perhaps that's more of a compliment than the masters suspect. He had a friendly word for every one of us, and we were all glad to think that Mrs. Brympton had a pleasant companionable gentleman like that to keep her company when the master was away. Mr. Ranford seemed on excellent terms with Mr. Brympton too; though I couldn't but wonder that two gentlemen so unlike each other should be so friendly. But then I knew how the real quality can keep their feelings to themselves.

As for Mr. Brympton, he came and went, never staying more than a day or two, cursing the dullness and the solitude, grumbling at everything, and (as I soon found out) drinking a deal more than was good for him. After Mrs. Brympton left the table he would sit half the night over the old Brympton port and madeira, and once, as I was leaving my mistress's room rather later than usual, I met him coming up the stairs in such a state that I turned sick to think of what some ladies have to endure and hold their tongues about.

The servants said very little about their master; but from what they let drop I could see it had been an unhappy match from the beginning. Mr. Brympton was coarse, loud, and pleasure-loving; my mistress quiet, retiring, and perhaps a trifle cold. Not that she was not always pleasant-spoken to him: I thought her wonderfully forbearing; but to a gentleman as free as Mr. Brympton I dare say she seemed a little offish.

Well, things went on quietly for several weeks. My mistress was kind, my duties were light, and I got on well with the other servants. In short, I had nothing to complain of; yet there was always a weight on me. I can't say why it was so, but I know it was not the loneliness that I felt. I soon got used to that; and being still languid from the fever, I was thankful for the quiet and the good country air. Nevertheless, I was never quite easy in my mind. My mistress, knowing I had been ill, insisted that I should take my walk regular, and often invented errands for me—a yard of ribbon to be fetched from the village, a letter posted, or a book returned to Mr. Ranford. As soon as I was out of doors my spirits rose, and I looked forward to my walks through the bare moist-smelling woods; but the moment I caught sight of the house again my heart dropped down like a stone in a well. It was not a gloomy house exactly, yet I never entered it but a feeling of gloom came over me.

Mrs. Brympton seldom went out in winter; only on the finest days did she walk an hour at noon on the south terrace. Excepting Mr. Ranford, we had no visitors but the doctor, who drove over from D—— about once a week. He sent for me once or twice to give me some trifling direction about my mistress, and though he never told me what her illness was, I thought, from a waxy look she had now and then of a morning, that it might be the heart that ailed her. The season was soft and unwholesome, and in January we had a long spell of rain. That was a sore trial to me, I own, for I couldn't go out, and sitting over my sewing all day, listening to the drip, drip of the eaves, I grew so nervous that the least sound made me jump. Somehow, the thought of that locked room across the passage began to weigh on me. Once or twice, in the long rainy nights, I fancied I heard noises there; but that was nonsense, of course, and the daylight drove such notions out of my head. Well, one morning Mrs. Brympton gave me quite a start of pleasure by telling me she wished me to go to town for some shopping. I hadn't known till then how low my spirits had fallen. I set off in high glee, and my first sight of the crowded streets and the cheerful-looking shops quite took me out of myself. Toward afternoon, however, the noise and confusion began to tire me, and I was actually looking forward to the quiet of Brympton, and thinking how I should enjoy the drive home through the dark woods, when I ran across an old acquaintance, a maid I had once been in service with. We had lost sight of each other for a number of years, and I had to stop and tell her what had happened to me in the interval. When I mentioned where I was living she rolled up her eyes and pulled a long face.

"What! The Mrs. Brympton that lives all the year at her place on the Hudson? My dear, you won't stay there three months."

"Oh, but I don't mind the country," says I, offended somehow at her tone. "Since the fever I'm glad to be quiet."

She shook her head. "It's not the country I'm thinking of. All I know is she's had four maids in the last six months, and the last one, who was a friend of mine, told me nobody could stay in the house."

"Did she say why?" I asked.

"No—she wouldn't give me her reason. But she says to me, *Mrs. Ansey,* she says, *if ever a young woman as you know of thinks of going there, you tell her it's not worth while to unpack her boxes.*"

"Is she young and handsome?" said I, thinking of Mr. Brympton.

"Not her! She's the kind that mothers engage when they've gay young gentlemen at college."

Well, though I knew the woman was an idle gossip, the words stuck in my head, and my heart sank lower than ever as I drove up to Brympton in the dusk. There *was* something about the house—I was sure of it now. . . .

When I went in to tea I heard that Mr. Brympton had arrived, and I saw at a glance that there had been a disturbance of some kind. Mrs. Blinder's hand shook so that she could hardly pour the tea, and Mr. Wace quoted the most dreadful texts full of brimstone. Nobody said a word to me then, but when I went up to my room Mrs. Blinder followed me.

"Oh, my dear," says she, taking my hand, "I'm so glad and thankful you've come back to us!"

That struck me as you may imagine. "Why," said I, "did you think I was leaving for good?"

"No, no, to be sure," said she, a little confused, "but I can't a-bear to have madam left alone for a day even." She pressed my hand hard, and, "Oh, Miss Hartley," says she, "be good to your mistress, as you're a Christian woman." And with that she hurried away, and left me staring.

A moment later Agnes called me to Mrs. Brympton. Hearing Mr. Brympton's voice in her room, I went round by the dressing-room, thinking I would lay out her dinner-gown before going in. The dressing-room is a large room with a window over the portico that looks toward the gardens. Mr. Brympton's apartments are beyond. When I went in, the door into the bedroom was ajar, and I heard Mr. Brympton saying angrily: "One would suppose he was the only person fit for you to talk to."

"I don't have many visitors in winter," Mrs. Brympton answered quietly.

"You have *me!*" he flung at her, sneeringly.

"You are here so seldom," said she.

"Well—whose fault is that? You make the place about as lively as the family vault——"

With that I rattled the toilet-things, to give my mistress warning, and she rose and called me in.

The two dined alone, as usual, and I knew by Mr. Wace's manner at supper that things must be going badly. He quoted the prophets something terrible, and worked on the kitchen-maid so that she declared she wouldn't go down alone to put the cold meat in the ice-box. I felt nervous myself, and after I had put my mistress to bed I was half tempted to go down again and persuade Mrs. Blinder to sit up awhile over a game of cards. But I heard her door closing for the night and so I went on to my own room. The rain had begun again, and the drip, drip, drip seemed to be dropping into my brain. I lay awake listening to it, and turning over what my friend in town had said. What puzzled me was that it was always the maids who left . . .

After a while I slept; but suddenly a loud noise wakened me. My bell had rung. I sat up, terrified by the unusual sound, which seemed to go on jangling through the darkness. My hands shook so that I couldn't find the matches. At length I struck a light and jumped out of bed. I began to think I must have been dreaming; but I looked at the bell against the wall, and there was the little hammer still quivering.

I was just beginning to huddle on my clothes when I heard another sound. This time it was the door of the locked room opposite mine softly opening and closing. I heard the sound distinctly, and it frightened me so that I stood stock still. Then I heard a footstep hurrying down the passage toward the main house. The floor being carpeted, the sound was very faint, but I was quite sure it was a woman's step. I turned cold with the thought of it, and for a minute or two I dursn't breathe or move. Then I came to my senses.

"Alice Hartley," says I to myself, "someone left that room just now and ran down the passage ahead of you. The idea isn't pleasant, but you may as well face it. Your mistress has rung for you, and to answer her bell you've got to go the way that other woman has gone."

Well—I did it. I never walked faster in my life, yet I thought I should never get to the end of the passage or reach Mrs. Brymton's room. On the way I heard nothing and saw nothing: all was dark and quiet as the grave. When I reached my mistress's door the silence was so deep that I began to think I must be dreaming, and was half minded to turn back. Then a panic seized me, and I knocked.

There was no answer, and I knocked again, loudly. To my astonishment the door was opened by Mr. Brympton. He started back when he saw me, and in the light of my candle his face looked red and savage.

"*You?*" he said, in a queer voice. *"How many of you are there, in God's name?"*

At that I felt the ground give under me; but I said to myself that he had been drinking, and answered as steadily as I could: "May I go in, sir? Mrs. Brympton has rung for me."

"You may all go in, for what I care," says he, and, pushing by me, walked down the hall to his own bedroom. I looked after him as he went, and to my surprise I saw that he walked as straight as a sober man.

I found my mistress lying very weak and still, but she forced a smile when she saw me, and signed me to pour out some drops for her. After that she lay without speaking, her breath coming quick, and her eyes closed. Suddenly she groped out with her hand, and *"Emma,"* says she, faintly.

"It's Hartley, madam," I said. "Do you want anything?"

She opened her eyes wide and gave me a startled look.

"I was dreaming," she said. "You may go, now, Hartley, and thank you kindly. I'm quite well again, you see." And she turned her face away from me.

III

THERE was no more sleep for me that night, and I was thankful when daylight came.

Soon afterward, Agnes called me to Mrs. Brympton. I was afraid she was ill again, for she seldom sent for me before nine, but I found her sitting up in bed, pale and drawn-looking, but quite herself.

"Hartley," says she quickly, "will you put on your things at once and go down to the village for me? I want this prescription made up" —here she hesitated a minute and blushed—"and I should like you to be back again before Mr. Brympton is up."

"Certainly, madam," I said.

"And—stay a moment"—she called me back as if an idea had just struck her—"while you're waiting for the,mixture, you'll have time to go on to Mr. Ranford's with this note."

It was a two-mile walk to the village, and on my way I had time to turn things over in my mind. It struck me as peculiar that my mistress should wish the prescription made up without Mr. Brympton's knowledge; and, putting this together with the scene of the night before, and with much else that I had noticed and suspected, I began to wonder if the poor lady was weary of her life, and had come to the mad resolve of ending it. The idea took such hold on me that I reached the village on a run, and dropped breathless into a chair before the chemist's counter. The good man, who was just taking down his shutters, stared at me so hard that it brought me to myself.

"Mr. Limmel," I says, trying to speak indifferent, "will you run your eye over this, and tell me if it's quite right?"

He put on his spectacles and studied the prescription.

"Why, it's one of Dr. Walton's," says he. "What should be wrong with it?"

"Well—is it dangerous to take?"

"Dangerous—how do you mean?"

I could have shaken the man for his stupidity.

"I mean—if a person was to take too much of it—by mistake of course—" says I, my heart in my throat.

"Lord bless you, no. It's only lime-water. You might feed it to a baby by the bottleful."

I gave a great sigh of relief and hurried on to Mr. Ranford's. But on the way another thought struck me. If there was nothing to conceal about my visit to the chemist's, was it my other errand that Mrs. Brympton wished me to keep private? Somehow, that thought frightened me worse than the other. Yet the two gentlemen seemed fast friends, and I would have staked my head on my mistress's goodness. I felt ashamed of my suspicions, and concluded that I was still disturbed by the strange events of the night. I left the note at Mr. Ranford's and, hurrying back to Brympton, slipped in by a side door without being seen, as I thought.

An hour later, however, as I was carrying in my mistress's breakfast, I was stopped in the hall by Mr. Brympton.

"What were you doing out so early?" he says, looking hard at me.

"Early—me, sir?" I said, in a tremble.

"Come, come," he says, an angry red spot coming out on his forehead, "didn't I see you scuttling home through the shrubbery an hour or more ago?"

I'm a truthful woman by nature, but at that a lie popped out readymade. "No, sir, you didn't," said I and looked straight back at him.

He shrugged his shoulders and gave a sullen laugh. "I suppose you think I was drunk last night?" he asked suddenly.

"No, sir, I don't," I answered, this time truthfully enough.

He turned away with another shrug. "A pretty notion my servants have of me!" I heard him mutter as he walked off.

Not till I had settled down to my afternoon's sewing did I realize how the events of the night had shaken me. I couldn't pass that locked door without a shiver. I knew I had heard someone come out of it, and walk down the passage ahead of me. I thought of speaking to Mrs. Blinder or to Mr. Wace, the only two in the house who appeared to have an inkling of what was going on, but I had a feeling that if I questioned them they would deny everything, and that I might learn more by holding my tongue and keeping my eyes open. The idea of spending another night opposite the locked room sickened me, and once I was seized with the notion of packing my trunk and taking the first train to town; but it wasn't in me to throw over a kind mistress in that manner, and I tried to go on with my sewing as if nothing had happened. I hadn't worked ten minutes before the sewing-machine broke down. It was one I had found in the house, a good machine, but a trifle out of order: Mrs. Blinder said it had never been used since Emma Saxon's death. I stopped to see what was wrong, and as I was working at the machine a drawer which I had never been able to open slid forward and a photograph fell out. I picked it up and sat looking at it in a maze. It was a woman's likeness, and I knew I had seen the face somewhere—the eyes had an asking look that I had felt on me before. And suddenly I remembered the pale woman in the passage.

I stood up, cold all over, and ran out of the room. My heart seemed to be thumping in the top of my head, and I felt as if I should never get away from the look in those eyes. I went straight to Mrs. Blinder. She was taking her afternoon nap, and sat up with a jump when I came in.

"Mrs. Blinder," said I, "who is that?" And I held out the photograph.

She rubbed her eyes and stared.

"Why, Emma Saxon," says she. "Where did you find it?"

I looked hard at her for a minute. "Mrs. Blinder," I said, "I've seen that face before."

Mrs. Blinder got up and walked over to the looking-glass. "Dear me! I must have been asleep," she says. "My front is all over one ear. And now do run along, Miss Hartley, dear, for I hear the clock striking four, and I must go down this very minute and put on the Virginia ham for Mr. Brympton's dinner."

I V

To all appearances, things went on as usual for a week or two. The only difference was that Mr. Brympton stayed on, instead of going off as he usually did, and that Mr. Ranford never showed himself. I heard Mr. Brympton remark on this one afternoon when he was sitting in my mistress's room before dinner:

"Where's Ranford?" says he. "He hasn't been near the house for a week. Does he keep away because I'm here?"

Mrs. Brympton spoke so low that I couldn't catch her answer.

"Well," he went on, "two's company and three's trumpery; I'm sorry to be in Ranford's way, and I suppose I shall have to take myself off again in a day or two and give him a show." And he laughed at his own joke.

The very next day, as it happened, Mr. Ranford called. The footman said the three were very merry over their tea in the library, and Mr. Brympton strolled down to the gate with Mr. Ranford when he left.

I have said that things went on as usual; and so they did with the rest of the household; but as for myself, I had never been the same since the night my bell had rung. Night after night I used to lie awake, listening for it to ring again, and for the door of the locked room to open stealthily. But the bell never rang, and I heard no sound across the passage. At last the silence began to be more dreadful to me than the most mysterious sounds. I felt that *someone* was cowering there, behind the locked door, watching and listening as I watched and listened, and I could almost have cried out: "Whoever you are, come out and let me see you face to face, but don't lurk there and spy on me in the darkness!"

Feeling as I did, you may wonder I didn't give warning. Once I very nearly did so; but at the last moment something held me back. Whether it was compassion for my mistress, who had grown more and more dependent on me, or unwillingness to try a new place, or some other feeling that I couldn't put a name to, I lingered on as if spellbound, though every night was dreadful to me, and the days but little better.

For one thing, I didn't like Mrs. Brympton's looks. She had never been the same since that night, no more than I had. I thought she would brighten up after Mr. Brympton left, but though she seemed easier in her mind, her spirits didn't revive, nor her strength either. She had grown attached to me, and seemed to like to have me about; and Agnes told me one day that, since Emma Saxon's death, I was the only maid her mistress had taken to. This gave me a warm feeling for the poor lady, though after all there was little I could do to help her.

After Mr. Brympton's departure, Mr. Ranford took to coming again, though less often than formerly. I met him once or twice in the grounds, or in the village, and I couldn't but think there was a change in him too; but I set it down to my disordered fancy.

The weeks passed, and Mr. Brympton had now been a month absent. We heard he was cruising with a friend in the West Indies, and Mr. Wace said that was a long way off, but though you had wings of a dove and went to the uttermost parts of the earth, you couldn't get away from the Almighty. Agnes said that as long as he stayed away from Brympton the Almighty might have him and welcome; and this raised a laugh, though Mrs. Blinder tried to look shocked, and Mr. Wace said the bears would eat us.

We were all glad to hear that the West Indies were a long way off, and I remember that, in spite of Mr. Wace's solemn looks, we had a very merry dinner that day in the hall. I don't know if it was because of my being in better spirits, but I fancied Mrs. Brympton looked better too, and seemed more cheerful in her manner. She had been for a walk in the morning, and after luncheon she lay down in her room, and I read aloud to her. When she dismissed me I went to my own room feeling quite bright and happy, and for the first time in weeks walked past the locked door without thinking of it. As I sat down to my work I looked out and saw a few snow-flakes falling. The sight was pleasanter than the eternal rain, and I pictured to myself how pretty the bare gardens would look in their white mantle. It seemed to me as if the snow would cover up all the dreariness, indoors as well as out.

The fancy had hardly crossed my mind when I heard a step at my side. I looked up, thinking it was Agnes.

"Well, Agnes—" said I, and the words froze on my tongue; for there, in the door, stood Emma Saxon.

I don't know how long she stood there. I only know I couldn't stir or take my eyes from her. Afterward I was terribly frightened, but at the time it wasn't fear I felt, but something deeper and quieter. She looked at me long and long, and her face was just one dumb prayer to me—but how in the world was I to help her? Suddenly she turned, and I heard her walk down the passage. This time I wasn't afraid to follow—I felt that I must know what she wanted. I sprang up and ran out. She was at the other end of the passage, and I expected her to take the turn toward my mistress's room; but instead of that she pushed open the door that led to the backstairs. I followed her down the stairs, and across the passageway to the back door. The kitchen and hall were empty at that hour, the servants being off duty, except for the footman, who was in the pantry. At the door she stood still a moment, with another look at me; then she turned the handle, and stepped out. For a minute I hesitated. Where was she leading me to? The door had closed softly after her, and I opened it and looked out, half expecting to find that she had disappeared. But I saw her a few yards off hurrying across the courtyard to the path through the woods. Her figure looked black and lonely in the snow, and for a second my heart failed me and I thought of turning back. But all the while she was drawing me after her; and catching up an old shawl of Mrs. Blinder's I ran out into the open.

Emma Saxon was in the wood-path now. She walked on steadily, and I followed at the same pace, till we passed out of the gates and reached the highroad. Then she struck across the open fields to the village. By this time the ground was white, and as she climbed the slope of a bare hill ahead of me I noticed that she left no foot-prints behind her. At sight of that my heart shrivelled up within me, and my knees were water. Somehow, it was worse here than indoors. She made the whole countryside seem lonely as the grave, with none but us two in it, and no help in the wide world.

Once I tried to go back; but she turned and looked at me, and it was as if she had dragged me with ropes. After that I followed her like a dog. We came to the village and she led me through it, past the church and the blacksmith's shop, and down the lane to Mr. Ranford's. Mr. Ranford's house stands close to the road: a plain old-fashioned building, with a flagged path leading to the door between box-borders. The lane was deserted, and as I turned into it I saw Emma Saxon pause under the old elm by the gate. And now another fear came over me. I saw that we had reached the end of our journey, and that it was my turn to act. All the way from Brympton I had been asking myself what she wanted of me, but I had followed in a trance, as it were, and not till I saw her stop at Mr. Ranford's gate did my brain begin to clear itself. I stood a little way off in the snow, my heart beating fit to strangle me, and my feet frozen to the ground; and she stood under the elm and watched me.

I knew well enough that she hadn't led me there for nothing. I felt there was something I ought to say or do—but how was I to guess what it was? I had never thought harm of my mistress and Mr. Ranford, but I was sure now that, from one cause or another, some dreadful thing hung over them. *She* knew what it was; she would tell me if she could; perhaps she would answer if I questioned her.

It turned me faint to think of speaking to her; but I plucked up heart and dragged myself across the few yards between us. As I did so, I heard the house-door open and saw Mr. Ranford approaching. He looked handsome and cheerful, as my mistress had looked that morning, and at sight of him the blood began to flow again in my veins.

"Why, Hartley," said he, "what's the matter? I saw you coming down the lane just now, and came out to see if you had taken root in the snow." He stopped and stared at me. "What are you looking at?" he says.

I turned toward the elm as he spoke, and his eyes followed me; but there was no one there. The lane was empty as far as the eye could reach.

A sense of helplessness came over me. She was gone, and I had not been able to guess what she wanted. Her last look had pierced me to the marrow; and yet it had not told me! All at once, I felt more desolate than when she had stood there watching me. It seemed as if she had left me all alone to carry the weight of the secret I couldn't guess. The snow went round me in great circles, and the ground fell away from me. . . .

A drop of brandy and the warmth of Mr. Ranford's fire soon brought me to, and I insisted on being driven back at once to Brympton. It was nearly dark, and I was afraid my mistress might be wanting me. I explained to Mr. Ranford that I had been out for a walk and had been taken with a fit of giddiness as I passed his gate. This was true enough; yet I never felt more like a liar than when I said it.

When I dressed Mrs. Brympton for dinner she remarked on my pale looks and asked what ailed me. I told her I had a headache, and she said she would not require me again that evening, and she advised me to go to bed.

It was a fact that I could scarcely keep on my feet; yet I had no fancy to spend a solitary evening in my room. I sat downstairs in the hall as long as I could hold my head up; but by nine I crept upstairs, too weary to care what happened if I could but get my head on a pillow. The rest of the household went to bed soon afterward; they kept early hours when the master was away, and before ten I heard Mrs. Blinder's door close, and Mr. Wace's soon after.

It was a very still night, earth and air all muffled in snow. Once in bed I felt easier, and lay quiet, listening to the strange noises that come out in a house after dark. Once I thought I heard a door open and close again below: it might have been the glass door that led to the gardens. I got up and peered out of the window; but it was in the dark of the moon, and nothing visible outside but the streaking of snow against the panes.

I went back to bed and must have dozed, for I jumped awake to the furious ringing of my bell. Before my head was clear I had sprung out of bed, and was dragging on my clothes. *It is going to happen now,* I heard myself saying; but what I meant I had no notion. My hands seemed to be covered with glue—I thought I should never get into my clothes. At last I opened my door and peered down the passage. As far as my candle-flame carried, I could see nothing unusual ahead of me. I hurried on, breathless; but as I pushed open the baize door leading to the main hall my heart stood still, for there at the head of the stairs was Emma Saxon, peering dreadfully down into the darkness.

For a second I couldn't stir; but my hand slipped from the door, and as it swung shut the figure vanished. At the same instant there came another sound from below stairs—a stealthy mysterious sound, as of a latch-key turning in the house-door. I ran to Mrs. Brympton's room and knocked.

There was no answer, and I knocked again. This time I heard someone moving in the room; the bolt slipped back and my mistress stood before me. To my surprise I saw that she had not undressed for the night. She gave me a startled look.

"What is this, Hartley?" she says in a whisper. "Are you ill? What are you doing here at this hour?"

"I am not ill, madam; but my bell rang."

At that she turned pale, and seemed about to fall.

"You are mistaken," she said harshly; "I didn't ring. You must have been dreaming." I had never heard her speak in such a tone. "Go back to bed," she said, closing the door on me.

But as she spoke I heard sounds again in the hall below: a man's step this time; and the truth leaped out on me.

"Madam," I said, pushing past her, "there is someone in the house——"

"Someone—?"

"Mr. Brympton, I think—I hear his step below——"

A dreadful look came over her, and without a word, she dropped flat at my feet. I fell on my knees and tried to lift her: by the way she breathed I saw it was no common faint. But as I raised her head there came quick steps on the stairs and across the hall: the door was flung open, and there stood Mr. Brympton, in his travelling-clothes, the snow dripping from him. He drew back with a start as he saw me kneeling by my mistress.

"What the devil is this?" he shouted. He was less high-coloured than usual, and the red spot came out on his forehead.

"Mrs. Brympton has fainted, sir," said I.

He laughed unsteadily and pushed by me. "It's a pity she didn't choose a more convenient moment. I'm sorry to disturb her, but——"

I raised myself up aghast at the man's action.

"Sir," said I, "are you mad? What are you doing?"

"Going to meet a friend," said he, and seemed to make for the dressing-room.

At that my heart turned over. I don't know what I thought or feared; but I sprang up and caught him by the sleeve.

"Sir, sir," said I, "for pity's sake look at your wife!"

He shook me off furiously.

"It seems that's done for me," says he, and caught hold of the dressing-room door.

At that moment I heard a slight noise inside. Slight as it was, he heard it too, and tore the door open; but as he did so he dropped back. On the threshold stood Emma Saxon. All was dark behind her, but I saw her plainly, and so did he. He threw up his hands as if to hide his face from her; and when I looked again she was gone.

He stood motionless, as if the strength had run out of him; and in the stillness my mistress suddenly raised herself and, opening her eyes, fixed a look on him. Then she fell back, and I saw the death-flutter pass over her. . . .

We buried her on the third day, in a driving snow-storm. There were few people in the church, for it was bad weather to come from town, and I've a notion my mistress was one that hadn't many near friends. Mr. Ranford was among the last to come, just before they carried her up the aisle. He was in black, of course, being such a friend of the family, and I never saw a gentleman so pale. As he passed me, I noticed that he leaned a trifle on a stick he carried; and I fancy Mr. Brympton noticed it too, for the red spot came out sharp on his forehead, and all through the service he kept staring across the church at Mr. Ranford, instead of following the prayers as a mourner should.

When it was over and we went out to the graveyard, Mr. Ranford had disappeared, and as soon as my poor mistress's body was underground, Mr. Brympton jumped into the carriage nearest the gate and drove off without a word to any of us. I heard him call out: "To the station," and we servants went back alone to the house.

AN AFTERWORD ON
"THE LADY'S MAID'S BELL"

WHEN, a few years ago, the late Edith Wharton published her memoirs, Dorothy Parker borrowed the title of a song then current on Broadway to make upon that autobiography the most telling as well as the most compact comment which it elicited. Instead of *A Backward Glance* it should, Mrs. Parker suggested, have been called *Edie Was a Lady*.

It was the irony of that long and distinguished, but severely restricted, life that, although in such works as *The House of Mirth* and *The Age of Innocence* Mrs. Wharton was the successful and richly rewarded chronicler of the great world into which she was born and in which she lived out her days, her best chance of being remembered rests on *Ethan Frome,* a venture into a world she had visited only in her imagination. And I suspect that one reason this tale of "The Lady's Maid's Bell" still lingers in the memory of anyone who first encountered it in *Scribner's* five-and-thirty years ago is that at least it was told from the viewpoint of the servants' quarters. Indeed, a provocative thesis could be written on the heightened effect all tales of dread and mystery take on by being related from below stairs. Mrs. Belloc Lowndes knew this infallibly when she sat down to write in *The Lodger* the best murder story in the English language. The same instinct guided Emily Brontë when she set to work on the novel her feckless brother had started. In no time she had dropped the colorless passer-by who was his narrator and so shifted the narrative that it became the reminiscent clack of an old goody who had been a housekeeper at Wuthering Heights. In the same fashion Mrs. Wharton imparted to this story of hers the priceless flavor of an old wives' tale.

"It is in the warm darkness of the pre-natal fluid, far below our conscious reason," said Mrs. Wharton, "that the faculty dwells with which we apprehend the ghosts we may not be endowed with the gift of seeing." I quote this from her preface to a collection of her ghost stories which was already scheduled for publication at the time of her death. For many years after its first appearance, "The Lady's Maid's Bell" could be found only at the tag end of a hideaway called *The Descent of Man* but now it is available not only here but in this new collection. Let me quote further from that preface:

Since I first dabbled in the inventing of ghost stories I have made the depressing discovery that the faculty required for their enjoyment has become almost atrophied in modern man. No one ever expected a Latin to understand a ghost, or shiver over it; to do that one must still have in one's ears the ancestral murmurs of the northern *Urwald* or the churning of dark seas on the outermost western isles. But when I first began to read, and then to write ghost stories, I was conscious of a common medium between myself and my readers, of their meeting me half-way among the primeval shadows, and filling in the gaps in my narrative with sensations and divinations akin to my own.

Deep within us northerners as the ghost instinct lurks, I seem to see it being gradually atrophied by those two world-wide enemies of the imagination, the wireless and the cinema. To a generation for whom everything which used to nourish the imagination because it had to be captured by an effort, and then slowly assimilated, is now served up cooked, seasoned, and chopped into little bits, the creative faculty (for reading as well as writing should be a creative act) is rapidly withering, together with the power of sustained attention; and the world which used to be *si grand à la clarté des lampes* is diminishing in inverse ratio to the new means of spanning it; so that the more we add to its material surface the smaller it becomes to the imagination.

Thus Mrs. Wharton in the autumnal preface which was doubtless one of the last things she wrote.

A. W.

JOE

by

GUSTAV ECKSTEIN

JOE

I

ONE night when he had had a glass or two of Burgundy he told of
something that had happened before he came to America, as a matter
of fact, before he came down from the farm to Lisbon. So he must
have been young, eighteen or nineteen, perhaps. A girl, not a bad girl,
had fallen in love and the man had made off, and at the birth of the
child she had drowned herself in a cistern. Because it was that way, the
priest did not want to bury her in sacred ground—priests in such small
country places are hard. Joe argued with the priest, and right out where
everybody could hear. Dogs came round and smelled the body. Joe
claimed such a body would spread disease. He was like that—once he
had an idea, it was not easy to get it out of his head. He and some
others talked the matter over, then presently he was up and off for his
shotgun, the rest of the village following along to see what would
happen. To defy the priest—it was like defying God. When they reached
the priest's house Joe called out the priest, told him he was performing
the service, and in his best manner, too. This the priest did, and the
girl was buried, but Joe knew what that meant, knew where even this
crowd, when the excitement was over, would stand. Better to go down
to Lisbon to live.

He was married and had a child or two. His mother and father
were dead, but his grandmother was alive and had given him her farm,
a small farm but in the rich grape country round Thomar, and close
enough to Lisbon to make it easy to cart things. A kind of ideal of pedi-
gree went with the farm—for instance, you might have only one pig,
but it would be the best variety of pig known.

Joe sold the farm and bought land and a house right in the heart of

Lisbon. The house was a two-story house with pepper trees around it. He lived on the first floor and rented out the second to a man who helped him work the land as a truck garden. That meant money. He soon felt that no one was better than he was, and a gay life he began to lead, had a way of not getting drunk and yet drinking enough, played the accordion and sang, and at the fiestas, when Lisbon dances from one end to the other, he was a regular dancing fool, jigged till the others dropped dead. His eyes were blue, and got bluer as he got gayer, but green as he got angry. In short, he danced, drank, gambled, and then there was a mortgage.

Meantime there had been more children, also rabbits, mice, rats, birds, and two dogs, and for a while a chimpanzee. The chimpanzee belonged to the man who lived in the place below, but twice broke its chain and climbed a twenty-five-foot wall to come up to Joe's place, the second time so scratched its owner that he wanted to kill it. Joe said that would be a shame, took the animal for himself, and soon taught it all kinds of useful things. It would jump on a certain board of a platform whenever anyone rang the bell, and the board would give, and that lift the latch that held the gate, and no one would have to go down to the gate to open it. Naturally the neighbor children saw this chance, and rang the bell and ran, but the chimpanzee then of its own accord thought out how to save itself being fooled by first creeping along the wall and looking over.

To show how stubborn Joe was—one day he went to market with his mule and a cart of cabbages, and the mule decided to stand still. He argued with the mule, then unhitched the cabbages so that the mule had absolutely no case, then said that that mule would move. A street-car was behind and clanking. Everybody behind the street-car was yelling. Joe beat the mule and kicked it, and it moved. Ladies were in the street-car, so he was sentenced to two days and three nights for cruelty to a mule. He would not have had to go to jail, but could not be made to turn a hand to save himself, said any intelligent man would have done as he did, and that he liked this bit of cruelty practiced on himself, came out of jail with grime on his body and bugs in his hair, and was pleased. His wife was so ashamed.

His money had grown less and less, so he took a job with the fire department, the big central division where all the mules were reshod. The fire chief lived there. The gymnasium was there. Joe was a daredevil in the gymnasium. Joe was everything—carpenter, mason, stableman. If lights were needed, he put them up. If sewer pipes had to be laid, he laid them. He started a division truck garden, which made two truck gardens, and that was possible because he could work at them in the day, then at night go on his duty of inspecting the theaters and that sort of thing. Also there were more fires in winter, and there was more gardening in summer. But most important, to make the good soil there was the manure of the mules. "Good si-ile is what you need." He was always saying that.

As for his fireman belongings, he liked his helmet most, had his photograph taken in his helmet, said you had to have a helmet because it protected your brains. If you broke any other part of you it practically made no difference, but of your brains you had to be careful. When the fire department bought nets to catch people leaping from burning buildings, he pushed himself forward to try out the idea, leaped safely from a second story, then must also from a third story, but perhaps did not land exactly in the middle of the net, because someone let go an end, and he, being in the sitting position, hurt what he thought was the tip of his spine. He was never real right after that. Later he rescued a woman, and someone else got the medal, and that finished things. That was something you could not do to Joe. He quit the fire department, quit though he had now four children and a fifth was coming —quit Lisbon, Portugal, Europe, took ship for America, was thorough in whatever he did. It was the fire chief gave Joe's son Gabriel his education.

II

Joe's ship put in at Fall River. He had given his last money to his wife, so had to do something, and began unloading lumber from a Portuguese freighter. The man in charge, a big Portuguese, guyed him, then abused him, then kicked him. At the moment the kick came he was lifting a plank, and it was easy just to continue the swing of the plank over his shoulder and down on the man's head. The man was taken to a hospital and for a time it was thought he would die.

Perhaps Joe did not care to stay with these Portuguese after this. When all is said he left Portugal to be rid of Portuguese. Then, too, this harbor with its ships and shipping was making him homesick, and it would be better to put temptation out of the way and go where he could not see the ocean. So he did some talking and got a letter, and went on unloading lumber till he had fare to a place off toward the middle of the country, Cincinnati, where there were no Portuguese, only one family half Portuguese that might help him.

The family had horses and he liked that. He was little, but felt big when he was on a horse. And he liked the manure, and soon had things growing round the house. A lady, a friend of the Portuguese family, got to talking to him, and the lady was not well, and he had had his troubles. Later he brought fresh cut flowers and left them in the room where the lady lay ill. The lady's name was Dabney—which he promptly changed to Davney—and her husband was Doctor Dabney, president of the university.

The grounds of the university back there in 1907 were bare clay. A long wood steps led from the street up to McMicken Hall, and there were no sidewalks, no flowers, and of course no trees. "But no university without trees." That was what the president said to Joe the first time they talked, though Joe's actual work when the university employed him was to lay sewer pipes. Mr. and Mrs. Kelch, also of the university, gave him a place to sleep to help him get started. He washed in the boiler-room.

Then he was formally made gardener, and right away the grounds began to change. His experiences in Portugal had been with vegetables, but he liked flowers, said he liked carnations most because over there they got so big and smelled so sweet. All flowers over there had more odor. It was the soil and the warm sea air and the regular rains.

In someone's weak moment he was told he might bring his belongings to the top floor of Cunningham. Next morning they came, tools, dirt, sand, manure. The manure he was going to let ripen up there in

Cunningham. He had a walk naturally brisk, but brisk in boots, and hour after hour now the boots went through the lower hall, up the two flights, and in over someone's laboratory. "Why ever did we let that fellow come there?" Everybody was asking and nobody knew. "I canno keep clean all the time. I have to work." That was his answer, and he took, besides, a mulish pleasure in this going among the great just as he was. He brought to the third floor hundreds of earthenware pots, planted first in the smallest, then transplanted into larger, and into larger, and so on and on.

He dropped in at the president's office, said he had to see the president, was told he could not because someone was there, then, before the secretary could stop him, was in. Then went to the business office, wanted to make arrangements for some new flowers, was told there were no funds, argued and argued and argued, and ended by being allowed to buy fifty tubers, and with the price of fifty went to a German and argued him out of a hundred and fifty. Afterward he discussed with the professor of botany what was to be done about a certain plant, and the professor of botany went to get a book, but Joe did not know much about books (there were none up there to the other side of Lisbon), and lost his temper. "You canno grow outa book, but outa ground."

A fern in the president's office was not doing well. Every day another leaf had to be pulled out. Joe was being teased about it. He pretended not to care, but his younger daughter, Peg, who was over on this side now, said he would make that fern grow if he had to crawl into it. He took it out of its pot, cleaned the roots and changed the earth. But that did no good. He tried north light. That did no good. He tried south light. And that did no good. At last he was so worried he thought of science, asked a man in the department of chemistry to analyze the earth. And that did no good. He carried the plant into a professor's room, set it on the professor's desk, and when the professor did not want it there said the sun and air on that desk were right and the plant would have to stay. Every morning and every evening he stood and looked at that plant. Then one evening in a rage he snatched it up, slammed it down on a radiator and cooked it, and then everybody did laugh, said he had lost his nerve and was going to kill it. Instead, it grew all over the place and no one knew what to do with it.

A bull broke loose down in the city, sauntered up Vine Street, wrecked a few shop windows. Joe saw the bull. The bull saw Joe. Joe started after the bull and there was a race of half a mile. Then a thing happened that people round the university were going to remember. A child ran across the path of the bull and the bull was in a goring state. Joe took one plunge and grabbed the bull's tail, hung to the tail, and at the right moment took another plunge and was on the bull's back, clutched its horns, twisted them, round, round, round, till both animal and man went down into the dirt, when he succeeded in slipping from under and tying it to a pole. The police came. He left. The police took charge. He grinned. He was 5 feet 4, and weighed 155 pounds.

Everybody over the hill now knew him—students, professors, deans, janitors. When he walked down Calhoun Street they called to him from every house. One liked him, one didn't—"kin go to hell." He would tell his son Gabriel, also on this side now, which professor it was worth almost dying for (mainly the president), which it was worth listening to, which was worth liking, and which was a hypocrite—"Every time that man he say something, I know he don't mean." When one came along, Joe was just too busy to see him, and when another, he was not busy at all. One absent-minded one he would call from his absent-minded walk, would point to some earth on which nothing was growing, and say that there the letters of the university would rise in blue flowers, and the absent-minded one not believe it, and this bit of dialogue be kept up every day till the blue flowers came.

He had by now flowers along McMicken, beds on either side toward Cunningham and Hanna, and around these buildings, and on the window-sills, and down where the steps divide, and where the students gave their plays. On the far side of the library he had a snake of coarse grass, the eyes pansies. Close against the walls he had his flowers tall, and in front of the tall ones some not so tall, and way in front short ones, the difference got in part simply by the different amounts of water he gave them. Then he would change the kinds, have tulips in the spring, and on the same beds when the students came back in the fall salvias and cosmos.

So there was this planting, and the cutting of the grass, and the sprinkling—everybody would have left the buildings, but Joe Reis would still be there. Long after midnight he would be changing sprinklers, would sleep an hour, come back, sleep another hour, come back, and many a night lay till morning on the university grass—from time to time played his Portuguese guitar.

He loved that guitar. It had got cracked on the ship and he had not been able to play it. Then a Mr. Kupka came to the university, and Joe nosed about where Mr. Kupka worked and saw how he worked, took him the instrument, asked him if he would repair it, said he had been afraid to leave it to a violin-maker he did not know because it might get exchanged or stolen. And Mr. Kupka glued the instrument, and when Joe saw the beautiful work, how you could not tell where the injured places were, he was overwhelmed and put a bed of flowers in front of Mr. Kupka's house.

Someone said Joe would have to stop his smoking in the university corridors. "No smoke, no work." That was what Joe said, shrugged his shoulders, smoked, and said again what he said, "I canno smoke, kin go to hell." He smoked not only in the corridors, but in the president's office. The president was helping him get ready for his naturalization examinations. "My frie-e-end, Pre-e-sident Davney." He also said that with a variation. "Pre-e-sident Davney, pre-e-sident inside the buildings, me outside."

In the middle of all this there would be a fire, and he was just like a child about a fire, the way he always had been. He got his wife, also on this side now, and Peg, and Peg's older brother, every one of them, out of bed to walk with him the three miles to Chester Park, and they did not come home till four in the morning because the flames looked so fine. "Could have saved that building." He said there was no system in America. In Portugal firemen drilled blindfolded—could not see when there was smoke, either! Once there was a fire down behind Mc-Micken, and he slipped into the building ahead of the firemen, crawled along on his belly, wanted to make his way to a trap-door, wanted that door open. And he was right. But the fire marshal did not like this interfering in his business and pitched him out.

At such a moment as this, when he was pitched out, you thought not of the size of his body, but of how it moved. You thought of that, too, when you saw him trim trees, sitting with his feet out a window. It might be necessary to sit that way, but certainly it was not necessary to climb from window to window on the outside of the building and on the third floor. People used to say he was like a cat, but no cat would do that. He would climb to the top of a tree, let his weight bend a branch, and drop on a roof, then remark that that was the way robbers did it in France.

III

HE went now to live on Denis Street. All his family was on this side now, only not his older daughter. His oldest son came two years after he came. His wife, his younger daughter, and his youngest son started to come two years after that, but the boy had something wrong with his eyes and was turned back at the Azores, so had to wait a year and a half for his other brother, the second of the three, Gabriel. Mrs. Kelch conducted a raffle to help Joe bring over his wife. The garden club also contributed a little.

His wife was sick from the day she came. She worked awhile in the university kitchen, and every time she leaned her abdomen against the sink she complained of pain. It was the last of September when she came. A little later there was snow, and she had never seen snow, and though the children got used to it quickly and liked it, she was afraid she would slip, and did slip, and broke her arm. She spoke no English, and the children spoke no English and were lonely. Then, too, they were living way over in Cumminsville, so Joe thought it would be better if they came to live nearer the university, and that is why they moved to Denis Street. She also had had the worry about the boy's eyes, and just when her arm was healed she fell on the ice and broke the arm again. It was late winter now. The pain in the abdomen was getting worse, and after a while Peg had to begin giving her morphine, and that was not easy on Peg either, Peg only thirteen.

Everything went wrong that next year and a half, and once when they were wrongest Joe got help from a church that was not his church, promptly went to his church and told the priest there were Christians also outside the church. He need not have done that, but he was apt to lose his temper about the church, might even call priests parasites. This feeling began back in Portugal with the burial of that girl, and was added to by other things he knew from the days before the king was killed and the queen ousted and the republic proclaimed. The feeling, of course, had nothing to do with his idea of God. He did not say much about God, but sometimes would ask Peg what she thought, and then might help her think. God was not in the sky, and not in any one kind of building, but much nearer perhaps, perhaps in the flowers, and in the sun that brought them. He said that was why he liked to get the flowers as big as he could, and, when he did, saw in that proof for his idea. When it came to such questions as confession and mass and praying on one's knees, each must make up his own mind. Nevertheless, in his talk he was very apt to mix confession and mass and hypocrisy.

One result was that when his wife was dying he would not allow the priest into the house, and when she was dead would not allow her to be buried from the church. The burial was set for early morning, in a small graveyard north a mile or two from the university, and only the daughter of the president and one or two others went with the body. Joe was not there, and none of the family, which was not because they were unfeeling, but because one doesn't go in Portugal. "We do all we kin for our people while they are alive, and when they are dead we are done with them." But when the burial party got to the graveyard—the graveyard now not of Joe's church, but of the other church—there was no one to open the chapel and no one to perform the service. The sexton was half-dressed and did not want to get dressed, and agreed to only when the daughter of the president paid him five dollars.

IV

AND now Joe wanted to live alone. It was hard for him to live with anybody, and hard for the other person too. Peg had always to be doing somersaults to find out how he was going to take a thing. Sometimes the way he acted was downright mean. She would have to go to school, but also would have to have the house just so, and by five o'clock, and the worst was he pretended not to trust her. She would visit across the street at Mrs. Beck's, and when he came home he would ask her where she had been, and she would tell him. She never lied—was not going to give him that sugar—and he knew she never lied, yet would go across the street and inquire, and that would make her want almost to kill him. Then he was so ready to give a good beating to anyone who disagreed with him. But this was not for the family only. A few plasterers working in the university basement teased him about his beard, and he asked Mr. Kelch to wait and witness while he went to slip an iron pipe into his basket. If one of those plasterers guyed him again he would settle the man. As for the beard, he was wearing that because he had told himself he would not shave for a certain length of time after his wife died. He told himself it would be for so long, and for so long it would be.

Where he went to live was in a shack back of the houses on Calhoun Street. It was near where, evenings, he pitched quoits—was good at quoits, perhaps better than anyone in the city, his team going even down into Kentucky. But what he now wanted of that quoit-field was to make it into a truck garden. As well to have something by the side, things at the university what they were. Really the ground belonged to the city, and the shack belonged to the city, originally was built for a tool-house.

The work on this garden would have to be at night, so the first thing he did was sink poles and string wires and lights. You could see his place from all around, and could now find him there any hour except perhaps for fifteen minutes when he was having lunch and a bit of conversation with the baker, even this apt to turn on the pla-a-ntes. He was interested in each single one of them, and if somebody he hated came to him and said there was a sick one off somewhere, he would go along, as a doctor might.

When it came to turning up the earth he did not use a pick, because he believed in taking out plenty at a time, and he did not use a plow, because you left too many large lumps with a plow. He used a peculiar pronged hoe that you swung over your head and that you had to know just how to use if you were not to hack off your own leg, which even he looked in danger of doing. The depth depended on the plant, and not on where the roots would go in the next two weeks, but on where they would have to go if you were to have the largest plant you could imagine. "The delicate pla-a-ntes must not be expected to push by themselves through the hard earth." And it was not enough to dig once, but you had to again and again so as to break the crust that formed on top when the sun dried the earth that the rain soaked. That is, you had to let in air. And you had to bring the rich minera-a-ls up to the roots. "You take a six-month baby, you canno expect he go get bottle milk. You must wait till he get strong, then you don't have to bother so much." He would read where a farmer with ten thousand acres had failed, and wonder why the man had not worked one acre well. You could make a good living out of one acre. "They think they kin grow the beautiful pla-a-ntes without work, but they canno. They put in the seed, then if the sun and rain come right they get a crop, otherwise they fail. What they think? In Portugal thirty acres is a big farm."

He would walk along a furrow, have a handful of one kind of seed, and at every ten inches drop three. Whoever was helping him would mean to drop three, but occasionally would drop four. Joe would see. And if instead of ten inches the seeds were dropped at eight inches or twelve inches, Joe would see. Joe himself would walk an even pace, not count, more nearly flip the seeds, and they would lie right there, and always at ten inches and out of a full hand.

He refused to tie a plant with a rag, said rag got diseased, or to tie it with string, said string cut the stems, but used raffia, said raffia was plant material and when it got wet it swelled and was stronger than before.

And he was the same about everything. Yet even if you knew this, there sometimes was something so astonishing in his results that they seemed unexplained. He had a friend, Mr. Masset, who helped him with his finances, and he gave Mrs. Masset a begonia with instructions how to take care of it, but in an English she did not understand. Later he came, and she was uneasy when she heard his boots, because the begonia was dead. That to Joe, to let a plant die, was a real sin, and when he found it out, though he did not know Mrs. Masset well, he scolded her hard and left the house. When he had got himself into a better humor he brought her another begonia, and this time she listened to what he said, and soon Mr. Masset had to be complaining that the begonia was less a flower than a tree. Joe brought an enormous pot, transplanted the flower, and it soon was even more a tree, and this notwithstanding it had only the sunlight that shone through a window. At last he agreed to cut it down, but it right away shot up from the bottom again.

So he had the work on his garden, and the work at the university, and the help he gave the teachers with their war gardens, and the help he gave his friends, nevertheless by the end of the first season had cleared four hundred dollars from truck products, and would have cleared more if he had not been so ready to give just everybody a gooda measure, as he called it. But he liked this idea of a treat with each sale, only carried the idea pretty far, would sell for twenty-five cents a quart what in market they were selling for seventy-five, and his vegetables were fresh because he simply could not be made to pick anything till the buyer was there and waiting. Mr. Masset would remind him how, when spring came, he never had money to buy seeds and had to borrow. Immediately he would argue—ah, you wrong!—would say that these were his friends he was selling to, or that his pleasure was not in money, but in showing what he could do with the earth, or that he did not trust the banks. "All these people save money, save money, save money, and they can't take it with them."

He grew a pumpkin unknown in this locality, and of the vines made a corridor to shelter the path to the shack, was proud of this pumpkin, took a sample to town and had it on show at a florist's, also had a photograph, himself and the pumpkin, the pumpkin looking like a bag of flour. People used to be afraid that one of those pumpkins would fall and somebody get killed, but Joe said the vine was strong enough and would take care.

Of his butter beans he likewise made a corridor, had this corridor lighted with electric lights, and there were overhead sprinklers, so that all he had to do was turn a faucet and in half an hour the vines were watered. When the beans came it was not a case of a pod here and a pod there, but of pod next pod as close as they could squeeze, seemed just crazy to come out for him. And they were the most gorgeous butter beans anyone on Calhoun Street had ever known. So there was another photograph, himself and three pods, the pods half as long as his arm, his cigar cocked toward heaven and something huge bulging in one pocket of his bulging trousers.

For his tomatoes he selected his own seeds—read what he could find of Luther Burbank, but said anyone with common sense and money could do the same. One sprout looked particularly strong, so he took all the others from the box where he was growing them, gave the whole earth to the one, added manure to the earth till manure and earth were half and half, worked the manure to the bottom, then built a trellis, telling everyone who watched that the usual bunching of branches was wrong, that you ought to place the branches so that each got the sun on both sides. This plant grew as the begonia grew, attained a spread of thirty feet and yielded 288 tomatoes—one plant! On another plant a single tomato weighed two and a half pounds. He grew a plant by his method as against a professor by a professor's method, and got twenty-five more tomatoes than the professor. He had a yellow variety as big as his red variety. His carrots, when he gathered them on a rainy chilly night, filled two wheelbarrows. He got as high as twelve ears of corn from one stalk. Besides, he had string beans, cabbages, radishes, potatoes, grapes, garlic, red beets, mangoes, was able to grow so many kinds because he had more than one kind in a bed, set a small plant next a large, had one growing low while the other was growing high, and both got the sun. Every space, no matter how small, had something on it. And all grew big, and all came from less than an acre that did not belong to him and that he had to work nights, and that he began to work in the first place because he was disillusioned.

The guarding of the shack, meantime, he left to his dog. This was the third dog since he reached America. The first stepped off a curb on McMillan Street and was killed. That dog had meant so much to Joe, having come right after his wife died and things were black, and Peg was there when he threw himself on the ground and wept. The second dog would go into his pocket and get out a ball, a small black dog who one day was lost, more probably stolen, and Joe gave advice to everybody to seize that dog no matter where found, in whoever's automobile or back yard, he to take all responsibility. He had called that dog Amigo. And he called the present one Amigo. All day Amigo was in and out of the shack, the shack full of dirt because both Joe and Amigo brought their belongings in. Joe always went half and half with a dog, had two places to sleep, and when the bedding in the one was changed, it was changed in the other also.

But he was not well. His son Gabriel came one night and found his father on the floor, unconscious, the alarm clock lying off in a corner as if thrown there. When finally he could be waked he remembered only that he had been winding the clock and perhaps had felt a bit dizzy. He said he had not been right since that day he jumped into the fire net and landed on the tip of his spine.

v

THEN it got about that Doctor Dabney meant to resign. "Doctor Dabney resign—Joe resign." That is what Joe said, and slapped down his hand, but perhaps was pretty close to resigning anyway.

He turned up at the Thomson estate. Doctor Dabney's daughter was a Thomson, the same woman who helped Joe bury his wife. "I come to work for you." He said that and nothing else, nothing about salary, nothing about what he planned to do or where he planned to stay, just kept repeating he would come. And came. He settled in a room on the second floor of the garage, locked the door, put the key into his pocket, and let no one in. "I positively can smell that room way down here." That is what Mrs. Thomson said to him one morning, and what he answered, after having drawn up and thrown back his head, was, "I didn't think you'd lie."

Besides his dog and his tools he had brought with him a three-legged cat. To the cat the Thomsons objected. A cat would kill birds. Joe said it would not, then when pressed said it would kill nothing but sparrows. But the Thomsons had had experiences with a cat, another cat, a Mister Peter, and nobody knew better than Joe what those experiences had been. Mister Peter, a beast so huge that Mr. Kelch had fled, thinking it had escaped from the Zoo, had killed two chicks under Mrs. Dabney's eyes, and there had been an important family conference at the end of which Joe had been consulted and had handed down his opinion. "Shame to kill that cat." (The exact words were, "ke-el that cat.") He said he would himself take the cat and lock it nights into a room at McMicken. Near a window of that room was a tree, and in a few days Mister Peter had got the habit of reaching out now and then to help himself to a sparrow, once reached too far and fell to the ground and was killed. Joe buried him on the spot where he died.

All this was now recalled apropos of the three-legged cat, and Joe listened, and again handed down his opinion. "I arrange that this here cat will not ke-el any bird." So the three-legged cat stayed. The dog stayed too.

The work on the estate had begun everywhere at once, things in a mess as always when he was beginning, because, though he worked at one point, he also was throwing up the ground at another. He felt that now at last he had what he always wanted—land enough and money enough. All that to the side of the house and beyond the first trees was pasture, and this he graded for a vast lawn. The operations were mammoth. He tore up trees, planted trees, laid down sod, and at the same time was starting flower-beds. Around the heavier-stalked flowers, as around the trees, as around every shrub, he dug a moat, the moat to be a kind of basin that he could regularly fill with water and so be sure that the deeper roots were really reached. Back of the garage he was starting a tennis-court. Back of the house he was starting the truck garden. For the truck garden he had literally to make the earth, laid it down load after load till the whole was on the level of the street. Much of all this had once more to be done at night, the lighting different from that on Calhoun Street—only a single lamp high over the middle of the garden, but so powerful that the neighbors at long distances complained of the way it glared into their sleeping-windows.

"Good si-ile is what you need." The old phrase was back on his tongue again. "Manures and water is what you need." He always pluralized the word manure, and the manure kept coming, but all he could think of was more manure. He said he knew of a stable where there was a great heap, and of a cart that he could buy for twenty-five dollars, and of a man from whom he could borrow a horse in a return for part-time use of the cart. Then through all the winter he hauled, cartload after cartload, till one day there was a terrible screaming back at the barn. The Portuguese was arguing with a German. Mrs. Thomson came running. The German was threatening to kill Joe and to sue the estate, said Joe had removed not only the manure bargained for, but had dug up the earth under the manure, and the holes had filled with water and drowned the chickens. Joe denied everything, and was incensed when a small settlement was made in favor of the German. "I try save you money, and that way you spend. He would not have ke-eled me and would not have sued you."

In winter Joe got up at 4:30, in summer at 3:30, worked till 7:30, then came in for a big breakfast. After breakfast he rested a half-hour, then worked till 11:30 or 12:30, depending on the heat, when he ate his dinner, began it with the invariable remark that he must have gasoline for his eng-i-ine. Then a siesta of two hours. After both dinner and supper he talked with his dog, an intimate, earnest conversation, the way a hard-working man may set aside a little regular time for his wife. Then the sprinkling, which took as long as it took, usually till 1 a.m. Mrs. Thomson had forever to be telling him to rest, and one reason she would give would be that the family also would like a little rest, at which he would agree to stop playing his guitar, but not to stop sprinkling.

He was preparing the inside of the garage for Halloween, had got it like an autumn garden with dried leaves, dried sheaves, dried branches, all the most wonderful colors. No doubt he worked too hard, because suddenly he was so sick he had to be carried to the second floor to his bed. Yet when the party was at its height he reappeared, slowly descended the steps, and began to dance as he always had for the children at their parties. It was an extraordinary dancing. Everybody laughed and shouted. Then, again suddenly, he was so sick he had to be carried to his bed.

Christmas day began cold and clear. He did not spend it at the Thomsons' but over near the university, walking with his dog. All his dogs walked just behind him and a little to the left. But today he was tossing a ball and the dog dashing after it, at a street corner dashed into an automobile and was killed. Next morning he brought the body to Mr. Kupka's shop, slunk in with the body thrown over the back of his neck, wanted Mr. Kupka to remove the hide, wanted to keep the hide for the memory. He was very broken.

Then spring came, and Mrs. Thomson offered to have the ground plowed to exactly the eighteen inches that he required. He would not hear of it even though he was sick, wanted to turn up his own ground, and all day could be seen half down in some ditch, swinging to left and right with the same pronged tool he used on Calhoun Street. When one of the prongs broke off he went to the blacksmith and stayed with the blacksmith hour after hour till the new tool was made, said he thought of putting the tool on the market, said it would dig five times as fast as any other tool, and that the laborers who claimed they could not use it were either stupid or lazy, but perhaps both. He was always discharging one and employing another.

As the spring advanced the estate was becoming what from the beginning he dreamed, one of the finest in the country. Sundays people visited from everywhere, and he liked it. But the old sore was giving him no peace. He was having trouble with his eyes, besides, some chronic affection for which he could not be made to go to a doctor. He said he was going to die, so why should he put himself to a course of treatment? Another man on the estate began having trouble with his eyes, and still Joe would not go to a doctor. Only when he was reminded that the children might begin having trouble with their eyes he went. The children loved him and feared him.

The eyes got better under treatment, but the old sore was worse and worse. He had now to lie down whether he wanted to or not, then had to go to a doctor, then to a hospital where he was kept weeks and told nothing. It was Mrs. Thomson herself had to tell him he had cancer. He took the news stoically. A few hours later he decided he must return to Portugal, and right away. Everything these last years had to be right away. He said the doctors there might help him, but what in his heart he wanted was to see Portugal once more. He drove everybody, Mrs. Thomson, Congressman Longworth, the immigration people, and actually was on the sea, from Cincinnati, five days after he made up his mind. He had caused such a commotion that those around him were angry with him, and when Mrs. Thomson got him to the railway station she told him so. "Death is master, not I." That was his answer. He was weeping.

He reached Portugal, but Portugal was not what he thought, and seven weeks after she parted with him Mrs. Thomson had a telegram saying he was back, was at Ellis Island, and had with him his daughter and his daughter's two children, and that he needed one hundred and ninety dollars. The daughter was the oldest, the one he had taught gymnastics back there in the big house in Lisbon, and it meant that he had them all, had moved them, as someone seeing them said, the way a dog moves a litter of pups.

The voyage had frightfully exhausted him. When he got to Cincinnati there was question of a blood transfusion, and he did not know where Peg was living, so advertised for her in a newspaper, and when she came even before the paper was on the street he broke down altogether. He blamed himself, said he had not been just to her when she was a girl and visited afternoons across the street at Mrs. Beck's. It was hard to see him that way. But in a few days he was better, called on Mrs. Thomson, had smuggled in for her some shoots of a Portuguese grape by sewing them into his clothes. He wanted her to advise him what to do about the operation, and she urged him to it. The Portuguese doctors also had urged him. In consequence he was admitted to the hospital on May 31st, was operated several days later, and discharged four months later, on October 5th. As usual, there had to be a photograph, himself and the surgeons who, as he exclaimed all day and to everyone, had saved his life.

Again he called on Mrs. Thomson, took it for granted he was to go on with the estate, and was stunned when he learned he was not. The surgeons had told her he must not do such heavy work again, but what he felt was that she had not been fully frank with him. "Why didn't you let me die? You had the chance to. You know that if I can't make things grow I have no life." After a time he pretended to understand, but something had come between them and he never again gave her his trust.

VI

WHAT he did was take a job at the university greenhouse. Really the greenhouse was built for him, and while it was building he talked, almost as when he was young, of the great things he would do. Here he saw for the first time desert plants and air-growing plants, and he threw into the work what strength he had left. But the place was small, and whatever he grew multiplied so fast that soon there was not a foot of space in which to put anything or to work. And the time was coming too, and quickly, when he could not work, and when, if it stormed in the night, it was Peg who had to get up and shut the greenhouse windows.

Then he must give up the greenhouse, and it came to be common talk that Portuguese Joe had not long to live. At the university it was realized something had to be done, and he was sent to the medical college as night watchman. He arrived with a few sick plants.

His life had been in the open air and close to the earth, and the idea that now at the end there should be a round of rooms with a time-clock was absurd. The clock kept getting out of order. "The clock is being

fixed, but it won't work." He said that, and his face gave away nothing. On a cold night he did not shut the cellar windows, and by morning the pipes were frozen. And another night there was a blizzard, and
by morning the snow had to be shoveled out of the seminar-room.
Concerning the last he said that the professor who used the room ought
to pull down the windows and not leave it to the night watchman, and
perhaps he was right. Commonly he started with mopping the basement. Then he made his rounds—one round. After all, if there were a
fire he was apt to smell it, had had experiences enough. So what he
did was just sit in the dark near the entrance, far back in the reclining
chair the professor of physiology had given him, his guitar in his hands,
the melody some Portuguese melody, the words any that came to his
head, of the walls, of the shadows, of the old country.

One night the professor of anatomy offered to bring him back a
Hamburger sandwich, but when the sandwich came he could not be
waked. His breathing was queer. His new dog was by his side, and
one could not be sure what the dog would do. After a time it was clear
that the dog understood and it was possible to shake Joe and slap the
bottoms of his feet, but still he did not wake. It struck the professor
that if the door-bell were rung, a sound that a night watchman's sleeping self might be expected to hear, he would wake. And he did, but it
was just as that day on Calhoun Street when the alarm clock lay off
in the corner. He was unaware that anything unusual had occurred.

He had said, when that last dog dashed into the automobile, that he
never would have another, but when another was given him took him.
This new one was a dreamy-eyed brute, stupid to look at, yet in a few
days obeyed Joe, talked with him, slept with him, and was liked by
everybody. Joe called him Amigo, as he had the others. Joe and Amigo
would come to the third floor, and mother rat be going back and forth
in the writing-desk. "Them is white rats—no touch." That is what Joe
would say, and Amigo's whole body would change, his snoot come
down on the desk, and his eyes quietly follow the movements. Or the
two would go to the basement where the rabbits were kept. "You ke-el
them, I ke-el you." Instantly Amigo would draw away, and you would
hear Joe's snicker. Or something would run along the hill opposite the

college, Amigo after it, and when he was all but on it, when his excitement was highest, remember, stop so short as almost to turn over, and look back timidly to hear what Joe was going to say. "Go ge-et 'em." Or the two would start to town, and the dog follow the street-car, Joe on the back platform, not worried in the least, till one day where the lines divide the dog got confused and took the wrong division. "When I reach McMillan he be there." But he was not. He was not at the medical college either, and did not come the next day, nor the day after, but on the third day came, and if Joe ever felt any uneasiness he showed nothing.

But not everybody liked the dog, and that was not the dog's fault. Joe would lock him nights into the best room of the college, the room that had the carpet, and not everything in that room was as it should be in the morning. And not everybody liked Joe. He had his enemies scattered back through the years. Furthermore, he was sick, and discouragement had brought him down, and he was not clean. Some nights he would rest his dirty fingers against the polished marble wall. Some mornings the washroom looked a "rum" place. One who worked with him burst out that he would kill that pig-Portuguese, another quickly suggesting that that might not pay because whoever did would hang for it. The pig-Portuguese had a good many friends on these hills.

Then one afternoon Joe and the dog were coming toward the college. The dog's feet were muddy. "You stay there." Joe punched his umbrella into the ground. The dog sat himself next the umbrella, and Joe went to find Clem. But Clem also was coming toward the building, had just got where the dog was watching the umbrella, a small crowd now gathered there because the dog was dead. No one had been by when death came, but everybody suspected foul play. Clem hurried to find Joe, met him in the hall, asked him if he knew, and Joe gave him an unforgettable look, a look three-quarters disbelief and one-quarter fear. "I think he would have lost his two sons more easily." A doctor drove up and, seeing the state Joe was in, took him away.

That night Joe came to the third floor. He had suffered, but the pain now was something else, and had he found who committed that crime, as he thought, he would not have waited on the courts. It was known he carried a knife sufficiently long to dig weeds if he liked. Next day he offered a reward of a hundred dollars. He talked so feelingly to a reporter of the *Post* that the reporter managed to get a full column onto the first page.

Joe was terribly shaken by this, and he was sick, but kept his job and was even thinking of something beyond. All along he had been much in the dean's office, had been trying to win the dean's sympathy for making the medical-college lawn into a garden. In the early days when he called on the president he kept on his hat, let his cigar droop from the corner of his mouth, came in with mud, hanging trousers, and all. But when now he called on the dean he washed his face, left his cigar outside, bowed, lifted his hat. And he had the dean's sympathy, but there were no funds and whatever was done had to be in a small way. This was hard because Joe could not now dig with his own hands. He complained and complained, at last one day simply took the whole of his own small salary and bought seeds (a part of this afterward repaid from a fund of the college stenographers).

The night of the day he bought the seeds he worked late, and next morning there were boxes and boxes, long low wooden boxes, earth in the boxes, manure on the earth, and thousands of seeds planted. The south corridor was wiped out, and in the middle corridor there was left only an aisle to allow the students into the dining-room. And in the following days he took the most feverish care, was forever moving the boxes one way or another so that they would catch the light. If a door was opened he screamed that there was a draft. The intention, of course, was to transplant to the front of the building as soon as the sprouts were strong enough. But it never came to that. The great campaign had a sudden end. Not everybody sees in the growing flower what Joe saw. One man summarized the matter with the fact that this was a college of medicine and not a college of botany. And Joe lost out.

He was rapidly losing in body too, nevertheless kept putting off the return to the hospital. Mr. and Mrs. Thomson learned they were apt to find him there in the dark near the entrance, and went to visit him, but he stood off from them and had little to say. He had less and less to say to anyone, mostly thrummed his guitar and sang of walls. And the summer came and went.

He was readmitted to the hospital late in October and operated on the 31st, a several-stage operation, the second stage on the 4th of November, and the major proceeding on the 23rd. All this he withstood pretty well. There was, of course, no thought of curing him, only of giving him relief for the short time he yet had to live. On the 13th the hospital notes report him somewhat better:

Joseph is up in a wheel chair, a little pale but still game. He seems to be back on the job and good for a few more months.

In the ward he always had a cigar or a pipe, someone each day thinking to bring him tobacco. Times past he would seem to be handing tobacco to just anyone, would half buy out a tobacconist at Christmas, and used to be scolded—to spend in a month what it took him three to earn.

Some days he was in his bed. Some days he was in his chair. Some days he was grim. Some days he was gloomy. He did not like that the nurses—those beautiful ladies—should be taking care of him. But some days he was gay and would write them verses. Then again he would say that things had been downhill for years, especially since the death of his wife. His flower-beds everywhere were in ruin or under sod. One bed at the university had had the form of a crescent, and though the flowers were gone, the form was still pushing up through the grass, like a thumb-mark somehow. He said that he always had had to fight for his right to garden, always could go only so far, always on one side or another met opposition, from the time he was a boy. Another disappointment was that none of his children had followed his profession. America needed flowers, and not out in California where any fool could throw down a few seeds and the plants spring up, but right here where the climate was difficult. Then his hope of a rock garden—a kind of place they had in Portugal, rocks and flowers, that he might have started over near Chester Park, and that would have paid for itself too —had come to nothing because he never could get either the money or the land. And his dogs, dead one after another. And people, they were not what he thought. Finally—cancer.

A friend brought a pot of flowers to the ward. He examined the flowers, worked his fingers into the dirt round the roots, thought that a little sand ought to be added to the dirt, and perhaps a little manure. But when it came time for the friend to leave the ward he must take the plant with him. "In this stinking air of sick people it would die— but when you come again tell me how it is doing."

Someone wanted to call a priest. "I have no money—maybe one hundred and fifty dollars—and perhaps I did not mop well the basement of the medical college, but I need no one to pray for me. I know my God He understand me."

On the 12th of January the notes reported him as having persecutory ideas, but as being otherwise the same. On the 16th the persecutory ideas had continued. What he imagined was that his friends were taking him for a spy on the university, and he said that that was something he could not bear. On that day he attempted to cut his throat. On the 26th he beat his head with an enamel hospital pan, but was too weak to accomplish what he meant. The pan was taken away. Next morning he was very low. Early in the afternoon the doctor was called, gave him a dose of caffeine, and at 3:25 his heart stopped. The funeral was from the chapel of the morgue. He had said to his daughter that he wanted flowers only as long as he could see them, and that none should be brought after he was dead. And none were. When the service was over, the body was taken to the department of anatomy, that too having been his wish.

AN AFTERWORD ON
"JOE"

THIS requiem—of "the truth, told lovingly" all compact—
was written by a teacher of physiology in the Cincinnati
medical school, where the grounds once flowered under
the magic of Joe's hands. Clearly, Joe had a green thumb—as the
English say of those for whom any plant will burgeon as from a
kind of loyalty. A kindred gift rewards certain other humans with
the immediate trust and lasting friendship of all animals. Just as
clearly, that gift must have been bestowed at birth on Gustav Eckstein. Eckstein's account of Joe was published in 1932—the book is
called *Lives*—as one of several biographies, the other unconsulted
subjects including a couple of turtles, a parrot, some mice that had
set up housekeeping in his desk, and a good many cockroaches
that shared with him the use of his laboratory. There is also a battered macaw that rides on his shoulder when he drives to work,
bawling out any traffic cop who may be hardy enough to impede
them. And a pigeon named Hato that traveled with Eckstein
everywhere, even attending the symphony concerts smuggled under his coat. Hato got lost one day in Japan. In vain the doctor
went from temple to temple, calling to her in the twilight.

Dr. Eckstein is most widely known, I suppose, as the author of
Noguchi. He is at work now on a companion piece—a life of the
great Pavlov—and at this writing a play of his called *The Ivory
Fan* is scheduled for production by Katharine Cornell. His most
recently published work is a unique and lovely monograph called

Canary—as important a book in its field as any that has appeared since Audubon.

Of recent years, a numerous tribe of canaries have had the free run of his laboratory, sharing it with him on such a patiently established basis of confidence that he has come in time not to enjoy them as pretty, fluttering, characterless songsters, but to know them as individual—highly individual—fellow-creatures. Their loves and their fears, their comedies and their tragedies, their loyalties and their treacheries, their traditions and their art, these he gets to know as it is given to few to know their neighbors. *Canary* is his report on his observations.

In that report he may tell you of the Sunday afternoons when Toscanini plays and the whole tribe form a fascinated golden horseshoe around the radio, either to hear the Maestro, or to accept the Ninth Symphony as an accompaniment and sing their fool heads off till the laboratory is drenched with such dawn-music as mortal ears seldom hear. Or he may tell you of the dreadful time when, through a careless window, the birds all vanished into the cold and peril of a February night. At last, by hopefully playing the piano, the little professor lured the patriarch back through the still open window. The patriarch did the rest. Father was the Caruso of the lot, and, planting himself on the sill, he took a good stance (in the manner of Mary Garden about to assault an aria) and sang as if his throat would burst, until, one by one, his children and grandchildren and great-grandchildren came hustling back out of the cold and dark to warmth and shelter. He *sang* them home. But no matter what the incident, you will, I think, enjoy Eckstein's offhand way of reporting it.

I must, however, confess a strong suspicion that the more austere scientists will shudder at his flagrant anthropomorphism, which is as marked (and as full of fond chuckles) as Uncle Remus's. He himself seems uncomfortably aware of this, rather in the manner of a small boy who knows he is doing something of which his elders will mysteriously disapprove, who regrets that fact, but who intends to go on doing it just the same. I hope he will. I am on his side in the matter. I believe that so, and only so, he can arrive by divination at knowledge inaccessible to those colder students who are rheumatically stiff from having been prostrate overlong before the inanimate.

When, in the coffee-strainer which Eckstein will have provided as a nest, the great moment approaches for the young to emerge from their shells, he is privileged to attend, as were the common people of France when their queen was brought to bed. But more considerate than they ever were—the secret of his relations with the canaries is a profound courtesy—he keeps his distance. Through a microphone built in to the nest he can hear, "inordinately loud and clear," the anvil chorus of the young bills hammering their way out. He himself may be scrupulous to credit a mechanically minded young friend with having perfected this device by which, far off at his desk, with earpieces adjusted, he can, without frightening the mother-bird (and without interrupting the work for which the school pays him), attend the eternal drama of the nest. But it is my own guess that a far more fruitful and important part of his equipment as an observer is something at once more sensitive, rarer, and less susceptible of fabrication. I mean the listening heart. If you must also have a name for the medium, the temperature, the conditioned atmosphere in which the observations are made, only one occurs to me. The word is "love."

Perhaps that might have gone without saying. The years have been many, and the distance from Assisi to Cincinnati is considerable, but Gustav Eckstein scarcely needs explanation in a world that still remembers that "divine demagogue" who long ago in Italy called the lark in the sky his sister and the donkey in the lane his brother. St. Francis made it easier for us to recognize the phenomenon of any man entering humbly and joyfully into the fellowship of creation. If you then make the sterile comment that Eckstein is, however, a poet rather than a scientist, I shall abstractedly agree with you, provided you do not also attempt to bootleg the implication that he is therefore any less likely to arrive at the truth.

A. W.

A CHRISTMAS GARLAND

Woven by

MAX BEERBOHM

A CHRISTMAS GARLAND
WOVEN BY MAX BEERBOHM
PUBLISHED 1912 BY E. P. DUTTON & CO., INC., NEW YORK

REPRINTED BY ARRANGEMENT WITH THE PUBLISHERS. NO PART OF THIS
WORK MAY BE REPRODUCED IN ANY FORM WITHOUT THE PERMISSION OF
THE PUBLISHERS

A CHRISTMAS GARLAND

THE MOTE IN THE MIDDLE DISTANCE
BY H*NRY J*M*S

IT was with the sense of a, for him, very memorable something that he peered now into the immediate future, and tried, not without compunction, to take that period up where he had, prospectively, left it. But just where the deuce *had* he left it? The consciousness of dubiety was, for our friend, not, this morning, quite yet clean-cut enough to outline the figures on what she had called his "horizon," between which and himself the twilight was indeed of a quality somewhat intimidating. He had run up, in the course of time, against a good number of "teasers"; and the function of teasing them back—of, as it were, giving them, every now and then, "what for"—was in him so much a habit that he would have been at a loss had there been, on the face of it, nothing to lose. Oh, he always had offered rewards, of course—had ever so liberally pasted the windows of his soul with staring appeals, minute descriptions, promises that knew no bounds. But the actual recovery of the article—the business of drawing and crossing the cheque, blotched though this were with tears of joy—had blankly appeared to him rather in the light of a sacrilege, casting, he sometimes felt, a palpable chill on the fervour of the next quest. It was just this fervour that was threatened as, raising himself on his elbow, he stared at the foot of his bed. That his eyes refused to rest there for more than the fraction of an instant, may be taken—*was,* even then, taken by Keith Tantalus—as a hint of his recollection that after all the phenomenon wasn't to be singular. Thus the exact repetition, at the foot of Eva's bed, of the shape pendulous at the foot of *his* was hardly enough to account for the fixity with which he envisaged it, and for which he was to find, some years later, a motive in the (as it turned out) hardly generous fear that Eva had already made the great investigation "on her own." Her very regular breathing presently reassured him that, if she *had* peeped into "her" stocking, she must have done so in sleep. Whether he should wake her now, or wait for their nurse to wake them both in due course, was a problem presently solved by a new development. It was plain that his sister was now watching him between her eyelashes. He had half expected that. She really was—he had often told her that she really was—magnificent; and her magnificence was never more obvious than in the pause that elapsed before she all of a sudden remarked "They so very indubitably *are,* you know!"

It occurred to him as befitting Eva's remoteness, which was a part of Eva's magnificence, that her voice emerged somewhat muffled by the bedclothes. She was ever, indeed, the most telephonic of her sex. In talking to Eva you always had, as it were, your lips to the receiver. If you didn't try to meet her fine eyes, it was that you simply couldn't hope to: there were too many dark, too many buzzing and bewildering and all frankly not negotiable leagues in between. Snatches of other voices seemed often to intertrude themselves in the parley; and your loyal effort not to overhear these was complicated by your fear of missing what Eva might be twittering. "Oh, you certainly haven't, my dear, the trick of propinquity!" was a thrust she had once parried by saying that, in that case, *he* hadn't—to which his unspoken rejoinder that she had caught her tone from the peevish young women at the Central seemed to him (if not perhaps in the last, certainly in the last but one, analysis) to lack finality. With Eva, he had found, it was always safest to "ring off." It was with a certain sense of his rashness in the matter, therefore, that he now, with an air of feverishly "holding the line," said "Oh, as to that!"

Had *she,* he presently asked himself, "rung off"? It was characteristic of our friend—was indeed "him all over"—that his fear of what she was going to say was as nothing to his fear of what she might be going to leave unsaid. He had, in his converse with her, been never so conscious as now of the intervening leagues; they had never so insistently beaten the drum of his ear; and he caught himself in the act of awfully computing, with a certain statistical passion, the distance between Rome and Boston. He has never been able to decide which of these points he was psychically the nearer to at the moment when Eva, replying "Well, one does, anyhow, leave a margin for the pretext, you know!" made him, for the first time in his life, wonder whether she were not more magnificent than even he had ever given her credit for being. Perhaps it was to test this theory, or perhaps merely to gain time, that he now raised himself to his knees, and, leaning with outstretched arm towards the foot of his bed, made as though to touch the stocking which Santa Claus had, overnight, left dangling there. His posture, as he stared obliquely at Eva, with a sort of beaming defiance, recalled to him something seen in an "illustration." This reminiscence, however—if such it was, save in the scarred, the poor dear old woebegone and so very beguilingly *not* refractive mirror of the moment—took a peculiar twist from Eva's behaviour. She had, with startling suddenness, sat bolt upright, and looked to him as if she were overhearing some tragedy at the other end of the wire, where, in the nature of things, she was unable to arrest it. The gaze she fixed on her extravagant kinsman was of a kind to make him wonder how he contrived to remain, as he beautifully did, rigid. His prop was possibly the reflection that flashed on him that, if *she* abounded in attenuations, well, hang it all, so did *he!* It was simply a difference of plane. Readjust the "values," as painters say, and there you were! He was to feel that he was only too crudely "there" when, leaning further forward, he laid a chubby forefinger on the stocking, causing that receptacle to rock ponderously to and fro. This effect was more expected than the tears which started to Eva's eyes, and the intensity with which "Don't you," she exclaimed, "see?"

"The mote in the middle distance?" he asked. "Did you ever, my dear, know me to see anything else? I tell you it blocks out everything. It's a cathedral, it's a herd of elephants, it's the whole habitable globe. Oh, it's, believe me, of an obsessiveness!" But his sense of the one thing it *didn't* block out from his purview enabled him to launch at Eva a speculation as to just how far Santa Claus had, for the particular occasion, gone. The gauge, for both of them, of this seasonable distance seemed almost blatantly suspended in the silhouettes of the two stockings. Over and above the basis of (presumably) sweetmeats in the toes and heels, certain extrusions stood for a very plenary fulfilment of desire. And, since Eva *had* set her heart on a doll of ample proportions and practicable eyelids—*had* asked that most admirable of her sex, their mother, for it with not less directness than he himself had put into his demand for a sword and helmet—her coyness now struck Keith as lying near to, at indeed a hardly measurable distance from, the borderline of his patience. If she didn't *want* the doll, why the deuce had she made such a point of getting it? He was perhaps on the verge of putting this question to her, when, waving her hand to include both stockings, she said "Of course, my dear, you *do* see. There they are, and you know I know you know we wouldn't, either of us, dip a finger into them." With a vibrancy of tone that seemed to bring her voice quite close to him, "One doesn't," she added, "violate the shrine—pick the pearl from the shell!"

Even had the answering question "Doesn't one just?" which for an instant hovered on the tip of his tongue, been uttered, it could not have obscured for Keith the change which her magnificence had wrought in him. Something, perhaps, of the bigotry of the convert was already discernible in the way that, averting his eyes, he said "One doesn't even peer." As to whether, in the years that have elapsed since he said this either of our friends (now adult) has, in fact, "peered," is a question which, whenever I call at the house, I am tempted to put to one or other of them. But any regret I may feel in my invariable failure to "come up to the scratch" of yielding to this temptation is balanced, for me, by my impression—my sometimes all but throned and anointed certainty—that the answer, if vouchsafed, would be in the negative.

P.C., X, 36

BY R*D**RD K*PL*NG

Then it's collar 'im tight,
  In the name o' the Lawd!
'Ustle 'im, shake 'im till 'e's sick!
  Wot, 'e *would,* would 'e? Well,
  Then yer've got ter give 'im 'Ell,
An' it's trunch, trunch, truncheon does the trick.

POLICE STATION DITTIES.

I HAD spent Christmas Eve at the Club, listening to a grand pow-wow between certain of the choicer sons of Adam. Then Slushby had cut in. Slushby is one who writes to newspapers and is theirs obediently "HUMANITARIAN." When Slushby cuts in, men remember they have to be up early next morning.

Sharp round a corner on the way home, I collided with something firmer than the regulation pillar-box. I righted myself after the recoil and saw some stars that were very pretty indeed. Then I perceived the nature of the obstruction.

"Evening, Judlip," I said sweetly, when I had collected my hat from the gutter. "Have I broken the law, Judlip? If so, I'll go quiet."

"Time yer was in bed," grunted X, 36. "Yer Ma'll be lookin' out for yer."

This from the friend of my bosom! It hurt. Many were the night-beats I had been privileged to walk with Judlip, imbibing curious lore that made glad the civilian heart of me. Seven whole 8 x 5 inch note-books had I pitmanised to the brim with Judlip. And now to be repulsed as one of the uninitiated! It hurt horrid.

There is a thing called Dignity. Small boys sometimes stand on it. Then they have to be kicked. Then they get down, weeping. I don't stand on Dignity.

"What's wrong, Judlip?" I asked, more sweetly than ever. "Drawn a blank tonight?"

"Yuss. Drawn a blank blank blank. 'Aven't 'ad so much as a kick at a lorst dorg. Christmas Eve ain't wot it was." I felt for my note-book. "Lawd! I remembers the time when the drunks and disorderlies down this street was as thick as flies on a fly-paper. One just picked 'em orf with one's finger and thumb. A bloomin' battew, that's wot it wos."

"The night's yet young, Judlip," I insinuated, with a jerk of my thumb at the flaring windows of the "Rat and Blood Hound." At that moment the saloon-door swung open, emitting a man and woman who walked with linked arms and exceeding great care.

Judlip eyed them longingly as they tacked up the street. Then he sighed. Now, when Judlip sighs the sound is like unto that which issues from the vent of a Crosby boiler when the cog-gauges are at 260° F.

"Come, Judlip!" I said. "Possess your soul in patience. You'll soon find someone to make an example of. Meanwhile"—I threw back my head and smacked my lips—"the usual, Judlip?"

In another minute I emerged through the swing-door, bearing a furtive glass of that same "usual," and nipped down the mews where my friend was wont to await these little tokens of esteem.

"To the Majesty of the Law, Judlip!"

When he had honoured the toast, I scooted back with the glass, leaving him wiping the beads off his beard-bristles. He was in his philosophic mood when I rejoined him at the corner.

"Wot am I?" he said, as we paced along. "A bloomin' cypher. Wot's the sarjint? 'E's got the Inspector over 'im. Over above the Inspector there's the Sooprintendent. Over above 'im's the old red-tape-masticatin' Yard. Over above that there's the 'Ome Sec. Wot's 'e? A cypher, like me. Why?" Judlip looked up at the stars. "Over above 'im's We Dunno Wot. Somethin' wot issues its horders an' regulations an' divisional injunctions, inscrootable like, but p'remptory; an' we 'as ter see as 'ow they're carried out, not arskin' no questions, but each man goin' about 'is dooty."

" 'Is dooty,' " said I, looking up from my note-book. "Yes, I've got that."

"Life ain't a bean-feast. It's a 'arsh reality. An' them as makes it a bean-feast 'as got to be 'arshly dealt with accordin'. That's wot the Force is put 'ere for from Above. Not as 'ow we ain't fallible. We makes our mistakes. An' when we makes 'em we sticks to 'em. For the honour o' the Force. Which same is the jool Britannia wears on 'er bosom as a charm against hanarchy. That's wot the brarsted old Beaks don't understand. Yer remember Smithers of our Div?"

I remembered Smithers—well. As fine, up-standing, square-toed, bullet-headed, clean-living a son of a gun as ever perjured himself in the box. There was nothing of the softy about Smithers. I took off my billicock to Smithers' memory.

"Sacrificed to public opinion? Yuss," said Judlip, pausing at a front door and flashing his 45 c.p. down the slot of a two-grade Yale. "Sacrificed to a parcel of screamin' old women wot ort ter 'ave gorn down on their knees an' thanked Gawd for such a protector. 'E'll be out in another 'alf year. Wot'll 'e do then, pore devil? Go a bust on 'is conduc' money an' throw in 'is lot with them same hexperts wot 'ad a 'oly terror of 'im." Then Judlip swore gently.

"What should you do, O Great One, if ever it were your duty to apprehend him?"

"Do? Why, yer blessed innocent, yer don't think I'd shirk a fair clean cop? Same time, I don't say as 'ow I wouldn't 'andle 'im tender like, for sake o' wot 'e wos. Likewise 'cos 'e'd be a stiff customer to tackle. Likewise 'cos——"

He had broken off, and was peering fixedly upwards at an angle of 85° across the moonlit street. " 'Ullo!" he said in a hoarse whisper.

Striking an average between the direction of his eyes—for Judlip, when on the job, has a soul-stirring squint—I perceived someone in the act of emerging from a chimney-pot.

Judlip's voice clove the silence. "Wot are yer doin' hup there?"

The person addressed came to the edge of the parapet. I saw then that he had a hoary white beard, a red ulster with the hood up, and what looked like a sack over his shoulder. He said something or other in a voice like a concertina that has been left out in the rain.

"I dessay," answered my friend. "Just you come down, an' we'll see about that."

The old man nodded and smiled. Then—as I hope to be saved—he came floating gently down through the moonlight, with the sack over his shoulder and a young fir-tree clasped to his chest. He alighted in a friendly manner on the curb beside us.

Judlip was the first to recover himself. Out went his right arm, and the airman was slung round by the scruff of the neck, spilling his sack in the road. I made a bee-line for his shoulder-blades. Burglar or no burglar, he was the best airman out, and I was muchly desirous to know the precise nature of the apparatus under his ulster. A back-hander from Judlip's left caused me to hop quickly aside. The prisoner was squealing and whimpering. He didn't like the feel of Judlip's knuckles at his cervical vertebræ.

"Wot wos yer doin' hup there?" asked Judlip, tightening the grip.

"I'm S-Santa Claus, Sir. P-please, Sir, let me g-go."

"Hold him," I shouted. "He's a German."

"It's my dooty ter caution yer that wotever yer say now may be used in hevidence against yer, yer old sinner. Pick up that there sack, an' come along o' me."

The captive snivelled something about peace on earth, good will to-ward men.

"Yuss," said Judlip. "That's in the Noo Testament, ain't it? The Noo Testament contains some uncommon nice readin' for old gents an' young ladies. But it ain't included in the librery o' the Force. We confine ourselves to the Old Testament—O.T., 'ot. An' 'ot you'll get it. Hup with that sack, an' quick march!"

I have seen worse attempts at a neck-wrench, but it was just not slippery enough for Judlip. And the kick that Judlip then let fly was a thing of beauty and a joy for ever.

"Frog's-march him!" I shrieked, dancing. "For the love of heaven, frog's-march him!"

Trotting by Judlip's side to the Station, I reckoned it out that if

Slushby had not been at the Club I should not have been here to see. Which shows that even Slushbys are put into this world for a purpose.

OUT OF HARM'S WAY

BY A. C. B*NS*N

CHAPTER XLII.—CHRISTMAS

MORE and more, as the tranquil years went by, Percy found himself able to draw a quiet satisfaction from the regularity, the even sureness, with which, in every year, one season succeeded to another. In boyhood he had felt always a little sad at the approach of autumn. The yellowing leaves of the lime trees, the creeper that flushed to so deep a crimson against the old grey walls, the chrysanthemums that shed so prodigally their petals on the smooth green lawn—all these things, beautiful and wonderful though they were, were somehow a little melancholy also, as being signs of the year's decay. Once, when he was fourteen or fifteen years old, he had overheard a friend of the family say to his father "How the days are drawing in!"—a remark which set him thinking deeply, with an almost morbid abandonment to gloom, for quite a long time. He had not then grasped the truth that in exactly the proportion in which the days draw in they will, in the fullness of time, draw out. This was a lesson that he mastered in later years. And, though the waning of summer never failed to touch him with the sense of an almost personal loss, yet it seemed to him a right thing, a wise ordination, that there should be these recurring changes. Those men and women of whom the poet tells us that they lived in "a land where it was always afternoon"—could they, Percy often wondered, have felt quite that thankfulness which on a fine afternoon is felt by us dwellers in ordinary climes? Ah, no! Surely it is because we are made acquainted with the grey sadness of twilight, the solemn majesty of the nighttime, the faint chill of the dawn, that we set so high a value on the more meridional hours. If there were no autumn, no winter, then spring and summer would lose, not all indeed, yet an appreciable part of their sweet savour for us. Thus, as his mind matured, Percy came to be very glad of the gradual changes of the year. He found in them *a rhythm,* as he once described it in his diary; and this he liked very much indeed. He was aware that in his own character, with its tendency to waywardness, to caprice, to disorder, there was an almost grievous lack of his *rhythmic* quality. In the sure and seemly progression of the months, was there not for him a desirable exemplar, a needed corrective? He was so liable to moods in which he rebelled against the performance of some quite simple duty, some appointed task—moods in which he said to himself "H-ng it! I will not do this," or "Oh, b-th-r! I shall not do that!" But it was clear that Nature herself never spoke thus. Even as a passenger in a frail barque on the troublous ocean will keep his eyes directed towards some upstanding rock on the far horizon, finding thus inwardly for himself, or hoping to find, a more stable equilibrium, a deeper tranquillity, than is his, so did Percy daily devote a certain portion of his time to quiet communion with the almanac.

There were times when he was sorely tempted to regret a little that some of the feasts of the Church were "moveable." True, they moved only within strictly prescribed limits, and in accordance with certain unalterable, wholly justifiable rules. Yet, in the very fact that they did move, there seemed—to use an expressive slang phrase of the day— "something not quite nice." It was therefore the fixed feasts that pleased Percy best, and on Christmas Day, especially, he experienced a temperate glow which would have perhaps surprised those who knew him only slightly.

By reason of the athletic exercises of his earlier years, Percy had retained in middle life a certain lightness and firmness of tread; and this on Christmas morning, between his rooms and the Cathedral, was always so peculiarly elastic that he might almost have seemed to be rather running than walking. The ancient fane, with its soarings of grey columns to the dimness of its embowed roof, the delicate traceries of the organ screen, the swelling notes of the organ, the mellow shafts of light filtered through the stained-glass windows whose hues were

as those of emeralds and rubies and amethysts, the stainless purity of
the surplices of clergy and choir, the sober richness of Sunday bonnets
in the transept, the faint yet heavy fragrance exhaled from the hot-
water pipes—all these familiar things, appealing, as he sometimes felt,
almost too strongly to that sensuous side of his nature which made him
so susceptible to the paintings of Mr. Leader, of Sir Luke Fildes, were
on Christmas morning more than usually affecting by reason of that
note of quiet joyousness, of peace and good will, that pervaded the
lessons of the day, the collect, the hymn, the sermon.

It was this spiritual aspect of Christmas that Percy felt to be hardly
sufficiently regarded, or at least dwelt on, nowadays, and he sometimes
wondered whether the modern Christmas had not been in some degree
inspired and informed by Charles Dickens. He had for that writer a
very sincere admiration, though he was inclined to think that his true
excellence lay not so much in faithful portrayal of the life of his times,
or in gift of sustained narration, or in those scenes of pathos which
have moved so many hearts in so many quiet homes, as in the power
of inventing highly fantastic figures, such as Mr. Micawber or Mr.
Pickwick. This view Percy knew to be somewhat heretical, and, consti-
tutionally averse from the danger of being suspected of "talking for
effect," he kept it to himself; but, had anyone challenged him to give
his opinion, it was thus that he would have expressed himself. In regard to Christmas, he could not help wishing that Charles Dickens had
laid more stress on its spiritual element. It was right that the feast
should be an occasion for good cheer, for the savoury meats, the steaming bowl, the blazing log, the traditional games. But was not the modern world, with its almost avowed bias towards materialism, too little
apt to think of Christmas as also a time for meditation, for taking
stock, as it were, of the things of the soul? Percy had heard that in
London nowadays there was a class of people who sate down to their
Christmas dinners in public hotels. He did not condemn this practice.
He never condemned a thing, but wondered, rather, whether it were
right, and could not help feeling that somehow it was not. In the course
of his rare visits to London he had more than once been inside of one
of the large new hotels that had sprung up—these "great caravanseries,"

as he described them in a letter to an old school-fellow who had been engaged for many years in Chinese mission work. And it seemed to him that the true spirit of Christmas could hardly be acclimatized in such places, but found its proper resting-place in quiet, detached homes, where were gathered together only those connected with one another by ties of kinship, or of long and tested friendship.

He sometimes blamed himself for having tended more and more, as the quiet, peaceful, tranquil years went by, to absent himself from even those small domestic gatherings. And yet, might it not be that his instinct for solitude at this season was a right instinct, at least for him, and that to run counter to it would be in some degree unacceptable to the Power that fashioned us? Thus he allowed himself to go, as it were, his own way. After morning service, he sate down to his Christmas fare alone, and then, when the simple meal was over, would sit and think in his accustomed chair, falling perhaps into one of those quiet dozes from which, because they seemed to be so natural a result, so seemly a consummation, of his thoughts, he did not regularly abstain. Later, he sallied forth, with a sense of refreshment, for a brisk walk among the fens, the sedges, the hedgerows, the reed-fringed pools, the pollard willows that would in due course be putting forth their tender shoots of palest green. And then, once more in his rooms, with the curtains drawn and the candles lit, he would turn to his bookshelves and choose from among them some old book that he knew and loved, or maybe some quite new book by that writer whose works were most dear to him because in them he seemed always to know so precisely what the author would say next, and because he found in their fine-spun repetitions a singular repose, a sense of security, an earnest of calm and continuity, as though he were reading over again one of those wise copy-books that he had so loved in boyhood, or were listening to the sounds made on a piano by some modest, very conscientious young girl with a pale red pig-tail, practising her scales, very gently, hour after hour, next door.

PERKINS AND MANKIND

BY H. G. W*LLS

CHAPTER XX

§ 1

It was the Christmas party at Heighton that was one of the turning-points in Perkins' life. The Duchess had sent him a three-page wire in the hyperbolical style of her class, conveying a vague impression that she and the Duke had arranged to commit suicide together if Perkins didn't "chuck" any previous engagement he had made. And Perkins had felt in a slipshod sort of way—for at this period he was incapable of ordered thought—he might as well be at Heighton as anywhere. . . .

The enormous house was almost full. There must have been upwards of fifty people sitting down to every meal. Many of these were members of the family. Perkins was able to recognize them by their unconvoluted ears—the well-known Grifford ear, transmitted from one generation to another. For the rest there were the usual lot from the Front Benches and the Embassies. Evesham was there, clutching at the lapels of his coat; and the Prescotts—he with his massive mask of a face, and she with her quick, hawk-like ways, talking about two things at a time; old Tommy Strickland, with his monocle and his dropped g's, telling you what he had once said to Mr. Disraeli; Boubou Seaforth and his American wife; John Pirram, ardent and elegant, spouting old French lyrics; and a score of others.

Perkins had got used to them by now. He no longer wondered what they were "up to," for he knew they were up to nothing whatever. He reflected, while he was dressing for dinner on Christmas night, how odd it was he had ever thought of Using them. He might as well have hoped to Use the Dresden shepherds and shepherdesses that grinned out in the last stages of refinement at him from the glazed cabinets in the drawing-rooms. . . . Or the Labour Members themselves. . . .

True there was Evesham. He had shown an exquisitely open mind about the whole thing. He had at once grasped the underlying principles, thrown out some amazingly luminous suggestions. Oh yes, Evesham was a statesman, right enough. But had even he ever really *believed* in the idea of a Provisional Government of England by the Female Foundlings?

To Perkins the whole thing had seemed so simple, so imminent—a thing that needed only a little general good-will to bring it about. And now . . . Suppose his Bill *had* passed its Second Reading, suppose it had become Law, would this poor old England be by way of functioning decently—after all? Foundlings were sometimes naughty. . . .

What was the matter with the whole human race? He remembered again those words of Scragson's that had had such a depressing effect on him at the Cambridge Union—"Look here, you know! It's all a huge nasty mess, and we're trying to swab it up with a pocket handkerchief." Well, he'd given up trying to do that. . . .

§ 2

During dinner his eyes wandered furtively up and down the endless ornate table, and he felt he had been, in a sort of way, right in thinking these people were the handiest instrument to prise open the national conscience with. The shining red faces of the men, the shining white necks and arms of the women, the fearless eyes, the general free-and-easiness and spaciousness, the look of late hours counteracted by fresh air and exercise and the best things to eat and drink—what mightn't be made of these people, if they'd only Submit?

Perkins looked behind them, at the solemn young footmen passing and repassing, noiselessly, in blue and white liveries. *They* had Submitted. And it was just because they had been able to that they were no good.

"Damn!" said Perkins, under his breath.

§ 3

One of the big conifers from the park had been erected in the hall, and this, after dinner, was found to be all lighted up with electric bulbs and hung with packages in tissue paper.

The Duchess stood, a bright, feral figure, distributing these packages to the guests. Perkins' name was called out in due course and the package addressed to him was slipped into his hand. He retired with it into a corner. Inside the tissue-paper was a small morocco leather case. Inside that was a set of diamond and sapphire sleeve-links—large ones.

He stood looking at them, blinking a little.

He supposed he must put them on. But something in him, some intractably tough bit of his old self, rose up protesting—frantically.

If he couldn't Use these people, at least they weren't going to Use *him!*

"No, damn it!" he said under his breath, and, thrusting the case into his pocket, slipped away unobserved.

§ 4

He flung himself into a chair in his bedroom and puffed a blast of air from his lungs. . . . Yes, it had been a narrow escape. He knew that if he had put those beastly blue and white things on he would have been a lost soul. . . .

"You've got to pull yourself together, d'you hear?" he said to himself. "You've got to do a lot of clear, steady, merciless thinking—now, tonight. You've got to persuade yourself somehow that, Foundlings or no Foundlings, this regeneration of mankind business may still be set going—and by *you.*"

He paced up and down the room, fuming. How recapture the generous certitudes that had one by one been slipping away from him? He found himself staring vacantly at the row of books on the little shelf by his bed. One of them seemed suddenly to detach itself—he could almost have sworn afterwards that he didn't reach out for it, but that it hopped down into his hand. . . .

"Sitting Up for the Dawn"! It was one of that sociological series by which H. G. Wells had first touched his soul to finer issues when he was at the 'Varsity.

He opened it with tremulous fingers. Could it re-exert its old sway over him now?

The page he had opened it at was headed "General Cessation Day," and he began to read. . . .

"The re-casting of the calendar on a decimal basis seems a simple enough matter at first sight. But even here there are details that will have to be thrashed out. . . .

"Mr. Edgar Dibbs, in his able pamphlet 'Ten to the Rescue,' [1] advocates a twenty-hour day, and has drawn up an ingenious scheme for accelerating the motion of this planet by four in every twenty-four hours, so that the alternations of light and darkness shall be re-adjusted to the new reckoning. I think such re-adjustment would be indispensable (though I know there is a formidable body of opinion against me). But I am far from being convinced of the feasibility of Mr. Dibbs' scheme. I believe the twenty-four hour day has come to stay—anomalous though it certainly will seem in the ten-day week, the fifty-day month, and the thousand-day year. I should like to have incorporated Mr. Dibbs' scheme in my vision of the Dawn. But, as I have said, the scope of this vision is purely practical. . . .

"Mr. Albert Baker, in a paper [2] read before the South Brixton Hebdomadals, pleads that the first seven days of the decimal week should retain their old names, the other three to be called provisionally Huxleyday, Marxday, and Tolstoiday. But, for reasons which I have set forth elsewhere,[3] I believe that the nomenclature which I had originally suggested [4]—Aday, Bday, and so on to Jday—would be really the

[1] Published by the Young Self-Helpers' Press, Ipswich.
[2] "Are We Going Too Fast?"
[3] "A Midwife for the Millennium." H. G. Wells.
[4] "How to Be Happy Though Yet Unborn." H. G. Wells.

simplest way out of the difficulty. Any fanciful way of naming the days would be bad, as too sharply differentiating one day from another. What we must strive for in the Dawn is that every day shall be as nearly as possible like every other day. We must help the human units —these little pink slobbering creatures of the Future whose cradle we are rocking—to progress not in harsh jerks, but with a beautiful unconscious rhythm. . . .

"There must be nothing corresponding to our Sunday. Sunday is a canker that must be cut ruthlessly out of the social organism. At present the whole community gets 'slack' on Saturday because of the paralysis that is about to fall on it. And then 'Black Monday'!—that day when the human brain tries to readjust itself—tries to realize that the shutters are down, and the streets are swept, and the stove-pipe hats are back in their band-boxes. . . .

"Yet of course there must be holidays. We can no more do without holidays than without sleep. For every man there must be certain stated intervals of repose—of recreation in the original sense of the word. My views on the worthlessness of classical education are perhaps pretty well known to you, but I don't underrate the great service that my friend Professor Ezra K. Higgins has rendered by his discovery[1] that the word recreation originally signified a re-creating—i.e.,[2] a time for the nerve-tissues to renew themselves in. The problem before us is how to secure for the human units in the Dawn—these giants of whom we are but the fœtuses—the holidays necessary for their full capacity for usefulness to the State, without at the same time disorganizing the whole community—and them.

"The solution is really very simple. The community will be divided into ten sections—Section A, Section B, and so on to Section J. And to every section one day of the decimal week will be assigned as a 'Cessation Day.' Thus, those people who fall under Section A will rest on Aday, those who fall under Section B will rest on Bday, and so on. On every day of the year one-tenth of the population will be resting, but

[1] "Words about Words." By Ezra K. Higgins. Professor of Etymology, Abraham Z. Stubbins University, Padua, Pa., U.S.A. (2 vols.).

[2] "*Id est*"—"That is."

the other nine-tenths will be at work. The joyous hum and clang of labour will never cease in the municipal workshops. . . .

"You figure the smokeless blue sky above London dotted all over with airships in which the holiday-making tenth are re-creating themselves for the labour of next week—looking down a little wistfully, perhaps, at the workshops from which they are temporarily banished. And here I scent a difficulty. So attractive a thing will labour be in the Dawn that a man will be tempted not to knock off work when his Cessation Day comes round, and will prefer to work for no wage rather than not at all. So that perhaps there will have to be a law making Cessation Day compulsory, and the Overseers will be empowered to punish infringement of this law by forbidding the culprit to work for ten days after the first offence, twenty after the second, and so on. But I don't suppose there will often be need to put this law in motion. The children of the Dawn, remember, will not be the puny self-ridden creatures that we are. They will not say, 'Is this what I want to do?' but 'Shall I, by doing this, be (*a*) harming or (*b*) benefiting—no matter in how infinitesimal a degree—the Future of the Race?'

"Sunday must go. And, as I have hinted, the progress of mankind will be steady proportionately to its own automatism. Yet I think there would be no harm in having one—just one—day in the year set aside as a day of universal rest—a day for the searching of hearts. Heaven—I mean the Future—forbid that I should be hide-bound by dry-as-dust logic, in dealing with problems of flesh and blood. The sociologists of the past thought the grey matter of their own brains all-sufficing. They forgot that flesh is pink and blood is red. That is why they could not convert people. . . .

"The five-hundredth and last day of each year shall be a General Cessation Day. It will correspond somewhat to our present Christmas Day. But with what a difference! It will not be, as with us, a mere opportunity for relatives to make up the quarrels they have picked with each other during the past year, and to eat and drink things that will make them ill well into next year. Holly and mistletoe there will be in the Municipal Eating Rooms, but the men and women who sit down there to General Cessation High-Tea will be glowing not with a facile affection for their kith and kin, but with communal anxiety for the welfare of the great-great-grand-children of people they have never met and are never likely to meet.

"The great event of the day will be the performance of the ceremony of 'Making Way.'

"In the Dawn, death will not be the haphazard affair that it is under the present anarchic conditions. Men will not be stumbling out of the world at odd moments and for reasons over which they have no control. There will always, of course, be a percentage of deaths by misadventure. But there will be no deaths by disease. Nor, on the other hand, will people die of old age. Every child will start life knowing that (barring misadventure) he has a certain fixed period of life before him —so much and no more, but not a moment less.

"It is impossible to foretell to what average age the children of the Dawn will retain the use of all their faculties—be fully vigorous mentally and physically. We only know they will be 'going strong' at ages when we have long ceased to be any use to the State. Let us, for sake of argument, say that on the average their faculties will have begun to decay at the age of ninety—a trifle over thirty-two, by the new reckoning. That, then, will be the period of life fixed for all citizens. Every man on fulfilling that period will avail himself of the Municipal Lethal Chamber. He will 'make way'. . . .

"I thought at one time that it would be best for every man to 'make way' on the actual day when he reaches the age-limit. But I see now that this would savour of private enterprise. Moreover, it would rule out that element of sentiment which, in relation to such a thing as death, we must do nothing to mar. The children and friends of a man on the brink of death would instinctively wish to gather round him. How could they accompany him to the lethal chamber, if it were an ordinary working-day, with every moment of the time mapped out for them?

"On General Cessation Day, therefore, the gates of the lethal chambers will stand open for all those who shall in the course of the past year have reached the age-limit. You figure the wide streets filled all day long with little solemn processions—solemn and yet not in the least unhappy. . . . You figure the old man walking with a firm step in the midst of his progeny, looking around him with a clear eye at this dear world which is about to lose him. He will not be thinking of himself. He will not be wishing the way to the lethal chamber was longer. He will be filled with joy at the thought that he is about to die for the good of the race—to 'make way' for the beautiful young breed of men and women who, in simple, artistic, antiseptic garments, are disporting themselves so gladly on this day of days. They pause to salute him as he passes. And presently he sees, radiant in the sunlight, the pleasant white-tiled dome of the lethal chamber. You figure him at the gate, shaking hands all round, and speaking perhaps a few well-chosen words about the Future. . . ."

§5

It was enough. The old broom hadn't lost its snap. It had swept clean the chambers of Perkins' soul—swished away the whole accumulation of nasty little cobwebs and malignant germs. Gone were the mean doubts that had formed in him, the lethargy, the cheap cynicism. Perkins was himself again.

He saw now how very stupid it was of him to have despaired just because his own particular panacea wasn't given a chance. That Provisional Government plan of his had been good, but it was only one of an infinite number of possible paths to the Dawn. He would try others —scores of others. . . .

He must get right away out of here—tonight. He must have his car brought round from the garage—now—to a side door. . . .

But first he sat down to the writing-table, and wrote quickly:

Dear Duchess,
I regret I am called away on urgent political business. . . .
Yours faithfully
J. Perkins. . . .

He took the morocco leather case out of his pocket and enclosed it, with the note, in a large envelope.

Then he pressed the electric button by his bedside, almost feeling that this was a signal for the Dawn to rise without more ado. . . .

SOME DAMNABLE ERRORS ABOUT CHRISTMAS

BY G. K. CH*ST*RT*N

THAT it is human to err is admitted by even the most positive of our thinkers. Here we have the great difference between latter-day thought and the thought of the past. If Euclid were alive today (and I dare say he is) he would not say, "The angles at the base of an isosceles triangle are equal to one another." He would say, "To me (a very frail and fallible being, remember) it does somehow seem that these two angles have a mysterious and awful equality to one another." The dislike of schoolboys for Euclid is unreasonable in many ways; but fundamentally it is entirely reasonable. Fundamentally it is the revolt from a man who was either fallible and therefore (in pretending to infallibility) an impostor, or infallible and therefore not human.

Now, since it is human to err, it is always in reference to those things which arouse in us the most human of all our emotions—I mean the emotion of love—that we conceive the deepest of our errors. Suppose we met Euclid on Westminster Bridge, and he took us aside and confessed to us that whilst he regarded parallelograms and rhomboids with an indifference bordering on contempt, for isosceles triangles he cherished a wild romantic devotion. Suppose he asked us to accompany him to the nearest music-shop, and there purchased a guitar in order that he might worthily sing to us the radiant beauty and the radiant goodness of isosceles triangles. As men we should, I hope, respect his enthusiasm, and encourage his enthusiasm, and catch his enthusiasm. But as seekers after truth we should be compelled to regard with a dark suspicion, and to check with the most anxious care, every fact that he told us about isosceles triangles. For adoration involves a glorious obliquity of vision. It involves more than that. We do not say of Love that he is short-sighted. We do not say of Love that he is myopic. We do not say of Love that he is astigmatic. We say quite simply, Love is blind. We might go further and say, Love is deaf. That would be a profound and obvious truth. We might go further still and say, Love is dumb. But that would be a profound and obvious lie. For love is always an extraordinarily fluent talker. Love is a wind-bag, filled with a gusty wind from Heaven.

It is always about the thing that we love most that we talk most. About this thing, therefore, our errors are something more than our deepest errors: they are our most frequent errors. That is why for nearly two thousand years mankind has been more glaringly wrong on the subject of Christmas than on any other subject. If mankind had hated Christmas, he would have understood it from the first. What would have happened then, it is impossible to say. For that which is hated, and therefore is persecuted, and therefore grows brave, lives on for ever, whilst that which is understood dies in the moment of our understanding of it—dies, as it were, in our awful grasp. Between the horns of this eternal dilemma shivers all the mystery of the jolly visible world, and of that still jollier world which is invisible. And it is because Mr. Shaw and the writers of his school cannot, with all their splendid sincerity and acumen, perceive that he and they and all of us are impaled on those horns as certainly as the sausages I ate for breakfast this morning had been impaled on the cook's toasting-fork—it is for this reason, I say, that Mr. Shaw and his friends seem to me to miss the basic principle that lies at the root of all things human and divine. By the way, not all things that are divine are human. But all things that are human are divine. But to return to Christmas.

I select at random two of the more obvious fallacies that obtain. One is that Christmas should be observed as a time of jubilation. This is (I admit) quite a recent idea. It never entered into the tousled heads of the shepherds by night, when the light of the angel of the Lord shone about them and they arose and went to do homage to the Child. It never entered into the heads of the Three Wise Men. They did not bring their gifts as a joke, but as an awful oblation. It never entered into the heads of the saints and scholars, the poets and painters, of the Middle Ages. Looking back across the years, they saw in that dark and ungarnished manger only a shrinking woman, a brooding man, and a child born to sorrow. The philomaths of the eighteenth century, looking back, saw nothing at all. It is not the least of the glories of the Victorian Era that it rediscovered Christmas. It is not the least of the mistakes of the Victorian Era that it supposed Christmas to be a feast.

The splendour of the saying, "I have piped unto you, and you have not danced; I have wept with you, and you have not mourned" lies in the fact that it might have been uttered with equal truth by any man who had ever piped or wept. There is in the human race some dark spirit of recalcitrance, always pulling us in the direction contrary to that in which we are reasonably expected to go. At a funeral, the slightest thing, not in the least ridiculous at any other time, will convulse us with internal laughter. At a wedding, we hover mysteriously on the brink of tears. So it is with the modern Christmas. I find myself in agreement with the cynics in so far that I admit that Christmas, as now observed, tends to create melancholy. But the reason for this lies solely in our own misconception. Christmas is essentially a *dies iræ*. If the cynics will only make up their minds to treat it as such, even the saddest and most atrabilious of them will acknowledge that he has had a rollicking day.

This brings me to the second fallacy. I refer to the belief that "Christmas comes but once a year." Perhaps it does, according to the calendar —a quaint and interesting compilation, but of little or no practical value to anybody. It is not the calendar, but the Spirit of Man that regulates the recurrence of feasts and fasts. Spiritually, Christmas Day recurs exactly seven times a week. When we have frankly acknowledged this, and acted on this, we shall begin to realize the Day's mystical and terrific beauty. For it is only every-day things that reveal themselves to us in all their wonder and their splendour. A man who happens one day to be knocked down by a motor-bus merely utters a curse and instructs his solicitor, but a man who has been knocked down by a motor-bus every day of the year will have begun to feel that he is taking part in an august and soul-cleansing ritual. He will await the diurnal stroke of fate with the same lowly and pious joy as animated the Hindoos awaiting Juggernaut. His bruises will be decorations, worn with the modest pride of the veteran. He will cry aloud, in the words of the late W. E. Henley, "My head is bloody but unbowed." He will add, "My ribs are broken but unbent."

I look for the time when we shall wish one another a Merry Christmas every morning; when roast turkey and plum-pudding shall be the staple of our daily dinner, and the holly shall never be taken down from the walls, and everyone will always be kissing everyone else under the mistletoe. And what is right as regards Christmas is right as regards all other so-called anniversaries. The time will come when we shall dance round the Maypole every morning before breakfast—a meal at which hot-cross buns will be a standing dish—and shall make April fools of one another every day before noon. The profound significance of All Fools' Day—the glorious lesson that we are all fools—is too apt at present to be lost. Nor is justice done to the sublime symbolism of Shrove Tuesday—the day on which all sins are shriven. Every day pancakes shall be eaten, either before or after the plum-pudding. They shall be eaten slowly and sacramentally. They shall be fried over fires tended and kept for ever bright by Vestals. They shall be tossed to the stars.

I shall return to the subject of Christmas next week.

A SEQUELULA TO "THE DYNASTS"[1]

BY TH*M*S H*RDY

The Void is disclosed. Our own Solar System is visible, distant by some two million miles.

Enter the Ancient Spirit and Chorus of the Years, the Spirit and Chorus of the Pities, the Spirit Ironic, the Spirit Sinister, Rumours, Spirit-Messengers, and the Recording Angel.

[1] *This has been composed from a scenario thrust on me by some one else. My philosophy of life saves me from sense of responsibility for any of my writings; but I venture to hold myself specially irresponsible for this one.*—TH*M*S H*RDY.

SPIRIT OF THE PITIES.

Yonder, that swarm of things insectual
Wheeling Nowhither in Particular—
What is it?

SPIRIT OF THE YEARS.

That? Oh that is merely one
Of those innumerous congeries
Of parasites by which, since time began,
Space has been interfested.

SPIRIT SINISTER.

What a pity
We have no means of stamping out these pests!

SPIRIT IRONIC.

Nay, but I like to watch them buzzing round,
Poor little trumpery ephaeonals!

CHORUS OF THE PITIES (aerial music).

Yes, yes!
What matter a few more or less?
Here and Nowhere plus
Whence and Why makes Thus.
Let these things be.
There's room in the world for them and us.

Nothing is,
Out in the vast immensities
Where these things flit,
Irrequisite
In a minor key
To the tune of the sempiternal It.

SPIRIT IRONIC.

The curious thing about them is that some
Have lesser parasites adherent to them—
Bipedular and quadrupedular
Infinitesimals. On close survey
You see these movesome. Do you not recall,
We once went in a party and beheld
All manner of absurd things happening
On one of those same—planets, don't you call them?

SPIRIT OF THE YEARS (screwing up his eyes at the Solar System).

One of that very swarm it was, if I mistake not.
It had a parasite that called itself
Napoléon. And lately, I believe,
Another parasite has had the impudence
To publish an elaborate account.
Of our (for so we deemed it) private visit.

SPIRIT SINISTER.

His name?

RECORDING ANGEL.

One moment.

(Turns over leaves.)

Hardy, Mr. Thomas,
Novelist. Author of "The Woodlanders,"
"Far from the Madding Crowd," "The Trumpet Major,"
"Tess of the D'Urbervilles," etcetera,
Etcetera. In 1895
"Jude the Obscure" was published, and a few
Hasty reviewers, having to supply
A column for the day of publication,
Filled out their space by saying that there were

Several passages that might have been
Omitted with advantage. Mr. Hardy
Saw that if that was so, well then, of course,
Obviously the only thing to do
Was to write no more novels and forthwith
Applied himself to drama, and to Us.

SPIRIT IRONIC.

Let us hear what he said about Us.

THE OTHER SPIRITS.

Let's.

RECORDING ANGEL (raising receiver of aerial telephone).
3 oh 4 oh oh 3 5, Space. . . . Hulloa.
Is that the Superstellar Library?
I'm the Recording Angel. Kindly send me
By Spirit-Messenger a copy of
"The Dynasts" by T. Hardy. Thank you.

A pause. Enter Spirit-Messenger, with copy of "The Dynasts."

Thanks.

Exit Spirit-Messenger. The Recording Angel reads "The Dynasts" aloud.

Just as the reading draws to a close, enter the Spirit of Mr. Clement Shorter and Chorus of Subtershorters. They are visible as small grey transparencies swiftly interpenetrating the brains of the spatial Spirits.

SPIRIT OF THE PITIES.

It is a book which, once you take it up,
You cannot readily lay down.

SPIRIT SINISTER.

There is

Not a dull page in it.

Spirit of the Years.

A bold conception
Outcarried with that artistry for which
The author's name is guarantee. We have
No hesitation in commending to our readers
A volume which—

The spirit of Mr. Clement Shorter and Chorus of Subtershorters are detected and expelled.

—we hasten to denounce
As giving an entirely false account
Of our impressions.

Spirit Ironic.

Hear, *hear!*

Spirit Sinister.

Hear, *hear!*

Spirit of the Pities.

Hear!

Spirit of the Years.

Intensive vision has this Mr. Hardy,
With a dark skill in weaving word-patterns
Of subtle ideographies that mark him
A man of genius. So am not I,
But a plain Spirit, simple and forthright,
With no damned philosophical fal-lals
About me. When I visited that planet
And watched the animalculae thereon,
I never said they were "automata"
And "jackaclocks," nor dared describe their deeds
As "Life's impulsion by Incognizance."

It may be that those mites have no free will,
But how should I know? Nay, how Mr. Hardy?
We cannot glimpse the origin of things,
Cannot conceive a Causeless Cause, albeit
Such a Cause must have been, and must be greater
Than we whose little wits cannot conceive it.
"Incognizance"! Why deem incognizant
An infinitely higher than ourselves?
How dare define its way with us? How know
Whether it leaves us free or holds us bond?

Spirit of the Pities.

Allow me to associate myself
With every word that's fallen from your lips.
The author of "The Dynasts" has indeed
Misused his undeniably great gifts
In striving to belittle things that are
Little enough already. I don't say
That the phrenetical behaviour
Of those aforesaid animalculae
Did, while we watched them, seem to indicate
Possession of free-will. But, bear in mind,
We saw them in peculiar circumstances—
At war, blinded with blood and lust and fear.
Is it not likely that at other times
They are quite decent midgets, capable
Of thinking for themselves, and also acting
Discreetly on their own initiative,
Not drilled and herded, yet gregarious—
A wise yet frolicsome community?

Spirit Ironic.

What are these "other times" though? I had thought
Those midgets whiled away the vacuous hours
After one war in training for the next.

And let me add that my contempt for them
Is not done justice to by Mr. Hardy.

SPIRIT SINISTER.

Nor mine. And I have reason to believe
Those midgets shone above their average
When we inspected them.

A RUMOUR (tactfully intervening).

Yet have I heard
(Though not on very good authority)
That once a year they hold a festival
And thereat all with one accord unite
In brotherly affection and good will.

SPIRIT OF THE YEARS (to Recording Angel).

Can you authenticate this Rumour?

RECORDING ANGEL.

Such festival they have, and call it "Christmas."

SPIRIT OF THE PITIES.

Then let us go and reconsider them
Next "Christmas."

SPIRIT OF THE YEARS (to Recording Angel).

When is that?

RECORDING ANGEL (consults terrene calendar).

This day three weeks.

SPIRIT OF THE YEARS.

On that day we will re-traject ourselves.
Meanwhile, 'twere well we should be posted up
In details of this feast.

SPIRIT OF THE PITIES (to Recording Angel).

Aye, tell us more.

RECORDING ANGEL.

I fancy you could best find what you need
In the Complete Works of the late Charles Dickens.
I have them here.

SPIRIT OF THE YEARS.

Read them aloud to us.

The Recording Angel reads aloud the Complete Works of Charles
Dickens.

RECORDING ANGEL (closing "Edwin Drood").

'Tis Christmas Morning.

SPIRIT OF THE YEARS.

Then must we away.

SEMICHORUS I. OF YEARS (aerial music).

'Tis time we press on to revisit
That dear little planet,
Today of all days to be seen at
Its brightest and best.
Now holly and mistletoe girdle
Its halls and its homesteads,
And every biped is beaming
With peace and good will.

SEMICHORUS II.

With good will and why not with free will?
If clearly the former
May nest in those bosoms, then why not
The latter as well?

Let's lay down no laws to trip up on,
  Our way is in darkness,
And not but by groping unhampered
  We win to the light.

The Spirit and Chorus of the Years traject themselves, closely followed
  by the Spirit and Chorus of the Pities, the Spirits and Choruses
  Sinister and Ironic, Rumours, Spirit Messengers, and the Recording Angel.

There is the sound of a rushing wind. The Solar System is seen for a
  few instants growing larger and larger—a whorl of dark, vastening
  orbs careering round the sun. All but one of these is lost to sight.
  The convex seas and continents of our planet spring into prominence.

The Spirit of Mr. Hardy is visible as a grey transparency swiftly interpenetrating the brain of the Spirit of the Years, and urging him
  in a particular direction, to a particular point.

The Aerial Visitants now hover in mid-air on the outskirts of Caster-
  bridge, Wessex, immediately above the County Gaol.

SPIRIT OF THE YEARS.

First let us watch the revelries within
This well-kept castle whose great walls connote
A home of the pre-eminently blest.

The roof of the gaol becomes transparent, and the whole interior is
  revealed, like that of a bee-hive under glass.

Warders are marching mechanically round the corridors of white stone,
  unlocking and clanging open the iron doors of the cells. Out from
  every door steps a convict, who stands at attention, his face to the
  wall.

At a word of command the convicts fall into gangs of twelve, and
  march down the stone stairs, out into the yard, where they line
  up against the walls.

Another word of command, and they file mechanically, but not more
  mechanically than their warders, into the Chapel.

SPIRIT OF THE PITIES.

Enough!

SPIRITS SINISTER AND IRONIC.

'Tis more than even we can bear.

SPIRIT OF THE PITIES.

Would we had never come!

SPIRIT OF THE YEARS.

Brother, 'tis well
To have faced a truth however hideous,
However humbling. Gladly I discipline
My pride by taking back those pettish doubts
Cast on the soundness of the central thought
In Mr. Hardy's drama. He was right.

Automata these animalculae
Are—puppets, pitiable jackaclocks.
Be't as it may elsewhere, upon this planet
There's no free will, only obedience
To some blind, deaf, unthinking despotry
That justifies the horridest pessimism.
Frankly acknowledging all this, I beat
A quick but not disorderly retreat.

He re-trajects himself into Space, followed closely by his Chorus, and
by the Spirit and Chorus of the Pities, the Spirits Sinister and
Ironic with their Choruses, Rumours, Spirit Messengers, and the
Recording Angel.

SHAKESPEARE AND CHRISTMAS

BY FR*NK H*RR*S

THAT Shakespeare hated Christmas—hated it with a venom utterly alien to the gentle heart in him—I take to be a proposition that establishes itself automatically. If there is one thing lucid-obvious in the Plays and Sonnets, it is Shakespeare's unconquerable loathing of Christmas. The Professors deny it, however, or deny that it is proven. With these gentlemen I will deal faithfully. I will meet them on their own parched ground, making them fertilize it by shedding there the last drop of the water that flows through their veins.

If you find, in the works of a poet whose instinct is to write about everything under the sun, one obvious theme untouched, or touched hardly at all, then it is at least presumable that there was some good reason for that abstinence. Such a poet was Shakespeare. It was one of the divine frailties of his genius that he must be ever flying off at a tangent from his main theme to unpack his heart in words about some frivolous-small irrelevance that had come into his head. If it could be shown that he never mentioned Christmas, we should have proof presumptive that he consciously avoided doing so. But if the fact is that he did mention it now and again, but in grudging fashion, without one spark of illumination—he, the arch-illuminator of all things—then we have proof positive that he detested it.

I see Dryasdust thumbing his Concordance. Let my memory save him the trouble. I will reel him off the one passage in which Shakespeare spoke of Christmas in words that rise to the level of mediocrity.

> Some say that ever 'gainst that season comes
> Wherein our Saviour's birth is celebrated,
> The bird of dawning singeth all night long:
> And then, they say, no spirit dare stir abroad;
> The nights are wholesome; then no planets strike,

No fairy takes, nor witch hath power to charm,
So hallowed and so gracious is the time.

So says Marcellus at Elsinore. This is the best our Shakespeare can vamp up for the birthday of the Man with whom he of all men had the most in common. And Dryasdust, eternally unable to distinguish chalk from cheese, throws up his hands in admiration of the marvellous poetry. If Dryasdust had written it, it would more than pass muster. But as coming from Shakespeare, how feeble-cold—aye, and sulky-sinister! The greatest praiser the world will ever know!—and all he can find in his heart to sing of Christmas is a stringing-together of old women's superstitions! Again and again he has painted Winter for us as it never has been painted since—never by Goethe even, though Goethe in more than one of the *Winter-Lieder* touched the hem of his garment. There was every external reason why he should sing, as only he could have sung, of Christmas. The Queen set great store by it. She and her courtiers celebrated it year by year with lusty-pious unction. And thus the ineradicable snob in Shakespeare had the most potent of all inducements to honour the feast with the full power that was in him. But he did not, because he would not. What is the key to the enigma?

For many years I hunted it vainly. The second time that I met Carlyle I tried to enlist his sympathy and aid. He sat pensive for a while and then said that it seemed to him "a goose-quest." I replied, "You have always a phrase for everything, Tom, but always the wrong one." He covered his face, and presently, peering at me through his gnarled fingers, said "Mon, ye're recht." I discussed the problem with Renan, with Emerson, with Disraeli, also with Cetewayo—poor Cetewayo, best and bravest of men, but intellectually a Professor, like the rest of them. It was borne in on me that if I were to win to the heart of the mystery I must win alone.

The solution, when suddenly it dawned on me, was so simple-stark that I was ashamed of the ingenious-clever ways I had been following. (I learned then—and perhaps it is the one lesson worth the learning of any man—that truth may be approached only through the logic of the heart. For the heart is eye and ear, and all excellent understanding abides there.) On Christmas Day, assuredly, Anne Hathaway was born.

In what year she was born I do not know nor care. I take it she was not less than thirty-eight when she married Shakespeare. This, however, is sheer conjecture, and in no way important-apt to our inquiry. It is not the year, but the day of the year, that matters. All we need bear in mind is that on Christmas Day that woman was born into the world.

If there be any doubting Thomas among my readers, let him not be afraid to utter himself. I am (with the possible exception of Shakespeare) the gentlest man that ever breathed, and I do but bid him study the Plays in the light I have given him. The first thing that will strike him is that Shakespeare's thoughts turned constantly to the birthdays of all his Fitton-heroines, as a lover's thoughts always do turn to the moment at which the loved one first saw the light. "There was a star danced, and under that" was born Beatrice. Juliet was born "on Lammas Eve." Marina tells us she derived her name from the chance of her having been "born at sea." And so on, throughout the whole gamut of women in whom Mary Fitton was bodied forth to us. But mark how carefully Shakespeare says never a word about the birthdays of the various shrews and sluts in whom, again and again, he gave us his wife. When and where was born Queen Constance, the scold? And Bianca? And Doll Tearsheet, and "Greasy Jane" in the song, and all the rest of them? It is of the last importance that we should know. Yet never a hint is vouchsafed us in the text. It is clear that Shakespeare cannot bring himself to write about Anne Hathaway's birthday—will not stain his imagination by thinking of it. That is entirely human-natural. But why should he loathe Christmas Day itself with precisely the same loathing? There is but one answer—and that inevitable-final. The two days were one.

Some soul-secrets are so terrible that the most hardened realist of us may well shrink from laying them bare. Such a soul-secret was this of Shakespeare's. Think of it! The gentlest spirit that ever breathed, raging and fuming endlessly in impotent-bitter spleen against the prettiest of festivals! Here is a spectacle so tragic-piteous that, try as we will, we shall not put it from us. And it is well that we should not, for in our plenary compassion we shall but learn to love the man the more.

[*Mr. Fr*nk H*rr*s is very much a man of genius, and I should be sorry if this adumbration of his manner made any one suppose that I do not rate his writings about Shakespeare higher than those of all "the Professors" together.—M. B.*]

SCRUTS

BY ARN*LD B*NN*TT

I

EMILY WRACKGARTH stirred the Christmas pudding till her right arm began to ache. But she did not cease for that. She stirred on till her right arm grew so numb that it might have been the right arm of some girl at the other end of Bursley. And yet something deep down in her whispered "It is *your* right arm! And you can do what you like with it!"

She did what she liked with it. Relentlessly she kept it moving till it reasserted itself as the arm of Emily Wrackgarth, prickling and tingling as with red-hot needles in every tendon from wrist to elbow. And still Emily Wrackgarth hardened her heart.

Presently she saw the spoon no longer revolving, but wavering aimlessly in the midst of the basin. Ridiculous! This must be seen to! In the down of dark hairs that connected her eyebrows there was a marked deepening of that vertical cleft which, visible at all times, warned you that here was a young woman not to be trifled with. Her brain dispatched to her hand a peremptory message—which miscarried. The spoon wobbled as though held by a baby. Emily knew that she herself as a baby had been carried into this very kitchen to stir the Christmas pudding. Year after year, as she grew up, she had been allowed to stir it "for luck." And those, she reflected, were the only cookery lessons she ever got. How like Mother!

Mrs. Wrackgarth had died in the past year, of a complication of ailments.[1] Emily still wore on her left shoulder that small tag of crape which is as far as the Five Towns go in the way of mourning. Her father had died in the year previous to that, of a still more curious and enthralling complication of ailments.[2] Jos, his son, carried on the Wrackgarth Works, and Emily kept house for Jos. She with her own hand had made this pudding. But for her this pudding would not have been. Fantastic! Utterly incredible! And yet so it was. She was grown-up. She was mistress of the house. She could make or unmake puddings at will. And yet she was Emily Wrackgarth. Which was absurd.

She would not try to explain, to reconcile. She abandoned herself to the exquisite mysteries of existence. And yet in her abandonment she kept a sharp look-out on herself, trying fiercely to make head or tail of her nature. She thought herself a fool. But the fact that she thought so was for her a proof of adult sapience. Odd! She gave herself up. And yet it was just by giving herself up that she seemed to glimpse sometimes her own inwardness. And these bleak revelations saddened her. But she savoured her sadness. It was the wine of life to her. And for her sadness she scorned herself, and in her conscious scorn she recovered her self-respect.

It is doubtful whether the people of southern England have even yet realized how much introspection there is going on all the time in the Five Towns.

Visible from the window of the Wrackgarths' parlour was that colossal statue of Commerce which rears itself aloft at the point where Oodge Lane is intersected by Blackstead Street. Commerce, executed in glossy Doultonware by some sculptor or sculptors unknown, stands pointing her thumb over her shoulder towards the chimneys of far Hanbridge. When I tell you that the circumference of that thumb is six inches, and the rest to scale, you will understand that the statue is one of the prime glories of Bursley. There were times when Emily Wrackgarth seemed to herself as vast and as lustrously impressive as it. There were other times when she seemed to herself as trivial and slav-

---

[1] See "The History of Sarah Wrackgarth," pp. 345-482.
[2] See "The History of Sarah Wrackgarth," pp. 231-344.

ish as one of those performing fleas she had seen at the Annual Ladies'
Evening Fête organized by the Bursley Mutual Burial Club. Extremist!

She was now stirring the pudding with her left hand. The ingredi-
ents had already been mingled indistinguishably in that rich, undulating mass of tawniness which proclaims perfection. But Emily was determined to give her left hand, not less than her right, what she called
"a doing." Emily was like that.

At mid-day, when her brother came home from the Works, she was
still at it.

"Brought those scruts with you?" she asked, without looking up.

"That's a fact," he said, dipping his hand into the sagging pocket of
his coat.

It is perhaps necessary to explain what scruts are. In the daily output
of every pot-bank there are a certain proportion of flawed vessels. These
are cast aside by the foreman, with a lordly gesture, and in due course
are hammered into fragments. These fragments, which are put to various uses, are called scruts; and one of the uses they are put to is a
sentimental one. The dainty and luxurious Southerner looks to find in
his Christmas pudding a wedding-ring, a gold thimble, a threepenny-
bit, or the like. To such fal-lals the Five Towns would say fie. A Christmas pudding in the Five Towns contains nothing but suet, flour,
lemon-peel, cinnamon, brandy, almonds, raisins—and two or three
scruts. There is a world of poetry, beauty, romance, in scruts—though
you have to have been brought up on them to appreciate it. Scruts have
passed into the proverbial philosophy of the district. "Him's a pudden
with more scruts than raisins to 'm" is a criticism not infrequently
heard. It implies respect, even admiration. Of Emily Wrackgarth herself people often said, in reference to her likeness to her father, "Her's
a scrut o' th' owd basin."

Jos had emptied out from his pocket on to the table a good three
dozen of scruts. Emily laid aside her spoon, rubbed the palms of her
hands on the bib of her apron, and proceeded to finger these scruts
with the air of a connoisseur, rejecting one after another. The pudding
was a small one, designed merely for herself and Jos, with remainder
to "the girl"; so that it could hardly accommodate more than two or

three scruts. Emily knew well that one scrut is as good as another. Yet she did not want her brother to feel that anything selected by him would necessarily pass muster with her. For his benefit she ostentatiously wrinkled her nose.

"By the by," said Jos, "you remember Albert Grapp? I've asked him to step over from Hanbridge and help eat our snack on Christmas Day."

Emily gave Jos one of her looks. "You've asked that Mr. Grapp?"

"No objection, I hope? He's not a bad sort. And he's considered a bit of a ladies' man, you know."

She gathered up all the scruts and let them fall in a rattling shower on the exiguous pudding. Two or three fell wide of the basin. These she added.

"Steady on!" cried Jos. "What's that for?"

"That's for your guest," replied his sister. "And if you think you're going to palm me off on to him, or on to any other young fellow, you're a fool, Jos Wrackgarth."

The young man protested weakly, but she cut him short.

"Don't think," she said, "I don't know what you've been after, just of late. Cracking up one young sawny and then another on the chance of me marrying him! I never heard of such goings on. But here I am, and here I'll stay, as sure as my name's Emily Wrackgarth, Jos Wrackgarth!"

She was the incarnation of the adorably feminine. She was exquisitely vital. She exuded at every pore the pathos of her young undirected force. It is difficult to write calmly about her. For her, in another age, ships would have been launched and cities besieged. But brothers are a race apart, and blind. It is a fact that Jos would have been glad to see his sister "settled"—preferably in one of the other four Towns.

She took up the spoon and stirred vigorously. The scruts grated and squeaked together around the basin, while the pudding feebly wormed its way up among them.

II

ALBERT GRAPP, ladies' man though he was, was humble of heart. Nobody knew this but himself. Not one of his fellow clerks in Clither's Bank knew it. The general theory in Hanbridge was "Him's got a stiff opinion o' hisself." But this arose from what was really a sign of humility in him. He made the most of himself. He had, for instance, a way of his own in the matter of dressing. He always wore a voluminous frock-coat, with a pair of neatly-striped vicuna trousers, which he placed every night under his mattress, thus preserving in perfection the crease down the centre of each. His collar was of the highest, secured in front with an aluminium stud, to which was attached by a patent loop a natty bow of dove-coloured sateen. He had two caps, one of blue serge, the other of shepherd's plaid. These he wore on alternate days. He wore them in a way of his own—well back from his forehead, so as not to hide his hair, and with the peak behind. The peak made a sort of half-moon over the back of his collar. Through a fault of his tailor, there was a yawning gap between the back of his collar and the collar of his coat. Whenever he shook his head, the peak of his cap had the look of a live thing trying to investigate this abyss. Dimly aware of the effect, Albert Grapp shook his head as seldom as possible.

On wet days he wore a mackintosh. This, as he did not yet possess a great-coat, he wore also, but with less glory, on cold days. He had hoped there might be rain on Christmas morning. But there was no rain. "Like my luck," he said as he came out of his lodgings and turned his steps to that corner of Jubilee Avenue from which the Hanbridge-Bursley trams start every half-hour.

Since Jos Wrackgarth had introduced him to his sister at the Hanbridge Oddfellows' Biennial Hop, when he danced two quadrilles with her, he had seen her but once. He had nodded to her, Five Towns fashion, and she had nodded back at him, but with a look that seemed to say "You needn't nod next time you see me. I can get along well enough without your nods." A frightening girl! And yet her brother had since told him she seemed "a bit gone, like" on him. Impossible! He, Albert Grapp, make an impression on the brilliant Miss Wrackgarth! Yet she had sent him a verbal invite to spend Christmas in her own home. And the time had come. He was on his way. Incredible that he should arrive! The tram must surely overturn, or be struck by lightning. And yet no! He arrived safely.

The small servant who opened the door gave him another verbal message from Miss Wrackgarth. It was that he must wipe his feet "well" on the mat. In obeying this order he experienced a thrill of satisfaction he could not account for. He must have stood shuffling his boots vigorously for a full minute. This, he told himself, was life. He, Albert Grapp, was alive. And the world was full of other men, all alive; and yet, because they were not doing Miss Wrackgarth's bidding, none of them really lived. He was filled with a vague melancholy. But his melancholy pleased him.

In the parlour he found Jos awaiting him. The table was laid for three.

"So you're here, are you?" said the host, using the Five Towns formula. "Emily's in the kitchen," he added. "Happen she'll be here directly."

"I hope she's tol-lol-ish?" asked Albert.

"She is," said Jos. "But don't you go saying that to her. She doesn't care about society airs and graces. You'll make no headway if you aren't blunt."

"Oh, right you are," said Albert, with the air of a man who knew his way about.

A moment later Emily joined them, still wearing her kitchen apron. "So you're here, are you?" she said, but did not shake hands. The servant had followed her in with the tray, and the next few seconds were occupied in the disposal of the beef and trimmings.

The meal began, Emily carving. The main thought of a man less infatuated than Albert Grapp would have been "This girl can't cook. And she'll never learn to." The beef, instead of being red and brown, was pink and white. Uneatable beef! And yet he relished it more than anything he had ever tasted. This beef was her own handiwork. Thus it was because she had made it so. . . . He warily refrained from complimenting her, but the idea of a second helping obsessed him.

"Happen I could do with a bit more, like," he said.

Emily hacked off the bit more and jerked it on to the plate he had held out to her.

"Thanks," he said; and then, as Emily's lip curled, and Jos gave him a warning kick under the table, he tried to look as if he had said nothing.

Only when the second course came on did he suspect that the meal was a calculated protest against his presence. This a Christmas pudding? The litter of fractured earthenware was hardly held together by the suet and raisins. All his pride of manhood—and there was plenty of pride mixed up with Albert Grapp's humility—dictated a refusal to touch that pudding. Yet he soon found himself touching it, though gingerly, with his spoon and fork.

In the matter of dealing with scruts there are two schools—the old and the new. The old school pushes its head well over its plate and drops the scrut straight from its mouth. The new school emits the scrut into the fingers of its left hand and therewith deposits it on the rim of the plate. Albert noticed that Emily was of the new school. But might she not despise as affectation in him what came natural to herself? On the other hand, if he showed himself as a prop of the old school, might she not set her face the more stringently against him? The chances were that whichever course he took would be the wrong one.

It was then that he had an inspiration—an idea of the sort that comes to a man once in his life and finds him, likely as not, unable to put it into practice. Albert was not sure he could consummate this idea of his. He had indisputably fine teeth—"a proper mouthful of grinders" in local phrase. But would they stand the strain he was going to impose on them? He could but try them. Without a sign of nervousness he raised his spoon, with one scrut in it, to his mouth. This scrut he put between two of his left-side molars, bit hard on it, and—eternity of that moment!—felt it and heard it snap in two. Emily also heard it. He was conscious that at sound of the percussion she started forward and stared at him. But he did not look at her. Calmly, systematically, with gradually diminishing crackles, he reduced that scrut to powder, and washed the powder down with a sip of beer. While he dealt with the second scrut he talked to Jos about the Borough Council's proposal to erect an electric power-station on the site of the old gas-works down Hillport way. He was aware of a slight abrasion inside his left cheek. No matter. He must be more careful. There were six scruts still to be negotiated. He knew that what he was doing was a thing grandiose, unique, epical; a history-making thing; a thing that would outlive marble and the gilded monuments of princes. Yet he kept his head. He did not hurry, nor did he dawdle. Scrut by scrut, he ground slowly but he ground exceeding small. And while he did so he talked wisely and well. He passed from the power-station to a first edition of Le-conte de Lisle's "Parnasse Contemporain" that he had picked up for sixpence in Liverpool, and thence to the Midland's proposal to drive a tunnel under the Knype Canal so as to link up the main-line with the Critchworth and Suddleford loop-line. Jos was too amazed to put in a word. Jos sat merely gaping—a gape that merged by imperceptible degrees into a grin. Presently he ceased to watch his guest. He sat watching his sister.

Not once did Albert himself glance in her direction. She was just a dim silhouette on the outskirts of his vision. But there she was, unmoving, and he could feel the fixture of her unseen eyes. The time was at hand when he would have to meet those eyes. Would he flinch? Was he master of himself?

The last scrut was powder. No temporizing! He jerked his glass to his mouth. A moment later, holding out his plate to her, he looked Emily full in the eyes. They were Emily's eyes, but not hers alone. They were collective eyes—that was it! They were the eyes of stark, staring womanhood. Her face had been dead white, but now suddenly up from her throat, over her cheeks, through the down between her eyebrows, went a rush of colour, up over her temples, through the very parting of her hair.

"Happen," he said without a quaver in his voice, "I'll have a bit more, like."

She flung her arms forward on the table and buried her face in them.

It was a gesture wild and meek. It was the gesture foreseen and yet incredible. It was recondite, inexplicable, and yet obvious. It was the only thing to be done—and yet, by gum, she had done it.

Her brother had risen from his seat and was now at the door. "Think I'll step round to the Works," he said, "and see if they banked up that furnace aright."

Note.—*The author has in preparation a series of volumes dealing with the life of Albert and Emily Grapp.*

ENDEAVOUR

BY J*HN G*LSW*RTHY

THE dawn of Christmas Day found London laid out in a shroud of snow. Like a body wasted by diseases that had triumphed over it at last, London lay stark and still now, beneath a sky that was as the closed leaden shell of a coffin. It was what is called an old-fashioned Christmas.

Nothing seemed to be moving except the Thames, whose embanked waters flowed on sullenly in their eternal act of escape to the sea. All along the wan stretch of Cheyne Walk the thin trees stood exanimate, with not a breath of wind to stir the snow that pied their soot-blackened branches. Here and there on the muffled ground lay a sparrow that had been frozen in the night, its little claws sticking up heavenward. But here and there also those tinier adventurers of the London air, smuts, floated vaguely and came to rest on the snow—signs that in the seeming death of civilization some housemaids at least survived, and some fires had been lit.

One of these fires, crackling in the grate of one of those dining-rooms which look fondly out on the river and tolerantly across to Battersea, was being watched by the critical eye of an aged canary. The cage in which this bird sat was hung in the middle of the bow-window. It contained three perches, and also a pendent hoop. The tray that was its floor had just been cleaned and sanded. In the embrasure to the right was a fresh supply of hemp-seed; in the embrasure to the left the bath-tub had just been refilled with clear water. Stuck between the bars was a large sprig of groundsel. Yet, though all was thus in order, the bird did not eat nor drink, nor did he bathe. With his back to Battersea, and his head sunk deep between his little sloping shoulders, he watched the fire. The windows had for a while been opened, as usual, to air the room for him; and the fire had not yet mitigated the chill. It was not his custom to bathe at so inclement an hour; and his appetite for food and drink, less keen than it had once been, required to be whetted by example—he never broke his fast before his master and mistress broke theirs. Time had been when, for sheer joy in life, he fluttered from perch to perch, though there were none to watch him, and even sang roulades, though there were none to hear. He would not do these things nowadays save at the fond instigation of Mr. and Mrs. Adrian Berridge. The housemaid who ministered to his cage, the parlourmaid who laid the Berridge's breakfast table, sometimes tried to incite him to perform for their own pleasure. But the sense of caste, strong in his protuberant little bosom, steeled him against these advances.

While the breakfast-table was being laid, he heard a faint tap against the window-pane. Turning round, he perceived on the sill a creature like to himself, but very different—a creature who, despite the pretensions of a red waistcoat in the worst possible taste, belonged evidently to the ranks of the outcast and the disinherited. In previous winters the sill had been strewn every morning with bread-crumbs. This winter, no bread-crumbs had been vouchsafed; and the canary, though he did not exactly understand why this was so, was glad that so it was. He had felt that his poor relations took advantage of the Berridge's kindness. Two or three of them, as pensioners, might not have been amiss. But they came in swarms, and they gobbled their food in a disgusting fashion, not trifling coquettishly with it as birds should. The reason for this, the canary knew, was that they were hungry; and of that he was sorry. He hated to think how much destitution there was in the world; and he could not help thinking about it when samples of it were thrust under his notice. That was the principal reason why he was glad that the window-sill was strewn no more and seldom visited.

He would much rather not have seen this solitary applicant. The two eyes fixed on his made him feel very uncomfortable. And yet, for fear of seeming to be outfaced, he did not like to look away.

The subdued clangour of the gong, sounded for breakfast, gave him an excuse for turning suddenly round and watching the door of the room.

A few moments later there came to him a faint odour of Harris tweed, followed immediately by the short, somewhat stout figure of his master—a man whose mild, fresh, pink, round face seemed to find salvation, as it were, at the last moment, in a neatly-pointed auburn beard.

Adrian Berridge paused on the threshold, as was his wont, with closed eyes and dilated nostrils, enjoying the aroma of complex freshness which the dining-room had at this hour. Pathetically a creature of habit, he liked to savour the various scents, sweet or acrid, that went to symbolize for him the time and the place. Here were the immediate scents of dry toast, of China tea, of napery fresh from the wash, together with that vague, super-subtle scent which boiled eggs give out through their unbroken shells. And as a permanent base to these there was the scent of much-polished Chippendale, and of bees'-waxed parquet, and of Persian rugs. Today, moreover, crowning the composition, there was the delicate pungency of the holly that topped the Queen Anne mirror and the Mantegna prints.

Coming forward into the room, Mr. Berridge greeted the canary. "Well, Amber, old fellow," he said, "a happy Christmas to you!" Affectionately he pushed the tip of a plump white finger between the bars. "Tweet!" he added.

"Tweet!" answered the bird, hopping to and fro along his perch.

"Quite an old-fashioned Christmas, Amber!" said Mr. Berridge, turning to scan the weather. At sight of the robin, a little spasm of pain contracted his face. A shine of tears came to his prominent pale eyes, and he turned quickly away. Just at that moment, heralded by a slight fragrance of old lace and of that peculiar, almost unseizable odour that uncut turquoises have, Mrs. Berridge appeared.

"What is the matter, Adrian?" she asked quickly. She glanced sideways into the Queen Anne mirror, her hand fluttering, like a pale moth, to her hair, which she always wore braided in a fashion she had derived from Pollaiuolo's St. Ursula.

"Nothing, Jacynth—nothing," he answered with a lightness that carried no conviction; and he made behind his back a gesture to frighten away the robin.

"Amber isn't unwell, is he?" She came quickly to the cage. Amber executed for her a roulade of great sweetness. His voice had not perhaps the fullness for which it had been noted in earlier years; but the art with which he managed it was as exquisite as ever. It was clear to his audience that the veteran artist was hale and hearty.

But Jacynth, relieved on one point, had a misgiving on another. "This groundsel doesn't look very fresh, does it?" she murmured, withdrawing the sprig from the bars. She rang the bell, and when the servant came in answer to it said, "Oh Jenny, will you please bring up another piece of groundsel for Master Amber? I don't think this one is quite fresh."

This formal way of naming the canary to the servants always jarred on her principles and on those of her husband. They tried to regard their servants as essentially equals of themselves, and lately had given Jenny strict orders to leave off calling them "Sir" and "Ma'am," and to call them simply "Adrian" and "Jacynth." But Jenny, after one or two efforts that ended in faint giggles, had reverted to the crude old nomenclature—as much to the relief as to the mortification of the Berridges. They did, it is true, discuss the possibility of redressing the balance by calling the parlourmaid "Miss." But, when it came to the point, their lips refused this office. And conversely their lips persisted in the social prefix to the bird's name.

Somehow that anomaly seemed to them symbolic of their lives. Both of them yearned so wistfully to live always in accordance to the nature of things. And this, they felt, ought surely to be the line of least resistance. In the immense difficulties it presented, and in their constant failures to surmount these difficulties, they often wondered whether the nature of things might not be, after all, something other than what they thought it. Again and again it seemed to be in as direct conflict with duty as with inclination; so that they were driven to wonder also whether what they conceived to be duty were not also a mirage—a marsh-light leading them on to disaster.

The fresh groundsel was brought in while Jacynth was pouring out the tea. She rose and took it to the cage; and it was then that she too saw the robin, still fluttering on the sill. With a quick instinct she knew that Adrian had seen it—knew what had brought that look to his face. She went and, bending over him, laid a hand on his shoulder. The disturbance of her touch caused the tweed to give out a tremendous volume of scent, making her feel a little dizzy.

"Adrian," she faltered, "mightn't we for once—it is Christmas Day— mightn't we, just today, sprinkle some bread-crumbs?"

He rose from the table, and leaned against the mantelpiece, looking down at the fire. She watched him tensely. At length, "Oh Jacynth," he groaned, "don't—don't tempt me."

"But surely, dear, surely——"

"Jacynth, don't you remember that long talk we had last winter, after the annual meeting of the Feathered Friends' League, and how we agreed that those sporadic doles could do no real good—must even degrade the birds who received them—and that we had no right to meddle in what ought to be done by collective action of the State?"

"Yes, and—oh my dear, I do still agree, with all my heart. But if the State will do nothing—nothing——"

"It won't, it daren't, go on doing nothing, unless we encourage it to do so. Don't you see, Jacynth, it is just because so many people take it on themselves to feed a few birds here and there that the State feels it can afford to shirk the responsibility?"

"All that is fearfully true. But just now—Adrian, the look in that robin's eyes——"

Berridge covered his own eyes, as though to blot out from his mind the memory of that look. But Jacynth was not silenced. She felt herself dragged on by her sense of duty to savour, and to make her husband savour, the full bitterness that the situation could yield for them both. "Adrian," she said, "a fearful thought came to me. Suppose—suppose it had been Amber!"

Even before he shuddered at the thought, he raised his finger to his lips, glancing round at the cage. It was clear that Amber had not over-heard Jacynth's remark, for he threw back his head and uttered one of his blithest trills. Adrian, thus relieved, was free to shudder at the thought just suggested.

"Sometimes," murmured Jacynth, "I wonder if we, holding the views we hold, are justified in keeping Amber."

"Ah, dear, we took him in our individualistic days. We cannot re-pudiate him now. It wouldn't be fair. Besides, you see, he isn't here on a basis of mere charity. He's not a parasite, but an artist. He gives us of his art."

"Yes, dear, I know. But you remember our doubts about the position of artists in the community—whether the State ought to sanction them at all."

"True. But we cannot visit those doubts on our old friend yonder, can we, dear? At the same time, I admit that when—when—Jacynth, if ever anything happens to Amber, we shall perhaps not be justified in keeping another bird."

"Don't, please don't talk of such things." She moved to the window. Snow, a delicate white powder, was falling on the coverlet of snow.

Outside, on the sill, the importunate robin lay supine, his little heart beating no more behind the shabby finery of his breast, but his glazing eyes half-open as though even in death he were still questioning. Above him and all around him brooded the genius of infinity, dispassionate, inscrutable, grey.

Jacynth turned and mutely beckoned her husband to the window.

They stood there, these two, gazing silently down.

Presently Jacynth said: "Adrian, are you sure that we, you and I, for all our theories, and all our efforts, aren't futile?"

"No, dear. Sometimes I am not sure. But—there's a certain comfort in not being sure. To die for what one knows to be true, as many saints have done—that is well. But to live, as many of us do nowadays, in service of what may, for aught we know, be only a half-truth or not true at all—this seems to me nobler still."

"Because it takes more out of us?"

"Because it takes more out of us."

Standing between the live bird and the dead, they gazed across the river, over the snow-covered wharves, over the dim, slender chimneys from which no smoke came, into the grey-black veil of the distance. And it seemed to them that the genius of infinity did not know—perhaps did not even care—whether they were futile or not, nor how much and to what purpose, if to any purpose, they must go on striving.

CHRISTMAS

BY G. S. STR**T

ONE likes it or not. This said, there is plaguy little else to say of Christmas, and I (though I doubt my sentiments touch you not at all) would rather leave that little unsaid. Did I confess a distaste for Christmas, I should incur your enmity. But if I find it, as I protest I do, rather agreeable than otherwise, why should I spoil my pleasure by stringing vain words about it? Swift and the broomstick—yes. But that essay was done at the behest of a clever woman, and to annoy the admirers of Robert Boyle. Besides, it was hardly—or do you think it was? —worth the trouble of doing it. There was no trouble involved? Possibly. But I am not the Dean. And anyhow the fact that he never did anything of the kind again may be taken to imply that he would not be bothered. So would not I, if I had a deanery.

That is an hypothesis I am tempted to pursue. I should like to fill my allotted space before reaching the tiresome theme I have set myself . . . A deanery, the cawing of rooks, their effect on the nervous system, Trollope's delineations of deans, the advantages of the Mid-Victorian novel . . . But your discursive essayist is a nuisance. Best come to the point. The bore is in finding a point to come to. Besides, the chances are that any such point will have long ago been worn blunt by a score of more active seekers. Alas!

Since I wrote the foregoing words, I have been out for a long walk, in search of inspiration, through the streets of what is called the West End. Snobbishly so called. Why draw these crude distinctions? We all know that Mayfair happens to lie a few miles further west than White-chapel. It argues a lack of breeding to go on calling attention to the fact. If the people of Whitechapel were less beautiful or less well-mannered or more ignorant than we, there might be some excuse. But they are not so. True, themselves talk about the East End, but this only makes the matter worse. To a sensitive ear their phrase has a ring of ironic humility that jars not less than our own coarse boastfulness. Heaven knows they have a right to be ironic, and who shall blame them for exercising it? All the same, this sort of thing worries me horribly.

I said that I found Christmas rather agreeable than otherwise. But I was speaking as one accustomed to live mostly in the past. The walk I have just taken, refreshing in itself, has painfully reminded me that I cannot hit it off with the present. My life is in the later days of the eighteenth and the earlier days of the nineteenth century. This twen-tieth affair is as a vision, dimly foreseen at odd moments, and put from me with a slight shudder. My actual Christmases are spent (say) in Holland House, which has but recently been built. Little Charles Fox is allowed by his father to join us for the earlier stages of dessert. I am conscious of patting him on the head and predicting for him a distin-guished future. A very bright little fellow, with his father's eyes! Or again, I am down at Newstead. Byron is in his wildest spirits, a shade too uproarious. I am glad to escape into the park and stroll a quiet hour on the arm of Mr. Hughes Ball. Years pass. The approach of Christ-mas finds one loath to leave one's usual haunts. One is on one's way to one's club to dine with Postumus and dear old "Wigsby" Pendennis, quietly at one's consecrated table near the fireplace. As one is crossing St. James's Street an ear-piercing grunt causes one to reel back just in time to be not run over by a motor-car. Inside is a woman who scowls down at one through the window—"Serve you right if we'd gone over you." Yes, I often have these awakenings to fact—or rather these provisions of what life might be if I survived into the twentieth century. Alas!

I have mentioned that woman in the motor-car because she is germane to my theme. She typifies the vices of the modern Christmas. For her, by the absurd accident of her wealth, there is no distinction between people who have not motor-cars and people who might as well be run over. But I wrong her. If we others were all run over, there would be no one before whom she could flaunt her loathsome air of superiority. And what would she do then, poor thing? I doubt she would die of boredom—painfully, one hopes. In the same way, if the shop-keepers in Bond Street knew there was no one who could not afford to buy the things in their windows, there would be an end to the display that makes those windows intolerable (to you and me) during the month of December. I had often suspected that the things there were not meant to be bought by people who could buy them, but merely to irritate the rest. This afternoon I was sure of it. Not in one window anything a sane person would give to any one not an idiot, but everywhere a general glossy grin out at people who are not plutocrats. This sort of thing lashes me to ungovernable fury. The lion is roused, and I recognize in myself a born leader of men. Be so good as to smash those windows for me.

One does not like to think that Christmas has been snapped up, docked of its old-world kindliness, and pressed into the service of an odious ostentation. But so it has. Alas! The thought of Father Christmas trudging through the snow to the homes of gentle and simple alike (forgive that stupid, snobbish phrase) was agreeable. But Father Christmas in red plush breeches, lounging on the doorstep of Sir Gorgius Midas—one averts one's eyes.

I have—now I come to think of it—another objection to the modern Christmas. It would be affectation to pretend not to know that there are many Jews living in England, and in London especially. I have always had a deep respect for that race, their distinction in intellect and in character. Being not one of them, I may in their behalf put a point which themselves would be the last to suggest. I hope they will acquit me of impertinence in doing this. You, in your turn, must acquit me of sentimentalism. The Jews are a minority, and as such must take their chances. But may not a majority refrain from pressing its rights to the utmost? It is well that we should celebrate Christmas heartily, and all that. But we could do so without an emphasis that seems to me, in the circumstances, 'tother side good taste. "Good taste" is a hateful phrase. But it escaped me in the heat of the moment. Alas!

THE FEAST

BY J*S*PH C*NR*D

THE hut in which slept the white man was on a clearing between the forest and the river. Silence, the silence murmurous and unquiet of a tropical night, brooded over the hut that, baked through by the sun, sweated a vapour beneath the cynical light of the stars. Mahamo lay rigid and watchful at the hut's mouth. In his upturned eyes, and along the polished surface of his lean body black and immobile, the stars were reflected, creating an illusion of themselves who are illusions.

The roofs of the congested trees, writhing in some kind of agony private and eternal, made tenebrous and shifty silhouettes against the sky, like shapes cut out of black paper by a maniac who pushes them with his thumb this way and that, irritably, on a concave surface of blue steel. Resin oozed unseen from the upper branches to the trunks swathed in creepers that clutched and interlocked with tendrils venomous, frantic and faint. Down below, by force of habit, the lush herbage went through the farce of growth—that farce old and screaming, whose trite end is decomposition.

Within the hut the form of the white man, corpulent and pale, was covered with a mosquito-net that was itself illusory like everything else, only more so. Flying squadrons of mosquitoes inside its meshes flickered and darted over him, working hard, but keeping silence so as not to excite him from sleep. Cohorts of yellow ants disputed him against cohorts of purple ants, the two kinds slaying one another in thousands. The battle was undecided when suddenly, with no such warning as it gives in some parts of the world, the sun blazed up over the horizon, turning night into day, and the insects vanished back into their camps.

The white man ground his knuckles into the corners of his eyes, emitting that snore final and querulous of a middle-aged man awakened rudely. With a gesture brusque but flaccid he plucked aside the net and peered around. The bales of cotton cloth, the beads, the brass wire, the bottles of rum, had not been spirited away in the night. So far so good. The faithful servant of his employers was now at liberty to care for his own interests. He regarded himself, passing his hands over his skin.

"Hi! Mahamo!" he shouted. "I've been eaten up."

The islander, with one sinuous motion, sprang from the ground, through the mouth of the hut. Then, after a glance, he threw high his hands in thanks to such good and evil spirits as had charge of his concerns. In a tone half of reproach, half of apology, he murmured——

"You white men sometimes say strange things that deceive the heart."

"Reach me that ammonia bottle, d'you hear?" answered the white man. "This is a pretty place you've brought me to!" He took a draught. "Christmas Day, too! Of all the— But I suppose it seems all right to you, you funny blackamoor, to be here on Christmas Day?"

"We are here on the day appointed, Mr. Williams. It is a feast-day of your people?"

Mr. Williams had lain back, with closed eyes, on his mat. Nostalgia was doing duty to him for imagination. He was wafted to a bedroom in Marylebone, where in honour of the Day he lay late dozing, with great contentment; outside, a slush of snow in the street, the sound of churchbells; from below a savour of especial cookery. "Yes," he said, "it's a feast-day of my people."

"Of mine also," said the islander humbly.

"Is it though? But they'll do business first?"

"They must first do that."

"And they'll bring their ivory with them?"

"Every man will bring ivory," answered the islander, with a smile gleaming and wide.

"How soon'll they be here?"

"Has not the sun risen? They are on their way."

"Well, I hope they'll hurry. The sooner we're off this cursed island of yours the better. Take all those things out," Mr. Williams added, pointing to the merchandise, "and arrange them—neatly, mind you!"

In certain circumstances it is right that a man be humoured in trifles. Mahamo, having borne out the merchandise, arranged it very neatly.

While Mr. Williams made his toilet, the sun and the forest, careless of the doings of white and black men alike, waged their warfare implacable and daily. The forest from its inmost depths sent forth perpetually its legions of shadows that fell dead in the instant of exposure to the enemy whose rays heroic and absurd its outposts annihilated. There came from those inilluminable depths the equable rumour of myriads of winged things and crawling things newly roused to the task of killing and being killed. Thence detached itself, little by little, an insidious sound of a drum beaten. This sound drew more near.

Mr. Williams, issuing from the hut, heard it, and stood gaping towards it.

"Is that them?" he asked.

"That is they," the islander murmured, moving away towards the edge of the forest.

Sounds of chanting were a now audible accompaniment to the drum.

"What's that they're singing?" asked Mr. Williams.

"They sing of their business," said Mahamo.

"Oh!" Mr. Williams was slightly shocked. "I'd have thought they'd be singing of their feast."

"It is of their feast they sing."

It has been stated that Mr. Williams was not imaginative. But a few years of life in climates alien and intemperate had disordered his nerves. There was that in the rhythms of the hymn which made bristle his flesh.

Suddenly, when they were very near, the voices ceased, leaving a legacy of silence more sinister than themselves. And now the black spaces between the trees were relieved by bits of white that were the eyeballs and teeth of Mahamo's brethren.

"It was of their feast, it was of you, they sang," said Mahamo.

"Look here," cried Mr. Williams in his voice of a man not to be trifled with. "Look here, if you've——"

He was silenced by sight of what seemed to be a young sapling sprung up from the ground within a yard of him—a young sapling tremulous, with a root of steel. Then a thread-like shadow skimmed the air, and another spear came impinging the ground within an inch of his feet.

As he turned in his flight he saw the goods so neatly arranged at his orders, and there flashed through him, even in the thick of the spears, the thought that he would be a grave loss to his employers. This—for Mr. Williams was, not less than the goods, of a kind easily replaced— was an illusion. It was the last of Mr. Williams' illusions.

A RECOLLECTION

BY EDM*ND G*SSE

"And let us strew
Twain wreaths of holly and of yew."
WALLER.

ONE out of many Christmas Days abides with peculiar vividness in my memory. In setting down, however clumsily, some slight record of it, I feel that I shall be discharging a duty not only to the two disparately illustrious men who made it so very memorable, but also to all young students of English and Scandinavian literature. My use of the first person singular, delightful though that pronoun is in the works of the truly gifted, jars unspeakably on me; but reasons of space balk my sober desire to call myself merely the present writer, or the infatuated go-between, or the cowed and imponderable young person who was in attendance.

In the third week of December 1878, taking the opportunity of a brief and undeserved vacation, I went to Venice. On the morning after my arrival, in answer to a most kind and cordial summons, I presented myself at the Palazzo Rezzonico. Intense as was the impression he always made even in London, I think that those of us who met Robert Browning only in the stress and roar of that metropolis can hardly have gauged the fullness of his potentialities for impressing. Venice, "so weak, so quiet," as Mr. Ruskin had called her, was indeed the ideal setting for one to whom neither of those epithets could by any possibility have been deemed applicable. The steamboats that now wake the echoes of the canals had not yet been imported; but the vitality of the imported poet was in some measure a preparation for them. It did not, however, find me quite prepared for itself, and I am afraid that some minutes must have elapsed before I could, as it were, find my feet in the torrent of his geniality and high spirits, and give him news of his friends in London.

He was at that time engaged in revising the proof-sheets of "Dramatic Idylls," and after luncheon, to which he very kindly bade me remain, he read aloud certain selected passages. The yellow haze of a wintry Venetian sunshine poured in through the vast windows of his *salone,* making an aureole around his silvered head. I would give much to live that hour over again. But it was vouchsafed in days before the Browning Society came and made everything so simple for us all. I am afraid that after a few minutes I sat enraptured by the sound rather than by the sense of the lines. I find, in the notes I made of the occasion, that I figured myself as plunging through some enchanted thicket on the back of an inspired bull.

That evening, as I was strolling in Piazza San Marco, my thoughts of Browning were all of a sudden scattered by the vision of a small, thick-set man seated at one of the tables in the Café Florian. This was —and my heart leapt like a young trout when I saw that it could be none other than—Henrik Ibsen. Whether joy or fear was the predominant emotion in me, I should be hard put to it to say. It had been my privilege to correspond extensively with the great Scandinavian, and to be frequently received by him, some years earlier than the date of which I write, in Rome. In that city haunted by the shades of so many Emperors and Popes I had felt comparatively at ease even in Ibsen's presence. But seated here in the homelier decay of Venice, closely buttoned in his black surcoat and crowned with his uncompromising top-hat, with the lights of the Piazza flashing back wanly from his gold-rimmed spectacles, and his lips tight-shut like some steel trap into which our poor humanity had just fallen, he seemed to constitute a menace under which the boldest might well quail. Nevertheless, I took my courage in both hands, and laid it as a kind of votive offering on the little table before him.

My reward was in the surprising amiability that he then and afterwards displayed. My travelling had indeed been doubly blessed, for, whilst my subsequent afternoons were spent in Browning's presence, my evenings fell with regularity into the charge of Ibsen. One of these evenings is for me "prouder, more laurel'd than the rest" as having been the occasion when he read to me the MS. of a play which he had just completed. He was staying at the Hôtel Danieli, an edifice famous for having been, rather more than forty years previously, the socket in which the flame of an historic *grande passion* had finally sunk and guttered out with no inconsiderable accompaniment of smoke and odour. It was there, in an upper room, that I now made acquaintance with a couple very different from George Sand and Alfred de Musset, though destined to become hardly less famous than they. I refer to Torvald and Nora Helmer. My host read to me with the utmost vivacity, standing in the middle of the apartment; and I remember that in the scene where Nora Helmer dances the tarantella her creator instinctively executed a few illustrative steps.

During those days I felt very much as might a minnow swimming to and fro between Leviathan on the one hand and Behemoth on the other—a minnow tremulously pleased, but ever wistful for some means of bringing his two enormous acquaintances together. On the afternoon of December 24th I confided to Browning my aspiration. He had never heard of this brother poet and dramatist, whose fame indeed was at that time still mainly Boreal; but he cried out with the greatest heartiness, "Capital! Bring him round with you at one o'clock tomorrow for turkey and plum-pudding!"

I betook myself straight to the Hôtel Danieli, hoping against hope that Ibsen's sole answer would not be a comminatory grunt and an instant rupture of all future relations with myself. At first he was indeed resolute not to go. He had never heard of this Herr Browning. (It was one of the strengths of his strange, crustacean genius that he never had heard of anybody.) I took it on myself to say that Herr Browning would send his private gondola, propelled by his two gondoliers, to conduct Herr Ibsen to the scene of the festivity. I think it was this prospect that made him gradually unbend, for he had already acquired that taste for pomp and circumstance which was so notable a characteristic of his later years. I hastened back to the Palazzo Rezzonico before he could change his mind. I need hardly say that Browning instantly consented to send the gondola. So large and lovable was his nature that, had he owned a thousand of those conveyances, he would not have hesitated to send out the whole fleet in honour of any friend of any friend of his.

Next day, as I followed Ibsen down the Danielian water-steps into the expectant gondola, my emotion was such that I was tempted to snatch from him his neatly-furled umbrella and spread it out over his head, like the umbrella beneath which the Doges of days gone by had made their appearances in public. It was perhaps a pity that I repressed this impulse. Ibsen seemed to be already regretting that he had unbent. I could not help thinking, as we floated along the Riva Schiavoni, that he looked like some particularly ruthless member of the Council of Ten. I did, however, try faintly to attune him in some sort to the spirit of our host and of the day of the year. I adumbrated Browning's outlook on life, translating into Norwegian, I will remember, the words "God's in His Heaven, all's right with the world." In fact I cannot charge myself with not having done what I could. I can only lament that it was not enough.

When we marched into the *salone,* Browning was seated at the piano, playing (I think) a Toccata of Galuppi's. On seeing us, he brought his hands down with a great crash on the keyboard, seemed to reach us in one astonishing bound across the marble floor, and clapped Ibsen loudly on either shoulder, wishing him "the Merriest of Merry Christmases."

Ibsen, under this sudden impact, stood firm as a rock, and it flitted through my brain that here at last was solved the old problem of what would happen if an irresistible force met an immovable mass. But it was obvious that the rock was not rejoicing in the moment of victory. I was tartly asked whether I had not explained to Herr Browning that his guest did not understand English. I hastily rectified my omission, and thenceforth our host spoke in Italian. Ibsen, though he understood that language fairly well, was averse to speaking it. Such remarks as he made in the course of the meal to which we presently sat down were made in Norwegian and translated by myself.

Browning, while he was carving the turkey, asked Ibsen whether he had visited any of the Venetian theatres. Ibsen's reply was that he never visited theatres. Browning laughed his great laugh, and cried "That's right! We poets who write plays must give the theatres as wide a berth as possible. We aren't wanted there!" "How so?" asked Ibsen. Browning looked a little puzzled, and I had to explain that in northern Europe Herr Ibsen's plays were frequently performed. At this I seemed to see on Browning's face a slight shadow—so swift and transient a shadow as might be cast by a swallow flying across a sunlit garden. An instant, and it was gone. I was glad, however, to be able to soften my statement by adding that Herr Ibsen had in his recent plays abandoned the use of verse.

The trouble was that in Browning's company he seemed practically to have abandoned the use of prose too. When, moreover, he did speak, it was always in a sense contrary to that of our host. The Risorgimento was a theme always very near to the great heart of Browning, and on this occasion he hymned it with more than his usual animation and resource (if indeed that were possible). He descanted especially on the vast increase that had accrued to the sum of human happiness in Italy since the success of that remarkable movement. When Ibsen rapped out the conviction that what Italy needed was to be invaded and conquered once and for all by Austria, I feared that an explosion was inevitable. But hardly had my translation of the inauspicious sentiment been uttered when the plum-pudding was borne into the room, flaming on its dish. I clapped my hands wildly at sight of it, in the English fashion, and was intensely relieved when the yet more resonant applause of Robert Browning followed mine. Disaster had been averted by a crowning mercy. But I am afraid that Ibsen thought us both quite mad.

The next topic that was started, harmless though it seemed at first, was fraught with yet graver peril. The world of scholarship was at that time agitated by the recent discovery of what might or might not prove to be a fragment of Sappho. Browning proclaimed his unshakable belief in the authenticity of these verses. To my surprise, Ibsen, whom I had been unprepared to regard as a classical scholar, said positively that they had not been written by Sappho. Browning challenged him to give a reason. A literal translation of the reply would have been "Because no woman ever was capable of writing a fragment of good poetry." Imagination reels at the effect this would have had on the recipient of "Sonnets from the Portuguese." The agonized interpreter, throwing honour to the winds, babbled some wholly fallacious version of the words. Again the situation had been saved; but it was of the kind that does not even in furthest retrospect lose its power to freeze the heart and constrict the diaphragm.

I was fain to thank heaven when, immediately after the termination of the meal, Ibsen rose, bowed to his host, and bade me express his thanks for the entertainment. Out on the Grand Canal, in the gondola which had again been placed at our disposal, his passion for "documents" that might bear on his work was quickly manifested. He asked me whether Herr Browning had ever married. Receiving an emphatically affirmative reply, he inquired whether Fru Browning had been happy. Loath though I was to cast a blight on his interest in the matter, I conveyed to him with all possible directness the impression that Elizabeth Barrett had assuredly been one of those wives who do not dance tarantellas nor slam front-doors. He did not, to the best of my recollection, make further mention of Browning, either then or afterwards.

Browning himself, however, thanked me warmly, next day, for having introduced my friend to him. "A capital fellow!" he exclaimed, and then, for a moment, seemed as though he were about to qualify this estimate, but ended by merely repeating "A capital fellow!"

Ibsen remained in Venice some weeks after my return to London. He was, it may be conjectured, bent on a specially close study of the Bride of the Adriatic because her marriage had been not altogether a happy one. But there appears to be no evidence whatsoever that he went again, either of his own accord or by invitation, to the Palazzo Rezzonico.

OF CHRISTMAS

BY H*L**RE B*LL*C

THERE was a man came to an Inn by night, and after he had called three times they should open him the door—though why three times, and not three times three, nor thirty times thirty, which is the number of the little stone devils that make mows at St. Aloesius of Ledera over against the marshes Gué-la-Nuce to this day, nor three hundred times three hundred (which is a bestial number), nor three thousand times three-and-thirty, upon my soul I know not, and nor do you— when, then, this jolly fellow had three times cried out, shouted, yelled, holloa'd, loudly besought, caterwauled, brayed, sung out, and roared, he did by the same token set himself to beat, hammer, bang, pummel, and knock at the door. Now the door was Oak. It had been grown in the forest of Boulevoise, hewn in Barre-le-Neuf, seasoned in South Hoxton, hinged nowhere in particular, and panelled—and that most abominably well—in Arque, where the peasants sell their souls for skill in such handicraft. But our man knew nothing of all this, which, had he known it, would have mattered little enough to him, for a reason which I propose to tell in the next sentence. The door was opened. As to the reasons why it was not opened sooner, these are most tediously set forth in Professor Sir T. K. Slibby's "Half-Hours With Historic Doors," as also in a fragment at one time attributed to Oleaginus Silo but now proven a forgery by Miss Evans. Enough for our purpose, merry reader of mine, that the door was opened.

The man, as men will, went in. And there, for God's sake and by the grace of Mary Mother, let us leave him; for the truth of it is that his strength was all in his lungs, and himself a poor, weak, clout-faced, wizen-bellied, pin-shanked bloke anyway, who at Trinity Hall had spent the most of his time in reading Hume (that was Satan's lackey) and after taking his degree did a little in the way of Imperial Finance. Of him it was that Lord Abraham Hart, that far-seeing statesman, said, "This young man has the root of the matter in him." I quote the epigram rather for its perfect form than for its truth. For once, Lord Abraham was deceived. But it must be remembered that he was at this time being plagued almost out of his wits by the vile (though cleverly engineered) agitation for the compulsory winding-up of the Rondoosdop Development Company. Afterwards, in Wormwood Scrubbs, his Lordship admitted that his estimate of his young friend had perhaps been pitched too high. In Dartmoor he has since revoked it altogether, with that manliness for which the Empire so loved him when he was at large.

Now the young man's name was Dimby—"Trot" Dimby—and his mother had been a Clupton, so that—but had I not already dismissed him? Indeed I only mentioned him because it seemed that his going to that Inn might put me on track of that One Great Ultimate and Final True Thing I am purposed to say about Christmas. Don't ask me yet what that Thing is. Truth dwells in no man, but is a shy beast you must hunt as you may in the forests that are round about the Walls of Heaven. And I do hereby curse, gibbet, and denounce *in execrationem perpetuam atque aeternam* the man who hunts in a crafty or calculating way—as, lying low, nosing for scents, squinting for trails, crawling noiselessly till he shall come near to his quarry and then taking careful aim. Here's to him who hunts Truth in the honest fashion of men, which is, going blindly at it, following his first scent (if such there be) or (if none) none, scrambling over boulders, fording torrents, winding his horn, plunging into thickets, skipping, firing off his gun in the air continually, and then ramming in some more ammunition anyhow, with a laugh and a curse if the charge explode in his own jolly face. The chances are he will bring home in his bag nothing but a field-mouse he trod on by accident. Not the less his is the true sport and the essential stuff of holiness.

As touching Christmas—but there is nothing like verse to clear the mind, heat the blood, and make very humble the heart. Rouse thee, Muse!

> One Christmas Night in Pontgibaud
>   (*Pom-pom, rub-a-dub-dub*)
> A man with a drum went to and fro
>   (*Two merry eyes, two cheeks chub*)
> Nor not a citril within, without,
> But heard the racket and heard the rout
> And marvelled what it was all about
>   (*And who shall shrive Beelzebub?*)
>
> He whacked so hard the drum was split
>   (*Pom-pom, rub-a-dub-dum*)
> Out lept Saint Gabriel from it
>   (*Praeclarissimus Omnium*)
> Who spread his wings and up he went
> Nor ever paused in his ascent
> Till he had reached the firmament
>   (*Benedicamus Dominum*).

That's what I shall sing (please God) at dawn tomorrow, standing on the high, green barrow at Storrington, where the bones of Athelstan's men are. Yea,

> At dawn tomorrow
>   On Storrington Barrow
> I'll beg or borrow
>   A bow and arrow
> And shoot sleek sorrow
>   Through the marrow.

The floods are out and the ford is narrow,
The stars hang dead and my limbs are lead,
  But ale is gold
  And there's good foot-hold
On the Cuckfield side of Storrington Barrow.

This too I shall sing, and other songs that are yet to write. In Pagham I shall sing them again, and again in Little Dewstead. In Hornside I shall rewrite them, and at the Scythe and Turtle in Liphook (if I have patience) annotate them. At Selsey they will be very damnably in the way, and I don't at all know what I shall do with them at Selsey.

Such then, as I see it, is the whole pith, mystery, outer form, common acceptation, purpose, usage usual, meaning and inner meaning, beauty intrinsic and extrinsic, and right character of Christmas Feast. *Habent urbs atque orbis revelationem.* Pray for my soul.

A STRAIGHT TALK

BY G**RGE B*RN*RD SH*W

(Preface to "Snt George. A Christmas Play.")

WHEN a public man lays his hand on his heart and declares that his conduct needs no apology, the audience hastens to put up its umbrellas against the particularly severe downpour of apologies in store for it. I won't give the customary warning. My conduct shrieks aloud for apology, and you are in for a thorough drenching.

Flatly, I stole this play. The one valid excuse for the theft would be mental starvation. That excuse I shant plead. I could have made a dozen better plays than this out of my own head. You dont suppose Shakespeare was so vacant in the upper story that there was nothing for it but to rummage through cinquecento romances, Townley Mysteries, and suchlike insanitary rubbish-heaps, in order that he might fish out enough scraps for his artistic fangs to fasten on. Depend on it, there were plenty of decent original notions seething behind yon marble brow. Why didnt our William use them? He was too lazy. And so am I. It is easier to give a new twist to somebody else's story that you take readymade than to perform that highly-specialized form of skilled labour which consists in giving artistic coherence to a story that you have conceived roughly for yourself. A literary gentleman once hoisted a theory that there are only thirty-six possible stories in the world. This—I say it with no deference at all—is bosh. There are as many possible stories in the world as there are microbes in the well-lined shelves of a literary gentleman's "den." On the other hand, it is perfectly true that only a baker's dozen of these have got themselves told. The reason lies in that bland, unalterable resolve to shirk honest work, by which you recognize the artist as surely as you recognize the leopard by his spots. In so far as I am an artist, I am a loafer. And if you expect me, in that line, to do anything but loaf, you will get the shock your romantic folly deserves. The only difference between me and my rivals past and present is that I have the decency to be ashamed of myself. So that if you are not too bemused and bedevilled by my "brilliancy" to kick me downstairs, you may rely on me to cheerfully lend a foot in the operation. But, while I have my share of judicial vindictiveness against crime, Im not going to talk the common judicial cant about brutality making a Better Man of the criminal. I havent the slightest doubt that I would thieve again at the earliest opportunity. Meanwhile be so good as to listen to the evidence on the present charge.

In the December after I was first cast ashore at Holyhead, I had to go down to Dorsetshire. In those days the more enterprising farm-labourers used still to annually dress themselves up in order to tickle the gentry into disbursing the money needed to supplement a local-minimum wage. They called themselves the Christmas Mummers, and performed a play entitled Snt George. As my education had been of the typical Irish kind, and the ideas on which I had been nourished were precisely the ideas that once in Tara's Hall were regarded as dangerous novelties, Snt George staggered me with the sense of being suddenly bumped up against a thing which lay centuries ahead of the time I had been born into. (Being, in point of fact, only a matter of five hundred years old, it would have the same effect today on the average London playgoer if it was produced in a west end theatre.) The plot was simple. It is set forth in Thomas Hardy's "Return of the Native"; but, as the people who read my books have no energy left over to cope with other authors, I must supply an outline of it myself.

Entered, first of all, the English Knight, announcing his determination to fight and vanquish the Turkish Knight, a vastly superior swordsman, who promptly made mincemeat of him. After the Saracen had celebrated his victory in verse, and proclaimed himself the world's champion, entered Snt George, who, after some preliminary patriotic flourishes, promptly made mincemeat of the Saracen—to the blank amazement of an audience which included several retired army officers. Snt George, however, saved his face by the usual expedient of the victorious British general, attributing to Providence a result which by no polite stretch of casuistry could have been traced to the operations of his own brain. But here the dramatist was confronted by another difficulty: there being no curtain to ring down, how were the two corpses to be got gracefully rid of? Entered therefore the Physician, and brought them both to life. (Any one objecting to this scene on the score of romantic improbability is hereby referred to the Royal College of Physicians, or to the directors of any accredited medical journal, who will hail with delight this opportunity of proving once and for all that re-vitalization is the child's-play of the Faculty.)

Such then is the play that I have stolen. For all the many pleasing æsthetic qualities you will find in it—dramatic inventiveness, humour and pathos, eloquence, elfin glamour and the like—you must bless the original author: of these things I have only the usufruct. To me the play owes nothing but the stiffening of civistic conscience that has been crammed in. Modest? Not a bit of it. It is my civistic conscience that makes a man of me and (incidentally) makes this play a masterpiece.

Nothing could have been easier for me (if I were some one else) than to perform my task in that God-rest-you-merry-gentlemen-may-nothing-you-dismay spirit which so grossly flatters the sensibilities of the average citizen by its assumption that he is sharp enough to be dismayed by what stares him in the face. Charles Dickens had lucid intervals in which he was vaguely conscious of the abuses around him; but his spasmodic efforts to expose these brought him into contact with realities so agonizing to his high-strung literary nerves that he invariably sank back into debauches of unsocial optimism. Even the Swan of Avon had his glimpses of the havoc of displacement wrought by Elizabethan romanticism in the social machine which had been working with tolerable smoothness under the prosaic guidance of Henry 8. The time was out of joint; and the Swan, recognizing that he was the last person to ever set it right, consoled himself by offering the world a soothing doctrine of despair. Not for me, thank you, that Swans-down pillow. I refuse as flatly to fuddle myself in the shop of "W. Shakespeare, Druggist," as to stimulate myself with the juicy joints of "C. Dickens, Family Butcher." Of these and suchlike pernicious establishments my patronage consists in weaving round the shopdoor a barbed-wire entanglement of dialectic and then training my moral machine-guns on the customers.

In this devilish function I have, as you know, acquired by practice a tremendous technical skill; and but for the more or less innocent pride I take in showing off my accomplishment to all and sundry, I doubt whether even my iron nerves would be proof against the horrors that have impelled me to thus perfect myself. In my nonage I believed humanity could be reformed if only it were intelligently preached at for a sufficiently long period. This first fine careless rapture I could no more recapture, at my age, than I could recapture hoopingcough or nettlerash. One by one, I have flung all political nostra overboard, till there remain only dynamite and scientific breeding. My touching faith in these saves me from pessimism: I believe in the future; but this only makes the present—which I foresee as going strong for a couple of million of years or so—all the more excruciating by contrast.

For casting into dramatic form a compendium of my indictments of the present from a purely political standpoint, the old play of Snt George occurred to me as having exactly the framework I needed. In the person of the Turkish Knight I could embody that howling chaos which does duty among us for a body-politic. The English Knight would accordingly be the Liberal Party, whose efforts (whenever it is in favour with the electorate) to reduce chaos to order by emulating in foreign politics the blackguardism of a Metternich or Bismarck, and in home politics the spirited attitudinizings to the Garibaldi or Cavour, are foredoomed to the failure which its inherent oldmaidishness must always win for the Liberal Party in all undertakings whatsoever. Snt George is, of course, myself. But here my very aptitude in controversy tripped me up as playwright. Owing to my knack of going straight to the root of the matter in hand and substituting, before you can say Jack Robinson, a truth for every fallacy and a natural law for every convention, the scene of Snt George (Bernard Shaw)'s victory over the Turkish Knight came out too short for theatrical purposes. I calculated that the play as it stood would not occupy more than five hours in performance. I therefore departed from the original scheme so far as to provide the Turkish Knight with three attendant monsters, severally named the Good, the Beyootiful, and the Ter-rew, and representing in themselves the current forms of Religion, Art, and Science. These three Snt George successively challenges, tackles, and flattens out—the first as lunacy, the second as harlotry, the third as witchcraft. But even so the play would not be long enough had I not padded a good deal of buffoonery into the scene where the five corpses are brought back to life.

The restorative Physician symbolizes that irresistible force of human stupidity by which the rottenest and basest institutions are enabled to thrive in the teeth of the logic that has demolished them. Thus, for the author, the close of the play is essentially tragic. But what is death to him is fun to you, and my buffooneries wont offend any of you. Bah!

FOND HEARTS ASKEW

BY M**R*CE H*WL*TT

To

WILLIAM ROBERTSON NICOLL
SAGE AND REVEREND
AND A TRUE KNIGHT
THIS ROMAUNT
OF DAYS EDVARDIAN

PROLOGUE

Too *strong a wine, belike, for some stomachs, for there's honey in it, and a dibbet of gore, with other condiments. Yet Mistress Clio (with whom, some say, Mistress Thalia, that sweet hoyden) brewed it: she, not I, who do but hand the cup round by her warrant and good favour. Her guests, not mine, you shall take it or leave it—spill it untasted or quaff a bellyful. Of a hospitable temper, she whose page I am; but a great lady, over self-sure to be dudgeoned by wry faces in the refectory. As for the little sister (if she did have finger in the concoction)—no fear of offence there! I dare vow, who know somewhat the fashion of her, she will but trill a pretty titter or so at your qualms.*

BENEDICTUS BENEDICAT.

I CRY you mercy for a lacuna at the outset. I know not what had knitted and blackened the brows of certain two speeding eastward through London, enhansomed, on the night of the feast of St. Box: *alter,* Geoffrey Dizzard, called "The Honourable," *lieu-tenant* in the Guards of Edward the Peace Getter; *altera,* the Lady Angelica Plantaganet, to him affianced. Devil take the cause of the bicker: enough that they were at sulks. Here's for a sight of the girl!

Johannes Sargent, that swift giant from the New World, had already flung her on canvas, with a brace of sisters. She outstands there, a virgin poplar-tall; hair like ravelled flax and coiffed in the fashion of the period; neck like a giraffe's; lips shaped for kissing rather than smiling; eyes like a giraffe's again; breasts like a boy's, and something of a dressed-up boy in the total aspect of her. She has arms a trifle long even for such height as hers; fingers very long, too, with red-pink nails trimmed to a point. She looks out slantwise, conscious of her beauty, and perhaps of certain other things. Fire under that ice, I conjecture— red corpuscles rampant behind that meek white mask of hers. *"Forsitan in hoc anno pulcherrima debutantium"* is the verdict of a contemporary journal. For *"forsitan"* read *"certe."* No slur, that, on the rest of the bevy.

Very much as Johannes had seen her did she appear now to the cits, as the cabriolet swung past them. Paramount there, she was still more paramount here. Yet this Geoffrey was not ill-looking. In the secret journal of Mary Jane, serving-wench in the palace of Geoffrey's father (who gat his barony by beer) note is made of his "lovely blue eyes; complexion like a blush rose; hands like a girl's; lips like a girl's again; yellow curls close cropped; and for moustachio (so young is he yet) such a shadow as amber might cast on water."

Here, had I my will, I would limn you Mary Jane herself, that parched nymph. Time urges, though. The cabrioleteer thrashes his horse (me with it) to a canter, and plunges into Soho. Some wagon athwart the path gives pause. Angelica, looking about her, bites lip. For this is the street of Wardour, wherein (say all the chronicles most absolutely) she and Geoffrey had first met and plit their troth.

"Methinks," cries she, loud and clear to the wagoner, and pointing finger at Geoffrey, "the Devil must be between your shafts, to make a mock of me in this conjunction, the which is truly of his own doing."

"Sweet madam," says Geoffrey (who was also called "The Ready"), "shall I help harness you at his side? Though, for my part, I doubt 'twere supererogant, in that he buckled you to his service or ever the priest dipped you."

A bitter jest, this; and the thought of it still tingled on the girl's cheek and clawed her heart when Geoffrey handed her down at the portico of Drury Lane Theatre. A new pantomime was afoot. Geoffrey's father (that bluff red baron) had chartered a box, was already there with his lady and others.

Lily among peonies, Angelica sat brooding, her eyes fastened on the stage, Geoffrey behind her chair, brooding by the same token. Presto, he saw a flood of pink rush up her shoulders to her ears. The "principal boy" had just skipped on to the stage. No boy at all (God be witness), but one Mistress Tina Vandeleur, very apt in masquerado, and seeming true boy enough to the guileless. Stout of leg, light-footed, with a tricksy plume to his cap, and the swagger of one who would beard the Saints for a wager, this Aladdin was just such a galliard as Angelica had often fondled in her dreams. He lept straight into the closet of her heart, and "Deus!" she cried, "maugre my maidenhood, I will follow those pretty heels round the earth!"

Cried Geoffrey "Yea! and will not I presently string his ham to save your panting?"

"*Tacete!*" cried the groundlings.

A moment after, Geoffrey forgot his spleen. Cupid had noosed him —bound him tight to the Widow Twankey. This was a woman most unlike to Angelica: poplar-tall, I grant you; but elm-wide into the bargain; deep-voiced, robustious, and puffed bravely out with hot vital essences. Seemed so to Geoffrey, at least, who had no smattering of theatres and knew not his cynosure to be none other than Master Willie Joffers, prime buffo of the day. Like Angelica, he had had fond visions; and lo here, the very lady of them!

Says he to Angelica, "I am heartset on this widow."

"By so much the better!" she laughs. "I to my peacock, you to your peahen, with a God-speed from each to other."

How to snare the birds? A pretty problem: the fowling was like to be delicate. So hale a strutter as Aladdin could not lack for bonamies,

"Will he deign me?" wondered meek Angelica. "This widow," thought Geoffrey, "is belike no widow at all, but a modest wife with a yea for no man but her lord." Head to head they took counsel, cudgelled their wits for some proper vantage. Of a sudden, Geoffrey clapped hand to thigh. Student of Boccaccio, Heveletius, and other sages, he had the clue in his palm. A whisper 'from him, a nod from Angelica, and the twain withdrew from the box into the corridor without.

There, back to back, they disrobed swiftly, each tossing to other every garment as it was doffed. Then a flurried toilet, and a difficult, for the man especially; but hotness of desire breeds dexterity. When they turned and faced each other, Angelica was such a boy as Aladdin would not spurn as page, Geoffrey such a girl as the widow might well covet as body-maid.

Out they hied under the stars, and sought way to the postern whereby the mummers would come when their work were done. Thereat they stationed themselves in shadow. A bitter night, with a lather of snow on the cobbles; but they were heedless of that: love and their dancing hearts warmed them.

They waited long. Strings of muffled figures began to file out, but never an one like to Aladdin or the Widow. Midnight tolled. Had these two had wind of the ambuscado and crept out by another door? Nay, patience!

At last! A figure showed in the doorway—a figure cloaked womanly, but topped with face of Aladdin. Trousered Angelica, with a cry, darted forth from the shadow. To Mistress Vandeleur's eyes she was as truly man as was Mistress Vandeleur to hers. Thus confronted, Mistress Vandeleur shrank back, blushing hot.

"Nay!" laughs Angelica, clipping her by the wrists. "Cold boy, you shall not so easily slip me. A pretty girl you make, Aladdin; but love pierces such disguise as a rapier might pierce lard."

"Madman! Unhandle me!" screams the actress.

"No madman I, as well you know," answers Angelica, "but a maid whom spurned love may yet madden. Kiss me on the lips."

While they struggle, another figure fills the postern, and in an instant Angelica is torn aside by Master Willie Joffers (well versed, for all his mumming, in matters of chivalry). "Kisses for such coward lips?" cries he. "Nay, but a swinge to silence them!" and would have struck trousered Angelica full on the mouth. But décolleté Geoffrey Dizzard, crying at him "Sweet termagant, think not to baffle me by these airs of manhood!" had sprung in the way and on his own nose received the blow.

. He staggered and, spurting blood, fell. Up go the buffo's hands, and "Now may the Saints whip me," cries he, "for a tapster of girl's blood!" and fled into the night, howling like a dog. Mistress Vandeleur had fled already. Down on her knees goes Angelica, to staunch Geoffrey's flux.

Thus far, straight history. Apocrypha, all the rest: you shall pick your own sequel. As for instance, some say Geoffrey bled to the death, whereby stepped Master Joffers to the scaffold, and Angelica (the Vandeleur too, like as not) to a nunnery. Others have it he lived, thanks to nurse Angelica, who, thereon wed, suckled him twin Dizzards in due season. Joffers, they say, had wife already, else would have wed the Vandeleur, for sake of symmetry.

DICKENS

BY G**RGE M**RE

I HAD often wondered why when people talked to me of Tintoretto I always found myself thinking of Turgéneff. It seemed to me strange that I should think of Turgéneff instead of thinking of Tintoretto; for at first sight nothing can be more far apart than the Slav mind and the Flemish. But one morning, some years ago, while I was musing by my fireplace in Victoria Street, Dolmetsch came to see me. He had a soiled roll of music under his left arm. I said, "How are you?" He said, "I am well. And you?" I said, "I, too, am well. What is that, my dear Dolmetsch, that you carry under your left arm?" He answered, "It is a Mass by Palestrina." "Will you read me the score?" I asked. I was afraid he would say no. But Dolmetsch is not one of those men who say no, and he read me the score. He did not read very well, but I had never heard it before, so when he finished I begged of him he would read it to me again. He said, "Very well, Moore, I will read it to you again." I remember his exact words, because they seemed to me at the time to be the sort of thing that only Dolmetsch could have said. It was a foggy morning in Victoria Street, and while Dolmetsch read again the first few bars, I thought how Renoir would have loved to paint in such an atmosphere the tops of the plane trees that flaccidly show above the wall of Buckingham Palace.... Why had I never been invited to Buckingham Palace? I did not want to go there, but it would have been nice to have been asked. ... How *brave gaillard* was Renoir, and how well he painted from that subfuse palette! ...

My roving thoughts were caught back to the divine score which Arnold Dolmetsch was reading to me. How well placed they were, those semibreves! Could anyone but Palestrina have placed them so nicely? I wondered what girl Palestrina was courting when he conceived them. She must have been blonde, surely, and with narrow flanks.... There are moments when one does not think of girls, are there not, dear reader? And I swear to you that such a moment came to me while Dolmetsch mumbled the last two bars of that Mass. The notes were "do, la, sol, do, fa, do, sol, la," and as he mumbled them I sat upright and stared into space, for it had become suddenly plain to me why when people talked of Tintoretto I always found myself thinking of Turgéneff.

I do not say that this story that I have told to you is a very good story, and I am afraid that I have not well told it. Some day, when I have time, I should like to re-write it. But meantime I let it stand, because without it you could not receive what is upmost in my thoughts, and which I wish you to share with me. Without it, what I am yearning to say might seem to you a hard saying; but now you will understand me.

There never was a writer except Dickens. Perhaps you have never heard say of him? No matter, till a few days past he was only a name to me. I remember that when I was a young man in Paris, I read a praise of him in some journal; but in those days I was kneeling at other altars, I was scrubbing other doorsteps. . . . So has it been ever since; always a false god, always the wrong doorstep. I am sick of the smell of the incense I have swung to this and that false god—Zola, Yeats, *et tous ces autres*. I am angry to have got housemaid's knee, because I got it on doorsteps that led to nowhere. There is but one doorstep worth scrubbing. The doorstep of Charles Dickens. . . .

Did he write many books? I know not, it does not greatly matter, he wrote the "Pickwick Papers"; that suffices. I have read as yet but one chapter, describing a Christmas party in a country house. Strange that anyone should have essayed to write about anything but that! Christmas—I see it now—is the only moment in which men and women are really alive, are really worth writing about. At other seasons they do not exist for the purpose of art. I spit on all seasons except Christmas . . . Is he not in all fiction the greatest figure, this Mr. Wardell, this old "squire" rosy-cheeked, who entertains this Christmas party at his house? He is more truthful, he is more significant, than any figure in Balzac. He is better than all Balzac's figures rolled into one . . . I used to kneel on that doorstep. Balzac wrote many books. But now it behoves me to ask myself whether he ever wrote a good book. One knows that he used to write for fifteen hours at a stretch, gulping down coffee all the while. But it does not follow that the coffee was good, nor does it follow that what he wrote was good. The Comédie Humaine is all chicory . . . I had wished for some years to say this, I am glad *d'avoir débarrassé ma poitrine de ça*.

To have described divinely a Christmas party is something, but it is not everything. The disengaging of the erotic motive is everything, is the only touchstone. If while that is being done we are soothed into a trance, a nebulous delirium of the nerves, then we know the novelist to be a supreme novelist. If we retain consciousness, he is not supreme, and to be less than supreme in art is to not exist . . . Dickens disengages the erotic motive through two figures, Mr. Winkle, a sportman, and Miss Arabella, "a young lady with fur-topped boots." They go skating, he helps her over a stile. Can one not well see her? She steps over the stile and her shin defines itself through her balbriggan stocking. She is a knock-kneed girl, and she looks at Mr. Winkle with that sensual regard that sometimes comes when the wind is north-west. Yes, it is a north-west wind that is blowing over this landscape that Hals or Winchoven might have painted—no, Winchoven would have fumbled it with rose-madder, but Hals would have done it well. Hals would have approved—would he not?—the pollard aspens, these pollard aspens deciduous and wistful, which the rime makes glistening. That field, how well ploughed it is, and are they not like petticoats, those clouds low-hanging? Yes, Hals would have stated them well, but only Manet could have stated the slope of the thighs of the girl—how does she call herself?—Arabella—it is a so hard name to remember—as she steps across the stile. Manet would have found pleasure in her cheeks also. They are a little chapped with the north-west wind that makes the pollard aspens to quiver. How adorable a thing it is, a girl's nose that the north-west wind renders red! We may tire of it sometimes, because we sometimes tire of all things, but Winkle does not know this. Is Arabella his mistress? If she is not, she has been, or at any rate she will be. How full she is of temperament, is she not? Her shoulder-blades seem a little carelessly modelled, but how good they are in intention! How well placed that smut on her left cheek!

Strange thoughts of her surge up vaguely in me as I watch her—thoughts that I cannot express in English. . . . Elle est plus vieille que les roches entre lesquelles elle s'est assise; comme le vampire elle a été fréquemment morte, et a appris les secrets du tombeau; et s'est plongée dans des mers profondes, et conserve autour d'elle leur jour ruiné; et, comme Lède, était mère d'Hélène de Troie, et, comme Sainte-Anne, mère de Maria; et tout cela n'a été pour elle que. . . . I desist, for not through French can be expressed the thoughts that surge in me. French is a stale language. So are all the European languages, one can say in them nothing fresh. . . . The stalest of them all is Erse. . . .

Deep down in my heart a sudden voice whispers me that there is only one land wherein art may reveal herself once more. Of what avail to await her anywhere else than in Mexico? Only there can the apocalypse happen. I will take a ticket for Mexico, I will buy a Mexican grammar, I will be a Mexican. . . . On a hillside, or beside some grey pool, gazing out across those plains poor and arid, I will await the first pale showings of the new dawn. . . .

EUPHEMIA CLASHTHOUGHT[1]

AN IMITATION OF MEREDITH

IN the heart of insular Cosmos, remote by some scores of leagues of Hodge-trod arable or pastoral, not more than a snuff-pinch for gaping tourist nostrils accustomed to inhalation of prairie winds, but enough for perspective, from those marginal sands, trident-scraped, we are to fancy, by a helmeted Dame Abstract familiarly profiled on disks of current bronze—price of a loaf for humbler maws disdainful of Gallic side-dishes for the titillation of choicer palates—stands Clashthought Park, a house of some pretension, mentioned at Runnymede, with the spreading exception of wings given to it in later times by Dædalean masters not to be balked of billiards or traps for Terpsichore, and owned for unbroken generations by a healthy line of procreant Clash-thoughts, to the undoing of collateral branches eager for the birth of a female. Passengers through cushioned space, flying top-speed or dally-ing with obscure stations not alighted at apparently, have had it pointed out to them as beheld dimly for a privileged instant before they sink back behind crackling barrier of instructive paper with a "Thank you, Sir," or "Madam," as the case may be. Guide-books praise it. I conceive they shall be studied for a cock-shy of rainbow epithets slashed in at the target of Landed Gentry, premonitorily. The tintinnabulation's enough. Periodical footings of Clashthoughts into Mayfair or the Tyrol, signalled by the slide from its mast of a crested index of Æolian caprice, blazon of their presence, give the curious a right to spin through the halls and galleries under a cackle of housekeeper guideship

---

[1] It were not, as a general rule, well to republish after a man's death the skit you made of his work while he lived. Meredith, however, was so transcendent that such skits must ever be harmless, and so lasting will his fame be that they can never lose what freshness they may have had at first. So I have put this thing in with the others, making improvements that were needed.—M. B.

—scramble for a chuck of the dainties, dog fashion. There is something to be said for the rope's twist. Wisdom skips.

It is recorded that the goblins of this same Lady Wisdom were all agog one Christmas morning between the doors of the house and the village church, which crouches on the outskirt of the park, with something of a lodge in its look, you might say, more than of celestial twinkles, even with Christmas hoar-frost bleaching the grey of it in sunlight, as one sees imaged on seasonable missives for amity in the trays marked "sixpence and upwards," here and there, on the counters of barter.

Be sure these goblins made obeisance to Sir Peter Clashthought, as he passed by, starched beacon of squirearchy, wife on arm, sons to heel. After him, certain members of the household—rose-chapped males and females, bearing books of worship. The pack of goblins glance up the drive with nudging elbows and whisperings of "Where is daughter Euphemia? Where Sir Rebus, her affianced?"

Off they scamper for a peep through the windows of the house. They throng the sill of the library, ears acock and eyelids twittering admiration of a prospect. Euphemia was in view of them—essence of her. Sir Rebus was at her side. Nothing slips the goblins.

"Nymph in the Heavy Dragoons" was Mrs. Cryptic-Sparkler's famous definition of her. The County took it for final—an uncut gem with a fleck in the heart of it. Euphemia condoned the imagery. She had breadth. Heels that spread ample curves over the ground she stood on, and hands that might floor you with a clench of them, were hers. Grey eyes looked out lucid and fearless under swelling temples that were lost in a ruffling copse of hair. Her nose was virginal, with hints of the Iron Duke at most angles. Square chin, cleft centrally, gave her throat the look of a tower with a gun protrudent at top. She was dressed for church evidently, but seemed no slave to Time. Her bonnet was pushed well back from her head, and she was fingering the ribbons. One saw she was a woman. She inspired deference.

"Forefinger for Shepherd's Crook" was what Mrs. Cryptic-Sparkler had said of Sir Rebus. It shall stand at that.

"You have Prayer Book?" he queried.

She nodded. Juno catches the connubial trick.

"Hymns?"

"Ancient and Modern."

"I may share with you?"

"I know by heart. Parrots sing."

"Philomel carols," he bent to her.

"Complaints spoil a festival."

He waved hand to the door. "Lady, your father has started."

"He knows the adage. Copy-books instil it."

"Inexorable truth in it."

"We may dodge the scythe."

"To be choked with the sands?"

She flashed a smile. "I would not," he said, "that my Euphemia were late for the Absolution."

She cast eyes to the carpet. He caught them at the rebound.

"It snows," she murmured, swimming to the window.

"A flake, no more. The season claims it."

"I have thin boots."

"Another pair?"

"My maid buttons. She is at church."

"My fingers?"

"Ten on each."

"Five," he corrected.

"Buttons."

"I beg your pardon."

She saw opportunity. She swam to the bell-rope and grasped it for a tinkle. The action spread feminine curves to her lover's eyes. He was a man.

Obsequiousness loomed in the doorway. Its mistress flashed an order for port—two glasses. Sir Rebus sprang a pair of eyebrows on her. Suspicion slid down the banisters of his mind, trailing a blue ribbon. Inebriates were one of his hobbies. For an instant she was sunset.

"Medicinal," she murmured.

"Forgive me, Madam. A glass, certainly. 'Twill warm us for worshipping."

The wine appeared, seemed to blink owlishly through the facets of its decanter, like some hoary captive dragged forth into light after years of subterraneous darkness—something querulous in the sudden liberation of it. Or say that it gleamed benignant from its tray, steady-borne by the hands of reverence, as one has seen Infallibility pass with uplifting of jewelled fingers through genuflexions to the Balcony. Port has this in it: that it compels obeisance, master of us; as opposed to brother and sister wines wooing us with a coy flush in the gold of them to a cursory tope or harlequin leap shimmering up the veins with a sly wink at us through eyelets. Hussy vintages swim to a cosset. We go to Port, mark you!

Sir Rebus sipped with an affectionate twirl of thumb at the glass's stem. He said "One scents the cobwebs."

"Catches in them," Euphemia flung at him.

"I take you. Bacchus laughs in the web."

"Unspun but for Pallas."

"A lady's jealousy."

"Forethought, rather."

"Brewed in the paternal pate. Grant it!"

"For a spring in accoutrements."

Sir Rebus inclined gravely. Port precludes prolongment of the riposte.

She replenished glasses. Depreciation yielded. "A step," she said, "and we are in time for the First Lesson."

"This," he agreed, "is a wine."

"There are blasphemies in posture. One should sit to it."

"Perhaps." He sank to commodious throne of leather indicated by her finger.

Again she filled for him. "This time, no heel-taps," she was imperative. "The Litany demands basis."

"True." He drained, not repelling the decanter placed at his elbow.

"It is a wine," he presently repeated with a rolling tongue over it.

"Laid down by my great-grandfather, Cloistral."

"Strange," he said, examining the stopper, "no date. Antediluvian. Sound, though."

He drew out his note-book. *"The senses,"* he wrote, *"are internecine.*

They shall have learned esprit de corps before they enslave us." This was one of his happiest flings to general from particular. *"Visual distraction cries havoc to ultimate delicacy of palate"* would but have pinned us a butterfly best ahover; nor even so should we have had truth of why the aphorist, closing note-book and nestling back of head against that of chair, closed eyes also.

As by some such law as lurks in meteorological toy for our guidance in climes close-knit with Irony for bewilderment, making egress of old woman synchronize inevitably with old man's ingress, or the other way about, the force that closed the aphorist's eyelids parted his lips in degree according. Thus had Euphemia, erect on hearth-rug, a cavern to gaze down into. Outworks of fortifying ivory cast but denser shadows into the inexplorable. The solitudes here grew murmurous. To and fro through secret passages in the recesses leading up deviously to lesser twin caverns of nose above, the gnomes Morphean went about their business, whispering at first, but presently bold to wind horns in unison —Rolandwise, not less.

Euphremia had an ear for it; whim also to construe lord and master relaxed but reboant and soaring above the verbal to harmonic truths of abstract or transcendental, to be hummed subsequently by privileged female audience of one bent on a hook-or-crook plucking out of pith for salvation.

She caught tablets pendent at her girdle. *"How long,"* queried her stilus, *"has our sex had humour? Jael hammered."*

She might have hitched speculation further. But Mother Earth, white-mantled, called to her.

Casting eye of caution at recumbence, she paddled across the carpet and anon swam out over the snow.

Pagan young womanhood, six foot of it, spanned eight miles before luncheon.

AN AFTERWORD ON
"A CHRISTMAS GARLAND"

IN 1898, Bernard Shaw, always a brittle mechanism, lay ill with a necrosis of the bone which had followed a fall from his bicycle. Meditating moodily on his impending funeral, he comforted himself with the thought that at least all the animals he had never eaten, walking two by two, might fitly follow his coffin through the streets of London. It was Mr. Chesterton who protested that many humans would also be proud to march in that cortège. He himself, for instance, would gladly and adequately replace one of the elephants.

Meanwhile, reviewing his past from his bed of pain, Shaw could find no justification for his having spent four irrevocable years as dramatic critic of the *Saturday Review,* to which dubious sinecure he had been appointed by the late Frank Harris. If he lived to walk once more, never again would he employ that talent for crossing the threshold of a theater. His valedictory piece for the *Saturday Review* worked itself up to this peroration:

Still, the gaiety of nations must not be eclipsed. The long string of beautiful ladies who are present in the square without, awaiting, under the supervision of two gallant policemen, their turn at my bedside, must be reassured when they protest, as they will, that the light of their life will go out if my dramatic articles cease. To each of them I will present the flower left by her predecessor, and assure her that there are as good fish in the sea as ever came out of it. The younger generation is knocking at the door; and as I open it there steps sprightly in the incomparable Max.

The incomparable Max was the younger brother of the ascendant Beerbohm Tree, who at that time had not yet come to full flower in the City of Dreadful Knights but had already built His Majesty's Theatre out of the profits of *Trilby*. In the late nineties, Max Beerbohm had achieved some fame as an infallible and malignant caricaturist, but it was not until after he, too, had cried out in pain and fled from the theater—he ran all the way to Rapallo still wearing, I believe, the evening pumps with which he had been shod when the impulse smote him—that he began turning his matchless gift of caricature into verbal expression. First came *Zuleika Dobson*. Its enchanted readers constitute a cult to which the editor of this anthology does not belong. Then —in 1912—came the uncannily accurate parodies that make up the volume here reprinted. These are masterpieces in a form to which I have been addicted ever since, at a tender age, I encountered Bret Harte's exuberant travesty of *Jane Eyre*. This was called "Miss Mix" and I hereby offer a sample:

I entered, overcome with conflicting emotions. I was dressed in a narrow gown of dark serge, trimmed with black bugles. A thick green shawl was pinned across my breast. My hands were encased with black half-mittens worked with steel beads; on my feet were large pattens, originally the property of my deceased grandmother. I carried a blue cotton umbrella. As I passed before a mirror I could not help glancing at it, nor could I disguise from myself the fact that I was not handsome.

Drawing a chair into a recess, I sat down with folded hands, calmly awaiting the arrival of my master. Once or twice a fearful yell rang through the house, or the rattling of chains, and curses uttered in a deep, manly voice broke upon the oppressive stillness. I began to feel my soul rising with the emergency of the moment.

"You look alarmed, miss. You don't hear anything, do you?" asked the housekeeper nervously.

"Nothing whatever," I remarked calmly, as a terrific scream, followed by the dragging of chairs and tables in the room above, drowned for a moment my reply. "It is the silence, on the contrary, which has made me foolishly nervous."

The housekeeper looked at me approvingly, and instantly made some tea for me.

I drank seven cups; as I was beginning the eighth I heard a crash, and the next moment a man leaped into the room through the broken window.

But the perfect sentence is the one in which Miss Mix makes this observation concerning Mr. Rawjester: "I saw from the way he wiped his feet on my dress that he had again forgotten my presence."

And speaking of parodies, there comes to mind a cluster of them I relished long ago in the Christmas issue of the defunct *Metropolitan Magazine*. They were by Franklin P. Adams, a journalist whose name (and, for that matter, whose initials, as well) was then unfamiliar to me. His parodies took potshots at such local targets as O. Henry, Mary E. Wilkins, William Allen White, and Robert W. Chambers. In particular I recall the goings-on of the wealthy and high-born man-about-town in the Chambers parody. To this, the mordant Boardman Robinson had contributed a wicked burlesque of a Wenzell illustration, in which the aforesaid man-about-town, in gleaming patent-leather shoon, was portrayed in dominant and virile juxtaposition to a lady in evening dress. I shall always remember the caption to that picture as one of the two most compact parodies ever written. The caption read as follows: "Women generally obeyed Bleeker Schuylkill." However, I refer to that forgotten triumph in this context only because of an odd coincidence. Mr. Adams's group in the *Metropolitan* was published in 1909—three years before the Beerbohm book. It was called, oddly enough, "A Christmas Garland."

A. W.

THE PORTRAIT
OF M. M.

D. H. LAWRENCE'S
INTRODUCTION TO
"MEMOIRS OF
THE FOREIGN LEGION"
BY M. M.

THE PORTRAIT OF M. M.

On a dark, wet, wintry evening in November 1919, I arrived in Florence, having just got back to Italy for the first time since 1914. My wife was in Germany, gone to see her mother, also for the first time since that fatal year 1914. We were poor; who was going to bother to publish me and to pay for my writings, in 1918 and 1919? I landed in Italy with nine pounds in my pocket and about twelve pounds lying in the bank in London. Nothing more. My wife, I hoped, would arrive in Florence with two or three pounds remaining. We should have to go very softly, if we were to house ourselves in Italy for the winter. But after the desperate weariness of the war, one could not bother.

So I had written to N—— D—— to get me a cheap room somewhere in Florence, and to leave a note at Cook's. I deposited my bit of luggage at the station, and walked to Cook's in the Via Tornabuoni. Florence was strange to me: seemed grim and dark and rather awful on the cold November evening. There was a note from D——, who has never left me in the lurch. I went down the Lung' Arno to the address he gave.

I had just passed the end of the Ponte Vecchio, and was watching the first lights of evening and the last light of day on the swollen river as I walked, when I heard D——'s voice:

"Isn't that Lawrence? Why, of course it is, of course it is, beard and all! Well, how are you, eh? You got my note? Well, now, my dear boy, you just go on to the Cavelotti—straight ahead, straight ahead—you've got the number. There's a room for you there. We shall be there in half an hour. Oh, let me introduce you to M——"

I had unconsciously seen the two men approaching, D—— tall and portly, the other man rather short and strutting. They were both buttoned up in their overcoats, and both had rather curly little hats. But

D—— was decidedly shabby and a gentleman, with his wicked red face and tufted eyebrows. The other man was almost smart, all in grey, and he looked at first sight like an actor-manager, common. There was a touch of down-on-his-luck about him too. He looked at me, buttoned up in my old thick overcoat, and with my beard bushy and raggy because of my horror of entering a strange barber's shop, and he greeted me in a rather fastidious voice, and a little patronizingly. I forgot to say I was carrying a small handbag. But I realized at once that I ought, in this little grey-sparrow man's eyes—he stuck his front out tubbily, like a bird, and his legs seemed to perch behind him, as a bird's do— I ought to be in a cab. But I wasn't. He eyed me in that shrewd and rather impertinent way of the world of actor-managers: cosmopolitan, knocking shabbily round the world.

He looked a man of about forty, spruce and youngish in his deportment, very pink-faced, and very clean, very natty, very alert, like a sparrow painted to resemble a tom-tit. He was just the kind of man I had never met: little smart man of the shabby world, very much on the spot, don't you know.

"How much does it cost?" I asked D——, meaning the room.

"Oh, my dear fellow, a trifle. Ten francs a day. Third rate, tenth rate, but not bad at the price. Pension terms of course—everything included—except wine."

"Oh, no, not at all bad for the money," said M——. "Well, now, shall we be moving? You want the postoffice, D——?" His voice was precise and a little mincing, and it had an odd high squeak.

"I do," said D——.

"Well, then, come down here—" M—— turned to a dark little alley.

"Not at all," said D——. "We turn down by the bridge."

"This is quicker," said M——. He had a twang rather than an accent in his speech—not definitely American.

He knew all the short cuts of Florence. Afterwards I found that he knew all the short cuts in all the big towns of Europe.

I went on to the Cavelotti and waited in an awful plush and gilt drawing-room, and was given at last a cup of weird muddy brown slush called tea, and a bit of weird brown mush called jam on some bits of bread. Then I was taken to my room. It was far off, on the third floor of the big, ancient, deserted Florentine house. There I had a big and lonely, stone-comfortless room looking on to the river. Fortunately it was not very cold inside, and I didn't care. The adventure of being back in Florence again after the years of war made one indifferent.

After an hour or so someone tapped. It was D—— coming in with his grandiose air—now a bit shabby, but still very courtly.

"Why, here you are—miles and miles from human habitation! I *told* her to put you on the second floor, where we are. What does she mean by it? Ring that bell. Ring it."

"No," said I, "I'm all right here."

"What!" cried D——. "In this Spitzbergen! Where's that bell?"

"Don't ring it," said I, who have a horror of chambermaids and explanations.

"Not ring it! Well, you're a man, you are! Come on then. Come on down to my room. Come on. Have you had some tea—filthy muck they call tea here? I never drink it."

I went down to D——'s room on the lower floor. It was a littered mass of books and typewriter and papers: D—— was just finishing his novel. M—— was resting on the bed, in his shirt sleeves: a tubby, fresh-faced little man in a suit of grey, faced cloth bound at the edges with grey silk braid. He had light blue eyes, tired underneath, and crisp, curly, dark brown hair just grey at the temples. But everything was neat and even finicking about his person.

"Sit down! Sit down!" said D——, wheeling up a chair. "Have a whisky?"

"Whisky!" said I.

"Twenty-four francs a bottle—and a find at that," moaned D——. I must tell that the exchange was then about forty-five lire to the pound.

"Oh, N——," said M——, "I didn't tell you. I was offered a bottle of 1913 Black and White for twenty-eight lire."

"Did you buy it?"

"No. It's your turn to buy a bottle."

"Twenty-eight francs—my dear fellow!" said D——, cocking up his eyebrows. "I shall have to starve myself to do it."

"Oh, no you won't, you'll eat here just the same," said M——.

"Yes, and I'm starved to death. Starved to death by the muck—the absolute muck they call food here. I can't face twenty eight francs, my dear chap—can't be done, on my honour."

"Well, look here, N——. We'll both buy a bottle. And you can get the one at twenty-two, and I'll buy the one at twenty-eight."

So it always was, M—— indulged D——, and spoilt him in every way. And of course D—— wasn't grateful. *Au contraire!* And M——'s pale blue smallish round eyes, in his cockatoo-pink face, would harden to indignation occasionally.

The room was dreadful. D—— never opened the windows: didn't believe in opening windows. He believed that a certain amount of nitrogen—I should say a great amount—is beneficial. The queer smell of a bedroom which is slept in, worked in, lived in, smoked in, and in which men drink their whiskies, was something new to me. But I didn't care. One had got away from the war.

We drank our whiskies before dinner. M—— was rather yellow under the eyes, and irritable; even his pink fattish face went yellowish.

"Look here," said D——. "Didn't you say there was a turkey for dinner? What? Have you been to the kitchen to see what they're doing to it?"

"Yes," said M—— testily. "I forced them to prepare it to roast."

"With chestnuts—stuffed with chestnuts?" said D——.

"They *said* so," said M——.

"Oh, but go down and see that they're doing it. Yes, you've got to keep your eye on them, got to. The most awful howlers if you don't. You go now and see what they're up to." D—— used his most irresistible grand manner.

"It's too late," persisted M——, testy.

"It's *never* too late. You just run down and absolutely prevent them from boiling that bird in the old soup-water," said D——. "If you need force, fetch me."

M—— went. He was a great epicure, and knew how things should be cooked. But of course his irruptions into the kitchen roused considerable resentment, and he was getting quaky. However, he went. He came back to say the turkey was being roasted, but without chestnuts. "What did I tell you! What did I tell you!" cried D——. "They are absolute—! If you don't hold them by the neck while they peel the chestnuts, they'll stuff the bird with old boots, to save themselves trouble. Of course, you should have gone down sooner, M——."

Dinner was always late, so the whisky was usually two whiskies. Then we went down, and were merry in spite of all things. That is, D—— always grumbled about the food. There was one unfortunate youth who was boots and porter and waiter and all. He brought the big dish to D——, and D—— always poked and pushed among the portions, and grumbled frantically, sotto voce, in Italian to the youth Beppo, getting into a nervous frenzy. Then M—— called the waiter to himself, picked the nicest bits off the dish and gave them to D——, then helped himself.

The food was not good, but with D—— it was an obsession. With the waiter he was terrible. *"Cos' è? Zuppa? Grazie. No, niente per me. No! No! Quest' acqua sporca non bevo io.* I don't drink this dirty water. What—What's that in it—a piece of dish clout? Oh, holy Dio, I can't eat another thing this evening——"

And he yelled for more bread—bread being war-rations and very limited in supply—so M—— in nervous distress gave him his piece, and D—— threw the crumb part on the floor, anywhere, and called for another litre. We always drank heavy dark red wine at three francs a litre. D—— drank two-thirds, M—— drank least. He loved his liquors, and did not care for wine. We were noisy and unabashed at table. The old Danish ladies at the other end of the room, and the rather impecunious young Duca and family not far off were not supposed to understand English. The Italians rather liked the noise, and the young signorina with the high-up yellow hair eyed us with profound interest. On we sailed, gay and noisy, D—— telling witty anecdotes and grumbling wildly and only half whimsically about the food. We sat on till most people had finished, then went up to more whisky—one more perhaps—in M——'s room.

When I came down in the morning I was called into M——'s room. He was like a little pontiff in a blue kimono-shaped dressing-gown with a broad border of reddish purple: the blue was a soft mid-blue, the material a dull silk. So he minced about, in *demi-toilette*. His room was very clean and neat, and slightly perfumed with essences. On his dressing-table stood many cut-glass bottles and silver-topped bottles with essences and pomades and powders, and heaven knows what. A very elegant little prayer book lay by his bed—and a life of St. Benedict. For M—— was a Roman Catholic convert. All he had was expensive and finicking: thick leather silver-studded suit-cases standing near the wall, trouser-stretcher all nice, hair-brushes and clothes-brush with old ivory backs. I wondered over him and his niceties and little pomposities. He was a new bird to me.

For he wasn't at all just the common person he looked. He was queer and sensitive as a woman with D——, and patient and fastidious. And yet he *was* common, his very accent was common, and D—— despised him.

And M—— rather despised me because I did not spend money. I paid for a third of the wine we drank at dinner, and bought the third bottle of whisky we had during M——'s stay. After all, he only stayed three days. But I would not spend for myself. I had no money to spend, since I knew I must live and my wife must live.

"Oh," said M——. "Why, that's the very time to spend money, when you've got none. If you've got none, why try to save it? That's been my philosophy all my life; when you've got no money, you may just as well spend it. If you've got a good deal, that's the time to look after it." Then he laughed his queer little laugh, rather squeaky. These were his exact words.

"Precisely," said D——. "Spend when you've nothing to spend, my boy. Spent *hard* then."

"No," said I. "If I can help it, I will never let myself be penniless while I live. I mistrust the world too much."

"But if you're going to live in fear of the world," said M——, "what's the good of living at all? Might as well die."

I think I give his words almost verbatim. He had a certain impatience of me and of my presence. Yet we had some jolly times—mostly in one or other of their bedrooms, drinking a whisky and talking. We drank a bottle a day—I had very little, preferring the wine at lunch and dinner, which seemed delicious after the war famine. D—— would bring up the remains of the second litre in the evening, to go on with before the coffee came.

I arrived in Florence on the Wednesday or Thursday evening; I think Thursday. M—— was due to leave for Rome on the Saturday. I asked D—— who M—— was. "Oh, you never know what he's at. He was manager for Isadora Duncan for a long time—knows all the capitals of Europe: St. Petersburg, Moscow, Tiflis, Constantinople, Berlin, Paris—knows them as you and I know Florence. He's been mostly in that line—theatrical. Then a journalist. He edited the *Roman Review* till the war killed it. Oh, a many-sided sort of fellow."

"But how do you know him?" said I.

"I met him in Capri years and years ago—oh, sixteen years ago—and clean forgot all about him till somebody came to me one day in Rome and said: 'You're N—— D——.' *I* didn't know who he was. But he'd never forgotten me. Seems to be smitten by me, somehow or other. All the better for me—ha-ha!—if he *likes* to run round for me. My dear fellow, I wouldn't prevent him, if it amuses him. Not for worlds."

And that was how it was. M—— ran D——'s errands, forced the other man to go to the tailor, to the dentist, and was almost a guardian angel to him.

"Look here!" cried D——. "I *can't* go to that damned tailor. Let the thing wait, I can't go."

"Oh, yes. Now look here, N——, if you don't get it done now while I'm here, you'll never get it done. I made the appointment for three o'clock——"

"To hell with you! Details! Details! I can't stand it, I tell you."

D—— chafed and kicked, but went.

"A little fussy fellow," he said. "Oh, yes, fussing about like a woman. Fussy, you know, fussy. I *can't stand* these fussy—" And D—— went off into improprieties.

Well, M—— ran round and arranged D——'s affairs and settled his little bills, and was so benevolent, and so impatient and nettled at the ungrateful way in which the benevolence was accepted. And D—— despised him all the time as a little busybody and an inferior. And I there between them just wondered. It seemed to me M—— would get very irritable and nervous at midday and before dinner, yellow around the eyes and played out. He wanted his whisky. He was tired after running round on a thousand errands and quests which I never understood. He always took his morning coffee at dawn, and was out to early Mass and pushing his affairs before eight o'clock in the morning. But what his affairs were I still do not know. Mass is all I am certain of.

However, it was his birthday on the Sunday, and D—— would not let him go. He had once said he would give a dinner for his birthday, and this he was not allowed to forget. It seemed to me M—— rather wanted to get out of it. But D—— was determined to have that dinner.

"You aren't going before you've given us that hare, don't you imagine it, my boy. I've got the smell of that hare in my imagination, and I've damned well got to set my teeth in it. Don't you imagine you're going without having produced that hare."

So poor M——, rather a victim, had to consent. We discussed what we should eat. It was decided the hare should have truffles, and a dish of champignons, and cauliflower, and zabaioni—and I forget what else. It was to be on Saturday evening. And M—— would leave on Sunday for Rome.

Early on the Saturday morning he went out, with the first daylight, to the old market, to get the hare and the mushrooms. He went himself because he was a connoisseur.

On the Saturday afternoon D—— took me wandering round to buy a birthday present.

"I shall have to buy him something—have to—have to—" he said fretfully. He only wanted to spend about five francs. We trailed over the Ponte Vecchio, looking at the jewellers' booths there. It was before the foreigners had come back, and things were still rather dusty and almost at pre-war prices. But we could see nothing for five francs except the little saint-medals. D—— wanted to buy one of those. It seemed to me infra dig. So at last coming down to the Mercato Nuovo we saw little bowls of Volterra marble, a natural amber colour, for four francs.

"Look, buy one of those," I said to D——, "and he can put his pins or studs or any trifle in, as he needs."

So we went in and bought one of the little bowls of Volterra marble. M—— seemed so touched and pleased with the gift.

"Thank you a thousand times, N——," he said. "That's charming! That's exactly what I want."

The dinner was quite a success, and, poorly fed as we were at the pension, we stuffed ourselves tight on the mushrooms and the hare and the zabaioni, and drank ourselves tight with the good red wine which swung in its straw flask in the silver swing on the table. A flask has two and a quarter litres. We were four persons, and we drank almost two flasks. D—— made the waiter measure the remaining half-litre and take it off the bill. But good, good food, and cost about twelve francs a head the whole dinner.

Well, next day was nothing but bags and suit-cases in M——'s room, and the misery of departure with luggage. He went on the midnight train to Rome—first class.

"I always travel first class," he said, "and I always shall, while I can buy the ticket. Why should I go second? It's beastly enough to travel at all."

"My dear fellow, I came up third the last time I came from Rome," said D——. "Oh, not bad, not bad. Damned fatiguing journey anyhow."

So the little outsider was gone, and I was rather glad. I don't think he liked me. Yet one day he said to me at table:

"How lovely your hair is—such a lovely colour! What do you dye it with?"

I laughed, thinking he was laughing too. But no, he meant it.

"It's got no particular colour at all," I said, "so I couldn't dye it that!"

"It's a lovely colour," he said. And I think he didn't believe me, that I didn't dye it. It puzzled me, and it puzzles me still.

But he was gone. D—— moved into M——'s room, and asked me to come down to the room he himself was vacating. But I preferred to stay upstairs.

M—— was a fervent Catholic, taking the religion, alas, rather unctu-

ously. He had entered the Church only a few years before. But he had
a bishop for a god-father, and seemed to be very intimate with the
upper clergy. He was very pleased and proud because he was a constant guest at the famous old monastery south of Rome. He talked of
becoming a monk, a monk in that aristocratic and well-bred order. But
he had not even begun his theological studies: or any studies of any
sort. And D—— said he only chose the Benedictines because they lived
better than any of the others.

But I had said to M——, that when my wife came and we moved
south, I would like to visit the monastery some time, if I might. "Certainly," he said. "Come when I am there. I shall be there in about a
month's time. Do come! Do be sure and come. It's a wonderful place—
oh, wonderful. It will make a great impression on you. Do come. Do
come. And I will tell Don Bernardo, who is my *greatest* friend, and
who is guest-master, about you. So that if you wish to go when I am
not there, write to Don Bernardo. But do come when I am there."

My wife and I were due to go into the mountains south of Rome,
and stay there some months. Then I was to visit the big, noble monastery that stands on a bluff hill like a fortress crowning a great
precipice, above the little town and the plain between the mountains.
But it was so icy cold and snowy among the mountains, it was un-
bearable. We fled south again, to Naples, and to Capri. Passing, I saw
the monastery crouching there above, world-famous, but it was impossible to call then.

I wrote and told M—— of my move. In Capri I had an answer from
him. It had a wistful tone—and I don't know what made me think
that he was in trouble, in monetary difficulty. But felt it acutely—a
kind of appeal. Yet he said nothing direct. And he wrote from an expensive hotel in Anzio, on the sea near Rome.

At the moment I had just received twenty pounds, unexpected and
joyful, from America—a gift too. I hesitated for some time, because I
felt unsure. Yet the curious appeal came out of the letter, though nothing was said. And I felt also I owed M—— that dinner, and I didn't
want to owe him anything, since he despised me a little for being
careful. So partly out of revenge, perhaps, and partly because I felt the

strange wistfulness of him appealing to me, I sent him five pounds, saying perhaps I was mistaken in imagining him very hard up, but if so, he wasn't to be offended.

It is strange to me even now, how I knew he was appealing to me. Because it was all as vague as I say. Yet I felt it so strongly. He replied: "Your cheque has saved my life. Since I last saw you I have fallen down an abyss. But I will tell you when I see you. I shall be at the monastery in three days. Do come—and come alone." I have forgotten to say that he was a rabid woman-hater.

This was just after Christmas. I thought his "saved my life" and "fallen down an abyss" was just the American touch of "very, very—" I wondered what on earth the abyss could be, and I decided it must be that he had lost his money or his hopes. It seemed to me that some of his old buoyant assurance came out again in this letter. But he was now very friendly, urging me to come to the monastery, and treating me with a curious little tenderness and protectiveness. He had a queer delicacy of his own, varying with a bounce and a commonness. He was a common little bounder. And then he had this curious delicacy and tenderness and wistfulness.

I put off going north. I had another letter urging me—and it seemed to me that, rather assuredly, he was expecting more money. Rather cockily, as if he had a right to it. And that made me not want to give him any. Besides, as my wife said, what right had I to give away the little money we had, and we there stranded in the south of Italy with no resources if once we were spent up? And I have always been determined *never* to come to my last shilling—if I have to reduce my spending almost to nothingness. I have always been determined to keep a few pounds between me and the world.

I did not send any money. But I wanted to go to the monastery, so wrote and said I would come for two days. I always remember getting up in the black dark of the January morning, and making a little coffee on the spirit-lamp, and watching the clock, the big-faced, blue old clock on the campanile in the piazza in Capri, to see I wasn't late. The electric light in the piazza lit up the face of the campanile. And we were then, a stone's throw away, high in the Palazzo Ferraro, opposite the bubbly roof of the little *duomo*. Strange dark winter morning, with the open sea beyond the roofs, seen through the side window, and the thin line of the lights of Naples twinkling far, far off.

At ten minutes to six I went down the smelly dark stone stairs of the old palazzo, out into the street. A few people were already hastening up the street to the terrace that looks over the sea to the bay of Naples. It was dark and cold. We slid down in the funicular to the shore, then in little boats were rowed out over the dark sea to the steamer that lay there showing her lights and hooting.

It was three long hours across the sea to Naples, with dawn coming slowly in the East, beyond Ischia, and flushing into lovely colours as our steamer pottered along the peninsula, calling at Massa and Sorrento and Piano. I always loved hanging over the side and watching the people come out in boats from the little places of the shore, that rose steep and beautiful. I love the movement of these watery Neapolitan people, and the naïve trustful way they clamber in and out the boats, and their softness, and their dark eyes. But when the steamer leaves the peninsula and begins to make away round Vesuvius to Naples, one is already tired, and cold, cold, cold in the wind that comes piercing from the snow-crests away there along Italy. Cold, and reduced to a kind of stony apathy by the time we come to the mole in Naples, at ten o'clock —or twenty past ten.

We were rather late, and I missed the train. I had to wait till two o'clock. And Naples is a hopeless town to spend three hours in. However, time passes. I remember I was calculating in my mind whether they had given me the right change at the ticket-window. They hadn't —and I hadn't counted in time. Thinking of this, I got in the Rome train. I had been there ten minutes when I heard a trumpet blow.

"Is this the Rome train?" I asked my fellow-traveller.

"*Si.*"

"The express?"

"No, it is the slow train."

"It leaves?"

"At ten past two."

I almost jumped through the window. I flew down the platform.

"The *diretto!*" I cried to a porter.

"*Parte! Eccolo la!*" he said, pointing to a big train moving inevitably away.

I flew with wild feet across the various railway lines and seized the end of the train as it travelled. I had caught it. Perhaps if I had missed it fate would have been different. So I sat still for about three hours. Then I had arrived.

There is a long drive up the hill from the station to the monastery. The driver talked to me. It was evident he bore the monks no good will.

"Formerly," he said, "if you went up to the monastery you got a glass of wine and a plate of macaroni. But now they kick you out of the door."

"Do they?" I said. "It is hard to believe."

"They kick you out of the gate," he vociferated.

We twisted up and up the wild hillside, past the old castle of the town, past the last villa, between trees and rocks. We saw no one. The whole hill belongs to the monastery. At last at twilight we turned the corner of the oak wood and saw the monastery like a huge square fortress-palace of the sixteenth century crowning the near distance. Yes, and there was M—— just stepping through the huge old gateway and hastening down the slope to where the carriage must stop. He was bareheaded, and walking with his perky, busy little stride, seemed very much at home in the place. He looked up to me with a ten-der, intimate look as I got down from the carriage. Then he took my hand.

"So *very* glad to see you," he said. "I'm so *pleased* you've come."

And he looked into my eyes with that wistful, watchful tenderness rather like a woman who isn't quite sure of her lover. He had a certain charm in his manner; and an odd pompous touch with it at this mo-ment, welcoming his guest at the gate of the vast monastery which reared above us from its buttresses in the rock, was rather becoming. His face was still pink, his eyes pale blue and sharp, but he looked greyer at the temples.

"Give me your bag," he said. "Yes, do—and come along. Don Bernardo is just at Evensong, but he'll be here in a little while. Well, now, tell me all the news."

"Wait," I said. "Lend me five francs to finish paying the driver—he has no change."

"Certainly, certainly," he said, giving the five francs.

I had no news, so asked him his.

"Oh, I have none either," he said. "Very short of money, that of course is *no* news." And he laughed his little laugh. "I'm so glad to be here," he continued. "The peace, and the rhythm of the life is so *beautiful!* I'm sure you'll love it."

We went up the slope under the big, tunnel-like entrance and were in the grassy courtyard, with the arched walk on the far sides, and one or two trees. It was like a grassy cloister, but still busy. Black monks were standing chatting, an old peasant was just driving two sheep from the cloister grass, and an old monk was darting into the little post-office which one recognized by the shield with the national arms over the doorway. From under the far arches came an old peasant carrying a two-handed saw.

And there was Don Bernardo, a tall monk in a black, well-shaped gown, young, good-looking, gentle, hastening forward with a quick smile. He was about my age, and his manner seemed fresh and subdued, as if he were still a student. One felt one was at college with one's college mates.

We went up the narrow stair and into the long, old, naked white corridor, high and arched. Don Bernardo had got the key of my room: two keys, one for the dark antechamber, one for the bedroom. A charming and elegant bedroom, with an engraving of English landscape, and outside the net curtain a balcony looking down on the garden, a narrow strip beneath the walls, and beyond, the clustered buildings of the farm, and the oak woods and arable fields of the hill summit; and beyond again, the gulf where the world's valley was, and all the mountains that stand in Italy on the plains as if God had just put them down ready made. The sun had already sunk, the snow on the mountains was full of a rosy glow, the valleys were full of shadow.

One heard, far below, the trains shunting, the world clinking in the cold air.

"Isn't it wonderful! Ah, the most wonderful place on earth!" said M——. "What now could you wish better than to end your days here? The peace, the beauty, the eternity of it." He paused and sighed. Then he put his hand on Don Bernardo's arm and smiled at him with that odd, rather wistful smirking tenderness that made him such a quaint creature in my eyes.

"But I'm going to enter the order. You're going to let me be a monk and be one of you, aren't you, Don Bernardo?"

"We will see," smiled Don Bernardo. "When you have begun your studies."

"It will take me two years," said M——. "I shall have to go to college in Rome. When I have got the money for the fees—" He talked away, like a boy planning a new role.

"But I'm sure Lawrence would like to drink a cup of tea," said Don Bernardo. He spoke English as if it were his native language. "Shall I tell them to make it in the kitchen, or shall we go to your room?"

"Oh, we'll go to my room. How thoughtless of me! Do forgive me, won't you?" said M——, laying his hand gently on my arm. "I'm so awfully sorry, you know. But we get so excited and enchanted when we talk of the monastery. But come along, come along, it will be ready in a moment on the spirit-lamp."

We went down to the end of the high, white, naked corridor. M—— had a quite sumptuous room, with a curtained bed in one part, and under the window his writing-desk with papers and photographs, and near by a sofa and an easy table, making a little sitting-room, while the bed and toilet things, pomades and bottles, were all in the distance, in the shadow. Night was fallen. From the window one saw the world far below, like a pool the flat plain, a deep pool of darkness with little twinkling lights, and rows and bunches of light that were the railway station.

I drank my tea, M—— drank a little liqueur, Don Bernardo in his black winter robe sat and talked with us. At least he did very little talking. But he listened and smiled and put in a word or two as we talked, seated round the table on which stood the green-shaded electric lamp.

The monastery was cold as the tomb. Couched there on the top of its hill, it is not much below the winter snow-line. Now by the end of January all the summer heat is soaked out of the vast, ponderous stone walls, and they become masses of coldness cloaking around. There is no heating apparatus whatsoever—none. Save the fire in the kitchen, for cooking, nothing. Dead, silent, stone cold everywhere.

At seven we went down to dinner. Capri in the daytime was hot, so I had brought only a thin old dust-coat. M—— therefore made me wear a big coat of his own, a coat made of thick, smooth black cloth, and lined with black sealskin, and having a collar of silky black seal-skin. I can still remember the feel of the silky fur. It was queer to have him helping me solicitously into this coat, and buttoning it at the throat for me.

"Yes, it's a beautiful coat. Of course!" he said. "I hope you find it warm."

"Wonderful," said I. "I feel as warm as a millionaire."

"I'm so glad you do," he laughed.

"You don't mind my wearing your grand coat?" I said.

"Of course not! Of course not! It's a pleasure to me if it will keep you warm. We don't want to die of cold in the monastery, do we? That's one of the mortifications we will do our best to avoid. What? Don't you think? Yes, I think this coldness is going almost too far. I had that coat made in New York fifteen years ago. Of course in Italy" he said It'ly—"I've never worn it, so it is as good as new. And it's a beautiful coat, fur and cloth of the very best. *And* the tailor." He laughed a little, self-approving laugh. He liked to give the impression that he dealt with the *best* shops, don't you know, and stayed in the *best* hotels, etc. I grinned inside the coat, detesting best hotels, best shops, and best overcoats. So off we went, he in his grey overcoat and I in my sealskin millionaire monster, down the dim corridor to the guests' refectory. It was a bare room with a long white table. M—— and I sat at the near end. Further down was another man, perhaps the

father of one of the boy students. There is a college attached to the
monastery.

We sat in the icy room, muffled up in our overcoats. A lay brother
with a bulging forehead and queer, fixed eyes waited on us. He might
easily have come from an old Italian picture. One of the adoring peasants. The food was abundant—but, alas, it had got cold in the long
cold transit from the kitchen. And it was roughly cooked, even if it
was quite wholesome. Poor M—— did not eat much, but nervously
nibbled his bread. I could tell the meals were a trial to him. He could
not bear the cold food in that icy, empty refectory. And his tisickiness
offended the lay brothers. I could see that his little pomposities and his
"superior" behaviour and his long stay made them have that old monastic grudge against him, silent but very obstinate and effectual—the
same now as six hundred years ago. We had a decanter of good red
wine—but he did not care for much wine. He was glad to be peeling
the cold orange which was dessert.

After dinner he took me down to see the church, creeping like two
thieves down the dimness of the great, prison-cold white corridors, on
the cold flag floors. Stone-cold: the monks must have invented the
term. These monks were at Complin. So we went by our two secret little selves into the tall dense nearly-darkness of the church. M——,
knowing his way about here as in the cities, led me, poor wondering
worldling, by the arm through the gulfs of the tomb-like place. He
found the electric light switches inside the church, and stealthily made
me a light as we went. We looked at the lily marble of the great floor,
at the pillars, at the Benvenuto Cellini casket, at the really lovely pillars and slabs of different coloured marbles, yellow and grey and rose
and green and lily-white, veined and mottled and splashed: lovely,
lovely stones— And Benvenuto had used pieces of lapis lazuli, blue as
cornflowers. Yes, yes, all very rich and wonderful.

We tiptoed about the dark church stealthily, from altar to altar, and
M—— whispered ecstasies in my ear. Each time we passed before an
altar, whether the high altar or the side chapels, he did a wonderful
reverence, which he must have practised for hours, bowing waxily
down and sinking till his one knee touched the pavement, then rising

like a flower that rises and unfolds again, till he had skipped to my side and was playing cicerone once more. Always in his grey overcoat, and in whispers; me in the black overcoat, millionairish. So we crept into the chancel and examined all the queer fat babies of the choir stalls, carved in wood and rolling on their little backs between monk's place and monk's place—queer things for the chanting monks to have between them, these shiny, polished, dark brown fat babies, all different, and all jolly and lusty. We looked at everything in the church— and then at everything in the ancient room at the side where surplices hang and monks can wash their hands.

Then we went down to the crypt, where the modern mosaics glow in wonderful colours, and sometimes in fascinating little fantastic trees and birds. But it was rather like a scene in a theatre, with M—— for the wizard and myself a sort of Parsifal in the New York coat. He switched on the lights, the gold mosaic of the vaulting glittered and bowed, the blue mosaic glowed out, the holy of holies gleamed theatrically, the stiff mosaic figures posed around us. To tell the truth, I was glad to get back to the normal human room and sit on a sofa huddled in my overcoat, and look at photographs which M—— showed me: photographs of everywhere in Europe. Then he showed me a wonderful photograph of a picture of a lovely lady, asked me what I thought of it, and seemed to expect me to be struck to bits by the beauty. His almost sanctimonious expectation made me tell the truth, that I thought it just a bit cheap, trivial. And then he said, dramatic:

"That's my mother."

It looked so unlike anybody's mother, much less M——'s, that I was startled. I realized that she was his great stunt, and that I had put my foot in it. So I just held my tongue. Then I said, for I felt he was going to be silent forever:

"There are so few portraits, unless by the really great artists, that aren't a bit cheap. She must have been a beautiful woman."

"Yes, she *was*," he said curtly. And we dropped the subject.

He locked all his drawers *very* carefully, and kept the keys on a chain. He seemed to give the impression that he had a great many secrets, perhaps dangerous ones, locked up in the drawers of his writing-table there. And I always wonder what the secrets can be, that are able to be kept so tight under lock and key.

Don Bernardo tapped and entered. We all sat round and sipped a funny liqueur which I didn't like. M—— lamented that the bottle was finished. I asked him to order another and let me pay for it. So he said he would tell the postman to bring it up next day from the town. Don Bernardo sipped his tiny glass with the rest of us, and he told me, briefly, his story—and we talked politics till nearly midnight. Then I came out of the black overcoat and we went to bed.

In the morning a fat, smiling, nice old lay brother brought me my water. It was a sunny day. I looked down on the farm cluster and the brown fields and the sere oak woods of the hill-crown, and the rocks and bushes savagely bordering it round. Beyond, the mountains with their snow were blue-glistery with sunshine, and seemed quite near, but across a sort of gulf. All was still and sunny. And the poignant grip of the past, the grandiose, violent past of the Middle Ages, when blood was strong and unquenched and life was flamboyant with splendours and horrible miseries, took hold of me till I could hardly bear it. It was really agony to me to be in the monastery and to see the old farm and the bullocks slowly working in the fields below, and the black pigs rooting among weeds, and to see a monk sitting on a parapet in the sun, and an old, old man in skin sandals and white bunched, swathed legs come driving an ass slowly to the monastery gate, slowly, with all that lingering nonchalance and wildness of the Middle Ages, and yet to know that I was myself, child of the present. It was so strange from M——'s window to look down on the plain and see the white road going straight past a mountain that stood like a loaf of sugar, the river meandering in loops, and the railway with glistening lines making a long black swoop across the flat and into the hills. To see trains come steaming, with white smoke flying. To see the station like a little harbour where trucks like shipping stood anchored in rows in the black bay of railway. To see trains stop in the station and tiny people swarming like flies! To see all this from the monastery, where the Middle Ages live on in a sort of agony, like Tithonus, and cannot die, this was almost a violation to my soul, made almost a wound.

Immediately after coffee we went down to Mass. It was celebrated in a small crypt chapel underground, because that was warmer. The twenty or so monks sat in their stalls, one monk officiating at the altar. It was quiet and simple, the monks sang sweetly and well, there was no organ. It seemed soon to pass by. M—— and I sat near the door. He was very devoted and scrupulous in his going up and down. I was an outsider. But it was pleasant—not too sacred. One felt the monks were very human in their likes and their jealousies. It was rather like a group of dons in the dons' room at Cambridge, a cluster of professors in any college. But during Mass they, of course, just sang their responses. Only I could tell some watched the officiating monk rather with ridicule—he was one of the ultra-punctilious sort, just like a don. And some boomed their responses with a grain of defiance against some brother monk who had earned dislike. It was human, and more like a university than anything. We went to Mass every morning, but I did not go to Evensong.

After Mass, M—— took me round and showed me everything of the vast monastery. We went into the Bramante Courtyard, all stone, with its great well in the centre, and the colonnades of arches going round, full of sunshine, gay and Renaissance, a little bit ornate but still so jolly and gay, sunny pale stone waiting for the lively people, with the great flight of pale steps sweeping up to the doors of the church, waiting for gentlemen in scarlet trunk-hose, slender red legs, and ladies in brocade gowns, and page-boys with fluffed golden hair. Splendid, sunny, gay Bramante Courtyard of lively stone. But empty. Empty of life. The gay red-legged gentry dead for ever. And when pilgrimages do come and throng in, it is horrible artisan excursions from the great town, and the sordidness of industrialism.

We climbed the little watchtower that is now an observatory, and saw the vague and unshaven Don Giovanni among all his dust and instruments. M—— was very familiar and friendly, chattering in his quaint Italian, which was more wrong than any Italian I have ever heard spoken; very familiar and friendly, and a tiny bit deferential to the monks, and yet, and yet—rather patronizing. His little pomposity and patronizing tone coloured even his deferential yearning to be admitted to the monastery. The monks were rather brief with him. They no doubt have their likes and dislikes greatly intensified by the monastic life.

We stood on the summit of the tower and looked at the world below: the town, the castle, the white roads coming straight as judgment out of the mountains north, from Rome, and piercing into the mountains south, toward Naples, traversing the flat, flat plain. Roads, railway, river, streams, a world in accurate and lively detail, with mountains sticking up abruptly and rockily, as the old painters painted it. I think there is no way of painting Italian landscape except that way— that started with Lorenzetti and ended with the sixteenth century.

We looked at the ancient cell away under the monastery, where all the sanctity started. We looked at the big library that belongs to the State, and at the smaller library that belongs still to the abbot. I was tired, cold, and sick among the books and illuminations. I could not bear it any more. I felt I must be outside, in the sun, and see the world below, and the way out.

That evening I said to M——:

"And what was the abyss, then?"

"Oh, well, you know," he said, "it was a cheque which I made out at Anzio. There should have been money to meet it, in my bank in New York. But it appears the money had never been paid in by the people that owed it me. So there was I in a very nasty hole, an unmet cheque, and no money at all in Italy. I really had to escape here. It is an *absolute* secret that I am here, and it must be, till I can get this business settled. Of course I've written to America about it. But as you see, I'm in a very nasty hole. That five francs I gave you for the driver was the last penny I had in the world: absolutely the last penny. I haven't even anything to buy a cigarette or a stamp." And he laughed chirpily, as if it were a joke. But he didn't really think it a joke. Nor was it a joke.

I had come with only two hundred lire in my pocket, as I was waiting to change some money at the bank. Of this two hundred I had one hundred left or one hundred and twenty-five. I should need a hundred to get home. I could only give M—— the twenty-five, for the bottle of drink. He was rather crestfallen. But I didn't want to give him money this time—because he expected it.

However, we talked about his plans: how he was to earn something. He told me what he had written. And I cast over in my mind where he might get something published in London, wrote a couple of letters on his account, told him where I thought he had best send his material. There wasn't a great deal of hope, for his smaller journalistic articles seemed to me very self-conscious and poor. He had one about the monastery, which I thought he might sell because of the photographs.

That evening he first showed me the Legion manuscript. He had got it rather raggedly typed out. He had a typewriter, but he felt he ought to have somebody to do his typing for him, as he hated it and did unwillingly. That evening and when I went to bed and when I woke in the morning I read this manuscript. It did not seem very good—vague and diffuse where it shouldn't have been—lacking in sharp detail and definite event. And yet there was something in it that made me want it done properly. So we talked about it, and discussed it carefully, and he unwillingly promised to tackle it again. He was curious, always talking about his work, even always working, but never *properly* doing anything.

We walked out in the afternoon through the woods and across the rocky bit of moorland which covers most of the hill-top. We were going to the ruined convent which lies on the other brow of the monastery hill, abandoned and sad among the rocks and heath and thorny bushes. It was sunny and warm. A barefoot little boy was tending a cow and three goats and a pony, a barefoot little girl had five geese in charge. We came to the convent and looked in. The further part of the courtyard was still entire, the place was a sort of farm, two rooms occupied by a peasant-farmer. We climbed about the ruins. Some creature was crying—crying, crying, crying with a strange, inhuman persistence, leaving off and crying again. We listened and listened—the sharp, poignant crying. Almost it might have been a sharp-voiced baby. We scrambled about, looking. And at last outside a little cave-like place found a blind black puppy crawling miserably on the floor, unable to walk, and crying incessantly. We put it back in the little cave-like shed, and went away. The place was deserted save for the crying puppy.

On the road outside, however, was a man, a peasant, just drawing up to the arched convent gateway with an ass under a load of brushwood. He was thin and black and dirty. He took off his hat, and we told him of the puppy. He said the bitch-mother had gone off with his son with the sheep. Yes, she had been gone all day. Yes, she would be back at sunset. No, the puppy had not drunk all day. Yes, the little beast cried, but the mother would come back to him.

They were the Old World peasants still about the monastery, with the hard, small bony heads and deep-lined faces and utterly blank minds, crying their speech as crows cry, and living their lives as lizards among the rocks, blindly going on with the little job in hand, the present moment cut off from all past and future, and having no idea and no sustained emotion, only that eternal will-to-live which makes a tortoise wake up once more in spring, and makes a grasshopper whistle on in the moonlight nights even of November. Only these peasants don't whistle much. The whistlers go to America. It is the hard, static, unhoping souls that persist in the old life. And still they stand back, as one passes them in the corridors of the great monastery, they press themselves back against the whitewashed walls of the still place, and drop their heads, as if some mystery were passing by, some God-mystery, the higher beings, which they must not look closely upon. So also this old peasant—he was not old, but deep-lined like a gnarled bough. He stood with his hat down in his hands as we spoke to him and answered short, hard, insentient answers, as a tree might speak.

"The monks keep their peasants humble," I said to M——.

"Of course!" he said. "Don't you think they are quite right? Don't you think they should be humble?" And he bridled like a little turkey-cock on his hind legs.

"Well," I said, "if there's any occasion for humility, I do."

"Don't you think there is occasion?" he cried. "If there's one thing worse than another, it's this *equality* that has come into the world. Do you believe in it yourself?"

"No," I said. "I don't believe in equality. But the problem is, wherein does superiority lie?"

"Oh," chirped M—— complacently. "It lies in many things. It lies in birth and in upbringing and so on, but it is chiefly in *mind*. Don't you think? Of course I don't mean that the physical qualities aren't *charming*. They are, and nobody appreciates them more than I do. Some of the peasants are *beautiful* creatures, perfectly beautiful. But that passes. And the mind endures."

I did not answer. M—— was not a man one talked far with. But I thought to myself, I *could* not accept M——'s superiority to the peasant. If I had really to live always under the same roof with either one of them, I would have chosen the peasant. Not because the peasant was wonderful and stored with mystic qualities. No, I don't give much for the wonderful mystic qualities in peasants. Money is their mystery of mysteries, absolutely. No, if I chose the peasant it would be for what he *lacked* rather than for what he had. He lacked that complacent mentality that M—— was so proud of, he lacked all the trivial trash of glib talk and more glib thought, all the conceit of our shallow consciousness. For his mindlessness I would have chosen the peasant, and for his strong blood-presence. M—— wearied me with his facility and his readiness to rush into speech, and for the exhaustive nature of his presence. As if he had no strong blood in him to sustain him, only this modern parasitic lymph which cries for sympathy all the time.

"Don't you think yourself that you are superior to that peasant?" he asked me, rather ironically. He half expected me to say no.

"Yes, I do," I replied. "But I think most middle-class, most so-called educated people are inferior to the peasant. I do that."

"Of course," said M—— readily. "In their *hypocrisy*—" He was great against hypocrisy—especially the English sort.

"And if I think myself superior to the peasant, it is only that I feel myself like the growing tip, or one of the growing tips of the tree, and him like a piece of the hard, fixed tissue of the branch or trunk. We're part of the same tree: and it's the same sap," said I.

"Why, exactly! Exactly!" cried M——. "Of course! The Church

would teach the same doctrine. We are all one in Christ—but between our souls and our duties there are great differences."

It is terrible to be agreed with, especially by a man like M——. All that one says, and means, turns to nothing.

"Yes," I persisted. "But it seems to me the so-called culture, education, the so-called leaders and leading-classes today, are only parasites—like a great flourishing bush of parasitic consciousness flourishing on top of the tree of life, and sapping it. The consciousness of today doesn't rise from the roots. It is just parasitic in the veins of life. And the middle and upper classes are just parasitic upon the body of life which still remains in the lower classes."

"What!" said M—— acidly. "Do you believe in the democratic lower classes?"

"Not a bit," said I.

"I should think not, indeed!" he cried complacently.

"No, I don't believe the lower classes can ever make life whole again, till they *do* become humble, like the old peasants, and yield themselves to real leaders. But not to great negators like Lloyd George or Lenin or Briand."

"Of course! Of course!" he cried. "What you need is the Church in power again. The Church has a place for everybody."

"You don't think the Church belongs to the past?" I asked.

"Indeed I don't, or I shouldn't be here. No," he said sententiously, "the Church is eternal. It puts people in their proper place. It puts women down into *their* proper place, which is the first thing to be done——"

He had a great dislike of women, and was very acid about them. Not because of their sins, but because of their virtues: their economies, their philanthropies, their spiritualities. Oh, how he loathed women! He had been married, but the marriage had not been a success. He smarted still. Perhaps his wife had despised him, and he had not *quite* been able to defeat her contempt.

So he loathed women, and wished for a world of men. "They talk about love between men and women," he said. "Why, it's all a *fraud*. The woman is just taking all and giving nothing, and feeling sanctified about it. All she tries to do is thwart a man in whatever he is doing. No, I have found my life in my *friendships*. Physical relationships are very attractive, of course, and one tries to keep them as decent and all that as one can. But one knows they will pass and be finished. But one's *mental* friendships last forever."

"With me, on the contrary," said I. "If there is no profound blood-sympathy, I know the mental friendship is trash. If there is real, deep blood-response, I will stick to that if I have to betray all the mental sympathies I ever made, or all the lasting spiritual loves I ever felt."

He looked at me, and his face seemed to fall. Round the eyes he was yellow and tired and nervous. He watched me for some time.

"Oh!" he said, in a queer tone, rather cold. "Well, my experience has been the opposite."

We were silent for some time.

"And you," I said, "even if you do manage to do all your studies and enter the monastery, do you think you will be satisfied?"

"If I can be so fortunate, I do really," he said. "Do you doubt it?"

"Yes," I said. "Your nature is worldly, more worldly than mine. Yet I should die if I had to stay up here."

"Why?" he asked, curiously.

"Oh, I don't know. The past, the past. The beautiful, the wonderful past, it seems to prey on my heart, I can't bear it."

He watched me closely.

"Really!" he said stoutly. "Do you feel like that? But don't you think it is a far preferable life up here than down there? Don't you think the past is far preferable to the future, with all this *socialismo* and these *communisti* and so on?"

We were seated, in the sunny afternoon, on the wild hill-top high above the world. Across the stretch of pale, dry, standing thistles that peopled the waste ground, and beyond the rocks was the ruined convent. Rocks rose behind us, the summit. Away on the left were the woods which hid us from the great monastery. This was the mountain top, the last foothold of the old world. Below we could see the plain, the straight white road, straight as a thought, and the more flexible black railway with the railway station. There swarmed the *ferrovieri*

like ants. There was democracy, industrialism, socialism, the red flag
of the communists and the red, white, and green tricolour of the fa-
scisti. That was another world. And how bitter, how barren a world!
Barren, like the black cinder-track of the railway, with its two steel
lines.

And here above, sitting with the little stretch of pale, dry thistles
around us, our back to a warm rock, we were in the Middle Ages.
Both worlds were agony to me. But here, on the mountain top, was
worst: the past, the poignancy of the not-quite-dead past.

"I think one's got to go through with the life down there—get somewhere beyond it. One can't go back," I said to him.

"But do you call the monastery going back?" he said. "I don't. The
peace, the eternity, the concern with things that matter. I consider it
the happiest fate that could happen to me. Of course it means putting
physical things aside. But when you've done that—why, it seems to me
perfect."

"No," I said. "You're too worldly."

"But the monastery is worldly too. We're not Trappists. Why, the
monastery is one of the centres of the world—one of the most active
centres."

"Maybe. But that impersonal activity, with the blood suppressed and
going sour—no, it's too late. It is too abstract—political maybe——"

"I'm sorry you think so," he said, rising. "I don't."

"Well," I said. "You'll never be a monk here, M——. You see if you
are."

"You don't think I shall?" he replied, turning to me. And there was
a catch of relief in his voice. Really, the monastic state must have been
like going to prison for him.

"You haven't a vocation," I said.

"I may not *seem* to have, but I hope I actually have."

"You haven't."

"Of course, if you're so sure," he laughed, putting his hand on my
arm.

He seemed to understand so much, round about the questions that
trouble one deepest. But the quick of the question he never felt. He

had no real middle, no real centre bit to him. Yet, round and round about all the questions, he was so intelligent and sensitive.

We went slowly back. The peaks of those Italian mountains in the sunset, the extinguishing twinkle of the plain away below, as the sun declined and grew yellow; the intensely powerful medieval spirit lingering on this wild hill summit, all the wonder of the medieval past; and then the huge mossy stones in the wintry wood that was once a sacred grove; the ancient path through the wood that led from temple to temple on the hill summit, before Christ was born; and then the great Cyclopean wall one passes at the bend of the road, built even before the pagan temples; all this overcame me so powerfully this afternoon, that I was almost speechless. That hill-top must have been one of man's intensely sacred places for three thousand years. And men die generation after generation, races die, but the new cult finds root in the old sacred place, and the quick spot of earth dies very slowly. Yet at last it too dies. But this quick spot is still not quite dead. The great monastery couchant there, half empty, but also not quite dead. And M—— and I walking across as the sun set yellow and the cold of the snow came into the air, back home to the monastery! And I feeling as if my heart had once more broken—I don't know why. And he feeling his fear of life, that haunted him, and his fear of his own self and its consequences, that never left him for long. And he seemed to walk close to me, very close. And we had neither of us anything more to say.

Don Bernardo was looking for us as we came up under the archway, he hatless in the cold evening, his black dress swinging voluminous. There were letters for M——. There was a small cheque for him from America—about fifty dollars—from some newspaper in the Middle West that had printed one of his articles. He had to talk with Don Bernardo about this.

I decided to go back the next day. I could not stay any longer. M—— was very disappointed, and begged me to remain. "I thought you would stay a week at least," he said. "Do stay over Sunday. Oh, do!" But I couldn't, I didn't want to. I could see that his days were a torture to him—the long, cold days in that vast quiet building, with the strange and exhausting silence in the air, and the sense of the past preying on one, and the sense of the silent, suppressed scheming struggle of life going on still in the sacred place.

It was a cloudy morning. In the green courtyard the big Don Anselmo had just caught the little Don Lorenzo round the waist and was swinging him over a bush, like lads before school. The prior was just hurrying somewhere, following his long fine nose. He bade me goodbye; pleasant, warm, jolly, with a touch of wistfulness in his deafness. I parted with real regret from Don Bernardo.

M—— was coming with me down the hill—not down the carriage road, but down the wide old paved path that swoops so wonderfully from the top of the hill to the bottom. It feels thousands of years old. M—— was quiet and friendly. We met Don Vincenzo, he who has the care of the land and crops, coming slowly, slowly uphill in his black cassock, treading slowly with his great thick boots. He was reading a little book. He saluted us as we passed. Lower down a strapping girl was watching three merino sheep among the bushes. One sheep came on its exquisite slender legs to smell of me, with that insatiable curiosity of a *pecora*. Her nose was silken and elegant as she reached it to sniff at me, and the yearning, wondering, inquisitive look in her eyes made me realize that the Lamb of God must have been such a sheep as this.

M—— was miserable at my going. Not so much at my going, as at being left alone up there. We came to the foot of the hill, on to the town highroad. So we went into a little cave of a wine-kitchen to drink a glass of wine. M—— chatted a little with the young woman. He chatted with everybody. She eyed us closely, and asked if we were from the monastery. We said we were. She seemed to have a little lurking antagonism round her nose, at the mention of the monastery. M—— paid for the wine—a franc. So we went out on the highroad, to part.

"Look," I said. "I can only give you twenty lire, because I shall need the rest for the journey——"

But he wouldn't take them. He looked at me wistfully. Then I went on down to the station, he turned away uphill. It was market in the town, and there were clusters of bullocks, and women cooking a little meal at a brazier under the trees, and goods spread out on the floor to sell, and sacks of beans and corn standing open, clustered round the trunks of the mulberry trees, and wagons with their shafts on the ground. The old peasants in their brown homespun frieze and skin sandals were watching for the world. And there again was the Middle Ages.

It began to rain, however. Suddenly it began to pour with rain, and my coat was wet through, and my trouser-legs. The train from Rome was late—I hoped not very late, or I should miss the boat. She came at last, and was full. I had to stand in the corridor. Then the man came to say dinner was served, so I luckily got a place and had my meal too. Sitting there in the dining-car, among the fat Neapolitans eating their macaroni, with the big glass windows steamed opaque and the rain beating outside, I let myself be carried away, away from the monastery, away from M——, away from everything.

At Naples there was a bit of sunshine again, and I had time to go on foot to the Immacolatella, where the little steamer lay. There on the steamer I sat in a bit of sunshine, and felt that again the world had come to an end for me, and again my heart was broken. The steamer seemed to be making its way away from the old world, that had come to another end in me.

It was after this I decided to go to Sicily. In February, only a few days after my return from the monastery, I was on the steamer for Palermo, and at dawn looking out on the wonderful coast of Sicily. Sicily, tall, forever rising up to her gem-like summits, all golden in dawn, and always glamorous, always hovering as if inaccessible, and yet so near, so distinct. Sicily, unknown to me, and amethystine-glamorous in the Mediterranean dawn: like the dawn of our day, the wonder-morning of our epoch.

I had various letters from M——. He had told me to go to Girgenti. But I arrived in Girgenti when there was a strike of sulphur-miners, and they threw stones. So I did not want to live in Girgenti. M—— hated Taormina—he had been everywhere, tried everywhere, and was not, I found, in any good odour in most places. He wrote, however, saying he hoped I would like it. And later he sent the Legion manuscript. I thought it was good, and told him so. It was offered to publishers in London, but rejected.

In early April I went with my wife to Syracuse for a few days: lovely, lovely days, with the purple anemones blowing in the Sicilian fields, and Adonis-blood red on the little ledges, and the corn rising strong and green in the magical, malarial places, and Etna flowing now to the northward, still with her crown of snow. The lovely, lovely journey from Catania to Syracuse, in spring, winding round the blueness of that sea, where the tall pink asphodel was dying, and the yellow asphodel like a lily showing her silk. Lovely, lovely Sicily, the dawnplace, Europe's dawn, with Odysseus pushing his ship out of the shadows into the blue. Whatever had died for me, Sicily had then not died: dawn-lovely Sicily, and the Ionian Sea.

We came back, and the world was lovely: our own house above the almond trees, and the sea in the cove below. Calabria glimmering like a changing opal away to the left, across the blue, bright straits, and all the great blueness of the lovely dawn-sea in front, where the sun rose with a splendour like trumpets every morning, and me rejoicing like a madness in this dawn, day-dawn, life-dawn, the dawn which is Greece, which is me.

Well, into this lyricism suddenly crept the serpent. It was a lovely morning, still early. I heard a noise on the stairs from the lower terrace, and went to look. M—— on the stairs, looking up at me with a frightened face.

"Why!" I said. "Is it you?"

"Yes," he replied. "A terrible thing has happened."

He waited on the stairs, and I went down. Rather unwillingly, because I detest terrible things, and the people to whom they happen. So we leaned on the creeper-covered rail of the terrace, under festoons of creamy bignonia flowers, and looked at the pale blue, ethereal sea.

"What terrible thing!" said I.

"When did you get back?" said he.

"Last evening."

"Oh! I came before. The *contadini* said they thought you would come yesterday evening. I've been here several days."

"Where are you staying?"

"At the San Domenico."

The San Domenico being then the most expensive hotel here, I thought he must have money. But I knew he wanted something of me.

"And are you staying some time?"

He paused a moment, and looked round cautiously.

"Is your wife there?" he asked, sotto voce.

"Yes, she's upstairs."

"Is there anyone who can hear?"

"No—only old Grazia down below, and she can't understand anyhow."

"Well," he said, stammering. "Let me tell you what's happened. I had to escape from the monastery. Don Bernardo. had a telephone message from the town below, that the carabinieri were looking for an Americano—my name— Of course you can guess how I felt, up there! Awful! Well—! I had to fly at a moment's notice. I just put two shirts in a handbag and went. I slipped down a path—or rather, it isn't a path—down the back of the hill. Ten minutes after Don Bernardo had the message I was running down the hill."

"But what did they want you for?" I asked dismayed.

"Well," he faltered. "I told you about the cheque at Anzio, didn't I? Well, it seems the hotel people applied to the police. Anyhow," he added hastily, "I couldn't let myself be arrested up there, could I? So awful for the monastery!"

"Did they know then that you were in trouble?" I asked.

"Don Bernardo knew I had no money," he said. "Of course he had to know. Yes—he knew I was in *difficulty*. But, of course, he didn't know—well—*everything*." He laughed a little, comical laugh over the *everything,* as if he was just a little bit naughtily proud of it: most ruefully also.

"No," he continued, "that's what I'm most afraid of—that they'll find out everything at the monastery. Of course it's *dreadful*—the Americano, been staying there for months, and everything so nice and

—well, you know how they are, they imagine every American is a millionaire, if not a multimillionaire. And suddenly to be wanted by the police! Of course it's *dreadful!* Anything rather than a scandal at the monastery—anything. Oh, how awful it was! I can tell you, in that quarter of an hour, I sweated blood. Don Bernardo lent me two hundred lire of the monastery money—which he'd no business to do. And I escaped down the back of the hill, I walked to the next station up the line, and took the next train—the slow train—a few stations up towards Rome. And there I changed and caught the *diretto* for Sicily. I came straight to you— Of course I was in *agony:* imagine it! I spent most of the time as far as Naples in the lavatory." He laughed his little jerky laugh.

"What class did you travel?"

"Second. All through the night. I arrived more dead than alive, not having had a meal for two days—only some sandwich stuff I bought on the platform."

"When did you come then?"

"I arrived on Saturday evening. I came out here on Sunday morning, and they told me you were away. Of course, imagine what it's like! I'm in torture every minute, in torture, of course. Why, just imagine!" And he laughed his little laugh.

"But how much money have you got?"

"Oh—I've just got twenty-five francs and five soldi." He laughed as if it was rather a naughty joke.

"But," I said, "if you've got no money, why do you go to the San Domenico? How much do you pay there?"

"Fifty lire a day. Of course it's *ruinous——*"

"But at the Bristol you only pay twenty-five—and at Fichera's only twenty."

"Yes, I know you do," he said. "But I stayed at the Bristol once, and I loathed the place. Such an offensive manager. And I couldn't touch the food at Fichera's."

"But who's going to pay for the San Domenico, then?" I asked.

"Well, I thought," he said, "you know all those manuscripts of mine? Well, you think they're some good, don't you? Well, I thought if I made them over to you, and you did what you could with them and just kept me going till I can get a new start—or till I can get away——"

I looked across the sea: the lovely morning-blue sea towards Greece.

"Where do you want to get away to?" I said.

"To Egypt. I know a man in Alexandria who owns newspapers there. I'm sure if I could get over there he'd give me an editorship or something. And of course money will come. I've written to ——, who was my *greatest* friend, in London. He will send me something——"

"And what else do you expect?"

"Oh, my article on the monastery was accepted by *Land and Water* —thanks to you and your kindness, of course. I thought if I might stay very quietly with you, for a time, and write some things I'm wanting to do, and collect a little money—and then get away to Egypt——"

He looked up into my face, as if he were trying all he could on me. First thing I knew was that I could not have him in the house with me; and even if I could have done it, my wife never could.

"You've got a lovely place here, perfectly beautiful," he said. "Of course, if it had to be Taormina, you've chosen far the best place here. I like this side so much better than the Etna side. Etna always there and people raving about it gets on my nerves. And a *charming* house, *charming*."

He looked round the loggia and along the other terrace.

"Is it all yours?" he said.

"We don't use the ground floor. Come in here."

So we went into the *salotta*.

"Oh, what a beautiful room," he cried. "But perfectly palatial. Charming! Charming! *Much* the nicest house in Taormina."

"No," I said, "as a house it isn't very grand, though I like it for myself. It's just what I want. And I love the situation. But I'll go and tell my wife you are here."

"Will you?" he said, bridling nervously. "Of course I've never met your wife." And he laughed the nervous, naughty, joky little laugh.

I left him, and ran upstairs to the kitchen. There was my wife, with wide eyes. She had been listening to catch the conversation. But M——'s voice was too hushed.

"M——!" said I softly. "The carabinieri wanted to arrest him at the monastery, so he has escaped here, and wants me to be responsible for him."

"Arrest him, what for?"

"Debts, I suppose. Will you come down and speak to him?"

M—— of course was very charming with my wife. He kissed her hand humbly, in the correct German fashion, and spoke with an air of reverence that infallibly gets a woman.

"Such a beautiful place you have here," he said, glancing through the open doors of the room, at the sea beyond. "So clever of you to find it."

"Lawrence found it," said she. "Well, and you are in all kinds of difficulty!"

"Yes, isn't it terrible!" he said, laughing as if it were a joke—rather a wry joke. "I felt dreadful at the monastery. So dreadful for them, if there was any sort of scandal. And after I'd been so well received there —and so much the Signor Americano— Dreadful, don't you think?" He laughed again, like a naughty boy.

We had an engagement to lunch that morning. My wife was dressed, so I went to get ready. Then we told M—— we must go out, and he accompanied us to the village. I gave him just the hundred francs I had in my pocket, and he said, could he come and see me that evening? I asked him to come next morning.

"You're so awfully kind," he said, simpering a little.

But by this time I wasn't feeling kind.

"He's quite nice," said my wife. "But he's rather an impossible little person. And you'll see, he'll be a nuisance. Whatever do you pick up such dreadful people for?"

"Nay," I said. "You can't accuse me of picking up dreadful people. He's the first. And even he isn't dreadful."

The next morning came a letter from Don Bernardo addressed to me, but only enclosing a letter to M——. So he was using my address. At ten o'clock he punctually appeared, slipping in as if to avoid notice. My wife would not see him, so I took him out on the terrace again.

"Isn't it beautiful here!" he said. "Oh, so beautiful! If only I had my peace of mind. Of course I sweat blood every time anybody comes through the door. You are splendidly private out here."

"Yes," I said. "But, M——, there isn't a room for you in the house. There isn't a spare room anyway. You'd better think of getting something cheaper in the village."

"But what can I get?" he snapped.

That rather took my breath away. Myself, I had never been near the San Domenico Hotel. I knew I simply could not afford it.

"What made you go to the San Domenico in the first place?" I said. "The most expensive hotel in the place!"

"Oh, I'd stayed there for two months, and they knew me, and I knew they'd ask no questions. I knew they wouldn't ask for a deposit or anything."

"But nobody dreams of asking for a deposit," I said.

"Anyhow, I shan't take my meals there. I shall just take coffee in the morning. I've had to eat there so far, because I was starved to death, and had no money to go out. But I had two meals in that little restaurant yesterday; disgusting food."

"And how much did that cost?"

"Oh, fourteen francs and fifteen francs, with a quarter of wine—and such a poor meal!"

Now I was annoyed, knowing that I myself should have bought bread and cheese for one franc, and eaten it in my room. But also I realized that the modern creed says, if you sponge, sponge thoroughly; and also that every man has a "right to live," and that if he can manage to live well, no matter at whose expense, all credit to him. This is the kind of talk one accepts in one's slipshod moments; now it was actually tried on me, I didn't like it at all.

"But who's going to pay your bill at the San Domenico?" I said.

"I thought you'd advance me the money on those manuscripts."

"It's no good talking about the money on the manuscripts," I said. "I should have to give it to you. And as a matter of fact, I've got just sixty pounds in the bank in England, and about fifteen hundred lire here. My wife and I have got to live on that. We don't spend as much in a week as you spend in three days at the San Domenico. It's no good your thinking I can advance money on the manuscripts. I can't.

If I was rich, I'd give you money. But I've got no money, and never have had any. Have you nobody you can go to?"

"I'm waiting to hear from ——. When I go back into the village, I'll telegraph to him," replied M——, a little crestfallen. "Of course I'm in torture night and day, or I wouldn't appeal to you like this. I know it's unpleasant for you"—he put his hand on my arm and looked up beseechingly—"but what am I to do?"

"You must get out of the San Domenico," I said. "That's the first thing."

"Yes," he said, a little piqued now. "I know it is. I'm going to ask Pancrazio Melenga to let me have a room in his house. He knows me quite well—he's an awfully nice fellow. He'll do *anything* for me— *anything*. I was just going there yesterday afternoon when you were coming from Timeo. He was out, so I left word with his wife, who is a charming little person. If he has a room to spare, I know he will let me have it. And he's a *splendid* cook—splendid. By far the nicest food in Taormina."

"Well," I said. "If you settle with Melenga, I will pay your bill at the San Domenico, but I can't do any more. I simply can't."

"But what am I to *do?*" he snapped.

"I don't know," I said. "You must think."

"I came here," he said, "thinking you would help me. What am I to do, if you won't? I shouldn't have come to Taormina at all, save for you. Don't be unkind to me—don't speak so coldly to me." He put his hand on my arm, and looked up at me with tears swimming in his eyes. Then he turned aside his face, overcome with tears. I looked away at the Ionian Sea, feeling my blood turn to ice and the sea go black. I loathe scenes such as this.

"Did you telegraph to ——?" I said.

"Yes. I have no answer yet. I hope you don't mind—I gave your address for a reply."

"Oh," I said. "There's a letter for you from Don Bernardo."

He went pale. I was angry at his having used my address in this manner.

"Nothing further has happened at the monastery," he said. "They rang up from the *questura,* from the police station, and Don Bernardo answered that the Americano had left for Rome. Of course I did take the train for Rome. And Don Bernardo wanted me to go to Rome. He advised me to do so. I didn't tell him I was here till I had got here. He thought I should have had more resources in Rome, and of course I should. I should certainly have gone there, if it hadn't been for *you here*——"

Well, I was getting tired and angry. I would not give him any more money at the moment. I promised if he would leave the hotel I would pay his bill, but he must leave it at once. He went off to settle with Melenga. He asked again if he could come in the afternoon. I said I was going out.

He came, nevertheless, while I was out. This time my wife found him on the stairs. She was for hating him, of course. So she stood immovable on the top stair, and he stood two stairs lower, and he kissed her hand in utter humility. And he pleaded with her, and as he looked up to her on the stairs the tears ran down his face and he trembled with distress. And her spine crept up and down with distaste and discomfort. But he broke into a few phrases of touching German, and I know he broke down her reserve and she promised him all he wanted. This part she would never confess, though. Only she was shivering with revulsion and excitement and even a sense of power, when I came home.

That was why M—— appeared more impertinent than ever, next morning. He had arranged to go to Melenga's house the following day, and to pay ten francs a day for his room, his meals extra. So that was something. He made a long tale about not eating any of his meals in the hotel now, but pretending he was invited out, and eating in the little restaurants where the food was so bad. And he had now only fifteen lire left in his pocket. But I was cold, and wouldn't give him any more. I said I would give him money next day, for his bill.

He had now another request, and a new tone.

"Won't you do *one more* thing for me?" he said. "Oh, do! Do do this one thing for me. I want you to go to the monastery and bring away my important papers and some clothes and my important trinkets. I have made a list of the things here—and where you'll find them in my writing-table and in the chest of drawers. I don't think you'll have any trouble. Don Bernardo has the keys. He will open everything for you. And I beg you, *in the name of God,* don't let anybody else see the things. Not even Don Bernardo. Don't, whatever you do, let him see the papers and manuscripts you are bringing. If he sees them, there's an end to me at the monastery. I can *never* go back there. I am ruined in their eyes for ever. As it is, although Don Bernardo is the best person in the world and my dearest friend, still—you know what people are, especially monks. A little curious, don't you know, a little inquisitive. Well, let us hope for the best as far as that goes. But you will do this for me, won't you? I shall be so eternally grateful."

Now a journey to the monastery meant a terrible twenty hours in the train each way—all that awful journey through Calabria to Naples and northwards. It meant mixing myself up in this man's affairs. It meant appearing as his accomplice at the monastery. It meant travelling with all his "compromising" papers and his valuables. And all this time, I never knew what mischiefs he had really been up to, and I didn't trust him, not for one single second. He would tell me nothing save that Anzio hotel cheque. I knew that wasn't all, by any means. So I mistrusted him. And with a feeling of utter mistrust goes a feeling of contempt and dislike— And finally, it would have cost me at least ten pounds sterling, which I simply did not want to spend in waste.

"I don't want to do that," I said.

"Why not?" he asked, sharp, looking green. He had planned it all out.

"No, I don't want to."

"Oh, but I *can't* remain here as I am. I've got no *clothes*—I've got nothing to *wear*. I *must* have my things from the monastery. What can I do? What can I do? I came to you, if it hadn't been for you I should have gone to Rome. I came to you— Oh, yes, you *will* go. You *will* go, won't you? You *will* go to the monastery for my things?" And again he put his hand on my arm, and the tears began to fall from his upturned eyes. I turned my head aside. Never had the Ionian Sea looked so sickening to me.

"I don't *want* to," said I.

"But you *will!* You will! You *will* go to the monastery for me, won't you? Everything else is no good if you won't. I've nothing to wear. I haven't got my manuscripts to work on, I can't do the things I am doing. Here I live in a sweat of anxiety. I try to work, and I can't settle. I can't do anything. It's dreadful. I shan't have a minute's peace till I have got those things from the monastery, till I know they can't get at my private papers. You will do this for me! You will, won't you? Please do! Oh, please do!" And again tears.

And I with my bowels full of bitterness, loathing the thought of that journey there and back, on such an errand. Yet not quite sure that I ought to refuse. And he pleaded and struggled, and tried to bully me with tears and entreaty and reproach, to do his will. And I couldn't quite refuse. But neither could I agree.

At last I said:

"I don't want to go, and I tell you. I won't promise to go. And I won't say that I will not go. I won't say until tomorrow. Tomorrow I will tell you. Don't come to the house. I will be in the Corso at ten o'clock."

"I didn't doubt for a minute you would do this for me," he said. "Otherwise I should never have come to Taormina." As if he had done me an honour in coming to Taormina; and as if I had betrayed *him*.

"Well," I said. "If you make these messes you'll have to get out of them yourself. I don't know why you are *in* such a mess."

"Any man may make a mistake," he said sharply, as if correcting me.

"Yes, a *mistake!*" said I. "If it's a question of a mistake."

So once more he went, humbly, beseechingly, and yet, one could not help but feel, with all that terrible insolence of the humble. It is the humble, the wistful, the would-be loving souls today who bully us with their charity-demanding insolence. They just make up their minds, these needful sympathetic souls, that one is there to do their will. Very good.

I decided in the day I would *not* go. Without reasoning it out, I knew I *really* didn't want to go. I plainly didn't want it. So I wouldn't go.

The morning came again hot and lovely. I set off to the village. But there was M—— watching for me on the path beyond the valley. He came forward and took my hand warmly, clingingly. I turned back, to remain in the country. We talked for a minute of his leaving the hotel—he was going that afternoon, he had asked for his bill. But·he was waiting for the other answer.

"And I have decided," I said, "I won't go to the monastery."

"You won't." He looked at me. I saw how yellow he was round the eyes, and yellow under his reddish skin.

"No," I said.

And it was final. He knew it. We went some way in silence. I turned in at the garden gate. It was a lovely, lovely morning of hot sun. But-terflies were flapping over the rosemary hedges and over a few little red poppies, the young vines smelt sweet in flower, very sweet, the corn was tall and green, and there were still some wild, rose-red gladiolus flowers among the watery green of the wheat. M—— had accepted my refusal. I expected him to be angry. But no, he seemed quieter, wist-fuller, and he seemed almost to love me for having refused him. I stood at a bend in the path. The sea was heavenly blue, rising up beyond the vines and olive leaves, lustrous pale lacquer blue as only the Ionian Sea can be. Away at the brook below the women were washing, and one could hear the chock-chock-chock of linen beating against the stones. I felt M—— then an intolerable weight and like a clot of dirt over everything.

"May I come in?" he said to me.

"No," I said. "Don't come to the house. My wife doesn't want it."

Even that he accepted without any offence, and seemed only to like me better for it. That was a puzzle to me. I told him I would leave a letter and a cheque for him at the bank in the Corso that afternoon.

I did so, writing a cheque for a few pounds, enough to cover his bill and leave a hundred lire or so over, and a letter to say I could *not* do any more, and I didn't want to see him any more.

So, there was an end of it for a moment. Yet I felt him looming in the village, waiting. I had rashly said I would go to tea with him to the villa of one of the Englishmen resident here, whose acquaintance I had not made. Alas, M—— kept me to the promise. As I came home he appealed to me again. He was rather insolent. What good to him, he said, were the few pounds I had given him? He had a hundred and fifty lire left. What good was that? I realized it really was not a solution, and said nothing. Then he spoke of his plans for getting to Egypt. The fare, he had found out, was thirty-five pounds. And where were thirty-five pounds coming from? Not from me.

I spent a week avoiding him, wondering what on earth the poor devil was doing, and yet *determined* he should not be a parasite on me. If I could have given him fifty pounds and sent him to Egypt to be a parasite on somebody else, I would have done so. Which is what we call charity. However, I couldn't.

My wife chafed, crying: "What have you done! We shall have him on our hands all our life. We can't let him starve. It is degrading, degrading, to have him hanging on to us."

"Yes," I said. "He must starve or work or something. I am not God who is responsible for him."

M—— was determined not to lose his status as a gentleman. In a way I sympathized with him. He would never be out at elbows. That is your modern rogue. He will not degenerate outwardly. Certain standards of a gentleman he *would* keep up: he would be well-dressed, he would be lavish with borrowed money, he would be as far as possible honourable in his small transactions of daily life. Well, very good. I sympathized with him to a certain degree. If he could find his own way out, well and good. Myself, I was not his way out.

Ten days passed. It was hot and I was going about the terrace in pyjamas and a big old straw hat, when, suddenly, a Sicilian, handsome, in the prime of life, and in his best black suit, smiling at me and taking off his hat!

And could he speak to me? I threw away my straw hat, and we went into the *salotta*. He handed me a note.

"*Il Signor M—— mi ha dato questa lettera per Lei!*" he began, and I knew what was coming. Melenga had been a waiter in good hotels, had saved money, built himself a fine house which he let to foreigners. He was a pleasant fellow, and at his best now, because he was in a rage. I must repeat M——'s letter from memory: "Dear Lawrence, would you do me another kindness? *Land and Water* sent a cheque for seven guineas for the article on the monastery, and Don Bernardo forwarded this to me under Melenga's name. But unfortunately he made a mistake, and put Orazio instead of Pancrazio, so the postoffice would not deliver the letter, and have returned it to the monastery. This morning Melenga insulted me, and I cannot stay in his house another minute. Will you be so kind as to advance me these seven guineas? I shall leave Taormina at once, for Malta."

I asked Melenga what had happened, and read him the letter. He was handsome in his rage, lifting his brows and suddenly smiling.

"Ma senta, signore! Signor M—— has been in my house for ten days, and lived well, and eaten well, and drunk well, and I have not seen a single penny of his money. I go out in the morning and buy all the things, all he wants, and my wife cooks it, and he is very pleased, very pleased, has never eaten such good food in his life, and everything is splendid, splendid. And he never pays a penny. Not a penny. Says he is waiting for money from England, from America, from India. But the money never comes. And I am a poor man, signore, I have a wife and child to keep. I have already spent three hundred lire for this Signor M——, and I never see a penny of it back. And he says the money is coming, it is coming. But when? He never says he has got no money. He says he is expecting. Tomorrow—always tomorrow. It will come tonight, it will come tomorrow. This makes me in a rage. Till at last this morning I said to him I would bring nothing in, and he shouldn't have not so much as a drop of coffee in my house until he paid for it. It displeases me, signore, to say such a thing. I have known Signor M—— for many years, and he has always had money, and always been pleasant, *molto bravo,* and also generous with his money. *Si, lo so!* And my wife, *poverina,* she cries and says if the man has no money he must eat. But he doesn't say he has no money. He says always it is coming, it is coming, today, tomorrow, today, tomorrow. *E non viene mai niente.* And this enrages me, signore. So I said that to

him this morning. And he said he wouldn't stay in my house, and that I had insulted him, and he sends me this letter to you, signore, and says you will send him the money. *Ecco come!*"

Between his rage he smiled at me. One thing, however, I could see: he was not going to lose his money, M—— or no M——.

"Is it true that a letter came which the post would not deliver?" I asked him.

"*Sì, signore, è vero*. It came yesterday, addressed to me. And why, signore, why do his letters come addressed in my name? Why? Unless he has done something—?"

He looked at me inquiringly. I felt already mixed up in shady affairs.

"Yes," I said, "there is something. But I don't know exactly what. I don't ask, because I don't want to know in these affairs. It is better not to know."

"*Già! Già! Molto meglio, signore*. There will be something. There will be something happened that he had to escape from that monastery. And it will be some affair of the police."

"Yes, I think so," said I. "Money and the police. Probably debts. I don't ask. He is only an acquaintance of mine, not a friend."

"Sure it will be an affair of the police," he said with a grimace. "If not, why does he use my name! Why don't his letters come in his own name? Do you believe, signore, that he has any money? Do you think this money will come?"

"I'm sure he's *got* no money," I said. "Whether anybody will send him any, I don't know."

The man watched me attentively.

"He's got nothing?" he said.

"No. At present he's got nothing."

Then Pancrazio exploded on the sofa.

"*Allora!* Well, then! Well, then, why does he come to my house, why does he come and take a room in my house, and ask me to buy food, good food as for a gentleman who can pay, and a flask of wine, and everything, if he has no money? If he has no money, why does he come to Taormina? It is many years that he has been in Italy—ten years, fifteen years. And he has no money. Where has he had his money from before? Where?"

"From his writing, I suppose."

"Well, then why doesn't he get money for his writing now? He writes. He writes, he works, he says it is for the big newspapers."

"It is difficult to sell things."

"Heh! Then why doesn't he live on what he made before? He hasn't a soldo. He hasn't a penny— But how! How did he pay his bill at the San Domenico?"

."I had to lend him money for that. He really hadn't a penny."

"You! You! Well, then, he has been in Italy all these years. How is it he has nobody that he can ask for a hundred lire or two? Why does he come to you? Why? Why has he nobody in Rome, in Florence, anywhere?"

"I wonder that myself."

"*Sicuro!* He's been all these years here. And why doesn't he speak proper Italian? After all these years, and speaks all upside-down, it isn't Italian, an ugly confusion. Why? Why? He passes for a signore, for a man of education. And he comes to take the bread out of my mouth. And I have a wife and child, I am a poor man, I have nothing to eat myself if everything goes to a mezzo-signore like him. Nothing! He owes me now three hundred lire. But he will not leave my house, he will not leave Taormina till he has paid. I will go to the *prefettura,* I will go to the *questura,* to the police. I will not be swindled by such a mezzo-signore. What does he want to do? If he has no money, what does he want to do?"

"To go to Egypt, where he says he can earn some," I replied briefly. But I was feeling bitter in the mouth. When the man called M—— a mezzo-signore, a half-gentleman, it was so true. And at the same time it was so cruel, and so rude. And Melenga—there I sat in my pyjamas and sandals—probably he would be calling me also a mezzo-signore, or a quarto-signore even. He was a Sicilian who feels he is being done out of his money—and that is saying everything.

"To Egypt! And who will pay for him to go? Who will give him money? But he must pay me first. He must pay me first."

"He says," I said, "that in the letter which went back to the monastery there was a cheque for seven pounds—some six hundred lire—and he asks me to send him this money, and when the letter is returned again I shall have the cheque that is in it."

Melenga watched me.

"Six hundred lire—" he said.

"Yes."

"Oh, well, then. If he pays me, he can stay—" he said; he almost added: "till the six hundred is finished." But he left it unspoken.

"But am I going to send the money? Am I sure that what he says is true?"

"I think it is true. I think it is true," said he. "The letter *did* come."

I thought for a while.

"First," I said, "I will write and ask him if it is quite true, and to give me a guarantee."

"Very well," said Melenga.

I wrote to M——, saying that if he could assure me that what he said about the seven guineas was quite correct, and if he would give me a note to the editor of *Land and Water,* saying that the cheque was to be paid to me, I would send the seven guineas.

Melenga was back in another half-hour. He brought a note which began:

"Dear Lawrence, I seem to be living in an atmosphere of suspicion. First Melenga this morning, and now you—" Those are the exact opening words. He went on to say that of course his word was true, and he enclosed a note to the editor, saying the seven guineas were to be transferred to me. He asked me please to send the money, as he could not stay another night at Melenga's house, but would leave for Catania, where, by the sale of some trinkets, he hoped to make some money and to see once more about a passage to Egypt. He had been to Catania once already—travelling *third class!*—but had failed to find any cargo boat that would take him to Alexandria. He would get away now to Malta. His things were being sent down to Syracuse from the monastery.

I wrote and said I hoped he would get safely away, and enclosed the cheque.

"This will be for six hundred lire," said Melenga.

"Yes," said I.

"Eh, va bene! If he pays the three hundred lire, he can stop in my house for thirty lire a day."

"He says he won't sleep in your house again."

"Ma! Let us see. If he likes to stay. He has always been a *bravo signore.* I have always liked him quite well. If he wishes to stay and pay me thirty lire a day——"

The man smiled at me rather greenly.

"I'm afraid he is offended," said I.

"Eh, va bene! Ma senta, signore. When he was here before—you know I have this house of mine to let. And you know the English signorina goes away in the summer. Oh, very well. Says M——, he writes for a newspaper, he owns a newspaper, I don't know what, in Rome. He will put in an advertisement advertising my villa. And so I shall get somebody to take it. Very well. And he put in the advertisement. He sent me the paper and I saw it there. But no one came to take my villa. *Va bene!* But after a year, in the January, that is, came a bill for me for twenty-two lire to pay for it. Yes, I had to pay the twenty-two lire, for nothing—for the advertisement which Signor M—— put in the paper."

"Bah!" said I.

He shook hands with me and left. The next day he came after me in the street, and said that M—— had departed the previous evening for Catania. As a matter of fact the post brought me a note of thanks from Catania. M—— was never indecent, and one could never dismiss him just as a scoundrel. He was not. He was one of these modern parasites who just assume their right to live and live well, leaving the payment to anybody who can, will, or must pay. The end is inevitably swindling.

There came also a letter from Rome, addressed to me. I opened it unthinking. It was for M——, from an Italian lawyer, stating that inquiry had been made about the writ against M——, and that it was for *qualche affare di truffa,* some affair of swindling: that the lawyer had seen this, that, and the other person, but nothing could be done. He regretted, etc., etc. I forwarded this letter to M—— at Syracuse, and hoped to God it was ended. Ah, I breathed free now he had gone.

But, no. A friend who was with us dearly wanted to go to Malta. It is only about eighteen hours' journey from Taormina—easier than going to Naples. So our friend invited us to take the trip with her, as her guests. This was rather jolly. I calculated that M——, who had been gone a week or so, would easily have got to Malta. I had had a friendly letter from him from Syracuse, thanking me for the one I had forwarded, and enclosing an I.O.U. for the various sums of money he had had.

So, on a hot, hot Thursday, we were sitting in the train again running south, the four and a half hours' journey to Syracuse. And M—— dwindled now into the past. If we should see him! But no, it was impossible. After all the wretchedness of that affair we were in holiday spirits.

The train ran into Syracuse station. We sat on, to go the few yards further into the port. A tout climbed on the foot-board: Were we going to Malta? Well, we couldn't. There was a strike of the steamers, we couldn't go. When would the steamer go? Who knows? Perhaps tomorrow.

We got down crestfallen. What should we do? There stood the express train about to start off back northwards. We could be home again that evening. But, no, it would be too much of a fiasco. We let the train go, and trailed off into the town, to the Grand Hotel, which is an old Italian place just opposite the port. It is rather a dreary hotel—and many bloodstains of squashed mosquitoes on the bedroom walls. Ah, vile mosquitoes!

However, nothing to be done. Syracuse port is fascinating too, a tiny port with the little Sicilian ships having the slanting eyes painted on the prow, to see the way, and a coal boat from Cardiff, and one American and two Scandinavian steamers—no more. But there were two torpedo boats in the harbour, and it was like a *festa,* a strange, lousy *festa.*

Beautiful the round harbour where the Athenian ships came. And wonderful, beyond, the long sinuous sky-line of the long flat-topped table-land hills which run along the southern coast, so different from the peaky, pointed, bunched effect of many-tipped Sicily in the north. The sun went down behind that lovely, sinuous sky-line, the harbour water was gold and red, the people promenaded in thick streams under the pomegranate trees and hibiscus trees. Arabs in white burnouses and fat Turks in red fezzes and black alpaca long coats strolled also—waiting for the steamer.

Next day it was very hot. We went to the consul and the steamer agency. There was real hope that the brute of a steamer might actually sail that night. So we stayed on, and wandered round the town on the island, the old solid town, and sat in the church looking at the grand Greek columns embedded there in the walls.

When I came in to lunch, the porter said there was a letter for me. Impossible! said I. But he brought me a note. Yes. M——! He was staying at the other hotel along the front. "Dear Lawrence, I saw you this morning, all three of you walking down the Via Nazionale, but you would not look at me. I have got my visés and everything ready. The strike of the steamboats has delayed me here. I am sweating blood. I have a last request to make of you. Can you let me have ninety lire, to make up what I need for my hotel bill? If I cannot have this I am lost. I hoped to find you at the hotel but the porter said you were out. I am at the Casa Politi, passing every half-hour in agony. If you can be so kind as to stretch your generosity to this last loan, of course I shall be eternally grateful. I can pay you back once I get to Malta——"

Well, here was a blow! The worst was that he thought I had cut him —a thing I wouldn't have done. So after luncheon behold me going through the terrific sun of that harbour front of Syracuse, an enormous and powerful sun, to the Casa Politi. The porter recognized me and looked inquiringly. M—— was out, and I said I would call again at four o'clock.

It happened we were in the town eating ices at four, so I didn't get to his hotel till half-past. He was out—gone to look for me. So I left a note saying I had not seen him in the Via Nazionale, that I had called twice, and that I should be in the Grand Hotel in the evening.

When we came in at seven, M—— in the hall, sitting, the picture of misery and endurance. He took my hand in both his, and bowed to the women, who nodded and went upstairs. He and I went and sat in the empty lounge. Then he told me the trials he had had—how his luggage had come, and the station had charged him eighteen lire a day for deposit; how he had had to wait on at the hotel because of the ship; how he had tried to sell his trinkets, and had today parted with his opal sleevelinks—so that now he only wanted seventy, not ninety lire. I gave him a hundred note, and he looked into my eyes, his own eyes swimming with tears, and he said he was sweating blood.

Well, the steamer went that night. She was due to leave at ten. We went on board after dinner. We were going second class. And so, for once, was M——. It was only an eight hours' crossing, yet, in spite of all the blood he had sweated, he would not go third class. In a way I admired him for sticking to his principles. I should have gone third myself, out of shame of spending somebody else's money. He would not give way to such weakness. He knew that as far as the world goes, you're a first-class gentleman if you have a first-class ticket; if you have a third, no gentleman at all. It behoved him to be a gentleman. I understood his point, but the women were indignant. And I was just rather tired of him and his gentlemanliness.

It amused me very much to lean on the rail of the upper deck and watch the people coming on board—first going into the little customs house with their baggage, then scuffling up the gangway on board. The tall Arabs in their ghostly white woollen robes came carrying their sacks: they were going on to Tripoli. The fat Turk in his fez and long black alpaca coat with white drawers underneath came beaming up to the second class. There was a great row in the customs house; and then, simply running like a beetle with rage, there came on board a little Maltese or Greek fellow, followed by a tall lantern-jawed fellow, both seedy-looking scoundrels suckled in scoundrelism. They raved and nearly threw their arms away into the sea, talking wildly in some weird language with the fat Turk, who listened solemnly, away below on the deck. Then they rushed to somebody else. Of course, we were dying with curiosity. Thank heaven I heard men talking in Italian. It appears the two seedy fellows were trying to smuggle silver coin in small sacks.

and rolls out of the country. They were detected. But they declared they had a right to take it away, as it was foreign specie, English florins and half-crowns, and South American dollars and Spanish money. The customs officer, however, detained the lot. The little enraged beetle of a fellow ran back and forth from the ship to the customs, from the customs to the ship, afraid to go without his money, afraid the ship would go without him.

At five minutes to ten, there came M——, very smart in his little grey overcoat and grey curly hat, walking very smart and erect and genteel, and followed by a porter with a barrow of luggage. They went into the customs, M—— in his grey suède gloves passing rapidly and smartly in, like the grandest gentleman on earth, and with his grey suède hands throwing open his luggage for inspection. From on board we could see the interior of the little customs shed.

Yes, he was through. Brisk, smart, superb, like the grandest little gentleman on earth, strutting because he was late, he crossed the bit of flagged pavement and came up the gangway, haughty as you can wish. The carabinieri were lounging by the foot of the gangway, fooling with one another. The little gentleman passed them with his nose in the air, came quickly on board, followed by his porter, and in a moment disappeared. After about five minutes the porter reappeared—a red-haired fellow, I knew him—he even saluted me from below, the brute. But M—— lay in hiding.

I trembled for him at every unusual stir. There on the quay stood the English consul with his bulldog, and various elegant young officers with yellow on their uniforms, talking to elegant young Italian ladies in black hats with stiff ospreys and bunchy furs, and gangs of porters and hotel people and onlookers. Then came a tramp-tramp-tramp of a squad of soldiers in red fezzes and baggy grey trousers. Instead of coming on board they camped on the quay. I wondered if all these had come for poor M——. But apparently not.

So the time passed, till nearly midnight, when one of the elegant young lieutenants began to call the names of the soldiers, and the soldiers answered, and one after another filed on board with his kit. So, they were on board, on their way to Africa.

Now somebody called out, and the visitors began to leave the boat. Barefooted sailors and a boy ran to raise the gangway. The last visitor or official with a bunch of papers stepped off the gangway. People on shore began to wave handkerchiefs. The red-fezzed soldiers leaned like so many flower-pots over the lower rail. There was a calling of farewells. The ship was fading into the harbour, the people on shore seemed smaller, under the lamp, in the deep night—without one's knowing why.

So, we passed out of the harbour, passed the glittering lights of Ortygia, past the two lighthouses, into the open Mediterranean. The noise of a ship in the open sea! It was a still night, with stars, only a bit chill. And the ship churned through the water.

Suddenly, like a revenant, appeared M—— near us, leaning on the rail and looking back at the lights of Syracuse sinking already forlorn and little on the low darkness. I went to him.

"Well," he said, with his little smirk of a laugh. "Good-bye, Italy!"

"Not a sad farewell either," said I.

"No, my word, not this time," he said. "But what an awful long time we were starting! A *brutta mezz'ora* for me, indeed. Oh, my word, I begin to breathe free for the first time since I left the monastery! How awful it's been! But of course, in Malta, I shall be all right. Don Bernardo has written to his friends there. They'll have everything ready for me that I want, and I can pay you back the money you so kindly lent me."

We talked for some time, leaning on the inner rail of the upper deck.

"Oh," he said, "there's Commander So-and-so, of the British fleet. He's stationed in Malta. I made his acquaintance in the hotel. I hope we're going to be great friends in Malta. I hope I shall have an opportunity to introduce you to him. Well, I suppose you will want to be joining your ladies. So long, then. Oh, for tomorrow morning! I never longed so hard to be in the British Empire—" He laughed, and strutted away.

In a few minutes we three, leaning on the rail of the second-class upper deck, saw our little friend large as life on the first-class deck, smoking a cigar and chatting in an absolutely first-class-ticket manner with the above mentioned Commander. He pointed us out to the Commander, and we felt the first-class passengers were looking across at us second-class passengers with pleasant interest. The women went behind a canvas heap to laugh, I hid my face under my hat-brim to grin and watch. Larger than any first-class ticketer leaned our little friend on the first-class rail, and whiffed at his cigar. So *dégagé* and so genteel he could be. Only I noticed he wilted a little when the officers of the ship came near.

He was still on the first-class deck when we went down to sleep. In the morning I came up soon after dawn. It was a lovely summer Mediterranean morning, with the sun rising up in a gorgeous golden rage, and the sea so blue, so fairy blue, as the Mediterranean is in summer. We were approaching quite near to a rocky, pale yellow island with some vineyards, rising magical out of the swift blue sea into the morning radiance. The rocks were almost as pale as butter, the islands were like golden shadows loitering in the midst of the Mediterranean, lonely among all the blue.

M—— came up to my side.

"Isn't it lovely! Isn't it beautiful!" he said, "I love approaching these islands in the early morning." He had almost recovered his assurance, and the slight pomposity and patronizing tone I had first known in him. "In two hours I shall be free! Imagine it! Oh, what a beautiful feeling!" I looked at him in the morning light. His face was a good deal broken by his last month's experience, older looking, and dragged. Now that the excitement was nearing its end, the tiredness began to tell on him. He was yellowish round the eyes, and the whites of his round, rather impudent blue eyes were discoloured.

Malta was drawing near. We saw the white fringe of the sea upon the yellow rocks, and a white road looping on the yellow rocky hillside. I thought of St. Paul, who must have been blown this way, must have struck the island from this side. Then we saw the heaped glitter of the square facets of houses, Valletta, splendid above the Mediterranean, and a tangle of shipping and dreadnoughts and watchtowers in the beautiful, locked-in harbour.

We had to go down to have passports examined. The officials sat in the long saloon. It was a horrible squash and squeeze of the first- and second-class passengers. M—— was a little ahead of me. I saw the American eagle on his passport. Yes, he passed all right. Once more he was free. As he passed away he turned and gave a condescending affable nod to me and to the Commander, who was just behind me.

The ship was lying in Valletta harbour. I saw M——, quite superb and brisk now, ordering a porter with his luggage into a boat. The great rocks rose above us, yellow and carved, cut straight by man. On top were all the houses. We got at last into a boat and were rowed ashore. Strange to be on British soil and to hear English. We got a carriage and drove up the steep highroad through the cutting in the rock, up to the town. There in the big square we had coffee, sitting out of doors. A military band went by, playing splendidly in the bright, hot morning. The Maltese lounged about, and watched. Splendid the band, and the soldiers! One felt the splendour of the British Empire, let the world say what it likes. But, alas, as one stayed on even in Malta, one felt the old lion had gone foolish and amiable. Foolish and amiable, with the weak amiability of old age.

We stayed in the Great Britain Hotel. Of course one could not be in Valletta for twenty-four hours without meeting M——. There he was, in the Strada Reale, strutting in a smart white duck suit, with a white piqué cravat. But, alas, he had no white shoes: they had got lost or stolen. He had to wear black boots with his summer finery.

He was staying in an hotel a little further down our street, and he begged me to call and see him, he begged me to come to lunch. I promised and went. We went into his bedroom, and he rang for more sodas.

"How wonderful it is to be here!" he said brightly. "Don't you like it immensely? And, oh, how wonderful to have a whisky and soda. Well, now, say when."

He finished one bottle of Black and White, and opened another. The waiter, a good-looking Maltese fellow, appeared with two siphons. M—— was very much the signore with him, and at the same time very familiar: as I should imagine a rich Roman of the merchant class might have been with a pet slave. We had quite a nice lunch, and whisky and soda and a bottle of French wine. And M—— was the charming and attentive host.

After lunch we talked again of manuscripts and publishers and how he might make money. I wrote one or two letters for him. He was anxious to get something under way. And yet the trouble of these arrangements was almost too much for his nerves. His face looked broken and old, but not like an old man's, like an old boy's, and he was really very irritable.

For my own part I was soon tired of Malta, and would gladly have left after three days. But there was the strike of steamers still, we had to wait on. M—— professed to be enjoying himself hugely, making excursions every day, to St. Paul's Bay and to the other islands. He had also made various friends or acquaintances. Particularly two young men, Maltese, who were friends of Don Bernardo. He introduced me to these two young men: one Gabriel Mazzaiba and the other Salonia. They had small businesses down on the wharf. Salonia asked M—— to go for a drive in a motor-car round the island, and M—— pressed me to go too. Which I did. And swiftly, on a Saturday afternoon, we dodged about in the car upon that dreadful island, first to some fearful and stony bay, arid, treeless, desert, a bit of stony desert by the sea, with unhappy villas and a sordid, scrap-iron front; then away inland up long and dusty roads, across a bone-dry, bone-bare, hideous landscape. True, there was ripening corn, but this was all of a colour with the dust-yellow, bone-bare island. Malta is all a pale, softish, yellowish rock, just like Bath brick: this goes into fathomless dust. And the island is stark as a corpse, no trees, no bushes even: a fearful landscape, cultivated, and weary with ages of weariness, and old weary houses here and there.

We went to the old capital in the centre of the island, and this is interesting. The town stands on a bluff of hill in the middle of the dreariness, looking at Valletta in the distance, and the sea. The houses are all pale yellow, and tall, and silent, as if forsaken. There is a cathedral, too, and a fortress outlook over the sun-blazed, sun-dried, disheartening island. Then we dashed off to another village and climbed a church-dome that rises like a tall blister on the plain, with houses round and corn beyond and dust that has no glamour, stale, weary, like bone-dust, and thorn hedges sometimes, and some tin-like prickly pears. In the dusk we came round by St. Paul's Bay, back to Valletta.

The young men were very pleasant, very patriotic for Malta, very Catholic. We talked politics and a thousand things. M—— was gently patronizing, and seemed, no doubt, to the two Maltese a very elegant and travelled and wonderful gentleman. They, who had never seen even a wood, thought how wonderful a forest must be, and M—— talked to them of Russia and of Germany.

But I was glad to leave that bone-dry, hideous island. M—— begged me to stay longer: but not for worlds! He was establishing himself securely: was learning the Maltese language, and cultivating a thorough acquaintance with the island. And he was going to establish himself. Mazzaiba was exceedingly kind to him, helping him in every way. In Rabato, the suburb of the old town—a quiet, forlorn little yellow street —he found a tiny house of two rooms and a tiny garden. This would cost five pounds a year. Mazzaiba lent the furniture—and when I left, M—— was busily skipping back and forth from Rabato to Valletta, arranging his little home, and very pleased with it. He was also being very Maltese, and rather anti-British, as is essential, apparently, when one is not a Britisher and finds oneself in any part of the British Empire. M—— was very much the American gentleman.

Well, I was thankful to be home again and to know that he was safely shut up in that beastly island. He wrote me letters, saying how he loved it all, how he would go down to the sea—five or six miles' walk—at dawn, and stay there all day, studying Maltese and writing for the newspapers. The life was fascinating, the summer was blisteringly hot, and the Maltese were *most* attractive, especially when they knew you were not British. Such good-looking fellows, too, and do anything you want. Wouldn't I come and spend a month? I did not answer—felt I had had enough. Came a postcard from M——: "I haven't had a letter from you, nor any news at all. I am afraid you are ill, and feel so anxious. Do write—" But, no, I didn't want to write.

During August and September and half October we were away in the north. I forgot my little friend; hoped he was gone out of my life. But I had that fatal sinking feeling that he *hadn't* really gone out of it yet.

In the beginning of November a little letter from Don Bernardo—did I know that M—— had committed suicide in Malta? Following that, a scrubby Maltese newspaper, posted by Salonia, with a marked notice: "The suicide of an American gentleman at Rabato. Yesterday the American M—— M——, a well-built man in the prime of life, was found dead in his bed in his house at Rabato. By the bedside was a bottle containing poison. The deceased had evidently taken his life by swallowing prussic acid. Mr. M—— had been staying for some months on the island, studying the language and the conditions, with a view to writing a book. It is understood that financial difficulties were the cause of this lamentable event."

Then Mazzaiba wrote asking me what I knew of M——, and saying the latter had borrowed money which he, Mazzaiba, would like to recover. I replied at once, and then received the following letter from Salonia:

"Valletta, 20 November 1920.

"My dear Mr. Lawrence,

"Some time back I mailed you our *Daily Malta Chronicle* which gave an account of the death of M——. I hope you have received same. As the statements therein given were very vague and not quite correct, please accept the latter part of this letter as a more correct version.

"The day before yesterday Mazzaiba received your letter, which he gave me to read. As you may suppose, we were very much astonished by its general purport. Mazzaiba will be writing to you in a few days; in the meantime I volunteered to give you the details you asked for.

"Mazzaiba and I have done all in our power to render M——'s stay here as easy and pleasant as possible from the time we first met him in your company at the Great Britain Hotel. [This is not correct. They were already quite friendly with M—— before that motor-drive, when I saw these two Maltese for the first time.] He lived in an embarrassed mood since then, and though we helped him as best we could both morally and financially, he never confided to us his troubles. To this very day we cannot but look on his coming here and his stay amongst us, to say the least of the way he left us, as a huge farce wrapped up in mystery, a painful experience unsolicited by either of us, and a cause of grief unrequited except by our own personal sense of duty toward a stranger.

"Mazzaiba out of mere respect did not tell me of his commitments toward M—— until about a month ago, and this he did in a most confidential and private manner merely to put me on my guard, thinking, and rightly, too, that M—— would be falling on me next time for funds; Mazzaiba having already given him about £55 and would not possibly commit himself any further. Of course, we found him all along a perfect gentleman. Naturally, he hated the very idea that we or anybody else in Malta should look upon him in any other light. He never asked directly, though Mazzaiba (later myself) was always quick enough to interpret rightly what he meant and obliged him forthwith.

"At this stage, to save the situation, he made up a scheme that the three of us should exploit the commercial possibilities in Morocco. It very nearly materialized, everything was ready, I was to go with him to Morocco, Mazzaiba to take charge of affairs here and to dispose of transactions we initiated there. Fortunately, for lack of the necessary funds the idea had to be dropped, and there it ended, thank God, after a great deal of trouble I had in trying to set it well on foot.

"Last July, the police, according to our law, advised him that he was either to find a surety or to deposit a sum of money with them, as otherwise at the expiration of his three months' stay he would be compelled to leave the place. Money he had none, so he asked Mazzaiba to stand as surety. Mazzaiba could not, as he was already guarantor for his alien cousins who were here at the time. Mazzaiba (not M——) asked me and I complied, thinking that the responsibility was just moral and only exacted as a matter of form.

"When, as stated before, Mazzaiba told me that M—— owed him £55 and that he owed his grocer and others at Notabile (the old town, of which Rabato is the suburb) over £10, I thought I might as well look up my guarantee and see if I was directly responsible for any debts he incurred here. The words of his declaration which I endorsed stated that 'I hereby solemnly promise that I will not be a burden to the inhabitants of these islands, etc.,' and deeming unpaid debts to be more or less a burden, I decided to withdraw my guarantee, which I did on the 23rd ult. The reason I gave to the police was that he was outliving his income and that I did not intend to shoulder any financial responsibility in the matter. On the same day I wrote to him up at Notabile, saying that for family reasons I was compelled to withdraw his surety. He took my letter in the sense implied and no way offended at my procedure.

"M——, in his resourceful way, knowing that he would with great difficulty find another guarantor, wrote at once to the police saying that he understood from Mr. Salonia that he (S) had withdrawn his guarantee, but as he (M) would be leaving the island in about three weeks' time (still intending to exploit Morocco) he begged the Commissioner to allow him this period of grace, without demanding a new surety. In fact he asked me to find him a cheap passage to Gib. in an ingoing tramp steamer. The police did not reply to his letter at all; no doubt they had everything ready and well thought out. He was alarmed in not receiving an acknowledgment, and, knowing full well what he imminently expected at the hands of the Italian police, he decided to prepare for the last act of his drama.

"We had not seen him for three or four days when he came to Mazzaiba's office on Wednesday, 3rd inst., in the forenoon. He stayed there for some time talking on general subjects and looking somewhat more excited than usual. He went up to town alone at noon as Mazzaiba went to Singlea. I was not with them in the morning, but in the afternoon about 4:30, whilst I was talking to Mazzaiba in his office, M—— again came in looking very excited, and, being closing time, we went up, the three of us, to town, and there left him in the company of a friend.

"On Thursday morning, 4th inst., at about 10 a.m., two detectives in plain clothes met him in a street at Notabile. One of them quite casually went up to him and said very civilly that the inspector of police wished to see him *re* a guarantee or something, and that he was to go with him to the police station. This was an excuse, as the detective had about him a warrant for his arrest for frauding an hotel in Rome, and that he was to be extradited at the request of the authorities in Italy. M—— replied that as he was in his sandals he would dress up and go with them immediately, and, accompanying him to his house at No. 1 Strada S. Pietro, they allowed him to enter. He locked the door behind him, leaving them outside.

"A few minutes later he opened his bedroom window and dropped a letter addressed to Don Bernardo which he asked a boy in the street to post for him, and immediately closed the window again. One of the detectives picked up the letter and we do not know to this day if same was posted at all. Some time elapsed and he did not come out. The detectives were by this time very uneasy and as another police official came up they decided to burst open the door. As the door did not give way they got a ladder and climbed over the roof, and there they found M—— in his bedroom dying from poisoning, outstretched on his bed and a glass of water close by. A priest was immediately called in who had just time to administer extreme unction before he died at 11:45 a.m.

"At 8:00 a.m. the next day his body was admitted for examination at the Floriana Civil Hospital and death was certified to be from poisoning with hydrocyanic acid. His age was given as 44, being buried on his birthday (7th Novr.), with R. Catholic rites at the expense of *his friends in Malta*.

"Addenda: Contents of Don Bernardo's letter:

" 'I leave it to you and to Gabriel Mazzaiba to arrange my affairs. I cannot live any longer. Pray for me.'

"Document found on his writing-table:

" 'In case of my unexpected death inform American consul.

" 'I want to be buried first class, my wife will pay.

" 'My little personal belongings to be delivered to my wife. (Address.)

" 'My best friend here, Gabriel Mazzaiba, inform him. (Address.)

" 'My literary executor N—— D——. (Address.)

"'All manuscripts and books for N—— D——. I leave my literary property to N—— D—— to whom half the results are to accrue. The other half my debts are to be paid with:

"'Furniture etc. belong to Coleiro, Floriana.

"'Silver spoons etc. belong to Gabriel Mazzaiba. (Address.)'

"The American Consul is in charge of all his personal belongings. I am sure he will be pleased to give you any further details you may require. By the way, his wife refused to pay his burial expenses, but five of his friends in Malta undertook to give him a decent funeral. His mourners were: the consul, the vice-consul, Mr. A., an American citizen, Gabriel Mazzaiba, and myself.

"Please convey to Mrs. Lawrence an expression of our sincere esteem and high regard and you will kindly accept equally our warmest respects, whilst soliciting any information you would care to pass on to us regarding the late M——.

"Believe me, my dear Mr. Lawrence, etc."

[Mrs. M—— refunded the burial expenses through the American consul about two months after her husband's death.]

When I had read this letter the world seemed to stand still for me. I knew that in my own soul I had said: "Yes, he must die if he cannot find his own way." But for all that, now I *realized* what it must have meant to be the hunted, desperate man: everything seemed to stand still. I could, by giving half my money, have saved his life. I had chosen not to save his life.

Now, after a year has gone by, I keep to my choice. I still would not save his life. I respect him for dying when he was cornered. And for this reason I feel still connected with him: still have this to discharge, to get his book published, and to give him his place, to present him just as he was as far as I knew him myself.

The worst thing I have against him is that he abused the confidence, the kindness, and the generosity of unsuspecting people like Mazzaiba. He did not *want* to, perhaps. But he did it. And he leaves Mazzaiba swindled, distressed, confused, and feeling sold in the best part of himself. What next? What is one to feel towards one's strangers, after having known M——? It is this Judas treachery to *ask* for sympathy and for generosity, to take it when given—and then: "Sorry, but anybody may make a mistake!" It is this betraying with a kiss which makes me still say: "He should have died sooner." No, I would not help to keep him alive, not if I had to choose again. I would let him go over into death. He shall and should die, and so should all his sort: and so they will. There are so many kiss-giving Judases. He was not a criminal: he was obviously well intentioned: but a Judas every time, selling the good feeling he had tried to arouse, and had aroused, for any handful of silver he could get. A little loving vampire!

Yesterday arrived the manuscript of the Legion, from Malta. It is exactly two years since I read it first in the monastery. Then I was moved and rather horrified. Now I am chiefly amused; because in my mind's eye is the figure of M—— in the red trousers and the blue coat with lappets turned up, swinging like a little indignant pigeon across the drill yards and into the canteen of Bel-Abbes. He *is* so indignant, so righteously and morally indignant, and so funny. All the horrors of the actuality fade before the indignation, his little, tuppenny indignation.

Oh, M—— is a prime hypocrite. *How* loudly he rails against the Boches! *How* great his enthusiasm for the pure, the spiritual Allied cause. Just so long as he is in Africa, and it suits his purpose! His scorn for the German tendencies of the German legionaries: even Count de R. secretly leans towards Germany. "Blood is thicker than water," says our hero glibly. Some blood, thank God. Apparently not his own. For according to all showing he was, by blood, pure German: father and mother: even Hohenzollern blood!!! Pure German! Even his speech, his *mother-tongue,* was German and not English! And then the little mongrel—!

But perhaps something happens to blood when once it has been taken to America.

And then, once he is in Valbonne, lo, a change! Where now is sacred France and the holy Allied Cause! Where is our hero's fervour? It is *worse than* Bel-Abbes! Yes, indeed, far less human, more hideously cold. One is driven by very rage to wonder if he was really a spy, a German spy whom Germany cast off because he was no good.

The little *gentleman!* God damn his white-blooded gentility. The legionaries must have been gentlemen, that they didn't kick him every day to the lavatory and back.

"You are a journalist?" said the colonel.

"No, a *littérateur*," said M—— perkily.

"That is something more?" said the Colonel.

Oh, I would have given a lot to have seen it and heard it. The *littérateur!* Well, I hope this book will establish his fame as such. I hope the editor, if it gets one, won't alter any more of the marvellously staggering sentences and the joyful French mistakes. The *littérateur!*—the impossible little pigeon!

But the Bel-Abbes part is alive and interesting. It should be read only by those who have the stomach. Ugly, foul—alas, it is no uglier and no fouler than the reality. M—— himself was near enough to being a scoundrel, thief, forger, etc., etc.—what lovely strings of names he hurls at them!—to be able to appreciate their company. He himself was such a liar, that he was not taken in. But his conceit as a gentleman *keeping up appearances* gave him a real standpoint from which to see the rest. The book is in its way a real creation. But I would hate it to be published and taken at its face value, with M—— as a spiritual dove among vultures of lust. Let us first put a pinch of salt on the tail of this dove. What he did do in the way of vice, even in Bel-Abbes, I never chose to ask him.

Yes, yes, he sings another note when he is planted right among the sacred Allies, with never a German near. Then the gorgeousness goes out of his indignation. He takes it off with the red trousers. Now he is just a sordid little figure in filthy corduroys. There is no vice to purple his indignation, the little holy liar. There is only sordidness and automatic, passionless, colourless awful mud. When all is said and done, mud, cold, hideous, foul, engulfing mud, up to the waist, this is the final symbol of the Great War. Hear some of the horrified young soldiers. They dare hardly speak of it yet.

The Valbonne part is worse, really, than the Bel-Abbes part. Passionless, barren, utterly, coldly foul and hopeless. The ghastly emptiness, and the slow mud-vortex, the brink of it.

Well, now M—— has gone himself. Yes, and he would be gone in the common mud and dust himself, if it were not that the blood still beats warm and hurt and kind in some few hearts. M—— "hinted" to Mazzaiba for money, in Malta, and Mazzaiba gave it to him, thinking him a man in distress. He thought him a gentleman, and lovable, and in trouble! And Mazzaiba—it isn't his real name, but there he is, real enough—still has this feeling of grief for M——. So much so that now he has had the remains taken from the public grave in Malta, and buried in his own, the Mazzaiba grave, so that they shall not be lost. For my part, I would have said that the sooner they mingled with the universal dust, the better. But one is glad to see a little genuine kindness and gentleness, even if it is wasted on the bones of that selfish little scamp of a M——. He despised his "physical friendships," though he didn't forgo them. So why should anyone rescue his physique from the public grave?

But there you are—there was his power: to arouse affection and a certain tenderness in the hearts of others, for himself. And on this he traded. One sees the trick working all the way through the Legion book. God knows how much warm kindness, generosity, was showered on him during the course of his forty-odd years. And selfish little scamp, he took it as a greedy boy takes cakes off a dish, quickly, to make the most of his opportunity while it lasted. And the cake once eaten: *buona sera!* He patted his own little paunch and felt virtuous. Merely physical feeling, you see! He had a way of saying "physical" —a sort of American way, as if it were spelt "fisacal"—that made me want to kick him.

Not that he was mean, while he was about it. No, he would give very freely: even a little ostentatiously, always feeling that he was being a *liberal gentleman*. Ach, the liberality and the gentility he prided himself on! *Ecco!* And he gave a large tip, with a little winsome smile. But in his heart of hearts it was always himself he was thinking of, while he did it. Playing his role of the gentleman who was awfully *nice* to everybody—so long as they were nice to him, or so long as it served his advantage. Just private charity!

Well, poor devil, he is dead: which is all the better. He had his points, the courage of his own terrors, quick-wittedness, sensitiveness to certain things in his surroundings. I prefer him, scamp as he is, to the ordinary respectable person. He ran his risks: he *had* to be running risks with the police, apparently. And he poisoned himself rather than fall into their clutches. I like him for that. And I like him for the sharp and quick way he made use of every one of his opportunities to get out of that beastly army. There I admire him: a courageous, isolated little devil, facing his risks, and like a good rat, *determined* not to be trapped. I won't forgive him for trading on the generosity of others, and so dropping poison into the heart of all warm-blooded faith. But I am glad after all that Mazzaiba has rescued his bones from the public grave. I wouldn't have done it myself, because I don't forgive him his "fisacal" impudence and parasitism. But I am glad Mazzaiba has done it. And, for my part, I will put his Legion book before the world if I can. Let him have his place in the world's consciousness.

Let him have his place, let his word be heard. He went through vile experiences: he looked them in the face, braved them through, and kept his manhood in spite of them. For manhood is a strange quality, to be found in human rats as well as in hot-blooded men. M—— carried the human consciousness through circumstances which would have been too much for me. I would have died rather than be so humiliated, I could never have borne it. Other men, I know, went through worse things in the war. But then, horrors, like pain, are their own anæsthetic. Men lose their normal consciousness, and go through in a sort of delirium. The bit of Stendhal which Dos Passos quotes in front of *Three Soldiers* is frighteningly true. There are certain things which are *so* bitter, *so* horrible, that the contemporaries just cannot know them, cannot contemplate them. So it is with a great deal of the late war. It was so foul, and humanity in Europe fell suddenly into such ignominy and inhuman ghastliness, that we shall *never* fully realize what it was. We just cannot bear it. We haven't the soul-strength to contemplate it.

And yet, humanity can only finally conquer by realizing. It is human destiny, since Man fell into consciousness and self-consciousness, that we can only go forward step by step through realization, full, bitter, conscious realization. This is true of all the great terrors and agonies and anguishes of life: sex, and war, and even crime. When Flaubert in his story—it is so long since I read it—makes his saint have to kiss the leper, and naked clasp the leprous awful body against his own, that is what we must at last do. It is the great command, *Know Thyself*. We've got to *know* what sex is, let the sentimentalists wiggle as they like. We've got to know the greatest and most shattering human passions, let the puritans squeal as they like for screens. And we've got to know humanity's criminal tendency, look straight at humanity's great deeds of crime against the soul. We have to fold this horrible leper against our naked warmth, because life and the throbbing blood and the believing soul are greater even than leprosy. Knowledge, true knowledge, is like vaccination. It prevents the continuing of ghastly moral disease.

And so it is with the war. Humanity in Europe fell horribly into a hatred of the living soul, in the war. There is no gainsaying it. We all fell. Let us not try to wriggle out of it. We fell into hideous depravity of hating the human soul; a purulent smallpox of the spirit we had. It was shameful, shameful, shameful, in every country and in all of us. Some tried to resist, and some didn't. But we were all drowned in shame. A purulent smallpox of the vicious spirit, vicious against the deep soul that pulses in the blood.

We haven't got over it. The smallpox sores are running yet in the spirit of mankind. And we have got to take this putrid spirit to our bosom. There's nothing else for it. Take the foul rotten spirit of mankind, full of the running sores of the war, to our bosom, and cleanse it there. Cleanse it not with blind love; ah, no, that won't help. But with bitter and wincing realization. We have to take the disease into our consciousness and let it go through our soul, like some virus. We have got to realize. And then we can surpass.

M—— went where I could never go. He carried the human consciousness unbroken through circumstances I could not have borne.

It is not heroism to rush on death. It is cowardice to accept a martyrdom today. That is the feeling one has at the end of Dos Passos's book. To let oneself be absolutely trapped? Never! I prefer M——. He drew himself out of the thing he loathed, despised, and feared. He fought it, for his own spirit and liberty. He fought it open-eyed. He went through. They were more publicly heroic, they won war medals. But the lonely terrified courage of the isolated spirit which grits its teeth and stares the horrors in the face and *will* not succumb to them, but fights its way through them, *knowing* that it must surpass them: this is the rarest courage. And this courage M—— had: and the man in the Dos Passos book didn't *quite* have it. And so, though M—— poisoned himself, and I would not wish him *not* to have poisoned himself; though as far as warm life goes, I don't forgive him; yet, as far as the eternal and unconquerable spirit of man goes, I am with him through eternity. I am grateful to him; he beat out for me boundaries of human experience which I could not have beaten out for myself. The *human* traitor he was. But he was not traitor to the spirit. In the great spirit of human consciousness he was a hero, little, quaking and heroic: a strange, quaking little star.

Even the dead ask only for *justice:* not for praise or exoneration. Who dares humiliate the dead with excuses for their living? I hope I may do M—— justice; and I hope his restless spirit may be appeased. I do not try to forgive. The living blood knows no forgiving. Only the overweening spirit takes on itself to dole out forgiveness. But justice is a sacred human right. The overweening spirit pretends to perch above justice. But I am a man, not a spirit, and men with blood that throbs and throbs and throbs can only live at length by being just, can only die in peace if they have justice. Forgiveness gives the whimpering dead no rest. Only deep, true justice.

There is M——'s manuscript then, like a map of the lower places of mankind's activities. There is the war: foul, foul, unutterably foul. As foul as M—— says. Let us make up our minds about it.

It is the only help: to realize, *fully,* and then make up our minds. The war was *foul*. As long as I am a man, I say it and assert it, and further I say, as long as I am a man such a war shall never occur again.

It shall not, and it shall not. All modern militarism is foul. It shall go. A man I am, and above machines, and it shall go, forever, because I have found it vile, vile, too vile ever to experience again. Cannons shall go. Never again shall trenches be dug. They *shall* not, for I am a man, and such things are within the power of man, to break and make. I have said it, and as long as blood beats in my veins, I mean it. Blood beats in the veins of many men who mean it as well as I.

Man perhaps *must* fight. Mars, the great god of war, will be a god for ever. Very well. Then if fight you must, fight you shall, and without engines, without machines. Fight if you like, as the Roman fought, with swords and spears, or like the Red Indian, with bows and arrows and knives and war paint. But never again shall you fight with the foul, base, fearful, monstrous machines of war which man invented for the last war. You shall not. The diabolic mechanisms are man's, and I am a man. Therefore they are mine. And I smash them into oblivion. With every means in my power, *except* the means of these machines, I smash them into oblivion. I am at war! I, a man, am at war! —with these foul machines and contrivances that men have conjured up. Men have conjured them up. I, a man, will conjure them down again. Won't I? But I will! I am not one man, I am many, I am most.

So much for the war! So much for M——'s manuscript. Let it be read. It is not this that will do harm, but sloppy sentiment and cant. Take the bitterness and cleanse the blood.

Now would you believe it, that little scamp M—— spent over a hundred pounds of borrowed money during his four months in Malta, when his expenses, he boasted to me, need not have been more than a pound a week, once he got into the little house in Notabile? That is, he spent at least seventy pounds too much. Heaven knows what he did with it, apart from "guzzling." And this hundred pounds must be paid back in Malta. Which it never will be, unless this manuscript pays it back. Pay the gentleman's last debts, if no others.

He had to be a gentleman. I didn't realize till after his death. I never suspected him of royal blood. But there you are, you never know where it will crop out. He was the grandson of an emperor. His mother was the illegitimate daughter of the German Kaiser;

D—— says, of the old Kaiser Wilhelm I, Don Bernardo says, of Kaiser Friedrich Wilhelm, father of the present ex-Kaiser. She was born in Berlin on October 31, 1845; and her portrait, by Paul, now hangs in a gallery in Rome. Apparently there had been some injustice against her in Berlin, for she seems once to have been in the highest society there, and to have attended at court. Perhaps she was discreetly banished by Wilhelm II, hence M——'s hatred of that monarch. She lies buried in the Protestant Cemetery in Rome, where she died in 1912, with the words *Filia Regis* on her tomb. M—— adored her, and she him. Part of his failings one can *certainly* ascribe to the fact that he was an only son, an adored son, in whose veins the mother imagined only royal blood. And she must have thought him so beautiful, poor thing! Ah, well, they are both dead. Let us be just and wish them Lethe.

M—— himself was born in New York, November 7, 1876; so at least it says on his passport. He entered the Catholic Church in England in 1902. His father was a Mr. L—— M——, married to the mother in 1867.

So poor M—— had Hohenzollern blood in his veins: close kin to the ex-Kaiser Wilhelm. Well, that itself excuses him a great deal: because of the cruel illusion of importance *manqué,* which it must have given him. He never breathed a word of this to me. Yet apparently it is accepted at the monastery, the great monastery which knows most European secrets of any political significance. And for myself, I believe it is true. And if he was a scamp and a treacherous little devil, he had also qualities of nerve and breeding undeniable. He faced his way through that Legion experience: royal nerves dragging themselves through the sewers, without giving way. But, alas for royal blood! Like most other blood, it has gradually gone white, during our spiritual era. Bunches of nerves! And whitish, slightly acid blood. And no bowels of deep compassion and kindliness. Only charity—a little more than kin, and less than kind.

Also, M——! Ich grüsse dich, in der Ewigkeit. Aber hier, im Herzblut, hast du Gift und Leid nachgelassen—to use your own romantic language.

AN AFTERWORD ON
"THE PORTRAIT OF M. M."

THE foregoing chronicle was first published as a preface to a manuscript left behind when Maurice Magnus, a rootless cosmopolite with an American passport, killed himself on the island of Malta. It appears to have been generally believed both by those who liked him and by those who did not that he was, under the bar sinister, a second cousin of the second Kaiser Wilhelm. In 1915, after sundry efforts to attach himself to the Red Cross service behind one or another of the Allied armies, he impulsively flung himself into the Foreign Legion. From the ranks of that outfit, after some distasteful months in barracks in Morocco and several more in training quarters at Valbonne near Lyons, he deserted without ever having met the enemy, seen a trench, or heard a gun fired in anger. While on leave in Paris, he nimbly shifted to civilian clothes, took train to Nice, and with considerable gumption walked unchallenged across the frontier at Ventimiglia, a defection from the Allied cause which appears to have gone uncomplained of. His report on these adventures Magnus committed to paper as early as 1917 under the title *Dregs* and it was this manuscript (considerably expurgated, Norman Douglas has since testified, in its references to "certain ultra-masculine peculiarities of legionary life") which Lawrence published seven years later, prefacing it with the contemptuous and coldly angry portrait of the author here reprinted. It is improbable that ever in any age or tongue was a posthumous work offered to the public with a foreword so conspicuously lacking in the elegiac note.

Here it has seemed best to follow Lawrence's text in pretending to mask the identities of Magnus and his friend, N. D., although as mysteries these, even at the first, were about as baffling as those brain-puzzlers of my youth, when we all stood a chance to win a diamond-frame bicycle if only we could contrive to supply the missing letters in LIL-IAN RUSS-LL or WIL-IAM JENNI-GS B-YAN. But if any chance readers could not for the life of them guess whom Lawrence had in mind when he introduced N. D. as an English novelist loose in Italy, the last gossamer veil was rent when the aforesaid Douglas, author of *South Wind,* entered the lists with an expostulatory pamphlet called "A Plea for Better Manners." The tone of this brochure was elaborately good-humored and with a "Come, come, little man" note it attempted—quite without success, I think—to achieve toward Lawrence the air of one looking down tolerantly as from a higher level. Douglas was at some pains to present Magnus as a man more generous, unworldly, gallant, and likable than anyone could have guessed from Lawrence's presentation of him. And he was at even greater pains to picture Lawrence himself as an unscrupulous romancer, in this instance especially disqualified for the biographer's role by his understandable irritation as an unappeased creditor. Mr. Douglas winds up his plea as follows:

I think a careful study of this Introduction will convince most readers that my young friend has not exalted himself to any great extent; that, on the contrary, in exposing the frailties of Maurice Magnus he has contrived, like a true Boswell, to expose his own. Be that as it may, it is worth noting that Mr. Mazzaiba himself, the long-suffering creditor for those fifty-five pounds, must have taken another and most singular view of this "Judas treachery," as Lawrence calls it. Despite his grievance against Maurice, he went to the expense of having his remains moved from the public grave at Malta and interred in his own burial-place; which says a good deal for both of them and proves, among other things, that some people can still be trusted to behave like gentlemen. And there he now lies, the poor devil; unconcerned about bailiffs —and biographers. *Requiescat.* Lawrence calls him an outsider; it is the mildest of some fifteen pretty names he bestows on him. An outsider. So be it. I wish we had a few more such outsiders on earth.

Douglas might pertinently have added that the hapless Magnus would have been more dispassionately examined as a specimen by one who was himself less troublingly preoccupied by the subject of virility. But when Douglas has advanced his brief for the defense, Lawrence's portrait of M. M. remains, subtly confirmed by the outraged self-importance of the memoirs themselves. If the breathing, speaking likeness was in any measure the product of what Douglas calls "the novelist's touch," it is strange that for no novel of his did Lawrence ever succeed in creating a character half so convincing as this wrathful sketch. Strange, too, it is that Magnus, though he wrote a good deal and though his mother's gravestone in Rome is marked by the legend "Filia Regis," will be remembered, if at all, because he sat for his portrait—perhaps wriggled would be the better word—wriggled for his portrait to a painter of genius who happened to despise him.

A. W.

TWO
FRIENDS

by

WILLA CATHER

TWO FRIENDS

EVEN in early youth, when the mind is so eager for the new and un-
tried, while it is still a stranger to faltering and fear, we yet like to
think that there are certain unalterable realities, somewhere at the bottom of things. These anchors may be ideas; but more often they are
merely pictures, vivid memories, which in some unaccountable and
very personal way give us courage. The sea-gulls, that seem so much
creatures of the free wind and waves, that are as homeless as the sea
(able to rest upon the tides and ride the storm, needing nothing but
water and sky), at certain seasons even they go back to something
they have known before; to remote islands and lonely ledges that are
their breeding-grounds. The restlessness of youth has such retreats,
even though it may be ashamed of them.

Long ago, before the invention of the motor-car (which has made
more changes in the world than the War, which indeed produced the
particular kind of war that happened just a hundred years after Water-
loo), in a little wooden town in a shallow Kansas river valley, there
lived two friends. They were "business men," the two most prosperous
and influential men in our community, the two men whose affairs
took them out into the world to big cities, who had "connexions" in St.
Joseph and Chicago. In my childhood they represented to me success
and power.

R. E. Dillon was of Irish extraction, one of the dark Irish, with glistening jet-black hair and moustache, and thick eyebrows. His skin was
very white, bluish on his shaven cheeks and chin. Shaving must have
been a difficult process for him, because there were no smooth ex-
panses for the razor to glide over. The bony structure of his face was

prominent and unusual; high cheek-bones, a bold Roman nose, a chin cut by deep lines, with a hard dimple at the tip, a jutting ridge over his eyes where his curly black eyebrows grew and met. It was a face in many planes, as if the carver had whittled and modelled and indented to see how far he could go. Yet on meeting him what you saw was an imperious head on a rather small, wiry man, a head held conspicuously and proudly erect, with a carriage unmistakably arrogant and consciously superior. Dillon had a musical, vibrating voice, and the changeable grey eye that is peculiarly Irish. His full name, which he never used, was Robert Emmet Dillon, so there must have been a certain feeling somewhere back in his family.

He was the principal banker in our town, and proprietor of the large general store next the bank; he owned farms up in the grass country, and a fine ranch in the green timbered valley of the Caw. He was, according to our standards, a rich man.

His friend, J. H. Trueman, was what we called a big cattleman. Trueman was from Buffalo; his family were old residents there, and he had come West as a young man because he was restless and unconventional in his tastes. He was fully ten years older than Dillon—in his early fifties, when I knew him; large, heavy, very slow in his movements, not given to exercise. His countenance was as unmistakably American as Dillon's was not—but American of that period, not of this. He did not belong to the time of efficiency and advertising and progressive methods. For any form of pushing or boosting he had a cold, unqualified contempt. All this was in his face—heavy, immobile, rather melancholy, not remarkable in any particular. But the moment one looked at him one felt solidity, an entire absence of anything mean or small, easy carelessness, courage, a high sense of honour.

These two men had been friends for ten years before I knew them, and I knew them from the time I was ten until I was thirteen. I saw them as often as I could, because they led more varied lives than the other men in our town; one could look up to them. Dillon, I believe, was the more intelligent. Trueman had, perhaps, a better tradition, more background.

Dillon's bank and general store stood at the corner of Main Street and a cross-street, and on this cross-street, two short blocks away, my family lived. On my way to and from school, and going on the countless errands that I was sent upon day and night, I always passed Dillon's store. Its long, red brick wall, with no windows except high overhead, ran possibly a hundred feet along the sidewalk of the cross-street. The front door and show windows were on Main Street, and the bank was next door. The board sidewalk along that red brick wall was wider than any other piece of walk in town, smoother, better laid, kept in perfect repair; very good to walk on in a community where most things were flimsy. I liked the store and the brick wall and the sidewalk because they were solid and well built, and possibly I admired Dillon and Trueman for much the same reason. They were secure and established. So many of our citizens were nervous little hopper men, trying to get on. Dillon and Trueman had got on; they stood with easy assurance on a deck that was their own.

In the daytime one did not often see them together—each went about his own affairs. But every evening they were both to be found at Dillon's store. The bank, of course, was locked and dark before the sun went down, but the store was always open until ten o'clock; the clerks put in a long day. So did Dillon. He and his store were one. He never acted as salesman, and he kept a cashier in the wire-screened office at the back end of the store; but he was there to be called on. The thrifty Swedes to the north, who were his best customers, usually came to town and did their shopping after dark—they didn't squander daylight hours in farming season. In these evening visits with his customers, and on his drives in his buckboard among the farms, Dillon learned all he needed to know about how much money it was safe to advance a farmer who wanted to feed cattle, or to buy a steam thrasher, or build a new barn.

Every evening in winter, when I went to the post-office after supper, I passed through Dillon's store instead of going round it—for the warmth and cheerfulness, and to catch sight of Mr. Dillon and Mr. Trueman playing chequers in the office behind the wire screening; both seated on high accountant's stools, with the chequer-board on the cashier's desk before them. I knew all Dillon's clerks, and if they were not busy, I often lingered about to talk to them; sat on one of the grocery counters and watched the chequer-players from a distance. I remember Mr. Dillon's hand used to linger in the air above the board before he made a move; a well-kept hand, white, marked with blue veins and streaks of strong black hair. Trueman's hands rested on his knees under the desk while he considered; he took a chequer, set it down, then dropped his hand on his knee again. He seldom made an unnecessary movement with his hands or feet. Each of the men wore a ring on his little finger. Mr. Dillon's was a large diamond solitaire set in a gold claw, Trueman's the head of a Roman soldier cut in onyx and set in pale twisted gold; it had been his father's, I believe.

Exactly at ten o'clock the store closed. Mr. Dillon went home to his wife and family, to his roomy, comfortable house with a garden and orchard and big stables. Mr. Trueman, who had long been a widower, went to his office to begin the day over. He led a double life, and until one or two o'clock in the morning entertained the poker-players of our town. After everything was shut for the night, a queer crowd drifted into Trueman's back office. The company was seldom the same on two successive evenings, but there were three tireless poker-players who always came: the billiard-hall proprietor, with green-gold moustache and eyebrows, and big white teeth; the horse-trader, who smelled of horses; the dandified cashier of the bank that rivalled Dillon's. The gamblers met in Trueman's place because a game that went on there was respectable, was a social game, no matter how much money changed hands. If the horse-trader or the crooked money-lender got over-heated and broke loose a little, a look or a remark from Mr. Trueman would freeze them up. And his remark was always the same:

"Careful of the language around here."

It was never "your" language, but "the" language—though he certainly intended no pleasantry. Trueman himself was not a lucky poker man; he was never ahead of the game on the whole. He played because he liked it, and he was willing to pay for his amusement. In general he was large and indifferent about money matters—always carried a few hundred-dollar bills in his inside coat-pocket, and left his coat hanging anywhere—in his office, in the bank, in the barber shop, in the cattle-sheds behind the freight yard.

Now, R. E. Dillon detested gambling, often dropped a contemptuous word about "poker bugs" before the horse-trader and the billiard-hall man and the cashier of the other bank. But he never made remarks of that sort in Trueman's presence. He was a man who voiced his prejudices fearlessly and cuttingly, but on this and other matters he held his peace before Trueman. His regard for him must have been very strong.

During the winter, usually in March, the two friends always took a trip together, to Kansas City and St. Joseph. When they got ready, they packed their bags and stepped aboard a fast Santa Fe train and went; the Limited was often signalled to stop for them. Their excursions made some of the rest of us feel less shut away and small-townish, just as their fur overcoats and silk shirts did. They were the only men in Singleton who wore silk shirts. The other business men wore white shirts with detachable collars, high and stiff or low and sprawling, which were changed much oftener than the shirts. Neither of my heroes was afraid of laundry bills. They did not wear waistcoats, but went about in their shirt-sleeves in hot weather; their suspenders were chosen with as much care as their neckties and handkerchiefs. Once when a bee stung my hand in the store (a few of them had got into the brown-sugar barrel), Mr. Dillon himself moistened the sting, put baking soda on it, and bound my hand up with his pocket handkerchief. It was of the smoothest linen, and in one corner was a violet square bearing his initials, R. E. D., in white. There were never any handkerchiefs like that in my family. I cherished it until it was laundered, and I returned it with regret.

It was in the spring and summer that one saw Mr. Dillon and Mr. Trueman at their best. Spring began early with us—often the first week of April was hot. Every evening when he came back to the store after supper, Dillon had one of his clerks bring two arm-chairs out to the wide sidewalk that ran beside the red brick wall—office chairs of the old-fashioned sort, with a low round back which formed a half-circle to enclose the sitter, and spreading legs, the front ones slightly higher. In those chairs the two friends would spend the evening. Dillon would sit down and light a good cigar. In a few moments Mr. Trueman would come across from Main Street, walking slowly, spaciously, as if he were used to a great deal of room. As he approached, Mr. Dillon would call out to him:

"Good evening, J. H. Fine weather."

J. H. would take his place in the empty chair.

"Spring in the air," he might remark, if it were April. Then he would relight a dead cigar which was always in his hand—seemed to belong there, like a thumb or finger.

"I drove up north today to see what the Swedes are doing," Mr. Dillon might begin. "They're the boys to get the early worm. They never let the ground go to sleep. Whatever moisture there is, they get the benefit of it."

"The Swedes are good farmers. I don't sympathize with the way they work their women."

"The women like it, J. H. It's the old-country way; they're accustomed to it, and they like it."

"Maybe. I don't like it," Trueman would reply with something like a grunt.

They talked very much like this all evening; or, rather, Mr. Dillon talked, and Mr. Trueman made an occasional observation. No one could tell just how much Mr. Trueman knew about anything, because he was so consistently silent. Not from diffidence, but from superiority; from a contempt for chatter, and a liking for silence, a taste for it. After they had exchanged a few remarks, he and Dillon often sat in an easy quiet for a long time, watching the passers-by, watching the wagons on the road, watching the stars. Sometimes, very rarely, Mr. Trueman told a long story, and it was sure to be an interesting and unusual one.

But on the whole it was Mr. Dillon who did the talking; he had a wide-awake voice with much variety in it. Trueman's was thick and low—his speech was rather indistinct and never changed in pitch or tempo. Even when he swore wickedly at the hands who were loading his cattle into freight cars, it was a mutter, a low, even growl. There was a curious attitude in men of his class and time, that of being rather above speech, as they were above any kind of fussiness or eagerness. But I knew he liked to hear Mr. Dillon talk—anyone did. Dillon had such a crisp, clear enunciation, and he could say things so neatly. People would take a reprimand from him they wouldn't have taken from anyone else, because he put it so well. His voice was never warm or soft—it had a cool, sparkling quality; but it could be very humorous, very kind and considerate, very teasing and stimulating. Every sentence he uttered was alive, never languid, perfunctory, slovenly, unaccented. When he made a remark, it not only meant something, but sounded like something—sounded like the thing he meant.

When Mr. Dillon was closeted with a depositor in his private room in the bank, and you could not hear his words through the closed door, his voice told you exactly the degree of esteem in which he held that customer. It was interested, encouraging, deliberative, humorous, satisfied, admiring, cold, critical, haughty, contemptuous, according to the deserts and pretensions of his listener. And one could tell when the person closeted with him was a woman; a farmer's wife, or a woman who was trying to run a little business, or a country girl hunting a situation. There was a difference; something peculiarly kind and encouraging. But if it were a foolish, extravagant woman, or a girl he didn't approve of, oh, then one knew it well enough! The tone was courteous, but cold; relentless as the multiplication table.

All these possibilities of voice made his evening talk in the spring dusk very interesting; interesting for Trueman and for me. I found many pretexts for lingering near them, and they never seemed to mind my hanging about. I was very quiet. I often sat on the edge of the sidewalk with my feet hanging down and played jacks by the hour when there was moonlight. On dark nights I sometimes perched on top of one of the big goods-boxes—we called them "store boxes"—there were usually several of these standing empty on the sidewalk against the red brick wall.

I liked to listen to those two because theirs was the only "conversation" one could hear about the streets. The older men talked of nothing but politics and their business, and the very young men's talk was entirely what they called "josh"; very personal, supposed to be funny, and really not funny at all. It was scarcely speech, but noises, snorts, giggles, yawns, sneezes, with a few abbreviated words and slang expressions which stood for a hundred things. The original Indians of the Kansas plains had more to do with articulate speech than had our promising young men.

To be sure, my two aristocrats sometimes discussed politics, and joked each other about the policies and pretensions of their respective parties. Mr. Dillon, of course, was a Democrat—it was in the very frosty sparkle of his speech—and Mr. Trueman was a Republican; his rear, as he walked about the town, looked a little like the walking elephant labelled "G. O. P." in *Puck*. But each man seemed to enjoy hearing his party ridiculed, took it as a compliment.

In the spring their talk was usually about weather and planting and pasture and cattle. Mr. Dillon went about the country in his light buckboard a great deal at that season, and he knew what every farmer was doing and what his chances were, just how much he was falling behind or getting ahead.

"I happened to drive by Oscar Ericson's place today, and I saw as nice a lot of calves as you could find anywhere," he would begin, and Ericson's history and his family would be pretty thoroughly discussed before they changed the subject.

Or he might come out with something sharp: "By the way, J. H., I saw an amusing sight today. I turned in at Sandy Bright's place to get water for my horse, and he had a photographer out there taking pictures of his house and barn. It would be more to the point if he had a picture taken of the mortgages he's put on that farm."

Trueman would give a short, mirthless response, more like a cough than a laugh.

Those April nights, when the darkness itself tasted dusty (or, by the special mercy of God, cool and damp), when the smell of burning grass was in the air, and a sudden breeze brought the scent of wild-plum blossoms—those evenings were only a restless preparation for the summer nights, nights of full liberty and perfect idleness. Then there was no school, and one's family never bothered about where one was. My parents were young and full of life, glad to have the children out of the way. All day long there had been the excitement that intense heat produces in some people—a mild drunkenness made of sharp contrasts: thirst and cold water, the blazing stretch of Main Street and the cool of the brick stores when one dived into them. By nightfall one was ready to be quiet. My two friends were always in their best form on those moonlit summer nights, and their talk covered a wide range.

I suppose there were moonless nights, and dark ones with but a silver shaving and pale stars in the sky, just as in the spring. But I remember them all as flooded by the rich indolence of a full moon, or a half-moon set in uncertain blue. Then Trueman and Dillon would sit with their coats off and have a supply of fresh handkerchiefs to mop their faces; they were more largely and positively themselves. One could distinguish their features, the stripes on their shirts, the flash of Mr. Dillon's diamond; but their shadows made two dark masses on the white sidewalk. The brick wall behind them, faded almost pink by the burning of successive summers, took on a carnelian hue at night. Across the street, which was merely a dusty road, lay an open space, with a few stunted box-elder trees, where the farmers left their wagons and teams when they came to town. Beyond this space stood a row of frail wooden buildings, due to be pulled down any day; tilted, crazy, with outside stairs going up to rickety second-story porches that sagged in the middle. They had once been white, but were now grey, with faded blue doors along the wavy upper porches. These abandoned buildings, an eyesore by day, melted together into a curious pile in the moonlight, became an immaterial structure of velvet-white and glossy blackness, with here and there a faint smear of blue door, or a tilted patch of sage-green that had once been a shutter.

The road, just in front of the sidewalk where I sat and played jacks, would be ankle-deep in dust, and seemed to drink up the moonlight like folds of velvet. It drank up sound, too; muffled the wagon-wheels and hoof-beats; lay soft and meek like the last residuum of material things—the soft bottom resting-place. Nothing in the world, not snow mountains or blue seas, is so beautiful in moonlight as the soft, dry summer roads in a farming country, roads where the white dust falls back from the slow wagon-wheel.

Wonderful things do happen even in the dullest places—in the cornfields and the wheatfields. Sitting there on the edge of the sidewalk one summer night, my feet hanging in the warm dust, I saw an occultation of Venus. Only the three of us were there. It was a hot night, and the clerks had closed the store and gone home. Mr. Dillon and Mr. Trueman waited on a little while to watch. It was a very blue night, breathless and clear, not the smallest cloud from horizon to horizon. Everything up there overhead seemed as usual, it was the familiar face of a summer-night sky. But presently we saw one bright star moving. Mr. Dillon called to me, told me to watch what was going to happen, as I might never chance to see it again in my lifetime.

That big star certainly got nearer and nearer the moon—very rapidly, too, until there was not the width of your hand between them—now the width of two fingers—then it passed directly into the moon at about the middle of its girth; absolutely disappeared. The star we had been watching was gone. We waited, I do not know how long, but it seemed to me about fifteen minutes. Then we saw a bright wart on the other edge of the moon, but for a second only—the machinery up there worked fast. While the two men were exclaiming and telling me to look, the planet swung clear of the golden disk, a rift of blue came between them and widened very fast. The planet did not seem to move, but that inky blue space between it and the moon seemed to spread. The thing was over.

My friends stayed on long past their usual time and talked about eclipses and such matters.

"Let me see," Mr. Trueman remarked slowly, "they reckon the moon's about two hundred and fifty thousand miles away from us. I wonder how far that star is."

"I don't know, J. H., and I really don't much care. When we can get the tramps off the railroad, and manage to run this town with one fancy house instead of two, and have a Federal Government that is as honest as a good banking business, then it will be plenty of time to turn our attention to the stars."

Mr. Trueman chuckled and took his cigar from between his teeth. "Maybe the stars will throw some light on all that, if we get the run of them," he said humorously. Then he added: "Mustn't be a reformer, R. E. Nothing in it. That's the only time you ever get off on the wrong foot. Life is what it always has been, always will be. No use to make a fuss." He got up, said: "Good night, R. E.," said good night to me, too, because this had been an unusual occasion, and went down the sidewalk with his wide, sailor-like tread, as if he were walking the deck of his own ship.

When Dillon and Trueman went to St. Joseph, or, as we called it, St. Joe, they stopped at the same hotel, but their diversions were very dissimilar. Mr. Dillon was a family man and a good Catholic; he behaved in St. Joe very much as if he were at home. His sister was Mother Superior of a convent there, and he went to see her often. The nuns made much of him, and he enjoyed their admiration and all the ceremony with which they entertained him. When his two daughters were going to the convent school, he used to give theatre parties for them, inviting all their friends.

Mr. Trueman's way of amusing himself must have tried his friend's patience—Dillon liked to regulate other people's affairs if they needed it. Mr. Trueman had a lot of poker-playing friends among the commission men in St. Joe, and he sometimes dropped a good deal of money. He was supposed to have rather questionable women friends there, too. The grasshopper men of our town used to say that Trueman was financial adviser to a woman who ran a celebrated sporting house. Mary Trent, her name was. She must have been a very unusual woman; she had credit with all the banks, and never got into any sort of trouble. She had formerly been head mistress of a girls' finishing school and knew how to manage young women. It was probably a fact that Trueman knew her and found her interesting, as did many another sound business man of that time. Mr. Dillon must have shut his ears to these rumours—a measure of the great value he put on Trueman's companionship.

Though they did not see much of each other on these trips, they immensely enjoyed taking them together. They often dined together at the end of the day, and afterwards went to the theatre. They both loved the theatre; not this play or that actor, but the theatre—whether they saw *Hamlet* or *Pinafore*. It was an age of good acting, and the drama held a more dignified position in the world than it holds today.

After Dillon and Trueman had come home from the city, they used sometimes to talk over the plays they had seen, recalling the great scenes and fine effects. Occasionally an item in the Kansas City *Star* would turn their talk to the stage.

"J. H., I see by the paper that Edwin Booth is very sick," Mr. Dillon announced one evening as Trueman came up to take the empty chair.

"Yes, I noticed." Trueman sat down and lit his dead cigar. "He's not a young man any more." A long pause. Dillon always seemed to know when the pause would be followed by a remark, and waited for it. "The first time I saw Edwin Booth was in Buffalo. It was in *Richard the Second,* and it made a great impression on me at the time." Another pause. "I don't know that I'd care to see him in that play again. I like tragedy, but that play's a little too tragic. Something very black about it. I think I prefer *Hamlet."*

They had seen Mary Anderson in St. Louis once, and talked of it for years afterwards. Mr. Dillon was very proud of her because she was a Catholic girl, and called her "our Mary." It was curious that a third person, who had never seen these actors or read the plays, could get so much of the essence of both from the comments of two business men who used none of the language in which such things are usually discussed, who merely reminded each other of moments here and there in the action. But they saw the play over again as they talked of it, and perhaps whatever is seen by the narrator as he speaks is sensed by the listener, quite irrespective of words. This transference of experience went further: in some way the lives of those two men came across to me as they talked, the strong, bracing reality of successful, large-minded men who had made their way in the world when business was still a personal adventure.

I I

MR. DILLON went to Chicago once a year to buy goods for his store. Trueman would usually accompany him as far as St. Joe, but no farther. He dismissed Chicago as "too big." He didn't like to be one of the crowd, didn't feel at home in a city where he wasn't recognized as J. H. Trueman.

It was one of these trips to Chicago that brought about the end—for me and for them—a stupid, senseless, commonplace end.

Being a Democrat, already somewhat "tainted" by the free-silver agitation, one spring Dillon delayed his visit to Chicago in order to be there for the Democratic Convention—it was the Convention that first nominated Bryan.

On the night after his return from Chicago, Mr. Dillon was seated in his chair on the sidewalk, surrounded by a group of men who wanted to hear all about the nomination of a man from a neighbour State. Mr. Trueman came across the street in his leisurely way, greeted Dillon, and asked him how he had found Chicago—whether he had had a good trip.

Mr. Dillon must have been annoyed because Trueman didn't mention the Convention. He threw back his head rather haughtily. "Well, J. H., since I saw you last, we've found a great leader in this country, and a great orator." There was a frosty sparkle in his voice that presupposed opposition—like the feint of a boxer getting ready.

"Great windbag!" muttered Trueman. He sat down in his chair, but I noticed that he did not settle himself and cross his legs as usual.

Mr. Dillon gave an artificial laugh. "It's nothing against a man to be a fine orator. All the great leaders have been eloquent. This Convention was a memorable occasion; it gave the Democratic party a rebirth."

"Gave it a black eye, and a blind spot, I'd say!" commented Trueman. He didn't raise his voice, but he spoke with more heat than I had ever heard from him. After a moment he added: "I guess Grover

Cleveland must be a sick man; must feel like he'd taken a lot of trouble for nothing."

Mr. Dillon ignored these thrusts and went on telling the group around him about the Convention, but there was a special nimbleness and exactness in his tongue, a chill politeness in his voice that meant anger. Presently he turned again to Mr. Trueman, as if he could now trust himself.

"It was one of the great speeches of history, J. H.; our grandchildren will have to study it in school, as we did Patrick Henry's."

"Glad I haven't got any grandchildren, if they'd be brought up on that sort of tall talk," said Mr. Trueman. "Sounds like a schoolboy had written it. Absolutely nothing back of it but an unsound theory."

Mr. Dillon's laugh made me shiver; it was like a thin glitter of danger. He arched his curly eyebrows provokingly.

"We'll have four years of currency reform, anyhow. By the end of that time, you old dyed-in-the-wool Republicans will be thinking differently. The under dog is going to have a chance."

Mr. Trueman shifted in his chair. "That's no way for a banker to talk." He spoke very low. "The Democrats will have a long time to be sorry they ever turned Pops. No use talking to you while your Irish is up. I'll wait till you cool off." He rose and walked away, less deliberately than usual, and Mr. Dillon, watching his retreating figure, laughed haughtily and disagreeably. He asked the grain-elevator man to take the vacated chair. The group about him grew, and he sat expounding the reforms proposed by the Democratic candidate until a late hour.

For the first time in my life I listened with breathless interest to a political discussion. Whomever Mr. Dillon failed to convince, he convinced me. I grasped it at once: that gold had been responsible for most of the miseries and inequalities of the world; that it had always been the club the rich and cunning held over the poor; and that "the free and unlimited coinage of silver" would remedy all this. Dillon declared that young Mr. Bryan had looked like the patriots of old when he faced and challenged high finance with: "You shall not press down upon the brow of labour this crown of thorns; you shall not crucify mankind upon a cross of gold." I thought that magnificent; I thought the cornfields would show them a thing or two, back there!

R. E. Dillon had never taken an aggressive part in politics. But from that night on, the Democratic candidate and the free-silver plank were the subject of his talks with his customers and depositors. He drove about the country convincing the farmers, went to the neighbouring towns to use his influence with the merchants, organized the Bryan Club and the Bryan Ladies' Quartette in our county, contributed largely to the campaign fund. This was all a new line of conduct for Mr. Dillon, and it sat unsteadily on him. Even his voice became unnatural; there was a sting of comeback in it. His new character made him more like other people and took away from his special personal quality. I wonder whether it was not Trueman, more than Bryan, who put such an edge on him.

While all these things were going on, Trueman kept to his own office. He came to Dillon's bank on business, but he did not "come back to the sidewalk," as I put it to myself. He waited and said nothing, but he looked grim. After a month or so, when he saw that this thing was not going to blow over, when he heard how Dillon had been talking to representative men all over the county, and saw the figure he had put down for the campaign fund, then Trueman remarked to some of his friends that a banker had no business to commit himself to a scatter-brained financial policy which would destroy credit.

The next morning Mr. Trueman went to the bank across the street, the rival of Dillon's, and wrote a cheque on Dillon's bank "for the amount of my balance." He wasn't the sort of man who would ever know what his balance was, he merely kept it big enough to cover emergencies. That afternoon the Merchants' National took the cheque over to Dillon on its collecting rounds, and by night the word was all over town that Trueman had changed his bank. After this there would be no going back, people said. To change your bank was one of the most final things you could do. The little, unsuccessful men were pleased, as they always are at the destruction of anything strong and fine.

All through the summer and the autumn of that campaign Mr. Dillon was away a great deal. When he was at home, he took his evening airing on the sidewalk, and there was always a group of men about him, talking of the coming election; that was the most exciting presidential campaign people could remember. I often passed this group on my way to the post-office, but there was no temptation to linger now. Mr. Dillon seemed like another man, and my zeal to free humanity from the cross of gold had cooled. Mr. Trueman I seldom saw. When he passed me on the street, he nodded kindly.

The election and Bryan's defeat did nothing to soften Dillon. He had been sure of a Democratic victory. I believe he felt almost as if Trueman were responsible for the triumph of Hanna and McKinley. At least he knew that Trueman was exceedingly well satisfied, and that was bitter to him. He seemed to me sarcastic and sharp all the time now.

I don't believe self-interest would ever have made a breach between Dillon and Trueman. Neither would have taken advantage of the other. If a combination of circumstances had made it necessary that one or the other should take a loss in money or prestige, I think Trueman would have pocketed the loss. That was his way. It was his code, moreover. A gentleman pocketed his gains mechanically, in the day's routine; but he pocketed losses punctiliously, with a sharp, if bitter, relish. I believe now, as I believed then, that this was a quarrel of "principle." Trueman looked down on anyone who could take the reasoning of the Populist party seriously. He was a perfectly direct man, and he showed his contempt. That was enough. It lost me my special pleasure of summer nights: the old stories of the early West that sometimes came to the surface; the minute biographies of the farming people; the clear, detailed, illuminating accounts of all that went on in the great crop-growing, cattle-feeding world; and the silence—the strong, rich, out-flowing silence between two friends, that was as full and satisfying as the moonlight. I was never to know its like again.

After that rupture nothing went well with either of my two great men. Things were out of true, the equilibrium was gone. Formerly, when they used to sit in their old places on the sidewalk, two black figures with patches of shadow below, they seemed like two bodies held steady by some law of balance, an unconscious relation like that between the earth and the moon. It was this mathematical harmony which gave a third person pleasure.

Before the next presidential campaign came round, Mr. Dillon died (a young man still) very suddenly, of pneumonia. We didn't know that he was seriously ill until one of his clerks came running to our house to tell us he was dead. The same clerk, half out of his wits—it looked like the end of the world to him—ran on to tell Mr. Trueman.

Mr. Trueman thanked him. He called his confidential man, and told him to order flowers from Kansas City. Then he went to his house, informed his housekeeper that he was going away on business, and packed his bag. That same night he boarded the Santa Fe Limited and didn't stop until he was in San Francisco. He was gone all spring. His confidential clerk wrote him letters every week about the business and the new calves, and got telegrams in reply. Trueman never wrote letters.

When Mr. Trueman at last came home, he stayed only a few months. He sold out everything he owned to a stranger from Kansas City; his feeding ranch, his barns and sheds, his house and town lots. It was a terrible blow to me; now only the common, everyday people would be left. I used to walk mournfully up and down before his office while all these deeds were being signed—there were usually lawyers and notaries inside. But once, when he happened to be alone, he called me in, asked me how old I was now, and how far along I had got in school. His face and voice were more than kind, but he seemed absent-minded, as if he were trying to recall something. Presently he took from his watch-chain a red seal I had always admired, reached for my hand, and dropped the piece of carnelian into my palm.

"For a keepsake," he said evasively.

When the transfer of his property was completed, Mr. Trueman left us for good. He spent the rest of his life among the golden hills of San Francisco. He moved into the Saint Francis Hotel when it was first built, and had an office in a high building at the top of what is now

Powell Street. There he read his letters in the morning and played poker at night. I've heard a man whose offices were next his tell how Trueman used to sit tilted back in his desk chair, a half-consumed cigar in his mouth, morning after morning, apparently doing nothing, watching the Bay and the ferry-boats, across a line of wind-racked eucalyptus trees. He died at the Saint Francis about nine years after he left our part of the world.

The breaking-up of that friendship between two men who scarcely noticed my existence was a real loss to me, and has ever since been a regret. More than once, in Southern countries where there is a smell of dust and dryness in the air and the nights are intense, I have come upon a stretch of dusty white road drinking up the moonlight beside a blind wall, and have felt a sudden sadness. Perhaps it was not until the next morning that I knew why—and then only because I had dreamed of Mr. Dillon or Mr. Trueman in my sleep. When that old scar is occasionally touched by chance, it rouses the old uneasiness; the feeling of something broken that could so easily have been mended; of something delightful that was senselessly wasted, of a truth that was accidentally distorted—one of the truths we want to keep.

AN AFTERWORD ON
"TWO FRIENDS"

THIS memory of Miss Cather's Nebraskan childhood was written in Pasadena in 1931. It was first published in July of the following year in the *Woman's Home Companion* and next reappeared as the third of the three stories that make up the volume called *Obscure Destinies*.

It is one of the additional arguments for such an anthology as this one that it is a set of signposts, that in it a reader may come upon an author for the first time and straightway hurry to the nearest library for all his other works. There is, for example, considerable evidence that the matchless novel called *A Handful of Dust,* which was published at the end of the first *Woollcott Reader,* sent many a prospective convert in quest of any and all other books by Evelyn Waugh. It is my guess and hope that in the same way Dr. Eckstein's "Joe" will send others looking for his incomparable *Canary.* Perhaps it will even be the fortune of "Two Friends" in its third advent to find some readers who, as it happens, have dwelt till now in that outer darkness which is the portion of those who know not Willa Cather.

At first glance this expectation may seem a piece of presumption on the part of the undersigned. Surely—as the president of the Women's Club always says (with a fine glow of improvisation) when she presents the speaker of the afternoon—Miss Cather needs no introduction. Nonsense! You have only to contrast the printings of, let us say, *Gone with the Wind* with those of *My Ántonia* to have some notion of the multitude of potential readers to whom even so established and honored an author as Willa Cather remains after all these years an unknown quantity. It is my own conviction that the largest contribution to that difference is chance, or rather a set of external factors with which the quality of *My Ántonia* and the appreciative capacity of the reading public have little or nothing to do. At all events, in *My Ántonia* and *Death Comes for the Archbishop* and *A Lost Lady* and *Shadows on the Rock* you will find as nourishing and comely and unfailingly distinguished a contribution to American letters as has been made by anyone in my lifetime. Mind you, my own addiction to her works is by no means limited to these four. There is some merit even in that novel of hers which won the Pulitzer Prize.

It has been my experience that many recall out of their first reading of "Two Friends" the lovely passage about the dust in the moonlight. One evening, by the way, that passage served to launch Thornton Wilder, Gertrude Stein, and myself, as we lingered over our cakes and ale in a Chicago tavern, on the good old parlor-game of discussing the difference between poetry and prose. From the poets themselves one gets only the hint that the key is in the physical reaction of the reader. The late A. E. Housman testified that he never dared let a line of poetry run through his mind while he was shaving, as it was sure to make his beard bristle under the razor. "If," said Emily Dickinson, "I read a book and it makes my whole body so cold no fire can ever warm me, I know that is poetry. If I feel physically as if the top of my head were taken off, I know that is poetry. These are the only ways I know it. Is there any other way?" Nor on this occasion was Miss Stein exactly helpful. "Poetry," she said, looking over my head and talking there too, "is addressed to the noun." Which left me about where I was. But, poetry or prose, one seldom thus catches Miss Cather in the act of fine writing. Not often can a passage of hers be taken out and held up to the light like a jewel. The serene and breath-taking beauty of many a scene in *Death Comes for the Arch-bishop* and *Shadows on the Rock* is as impalpable as a perfume. And as undebatable.

A. W.

CAKES AND ALE:

OR
THE SKELETON IN
THE CUPBOARD

by

W. SOMERSET MAUGHAM

CAKES AND ALE:
or The Skeleton in the Cupboard

I

I HAVE noticed that when someone asks for you on the telephone and, finding you out, leaves a message begging you to call him up the moment you come in, and it's important, the matter is more often important to him than to you. When it comes to making you a present or doing you a favour most people are able to hold their impatience within reasonable bounds. So when I got back to my lodgings with just enough time to have a drink, a cigarette, and to read my paper before dressing for dinner, and was told by Miss Fellows, my landlady, that Mr. Alroy Kear wished me to ring him up at once, I felt that I could safely ignore his request.

"Is that the writer?" she asked me.

"It is."

She gave the telephone a friendly glance.

"Shall I get him?"

"No, thank you."

"What shall I say if he rings again?"

"Ask him to leave a message."

"Very good, sir."

She pursed her lips. She took the empty siphon, swept the room with a look to see that it was tidy, and went out. Miss Fellows was a great novel reader. I was sure that she had read all Roy's books. Her disapproval of my casualness suggested that she had read them with admiration. When I got home again, I found a note in her bold, legible writing on the sideboard.

Mr. Kear rang up twice. Can you lunch with him tomorrow? If not what day will suit you?

I raised my eyebrows. I had not seen Roy for three months and then only for a few minutes at a party; he had been very friendly—he always was—and when we separated he had expressed his hearty regret that we met so seldom.

"London's awful," he said. "One never has time to see any of the people one wants to. Let's lunch together one day next week, shall we?"

"I'd like to," I replied.

"I'll look at my book when I get home and ring you up."

"All right."

I had not known Roy for twenty years without learning that he always kept in the upper left-hand pocket of his waistcoat the little book in which he put down his engagements; I was therefore not surprised when I heard from him no further. It was impossible for me now to persuade myself that this urgent desire of his to dispense hospitality was disinterested. As I smoked a pipe before going to bed I turned over in my mind the possible reasons for which Roy might want me to lunch with him. It might be that an admirer of his had pestered him to introduce me to her or that an American editor, in London for a few days, had desired Roy to put me in touch with him; but I could not do my old friend the injustice of supposing him so barren of devices as not to be able to cope with such a situation. Besides, he told me to choose my own day, so it could hardly be that he wished me to meet anyone else.

Than Roy no one could show a more genuine cordiality to a fellow novelist whose name was on everybody's lips, but no one could more genially turn a cold shoulder on him when idleness, failure, or someone else's success had cast a shade on his notoriety. The writer has his ups and downs, and I was but too conscious that at the moment I was not in the public eye. It was obvious that I might have found excuses without affront to refuse Roy's invitation, though he was a determined fellow and if he was resolved for purposes of his own to see me, I well

knew that nothing short of a downright "go to hell" would check his
persistence; but I was beset by curiosity. I had also a considerable affection for Roy.

I had watched with admiration his rise in the world of letters. His
career might well have served as a model for any young man entering
upon the pursuit of literature. I could think of no one among my contemporaries who had achieved so considerable a position on so little
talent. This, like the wise man's daily dose of Bemax, might have gone
into a heaped-up tablespoon. He was perfectly aware of it, and it must
have seemed to him sometimes little short of a miracle that he had
been able with it to compose already some thirty books. I cannot but
think that he saw the white light of revelation when first he read that
Charles Dickens in an after-dinner speech had stated that genius was
an infinite capacity for taking pains. He pondered the saying. If that
was all, he must have told himself, he could be a genius like the rest;
and when the excited reviewer of a lady's paper, writing a notice of
one of his works, used the word (and of late the critics have been doing
it with agreeable frequency) he must have sighed with the satisfaction
of one who after long hours of toil has completed a cross-word puzzle.
No one who for years had observed his indefatigable industry could
deny that at all events he deserved to be a genius.

Roy started with certain advantages. He was the only son of a civil
servant who, after being Colonial Secretary for many years in Hong-
Kong, ended his career as Governor of Jamaica. When you looked up
Alroy Kear in the serried pages of *Who's Who* you saw *o.s.* of Sir Ray-
mond Kear, K.C.M.G., K.C.V.O., *q.v.*, and of Emily, *y.d.* of the late
Major General Percy Camperdown, Indian Army. He was educated at
Winchester and at New College, Oxford. He was president of the
Union and but for an unfortunate attack of measles might very well
have got his rowing blue. His academic career was respectable rather
than showy, and he left the university without a debt in the world.
Roy was even then of a thrifty habit, without any inclination to un-
profitable expense, and he was a good son. He knew that it had been
a sacrifice to his parents to give him so costly an education. His father,
having retired, lived in an unpretentious, but not mean, house near

Stroud in Gloucestershire, but at intervals went to London to attend official dinners connected with the colonies he had administered, and on these occasions was in the habit of visiting the Athenæum, of which he was a member. It was through an old crony at this club that he was able to get his son, when he came down from Oxford, appointed private secretary to a politician who, after having made a fool of himself as Secretary of State in two Conservative administrations, had been rewarded with a peerage. This gave Roy a chance to become acquainted at an early age with the great world. He made good use of his opportunities. You will never find in his works any of the solecisms that disfigure the productions of those who have studied the upper circles of society only in the pages of the illustrated papers. He knew exactly how dukes spoke to one another, and the proper way they should be addressed respectively by a member of Parliament, an attorney, a bookmaker, and a valet. There is something captivating in the jauntiness with which in his early novels he handles viceroys, ambassadors, prime ministers, royalties, and great ladies. He is friendly without being patronizing and familiar without being impertinent. He does not let you forget their rank, but shares with you his comfortable feeling that they are of the same flesh as you and I. I always think it a pity that, fashion having decided that the doings of the aristocracy are no longer a proper subject for serious fiction, Roy, always keenly sensitive to the tendency of the age, should in his later novels have confined himself to the spiritual conflicts of solicitors, chartered accountants, and produce brokers. He does not move in these circles with his old assurance.

I knew him first soon after he resigned his secretaryship to devote himself exclusively to literature, and he was then a fine, upstanding young man, six feet high in his stockinged feet and of an athletic build, with broad shoulders and a confident carriage. He was not handsome, but in a manly way agreeable to look at, with wide blue frank eyes and curly hair of a lightish brown; his nose was rather short and broad, his chin square. He looked honest, clean, and healthy. He was something of an athlete. No one who has read in his early books the descriptions of a run with the hounds, so vivid, and so accurate, can doubt that he wrote from personal experience; and until quite lately he was willing now and then to desert his desk for a day's hunting. He published his first novel at the period when men of letters, to show their virility, drank beer and played cricket, and for some years there was seldom a literary eleven in which his name did not figure. This particular school, I hardly know why, has lost its bravery, their books are neglected, and cricketers though they have remained, they find difficulty in placing their articles. Roy ceased playing cricket a good many years ago and he has developed a fine taste for claret.

Roy was very modest about his first novel. It was short, neatly written, and, as is everything he has produced since, in perfect taste. He sent it with a pleasant letter to all the leading writers of the day, and in this he told each one how greatly he admired his works, how much he had learned from his study of them, and how ardently he aspired to follow, albeit at a humble distance, the trail his correspondent had blazed. He laid his book at the feet of a great artist as the tribute of a young man entering upon the profession of letters to one whom he would always look up to as his master. Deprecatingly, fully conscious of his audacity in asking so busy a man to waste his time on a neophyte's puny effort, he begged for criticism and guidance. Few of the replies were perfunctory. The authors he wrote to, flattered by his praise, answered at length. They commended his book; many of them asked him to luncheon. They could not fail to be charmed by his frankness and warmed by his enthusiasm. He asked for their advice with a humility that was touching and promised to act upon it with a sincerity that was impressive. Here, they felt, was someone worth taking a little trouble over.

His novel had a considerable success. It made him many friends in literary circles and in a very short while you could not go to a tea party in Bloomsbury, Campden Hill, or Westminster without finding him handing round bread and butter or disembarrassing an elderly lady of an empty cup. He was so young, so bluff, so gay, he laughed so merrily at other people's jokes, that no one could help liking him. He joined dining clubs where in the basement of a hotel in Victoria Street or Holborn men of letters, young barristers, and ladies in Liberty silks and strings of beads ate a three-and-sixpenny dinner and discussed art and literature. It was soon discovered that he had a pretty gift for after-dinner speaking. He was so pleasant that his fellow writers, his rivals and contemporaries, forgave him even the fact that he was a gentleman. He was generous in his praise of their fledgeling works, and when they sent him manuscripts to criticize could never find a thing amiss. They thought him not only a good sort, but a sound judge.

He wrote a second novel. He took great pains with it and he profited by the advice his elders in the craft had given him. It was only just that more than one should at his request write a review for a paper with whose editor Roy had got into touch and only natural that the review should be flattering. His second novel was successful, but not so successful as to arouse the umbrageous susceptibilities of his competitors. In fact it confirmed them in their suspicions that he would never set the Thames on fire. He was a jolly good fellow; no side, or anything like that: they were quite content to give a leg up to a man who would never climb so high as to be an obstacle to themselves. I know some who smile bitterly now when they reflect on the mistake they made.

But when they say that he is swollen-headed they err. Roy has never lost the modesty which in his youth was his most engaging trait.

"I know I'm not a great novelist," he will tell you. "When I compare myself with the giants I simply don't exist. I used to think that one day I should write a really great novel, but I've long ceased even to hope for that. All I want people to say is that I do my best. I do work. I never let anything slipshod get past me. I think I can tell a good story and I can create characters that ring true. And after all the proof of the pudding is in the eating: *The Eye of the Needle* sold thirty-five thousand in England and eighty thousand in America, and for the serial rights of my next book I've got the biggest terms I've ever had yet."

And what, after all, can it be other than modesty that makes him even now write to the reviewers of his books, thanking them for their praise, and ask them to luncheon? Nay, more: when someone has written a stinging criticism and Roy, especially since his reputation became so great, has had to put up with some very virulent abuse, he does not, like most of us, shrug his shoulders, fling a mental insult at the ruffian

who does not like our work, and then forget about it; he writes a long
letter to his critic, telling him that he is very sorry he thought his book
bad, but his review was so interesting in itself, and, if he might venture
to say so, showed so much critical sense and so much feeling for words,
that he felt bound to write to him. No one is more anxious to improve
himself than he and he hopes he is still capable of learning. He does
not want to be a bore, but if the critic has nothing to do on Wednesday
or Friday will he come and lunch at the Savoy and tell him why exactly he thought his book so bad? No one can order a lunch better than
Roy, and generally by the time the critic has eaten half a dozen oysters
and a cut from a saddle of baby lamb, he has eaten his words too. It is
only poetic justice that when Roy's next novel comes out the critic
should see in the new work a very great advance.

One of the difficulties that a man has to cope with as he goes through
life is what to do about the persons with whom he has once been intimate and whose interest for him has in due course subsided. If both
parties remain in a modest station the break comes about naturally,
and no ill feeling subsists, but if one of them achieves eminence the
position is awkward. He makes a multitude of new friends, but the
old ones are inexorable; he has a thousand claims on his time, but they
feel that they have the first right to it. Unless he is at their beck and
call they sigh and with a shrug of the shoulders say:

"Ah, well, I suppose you're like everyone else. I must expect to be
dropped now that you're a success."

That of course is what he would like to do if he had the courage.
For the most part he hasn't. He weakly accepts an invitation to supper
on Sunday evening. The cold roast beef is frozen and comes from Australia and was over-cooked at middle day; and the burgundy—ah, why
will they call it burgundy? Have they never been to Beaune and stayed
at the Hôtel de la Poste? Of course it is grand to talk of the good old
days when you shared a crust of bread in a garret together, but it is a
little disconcerting when you reflect how near to a garret is the room
you are sitting in. You feel ill at ease when your friend tells you that
his books don't sell and that he can't place his short stories; the managers won't even read his plays, and when he compares them with

some of the stuff that's put on (here he fixes you with an accusing eye) it really does seem a bit hard. You are embarrassed and you look away. You exaggerate the failures you have had in order that he may realize that life has its hardships for you too. You refer to your work in the most disparaging way you can and are a trifle taken aback to find that your host's opinion of it is the same as yours. You speak of the fickleness of the public so that he may comfort himself by thinking that your popularity cannot last. He is a friendly but severe critic.

"I haven't read your last book," he says, "but I read the one before. I've forgotten its name."

You tell him.

"I was rather disappointed in it. I didn't think it was quite so good as some of the things you've done. Of course you know which my favourite is."

And you, having suffered from other hands than his, answer at once with the name of the first book you ever wrote; you were twenty then, and it was crude and ingenuous, and on every page was written your inexperience.

"You'll never do anything so good as that," he says heartily, and you feel that your whole career has been a long decadence from that one happy hit. "I always think you've never *quite* fulfilled the promise you showed then."

The gas fire roasts your feet, but your hands are icy. You look at your wrist watch surreptitiously and wonder whether your old friend would think it offensive if you took your leave as early as ten. You have told your car to wait round the corner so that it should not stand outside the door and by its magnificence affront his poverty, but at the door he says:

"You'll find a bus at the bottom of the street. I'll just walk down with you."

Panic seizes you and you confess that you have a car. He finds it very odd that the chauffeur should wait round the corner. You answer that this is one of his idiosyncrasies. When you reach it your friend looks at it with tolerant superiority. You nervously ask him to dinner with you one day. You promise to write to him and you drive away wondering whether when he comes he will think you are swanking if you ask him to Claridge's or mean if you suggest Soho.

Roy Kear suffered from none of these tribulations. It sounds a little brutal to say that when he had got all he could out of people he dropped them; but it would take so long to put the matter more delicately, and would need so subtle an adjustment of hints, half-tones, and allusions, playful or tender, that such being at bottom the fact, I think it as well to leave it at that. Most of us when we do a caddish thing harbour resentment against the person we have done it to, but Roy's heart, always in the right place, never permitted him such pettiness. He could use a man very shabbily without afterward bearing him the slightest ill-will.

"Poor old Smith," he would say. "He is a dear; I'm so fond of him. Pity he's growing so bitter. I wish one could do something for him. No, I haven't seen him for years. It's no good trying to keep up old friendships. It's painful for both sides. The fact is, one grows out of people, and the only thing is to face it."

But if he ran across Smith at some gathering like the private view of the Royal Academy, no one could be more cordial. He wrung his hand and told him how delighted he was to see him. His face beamed. He shed good fellowship as the kindly sun its rays. Smith rejoiced in the glow of this wonderful vitality and it was damned decent of Roy to say he'd give his eye-teeth to have written a book half as good as Smith's last. On the other hand, if Roy thought Smith had not seen him, he looked the other way; but Smith *had* seen him, and Smith resented being cut. Smith was very acid. He said that in the old days Roy had been glad enough to share a steak with him in a shabby restaurant and spend a month's holiday in a fisherman's cottage at St. Ives. Smith said that Roy was a time server. He said he was a snob. He said he was a humbug.

Smith was wrong here. The most shining characteristic of Alroy Kear was his sincerity. No one can be a humbug for five-and-twenty years. Hypocrisy is the most difficult and nerve-racking vice that any man can pursue; it needs an unceasing vigilance and a rare detachment of spirit. It cannot, like adultery or gluttony, be practised at spare moments; it is a whole-time job. It needs also a cynical humour; although Roy laughed so much I never thought he had a very quick sense of humour, and I am quite sure that he was incapable of cynicism. Though I have finished few of his novels, I have begun a good many, and to my mind his sincerity is stamped on every one of their multitudinous pages. This is clearly the chief ground of his stable popularity. Roy has always sincerely believed what everyone else believed at the moment. When he wrote novels about the aristocracy he sincerely believed that its members were dissipated and immoral, and yet had a certain nobility and an innate aptitude for governing the British Empire; when later he wrote of the middle classes he sincerely believed that they were the backbone of the country. His villains have always been villainous, his heroes heroic, and his maidens chaste.

When Roy asked the author of a flattering review to lunch it was because he was sincerely grateful to him for his good opinion, and when he asked the author of an unflattering one it was because he was sincerely concerned to improve himself. When unknown admirers from Texas or Western Australia came to London it was not only to cultivate his public that he took them to the National Gallery, it was because he was sincerely anxious to observe their reactions to art. You had only to hear him lecture to be convinced of his sincerity.

When he stood on the platform, in evening dress admirably worn, or in a loose, much used, but perfectly cut lounge suit if it better fitted the occasion, and faced his audience seriously, frankly, but with an engaging diffidence, you could not but realize that he was giving himself up to his task with complete earnestness. Though now and then he pretended to be at a loss for a word, it was only to make it more effective when he uttered it. His voice was full and manly. He told a story well. He was never dull. He was fond of lecturing upon the younger writers of England and America, and he explained their merits to his audience with an enthusiasm that attested his generosity. Perhaps he told almost too much, for when you had heard his lecture you felt that you really knew all you wanted to about them and it was quite unnecessary to read their books. I suppose that is why when Roy had lectured in some provincial town not a single copy of the books of the authors he had spoken of was ever asked for, but there was always a run on his own. His energy was prodigious. Not only did he make successful tours of the United States, but he lectured up and down Great Britain. No club was so small, no society for the self-improvement of its members so insignificant, that Roy disdained to give it an hour of his time. Now and then he revised his lectures and issued them in neat little books. Most people who are interested in these things have at least looked through the works entitled *Modern Novelists, Russian Fiction,* and *Some Writers;* and few can deny that they exhibit a real feeling for literature and a charming personality.

But this by no means exhausted his activities. He was an active member of the organizations that have been founded to further the interests of authors or to alleviate their hard lot when sickness or old age has brought them to penury. He was always willing to give his help when matters of copyright were the subject of legislation and he was never unprepared to take his place in those missions to a foreign country which are devised to establish amicable relations between writers of different nationalities. He could be counted on to reply for literature at a public dinner and he was invariably on the reception committee formed to give a proper welcome to a literary celebrity from overseas. No bazaar lacked an autographed copy of at least one of his books. He never refused to grant an interview. He justly said that no one knew better than he the hardships of the author's trade and if he could help a struggling journalist to earn a few guineas by having a pleasant chat with him he had not the inhumanity to refuse. He generally asked his interviewer to luncheon and seldom failed to make a good impression on him. The only stipulation he made was that he should see the article before it was published. He was never impatient with the persons who call up the celebrated on the telephone at inconvenient moments to ask them for the information of newspaper readers whether they believe in God or what they eat for breakfast. He figured in every symposium and the public knew what he thought of prohibition, vegetarianism, jazz, garlic, exercise, marriage, politics, and the place of women in the home.

His views on marriage were abstract, for he had successfully evaded the state which so many artists have found difficult to reconcile with the arduous pursuit of their calling. It was generally known that he had for some years cherished a hopeless passion for a married woman of rank, and though he never spoke of her but with chivalrous admiration, it was understood that she had treated him with harshness. The novels of his middle period reflected in their unwonted bitterness the strain to which he had been put. The anguish of spirit he had passed through then enabled him without offence to elude the advances of ladies of little reputation, frayed ornaments of a hectic circle, who were willing to exchange an uncertain present for the security of marriage with a successful novelist. When he saw in their bright eyes the shadow of the registry office, he told them that the memory of his one great love would always prevent him from forming any permanent tie. His quixotry might exasperate, but could not affront, them. He sighed a little when he reflected that he must be for ever denied the joys of domesticity and the satisfaction of parenthood, but it was a sacrifice that he was prepared to make not only to his ideal, but also to the possible partner of his joys. He had noticed that people really do not want to be bothered with the wives of authors and painters. The artist who insisted on taking his wife wherever he went only made himself a nuisance and indeed was in consequence often not asked to places he would have liked to go to; and if he left his wife at home, he was on his return exposed to recriminations that shattered the repose so essential for him to do the best that was in him. Alroy Kear was a bachelor and now at fifty was likely to remain one.

He was an example of what an author can do, and to what heights he can rise, by industry, common sense, honesty, and the efficient combination of means and ends. He was a good fellow and none but a cross-grained carper could grudge him his success. I felt that to fall asleep with his image in my mind would ensure me a good night. I scribbled a note to Miss Fellows, knocked the ashes out of my pipe, put out the light in my sitting room, and went to bed.

11

WHEN I rang for my letters and the papers next morning a message
was delivered to me, in answer to my note to Miss Fellows, that Mr.
Alroy Kear expected me at one-fifteen at his club in St. James's Street;
so a little before one I strolled round to my own and had the cocktail
which I was pretty sure Roy would not offer me. Then I walked down
St. James's Street, looking idly at the shop windows, and since I had
still a few minutes to spare (I did not want to keep my appointment
too punctually) I went into Christie's to see if there was anything I
liked the look of. The auction had already begun and a group of dark,
small men were passing round to one another pieces of Victorian silver, while the auctioneer, following their gestures with bored eyes, muttered in a drone: "Ten shillings offered, eleven, eleven and six . . ." It
was a fine day, early in June, and the air in King Street was bright.
It made the pictures on the walls of Christie's look very dingy. I went
out. The people in the street walked with a kind of nonchalance, as
though the ease of the day had entered into their souls and in the
midst of their affairs they had a sudden and surprised inclination to
stop and look at the picture of life.

Roy's club was sedate. In the ante-chamber were only an ancient
porter and a page; and I had a sudden and melancholy feeling that
the members were all attending the funeral of the head waiter. The
page, when I had uttered Roy's name, led me into an empty passage
to leave my hat and stick and then into an empty hall hung with life-
sized portraits of Victorian statesmen. Roy got up from a leather sofa
and warmly greeted me.

"Shall we go straight up?" he said.

I was right in thinking that he would not offer me a cocktail and I
commended my prudence. He led me up a noble flight of heavily carpeted stairs, and we passed nobody on the way; we entered the strangers' dining room, and we were its only occupants. It was a room of

some size, very clean and white, with an Adam window. We sat down by it and a demure waiter handed us the bill of fare. Beef, mutton and lamb, cold salmon, apple tart, rhubarb tart, gooseberry tart. As my eye travelled down the inevitable list I sighed as I thought of the restaurants round the corner where there was French cooking, the clatter of life, and pretty painted women in summer frocks.

"I can recommend the veal-and-ham pie," said Roy.

"All right."

"I'll mix the salad myself," he told the waiter in an off-hand and yet commanding way, and then, casting his eye once more on the bill of fare, generously: "And what about some asparagus to follow?"

"That would be very nice."

His manner grew a trifle grander.

"Asparagus for two and tell the chef to choose them himself. Now what would you like to drink? What do you say to a bottle of hock? We rather fancy our hock here."

When I had agreed to this he told the waiter to call the wine steward. I could not but admire the authoritative and yet perfectly polite manner in which he gave his orders. You felt that thus would a well-bred king send for one of his field marshals. The wine steward, portly in black, with the silver chain of his office round his neck, bustled in with the wine list in his hand. Roy nodded to him with curt familiarity.

"Hullo, Armstrong, we want some of the Liebfraumilch, the '21."

"Very good, sir."

"How's it holding up? Pretty well? We shan't be able to get any more of it, you know."

"I'm afraid not, sir."

"Well, it's no good meeting trouble half-way, is it, Armstrong?"

Roy smiled at the steward with breezy cordiality. The steward saw from his long experience of members that the remark needed an answer.

"No, sir."

Roy laughed and his eye sought mine. Quite a character, Armstrong.

"Well, chill it, Armstrong; not too much, you know, but just right.

I want my guest to see that we know what's what here." He turned to me. "Armstrong's been with us for eight-and-forty years." And when the wine steward had left us: "I hope you don't mind coming here. It's quiet and we can have a good talk. It's ages since we did. You're looking very fit."

This drew my attention to Roy's appearance.

"Not half so fit as you," I answered.

"The result of an upright, sober, and godly life," he laughed. "Plenty of work. Plenty of exercise. How's the golf? We must have a game one of these days."

I knew that Roy was scratch and that nothing would please him less than to waste a day with so indifferent a player as myself. But I felt I was quite safe in accepting so vague an invitation. He looked the picture of health. His curly hair was getting very grey, but it suited him and made his frank, sunburned face look younger. His eyes, which looked upon the world with such a hearty candour, were bright and clear. He was not so slim as in his youth and I was not surprised that when the waiter offered us rolls he asked for Rye-Vita. His slight corpulence only added to his dignity. It gave weight to his observations. Because his movements were a little more deliberate than they had been you had a comfortable feeling of confidence in him; he filled his chair with so much solidity that you had almost the impression that he sat upon a monument.

I do not know whether, as I wished, I have indicated by my report of his dialogue with the waiter that his conversation was not as a rule brilliant or witty, but it was easy and he laughed so much that you sometimes had the illusion that what he said was funny. He was never at a loss for a remark and he could discourse on the topics of the day with an ease that prevented his hearers from experiencing any sense of strain.

Many authors from their preoccupation with words have the bad habit of choosing those they use in conversation too carefully. They form their sentences with unconscious care and say neither more nor less than they mean. It makes intercourse with them somewhat formidable to persons in the upper ranks of society whose vocabulary is limited by their simple spiritual needs, and their company consequently is sought only with hesitation. No constraint of this sort was ever felt with Roy. He could talk with a dancing guardee in terms that were perfectly comprehensible to him and with a racing countess in the language of her stable boys. They said of him with enthusiasm and relief that he was not a bit like an author. No compliment pleased him better. The wise always use a number of ready-made phrases (at the moment I write, "nobody's business" is the most common), popular adjectives (like "divine" or "shy-making"), verbs that you only know the meaning of if you live in the right set (like "dunch"), which give ease and a homely sparkle to small talk and avoid the necessity of thought. The Americans, who are the most efficient people on the earth, have carried this device to such a height of perfection and have invented so wide a range of pithy and hackneyed phrases that they can carry on an amusing and animated conversation without giving a moment's reflection to what they are saying and so leave their minds free to consider the more important matters of big business and fornication. Roy's repertory was extensive and his scent for the word of the minute unerring; it peppered his speech, but aptly, and he used it each time with a sort of bright eagerness, as though his fertile brain had just minted it.

Now he talked of this and that, of our common friends and the latest books, of the opera. He was very breezy. He was always cordial, but today his cordiality took my breath away. He lamented that we saw one another so seldom and told me with the frankness that was one of his pleasantest characteristics how much he liked me and what a high opinion he had of me. I felt I must not fail to meet this friendliness half-way. He asked me about the book I was writing, I asked him about the book he was writing. We told one another that neither of us had had the success he deserved. We ate the veal-and-ham pie and Roy told me how he mixed a salad. We drank the hock and smacked appreciative lips.

And I wondered when he was coming to the point.

I could not bring myself to believe that at the height of the London season Alroy Kear would waste an hour on a fellow writer who was not a reviewer and had no influence in any quarter whatever in order to talk of Matisse, the Russian Ballet, and Marcel Proust. Besides, at the back of his gaiety I vaguely felt a slight apprehension. Had I not known that he was in a prosperous state I should have suspected that he was going to borrow a hundred pounds from me. It began to look as though luncheon would end without his finding the opportunity to say what he had in mind. I knew he was cautious. Perhaps he thought that this meeting, the first after so long a separation, had better be employed in establishing friendly relations, and was prepared to look upon the pleasant, substantial meal merely as ground bait.

"Shall we go and have our coffee in the next room?" he said.

"If you like."

"I think it's more comfortable."

I followed him into another room, much more spacious, with great leather armchairs and huge sofas; there were papers and magazines on the tables. Two old gentlemen in a corner were talking in undertones. They gave us a hostile glance, but this did not deter Roy from offering them a cordial greeting.

"Hullo, General," he cried, nodding breezily.

I stood for a moment at the window, looking at the gaiety of the day, and wished I knew more of the historical associations of St. James's Street. I was ashamed that I did not even know the name of the club across the way and was afraid to ask Roy lest he should despise me for not knowing what every decent person knew. He called me back by asking me whether I would have a brandy with my coffee, and when I refused, insisted. The club's brandy was famous. We sat side by side on a sofa by the elegant fireplace and lit cigars.

"The last time Edward Driffield ever came to London he lunched with me here," said Roy casually. "I made the old man try our brandy and he was delighted with it. I was staying with his widow over last week-end."

"Were you?"

"She sent you all sorts of messages."

"That's very kind of her. I shouldn't have thought she remembered me."

"Oh, yes, she does. You lunched there about six years ago, didn't you? She says the old man was so glad to see you."

"I didn't think *she* was."

"Oh, you're quite wrong. Of course she had to be very careful. The old man was pestered with people who wanted to see him and she had to husband his strength. She was always afraid he'd do too much. It's a wonderful thing if you come to think of it that she should have kept him alive and in possession of all his faculties to the age of eighty-four. I've been seeing a good deal of her since he died. She's awfully lonely. After all, she devoted herself to looking after him for twenty-five years. Othello's occupation, you know. I really feel sorry for her."

"She's still comparatively young. I dare say she'll marry again."

"Oh, no, she couldn't do that. That would be dreadful."

There was a slight pause while we sipped our brandy.

"You must be one of the few persons still alive who knew Driffield when he was unknown. You saw quite a lot of him at one time, didn't you?"

"A certain amount. I was almost a small boy and he was a middle-aged man. We weren't boon companions, you know."

"Perhaps not, but you must know a great deal about him that other people don't."

"I suppose I do."

"Have you ever thought of writing your recollections of him?"

"Good heavens, no!"

"Don't you think you ought to? He was one of the greatest novelists of our day. The last of the Victorians. He was an enormous figure. His novels have as good a chance of surviving as any that have been written in the last hundred years."

"I wonder. I've always thought them rather boring."

Roy looked at me with eyes twinkling with laughter.

"How like you that is! Anyhow you must admit that you're in the minority. I don't mind telling you that I've read his novels not once or twice, but half a dozen times, and every time I read them I think they're finer. Did you read the articles that were written about him at his death?"

"Some of them."

"The consensus of opinion was absolutely amazing. I read every one."

"If they all said the same thing, wasn't that rather unnecessary?"

Roy shrugged his massive shoulders good-humouredly, but did not answer my question.

"I thought the *Times Lit. Sup.* was splendid. It would have done the old man good to read it. I hear that the quarterlies are going to have articles in their next numbers."

"I still think his novels rather boring."

Roy smiled indulgently.

"Doesn't it make you slightly uneasy to think that you disagree with everyone whose opinion matters?"

"Not particularly. I've been writing for thirty-five years now, and you can't think how many geniuses I've seen acclaimed, enjoy their hour or two of glory, and vanish into obscurity. I wonder what's happened to them. Are they dead, are they shut up in madhouses, are they hidden away in offices? I wonder if they furtively lend their books to the doctor and the maiden lady in some obscure village. I wonder if they are still great men in some Italian pension."

"Oh, yes, they're the flash in the pans. I've known them."

"You've even lectured about them."

"One has to. One wants to give them a leg up if one can and one knows they won't amount to anything. Hang it all, one can afford to be generous. But after all, Driffield wasn't anything like that. The collected edition of his works is in thirty-seven volumes and the last set that came up at Sotheby's sold for seventy-eight pounds. That speaks for itself. His sales have increased steadily every year and last year was the best he ever had. You can take my word for that. Mrs. Driffield showed me his accounts last time I was down there. Driffield has come to stay all right."

"Who can tell?"

"Well, you think you can," replied Roy acidly.

I was not put out. I knew I was irritating him and it gave me a pleasant sensation.

"I think the instinctive judgments I formed when I was a boy were right. They told me Carlyle was a great writer and I was ashamed that I found the *French Revolution* and *Sartor Resartus* unreadable. Can anyone read them now? I thought the opinions of others must be better than mine and I persuaded myself that I thought George Meredith magnificent. In my heart I found him affected, verbose, and insincere. A good many people think so too now. Because they told me that to admire Walter Pater was to prove myself a cultured young man, I admired Walter Pater, but, heavens, how Marius bored me!"

"Oh, well, I don't suppose anyone reads Pater now, and of course Meredith has gone all to pot and Carlyle was a pretentious windbag."

"You don't know how secure of immortality they all looked thirty years ago."

"And have you never made mistakes?"

"One or two. I didn't think half as much of Newman as I do now, and I thought a great deal more of the tinkling quatrains of Fitz-Gerald. I could not read Goethe's *Wilhelm Meister;* now I think it his masterpiece."

"And what did you think much of then that you think much of still?"

"Well, *Tristram Shandy* and *Amelia* and *Vanity Fair. Madame Bovary, La Chartreuse de Parme,* and *Anna Karenina.* And Wordsworth and Keats and Verlaine."

"If you don't mind my saying so, I don't think that's particularly original."

"I don't mind your saying so at all. I don't think it is. But you asked me why I believed in my own judgment, and I was trying to explain to you that, whatever I said out of timidity and in deference to the cultured opinion of the day, I didn't really admire certain authors who were then thought admirable and the event seems to show that I was right. And what I honestly and instinctively liked then has stood the test of time with me and with critical opinion in general."

Roy was silent for a moment. He looked in the bottom of his cup, but whether to see if there were any more coffee in it or to find something to say, I did not know. I gave the clock on the chimney-piece a glance. In a minute it would be fitting for me to take my leave. Perhaps I had been wrong and Roy had invited me only that we might idly chat of Shakespeare and the musical glasses. I chid myself for the uncharitable thoughts I had had of him. I looked at him with concern. If that was his only object it must be that he was feeling tired or discouraged. If he was disinterested it could only be that for the moment at least the world was too much for him. But he caught my look at the clock and spoke.

"I don't see how you can deny that there must be something in a man who's able to carry on for sixty years, writing book after book, and who's able to hold an ever-increasing public. After all, at Ferne Court there are shelves filled with the translations of Driffield's books into every language of civilized people. Of course I'm willing to admit that a lot he wrote seems a bit old-fashioned nowadays. He flourished in a bad period and he was inclined to be longwinded. Most of his plots are melodramatic; but there's one quality you must allow him: beauty."

"Yes?" I said.

"When all's said and done, that's the only thing that counts, and Driffield never wrote a page that wasn't instinct with beauty."

"Yes?" I said.

"I wish you'd been there when we went down to present him with his portrait on his eightieth birthday. It really was a memorable occasion."

"I read about it in the papers."

"It wasn't only writers, you know, it was a thoroughly representative gathering—science, politics, business, art, the world; I think you'd have to go a long way to find gathered together such a collection of distinguished people as got out from that train at Blackstable. It was awfully moving when the P.M. presented the old man with the Order of Merit. He made a charming speech. I don't mind telling you there were tears in a good many eyes that day."

"Did Driffield cry?"

"No, he was singularly calm. He was like he always was, rather shy, you know, and quiet, very well mannered, grateful, of course, but a little dry. Mrs. Driffield didn't want him to get overtired and when we went into lunch he stayed in his study, and she sent him something in on a tray. I slipped away while the others were having their coffee. He was smoking his pipe and looking at the portrait. I asked him what he thought of it. He wouldn't tell me, he just smiled a little. He asked me if I thought he could take his teeth out and I said, No, the deputation would be coming in presently to say good-bye to him. Then I asked him if he didn't think it was a wonderful moment. 'Rum,' he said, 'very rum.' The fact is, I suppose, he was shattered. He was a messy eater in his later days and a messy smoker—he scattered the tobacco all over himself when he filled his pipe; Mrs. Driffield didn't like people to see him when he was like that, but of course she didn't mind me; I tidied him up a bit and then they all came in and shook hands with him, and we went back to town."

I got up.

"Well, I really must be going. It's been awfully nice seeing you."

"I'm just going along to the private view at the Leicester Galleries. I know the people there. I'll take you in if you like."

"It's very kind of you, but they sent me a card. No, I don't think I'll come."

We walked down the stairs and I got my hat. When we came out into the street and I turned toward Piccadilly, Roy said:

"I'll just walk up to the top with you." He got into step with me. "You knew his first wife, didn't you?"

"Whose?"

"Driffield's."

"Oh!" I had forgotten him. "Yes."

"Well?"

"Fairly."

"I suppose she was awful."

"I don't recollect that."

"She must have been dreadfully common. She was a barmaid, wasn't she?"

"Yes."

"I wonder why the devil he married her. I've always been given to understand that she was extremely unfaithful to him."

"Extremely."

"Do you remember at all what she was like?"

"Yes, very distinctly," I smiled. "She was sweet."

Roy gave a short laugh.

"That's not the general impression."

I did not answer. We had reached Piccadilly and, stopping, I held out my hand to Roy. He shook it, but I fancied without his usual heartiness. I had the impression that he was disappointed with our meeting. I could not imagine why. Whatever he had wanted of me I had not been able to do, for the reason that he had given me no inkling of what it was, and as I strolled under the arcade of the Ritz Hotel and along the park railings till I came opposite Half Moon Street I wondered if my manner had been more than ordinarily forbidding. It was quite evident that Roy had felt the moment inopportune to ask me to grant him a favour.

I walked up Half Moon Street. After the gay tumult of Piccadilly it had a pleasant silence. It was sedate and respectable. Most of the houses let apartments, but this was not advertised by the vulgarity of a card; some had a brightly polished brass plate, like a doctor's, to announce the fact and others the word *Apartments* neatly painted on the fanlight. One or two with an added discretion merely gave the name of the proprietor, so that if you were ignorant you might have thought it a tailor's or a money-lender's. There was none of the congested traffic of Jermyn Street, where also they let rooms, but here and there a smart car, unattended, stood outside a door and occasionally at another a taxi deposited a middle-aged lady. You had the feeling that the people who lodged here were not gay and a trifle disreputable as in Jermyn Street, racing men who rose in the morning with headaches and asked for a hair of the dog that bit them, but respectable women from the country who came up for six weeks for the London season and elderly gentlemen who belonged to exclusive clubs. You felt that they came year after year to the same house and perhaps had known the proprietor when he was still in private service. My own Miss Fellows had been cook in some very good places, but you would never have guessed it had you seen her walking along to do her shopping in Shepherd's Market. She was not stout, red-faced, and blousy as one expects a cook to be; she was spare and very upright, neatly but fashionably dressed, a woman of middle age, with determined features; her lips were rouged and she wore an eyeglass. She was businesslike, quiet, coolly cynical, and very expensive.

The rooms I occupied were on the ground floor. The parlour was papered with an old marbled paper and on the walls were water colours of romantic scenes, cavaliers bidding good-bye to their ladies and knights of old banqueting in stately halls; there were large ferns in pots, and the armchairs were covered with faded leather. There was about the room an amusing air of the eighteen eighties, and when I looked out of the window I expected to see a private hansom rather than a Chrysler. The curtains were of a heavy red rep.

III

I HAD a good deal to do that afternoon, but my conversation with Roy and the impression of the day before yesterday, the sense of a past that still dwelt in the minds of men not yet old, that my room, I could not tell why, had given me even more strongly than usual as I entered it, inveigled my thoughts to saunter down the road of memory. It was as though all the people who had at one time and another inhabited my lodging pressed upon me with their old-fashioned ways and odd clothes, men with mutton-chop whiskers in frock coats and women in bustles and flounced skirts. The rumble of London, which I did not know if I imagined or heard (my house was at the top of Half Moon Street), and the beauty of the sunny June day (*le vierge, le vivace, et le bel aujourd'hui*), gave my reveries a poignancy which was not quite painful. The past I looked at seemed to have lost its reality and I saw it as though it were a scene in a play and I a spectator in the back row of a dark gallery. But it was all very clear as far as it went. It was not misty like life as one leads it when the ceaseless throng of impressions seems to rob them of outline, but sharp and definite like a landscape painted in oils by a painstaking artist of the middle-Victorian era.

I fancy that life is more amusing now than it was forty years ago and I have a notion that people are more amiable. They may have been worthier then, possessed of more solid virtue as, I am told, they were possessed of more substantial knowledge; I do not know. I know they were more cantankerous; they ate too much, many of them drank too much, they took too little exercise. Their livers were out of order and their digestions often impaired. They were irritable. I do not speak of London of which I knew nothing till I was grown up, nor of grand people who hunted and shot, but of the countryside and of the modest persons, gentlemen of small means, clergymen, retired officers, and such like who made up the local society. The dullness of their lives was almost incredible. There were no golf links; at a few houses was an ill-kept tennis court, but it was only the very young who played; there was a dance once a year in the Assembly Rooms; carriage folk went for a drive in the afternoon; the others went for a "constitutional"! You may say that they did not miss amusements they had never thought of, and that they created excitement for themselves from the small entertainment (tea when you were asked to bring your music and you sang the songs of Maude Valerie White and Tosti) which at infrequent intervals they offered one another; the days were very long; they were bored. People who were condemned to spend their lives within a mile of one another quarrelled bitterly, and seeing each other every day in the town cut one another for twenty years. They were vain, pig-headed, and odd. It was a life that perhaps formed queer characters; people were not so like one another as now and they acquired a small celebrity by their idiosyncrasies, but they were not easy to get on with. It may be that we are flippant and careless, but we accept one another without the old suspicion; our manners, rough and ready, are kindly; we are more prepared to give and take and we are not so crabbed.

I lived with an uncle and aunt on the outskirts of a little Kentish town by the sea. It was called Blackstable and my uncle was the vicar. My aunt was a German. She came of a very noble but impoverished family, and the only portion she brought her husband was a marquetry writing desk, made for an ancestor in the seventeenth century, and a set of tumblers. Of these only a few remained when I entered upon the scene and they were used as ornaments in the drawing room. I liked the grand coat-of-arms with which they were heavily engraved. There were I don't know how many quarterings, which my aunt used demurely to explain to me, and the supporters were fine and the crest emerging from a crown incredibly romantic. She was a simple old lady, of a meek and Christian disposition, but she had not, though married for more than thirty years to a modest parson with very little income beyond his stipend, forgotten that she was *hochwohlgeboren*. When a rich banker from London, with a name that in these days is famous in financial circles, took a neighbouring house for the summer holidays, though my uncle called on him (chiefly, I surmise, to get a subscription to the Additional Curates Society), she refused to do so because he was in trade. No one thought her a snob. It was accepted as perfectly reasonable. The banker had a little boy of my own age, and, I forget how, I became acquainted with him. I still remember the discussion that ensued when I asked if I might bring him to the vicarage; permission was reluctantly given me, but I was not allowed to go in return to his house. My aunt said I'd be wanting to go to the coal merchant's next, and my uncle said:

"Evil communications corrupt good manners."

The banker used to come to church every Sunday morning, and he always put half a sovereign in the plate, but if he thought his generosity made a good impression he was much mistaken. All Blackstable knew, but only thought him purse-proud.

Blackstable consisted of a long winding street that led to the sea, with little two-story houses, many of them residential but with a good many shops; and from this ran a certain number of short streets, recently built, that ended on one side in the country and on the other in the marshes. Round about the harbour was a congeries of narrow winding alleys. Colliers brought coal from Newcastle to Blackstable and the harbour was animated. When I was old enough to be allowed out by myself I used to spend hours wandering about there looking at the rough grimy men in their jerseys and watching the coal being unloaded.

It was at Blackstable that I first met Edward Driffield. I was fifteen and had just come back from school for the summer holidays. The morning after I got home I took a towel and bathing drawers and went down to the beach. The sky was unclouded and the air hot and bright, but the North Sea gave it a pleasant tang so that it was a delight just to live and breathe. In winter the natives of Blackstable walked down the empty street with a hurried gait, screwing themselves up in order to expose as little surface as possible to the bitterness of the east wind, but now they dawdled; they stood about in groups in the space between the Duke of Kent and the Bear and Key. You heard a hum of their East Anglian speech, drawling a little with an accent that may be ugly, but in which from old association I still find a leisurely charm. They were fresh-complexioned, with blue eyes and high cheek-bones, and their hair was light. They had a clean, honest, and ingenuous look. I do not think they were very intelligent, but they were guileless. They looked healthy, and though not tall for the most part were strong and active. There was little wheeled traffic in Blackstable in those days and the groups that stood about the road chatting seldom had to move for anything but the doctor's dogcart or the baker's trap.

Passing the bank, I called in to say how-do-you-do to the manager, who was my uncle's churchwarden, and when I came out met my uncle's curate. He stopped and shook hands with me. He was walking with a stranger. He did not introduce me to him. He was a smallish man with a beard and he was dressed rather loudly in a bright brown knickerbocker suit, the breeches very tight, with navy blue stockings, black boots, and a billycock hat. Knickerbockers were uncommon then, at least in Blackstable, and being young and fresh from school I immediately set the fellow down as a cad. But while I chatted with the curate he looked at me in a friendly way, with a smile in his pale blue eyes. I felt that for two pins he would have joined in the conversation and I assumed a haughty demeanour. I was not going to run the risk of being spoken to by a chap who wore knickerbockers like a game-keeper and I resented the familiarity of his good-humoured expression. I was myself faultlessly dressed in white flannel trousers, a blue blazer with the arms of my school on the breast pocket, and a black-and-white straw hat with a very wide brim. The curate said that he must be getting on (fortunately, for I never knew how to break away from a meeting in the street and would endure agonies of shyness while I looked in vain for an opportunity), but said that he would be coming up to the vicarage that afternoon and would I tell my uncle. The stranger nodded and smiled as we parted, but I gave him a stony stare. I supposed he was a summer visitor and in Blackstable we did not mix with the summer visitors. We thought London people vulgar. We said it was horrid to have all that rag-tag and bobtail down from town every year, but of course it was all right for the tradespeople. Even they, however, gave a faint sigh of relief when September came to an end and Blackstable sank back into its usual peace.

When I went home to dinner, my hair insufficiently dried and cling-ing lankly to my head, I remarked that I had met the curate and he was coming up that afternoon.

"Old Mrs. Shepherd died last night," said my uncle in explanation.

The curate's name was Galloway; he was a tall thin ungainly man with untidy black hair and a small sallow dark face. I suppose he was quite young, but to me he seemed middle-aged. He talked very quickly and gesticulated a great deal. This made people think him rather queer and my uncle would not have kept him but that he was very energetic, and my uncle, being extremely lazy, was glad to have someone to take so much work off his shoulders. After he had finished the business that had brought him to the vicarage Mr. Galloway came in to say how-do-you-do to my aunt and she asked him to stay to tea.

"Who was that you were with this morning?" I asked him as he sat down.

"Oh, that was Edward Driffield. I didn't introduce him. I wasn't sure if your uncle would wish you to know him."

"I think it would be most undesirable," said my uncle.

"Why, who is he? He's not a Blackstable man, is he?"

"He was born in the parish," said my uncle. "His father was old Miss Wolfe's bailiff at Ferne Court. But they were chapel people."

"He married a Blackstable girl," said Mr. Galloway.

"In church, I believe," said my aunt. "Is it true that she was a barmaid at the Railway Arms?"

"She looks as if she might have been something like that," said Mr. Galloway, with a smile.

"Are they going to stay long?"

"Yes, I think so. They've taken one of those houses in that street where the Congregational chapel is," said the curate.

At that time in Blackstable, though the new streets doubtless had names, nobody knew or used them.

"Is he coming to church?" asked my uncle.

"I haven't actually talked to him about it yet," answered Mr. Galloway. "He's quite an educated man, you know."

"I can hardly believe that," said my uncle.

"He was at Haversham School, I understand, and he got any number of scholarships and prizes. He got a scholarship at Wadham, but he ran away to sea instead."

"I'd heard he was rather a harum-scarum," said my uncle.

"He doesn't look much like a sailor," I remarked.

"Oh, he gave up the sea many years ago. He's been all sorts of things since then."

"Jack of all trades and master of none," said my uncle.

"Now, I understand, he's a writer."

"That won't last long," said my uncle.

I had never known a writer before; I was interested.

"What does he write?" I asked. "Books?"

"I believe so," said the curate, "and articles. He had a novel published last spring. He's promised to lend it me."

"I wouldn't waste my time on rubbish in your place," said my uncle, who never read anything but the *Times* and the *Guardian*.

"What's it called?" I asked.

"He told me the title, but I forget it."

"Anyhow, it's quite unnecessary that you should know," said my uncle. "I should very much object to your reading trashy novels. During your holidays the best thing you can do is to keep out in the open air. And you have a holiday task, I presume?"

I had. It was *Ivanhoe*. I had read it when I was ten, and the notion of reading it again and writing an essay on it bored me to distraction.

When I consider the greatness that Edward Driffield afterward achieved I cannot but smile as I remember the fashion in which he was discussed at my uncle's table. When he died a little while ago and an agitation arose among his admirers to have him buried in Westminster Abbey the present incumbent at Blackstable, my uncle's successor twice removed, wrote to the *Daily Mail* pointing out that Driffield was born in the parish and not only had passed long years, especially the last twenty-five of his life, in the neighbourhood, but had laid there the scene of some of his most famous books; it was only becoming then that his bones should rest in the churchyard where under the Kentish elms his father and mother dwelt in peace. There was relief in Blackstable when, the Dean of Westminster having somewhat curtly refused the Abbey, Mrs. Driffield sent a dignified letter to the press in which she expressed her confidence that she was carrying out the dearest wishes of her dead husband in having him buried among the simple people he knew and loved so well. Unless the notabilities of Blackstable have very much changed since my day I do not believe they very much liked that phrase about "simple people," but, as I afterward learnt, they had never been able to "abide" the second Mrs. Driffield.

IV

To my surprise, two or three days after I lunched with Alroy Kear I received a letter from Edward Driffield's widow. It ran as follows:

DEAR FRIEND,

I hear that you had a long talk with Roy last week about Edward Driffield and I am so glad to know that you spoke of him so nicely. He often talked to me of you. He had the greatest admiration for your

*talent and he was so very pleased to see you when you came to lunch
with us. I wonder if you have in your possession any letters that he
wrote to you and if so whether you would let me have copies of them.
I should be very pleased if I could persuade you to come down for two
or three days and stay with me. I live very quietly now and have no
one here, so please choose your own time. I shall be delighted to see
you again and have a talk of old times. I have a particular service I
want you to do me and I am sure that for the sake of my dear dead
husband you will not refuse.*

Yours ever sincerely,
AMY DRIFFIELD.

I had seen Mrs. Driffield only once and she but mildly interested me;
I do not like being addressed as "dear friend"; that alone would have
been enough to make me decline her invitation; and I was exasperated
by its general character which, however ingenious an excuse I invented,
made the reason I did not go quite obvious, namely, that I did not
want to. I had no letters of Driffield's. I suppose years ago he had written to me several times, brief notes, but he was then an obscure scrib-
bler and even if I ever kept letters it would never have occurred to me
to keep his. How was I to know that he was going to be acclaimed as
the greatest novelist of our day? I hesitated only because Mrs. Driffield
said she wanted me to do something for her. It would certainly be a
nuisance, but it would be churlish not to do it if I could, and after all
her husband was a very distinguished man.

The letter came by the first post and after breakfast I rang up Roy.
As soon as I mentioned my name I was put through to him by his
secretary. If I were writing a detective story I should immediately have
suspected that my call was awaited, and Roy's virile voice calling hullo
would have confirmed my suspicion. No one could naturally be quite
so cheery so early in the morning.

"I hope I didn't wake you," I said.

"Good God, no." His healthy laugh rippled along the wires. "I've
been up since seven. I've been riding in the park. I'm just going to
have breakfast. Come along and have it with me."

"I have a great affection for you, Roy," I answered, "but I don't think you're the sort of person I'd care to have breakfast with. Besides, I've already had mine. Look here, I've just had a letter from Mrs. Driffield asking me to go down and stay."

"Yes, she told me she was going to ask you. We might go down together. She's got quite a good grass court and she does one very well. I think you'd like it."

"What is it that she wants me to do?"

"Ah, I think she'd like to tell you that herself."

There was a softness in Roy's voice such as I imagined he would use if he were telling a prospective father that his wife was about to gratify his wishes. It cut no ice with me.

"Come off it, Roy," I said. "I'm too old a bird to be caught with chaff. Spit it out."

There was a moment's pause at the other end of the telephone. I felt that Roy did not like my expression.

"Are you busy this morning?" he asked suddenly. "I'd like to come and see you."

"All right, come on. I shall be in till one."

"I'll be round in about an hour."

I replaced the receiver and relit my pipe. I gave Mrs. Driffield's letter a second glance.

I remembered vividly the luncheon to which she referred. I happened to be staying for a long week-end not far from Tercanbury with a certain Lady Hodmarsh, the clever and handsome American wife of a sporting baronet with no intelligence and charming manners. Perhaps to relieve the tedium of domestic life she was in the habit of entertaining persons connected with the arts. Her parties were mixed and gay. Members of the nobility and gentry mingled with astonishment and an uneasy awe with painters, writers, and actors. Lady Hodmarsh neither read the books nor looked at the pictures of the people to whom she offered hospitality, but she liked their company and enjoyed the feeling it gave her of being in the artistic know. When on this occasion the conversation happened to dwell for a moment on Edward Driffield, her most celebrated neighbour, and I mentioned that I had at one time known him very well, she proposed that we should go over and lunch with him on Monday when a number of her guests were going back to London. I demurred, for I had not seen Driffield for five-and-thirty years and I could not believe that he would remember me; and if he did (though this I kept to myself) I could not believe that it would be with pleasure. But there was a young peer there, a certain Lord Scallion, with literary inclinations so violent that, instead of ruling this country as the laws of man and nature have decreed, he devoted his energy to the composition of detective novels. His curiosity to see Driffield was boundless and the moment Lady Hodmarsh made her suggestion he said it would be too divine. The star guest of the party was a big young fat duchess and it appeared that her admiration for the celebrated writer was so intense that she was prepared to cut an engagement in London and not go up till the afternoon.

"That would make four of us," said Lady Hodmarsh. "I don't think they could manage more than that. I'll wire to Mrs. Driffield at once."

I could not see myself going to see Driffield in that company and tried to throw cold water on the scheme.

"It'll only bore him to death," I said. "He'll hate having a lot of strangers barging in on him like this. He's a very old man."

"That's why if they want to see him they'd better see him now. He can't last much longer. Mrs. Driffield says he likes to meet people. They never see anybody but the doctor and the parson and it's a change for them. Mrs. Driffield said I could always bring anyone interesting. Of course she has to be very careful. He's pestered by all sorts of people who want to see him just out of idle curiosity, and interviewers and authors who want him to read their books, and silly hysterical women. But Mrs. Driffield is wonderful. She keeps everyone away from him but those she thinks he ought to see. I mean, he'd be dead in a week if he saw everyone who wants to see him. She has to think of his strength. Naturally we're different."

Of course I thought I was; but as I looked at them I perceived that the duchess and Lord Scallion thought they were too; so it seemed best to say no more.

We drove over in a bright yellow Rolls. Ferne Court was three miles from Blackstable. It was a stucco house built, I suppose, about 1840, plain and unpretentious, but substantial; it was the same back and front, two large bows on each side of a flat piece in which was the front door, and there were two large bows on the first floor. A plain parapet hid the low roof. It stood in about an acre of garden, somewhat overgrown with trees, but neatly tended, and from the drawing-room window you had a pleasant view of woods and green downland. The drawing room was furnished so exactly as you felt a drawing room in a country house of modest size should be furnished that it was slightly disconcerting. Clean bright chintzes covered the comfortable chairs and the large sofa, and the curtains were of the same bright clean chintz. On little Chippendale tables stood large Oriental bowls filled with pot-pourri. On the cream-coloured walls were pleasant water colours by painters well known at the beginning of this century. There were great masses of flowers charmingly arranged, and on the grand piano in silver frames photographs of celebrated actresses, deceased authors, and minor royalties.

It was no wonder that the duchess cried out that it was a lovely room. It was just the kind of room in which a distinguished writer should spend the evening of his days. Mrs. Driffield received us with modest assurance. She was a woman of about five-and-forty, I judged, with a small sallow face and neat, sharp features. She had a black cloche hat pressed tight down on her head and wore a grey coat and skirt. Her figure was slight and she was neither tall nor short, and she looked trim, competent, and alert. She might have been the squire's widowed daughter, who ran the parish and had a peculiar gift for organization. She introduced us to a clergyman and a lady, who got up as we were shown in. They were the vicar of Blackstable and his wife. Lady Hodmarsh and the duchess immediately assumed that cringing affability that persons of rank assume with their inferiors in order to show them that they are not for a moment aware that there is any difference of station between them.

Then Edward Driffield came in. I had seen portraits of him from time to time in the illustrated papers but it was with dismay that I saw him in the flesh. He was smaller than I remembered and very thin, his head was barely covered with fine silvery hair, he was clean-shaven, and his skin was almost transparent. His blue eyes were very pale and the rims of his eyelids red. He looked an old, old man, hanging on to mortality by a thread; he wore very white false teeth and they made his smile seem forced and stiff. I had never seen him but bearded and his lips were thin and pallid. He was dressed in a new, well-cut suit of blue serge and his low collar, two or three sizes too large for him, showed a wrinkled, scraggy neck. He wore a neat black tie with a pearl in it. He looked a little like a dean in mufti on his summer holiday in Switzerland.

Mrs. Driffield gave him a quick glance as he came in and smiled encouragingly; she must have been satisfied with the neatness of his appearance. He shook hands with his guests and to each one said something civil. When he came to me he said:

"It's very good of a busy and successful man like you to come all this way to see an old fogy."

I was a trifle taken aback, for he spoke as though he had never seen me before, and I was afraid my friends would think I had been boasting when I claimed at one time to have known him intimately. I wondered if he had completely forgotten me.

"I don't know how many years it is since we last met," I said, trying to be hearty.

He looked at me for what I suppose was no more than a few seconds, but for what seemed to me quite a long time, and then I had a sudden shock; he gave me a little wink. It was so quick that nobody but I could have caught it, and so unexpected in that distinguished old face that I could hardly believe my eyes. In a moment his face was once more composed, intelligently benign, and quietly observant. Luncheon was announced and we trooped into the dining room.

This also was in what can only be described as the acme of good taste. On the Chippendale sideboard were silver candlesticks. We sat on Chippendale chairs and ate off a Chippendale table. In a silver bowl in the middle were roses and round this were silver dishes with chocolates in them and peppermint creams; the silver salt cellars were brightly polished and evidently Georgian. On the cream-coloured walls were

mezzotints of ladies painted by Sir Peter Lely and on the chimney-piece
a garniture of blue delft. The service was conducted by two maids in
brown uniform and Mrs. Driffield in the midst of her fluent conversation kept a wary eye on them. I wondered how she had managed to
train these buxom Kentish girls (their healthy colour and high cheek-
bones betrayed the fact that they were "local") to such a pitch of efficiency. The lunch was just right for the occasion, smart but not showy,
fillets of sole rolled up and covered with a white sauce, roast chicken,
with new potatoes and green peas, asparagus and gooseberry fool. It
was the dining room and the lunch and the manner which you felt
exactly fitted a literary gent of great celebrity but moderate wealth.

Mrs. Driffield, like the wives of most men of letters, was a great
talker and she did not let the conversation at her end of the table flag;
so that, however much we might have wanted to hear what her husband was saying at the other, we had no opportunity. She was gay and
sprightly. Though Edward Driffield's indifferent health and great age
obliged her to live most of the year in the country, she managed notwithstanding to run up to town often enough to keep abreast of what
was going on and she was soon engaged with Lord Scallion in an
animated discussion of the plays in the London theatres and the terrible
crowd at the Royal Academy. It had taken her two visits to look at all
the pictures and even then she had not had time to see the water colours. She liked water colours so much; they were unpretentious; she
hated things to be pretentious.

So that host and hostess should sit at the head and foot of the table,
the vicar sat next to Lord Scallion and his wife next to the duchess.
The duchess engaged her in conversation on the subject of working-
class dwellings, a subject on which she seemed to be much more at
home than the parson's lady, and my attention being thus set free I
watched Edward Driffield. He was talking to Lady Hodmarsh. She
was apparently telling him how to write a novel and giving him a list
of a few that he really ought to read. He listened to her with what
looked like polite interest, putting in now and then a remark in a voice
too low for me to catch, and when she made a jest (she made them
frequently and often good ones) he gave a little chuckle and shot her

a quick look that seemed to say: this woman isn't such a damned fool after all. Remembering the past, I asked myself curiously what he thought of this grand company, his neatly turned out wife, so competent and discreetly managing, and the elegant surroundings in which he lived. I wondered if he regretted his early days of adventure. I wondered if all this amused him or if the amiable civility of his manner masked a hideous boredom. Perhaps he felt my eyes upon him, for he raised his. They rested on me for a while with a meditative look, mild and yet oddly scrutinizing, and then suddenly, unmistakably this time, he gave me another wink. The frivolous gesture in that old, withered face was more than startling, it was embarrassing; I did not know what to do. My lips outlined a dubious smile.

But the duchess joining in the conversation at the head of the table, the vicar's wife turned to me.

"You knew him many years ago, didn't you?" she asked me in a low tone.

"Yes."

She gave the company a glance to see that no one was attending to us.

"His wife is anxious that you shouldn't call up old memories that might be painful to him. He's very frail, you know, and the least thing upsets him."

"I'll be very careful."

"The way she looks after him is simply wonderful. Her devotion is a lesson to all of us. She realizes what a precious charge it is. Her unselfishness is beyond words." She lowered her voice a little more. "Of course he's a very old man and old men sometimes are a little trying; I've never seen her out of patience. In her way she's just as wonderful as he is."

These were the sort of remarks to which it was difficult to find a reply, but I felt that one was expected of me.

"Considering everything, I think he looks very well," I murmured.

"He owes it all to her."

At the end of luncheon we went back into the drawing room and after we had been standing about for two or three minutes Edward

Driffield came up to me. I was talking with the vicar and for want of anything better to say was admiring the charming view. I turned to my host.

"I was just saying how picturesque that little row of cottages is down there."

"From here." Driffield looked at their broken outline and an ironic smile curled his thin lips. "I was born in one of them. Rum, isn't it?"

But Mrs. Driffield came up to us with bustling geniality. Her voice was brisk and melodious.

"Oh, Edward, I'm sure the duchess would like to see your writing room. She has to go almost immediately."

"I'm so sorry, but I must catch the three-eighteen from Tercanbury," said the duchess.

We filed into Driffield's study. It was a large room on the other side of the house, looking out on the same view as the dining room, with a bow window. It was the sort of room that a devoted wife would evidently arrange for her literary husband. It was scrupulously tidy and large bowls of flowers gave it a feminine touch.

"This is the desk at which he's written all his later works," said Mrs. Driffield, closing a book that was open face downward on it. "It's the frontispiece in the third volume of the *edition de luxe*. It's a period piece."

We all admired the writing table and Lady Hodmarsh, when she thought no one was looking, ran her fingers along its under edge to see if it was genuine. Mrs. Driffield gave us a quick, bright smile.

"Would you like to see one of his manuscripts?"

"I'd love to," said the duchess, "and then I simply must bolt."

Mrs. Driffield took from a shelf a manuscript bound in blue morocco, and while the rest of the party reverently examined it I had a look at the books with which the room was lined. As authors will, I ran my eye round quickly to see if there were any of mine, but could not find one; I saw, however, a complete set of Alroy Kear's and a great many novels in bright bindings, which looked suspiciously unread; I guessed that they were the works of authors who had sent them to the master in homage to his talent and perhaps the hope of a few words of eulogy that could be used in the publisher's advertisements. But all the books were so neatly arranged, they were so clean, that I had the impression they were very seldom read. There was the *Oxford Dictionary* and there were standard editions in grand bindings of most of the English classics, Fielding, Boswell, Hazlitt, and so on, and there were a great many books on the sea; I recognized the variously coloured, untidy volumes of the sailing directions issued by the Admiralty, and there were a number of works on gardening. The room had the look not of a writer's workshop, but of a memorial to a great name, and you could almost see already the desultory tripper wandering in for want of something better to do and smell the rather musty, close smell of a museum that few visited. I had a suspicion that nowadays if Driffield read anything at all it was the *Gardeners' Chronicle* or the *Shipping Gazette,* of which I saw a bundle on a table in the corner.

When the ladies had seen all they wanted we bade our hosts farewell. But Lady Hodmarsh was a woman of tact and it must have occurred to her that I, the excuse for the party, had scarcely had a word with Edward Driffield, for at the door, enveloping me with a friendly smile, she said to him:

"I was so interested to hear that you and Mr. Ashenden had known one another years and years ago. Was he a nice little boy?"

Driffield looked at me for a moment with that level, ironic gaze of his. I had the impression that if there had been nobody there he would have put his tongue out at me.

"Shy," he replied. "I taught him to ride a bicycle."

We got once more into the huge yellow Rolls and drove off.

"He's too sweet," said the duchess. "I'm so glad we went."

"He has such nice manners, hasn't he?" said Lady Hodmarsh.

"You didn't really expect him to eat his peas with a knife, did you?" I asked.

"I wish he had," said Scallion. "It would have been so picturesque."

"I believe it's very difficult," said the duchess. "I've tried over and over again and I can never get them to stay on."

"You have to spear them," said Scallion.

"Not at all," retorted the duchess. "You have to balance them on the flat, and they roll like the devil."

"What did you think of Mrs. Driffield?" asked Lady Hodmarsh.

"I suppose she serves her purpose," said the duchess.

"He's so old, poor darling, he must have someone to look after him. You know she was a hospital nurse?"

"Oh, was she?" said the duchess. "I thought perhaps she'd been his secretary or typist or something."

"She's quite nice," said Lady Hodmarsh, warmly defending a friend.

"Oh, quite."

"He had a long illness about twenty years ago, and she was his nurse then, and after he got well he married her."

"Funny how men will do that. She must have been years younger than him. She can't be more than—what?—forty or forty-five."

"No, I shouldn't think so. Forty-seven, say. I'm told she's done a great deal for him. I mean, she's made him quite presentable. Alroy Kear told me that before that he was almost too bohemian."

"As a rule authors' wives are odious."

"It's such a bore having to have them, isn't it?"

"Crushing. I wonder they don't see that themselves."

"Poor wretches, they often suffer from the delusion that people find them interesting," I murmured.

We reached Tercanbury, dropped the duchess at the station, and drove on.

v

IT was true that Edward Driffield had taught me to bicycle. That was indeed how I first made his acquaintance. I do not know how long the safety bicycle had been invented, but I know that it was not common in the remote part of Kent in which I lived and when you saw someone speeding along on solid tires you turned round and looked till he was out of sight. It was still a matter for jocularity on the part of middle-aged gentlemen who said Shanks's pony was good enough for them, and for trepidation on the part of elderly ladies who made a dash for the side of the road when they saw one coming. I had been for some time filled with envy of the boys whom I saw riding into the school grounds on their bicycles, and it gave a pretty opportunity for showing off when you entered the gateway without holding on to the handles. I had persuaded my uncle to let me have one at the beginning of the summer holidays, and though my aunt was against it, since she said I should only break my neck, he had yielded to my pertinacity more willingly because I was of course paying for it out of my own money. I ordered it before school broke up and a few days later the carrier brought it over from Tercanbury.

I was determined to learn to ride it by myself and chaps at school had told me that they had learned in half an hour. I tried and tried and at last came to the conclusion that I was abnormally stupid (I am inclined now to think that I was exaggerating), but even after my pride was sufficiently humbled for me to allow the gardener to hold me up I seemed at the end of the first morning no nearer to being able to get on by myself than at the beginning. Next day, however, thinking that the carriage drive at the vicarage was too winding to give a fellow a proper chance, I wheeled the bicycle to a road not far away which I knew was perfectly flat and straight and so solitary that no one would see me making a fool of myself. I tried several times to mount, but fell off each time. I barked my shins against the pedals and got very hot and bothered. After I had been doing this for about an hour, though I began to think that God did not intend me to ride a bicycle, but was determined (unable to bear the thought of the sarcasms of my uncle, his representative at Blackstable) to do so all the same, to my disgust I saw two people on bicycles coming along the deserted road. I immediately wheeled my machine to the side and sat down on a stile, looking out to sea in a nonchalant way as though I had been for a ride and were just sitting there rapt in contemplation of the vasty ocean. I kept my eyes dreamily averted from the two persons who were advancing toward me, but I felt that they were coming nearer, and through the corner of my eye I saw that they were a man and a woman. As they passed me the woman swerved violently to my side of the road and, crashing against me, fell to the ground.

"Oh, I'm sorry," she said. "I knew I should fall off the moment I saw you."

It was impossible under the circumstances to preserve my appearance of abstraction and, blushing furiously, I said that it didn't matter at all.

The man had got off as she fell.

"You haven't hurt yourself?" he asked.

"Oh, no."

I recognized him then as Edward Driffield, the author I had seen walking with the curate a few days before.

"I'm just learning to ride," said his companion. "And I fall off whenever I see anything in the road."

"Aren't you the vicar's nephew?" said Driffield. "I saw you the other day. Galloway told me who you were. This is my wife."

She held out her hand with an oddly frank gesture and when I took it gave mine a warm and hearty pressure. She smiled with her lips and with her eyes and there was in her smile something that even then I recognized as singularly pleasant. I was confused. People I did not know made me dreadfully self-conscious, and I could not take in any of the details of her appearance. I just had an impression of a rather large blond woman. I do not know if I noticed then or only remembered afterward that she wore a full skirt of blue serge, a pink shirt with a starched front and a starched collar, and a straw hat, called in those days, I think, a boater, perched on the top of a lot of golden hair.

"I think bicycling's lovely, don't you?" she said, looking at my beautiful new machine which leaned against the stile. "It must be wonderful to be able to ride well."

I felt that this inferred an admiration for my proficiency.

"It's only a matter of practice," I said.

"This is only my third lesson. Mr. Driffield says I'm coming on wonderful, but I feel so stupid I could kick myself. How long did it take you before you could ride?"

I blushed to the roots of my hair. I could hardly utter the shameful words.

"I can't ride," I said. "I've only just got this bike and this is the first time I've tried."

I equivocated a trifle there, but I made it all right with my conscience by adding the mental reservation: except yesterday at home in the garden.

"I'll give you a lesson if you like," said Driffield in his good-humoured way. "Come on."

"Oh, no," I said. "I wouldn't dream of it."

"Why not?" asked his wife, her blue eyes still pleasantly smiling. "Mr. Driffield would like to and it'll give me a chance to rest."

Driffield took my bicycle, and I, reluctant but unable to withstand his friendly violence, clumsily mounted. I swayed from side to side, but he held me with a firm hand.

"Faster," he said.

I pedalled and he ran by me as I wabbled from side to side. We were both very hot when, notwithstanding his struggles, I at last fell off. It was very hard under such circumstances to preserve the standoffishness befitting the vicar's nephew with the son of Miss Wolfe's bailiff, and when I started back again and for thirty or forty thrilling yards actually rode by myself and Mrs. Driffield ran into the middle of the road with her arms akimbo shouting: "Go it, go it, two to one on the favourite," I was laughing so much that I positively forgot all about my social status. I got off of my own accord, my face no doubt wearing an air of immodest triumph, and received without embarrassment the Driffields' congratulation on my cleverness in riding a bicycle the very first day I tried.

"I want to see if I can get on by myself," said Mrs. Driffield, and I sat down again on the stile while her husband and I watched her unavailing struggles.

Then, wanting to rest again, disappointed but cheerful, she sat down beside me. Driffield lit his pipe. We chatted. I did not of course realize it then, but I know now that there was a disarming frankness in her manner that put one at one's ease. She talked with a kind of eagerness, like a child bubbling over with the zest of life, and her eyes were lit all the time by her engaging smile. I did not know why I liked it. I should say it was a little sly, if slyness were not a displeasing quality; it was too innocent to be sly. It was mischievous rather, like that of a child who has done something that he thinks funny, but is quite well aware that you will think rather naughty; he knows all the same that you won't be really cross and if you don't find out about it quickly he'll come and tell you himself. But of course then I only knew that her smile made me feel at home.

Presently Driffield, looking at his watch, said that they must be going and suggested that we should all ride back together in style. It was just the time that my aunt and uncle would be coming home from their daily walk down the town and I did not like to run the risk of being seen with people whom they would not at all approve of; so I asked them to go on first, as they would go more quickly than I. Mrs. Driffield would not hear of it, but Driffield gave me a funny, amused little look, which made me think that he saw through my excuse so that I blushed scarlet, and he said:

"Let him go by himself, Rosie. He can manage better alone."

"All right. Shall you be here tomorrow? We're coming."

"I'll try to," I answered.

They rode off, and in a few minutes I followed. Feeling very much pleased with myself, I rode all the way to the vicarage gates without falling. I think I boasted a good deal at dinner, but I did not say that I had met the Driffields.

Next day at about eleven I got my bicycle out of the coach-house. It was so called though it held not even a pony trap and was used by the gardener to keep the mower and the roller, and by Mary-Ann for her sack of meal for the chickens. I wheeled it down to the gate and, mounting none too easily, rode along the Tercanbury Road till I came to the old turnpike and turned into Joy Lane.

The sky was blue and the air, warm and yet fresh, crackled, as it were, with the heat. The light was brilliant without harshness. The sun's beams seemed to hit the white road with a directed energy and bounce back like a rubber ball.

I rode backward and forward, waiting for the Driffields, and presently saw them come. I waved to them and turned round (getting off

to do so) and we pedalled along together. Mrs. Driffield and I complimented one another on our progress. We rode anxiously, clinging like
grim death to the handle-bars, but exultant, and Driffield said that as
soon as we felt sure of ourselves we must go for rides all over the
country.

"I want to get rubbings of one or two brasses in the neighbourhood,"
he said.

I did not know what he meant, but he would not explain.

"Wait and I'll show you," he said. "Do you think you could ride
fourteen miles tomorrow, seven there and seven back?"

"Rather," I said.

"I'll bring a sheet of paper for you and some wax and you can make
a rubbing. But you'd better ask your uncle if you can come."

"I needn't do that."

"I think you'd better all the same."

Mrs. Driffield gave me that peculiar look of hers, mischievous and
yet friendly, and I blushed scarlet. I knew that if I asked my uncle he
would say no. It would be much better to say nothing about it. But
as we rode along I saw coming toward us the doctor, in his dogcart. I
looked straight in front of me as he passed in the vain hope that if I
did not look at him he would not look at me. I was uneasy. If he had
seen me the fact would quickly reach the ears of my uncle or my aunt
and I considered whether it would not be safer to disclose myself a
secret that could no longer be concealed. When we parted at the vicarage gates (I had not been able to avoid riding as far as this in their
company) Driffield said that if I found I could come with them next
day I had better call for them as early as I could.

"You know where we live, don't you? Next door to the Congregational Church. It's called Lime Cottage."

When I sat down to dinner I looked for an opportunity to slip in
casually the information that I had by accident run across the Driffields; but news travelled fast in Blackstable.

"Who were those people you were bicycling with this morning?"
asked my aunt. "We met Dr. Anstey in the town and he said he'd
seen you."

My uncle, chewing his roast beef with an air of disapproval, looked sullenly at his plate.

"The Driffields," I said with nonchalance. "You know, the author. Mr. Galloway knows them."

"They're most disreputable people," said my uncle. "I don't wish you to associate with them."

"Why not?" I asked.

"I'm not going to give you my reasons. It's enough that I don't wish it."

"How did you ever get to know them?" asked my aunt.

"I was just riding along and they were riding along, and they asked me if I'd like to ride with them," I said, distorting the truth a little.

"I call it very pushing," said my uncle.

I began to sulk. And to show my indignation when the sweet was put on the table, though it was raspberry tart which I was extremely fond of, I refused to have any. My aunt asked me if I was not feeling very well.

"Yes," I said, as haughtily as I could, "I'm feeling all right."

"Have a little bit," said my aunt.

"I'm not hungry," I answered.

"Just to please me."

"He must know when he's had enough," said my uncle.

I gave him a bitter look.

"I don't mind having a small piece," I said.

My aunt gave me a generous helping, which I ate with the air of one who, impelled by a stern sense of duty, performs an act that is deeply distasteful to him. It was a beautiful raspberry tart. Mary-Ann made short pastry that melted in the mouth. But when my aunt asked me whether I could not manage a little more I refused with cold dignity. She did not insist. My uncle said grace and I carried my outraged feelings into the drawing room.

But when I reckoned that the servants had finished their dinner I went into the kitchen. Emily was cleaning the silver in the pantry. Mary-Ann was washing up.

"I say, what's wrong with the Driffields?" I asked her.

Mary-Ann had come to the vicarage when she was eighteen. She had bathed me when I was a small boy, given me powders in plum jam when I needed them, packed my box when I went to school, nursed me when I was ill, read to me when I was bored, and scolded me when I was naughty. Emily, the housemaid, was a flighty young thing, and Mary-Ann didn't know whatever would become of me if *she* had the looking after of me. Mary-Ann was a Blackstable girl. She had never been to London in her life and I do not think she had been to Tercanbury more than three or four times. She was never ill. She never had a holiday. She was paid twelve pounds a year. One evening a week she went down the town to see her mother, who did the vicarage washing; and on Sunday evenings she went to church. But Mary-Ann knew everything that went on in Blackstable. She knew who everybody was, who had married whom, what anyone's father had died of, and how many children, and what they were called, any woman had had.

I asked Mary-Ann my question and she slopped a wet clout noisily into the sink.

"I don't blame your uncle," she said. "I wouldn't let you go about with them, not if you was my nephew. Fancy their askin' you to ride your bicycle with them! Some people will do anything."

I saw that the conversation in the dining room had been repeated to Mary-Ann.

"I'm not a child," I said.

"That makes it all the worse. The impudence of their comin' 'ere at all!" Mary-Ann dropped her aitches freely. "Takin' a house and pretendin' to be ladies and gentlemen. Now leave that pie alone."

The raspberry tart was standing on the kitchen table and I broke off a piece of crust with my fingers and put it in my mouth.

"We're goin' to eat that for our supper. If you'd wanted a second 'elpin' why didn't you 'ave one when you was 'avin' your dinner? Ted Driffield never could stick to anything. He 'ad a good education, too. The one I'm sorry for is his mother. He's been a trouble to 'er from the day he was born. And then to go an' marry Rosie Gann. They tell me that when he told his mother what he was goin' to do she took to 'er bed and stayed there for three weeks and wouldn't talk to anybody."

"Was Mrs. Driffield Rosie Gann before she married? Which Ganns were those?"

Gann was one of the commonest names at Blackstable. The churchyard was thick with their graves.

"Oh, you wouldn't 'ave known them. Old Josiah Gann was her father. He was a wild one, too. He went for a soldier and when he come back he 'ad a wooden leg. He used to go out doing painting, but he was out of work more often than not. They lived in the next 'ouse to us in Rye Lane. Me an' Rosie used to go to Sunday school together."

"But she's not as old as you are," I said with the bluntness of my age.

"She'll never see thirty again."

Mary-Ann was a little woman with a snub nose and decayed teeth, but fresh-coloured, and I do not suppose she could have been more than thirty-five.

"Rosie ain't more than four or five years younger than me, whatever she may pretend she is. They tell me you wouldn't know her now all dressed up and everything."

"Is it true that she was a barmaid?" I asked.

"Yes, at the Railway Arms and then at the Prince of Wales's Feathers at Haversham. Mrs. Reeves 'ad her to 'elp in the bar at the Railway Arms, but it got so bad she had to get rid of her."

The Railway Arms was a very modest little public house just opposite the station of the London, Chatham & Dover Railway. It had a sort of sinister gaiety. On a winter's night as you passed by you saw through the glass doors men lounging about the bar. My uncle very much disapproved of it, and had for years been trying to get its licence taken away. It was frequented by the railway porters, colliers, and farm labourers. The respectable residents of Blackstable would have disdained to enter it and, when they wanted a glass of bitter, went to the Bear and Key or the Duke of Kent.

"Why, what did she do?" I asked, my eyes popping out of my head.

"What didn't she do?" said Mary-Ann. "What d'you think your uncle would say if he caught me tellin' you things like that? There wasn't a man who come in to 'ave a drink that she didn't carry on with. No matter who they was. She couldn't stick to anybody, it was

just one man after another. They tell me it was simply 'orrible. That
was when it begun with Lord George. It wasn't the sort of place he
was likely to go to, he was too grand for that, but they say he went in
accidental like one day when his train was late, and he saw her. And
after that he was never out of the place, mixin' with all them common
rough people, and of course they all knew what he was there for, and
him with a wife and three children. Oh, I was sorry for her! And the
talk it made. Well, it got so Mrs. Reeves said she wasn't going to put
up with it another day and she gave her her wages and told her to pack
her box and go. Good riddance to bad rubbish, that's what I said."

I knew Lord George very well. His name was George Kemp and
the title by which he was always known had been given him ironically
owing to his grand manner. He was our coal merchant, but he also
dabbled in house property, and he owned a share in one or two colliers. He lived in a new brick house that stood in its own grounds and
he drove his own trap. He was a stoutish man with a pointed beard,
florid, with a high colour and bold blue eyes. Remembering him, I
think he must have looked like some jolly rubicund merchant in an old
Dutch picture. He was always very flashily dressed and when you saw
him driving at a smart pace down the middle of the High Street in a
fawn-coloured covert-coat with large buttons, his brown bowler on the
side of his head and a red rose in his button hole, you could not but
look at him. On Sunday he used to come to church in a lustrous topper
and a frock coat. Everyone knew that he wanted to be made churchwarden, and it was evident that his energy would have made him useful, but my uncle said not in his time, and though Lord George as a
protest went to chapel for a year my uncle remained obdurate. He cut
him dead when he met him in the town. A reconciliation was effected
and Lord George came to church again, but my uncle only yielded so
far as to appoint him sidesman. The gentry thought him extremely
vulgar and I have no doubt that he was vain and boastful. They complained of his loud voice and his strident laugh—when he was talking
to somebody on one side of the street you heard every word he said
from the other—and they thought his manners dreadful. He was much
too friendly; when he talked to them it was as though he were not in

trade at all; they said he was very pushing. But if he thought his hail-fellow-well-met air, his activity in public works, his open purse when subscriptions were needed for the annual regatta or for the harvest festival, his willingness to do anyone a good turn were going to break the barriers at Blackstable he was mistaken. His efforts at sociability were met with blank hostility.

I remember once that the doctor's wife was calling on my aunt and Emily came in to tell my uncle that Mr. George Kemp would like to see him.

"But I heard the front door ring, Emily," said my aunt.

"Yes'm, he came to the front door."

There was a moment's awkwardness. Everyone was at a loss to know how to deal with such an unusual occurrence, and even Emily, who knew who should come to the front door, who should go to the side door, and who to the back, looked a trifle flustered. My aunt, who was a gentle soul, I think felt honestly embarrassed that anyone should put himself in such a false position; but the doctor's wife gave a little sniff of contempt. At last my uncle collected himself.

"Show him into the study, Emily," he said. "I'll come as soon as I've finished my tea."

But Lord George remained exuberant, flashy, loud, and boisterous. He said the town was dead and he was going to wake it up. He was going to get the company to run excursion trains. He didn't see why it shouldn't become another Margate. And why shouldn't they have a mayor? Ferne Bay had one.

"I suppose he thinks he'd be mayor himself," said the people of Blackstable. They pursed their lips. "Pride goeth before a fall," they said.

And my uncle remarked that you could take a horse to the water but you couldn't make him drink.

I should add that I looked upon Lord George with the same scornful derision as everyone else. It outraged me that he should stop me in the street and call me by my Christian name and talk to me as though there were no social difference between us. He even suggested that I should play cricket with his sons, who were of about the same age as myself. But they went to the grammar school at Haversham and of course I couldn't possibly have anything to do with them.

I was shocked and thrilled by what Mary-Ann told me, but I had difficulty in believing it. I had read too many novels and had learnt too much at school not to know a good deal about love, but I thought it was a matter that only concerned young people. I could not conceive that a man with a beard, who had sons as old as I, could have any feelings of that sort. I thought when you married all that was finished. That people over thirty should be in love seemed to me rather disgusting.

"You don't mean to say they did anything?" I asked Mary-Ann.

"From what I hear there's very little that Rosie Gann didn't do. And Lord George wasn't the only one."

"But, look here, why didn't she have a baby?"

In the novels I had read whenever lovely woman stooped to folly she had a baby. The cause was put with infinite precaution, sometimes indeed suggested only by a row of asterisks, but the result was inevitable.

"More by good luck than by good management, I lay," said Mary-Ann. Then she recollected herself and stopped drying the plates she was busy with. "It seems to me you know a lot more than you ought to," she said.

"Of course I know," I said importantly. "Hang it all, I'm practically grown up, aren't I?"

"All I can tell you," said Mary-Ann, "is that when Mrs. Reeves gave her the sack, Lord George got her a job at the Prince of Wales's Feathers at Haversham and he was always poppin' over there in his trap. You can't tell me the ale's any different over there from what it is here."

"Then why did Ted Driffield marry her?" I asked.

"Ask me another," said Mary-Ann. "It was at the Feathers he saw her. I suppose he couldn't get anyone else to marry him. No respectable girl would 'ave 'ad 'im."

"Did he know about her?"

"You'd better ask him."

I was silent. It was all very puzzling.

"What does she look like now?" asked Mary-Ann. "I never seen her since she married. I never even speak to 'er after I 'eard what was goin' on at the Railway Arms."

"She looks all right," I said.

"Well, you ask her if she remembers me and see what she says."

VI

I HAD quite made up my mind that I was going out with the Driffields next morning, but knew that it was no good asking my uncle if I might. If he found out that I had been and made a row it couldn't be helped, and if Ted Driffield asked me whether I had got my uncle's permission I was quite prepared to say I had. But I had after all no need to lie. In the afternoon, the tide being high, I walked down to the beach to bathe and my uncle, having something to do in the town, walked part of the way with me. Just as we were passing the Bear and Key, Ted Driffield stepped out of it. He saw us and came straight up to my uncle. I was startled at his coolness.

"Good afternoon, Vicar," he said. "I wonder if you remember me. I used to sing in the choir when I was a boy. Ted Driffield. My old governor was Miss Wolfe's bailiff."

My uncle was a very timid man, and he was taken aback.

"Oh, yes, how do you do? I was sorry to hear your father died."

"I've made the acquaintance of your young nephew. I was wondering if you'd let him come for a ride with me tomorrow. It's rather dull for him riding alone, and I'm going to do a rubbing of one of the brasses at Ferne Church."

"It's very kind of you, but——"

My uncle was going to refuse, but Driffield interrupted him.

"I'll see he doesn't get up to any mischief. I thought he might like to make a rubbing himself. It would be an interest for him. I'll give him some paper and wax so that it won't cost him anything."

My uncle had not a consecutive mind and the suggestion that Ted

Driffield should pay for my paper and wax offended him so much that he quite forgot his intention to forbid me to go at all.

"He can quite well get his own paper and wax," he said. "He has plenty of pocket money, and he'd much better spend it on something like that than on sweets and make himself sick."

"Well, if he goes to Hayward, the stationer's, and says he wants the same paper as I got and the wax they'll let him have it."

"I'll go now," I said, and to prevent any change of mind on my uncle's part dashed across the road.

VII

I DO not know why the Driffields bothered about me unless it was from pure kindness of heart. I was a dull little boy, not very talkative, and if I amused Ted Driffield at all it must have been unconsciously. Perhaps he was tickled by my attitude of superiority. I was under the impression that it was condescension on my part to consort with the son of Miss Wolfe's bailiff, and he what my uncle called a penny-a-liner; and when, perhaps with a trace of superciliousness, I asked him to lend me one of his books and he said it wouldn't interest me I took him at his word and did not insist. After my uncle had once consented to my going out with the Driffields he made no further objection to my association with them. Sometimes we went for sails together, sometimes we went to some picturesque spot and Driffield painted a little water colour. I do not know if the English climate was better in those days or if it is only an illusion of youth, but I seem to remember that all through that summer the sunny days followed one another in an unbroken line. I began to feel a curious affection for the undulating, opulent, and gracious country. We went far afield, to one church after another, taking rubbings of brasses, knights in armour and ladies in stiff farthingales. Ted Driffield fired me with his own enthusiasm for this naïve pursuit and I rubbed with passion. I showed my uncle proudly the results of my industry, and I suppose he thought that whatever my company, I could not come to much harm when I was occupied in church. Mrs. Driffield used to remain in the churchyard while we were at work, not reading or sewing, but just mooning about; she seemed able to do nothing for an indefinite time without feeling bored. Sometimes I would go out and sit with her for a little on the grass. We chattered about my school, my friends there and my masters, about the people at Blackstable, and about nothing at all. She gratified me by calling me Mr. Ashenden. I think she was the first person who had ever done so and it made me feel grown up. I resented it vastly when people called me Master Willie. I thought it a ridiculous name for anyone to have. In fact I did not like either of my names and spent much time inventing others that would have suited me better. The ones I preferred were Roderic Ravensworth and I covered sheets of paper with this signature in a suitably dashing hand. I did not mind Ludovic Montgomery either.

I could not get over what Mary-Ann had told me about Mrs. Driffield. Though I knew theoretically what people did when they were married, and was capable of putting the facts in the bluntest language, I did not really understand it. I thought it indeed rather disgusting and I did not quite, quite believe it. After all, I was aware that the earth was round, but I *knew* it was flat. Mrs. Driffield seemed so frank, her laugh was so open and simple, there was in her demeanour something so young and childlike, that I could not see her "going with" sailors and above all anyone so gross and horrible as Lord George. She was not at all the type of the wicked woman I had read of in novels. Of course I knew she wasn't "good form" and she spoke with the Blackstable accent, she dropped an aitch now and then, and sometimes her grammar gave me a shock, but I couldn't help liking her. I came to the conclusion that what Mary-Ann had told me was a pack of lies.

One day I happened to tell her that Mary-Ann was our cook.

"She says she lived next door to you in Rye Lane," I added, quite prepared to hear Mrs. Driffield say that she had never even heard of her.

But she smiled and her blue eyes gleamed.

"That's right. She used to take me to Sunday school. She used to have a rare job keeping me quiet. I heard she'd gone to service at the vicarage. Fancy her being there still! I haven't seen her for donkey's years. I'd like to see her again and have a chat about old days. Remember me to her, will you, and ask her to look in on her evening out. I'll give her a cup of tea."

I was taken aback at this. After all, the Driffields lived in a house that they were talking of buying and they had a "general." It wouldn't be at all the thing for them to have Mary-Ann to tea, and it would make it very awkward for me. They seemed to have no sense of the things one could do and the things one simply couldn't. It never ceased to embarrass me, the way in which they talked of incidents in their past that I should have thought they would not dream of mentioning. I do not know that the people I lived among were pretentious in the sense of making themselves out to be richer or grander than they really were, but looking back it does seem to me that they lived a life full of pretences. They dwelt behind a mask of respectability. You never caught them in their shirt sleeves with their feet on the table. The ladies put on afternoon dresses and were not visible till then; they lived privately with rigid economy so that you could not drop in for a casual meal, but when they entertained their tables groaned with food. Though catastrophe overwhelmed the family, they held their heads high and ignored it. One of the sons might have married an actress, but they never referred to the calamity, and though the neighbours said it was dreadful, they took ostentatious care not to mention the theatre in the presence of the afflicted. We all knew that the wife of Major Greencourt who had taken the Three Gables was connected with trade, but neither she nor the major ever so much as hinted at the discreditable secret; and though we sniffed at them behind their backs, we were too polite even to mention crockery (the source of Mrs. Greencourt's adequate income) in their presence. It was still not unheard of for an angry parent to cut off his son with a shilling or to tell his daughter (who like my own mother had married a solicitor) never to darken his doors again. I was used to all this and it seemed to me perfectly natural. What did shock me was to hear Ted Driffield speak of being a waiter in a restaurant in Holborn as though it were the most ordinary thing in the world. I knew he had run away to sea, that was romantic; I knew that boys, in books at all events, often did this and had thrilling adventures before they married a fortune and an earl's daughter; but Ted Driffield had driven a cab at Maidstone and had been clerk in a booking office at Birmingham. Once when we bicycled past the Railway Arms, Mrs. Driffield mentioned quite casually, as though it were something that anyone might have done, that she had worked there for three years.

"It was my first place," she said. "After that I went to the Feathers at Haversham. I only left there to get married."

She laughed as though she enjoyed the recollection. I did not know what to say; I did not know which way to look; I blushed scarlet. Another time when we were going through Ferne Bay on our way back from a long excursion, it being a hot day and all of us thirsty, she suggested that we should go into the Dolphin and have a glass of beer. She began talking to the girl behind the bar and I was horrified to hear her remark that she had been in the business herself for five years. The landlord joined us and Ted Driffield offered him a drink, and Mrs. Driffield said that the barmaid must have a glass of port, and for some time they all chatted amiably about trade and tied houses and how the price of everything was going up. Meanwhile, I stood, hot and cold all over, and not knowing what to do with myself. As we went out Mrs. Driffield remarked:

"I took quite a fancy to that girl, Ted. She ought to do well for herself. As I said to her, it's a hard life but a merry one. You do see a bit of what's going on and if you play your cards right you ought to marry well. I noticed she had an engagement ring on, but she told me she just wore that because it gave the fellows a chance to tease her."

Driffield laughed. She turned to me.

"I had a rare old time when I was a barmaid, but of course you can't go on for ever. You have to think of your future."

But a greater jolt awaited me. It was half-way through September and my holidays were drawing to an end. I was very full of the Driffields, but my desire to talk about them at home was snubbed by my uncle.

"We don't want your friends pushed down our throats all day long," said he. "There are other topics of conversation that are more suitable. But I do think that, as Ted Driffield was born in the parish and is seeing you almost every day, he might come to church occasionally."

One day I told Driffield: "My uncle wants you to come to church."

"All right. Let's go to church next Sunday night, Rosie."

"I don't mind," she said.

I told Mary-Ann they were going. I sat in the vicarage pew just behind the squire's and I could not look round, but I was conscious by the behaviour of my neighbours on the other side of the aisle that they were there, and as soon as I had a chance next day I asked Mary-Ann if she had seen them.

"I see 'er all right," said Mary-Ann grimly.

"Did you speak to her afterward?"

"Me?" She suddenly burst into anger. "You get out of my kitchen. What d'you want to come bothering me all day long? How d'you expect me to do my work with you getting in my way all the time?"

"All right," I said. "Don't get in a wax."

"I don't know what your uncle's about lettin' you go all over the place with the likes of them. All them flowers in her 'at. I wonder she ain't ashamed to show her face. Now run along, I'm busy."

I did not know why Mary-Ann was so cross. I did not mention Mrs. Driffield again. But two or three days later I happened to go into the kitchen to get something I wanted. There were two kitchens at the vicarage, a small one in which the cooking was done and a large one, built I suppose for a time when country clergymen had large families and gave grand dinners to the surrounding gentry, where Mary-Ann sat and sewed when her day's work was over. We had cold supper at eight so that after tea she had little to do. It was getting on for seven and the day was drawing in. It was Emily's evening out and I expected to find Mary-Ann alone, but as I went along the passage I heard voices and the sound of laughter. I supposed Mary-Ann had someone in to see her. The lamp was lit, but it had a thick green shade and the kitchen was almost in darkness. I saw a teapot and cups on the table.

Mary-Ann was having a late cup of tea with her friend. The conversation stopped as I opened the door, then I heard a voice.

"Good evening."

With a start I saw that Mary-Ann's friend was Mrs. Driffield. Mary-Ann laughed a little at my surprise.

"Rosie Gann dropped in to have a cup of tea with me," she said.

"We've been having a talk about old times."

Mary-Ann was a little shy at my finding her thus, but not half so shy as I. Mrs. Driffield gave me that childlike, mischievous smile of hers; she was perfectly at her ease. For some reason I noticed her dress. I suppose because I had never seen her so grand before. It was of pale blue cloth, very tight at the waist, with high sleeves and a long skirt with a flounce at the bottom. She wore a large black straw hat with a great quantity of roses and leaves and bows on it. It was evidently the hat she had worn in church on Sunday.

"I thought if I went on waiting till Mary-Ann came to see me I'd have to wait till doomsday, so I thought the best thing I could do was to come and see her myself."

Mary-Ann grinned self-consciously, but did not look displeased. I asked for whatever it was I wanted and as quickly as I could left them. I went out into the garden and wandered about aimlessly. I walked down to the road and looked over the gate. The night had fallen. Presently I saw a man strolling along. I paid no attention to him, but he passed backward and forward and it looked as though he were waiting for someone. At first I thought it might be Ted Driffield and I was on the point of going out when he stopped and lit a pipe; I saw it was Lord George. I wondered what he was doing there and at the same moment it struck me that he was waiting for Mrs. Driffield. My heart began to beat fast, and though I was hidden by the darkness I withdrew into the shade of the bushes. I waited a few minutes longer, then I saw the side door open and Mrs. Driffield let out by Mary-Ann. I heard her footsteps on the gravel. She came to the gate and opened it. It opened with a little click. At the sound Lord George stepped across the road and before she could come out slipped in. He took her in his arms and gave her a great hug. She gave a little laugh.

"Take care of my hat," she whispered.

I was not more than three feet away from them and I was terrified lest they should notice me. I was so ashamed for them. I was trembling with agitation. For a minute he held her in his arms.

"What about the garden?" he said, still in a whisper.

"No, there's that boy. Let's go in the fields."

They went out by the gate, he with his arm round her waist, and were lost in the night. Now I felt my heart pounding against my chest so that I could hardly breathe. I was so astonished at what I had seen that I could not think sensibly. I would have given anything to be able to tell someone, but it was a secret and I must keep it. I was thrilled with the importance it gave me. I walked slowly up to the house and let myself in by the side door. Mary-Ann, hearing it open, called me.

"Is that you, Master Willie?"

"Yes."

I looked in the kitchen. Mary-Ann was putting the supper on a tray to take it into the dining room.

"I wouldn't say anything to your uncle about Rosie Gann 'avin' been here," she said.

"Oh, no."

"It was a surprisement to me. When I 'eard a knock at the side door and opened it and saw Rosie standing there, you could 'ave knocked me down with a feather. 'Mary-Ann,' she says, an' before I knew what she was up to she was kissing me all over me face. I couldn't but ask 'er in and when she was in I couldn't but ask her to 'ave a nice cup of tea."

Mary-Ann was anxious to excuse herself. After all she had said of Mrs. Driffield it must seem strange to me that I should find them sitting there together chatting away and laughing. I did not want to crow.

"She's not so bad, is she?" I said.

Mary-Ann smiled. Notwithstanding her black decayed teeth there was in her smile something sweet and touching.

"I don't 'ardly know what it is, but there's somethin' you can't 'elp likin' about her. She was 'ere the best part of an hour and I will say that for 'er, she never once give 'erself airs. And she told me with 'er own lips the material of that dress she 'ad on cost thirteen and eleven a yard and I believe it. She remembers everything, how I used to brush her 'air for her when she was a tiny tot and how I used to make her wash her little 'ands before tea. You see, sometimes her mother used to send 'er in to 'ave her tea with us. She was as pretty as a picture in them days."

Mary-Ann looked back into the past and her funny crumpled face grew wistful.

"Oh, well," she said after a pause, "I dare say she's been no worse than plenty of others if the truth was only known. She 'ad more temptation than most, and I dare say a lot of them as blame her would 'ave been no better than what she was if they'd 'ad the opportunity."

VIII

THE weather broke suddenly; it grew chilly and heavy rain fell. It put an end to our excursions. I was not sorry, for I did not know how I could look Mrs. Driffield in the face now that I had seen her meeting with George Kemp. I was not so much shocked as astonished. I could not understand how it was possible for her to like being kissed by an old man, and the fantastic notion passed through my mind, filled with the novels I had read, that somehow Lord George held her in his power and forced her by his knowledge of some fearful secret to submit to his loathsome embraces. My imagination played with terrible possibilities. Bigamy, murder, and forgery. Very few villains in books failed to hold the threat of exposure of one of these crimes over some hapless female. Perhaps Mrs. Driffield had backed a bill; I never could quite understand what this meant, but I knew that the consequences were disastrous. I toyed with the fancy of her anguish (the long sleepless nights when she sat at her window in her nightdress, her long fair hair hanging to her knees, and watched hopelessly for the dawn) and saw myself (not a boy of fifteen with sixpence a week pocket money, but a tall man with a waxed moustache and muscles of steel in faultless evening dress) with a happy blend of heroism and dexterity rescuing her from the toils of the rascally blackmailer. On the other hand, it had not looked as though she had yielded quite unwillingly to Lord George's fondling and I could not get out of my ears the sound of her laugh. It had a note that I had never heard before. It gave me a queer feeling of breathlessness.

During the rest of my holidays, I only saw the Driffields once more. I met them by chance in the town and they stopped and spoke to me. I suddenly felt very shy again, but when I looked at Mrs. Driffield I could not help blushing with embarrassment, for there was nothing in her countenance that indicated a guilty secret. She looked at me with those soft blue eyes of hers in which there was a child's playful naughtiness. She often held her mouth a little open, as though it were just going to break into a smile, and her lips were full and red. There was honesty and innocence in her face and an ingenuous frankness and though then I could not have expressed this, I felt it quite strongly. If I had put it into words at all I think I should have said: She looks as straight as a die. It was impossible that she could be "carrying on" with Lord George. There must be an explanation; I did not believe what my eyes had seen.

Then the day came when I had to go back to school. The carter had taken my trunk and I walked to the station by myself. I had refused to let my aunt see me off, thinking it more manly to go alone, but I felt rather low as I walked down the street. It was a small branch line to Tercanbury and the station was at the other end of the town near the beach. I took my ticket and settled myself in the corner of a third-class carriage. Suddenly I heard a voice: "There he is"; and Mr. and Mrs. Driffield bustled gaily up.

"We thought we must come and see you off," she said. "Are you feeling miserable?"

"No, of course not."

"Oh, well, it won't last long. We'll have no end of a time when you come back for Christmas. Can you skate?"

"No."

"I can. I'll teach you."

Her high spirits cheered me, and at the same time the thought that they had come to the station to say good-bye to me gave me a lump in my throat. I tried hard not to let the emotion I felt appear on my face.

"I expect I shall be playing a lot of football this term," I said. "I ought to get into the second fifteen."

She looked at me with kindly shining eyes, smiling with her full red lips. There was something in her smile I had always rather liked, and her voice seemed almost to tremble with a laugh or a tear. For one horrible moment I was afraid that she was going to kiss me. I was scared out of my wits. She talked on, she was mildly facetious as grown-up people are with schoolboys, and Driffield stood there without saying anything. He looked at me with a smile in his eyes and pulled his beard. Then the guard blew a cracked whistle and waved a red flag. Mrs. Driffield took my hand and shook it. Driffield came forward.

"Good-bye," he said. "Here's something for you."

He pressed a tiny packet into my hand and the train steamed off. When I opened it I found that it was two half-crowns wrapped in a piece of toilet paper. I blushed to the roots of my hair. I was glad enough to have an extra five shillings, but the thought that Ted Driffield had dared to give me a tip filled me with rage and humiliation. I could not possibly accept anything from him. It was true that I had bicycled with him and sailed with him, but he wasn't a sahib (I had got that from Major Greencourt) and it was an insult to me to give me five shillings. At first I thought of returning the money without a word, showing by my silence how outraged I was at the solecism he had committed, then I composed in my head a dignified and frigid letter in which I thanked him for his generosity, but said that he must see how impossible it was for a gentleman to accept a tip from someone who was practically a stranger. I thought it over for two or three days and every day it seemed more difficult to me to part with the two half-crowns. I felt sure that Driffield had meant it kindly, and of course he was very bad form and didn't know about things; it would be rather hard to hurt his feelings by sending the money back, and finally I spent it. But I assuaged my wounded pride by not writing to thank Driffield for his gift.

When Christmas came, however, and I went back to Blackstable for the holidays, it was the Driffields I was most eager to see. In that stagnant little place they alone seemed to have a connexion with the outside world which already was beginning to touch my daydreams with anxious curiosity. But I could not overcome my shyness enough to go to their house and call, and I hoped that I should meet them in the town. But the weather was dreadful, a boisterous wind whistled down the street, piercing you to the bone, and the few women who had an errand were swept along by their full skirts like fishing boats in half a gale. The cold rain scudded in sudden squalls and the sky, which in summer had enclosed the friendly country so snugly, now was a great pall that pressed upon the earth with sullen menace. There was small hope of meeting the Driffields by chance and at last I took my courage in both hands and one day after tea slipped out. As far as the station the road was pitch dark, but there the street lamps, few and dim, made it easier to keep to the pavement. The Driffields lived in a little two-story house in a side street; it was of dingy yellow brick and had a bow window. I knocked and presently a little maid opened the door; I asked if Mrs. Driffield was in. She gave me an uncertain look and, saying she would go and see, left me standing in the passage. I had already heard voices in the next room, but they were stilled as she opened the door and, entering, shut it behind her. I had a faint impression of mystery; in the houses of my uncle's friends, even if there was no fire and the gas had to be lit as you went in, you were shown into the drawing room when you called. But the door was opened and Driffield came out. There was only a speck of light in the passage and at first he could not see who it was; but in an instant he recognized me.

"Oh, it's you. We wondered when we were going to see you." Then he called out: "Rosie, it's young Ashenden."

There was a cry and before you could say knife Mrs. Driffield had come into the passage and was shaking my hands.

"Come in, come in. Take off your coat. Isn't it awful, the weather? You must be perishing."

She helped me with my coat and took off my muffler and snatched my cap out of my hand and drew me into the room. It was hot and stuffy, a tiny room full of furniture, with a fire burning in the grate; they had gas there, which we hadn't at the vicarage, and the three burners in round globes of frosted glass filled the room with harsh light. The air was grey with tobacco smoke. At first, dazzled and then taken aback by my effusive welcome, I did not see who the two men were who got up as I came in. Then I saw they were the curate, Mr. Galloway, and Lord George Kemp. I fancied that the curate shook my hand with constraint.

"How are you? I just came in to return some books that Mrs. Driffield had lent me and Mrs. Driffield very kindly asked me to stay to tea."

I felt rather than saw the quizzical look that Driffield gave him. He said something about the mammon of unrighteousness, which I recognized as a quotation, but did not gather the sense of. Mr. Galloway laughed.

"I don't know about that," he said. "What about the publicans and sinners?"

I thought the remark in very bad taste, but I was immediately seized upon by Lord George. There was no constraint about him.

"Well, young fellow, home for the holidays? My word, what a big chap you're growing."

I shook hands with him rather coldly. I wished I had not come.

"Let me give you a nice strong cup of tea," said Mrs. Driffield.

"I've already had tea."

"Have some more," said Lord George, speaking as though he owned the place (that was just like him). "A big fellow like you can always tuck away another piece of bread and butter and jam and Mrs. D. will cut you a slice with her own fair hands."

The tea things were still on the table and they were sitting round it. A chair was brought up for me and Mrs. Driffield gave me a piece of cake.

"We were just trying to persuade Ted to sing us a song," said Lord George. "Come on, Ted."

"Sing 'All Through Stickin' to a Soljer,' Ted," said Mrs. Driffield. "I love that."

"No, sing 'First We Mopped the Floor with Him.' "

"I'll sing 'em both if you're not careful," said Driffield.

He took his banjo, which was lying on the top of the cottage piano, tuned it, and began to sing. He had a rich baritone voice. I was quite used to people singing songs. When there was a tea party at the vicarage, or I went to one of the major's or the doctor's, people always brought their music with them. They left it in the hall, so that it should not seem that they wanted to be asked to play or sing; but after tea the hostess asked them if they had brought it. They shyly admitted that they had, and if it was at the vicarage I was sent to fetch it. Sometimes a young lady would say that she had quite given up playing and hadn't brought anything with her, and then her mother would break in and say that *she* had brought it. But when they sang it was not comic songs; it was "I'll Sing Thee Songs of Araby," or "Good Night, Beloved," or "Queen of My Heart." Once at the annual concert at the Assembly Rooms, Smithson, the draper, had sung a comic song, and though the people at the back of the hall had applauded a great deal, the gentry had seen nothing funny in it. Perhaps there wasn't. Anyhow, before the next concert he was asked to be a little more careful about what he sang ("Remember there are ladies present, Mr. Smithson") and so gave "The Death of Nelson." The next ditty that Driffield sang had a chorus and the curate and Lord George joined in lustily. I heard it a good many times afterward, but I can only remember four lines:

> *First we mopped the floor with him;*
> *Dragged him up and down the stairs;*
> *Then we lugged him round the room,*
> *Under tables, over chairs.*

When it was finished, assuming my best company manners, I turned to Mrs. Driffield.

"Don't you sing?" I asked.

"I do, but it always turns the milk, so Ted doesn't encourage me."

Driffield put down his banjo and lit a pipe.

"Well, how's the old book getting along, Ted?" said Lord George heartily.

"Oh, all right. I'm working away, you know."

"Good old Ted and his books," Lord George laughed. "Why don't you settle down and do something respectable for a change? I'll give you a job in my office."

"Oh, I'm all right."

"You let him be, George," said Mrs. Driffield. "He likes writing, and what I say is, as long as it keeps him happy why shouldn't he?"

"Well, I don't pretend to know anything about books," began George Kemp.

"Then don't talk about them," interrupted Driffield with a smile.

"I don't think anyone need be ashamed to have written *Fairhaven*," said Mr. Galloway, "and I don't care what the critics said."

"Well, Ted, I've known you since I was a boy and *I* couldn't read it, try as I would."

"Oh, come on, we don't want to start talking about books," said Mrs. Driffield. "Sing us another song, Ted."

"I must be going," said the curate. He turned to me. "We might walk along together. Have you got anything for me to read, Driffield?"

Driffield pointed to a pile of new books that were heaped up on a table in the corner.

"Take your pick."

"By Jove, what a lot!" I said, looking at them greedily.

"Oh, it's all rubbish. They're sent down for review."

"What d'you do with them?"

"Take 'em into Tercanbury and sell 'em for what they'll fetch. It all helps to pay the butcher."

When we left, the curate and I, he with three or four books under his arm, he asked me:

"Did you tell your uncle you were coming to see the Driffields?"

"No, I just went out for a walk and it suddenly occurred to me that I might look in."

This of course was some way from the truth, but I did not care to tell Mr. Galloway that, though I was practically grown up, my uncle realized the fact so little that he was quite capable of trying to prevent me from seeing people he objected to.

"Unless you have to I wouldn't say anything about it in your place. The Driffields are perfectly all right, but your uncle doesn't quite approve of them."

"I know," I said. "It's such rot."

"Of course they're rather common, but he doesn't write half badly, and when you think what he came from it's wonderful that he writes at all."

I was glad to know how the land lay. Mr. Galloway did not wish my uncle to know that he was on friendly terms with the Driffields. I could feel sure at all events that he would not give me away.

The patronizing manner in which my uncle's curate spoke of one who has been now so long recognized as one of the greatest of the later Victorian novelists must arouse a smile; but it was the manner in which he was generally spoken of at Blackstable. One day we went to tea at Mrs. Greencourt's, who had staying with her a cousin, the wife of an Oxford don, and we had been told that she was very cultivated. She was a Mrs. Encombe, a little woman with an eager wrinkled face; she surprised us very much because she wore her grey hair short and a black serge skirt that only just came down below the tops of her square-toed boots. She was the first example of the New Woman that had ever been seen in Blackstable. We were staggered and immediately on the defensive, for she looked intellectual and it made us feel shy. (Afterward we all scoffed at her, and my uncle said to my aunt: "Well, my dear, I'm thankful you're not clever, at least I've been spared that"; and my aunt in a playful mood put my uncle's slippers which were warming for him by the fire over her boots and said: "Look, I'm the new woman." And then we all said: "Mrs. Greencourt is very funny; you never know what she'll do next. But of course she isn't quite quite." We could hardly forget that her father made china and that her grandfather had been a factory hand.)

But we all found it very interesting to hear Mrs. Encombe talk of the people she knew. My uncle had been at Oxford, but everyone he

asked about seemed to be dead. Mrs. Encombe knew Mrs. Humphry
Ward and admired *Robert Elsmere*. My uncle considered it a scandalous work, and he was surprised that Mr. Gladstone, who at least
called himself a Christian, had found a good word to say for it. They
had quite an argument about it. My uncle said he thought it would
unsettle people's opinions and give them all sorts of ideas that they
were much better without. Mrs. Encombe answered that he wouldn't
think that if he knew Mrs. Humphry Ward. She was a woman of the
very highest character, a niece of Mr. Matthew Arnold, and whatever
you might think of the book itself (and she, Mrs. Encombe, was quite
willing to admit that there were parts which had better have been
omitted) it was quite certain that she had written it from the very
highest motives. Mrs. Encombe knew Miss Broughton too. She was
of very good family and it was strange that she wrote the books she
did.

"I don't see any harm in them," said Mrs. Hayforth, the doctor's wife.
"I enjoy them, especially *Red as a Rose Is She.*"

"Would you like your girls to read them?" asked Mrs. Encombe.

"Not just yet perhaps," said Mrs. Hayforth. "But when they're married I should have no objection."

"Then it might interest you to know," said Mrs. Encombe, "that
when I was in Florence last Easter I was introduced to Ouida."

"That's quite another matter," returned Mrs. Hayforth. "I can't believe that any lady would read a book by Ouida."

"I read one out of curiosity," said Mrs. Encombe. "I must say, it's
more what you'd expect from a Frenchman than from an English
gentlewoman."

"Oh, but I understand she isn't really English. I've always heard her
real name is Mademoiselle de la Ramée."

It was then that Mr. Galloway mentioned Edward Driffield.

"You know we have an author living here," he said.

"We're not very proud of him," said the major. "He's the son of old
Miss Wolfe's bailiff and he married a barmaid."

"Can he write?" asked Mrs. Encombe.

"You can tell at once that he's not a gentleman," said the curate, "but when you consider the disadvantages he's had to struggle against it's rather remarkable that he should write as well as he does."

"He's a friend of Willie's," said my uncle.

Everyone looked at me, and I felt very uncomfortable.

"They bicycled together last summer, and after Willie had gone back to school I got one of his books from the library to see what it was like. I read the first volume and then I sent it back. I wrote a pretty stiff letter to the librarian and I was glad to hear that he'd withdrawn it from circulation. If it had been my own property I should have put it promptly in the kitchen stove."

"I looked through one of his books myself," said the doctor. "It interested me because it was set in this neighbourhood and I recognized some of the people. But I can't say I liked it; I thought it unnecessarily coarse."

"I mentioned that to him," said Mr. Galloway, "and he said the men in the colliers that run up to Newcastle and the fishermen and farm hands don't behave like ladies and gentlemen and don't talk like them."

"But why write about people of that character?" said my uncle.

"That's what I say," said Mrs. Hayforth. "We all know that there are coarse and wicked and vicious people in the world, but I don't see what good it does to write about them."

"I'm not defending him," said Mr. Galloway. "I'm only telling you what explanation he gives himself. And then of course he brought up Dickens."

"Dickens is quite different," said my uncle. "I don't see how anyone can object to the *Pickwick Papers.*"

"I suppose it's a matter of taste," said my aunt. "I always found Dickens very coarse. I don't want to read about people who drop their aitches. I must say I'm very glad the weather's so bad now and Willie can't take any more rides with Mr. Driffield. I don't think he's quite the sort of person he ought to associate with."

Both Mr. Galloway and I looked down our noses.

IX

As often as the mild Christmas gaieties of Blackstable allowed me I went to the Driffields' little house next door to the Congregational chapel. I always found Lord George and often Mr. Galloway. Our conspiracy of silence had made us friends and when we met at the vicarage or in the vestry after church we looked at one another archly. We did not talk about our secret, but we enjoyed it; I think it gave us both a good deal of satisfaction to know that we were making a fool of my uncle. But once it occurred to me that George Kemp, meeting my uncle in the street, might remark casually that he had been seeing a lot of me at the Driffields'.

"What about Lord George?" I said to Mr. Galloway.

"Oh, I made that all right."

We chuckled. I began to like Lord George. At first I was very cold with him and scrupulously polite, but he seemed so unconscious of the social difference between us that I was forced to conclude that my haughty courtesy failed to put him in his place. He was always cordial, breezy, even boisterous; he chaffed me in his common way and I answered him back with schoolboy wit; we made the others laugh and this disposed me kindly toward him. He was for ever bragging about the great schemes he had in mind, but he took in good part my jokes at the expense of his grandiose imaginations. It amused me to hear him tell stories about the swells of Blackstable that made them look foolish and when he mimicked their oddities I roared with laughter. He was blatant and vulgar and the way he dressed was always a shock to me (I had never been to Newmarket nor seen a trainer, but that was my idea of how a Newmarket trainer dressed) and his table manners were offensive, but I found myself less and less affronted by him. He gave me the *Pink 'Un* every week and I took it home, carefully tucked away in my greatcoat pocket, and read it in my bedroom.

I never went to the Driffields' till after tea at the vicarage, but I always managed to make a second tea when I got there. Afterward Ted

Driffield sang comic songs, accompanying himself sometimes on the banjo and sometimes on the piano. He would sing, peering at the music with his rather short-sighted eyes, for an hour at a time; there was a smile on his lips and he liked us all to join in the chorus. We played whist. I had learned the game when I was a child and my uncle and aunt and I used to play at the vicarage during the long winter evenings. My uncle always took dummy, and though of course we played for love, when my aunt and I lost I used to retire under the dining-room table and cry. Ted Driffield did not play cards, he said he had no head for them, and when we started a game he would sit down by the fire and, pencil in hand, read one of the books that had been sent down to him from London to review. I had never played with three people before and of course I did not play well, but Mrs. Driffield had a natural card sense. Her movements as a rule were rather deliberate, but when it came to playing cards she was quick and alert. She played the rest of us right off our heads. Ordinarily she did not speak very much and then slowly, but when, after a hand was played, she took the trouble good-humouredly to point out to me my mistakes, she was not only lucid but voluble. Lord George chaffed her as he chaffed everybody; she would smile at his banter, for she very seldom laughed, and sometimes make a neat retort. They did not behave like lovers, but like familiar friends, and I should have quite forgotten what I had heard about them and what I had seen but that now and then she gave him a look that embarrassed me. Her eyes rested on him quietly, as though he were not a man but a chair or a table, and in them was a mischievous, childlike smile. Then I would notice that his face seemed suddenly to swell and he moved uneasily in his chair. I looked quickly at the curate, afraid that he would notice something, but he was intent on the cards or else was lighting his pipe.

The hour or two I spent nearly every day in that hot, poky, smoke-laden room passed like lightning, and as the holidays drew nearer to their end I was seized with dismay at the thought that I must spend the next three months dully at school.

"I don't know what we shall do without you," said Mrs. Driffield. "We shall have to play dummy."

I was glad that my going would break up the game. While I was doing prep I did not want to think that they were sitting in that little room and enjoying themselves just as if I did not exist.

"How long do you get at Easter?" asked Mr. Galloway.

"About three weeks."

"We'll have a lovely time then," said Mrs. Driffield. "The weather ought to be all right. We can ride in the mornings and then after tea we'll play whist. You've improved a lot. If we play three or four times a week during your Easter holidays you won't need to be afraid to play with anybody."

x

But the term came to an end at last. I was in high spirits when once more I got out of the train at Blackstable. I had grown a little and I had had a new suit made at Tercanbury, blue serge and very smart, and I had bought a new tie. I meant to go and see the Driffields immediately I had swallowed my tea and I was full of hope that the carrier would have brought my box in time for me to put the new suit on. It made me look quite grown up. I had already begun putting vaseline on my upper lip every night to make my moustache grow. On my way through the town I looked down the street in which the Driffields lived in the hope of seeing them. I should have liked to go in and say how-do-you-do, but I knew that Driffield wrote in the morning and Mrs. Driffield was not "presentable." I had all sorts of exciting things to tell them. I had won the hundred-yard race in the sports and I had been second in the hurdles. I meant to have a shot for the history prize in the summer and I was going to swot up my English history during the holidays. Though there was an east wind blowing, the sky was blue and there was a feeling of spring in the air. The High Street, with its colours washed clean by the wind and its lines sharp as though drawn with a new pen, looked like a picture by Samuel Scott, quiet and naïve and cosy: now, looking back; then it looked like nothing but High Street, Blackstable. When I came to the railway bridge I noticed that two or three houses were being built.

"By Jove," I said, "Lord George *is* going it."

In the fields beyond, little white lambs were gambolling. The elm trees were just beginning to turn green. I let myself in by the side door. My uncle was sitting in his armchair by the fire reading the *Times*. I shouted to my aunt and she came downstairs, a pink spot from the excitement of seeing me on each of her withered cheeks, and threw her thin old arms round my neck. She said all the right things.

"How you've grown!" and "Good gracious me, you'll be getting a moustache soon!"

I kissed my uncle on his bald forehead and I stood in front of the fire, with my legs well apart and my back to it, and was extremely grown up and rather condescending. Then I went upstairs to say how-do-you-do to Emily, and into the kitchen to shake hands with Mary-Ann, and out in the garden to see the gardener.

When I sat down hungrily to dinner and my uncle carved the leg of mutton I asked my aunt:

"Well, what's happened at Blackstable since I was here?"

"Nothing very much. Mrs. Greencourt went down to Mentone for six weeks, but she came back a few days ago. The major had an attack of gout."

"And your friends the Driffields have bolted," added my uncle.

"They've done what?" I cried.

"Bolted. They took their luggage away one night and just went up to London. They've left bills all over the place. They hadn't paid their rent and they hadn't paid for their furniture. They owed Harris the butcher the best part of thirty pounds."

"How awful," I said.

"That's bad enough," said my aunt, "but it appears they hadn't even paid the wages of the maid they had for three months."

I was flabbergasted. I thought I felt a little sick.

"I think in future," said my uncle, "you would be wiser not to consort with people whom your aunt and I don't think proper associates for you."

"One can't help feeling sorry for all those tradesmen they cheated," said my aunt.

"It serves them right," said my uncle. "Fancy giving credit to people like that! I should have thought anyone could see they were nothing but adventurers."

"I always wonder why they came down here at all."

"They just wanted to show off, and I suppose they thought as people knew who they were here it would be easier to get things on credit."

I did not think this quite reasonable, but was too much crushed to argue.

As soon as I had the chance I asked Mary-Ann what she knew of the incident. To my surprise she did not take it at all in the same way as my uncle and aunt. She giggled.

"They let everyone in proper," she said. "They was as free as you like with their money and everyone thought they 'ad plenty. It was always the best end of the neck for them at the butcher's and when they wanted a steak nothing would do but the undercut. Asparagus and grapes and I don't know what all. They ran up bills in every shop in the town. I don't know 'ow people can be such fools."

But it was evidently of the tradesmen she was speaking and not of the Driffields.

"But how did they manage to bunk without anyone knowing?" I asked.

"Well, that's what everybody's askin'. They do say it was Lord George 'elped them. How did they get their boxes to the station, I ask you, if 'e didn't take them in that there trap of 'is?"

"What does he say about it?"

"He says 'e knows no more about it than the man in the moon. There was a rare to-do all over the town when they found out the Driffields had shot the moon. It made me laugh. Lord George says 'e never knew they was broke, and 'e makes out 'e was as surprised as anybody. But I for one don't believe a word of it. We all knew about 'im and Rosie before she was married, and between you and me and the gatepost I don't know that it ended there. They do say they was seen walkin' about the fields together last summer and 'e was in and out of the 'ouse pretty near every day."

"How did people find out?"

"Well, it's like this. They 'ad a girl there and they told 'er she could go 'ome and spend the night with her mother, but she wasn't to be back later than eight o'clock in the morning. Well, when she come back she couldn't get in. She knocked and she rung but nobody answered, and so she went in next door and asked the lady there what she'd better do, and the lady said she'd better go to the police station. The sergeant come back with 'er and 'e knocked and 'e rung, but 'e couldn't get no answer. Then he asked the girl 'ad they paid 'er 'er wages, and she said no, not for three months, and then 'e said, you take my word for it, they've shot the moon, that's what they've done. An' when they come to get inside they found they'd took all their clothes, an' their books—they say as Ted Driffield 'ad a rare lot of books—an' every blessed thing that belonged to them."

"And has nothing been heard of them since?"

"Well, not exactly, but when they'd been gone about a week the girl got a letter from London, and when she opened it there was no letter or anything, but just a postal order for 'er wages. An' if you ask me, I call that very 'andsome not to do a poor girl out of her wages."

I was much more shocked than Mary-Ann. I was a very respectable youth. The reader cannot have failed to observe that I accepted the conventions of my class as if they were the laws of Nature, and though debts on the grand scale in books had seemed to me romantic, and duns and money-lenders were familiar figures to my fancy, I could not but think it mean and paltry not to pay the tradesmen's books. I listened with confusion when people talked in my presence of the Driffields, and when they spoke of them as my friends I said: "Hang it all, I just knew them"; and when they asked: "Weren't they fearfully common?" I said: "Well, after all they didn't exactly suggest the Vere de Veres, you know." Poor Mr. Galloway was dreadfully upset.

"Of course I didn't think they were wealthy," he told me, "but I thought they had enough to get along. The house was very nicely furnished and the piano was new. It never struck me that they hadn't paid for a single thing. They never stinted themselves. What hurts me is the deceit. I used to see quite a lot of them and I thought they liked me.

They always made one welcome. You'd hardly believe it, but the last time I saw them when they shook hands with me Mrs. Driffield asked me to come next day and Driffield said: 'Muffins for tea tomorrow.' And all the time they had everything packed upstairs and that very night they took the last train to London."

"What does Lord George say about it?"

"To tell you the truth I haven't gone out of my way to see him lately. It's been a lesson to me. There's a little proverb about evil communications which I've thought well to bear in mind."

I felt very much the same about Lord George, and I was a little nervous, too. If he took it into his head to tell people that at Christmas I had been going to see the Driffields almost every day, and it came to my uncle's ears, I foresaw an unpleasant fuss. My uncle would accuse me of deceit and prevarication and disobedience and of not behaving like a gentleman, and I did not at the moment see what answer I could make. I knew him well enough to be aware that he would not let the matter drop, and that I should be reminded of my transgression for years. I was just as glad not to see Lord George. But one day I ran into him face to face in the High Street.

"Hullo, youngster," he cried, addressing me in a way I particularly resented. "Back for the holidays, I suppose."

"You suppose quite correctly," I answered with what I thought withering sarcasm.

Unfortunately he only bellowed with laughter.

"You're so sharp you'll cut yourself if you don't look out," he answered heartily. "Well, it looks as if there was no more whist for you and me just yet. Now you see what comes of living beyond your means. What I always say to my boys is, if you've got a pound and you spend nineteen and six you're a rich man, but if you spend twenty shillings and sixpence you're a pauper. Look after the pence, young fellow, and the pounds'll look after themselves."

But though he spoke after this fashion there was in his voice no note of disapproval, but a bubble of laughter as though in his heart he were tittering at these admirable maxims.

"They say you helped them to bunk," I remarked.

"Me?" His face assumed a look of extreme surprise, but his eyes glittered with sly mirth. "Why, when they came and told me the Driffields had shot the moon you could have knocked me down with a feather. They owed me four pounds seventeen and six for coal. We've all been let in, even poor old Galloway, who never got his muffins for tea."

I had never thought Lord George more blatant. I should have liked to say something final and crushing, but as I could not think of anything I just said that I must be getting along and with a curt nod left him.

XI

MUSING thus over the past, while I waited for Alroy Kear, I chuckled when I considered this shabby incident of Edward Driffield's obscurity in the light of the immense respectability of his later years. I wondered whether it was because, in my boyhood, he was as a writer held in such small esteem by the people about me that I had never been able to see in him the astonishing merit that the best critical opinion eventually ascribed to him. He was for long thought to write very bad English, and indeed he gave you the impression of writing with the stub of a blunt pencil; his style was laboured, an uneasy mixture of the classical and the slangy, and his dialogue was such as could never have issued from the mouth of a human being. Toward the end of his career, when he dictated his books, his style, acquiring a conversational ease, became flowing and limpid; and then the critics, going back to the novels of his maturity, found that their English had a nervous, racy vigour that eminently suited the matter. His prime belonged to a period when the purple patch was in vogue and there are descriptive passages in his works that have found their way into all the anthologies of English prose. His pieces on the sea, and spring in the Kentish woods, and sunset on the lower reaches of the Thames are famous. It should be a mortification to me that I cannot read them without discomfort.

When I was a young man, though his books sold but little and one or two were banned by the libraries, it was very much a mark of culture to admire them. He was thought boldly realistic. He was a very good stick to beat the Philistines with. Somebody's lucky inspiration discovered that his sailors and peasants were Shakespearian, and when the advanced got together they uttered shrill cries of ecstasy over the dry and spicy humour of his yokels. This was a commodity that Edward Driffield had no difficulty in supplying. My own heart sank when he led me into the forecastle of a sailing ship or the taproom of a public house and I knew I was in for half a dozen pages in dialect of facetious comment on life, ethics, and immortality. But, I admit, I have always thought the Shakespearian clowns tedious and their innumerable progeny insupportable.

Driffield's strength lay evidently in his depiction of the class he knew best, farmers and farm labourers, shopkeepers and bartenders, skippers of sailing ships, mates, cooks, and able seamen. When he introduces characters belonging to a higher station in life even his warmest admirers, one would have thought, must experience a certain malaise; his fine gentlemen are so incredibly fine, his high-born ladies are so good, so pure, so noble that you are not surprised that they can only express themselves with polysyllabic dignity. His women difficultly come to life. But here again I must add that this is only my own opinion; the world at large and the most eminent critics have agreed that they are very winsome types of English womanhood, spirited, gallant, high-souled, and they have been often compared with the heroines of Shakespeare. We know of course that women are habitually constipated, but to represent them in fiction as being altogether devoid of a back passage seems to me really an excess of chivalry. I am surprised that they care to see themselves thus limned.

The critics can force the world to pay attention to a very indifferent writer, and the world may lose its head over one who has no merit at all, but the result in neither case is lasting; and I cannot help thinking that no writer can hold the public for as long as Edward Driffield without considerable gifts. The elect sneer at popularity; they are inclined even to assert that it is a proof of mediocrity; but they forget that posterity makes its choice not from among the unknown writers of a period, but from among the known. It may be that some great masterpiece which deserves immortality has fallen still-born from the press, but posterity will never hear of it; it may be that posterity will scrap all the best-sellers of our day, but it is among them that it must choose. At all events Edward Driffield is in the running. His novels happen to bore me; I find them long; the melodramatic incidents with which he sought to stir the sluggish reader's interest leave me cold; but he certainly had sincerity. There is in his best books the stir of life, and in none of them can you fail to be aware of the author's enigmatic personality. In his earlier days he was praised or blamed for his realism; according to the idiosyncracy of his critics he was extolled for his truth or censured for his coarseness. But realism has ceased to excite remark, and the library reader will take in his stride obstacles at which a generation back he would have violently shied. The cultured reader of these pages will remember the leading article in the Literary Supplement of the *Times* which appeared at the moment of Driffield's death. Taking the novels of Edward Driffield as his text, the author wrote what was very well described as a hymn to beauty. No one who read it could fail to be impressed by those swelling periods, which reminded one of the noble prose of Jeremy Taylor, by that reverence and piety, by all those high sentiments, in short, expressed in a style that was ornate without excess and dulcet without effeminacy. It was itself a thing of beauty. If some suggested that Edward Driffield was by way of being a humorist and that a jest would here and there have lightened this eulogious article it must be replied that after all it was a funeral oration. And it is well known that Beauty does not look with a good grace on the timid advances of Humour. Roy Kear, when he was talking to me of Driffield, claimed that, whatever his faults, they were redeemed by the beauty that suffused his pages. Now I come to look back on our conversation, I think it was this remark that had most exasperated me.

Thirty years ago in literary circles God was all the fashion. It was good form to believe and journalists used him to adorn a phrase or balance a sentence; then God went out (oddly enough with cricket and beer) and Pan came in. In a hundred novels his cloven hoof left its imprint on the sward; poets saw him lurking in the twilight on Lon-

don commons, and literary ladies in Surrey and New England, nymphs
of an industrial age, mysteriously surrendered their virginity to his
rough embrace. Spiritually they were never the same again. But Pan
went out and now beauty has taken his place. People find it in a phrase,
or a turbot, a dog, a day, a picture, an action, a dress. Young women in
cohorts, each of whom has written so promising and competent a novel,
prattle of it in every manner from allusive to arch, from intense to
charming; and the young men, more or less recently down from Oxford,
but still trailing its clouds of glory, who tell us in the weekly papers what
we should think of art, life, and the universe, fling the word with a
pretty negligence about their close-packed pages. It is sadly frayed.
Gosh, they have worked it hard! The ideal has many names and beauty
is but one of them. I wonder if this clamour is anything more than the
cry of distress of those who cannot make themselves at home in our
heroic world of machines, and I wonder if their passion for beauty,
the Little Nell of this shamefaced day, is anything more than sentimentality. It may be that another generation, accommodating itself
more adequately to the stress of life, will look for inspiration not in a
flight from reality, but in an eager acceptance of it.

I do not know if others are like myself, but I am conscious that I
cannot contemplate beauty long. For me no poet made a falser statement than Keats when he wrote the first line of "Endymion." When
the thing of beauty has given me the magic of its sensation my mind
quickly wanders; I listen with incredulity to the persons who tell me
that they can look with rapture for hours at a view or a picture. Beauty
is an ecstasy; it is as simple as hunger. There is really nothing to be said
about it. It is like the perfume of a rose: you can smell it and that is all:
that is why the criticism of art, except in so far as it is unconcerned
with beauty and therefore with art, is tiresome. All the critic can tell
you with regard to Titian's *Entombment of Christ,* perhaps of all the
pictures in the world that which has most pure beauty, is to go and
look at it. What else he has to say is history, or biography, or what not.
But people add other qualities to beauty—sublimity, human interest,
tenderness, love—because beauty does not long content them. Beauty is
perfect, and perfection (such is human nature) holds our attention but

for a little while. The mathematician who after seeing *Phèdre* asked: "*Qu'est-ce que ça prouve?*" was not such a fool as he has been generally made out. No one has ever been able to explain why the Doric temple of Pæstum is more beautiful than a glass of cold beer except by bringing in considerations that have nothing to do with beauty. Beauty is a blind alley. It is a mountain peak which once reached leads nowhere. That is why in the end we find more to entrance us in El Greco than in Titian, in the incomplete achievement of Shakespeare than in the consummate success of Racine. Too much has been written about beauty. That is why I have written a little more. Beauty is that which satisfies the æsthetic instinct. But who wants to be satisfied? It is only to the dullard that enough is as good as a feast. Let us face it: beauty is a bit of a bore.

But of course what the critics wrote about Edward Driffield was eyewash. His outstanding merit was not the realism that gave vigour to his work, nor the beauty that informed it, nor his graphic portraits of seafaring men, nor his poetic descriptions of salty marshes, of storm and calm and of nestling hamlets; it was his longevity. Reverence for old age is one of the most admirable traits of the human race and I think it may safely be stated that in no other country than ours is this trait more marked. The awe and love with which other nations regard old age is often platonic; but ours is practical. Who but the English would fill Covent Garden to listen to an aged prima donna without a voice? Who but the English would pay to see a dancer so decrepit that he can hardly put one foot before the other and say to one another admiringly in the intervals: "By George, sir, d'you know he's a long way past sixty?" But compared with politicians and writers these are but striplings, and I often think that a *jeune premier* must be of a singularly amiable disposition if it does not make him bitter to consider that when at the age of seventy he must end his career the public man and the author are only at their prime. A man who is a politician at forty is a statesman at three score and ten. It is at this age, when he would be too old to be a clerk or a gardener or a police-court magistrate, that he is ripe to govern a country. This is not so strange when you reflect that from the earliest times the old have rubbed it into the young that they

are wiser than they, and before the young had discovered what nonsense this was they were old too, and it profited them to carry on the
imposture; and besides, no one can have moved in the society of politicians without discovering that (if one may judge by results) it requires
little mental ability to rule a nation. But why writers should be more
esteemed the older they grow, has long perplexed me. At one time I
thought that the praise accorded to authors when they had ceased for
twenty years to write anything of interest was largely due to the fact
that the younger men, having no longer to fear their competition, felt
it safe to extol their merit; and it is well known that to praise someone
whose rivalry you do not dread is often a very good way of putting a
spoke in the wheel of someone whose rivalry you do. But this is to take
a low view of human nature and I would not for the world lay myself
open to a charge of cheap cynicism. After mature consideration I have
come to the conclusion that the real reason for the universal applause
that comforts the declining years of the author who exceeds the common span of man is that intelligent people after the age of thirty read
nothing at all. As they grow older the books they read in their youth
are lit with its glamour and with every year that passes they ascribe
greater merit to the author that wrote them. Of course he must go on;
he must keep in the public eye. It is no good his thinking that it is
enough to write one or two masterpieces; he must provide a pedestal
for them of forty or fifty works of no particular consequence. This
needs time. His production must be such that if he cannot captivate a
reader by his charm he can stun him by his weight.

If, as I think, longevity is genius, few in our time have enjoyed it in
a more conspicuous degree than Edward Driffield. When he was a
young fellow in the sixties (the cultured having had their way with
him and passed him by) his position in the world of letters was only
respectable; the best judges praised him, but with moderation; the
younger men were inclined to be frivolous at his expense. It was agreed
that he had talent, but it never occurred to anyone that he was one of
the glories of English literature. He celebrated his seventieth birthday;
an uneasiness passed over the world of letters, like a ruffling of the

waters when on an Eastern sea a typhoon lurks in the distance, and it grew evident that there had lived among us all these years a great novelist and none of us had suspected it. There was a rush for Driffield's books in the various libraries and a hundred busy pens, in Bloomsbury, in Chelsea, and in other places where men of letters congregate, wrote appreciations, studies, essays, and works, short and chatty or long and intense, on his novels. These were reprinted, in complete editions, in select editions, at a shilling and three and six and five shillings and a guinea. His style was analysed, his philosophy was examined, his technique was dissected. At seventy-five everyone agreed that Edward Driffield had genius. At eighty he was the Grand Old Man of English Letters. This position he held till his death.

Now we look about and think sadly that there is no one to take his place. A few septuagenarians are sitting up and taking notice, and they evidently feel that they could comfortably fill the vacant niche. But it is obvious that they lack something.

Though these recollections have taken so long to narrate they took but a little while to pass through my head. They came to me higgledy-piggledy, an incident and then a scrap of conversation that belonged to a previous time, and I have set them down in order for the convenience of the reader and because I have a neat mind. One thing that surprised me was that even at that far distance I could remember distinctly what people looked like and even the gist of what they said, but only with vagueness what they wore. I knew of course that the dress, especially of women, was quite different forty years ago from what it was now, but if I recalled it at all it was not from life but from pictures and photographs that I had seen much later.

I was still occupied with my idle fancies when I heard a taxi stop at the door, the bell ring, and in a moment Alroy Kear's booming voice telling the butler that he had an appointment with me. He came in, big, bluff, and hearty; his vitality shattered with a single gesture the frail construction I had been building out of the vanished past. He brought in with him, like a blustering wind in March, the aggressive and inescapable present.

"I was just asking myself," I said, "who could possibly succeed Edward Driffield as the Grand Old Man of English Letters and you arrive to answer my question."

He broke into a jovial laugh, but into his eyes came a quick look of suspicion.

"I don't think there's anybody," he said.

"How about yourself?"

"Oh, my dear boy, I'm not fifty yet. Give me another twenty-five years." He laughed, but his eyes held mine keenly. "I never know when you're pulling my leg." He looked down suddenly. "Of course one can't help thinking about the future sometimes. All the people who are at the top of the tree now are anything from fifteen to twenty years older than me. They can't last for ever, and when they're gone who is there? Of course there's Aldous; he's a good deal younger than me, but he's not very strong and I don't believe he takes great care of himself. Barring accidents, by which I mean barring some genius who suddenly springs up and sweeps the board, I don't quite see how in another twenty or twenty-five years I can help having the field pretty well to myself. It's just a question of pegging away and living on longer than the others."

Roy sank his virile bulk into one of my landlady's armchairs and I offered him a whisky and soda.

"No, I never drink spirits before six o'clock," he said. He looked about him. "Jolly, these digs are."

"I know. What have you come to see me about?"

"I thought I'd better have a little chat with you about Mrs. Driffield's invitation. It was rather difficult to explain over the telephone. The truth of the matter is that I've arranged to write Driffield's life."

"Oh! Why didn't you tell me the other day?"

I felt friendly disposed toward Roy. I was happy to think that I had not misjudged him when I suspected that it was not merely for the pleasure of my company that he had asked me to luncheon.

"I hadn't entirely made up my mind. Mrs. Driffield is very keen on my doing it. She's going to help me in every way she can. She's giving me all the material she has. She's been collecting it for a good many years. It's not an easy thing to do and of course I can't afford not to do it well. But if I can make a pretty good job of it, it can't fail to do me a lot of good. People have so much more respect for a novelist if he writes something serious now and then. Those critical works of mine were an awful sweat, and they sold nothing, but I don't regret them for a moment. They've given me a position I could never have got without them."

"I think it's a very good plan. You've known Driffield more intimately than most people for the last twenty years."

"I think I have. But of course he was over sixty when I first made his acquaintance. I wrote and told him how much I admired his books and he asked me to go and see him. But I know nothing about the early part of his life. Mrs. Driffield used to try to get him to talk about those days and she made very copious notes of all he said, and then there are diaries that he kept now and then, and of course a lot of the stuff in the novels is obviously autobiographical. But there are immense lacunæ. I'll tell you the sort of book I want to write, a sort of intimate life, with a lot of those little details that make people feel warm inside, you know, and then woven in with this a really exhaustive criticism of his literary work, not ponderous, of course, but although sympathetic, searching and . . . subtle. Naturally it wants doing, but Mrs. Driffield seems to think I can do it."

"I'm sure you can," I put in.

"I don't see why not," said Roy. "I am a critic, and I'm a novelist. It's obvious that I have certain literary qualifications. But I can't do anything unless everyone who can is willing to help me."

I began to see where I came in. I tried to make my face look quite blank. Roy leaned forward.

"I asked you the other day if you were going to write anything about Driffield yourself and you said you weren't. Can I take that as definite?"

"Certainly."

"Then have you got any objection to giving me your material?"

"My dear boy, I haven't got any."

"Oh, that's nonsense," said Roy good-humouredly, with the tone of a doctor who is trying to persuade a child to have its throat examined. "When he was living at Blackstable you must have seen a lot of him."

"I was only a boy then."

"But you must have been conscious of the unusual experience. After all, no one could be for half an hour in Edward Driffield's society without being impressed by his extraordinary personality. It must have been obvious even to a boy of sixteen, and you were probably more observant and sensitive than the average boy of that age."

"I wonder if his personality would have seemed extraordinary without the reputation to back it up. Do you imagine that if you went down to a spa in the west of England as Mr. Atkins, a chartered accountant taking the waters for his liver, you would impress the people you met there as a man of immense character?"

"I imagine they'd soon realize that I was not quite the common or garden chartered accountant," said Roy, with a smile that took from his remark any appearance of self-esteem.

"Well, all I can tell you is that what chiefly bothered me about Driffield in those days was that the knickerbocker suit he wore was dreadfully loud. We used to bicycle a lot together and it always made me feel a trifle uncomfortable to be seen with him."

"It sounds comic now. What did he talk about?"

"I don't know; nothing very much. He was rather keen on architecture, and he talked about farming, and if a pub looked nice he generally suggested stopping for five minutes and having a glass of bitter, and then he would talk to the landlord about the crops and the price of coal and things like that."

I rambled on, though I could see by the look of Roy's face that he was disappointed with me; he listened, but he was a trifle bored, and it struck me that when he was bored he looked peevish. But though I couldn't remember that Driffield had ever said anything significant during those long rides of ours, I had a very acute recollection of the *feel* of them. Blackstable was peculiar in this, that though it was on the sea, with a long shingly beach and marshland at the back, you had only to go about half a mile inland to come into the most rural country in Kent. Winding roads that ran between the great fat green fields and clumps of huge elms, substantial and with a homely stateliness like good old Kentish farmers' wives, high-coloured and robust, who had grown portly on good butter and home-made bread and cream and fresh eggs. And sometimes the road was only a lane, with thick hawthorn hedges, and the green elms overhung it on either side so that when you looked up there was only a strip of blue sky between. And as you rode along in the warm, keen air you had a sensation that the world was standing still and life would last for ever. Although you were pedalling with such energy you had a delicious feeling of laziness. You were quite happy when no one spoke, and if one of the party from sheer high spirits suddenly put on speed and shot ahead it was a joke that everyone laughed at and for a few minutes you pedalled as hard as you could. And we chaffed one another innocently and giggled at our own humour. Now and then one would pass cottages with little gardens in front of them and in the gardens were hollyhocks and tiger lilies; and a little way from the road were farmhouses, with their spacious barns and oasthouses; and one would pass through hopfields with the ripening hops hanging in garlands. The public houses were friendly and informal, hardly more important than cottages, and on the porches often honeysuckle would be growing. The names they bore were usual and familiar: the Jolly Sailor, the Merry Ploughman, the Crown and Anchor, the Red Lion.

But of course all that could matter nothing to Roy, and he interrupted me.

"Did he never talk of literature?" he asked.

"I don't think so. He wasn't that sort of writer. I suppose he thought about his writing, but he never mentioned it. He used to lend the curate books. In the winter, one Christmas holidays, I used to have tea at his house nearly every day and sometimes the curate and he would talk about books, but we used to shut them up."

"Don't you remember anything he said?"

"Only one thing. I remember it because I hadn't ever read the things he was talking about and what he said made me do so. He said that when Shakespeare retired to Stratford-on-Avon and became respectable, if he ever thought of his plays at all, probably the two that he remembered with most interest were *Measure for Measure* and *Troilus and Cressida.*"

"I don't think that's very illuminating. Didn't he say anything about anyone more modern than Shakespeare?"

"Well, not then, that I can remember; but when I was lunching with the Driffields a few years ago I overheard him saying that Henry James had turned his back on one of the great events of the world's history, the rise of the United States, in order to report tittle-tattle at tea parties in English country houses. Driffield called it *il gran rifiuto*. I was surprised at hearing the old man use an Italian phrase and amused because a great big bouncing duchess who was there was the only person who knew what the devil he was talking about. He said: 'Poor Henry, he's spending eternity wandering round and round a stately park and the fence is just too high for him to peep over and they're having tea just too far for him to hear what the countess is saying.'"

Roy listened to my little anecdote with attention. He shook his head reflectively.

"I don't think I could use that. I'd have the Henry James gang down on me like a thousand of bricks. . . . But what used you to do during those evenings?"

"Well, we played whist while Driffield read books for review, and he used to sing."

"That's interesting," said Roy, leaning forward eagerly. "Do you remember what he sang?"

"Perfectly. 'All Through Stickin' to a Soljer' and 'Come Where the Booze Is Cheaper' were his favourites."

"Oh!"

I could see that Roy was disappointed.

"Did you expect him to sing Schumann?" I asked.

"I don't know why not. It would have been rather a good point. But I think I should have expected him to sing sea chanties or old English country airs, you know, the sort of thing they used to sing at fairings—blind fiddlers and the village swains dancing with the girls on the threshing floor and all that sort of thing. I might have made something rather beautiful out of that, but I can't *see* Edward Driffield singing music-hall songs. After all, when you're drawing a man's portrait you must get the values right; you only confuse the impression if you put in stuff that's all out of tone."

"You know that shortly after this he shot the moon. He let everybody in."

Roy was silent for fully a minute and he looked down at the carpet reflectively.

"Yes, I knew there'd been some unpleasantness. Mrs. Driffield mentioned it. I understand everything was paid up later before he finally bought Ferne Court and settled down in the district. I don't think it's necessary to dwell on an incident that is not really of any importance in the history of his development. After all, it happened nearly forty years ago. You know, there were some very curious sides to the old man. One would have thought that after a rather sordid little scandal like that the neighbourhood of Blackstable would be the last place he'd choose to spend the rest of his life in when he'd become celebrated, especially when it was the scene of his rather humble origins; but he didn't seem to mind a bit. He seemed to think the whole thing rather a good joke. He was quite capable of telling people who came to lunch about it and it was very embarrassing for Mrs. Driffield. I should like you to know Amy better. She's a very remarkable woman. Of course the old man had written all his great books before he ever set eyes on her, but I don't think anyone can deny that it was she who created the rather imposing and dignified figure that the world saw for the last twenty-five years of his life. She's been very frank with me. She didn't have such an easy job of it. Old Driffield had some very queer ways and she had to use a good deal of tact to get him to behave decently. He was very obstinate in some things and I think a woman of less character would have been discouraged. For instance, he had a habit that poor Amy had a lot of trouble to break him of: after he'd finished his meat and vegetables he'd take a piece of bread and wipe the plate clean with it and eat it."

"Do you know what that means?" I said. "It means that for long he had so little to eat that he couldn't afford to waste any food he could get."

"Well, that may be, but it's not a very pretty habit for a distinguished man of letters. And then, he didn't exactly tipple, but he was rather fond of going down to the Bear and Key at Blackstable and having a few beers in the public bar. Of course there was no harm in it, but it did make him rather conspicuous, especially in summer when the place was full of trippers. He didn't mind who he talked to. He didn't seem able to realize that he had a position to keep up. You can't deny it was rather awkward after they'd been having a lot of interesting people to lunch—people like Edmund Gosse, for instance, and Lord Curzon—that he should go down to a public house and tell the plumber and the baker and the sanitary inspector what he thought about them. But of course that could be explained away. One could say that he was after local colour and was interested in types. But he had some habits that really were rather difficult to cope with. Do you know that it was with the greatest difficulty that Amy Driffield could ever get him to take a bath?"

"He was born at a time when people thought it unhealthy to take too many baths. I don't suppose he ever lived in a house that had a bathroom till he was fifty."

"Well, he said he never had had a bath more than once a week and he didn't see why he should change his habits at his time of life. Then Amy said that he must change his under linen every day, but he objected to that too. He said he'd always been used to wearing his vest and drawers for a week and it was nonsense, it only wore them out to have them washed so often. Mrs. Driffield did everything she could to tempt him to have a bath every day, with bath salts and perfumes, you know, but nothing would induce him to, and as he grew older he wouldn't even have one once a week. She tells me that for the last three years of his life he never had a bath at all. Of course, all this is between ourselves; I'm merely telling it to show you that in writing his life I shall have to use a good deal of tact. I don't see how one can deny that he was just a wee bit unscrupulous in money matters and he had a kink in him that made him take a strange pleasure in the society of his inferiors and some of his personal habits were rather disagreeable, but I don't think that side of him was the most significant. I don't want to say anything that's untrue, but I do think there's a certain amount that's better left unsaid."

"Don't you think it would be more interesting if you went the whole hog and drew him warts and all?"

"Oh, I couldn't. Amy Driffield would never speak to me again. She only asked me to do the life because she felt she could trust my discretion. I must behave like a gentleman."

"It's very hard to be a gentleman and a writer."

"I don't see why. And besides, you know what the critics are. If you tell the truth they only say you're cynical and it does an author no good to get a reputation for cynicism. Of course I don't deny that if I were thoroughly unscrupulous I could make a sensation. It would be rather amusing to show the man with his passion for beauty and his careless treatment of his obligations, his fine style and his personal hatred for soap and water, his idealism and his tippling in disreputable pubs; but honestly, would it pay? They'd only say I was imitating Lytton Strachey. No, I think I shall do much better to be allusive and charming and rather subtle, you know the sort of thing, and tender. I think one ought always to *see* a book before one starts it. Well, I see this rather like a portrait of Van Dyck, with a good deal of atmosphere, you know, and a certain gravity, and with a sort of aristocratic distinction. Do you know what I mean? About eighty thousand words."

He was absorbed for a moment in the ecstasy of æsthetic contemplation. In his mind's eye he saw a book, in royal octavo, slim and light in the hand, printed with large margins on handsome paper in a type that was both clear and comely, and I think he saw a binding in smooth black cloth with a decoration in gold and gilt lettering. But being human, Alroy Kear could not, as I suggested a few pages back, hold the ecstasy that beauty yields for more than a little while. He gave me a candid smile.

"But how the devil am I to get over the first Mrs. Driffield?"

"The skeleton in the cupboard," I murmured.

"She is damned awkward to deal with. She was married to Driffield for a good many years. Amy has very decided views on the subject, but I don't see how I can possibly meet them. You see, her attitude is that Rose Driffield exerted a most pernicious influence on her husband, and that she did everything possible to ruin him morally, physically, and financially; she was beneath him in every way, at least intellectually and spiritually, and it was only because he was a man of immense force and vitality that he survived. It was of course a very unfortunate marriage. It's true that she's been dead for ages and it seems a pity to rake up old scandals and wash a lot of dirty linen in public; but the fact remains that all Driffield's greatest books were written when he was living with her. Much as I admire the later books, and no one is more conscious of their genuine beauty than I am, and they have a restraint and a sort of classical sobriety which are admirable, I must admit that they haven't the tang and the vigour and the smell and bustle of life of the early ones. It does seem to me that you can't altogether ignore the influence his first wife had on his work."

"What are you going to do about it?" I asked.

"Well, I can't see why all that part of his life shouldn't be treated with the greatest possible reserve and delicacy, so as not to offend the most exacting susceptibility, and yet with a sort of manly frankness, if you understand what I mean, that would be rather moving."

"It sounds a very tall order."

"As I see it, there's no need to dot the i's or to cross the t's. It can only be a question of getting just the right touch. I wouldn't state more than I could help, but I would suggest what was essential for the reader to realize. You know, however gross a subject is you can soften its unpleasantness if you treat it with dignity. But I can do nothing unless I am in complete possession of the facts."

"Obviously you can't cook them unless you have them."

Roy had been expressing himself with a fluent ease that revealed the successful lecturer. I wished (a) that I could express myself with so much force and aptness, never at a loss for a word, rolling off the sentences without a moment's hesitation; and (b) that I did not feel so miserably incompetent with my one small insignificant person to represent the large and appreciative audience that Roy was instinctively addressing. But now he paused. A genial look came over his face, which his enthusiasm had reddened and the heat of the day caused to perspire, and the eyes that had held me with a dominating brilliance softened and smiled.

"This is where you come in, old boy," he said pleasantly.

I have always found it a very good plan in life to say nothing when I had nothing to say and when I do not know how to answer a remark to hold my tongue. I remained silent and looked back at Roy amiably.

"You know more about his life at Blackstable than anybody else."

"I don't know about that. There must be a number of people at Blackstable who saw as much of him in the old days as I did."

"That may be, but after all they're presumably not people of any importance, and I don't think they matter very much."

"Oh, I see. You mean that I'm the only person who might blow the gaff."

"Roughly, that is what I do mean, if you feel that you must put it in a facetious way."

I saw that Roy was not inclined to be amused. I was not annoyed, for I am quite used to people not being amused at my jokes. I often think that the purest type of the artist is the humorist who laughs alone at his own jests.

"And you saw a good deal of him later on in London, I believe."

"Yes."

"That is when he had an apartment somewhere in Lower Belgravia."

"Well, lodgings in Pimlico."

Roy smiled dryly.

"We won't quarrel about the exact designation of the quarter of London in which he lived. You were very intimate with him then."

"Fairly."

"How long did that last?"

"About a couple of years."

"How old were you then?"

"Twenty."

"Now look here, I want you to do me a great favour. It won't take you very long and it will be of quite inestimable value to me. I want you to jot down as fully as you can all your recollections of Driffield, and all you remember about his wife and his relations with her and so on, both at Blackstable and in London."

"Oh, my dear fellow, that's asking a great deal. I've got a lot of work to do just now."

"It needn't take you very long. You can write it quite roughly, I mean. You needn't bother about style, you know, or anything like that. I'll put the style in. All I want are the facts. After all, you know them and nobody else does. I don't want to be pompous or anything like that, but Driffield was a great man and you owe it to his memory and to English literature to tell everything you know. I shouldn't have asked you, but you told me the other day that you weren't going to write anything about him yourself. It would be rather like a dog in a manger to keep to yourself a whole lot of material that you have no intention of using."

Thus Roy appealed at once to my sense of duty, my indolence, my generosity, and my rectitude.

"But why does Mrs. Driffield want me to go down and stay at Ferne Court?" I asked.

"Well, we talked it over. It's a very jolly house to stay in. She does one very well, and it ought to be divine in the country just now. She thought it would be very nice and quiet for you if you felt inclined to write your recollections there; of course, I said I couldn't promise that, but naturally being so near Blackstable would remind you of all sorts of things that you might otherwise forget. And then, living in his house, among his books and things, it would make the past seem much more real. We could all talk about him, and you know how in the heat of conversation things come back. Amy's very quick and clever. She's been in the habit of making notes of Driffield's talk for years, and after all it's quite likely that you'll say things on the spur of the moment that you wouldn't think of writing and she can just jot them down afterward. And we can play tennis and bathe."

"I'm not very fond of staying with people," I said. "I hate getting up for a nine-o'clock breakfast to eat things I have no mind to. I don't like going for walks, and I'm not interested in other people's chickens."

"She's a lonely woman now. It would be a kindness to her and it would be a kindness to me too."

I reflected.

"I'll tell you what I'll do: I'll go down to Blackstable, but I'll go down on my own. I'll put up at the Bear and Key and I'll come over and see Mrs. Driffield while you're there. You can both talk your heads off about Edward Driffield, but I shall be able to get away when I'm fed up with you."

Roy laughed good-naturedly.

"All right. That'll do. And will you jot down anything you can remember that you think will be useful to me?"

"I'll try."

"When will you come? I'm going down on Friday."

"I'll come with you if you'll promise not to talk to me in the train."

"All right. The five-ten's the best one. Shall I come and fetch you?"

"I'm capable of getting to Victoria by myself. I'll meet you on the platform."

I don't know if Roy was afraid of my changing my mind, but he got up at once, shook my hand heartily, and left. He begged me on no account to forget my tennis racket and bathing suit.

XII

My promise to Roy sent my thoughts back to my first years in London. Having nothing much to do that afternoon, it occurred to me to stroll along and have a cup of tea with my old landlady. Mrs. Hudson's name had been given to me by the secretary of the medical school at St. Luke's when, a callow youth just arrived in town, I was looking for lodgings. She had a house in Vincent Square. I lived there for five years, in two rooms on the ground floor, and over me on the drawing-room floor lived a master at Westminster School. I paid a pound a week for my rooms and he paid twenty-five shillings. Mrs. Hudson was a little, active, bustling woman, with a sallow face, a large aquiline nose, and the brightest, the most vivacious, black eyes that I ever saw.

She had a great deal of very dark hair, in the afternoons and all day on Sunday arranged in a fringe on the forehead with a bun at the nape of the neck as you may see in old photographs of the Jersey Lily. She had a heart of gold (though I did not know it then, for when you are young you take the kindness people show you as your right) and she was an excellent cook. No one could make a better *omelette soufflée* than she. Every morning she was up betimes to get the fire lit in her gentlemen's sitting room so that they needn't eat their breakfasts simply perishin' with the cold, my word it's bitter this morning; and if she didn't hear you having your bath, a flat tin bath that slipped under the bed, the water put in the night before to take the chill off, she'd say: "There now, there's my dining-room floor not up yet, 'e'll be late for his lecture again," and she would come tripping upstairs and thump on the door and you would hear her shrill voice: "If you don't get up at once you won't 'ave time to 'ave breakfast, an' I've got a lovely 'addick for you." She worked all day long and she sang at her work and she was gay and happy and smiling. Her husband was much older than she. He had been a butler in very good families, and wore side-whiskers and a perfect manner; he was verger at a neighbouring church, highly respected, and he waited at table and cleaned the boots and helped with the washing-up. Mrs. Hudson's only relaxation was to come up after she had served the dinners (I had mine at half-past six and the schoolmaster at seven) and have a little chat with her gentlemen. I wish to goodness I had had the sense (like Amy Driffield with her celebrated husband) to take notes of her conversation, for Mrs. Hudson was a mistress of Cockney humour. She had a gift of repartee that never failed her, she had a racy style and an apt and varied vocabulary, she was never at a loss for the comic metaphor or the vivid phrase. She was a pattern of propriety and she would never have women in her house, you never knew what they were up to ("It's men, men, men all the time with them, and afternoon tea and thin bread and butter, and openin' the door and ringin' for 'ot water and I don't know what all"); but in conversation she did not hesitate to use what was called in those days the blue bag. One could have said of her what she said of Marie Lloyd: "What I like about 'er is that she gives you a good laugh. She goes pretty near the knuckle sometimes, but she never jumps over the fence." Mrs. Hudson enjoyed her own humour and I think she talked more willingly to her lodgers because her husband was a serious man ("It's as it should be," she said, " 'im bein' a verger and attendin' weddings and funerals and what all") and wasn't much of a one for a joke. "Wot I says to 'Udson is, laugh while you've got the chance, you won't laugh much when you're dead and buried."

Mrs. Hudson's humour was cumulative and the story of her feud with Miss Butcher who let lodgings at number fourteen was a great comic saga that went on year in and year out.

"She's a disagreeable old cat, but I give you my word I'd miss 'er if the Lord took 'er one fine day. Though what 'e'd do with 'er when 'e got 'er I can't think. Many's the good laugh she's give me in 'er time."

Mrs. Hudson had very bad teeth and the question whether she should have them taken out and have false ones was discussed by her two or three years with an unimaginable variety of comic invention.

"But as I said to 'Udson on'y last night, when he said: 'Oh, come on, 'ave 'em out and 'ave done with it,' I shouldn't 'ave anythin' to talk about."

I had not seen Mrs. Hudson for two or three years. My last visit had been in answer to a little letter in which she asked me to come and drink a nice strong cup of tea with her and announced: "Hudson died three months ago next Saturday, aged seventy-nine, and George and Hester send their respectful compliments." George was the issue of her marriage with Hudson. He was now a man approaching middle age who worked at Woolwich Arsenal, and his mother had been repeating for twenty years that George would be bringing a wife home one of these days. Hester was the maid-of-all-work she had engaged toward the end of my stay with her, and Mrs. Hudson still spoke of her as "that dratted girl of mine." Though Mrs. Hudson must have been well over thirty when I first took her rooms, and that was five-and-thirty years ago, I had no feeling as I walked leisurely through the Green Park that I should not find her alive. She was as definitely part of the recollections of my youth as the pelicans that stood at the edge of the ornamental water.

I walked down the area steps and the door was opened to me by Hester, a woman getting on for fifty now and stoutish, but still bearing on her shyly grinning face the irresponsibility of the dratted girl. Mrs. Hudson was darning George's socks when I was shown into the front room of the basement and she took off her spectacles to look at me.

"Well, if that isn't Mr. Ashenden! Who ever thought of seeing you? Is the water boiling, 'Ester? You will 'ave a nice cup of tea, won't you?"

Mrs. Hudson was a little heavier than when I first knew her and her movements were more deliberate, but there was scarcely a white hair on her head, and her eyes, as black and shining as buttons, sparkled with fun. I sat down in a shabby little armchair covered with maroon leather.

"How are you getting on, Mrs. Hudson?" I asked.

"Oh, I've got nothin' much to complain of except that I'm not so young as I used to was," she answered. "I can't do so much as I could when you was 'ere. I don't give my gentlemen dinner now, only break-fast."

"Are all your rooms let?"

"Yes, I'm thankful to say."

Owing to the rise of prices Mrs. Hudson was able to get more for her rooms than in my day, and I think in her modest way she was quite well off. But of course people wanted a lot nowadays.

"You wouldn't believe it, first I 'ad to put in a bathroom, and then I 'ad to put in the electric light, and then nothin' would satisfy them but I must 'ave a telephone. What they'll want next I can't think."

"Mr. George says it's pretty near time Mrs. 'Udson thought of retir-ing," said Hester, who was laying the tea.

"You mind your own business, my girl," said Mrs. Hudson tartly. "When I retire it'll be to the cemetery. Fancy me livin' all alone with George and 'Ester without nobody to talk to."

"Mr. George says she ought to take a little 'ouse in the country an' take care of 'erself," said Hester, unperturbed by the reproof.

"Don't talk to me about the country. The doctor said I was to go there for six weeks last summer. It nearly killed me, I give you my word. The noise of it. All them birds singin' all the time, and the cocks crowin' and the cows mooin'. I couldn't stick it. When you've lived all the years I 'ave in peace and quietness you can't get used to all that racket goin' on all the time."

A few doors away was the Vauxhall Bridge Road and down it trams were clanging, ringing their bells as they went, motor buses were lumbering along, taxis were tooting their horns. If Mrs. Hudson heard it, it was London she heard, and it soothed her as a mother's crooning soothes a restless child.

I looked round the cosy, shabby, homely little parlour in which Mrs. Hudson had lived so long. I wondered if there was anything I could do for her. I noticed that she had a gramophone. It was the only thing I could think of.

"Is there anything you want, Mrs. Hudson?" I asked.

She fixed her beady eyes on me reflectively.

"I don't know as there is, now you come to speak of it, except me 'ealth and strength for another twenty years so as I can go on workin'."

I do not think I am a sentimentalist, but her reply, unexpected but so characteristic, made a sudden lump come to my throat.

When it was time for me to go I asked if I could see the rooms I had lived in for five years.

"Run upstairs, 'Ester, and see if Mr. Graham's in. If he ain't, I'm sure 'e wouldn't mind you 'avin' a look at them."

Hester scurried up, and in a moment, slightly breathless, came down again to say that Mr. Graham was out. Mrs. Hudson came with me. The bed was the same narrow iron bed that I had slept in and dreamed in and there was the same chest of drawers and the same washing stand. But the sitting room had the grim heartiness of the athlete; on the walls were photographs of cricket elevens and rowing men in shorts; golf clubs stood in the corner and pipes and tobacco jars, ornamented with the arms of a college, were littered on the chimney-piece. In my day we believed in art for art's sake and this I exemplified by draping the chimney-piece with a Moorish rug, putting up curtains of art serge and a bilious green, and hanging on the walls autotypes of pictures by Perugino, Van Dyck, and Hobbema.

"Very artistic you was, wasn't you?" Mrs. Hudson remarked, not without irony.

"Very," I murmured.

I could not help feeling a pang as I thought of all the years that had passed since I inhabited that room, and of all that had happened to me. It was at that same table that I had eaten my hearty breakfast and my frugal dinner, read my medical books and written my first novel. It was in that same armchair that I had read for the first time Wordsworth and Stendhal, the Elizabethan dramatists and the Russian novelists, Gibbon, Boswell, Voltaire, and Rousseau. I wondered who had used them since. Medical students, articled clerks, young fellows making their way in the city, and elderly men retired from the colonies or thrown unexpectedly upon the world by the break-up of an old home. The room made me, as Mrs. Hudson would have put it, go queer all over. All the hopes that had been cherished there, the bright visions of the future, the flaming passion of youth; the regrets, the disillusion, the weariness, the resignation; so much had been felt in that room, by so many, the whole gamut of human emotion, that it seemed strangely to have acquired a troubling and enigmatic personality of its own. I have no notion why, but it made me think of a woman at a crossroad with a finger on her lips, looking back and with her other hand beckoning. What I obscurely (and rather shamefacedly) felt, communicated itself to Mrs. Hudson, for she gave a laugh and with a characteristic gesture rubbed her prominent nose.

"My word, people are funny," she said. "When I think of all the gentlemen I've 'ad here, I give you my word you wouldn't believe it if I told you some of the things I know about them. One of them's funnier than the other. Sometimes I lie abed thinkin' of them, and *laugh*. Well, it would be a bad world if you didn't get a good laugh now and then, but, lor', lodgers really are the limit."

XIII

I LIVED with Mrs. Hudson for nearly two years before I met the Driffields again. My life was very regular. I spent all day at the hospital and about six walked back to Vincent Square. I bought the *Star* at Lambeth Bridge and read it till my dinner was served. Then I read seriously for an hour or two, works to improve my mind, for I was a strenuous, earnest, and industrious youth, and after that wrote novels and plays till bedtime. I do not know for what reason it was that one day toward the end of June, happening to leave the hospital early, I thought I would walk down the Vauxhall Bridge Road. I liked it for its noisy bustle. It had a sordid vivacity that was pleasantly exciting and you felt that at any moment an adventure might there befall you. I strolled along in a daydream and was surprised suddenly to hear my name. I stopped and looked, and there to my astonishment stood Mrs. Driffield. She was smiling at me.

"Don't you know me?" she cried.

"Yes. Mrs. Driffield."

And though I was grown up I was conscious that I was blushing as furiously as when I was sixteen. I was embarrassed. With my lamentably Victorian notions of honesty I had been much shocked by the Driffields' behaviour in running away from Blackstable without paying their bills. It seemed to me very shabby. I felt deeply the shame I thought they must feel and I was astounded that Mrs. Driffield should speak to someone who knew of the discreditable incident. If I had seen her coming I should have looked away, my delicacy presuming that she would wish to avoid the mortification of being seen by me; but she held out her hand and shook mine with obvious pleasure.

"I am glad to see a Blackstable face," she said. "You know we left there in a hurry."

She laughed and I laughed too; but her laugh was mirthful and childlike, while mine, I felt, was strained.

"I hear there *was* a to-do when they found out we'd skipped. I thought Ted would never stop laughing when he heard about it. What did your uncle say?"

I was quick to get the right tone. I wasn't going to let her think that I couldn't see a joke as well as anyone.

"Oh, you know what he is. He's very old-fashioned."

"Yes, that's what's wrong with Blackstable. They want waking up." She gave me a friendly look. "You've grown a lot since I saw you last. Why, you're growing a moustache."

"Yes," I said, giving it as much of a twirl as its size allowed me. "I've had that for ages."

"How time does fly, doesn't it? You were just a boy four years ago and now you're a man."

"I ought to be," I replied somewhat haughtily. "I'm nearly twenty-one."

I was looking at Mrs. Driffield. She wore a very small hat with feathers in it, and a pale grey dress with large leg-of-mutton sleeves and a long train. I thought she looked very smart. I had always thought that she had a nice face, but I noticed now, for the first time, that she was pretty. Her eyes were bluer than I remembered and her skin was like ivory.

"You know we live just round the corner," she said.

"So do I."

"We live in Limpus Road. We've been there almost ever since we left Blackstable."

"Well, I've been in Vincent Square for nearly two years."

"I knew you were in London. George Kemp told me so, and I often wondered where you were. Why don't you walk back with me now? Ted will be so pleased to see you."

"I don't mind," I said.

As we walked along she told me that Driffield was now literary editor of a weekly paper; his last book had done much better than any of his others and he was expecting to get quite a bit as an advance on royalties for the next one. She seemed to know most of the Blackstable news, and I remembered how it had been suspected that Lord George had helped the Driffields in their flight. I guessed that he wrote to them now and then. I noticed as we walked along that sometimes the men who passed us stared at Mrs. Driffield. It occurred to me presently that they must think her pretty too. I began to walk with a certain swagger.

Limpus Road was a long wide straight street that ran parallel with the Vauxhall Bridge Road. The houses were all alike, of stucco, dingily painted, solid, and with substantial porticoes. I suppose they had been built to be inhabited by men of standing in the city of London, but the street had gone down in the world or had never attracted the right sort of tenant; and its decayed respectability had an air at once furtive and shabbily dissipated, that made you think of persons who had seen better days and now, genteelly fuddled, talked of the social distinction of their youth. The Driffields lived in a house painted a dull red, and Mrs. Driffield, letting me into a narrow dark hall, opened a door and said:

"Go in. I'll tell Ted you're here."

She walked down the hall and I entered the sitting room. The Driffields had the basement and the ground floor of the house, which they rented from the lady who lived in the upper part. The room into which I went looked as if it had been furnished with the scourings of auction sales. There were heavy velvet curtains with great fringes, all loops and festoons, and a gilt suite, upholstered in yellow damask, heavily buttoned; and there was a great pouf in the middle of the room. There were gilt cabinets in which were masses of little articles, pieces of china, ivory figures, wood carvings, bits of Indian brass; and on the walls hung large oil paintings of highland glens and stags and gillies. In a moment Mrs. Driffield brought her husband and he greeted me warmly. He wore a shabby alpaca coat and grey trousers; he had shaved his beard and wore now a moustache and a small imperial. I noticed for the first time how short he was; but he looked more distinguished than he used to. There was something a trifle foreign in his appearance and I thought this was much more what I should expect an author to look like.

"Well, what do you think of our new abode?" he asked. "It looks rich, doesn't it? I think it inspires confidence."

He looked round him with satisfaction.

"And Ted's got his den at the back where he can write, and we've got a dining room in the basement," said Mrs. Driffield. "Miss Cowley was companion for many years to a lady of title and when she died she left her all her furniture. You can see everything's good, can't you? You can see it came out of a gentleman's house."

"Rosie fell in love with the place the moment we saw it," said Driffield.

"You did too, Ted."

"We've lived in sordid circumstances so long; it's a change to be surrounded by luxury. Madame de Pompadour and all that sort of thing."

When I left them it was with a very cordial invitation to come again. It appeared that they were at home every Saturday afternoon and all sorts of people whom I would like to meet were in the habit of dropping in.

XIV

I WENT. I enjoyed myself. I went again. When the autumn came and I returned to London for the winter session at St. Luke's I got into the habit of going every Saturday. It was my introduction into the world of art and letters; I kept it a profound secret that in the privacy of my lodgings I was busily writing; I was excited to meet people who were writing also and I listened entranced to their conversation. All sorts of persons came to these parties: at that time week-ends were rare, golf was still a subject for ridicule, and few had much to do on Saturday afternoons. I do not think anyone came who was of any great importance; at all events, of all the painters, writers, and musicians I met at the Driffields' I cannot remember one whose reputation has endured; but the effect was cultured and animated. You found young actors who were looking for parts and middle-aged singers who deplored the fact that the English were not a musical race, composers who played their compositions on the Driffields' cottage piano and complained in a whispered aside that they sounded nothing except on a concert grand, poets who on pressure consented to read a little thing that they had just written, and painters who were looking for commissions. Now and then a person of title added a certain glamour; seldom, however, for in those days the aristocracy had not yet become bohemian and if a person of quality cultivated the society of artists it was generally because a notorious divorce or a little difficulty over cards had made life in his own station (or hers) a bit awkward. We have changed all that. One of the greatest benefits that compulsory education has conferred upon the world is the wide diffusion among the nobility and gentry of the practice of writing. Horace Walpole once wrote a *Catalogue of Royal and Noble Authors;* such a work now would have the dimensions of an encyclopædia. A title, even a courtesy one, can make a well-known author of almost anyone and it may be safely asserted that there is no better passport to the world of letters than rank.

I have indeed sometimes thought that now that the House of Lords must inevitably in a short while be abolished, it would be a very good plan if the profession of literature were by law confined to its members and their wives and children. It would be a graceful compensation that the British people might offer the peers in return for the surrender of their hereditary privileges. It would be a means of support for those (too many) whom devotion to the public cause in keeping chorus girls and race horses and playing *chemin de fer* has impoverished, and a pleasant occupation for the rest who by the process of natural selection have in the course of time become unfit to do anything but govern the British Empire. But this is an age of specialization and if my plan is adopted it is obvious that it cannot but be to the greater glory of English literature that its various provinces should be apportioned among the various ranks of the nobility. I would suggest, therefore, that the humbler branches of literature should be practised by the lower orders of the peerage and that the barons and viscounts should devote themselves exclusively to journalism and the drama. Fiction might be the privileged demesne of the earls. They have already shown their aptitude for this difficult art and their numbers are so great that they would very competently supply the demand. To the marquises might safely be left the production of that part of literature which is known (I have never quite seen why) as *belles lettres*. It is perhaps not very profitable from a pecuniary standpoint, but it has a distinction that very well suits the holders of this romantic title.

The crown of literature is poetry. It is its end and aim. It is the sublimest activity of the human mind. It is the achievement of beauty. The writer of prose can only step aside when the poet passes; he makes the best of us look like a piece of cheese. It is evident then that the writing of poetry should be left to the dukes, and I should like to see their rights protected by the most severe pains and penalties, for it is intolerable that the noblest of arts should be practised by any but the noblest of men. And since here, too, specialization must prevail, I foresee that the dukes (like the successors of Alexander) will divide the realm of poetry between them, each confining himself to that aspect with which hereditary influence and natural bent have rendered him competent to deal: thus I see the dukes of Manchester writing poems of a didactic and moral character, the dukes of Westminster composing stirring odes on Duty and the Responsibilities of Empire; whereas I imagine that the dukes of Devonshire would be more likely to write love lyrics and elegies in the Propertian manner, while it is almost inevitable that the dukes of Marlborough should pipe in an idyllic strain on such subjects as domestic bliss, conscription, and content with modest station.

But if you say that this is somewhat formidable and remind me that the muse does not only stalk with majestic tread, but on occasion trips on a light fantastic toe; if, recalling the wise person who said that he did not care who made a nation's laws so long as he wrote its songs, you ask me (thinking rightly that it would ill become the dukes to do so) who shall twang those measures on the lyre that the diverse and inconstant soul of man occasionally hankers after—I answer (obviously enough, I should have thought) the duchesses. I recognize that the day is past when the amorous peasants of the Romagna sang to their sweethearts the verses of Torquato Tasso and Mrs. Humphry Ward crooned over young Arnold's cradle the choruses of *Œdipus in Colonus*. The age demands something more up-to-date. I suggest, therefore, that the more domestic duchesses should write our hymns and our nursery rhymes; while the skittish ones, those who incline to mingle vine leaves with the strawberry, should write the lyrics for musical comedies, humorous verse for the comic papers, and mottoes for Christmas cards and crackers. Thus would they retain in the hearts of the British public that place which they have held hitherto only on account of their exalted station.

It was at these parties on Saturday afternoon that I discovered very much to my surprise that Edward Driffield was a distinguished person. He had written something like twenty books, and though he had never made more than a pittance out of them his reputation was considerable. The best judges admired them and the friends who came to his house were agreed that one of these days he would be recognized. They rated the public because it would not see that here was a great writer, and since the easiest way to exalt one man is to kick another in the pants, they reviled freely all the novelists whose contemporary fame obscured his. If, indeed, I had known as much of literary circles as I learned later I should have guessed by the not infrequent visits of Mrs. Barton Trafford that the time was approaching when Edward Driffield, like a runner in a long-distance race breaking away suddenly from the little knot of plodding athletes, must forge ahead. I admit that when first I was introduced to this lady her name meant nothing to me. Driffield presented me as a young neighbour of his in the country and told her that I was a medical student. She gave me a mellifluous smile, murmured in a soft voice something about Tom Sawyer, and, accepting the bread and butter I offered her, went on talking with her host. But I noticed that her arrival had made an impression and the conversation, which had been noisy and hilarious, was hushed. When in an undertone I asked who she was, I found that my ignorance was amazing; I was told that she had "made" So and So and So and So. After half an hour she rose, shook hands very graciously with such of the people as she was acquainted with, and with a sort of lithe sweetness sidled out of the room. Driffield accompanied her to the door and put her in a hansom.

Mrs. Barton Trafford was then a woman of about fifty; she was small and slight, but with rather large features, which made her head look a little too big for her body; she had crisp white hair which she wore like the Venus of Milo, and she was supposed in her youth to have been very comely. She dressed discreetly in black silk, and wore round her neck jangling chains of beads and shells. She was said to have been unhappily married in early life, but now for many years had been congenially united to Barton Trafford, a clerk in the Home Office and a well-known authority on prehistoric man. She gave you the curious impression of having no bones in her body and you felt that if you pinched her shin (which of course my respect for her sex as well as something of quiet dignity in her appearance would have never allowed me to do) your fingers would meet. When you took her hand it was like taking a fillet of sole. Her face, notwithstanding its large features, had something fluid about it. When she sat it was as though she had no backbone and were stuffed, like an expensive cushion, with swansdown.

Everything was soft about her, her voice, her smile, her laugh; her eyes, which were small and pale, had the softness of flowers; her manner was as soft as the summer rain. It was this extraordinary, and charming, characteristic that made her the wonderful friend she was. It was this that had gained her the celebrity that she now enjoyed. The whole world was aware of her friendship with the great novelist whose death a few years back had come as such a shock to the English-speaking peoples. Everyone had read the innumerable letters which he had written to her and which she was induced to publish shortly after his demise. Every page revealed his admiration for her beauty and his respect for her judgment; he could never say often enough how much he owed to her encouragement, her ready sympathy, her tact, her taste; and if certain of his expressions of passion were such as some persons might think would not be read by Mr. Barton Trafford with unmixed feelings, that only added to the human interest of the work. But Mr. Barton Trafford was above the prejudices of vulgar men (his misfortune, if such it was, was one that the greatest personages in history have endured with philosophy) and, abandoning his studies of aurignacian flints and neolithic ax heads he consented to write a Life of the deceased novelist in which he showed quite definitely how great a part of the writer's genius was due to his wife's influence.

But Mrs. Barton Trafford's interest in literature, her passion for art, were not dead because the friend for whom she had done so much had become part, with her far from negligible assistance, of posterity. She was a great reader. Little that was noteworthy escaped her attention and she was quick to establish personal relations with any young writer who showed promise. Her fame, especially since the Life, was now such that she was sure that no one would hesitate to accept the sympathy she was prepared to offer. It was inevitable that Mrs. Barton Trafford's genius for friendship should in due course find an outlet. When she read something that struck her, Mr. Barton Trafford, himself no mean critic, wrote a warm letter of appreciation to the author and asked him to luncheon. After luncheon, having to get back to the Home Office, he left him to have a chat with Mrs. Barton Trafford. Many were called. They all had *something,* but that was not enough. Mrs. Barton Trafford had a *flair,* and she trusted her *flair;* her *flair* bade her wait.

She was so cautious indeed that with Jasper Gibbons she almost missed the bus. The records of the past tell us of writers who grew famous in a night, but in our more prudent day this is unheard of. The critics want to see which way the cat will jump, and the public has been sold a pup too often to take unnecessary chances. But in the case of Jasper Gibbons it is almost the exact truth that he did thus jump into celebrity. Now that he is so completely forgotten and the critics who praised him would willingly eat their words if they were not carefully guarded in the files of innumerable newspaper offices, the sensation he made with his first volume of poems is almost unbelievable. The most important papers gave to reviews of them as much space as they would have to the report of a prize fight; the most influential critics fell over one another in their eagerness to welcome him. They likened him to Milton (for the sonority of his blank verse), to Keats (for the opulence of his sensuous imagery), and to Shelley (for his airy fantasy); and, using him as a stick to beat idols of whom they were weary, they gave in his name many a resounding whack on the emaciated buttocks of Lord Tennyson and a few good husky smacks on the bald pate of Robert Browning. The public fell like the walls of Jericho. Edition after edition was sold, and you saw Jasper Gibbons's handsome volume in the boudoirs of countesses in Mayfair, in vicarage drawing rooms from Land's End to John o' Groat's, and in the parlours of many an honest but cultured merchant in Glasgow, Aberdeen, and Belfast. When it became known that Queen Victoria had accepted a specially bound copy of the book from the hands of the loyal publisher, and had given him (not the poet, the publisher) a copy of *Leaves from a Journal in the Highlands* in exchange, the national enthusiasm knew no bounds.

And all this happened as it were in the twinkling of an eye. Seven cities in Greece disputed the honour of having given birth to Homer, and though Jasper Gibbons's birthplace (Walsall) was well known, twice seven critics claimed the honour of having discovered him; eminent judges of literature who for twenty years had written eulogies of one another's works in the weekly papers quarrelled so bitterly over this matter that one cut the other dead in the Athenæum. Nor was the great world remiss in giving him its recognition. Jasper Gibbons was asked to luncheon and invited to tea by dowager duchesses, the wives of cabinet ministers, and the widows of bishops. It is said that Harrison Ainsworth was the first English man of letters to move in English society on terms of equality (and I have sometimes wondered that an enterprising publisher on this account has not thought of bringing out a complete edition of his works); but I believe that Jasper Gibbons was the first poet to have his name engraved at the bottom of an At Home card as a draw as enticing as an opera singer or a ventriloquist.

It was out of the question then for Mrs. Barton Trafford to get in on the ground floor. She could only buy in the open market. I do not know what prodigious strategy she employed, what miracles of tact, what tenderness, what exquisite sympathy, what demure blandishments; I can only surmise and admire; she nobbled Jasper Gibbons. In a little while he was eating out of her soft hand. She was admirable. She had him to lunch to meet the right people; she gave At Homes where he recited his poems before the most distinguished persons in England; she introduced him to eminent actors who gave him commissions to write plays; she saw that his poems should only appear in the proper places; she dealt with the publishers and made contracts for him that would have staggered even a cabinet minister; she took care that he should accept only the invitations of which she approved; she even went so far as to separate him from the wife with whom he had lived happily for ten years, since she felt that a poet to be true to himself and his art must not be encumbered with domestic ties. When the crash came Mrs. Barton Trafford, had she chosen, might have said that she had done everything for him that it was humanly possible to do.

For there was a crash. Jasper Gibbons brought out another volume of poetry; it was neither better nor worse than the first; it was very much like the first; it was treated with respect, but the critics made reservations; some of them even carped. The book was a disappointment. Its sale also. And unfortunately Jasper Gibbons was inclined to tipple. He had never been accustomed to having money to spend, he was quite unused to the lavish entertainments that were offered him, perhaps he missed his homely, common little wife; once or twice he came to dinner at Mrs. Barton Trafford's in a condition that anyone less worldly, less simple-minded than she, would have described as blind to the world. She told her guests gently that the bard was not quite himself that evening. His third book was a failure. The critics tore him limb from limb, they knocked him down and stamped on him, and, to quote one of Edward Driffield's favourite songs, then they lugged him round the room and then they jumped upon his face: they were quite naturally annoyed that they had mistaken a fluent versifier for a deathless poet and were determined that he should suffer for their error. Then Jasper Gibbons was arrested for being drunk and disorderly in Piccadilly and Mr. Barton Trafford had to go to Vine Street at midnight to bail him out.

Mrs. Barton Trafford at this juncture was perfect. She did not repine. No harsh word escaped her lips. She might have been excused if she had felt a certain bitterness because this man for whom she had done so much had let her down. She remained tender, gentle, and sympathetic. She was the woman who understood. She dropped him, but not like a hot brick, or a hot potato. She dropped him with infinite gentleness, as softly as the tear that she doubtless shed when she made up her mind to do something so repugnant to her nature; she dropped him with so much tact, with such sensibility, that Jasper Gibbons perhaps hardly knew he was dropped. But there was no doubt about it. She would say nothing against him, indeed she would not discuss him at all, and when mention was made of him she merely smiled, a little sadly, and sighed. But her smile was the *coup de grâce,* and her sigh buried him deep.

Mrs. Barton Trafford had a passion for literature too sincere to allow a setback of this character long to discourage her; and however great her disappointment she was a woman of too disinterested a nature to let the gifts of tact, sympathy, and understanding with which she was blessed by nature lie fallow. She continued to move in literary circles, going to tea parties here and there, to soirées, and to At Homes, charming always and gentle, listening intelligently, but watchful, critical, and determined (if I may put it crudely) next time to back a winner. It was then that she met Edward Driffield and formed a favourable opinion of his gifts. It is true that he was not young, but then he was unlikely like Jasper Gibbons to go to pieces. She offered him her friendship. He could not fail to be moved when, in that gentle way of hers, she told him that it was a scandal that his exquisite work remained known only in a narrow circle. He was pleased and flattered. It is always pleasant to be assured that you are a genius. She told him that Barton Trafford was reflecting on the possibility of writing an important article on him for the *Quarterly Review.* She asked him to luncheon to meet people who might be useful to him. She wanted him to know his intellectual equals. Sometimes she took him for a walk on the Chelsea Embankment and they talked of poets dead and gone and love and friendship, and had tea in an A.B.C. shop. When Mrs. Barton Trafford came to Limpus Road on Saturday afternoon she had the air of the queen bee preparing herself for the nuptial flight.

Her manner with Mrs. Driffield was perfect. It was affable, but not condescending. She always thanked her very prettily for having allowed her to come and see her and complimented her on her appearance. If she praised Edward Driffield to her, telling her with a little envy in her tone what a privilege it was to enjoy the companionship of such a great man, it was certainly from pure kindness, and not because she knew that there is nothing that exasperates the wife of a literary man more than to have another woman tell her flattering things about him. She talked to Mrs. Driffield of the simple things her simple nature might be supposed to be interested in, of cooking and servants and Edward's health and how careful she must be with him. Mrs. Barton Trafford treated her exactly as you would expect a woman of very good Scotch family, which she was, to treat an ex-barmaid with whom a distinguished man of letters had made an unfortunate marriage. She was cordial, playful, and gently determined to put her at her ease.

It was strange that Rosie could not bear her; indeed, Mrs. Barton Trafford was the only person that I ever knew her dislike. In those days even barmaids did not habitually use the "bitches" and "bloodys" that are part and parcel of the current vocabulary of the best-brought-up young ladies, and I never heard Rosie use a word that would have shocked my Aunt Sophie. When anyone told a story that was a little near the knuckle she would blush to the roots of her hair. But she referred to Mrs. Barton Trafford as "that damned old cat." It needed the most urgent persuasions of her more intimate friends to induce her to be civil to her.

"Don't be a fool, Rosie," they said. They all called her Rosie and presently I, though very shyly, got in the habit of doing so too. "If she wants to she can make him. He must play up to her. She can work the trick if anyone can."

Though most of the Driffields' visitors were occasional, appearing every other Saturday, say, or every third, there was a little band that, like myself, came almost every week. We were the stand-bys; we arrived early and stayed late. Of these the most faithful were Quentin Forde, Harry Retford, and Lionel Hillier.

Quentin Forde was a stocky little man with a fine head of the type that was afterward for a time much admired in the moving pictures, a straight nose and handsome eyes, neatly cropped grey hair, and a black moustache; if he had been four or five inches taller he would have been the perfect type of the villain of melodrama. He was known to be very "well connected," and he was affluent; his only occupation was to cultivate the arts. He went to all the first nights and all the private views. He had the amateur's severity, and cherished for the productions of his contemporaries a polite but sweeping contempt. I discovered that he did not come to the Driffields' because Edward was a genius, but because Rosie was beautiful.

Now that I look back I cannot get over my surprise that I should have had to be told what was surely so obvious. When I first knew her it never occurred to me to ask myself whether she was pretty or plain, and when, seeing her again after five years, I noticed for the first time that she was very pretty, I was interested but did not trouble to think much about it. I took it as part of the natural order of things, just as I took the sun setting over the North Sea or the towers of Tercanbury Cathedral. I was quite startled when I heard people speak of Rosie's beauty, and when they complimented Edward on her looks and his eyes rested on her for a moment, mine followed his. Lionel Hillier was a painter and he asked her to sit for him. When he talked of the picture he wanted to paint and told me what he saw in her, I listened to him stupidly. I was puzzled and confused. Harry Retford knew one of the fashionable photographers of the period and, arranging special terms, he took Rosie to be photographed. A Saturday or two later the proofs were there and we all looked at them. I had never seen Rosie in evening dress. She was wearing a dress of white satin, with a long train and puffy sleeves, and it was cut low; her hair was more elaborately done than usual. She looked very different from the strapping young woman I had first met in Joy Lane in a boater and a starched shirt. But Lionel Hillier tossed the photographs aside impatiently.

"Rotten," he said. "What can a photograph give of Rosie? The thing about her is her colour." He turned to her. "Rosie, don't you know that your colour is *the* great miracle of the age?"

She looked at him without answering, but her full red lips broke into their childlike, mischievous smile.

"If I can only get a suggestion of it I'm made for life," he said. "All the rich stockbrokers' wives will come on their bended knees and beg me to paint them like you."

Presently I learned that Rosie was sitting to him, but when, never having been in a painter's studio and looking upon it as the gateway of romance, I asked if I might not come one day and see how the picture was getting on, Hillier said that he did not want anyone to see it yet. He was a man of five-and-thirty and of a flamboyant appearance. He looked like a portrait of Van Dyck in which the distinction had been replaced by good humour. He was slightly above the middle height, slim; and he had a fine mane of black hair and flowing moustaches and a pointed beard. He favoured broad-brimmed sombreros and Spanish capes. He had lived a long time in Paris and talked admiringly of painters, Monet, Sisley, Renoir, of whom we had never heard, and with contempt of Sir Frederick Leighton and Mr. Alma-Tadema and Mr. G. F. Watts, whom in our heart of hearts we very much admired. I have often wondered what became of him. He spent a few years in London trying to make his way, failed, I suppose, and then drifted to Florence. I was told that he had a drawing school there, but when, years later, chancing to be in that city, I asked about him, I could find no one who had ever heard of him. I think he must have had some talent, for I have even now a very vivid recollection of the portrait he painted of Rosie Driffield. I wonder what has happened to it. Has it been destroyed or is it hidden away, its face to the wall, in the attic of a junk shop in Chelsea? I should like to think that it has at least found a place on the walls of some provincial gallery.

When I was at last allowed to come and see it, I put my foot in it fine and proper. Hillier's studio was in the Fulham Road, one of a group at the back of a row of shops, and you went in through a dark and smelly passage. It was a Sunday afternoon in March, a fine blue day, and I walked from Vincent Square through deserted streets. Hillier lived in his studio; there was a large divan on which he slept, and a tiny little room at the back where he cooked his breakfast, washed his brushes, and, I suppose, himself.

When I arrived Rosie still wore the dress in which she had been sitting and they were having a cup of tea. Hillier opened the door for me and, still holding my hand, led me up to the large canvas.

"There she is," he said.

He had painted Rosie full length, just a little less than life-size, in an evening dress of white silk. It was not at all like the academy portraits I was accustomed to. I did not know what to say, so I said the first thing that came into my head.

"When will it be finished?"

"It is finished," he answered.

I blushed furiously. I felt a perfect fool. I had not then acquired the technique that I flatter myself now enables me to deal competently with the works of modern artists. If this were the place I could write a very neat little guide to enable the amateur of pictures to deal to the satisfaction of their painters with the most diverse manifestations of the creative instinct. There is the intense "By God" that acknowledges the power of the ruthless realist, the "It's so awfully sincere" that covers your embarrassment when you are shown the coloured photograph of an alderman's widow, the low whistle that exhibits your admiration for the post-impressionist, the "Terribly amusing" that expresses what you feel about the cubist, the "Oh!" of one who is overcome, the "Ah!" of him whose breath is taken away.

"It's awfully like," was all that then I could lamely say.

"It's not chocolate-boxy enough for you," said Hillier.

"I think it's awfully good," I answered quickly, defending myself. "Are you going to send it to the Academy?"

"Good God, no! I might send it to the Grosvenor."

I looked from the painting to Rosie and from Rosie to the painting.

"Get into the pose, Rosie," said Hillier, "and let him see you."

She got up on to the model stand. I stared at her and I stared at the picture. I had such a funny little feeling in my heart. It was as though someone softly plunged a sharp knife into it, but it was not an unpleasant sensation at all, painful but strangely agreeable; and then suddenly I felt quite weak at the knees. But now I do not know if I remember Rosie in the flesh or in the picture. For when I think of her it is not in the shirt and boater that I first saw her in, nor in any of the other dresses I saw her in then or later, but in the white silk that Hillier painted, with a black velvet bow in her hair, and in the pose he had made her take.

I never exactly knew Rosie's age, but reckoning the years out as well as I can, I think she must have been thirty-five. She did not look anything like it. Her face was quite unlined and her skin as smooth as a child's. I do not think she had very good features. They certainly had none of the aristocratic distinction of the great ladies whose photographs were then sold in all the shops; they were rather blunt. Her short nose was a little thick, her eyes were smallish, her mouth was large; but her eyes had the blue of cornflowers, and they smiled with her lips, very red and sensual, and her smile was the gayest, the most friendly, the sweetest thing I ever saw. She had by nature a heavy, sullen look, but when she smiled this sullenness became on a sudden infinitely attractive. She had no colour in her face; it was of a very pale brown except under the eyes, where it was faintly blue. Her hair was pale gold and it was done in the fashion of the day high on the head with an elaborate fringe.

"She's the very devil to paint," said Hillier, looking at her and at his picture. "You see, she's all gold, her face and her hair, and yet she doesn't give you a golden effect, she gives you a silvery effect."

I knew what he meant. She glowed, but palely, like the moon rather than the sun, or if it was like the sun it was like the sun in the white mist of dawn. Hillier had placed her in the middle of his canvas and she stood, with her arms by her sides, the palms of her hands toward you and her head a little thrown back, in an attitude that gave value to the pearly beauty of her neck and bosom. She stood like an actress taking a call, confused by unexpected applause, but there was something so virginal about her, so exquisitely springlike, that the comparison was absurd. This artless creature had never known grease paint or footlights. She stood like a maiden apt for love offering herself guilelessly, because she was fulfilling the purposes of Nature, to the embraces of a lover. She belonged to a generation that did not fear a certain opulence of line, she was slender, but her breasts were ample and her lips well marked. When, later, Mrs. Barton Trafford saw the picture she said it reminded her of a sacrificial heifer.

XV

EDWARD DRIFFIELD worked at night, and Rosie, having nothing to do, was glad to go out with one or other of her friends. She liked luxury and Quentin Forde was well-to-do. He would fetch her in a cab and take her to dine at Kettner's or the Savoy, and she would put on her grandest clothes for him; and Harry Retford, though he never had a bob, behaved as if he had, and took her about in hansoms too and gave her dinner at Romano's or in one or other of the little restaurants that were becoming modish in Soho. He was an actor and a clever one, but he was difficult to suit and so was often out of work. He was about thirty, a man with a pleasantly ugly face and a clipped way of speaking that made what he said sound funny. Rosie liked his devil-may-care attitude toward life, the swagger with which he wore clothes made by the best tailor in London and unpaid for, the recklessness with which he would put a fiver he hadn't got on a horse, and the generosity with which he flung his money about when a lucky win put him in funds. He was gay, charming, vain, boastful, and unscrupulous. Rosie told me that once he had pawned his watch to take her out to dinner and then borrowed a couple of pounds from the actor manager who had given them seats for the play in order to take him out to supper with them afterward.

But she was just as well pleased to go with Lionel Hillier to his studio and eat a chop that he and she cooked between them and spend the evening talking, and it was only very rarely that she would dine with me at all. I used to fetch her after I had had my dinner in Vincent Square and she hers with Driffield, and we would get on a bus and go to a music hall. We went here and there, to the Pavilion or the Tivoli, sometimes to the Metropolitan if there was a particular turn we wanted to see; but our favourite was the Canterbury. It was cheap and the show was good. We ordered a couple of beers and I smoked my pipe.

Rosie looked round with delight at the great dark smoky house, crowded to the ceiling with the inhabitants of South London.

"I like the Canterbury," she said. "It's so homy."

I discovered that she was a great reader. She liked history, but only history of a certain kind, the lives of queens and of mistresses of royal personages; and she would tell me with a childlike wonder of the strange things she read. She had a wide acquaintance with the six consorts of King Henry VIII and there was little she did not know about Mrs. Fitzherbert and Lady Hamilton. Her appetite was prodigious and she ranged from Lucrezia Borgia to the wives of Philip of Spain; then there was the long list of the royal mistresses of France. She knew them all, and all about them, from Agnès Sorel down to Madame du Barry.

"I like to read about real things," she said. "I don't much care about novels."

She liked to gossip about Blackstable and I thought it was on account of my connexion with it that she liked to come out with me. She seemed to know all that was going on there.

"I go down every other week or so to see my mother," she said. "Just for the night, you know."

"To Blackstable?"

I was surprised.

"No, not to Blackstable," Rosie smiled. "I don't know that I'd care to go there just yet. To Haversham. Mother comes over to meet me. I stay at the hotel where I used to work."

She was never a great talker. Often when, the night being fine, we decided to walk back from the music hall at which we had been spending the evening, she never opened her mouth. But her silence was intimate and comfortable. It did not exclude you from thoughts that engaged her apart from you; it included you in a pervasive well-being.

I was talking about her once to Lionel Hillier and I said to him that I could not understand how she had turned from the fresh pleasant-looking young woman I had first known at Blackstable into the lovely creature whose beauty now practically everyone acknowledged. (There were people who made reservations. "Of course she has a very good figure," they said, "but it's not the sort of face I very much admire personally." And others said: "Oh, yes, of course, a very pretty woman; but it's a pity she hasn't a little more distinction.")

"I can explain that to you in half a jiffy," said Lionel Hillier. "She was only a fresh, buxom wench when you first met her. *I* made her beauty."

I forget what my answer was, but I know it was ribald.

"All right. That just shows you don't know anything about beauty. No one ever thought very much of Rosie till I saw her like the sun shining silver. It wasn't till I painted it that anyone knew that her hair was the most lovely thing in the world."

"Did you make her neck and her breasts and her carriage and her bones?" I asked.

"Yes, damn you, that's just what I did do."

When Hillier talked of Rosie in front of her she listened to him with a smiling gravity. A little flush came into her pale cheeks. I think that at first when he spoke to her of her beauty she believed he was just making game of her; but when she found out that he wasn't, when he painted her silvery gold, it had no particular effect on her. She was a trifle amused, pleased of course, and a little surprised, but it did not turn her head. She thought him a little mad. I often wondered whether there was anything between them. I could not forget all I had heard of Rosie at Blackstable and what I had seen in the vicarage garden; I wondered about Quentin Forde, too, and Harry Retford. I used to watch them with her. She was not exactly familiar with them, comradely rather; she used to make her appointments with them quite openly in anybody's hearing; and when she looked at them it was with that mischievous, childlike smile which I had now discovered held such a mysterious beauty. Sometimes when we were sitting side by side in a music hall I looked at her face; I do not think I was in love with her, I merely enjoyed the sensation of sitting quietly beside her and looking at the pale gold of her hair and the pale gold of her skin. Of course Lionel Hillier was right; the strange thing was that this gold did give one a strange moonlight feeling. She had the serenity of a summer evening when the light fades slowly from the unclouded sky. There was nothing dull in her immense placidity; it was as living as the sea when under the August sun it lay calm and shining along the Kentish coast. She reminded me of a sonation by an old Italian composer with its wistfulness in which there is yet an urbane flippancy and its light rippling gaiety in which echoes still the trembling of a sigh. Sometimes, feeling my eyes on her, she would turn round and for a moment or two look me full in the face. She did not speak. I did not know of what she was thinking.

Once, I remember, I fetched her at Limpus Road, and the maid, telling me she was not ready, asked me to wait in the parlour. She came in. She was in black velvet, with a picture hat covered with ostrich feathers (we were going to the Pavilion and she had dressed up for it) and she looked so lovely that it took my breath away. I was staggered. The clothes of that day gave a woman dignity and there was something amazingly attractive in the way her virginal beauty (sometimes she looked like the exquisite statue of Psyche in the museum at Naples) contrasted with the stateliness of her gown. She had a trait that I think must be very rare: the skin under her eyes, faintly blue, was all dewy. Sometimes I could not persuade myself that it was natural, and once I asked her if she had rubbed vaseline under her eyes. That was just the effect it gave. She smiled, took a handkerchief and handed it to me.

"Rub them and see," she said.

Then one night when we had walked home from the Canterbury, and I was leaving her at her door, when I held out my hand she laughed a little, a low chuckle it was, and leaned forward.

"You old silly," she said.

She kissed me on the mouth. It was not a hurried peck, nor was it a kiss of passion. Her lips, those very full red lips of hers, rested on mine long enough for me to be conscious of their shape and their warmth and their softness. Then she withdrew them, but without hurry, in silence pushed open the door, slipped inside, and left me. I was so startled that I had not been able to say anything. I accepted her kiss stupidly. I remained inert. I turned away and walked back to my lodg-

ings. I seemed to hear still in my ears Rosie's laughter. It was not contemptuous or wounding, but frank and affectionate; it was as though
she laughed because she was fond of me.

XVI

I DID not go out with Rosie again for more than a week. She was
going down to Haversham to spend a night with her mother. She had
various engagements in London. Then she asked me if I would go to
the Haymarket Theatre with her. The play was a success and free
seats were not to be had, so we made up our minds to go in the pit.
We had a steak and a glass of beer at the Café Monico and then stood
with the crowd. In those days there was no orderly queue and when
the doors were opened there was a mad rush and scramble to get in.
We were hot and breathless and somewhat battered when at last we
pushed our way into our seats.

We walked back through St. James's Park. The night was so lovely
that we sat down on a bench. In the starlight Rosie's face and her fair
hair glowed softly. She was suffused, as it were (I express it awkwardly, but I do not know how to describe the emotion she gave me)
with a friendliness at once candid and tender. She was like a silvery
flower of the night that only gave its perfume to the moonbeams. I
slipped my arm round her waist and she turned her face to mine. This
time it was I who kissed. She did not move; her soft red lips submitted
to the pressure of mine with a calm, intense passivity as the water of a
lake accepts the lights of the moon. I don't know how long we stayed
there.

"I'm awfully hungry," she said suddenly.

"So am I," I laughed.

"Couldn't we go and have some fish and chips somewhere?"

"Rather."

In those days I knew my way very well about Westminster, not yet
a fashionable quarter for parliamentary and otherwise cultured persons,
but slummy and down-at-heel; and after we had come out of the park,

crossing Victoria Street, I led Rosie to a fried-fish shop in Horseferry Row. It was late and the only other person there was the driver of a four-wheeler waiting outside. We ordered our fish and chips and a bottle of beer. A poor woman came in and bought two penn'orth of mixed and took it away with her in a piece of paper. We ate with appetite.

Our way back to Rosie's led through Vincent Square and as we passed my house I asked her:

"Won't you come in for a minute? You've never seen my rooms."

"What about your landlady? I don't want to get you into trouble."

"Oh, she sleeps like a rock."

"I'll come in for a little."

I slipped my key into the lock and because the passage was dark took Rosie's hand to lead her in. I lit the gas in my sitting room. She took off her hat and vigorously scratched her head. Then she looked for a glass, but I was very artistic and had taken down the mirror that was over the chimney-piece and there was no means in the room for anyone to see what he looked like.

"Come into my bedroom," I said. "There's a glass there."

I opened the door and lit the candle. Rosie followed me in and I held it up so that she should be able to see herself. I looked at her in the glass as she arranged her hair. She took two or three pins out, which she put in her mouth, and taking one of my brushes, brushed her hair up from the nape of the neck. She twisted it, patted it, and put back the pins, and as she was intent on this her eyes caught mine in the glass and she smiled at me. When she had replaced the last pin she turned and faced me; she did not say anything; she looked at me tranquilly, still with that little friendly smile in her blue eyes. I put down the candle. The room was very small and the dressing table was by the bed. She raised her hand and softly stroked my cheek.

I wish now that I had not started to write this book in the first person singular. It is all very well when you can show yourself in an amiable or touching light; and nothing can be more effective than the modest heroic or pathetic humorous which in this mode is much cultivated; it is charming to write about yourself when you see on the reader's eyelash the glittering tear and on his lips the tender smile; but it is not so nice when you have to exhibit yourself as a plain damned fool.

A little while ago I read in the *Evening Standard* an article by Mr. Evelyn Waugh in the course of which he remarked that to write novels in the first person was a contemptible practice. I wish he had explained why, but he merely threw out the statement with just the same take-it-or-leave-it casualness as Euclid used when he made his celebrated observation about parallel straight lines. I was much concerned and forthwith asked Alroy Kear (who reads everything, even the books he writes prefaces for) to recommend to me some works on the art of fiction. On his advice I read *The Craft of Fiction* by Mr. Percy Lubbock, from which I learned that the only way to write novels was like Henry James; after that I read *Aspects of the Novel* by Mr. E. M. Forster, from which I learned that the only way to write novels was like Mr. E. M. Forster; then I read *The Structure of the Novel* by Mr. Edwin Muir, from which I learned nothing at all. In none of them could I discover anything to the point at issue. All the same I can find one reason why certain novelists, such as Defoe, Sterne, Thackeray, Dickens, Emily Brontë, and Proust, well known in their day but now doubtless forgotten, have used the method that Mr. Evelyn Waugh reprehends. As we grow older we become more conscious of the complexity, incoherence, and unreasonableness of human beings; this indeed is the only excuse that offers for the middle-aged or elderly writer, whose thoughts should more properly be turned to graver matters, occupying himself with the trivial concerns of imaginary people. For if the proper study of mankind is man it is evidently more sensible to occupy yourself with the coherent, substantial, and significant creatures of fiction than with the irrational and shadowy figures of real life. Sometimes the novelist feels himself like God and is prepared to tell you everything about his characters; sometimes, however, he does not; and then he tells you not everything that is to be known about them but the little he knows himself; and since as we grow older we feel ourselves less and less like God I should not be surprised to learn that with advancing years the novelist grows less and less inclined to de-

scribe more than his own experience has given him. The first person
singular is a very useful device for his limited purpose.

Rosie raised her hand and softly stroked my face. I do not know why
I should have behaved as I then did; it was not at all how I had seen
myself behaving on such an occasion. A sob broke from my tight
throat. I do not know whether it was because I was shy and lonely
(not lonely in the body, for I spent all day at the hospital with all
kinds of people, but lonely in the spirit) or because my desire was so
great, but I began to cry. I felt terribly ashamed of myself; I tried to
control myself, I couldn't; the tears welled up in my eyes and poured
down my cheeks. Rosie saw them and gave a little gasp.

"Oh, honey, what is it? What's the matter? Don't. Don't!"

She put her arms round my neck and began to cry too, and she
kissed my lips and my eyes and my wet cheeks. She undid her bodice
and lowered my head till it rested on her bosom. She stroked my
smooth face. She rocked me back and forth as though I were a child
in her arms. I kissed her breasts and I kissed the white column of her
neck; and she slipped out of her bodice and out of her skirt and her
petticoats and I held her for a moment by her corseted waist; then she
undid it, holding her breath for an instant to enable her to do so, and
stood before me in her shift. When I put my hands on her sides I could
feel the ribbing of the skin from the pressure of the corsets.

"Blow out the candle," she whispered.

It was she who awoke me when the dawn peering through the curtains revealed the shape of the bed and of the wardrobe against the
darkness of the lingering night. She woke me by kissing me on the
mouth and her hair falling over my face tickled me.

"I must get up," she said. "I don't want your landlady to see me."

"There's plenty of time."

Her breasts when she leaned over me were heavy on my chest. In a
little while she got out of bed. I lit the candle. She turned to the glass
and tied up her hair and then she looked for a moment at her naked
body. Her waist was naturally small; though so well developed she was
very slender; her breasts were straight and firm and they stood out

from the chest as though carved in marble. It was a body made for the act of love. In the light of the candle, struggling now with the increasing day, it was all silvery gold; and the only colour was the rosy pink of the hard nipples.

We dressed in silence. She did not put on her corsets again, but rolled them up and I wrapped them in a piece of newspaper. We tiptoed along the passage and when I opened the door and we stepped out into the street the dawn ran to meet us like a cat leaping up the steps. The square was empty; already the sun was shining on the eastern windows. I felt as young as the day. We walked arm in arm till we came to the corner of Limpus Road.

"Leave me here," said Rosie. "One never knows."

I kissed her and I watched her walk away. She walked rather slowly, with the firm tread of the country woman who likes to feel the good earth under her feet, and held herself erect. I could not go back to bed. I strolled on till I came to the Embankment. The river had the bright hues of the early morning. A brown barge came downstream and passed under Vauxhall Bridge. In a dinghy two men were rowing close to the side. I was hungry.

XVII

AFTER that for more than a year whenever Rosie came out with me she used on the way home to drop into my room, sometimes for an hour, sometimes till the breaking day warned us that the slaveys would soon be scrubbing the doorsteps. I have a recollection of warm sunny mornings when the tired air of London had a welcome freshness, and of our footfalls that seemed so noisy in the empty streets, and then of scurrying along huddled under an umbrella, silent but gay, when the winter brought cold and rain. The policeman on point duty gave us a stare as we passed, sometimes of suspicion; but sometimes also there was a twinkle of comprehension in his eyes. Now and then we would see a homeless creature huddled up asleep in a portico and Rosie gave my arm a friendly little pressure when (chiefly for show and because I wanted to make a good impression on her, for my shillings were scarce) I placed a piece of silver on a shapeless lap or in a skinny fist. Rosie made me very happy. I had a great affection for her. She was easy and comfortable. She had a placidity of temper that communicated itself to the people she was with; you shared her pleasure in the passing moment.

Before I became her lover I had often asked myself if she was the mistress of the others, Forde, Harry Retford, and Hillier, and afterward I questioned her. She kissed me.

"Don't be so silly. I like them, you know that. I like to go out with them, but that's all."

I wanted to ask her if she had been the mistress of George Kemp, but I did not like to. Though I had never seen her in a temper, I had a notion that she had one and I vaguely felt that this was a question that might anger her. I did not want to give her the opportunity of saying things so wounding that I could not forgive her. I was young, only just over one-and-twenty. Quentin Forde and the others seemed old to me; it did not seem unnatural to me that to Rosie they were only friends. It gave me a little thrill of pride to think that I was her lover. When I used to look at her chatting and laughing with all and sundry at tea on Saturday afternoons, I glowed with self-satisfaction. I thought of the nights we passed together and I was inclined to laugh at the people who were so ignorant or my great secret. But sometimes I thought that Lionel Hillier looked at me in a quizzical way, as if he were enjoying a good joke at my expense, and I asked myself uneasily if Rosie had told him that she was having an affair with me. I wondered if there was anything in my manner that betrayed me. I told Rosie that I was afraid Hillier suspected something; she looked at me with those blue eyes of hers that always seemed ready to smile.

"Don't bother about it," she said. "He's got a nasty mind."

I had never been intimate with Quentin Forde. He looked upon me as a dull and insignificant young man (which of course I was) and though he had always been civil he had never taken any notice of me. I thought it could only be my fancy that now he began to be a little more frigid with me than before. But one day Harry Retford to my surprise asked me to dine with him and go to the play. I told Rosie.

"Oh, of course you must go. He'll give you an awfully good time. Good old Harry, he always makes me laugh."

So I dined with him. He made himself very pleasant and I was impressed to hear him talk of actors and actresses. He had a sarcastic humour and was very funny at the expense of Quentin Forde, whom he did not like; I tried to get him to talk of Rosie, but he had nothing to say of her. He seemed to be a gay dog. With leers and laughing innuendoes he gave me to understand that he was a devil with the girls. I could not but ask myself if he was standing me this dinner because he knew I was Rosie's lover and so felt friendly disposed toward me. But if he knew, of course the others knew too. I hope I did not show it, but in my heart I certainly felt somewhat patronizing toward them.

Then in winter, toward the end of January, someone new appeared at Limpus Road. This was a Dutch Jew named Jack Kuyper, a diamond merchant from Amsterdam, who was spending a few weeks in London on business. I do not know how he had come to know the Driffields and whether it was esteem for the author that brought him to the house, but it was certainly not that which caused him to come again. He was a tall, stout, dark man with a bald head and a big hooked nose, a man of fifty, but of a powerful appearance, sensual, determined, and jovial. He made no secret of his admiration for Rosie. He was rich apparently, for he sent her roses every day; she chid him for his extravagance, but was flattered. I could not bear him. He was blatant and loud. I hated his fluent conversation in perfect but foreign English; I hated the extravagant compliments he paid Rosie; I hated the heartiness with which he treated her friends. I found that Quentin Forde liked him as little as I; we almost became cordial with one another.

"Mercifully he's not staying long." Quentin Forde pursed his lips and raised his black eyebrows; with his white hair and long sallow face he looked incredibly gentlemanly. "Women are always the same; they adore a bounder."

"He's so frightfully vulgar," I complained.

"That is his charm," said Quentin Forde.

For the next two or three weeks I saw next to nothing of Rosie. Jack Kuyper took her out night after night, to this smart restaurant and that, to one play after another. I was vexed and hurt.

"He doesn't know anyone in London," said Rosie, trying to soothe my ruffled feelings. "He wants to see everything he can while he's here. It wouldn't be very nice for him to go alone all the time. He's only here for a fortnight more."

I did not see the object of this self-sacrifice on her part.

"But don't you think he's awful?" I said.

"No. I think he's fun. He makes me laugh."

"Don't you know that he's absolutely gone on you?"

"Well, it pleases him and it doesn't do me any harm."

"He's old and fat and horrible. It gives me the creeps to look at him."

"I don't think he's so bad," said Rosie.

"You couldn't have anything to do with him," I protested. "I mean, he's such an awful cad."

Rosie scratched her head. It was an unpleasant habit of hers.

"It's funny how different foreigners are from English people," she said.

I was thankful when Jack Kuyper went back to Amsterdam. Rosie had promised to dine with me the day after and as a treat we arranged to dine in Soho. She fetched me in a hansom and we drove on.

"Has your horrible old man gone?" I asked.

"Yes," she laughed.

I put my arm round her waist. (I have elsewhere remarked how much more convenient the hansom was for this pleasant and indeed almost essential act in human intercourse than the taxi of the present day, so unwillingly refrain from labouring the point.) I put my arm round her waist and kissed her. Her lips were like spring flowers. We arrived. I hung my hat and my coat (it was very long and tight at the waist, with a velvet collar and velvet cuffs; very smart) on a peg and asked Rosie to give me her cape.

"I'm going to keep it on," she said.

"You'll be awfully hot. You'll only catch cold when we go out."

"I don't care. It's the first time I've worn it. Don't you think it's lovely? And look: the muff matches."

I gave the cape a glance. It was of fur. I did not know it was sable. "It looks awfully rich. How did you get that?"

"Jack Kuyper gave it to me. We went and bought it yesterday just before he went away." She stroked the smooth fur; she was as happy with it as a child with a toy. "How much d'you think it cost?"

"I haven't an idea."

"Two hundred and sixty pounds. Do you know I've never had anything that cost so much in my life? I told him it was far too much, but he wouldn't listen. He made me have it."

Rosie chuckled with glee and her eyes shone. But I felt my face go stiff and a shiver run down my spine.

"Won't Driffield think it's rather funny, Kuyper giving you a fur cape that costs all that?" said I, trying to make my voice sound natural.

Rosie's eyes danced mischievously.

"You know what Ted is, he never notices anything; if he says anything about it I shall tell him I gave twenty pounds for it in a pawnshop. He won't know any better." She rubbed her face against the collar. "It's so soft. And everyone can see it cost money."

I tried to eat and in order not to show the bitterness in my heart I did my best to keep the conversation going on one topic or another. Rosie did not much mind what I said. She could only think of her new cape and every other minute her eyes returned to the muff that she insisted on holding on her lap. She looked at it with an affection in which there was something lazy, sensual, and self-complacent. I was angry with her. I thought her stupid and common.

"You look like a cat that's swallowed a canary," I could not help snapping.

She only giggled.

"That's what I feel like."

Two hundred and sixty pounds was an enormous sum to me. I did not know one *could* pay so much for a cape. I lived on fourteen pounds a month and not at all badly either; and in case any reader is not a ready reckoner I will add that this is one hundred and sixty-eight pounds a year. I could not believe that anyone would make as expensive a present as that from pure friendship; what did it mean but that Jack Kuyper had been sleeping with Rosie, night after night, all the time he was in London, and now when he went away was paying her? How could she accept it? Didn't she see how it degraded her? Didn't she see how frightfully vulgar it was of him to give her a thing that cost so much? Apparently not, for she said to me:

"It was nice of him, wasn't it? But then Jews are always generous."

"I suppose he could afford it," I said.

"Oh, yes, he's got lots of money. He said he wanted to give me something before he went away and asked me what I wanted. Well, I said, I could do with a cape and a muff to match, but I never thought he'd buy me anything like this. When we went into the shop I asked them to show me something in astrakhan, but he said: No, sable, and the best money can buy. And when we saw this he absolutely insisted on my having it."

I thought of her with her white body, her skin so milky, in the arms of that old fat gross man and his thick loose lips kissing hers. And then I knew that the suspicion that I had refused to believe was true; I knew that when she went out to dinner with Quentin Forde and Harry Retford and Lionel Hillier she went to bed with them just as she came to bed with me. I could not speak; I knew that if I did I should insult her. I do not think I was jealous so much as mortified. I felt that she had been making a damned fool of me. I used all my determination to prevent the bitter gibes from passing my lips.

We went on to the theatre. I could not listen to the play. I could only feel against my arm the smoothness of the sable cape; I could only see her fingers for ever stroking the muff. I could have borne the thought of the others; it was Jack Kuyper who horrified me. How could she? It was abominable to be poor. I longed to have enough money to tell her that if she would send the fellow back his beastly furs I would give her better ones instead. At last she noticed that I did not speak.

"You're very silent tonight."

"Am I?"

"Aren't you well?"

"Perfectly."

She gave me a sidelong look. I did not meet her eyes, but I knew they were smiling with that smile at once mischievous and childlike that I knew so well. She said nothing more. At the end of the play, since it was raining, we took a hansom and I gave the driver her address in Limpus Road. She did not speak till we got to Victoria Street, then she said:

"Don't you want me to come home with you?"

"Just as you like."

She lifted up the trap and gave the driver my address. She took my hand and held it, but I remained inert. I looked straight out of the window with angry dignity. When we reached Vincent Square I handed her out of the cab and let her into the house without a word. I took off my hat and coat. She threw her cape and her muff on the sofa.

"Why are you so sulky?" she asked, coming up to me.

"I'm not sulky," I answered, looking away.

She took my face in her two hands.

"How can you be so silly? Why should you be angry because Jack Kuyper gives me a fur cape? You can't afford to give me one, can you?"

"Of course I can't."

"And Ted can't either. You can't expect me to refuse a fur cape that cost two hundred and sixty pounds. I've wanted a fur cape all my life. It means nothing to Jack."

"You don't expect me to believe that he gave it you just out of friendship."

"He might have. Anyhow, he's gone back to Amsterdam, and who knows when he'll come back?"

"He isn't the only one, either."

I looked at Rosie now, with angry, hurt, resentful eyes; she smiled at me, and I wish I knew how to describe the sweet kindliness of her beautiful smile; her voice was exquisitely gentle.

"Oh, my dear, why d'you bother your head about any others? What harm does it do you? Don't I give you a good time? Aren't you happy when you're with me?"

"Awfully."

"Well, then. It's so silly to be fussy and jealous. Why not be happy with what you can get? Enjoy yourself while you have the chance, I say; we shall all be dead in a hundred years and what will anything matter then? Let's have a good time while we can."

She put her arms round my neck and pressed her lips against mine. I forgot my wrath. I only thought of her beauty and her enveloping kindness.

"You must take me as I am, you know," she whispered.

"All right," I said.

XVIII

DURING all this time I saw really very little of Driffield. His editorship occupied much of his day and in the evening he wrote. He was, of course, there every Saturday afternoon, amiable and ironically amusing; he appeared glad to see me and chatted with me for a little while pleasantly of indifferent things; but naturally most of his attention was given to guests older and more important than I. But I had a feeling that he was growing more aloof; he was no longer the jolly, rather vulgar companion that I had known at Blackstable. Perhaps it was only my increasing sensibility that discerned as it were an invisible barrier that existed between him and the people he chaffed and joked with. It was as though he lived a life of the imagination that made the life of every day a little shadowy. He was asked to speak now and then at public dinners. He joined a literary club. He began to know a good many people outside the narrow circle into which his writing had drawn him, and he was increasingly asked to luncheon and tea by the ladies who like to gather about them distinguished authors. Rosie was asked too, but seldom went; she said she didn't care for parties, and after all they didn't want her, they only wanted Ted. I think she was shy and felt out of it. It may be that hostesses had more than once let her see how tiresome they thought it that she must be included; and after inviting her because it was polite, ignored her because to be polite irked them.

It was just about then that Edward Driffield published *The Cup of Life*. It is not my business to criticize his works, and of late as much has been written about them as must satisfy the appetite of any ordinary reader; but I will permit myself to say that *The Cup of Life*, though certainly not the most celebrated of his books, nor the most popular, is to my mind the most interesting. It has a cold ruthlessness that in all the sentimentality of English fiction strikes an original note. It is refreshing and astringent. It tastes of tart apples. It sets your teeth on edge, but it has a subtle, bitter-sweet savour that is very agreeable to the palate. Of all Driffield's books it is the only one I should like to have written. The scene of the child's death, terrible and heart-rending, but written without slop or sickliness, and the curious incident that follows it, cannot easily be forgotten by anyone who has read them.

It was this part of the book that caused the sudden storm that burst on the wretched Driffield's head. For a few days after publication it looked as though it would run its course like the rest of his novels, namely that it would have substantial reviews, laudatory on the whole but with reservations, and that the sales would be respectable, but modest. Rosie told me that he expected to make three hundred pounds out of it and was talking of renting a house on the river for the summer. The first two or three notices were noncommittal; then in one of the morning papers appeared a violent attack. There was a column of it. The book was described as gratuitously offensive, obscene, and the publishers were rated for putting it before the public. Harrowing pictures were drawn of the devastating effect it must have on the youth of England. It was described as an insult to womanhood. The reviewer protested against the possibility of such a work falling into the hands of young boys and innocent maidens. Other papers followed suit. The more foolish demanded that the book should be suppressed and some asked themselves gravely if this was not a case where the public prosecutor might with fitness intervene. Condemnation was universal; if here and there a courageous writer, accustomed to the more realistic tone of continental fiction, asserted that Edward Driffield had never written anything better, he was ignored. His honest opinion was ascribed to a base desire to play to the gallery. The libraries barred the book and the lessors of the railway bookstalls refused to stock it.

All this was naturally very unpleasant for Edward Driffield, but he bore it with philosophic calm. He shrugged his shoulders.

"They say it isn't true," he smiled. "They can go to hell. It is true."

He was supported in this trial by the fidelity of his friends. To admire *The Cup of Life* became a mark of æsthetic acumen: to be shocked by it was to confess yourself a Philistine. Mrs. Barton Trafford had no hesitation in saying that it was a masterpiece, and though this wasn't quite the moment for Barton's article in the *Quarterly,* her faith in Edward Driffield's future remained unshaken. It is strange (and instructive) to read now the book that created such a sensation; there is not a word that could bring a blush to the cheek of the most guileless, not an episode that could cause the novel reader of the present day to turn a hair.

X I X

ABOUT six months later, when the excitement over *The Cup of Life* had subsided and Driffield had already begun the novel which he published under the name of *By Their Fruits,* I, being then an in-patient dresser and in my fourth year, in the course of my duties went one day into the main hall of the hospital to await the surgeon whom I was accompanying on his round of the wards. I glanced at the rack in which letters were placed, for sometimes people, not knowing my address in Vincent Square, wrote to me at the hospital. I was surprised to find a telegram for me. It ran as follows:

Please come and see me at five o'clock this afternoon without fail. Important.

ISABEL TRAFFORD

I wondered what she wanted me for. I had met her perhaps a dozen times during the last two years, but she had never taken any notice of me, and I had never been to her house. I knew that men were scarce at teatime and a hostess, short of them at the last moment, might think that a young medical student was better than nothing; but the wording of the telegram hardly suggested a party.

The surgeon for whom I dressed was prosy and verbose. It was not till past five that I was free and then it took me a good twenty minutes to get down to Chelsea. Mrs. Barton Trafford lived in a block of flats on the Embankment. It was nearly six when I rang at her door and asked if she was at home. But when I was ushered into her drawing room and began to explain why I was late she cut me short.

"We supposed you couldn't get away. It doesn't matter."

Her husband was there.

"I expect he'd like a cup of tea," he said.

"Oh, I think it's rather late for tea, isn't it?" she looked at me gently, her mild, rather fine eyes full of kindness. "You don't want any tea, do you?"

I was thirsty and hungry, for my lunch consisted of a scone and butter and a cup of coffee, but I did not like to say so. I refused tea.

"Do you know Allgood Newton?" asked Mrs. Barton Trafford, with a gesture toward a man who had been sitting in a big armchair when I was shown in, and now got up. "I expect you've met him at Edward's."

I had. He did not come often, but his name was familiar to me and I remembered him. He made me very nervous and I do not think I had ever spoken to him. Though now completely forgotten, in those days he was the best-known critic in England. He was a large, fat, blond man, with a fleshy white face, pale blue eyes, and greying fair hair. He generally wore a pale blue tie to bring out the colour of his eyes. He was very amiable to the authors he met at Driffield's and said charming and flattering things to them, but when they were gone he was very amusing at their expense. He spoke in a low, even voice, with an apt choice of words: no one could with more point tell a malicious story about a friend.

Allgood Newton shook hands with me and Mrs. Barton Trafford, with her ready sympathy, anxious to put me at my ease, took me by the hand and made me sit on the sofa beside her. The tea was still on the table and she took a jam sandwich and delicately nibbled it.

"Have you seen the Driffields lately?" she asked me as though making conversation.

"I was there last Saturday."

"You haven't seen either of them since?"

"No."

Mrs. Barton Trafford looked from Allgood Newton to her husband and back again as though mutely demanding their help.

"Nothing will be gained by circumlocution, Isabel," said Newton, a faintly malicious twinkle in his eye, in his fat precise way.

Mrs. Barton Trafford turned to me.

"Then you don't know that Mrs. Driffield has run away from her husband."

"What!"

I was flabbergasted. I could not believe my ears.

"Perhaps it would be better if you told him the facts, Allgood," said Mrs. Trafford.

The critic leaned back in his chair and placed the tips of the fingers of one hand against the tips of the fingers of the other. He spoke with unction.

"I had to see Edward Driffield last night about a literary article that I am doing for him and after dinner, since the night was fine, I thought I would walk round to his house. He was expecting me; and I knew besides that he never went out at night except for some function as important as the Lord Mayor's banquet or the Academy dinner. Imagine my surprise then, nay, my utter and complete bewilderment, when as I approached I saw the door of his house open and Edward in person emerge. You know of course that Immanuel Kant was in the habit of taking his daily walk at a certain hour with such punctuality that the inhabitants of Königsberg were accustomed to set their watches by the event and when once he came out of his house an hour earlier than usual they turned pale, for they knew that this could only mean that some terrible thing had happened. They were right; Immanuel Kant had just received intelligence of the fall of the Bastille."

Allgood Newton paused for a moment to mark the effect of his anecdote. Mrs. Barton Trafford gave him her understanding smile.

"I did not envisage so world-shaking a catastrophe as this when I saw Edward hurrying toward me, but it immediately occurred to me that something untoward was afoot. He carried neither cane nor gloves. He wore his working coat, a venerable garment in black alpaca, and a wide-awake hat. There was something wild in his mien and distraught in his bearing. I asked myself, knowing the vicissitudes of the conjugal state, whether a matrimonial difference had driven him headlong from the house or whether he was hastening to a letter box in order to post a letter. He sped like Hector flying, the noblest of the Greeks. He did not seem to see me and the suspicion flashed across my mind that he did not want to. I stopped him. 'Edward,' I said. He looked startled. For a moment I could have sworn he did not know who I was. 'What avenging furies urge you with such hot haste through the rakish purlieus of Pimlico?' I asked. 'Oh, it's you,' he said. 'Where are you going?' I asked. 'Nowhere,' he replied.'"

At this rate I thought Allgood Newton would never finish his story and Mrs. Hudson would be vexed with me for turning up to dinner half an hour late.

"I told him on what errand I had come, and proposed that we should return to his house where he could more conveniently discuss the question that perturbed me. 'I'm too restless to go home,' he said; 'let's walk. You can talk to me as we go along.' Assenting, I turned round and we began to walk; but his pace was so rapid that I had to beg him to moderate it. Even Dr. Johnson could not have carried on a conversation when he was walking down Fleet Street at the speed of an express train. Edward's appearance was so peculiar and his manner so agitated that I thought it wise to lead him through the less frequented streets. I talked to him of my article. The subject that occupied me was more copious than had at first sight appeared, and I was doubtful whether after all I could do justice to it in the columns of a weekly journal. I put the matter before him fully and fairly and asked him his opinion. 'Rosie has left me,' he answered. For a moment I did not know what he was talking about, but in a trice it occurred to me that he was speaking of the buxom and not unprepossessing female from whose hands I had on occasion accepted a cup of tea. From his tone I divined that he expected condolence from me rather than felicitation."

Allgood Newton paused again and his blue eyes twinkled.

"You're wonderful, Allgood," said Mrs. Barton Trafford.

"Priceless," said her husband.

"Realizing that the occasion demanded sympathy, I said: 'My dear fellow.' He interrupted me. 'I had a letter by the last post,' he said. 'She's run away with Lord George Kemp.' "

I gasped, but said nothing. Mrs. Trafford gave me a quick look.

" 'Who is Lord George Kemp?' 'He's a Blackstable man,' he replied. I had little time to think. I determined to be frank. 'You're well rid of her,' I said. 'Allgood!' he cried. I stopped and put my hand on his arm. 'You must know that she was deceiving you with all your friends. Her behaviour was a public scandal. My dear Edward, let us face the fact: your wife was nothing but a common strumpet.' He snatched his arm away from me and gave a sort of low roar, like an orang-utan in the forests of Borneo forcibly deprived of a coconut, and before I could stop him he broke away and fled. I was so startled that I could do nothing but listen to his cries and his hurrying footsteps."

"You shouldn't have let him go," said Mrs. Barton Trafford. "In the state he was he might have thrown himself in the Thames."

"The thought occurred to me, but I noticed that he did not run in the direction of the river, but plunged into the meaner streets of the neighbourhood in which we had been walking. And I reflected also that there is no example in literary history of an author committing suicide while engaged on the composition of a literary work. Whatever his tribulations, he is unwilling to leave to posterity an uncompleted opus."

I was astounded at what I heard and shocked and dismayed; but I was worried too because I could not make out why Mrs. Trafford had sent for me. She knew me much too little to think that the story could be of any particular interest to me; nor would she have troubled to let me hear it as a piece of news.

"Poor Edward," she said. "Of course no one can deny that it is a blessing in disguise, but I'm afraid he'll take it very much to heart. Fortunately he's done nothing rash." She turned to me. "As soon as Mr. Newton told us about it I went round to Limpus Road. Edward was out, but the maid said he'd only just gone; that means that he must have gone home between the time he ran away from Allgood and this morning. You'll wonder why I asked you to come and see me."

I did not answer. I waited for her to go on.

"It was at Blackstable you first knew the Driffields, wasn't it? You can tell us who is this Lord George Kemp. Edward said he was a Blackstable man."

"He's middle-aged. He's got a wife and two sons. They're as old as I am."

"But I don't understand who he can be. I can't find him either in *Who's Who* or in Debrett."

I almost laughed.

"Oh, he's not really a lord. He's the local coal merchant. They call him Lord George at Blackstable because he's so grand. It's just a joke."

"The quiddity of bucolic humour is often a trifle obscure to the un-initiated," said Allgood Newton.

"We must all help dear Edward in every way we can," said Mrs. Barton Trafford. Her eyes rested on me thoughtfully. "If Kemp has run away with Rosie Driffield he must have left his wife."

"I suppose so," I replied.

"Will you do something very kind?"

"If I can."

"Will you go down to Blackstable and find out exactly what has hap-pened? I think we ought to get in touch with the wife."

I have never been very fond of interfering in other people's affairs.

"I don't know how I could do that," I answered.

"Couldn't you see her?"

"No, I couldn't."

If Mrs. Barton Trafford thought my reply blunt she did not show it. She smiled a little.

"At all events that can be left over. The urgent thing is to go down and find out about Kemp. I shall try to see Edward this evening. I can't bear the thought of his staying on in that odious house by himself. Barton and I have made up our minds to bring him here. We have a spare room and I'll arrange it so that he can work there. Don't you agree that that would be the best thing for him, Allgood?"

"Absolutely."

"There's no reason why he shouldn't stay here indefinitely, at all events for a few weeks, and then he can come away with us in the summer. We're going to Brittany. I'm sure he'd like that. It would be a thorough change for him."

"The immediate question," said Barton Trafford, fixing on me an eye nearly as kindly as his wife's, "is whether this young sawbones will go to Blackstable and find out what he can. We must know where we are. That is essential."

Barton Trafford excused his interest in archæology by a hearty manner and a jocose, even slangy way of speech.

"He couldn't refuse," said his wife, giving me a soft, appealing glance. "You won't refuse, will you? It's so important and you're the only person who can help us."

Of course she did not know that I was as anxious to find out what had happened as she; she could not tell what a bitter jealous pain stabbed my heart.

"I couldn't possibly get away from the hospital before Saturday," I said.

"That'll do. It's very good of you. All Edward's friends will be grateful to you. When shall you return?"

"I have to be back in London early on Monday morning."

"Then come and have tea with me in the afternoon. I shall await you with impatience. Thank God, that's settled. Now I must try and get hold of Edward."

I understood that I was dismissed. Allgood Newton took his leave and came downstairs with me.

"Our Isabel has *un petit air* of Catherine of Aragon today that I find vastly becoming," he murmured when the door was closed behind us. "This is a golden opportunity and I think we may safely trust our friend not to miss it. A charming woman with a heart of gold. *Vénus toute entière à sa proie attachée.*"

I did not understand what he meant, for what I have already told the reader about Mrs. Barton Trafford I only learned much later, but I realized that he was saying something vaguely malicious about her, and probably amusing, so I sniggered.

"I suppose your youth inclines you to what my good Dizzy named in an unlucky moment the gondola of London."

"I'm going to take a bus," I answered.

"Oh? Had you proposed to go by hansom I was going to ask you to be good enough to drop me on your way, but if you are going to use the homely conveyance which I in my old-fashioned manner still prefer to call an omnibus, I shall hoist my unwieldly carcass into a four-wheeler."

He signalled to one and gave me two flabby fingers to shake.

"I shall come on Monday to hear the result of what dear Henry would call your so exquisitely delicate mission."

xx

But it was years before I saw Allgood Newton again, for when I got to Blackstable I found a letter from Mrs. Barton Trafford (who had taken the precaution to note my address) asking me, for reasons that she would explain when she saw me, not to come to her flat but to meet her at six o'clock in the first-class waiting room at Victoria Station. As soon then as I could get away from the hospital on Monday I made my way there, and after waiting for a while saw her come in. She came toward me with little tripping steps.

"Well, have you anything to tell me? Let us find a quiet corner and sit down."

We sought a place and found it.

"I must explain why I asked you to come here," she said. "Edward is staying with me. At first he did not want to come, but I persuaded him. But he's nervous and ill and irritable. I did not want to run the risk of his seeing you."

I told Mrs. Trafford the bare facts of my story and she listened attentively. Now and then she nodded her head. But I could not hope to make her understand the commotion I had found at Blackstable. The town was beside itself with excitement. Nothing so thrilling had happened there for years and no one could talk of anything else. Humpty-Dumpty had had a great fall. Lord George Kemp had absconded. About a week before he had announced that he had to go up to London on business, and two days later a petition in bankruptcy was filed against him. It appeared that his building operations had not been successful, his attempt to make Blackstable into a frequented seaside resort meeting with no response, and he had been forced to raise money in every way he could. All kinds of rumours ran through the little town. Quite a number of small people who had entrusted their savings to him were faced with the loss of all they had. The details were vague, for neither my uncle nor my aunt knew anything of business matters, nor had I the knowledge to make what they told me comprehensible. But there was a mortgage on George Kemp's house and a bill of sale on his furniture. His wife was left without a penny. His two sons, lads of twenty and twenty-one, were in the coal business, but that, too, was involved in the general ruin. George Kemp had gone off with all the cash he could lay hands on, something like fifteen hundred pounds, they said, though how they knew I cannot imagine; and it was reported that a warrant had been issued for his arrest. It was supposed that he had left the country; some said he had gone to Australia and some to Canada.

"I hope they catch him," said my uncle. "He ought to get penal servitude for life."

The indignation was universal. They could not forgive him because he had always been so noisy and boisterous, because he had chaffed them and stood them drinks and given them garden parties, because he had driven such a smart trap and worn his brown billycock hat at such a rakish angle. But it was on Sunday night after church in the vestry that the churchwarden told my uncle the worst. For the last two years he had been meeting Rosie Driffield at Haversham almost every week and they had been spending the night together at a public house. The licensee of this had put money into one of Lord George's wildcat schemes, and on discovering that he had lost it blurted out the whole story. He could have borne it if Lord George had defrauded others, but that he should defraud him who had done him a good turn and whom he looked upon as a chum, that was the limit.

"I expect they've run away together," said my uncle.

"I shouldn't be surprised," said the churchwarden.

After supper, while the housemaid was clearing away, I went into the kitchen to talk to Mary-Ann. She had been at church and had heard the story too. I cannot believe that the congregation had listened very attentively to my uncle's sermon.

"The vicar says they've run away together," I said. I had not breathed a word of what I knew.

"Why, of course they 'ave," said Mary-Ann. "He was the only man she ever really fancied. He only 'ad to lift 'is finger and she'd leave anyone no matter who it was."

I lowered my eyes. I was suffering from bitter mortification; and I was angry with Rosie: I thought she had behaved very badly to me.

"I suppose we shall never see her again," I said. It gave me a pang to utter the words.

"I don't suppose we shall," said Mary-Ann cheerfully.

When I had told Mrs. Barton Trafford as much of this story as I thought she need know, she sighed, but whether from satisfaction or distress I had no notion.

"Well, that's the end of Rosie at all events," she said. She got up and held out her hand. "Why will these literary men make these unfortunate marriages? It's all very sad, very sad. Thank you so much for what you've done. We know where we are now. The great thing is that it shouldn't interfere with Edward's work."

Her remarks seemed a trifle disconnected to me. The fact was, I have no doubt, that she was giving me not the smallest thought. I led her out of Victoria Station and put her into a bus that went down the King's Road, Chelsea; then I walked back to my lodgings.

XXI

I LOST touch with Driffield. I was too shy to seek him out; I was busy with my examinations, and when I had passed them I went abroad. I remembered vaguely to have seen in the paper that he had divorced Rosie. Nothing more was heard of her. Small sums reached her mother occasionally, ten or twenty pounds, and they came in a registered letter with a New York postmark; but no address was given, no message enclosed, and they were presumed to come from Rosie only because no one else could possibly send Mrs. Gann money. Then in the fullness of years Rosie's mother died, and it may be supposed that in some way the news reached her, for the letters ceased to come.

XXII

ALROY KEAR and I, as arranged, met on Friday at Victoria Station to catch the five-ten to Blackstable. We made ourselves comfortable in opposite corners of a smoking compartment. From him I now learned roughly what had happened to Driffield after his wife ran away from him. Roy had in due course become very intimate with Mrs. Barton Trafford. Knowing him and remembering her, I realized that this was inevitable. I was not surprised to hear that he had travelled with her and Barton on the continent, sharing with them to the full their passion for Wagner, post-impressionist painting, and baroque architecture. He had lunched assiduously at the flat in Chelsea and when advancing years and failing health had imprisoned Mrs. Trafford to her drawing room, notwithstanding the many claims on his time he had gone regularly once a week to sit with her. He had a good heart. After her death he wrote an article about her in which with admirable emotion he did justice to her great gifts of sympathy and discrimination.

It pleased me to think that his kindliness should receive its due and unexpected reward, for Mrs. Barton Trafford had told him much about

Edward Driffield that could not fail to be of service to him in the work of love in which he was now engaged. Mrs. Barton Trafford, exercising a gentle violence, not only took Edward Driffield into her house when the flight of his faithless wife left him what Roy could only describe by the French word *désemparé,* but persuaded him to stay for nearly a year. She gave him the loving care, the unfailing kindness, and the intelligent understanding of a woman who combined feminine tact with masculine vigour, a heart of gold with an unerring eye for the main chance. It was in her flat that he finished *By Their Fruits.* She was justified in looking upon it as her book and the dedication to her is a proof that Driffield was not unmindful of his debt. She took him to Italy (with Barton of course, for Mrs. Trafford knew too well how malicious people were, to give occasion for scandal) and with a volume of Ruskin in her hand revealed to Edward Driffield the immortal beauties of that country. Then she found him rooms in the Temple and arranged little luncheons there, she acting very prettily the part of hostess, where he could receive the persons whom his increasing reputation attracted.

It must be admitted that this increasing reputation was very largely due to her. His great celebrity came only during his last years when he had long ceased to write, but the foundations of it were undoubtedly laid by Mrs. Trafford's untiring efforts. Not only did she inspire (and perhaps write not a little, for she had a dexterous pen) the article that Barton at last contributed to the *Quarterly* in which the claim was first made that Driffield must be ranked with the masters of British fiction, but as each book came out she organized its reception. She went here and there, seeing editors and, more important still, proprietors of influential organs; she gave soirées to which everyone was invited who could be of use. She persuaded Edward Driffield to give readings at the houses of the very great for charitable purposes; she saw to it that his photographs should appear in the illustrated weeklies; she revised personally any interview he gave. For ten years she was an indefatigable press agent. She kept him steadily before the public.

Mrs. Barton Trafford had a grand time, but she did not get above herself. It was useless indeed to ask him to a party without her; he re-

fused. And when she and Barton and Driffield were invited anywhere
to dinner they came together and went together. She never let him
out of her sight. Hostesses might rave; they could take it or leave it.
As a rule they took it. If Mrs. Barton Trafford happened to be a little
out of temper it was through him she showed it, for while she remained
charming, Edward Driffield would be uncommonly gruff. But she
knew exactly how to draw him out and when the company was distinguished could make him brilliant. She was perfect with him. She
never concealed from him her conviction that he was the greatest writer
of his day; she not only referred to him invariably as the master, but,
perhaps a little playfully and yet how flatteringly, addressed him always
as such. To the end she retained something kittenish.

Then a terrible thing happened. Driffield caught pneumonia and was
extremely ill; for some time his life was despaired of. Mrs. Barton
Trafford did everything that such a woman could do, and would willingly have nursed him herself, but she was frail, she was indeed over
sixty, and he had to have professional nurses. When at last he pulled
through, the doctors said that he must go into the country, and since
he was still extremely weak insisted that a nurse should go with him.
Mrs. Trafford wanted him to go to Bournemouth so that she could run
down for week-ends and see that everything was well with him, but
Driffield had a fancy for Cornwall, and the doctors agreed that the mild
airs of Penzance would suit him. One would have thought that a woman
of Isabel Trafford's delicate intuition would have had some forboding
of ill. No. She let him go. She impressed on the nurse that she entrusted
her with a grave responsibility; she placed in her hands, if not the
future of English literature, at least the life and welfare of its most distinguished living representative. It was a priceless charge.

Three weeks later Edward Driffield wrote and told her that he had
married his nurse by special licence.

I imagine that never did Mrs. Barton Trafford exhibit more pre-
eminently her greatness of soul than in the manner in which she met
this situation. Did she cry, Judas, Judas? Did she tear her hair and fall
on the floor and kick her heels in an attack of hysterics? Did she turn
on the mild and learned Barton and call him a blithering old fool?

Did she inveigh against the faithlessness of men and the wantonness of women or did she relieve her wounded feelings by shouting at the top of her voice a string of those obscenities with which the alienists tell us the chastest females are surprisingly acquainted? Not at all. She wrote a charming letter of congratulation to Driffield and she wrote to his bride telling her that she was glad to think that now she would have two loving friends instead of one. She begged them both to come and stay with her on their return to London. She told everyone she met that the marriage had made her very, very happy, for Edward Driffield would soon be an old man and must have someone to take care of him; who could do this better than a hospital nurse? She never had anything but praise for the new Mrs. Driffield; she was not exactly pretty, she said, but she had a very nice face; of course she wasn't quite, quite a lady, but Edward would only have been uncomfortable with anyone too grand. She was just the sort of wife for him. I think it may be not unjustly said that Mrs. Barton Trafford fairly ran over with the milk of human kindness, but all the same I have an inkling that if ever the milk of human kindness was charged with vitriol, here was a case in point.

XXIII

WHEN we arrived at Blackstable, Roy and I, a car, neither ostentatiously grand nor obviously cheap, was waiting for him and the chauffeur had a note for me asking me to lunch with Mrs. Driffield next day. I got into a taxi and went to the Bear and Key. I had learned from Roy that there was a new Marine Hotel on the front, but I did not propose for the luxuries of civilization to abandon a resort of my youth. Change met me at the railway station, which was not in its old place, but up a new road, and of course it was strange to be driven down the High Street in a car. But the Bear and Key was unaltered. It received me with its old churlish indifference: there was no one at the entrance, the driver put my bag down and drove away; I called, no one answered; I went into the bar and found a young lady with shingled hair reading a book by Mr. Compton Mackenzie. I asked her if I could have a room.

She gave me a slightly offended look and said she thought so, but as that seemed to exhaust her interest in the matter I asked politely whether there was anyone who could show it to me. She got up and, opening a door, in a shrill voice called: "Katie."

"What is it?" I heard.

"There's a gent wants a room."

In a little while appeared an ancient and haggard female in a very dirty print dress, with an untidy mop of grey hair, and showed me, two flights up, a very small grubby room.

"Can't you do something better than that for me?" I asked.

"It's the room commercials generally 'ave," she answered with a sniff.

"Haven't you got any others?"

"Not single."

"Then give me a double room."

"I'll go and ask Mrs. Brentford."

I accompanied her down to the first floor and she knocked at a door. She was told to come in, and when she opened it I caught sight of a stout woman with grey hair elaborately marcelled. She was reading a book. Apparently everyone at the Bear and Key was interested in literature. She gave me an indifferent look when Katie said I wasn't satisfied with number seven.

"Show him number five," she said.

I began to feel that I had been a trifle rash in declining so haughtily Mrs. Driffield's invitation to stay with her and then putting aside in my sentimental way Roy's wise suggestion that I should stay at the Marine Hotel. Katie took me upstairs again and ushered me into a largish room looking on the High Street. Most of its space was occupied by a double bed. The windows had certainly not been opened for a month.

I said that would do and asked about dinner.

"You can 'ave what you like," said Katie. "We 'aven't got nothing in, but I'll run round and get it."

Knowing English inns, I ordered a fried sole and a grilled chop. Then I went for a stroll. I walked down to the beach and found that they had built an esplanade and there was a row of bungalows and villas where I remembered only windswept fields. But they were seedy and bedraggled and I guessed that even after all these years Lord George's dream of turning Blackstable into a popular seaside resort had not come true. A retired military man, a pair of elderly ladies walked along the crumbling asphalt. It was incredibly dreary. A chill wind was blowing and a light drizzle swept over from the sea.

I went back into town and here, in the space between the Bear and Key and the Duke of Kent, were little knots of men standing about notwithstanding the inclement weather; and their eyes had the same pale blue, their high cheek-bones the same ruddy colour as that of their fathers before them. It was strange to see that some of the sailors in blue jerseys still wore little gold rings in their ears; and not only old ones but boys scarcely out of their teens. I sauntered down the street and there was the bank re-fronted, but the stationery shop where I had bought paper and wax to make rubbings with an obscure writer whom I had met by chance was unchanged; there were two or three cinemas and their garish posters suddenly gave the prim street a dissipated air so that it looked like a respectable elderly woman who had taken a drop too much.

It was cold and cheerless in the commercial room where I ate my dinner alone at a large table laid for six. I was served by the slatternly Katie. I asked if I could have a fire.

"Not in June," she said. "We don't 'ave fires after April."

"I'll pay for it," I protested.

"Not in June. In October, yes, but not in June."

When I had finished I went into the bar to have a glass of port.

"Very quiet," I said to the shingled barmaid.

"Yes, it is quiet," she answered.

"I should have thought on a Friday night you'd have quite a lot of people in here."

"Well, one would think that, wouldn't one?"

Then a stout red-faced man with a close-cropped head of grey hair came in from the back and I guessed that this was my host.

"Are you Mr. Brentford?" I asked him.

"Yes, that's me."

"I knew your father. Will you have a glass of port?"

I told him my name, in the days of his boyhood better known than any other at Blackstable, but somewhat to my mortification I saw that it aroused no echo in his memory. He consented, however, to let me stand him a glass of port.

"Down here on business?" he asked me. "We get quite a few commercial gents at one time and another. We always like to do what we can for them."

I told him that I had come down to see Mrs. Driffield and left him to guess on what errand.

"I used to see a lot of the old man," said Mr. Brentford. "He used to be very partial to dropping in here and having his glass of bitter. Mind you, I don't say he ever got tiddly, but he used to like to sit in the bar and talk. My word, he'd talk by the hour and he never cared who he talked to. Mrs. Driffield didn't half like his coming here. He'd slip away, out of the house, without saying a word to anybody, and come toddling down. You know it's a bit of a walk for a man of that age. Of course when they missed him Mrs. Driffield knew where he was, and she used to telephone and ask if he was here. Then she'd drive over in the car and go in and see my wife. 'You go in and fetch him, Mrs. Brentford,' she'd say; 'I don't like to go in the bar meself, not with all those men hanging about'; so Mrs. Brentford would come in and she'd say: 'Now, Mr. Driffield, Mrs. Driffield's come for you in the car, so you'd better finish your beer and let her take you home.' He used to ask Mrs. Brentford not to say he was here when Mrs. Driffield rang up, but of course we couldn't do that. He was an old man and all that and we didn't want to take the responsibility. He was born in this parish, you know, and his first wife, she was a Blackstable girl. She's been dead these many years. I never knew her. He was a funny old fellow. No side, you know; they tell me they thought a rare lot of him in London and when he died the papers were full of him; but you'd never have known it to talk to him. He might have been just nobody like you and me. Of course we always tried to make him comfortable; we tried to get him to sit in one of them easy chairs, but no, he must sit up at the bar; he said he liked to feel his feet on a rail. My belief is he was happier here than anywhere. He always said he liked a bar parlour. He said you saw life there and he said he'd always loved life. Quite a character he was. Reminded me of my father, except that my old governor never read a book in his life and he drank a bottle of French brandy a day and he was seventy-eight when he died and his last illness was his first. I quite missed old Driffield when he popped off. I was only saying to Mrs. Brentford the other day, I'd like to read one of his books some time. They tell me he wrote several about these parts."

X X I V

NEXT morning it was cold and raw, but it was not raining, and I walked down the High Street toward the vicarage. I recognized the names over the shops, the Kentish names that have been borne for centuries—the Ganns, the Kemps, the Cobbs, the Igguldens—but I saw no one that I knew. I felt like a ghost walking down the street where I had once known nearly everyone, if not to speak to, at least by sight. Suddenly a very shabby little car passed me, stopped, and backed, and I saw someone looking at me curiously. A tall, heavy elderly man got out and came toward me.

"Aren't you Willie Ashenden?" he asked.

Then I recognized him. He was the doctor's son, and I had been at school with him; we had passed from form to form together, and I knew that he had succeeded his father in his practice.

"Hullo, how are you?" he asked. "I've just been along to the vicarage to see my grandson. It's a preparatory school now, you know, and I put him there at the beginning of this term."

He was shabbily dressed and unkempt, but he had a fine head and I saw that in youth he must have had unusual beauty. It was funny that I had never noticed it.

"Are you a grandfather?" I asked.

"Three times over," he laughed.

It gave me a shock. He had drawn breath, walked the earth, and presently grown to man's estate, married, had children, and they in turn had had children; I judged from the look of him that he had lived, with incessant toil, in penury. He had the peculiar manner of the country doctor, bluff, hearty, and unctuous. His life was over. I had plans in my head for books and plays, I was full of schemes for the future; I felt that a long stretch of activity and fun still lay before me; and yet, I supposed, to others I must seem the elderly man that he seemed to me. I was so shaken that I had not the presence of mind to ask about his brothers whom as a child I had played with, or about the old friends who had been my companions; after a few foolish remarks I left him. I walked on to the vicarage, a roomy, rambling house too far out of the way for the modern incumbent who took his duties more seriously than did my uncle and too large for the present cost of living. It stood in a big garden and was surrounded by green fields. There was a great square notice board that announced that it was a preparatory school for the sons of gentlemen and gave the name and the degrees of the head master. I looked over the paling; the garden was squalid and untidy and the pond in which I used to fish for roach was choked up. The glebe fields had been cut up into building lots. There were rows of little brick houses with bumpy ill-made roads. I walked along Joy Lane and there were houses here too, bungalows facing the sea; and the old turnpike house was a trim tea shop.

I wandered about here and there. There seemed innumerable streets of little houses of yellow brick, but I do not know who lived in them for I saw no one about. I went down to the harbour. It was deserted. There was but one tramp lying a little way out from the pier. Two or three sailormen were sitting outside a warehouse and they stared at me as I passed. The bottom had fallen out of the coal trade and colliers came to Blackstable no longer.

Then it was time for me to go to Ferne Court and I went back to the Bear and Key. The landlord had told me that he had a Daimler for hire and I had arranged that it should take me to my luncheon. It stood at the door when I came up, a brougham, but the oldest, most dilapidated car of its make that I had ever seen; it panted along with squeaks and thumps and rattlings, with sudden angry jerks, so that I wondered if I should ever reach my destination. But the extraordinary, the amazing thing about it was that it smelled exactly like the old landau which my uncle used to hire every Sunday morning to go to church in. This was a rank odour of stables and of stale straw that lay at the bottom of the carriage; and I wondered in vain why, after all these years, the motor car should have it too. But nothing can bring back the past like a perfume or a stench, and, oblivious to the country I was trundling through, I saw myself once more a little boy on the front seat with the communion plate beside me and, facing me, my aunt, smelling slightly of clean linen and eau-de-Cologne, in her black silk cloak and her little bonnet with a feather, and my uncle in his cassock, a broad band of ribbed silk round his ample waist and a gold cross hanging over his stomach from the gold chain round his neck.

"Now, Willie, mind you behave nicely today. You're not to turn round, and sit up properly in your seat. The Lord's House isn't the place to loll in and you must remember that you should set an example to other little boys who haven't had your advantages."

When I arrived at Ferne Court, Mrs. Driffield and Roy were walking round the garden and they came up to me as I got out of the car.

"I was showing Roy my flowers," said Mrs. Driffield, as she shook hands with me. And then with a sigh: "They're all I have now."

She looked no older than when last I saw her six years before. She wore her weeds with quiet distinction. At her neck was a collar of white crêpe and at her wrists cuffs of the same. Roy, I noticed, wore with his neat blue suit a black tie; I supposed it was a sign of respect for the illustrious dead.

"I'll just show you my herbaceous borders," said Mrs. Driffield, "and then we'll go in to lunch."

We walked round and Roy was very knowledgeable. He knew what all the flowers were called, and the Latin names tripped off his tongue like cigarettes out of a cigarette-making machine. He told Mrs. Driffield where she ought to get certain varieties that she absolutely must have and how perfectly lovely were certain others.

"Shall we go in through Edward's study?" suggested Mrs. Driffield. "I keep it exactly as it was when he was here. I haven't changed a thing. You'd be surprised how many people come over to see the

house, and of course above all they want to see the room he worked
in."

We went in through an open window. There was a bowl of roses
on the desk and on a little round table by the side of the armchair a
copy of the *Spectator*. In the ash trays were the master's pipes and there
was ink in the inkstand. The scene was perfectly set. I do not know
why the room seemed so strangely dead; it had already the mustiness
of a museum. Mrs. Driffield went to the bookshelves and with a little
smile, half playful, half sad, passed a rapid hand across the back of half
a dozen volumes bound in blue.

"You know that Edward admired your work so much," said Mrs.
Driffield. "He reread your books quite often."

"I'm very glad to think that," I said politely.

I knew very well that they had not been there on my last visit and
in a casual way I took one of them out and ran my fingers along the
top to see whether there was dust on it. There was not. Then I took
another book down, one of Charlotte Brontë's, and making a little
plausible conversation tried the same experiment. No, there was no
dust there either. All I learned was that Mrs. Driffield was an excellent
housekeeper and had a conscientious maid.

We went in to luncheon, a hearty British meal of roast beef and
Yorkshire pudding, and we talked of the work on which Roy was
engaged.

"I want to spare dear Roy all the labour I can," said Mrs. Driffield,
"and I've been gathering together as much of the material as I could
myself. Of course it's been rather painful, but it's been very interesting, too. I came across a lot of old photographs that I must show you."

After luncheon we went into the drawing room and I noticed again
with what perfect tact Mrs. Driffield had arranged it. It suited the
widow of a distinguished man of letters almost more than it had
suited the wife. Those chintzes, those bowls of pot-pourri, those Dresden china figures—there was about them a faint air of regret; they
seemed to reflect pensively upon a past of distinction. I could have
wished on this chilly day that there were a fire in the grate, but the
English are a hardy as well as a conservative race; and it is not difficult

for them to maintain their principles at the cost of the discomfort of others. I doubted whether Mrs. Driffield would have conceived the possibility of lighting a fire before the first of October. She asked me whether I had lately seen the lady who had brought me to lunch with the Driffields, and I surmised from her faint acerbity that since the death of her eminent husband the great and fashionable had shown a distinct tendency to take no further notice of her. We were just settling down to talk about the defunct; Roy and Mrs. Driffield were putting artful questions to incite me to disclose my recollections and I was gathering my wits about me so that I should not in an unguarded moment let slip anything that I had made up my mind to keep to myself; when suddenly the trim parlour-maid brought in two cards on a small salver.

"Two gentlemen in a car, mum, and they say, could they look at the house and garden?"

"What a bore!" cried Mrs. Driffield, but with astonishing alacrity. "Isn't it funny I should have been speaking just now about the people who want to see the house? I never have a moment's peace."

"Well, why don't you say you're sorry you can't see them?" said Roy, with what I thought a certain cattiness.

"Oh, I couldn't do that. Edward wouldn't have liked me to." She looked at the cards. "I haven't got my glasses on me."

She handed them to me, and on one I read "Henry Beard Mac-Dougal, University of Virginia"; and in pencil was written: "Assistant Professor in English Literature." The other was "Jean-Paul Underhill" and there was at the bottom an address in New York.

"Americans," said Mrs. Driffield. "Say I shall be very pleased if they'll come in."

Presently the maid ushered the strangers in. They were both tall young men and broad-shouldered, with heavy, clean-shaven, swarthy faces, and handsome eyes; they both wore horn-rimmed spectacles and they both had thick black hair combed straight back from their foreheads. They both wore English suits that were evidently brand new; they were both slightly embarrassed, but verbose and extremely civil. They explained that they were making a literary tour of England and, being admirers of Edward Driffield, had taken the liberty of stopping off on their way to Rye to visit Henry James's house in the hope that they would be permitted to see a spot sanctified by so many associations. The reference to Rye did not go down very well with Mrs. Driffield.

"I believe they have some very good links there," she said.

She introduced the Americans to Roy and me. I was filled with admiration for the way in which Roy rose to the occasion. It appeared that he had lectured before the University of Virginia and had stayed with a distinguished member of the faculty. It had been an unforgettable experience. He did not know whether he had been more impressed by the lavish hospitality with which those charming Virginians had entertained him or by their intelligent interest in art and literature. He asked how So and So was, and So and So; he had made lifelong friends there, and it looked as though everyone he had met was good and kind and clever. Soon the young professor was telling Roy how much he liked his books, and Roy was modestly telling him what in this one and the other his aim had been and how conscious he was that he had come far short of achieving it. Mrs. Driffield listened with smiling sympathy, but I had a feeling that her smile was growing a trifle strained. It may be that Roy had too, for he suddenly broke off.

"But you don't want me to bore you with my stuff," he said in his loud hearty way. "I'm only here because Mrs. Driffield has entrusted to me the great honour of writing Edward Driffield's Life."

This of course interested the visitors very much.

"It's some job, believe me," said Roy, playfully American. "Fortunately I have the assistance of Mrs. Driffield, who was not only a perfect wife, but an admirable amanuensis and secretary; the materials she has placed at my disposal are so amazingly full that really little remains for me to do but take advantage of her industry and her—her affectionate zeal."

Mrs. Driffield looked down demurely at the carpet and the two young Americans turned on her their large dark eyes in which you could read their sympathy, their interest, and their respect. After a little more conversation—partly literary but also about golf, for the visitors admitted that they hoped to get a round or two at Rye, and here again Roy was on the spot, for he told them to look out for such and such a bunker and when they came to London hoped they would play with him at Sunningdale; after this, I say, Mrs. Driffield got up and offered to show them Edward's study and bedroom, and of course the garden. Roy rose to his feet, evidently bent on accompanying them, but Mrs. Driffield gave him a little smile; it was pleasant but firm.

"Don't you bother to come, Roy," she said. "I'll take them round. You stay here and talk to Mr. Ashenden."

"Oh, all right. Of course."

The strangers bade us farewell and Roy and I settled down again in the chintz armchairs.

"Jolly room this is," said Roy.

"Very."

"Amy had to work hard to get it. You know the old man bought this house two or three years before they were married. She tried to make him sell it, but he wouldn't. He was very obstinate in some ways. You see, it belonged to a certain Miss Wolfe, whose bailiff his father was, and he said that when he was a little boy his one idea was to own it himself and now he'd got it he was going to keep it. One would have thought the last thing he'd want to do was to live in a place where everyone knew all about his origins and everything. Once poor Amy very nearly engaged a housemaid before she discovered she was Edward's great niece. When Amy came here the house was furnished from attic to cellar in the best Tottenham Court Road manner; you know the sort of thing, Turkey carpets and mahogany sideboards, and a plush-covered suite in the drawing room, and modern marquetry. It was his idea of how a gentleman's house should be furnished. Amy says it was simply awful. He wouldn't let her change a thing and she had to go to work with the greatest care; she says she simply couldn't have lived in it and she was determined to have things right, so she had to change things one by one so that he didn't pay any attention. She told me the hardest job she had was with his writing desk. I don't know whether you've noticed the one there is in his study now. It's a very good period piece; I wouldn't mind having it myself. Well, he had a horrible American roll-top desk. He'd had it for years and he'd written a dozen books on it and he simply wouldn't part with it, he had no feeling for things like that; he just happened to be attached to it because he'd had it so long. You must get Amy to tell you the story how she managed to get rid of it in the end. It's really priceless. She's a remarkable woman, you know; she generally gets her own way."

"I've noticed it," I said.

It had not taken her long to dispose of Roy when he showed signs of wishing to go over the house with the visitors. He gave me a quick look and laughed. Roy was not stupid.

"You don't know America as well as I do," he said. "They always prefer a live mouse to a dead lion. That's one of the reasons why I like America."

XXV

When Mrs. Driffield, having sent the pilgrims on their way, came back she bore under her arm a portfolio.

"What very nice young men!" she said. "I wish young men in England took such a keen interest in literature. I gave them that photo of Edward when he was dead and they asked me for one of mine, and I signed it for them." Then very graciously: "You made a great impression on them, Roy. They said it was a real privilege to meet you."

"I've lectured in America so much," said Roy, with modesty.

"Oh, but they've read your books. They say that what they like about them is that they're so virile."

The portfolio contained a number of old photographs, groups of schoolboys among whom I recognized an urchin with untidy hair as Driffield only because his widow pointed him out. Rugby fifteens with Driffield a little older, and then one of a young sailor in a jersey and a reefer jacket, Driffield when he ran away to sea.

"Here's one taken when he was first married," said Mrs. Driffield.

He wore a beard and black-and-white cheque trousers; in his buttonhole was a large white rose backed by maidenhair and on the table beside him a chimney-pot hat.

"And here is the bride," said Mrs. Driffield, trying not to smile.

Poor Rosie, seen by a country photographer over forty years ago, was grotesque. She was standing very stiffly against a background of baronial hall, holding a large bouquet; her dress was elaborately draped, pinched at the waist, and she wore a bustle. Her fringe came down to her eyes. On her head was a wreath of orange blossoms, perched high on a mass of hair, and from it was thrown back a long veil. Only I knew how lovely she must have looked.

"She looks fearfully common," said Roy.

"She was," murmured Mrs. Driffield.

We looked at more photographs of Edward, photographs that had been taken of him when he began to be known, photographs when he wore only a moustache and others, all the later ones, when he was clean-shaven. You saw his face grown thinner and more lined. The stubborn commonplace of the early portraits melted gradually into a weary refinement. You saw the change in him wrought by experience, thought, and achieved ambition. I looked again at the photograph of the young sailorman and fancied that I saw in it already a trace of that aloofness that seemed to me so marked in the older ones and that I had had years before the vague sensation of in the man himself. The face you saw was a mask and the actions he performed without significance. I had an impression that the real man, to his death unknown and lonely, was a wraith that went a silent way unseen between the writer of his books and the fellow who led his life, and smiled with ironical detachment at the two puppets that the world took for Edward Driffield. I am conscious that in what I have written of him I have not presented a living man, standing on his feet, rounded, with comprehensible motives and logical activities; I have not tried to: I am glad to leave that to the abler pen of Alroy Kear.

I came across the photographs that Harry Retford, the actor, had taken of Rosie, and then a photograph of the picture that Lionel Hillier had painted of her. It gave me a pang. That was how I best remembered her. Notwithstanding the old-fashioned gown, she was alive there and tremulous with the passion that filled her. She seemed to offer herself to the assault of love.

"She gives you the impression of a hefty wench," said Roy.

"If you like the milkmaid type," answered Mrs. Driffield. "I've always thought she looked rather like a white nigger."

That was what Mrs. Barton Trafford had been fond of calling her, and with Rosie's thick lips and broad nose there was indeed a hateful truth in the criticism. But they did not know how silvery golden her hair was, nor how golden silver her skin; they did not know her enchanting smile.

"She wasn't a bit like a white nigger," I said. "She was virginal like the dawn. She was like Hebe. She was like a white rose."

Mrs. Driffield smiled and exchanged a meaning glance with Roy.

"Mrs. Barton Trafford told me a great deal about her. I don't wish to seem spiteful, but I'm afraid I don't think that she can have been a very nice woman."

"That's where you make a mistake," I replied. "She was a very nice woman. I never saw her in a bad temper. You only had to say you wanted something for her to give it to you. I never heard her say a disagreeable thing about anyone. She had a heart of gold."

"She was a terrible slattern. Her house was always in a mess; you didn't like to sit down in a chair because it was so dusty and you dared not look in the corners. And it was the same with her person. She could never put a skirt on straight and you'd see about two inches of petticoat hanging down on one side."

"She didn't bother about things like that. They didn't make her any the less beautiful. And she was as good as she was beautiful."

Roy burst out laughing and Mrs. Driffield put her hand up to her mouth to hide her smile.

"Oh, come, Mr. Ashenden, that's really going too far. After all, let's face it, she was a nymphomaniac."

"I think that's a very silly word," I said.

"Well, then, let me say that she can hardly have been a very good woman to treat poor Edward as she did. Of course it was a blessing in disguise. If she hadn't run away from him he might have had to bear that burden for the rest of his life, and with such a handicap he could never have reached the position he did. But the fact remains that she was notoriously unfaithful to him. From what I hear she was absolutely promiscuous."

"You don't understand," I said. "She was a very simple woman. Her instincts were healthy and ingenuous. She loved to make people happy. She loved love."

"Do you call that love?"

"Well, then, the act of love. She was naturally affectionate. When she liked anyone it was quite natural for her to go to bed with him. She never thought twice about it. It was not vice; it wasn't lasciviousness; it was her nature. She gave herself as naturally as the sun gives heat or the flowers their perfume. It was a pleasure to her and she liked to give pleasure to others. It had no effect on her character; she remained sincere, unspoiled, and artless."

Mrs. Driffield looked as though she had taken a dose of castor oil and had just been trying to get the taste of it out of her mouth by sucking a lemon.

"I don't understand," she said. "But then I'm bound to admit that I never understood what Edward saw in her."

"Did he know that she was carrying on with all sorts of people?" asked Roy.

"I'm sure he didn't," she replied quickly.

"You think him a bigger fool than I do, Mrs. Driffield," I said.

"Then why did he put up with it?"

"I think I can tell you. You see, she wasn't a woman who ever inspired love. Only affection. It was absurd to be jealous over her. She was like a clear deep pool in a forest glade into which it's heavenly to plunge, but it is neither less cool nor less crystalline because a tramp and a gipsy and a gamekeeper have plunged into it before you."

Roy laughed again and this time Mrs. Driffield without concealment smiled thinly.

"It's comic to hear you so lyrical," said Roy.

I stifled a sigh. I have noticed that when I am most serious people are apt to laugh at me, and indeed when after a lapse of time I have read passages that I wrote from the fullness of my heart I have been tempted to laugh at myself. It must be that there is something naturally absurd in a sincere emotion, though why there should be I cannot imagine, unless it is that man, the ephemeral inhabitant of an insignificant planet, with all his pain and all his striving is but a jest in an eternal mind.

I saw that Mrs. Driffield wished to ask me something. It caused her a certain embarrassment.

"Do you think he'd have taken her back if she'd been willing to come?"

"You knew him better than I. I should say no. I think that when he had exhausted an emotion he took no further interest in the person who had aroused it. I should say that he had a peculiar combination of strong feeling and extreme callousness."

"I don't know how you can say that," cried Roy. "He was the kindest man I ever met."

Mrs. Driffield looked at me steadily and then dropped her eyes.

"I wonder what happened to her when she went to America?" he asked.

"I believe she married Kemp," said Mrs. Driffield. "I heard they had taken another name. Of course they couldn't show their faces over here again."

"When did she die?"

"Oh, about ten years ago."

"How did you hear?" I asked.

"From Harold Kemp, the son; he's in some sort of business at Maidstone. I never told Edward. She'd been dead to him for many years and I saw no reason to remind him of the past. It always helps you if you put yourself in other people's shoes and I said to myself that if I were he I shouldn't want to be reminded of an unfortunate episode of my youth. Don't you think I was right?"

XXVI

Mrs. Driffield very kindly offered to send me back to Blackstable in her car, but I preferred to walk. I promised to dine at Ferne Court next day and meanwhile to write down what I could remember of the two periods during which I had been in the habit of seeing Edward Driffield. As I walked along the winding road, meeting no one by the way, I mused upon what I should say. Do they not tell us that style is the art of omission? If that is so I should certainly write a very pretty piece, and it seemed almost a pity that Roy should use it only as material. I chuckled when I reflected what a bombshell I could throw if I chose. There was one person who could tell them all they wanted to know about Edward Driffield and his first marriage; but this fact I proposed to keep to myself. They thought Rosie was dead; they erred; Rosie was very much alive.

Being in New York for the production of a play and my arrival having been advertised to all and sundry by my manager's energetic press representative, I received one day a letter addressed in a handwriting I knew but could not place. It was large and round, firm but uneducated. It was so familiar to me that I was exasperated not to remember whose it was. It would have been more sensible to open the letter at once, but instead I looked at the envelope and racked my brain. There are handwritings I cannot see without a little shiver of dismay and some letters that look so tiresome that I cannot bring myself to open them for a week. When at last I tore open the envelope what I read gave me a strange feeling. It began abruptly:

I have just seen that you are in New York and would like to see you again. I am not living in New York any more, but Yonkers is quite close and if you have a car you can easily do it in half an hour. I expect you are very busy so leave it to you to make a date. Although it is many years since we last met I hope you have not forgotten your old friend

ROSE IGGULDEN (*formerly Driffield*)

I looked at the address; it was the Albemarle, evidently a hotel or an apartment house, then there was the name of a street, and Yonkers. A shiver passed through me as though someone had walked over my grave. During the years that had passed I had sometimes thought of Rosie, but of late I had said to myself that she must surely be dead. I was puzzled for a moment by the name. Why Iggulden and not Kemp? Then it occurred to me that they had taken this name, a Kentish one too, when they fled from England. My first impulse was to make an excuse not to see her; I am always shy of seeing again people I have not seen for a long time; but then I was seized with curiosity. I wanted to see what she was like and to hear what had happened to her. I was going down to Dobbs Ferry for the week-end, to reach which I had to pass through Yonkers, and so answered that I would come at about four on the following Saturday.

The Albemarle was a huge block of apartments, comparatively new, and it looked as though it were inhabited by persons in easy circumstances. My name was telephoned up by a Negro porter in uniform and I was taken up in the elevator by another. I felt uncommonly nervous. The door was opened for me by a coloured maid.

"Come right in," she said. "Mrs. Iggulden's expecting you."

I was ushered into a living room that served also as dining room, for at one end of it was a square table of heavily carved oak, a dresser, and four chairs of the kind that the manufacturers in Grand Rapids would certainly describe as Jacobean. But the other end was furnished with a Louis XV suite, gilt and upholstered in pale blue damask; there were a great many small tables, richly carved and gilt, on which stood Sèvres vases with ormolu decorations and nude bronze ladies with draperies flowing as though in a howling gale that artfully concealed those parts of their bodies that decency required; and each one held at the end of a playfully outstretched arm an electric lamp. The gramophone was the grandest thing I had ever seen out of a shop window, all gilt and shaped like a sedan chair and painted with Watteau courtiers and their ladies.

After I had waited for about five minutes a door was opened and Rosie came briskly in. She gave me both her hands.

"Well, this is a surprise," she said. "I hate to think how many years it is since we met. Excuse me one moment." She went to the door and called: "Jessie, you can bring the tea in. Mind the water's boiling properly." Then, coming back: "The trouble I've had to teach that girl to make tea properly, you'd never believe."

Rosie was at least seventy. She was wearing a very smart sleeveless frock of green chiffon, heavily *diamanté,* cut square at the neck and very short; it fitted like a bursting glove. By her shape I gathered that she wore rubber corsets. Her nails were blood-coloured and her eyebrows plucked. She was stout, and she had a double chin; the skin of her bosom, although she had powdered it freely, was red, and her face was red too. But she looked well and healthy and full of beans. Her hair was still abundant, but it was quite white, shingled and permanently waved. As a young woman she had had soft, naturally waving hair and these stiff undulations, as though she had just come out of a hairdresser's, seemed more than anything else to change her. The only thing that remained was her smile, which had still its old childlike and mischievous sweetness. Her teeth had never been very good, irregular and of bad shape; but these now were replaced by a set of perfect evenness and snowy brilliance; they were obviously the best that money could buy.

The coloured maid brought in an elaborate tea with *pâté* sandwiches and cookies and candy and little knives and forks and tiny napkins. It was all very neat and smart.

"That's one thing I've never been able to do without—my tea," said Rosie, helping herself to a hot buttered scone. "It's my best meal, really, though I know I shouldn't eat it. My doctor keeps on saying to me: 'Mrs. Iggulden, you can't expect to get your weight down if you will eat half a dozen cookies at tea.' " She gave me a smile, and I had a sudden inkling that, notwithstanding the marcelled hair and the powder and the fat, Rosie was the same as ever. "But what I say is: A little of what you fancy does you good."

I had always found her easy to talk to. Soon we were chatting away as though it were only a few weeks since we had last seen one another.

"Were you surprised to get my letter? I put Driffield so as you should know who it was from. We took the name of Iggulden when we came to America. George had a little unpleasantness when he left Blackstable, perhaps you heard about it, and he thought in a new country he'd better start with a new name, if you understand what I mean."

I nodded vaguely.

"Poor George, he died ten years ago, you know."

"I'm sorry to hear that."

"Oh, well, he was getting on in years. He was past seventy though you'd never have guessed it to look at him. It was a great blow to me. No woman could want a better husband than what he made me. Never a cross word from the day we married till the day he died. And I'm pleased to say he left me very well provided for."

"I'm glad to know that."

"Yes, he did very well over here. He went into the building trade, he always had a fancy for it, and he got in with Tammany. He always said the greatest mistake he ever made was not coming over here twenty years before. He liked the country from the first day he set foot in it. He had plenty of go and that's what you want here. He was just the sort to get on."

"Have you never been back to England?"

"No, I've never wanted to. George used to talk about it sometimes, just for a trip, you know, but we never got down to it, and now he's gone I haven't got the inclination. I expect London would seem very dead and alive to me after New York. We used to live in New York, you know. I only came here after his death."

"What made you choose Yonkers?"

"Well, I always fancied it. I used to say to George, when we retire we'll go and live at Yonkers. It's like a little bit of England to me; you know, Maidstone or Guildford or some place like that."

I smiled, but I understood what she meant. Notwithstanding its trams and its tootling cars, its cinemas and electric signs, Yonkers, with its winding main street, has a faint air of an English market town gone jazz.

"Of course I sometimes wonder what's happened to all the folks at Blackstable. I suppose they're most of them dead by now and I expect they think I am too."

"I haven't been there for thirty years."

I did not know then that the rumour of Rosie's death had reached Blackstable. I dare say that someone had brought back the news that George Kemp was dead and thus a mistake had arisen.

"I suppose nobody knows here that you were Edward Driffield's first wife?"

"Oh, no; why, if they had, I should have had the reporters buzzing around my apartment like a swarm of bees. You know sometimes I've hardly been able to help laughing when I've been out somewhere playing bridge and they've started talking about Ted's books. They like him no end in America. I never thought so much of them myself."

"You never were a great novel reader, were you?"

"I used to like history better, but I don't seem to have much time for reading now. Sunday's my great day. I think the Sunday papers over here are lovely. You don't have anything like them in England. Then of course I play a lot of bridge; I'm crazy about contract."

I remembered that when as a young boy I had first met Rosie her uncanny skill at whist had impressed me. I felt that I knew the sort of bridge player she was, quick, bold, and accurate: a good partner and a dangerous opponent.

"You'd have been surprised at the fuss they made over here when Ted died. I knew they thought a lot of him, but I never knew he was such a big bug as all that. The papers were full of him, and they had pictures of him and Ferne Court; he always said he meant to live in that house some day. Whatever made him marry that hospital nurse? I always thought he'd marry Mrs. Barton Trafford. They never had any children, did they?"

"No."

"Ted would have liked to have some. It was a great blow to him that I couldn't have any more after the first."

"I didn't know you'd ever had a child," I said with surprise.

"Oh, yes. That's why Ted married me. But I had a very bad time when it came and the doctors said I couldn't have another. If she'd lived, poor little thing, I don't suppose I'd ever have run away with George. She was six when she died. A dear little thing she was and as pretty as a picture."

"You never mentioned her."

"No, I couldn't bear to speak about her. She got meningitis and we took her to the hospital. They put her in a private room and they let

us stay with her. I shall never forget what she went through, screaming, screaming all the time, and nobody able to do anything."

Rosie's voice broke.

"Was it that death Driffield described in *The Cup of Life?*"

"Yes, that's it. I always thought it so funny of Ted. He couldn't bear
to speak of it, any more than I could, but he wrote it all down; he
didn't leave out a thing; even little things I hadn't noticed at the time
he put in and then I remembered them. You'd think he was just heartless, but he wasn't, he was upset just as much as I was. When we used
to go home at night he'd cry like a child. Funny chap, wasn't he?"

It was *The Cup of Life* that had raised such a storm of protest; and
it was the child's death and the episode that followed it that had especially brought down on Driffield's head such virulent abuse. I remembered the description very well. It was harrowing. There was nothing
sentimental in it; it did not excite the reader's tears, but his anger
rather that such cruel suffering should be inflicted on a little child.
You felt that God at the Judgment Day would have to account for such
things as this. It was a very powerful piece of writing. But if this incident was taken from life was the one that followed it also? It was this
that had shocked the public of the nineties and this that the critics had
condemned as not only indecent but incredible. In *The Cup of Life*
the husband and wife (I forget their names now) had come back from
the hospital after the child's death—they were poor people and they
lived from hand to mouth in lodgings—and had their tea. It was latish:
about seven o'clock. They were exhausted by the strain of a week's
ceaseless anxiety and shattered by their grief. They had nothing to say
to one another. They sat in a miserable silence. The hours passed. Then
on a sudden the wife got up and going into their bedroom put on her
hat.

"I'm going out," she said.

"All right."

They lived near Victoria Station. She walked along the Buckingham
Palace Road and through the park. She came into Piccadilly and went
slowly toward the Circus. A man caught her eye, paused, and turned
round.

"Good evening," he said.

"Good evening."

She stopped and smiled.

"Will you come and have a drink?" he asked.

"I don't mind if I do."

They went into a tavern in one of the side streets of Piccadilly, where harlots congregated and men came to pick them up, and they drank a glass of beer. She chatted with the stranger and laughed with him. She told him a cock-and-bull story about herself. Presently he asked if he could go home with her; no, she said, she couldn't do that, but they could go to a hotel. They got into a cab and drove to Bloomsbury and there they took a room for the night. And next morning she took a bus to Trafalgar Square and walked through the park; when she got home her husband was just sitting down to breakfast. After breakfast they went back to the hospital to see about the child's funeral.

"Will you tell me something, Rosie?" I asked. "What happened in the book after the child's death—did that happen too?"

She looked at me for a moment doubtfully; then her lips broke into her still beautiful smile.

"Well, it's all so many years ago, what odds does it make? I don't mind telling you. He didn't get it quite right. You see, it was only guesswork on his part. I was surprised that he knew as much as he did; I never told him anything."

Rosie took a cigarette and pensively tapped its end on the table, but she did not light it.

"We came back from the hospital just like he said. We walked back; I felt I couldn't sit still in a cab, and I felt all dead inside me. I'd cried so much I couldn't cry any more, and I was tired. Ted tried to comfort me, but I said: 'For God's sake shut up.' After that he didn't say any more. We had rooms in the Vauxhall Bridge Road then, on the second floor, just a sitting room and a bedroom, that's why we'd had to take the poor little thing to the hospital; we couldn't nurse her in lodgings; besides, the landlady said she wouldn't have it, and Ted said she'd be looked after better at the hospital. She wasn't a bad sort, the landlady; she'd been a tart and Ted used to talk to her by the hour together. She came up when she heard us come in.

" 'How's the little girl tonight?' she said.

" 'She's dead,' said Ted.

"I couldn't say anything. Then she brought up the tea. I didn't want anything, but Ted made me eat some ham. Then I sat at the window. I didn't look round when the landlady came up to clear away, I didn't want anyone to speak to me. Ted was reading a book; at least he was pretending to, but he didn't turn the pages, and I saw the tears dropping on it. I kept on looking out of the window. It was the end of June, the twenty-eighth, and the days were long. It was just near the corner where we lived and I looked at the people going in and out of the public house and the trams going up and down. I thought the day would never come to an end; then all of a sudden I noticed that it was night. All the lamps were lit. There were an awful lot of people in the street. I felt so tired. My legs were like lead.

" 'Why don't you light the gas?' I said to Ted.

" 'Do you want it?' he said.

" 'It's no good sitting in the dark,' I said.

"He lit the gas. He began smoking his pipe. I knew that would do him good. But I just sat and looked at the street. I don't know what came over me. I felt that if I went on sitting in that room I'd go mad. I wanted to go somewhere where there were lights and people. I wanted to get away from Ted; no, not so much that, I wanted to get away from all that Ted was thinking and feeling. We only had two rooms. I went into the bedroom; the child's cot was still there, but I wouldn't look at it. I put on my hat and a veil and I changed my dress and then I went back to Ted.

" 'I'm going out,' I said.

"Ted looked at me. I dare say he noticed I'd got my new dress on and perhaps something in the way I spoke made him see I didn't want him.

" 'All right,' he said.

"In the book he made me walk through the park, but I didn't do that really. I went down to Victoria and I took a hansom to Charing Cross. It was only a shilling fare. Then I walked up the Strand. I'd made up my mind what I wanted to do before I came out. Do you remember Harry Retford? Well, he was acting at the Adelphi then, he had the second comedy part. Well, I went to the stage door, and sent up my name. I always liked Harry Retford. I expect he was a bit unscrupulous and he was rather funny over money matters, but he could make you laugh and with all his faults he was a rare good sort. You know he was killed in the Boer War, don't you?"

"I didn't. I only knew he'd disappeared and one never saw his name on playbills; I thought perhaps he'd gone into business or something."

"No, he went out at once. He was killed at Ladysmith. After I'd been waiting a bit he came down and I said: 'Harry, let's go on the razzle tonight. What about a bit of supper at Romano's?' 'Not 'alf,' he said. 'You wait here and the minute the show's over and I've got my make-up off I'll come down.' It made me feel better just to see him; he was playing a racing tout and it made me laugh just to look at him in his cheque suit and his billycock hat and his red nose. Well, I waited till the end of the show and then he came down and we walked along to Romano's.

" 'Are you hungry?' he said to me.

" 'Starving,' I said; and I was.

" 'Let's have the best,' he said, 'and blow the expense. I told Bill Terris I was taking my best girl out to supper and I touched him for a couple of quid.'

" 'Let's have champagne,' I said.

" 'Three cheers for the widow!' he said.

"I don't know if you ever went to Romano's in the old days. It was fine. You used to see all the theatrical people and the racing men, and the girls from the Gaiety used to go there. It was *the* place. And the Roman. Harry knew him and he came up to our table; he used to talk in funny broken English; I believe he put it on because he knew it made people laugh. And if someone he knew was down and out he'd always lend him a fiver.

" 'How's the kid?' said Harry.

" 'Better,' I said.

"I didn't want to tell him the truth. You know how funny men are; they don't understand some things. I knew Harry would think it dreadful of me to come out to supper when the poor child was lying dead in the hospital. He'd be awfully sorry and all that, but that's not what I wanted; I wanted to laugh."

Rosie lit the cigarette that she had been playing with.

"You know how when a woman is having a baby, sometimes the husband can't stand it any more and he goes out and has another woman. And then when she finds out, and it's funny how often she does, she kicks up no end of a fuss; she says, that the man should go and do it just then, when she's going through hell, well, it's the limit. I always tell her not to be silly. It doesn't mean he doesn't love her, and isn't terribly upset, it doesn't mean anything, it's just nerves; if he weren't so upset he wouldn't think of it. I know, because that's how I felt then.

"When we'd finished our supper Harry said: 'Well, what about it?'

" 'What about what?' I said.

"There wasn't any dancing in those days and there was nowhere we could go.

" 'What about coming round to my flat and having a look at my photograph album?' said Harry.

" 'I don't mind if I do,' I said.

"He had a little bit of a flat in the Charing Cross Road, just two rooms and a bath and a kitchenette, and we drove round there, and I stayed the night.

"When I got back next morning the breakfast was already on the table and Ted had just started. I'd made up my mind that if he said anything I was going to fly out at him. I didn't care what happened. I'd earned my living before, and I was ready to earn it again. For two pins I'd have packed my box and left him there and then. But he just looked up as I came in.

" 'You've just come in time,' he said. 'I was going to eat your sausage.'

"I sat down and poured him out his tea. And he went on reading the paper. After we'd finished breakfast we went to the hospital. He never asked me where I'd been. I didn't know what he thought. He was terribly kind to me all that time. I was miserable, you know. Some-how I felt that I just couldn't get over it, and there was nothing he didn't do to make it easier for me."

"What did you think when you read the book?" I asked.

"Well, it did give me a turn to see that he did know pretty well what had happened that night. What beat me was his writing it at all. You'd have thought it was the last thing he'd put in a book. You're queer fish, you writers."

At that moment the telephone bell rang. Rosie took up the receiver and listened.

"Why, Mr. Vanuzzi, how very nice of you to call me up! Oh, I'm pretty well, thank you. Well, pretty and well, if you like. When you're my age you take all the compliments you can get."

She embarked upon a conversation which, I gathered from her tone, was of a facetious and even flirtatious character. I did not pay much attention, and since it seemed to prolong itself I began to meditate upon the writer's life. It is full of tribulation. First he must endure poverty and the world's indifference; then, having achieved a measure of success, he must submit with a good grace to its hazards. He depends upon a fickle public. He is at the mercy of journalists who want to interview him and photographers who want to take his picture, of editors who harry him for copy and tax gatherers who harry him for income tax, of persons of quality who ask him to lunch and secretaries of institutes who ask him to lecture, of women who want to marry him and women who want to divorce him, of youths who want his autograph, actors who want parts and strangers who want a loan, of gushing ladies who want advice on their matrimonial affairs and earnest young men who want advice on their compositions, of agents, publishers, managers, bores, admirers, critics, and his own conscience. But he has one compensation. Whenever he has anything on his mind, whether it be a harassing reflection, grief at the death of a friend, unrequited love, wounded pride, anger at the treachery of someone to whom he has shown kindness, in short any emotion or any perplexing thought, he has only to put it down in black and white, using it as the theme of a story or the decoration of an essay, to forget all about it. He is the only free man.

Rosie put back the receiver and turned to me.

"That was one of my beaux. I'm going to play bridge tonight and he rang up to say he'd call round for me in his car. Of course he's a Wop, but he's real nice. He used to run a big grocery store downtown, in New York, but he's retired now."

"Have you never thought of marrying again, Rosie?"

"No." She smiled. "Not that I haven't had offers. I'm quite happy as I am. The way I look on it is this, I don't want to marry an old man, and it would be silly at my age to marry a young one. I've had my time and I'm ready to call it a day."

"What made you run away with George Kemp?"

"Well, I'd always liked him. I knew him long before I knew Ted, you know. Of course I never thought there was any chance of marrying him. For one thing he was married already and then he had his position to think of. And then when he came to me one day and said that everything had gone wrong and he was bust and there'd be a warrant out for his arrest in a few days and he was going to America and would I go with him, well, what could I do? I couldn't let him go all that way by himself, with no money perhaps, and him having been always so grand and living in his own house and driving his own trap. It wasn't as if I was afraid of work."

"I sometimes think he was the only man you ever cared for," I suggested.

"I dare say there's some truth in that."

"I wonder what it was you saw in him."

Rosie's eyes travelled to a picture on the wall that for some reason had escaped my notice. It was an enlarged photograph of Lord George in a carved gilt frame. It looked as if it might have been taken soon after his arrival in America; perhaps at the time of their marriage. It was a three-quarter length. It showed him in a long frock coat, tightly buttoned, and a tall silk hat cocked rakishly on one side of his head; there was a large rose in his buttonhole; under one arm he carried a silver-headed cane and smoke curled from a big cigar that he held in his right hand. He had a heavy moustache, waxed at the ends, a saucy look in his eye, and in his bearing an arrogant swagger. In his tie was a horseshoe in diamonds. He looked like a publican dressed up in his best to go to the Derby.

"I'll tell you," said Rosie. "He was always such a perfect gentleman."

AN AFTERWORD ON "CAKES AND ALE: or THE SKELETON IN THE CUPBOARD"

O N the dust-jacket of *Cakes and Ale: or The Skeleton in the Cupboard* in its current American edition, Mr. Maugham's publishers print the following paragraph:

Rosie, the barmaid, was the skeleton in the cupboard, who by her zest for living raised the lives of her lovers to higher and more vivid levels.

Which succinct summary might strike the captious as leaving certain odds and ends of the novel's substance unaccounted for. It strikes even the not overly critical compiler of these footnotes as leaving something still to be said. To be sure, a good deal *was* said when the book was first published in 1930, except, as far as I know, the salient thing—that, as an example of the storyteller's art, *Cakes and Ale* is a masterpiece unsurpassed in our language in our time.

When Boswell's now hallowed life of Dr. Johnson was new, it seemed so freshly topical, so personal and even sensational a work that only after the dust had settled, did many appreciate it as a biography not without merit. In somewhat the same way, *Cakes and Ale*—particularly in its own London—was so promptly identified as a *roman à clef* and as such caused so many outbursts of wrath, so many gusts of nervous and malicious laughter, that its brilliance as a novel—its astounding technical dexterity and its brimming charm—were, for a time, lost sight of. It was surely inevitable that Driffield's achievement of literary fame by sheer longevity should bring to mind Thomas Hardy, that Mrs. Whiffen of English letters, who only two years before had to a great extent—his heart was taken out and buried elsewhere—been laid to rest in Westminster Abbey. Wherefore Hardy's friends were filled with grief in the not unreasonable fear that readers who did not know any better might think of Ted Driffield's personal life—particularly the early part with all its unseemly skullduggery—as having also been patterned after Hardy's. Then all the wiseacres felt sure they knew at whom Mr. Maugham was pointing when he etched with acid his portrait of Alroy Kear. Indeed, one British novelist, promptly suspected by his friends of having inspired the character, was kept for some months under their surveillance, though whether in fear that he would do damage to himself or to Mr. Maugham I am not sure. Finally, under the palpable pseudonym of A. Riposte, somebody since identified as one Elinor Mordaunt, who up to that time had taken no part in the conversation, dashed off for publication the following year a feeble tale called *Gin and Bitters* of which the central figure—also, oddly enough, a novelist—was an unscrupulous and uncivil opportunist pictured as behaving shabbily in various outposts of the empire. If this was intended as a solace to those whom *Cakes and Ale* had outraged, it proved unequal to a task for which, with all the bad will in the world, A. Riposte was otherwise ill equipped. In sporting circles, the effect was as if the editor of this anthology had asked Mr. Dempsey to step outside and take off his coat.

One aspect of *Cakes and Ale* puzzles me considerably. The author of *The Moon and Sixpence,* "Miss Thompson," the superb novel called *Of Human Bondage* and many a triumphant play has enjoyed, one would think, all the rewards from without—fame, critical appreciation, popular success, abundant financial return—which can ever be a writer's portion in his own lifetime. Yet on all the topics that eternally agitate New Grub Street, *Cakes and Ale* is filled with as much tacit and smoldering resentment as if it had been written by Maxwell Bodenheim.

Incidentally, Mr. Maugham indulged some years ago in an anthology of his own called *The Traveller's Library*. At the time when I was cabling for his authorization to include *Cakes and Ale* in this volume, the eavesdropping George S. Kaufman started the baseless rumor that I was trying to get Mr. Maugham's permission to include *his* anthology in mine. At that it might have simplified my task.

Finally, in all my admiration for *Cakes and Ale,* for the delicate dance of its shuttle between past and present, for the uncanny art whereby all its contrasting milieus are evoked—the vicarage, the Driffields' hangout at Blackstable, Mrs. Hudson's lodging-house, and above all the shiny *décor* for the apotheosis of Rosie in Yonkers—I would not for the world have it thought that I condone Mr. Maugham's use at one point of "infer" when he means "imply."

A. W.

BOSWELL
AND THE GIRL
FROM BOTANY BAY

by

FREDERICK A. POTTLE

TO

WILLIAM LYON PHELPS

TEACHER, COLLEAGUE, FRIEND

I dare not give, nor yet present,
But render part of that's thy own.
My mind and heart shall still invent
To seek out Treasure still unknown.

BOSWELL AND THE GIRL
FROM BOTANY BAY

THE editor of old journals and letters has one of the most absorbing tasks permitted to man, but I venture to think that when he opens the publisher's parcel and sees his work irrevocably fixed within the bounds of the printed page, his feelings partake less of satisfaction than of disappointment and frustration. He began with a clutter of obscure and untidy scrawls, the chronology of which was uncertain and the text doubtful. It was nothing but a heap of old sheets of paper with queer marks on them. His first task was the purely mechanical one of finding out what words the marks stood for, with no regard to sense. He puzzled over blotted and erased passages; he spent hours filling in lacunæ so as to take into account all the minute evidences of the manuscript; he weighed the chances whether his author really meant to write *adwise,* as the manuscript seems to indicate, or whether his pen slipped when he made the "d." Finally that part of the work is done, at least to his partial satisfaction. The text is there, stretched and ironed into shape, with all its foot-note array of *sics* and "doubtfuls." But by this time, if the editor has performed his textual labours manfully, he has far more than a mere copy. The pages of his transcript are to him windows opening into the past, revealing, now dimly and confusedly, now sharply and clearly, scenes of a vanished age. For you cannot make a really final text of any difficult document without having read nearly all the books in the world. Is that man's name Richson or Rickson? You will have to pore over many volumes to be sure. What did your author, in the midst of notes on Bristol and Chatterton, mean by the word "cranes," isolated from everything that follows and everything that precedes? You can find out, but it will not be by asking your friends.

Having, as you say, "established your text," you proceed to "annotate" it. It is then that the sense of futility begins to weigh you down. You feel like a reservoir filled to overflowing with sparkling information. There is so much in your head about that half-page, but it would fill two pages of fine print if you wrote it out, and even if you spent days on it, you know that it would be so dull that nobody but a professional student would ever read it. You are inhibited by the convention that foot-notes must be written in a style devoid of all personality, and by the more pertinent fact, which your own experience has demonstrated, that if foot-notes swell to too great proportions, they overwhelm the text and the result is chaos. You finally content yourself with a few crabbed lines on each page informing your reader that Samuel Johnson died in 1784 and that "Young" was Edward Young (1683–1765) who wrote *Night Thoughts*. As though that did anybody any good! And you feel precisely as though you had thrown a net around a river; you have slowed up the current a little but the water has all gone through.

This is particularly true of what may be called the annotation of human interest. It is your admitted privilege to erect neat little tombstones for the most prominent persons mentioned in your text, but how far dare you to go in giving extensive information about the utterly obscure ones? It is precisely the obscure ones that need it, for the others are in the *Dictionary of National Biography*. But this person who passes once across the page, whose name will evoke no echo of recollection in any reader—will you tell his story at length and point out the rich significance of that casual encounter? Only rarely, and when you do you will be scolded by your peers for having no sense of proportion. You will finally come to see that, do what you may, nobody else will ever understand that document as you do unless he edits it himself. Your best labours go unrecorded and die with you. You seek only the relief of cornering your friends occasionally and forcing them to listen to your rejected foot-notes.

What follows is an inordinately long foot-note: first, to Professor

Tinker's edition of Boswell's letters; secondly, to Mr. Lewis Bettany's edition of the diaries of Boswell's intimate friend, William Johnson Temple; thirdly, to Messrs. Nordhoff and Hall's *Mutiny on the Bounty;* finally, to Boswell's own Journal. It is a note which will take us from Scotland to Cornwall, from London to Rio de Janeiro, from the Cape of Good Hope to Australia, from Botany Bay to Timor in the Dutch East Indies, from Java back to England. And it will end at Fowey in Cornwall.

On 13 October 1794, when Boswell was within seven months of his end, he wrote a letter from his estate of Auchinleck in Ayrshire to his brother David in London; a letter filled with laments at his wretchedness in this, the last visit he was ever to make to his ancestral mansion, and with thoughtful and precise directions concerning his financial affairs. We are concerned only with the following sentences: "Be so good as to give Mrs. Bruce five pounds more and Betsy a guinea, and put into the Banking shop of Mr. Devaynes & Co. five pounds from me to the account of the Rev. Mr. Baron at Lestwithiel, Cornwall, and write to him that you have done so. He takes charge of paying the gratuity to Mary Broad." Mrs. Bruce was his housekeeper; Betsy, his youngest daughter. But who was Mary Broad, why should Boswell be paying her a "gratuity," and why should he enlist the services of a Cornish clergyman in the matter?

The diaries of William Johnson Temple remained unpublished until 1929. The passage I have just quoted naturally caught the eye of Mr. Bettany when he was editing them, for Temple was also a clergyman in Cornwall, and was a friend of the Rev. John Baron of Lostwithiel. In the summer of 1792 Boswell, with his two eldest daughters, had visited Temple at St. Gluvias, and had met Baron at that time. "But why," queried Mr. Bettany, "should he request a new acquaintance like Baron, who lived in so remote a place as Lostwithiel, to undertake the business of paying a gratuity? It all looks extremely odd and unaccountable; and one cannot help wondering what the real object was in this strange manœuvre. Irons in the fire, of course; but what use did Boswell expect to make of them?"

Mr. Bettany, it is only fair to state, is not to be blamed for not iden-tifying Mary Broad and so clearing up the whole mystery. Without the clues furnished by Boswell's Journal, which was not published when Mr. Bettany wrote, it would have been only by a stroke of luck that anyone could have identified her. But he might perhaps have drawn the conclusion that Mr. Baron was asked to pay the gratuity to Mary Broad because she lived somewhere in his vicinity; and Boswellians (a jealous fraternity) will think that he deserves mild reproof for his as-sumption that Boswell always had irons in the fire when he performed acts of kindness. For there exists, scattered through the two volumes of Boswell's letters, abundant evidence to the contrary.

I reviewed Mr. Bettany's book in 1929, soon after I assumed the editorship of the Boswell Papers. I find that in the margin opposite the name "Mary Broad" I scrawled, "Yes, Journal," and opposite the sentence about irons in the fire, "Can I discover?" I can now answer "Yes" to that query. But instead of recounting the series of false starts and lucky chances by which I pieced the narrative together from bits gained here and there, I shall simply tell in straightforward fashion the story of Mary Broad, citing my sources only when I make direct quo-tations.

When the American Colonies revolted from the Crown and suc-ceeded in establishing their independence, the ministers in charge of the destinies of Great Britain were faced by two urgent problems: how could they acquire new colonies to restore their country's prestige, and how could they provide a dumping ground for the hordes of con-victed felons who had been crowding the jails ever since the outbreak of the American War? It must not be forgotten that, from the reign of James the First, transportation beyond seas had been an essential feature of the penal administration of Great Britain. There were then no penitentiaries in the modern sense of the term. Criminals might be sentenced to corporal punishment or brief terms in houses of correc-tion, but if their crimes were of any magnitude according to the savage code of the day, they were either hanged out of hand or transported to the colonies, where their services were sold to the planters for longer or shorter periods at a rate of as much as twenty pounds a head. For

some years before the War of Independence this compulsory emigra-
tion had been bringing each year about two thousand unwilling Founders of First Families to the American shores.

A solution to both problems was immediately proposed: Australia.
The Portuguese and Spaniards were the first to sight that great continent; the Dutch first explored it and gave it the name, New Holland,
under which it was generally known throughout the eighteenth century; Dampier made it the object of a voyage of discovery. But it was
Captain James Cook who in 1770 first carefully charted one of the
coasts. He had been sent with Sir Joseph Banks in the *Endeavour* on a
strictly scientific quest: he was to go to Tahiti to observe the transit of
Venus, and then proceed southward to look for the Terra Australis
Incognita, a great continent supposed to extend to the South Pole. If he
failed to find it (as of course he did), he was to explore New Zealand,
and then come home by any route he thought proper. Having surveyed New Zealand, he touched near Cape Howe, at the south-east
corner of Australia, and then proceeded up the east coast, giving many
of the bays and promontories the names they still bear. Botany Bay
was so christened because of the abundance of flowers found there by
Banks. It was but natural that twelve years later, when it became clear
that America was lost, the thoughts of British statesmen should turn to
the vast island reported by Cook. He had, indeed, recommended it as
a penal colony as early as 1779.

On 18 August 1786 Lord Sydney wrote an epoch-making letter to
the Lords Commissioners of the Treasury. It begins as follows:

"My Lords:
The several gaols and places for the confinement of felons in this
kingdom being in so crowded a state that the greatest danger is to be
apprehended, not only from their escape, but from infectious distem-
pers . . . his Majesty, desirous of preventing by every possible means the
ill consequences which might happen from either of these causes, has
been pleased to signify to me his royal commands that measures should
immediately be pursued for sending out of this kingdom such of the
convicts as are under sentence or order of transportation."

He then goes on to say that the sloop *Nautilus,* having been sent out on the recommendation of a Committee of the House of Commons, reports that the southern coast of Africa, which it had been hoped would prove an eligible spot, was quite unfitted for a penal colony, and therefore "his Majesty has thought it advisable to fix upon Botany Bay, situated on the coast of New South Wales . . . which, according to the accounts given by the late Captain Cook . . . is looked upon as a place likely to answer the above purposes."

The order for the First Fleet then follows. Seven hundred and fifty convicts are to be sent with a guard of marines; they are to carry with them two years' provisions and touch at the Cape of Good Hope for seeds and live-stock. Since there will be many more male convicts than female, it is suggested that the tender which is to accompany the convoy "be employed in conveying to the new settlement a further number of women from the Friendly Islands, New Caledonia, etc., which are contiguous thereto, and from whence any number may be procured without difficulty; and without a sufficient number of that sex it is well-known that it would be impossible to preserve the settlement from gross irregularities and disorders." It is only fair to add at once that this last repulsive recommendation was not carried into effect.

It was nearly a year before the convoy actually sailed, a delay which can hardly be considered excessive in view of the magnitude of the undertaking. First of all the Government had to select a leader for the expedition. It would have been difficult to fix upon a better man than the one chosen: Arthur Phillip, a man trained to the sea, who had seen service in the war with France. The abuses of the first voyage were terrible enough, but they would have been far worse if it had not been for Phillip's vigilant and humane oversight of every detail of the fitting out of the fleet. In much he was overruled, but one of his stipulations was honoured: there should be no slavery in the new country. The Public Record Office contains a large *dossier* of his letters to the Commissioners. He protested at the shortness of the rations allowed by the contractors, the absence of anti-scorbutics and surgical supplies, and the crowding of the convicts. On 12 March 1787, having failed to induce the Navy Board to make any alteration in the contracts, he asked

Lord Sydney to put him on record as having declined responsibility for the deaths which might ensue. Six days later he wrote indignantly to Under-Secretary Nepean, "The situation in which the magistrates sent the women on board the *Lady Penrhyn* stamps them with infamy —tho' almost naked, and so very filthy that nothing but clothing them could have prevented them from perishing, and which could not be done in time to prevent a fever, which is still on board that ship. . . . There is a necessity for doing something for the young man who is on board that ship as surgeon, or I fear we shall lose him, and then a hundred women will be left without any assistance, several of them with child. Let me repeat my desire that orders immediately may be given to increase the convict allowance of bread. Sixteen pounds of bread for forty-two days is very little." On 11 April he complained in a postscript, "By some mistake 109 women and children are put on board the *Lady Penrhyn,* tho' that ship was only intended to carry 102, and with propriety should not have more than two-thirds of that number." He continued to beg for clothing for the women. He got little comfort from the Navy Board, which had already let the contracts for fitting out the fleet. As to short rations, he was informed that "when it is considered that the confinement on shipboard will not admit of much exercise, this allowance will be found more advantageous to the health of the convicts than full allowance," and the clothing never did come on board.

The fleet sailed on 13 May 1787: the man-of-war *Sirius* and the armed tender *Supply;* three storeships; and six transports carrying the convicts and the marines. There were 757 convicts in the convoy, of whom upwards of two hundred were women.

Among these wretched people we shall distinguish only two: William Bryant, age unknown, a Cornish fisherman, sentenced at the Launceston assizes in 1784 to seven years' transportation "for resisting the revenue officers, who attempted to seize some smuggled property he had," and Mary Broad, a girl of twenty-two, who had been capitally convicted at the Exeter assizes in 1786 for participating with two other women in a street robbery at Plymouth and stealing a cloak. Concerning her earlier history we know nothing except that she came of a poor but respectable family of Fowey in Cornwall, that her father, William Broad, was a "mariner," and that she was baptized in Fowey church on 1 May 1765.

It is not my intention in this paper to indulge in romance. I prefer (and I think my readers will prefer) the bare but authentic evidence of the contemporary documents. The space at my disposal is, however, limited; and I have chosen to give a sample of full documentation, and then to move forward with a rapid summary. From this point up to the spring of 1791 I shall present little detail. The reader should remind himself, however, that the period involved is no less than four years.

The fleet touched at Teneriffe, and then sailed for Rio de Janeiro, which was reached on 5 August. On 13 October it anchored at the Cape of Good Hope, and by 20 January 1788 the whole convoy was in Botany Bay. The trip had lasted more than eight months, and had carried the convicts three-fourths of the way around the globe. Forty-eight of them had died in the passage, a mortality of six per cent, which under the circumstances must be regarded as low, for many of them had been ill when the fleet sailed. The later convoys had a much worse record.

It is hard for us today to realize clearly the reckless temerity of the undertaking. No preparation whatever had been made for the reception of the convicts in Australia. Phillip was expected to land in a new and savage country at eight months' sailing distance from his source of supplies, and there within two years to establish a self-supporting colony. It would have been touch-and-go if the colonists had been farmers, artisans, and frontiersmen, carefully selected for strength, skill, and integrity. Phillip's colonists were actually the most vicious off-scourings of England. They were nearly all townsmen and knew no manual trade. In the whole First Fleet there were only twelve men who could handle carpenters' tools, though it must have been obvious before the Fleet sailed that as soon as the convicts landed, buildings would have to be erected to house them. The farming implements furnished by the profiteering contractors turned out to be almost useless, and nearly all the seed-wheat failed to grow. No new clothes had been provided, and there were no needles and no thread to mend the old ones. The land about Sydney Cove may have delighted a botanist like Banks, but it was ill suited for agriculture, even if the convicts had been better farmers. The colony was threatened with famine almost from the beginning.

The Fleet had brought provisions calculated to be sufficient for two years. Two years passed, and no relief came from home. In fairness to Parliament, it must be said that a supply ship was sent in 1789, but it struck on an ice-berg near the Cape of Good Hope, and had to be abandoned. The *Sirius* made one trip to the Cape for provisions, returning seven months later with some flour, but in March 1790 she was wrecked on one of the reefs with which the South Seas abound. The little tender, the *Supply,* now the sole hope of the colony, sailed for Batavia. Everybody, including the Governor, went on famine allowance. Men began to die of starvation. No fewer than 140 members of the colony died from various causes during this year.

One day in June 1790 the look-out raised a great shout, and men and women came running with tears and laughter to see a ship bearing into the bay. She proved to be the *Lady Juliana,* no supply ship at all, but a transport bringing a fresh detachment of female convicts. She was, in fact, the forerunner of the "Second Fleet," which finally straggled in, each vessel with its quota of felons. Eleven hundred had sailed, of whom 267 had died on the voyage, while 488 had to be put into hospital on their arrival. The newcomers had not brought enough food to maintain themselves. And the summer of 1790 was a long drought.

Meanwhile William Bryant had married Mary Broad, and she had borne him two children. He had been made fisherman for the Colony, and consequently had access to the Governor's boat, an open cutter fitted for a lug-sail and six oars. In December 1790 a Dutch schooner touched at Sydney Cove with a small store of provisions which had been purchased at exorbitant prices at Batavia for the Colony. Bryant, whose sentence had expired, but who saw no prospect of ever being sent back to England, resolved upon a plan of escape so desperate that one thinks it could have been prompted only by despair. The convicts had some money which they had brought with them from home, and which they naturally found of little use at Botany Bay. Bryant bought surreptitiously from the Dutch captain one hundred pounds of rice and fourteen pounds of pork, and bribed the baker of the Colony to give him one hundred pounds of flour. He also procured a quadrant, a chart, a compass, and two old muskets from the Dutch captain. At ten o'clock on the night of 28 March 1791, he, his wife Mary, their little boy Emanuel (aged three), their daughter Charlotte (a baby at the breast), and seven other convicts named John Simms, William Morton, James Cox, James Martin, John Butcher, William Allen, and Nathaniel Lilley, slipped away from their quarters and made for the Governor's boat. In their haste they dropped some of their rice, a net, and some tools which they had intended to carry with them. But they made good their escape, though pursued; pushed their craft out of the harbour, and headed northward, their goal being the Dutch island of Timor, more than three thousand miles away, or approximately the distance from New York to Southampton.

We have, alas, no log of their voyage. Our sources of information concerning it are two: an intelligent, though perhaps not altogether accurate, account written by a newspaper reporter who interviewed the survivors more than a year later, and the journal kept by Watkin Tench, officer of marines at Botany Bay, who had the singular fortune to have gone out on the same ship with Mary Bryant, to have been at the penal colony when she made her escape, and to have met her again under circumstances which I shall later describe. I shall avoid the temptation to sentimentalize the story, by quoting directly from these matter-of-fact narratives.

[*London Chronicle,* June 30–July 3, 1792.] "The monsoon had just set in, and the wind was contrary. . . . They were forced to keep along the coast as much as they could, for the convenience of procuring supplies of fresh water; and on these occasions, and when the weather was extremely tempestuous, they would sometimes sleep on shore, hauling their boat on the land. The savage natives, wherever they put on shore, came down in vast numbers with intent to murder them. They now found two old musquets, and a small quantity of powder, which Capt. Smyth [the Dutch captain] had given them, particularly serviceable, by firing over the heads of these multitudes, on which they ran off with great precipitation; but they were always forced to keep a strict watch.

. . . In lat. 26.27 [they] discovered a small island, on which no inhabitants were; here was great plenty of turtles, that proved a great relief to them; but they were very near being lost in landing. At this island they dried as much turtle as they could carry, which lasted them ten days. During the first five weeks of their voyage they had continual rains; and being obliged, in order to lighten the boat, to throw overboard all their wearing apparel, etc., were for that time continually wet. They were once eight days out of sight of land."

[Tench, *Complete Narrative*.] "They coasted the shore of New Holland, putting occasionally into different harbours which they found in going along. One of these harbours, in the latitude of 30° south, they described to be of superior excellence and capacity. Here they hauled their bark ashore, paid her seams with tallow, and repaired her. But it was with difficulty they could keep off the attacks of the Indians. These people continued to harras them so much that they quitted the main land and retreated to a small island in the harbour, where they completed their design. Between the latitude of 26° and 27°, they were driven by a current 30 leagues from the shore, among some islands, where they found plenty of large turtles. Soon after they closed again with the continent, when the boat got entangled in the surf, and was driven on shore, and they had all well nigh perished. They passed through the straits of Endeavour, and beyond the gulf of Carpentaria found a large fresh water river, which they entered, and filled from it their empty casks. Until they reached the gulf of Carpentaria, they saw no natives, or canoes, differing from those about Port Jackson. But now they were chased by large canoes, fitted with sails and fighting stages, and capable of holding thirty men each. They escaped by dint of rowing to windward."

On 5 June 1791 they came safe into Kupang at Timor, without the loss of a life, having been ten weeks in the passage.

Timor must have come to regard such casual apparitions of Britons in open boats as a thing to be expected of that enterprising race. Just two years before, Captain William Bligh of the *Bounty* had been set adrift by his mutinous crew near Tofoa in the Friendly Islands; set adrift in an open six-oared boat with eighteen loyal members of his crew. By use of compass, quadrant, and his memory of the South Seas (for the mutineers allowed him no chart) he brought his party safely four thousand miles across the sea to Timor. When the mutiny was reported at home, the Government sent Captain Edward Edwards to the South Seas in the *Pandora* to apprehend the mutineers. He took several of them at Tahiti, but in his way back through Endeavour Straits, the *Pandora* was wrecked, and the survivors, with some of the mutineers still in their clutches, made *their* way to Timor in the boats. All this has been told, and splendidly told, in Nordhoff and Hall's *Mutiny on the Bounty* and *Men Against the Sea*. The exploits of Bligh and Edwards have been widely and deservedly heralded, for the simple reason that Bligh published a book about his adventures, and Edwards turned in a report to the Admiralty, whereas it is probable that not one of Bryant's party could write. Of the three, it seems to me that Bryant's voyage was the most remarkable, for he had on board a woman and two little children, there was no professional navigator in the party, and of the entire crew only he and one other convict are known to have been familiar with the sea.

At Kupang, Fate made them the object of one of its pleasant ironies. They were kindly treated by the Dutch Governor, who believed their story that they were the passengers and part of the crew of an English brig which had suffered shipwreck, and that their boat had become separated from another bearing their Captain and the rest of the crew. For some time they lived at peace, no doubt taking a malicious pleasure in the knowledge that their bills were being charged against the British Government. But their behaviour gave "rise to suspicion; they were watched, and one of them at last, in a moment of intoxication, betrayed the secret." The Governor immediately arrested them and put them in prison. On 17 September Edwards came paddling in with the genuine castaways from the *Pandora*. The Governor delivered the convicts into his custody. Edwards clapped the party in irons, added them to his mutineers, and started for England with them in a vessel belonging to the Dutch East India Company. The climate was peculiarly dangerous to Europeans, and there was great sickness on board. Batavia was reached on 7 November, and three weeks later the little boy,

Emanuel, died in the hospital. On 22 December his father followed him. Between Batavia and the Cape of Good Hope, William Morton and John Simms succumbed to the prevalent infection, and James Cox jumped overboard. Edwards says he was drowned; his surgeon, George Hamilton, says that he swam safe to shore. Edwards appears to be more reliable than Hamilton, and as the poor man almost certainly had an iron shackle on his leg, it is highly doubtful that he managed to escape. At the Cape of Good Hope, Edwards found H.M.S. *Gorgon,* which had carried convicts to Botany Bay and was now on its return voyage. On board was the marine captain Tench whose account of the escape I have already cited.

"It was my fate," he says, "to fall in again with part of this little band of adventurers. In March 1792, when I arrived in the *Gorgon,* at the Cape of Good Hope, six of these people, including the woman and one child, were put on board of us, to be carried to England. [Here follows the account of their adventures quoted above.] I confess that I never looked at these people without pity and astonishment. They had miscarried in a heroic struggle for liberty, after having combated every hardship, and conquered every difficulty. The woman and one of the men had gone out to Port Jackson in the ship which had transported me thither. They had both of them been always distinguished for good behaviour."

The *Gorgon* sailed for home on 6 April 1792. Just one month later, somewhere on the high seas, the little girl, Charlotte Bryant, died. In the log of the *Gorgon* she is somewhat unhumorously described as "a supposed deserted convict from Port Jackson." When Mary Bryant was brought before Nicholas Bond, Esq., of the Public Office in Bow Street on 30 June 1792, she had lost husband and children; she had passed through such adventures as no other English woman of her time had experienced; and she was twenty-seven years old. Consider for a moment the pathos of the description still preserved in the manuscript register of Newgate Prison; it tells you all you are likely ever to know of her personal appearance: "Mary Bryant, *alias* Broad. Age 25 [it should be 27], height 5' 4", grey eyes, brown hair, sallow complexion, born in Cornwall, widow."

It will not do, in the light of what we know about Mary, to make her out the victim of a monstrous miscarriage of justice. The punishments meted out to lawbreakers in the eighteenth century were severe, but the courts were remarkably fair. A girl convicted in 1786 of stealing on the highway is more likely to have been a Moll Flanders than a Clarissa Harlowe. But whatever her past may have been, I fancy that both she and Bryant (whose crime of smuggling was almost respectable) were by no means incapable of reform; that both of them asked nothing better than a chance to make a new start and earn an honest living in Australia, and that they fled from the Colony only because they feared that they and their children would starve. It speaks well for them that they endangered the success of an already desperate venture by taking these children with them. It would be possible to cite instances of very respectable—even noble—persons who thought the desertion of an infant or two a small matter where their own lives were concerned.

I have, as I say, avoided sentiment. But as I ponder the story of Mary Bryant, two imaginary pictures of her rise in my mind, and since they have come without prompting, I give them to you. In one she sits at the tiller of the boat, steering it, under a light breeze, through the night. Bryant stands at the prow, scanning the sea for shoals; all the other convicts lie stretched in the bottom of the boat. Her little boy sleeps beside her knee; her baby slumbers in her lap. The great tropical stars are mirrored in her hopeful eyes, and the breeze stirs her hair gently. In the other she stands in the hard light of day on the deck of the *Gorgon,* haggard, unlovely in her tattered, filthy clothes. The Captain, very stiff and smart, is just closing the prayer-book, and two sailors are dropping over the side the little canvas sack that holds the body of her baby. Her hands grip each other tightly, but she makes no outcry.

In this summer of 1792, James Boswell, bibulous and erratic Scottish lawyer, was wearing out his dreary existence in London, whither he had brought his family in 1786, lured by impractical dreams of making a name and fortune at the English Bar. The *Journal of a Tour to the Hebrides* and the *Life of Samuel Johnson* had both appeared and had both enjoyed great success, but neither had sufficed to appease the restless ambition which tore the heart of their author. The recovery of Boswell's Journal does not change in many respects the view of his character which serious students of his life have always held, but it does overthrow completely a thesis which I once maintained, not without eloquence: namely, that the chief object of his ambition was literary fame. For the Laird of Auchinleck, descendant of a line which had maintained its ancestral mansion for 250 years, eighth cousin of His Majesty George III, it was not enough to have been "an humble attendant on an Authour" and to have written the *Life of Johnson*. That great book, we now know, was written in despair and published in misery, and its publication brought its author no lasting satisfaction. What James Boswell thirsted after more than the juice of the grape was to make speeches in the House of Commons or to sit on the woolsack. Seeing little chance of gaining prominence at the Scottish Bar, and, in truth, scorning all the prominence it offered, he came to London in his forty-sixth year, was admitted a barrister of the Inner Temple, and trudged off to King's Bench like a schoolboy, with a little notebook in which, merely by listening, he hoped to garner the legal knowledge which other men had acquired by years of grinding toil. When already past middle age he went as Junior on the circuits, the butt of practical jokes devised by cubs twenty years younger than himself. His beloved wife had died, after many years' struggle with tuberculosis, leaving him with five children whom he loved but whom he felt unable to care for properly. Lord Lonsdale, who had raised his hopes of Parliamentary fame to fever-pitch by making him Recorder of Carlisle, had turned upon him with shocking brutality, and had given him a description of his abilities and character which Macaulay might have envied.

An idle, unhappy, dissipated man, but a man who in his feckless wandering through life had managed to perform more acts of kindness than the majority of his successful colleagues. Since he had been admitted to the English Bar he could have counted his fees on the fingers of his two hands. But he still had some legal business. From the first of his professional life he had shown extraordinary interest in poor criminals whom no one else would defend, and this interest he kept to the end of his life. It was inevitable that when early in July 1792 he read in his newspaper of the Botany Bay convicts, he should at once have roused himself from his lethargy of woe and hurried down to Newgate to interview them. He kept no journal during this period, but we know from later references that he at once became very zealous in their behalf, and that they looked to him as their sole advocate. Since there was no trial, he had no opportunity to display his forensic eloquence. The man finally responsible for their fate was his old collegemate and enemy, Henry Dundas, then Secretary of State. On the last occasion that correspondence had passed between them, Boswell had reminded Dundas of a promise the great man had made him years before, and had asked for its fulfilment. Dundas had replied by complimenting him on his lively fancy. We may be sure that Boswell would have found any further appeal distasteful, but he set his private feelings aside. Dundas set a day to see him, and Boswell deferred a long-projected trip into Cornwall to keep the appointment. Dundas failed to appear. Boswell went home and wrote a letter: "The only *solatium* you can give me for this unpleasant disappointment is to favour me with two lines directed *Penryhn, Cornwall,* assuring me that nothing harsh shall be done to the unfortunate adventurers from New South Wales, for whom I interest myself. . . . A *negative* promise from a Secretary of State I hope will not be with-held, especially when you are the Secretary, and the request is for compassion." We know also that he importuned Evan Nepean, the Under-Secretary, and a "Mr. Pollock," Chief Clerk in the Secretary of State's office.

On 7 July 1792 Mary Bryant, James Martin, John Butcher, William Allen, and Nathaniel Lilley were put to the bar of the Old Bailey and ordered "to remain on their former sentence, until they should be discharged by due course of law." The legal penalty for escape from transportation was death, but the Government had no desire in this case to proceed with the full rigour of the law. As Nepean later told Boswell, "Government would not treat them with harshness, but at the same

time would not do a kind thing to them, as that might give encouragement to others to escape." They were accordingly sent to Newgate under an indeterminate sentence. It is some comfort to learn from the
newspapers that they considered "the prison a paradise, compared with
the dreadful sufferings they endured on their voyage."

Ten months later Dundas thought it safe to move in the case of
Mary Bryant. On 2 May 1793 "by His Majesty's command" he set his
hand to a free and unconditional pardon for her, in which the King is
made to say that "some favourable circumstances have been humbly
represented to us in her behalf inducing us to extend our Grace and
Mercy unto her." Unfortunately Boswell's Journal has again lapsed,
and we know none of the details of that affecting scene when Mary
Bryant stepped into the air again a free woman. But we do know that
she settled in Little Titchfield Street, London, and that Boswell supplied her with funds. He tried to get her gifts from other sources. Soon
after her discharge he called without an invitation to breakfast with
the former Lord Chancellor, Thurlow. "I asked him," he says, "to give
something to Mary Broad. He exclaimed, 'Damn her blood, let her go
to day's work.' But when I described her hardships and heroism, he
owned I was a good Advocate for her, and said he would give something if I desired it."

On the night of 5 June, as we learn from the *London Chronicle*,
Boswell, while coming home drunk, was attacked in Titchfield Street
by footpads, knocked down and nearly killed, robbed and left senseless
in the street. He may have been returning from a call on Mary, but it
is quite as likely that he had been to see his brother David, who lived
in Titchfield Street.

The Journal opens again on 1 August 1793, and it is in this, the last
journal Boswell kept, that we find extended references to Mary Bryant, or Broad, as Boswell always calls her. I wish to present these pretty
much without abridgement. The pen which drew the portrait of Dr.
Johnson loses none of its cunning in depicting this poor waif from the
Antipodes.

On 18 August he writes, "This morning there called on me Mr. Castel at No. 12 Cross Street, Carnaby Market, a Glazier, who told me that

he was a native of Fowey and knew all the relations of Mary Broad very well, and had received a letter from one of them directing him to me; that he wished to see her and inform them about her, and also to introduce her sister Dolly to her, who was in service in London. He mentioned that a large sum of money had been left to Mary Broad's Father and three or four more—no less than three hundred thousand pounds. I had a suspicion that he might be an impostor. However, I carried him to see her, and from his conversation it appeared that he really knew her relations. She did not recollect him, but he had seen her in her younger days. I was pleased with her good sense in being shy to him and not being elated by the sound of the great fortune. He said he would bring her sister Dolly to her in the evening. I walked away with him nearly to Oxford Street, and then returned to Mary and cautioned her not to put any trust in any thing he said till he had brought her sister. I sauntered restlessly. . . . Called on Mary in my way home, and found that Castel had actually brought her sister Dolly to her, a fine girl of twenty, who had been in great concern about her, and shewed the most tender affection."

The next day he went to see the four men still in Newgate to "assure them personally that I was doing all in my power for them."

On 25 August he met Dolly. "In the evening I went to Mary Broad's to meet her sister Dolly, who was very desireous to see me and thank me for my kindness to Mary. I found her to be a very fine, sensible young woman, and of such tenderness of heart that she yet cried and held her sister's hand. She expressed herself very gratefully to me, and said if she got money as was said, she would give me a thousand pounds. Poor girl, her behaviour pleased me much. She gave me, on my inquiring, her whole history since she came to London, from which it appeared that she had most meritoriously supported herself by good service. She was now Cook at Mr. Morgan's in Charlotte Street, Bedford Square, but the work was much too hard for her, a young and slender girl. I resolved to exert myself to get her a place more fit for her. It was now fixed that Mary should go by the first vessel to Fowey to visit her relations, her sister there having written to me that she would be kindly received. She had said to me as soon as she heard of the fortune that if she got a share she would reward me for all my trouble."

There is no further mention of Mary until 12 October: "I had fixed that Mary Broad should sail for Fowey in the *Ann and Elizabeth,* Job Moyse, Master, and it was necessary she should be on board this night, as the vessel was to be afloat early next morning. Having all along taken a very attentive charge of her, I had engaged to see her on board, and in order to do it, I this day refused invitations to dinner, both from Mr. Ross Mckye and Mr. Malone. I went to her in the forenoon and wrote two sheets of paper of her curious account of the escape from Botany bay."

These sheets, alas! have not been recovered; I can only hope that they still exist, and will one day see the light. But in his search of the manuscripts at Malahide Castle in March of this year (1937), Colonel Isham had the happiness to light upon a small packet endorsed by Boswell, "Leaves from Botany Bay used as Tea." Inside, just as Boswell placed them there, were a handful of heavily veined brown leaves—probably the only material relic of Mary Bryant now existing. Strange dark river, which quenches the bright flame of life, buries in oblivion the agony and heroism of human hearts, and casts at our feet a packet of withered leaves!

"I dined at home," Boswell continues, "and then went in a hackney coach to her room in little Titchfield street and took her and her box. My son James accompanied me, and was to wait at Mr. Dilly's till I returned from Beale's Wharf, Southwark, where she was to embark. I sat with her almost two hours, first in the kitchen and then in the bar of the Publick house at the Wharf, and had a bowl of punch, the landlord and the Captain of the vessel having taken a glass with us at last. She said her spirits were low; she was sorry to leave me; she was sure her relations would not treat her well. I consoled her by observing that it was her duty to go and see her aged Father and other relations; and it *might* be her interest in case it should be true that money to a considerable extent had been left to her father; that she might make her mind easy, for I assured her of ten pounds yearly as long as she behaved well, being resolved to make it up to her myself in so far as subscriptions should fail; and that being therefore independent, she might quit her relations whenever she pleased. Unluckily she could not write. I made her leave me a signature 'M.B.' similar to one which she carried with her, and this was to be a test of the authenticity of her letters to me, which she was to employ other hands to write. I saw her fairly into the cabin, and bid adieu to her with sincere good will. James had tired at Dilly's waiting so long and was gone home. I followed him. I paid her passage and entertainment on the voyage, and gave her an allowance till 1 November and £5 as the first half year's allowance per advance, the days of payment to be 1 November and 1 May."

The letter which puzzled Mr. Bettany shows Boswell a year later punctiliously fulfilling his promise, and makes clear that subscriptions *had* failed, and that he was paying the entire sum himself. So much for "irons in the fire."

On 2 November Boswell called on Mr. Pollock, and ("as I had often done before," he adds) urged clemency for the four men still in Newgate. James Martin's time had expired, and Boswell left the certificate of his conviction, which he had procured by a call on "Mr. Follet, Clerk of Assize on the Western Circuit." On his coming home to dinner he found that all four men had been freed by proclamation and had come directly to his door. With the entry for the next day they disappear for ever from the Journal. Nor can I tell you anything more about Mary Bryant's life from the day that Boswell parted with her at Beale's Wharf, except that she must have been living in Fowey or the vicinity a year later. The parish registers of Fowey and Lostwithiel contain no record of her remarriage or burial. A woman named Mary Bryant was married to one Richard Thomas at St. Breage parish in 1807; that may be our Mary, who would then have been only forty-two, but I doubt it. I am sure that we shall find out more about her. I hope that it will prove that she emigrated to America and became the ancestress of someone now reading this book. I can say with complete sincerity that I know of no one whom I should more proudly claim as my forbear than that heroic girl who escaped from Botany Bay and was befriended by James Boswell.

AN AFTERWORD ON
"BOSWELL AND THE GIRL
FROM BOTANY BAY"

IT is part of the province of such an anthology as this to make easily accessible certain works of good repute and quality which are either out of print or, for some other reason, difficult for a new generation to come by. The foregoing oddity has until now been familiar only to those who, in the spring of 1932, heard it as a lecture before the Elizabethan Club at New Haven, plus the inconsiderably larger number who have since had access to one or another of the five hundred copies which, with some amendment, have recently been printed. Professor Pottle's material had come to him as a rewarding by-product of his labors in editing the Boswell papers—a grateful but exacting task that fell to him on the untimely death of Geoffrey Scott. Those papers—diaries, manuscripts, letters received, letters written—are the ones which, almost a century and a half after James Boswell's death, emerged reluctantly from the purlieus of Malahide Castle, a small and comely twelfth-century fortress which the family still occupies just down the road from Dublin.

While there is abundant reason to believe that many a muniment room in the British Isles is still unexplored territory, a special set of circumstances explains the long sequestration of the Boswell papers. First, it must be recalled that the Boswells of Auchinleck—the name was originally Boisville—were gentry of Norman blood who regarded as more than a little deplorable this strange tendency of a son of their house to frequent low company like that of Dr. Johnson and such cattle. They thought of him as slumming. Then, when half a century had sanctified these relics, a grand-daughter, on venturing to examine them, chanced first on a page of unpublished diary. In it Boswell noted that he had asked what, after all, the great lexicographer considered the greatest pleasure in life. He also noted the reply. On reading it, his less robust descendant turned pale and in that book she read no more that day. Finally, when, after another generation or so, Auchinleck itself and all its contents were inherited by Lord Talbot de Malahide through his marriage to a Miss Boswell, the papers merely shifted into the possession of a line no more likely to set great store by them. After all, no documents only a century old could impress a man in whose muniment room the deeds and inventories spanned a millennium, and, besides, the lords of Malahide Castle were never men of a sort to be described as bookish.

Indeed, at Malahide there was so little disposition to boast of this enviable family treasure that not until 1925 did even so devout a student of the period as Chauncey B. Tinker of Yale learn that the papers still existed. Then, as the word spread, there was agitation among the collectors and it is said that Dr. Rosenbach, the Philadelphia dealer, startled and puzzled Lord Talbot by cabling an offer of fifty thousand pounds for the papers, sight unseen. They were finally sold to Lt.-Colonel Ralph H. Isham, the American bibliophile, and by him transferred from Malahide Castle to his own house near Glen Cove on Long Island.

Lord Talbot had agreed to part with them at all only on condition that his good lady should go through them first and assure him that nothing discreditable to the family would thereby get into circulation. This restriction led to one painful moment while her ladyship was explaining to Colonel Isham the difficulty of her task. Here, for example, was a letter from Boswell to his friend Temple, written after he had consoled poor Rousseau, lonely in his London exile, by promising to fetch his girl from Paris. At every stop of the diligence on the road to Calais, the amorous escort had collected his fee. Really, ought one to release for publication such goings-on of a scandalous great-great-grandfather? No. And Lady Talbot threw the letter into the fire. At this Colonel Isham's monocle—the only one, I believe, ever worn by a native son of Elizabeth, N. J.—is said to have leaped from its offended moorings. With perfect aplomb, however, he then tactfully persuaded Lady Talbot to adopt an editorial method less drastic. But that is another story.

The point is that here were riches unforeseen. Journals and manuscripts. Here were the answers to many a question which had puzzled Professor Tinker in the writing of *Young Boswell* and here, incidentally, was astonishing confirmation of many a brilliant guess Geoffrey Scott had made in writing *The Story of Zélide*. Letters. Letters from Voltaire, Burns, Goldsmith. Boswell's own love-letters, all neatly docketed. Like his celebrated compatriot, Madeleine Smith—in the case of Miss Smith's *billets-doux* to the exigent young man whose attentions she eventually discouraged by putting arsenic in his cocoa, the later missives were full of her wily efforts to recapture the whole tell-tale correspondence—like the fair Madeleine, Boswell wound up each romance with such tactics as would end it with all his letters back in his own hands. He, however, sought less to avoid embarrassment than to ensure their being left in good order for the convenience of an appreciative posterity.

Three years after Colonel Isham had started publication of the papers, a second batch came to light at Malahide—in a croquet-box. These included the manuscript of the *Journal of a Tour to the Hebrides,* the first full publication of which was thereby made possible a hundred and sixty-three years after it was written. Then, only this year, in a final combing of the premises, Colonel Isham came upon the eloquent little packet of withered vegetation which confirmed the tale of Mary Broad as Professor Pottle had told it at the Elizabethan Club five years before. A memento brown, desiccated, as brittle as old parchment, but able to tell its story just as black notes on white paper can lock up and cherish a melody for the delight of him who can read them. Leaves which Boswell had saved at all only because they had come all the way from Botany Bay and been put in his hands by a woman whose courage and tragic distress had deeply moved him.

A. W.

THE
GOLDEN
AGE

by

KENNETH GRAHAME

THE GOLDEN AGE

PROLOGUE: THE OLYMPIANS

Looking back to those days of old, ere the gate shut to behind me, I can see now that to children with a proper equipment of parents these things would have worn a different aspect. But to those whose nearest were aunts and uncles, a special attitude of mind may be allowed. They treated us, indeed, with kindness enough as to the needs of the flesh, but after that with indifference (an indifference, as I recognize, the result of a certain stupidity), and therewith the commonplace conviction that your child is merely animal. At a very early age I remember realizing in a quite impersonal and kindly way the existence of that stupidity, and its tremendous influence in the world; while there grew up in me, as in the parallel case of Caliban upon Setebos, a vague sense of a ruling power, wilful, and freakish, and prone to the practice of vagaries—"just choosing so": as, for instance, the giving of authority over us to these hopeless and incapable creatures, when it might far more reasonably have been given to ourselves over them. These elders, our betters by a trick of chance, commanded no respect, but only a certain blend of envy—of their good luck—and pity—for their inability to make use of it. Indeed, it was one of the most hopeless features in their character (when we troubled ourselves to waste a thought on them: which wasn't often) that, having absolute licence to indulge in the pleasures of life, they could get no good of it. They might dabble in the pond all day, hunt the chickens, climb trees in the most uncompromising Sunday clothes; they were free to issue forth and buy gun powder in the full eye of the sun—free to fire cannons and explode mines on the lawn: yet they never did any one of these things. No irresistible Energy haled them to church o' Sundays; yet they went there regularly of their own accord, though they betrayed no greater delight in the experience than ourselves.

On the whole, the existence of these Olympians seemed to be entirely void of interests, even as their movements were confined and slow, and their habits stereotyped and senseless. To anything but appearances they were blind. For them the orchard (a place elf-haunted, wonderful!) simply produced so many apples and cherries: or it didn't—when the failures of Nature were not infrequently ascribed to us. They never set foot within fir-wood or hazel-copse, nor dreamt of the marvels hid therein. The mysterious sources, sources as of old Nile, that fed the duck-pond had no magic for them. They were unaware of Indians, nor recked they anything of bisons or of pirates (with pistols!), though the whole place swarmed with such portents. They cared not to explore for robbers' caves, nor dig for hidden treasure. Perhaps, indeed, it was one of their best qualities that they spent the greater part of their time stuffily indoors.

To be sure there was an exception in the curate, who would receive, unblenching, the information that the meadow beyond the orchard was a prairie studded with herds of buffalo, which it was our delight, moccasined and tomahawked, to ride down with those whoops that announce the scenting of blood. He neither laughed nor sneered, as the Olympians would have done; but, possessed of a serious idiosyncrasy, he would contribute such lots of valuable suggestion as to the pursuit of this particular sort of big game that, as it seemed to us, his mature age and eminent position could scarce have been attained without a practical knowledge of the creature in its native lair. Then, too, he was always ready to constitute himself a hostile army or a band of marauding Indians on the shortest possible notice: in brief, a distinctly able man, with talents, so far as we could judge, immensely above the majority. I trust he is a bishop by this time. He had all the necessary qualifications, as we knew.

These strange folk had visitors sometimes—stiff and colourless Olympians like themselves, equally without vital interests and intelligent pursuits: emerging out of the clouds, and passing away again to drag on an aimless existence somewhere beyond our ken. Then brute force was pitilessly applied. We were captured, washed, and forced into clean collars: silently submitting as was our wont, with more contempt than anger. Anon, with unctuous hair and faces stiffened in a conventional grin, we sat and listened to the usual platitudes. How could reasonable people spend their precious time so? That was ever our wonder as we bounded forth at last: to the old clay-pit to make pots, or to hunt bears among the hazels.

It was perennial matter for amazement how these Olympians would talk over our heads—during meals, for instance—of this or the other social or political inanity, under the delusion that these pale phantasms of reality were among the importances of life. We, *illuminati,* eating silently, our heads full of plans and conspiracies, could have told them what real life was. We had just left it outside, and were all on fire to get back to it. Of course we didn't waste the revelation on them: the futility of imparting our ideas had long been demonstrated. One in thought and purpose, linked by the necessity of combating one hostile fate, a power antagonistic ever— a power we lived to evade—we had no confidants save ourselves. This strange anæmic order of beings was further removed from us, in fact, than the kindly beasts who shared our natural existence in the sun. The estrangement was fortified by an abiding sense of injustice, arising from the refusal of the Olympians ever to defend, to retract, to admit themselves in the wrong, or to accept similar concessions on our part. For instance, when I flung the cat out of an upper window (though I did it from no ill-feeling, and it didn't hurt the cat), I was ready, after a moment's reflection, to own I was wrong, as a gentleman should. But was the matter allowed to end there? I trow not. Again, when Harold was locked up in his room all day, for assault and battery upon a neighbour's pig —an action he would have scorned: being indeed on the friendliest terms with the porker in question—there was no handsome expression of regret on the discovery of the real culprit. What Harold had felt was not so much the imprisonment—indeed, he had very soon escaped by the window, with assistance from his allies, and had only gone back in time for his release—as the Olympian habit. A word would have set all right; but of course that word was never spoken.

Well! The Olympians are all past and gone. Somehow the sun does not seem to shine so brightly as it used; the trackless meadows of old time have shrunk and dwindled away to a few poor acres. A saddening doubt, a dull suspicion, creeps over me. *Et in Arcadia ego*—I certainly did once inhabit Arcady. Can it be that I also have become an Olympian?

A HOLIDAY

THE masterful wind was up and out, shouting and chasing, the lord of the morning. Poplars swayed and tossed with a roaring swish; dead leaves sprang aloft, and whirled into space; and all the clear-swept heaven seemed to thrill with sound like a great harp. It was one of the first awakenings of the year. The earth stretched herself, smiling in her sleep; and everything leapt and pulsed to the stir of the giant's movement. With us it was a whole holiday; the occasion a birthday—it matters not whose. Some one of us had had presents, and pretty conventional speeches, and had glowed with that sense of heroism which is no less sweet that nothing has been done to deserve it. But the holiday was for all, the rapture of awakening Nature for all, the various outdoor joys of puddles and sun and hedge-breaking for all. Colt-like I ran through the meadows, frisking happy heels in the face of Nature laughing responsive. Above, the sky was bluest of the blue; wide pools left by the winter's floods flashed the colour back, true and brilliant; and the soft air thrilled with the germinating touch that seems to kindle something in my own small person as well as in the rash primrose already lurking in sheltered haunts. Out into the brimming sun-bathed world I sped, free of lessons, free of discipline and correction, for one day at least. My legs ran of themselves, and though I heard my name called faint and shrill behind, there was no stopping for me. It was only Harold, I concluded, and his legs, though shorter than mine, were good for a longer spurt than this. Then I heard it called again, but this time more faintly, with a pathetic break in the middle; and I pulled up short, recognizing Charlotte's plaintive note.

She panted up anon, and dropped on the turf beside me. Neither had any desire for talk; the glow and the glory of existing on this perfect morning were satisfaction full and sufficient.

"Where's Harold?" I asked presently.

"Oh, he's just playin' muffin-man, as usual," said Charlotte with petulance. "Fancy wanting to be a muffin-man on a whole holiday!"

It was a strange craze, certainly; but Harold, who invented his own games and played them without assistance, always stuck staunchly to a new fad, till he had worn it quite out. Just at present he was a muffin-man, and day and night he went through passages and up and down staircases, ringing a noiseless bell and offering phantom muffins to invisible wayfarers. It sounds a poor sort of sport; and yet—to pass along busy streets of your own building, for ever ringing an imaginary bell and offering airy muffins of your own make to a bustling thronging crowd of your own creation—there were points about the game, it cannot be denied, though it seemed scarce in harmony with this radiant wind-swept morning!

"And Edward, where is he?" I questioned again.

"He's coming along by the road," said Charlotte. "He'll be crouching in the ditch when we get there, and he's going to be a grizzly bear and spring out on us, only you mustn't say I told you, 'cos it's to be a surprise."

"All right," I said magnanimously. "Come on and let's be surprised." But I could not help feeling that on this day of days even a grizzly felt misplaced and common.

Sure enough an undeniable bear sprang out on us as we dropped into the road; then ensued shrieks, growlings, revolver-shots, and unrecorded heroisms, till Edward condescended at last to roll over and die, bulking large and grim, an unmitigated grizzly. It was an understood thing, that whoever took upon himself to be a bear must eventually die, sooner or later, even if he were the eldest born; else, life would have been all strife and carnage, and the Age of Acorns have displaced our hard-won civilization. This little affair concluded with satisfaction to all parties concerned, we rambled along the road, picking up the defaulting Harold by the way, muffinless now and in his right and social mind.

"What would you do," asked Charlotte presently, the book of the moment always dominating her thoughts until it was sucked dry and cast aside, "what would you do if you saw two lions in the road, one on each side, and you didn't know if they was loose or if they was chained up?"

"Do?" shouted Edward valiantly. "I should—I should—I should—" His boastful accents died away into a mumble: "Dunno what I should do."

"Shouldn't do anything," I observed after consideration; and really, it would be difficult to arrive at a wiser conclusion.

"If it came to *doing*," remarked Harold reflectively, "the lions would do all the doing there was to do, wouldn't they?"

"But if they was *good* lions," rejoined Charlotte, "they would do as they would be done by."

"Ah, but how are you to know a good lion from a bad one?" said Edward. "The books don't tell you at all, and the lions ain't marked any different."

"Why, there aren't any good lions," said Harold hastily.

"Oh, yes, there are, heaps and heaps," contradicted Edward. "Nearly all the lions in the story-books are good lions. There was Androcles' lion, and St. Jerome's lion, and—and—and the Lion and the Unicorn——"

"He beat the Unicorn," observed Harold dubiously, "all round the town."

"That *proves* he was a good lion," cried Edward triumphantly. "But the question is, how are you to tell 'em when you see 'em?"

"*I* should ask Martha," said Harold of the simple creed.

Edward snorted contemptuously, then turned to Charlotte. "Look here," he said; "let's play at lions, anyhow, and I'll run on to that corner and be a lion—I'll be two lions, one on each side of the road—and you'll come along, and you won't know whether I'm chained up or not, and that'll be the fun!"

"No, thank you," said Charlotte firmly; "you'll be chained till I'm quite close to you, and then you'll be loose, and you'll tear me in pieces, and make my frock all dirty, and p'raps you'll hurt me as well. *I know* your lions!"

"No, I won't, I swear I won't," protested Edward. "I'll be quite a new lion at this—something you can't imagine." And he raced off to his post. Charlotte hesitated—then she went timidly on, at each step growing less Charlotte, the mummer of a minute, and more the anxious Pilgrim of all time. The lion's wrath waxed terrible at her approach; his roaring filled the startled air. I waited until they were both thoroughly absorbed, and then I slipped through the hedge out of the trodden highway, into the vacant meadow spaces. It was not that I was unsociable, nor that I knew Edward's lions to the point of satiety; but the passion and the call of the divine morning were high in my blood. Earth to earth! That was the frank note, the joyous summons of the day; and they could not but jar and seem artificial, these human discussions and pretences, when boon Nature, reticent no more, was singing that full-throated song of hers that thrills and claims control of every fibre. The air was wine, the moist earth-smell wine, the lark's song, the wafts from the cow-shed at top of the field, the pant and smoke of a distant train—all were wine—or song, was it, or odour, this unity they all blent into? I had no words then to describe it, that earth-effluence of which I was so conscious; nor, indeed, have I found words since. I ran sideways, shouting; I dug glad heels into the squelching soil; I splashed diamond showers from puddles with a stick; I hurled clods skyward at random, and presently I somehow found myself singing. The words were mere nonsense—irresponsible babble; the tune was an improvisation, a weary, unrhythmic thing of rise and fall: and yet it seemed to me a genuine utterance, and just at that moment the one thing fitting and right and perfect. Humanity would have rejected it with scorn. Nature, everywhere singing in the same key, recognized and accepted it without a flicker of dissent.

All the time the hearty wind was calling to me companionably from where he swung and bellowed in the tree-tops. "Take me for guide today," he seemed to plead. "Other holidays you have tramped it in the track of the stolid, unswerving sun; a belated truant, you have dragged a weary foot homeward with only a pale, expressionless moon for company. Today why not I, the trickster, the hypocrite? I who whip round corners and bluster, relapse and evade, then rally and pursue! I can lead you the best and rarest dance of any; for I am the strong capricious one, the lord of misrule, and I alone am irresponsible and unprincipled, and obey no law." And for me, I was ready enough to fall in with the fellow's humour; was not this a whole holiday? So we sheered off together, arm-in-arm, so to speak; and with fullest confidence I took the jigging, thwartwise course my chainless pilot laid for me.

A whimsical comrade I found him, ere he had done with me. Was it in jest, or with some serious purpose of his own, that he brought me plump upon a pair of lovers, silent, face to face o'er a discreet unwinking stile? As a rule this sort of thing struck me as the most pitiful tomfoolery. Two calves rubbing noses through a gate were natural and right and within the order of things; but that human beings, with salient interests and active pursuits beckoning them on from every side, could thus—! Well, it was a thing to hurry past, shamed of face, and think on no more. But this morning everything I met seemed to be accounted for and set in tune by that same magical touch in the air; and it was with a certain surprise that I found myself regarding these fatuous ones with kindliness instead of contempt, as I rambled by, unheeding of them. There was indeed some reconciling influence abroad, which could bring the like antics into harmony with bud and growth and the frolic air.

A puff on the right cheek from my wilful companion sent me off at a fresh angle, and presently I came in sight of the village church, sitting solitary within its circle of elms. From forth the vestry window projected two small legs, gyrating, hungry for foothold, with larceny—not to say sacrilege—in their every wriggle: a godless sight for a supporter of the Establishment. Though the rest was hidden, I knew the legs well enough; they were usually attached to the body of Bill Saunders, the peerless bad boy of the village. Bill's coveted booty, too, I could easily guess at that; it came from the Vicar's store of biscuits, kept (as I knew) in a cupboard along with his official trappings. For a moment I hesitated; then I passed on my way. I protest I was not on Bill's side; but then, neither was I on the Vicar's, and there was something in this immoral morning which seemed to say that perhaps, after all, Bill had as much right to the biscuits as the Vicar, and would certainly enjoy them better; and anyhow it was a disputable point, and no business of mine. Nature, who had accepted me for ally, cared little who had the world's biscuits, and assuredly was not going to let any friend of hers waste his time in playing policeman for Society.

He was tugging at me anew, my insistent guide; and I felt sure, as I rambled off in his wake, that he had more holiday matter to show me. And so, indeed, he had; and all of it was to the same lawless tune. Like a black pirate flag on the blue ocean of air, a hawk hung ominous; then, plummet-wise, dropped to the hedgerow, whence there rose, thin and shrill, a piteous voice of squealing. By the time I got there a whisk of feathers on the turf—like scattered playbills—was all that remained to tell of the tragedy just enacted. Yet Nature smiled and sang on, pitiless, gay, impartial. To her, who took no sides, there was every bit as much to be said for the hawk as for the chaffinch. Both were her children, and she would show no preferences.

Further on, a hedgehog lay dead athwart the path—nay, more than dead; decadent, distinctly; a sorry sight for one that had known the fellow in more bustling circumstances. Nature might at least have paused to shed one tear over this rough-jacketed little son of hers, for his wasted aims, his cancelled ambitions, his whole career of usefulness cut suddenly short. But not a bit of it! Jubilant as ever, her song went bubbling on, and "Death-in-Life" and again "Life-in-Death" were its alternate burdens. And looking round, and seeing the sheep-nibbled heels of turnips that dotted the ground, their hearts eaten out of them in frost-bound days now over and done, I seemed to discern, faintly, a something of the stern meaning in her valorous chant.

My invisible companion was singing also, and seemed at times to be chuckling softly to himself—doubtless at thought of the strange new lessons he was teaching me; perhaps, too, at a special bit of waggishness he had still in store. For when at last he grew weary of such insignificant earth-bound company, he deserted me at a certain spot I knew; then dropped, subsided, and slunk away into nothingness. I raised my eyes, and before me, grim and lichened, stood the ancient whipping-post of the village; its sides fretted with the initials of a generation that scorned its mute lesson, but still clipped by the stout rusty shackles that had tethered the wrists of such of that generation's ancestors as had dared to mock at order and law. Had I been an infant Sterne, here was a grand chance for sentimental output! As things were, I could only hurry homewards, my moral tail well between my legs, with an uneasy feeling, as I glanced back over my shoulder, that there was more in this chance than met the eye.

And outside our gate I found Charlotte, alone and crying. Edward, it seemed, had persuaded her to hide, in the full expectation of being duly found and ecstatically pounced upon; then he had caught sight of the butcher's cart, and, forgetting his obligations, had rushed off for a ride. Harold, it further appeared, greatly coveting tadpoles, and top-heavy with the eagerness of possession, had fallen into the pond. This, in itself, was nothing; but on attempting to sneak in by the back-door, he had rendered up his duckweed-bedabbled person into the hands of an aunt, and had been promptly sent off to bed; and this, on a holiday, was very much. The moral of the whipping-post was working itself out; and I was not in the least surprised when, on reaching home, I was seized upon and accused of doing something I had never even thought of. And my frame of mind was such, that I could only wish most heartily that I had done it.

A WHITE-WASHED UNCLE

In our small lives that day was eventful when another uncle was to come down from town, and submit his character and qualifications (albeit unconsciously) to our careful criticism. Earlier uncles had been weighed in the balance, and—alas!—found grievously wanting. There was Uncle Thomas—a failure from the first. Not that his disposition was malevolent, nor were his habits such as to unfit him for decent society; but his rooted conviction seemed to be that the reason of a child's existence was to serve as a butt for senseless adult jokes—or what, from the accompanying guffaws of laughter, appeared to be intended for jokes. Now, we were anxious that he should have a perfectly fair trial; so in the tool-house, between breakfast and lessons, we discussed and examined all his witticisms one by one, calmly, critically, dispassionately. It was no good! We could not discover any salt in them. And as only a genuine gift of humour could have saved Uncle Thomas—for he pretended to naught besides—he was reluctantly writ down a hopeless impostor.

Uncle George—the youngest—was distinctly more promising. He accompanied us cheerly round the establishment—suffered himself to be introduced to each of the cows—held out the right hand of fellowship to the pig—and even hinted that a pair of pink-eyed Himalayan rabbits might arrive—unexpectedly—from town some day. We were just considering whether in this fertile soil an apparently accidental remark on the solid qualities of guinea-pigs or ferrets might haply blossom and bring forth fruit, when our governess appeared on the scene. Uncle George's manner at once underwent a complete and contemptible change. His interest in rational topics seemed, "like a fountain's sickening pulse," to flag and ebb away; and though Miss Smedley's ostensible purpose was to take Selina for her usual walk, I can vouch for it that Selina spent her morning ratting, along with the keeper's boy and me; while if Miss Smedley walked with anyone, it would appear to have been with Uncle George.

But, despicable as his conduct had been, he underwent no hasty condemnation. The defection was discussed in all its bearings, but it seemed sadly clear at last that this uncle must possess some innate badness of character and fondness for low company. We who from daily experience knew Miss Smedley like a book—were we not only too well aware that she had neither accomplishments nor charms, no characteristic, in fact, but an inbred viciousness of temper and disposition? True, she knew the dates of the English kings by heart; but how could that profit Uncle George, who, having passed into the army, had ascended beyond the need of useful information? Our bows and arrows, on the other hand, had been freely placed at his disposal; and a soldier should not have hesitated in his choice a moment. No; Uncle George had fallen from grace, and was unanimously damned. And the non-arrival of the Himalayan· rabbits was only another nail in his coffin. Uncles, therefore, were just then a heavy and lifeless market, and there was little inclination to deal. Still it was agreed that Uncle William, who had just returned from India, should have as fair a trial as the others; more especially as romantic possibilities might well be embodied in one who had held the gorgeous East in fee.

Selina had kicked my shins—like the girl she is!—during a scuffle in the passage, and I was still rubbing them with one hand when I found that the uncle-on-approbation was half-heartedly shaking the other. A florid, elderly man, quite unmistakably nervous, he let drop one grimy paw after another, and, turning very red, with an awkward simulation of heartiness, "Well, h'are y'all?" he said. "Glad to see me, eh?" As we could hardly, in justice, be expected to have formed an opinion on him at that early stage, we could but look at each other in silence; which scarce served to relieve the tension of the situation. Indeed, the cloud never really lifted during his stay. In talking things over later, someone put forward the suggestion that he must at some time or other have committed a stupendous crime. But I could not bring myself to believe that the man, though evidently unhappy, was really guilty of anything; and I caught him once or twice looking at us with evident kindliness, though, seeing himself observed, he blushed and turned away his head.

When at last the atmosphere was clear of his depressing influence, we met despondently in the potato-cellar, all of us, that is, but Harold, who had been told off to accompany his relative to the station; and the feeling was unanimous that, as an uncle, William could not be allowed to pass. Selina roundly declared him a beast, pointing out that he had not even got us a half-holiday; and, indeed, there seemed little to do but to pass sentence. We were about to put it to the vote, when Harold appeared on the scene; his red face, round eyes, and mysterious demeanour, hinting at awful portents. Speechless he stood a space; then, slowly drawing his hand from the pocket of his knickerbockers, he displayed on a dirty palm one—two—three—four half-crowns! We could but gaze—tranced, breathless, mute. Never had any of us seen, in the aggregate, so much bullion before. Then Harold told his tale.

"I took the old fellow to the station," he said, "and as we went along I told him all about the stationmaster's family, and how I had seen the porter kissing our housemaid, and what a nice fellow he was, with no airs or affectation about him, and anything I thought would be of interest; but he didn't seem to pay much attention, but walked along puffing his cigar, and once I thought—I'm not certain, but I *thought* —I heard him say, 'Well, thank God, that's over!' When we got to the station he stopped suddenly, and said, 'Hold on a minute!' Then he shoved these into my hand in a frightened sort of way, and said, 'Look here, youngster! These are for you and the other kids. Buy what you like—make little beasts of yourselves—only don't tell the old people, mind! Now cut away home!' So I cut."

A solemn hush fell on the assembly, broken first by the small Charlotte. "I didn't know," she observed dreamily, "that there were such good men anywhere in the world. I hope he'll die tonight, for then he'll go straight to heaven!" But the repentant Selina bewailed herself with tears and sobs, refusing to be comforted; for that in her haste she had called this white-souled relative a beast.

"I'll tell you what we'll do," said Edward, the master-mind, rising —as he always did—to the situation; "we'll christen the piebald pig after him—the one that hasn't got a name yet. And that'll show we're sorry for our mistake!"

"I—I christened that pig this morning," Harold guiltily confessed; "I christened it after the curate. I'm very sorry—but he came and bowled to me last night, after you others had all been sent to bed early —and somehow I felt I *had* to do it!"

"Oh, but that doesn't count," said Edward hastily, "because we weren't all there. We'll take that christening off, and call it Uncle William. And you can save up the curate for the next litter!"

And the motion being agreed to without a division, the House went into Committee of Supply.

ALARUMS AND EXCURSIONS

"LET's pretend," suggested Harold, "that we're Cavaliers and Round-heads; and *you* be a Roundhead!"

"Oh, bother," I replied drowsily, "we pretended that yesterday; and it's not my turn to be a Roundhead, anyhow." The fact is, I was lazy, and the call to arms fell on indifferent ears. We three younger ones were stretched at length in the orchard. The sun was hot, the season merry June, and never (I thought) had there been such wealth and riot of buttercups throughout the lush grass. Green-and-gold was the dominant key that day. Instead of active "pretence" with its shouts and its perspiration, how much better—I held—to lie at ease and pretend to one's self, in green and golden fancies, slipping the husk and pass-ing, a careless lounger, through a sleepy imaginary world all gold and green! But the persistent Harold was not to be fobbed off.

"Well then," he began afresh, "let's pretend we're Knights of the Round Table; and" (with a rush) *"I'll* be Lancelot!"

"I won't play unless I'm Lancelot," I said. I didn't mean it really, but the game of Knights always began with this particular contest.

"Oh, *please,*" implored Harold. "You know when Edward's here I never get a chance of being Lancelot. I haven't been Lancelot for weeks!"

Then I yielded gracefully. "All right," I said. "I'll be Tristram."

"Oh, but you can't," cried Harold again. "Charlotte has always been Tristram. She won't play unless she's allowed to be Tristram! Be some-body else this time."

Charlotte said nothing, but breathed hard, looking straight before her. The peerless hunter and harper was her special hero of romance, and rather than see the part in less appreciative hands, she would have gone back in tears to the stuffy schoolroom.

"I don't care," I said. "I'll be anything. I'll be Sir Kay. Come on!"

Then once more in this country's story the mail-clad knights paced through the greenwood shaw, questing adventure, redressing wrong;

and bandits, five to one, broke and fled discomfited to their caves. Once more were damsels rescued, dragons disembowelled, and giants, in every corner of the orchard, deprived of their already superfluous number of heads; while Palomides the Saracen waited for us by the well, and Sir Breuse Saunce Pitié vanished in craven flight before the skilled spear that was his terror and his bane. Once more the lists were dight in Camelot, and all was gay with shimmer of silk and gold; the earth shook with thunder of hoofs, ash-staves flew in splinters, and the firmament rang to the clash of sword on helm. The varying fortune of the day swung doubtful—now on this side, now on that; till at last Lancelot, grim and great, thrusting through the press, unhorsed Sir Tristram (an easy task), and bestrode her, threatening doom; while the Cornish knight, forgetting hard-won fame of old, cried piteously, "You're hurting me, I tell you! And you're tearing my frock!" Then it happened that Sir Kay, hurtling to the rescue, stopped short in his stride, catching sight suddenly, through apple-boughs, of a gleam of scarlet afar off; while the confused tramp of many horses, mingled with talk and laughter, was borne to the ears of his fellow-champions and himself.

"What is it?" inquired Tristram, sitting up and shaking out her curls; while Lancelot forsook the clanging lists and trodded nimbly to the boundary-hedge.

I stood spell-bound for a moment longer, and then, with a cry of "Soldiers!" I was off to the hedge, Sir Tristram picking herself up and scurrying after us.

Down the road they came, two and two, at an easy walk; scarlet flamed in the eye, bits jingled and saddles squeaked delightfully; while the men, in a halo of dust, smoked their short clays like the heroes they were. In a swirl of intoxicating glory the troop clinked and clattered by, while we shouted and waved jumping up and down, and the big jolly horsemen acknowledged the salute with easy condescension. The moment they were past we were through the hedge and after them. Soldiers were not the common stuff of everyday life. There had been nothing like this since the winter before last, when on a certain afternoon—bare of leaf and monochromatic in its hue of sodden fallow and frost-nipt copse—suddenly the hounds had burst through the fence with their mellow cry, and all the paddock was for the minute reverberant of thudding hoof and dotted with glancing red. But this was better, since it could only mean that blows and bloodshed were in the air.

"Is there going to be a battle?" panted Harold, hardly able to keep up for excitement.

"Of course there is," I replied. "We're just in time. Come on!"

Perhaps I ought to have known better; and yet—? The pigs and poultry, with whom we chiefly consorted, could instruct us little concerning the peace that lapped in these latter days our seagirt realm. In the schoolroom we were just now dallying with the Wars of the Roses; and did not legends of the countryside inform us how cavaliers had once galloped up and down these very lanes from their quarters in the village? Here, now, were soldiers unmistakable; and if their business was not fighting, what was it? Sniffing the joy of battle, we followed hard in their tracks.

"Won't Edward be sorry," puffed Harold, "that he's begun that beastly Latin?"

It did, indeed, seem hard. Edward, the most martial spirit of us all, was drearily conjugating *amo* (of all verbs!) between four walls; while Selina, who ever thrilled ecstatic to a red coat, was struggling with the uncouth German tongue. "Age," I reflected, "carries its penalties."

It was a grievous disappointment to us that the troop passed through the village unmolested. Every cottage, I pointed out to my companions, ought to have been loopholed, and strongly held. But no opposition was offered to the soldiers, who, indeed, conducted themselves with a recklessness and a want of precaution that seemed simply criminal.

At the last cottage a transitory gleam of common sense flickered across me, and, turning on Charlotte, I sternly ordered her back. The small maiden, docile but exceedingly dolorous, dragged reluctant feet homewards, heavy at heart that she was to behold no stout fellows slain that day; but Harold and I held steadily on, expecting every instant to see the environing hedges crackle and spit forth the leaden death.

"Will they be Indians," asked my brother (meaning the enemy), "or Roundheads, or what?"

I reflected. Harold always required direct straightforward answers—not faltering suppositions.

"They won't be Indians," I replied at last; "nor yet Roundheads. There haven't been any Roundheads seen about here for a long time. They'll be Frenchmen."

Harold's face fell. "All right," he said, "Frenchmen'll do; but I did hope they'd be Indians."

"If they were going to be Indians," I explained, "I—I don't think I'd go on. Because when Indians take you prisoner they scalp you first, and then burn you at the stake. But Frenchmen don't do that sort of thing."

"Are you quite sure?" asked Harold doubtfully.

"Quite," I replied. "Frenchmen only shut you up in a thing called the Bastille; and then you get a file sent in to you in a loaf of bread, and saw the bars through, and slide down a rope, and they all fire at you—but they don't hit you—and you run down to the seashore as hard as you can, and swim off to a British frigate, and there you are!"

Harold brightened up again. The programme was rather attractive. "If they try to take us prisoner," he said, "we—we won't run, will we?"

Meanwhile, the craven foe was a long time showing himself; and we were reaching strange outland country, uncivilized, wherein lions might be expected to prowl at nightfall. I had a stitch in my side, and both Harold's stockings had come down. Just as I was beginning to have gloomy doubts of the proverbial courage of Frenchmen, the officer called out something, the men closed up, and, breaking into a trot, the troops—already far ahead—vanished out of our sight. With a sinking at the heart, I began to suspect we had been fooled.

"Are they charging?" cried Harold, very weary, but rallying gamely.

"I think not," I replied doubtfully. "When there's going to be a charge, the officer always makes a speech, and then they draw their swords and the trumpets blow, and—but let's try a short cut. We may catch them up yet."

So we struck across the fields and into another road, and pounded down that, and then over more fields, panting, down-hearted, yet hoping for the best. The sun went in, and a thin drizzle began to fall; we were muddy, breathless, almost dead-beat; but we blundered on, till at last we struck a road more brutally, more callously unfamiliar than any road I ever looked upon. Not a hint nor a sign of friendly direction or assistance on the dogged white face of it! There was no longer any disguising it: we were hopelessly lost. The small rain continued steadily, the evening began to come on. Really there are moments when a fellow is justified in crying; and I would have cried too, if Harold had not been there. That right-minded child regarded an elder brother as a veritable god; and I could see that he felt himself as secure as if a whole Brigade of Guards had hedged him round with protecting bayonets. But I dreaded sore lest he should begin again with his questions.

As I gazed in dumb appeal on the fact of unresponsive Nature, the sound of nearing wheels sent a pulse of hope through my being; increasing to rapture as I recognized in the approaching vehicle the familiar carriage of the old doctor. If ever a god emerged from a machine, it was when this heaven-sent friend, recognizing us, stopped and jumped out with a cheery hail. Harold rushed up to him at once. "Have you been there?" he cried. "Was it a jolly fight? Who beat? Were there many people killed?"

The doctor appeared puzzled. I briefly explained the situation.

"I see," said the doctor, looking grave and twisting his face this way and that. "Well, the fact is, there isn't going to be any battle today. It's been put off, on account of the change in the weather. You will have due notice of the renewal of hostilities. And now you'd better jump in and I'll drive you home. You've been running a fine rig! Why, you might have both been taken and shot as spies!"

This special danger had never even occurred to us. The thrill of it accentuated the cosy homelike feeling of the cushions we nestled into as we rolled homewards. The doctor beguiled the journey with blood-curdling narratives of personal adventure in the tented field, he having followed the profession of arms (so it seemed) in every quarter of the globe. Time, the destroyer of all things beautiful, subsequently revealed the baselessness of these legends; but what of that? There are higher things than truth; and we were almost reconciled, by the time we were put down at our gate, to the fact that the battle had been postponed.

THE FINDING OF THE PRINCESS

It was the day I was promoted to a toothbrush. The girls, irrespective of age, had been thus distinguished some time before; why, we boys could never rightly understand, except that it was part and parcel of a system of studied favouritism on behalf of creatures both physically inferior to and (as was shown by a fondness for tale-bearing) of weaker mental fibre than us boys. It was not that we yearned after these strange instruments in themselves. Edward, indeed, applied his to the scrubbing-out of his squirrel's cage, and for personal use, when a superior eye was grim on him, borrowed Harold's or mine, indifferently. But the nimbus of distinction that clung to them—that we coveted exceedingly. What more, indeed, was there to ascend to, before the remote, but still possible, razor and strop?

Perhaps the exaltation had mounted to my head; or Nature and the perfect morning joined to hint at disaffection. Anyhow, having breakfasted, and triumphantly repeated the collect I had broken down in the last Sunday—'twas one without rhythm or alliteration: a most objectionable collect—having achieved thus much, the small natural man in me rebelled, and I vowed, as I straddled and spat about the stable-yard in feeble imitation of the coachman, that lessons might go to the Inventor of them. It was only geography that morning, anyway: and the practical thing was worth any quantity of bookish theoric. As for me, I was going on my travels, and imports and exports, populations and capitals, might very well wait while I explored the breathing coloured world outside.

True, a fellow-rebel was wanted; and Harold might, as a rule, have been counted on with certainty. But just then Harold was very proud. The week before he had "gone into tables," and had been endowed with a new slate, having a miniature sponge attached wherewith we washed the faces of Charlotte's dolls, thereby producing an unhealthy pallor which struck terror into the child's heart, always timorous regarding epidemic visitations. As to "tables," nobody knew exactly what they were, least of all Harold; but it was a step over the heads of the rest, and therefore a subject of self-adulation and—generally speaking —airs; so that Harold, hugging his slate and his chains, was out of the question now. In such a matter, girls were worse than useless, as wanting the necessary tenacity of will and contempt for self-constituted authority. So eventually I slipped through the hedge a solitary protestant, and issued forth on the lane what time the rest of the civilized world was sitting down to lessons.

The scene was familiar enough; and yet, this morning how different it all seemed! The act, with its daring, tinted everything with new strange hues; affecting the individual with a sort of bruised feeling just below the pit of the stomach, that was intensified whenever his thoughts flew back to the ink-stained smelly schoolroom. And could this be really me? Or was I only contemplating, from the schoolroom aforesaid, some other jolly young mutineer, faring forth under the genial sun? Anyhow, here was the friendly well, in its old place, half-way up the lane. Hither the yoke-shouldering village-folk were wont to come to fill their clinking buckets; when the drippings made worms of wet in the thick dust of the road. They had flat wooden crosses inside each pail, which floated on the top and (we were instructed) served to prevent the water from slopping over. We used to wonder by what magic this strange principle worked, and who first invented the crosses, and whether he got a peerage for it. But indeed the well was a centre of mystery, for a hornets' nest was somewhere hard by, and the very thought was fearsome. Wasps we knew well and disdained, storming them in their fastnesses. But these great Beasts, vestured in angry orange, three stings from which—so 'twas averred—would kill a horse, these were of a different kidney, and their dreadful drone suggested prudence and retreat. At this time neither villagers nor hornets encroached on the stillness: lessons, apparently, pervaded all Nature. So, after dabbling awhile in the well—what boy has ever passed a bit of water without messing in it?—I scrambled through the hedge, shunning the hornet-haunted side, and struck into the silence of the copse.

If the lane had been deserted, this was loneliness become personal. Here mystery lurked and peeped; here brambles caught and held you with a purpose of their own; here saplings whipped your face with hu-man spite. The copse, too, proved vaster in extent, more direfully drawn out, than one would ever have guessed from its frontage on the lane; and I was really glad when at last the wood opened and sloped down to a streamlet brawling forth into the sunlight. By this cheery compan-ion I wandered along, conscious of little but that Nature, in providing store of water-rats, had thoughtfully furnished provender of right-sized stones. Rapids, also, there were, telling of canoes and portages, crin-kling bays and inlets, caves for pirates and hidden treasures—the wise Dame had forgotten nothing—till at last, after what lapse of time I know not, my further course, though not the stream's, was barred by some six feet of stout wire netting, stretched from side to side just where a thick hedge, arching till it touched, forbade all further view.

The excitement of the thing was becoming thrilling. A Black Flag must surely be fluttering close by? Here was most plainly a malignant contrivance of the Pirates, designed to baffle our gunboats when we dashed upstream to shell them from their lair! A gunboat, indeed, might well have hesitated, so stout was the netting, so close the hedge. But I spied where a rabbit was wont to pass, close down by the water's edge; where a rabbit could go a boy could follow, howbeit stomach-wise and with one leg in the stream; so the passage was achieved, and I stood inside, safe but breathless at the sight.

Gone was the brambled waste, gone the flickering tangle of wood-land. Instead, terrace after terrace of shaven sward, stone-edged, urn-cornered, stepped delicately down to where the stream, now tamed and educated, passed from one to another marble basin, in which on occa-sion gleams of red hinted at goldfish poised among the spreading water-lilies. The scene lay silent and slumbrous in the brooding noon-day sun: the drowsing peacock squatted humped on the lawn, no fish leapt in the pools, no bird declared himself from the trim secluding hedges. Self-confessed it was here, then, at last, the Garden of Sleep!

Two things, in those old days, I held in especial distrust: gamekeepers and gardeners. Seeing, however, no baleful apparitions of either quality, I pursued my way between rich flower-beds, in search of the necessary Princess. Conditions declared her presence patently as trumpets; without this centre such surroundings could not exist. A pavilion gold-topped, wreathed with lush jessamine, beckoned with a special significance over close-set shrubs. There, if anywhere, She should be enshrined. Instinct, and some knowledge of the habits of princesses, triumphed; for (indeed) there She was! In no tranced repose, however, but laughingly, struggling to disengage her hand from the grasp of a grown-up man who occupied the marble bench with her. (As to age, I suppose now that the two swung in respective scales that pivoted on twenty. But children heed no minor distinctions. To them, the inhabited world is composed of the two main divisions: children and upgrown people; the latter in no way superior to the former—only hopelessly different. These two, then, belonged to the grown-up section.) I paused, thinking it strange they should prefer seclusion when there were fish to be caught, and butterflies to hunt in the sun outside; and as I cogitated thus, the grown-up man caught sight of me.

"Hallo, sprat!" he said with some abruptness. "Where do you spring from?"

"I came up the stream," I explained politely and comprehensively, "and I was only looking for the Princess."

"Then you are a water-baby," he replied. "And what do you think of the Princess, now that you've found her?"

"I think she is lovely," I said (and doubtless I was right, having never learned to flatter). "But she's wide awake, so I suppose somebody has kissed her!"

This very natural deduction moved the grown-up man to laughter; but the Princess, turning red and jumping up, declared that it was time for lunch.

"Come along, then," said the grown-up man; "and you too, water-baby. Come and have something solid. You must want it."

I accompanied them without any feeling of false delicacy. The world, as known to me, was spread with food each several midday, and the particular table one sat at seemed a matter of no importance. The palace was very sumptuous and beautiful, just what a palace ought to be; and we were met by a stately lady, rather more grown-up than the Princess—apparently her mother. My friend the Man was very kind, and introduced me as the Captain, saying I had just run down from Aldershot. I didn't know where Aldershot was, but I had no manner of doubt that he was perfectly right. As a rule, indeed, grown-up people are fairly correct on matters of fact; it is in the higher gift of imagination that they are so sadly to seek.

The lunch was excellent and varied. Another gentleman in beautiful clothes—a lord presumably—lifted me into a high carved chair, and stood behind it, brooding over me like a Providence. I endeavoured to explain who I was and where I had come from, and to impress the company with my own toothbrush and Harold's tables; but either they were stupid—or is it a characteristic of Fairyland that everyone laughs at the most ordinary remarks? My friend the Man said good-naturedly, "All right, water-baby; you came up the stream, and that's good enough for us." The lord—a reserved sort of man, I thought—took no share in the conversation.

After lunch I walked on the terrace with the Princess and my friend the Man, and was very proud. And I told him what I was going to be, and he told me what he was going to be; and then I remarked, "I suppose you two are going to get married?" He only laughed after the Fairy fashion. "Because if you aren't," I added, "you really ought to," meaning that only a man who discovered a Princess, living in the right sort of palace like this, and didn't marry her there and then, was false to all recognized tradition.

They laughed again, and my friend suggested I should go down to the pond and look at the goldfish, while they went for a stroll. I was sleepy, and assented; but before they left me, the grown-up Man put two half-crowns in my hand, for the purpose, he explained, of treating the other water-babies. I was so touched by this crowning mark of friendship that I nearly cried; and I thought much more of his generosity than of the fact that the Princess, ere she moved away, stooped down and kissed me.

I watched them disappear down the path—how naturally arms seem to go round waists in Fairyland!—and then, my cheek on the cool marble, lulled by the trickle of water, I slipped into dreamland out of real and magic world alike. When I woke, the sun had gone in, a chill wind set all the leaves a-whispering, and the peacock on the lawn was harshly calling up the rain. A wild unreasoning panic possessed me, and I sped out of the garden like a guilty thing, wriggled through the rabbit-run, and threaded my doubtful way homewards, hounded by nameless terrors. The half-crowns happily remained solid and real to the touch; but could I hope to bear such treasure safely through the brigand-haunted wood? It was a dirty, weary little object that entered its home, at nightfall, by the unassuming aid of the scullery window: and only to be sent tealess to bed seemed infinite mercy to him. Officially tealess, that is; for, as was usual after such escapades, a sympathetic housemaid, coming delicately by backstairs, stayed him with chunks of cold pudding and condolence, till his small skin was tight as any drum. Then, Nature asserting herself, I passed into the comforting kingdom of sleep, where, a golden carp of fattest build, I oared it in translucent waters with a new half-crown snug under right fin and left; and thrust up a nose through water-lily leaves to be kissed by a rose-flushed Princess.

SAWDUST AND SIN

A BELT of rhododendrons grew close down to one side of our pond; and along the edge of it many things flourished rankly. If you crept through the undergrowth and crouched by the water's rim, it was easy —if your imagination were in healthy working order—to transport yourself in a trice to the heart of a tropical forest. Overhead the monkeys chattered, parrots flashed from bough to bough, strange large blossoms shone all round you, and the push and rustle of great beasts moving unseen thrilled you deliciously. And if you lay down with your nose an inch or two from the water, it was not long ere the old sense of proportion vanished clean away. The glittering insects that darted to and fro on its surface became sea-monsters dire, the gnats that hung above them swelled to albatrosses, and the pond itself stretched out into a vast inland sea, whereon a navy might ride secure, and whence at any moment the hairy scalp of a sea-serpent might be seen to emerge. It is impossible, however, to play at tropical forests properly, when homely accents of the human voice intrude; and all my hopes of see-ing a tiger seized by a crocodile while drinking (*vide* picture-books, *passim*) vanished abruptly, and earth resumed her old dimensions, when the sound of Charlotte's prattle somewhere hard by broke in on my primeval seclusion. Looking out from the bushes, I saw her trot-ting towards an open space of lawn the other side the pond, chattering to herself in her accustomed fashion, a doll tucked under either arm, and her brow knit with care. Propping up her double burden against a friendly stump, she sat down in front of them, as full of worry and anxiety as a Chancellor on a Budget night.

Her victims, who stared resignedly in front of them, were recog-nizable as Jerry and Rosa. Jerry hailed from far Japan: his hair was straight and black, his one garment cotton of a simple blue; and his reputation was distinctly bad. Jerome was his proper name, from his supposed likeness to the holy man who hung in a print on the stair-case; though a shaven crown was the only thing in common 'twixt Western saint and Eastern sinner. Rosa was typical British, from her flaxen poll to the stout calves she displayed so liberally; and in charac-ter she was of the blameless order of those who have not yet been found out.

I suspected Jerry from the first. There was a latent devilry in his slant eyes as he sat there moodily; and knowing what he was capable of, I scented trouble in store for Charlotte. Rosa I was not so sure about; she sat demurely and upright, and looked far away into the tree-tops in a visionary, world-forgetting sort of way; yet the prim purse of her mouth was somewhat overdone, and her eyes glittered un-naturally.

"Now, I'm going to begin where I left off," said Charlotte, regard-less of stops, and thumping the turf with her fist excitedly, "and you must pay attention, 'cos this is a treat, to have a story told you before you're put to bed. Well, so the White Rabbit scuttled off down the pas-sage and Alice hoped he'd come back 'cos he had a waistcoat on and her flamingo flew up a tree—but we haven't got to that part yet, you must wait a minute, and—where had I got to?"

Jerry remained passive only until Charlotte had got well under way, and then began to heel over quietly in Rosa's direction. His head fell on her plump shoulder, causing her to start nervously.

Charlotte seized and shook him with vigour. "Oh, Jerry," she cried piteously, "if you're not going to be good, how ever shall I tell you my story?"

Jerry's face was injured innocence itself. "Blame if you like, Madam," he seemed to say, "the eternal laws of gravitation, but not a helpless puppet, who is also an orphan and a stranger in the land."

"Now we'll go on," began Charlotte once more. "So she got into the garden at last—I've left out a lot but you won't care, I'll tell you some other time—and they were all playing croquet, and that's where the flamingo comes in, and the Queen shouted out, 'Off with her head!'"

At this point Jerry collapsed forward, suddenly and completely, his bald pate between his knees. Charlotte was not very angry this time. The sudden development of tragedy in the story had evidently been too much for the poor fellow. She straightened him out, wiped his nose, and, after trying him in various positions, to which he refused to adapt himself, she propped him against the shoulder of the (apparently) unconscious Rosa. Then my eyes were opened, and the full measure of Jerry's infamy became apparent. This, then, was what he had been playing up for! The rascal had designs, had he? I resolved to keep him under close observation.

"If you'd been in the garden," went on Charlotte reproachfully, "and flopped down like that when the Queen said, 'Off with his head!' she'd have offed with your head; but Alice wasn't that sort of girl at all. She just said, 'I'm not afraid of you, you're nothing but a pack of cards'— Oh, dear! I've got to the end already, and I hadn't begun hardly! I never can make my stories last out! Never mind, I'll tell you another one."

Jerry didn't seem to care, now he had gained his end, whether the stories lasted out or not. He was nestling against Rosa's plump form with a look of satisfaction that was simply idiotic; and one arm had disappeared from view—was it round her waist? Rosa's natural blush seemed deeper than usual, her head inclined shyly—it must have been round her waist.

"If it wasn't so near your bedtime," continued Charlotte reflectively, "I'd tell you a nice story with a bogy in it. But you'd be frightened, and you'd dream of bogies all night. So I'll tell you one about a White Bear, only you mustn't scream when the bear says 'Wow,' like I used to, 'cos he's a good bear really——"

Here Rosa fell flat on her back in the deadest of faints. Her limbs were rigid, her eyes glassy. What had Jerry been doing? It must have been something very bad, for her to take on like that. I scrutinized him carefully, while Charlotte ran to comfort the damsel. He appeared to be whistling a tune and regarding the scenery. If I only possessed Jerry's command of feature, I thought to myself, half regretfully, I would never be found out in anything.

"It's all your fault, Jerry," said Charlotte reproachfully, when the lady had been restored to consciousness. "Rosa's as good as gold except when you make her wicked. I'd put you in the corner, only a stump hasn't got a corner—wonder why that is? Thought everything had corners. Never mind, you'll have to sit with your face to the wall —so. Now you can sulk if you like!"

Jerry seemed to hesitate a moment between the bliss of indulgence in sulks with a sense of injury, and the imperious summons of beauty waiting to be wooed at his elbow; then, overmastered by his passion, he fell sideways across Rosa's lap. One arm stuck stiffly upwards, as in passionate protestation; his amorous countenance was full of entreaty. Rosa hesitated—wavered—yielded, crushing his slight frame under the weight of her full-bodied surrender.

Charlotte had stood a good deal, but it was possible to abuse even her patience. Snatching Jerry from his lawless embraces, she reversed him across her knee, and then—the outrage offered to the whole superior sex in Jerry's hapless person was too painful to witness; but though I turned my head away the sound of brisk slaps continued to reach my tingling ears. When I dared to look again, Jerry was sitting up as before; his garment, somewhat crumpled, was restored to its original position; but his pallid countenance was set hard. Knowing as I did, only too well, what a volcano of passion and shame must be seething under that impassive exterior, for the moment I felt sorry for him.

Rosa's face was still buried in her frock; it might have been shame, it might have been grief for Jerry's sufferings. But the callous Japanese never even looked her way. His heart was exceeding bitter within him. In merely following up his natural impulses he had run his head against convention, and learned how hard a thing it was; and the sunshiny world was all black to him. Even Charlotte softened somewhat at the sight of his rigid misery. "If you'll say you're sorry, Jerome," she said, "I'll say I'm sorry, too."

Jerry only dropped his shoulders against the stump and stared out in the direction of his dear native Japan, where love was no sin, and smacking had not been introduced. Why had he ever left it? He would go back tomorrow! And yet there were obstacles: another grievance. Nature, in endowing Jerry with every grace of form and feature, along with a sensitive soul, had somehow forgotten the gift of locomotion.

There was a crackling in the bushes behind me, with sharp short pants as of a small steam-engine, and Rollo, the black retriever, just released from his chain by some friendly hand, burst through the underwood seeking congenial company. I joyfully hailed him to stop being a panther, but he sped away round the pond, upset Charlotte with a boisterous caress, and seizing Jerry by the middle, disappeared with him down the drive. Charlotte, panting, raved behind the swift-footed avenger of crime; Rosa lay dishevelled, bereft of consciousness; Jerry himself spread helpless arms to heaven, and I almost thought I heard a cry for mercy, a tardy promise of amendment. But it was too late. The Black Man had got Jerry at last; and though the tear of sensibility might bedew an eye or two for his lost sake, no one who really knew him could deny the justice of his fate.

"YOUNG ADAM CUPID"

Nobody would have suspected Edward of being in love, had it not been that after breakfast, with an overacted carelessness, "Anybody who likes," he said, "can feed my rabbits," and he disappeared, with a jauntiness that deceived nobody, in the direction of the orchard. Now kingdoms might totter and reel, and convulsions play skittles with the map of Europe; but the iron unwritten law prevailed, that each boy severely fed his own rabbits. There was good ground, then, for suspicion and alarm; and while the lettuce leaves were being drawn through the wires, Harold and I conferred seriously on the situation.

It may be thought that the affair was none of our business; and indeed we cared little as individuals. We were only concerned as members of a corporation, for each of whom the mental or physical ailment of one of his fellows might have far-reaching effects. It was thought best that Harold, as least open to suspicion of motive, should be dispatched to probe and peer. His instructions were, to proceed by a report on the health of our rabbits in particular; to glide gently into a discussion concerning rabbits in general, their customs, practices, and vices; and to pass thence, by a natural transition, to the female sex, the inherent flaws in its composition, and the reasons for regarding it (speaking broadly) as dirt. He was especially to be very diplomatic, and then to return and report progress. He departed on his mission gaily; but his absence was short, and his return, discomfited and in tears, seemed to betoken some want of parts for diplomacy. He had found Edward, it appeared, pacing the orchard, with the sort of set smile that mountebanks wear in their precarious antics, fixed painfully on his face, as with pins. Harold had opened well, on the rabbit subject, but, with a fatal confusion between the abstract and the concrete, had then gone on to remark that Edward's lop-eared doe, with her long hindlegs and contemptuous twitch of the nose, always reminded him of Sabina Larkin (a nine-year-old damsel, child of a neighbouring farmer); at which point Edward, it would seem, had turned upon and savagely maltreated him, twisting his arm and punching him in the short ribs. So that Harold returned to the rabbit-hutches preceded by long-drawn wails; anon wishing, with tears and sobs, that he were a man, to kick his lovelorn brother; anon lamenting that ever he had been born.

I was not big enough to stand up to Edward personally, so I had to console the sufferer by allowing him to grease the wheels of the donkey-cart—a luscious treat that had been specially reserved for me, a week past, by the gardener's boy, for putting in a good word on his behalf with the new kitchenmaid. Harold was soon all smiles and grease; and I was not, on the whole, dissatisfied with the significant hint that had been gained as to the *fons et origo mali*.

Fortunately, means were at hand for resolving any doubts on the subject, since the morning was Sunday, and already the bells were ringing for church. Lest the connexion may not be evident at first sight, I should explain that the gloomy period of church-time, with its enforced inaction and its lack of real interest—passed, too, within sight of all that the village held of fairest—was just the one when a young man's fancies lightly turned to thoughts of love. The rest of the week afforded no leisure for such trifling; but in church—well, there was really nothing else to do! True, noughts-and-crosses might be indulged in on flyleaves of prayer-books while the Litany dragged its slow length along; but what balm or what solace could be found for the sermon? Naturally the eye, wandering here and there among the serried ranks, made bold untrammelled choice among our fair fellow-supplicants. It was in this way that, some months earlier, under the exceptional strain of the Athanasian Creed, my roving fancy had settled upon the baker's wife as a fit object for a life-long devotion. Her riper charms had conquered a heart which none of her bemuslined tittering juniors had been able to subdue; and that she was already wedded had never occurred to me as any bar to my affection. Edward's general demeanour, then, during morning service was safe to convict him; but there was also a special test for the particular case. It happened that we sat in a transept, and, the Larkins being behind us, Edward's only chance of feasting on Sabina's charms was in the all-too-fleeting interval when we swung round eastwards. I was not mistaken. During the singing of the Benedictus the impatient one made several false starts, and at last he slewed fairly round before "As it was in the beginning, is now, and ever shall be" was half finished. The evidence was conclusive: a court of law could have desired no better.

The fact being patent, the next thing was to grapple with it; and my mind was fully occupied during the sermon. There was really nothing unfair or unbrotherly in my attitude. A philosophic affection such as

mine own, which clashed with nothing, was (I held) permissible; but
the volcanic passions in which Edward indulged about once a quarter
were a serious interference with business. To make matters worse, next
week there was a circus coming to the neighbourhood, to which we
had all been strictly forbidden to go; and without Edward no visit in
contempt of law and orders could be successfully brought off. I had
sounded him as to the circus on our way to church, and he had replied
briefly that the very thought of a clown made him sick. Morbidity
could no further go. But the sermon came to an end without any line
of conduct having suggested itself; and I walked home in some depression, feeling sadly that Venus was in the ascendant and in direful opposition, while Auriga—the circus star—drooped declinant, perilously
near the horizon.

By the irony of fate, Aunt Eliza, of all people, turned out to be the
Dea ex machina. The thing fell out in this wise. It was that lady's ob-
noxious practice to issue forth, of a Sunday afternoon, on a visit of
state to such farmers and cottagers as dwelt at hand; on which occasion she was wont to hale a reluctant boy along with her, from the
mixed motives of propriety and his soul's health. Much cudgelling of
brains, I suppose, had on that particular day made me torpid and unwary. Anyhow, when a victim came to be sought for, I fell an easy
prey, while the others fled scathless and whooping. Our first visit was
to the Larkins. Here ceremonial might be viewed in its finest flower,
and we conducted ourselves like Queen Elizabeth when she trod the
measure, "high and disposedly." In the low oak-panelled parlour, cake
and currant wine were set forth, and, after courtesies and compliments
exchanged, Aunt Eliza, greatly condescending, talked the fashions with
Mrs. Larkin; while the farmer and I, perspiring with the unusual effort, exchanged remarks on the mutability of the weather and the
steady fall in the price of corn. (Who would have thought, to hear us,
that only two short days ago we had confronted each other on either
side of a hedge? I triumphant, provocative, derisive? He flushed,
wroth, cracking his whip, and volleying forth profanity? So powerful
is all-subduing ceremony!) Sabina the while, demurely seated with a
Pilgrim's Progress on her knee, and apparently absorbed in a brightly

coloured presentment of "Apollyon Straddling Right across the Way,"
eyed me at times with shy interest; but repelled all Aunt Eliza's advances with a frigid politeness for which I could not sufficiently admire her.

"It's surprising to me," I heard my aunt remark presently, "how my
eldest nephew, Edward, despises little girls. I heard him tell Charlotte
the other day that he wished he could exchange her for a pair of Japanese guinea-pigs. It made the poor child cry. Boys are so heartless!"
(I saw Sabina stiffen as she sat, and her tip-tilted nose twitched scornfully.) "Now this boy here—" (My soul descended into my very boots.
Could the woman have intercepted any of my amorous glances at the
baker's wife?) "Now this boy," my aunt went on, "is more human altogether. Only yesterday he took his sister to the baker's shop, and
spent his only penny buying her sweets. I thought it showed such a
nice disposition. I wish Edward were more like him!"

I breathed again. It was unnecessary to explain my real motives for
that visit to the baker's. Sabina's face softened, and her contemptuous
nose descended from its altitude of scorn; she gave me one shy glance
of kindness, and then concentrated her attention upon Mercy knocking
at the Wicket Gate. I felt awfully mean as regarded Edward; but
what could I do? I was in Gaza, gagged and bound; the Philistines
hemmed me in.

The same evening the storm burst, the bolt fell, and—to continue the
metaphor—the atmosphere grew serene and clear once more. The evening service was shorter than usual, the vicar, as he ascended the pulpit
steps, having dropped two pages out of his sermon-case—unperceived
by any but ourselves, either at the moment or subsequently when the
hiatus was reached; so, as we joyfully shuffled out I whispered Edward
that by racing home at top speed we should make time to assume our
bows and arrows (laid aside for the day) and play at Indians and buffaloes with Aunt Eliza's fowls—already strolling roostwards, regard-
less of their doom—before that sedately stepping lady could return.
Edward hung at the door, wavering; the suggestion had unhallowed
charms. At that moment Sabina issued primly forth, and, seeing Ed-

ward, put out her tongue at him in the most exasperating manner conceivable; then passed on her way, her shoulders rigid, her dainty head held high. A man can stand very much in the cause of love: poverty, aunts, rivals, barriers of every sort; all these only serve to fan the flame. But personal ridicule is a shaft that reaches the very vitals. Edward led the race home at a speed which one of Ballantyne's heroes might have equalled but never surpassed; and that evening the Indians dispersed Aunt Eliza's fowls over several square miles of country, so that the tale of them remaineth incomplete unto this day. Edward himself, cheering wildly, pursued the big Cochin-China cock till the bird sank gasping under the drawing-room window, whereat its mistress stood petrified; and after supper, in the shrubbery, smoked a half-consumed cigar he had picked up in the road, and declared to an awe-stricken audience his final, his immitigable resolve to go into the army.

The crisis was past, and Edward was saved! . . . And yet . . . *sunt lachrymæ rerum* . . . to me watching the cigar-stub alternately pale and glow against the dark background of laurel, a vision of a tip-tilted nose, of a small head poised scornfully, seemed to hover on the gathering gloom—seemed to grow and fade and grow again, like the grin of the Cheshire cat—pathetically, reproachfully even; and the charms of the baker's wife slipped from my memory like snow-wreaths in thaw. After all, Sabina was nowise to blame: why should the child be punished? Tomorrow I would give them the slip, and stroll round by her garden promiscuous-like, at a time when the farmer was safe in the rick-yard. If nothing came of it, there was no harm done, and if on the contrary . . . !

THE BURGLARS

It was much too fine a night to think of going to bed at once, and so, although the witching hour of nine p.m. had struck, Edward and I were still leaning out of the open window in our night-shirts, watching the play of the cedar-branch shadows on the moonlit lawn, and planning schemes of fresh devilry for the sunshiny morrow. From below, strains of the jocund piano declared that the Olympians were enjoying themselves in their listless impotent way; for the new curate had been bidden to dinner that night, and was at the moment unclerically proclaiming to all the world that he feared no foe. His discordant vociferations doubtless started a train of thought in Edward's mind, for he presently remarked, apropos of nothing whatever that had been said before, "I believe the new curate's rather gone on Aunt Maria."

I scouted the notion. "Why, she's quite old," I said. (She must have seen some five-and-twenty summers.)

"Of course she is," replied Edward scornfully. "It's not her, it's her money he's after, you bet!"

"Didn't know she had any money," I observed timidly.

"Sure to have," said my brother with confidence. "Heaps and heaps."

Silence ensued, both our minds being busy with the new situation thus presented: mine, in wonderment at this flaw that so often declared itself in enviable natures of fullest endowment—in a grown-up man and a good cricketer, for instance, even as this curate; Edward's (apparently) in the consideration of how such a state of things, supposing it existed, could be best turned to his own advantage.

"Bobby Ferris told me," began Edward in due course, "that there was a fellow spooning his sister once——"

"What's spooning?" I asked meekly.

"Oh, *I* dunno," said Edward indifferently. "It's—it's—it's just a thing they do, you know. And he used to carry notes and messages and things between 'em, and he got a shilling almost every time."

"What, from each of 'em?" I innocently inquired.

Edward looked at me with scornful pity. "Girls never have any money," he briefly explained. "But she did his exercises, and got him out of rows, and told stories for him when he needed it—and much better ones than he could have made up for himself. Girls are useful in some ways. So he was living in clover, when unfortunately they went and quarrelled about something."

"Don't see what that's got to do with it," I said.

"Nor don't I," rejoined Edward. "But anyhow the notes and things stopped, and so did the shillings. Bobby was fairly cornered, for he had bought two ferrets on tick, and promised to pay a shilling a week, thinking the shillings were going on for ever, the silly young ass. So when the week was up, and he was being dunned for the shilling, he went off to the fellow and said, 'Your broken-hearted Bella implores you to meet her at sundown. By the hollow oak as of old, be it only for a moment. Do not fail!' He got all that out of some rotten book, of course. The fellow looked puzzled and said:

" 'What hollow oak? I don't know any hollow oak.'

" 'Perhaps it was the Royal Oak?' said Bobby promptly, 'cos he saw he had made a slip, through trusting too much to the rotten book; but this didn't seem to make the fellow any happier."

"Should think not," I said; "the Royal Oak's an awful low sort of pub."

"I know," said Edward. "Well, at last the fellow said, 'I think I know what she means: the hollow tree in your father's paddock. It happens to be an elm, but she wouldn't know the difference. All right: say I'll be there.' Bobby hung about a bit, for he hadn't got his money. 'She was crying awfully,' he said. Then he got his shilling."

"And wasn't the fellow riled," I inquired, "when he got to the place and found nothing?"

"He found Bobby," said Edward indignantly. "Young Ferris was a gentleman, every inch of him. He brought the fellow another message from Bella: 'I dare not leave the house. My cruel parents immure me closely. If you only knew what I suffer. Your broken-hearted Bella.' Out of the same rotten book. This made the fellow a little suspicious, 'cos it was the old Ferrises who had been keen about the thing all through. The fellow, you see, had tin."

"But what's that got to—" I began again.

"Oh, *I* dunno," said Edward impatiently. "I'm telling you just what Bobby told me. He got suspicious, anyhow, but he couldn't exactly call Bella's brother a liar, so Bobby escaped for the time. But when he was in a hole next week, over a stiff French exercise, and tried the same sort of a game on his sister, she was too sharp for him, and he got caught out. Somehow women seem more mistrustful than men. They're so beastly suspicious by nature, you know."

"*I* know," said I. "But did the two—the fellow and the sister—make it up afterwards?"

"I don't remember about that," replied Edward indifferently; "but Bobby got packed off to school a whole year earlier than his people meant to send him. Which was just what he wanted. So you see it all came right in the end!"

I was trying to puzzle out the moral of this story—it was evidently meant to contain one somewhere—when a flood of golden lamplight mingled with the moon-rays on the lawn, and Aunt Maria and the new curate strolled out on the grass below us, and took the direction of a garden-seat which was backed by a dense laurel shrubbery reaching round in a half-circle to the house. Edward meditated moodily. "If we only knew what they were talking about," said he, "you'd soon see whether I was right or not. Look here! Let's send the kid down by the porch to reconnoitre!"

"Harold's asleep," I said; "it seems rather a shame——"

"Oh, rot!" said my brother; "he's the youngest, and he's got to do as he's told!"

So the luckless Harold was hauled out of bed and given his sailing-orders. He was naturally rather vexed at being stood up suddenly on the cold floor, and the job had no particular interest for him; but he was both staunch and well disciplined. The means of exit was simple enough. A porch of iron trellis came up to within easy reach of the window, and was habitually used by all three of us, when modestly anxious to avoid public notice. Harold climbed deftly down the porch like a white rat, and his night-gown glimmered a moment on the gravel walk ere he was lost to sight in the darkness of the shrubbery. A brief interval of silence ensued; broken suddenly by a sound of scuffle, and then a shrill long-drawn squeal, as of metallic surfaces in friction. Our scout had fallen into the hands of the enemy!

Indolence alone had made us devolve the task of investigation on our younger brother. Now that danger had declared itself, there was no hesitation. In a second we were down the side of the porch, and crawling Cherokee-wise through the laurels to the back of the garden-seat. Piteous was the sight that greeted us. Aunt Maria was on the seat, in a white evening frock, looking—for an aunt—really quite nice. On the lawn stood an incensed curate, grasping our small brother by a large ear, which—judging from the row he was making—seemed on the point of parting company with the head it completed and adorned. The gruesome noise he was emitting did not really affect us otherwise than æsthetically. To one who has tried both, the wail of genuine physical anguish is easily distinguishable from the pumped-up *ad misericordiam* blubber. Harold's could clearly be recognized as belonging to the latter class. "Now, you young ——" (whelp, *I* think it was, but Edward stoutly maintains it was devil), said the curate sternly, "tell us what you mean by it!"

"Well, leggo of my ear then," shrilled Harold, "and I'll tell you the solemn truth!"

"Very well," agreed the curate, releasing him; "now go ahead, and don't lie more than you can help."

We abode the promised disclosure without the least misgiving; but even we had hardly given Harold due credit for his fertility of resource and powers of imagination.

"I had just finished saying my prayers," began that young gentleman slowly, "when I happened to look out of the window, and on the lawn I saw a sight which froze the marrow in my veins! A burglar was approaching the house with snake-like tread! He had a scowl and a dark lantern, and he was armed to the teeth!"

We listened with interest. The style, though unlike Harold's native notes, seemed strangely familiar.

"Go on," said the curate grimly.

"Pausing in his stealthy career," continued Harold, "he gave a low whistle. Instantly the signal was responded to, and from the adjacent shadows two more figures glided forth. The miscreants were both armed to the teeth."

"Excellent," said the curate; "proceed."

"The robber chief," pursued Harold, warming to his work, "joined his nefarious comrades, and conversed with them in silent tones. His expression was truly ferocious, and I ought to have said that he was armed to the t——"

"There, never mind his teeth," interrupted the curate rudely; "there's too much jaw about you altogether. Hurry up and have done."

"I was in a frightful funk," continued the narrator, warily guarding his ear with his hand, "but just then the drawing-room window opened, and you and Aunt Maria came out—I mean emerged. The burglars vanished silently into the laurels, with horrid implications!"

The curate looked slightly puzzled. The tale was well sustained, and certainly circumstantial. After all, the boy might really have seen something. How was the poor man to know—though the chaste and lofty diction might have supplied a hint—that the whole yarn was a free adaptation from the last penny dreadful lent us by the knife-and-boot boy?

"Why did you not alarm the house?" he asked.

"'Cos I was afraid," said Harold sweetly, "that p'raps they mightn't believe me!"

"But how did you get down here, you naughty little boy?" put in Aunt Maria.

Harold was hard pressed—by his own flesh and blood, too!

At that moment Edward touched me on the shoulder and glided off through the laurels. When some ten yards away he gave a low whistle. I replied with another. The effect was magical. Aunt Maria started up with a shriek. Harold gave one startled glance around, and then fled like a hare, made straight for the back-door, burst in upon the servants at supper, and buried himself in the broad bosom of the cook, his special ally. The curate faced the laurels—hesitatingly. But Aunt Maria flung herself on him. "Oh, Mr. Hodgitts!" I heard her cry. "You are brave; for my sake do not be rash!" He was not rash. When I peeped out a second later the coast was entirely clear.

By this time there were sounds of a household timidly emerging; and Edward remarked to me that perhaps we had better be off. Retreat was an easy matter. A stunted laurel gave a leg-up on to the garden wall, which led in its turn to the roof of an outhouse, up which, at a dubious angle, we could crawl to the window of the box-room. This overland route had been revealed to us one day by the domestic cat, when hard pressed in the course of an otter-hunt, in which the cat

—somewhat unwillingly—was filling the title role; and it had proved distinctly useful on occasions like the present. We were snug in bed—minus some cuticle from knees and elbows—and Harold, sleepily chewing something sticky, had been carried up in the arms of the friendly cook, ere the clamour of the burglar-hunters had died away.

The curate's undaunted demeanour, as reported by Aunt Maria, was generally supposed to have terrified the burglars into flight, and much kudos accrued to him thereby. Some days later, however, when he had dropped in to afternoon tea, and was making a mild curatorial joke about the moral courage required for taking the last piece of bread-and-butter, I felt constrained to remark dreamily, and as it were to the universe at large, "Mr. Hodgitts! You are brave; for my sake do not be rash!"

Fortunately for me, the vicar also was a caller on that day; and it was always a comparatively easy matter to dodge my long-coated friend in the open.

A HARVESTING

The year was in its yellowing time, and the face of Nature a study in old gold. "A field *or, semé* with garbs of the same study": it may be false Heraldry—Nature's generally is—but it correctly blazons the display that Edward and I considered from the rick-yard gate. Harold was not on in this scene, being stretched upon the couch of pain: the special disorder stomachic, as usual. The evening before, Edward, in a fit of unwonted amiability, had deigned to carve me out a turnip lantern, an art-and-craft he was peculiarly deft in; and Harold, as the interior of the turnip flew out in scented fragments under the hollowing knife, had eaten largely thereof: regarding all such jetsam as his special perquisite. Now he was dreeing his weird, with such assistance as the chemist could afford. But Edward and I, knowing that this particular field was to be carried today, were revelling in the privilege of riding in the empty wagons from the rick-yard back to the sheaves, whence we returned toilfully on foot, to career it again over the billowy acres in these great galleys of a stubble sea. It was the nearest approach to sailing that we inland urchins might compass; and hence it ensued, that such stirring scenes as Sir Richard Grenville on the *Revenge,* the smoke-wreathed Battle of the Nile, and the Death of Nelson, had all been enacted in turn on these dusty quarter-decks, as they swayed and bumped afield.

Another wagon had shot its load, and was jolting out through the rick-yard gate, as we swung ourselves in, shouting, over its tail. Edward was the first up, and, as I gained my feet, he clutched me in a death-grapple. I was a privateersman, he proclaimed, and he the captain of the British frigate *Terpsichore,* of—I forget the precise number of guns. Edward always collared the best parts to himself; but I was holding my own gallantly, when I suddenly discovered that the floor we battled on was swarming with earwigs. Shrieking, I hurled free of him, and rolled over the tail-board on to the stubble. Edward executed a war-dance of triumph on the deck of the retreating galleon; but I cared little for that. I knew *he* knew that I wasn't afraid of him, but that I was—and terribly—of earwigs: "those mortal bugs o' the field." So I let him disappear, shouting lustily for all hands to repel boarders, while I strolled inland, down the village.

There was a touch of adventure in the expedition. This was not our own village, but a foreign one, distant at least a mile. One felt that sense of mingled distinction and insecurity which is familiar to the traveller: distinction, in that folk turned the head to note you curiously; insecurity, by reason of the ever-present possibility of missiles on the part of the younger inhabitants, a class eternally Conservative. Elated with isolation, I went even more nose-in-air than usual; and "even so," I mused, "might Mungo Park have threaded the trackless African forest and . . ." Here I plumped against a soft, but resisting body.

Recalled to my senses by the shock, I fell back in the attitude every boy under these circumstances instinctively adopts—both elbows well up over your ears. I found myself facing a tall elderly man, clean-shaven, clad in well-worn black—a clergyman evidently; and I noted at once a far-away look in his eyes, as if they were used to another plane of vision, and could not instantly focus things terrestrial, being suddenly recalled thereto. His figure was bent in apologetic protest. "I ask a thousand pardons, Sir," he said; "I am really so very absent-minded. I trust you will forgive me."

Now most boys would have suspected chaff under this courtly style of address. I take infinite credit to myself for recognizing at once the natural attitude of a man to whom his fellows were gentlemen all, neither Jew nor Gentile, clean nor unclean. Of course, I took the blame on myself; adding, that I was very absent-minded too. Which was indeed the case.

"I perceive," he said pleasantly, "that we have something in common. I, an old man, dream dreams; you, a young one, see visions. Your lot is the happier. And now"—his hand had been resting all this time on a wicket-gate—"you are. hot, it is easily seen—the day is advanced. Virgo is the zodiacal sign. Perhaps I may offer you some poor refreshment, if your engagements will permit?"

My only engagement that afternoon was an arithmetic lesson, and I had not intended to keep it in any case; so I passed in, while he held the gate open politely, murmuring, *"Venit Hesperus, ite capellæ:* come, little kid!" and then apologizing abjectly for a familiarity which (he said) was less his than the Roman poet's. A straight flagged walk led up to the cool-looking old house, and my host, lingering in his progress at this rose tree and that, forgot all about me at least twice, waking up and apologizing humbly after each lapse. During these intervals I put two and two together, and identified him as the rector: a bachelor, eccentric, learned exceedingly, round whom the crust of legend was already beginning to form; to myself an object of special awe, in that he was alleged to have written a real book. "Heaps o' books," Martha, my informant, said; but I knew the exact rate of discount applicable to Martha's statements.

We passed eventually through a dark hall into a room which struck me at once as the ideal I had dreamed but failed to find. None of your feminine fripperies here! None of your chair-backs and tidies! This man, it was seen, groaned under no aunts. Stout volumes in calf and vellum lined three sides; books sprawled or hunched themselves on chairs and tables; books diffused the pleasant odour of printers' ink and bindings; topping all, a faint aroma of tobacco cheered and heartened exceedingly, as under foreign skies the flap and rustle over the wayfarer's head of the Union Jack—the old flag of emancipation! And in one corner, book-piled like the rest of the furniture, stood a piano.

This I hailed with a squeal of delight. "Want to strum?" inquired my friend, as if it was the most natural wish in the world—his eyes were already straying towards another corner, where bits of writing-table peeped out from under a sort of Alpine system of book and foolscap.

"Oh, but may I?" I asked in doubt. "At home I'm not allowed to— only beastly exercises!"

"Well, you can strum here, at all events," he replied; and murmuring absently, *"Age, dic Latinum, barbite, carmen,"* he made his way, mechanically guided as it seemed, to the irresistible writing-table. In ten seconds he was out of sight and call. A great book open on his knee, another propped up in front, a score or so disposed within easy reach, he read and jotted with an absorption almost passionate. I might have been in Bœotia, for any consciousness he had of me. So with a light heart I turned to and strummed.

Those who painfully and with bleeding feet have scaled the crags of mastery over musical instruments have yet their loss in this: that the wild joy of strumming has become a vanished sense. Their happiness comes from the concord and the relative value of the notes they handle: the pure, absolute quality and nature of each note in itself are only appreciated by the strummer. For some notes have all the sea in them, and some cathedral bells; others a woodland joyance and a smell of greenery; in some fauns dance to the merry reed, and even the grave centaurs peep out from their caves. Some bring moonlight, and some the deep crimson of a rose's heart; some are blue, some red, while others will tell of an army with silken standards and march-music. And throughout all the sequence of suggestion, up above, the little white men leap and peep, and strive against the imprisoning wires; and all the big rosewood box hums as it were full of hiving bees.

Spent with the rapture, I paused a moment and caught my friend's eye over the edge of a folio. "But as for these Germans," he began abruptly, as if we had been in the middle of a discussion, "the scholar-ship is there, I grant you; but the spark, the fine perception, the happy intuition, where is it? They get it all from us!"

"They get nothing whatever from *us*," I said decidedly: the word German only suggesting Bands, to which Aunt Eliza was bitterly hostile.

"You think not?" he rejoined doubtfully, getting up and walking about the room. "Well, I applaud such fairness and temperance in so young a critic. They are qualities—in youth—as rare as they are pleas-ing. But just look at Schrumpffius, for instance—how he struggles and wrestles with a simple γάρ in this very passage here!"

I peeped fearfully through the open door, half dreading to see some sinuous and snark-like conflict in progress on the mat; but all was still. I saw no trouble at all in the passage, and I said so.

"Precisely," he cried, delighted. "To you, who possess the natural scholar's faculty in so happy a degree, there is no difficulty at all. But to this Schrumpffius—" But here, luckily for me, in came the house-keeper, a clean-looking woman of staid aspect.

"Your tea is in the garden," she said severely, as if she were correct-ing a faulty emendation. "I've put some cakes and things for the little gentleman; and you'd better drink it before it gets cold."

He waved her off and continued his stride, brandishing an aorist over my devoted head. The housekeeper waited unmoved till there fell a moment's break in his descant; and then, "You'd better drink it be-fore it gets cold," she observed again, impassively. The wretched man cast a deprecating look at me. "Perhaps a little tea would be rather nice," he observed feebly; and to my great relief he led the way into the garden. I looked about for the little gentleman, but, failing to dis-cover him, I concluded he was absent-minded too, and attacked the "cakes and things" with no misgivings.

After a most successful and most learned tea a something happened which, small as I was, never quite shook itself out of my memory. To us at parley in an arbour over the high road, there entered, slouching into view, a dingy tramp, satellited by a frowsy woman and a pariah dog; and, catching sight of us, he set up his professional whine; and I looked at my friend with the heartiest compassion, for I knew well from Martha—it was common talk—that at this time of day he was certainly and surely penniless. Morn by morn he started forth with pockets lined; and each returning evening found him with never a sou. All this he proceeded to explain at length to the tramp, courteously and even shamefacedly, as one who was in the wrong; and at last the gentleman of the road, realizing the hopelessness of his case, set to and cursed him with gusto, vocabulary, and abandonment. He reviled his eyes, his features, his limbs, his profession, his relatives and surroundings; and then slouched off, still oozing malice and filth. We watched the party to a turn in the road, where the woman, plainly weary, came to a stop. Her lord, after some conventional expletives demanded of him by his position, relieved her of her bundle, and caused her to hang on his arm with a certain rough kindness of tone, and in action even a dim approach to tenderness; and the dingy dog crept up for one lick of her hand.

"See," said my friend, bearing somewhat on my shoulder, "how this strange thing, this love of ours, lives and shines out in the unlikeliest of places! You have been in the fields in early morning? Barren acres, all! But only stoop—catch the light thwartwise—and all is a silver network of gossamer! So the fairy filaments of this strange thing underrun and link together the whole world. Yet it is not the old imperious god of the fatal bow—ἔρως ἀνίκατε μάχαν—not that—nor even the placid respectable στοργή—but something still unnamed, perhaps more mysterious, more divine! Only one must stoop to see it, old fellow, one must stoop!"

The dew was falling, the dusk closing, as I trotted briskly homewards down the road. Lonely spaces everywhere, above and around. Only Hesperus hung in the sky, solitary, pure, ineffably far-drawn and remote; yet infinitely heartening, somehow, in his valorous isolation.

SNOWBOUND

TWELFTH-NIGHT had come and gone, and life next morning seemed a trifle flat and purposeless. But yestereve, and the mummers were here! They had come striding into the old kitchen, powdering the red brick floor with snow from their barbaric bedizenments; and stamping, and crossing, and declaiming, till all was whirl and riot and shout. Harold was frankly afraid: unabashed, he buried himself in the cook's ample bosom. Edward feigned a manly superiority to illusion, and greeted these awful apparitions familiarly, as Dick and Harry and Joe. As for me, I was too big to run, too rapt to resist the magic surprise. Whence came these outlanders, breaking in on us with song and ordered masque and a terrible clashing of wooden swords? And after these, what strange visitants might we not look for any quiet night, when the chestnuts popped in the ashes, and the old ghost stories drew the awe-stricken circle close? Old Merlin, perhaps, "all furred in black sheep-skins, and a russet gown, with a bow and arrows, and bearing wild geese in his hand!" Or stately Ogier the Dane, recalled from Faëry, asking his way to the land that once had need of him! Or even, on some white night, the Snow-Queen herself, with a chime of sleigh-bells and the patter of reindeer's feet, halting of a sudden at the door flung wide, while aloft the Northern Lights went shaking attendant spears among the quiet stars!

This morning, house-bound by the relentless indefatigable snow, I was feeling the reaction. Edward, on the contrary, being violently stage-struck on this his first introduction to the real Drama, was striding up and down the floor, proclaiming, "Here be I, King Gearge the Third," in a strong Berkshire accent. Harold, accustomed, as the youngest, to lonely antics and to sports that asked no sympathy, was absorbed in "clubmen," a performance consisting in a measured progress round the room arm-in-arm with an imaginary companion of reverend years, with occasional halts at imaginary clubs, where—imaginary steps being leisurely ascended—imaginary papers were glanced at, imaginary scandal was discussed with elderly shakings of the head, and—regrettable to say—imaginary glasses were lifted lipwards. Heaven only knows how the germ of this dreary pastime first found way into his small-boyish being. It was his own invention, and he was proportionately proud of it. Meanwhile Charlotte and I, crouched in the window-seat, watched, spell-stricken, the whirl and eddy and drive of the innumerable snow-flakes, wrapping our cheery little world in an uncanny uniform, ghastly in line and hue.

Charlotte was sadly out of spirits. Having "countered" Miss Smedley at breakfast, during some argument or other, by an apt quotation from her favourite classic (*The Fairy Book*), she had been gently but firmly informed that no such things as fairies ever really existed. "Do you mean to say it's all lies?" asked Charlotte bluntly. Miss Smedley deprecated the use of any such unladylike words in any connexion at all. "These stories had their origin, my dear," she explained, "in a mistaken anthropomorphism in the interpretation of Nature. But though we are now too well informed to fall into similar errors, there are still many beautiful lessons to be learned from these myths——"

"But how can you learn anything," persisted Charlotte, "from what doesn't exist?" And she left the table defiant, howbeit depressed.

"Don't you mind *her*," I said consolingly; "how can she know anything about it? Why, she can't even throw a stone properly!"

"Edward says they're all rot, too," replied Charlotte doubtfully.

"Edward says everything's rot," I explained, "now he thinks he's going into the Army. If a thing's in a book it *must* be true, so that settles it!"

Charlotte looked almost reassured. The room was quieter now, for Edward had got the dragon down and was boring holes in him with a purring sound; Harold was ascending the steps of the Athenæum with a jaunty air—suggestive rather of the Junior Carlton. Outside, the tall elm-tops were hardly to be seen through the feathery storm. "The sky's a-falling," quoted Charlotte softly; "I must go and tell the king." The quotation suggested a fairy story, and I offered to read to her, reaching out for the book. But the Wee Folk were under a cloud; sceptical hints had embittered the chalice. So I was fain to fetch *Arthur*

—second favourite with Charlotte for his dames riding errant, and an easy first with us boys for his spear-splintering crash of tourney and hurtle against hopeless odds. Here again, however, I proved unfortunate; what ill-luck made the book open at the sorrowful history of Balin and Balan? "And he vanished anon," I read, "and so he heard an horne blow, as it had been the death of a beast. 'That blast,' said Balin, 'is blowen for me, for I am the prize, and yet I am not dead.'" Charlotte began to cry: she knew the rest too well. I shut the book in despair. Harold emerged from behind the armchair. He was sucking his thumb (a thing which members of the Reform are seldom seen to do), and he stared wide-eyed at his tear-stained sister. Edward put off his histrionics, and rushed up to her as the consoler—a new part for him.

"I know a jolly story," he began. "Aunt Eliza told it to me. It was when she was somewhere over in that beastly abroad" (he had once spent a black month of misery at Dinan) "and there was a fellow there who had got two storks. And one stork died—it was the she-stork." ("What did it die of?" put in Harold.) "And the other stork was quite sorry, and moped, and went on, and got very miserable. So they looked about and found a duck, and introduced it to the stork. The duck was a drake, but the stork didn't mind, and they loved each other and were as jolly as could be. By and by another duck came along—a real she-duck this time—and when the drake saw her he fell in love, and left the stork, and went and proposed to the duck; for she was very beautiful. But the poor stork who was left, he said nothing at all to anybody, but just pined and pined and pined away, till one morning he was found quite dead. But the ducks lived happily ever afterwards!"

This was Edward's idea of a jolly story! Down again went the corners of poor Charlotte's mouth. Really, Edward's stupid inability to see the real point in anything was *too* annoying! It was always so. Years before, it being necessary to prepare his youthful mind for a domestic event that might lead to awkward questionings at a time when there was little leisure to invent appropriate answers, it was delicately inquired of him whether he would like to have a little brother, or perhaps a little sister? He considered the matter carefully in all its bearings, and finally declared for a Newfoundland pup. Any boy more "gleg at the uptak" would have met his parents half-way, and eased their burden. As it was, the matter had to be approached all over again from a fresh standpoint. And now, while Charlotte turned away sniffingly, with a hic_up that told of an overwrought soul, Edward, unconscious (like Sir Isaac's Diamond) of the mischief he had done, wheeled round on Harold with a shout.

"I want a live dragon," he announced. "You've got to be my dragon!"

"Leave me go, will you?" squealed Harold, struggling stoutly. "I'm playin' at something else. How can I be a dragon and belong to all the clubs?"

"But wouldn't you like to be a nice scaly dragon, all green," said Edward, trying persuasion, "with a curly tail and red eyes, and breathing real smoke and fire?"

Harold wavered an instant: Pall Mall was still strong in him. The next he was grovelling on the floor. No saurian ever swung a tail so scaly and so curly as his. Clubland was a thousand years away. With horrific pants he emitted smokiest smoke and fiercest fire.

"Now I want a Princess," cried Edward, clutching Charlotte ecstatically; "and *you* can be the Doctor, and heal me from the dragon's deadly wound."

Of all professions I held the sacred art of healing in worst horror and contempt. Cataclysmal memories of purge and draught crowded thick on me, and with Charlotte—who courted no barren honours—I made a break for the door. Edward did likewise, and the hostile forces clashed together on the mat, and for a brief space things were mixed and chaotic and Arthurian. The silvery sound of the luncheon-bell restored an instant peace, even in the teeth of clenched antagonisms like ours. The Holy Grail itself, "sliding athwart a sunbeam," never so effectually stilled a riot of warring passions into sweet and quiet accord.

WHAT THEY TALKED ABOUT

EDWARD was standing ginger-beer like a gentleman, happening, as the one that had last passed under the dentist's hands, to be the capitalist of the flying hour. As in all well-regulated families, the usual tariff obtained in ours: half a crown a tooth; one shilling only if the molar were a loose one. This one, unfortunately—in spite of Edward's interested affectation of agony—had been shakiness undisguised; but the event was good enough to run to ginger-beer. As financier, however, Edward had claimed exemption from any servial duties of procurement, and had swaggered about the garden while I fetched from the village post-office, and Harold stole a tumbler from the pantry. Our preparations complete, we were sprawling on the lawn; the staidest and most self-respecting of the rabbits had been let loose to grace the feast, and was lopping demurely about the grass, selecting the juiciest plantains; while Selina, as the eldest lady present, was toying, in her affecting way, with the first full tumbler, daintily fishing for bits of broken cork.

"Hurry up, can't you?" growled our host. "What are you girls always so beastly particular for?"

"Martha says," explained Harold (thirsty too, but still just), "that if you swallow a bit of cork, it swells, and it swells, and it swells inside you, till you——"

"Oh, bosh!" said Edward, draining the glass with a fine pretence of indifference to consequences, but all the same (as I noticed) dodging the floating cork fragments with skill and judgment.

"Oh, it's all very well to say bosh," replied Harold, nettled, "but everyone knows it's true but you. Why, when Uncle Thomas was here last, and they got up a bottle of wine for him, he took just one tiny sip out of his glass, and then he said, 'Poo, my goodness, that's corked!' And he wouldn't touch it. And they had to get a fresh bottle up. The funny part was, though, I looked in his glass afterwards, when it was brought out into the passage, and there wasn't any cork in it at all! So I drank it all off, and it was very good!"

"You'd better be careful, young man!" said his elder brother, regarding him severely. "D'you remember that night when the mummers were here, and they had mulled port, and you went round and emptied all the glasses after they had gone away?"

"Ow! I did feel funny that night," chuckled Harold. "Thought the house was comin' down, it jumped about so; and Martha had to carry me up to bed, 'cos the stairs was goin' all waggity!"

We gazed searchingly at our graceless junior; but it was clear that he viewed the matter in the light of a phenomenon rather than of a delinquency.

A third bottle was by this time circling; and Selina, who had evidently waited for it to reach her, took a most unfairly long pull, and then, jumping up and shaking out her frock, announced that she was going for a walk. Then she fled like a hare; for it was the custom of our Family to meet with physical coercion any independence of action in individuals.

"She's off with those Vicarage girls again," said Edward, regarding Selina's long black legs twinkling down the path. "She goes out with them every day now; and as soon as ever they start, all their heads go together and they chatter, chatter, chatter the whole blessed time! I can't make out what they find to talk about. They never stop; it's gabble, gabble, gabble right along, like a nest of young rooks!"

"P'raps they talk about birds' eggs," I suggested sleepily (the sun was hot, the turf soft, the ginger-beer potent); "and about ships, and buffaloes, and desert islands; and why rabbits have white tails; and whether they'd sooner have a schooner or a cutter; and what they'll be when they're men—at least, I mean there's lots of things to talk about, if you *want* to talk."

"Yes; but they don't talk about those sort of things at all," persisted Edward. "How *can* they? They don't *know* anything; they can't *do* anything—except play the piano, and nobody would want to talk about *that;* and they don't care about anything—anything sensible, I mean. So what *do* they talk about?"

"I asked Martha once," put in Harold; "and she said, 'Never *you* mind; young ladies has lots of things to talk about that young gentlemen can't understand.'"

"I don't believe it," Edward growled.

"Well, that's what she *said,* anyway," rejoined Harold indifferently. The subject did not seem to him of first-class importance, and it was hindering the circulation of the ginger-beer.

We heard the click of the front-gate. Through a gap in the hedge we could see the party setting off down the road. Selina was in the middle; a Vicarage girl had her by either arm; their heads were together, as Edward had described; and the clack of their tongues came down the breeze like the busy pipe of starlings on a bright March morning.

"What *do* they talk about, Charlotte?" I inquired, wishing to pacify Edward. "You go out with them sometimes."

"I don't know," said poor Charlotte dolefully. "They make me walk behind, 'cos they say I'm too little, and mustn't hear. And I *do* want to so," she added.

"When any lady comes to see Aunt Eliza," said Harold, "they both talk at once all the time. And yet each of 'em seems to hear what the other one's saying. I can't make out how they do it. Grown-up people are so clever!"

"The curate's the funniest man," I remarked. "He's always saying things that have no sense in them at all, and then laughing at them as if they were jokes. Yesterday, when they asked him if he'd have some more tea, he said, 'Once more unto the breach, dear friends, once more,' and then sniggered all over. I didn't see anything funny in that. And then somebody asked him about his buttonhole, and he said, ''Tis but a little faded flower,' and exploded again. I thought it very stupid."

"Oh, *him,*" said Edward contemptuously; "he can't help it, you know; it's a sort of way he's got. But it's these girls I can't make out. If they've anything really sensible to talk about, how is it nobody knows what it is? And if they haven't—and we know they *can't* have, naturally—why don't they shut up their jaw? This old rabbit

here—*he* doesn't want to talk. He's got something better to do." And
Edward aimed a ginger-beer cork at the unruffled beast, who never
budged.

"Oh, but rabbits *do* talk," interposed Harold. "I've watched them
often in their hutch. They put their heads together and their noses go
up and down, just like Selina's and the Vicarage girls'. Only of course
I can't hear what they're saying."

"Well, if they do," said Edward unwillingly, "I'll bet they don't
talk such rot as those girls do!" Which was ungenerous, as well as
unfair; for it had not yet transpired—nor has it to this day—*what*
Selina and her friends talked about.

THE ARGONAUTS

The advent of strangers, of whatever sort, into our circle had always
been a matter of grave dubiety and suspicion. Indeed, it was generally
a signal for retreat into caves and fastnesses of the earth, into un-
threaded copses or remote outlying cow-sheds, whence we were only
to be extricated by wily nursemaids, rendered familiar by experience
with our secret runs and refuges. It was not surprising, therefore, that
the heroes of classic legend, when first we made their acquaintance,
failed to win our entire sympathy at once. "Confidence," says somebody, "is a plant of slow growth"; and these stately dark-haired demi-
gods, with names hard to master and strange accoutrements, had to
win a citadel already strongly garrisoned with a more familiar soldiery.
Their chill foreign goddesses had no such direct appeal for us as the
mocking malicious fairies and witches of the North. We missed the
pleasant alliance of the animal—the fox who spread the bushiest of
tails to convey us to the enchanted castle, the frog in the well, the
raven who croaked advice from the tree; and—to Harold especially—
it seemed entirely wrong that the hero should ever be other than the
youngest brother of three. This belief, indeed, in the special fortune
that ever awaited the youngest brother, as such—the "Borough-

English" of Faëry—had been of baleful effect on Harold, producing a certain self-conceit and perkiness that called for physical correction. But even in our admonishment we were on his side; and as we distrustfully eyed these new arrivals, old Saturn himself seemed something of a *parvenu*.

Even strangers, however, if they be good fellows at heart, may develop into sworn comrades; and these gay swordsmen, after all, were of the right stuff. Perseus, with his cap of darkness and his wonderful sandals, was not long in winging his way to our hearts. Apollo knocked at Admetus's gate in something of the right fairy fashion. Psyche brought with her an orthodox palace of magic, as well as helpful birds and friendly ants. Ulysses, with his captivating shifts and strategies, broke down the final barrier, and henceforth the band was adopted and admitted into our freemasonry.

I had been engaged in chasing Farmer Larkin's calves—his special pride—round the field, just to show the man we hadn't forgotten him, and was returning through the kitchen-garden with a conscience at peace with all men, when I happened upon Edward, grubbing for worms in the dung-heap. Edward put his worms into his hat, and we strolled along together, discussing high matters of state. As we reached the tool-shed, strange noises arrested our steps; looking in, we perceived Harold, alone, rapt, absorbed, immersed in the special game of the moment. He was squatting in an old pig-trough that had been brought in to be tinkered; and as he rhapsodized, anon he waved a shovel over his head, anon dug it into the ground with the action of those who would urge Canadian canoes. Edward strode in upon him.

"What rot are you playing at now?" he demanded sternly.

Harold flushed up, but stuck to his pig-trough like a man. "I'm Jason," he replied defiantly; "and this is the Argo. The other fellows are here too, only you can't see them; and we're just going through the Hellespont, so don't you come bothering." And once more he plied the wine-dark sea.

Edward kicked the pig-trough contemptuously. "Pretty sort of Argo you've got!" said he.

Harold began to get annoyed. "I can't help it," he retorted. "It's the best sort of Argo I can manage, and it's all right if you only pretend enough. But *you* never could pretend one bit."

Edward reflected. "Look here," he said presently. "Why shouldn't we get hold of Farmer Larkin's boat, and go right away up the river in a real Argo, and look for Medea, and the Golden Fleece, and everything? And I'll tell you what, I don't mind your being Jason, as you thought of it first."

Harold tumbled out of the trough in the excess of his emotion. "But we aren't allowed to go on the water by ourselves," he cried.

"No," said Edward, with fine scorn, "we aren't allowed; and Jason wasn't allowed either, I dare say. But he *went!*"

Harold's protest had been merely conventional: he only wanted to be convinced by sound argument. The next question was, How about the girls? Selina was distinctly handy in a boat; the difficulty about her was, that if she disapproved of the expedition—and, morally considered, it was not exactly a Pilgrim's Progress—she might go and tell, she having just reached that disagreeable age when one begins to develop a conscience. Charlotte, for her part, had a habit of daydreams, and was as likely as not to fall overboard in one of her rapt musings. To be sure, she would dissolve in tears when she found herself left out; but even that was better than a watery tomb. In fine, the public voice—and rightly, perhaps—was against the admission of the skirted animal: despite the precedent of Atalanta, who was one of the original crew.

"And now," said Edward, "who's to ask Farmer Larkin? *I* can't; last time I saw him he said when he caught me again he'd smack my head. *You'll* have to."

I hesitated, for good reasons. "You know those precious calves of his?" I began.

Edward understood at once. "All right," he said; "then we won't ask him at all. It doesn't much matter. He'd only be annoyed, and that would be a pity. Now let's set off."

We made our way down to the stream, and captured the farmer's boat without let or hindrance, the enemy being engaged in the hayfields. This "river," so called, could never be discovered by us in any atlas; indeed our Argo could hardly turn in it without risk of ship-wreck. But to us 'twas Orinoco, and the cities of the world dotted its shores. We put the Argo's head upstream, since that led away from the Larkin province; Harold was faithfully permitted to be Jason, and we shared the rest of the heroes among us. Then, quitting Thessaly, we threaded the Hellespont with shouts, breathlessly dodged the Clashing Rocks, and coasted under the lee of the Siren-haunted isles. Lemnos was fringed with meadow-sweet, dog-roses dotted the Mysian shore, and the cheery call of the haymaking folk sounded along the coast of Thrace.

After some hour or two's seafaring, the prow of the Argo embedded itself in the mud of a landing-place, plashy with the tread of cows and giving on to a lane that led towards the smoke of human habitations. Edward jumped ashore, alert for exploration, and strode off without waiting to see if we followed; but 'I lingered behind, having caught sight of a moss-grown water-gate hard by, leading into a garden that, from the brooding quiet lapping it round, appeared to portend magical possibilities.

Indeed the very air within seemed stiller, as we circumspectly passed through the gate; and Harold hung back shamefaced, as if we were crossing the threshold of some private chamber, and ghosts of old days were hustling past us. Flowers there were, everywhere; but they drooped and sprawled in an overgrowth hinting at indifference; the scent of heliotrope possessed the place as if actually hung in solid festoons from tall untrimmed hedge to hedge. No basket-chairs, shawls, or novels dotted the lawn with colour; and on the garden-front of the house behind, the blinds were mostly drawn. A grey old sun-dial dominated the central sward, and we moved towards it in-stinctively, as the most human thing in sight. An antick motto ran round it, and with eyes and fingers we struggled at the decipher-ment.

TIME: TRYETH: TROTHE, spelt out Harold at last. "I wonder what that means?"

I could not enlighten him, nor meet his further questions as to the inner mechanism of the thing, and where you wound it up. I had seen these instruments before, of course; but had never fully understood their manner of working.

We were still puzzling our heads over the contrivance, when I became aware that Medea herself was moving down the path from the house. Dark-haired, supple, of a figure lightly poised and swayed, but pale and listless—I knew her at once, and, having come out to find her, naturally felt no surprise at all. But Harold, who was trying to climb on to the top of the sun-dial, having a cat-like fondness for the summit of things, started and fell prone, barking his chin and filling the pleasance with lamentation.

Medea skimmed the ground swallow-like, and in a moment was on her knees comforting him, wiping the dirt out of his chin with her own dainty handkerchief, and vocal with soft murmur of consolation.

"You needn't take on so about him," I observed politely. "He'll cry for just one minute, and then he'll be all right."

My estimate was justified. At the end of his regulation time Harold stopped crying suddenly, like a clock that had struck its hour; and with a serene and cheerful countenance wriggled out of Medea's embrace, and ran for a stone to throw at an intrusive blackbird.

"Oh, you boys!" cried Medea, throwing wide her arms with abandonment. "Where have you dropped from? How dirty you are! I've been shut up here for a thousand years, and all that time I've never seen anyone under a hundred and fifty! Let's play at something, at once!"

"Rounders is a good game," I suggested. "Girls can play at rounders. And we could serve up to the sun-dial here. But you want a bat and a ball, and some more people."

She struck her hands together tragically. "I haven't a bat," she cried, "or a ball, or more people, or anything sensible whatever. Never mind; let's play at hide-and-seek in the kitchen-garden. And we'll race there, up to that walnut tree; I haven't run for a century!"

She was so easy a victor, nevertheless, that I began to doubt, as I panted behind whether she had not exaggerated her age by a year or two. She flung herself into hide-and-seek with all the gusto and abandonment of the true artist; and as she flitted away and reappeared, flushed and laughing divinely, the pale witch-maiden seemed to fall away from her, and she moved rather as that other girl I had read about, snatched from fields of daffodil to reign in shadow below, yet permitted now and again to revisit earth and light and the frank, caressing air.

Tired at last, we strolled back to the old sun-dial, and Harold, who never relinquished a problem unsolved, began afresh, rubbing his finger along the faint incisions. *"Time tryeth trothe.* Please, I want to know what that means?"

Medea's face dropped low over the sun-dial, till it was almost hidden in her fingers. "That's what I'm here for," she said presently in quite a changed, low voice. "They shut me up here—they think I'll forget— but I never will—never, never! And he, too—but I don't know—it is so long—I don't know!"

Her face was quite hidden now. There was silence again in the old garden. I felt clumsily helpless and awkward. Beyond a vague idea of kicking Harold, nothing remedial seemed to suggest itself.

None of us had noticed the approach of another she-creature—one of the angular and rigid class—how different from our dear comrade! The years Medea had claimed might well have belonged to her; she wore mittens, too—a trick I detested in woman. "Lucy!" she said sharply, in a tone with *aunt* writ large over it; and Medea started up guiltily.

"You've been crying," said the newcomer, grimly regarding her through spectacles. "And, pray, who are these exceedingly dirty little boys?"

"Friends of mine, Aunt," said Medea promptly, with forced cheerfulness. "I—I've known them a long time. I asked them to come."

The aunt sniffed suspiciously. "You must come indoors, dear," she said, "and lie down. The sun will give you a headache. And you little boys had better run away home to your tea. Remember, you should not come to pay visits without your nursemaid."

Harold had been tugging nervously at my jacket for some time, and I only waited till Medea turned and kissed a white hand to us as she was led away. Then I ran. We gained the boat in safety; and "What an old dragon!" said Harold.

"Wasn't she a beast!" I replied. "Fancy the sun giving anyone a headache! But Medea was a real brick. Couldn't we carry her off?"

"We could if Edward was here," said Harold confidently.

The question was, What had become of that defaulting hero? We were not left long in doubt. First, there came down the lane the shrill and wrathful clamour of a female tongue; then Edward, running his best; and then an excited woman hard on his heel. Edward tumbled into the bottom of the boat, gasping, "Shove her off!" And shove her off we did, mightily, while the dame abused us from the bank in the self-same accents in which Alfred hurled defiance at the marauding Dane.

"That was just like a bit out of *Westward Ho!*" I remarked approvingly, as we sculled down the stream. "But what had you been doing to her?"

"Hadn't been doing anything," panted Edward, still breathless. "I went up into the village and explored, and it was a very nice one, and the people were very polite. And there was a blacksmith's forge there, and they were shoeing horses, and hoofs fizzled and smoked, and smelt so jolly! I stayed there quite a long time. Then I got thirsty, so I asked that old woman for some water, and while she was getting it her cat came out of the cottage, and looked at me in a nasty sort of way, and said something I didn't like. So I went up to it just to—to teach it manners, and somehow or other, next minute it was up an apple tree, spitting, and I was running down the lane with that old thing after me."

Edward was so full of his personal injuries that there was no interesting him in Medea at all. Moreover, the evening was closing in, and it was evident that this cutting-out expedition must be kept for another day. As we neared home, it gradually occurred to us that perhaps the greatest danger was yet to come; for the farmer must have missed his boat ere now, and would probably be lying in wait for us near the landing-place. There was no other spot admitting of debarcation on the home side; if we got out on the other and made for the bridge, we

should certainly be seen and cut off. Then it was that I blessed my
stars that our elder brother was with us that day. He might be little
good at pretending, but in grappling with the stern facts of life he had
no equal. Enjoining silence, he waited till we were but a little way
from the fated landing-place, and then brought us in to the opposite
bank. We scrambled out noiselessly and—the gathering darkness
favouring us—crouched behind a willow, while Edward pushed off
the empty boat with his foot. The old Argo, borne down by the gentle
current, slid and grazed along the rushy bank; and when she came opposite the suspected ambush, a stream of imprecation told us that our
precaution had not been wasted. We wondered, as we listened, where
Farmer Larkin, who was bucolically bred and reared, had acquired
such range and wealth of vocabulary. Fully realizing at last that his
boat was derelict, abandoned, at the mercy of wind and wave—as well
as out of his reach—he strode away to the bridge, about a quarter of
a mile further down; and as soon as we heard his boots clumping on
the planks we nipped out, recovered the craft, pulled across, and made
the faithful vessel fast to her proper moorings. Edward was anxious
to wait and exchange courtesies and compliments with the disappointed farmer, when he should confront us on the opposite bank;
but wiser counsels prevailed. It was possible that the piracy was not
yet laid at our particular door: Ulysses, I reminded him, had reason to
regret a similar act of bravado, and—were he here—would certainly
advise a timely retreat. Edward held but a low opinion of me as a
counsellor; but he had a very solid respect for Ulysses.

THE ROMAN ROAD

ALL the roads of our neighbourhood were cheerful and friendly,
having each of them pleasant qualities of their own; but this one
seemed different from the others in its masterful suggestion of a serious
purpose, speeding you along with a strange uplifting of the heart. The
others tempted chiefly with their treasures of hedge and ditch; the
rapt surprise of the first lords-and-ladies, the rustle of a field-mouse,

the splash of a frog; while cool noses of brother-beasts were pushed at you through gate or gap. A loiterer you had need to be, did you choose one of them; so many were the tiny hands thrust out to detain you, from this side and that. But this one was of a sterner sort, and even in its shedding off of bank and hedgerow as it marched straight and full for the open downs, it seemed to declare its contempt for adventitious trappings to catch the shallow-pated. When the sense of injustice or disappointment was heavy on me, and things were very black within, as on this particular day, the road of character was my choice for that solitary ramble when I turned my back for an afternoon on a world that had unaccountably declared itself against me.

"The Knights' Road" we children had named it, from a sort of feeling that, if from any quarter at all, it would be down this track we might some day see Lancelot and his peers come pacing on their great war-horses; supposing that any of the stout band still survived, in nooks and unexplored places. Grown-up people sometimes spoke of it as the "Pilgrims' Way"; but I didn't know much about pilgrims —except Walter in the Hörselberg story. Him I sometimes saw breaking with haggard eyes out of yonder copse, and calling to the pilgrims as they hurried along on their desperate march to the Holy City, where peace and pardon were awaiting them. "All roads lead to Rome," I had once heard somebody say; and I had taken the remark very seriously, of course, and puzzled over it many days. There must have been some mistake, I concluded at last; but of one road at least I intuitively felt it to be true. And my belief was clinched by something that fell from Miss Smedley during a history lesson, about a strange road that ran right down the middle of England till it reached the coast, and then began again in France, just opposite, and so on undeviating, through city and vineyard, right from the misty Highlands to the Eternal City. Uncorroborated, any statement of Miss Smedley's usually fell on incredulous ears; but here, with the road itself in evidence, she seemed, once in a way, to have strayed into truth.

Rome! It was fascinating to think that it lay at the other end of this white ribbon that rolled itself off from my feet over the distant downs.

I was not quite so uninstructed as to imagine I could reach it that afternoon; but some day, I thought, if things went on being as unpleasant as they were now—some day, when Aunt Eliza had gone on a visit—some day, we would see.

I tried to imagine what it would be like when I got there. The Coliseum I knew, of course, from a woodcut in the history-book; so to begin with I plumped that down in the middle. The rest had to be patched up from the little grey market-town where twice a year we went to have our hair cut; hence, in the result, Vespasian's amphitheatre was approached by muddy little streets, wherein the Red Lion and the Blue Boar, with Somebody's Entire along their front, and "Commercial Room" on their windows; the doctor's house, of substantial red brick; and the façade of the New Wesleyan chapel, which we thought very fine, were the chief architectural ornaments; while the Roman populace pottered about in smocks and corduroys, twisting the tails of Roman calves and inviting each other to beer in musical Wessex. From Rome I drifted on to other cities, faintly heard of— Damascus, Brighton (Aunt Eliza's ideal), Athens, and Glasgow, whose glories the gardener sang; but there was a certain sameness in my conception of all of them: that Wesleyan chapel would keep cropping up everywhere. It was easier to go a-building among those dream-cities where no limitations were imposed, and one was sole architect, with a free hand. Down a delectable street of cloud-built palaces I was mentally pacing, when I happened upon the Artist.

He was seated at work by the roadside, at a point whence the cool large spaces of the downs, juniper-studded, swept grandly westwards. His attributes proclaimed him of the artist tribe; besides, he wore knickerbockers like myself, a garb confined, I was aware, to boys and artists. I knew I was not to bother him with questions, nor look over his shoulder and breathe in his ear—they didn't like it, this *genus irritabile*. But there was nothing about staring in my code of instructions, the point having somehow been overlooked; so, squatting down on the grass, I devoted myself to the passionate absorbing of every detail. At the end of five minutes there was not a button on him that I could not have passed an examination in; and the wearer himself of that homespun suit was probably less familiar with its pattern and texture than I was. Once he looked up, nodded, half held out his tobacco pouch, mechanically as it were, then, returning it to his pocket, resumed his work, and I my mental photography.

After another five minutes or so had passed, he remarked, without looking my way, "Fine afternoon we're having; going far today?"

"No, I'm not going any farther than this," I replied; "I *was* thinking of going on to Rome, but I've put it off."

"Pleasant place, Rome," he murmured; "you'll like it." It was some minutes later that he added, "But I wouldn't go just now, if I were you: too jolly hot."

"*You* haven't been to Rome, have you?" I inquired.

"Rather," he replied briefly. "I live there."

This was too much, and my jaw dropped as I struggled to grasp the fact that I was sitting there talking to a fellow who lived in Rome. Speech was out of the question; besides, I had other things to do. Ten solid minutes had I already spent in an examination of him as a mere stranger and artist; and now the whole thing had to be done over again, from the changed point of view. So I began afresh, at the crown of his soft hat, and worked down to the solid British shoes, this time investing everything with the new Roman halo; and at last I managed to get out, "But you don't really live there, do you?" never doubting the fact, but wanting to hear it repeated.

"Well," he said, good-naturedly overlooking the slight rudeness of my query, "I live there as much as I live anywhere. About half the year sometimes. I've got a sort of a shanty there. You must come and see it some day."

"But do you live anywhere else as well?" I went on, feeling the forbidden tide of questions surging up within me.

"Oh, yes, all over the place," was his vague reply. "And I've got a diggings somewhere off Piccadilly."

"Where's that?" I inquired.

"Where's what?" said he. "Oh, Piccadilly! It's in London."

"Have you a large garden?" I asked. "And how many pigs have you got?"

"I've got no garden at all," he replied sadly, "and they don't allow me to keep pigs, though I'd like to, awfully. It's very hard."

"But what do you do all day, then," I cried, "and where do you go and play, without any garden, or pigs, or things?"

"When I want to play," he said gravely, "I have to go and play in the street; but it's poor fun, I grant you. There's a goat, though, not far off and sometimes I talk to him when I'm feeling lonely; but he's very proud."

"Goats *are* proud," I admitted. "There's one lives near here, and if you say anything to him at all, he hits you in the wind with his head. You know what it feels like when a fellow hits you in the wind?"

"I do, well," he replied, in a tone of proper melancholy, and painted on.

"And have you been to any other places," I began again presently, "besides Rome and Piccy-what's-his-name?"

"Heaps," he said. "I'm a sort of Ulysses—seen men and cities, you know. In fact, about the only place I never got to was the Fortunate Island."

I began to like this man. He answered your questions briefly and to the point, and never tried to be funny. I felt I could be confidential with him.

"Wouldn't you like," I inquired, "to find a city without any people in it at all?"

He looked puzzled. "I'm afraid I don't quite understand," said he.

"I mean," I went on eagerly, "a city where you walk in at the gates, and the shops are all full of beautiful things, and the houses furnished as grand as can be, and there isn't anybody there whatever! And you go into the shops, and take anything you want—chocolates and magic-lanterns and injirubber balls—and there's nothing to pay; and you choose your own house and live there and do just as you like, and never go to bed unless you want to!"

The artist laid down his brush. "That *would* be a nice city," he said. "Better than Rome. You can't do that sort of thing in Rome—or Piccadilly either. But I fear it's one of the places I've never been to."

"And you'd ask your friends," I went on, warming to my subject;

"only those you really like, of course; and they'd each have a house to themselves—there'd be lots of houses—and there wouldn't be any relations at all, unless they promised they'd be pleasant; and if they weren't, they'd have to go."

"So you wouldn't have any relations?" said the artist. "Well, perhaps you're right. We have tastes in common, I see."

"I'd have Harold," I said reflectively, "and Charlotte. They'd like it awfully. The others are getting too old. Oh, and Martha—I'd have Martha to cook and wash up and do things. You'd like Martha. She's ever so much nicer than Aunt Eliza. She's my idea of a real lady."

"Then I'm sure I should like her," he replied heartily, "and when I come to—what do you call this city of yours? Nephelo—something, did you say?"

"I—I don't know," I replied timidly. "I'm afraid it hasn't got a name —yet."

The artist gazed out over the downs. " 'The poet says, dear city of Cecrops,' " he said softly to himself, " 'and wilt not thou say, dear city of Zeus?' That's from Marcus Aurelius," he went on, turning again to his work. "You don't know him, I suppose; you will some day."

"Who's he?" I inquired.

"Oh, just another fellow who lived in Rome," he replied, dabbing away.

"Oh, dear!" I cried disconsolately. "What a lot of people seem to live at Rome, and I've never even been there! But I think I'd like *my* city best."

"And so would I," he replied with unction. "But Marcus Aurelius wouldn't, you know."

"Then we won't invite him," I said; "will we?"

"*I* won't if you won't," said he. And that point being settled, we were silent for a while.

"Do you know," he said presently, "I've met one or two fellows from time to time, who have been to a city like yours—perhaps it was the same one. They won't talk much about it—only broken hints, now and then; but they've been there, sure enough. They don't seem to care about anything in particular—and everything's the same to them, rough or smooth; and sooner or later they slip off and disappear; and you never see them again. Gone back, I suppose."

"Of course," said I. "Don't see what they ever came away for; *I* wouldn't. To be told you've broken things when you haven't, and stopped having tea with the servants in the kitchen, and not allowed to have a dog to sleep with you. But *I've* known people, too, who've gone there."

The artist stared, but without incivility.

"Well, there's Lancelot," I went on. "The book says he died, but it never seemed to read right, somehow. He just went away, like Arthur. And Crusoe, when he got tired of wearing clothes and being respectable. And all the nice men in the stories who don't marry the Princess, 'cos only one man ever gets married in a book, you know. They'll be there!"

"And the men who never come off," he said, "who try like the rest, but get knocked out, or somehow miss—or break down or get bowled over in the mêlée—and get no Princess, nor even a second-class kingdom—some of them'll be there, I hope?"

"Yes, if you like," I replied, not quite understanding him; "if they're friends of yours, we'll ask 'em, of course."

"What a time we shall have!" said the artist reflectively. "And how shocked old Marcus Aurelius will be!"

The shadows had lengthened uncannily, a tide of golden haze was flooding the grey-green surface of the downs, and the artist began to put his traps together, preparatory to a move. I felt very low: we would have to part, it seemed, just as we were getting on so well together. Then he stood up, and he was very straight and tall, and the sunset was in his hair and beard as he stood there, high over me. He took my hand like an equal. "I've enjoyed our conversation very much," he said. "That was an interesting subject you started, and we haven't half exhausted it. We shall meet again, I hope?"

"Of course we shall," I replied, surprised that there should be any doubt about it.

"In Rome perhaps?" said he.

"Yes, in Rome," I answered; "or Piccy-the-other-place, or somewhere."

"Or else," said he, "in that other city—when we've found the way there. And I'll look out for you, and you'll sing out as soon as you see me. And we'll go down the street arm-in-arm, and into all the shops, and then I'll choose my house, and you'll choose your house, and we'll live there like princes and good fellows."

"Oh, but you'll stay in my house, won't you?" I cried. "I wouldn't ask everybody; but I'll ask *you*."

He affected to consider a moment; then, "Right!" he said; "I believe you mean it, and I *will* come and stay with you. I won't go to anybody else, if they ask me ever so much. And I'll stay quite a long time, too, and I won't be any trouble."

Upon this compact we parted, and I went down-heartedly from the man who understood me, back to the house where I never could do anything right. How was it that everything seemed natural and sensible to him, which these uncles, vicars, and other grown-up men took for the merest tomfoolery? Well, he would explain this, and many another thing, when we met again. The Knights' Road! How it always brought consolation! Was he possibly one of those vanished knights I had been looking for so long? Perhaps he would be in armour next time—why not? He would look well in armour, I thought. And I would take care to get there first, and see the sunlight flash and play on his helmet and shield, as he rode up the High Street of the Golden City.

Meantime, there only remained the finding it. An easy matter.

THE SECRET DRAWER

It must surely have served as a boudoir for the ladies of old time, this little used, rarely entered chamber where the neglected old bureau stood. There was something very feminine in the faint hues of its faded brocades, in the rose and blue of such bits of china as yet remained, and in the delicate old-world fragrance of pot-pourri from the great bowl, —blue and white, with funny holes in its cover—that stood on the bureau's flat top. Modern aunts disdained this out-of-the-way, back-water, upstairs room, preferring to do their accounts and grapple with their correspondence in some central position more in the whirl of things, whence one eye could be kept on the carriage-drive, while the other was alert for malingering servants and marauding children. Those aunts of a former generation—I sometimes felt—would have suited our habits better. But even by us children, to whom few places were private or reserved, the room was visited but rarely. To be sure, there was nothing particular in it that we coveted or required. Only a few spindle-legged, gilt-backed chairs; an old harp on which, so that legend ran, Aunt Eliza herself used once to play, in years remote, unchronicled; a corner cupboard with a few pieces of china; and the old bureau. But one other thing the room possessed, peculiar to itself: a certain sense of privacy—a power of making the intruder feel that he *was* intruding—perhaps even a faculty of hinting that someone might have been sitting on those chairs, writing at the bureau, or fingering the china, just a second before one entered. No such violent word as "haunted" could possibly apply to this pleasant old-fashioned chamber, which indeed we all rather liked; but there was no doubt it was reserved and stand-offish, keeping itself to itself.

Uncle Thomas was the first to draw my attention to the possibilities of the old bureau. He was pottering about the house one afternoon, having ordered me to keep at his heels for company—he was a man who hated to be left one minute alone—when his eye fell on it. "H'm! Sheraton!" he remarked. (He had a smattering of most things, this uncle, especially the vocabularies.) Then he let down the flap, and examined the empty pigeon-holes and dusty panelling. "Fine bit of inlay," he went on; "good work, all of it. I know the sort. There's a secret drawer in there somewhere." Then as I breathlessly drew near, he suddenly exclaimed, "By Jove, I do want to smoke!" And, wheeling round, he abruptly fled for the garden, leaving me with the cup dashed from my lips. What a strange thing, I mused, was this smoking, that takes a man suddenly, be he in the court, the camp, or the grove, grips him like an afreet, and whirls him off to do its imperious behests! Would it be even so with myself, I wondered, in those unknown grown-up years to come?

But I had no time to waste in vain speculations. My whole being was

still vibrating to those magic syllables "secret drawer"; and that particular chord had been touched that never fails to thrill responsive to
such words as *cave, trap-door, sliding-panel, bullion, ingots,* or *Spanish
dollars.* For, besides its own special bliss, who ever heard of a secret
drawer with nothing in it? And, oh, I did want money so badly! I
mentally ran over the list of demands which were pressing me the
most imperiously.

First, there was the pipe I wanted to give George Jannaway. George,
who was Martha's young man, was a shepherd, and a great ally of
mine; and the last fair he was at, when he bought his sweetheart fairings, as a right-minded shepherd should, he had purchased a lovely
snake expressly for me; one of the wooden sort, with joints, waggling
deliciously in the hand; with yellow spots on a green ground, sticky
and strong-smelling, as a fresh-painted snake ought to be; and with a
red-flannel tongue pasted cunningly into its jaws. I loved it much, and
took it to bed with me every night, till what time its spinal cord was
loosed and it fell apart, and went the way of all mortal joys. I thought
it very nice of George to think of me at the fair, and that's why I
wanted to give him a pipe. When the young year was chill and lamb-
ing-time was on, George inhabited a little wooden house on wheels,
far out on the wintry downs, and saw no faces but such as were sheep-
ish and woolly and mute; and when he and Martha were married, she
was going to carry his dinner out to him every day, two miles; and
after it, perhaps he would smoke my pipe. It seemed an idyllic sort of
existence, for both the parties concerned; but a pipe of quality, a pipe
fitted to be part of a life such as this, could not be procured (so Martha
informed me) for a smaller sum than eighteenpence. And meantime—!

Then there was the fourpence I owed Edward; not that he was bothering me for it, but I knew he was in need of it himself, to pay back
Selina, who wanted it to make up a sum of two shillings, to buy Harold
an ironclad for his approaching birthday—H.M.S. *Majestic,* now lying
uselessly careened in the toyshop window, just when her country had
such sore need of her.

And then there was that boy in the village who had caught a young
squirrel, and I had never yet possessed one, and he wanted a shilling

for it, but I knew that for ninepence in cash—but what was the good of these sorry threadbare reflections? I had wants enough to exhaust any possible find of bullion, even if it amounted to half a sovereign. My only hope now lay in the magic drawer, and here I was, standing and letting the precious minutes slip by! Whether "findings" of this sort could, morally speaking, be considered "keepings," was a point that did not occur to me.

The room was very still as I approached the bureau; possessed, it seemed to be, by a sort of hush of expectation. The faint odour of orris-root that floated forth as I let down the flap seemed to identify itself with the yellows and browns of the old wood, till hue and scent were of one quality and interchangeable. Even so, ere this, the pot-pourri had mixed itself with the tints of the old brocade, and brocade and pot-pourri had long been one. With expectant fingers I explored the empty pigeon-holes and sounded the depths of the softly sliding drawers. No books that I knew of gave any general recipe for a quest like this; but the glory, should I succeed unaided, would be all the greater.

To him who is destined to arrive, the fates never fail to afford, on the way, their small encouragements. In less than two minutes, I had come across a rusty button-hook. This was truly magnificent. In the nursery there existed, indeed, a general button-hook, common to either sex; but none of us possessed a private and special button-hook, to lend or to refuse as suited the high humour of the moment. I pocketed the treasure carefully, and proceeded. At the back of another drawer, three old foreign stamps told me I was surely on the highroad to fortune.

Following on these bracing incentives, came a dull blank period of unrewarding search. In vain I removed all the drawers and felt over every inch of the smooth surfaces, from front to back. Never a knob, spring, or projection met the thrilling fingertips; unyielding the old bureau stood, stoutly guarding its secret, if secret it really had. I began to grow weary and disheartened. This was not the first time that Uncle Thomas had proved shallow, uninformed, a guide into blind alleys where the echoes mocked you. Was it any good persisting longer? Was anything any good whatever? In my mind I began to review past disappointments, and life seemed one long record of failure and of non-arrival. Disillusioned and depressed, I left my work and went to the window. The light was ebbing from the room, and seemed outside to be collecting itself on the horizon for its concentrated effort of sunset. Far down the garden, Uncle Thomas was holding Edward in the air reversed, and smacking him. Edward, gurgling hysterically, was striking blind fists in the direction where he judged his stomach should rightly be; the contents of his pockets—a motley show—were strewing the lawn. Somehow, though I had been put through a similar performance myself an hour or two ago, it all seemed very far away and cut off from me.

Westwards the clouds were massing themselves in a low, violent bank; below them, to north and south, as far round as eye could reach, a narrow streak of gold ran out and stretched away, straight along the horizon. Somewhere very far off, a horn was blowing, clear and thin; it sounded like the golden streak grown audible, while the gold seemed the visible sound. It pricked my ebbing courage, this blended strain of music and colour. I turned for a last effort; and Fortune thereupon, as if half ashamed of the unworthy game she had been playing with me, relented, opening her clenched fist. Hardly had I put my hand once more to the obdurate wood, when with a sort of small sigh, almost a sob—as it were—of relief, the secret drawer sprang open.

I drew it out and carried it to the window, to examine it in the failing light. Too hopeless had I gradually grown, in my dispiriting search, to expect very much; and yet at a glance I saw that my basket of glass lay in shivers at my feet. No ingots nor dollars were here, to crown me the little Monte Cristo of a week. Outside, the distant horn had ceased its gnat-song, the gold was paling to primrose, and everything was lonely and still. Within, my confident little castles were tumbling down like so many card-houses, leaving me stripped of estate, both real and personal, and dominated by the depressing reaction.

And yet, as I looked again at the small collection that lay within that drawer of disillusions, some warmth crept back to my heart as I recognized that a kindred spirit to my own had been at the making of it. Two tarnished gilt buttons, naval, apparently; a portrait of a monarch unknown to me, cut from some antique print and deftly coloured by hand in just my own bold style of brushwork; some foreign copper coins, thicker and clumsier of make than those I hoarded myself; and a list of birds' eggs, with names of the places where they had been found. Also, a ferret's muzzle, and a twist of tarry string, still faintly aromatic! It was a real boy's hoard, then, that I had happened upon. He too had found out the secret drawer, this happy-starred young person; and here he had stowed away his treasures, one by one, and had cherished them secretly awhile; and then—what? Well, one would never know now the reason why these priceless possessions still lay here unclaimed; but across the void stretch of years I seemed to touch hands a moment with my little comrade of seasons—how many seasons?— long since dead.

I restored the drawer, with its contents, to the trusty bureau, and heard the spring click with a certain satisfaction. Some other boy, perhaps, would some day release that spring again. I trusted he would be equally appreciative. As I opened the door to go, I could hear, from the nursery at the end of the passage, shouts and yells, telling that the hunt was up. Bears, apparently, or bandits, were on the evening bill of fare, judging by the character of the noises. In another minute I would be in the thick of it, in all the warmth and light and laughter. And yet —what a long way off it all seemed, both in space and time, to me yet lingering on the threshold of that old-world chamber!

"EXIT TYRANNUS"

THE eventful day had arrived at last, the day which, when first named, had seemed—like all golden dates that promise anything definite—so immeasurably remote. When it was first announced, a fortnight before, that Miss Smedley was really going, the resultant ecstasies had occupied a full week, during which we blindly revelled in the contemplation and discussion of her past tyrannies, crimes, malignities; in recalling to each other this or that insult, dishonour, or physical assault, sullenly endured at a time when deliverance was not even a small star on the horizon; and in mapping out the shining days to come, with special new troubles of their own, no doubt—since this is but a workaday world!—but at least free from one familiar scourge. The time that remained had been taken up by the planning of practical expressions of the popular sentiment. Under Edward's masterly direction, arrangements had been made for a flag to be run up over the hen-house at the very moment when the fly, with Miss Smedley's boxes on top and the grim oppressor herself inside, began to move off down the drive. Three brass cannons, set on the brow of the sunk-fence, were to proclaim our deathless sentiments in the ears of the retreating foe; the dogs were to wear ribbons; and later—but this depended on our powers of evasiveness and dissimulation—there might be a small bonfire, with a cracker or two if the public funds could bear the unwonted strain.

I was awakened by Harold digging me in the ribs, and "She's going today!" was the morning hymn that scattered the clouds of sleep. Strange to say, it was with no corresponding jubilation of spirits that I slowly realized the momentous fact. Indeed, as I dressed, a dull disagreeable feeling that I could not define grew up in me—something like a physical bruise. Harold was evidently feeling it too, for after repeating, "She's going today!" in a tone more befitting the Litany, he looked hard in my face for direction as to how the situation was to be taken. But I crossly bade him look sharp and say his prayers and not bother me. What could this gloom portend, that on a day of days like the present seemed to hang my heavens with black?

Down at last and out in the sun, we found Edward before us, swinging on a gate and chanting a farmyard ditty in which all the beasts appear in due order, jargoning in their several tongues, and every verse begins with the couplet:

> Now, my lads, come with me,
> Out in the morning early!

The fateful exodus of the day had evidently slipped his memory entirely. I touched him on the shoulder. "She's going today!" I said. Edward's carol subsided like a water-tap turned off. "So she is!" he replied, and got down at once off the gate. And we returned to the house without another word.

At breakfast Miss Smedley behaved in a most mean and uncalled-for manner. The right divine of governesses to govern wrong includes no right to cry. In thus usurping the prerogative of their victims they ignore the rules of the ring, and hit below the belt. Charlotte was crying, of course; but that counted for nothing. Charlotte even cried when the pigs' noses were ringed in due season; thereby evoking the cheery contempt of the operators, who asserted they liked it, and doubtless knew. But when the cloud-compeller, her bolts laid aside, resorted to tears, mutinous humanity had a right to feel aggrieved, and think itself placed in a false and difficult position. What would the Romans have done, supposing Hannibal had cried? History has not even considered the possibility. Rules and precedents should be strictly observed on both sides. When they are violated, the other party is justified in feeling injured.

There were no lessons that morning, naturally—another grievance! The fitness of things required that we should have struggled to the last in a confused medley of moods and tenses, and parted for ever, flushed with hatred, over the dismembered corpse of the multiplication-table. But this thing was not to be; and I was free to stroll by myself through the garden, and combat, as best I might, this growing feeling of depression. It was a wrong system altogether, I thought, this going of people one had got used to. Things ought always to continue as they had been. Change there must be, of course; pigs, for instance, came and went with disturbing frequency—

> Fired their ringing shot and passed,
> Hotly charged and sank at last—

but Nature had ordered it so, and in requital had provided for rapid successors. Did you come to love a pig, and he was taken from you, grief was quickly assuaged in the delight of selection from the new litter. But now, when it was no question of a peerless pig, but only of a governess, Nature seemed helpless, and the future held no litter of oblivion. Things might be better, or they might be worse, but they would never be the same; and the innate conservatism of youth asks neither poverty nor riches, but only immunity from change.

Edward slouched up alongside of me presently, with a hangdog look on him, as if he had been caught stealing jam. "What a lark it'll be when she's really gone!" he observed, with a swagger obviously assumed.

"Grand fun!" I replied dolorously; and conversation flagged.

We reached the hen-house, and contemplated the banner of freedom lying ready to flaunt the breezes at the supreme moment.

"Shall you run it up," I asked, "when the fly starts, or—or wait a little till it's out of sight?"

Edward gazed round him dubiously. "We're going to have some rain, I think," he said; "and—and it's a new flag. It would be a pity to spoil it. P'raps I won't run it up at all."

Harold came round the corner like a bison pursued by Indians. "I've polished up the cannons," he cried, "and they look grand! Mayn't I load 'em now?"

"You leave 'em alone," said Edward severely, "or you'll be blowing yourself up." (Consideration for others was not usually Edward's strong point.) "Don't touch the gunpowder till you're told, or you'll get your head smacked."

Harold fell behind, limp, squashed, obedient. "She wants me to write to her," he began presently. "Says she doesn't mind the spelling, if I'll only write. Fancy her saying that!"

"Oh, shut up, will you?" said Edward savagely; and once more we were silent, with only our thoughts for sorry company.

"Let's go off to the copse," I suggested timidly, feeling that something had to be done to relieve the tension, "and cut more new bows and arrows."

"She gave me a knife my last birthday," said Edward moodily, never budging. "It wasn't much of a knife—but I wish I hadn't lost it!"

"When my legs used to ache," I said, "she sat up half the night, rubbing stuff on them. I forgot all about that till this morning."

"There's the fly!" cried Harold suddenly. "I can hear it scrunching on the gravel."

Then for the first time we turned and stared each other in the face.

The fly and its contents had finally disappeared through the gate, the rumble of its wheels had died away. Yet no flag floated defiantly in the sun, no cannons proclaimed the passing of a dynasty. From out the frosted cake of our existence Fate had cut an irreplaceable segment; turn which way we would, the void was present. We sneaked off in different directions, mutually undesirous of company; and it seemed borne in upon me that I ought to go and dig my garden right over, from end to end. It didn't actually want digging; on the other hand no amount of digging could affect it, for good or for evil; so I worked steadily, strenuously, under the hot sun, stifling thought in action. At the end of an hour or so, I was joined by Edward.

"I've been chopping up wood," he explained, in a guilty sort of way, though nobody had called on him to account for his doings.

"What for?" I inquired stupidly. "There's piles and piles of it chopped up already."

"I know," said Edward, "but there's no harm in having a bit over. You never can tell what may happen. But what have you been doing all this digging for?"

"You said it was going to rain," I explained hastily. "So I thought I'd get the digging done before it came. Good gardeners always tell you that's the right thing to do."

"It did look like rain at one time," Edward admitted; "but it's passed off now. Very queer weather we're having. I suppose that's why I've felt so funny all day."

"Yes, I suppose it's the weather," I replied. "*I've* been feeling funny too."

The weather had nothing to do with it, as we well knew. But we would both have died rather than admit the real reason.

THE BLUE ROOM

THAT Nature has her moments of sympathy with man has been noted often enough—and generally as a new discovery. To us, who had never known any other condition of things, it seemed entirely right and fitting that the wind sang and sobbed in the poplar tops, and, in the lulls of it, sudden spurts of rain spattered the already dusty roads, on that blusterous March day when Edward and I awaited, on the station platform, the arrival of the new tutor. Needless to say, this arrangement had been planned by an aunt, from some fond idea that our shy, innocent young natures would unfold themselves during the walk from the station, and that, on the revelation of each other's more solid qualities that must inevitably ensue, an enduring friendship, springing from mutual respect, might be firmly based. A pretty dream—nothing more. For Edward, who foresaw that the brunt of tutorial oppression would have to be borne by him, was sulky, monosyllabic, and determined to be as negatively disagreeable as good manners would permit. It was therefore evident that I would have to be spokesman and purveyor of hollow civilities, and I was none the more amiable on that account; all courtesies, welcomes, explanations, and other court-chamberlain kind of business, being my special aversion. There was much of the tempestuous March weather in the hearts of both of us, as we sullenly glowered along the carriage windows of the slackening train.

One is apt, however, to misjudge the special difficulties of a situation; and the reception proved, after all, an easy and informal matter. In a trainful so uniformly bucolic, a tutor was readily recognizable; and his portmanteau had been consigned to the luggage-cart, and his person conveyed into the lane, before I had discharged one of my carefully considered sentences. I breathed more easily and, looking up at our new friend as we stepped out together, remembered that we had been counting on something altogether more arid, scholastic, and severe. A boyish eager face and a petulant pince-nez, untidy hair, a head of constant quick turns like a robin's, and a voice that kept breaking into alto—

these were all very strange and new, but not in the least terrible.

He proceeded jerkily through the village, with glances on this side and that; and, "Charming," he broke out presently; "quite too charming and delightful!"

I had not counted on this sort of thing, and glanced for help to Edward, who, hands in pockets, looked grimly down his nose. He had taken his line, and meant to stick to it.

Meantime our friend had made an imaginary spy-glass out of his fist, and was squinting through it at something I could not perceive. "What an exquisite bit!" he burst out. "Fifteenth century—no—yes, it is!"

I began to feel puzzled, not to say alarmed. It reminded me of the butcher in *The Arabian Nights,* whose common joints, displayed on the shop-front, took to a startled public the appearance of dismembered humanity. This man seemed to see the strangest things in our dull, familiar surroundings.

"Ah!" he broke out again, as we jogged on between hedgerows. "And that field now, backed by the downs, with the rain-cloud brooding over it—that's all David Cox, every bit of it!"

"That field belongs to Farmer Larkin," I explained politely; for of course he could not be expected to know. "I'll take you over to Farmer Cox's tomorrow, if he's a friend of yours; but there's nothing to see there."

Edward, who was hanging sullenly behind, made a face at me, as if to say, "What sort of lunatic have we got here?"

"It has the true pastoral character, this country of yours," went on our enthusiast, "with just that added touch in cottage and farmstead, relics of a bygone art, which makes our English landscape so divine, so unique!"

Really this grasshopper was becoming a burden! These familiar fields and farms, of which we knew every blade and stick, had done nothing that I knew of to be bespattered with adjectives in this way. I had never thought of them as divine, unique, or anything else. They were—well, they were just themselves, and there was an end of it. Despairingly I jogged Edward in the ribs, as a sign to start rational conversation, but he only grinned and continued obdurate.

"You can see the house now," I remarked presently; "and that's Selina, chasing the donkey in the paddock. Or is it the donkey chasing Selina? I can't quite make out; but it's *them,* anyhow."

Needless to say, he exploded with a full charge of adjectives. "Exquisite!" he rapped out. "So mellow and harmonious, and so entirely in keeping!" (I could see from Edward's face that he was thinking who ought to be in keeping.) "Such possibilities of romance, now, in those old gables!"

"If you mean the garrets," I said, "there's a lot of old furniture in them; and one is generally full of apples; and the bats get in sometimes, under the eaves, and flop about till we go up with hairbrushes and things and drive 'em out; but there's nothing else in them that I know of."

"Oh, but there must be more than bats!" he cried. "Don't tell me there are no ghosts. I shall be deeply disappointed if there aren't any ghosts."

I did not think it worth while to reply, feeling really unequal to this sort of conversation. Besides, we were nearing the house, when my task would be ended. Aunt Eliza met us at the door, and in the cross-fire of adjectives that ensued—both of them talking at once, as grown-up folk have a habit of doing—we two slipped round to the back of the house, and speedily put several broad acres between us and civilization, for fear of being ordered in to tea in the drawing-room. By the time we returned, our new importation had gone up to dress for dinner, so till the morrow at least we were free of him.

Meanwhile the March wind, after dropping a while at sundown, had been steadily increasing in volume; and although I fell asleep at my usual hour, about midnight I was awakened by the stress and the cry of it. In the bright moonlight, wind strung branches tossed and swayed eerily across the blinds; there was rumbling in chimneys, whistling in keyholes, and everywhere a clamour and a call. Sleep was out of the question, and, sitting up in bed, I looked round. Edward sat up too. "I was wondering when you were going to wake," he said. "It's no good trying to sleep through this. I vote we get up and do something."

"I'm game," I replied. "Let's play at being in a ship at sea" (the plaint of the old house under the buffeting wind suggested this, naturally); "and we can be wrecked on an island, or left on a raft, whichever you choose; but I like an island best myself, because there's more things on it."

Edward on reflection negatived the idea. "It would make too much noise," he pointed out. "There's no fun playing at ships, unless you can make a jolly good row."

The door creaked, and a small figure in white slipped cautiously in. "Thought I heard you talking," said Charlotte. "We don't like it; we're afraid—Selina, too! She'll be here in a minute. She's putting on her new dressing-gown she's so proud of it."

His arms round his knees, Edward cogitated deeply until Selina appeared, barefooted, and looking slim and tall in the new dressing-gown. Then, "Look here," he exclaimed; "now we're all together, I vote we go and explore!"

"You're always wanting to explore," I said. "What on earth is there to explore for in this house?"

"Biscuits!" said the inspired Edward.

"Hooray! Come on!" chimed in Harold, sitting up suddenly. He had been awake all the time, but had been shamming sleep, lest he should be fagged to do anything.

It was indeed a fact, as Edward had remembered, that our thoughtless elders occasionally left the biscuits out, a prize for the night-walking adventurer with nerves of steel.

Edward tumbled out of bed and pulled a baggy old pair of knickerbockers over his bare shanks. Then he girt himself with a belt, into which he thrust, on the one side a large wooden pistol, on the other an old single-stick; and finally he donned a big slouch-hat—once an uncle's —that we used for playing Guy Fawkes and Charles-the-Second-up-a-tree in. Whatever the audience, Edward, if possible, always dressed for his parts with care and conscientiousness; while Harold and I, true Elizabethans, cared little about the mounting of the piece, so long as the real dramatic heart of it beat sound.

Our commander now enjoined on us a silence deep as the grave, reminding us that Aunt Eliza usually slept with an open door, past which we had to file.

"But we'll take the short cut through the Blue Room," said the wary Selina.

"Of course," said Edward approvingly. "I forgot about that. Now, then! You lead the way!"

The Blue Room had in prehistoric times been added to by taking in a superfluous passage, and so not only had the advantage of two doors, but also enabled us to get to the head of the stairs without passing the chamber wherein our dragon-aunt lay couched. It was rarely occupied, except when a casual uncle came down for the night. We entered in noiseless file, the room being plunged in darkness, except for a bright strip of moonlight on the floor, across which we must pass for our exit. On this our leading lady chose to pause, seizing the opportunity to study the hang of her new dressing-gown. Greatly satisfied thereat, she proceeded, after the feminine fashion, to peacock and to pose, pacing a minuet down the moonlit patch with an imaginary partner. This was too much for Edward's histrionic instincts, and after a moment's pause he drew his single-stick, and, with flourishes meet for the occasion, strode on to the stage. A struggle ensued on approved lines, at the end of which Selina was stabbed slowly and with unction, and her corpse borne from the chamber by the ruthless cavalier. The rest of us rushed after in a clump, with capers and gesticulations of delight; the special charm of the performance lying in the necessity for its being carried out with the dumbest of dumb shows.

Once out on the dark landing, the noise of the storm without told us that we had exaggerated the necessity for silence; so, grasping the tails of each other's night-gowns, even as Alpine climbers rope themselves together in perilous places, we fared stoutly down the staircase-moraine, and across the grim glacier of the hall, to where a faint glimmer from the half-open door of the drawing room beckoned to us like friendly hostel-lights. Entering, we found that our thriftless seniors had left the sound red heart of a fire, easily coaxed into a cheerful blaze; and biscuits—a plateful—smiled at us in an encouraging sort of way, together with the halves of a lemon, already squeezed, but still suckable. The biscuits were righteously shared, the lemon segments passed from mouth to mouth; and as we squatted round the fire, its genial warmth consoling our unclad limbs, we realized that so many nocturnal perils had not been braved in vain.

"It's a funny thing," said Edward, as we chatted, "how I hate this room in the daytime. It always means having your face washed, and your hair brushed, and talking silly company talk. But tonight it's really quite jolly. Looks different, somehow."

"I never can make out," I said, "what people come here to tea for. They can have their own tea at home if they like—they're not poor people—with jam and things, and drink out of their saucer, and suck their fingers, and enjoy themselves; but they come here from a long way off, and sit up straight with their feet off the bars of their chairs, and have one cup, and talk the same sort of stuff every time."

Selina sniffed disdainfully. "You don't know anything about it," she said. "In society you have to call on each other. It's the proper thing to do."

"Pooh! *You're* not in society," said Edward politely; "and, what's more, you never will be."

"Yes, I shall, some day," retorted Selina; "but I shan't ask you to come and see me, so there!"

"Wouldn't come if you did," growled Edward.

"Well, you won't get the chance," rejoined our sister, claiming her right of the last word. There was no heat about these little amenities, which made up—as understood by us—the art of polite conversation.

"I don't like society people," put in Harold from the sofa, where he was sprawling at full length—a sight the daylight hours would have blushed to witness. "There were some of 'em here this afternoon, when you two had gone off to the station. Oh, and I found a dead mouse on the lawn, and I wanted to skin it, but I wasn't sure I knew how, by myself; and they came out into the garden, and patted my head—I wish people wouldn't do that—and one of 'em asked me to pick her a flower. Don't know why she couldn't pick it herself; but I said, 'All right, I will if you'll hold my mouse.' But she screamed, and threw it away; and Augustus (the cat) got it, and ran away with it. I believe it was really his mouse all the time, 'cos he'd been looking about as if he had lost something, so I wasn't angry with *him*. But what did *she* want to throw away my mouse for?"

"You have to be careful with mice," reflected Edward; "they're such slippery things. Do you remember we were playing with a dead mouse once on the piano, and the mouse was Robinson Crusoe, and the piano was the island, and somehow Crusoe slipped down inside the island, into its works, and we couldn't get him out, though we tried rakes and all sorts of things, till the tuner came. And that wasn't till a week after, and then——"

Here Charlotte, who had been nodding solemnly, fell over into the fender; and we realized that the wind had dropped at last, and the house was lapped in a great stillness. Our vacant beds seemed to be calling to us imperiously; and we were all glad when Edward gave the signal for retreat. At the top of the staircase Harold unexpectedly turned mutinous, insisting on his right to slide down the banisters in a free country. Circumstances did not allow of argument; I suggested frog's-marching instead, and accordingly frog's-marched he was, the procession passing solemnly across the moonlit Blue Room, with Harold horizontal and limply submissive. Snug in bed at last, I was just slipping off into slumber when I heard Edward explode, with chuckle and snort.

"By Jove!" he said. "I forgot all about it. The new tutor's sleeping in the Blue Room!"

"Lucky he didn't wake up and catch us," I grunted drowsily; and, without another thought on the matter, we both sank into well-earned repose.

Next morning, coming down to breakfast braced to grapple with fresh adversity, we were surprised to find our garrulous friend of the previous day—he was late in making his appearance—strangely silent and (apparently) preoccupied. Having polished off our porridge, we ran out to feed the rabbits, explaining to them that a beast of a tutor would prevent their enjoying so much of our society as formerly.

On returning to the house at the fated hour appointed for study, we were thunderstruck to see the station-cart disappearing down the drive, freighted with our new acquaintance. Aunt Eliza was brutally uncommunicative; but she was overheard to remark casually that she thought the man must be a lunatic. In this theory we were only too ready to concur, dismissing thereafter the whole matter from our minds.

Some weeks later it happened that Uncle Thomas, while paying us a flying visit, produced from his pocket a copy of the latest weekly, *Psyche: A Journal of the Unseen;* and proceeded laboriously to rid himself of much incomprehensible humour, apparently at our expense. We bore it patiently, with the forced grin demanded by convention, anxious to get at the source of inspiration, which it presently appeared lay in a paragraph circumstantially describing our modest and humdrum habitation. "Case III.," it began. "The following particulars were communicated by a young member of the Society, of undoubted probity and earnestness, and are a chronicle of actual and recent experience." A fairly accurate description of the house followed, with details that were unmistakable; but to this there succeeded a flood of meaningless drivel about apparitions, nightly visitants, and the like, writ in a manner betokening a disordered mind, coupled with a feeble imagination. The fellow was not even original. All the old material was there—the storm at night, the haunted chamber, the white lady, the murder re-enacted, and so on—already worn threadbare in many a Christmas Number. No one was able to make head or tail of the stuff, or of its connexion with our quiet mansion; and yet Edward, who had always suspected the fellow, persisted in maintaining that our tutor of a brief span was, somehow or other, at the bottom of it.

A FALLING OUT

HAROLD told me the main facts of this episode some time later— in bits and with reluctance. It was not a recollection he cared to talk about. The crude blank misery of a moment is apt to leave a dull bruise which is slow to depart, if it ever do so entirely; and Harold confesses to a twinge or two, still, at times, like the veteran who brings home a bullet inside him from martial plains over the sea.

He knew he was a brute the moment he had done it. Selina had not meant to worry, only to comfort and assist. But his soul was one raw sore within him, when he found himself shut up in the school-room after hours, merely for insisting that 7 times 7 amounted to 47. The injustice of it seemed so flagrant. Why not 47 as much as 49? One number was no prettier than the other to look at, and it was evidently only a matter of arbitrary taste and preference, and, anyhow, it had always been 47 to him, and would be to the end of time. So when Selina came in out of the sun, leaving the Trappers of the Far West behind her, and putting off the glory of being an Apache squaw in order to hear him his tables and win his release, Harold turned on her venomously, rejected her kindly overtures, and even drove his elbow into her sympathetic ribs, in his determination to be left alone in the glory of sulks. The fit passed directly, his eyes were opened, and his soul sat in the dust as he sorrowfully began to cast about for some atonement heroic enough to salve the wrong.

Of course poor Selina looked for no sacrifice nor heroics whatever; she didn't even want him to say he was sorry. If he would only make it up, she would have done the apologizing part herself. But that was not a boy's way. Something solid, Harold felt, was due from him; and until that was achieved, making up must not be thought of, in order that the final effect might not be spoilt. Accordingly, when his release came, and Selina hung about trying to catch his eye, Harold, pos-sessed by the demon of distorted motive, avoided her steadily—though he was bleeding inwardly at every minute of delay—and came to me instead. Needless to say, I warmly approved his plan. It was so much more high-toned than just going and making up tamely, which anyone could do; and a girl who had been jabbed in the ribs by a hostile elbow could not be expected for a moment to overlook it, without the lini-ment of an offering to soothe her injured feelings.

"I know what she wants most," said Harold. "She wants that set of tea-things in the toyshop window, with the red and blue flowers on 'em; she's wanted it for months, 'cos her dolls are getting big enough to have real afternoon tea; and she wants it so badly that she won't walk that side of the street when we go into town. But it costs five shillings!"

Then we set to work seriously, and devoted the afternoon to a realization of assets and the composition of a Budget that might have been dated without shame from Whitehall. The result worked out as follows:

	s.	*d.*
By one uncle, unspent through having been lost for nearly a week—turned up at last in the straw of the dog-kennel	2	6
By advance from me on security of next uncle, and failing that, to be called in at Christmas	1	0
By shaken out of missionary-box with the help of a knife-blade. (They were our own pennies and a forced levy) .	0	4
By bet due from Edward, for walking across the field where Farmer Larkin's bull was, and Edward bet him two-pence he wouldn't—called in with difficulty	0	2
By advance from Martha, on no security at all, only you mustn't tell your aunt	1	0
Total	5	0

and at last we breathed again.

The rest promised to be easy. Selina had a tea-party at five on the morrow, with the chipped old wooden tea-things that had served her successive dolls from babyhood. Harold would slip off directly after dinner, going alone, so as not to arouse suspicion, as we were not allowed to go into town by ourselves. It was nearly two miles to our small metropolis, but there would be plenty of time for him to go and return, even laden with the olive-branch neatly packed in shavings. Besides, he might meet the butcher, who was his friend and would give him a lift. Then, finally, at five, the rapture of the new tea-service, descended from the skies; and, retribution made, making up at last, without loss of dignity. With the event before us, we thought it a small thing that twenty-four hours more of alienation and pretended sulks must be kept up on Harold's part; but Selina, who naturally knew nothing of the treat in store for her, moped for the rest of the evening, and took a very heavy heart to bed.

Next day, when the hour for action arrived, Harold evaded Olympian attention with an easy modesty born of long practice, and made off for the front gate. Selina, who had been keeping her eye upon him, thought he was going down to the pond to catch frogs, a joy they had planned to share together, and made after him. But Harold, though he heard her footsteps, continued sternly on his high mission, without even looking back; and Selina was left to wander disconsolately among flower-beds that had lost—for her—all scent and colour. I saw it all, and, although cold reason approved our line of action, instinct told me we were brutes.

Harold reached the town—so he recounted afterwards—in record time, having run most of the way for fear the tea-things, which had reposed six months in the window, should be snapped up by some other conscience-stricken lacerator of a sister's feelings; and it seemed hardly credible to find them still there, and their owner willing to part with them for the price marked on the ticket. He paid his money down at once, that there should be no drawing back from the bargain; and then, as the things had to be taken out of the window and packed, and the afternoon was yet young, he thought he might treat himself to a taste of urban joys and the *vie de bohème*. Shops came first, of course, and he flattened his nose successively against the window with the india-rubber balls in it, and the clockwork locomotive; and against the barber's window, with the wigs on blocks, reminding him of uncles, and shaving-cream that looked so good to eat; and the grocer's window, displaying more currants than the whole British population could possibly consume without a special effort; and the window of the bank, wherein gold was thought so little of that it was dealt about in shovels. Next there was the market-place, with all its clamorous joys; and when a runaway calf came down the street like a cannon-ball, Harold felt that he had not lived in vain. The whole place was so brimful of excitement that he had quite forgotten the why and the wherefore of his being there, when a sight of the church clock recalled him to his better self, and sent him flying out of the town, as he realized he had only just time enough left to get back in. If he were after his appointed hour, he would not only miss his high triumph, but probably would be detected as a transgressor of bounds—a crime before which a private opinion on multiplication sank to nothingness. So he jogged along on his homeward way, thinking of many things and probably talking to himself a good deal, as his habit was. He had covered nearly half the distance, when suddenly—a deadly sinking in the pit of his stomach—a paralysis of every limb—around him a world extinct of light and music—a black sun and a reeling sky—he had forgotten the tea-things!

It was useless, it was hopeless, all was over, and nothing could now be done. Nevertheless he turned and ran back wildly, blindly, choking with the big sobs that evoked neither pity nor comfort from a merciless mocking world around; a stitch in his side, dust in his eyes, and black despair clutching at his heart. So he stumbled on, with leaden legs and bursting sides, till—as if Fate had not yet dealt him her last worst buffet of all—on turning a corner in the road he almost ran under the wheels of a dogcart, in which, as it pulled up, was apparent the portly form of Farmer Larkin, the arch-enemy, at whose ducks he had been shying stones that very morning!

Had Harold been in his right and unclouded senses, he would have vanished through the hedge some seconds earlier, rather than pain the farmer by any unpleasant reminiscences which his appearance might recall; but, as things were, he could only stand and blubber hopelessly, caring, indeed, little now what further misery might befall him. The farmer, for his part, surveyed the desolate figure with some astonishment, calling out in no unfriendly accents. "Why, Master Harold! Whatever be the matter? Baint runnin' away, be ee?"

Then Harold, with the unnatural courage born of desperation, flung himself on the step, and, climbing into the cart, fell in the straw at the bottom of it, sobbing out that he wanted to go back, go back! The situation had a vagueness; but the farmer, a man of action rather than of words, swung his horse round smartly, and they were in the town again by the time Harold had recovered himself sufficiently to furnish details. As they drove up to the shop, the woman was waiting at the door with the parcel; and hardly a minute seemed to have elapsed since the black crisis, ere they were bowling along swiftly home, the precious parcel hugged in a close embrace.

And now the farmer came out in quite a new and unexpected light. Never a word did he say of broken fences and hurdles, of trampled crops and harried flocks and herds. One would have thought the man had never possessed a head of livestock in his life. Instead, he was deeply interested in the whole dolorous quest of the tea-things, and sympathized with Harold on the disputed point in mathematics as if he had been himself at the same stage of education. As they neared home, Harold found himself, to his surprise, sitting up and chatting to his new friend like man to man; and before he was set down at a convenient gap in the garden hedge, he had promised that when Selina gave her first public tea-party, little Miss Larkin should be invited to come and bring her whole sawdust family along with her; and the farmer appeared as pleased and proud as if he had won a gold medal at the Agricultural Show, and really, when I heard the story, it began to dawn upon me that those Olympians must have certain good points, far down in them, and that I should have to leave off abusing them some day.

At the hour of five, Selina, having spent the afternoon searching for Harold in all his accustomed haunts, sat down disconsolately to tea with her dolls, who ungenerously refused to wait beyond the appointed hour. The wooden tea-things seemed more chipped than usual; and the dolls themselves had more of wax and sawdust, and less of human colour and intelligence about them, than she ever remembered before. It was then that Harold burst in, very dusty, his stockings at his heels, and the channels ploughed by tears still showing on his grimy cheeks; and Selina was at last permitted to know that he had been thinking of her ever since his ill-judged exhibition of temper, and that his sulks had not been the genuine article, nor had he gone frogging by himself. It was a very happy hostess who dispensed hospitality that evening to a glassy-eyed, stiff-kneed circle; and many a dollish *gaucherie,* that would have been severely checked on ordinary occasions, was as much overlooked as if it had been a birthday.

But Harold and I, in what I was afterwards given to understand was our stupid masculine way, thought all her happiness sprang from possession of the long-coveted tea-service.

"LUSISTI SATIS"

AMONG the many fatuous ideas that possessed the Olympian noddle, this one was pre-eminent: that, being Olympians, they could talk quite freely in our presence on subjects of the closest import to us, so long as names, dates, and other landmarks were ignored. We were supposed to be denied the faculty for putting two and two together; and like the monkeys, who very sensibly refrain from speech lest they should be set to earn their livings, we were careful to conceal our capabilities for a simple syllogism. Thus we were rarely taken by surprise, and so were considered by our disappointed elders to be apathetic and to lack the divine capacity for wonder.

Now the daily output of the letter-bag, with the mysterious discussions that ensued thereon, had speedily informed us that Uncle Thomas was entrusted with a mission—a mission, too, affecting ourselves. Uncle Thomas's missions were many and various. A self-important man, one liking the business while protesting that he sank under the burden, he was the missionary, so to speak, of our remote habitation. The matching a ribbon, the running down to the stores, the interviewing a cook—these and similar duties lent constant colour and variety to his vacant life in London, and helped to keep down his figure. When the matter, however, had in our presence to be referred to with nods and pronouns, with significant hiatuses and interpolations in the French tongue, then the red flag was flown, the storm-cone hoisted, and by a studious pretence of inattention we were not long in plucking out the heart of the mystery.

To clinch our conclusion, we descended suddenly and together on Martha; proceeding, however, not by simple inquiry as to facts—that would never have done—but by informing her that the air was full of school and that we knew all about it, and then challenging denial. Martha was a trusty soul, but a bad witness for the defence, and we soon had it all out of her. The word had gone forth, the school had been selected; the necessary sheets were hemming even now, and Edward was the designated and appointed victim.

It had always been before us as an inevitable bourne, this strange unknown thing called school; and yet—perhaps I should say consequently—we had never seriously set ourselves to consider what it really meant. But now that the grim spectre loomed imminent, stretching lean hands for one of our flock, it behoved us to face the situation, to take soundings in this uncharted sea and find out whither we were drifting. Unfortunately the data in our possession were absolutely insufficient, and we knew not whither to turn for exact information. Uncle Thomas could have told us all about it, of course; he had been there himself, once, in the dim and misty past. But an unfortunate conviction, that Nature had intended him for a humorist, tainted all his evidence, besides making it wearisome to hear. Again, of such among our contemporaries as we had approached, the trumpets gave forth an uncertain sound. According to some it meant larks, revels, emancipation, and a foretaste of the bliss of manhood. According to others—the majority, alas!—it was a private and peculiar Hades, that could give the original institution points and a beating. When Edward was observed to be swaggering round with a jaunty air and his chest stuck out, I knew that he was contemplating his future from the one point of view. When, on the contrary, he was subdued and unaggressive, and sought the society of his sisters, I recognized that the other aspect was in the ascendant. "You can always run away, you know," I used to remark consolingly on these latter occasions; and Edward would brighten up wonderfully at the suggestion, while Charlotte melted into tears before her vision of a brother with blistered feet and an empty belly, passing nights of frost 'neath the lee of windy haystacks.

It was to Edward, of course, that the situation was chiefly productive of anxiety; and yet the ensuing change in my own circumstances and position furnished me also with food for grave reflection. Hitherto I had acted mostly to orders. Even when I had devised and counselled any particular devilry, it had been carried out on Edward's approbation, and—as eldest—at his special risk. Henceforward I began to be anxious of the bugbear Responsibility, and to realize what a soul-throttling thing it is. True, my new position would have its compensations. Edward had been masterful exceedingly, imperious, perhaps a little narrow; impassioned for hard facts, and with scant sympathy for make-believe. I should now be free and untrammelled; in the conception and the carrying out of a scheme, I could accept and reject to better artistic purpose.

It would, moreover, be needless to be a Radical any more. Radical I never was, really, by nature or by sympathy. The part had been thrust on me one day, when Edward proposed to foist the House of Lords on our small republic. The principles of the thing he set forth learnedly and well, and it all sounded promising enough, till he went on to explain that, for the present at least, he proposed to be the House of Lords himself. We others were to be the Commons. There would be promotions, of course, he added, dependent on service and on fitness, and open to both sexes; and to me in especial he held out hopes of speedy advancement. But in its initial stages the thing wouldn't work properly unless he were first and only Lord. Then I put my foot down promptly, and said it was all rot, and I didn't see the good of any House of Lords at all. "Then you must be a low Radical!" said Edward, with fine contempt. The inference seemed hardly necessary, but what could I do? I accepted the situation, and said firmly, Yes, I was a low Radical. In this monstrous character I had been obliged to masquerade ever since; but now I could throw it off, and look the world in the face again.

And yet, did this and other gains really outbalance my losses? Henceforth I should, it was true, be leader and chief; but I should also be the buffer between the Olympians and my little clan. To Edward this had been nothing; he had withstood the impact of Olympus without flinching, like Tenerife or Atlas unremoved. But was I equal to the task? And was there not rather a danger that for the sake of peace and quietness I might be tempted to compromise, compound, and make terms, sinking thus, by successive lapses, into the Blameless Prig? I don't mean, of course, that I thought out my thoughts to the exact point here set down. In those fortunate days of old, one was free from the hard necessity of transmuting the vague idea into the mechanical inadequate medium of words. But the feeling was there, that I might not possess the qualities of character for so delicate a position.

The unnatural halo round Edward got more pronounced, his own demeanour more responsible and dignified, with the arrival of his new clothes. When his trunk and play-box were sent in, the approaching cleavage between our brother, who now belonged to the future, and ourselves, still claimed by the past, was accentuated indeed. His name was painted on each of them, in large letters, and after their arrival their owner used to disappear mysteriously, and be found eventually wandering round his luggage, murmuring to himself, "Edward ——," in a rapt, remote sort of way. It was a weakness, of course, and pointed to a soft spot in his character; but those who can remember the sensation of first seeing their names in print will not think hardly of him.

As the short days sped by and the grim event cast its shadow longer and longer across the threshold, an unnatural politeness, a civility scarce canny, began to pervade the air. In those latter hours Edward himself was frequently heard to say, "Please," and also, "Would you mind fetchin' that ball?" while Harold and I would sometimes actually find ourselves trying to anticipate his wishes. As for the girls, they simply grovelled. The Olympians, too, in their uncouth way, by gift of carnal delicacies and such-like indulgence, seemed anxious to demonstrate that they had hitherto misjudged this one of us. Altogether the situation grew strained and false, and I think a general relief was felt when the end came.

We all trooped down to the station, of course; it is only in later years that the farce of "seeing people off" is seen in its true colours. Edward was the life and soul of the party; and if his gaiety struck one at times as being a trifle overdone, it was not a moment to be critical. As we tramped along, I promised him I would ask Farmer Larkin not to kill any more pigs till he came back for the holidays, and he said he would send me a proper catapult—the real lethal article, not a kid's plaything. Then suddenly, when we were about half-way down, one of the girls fell a-snivelling.

The happy few who dare to laugh at the woes of seasickness will perhaps remember how, on occasion, the sudden collapse of a fellow-voyager before their very eyes has caused them hastily to revise their self-confidence and resolve to walk more humbly for the future. Even so it was with Edward, who turned his head aside, feigning an interest in the landscape. It was but for a moment; then he recollected the hat he was wearing—a hard bowler, the first of that sort he had ever owned. He took it off, examined it, and felt it over. Something about it seemed to give him strength, and he was a man once more.

At the station, Edward's first care was to dispose his boxes on the platform so that everyone might see the labels and the letters thereon. One did not go to school for the first time every day! Then he read both sides of his ticket carefully; shifted it to every one of his pockets in turn; and finally fell to chinking of his money, to keep his courage up. We were all dry of conversation by this time, and could only stand round and stare in silence at the victim decked for the altar. And, as I looked at Edward, in new clothes of a manly cut, with a hard hat upon his head, a railway ticket in one pocket and money of his own in the other—money to spend as he liked and no questions asked!—I began to feel dimly how great was the gulf already yawning betwixt us. Fortunately I was not old enough to realize, further, that here on this little platform the old order lay at its last gasp, and that Edward might come back to us, but it would not be the Edward of yore, nor could things ever be the same again.

When the train steamed up at last, we all boarded it impetuously with the view of selecting the one peerless carriage to which Edward might be entrusted with the greatest comfort and honour; and as each one found the ideal compartment at the same moment, and vociferously maintained its merits, he stood some chance for a time of being left behind. A porter settled the matter by heaving him through the nearest door; and as the train moved off, Edward's head was thrust out of the window, wearing on it an unmistakable first-quality grin that he had been saving up somewhere for the supreme moment. Very small and white his face looked, on the long side of the retreating train. But the grin was visible, undeniable, stoutly maintained; till a curve swept him from our sight, and he was borne away in the dying rumble, out of our placid backwater, out into the busy world of rubs and knocks and competition, out into the New Life.

When a crab has lost a leg, his gait is still more awkward than his wont, till Time and healing Nature make him *totus teres atque rotundus* once more. We straggled back from the station disjointedly; Harold, who was very silent, sticking close to me, his last slender prop, while the girls in front, their heads together, were already reckoning up the weeks to the holidays. Home at last, Harold suggested one or two occupations of a spicy and contraband flavour, but though we did our manful best, there was no knocking any interest out of them. Then I suggested others, with the same want of success. Finally we found ourselves sitting silent on an upturned wheelbarrow, our chins on our fists, staring haggardly into the raw new conditions of our changed life, the ruins of a past behind our backs.

And all the while Selina and Charlotte were busy stuffing Edward's rabbits with unwonted forage, bilious and green; polishing up the cage of his mice till the occupants raved and swore like householders in the springtime; and collecting materials for new bows and arrows, whips, boats, guns, and four-in-hand harness, against the return of Ulysses. Little did they dream that the hero, once back from Troy and all its onsets, would scornfully condemn their clumsy but laborious armoury as rot and humbug and only fit for kids! This, with many another like awakening, was mercifully hidden from them. Could the veil have been lifted, and the girls permitted to see Edward as he would appear a short three months hence, ragged of attire and lawless of tongue, a scorner of tradition and an adept in strange new physical tortures, one who would in the same half-hour dismember a doll and shatter a hallowed belief—in fine, a sort of swaggering Captain, fresh from the Spanish Main—could they have had the least hint of this, well, then perhaps . . . But which of us is of mental fibre to stand the test of a glimpse into futurity? Let us only hope that, even with certain disillusionment ahead, the girls would have acted precisely as they did.

And perhaps we have reason to be very grateful that, both as children and long afterwards, we are never allowed to guess how the absorbing pursuit of the moment will appear not only to others but to ourselves, a very short time hence. So we pass, with a gusto and a heartiness that to an onlooker would seem almost pathetic, from one droll devotion to another misshapen passion; and who shall dare to play Rhadamanthus, to appraise the record, and to decide how much of it is solid achievement, and how much the merest child's play?

AN AFTERWORD ON
"THE GOLDEN AGE"

IN 1895, a year in which my own reading was pretty much confined to *Tom Sawyer*—after sundown I was under orders to skip the chapter on Injun Joe and the murder in the graveyard because it invariably led me to disturb the family by screaming in my sleep—in that distant era, the Olympians around me had sated themselves on the disturbing delights of *Trilby* and turned to this gentle and delicate masterpiece which had just come out of England. For some years thereafter, *The Golden Age* and its sequel *Dream Days* could be found within reach in every house in England and America where there were any books at all. *The Golden Age* even underwent the experience of being illustrated by Maxfield Parrish. It was read aloud to all the little wide-eyed Roosevelts in the White House, and the Kaiser kept a copy aboard his yacht. One seldom sees it anywhere nowadays, and to my notion such an anthology as this comes nearest to justifying its existence when it introduces an old friend to a new generation. All around me now are youngsters who have never read "The Roman Road" nor heard the burglars vanish into the shrubbery with horrid implications.

If in this volume there are as many as three pieces of perfection, surely *The Golden Age* is one of them. Its inconsequent chapters were the holiday fantasies of a seemly banker chap who became in due time the Secretary of the Bank of England—this Kenneth

Grahame who was born in Edinburgh in 1859 and died in 1932. The haze-hung prelude called "The Olympians" and several other chapters were wrung from him as contributions to the *National Observer,* a weekly of which the stormy editor, William Ernest Henley, tried in vain to persuade this promising pen to abandon the Old Lady of Threadneedle Street altogether. But it was Grahame's own notion that he was a spring and not a pump. Editors would be wise not to count on him. Oddly enough, the bulk of the papers which make up *The Golden Age* first appeared (along with the drawings of Aubrey Beardsley and other agitating ephemera of the mauve decade) in that short-lived periodical called the *Yellow Book.*

After thus momentously "commencing" author, Grahame then took on such exacting work at the bank that some years passed without a word from him. Indeed, he might never have been heard from again had he not married and found himself with a small exigent son—Alastair Grahame, who was known around the house as Mouse. Mouse demanded a story every night before he would go to sleep. One May evening in 1904, Mouse's mother, waiting for her husband to escort her to a dinner engagement, stood tapping her foot in the hallway. "Where is Mr. Grahame, Louise?" Her maid, standing with fan, shawl, and cloak held in readiness, replied with a sniff of disapproval: "He's with Master Mouse, madam. He's telling him some ditty or other about a toad." This was the first announcement of *The Wind in the Willows.* For even when Mouse was shipped off with his governess for a summer at Littlehampton, the story had to be continued by post and it was from these fifteen letters, which the governess had the wit to save, that the book was put together. Ever since the first success of *The Golden Age,* all American editors had been beseeching Grahame for copy. Wherefore when *The Wind in the Willows* was ready for print he sent it to the editor of *Every-*

body's Magazine who turned it down. All that was long ago. *Everybody's* is no more and Mouse himself was killed at a railway crossing when he was an undergraduate at Oxford.

A. W.

PETER RUGG

THE
MISSING MAN

by

WILLIAM AUSTIN

PETER RUGG, THE MISSING MAN

FROM JONATHAN DUNWELL OF NEW YORK TO
MR. HERMAN KRAUFF

SIR,—Agreeably to my promise, I now relate to you all the particulars of the lost man and child which I have been able to collect. It is entirely owing to the humane interest you seemed to take in the report, that I have pursued the inquiry to the following result.

You may remember that business called me to Boston in the summer of 1820. I sailed in the packet to Providence, and when I arrived there I learned that every seat in the stage was engaged. I was thus obliged either to wait a few hours or accept a seat with the driver, who civilly offered me that accommodation. Accordingly, I took my seat by his side, and soon found him intelligent and communicative. When we had travelled about ten miles, the horses suddenly threw their ears on their necks, as flat as a hare's. Said the driver, "Have you a surtout with you?"

"No," said I; "why do you ask?"

"You will want one soon," said he. "Do you observe the ears of all the horses?"

"Yes; and was just about to ask the reason."

"They see the storm-breeder, and we shall see him soon."

At this moment there was not a cloud visible in the firmament. Soon after, a small speck appeared in the road.

"There," said my companion, "comes the storm-breeder. He always leaves a Scotch mist behind him. By many a wet jacket do I remember him. I suppose the poor fellow suffers much himself—much more than is known to the world."

Presently a man with a child beside him, with a large black horse, and a weather-beaten chair, once built for a chaise-body, passed in great haste, apparently at the rate of twelve miles an hour. He seemed to grasp the reins of his horse with firmness, and appeared to anticipate his speed. He seemed dejected, and looked anxiously at the passengers, particularly at the stage-driver and myself. In a moment after he passed us, the horses' ears were up, and bent themselves forward so that they nearly met.

"Who is that man?" said I. "He seems in great trouble."

"Nobody knows who he is, but his person and the child are familiar to me. I have met him more than a hundred times, and have been so often asked the way to Boston by that man, even when he was travelling directly from that town, that of late I have refused any communication with him; and that is the reason he gave me such a fixed look."

"But does he never stop anywhere?"

"I have never known him to stop anywhere longer than to inquire the way to Boston; and let him be where he may, he will tell you he cannot stay a moment, for he must reach Boston that night."

We were now ascending a high hill in Walpole; and as we had a fair view of the heavens, I was rather disposed to jeer the driver for thinking of his surtout, as not a cloud as big as a marble could be discerned.

"Do you look," said he, "in the direction whence the man came; that is the place to look. The storm never meets him; it follows him."

We presently approached another hill; and when at the height, the driver pointed out in an eastern direction a little black speck about as big as a hat. "There," said he, "is the seed-storm. We may possibly reach Polley's before it reaches us, but the wanderer and his child will go to Providence through rain, thunder, and lightning."

And now the horses, as though taught by instinct, hastened with increased speed. The little black cloud came on rolling over the turnpike, and doubled and trebled itself in all directions. The appearance of this cloud attracted the notice of all the passengers, for after it had spread itself to a great bulk it suddenly became more limited in circumference, grew more compact, dark, and consolidated. And now the successive flashes of chain lightning caused the whole cloud to appear like a sort of irregular network, and displayed a thousand fantastic images. The driver bespoke my attention to a remarkable configuration in the cloud. He said every flash of lightning near its centre discovered to him, distinctly, the form of a man sitting in an open carriage drawn by a black horse. But in truth I saw no such thing; the man's fancy was doubtless at fault. It is a very common thing for the imagination to paint for the senses, both in the visible and invisible world.

In the meantime the distant thunder gave notice of a shower at hand; and just as we reached Polley's tavern the rain poured down in torrents. It was soon over, the cloud passing in the direction of the turnpike toward Providence. In a few moments after, a respectable-looking man in a chaise stopped at the door. The man and child in the chair having excited some little sympathy among the passengers, the gentleman was asked if he had observed them. He said he had met them; that the man seemed bewildered, and inquired the way to Boston; that he was driving at great speed, as though he expected to outstrip the tempest; that the moment he had passed him, a thunderclap broke directly over the man's head, and seemed to envelop both man and child, horse and carriage. "I stopped," said the gentleman, "supposing the lightning had struck him; but the horse only seemed to loom up and increase his speed; and as well as I could judge, he travelled just as fast as the thunder-cloud."

While this man was speaking, a pedlar with a cart of tin merchandise came up, all dripping; and on being questioned, he said he had met that man and carriage, within a fortnight, in four different states; that at each time he had inquired the way to Boston; and that a thunder-shower like the present had each time deluged his wagon and his wares, setting his tin pots, etc., afloat, so that he had determined to get a marine insurance for the future. But that which excited his surprise most was the strange conduct of his horse, for long before he could distinguish the man in the chair his own horse stood still in the road, and flung back his ears. "In short," said the pedlar, "I wish never to see that man and horse again; they do not look to me as though they belonged to this world."

This was all I could learn at that time; and the occurrence soon after would have become with me "like one of those things which had never happened," had I not, as I stood recently on the door-step of Bennett's hotel in Hartford, heard a man say, "There goes Peter Rugg and his child! He looks wet and weary, and farther from Boston than ever." I was satisfied it was the same man I had seen more than three years before; for whoever has once seen Peter Rugg can never after be deceived as to his identity.

"Peter Rugg!" said I. "And who is Peter Rugg?"

"That," said the stranger, "is more than anyone can tell exactly. He is a famous traveller, held in light esteem by all innholders, for he never stops to eat, drink, or sleep. I wonder why the government does not employ him to carry the mail."

"Aye," said a bystander, "that is a thought bright only on one side; how long would it take in that case to send a letter to Boston? for Peter has already, to my knowledge, been more than twenty years travelling to that place."

"But," said I, "does the man never stop anywhere; does he never converse with anyone? I saw the same man more than three years since, near Providence, and I heard a strange story about him. Pray, sir, give me some account of this man."

"Sir," said the stranger, "those who know the most respecting that man say the least. I have heard it asserted that Heaven sometimes sets a mark on a man, either for judgment or a trial. Under which Peter Rugg now labours, I cannot say; therefore I am rather inclined to pity than to judge."

"You speak like a humane man," said I; "and if you have known him so long, I pray you will give me some account of him. Has his appearance much altered in that time?"

"Why, yes. He looks as though he never ate, drank, or slept; and his child looks older than himself, and he looks like time broken off from eternity, and anxious to gain a resting-place."

"And how does his horse look?" said I.

"As for his horse, he looks fatter and gayer, and shows more animation and courage than he did twenty years ago. The last time Rugg spoke to me he inquired how far it was to Boston. I told him just one hundred miles.

" 'Why,' said he, 'how can you deceive me so? It is cruel to mislead a traveller. I have lost my way; pray direct me the nearest way to Boston.'

"I repeated, it was one hundred miles.

" 'How can you say so?' said he. 'I was told last evening it was but fifty, and I have travelled all night.'

" 'But,' said I, 'you are now travelling from Boston. You must turn back.'

" 'Alas,' said he, 'it is all turn back! Boston shifts with the wind, and plays all around the compass. One man tells me it is to the east, another to the west; and the guide-posts too, they all point the wrong way.'

" 'But will you not stop and rest?' said I. 'You seem wet and weary.'

" 'Yes,' said he, 'it has been foul weather since I left home.'

" 'Stop, then, and refresh yourself.'

" 'I must not stop; I must reach home tonight, if possible: though I think you must be mistaken in the distance to Boston.'

"He then gave the reins to his horse, which he restrained with difficulty, and disappeared in a moment. A few days afterward I met the man a little this side of Claremont, winding around the hills in Unity, at the rate, I believe, of twelve miles an hour."

"Is Peter Rugg his real name, or has he accidentally gained that name?"

"I know not, but presume he will not deny his name; you can ask him—for see, he has turned his horse, and is passing this way."

In a moment a dark-coloured, high-spirited horse approached, and would have passed without stopping, but I had resolved to speak to Peter Rugg, or whoever the man might be. Accordingly I stepped into the street; and as the horse approached, I made a feint of stopping him. The man immediately reined in his horse. "Sir," said I, "may I be so bold as to inquire if you are not Mr. Rugg? For I think I have seen you before."

"My name is Peter Rugg," said he. "I have unfortunately lost my way; I am wet and weary, and will take it kindly of you to direct me to Boston."

"You live in Boston, do you; and in what street?"

"In Middle Street."

"When did you leave Boston?"

"I cannot tell precisely; it seems a considerable time."

"But how did you and your child become so wet? It has not rained here today."

"It has just rained a heavy shower up the river. But I shall not reach Boston tonight if I tarry. Would you advise me to take the old road or the turnpike?"

"Why, the old road is one hundred and seventeen miles, and the turnpike is ninety-seven."

"How can you say so? You impose on me; it is wrong to trifle with a traveller; you know it is but forty miles from Newburyport to Boston."

"But this is not Newburyport; this is Hartford."

"Do not deceive me, sir. Is not this town Newburyport, and the river that I have been following the Merrimack?"

"No, sir; this is Hartford, and the river, the Connecticut."

He wrung his hands and looked incredulous. "Have the rivers, too, changed their courses, as the cities have changed places? But see! The clouds are gathering in the south, and we shall have a rainy night. Ah, that fatal oath!"

He would tarry no longer; his impatient horse leaped off, his hind flanks rising like wings; he seemed to devour all before him, and to scorn all behind.

I had now, as I thought, discovered a clue to the history of Peter Rugg; and I determined, the next time my business called me to Boston, to make a further inquiry. Soon after, I was enabled to collect the following particulars from Mrs. Croft, an aged lady in Middle Street, who has resided in Boston during the last twenty years. Her narration is this:

Just at twilight last summer a person stopped at the door of the late Mrs. Rugg. Mrs. Croft on coming to the door perceived a stranger, with a child by his side, in an old weather-beaten carriage, with a black horse. The stranger asked for Mrs. Rugg, and was informed that Mrs. Rugg had died at a good old age, more than twenty years before that time.

The stranger replied, "How can you deceive me so? Do ask Mrs. Rugg to step to the door."

"Sir, I assure you Mrs. Rugg has not lived here these twenty years; no one lives here but myself, and my name is Betsy Croft."

The stranger paused, looked up and down the street, and said, "Though the paint is rather faded, this looks like my house."

"Yes," said the child, "that is the stone before the door that I used to sit on to eat my bread-and-milk."

"But," said the stranger, "it seems to be on the wrong side of the street. Indeed, everything here seems to be misplaced. The streets are all changed, the people are all changed, the town seems changed, and what is strangest of all, Catherine Rugg has deserted her husband and child. Pray," continued the stranger, "has John Foy come home from sea? He went a long voyage; he is my kinsman. If I could see him, he could give me some account of Mrs. Rugg."

"Sir," said Mrs. Croft, "I never heard of John Foy. Where did he live?"

"Just above here, in Orange-tree Lane."

"There is no such place in this neighbourhood."

"What do you tell me! Are the streets gone? Orange-tree Lane is at the head of Hanover Street, near Pemberton's Hill."

"There is no such lane now."

"Madam, you cannot be serious! But you doubtless know my brother, William Rugg. He lives in Royal Exchange Lane, near King Street."

"I know of no such lane; and I am sure there is no such street as King Street in this town."

"No such street as King Street! Why, woman, you mock me! You may as well tell me there is no King George. However, madam, you see I am wet and weary, I must find a resting-place. I will go to Hart's tavern, near the market."

"Which market, sir? for you seem perplexed; we have several markets."

"You know there is but one market near the town dock."

"Oh, the old market; but no such person has kept there these twenty years."

Here the stranger seemed disconcerted, and uttered to himself quite audibly, "Strange mistake; how much this looks like the town of Boston! It certainly has a great resemblance to it; but I perceive my mistake now. Some other Mrs. Rugg, some other Middle Street. Then," said he, "madam, can you direct me to Boston?"

"Why, this is Boston, the city of Boston; I know of no other Boston."

"City of Boston it may be; but it is not the Boston where I live. I recollect now, I came over a bridge instead of a ferry. Pray, what bridge is that I just came over?"

"It is Charles River bridge."

"I perceive my mistake; there is a ferry between Boston and Charlestown; there is no bridge. Ah, I perceive my mistake. If I were in Boston my horse would carry me directly to my own door. But my horse shows by his impatience that he is in a strange place. Absurd, that I should have mistaken this place for the old town of Boston! It is a much finer city than the town of Boston. It has been built long since Boston. I fancy Boston must lie at a distance from this city, as the good woman seems ignorant of it."

At these words his horse began to chafe, and strike the pavement with his forefeet. The stranger seemed a little bewildered, and said, "No home tonight"; and giving the reins to his horse, passed up the street, and she saw no more of him.

It was evident that the generation to which Peter Rugg belonged had passed away.

This was all the account of Peter Rugg I could obtain from Mrs. Croft; but she directed me to an elderly man, Mr. James Felt, who lived near her, and who had kept a record of the principal occurrences for the last fifty years. At my request she sent for him; and after I had related to him the object of my inquiry, Mr. Felt told me he had known Rugg in his youth, and that his disappearance had caused some surprise; but as it sometimes happens that men run away—sometimes to be rid of others, and sometimes to be rid of themselves—and Rugg took his child with him, and his own horse and chair, and as it did not appear that any creditors made a stir, the occurrence soon mingled itself in the stream of oblivion; and Rugg and his child, horse, and chair were soon forgotten.

"It is true," said Mr. Felt, "sundry stories grew out of Rugg's affair, whether true or false I cannot tell; but stranger things have happened in my day, without even a newspaper notice."

"Sir," said I, "Peter Rugg is now living. I have lately seen Peter Rugg and his child, horse, and chair; therefore I pray you to relate to me all you know or ever heard of him."

"Why, my friend," said James Felt, "that Peter Rugg is now a living man, I will not deny; but that you have seen Peter Rugg and his child, is impossible, if you mean a small child; for Jenny Rugg, if living, must be at least—let me see—Boston massacre, 1770—Jenny Rugg, was about ten years old. Why, sir, Jenny Rugg, if living, must be more than sixty years of age. That Peter Rugg is living, is highly probable, as he was only ten years older than myself, and I was only eighty last March; and I am as likely to live twenty years longer as any man."

Here I perceived that Mr. Felt was in his dotage, and I despaired of gaining any intelligence from him on which I could depend.

I took my leave of Mrs. Croft, and proceeded to my lodgings at the Marlborough Hotel.

"If Peter Rugg," thought I, "has been travelling since the Boston massacre, there is no reason why he should not travel to the end of time. If the present generation know little of him, the next will know less, and Peter and his child will have no hold on this world."

In the course of the evening, I related my adventure in Middle Street.

"Ha," said one of the company, smiling, "do you really think you have seen Peter Rugg? I have heard my grandfather speak of him, as though he seriously believed his own story."

"Sir," said I, "pray let us compare your grandfather's story of Mr. Rugg with my own."

"Peter Rugg, sir—if my grandfather was worthy of credit—once lived in Middle Street, in this city. He was a man in comfortable circumstances, had a wife and one daughter, and was generally esteemed for his sober life and manners. But unhappily, his temper, at times, was altogether ungovernable, and then his language was terrible. In these fits of passion, if a door stood in his way, he would never do less than kick a panel through. He would sometimes throw his heels over his head, and come down on his feet, uttering oaths in a circle; and thus in a rage, he was the first who performed a somersault, and did what others have since learned to do for merriment and money. Once Rugg was seen to bite a tenpenny nail in halves. In those days everybody, both men and boys, wore wigs; and Peter, at these moments of violent passion, would become so profane that his wig would rise up from his head. Some said it was on account of his terrible language; others accounted for it in a more philosophical way, and said it was caused by the expansion of his scalp, as violent passion, we know, will swell the veins and expand the head. While these fits were on him, Rugg had no respect for heaven or earth. Except this infirmity, all agreed that Rugg was a good sort of a man; for when his fits were over, nobody was so ready to commend a placid temper as Peter.

"One morning, late in autumn, Rugg, in his own chair, with a fine large bay horse, took his daughter and proceeded to Concord. On his return a violent storm overtook him. At dark he stopped in Menotomy, now West Cambridge, at the door of a Mr. Cutter, a friend of his, who urged him to tarry the night. On Rugg's declining to stop, Mr. Cutter urged him vehemently. 'Why, Mr. Rugg,' said Cutter, 'the storm is overwhelming you. The night is exceedingly dark. Your little daughter will perish. You are in an open chair, and the tempest is increasing.' '*Let the storm increase,*' said Rugg, with a fearful oath, '*I will see home tonight, in spite of the last tempest, or may I never see home!*' At these words he gave his whip to his high-spirited horse and disappeared in a moment. But Peter Rugg did not reach home that night, nor the next; nor, when he became a missing man, could he ever be traced beyond Mr. Cutter's, in Menotomy.

"For a long time after, on every dark and stormy night the wife of

Peter Rugg would fancy she heard the crack of a whip, and the fleet tread of a horse, and the rattling of a carriage passing her door. The neighbours, too, heard the same noises, and some said they knew it was Rugg's horse; the tread on the pavement was perfectly familiar to them. This occurred so repeatedly that at length the neighbours watched with lanterns, and saw the real Peter Rugg, with his own horse and chair and the child sitting beside him, pass directly before his own door, his head turned towards his house, and himself making every effort to stop his horse, but in vain.

"The next day the friends of Mrs. Rugg exerted themselves to find her husband and child. They inquired at every public-house and stable in town; but it did not appear that Rugg made any stay in Boston. No one, after Rugg had passed his own door, could give any account of him, though it was asserted by some that the clatter of Rugg's horse and carriage over the pavements shook the houses on both sides of the streets. And this is credible, if indeed Rugg's horse and carriage did pass on that night; for at this day, in many of the streets, a loaded truck or team in passing will shake the houses like an earthquake. However, Rugg's neighbours never afterward watched. Some of them treated it all as a delusion, and thought no more of it. Others of a different opinion shook their heads and said nothing.

"Thus Rugg and his child, horse, and chair were soon forgotten; and probably many in the neighbourhood never heard a word on the subject.

"There was indeed a rumour that Rugg was seen afterward in Connecticut, between Suffield and Hartford, passing through the country at headlong speed. This gave occasion to Rugg's friends to make further inquiry; but the more they inquired, the more they were baffled. If they heard of Rugg one day in Connecticut, the next they heard of him winding round the hills in New Hampshire; and soon after a man in a chair, with a small child, exactly answering the description of Peter Rugg, would be seen in Rhode Island inquiring the way to Boston.

"But that which chiefly gave a colour of mystery to the story of Peter Rugg was the affair at Charlestown bridge. The toll-gatherer asserted that sometimes, on the darkest and most stormy nights, when no object could be discerned, about the time Rugg was missing, a horse and wheel-carriage, with a noise equal to a troop, would at midnight, in utter contempt of the rates of toll, pass over the bridge. This occurred so frequently that the toll-gatherer resolved to attempt a discovery. Soon after, at the usual time, apparently the same horse and carriage approached the bridge from Charlestown Square. The toll-gatherer, prepared, took his stand as near the middle of the bridge as he dared, with a large three-legged stool in his hand; as the appearance passed, he threw the stool at the horse, but heard nothing except the noise of the stool skipping across the bridge. The toll-gatherer on the next day asserted that the stool went directly through the body of the horse, and he persisted in that belief ever after. Whether Rugg, or whoever the person was, ever passed the bridge again, the toll-gatherer would never tell; and when questioned, seemed anxious to waive the subject. And thus Peter Rugg and his child, horse, and carriage, remain a mystery to this day."

This, sir, is all that I could learn of Peter Rugg in Boston.

FURTHER ACCOUNT OF PETER RUGG

By *Jonathan Dunwell*

In the autumn of 1825 I attended the races at Richmond in Virginia. As two new horses of great promise were run, the race-ground was never better attended, nor was expectation ever more deeply excited. The partisans of Dart and Lightning, the two racehorses, were equally anxious and equally dubious of the result. To an indifferent spectator, it was impossible to perceive any difference. They were equally beautiful to behold, alike in colour and height, and as they stood side by side they measured from heel to forefeet within half an inch of each other. The eyes of each were full, prominent, and resolute; and when at times they regarded each other, they assumed a lofty demeanour, seemed to shorten their necks, project their eyes, and rest their bodies equally on their four hoofs. They certainly showed signs of intelligence, and displayed a courtesy to each other unusual even with statesmen.

It was now nearly twelve o'clock, the hour of expectation, doubt, and anxiety. The riders mounted their horses; and so trim, light, and airy they sat on the animals as to seem a part of them. The spectators, many deep in a solid column, had taken their places, and as many thousand breathing statues were there as spectators. All eyes were turned to Dart and Lightning and their two fairy riders. There was nothing to disturb this calm except a busy woodpecker on a neighbouring tree. The signal was given, and Dart and Lightning answered it with ready intelligence. At first they proceed at a slow trot, then they quicken to a canter, and then a gallop; presently they sweep the plain. Both horses lay themselves flat on the ground, their riders bending forward and resting their chins between their horses' ears. Had not the ground been perfectly level, had there been any undulation, the least rise and fall, the spectator would now and then have lost sight of both horses and riders.

While these horses, side by side, thus appeared, flying without wings, flat as a hare, and neither gaining on the other, all eyes were diverted to a new spectacle. Directly in the rear of Dart and Lightning, a majestic black horse of unusual size, drawing an old weather-beaten chair, strode over the plain; and although he appeared to make no effort, for he maintained a steady trot, before Dart and Lightning approached the goal the black horse and chair had overtaken the racers, who, on perceiving this new competitor pass them, threw back their ears, and suddenly stopped in their course. Thus neither Dart nor Lightning carried away the purse.

The spectators now were exceedingly curious to learn whence came the black horse and chair. With many it was the opinion that nobody was in the vehicle. Indeed, this began to be the prevalent opinion; for those at a short distance, so fleet was the black horse, could not easily discern who, if anybody, was in the carriage. But both the riders, very near to whom the black horse passed, agreed in this particular—that a sad-looking man and a little girl were in the chair. When they stated this I was satisfied that the man was Peter Rugg. But what caused no little surprise, John Spring, one of the riders (he who rode Lightning), asserted that no earthly horse without breaking his trot could, in a carriage, outstrip his racehorse, and he persisted, with some passion, that it was not a horse—or, he was sure it was not a horse, but a large black ox. "What a great black ox can do," said John, "I cannot pretend to say; but no racehorse, not even flying Childers, could out-trot Lightning in a fair race."

This opinion of John Spring excited no little merriment, for it was obvious to everyone that it was a powerful black horse that interrupted the race; but John Spring, jealous of Lightning's reputation as a horse, would rather have it thought that any other beast, even an ox, had been the victor. However, the "horse-laugh" at John Spring's expense was soon suppressed; for as soon as Dart and Lightning began to breathe more freely, it was observed that both of them walked deliberately to the track of the race-ground, and putting their heads to the earth, suddenly raised them again and began to snort. They repeated this till John Spring said, "These horses have discovered something strange; they suspect foul play. Let me go and talk with Lightning."

He went up to Lightning and took hold of his mane; and Lightning put his nose toward the ground and smelt of the earth without touching it, then reared his head very high, and snorted so loudly that the sound echoed from the next hill. Dart did the same. John Spring stooped down to examine the spot where Lightning had smelled. In a moment he raised himself up, and the countenance of the man was changed. His strength failed him, and he sidled against Lightning.

At length John Spring recovered from his stupor, and exclaimed, "It was an ox! I told you it was an ox. No real horse ever yet beat Lightning."

And, now, on a close inspection of the black horse's tracks in the path, it was evident to everyone that the forefeet of the black horse were cloven. Notwithstanding these appearances, to me it was evident that the strange horse was in reality a horse. Yet when the people left the race-ground, I presume one-half of all those present would have testified that a large black ox had distanced two of the fleetest coursers that ever trod the Virginia turf. So uncertain are all things called historical facts.

While I was proceeding to my lodgings, pondering on the events of the day, a stranger rode up to me, and accosted me thus, "I think your name is Dunwell, sir."

"Yes, sir," I replied.

"Did I not see you a year or two since in Boston, at the Marlborough Hotel?"

"Very likely, sir, for I was there."

"And you heard a story about one Peter Rugg?"

"I recollect it all," said I.

"The account you heard in Boston must be true, for here he was to-day. The man has found his way to Virginia, and for aught that appears, has been to Cape Horn. I have seen him before today, but never saw him travel with such fearful velocity. Pray, sir, where does Peter Rugg spend his winters, for I have seen him only in summer, and always in foul weather except this time?"

I replied, "No one knows where Peter Rugg spends his winters; where or when he eats, drinks, sleeps, or lodges. He seems to have an indistinct idea of day and night, time and space, storm and sunshine. His only object is Boston. It appears to me that Rugg's horse has some control of the chair; and that Rugg himself is, in some sort, under the control of his horse."

I then inquired of the stranger where he first saw the man and horse.

"Why, sir," said he, "in the summer of 1824, I travelled to the North for my health; and soon after I saw you at the Marlborough Hotel I returned homeward to Virginia, and, if my memory is correct, I saw this man and horse in every state between here and Massachusetts. Sometimes he would meet me, but oftener overtake me. He never spoke but once, and that once was in Delaware. On his approach he checked his horse with some difficulty. A more beautiful horse I never saw; his hide was as fair and rotund and glossy as the skin of a Congo beauty. When Rugg's horse approached mine he reined in his neck, bent his ears forward until they met, and looked my horse full in the face. My horse immediately withered into half a horse, his hide curling up like a piece of burnt leather; spellbound, he was fixed to the earth as though a nail had been driven through each hoof.

" 'Sir,' said Rugg, 'perhaps you are travelling to Boston; and if so, I should be happy to accompany you, for I have lost my way, and I must reach home tonight. See how sleepy this little girl looks; poor thing, she is a picture of patience.'

" 'Sir,' said I, 'it is impossible for you to reach home tonight, for you are in Concord, in the county of Sussex, in the state of Delaware.'

" 'What do you mean,' said he, 'by state of Delaware? If I were in Concord, that is only twenty miles from Boston, and my horse Lightfoot could carry me to Charlestown ferry in less than two hours. You mistake, sir; you are a stranger here; this town is nothing like Concord. I am well acquainted with Concord. I went to Concord when I left Boston.'

" 'But,' said I, 'you are in Concord, in the state of Delaware.'

" 'What do you mean by state?' said Rugg.

" 'Why, one of the United States.'

" 'States!' said he, in a low voice; 'the man is a wag, and would persuade me I am in Holland.' Then, raising his voice, he said, 'You seem, sir, to be a gentleman, and I entreat you to mislead me not; tell me, quickly, for pity's sake, the right road to Boston, for you see my horse will swallow his bits; he has eaten nothing since I left Concord.'

" 'Sir,' said I, 'this town is Concord—Concord in Delaware, not Concord in Massachusetts; and you are now five hundred miles from Boston.'

"Rugg looked at me for a moment, more in sorrow than resentment, and then repeated, 'Five hundred miles! Unhappy man, who would have thought him deranged; but nothing in this world is so deceitful as appearances. Five hundred miles! This beats Connecticut River.'

"What he meant by Connecticut River, I know not; his horse broke away, and Rugg disappeared in a moment."

I explained to the stranger the meaning of Rugg's expression, "Connecticut River," and the incident respecting him that occurred at Hartford, as I stood on the door-stone of Mr. Bennett's excellent hotel. We both agreed that the man we had seen that day was the true Peter Rugg.

Soon after, I saw Rugg again, at the toll-gate on the turnpike between Alexandria and Middleburgh. While I was paying the toll, I observed to the toll-gatherer that the drought was more severe in his vicinity than farther south.

"Yes," said he, "the drought is excessive; but if I had not heard yesterday, by a traveller, that the man with the black horse was seen in Kentucky a day or two since, I should be sure of a shower in a few minutes."

I looked all around the horizon, and could not discern a cloud that could hold a pint of water.

"Look, sir," said the toll-gatherer, "you perceive to the eastward, just above that hill, a small black cloud not bigger than a blackberry, and while I am speaking it is doubling and trebling itself, and rolling up the turnpike steadily, as if its sole design was to deluge some object."

"True," said I, "I do perceive it; but what connexion is there between a thunder-cloud and a man and horse?"

"More than you imagine, or I can tell you; but stop a moment, sir, I may need your assistance. I know that cloud; I have seen it several times before, and can testify to its identity. You will soon see a man and black horse under it."

While he was speaking, true enough, we began to hear the distant thunder, and soon the chain lightning performed all the figures of a country-dance. About a mile distant we saw the man and black horse under the cloud; but before he arrived at the toll-gate, the thunder-cloud had spent itself, and not even a sprinkle fell near us.

As the man, whom I instantly knew to be Rugg, attempted to pass, the toll-gatherer swung the gate across the road, seized Rugg's horse by the reins, and demanded two dollars.

Feeling some little regard for Rugg, I interfered, and began to question the toll-gatherer, and requested him not to be wroth with the man. The toll-gatherer replied that he had just cause, for the man had run his toll ten times, and moreover that the horse had discharged a cannon-ball at him, to the great danger of his life; that the man had always before approached so rapidly that he was too quick for the rusty hinges of the toll-gate; "but now I will have full satisfaction."

Rugg looked wistfully at me, and said, "I entreat you, sir, to delay me not; I have found at length the direct road to Boston, and shall not reach home before night if you detain me. You see I am dripping wet, and ought to change my clothes."

The toll-gatherer then demanded why he had run his toll so many times.

"Toll! Why," said Rugg, "do you demand toll? There is no toll to pay on the king's highway."

"King's highway! Do you not perceive this is a turnpike?"

"Turnpike! There are no turnpikes in Massachusetts."

"That may be, but we have several in Virginia."

"Virginia! Do you pretend I am in Virginia?"

Rugg then, appealing to me, asked how far it was to Boston.

Said I, "Mr. Rugg, I perceive you are bewildered, and am sorry to see you so far from home; you are, indeed, in Virginia."

"You know me, then, sir, it seems; and you say I am in Virginia. Give me leave to tell you, sir, you are the most impudent man alive; for I was never forty miles from Boston, and I never saw a Virginian in my life. This beats Delaware!"

"Your toll, sir, your toll!"

"I will not pay you a penny," said Rugg; "you are both of you highway robbers. There are no turnpikes in this country. Take toll on the king's highway! Robbers take toll on the king's highway!" Then in a low tone he said, "Here is evidently a conspiracy against me; alas, I shall never see Boston! The highways refuse me a passage, the rivers change their courses, and there is no faith in the compass."

But Rugg's horse had no idea of stopping more than one minute; for in the midst of this altercation, the horse, whose nose was resting on the upper bar of the turnpike-gate, seized it between his teeth, lifted it gently off its staples, and trotted off with it. The toll-gatherer, confounded, strained his eyes after his gate.

"Let him go," said I, "the horse will soon drop your gate, and you will get it again."

I then questioned the toll-gatherer respecting his knowledge of this man; and he related the following particulars:

"The first time," said he, "that man ever passed this toll-gate was in the year 1806, at the moment of the great eclipse. I thought the horse was frightened at the sudden darkness, and concluded he had run away with the man. But within a few days after, the same man and horse repassed with equal speed, without the least respect to the toll-gate or to me, except by a vacant stare. Some few years afterward, during the late war, I saw the same man approaching again, and I resolved to check his career. Accordingly I stepped into the middle of the road, and stretched wide both my arms, and cried, 'Stop, sir, on your peril!' At this the man said, 'Now, Lightfoot, confound the robber!' At the same time he gave the whip liberally to the flank of his horse, which bounded off with such force that it appeared to me two such horses, give them a place to stand, would overcome any check man could devise. An ammunition wagon which had just passed on to Baltimore had dropped an eighteen-pounder in the road; this unlucky ball lay in the way of the horse's heels, and the beast, with the sagacity of a demon, clinched it with of his heels and hurled it behind him. I feel dizzy in relating the fact, but so nearly did the ball pass my head, that the wind thereof blew off my hat; and the ball embedded itself in that gate-post, as you may see if you will cast your eye on the post. I have permitted it to remain there in memory of the occurrence—as the people of Boston, I am told, preserve the eighteen-pounder which is now to be seen half embedded in Brattle Street church."

I then took leave of the toll-gatherer, and promised him if I saw or heard of his gate I would send him notice.

A strong inclination had possessed me to arrest Rugg and search his pockets, thinking great discoveries might be made in the examination; but what I saw and heard that day convinced me that no human force could detain Peter Rugg against his consent. I therefore determined if I ever saw Rugg again to treat him in the gentlest manner.

In pursuing my way to New York, I entered on the turnpike in Trenton; and when I arrived at New Brunswick, I perceived the road was newly macadamized. The small stones had just been laid thereon. As I passed this piece of road, I observed that, at regular distances of about eight feet, the stones were entirely displaced from spots as large as the circumference of a half-bushel measure. This singular appearance induced me to inquire the cause of it at the turnpike-gate.

"Sir," said the toll-gatherer, "I wonder not at the question, but I am unable to give you a satisfactory answer. Indeed, sir, I believe I am bewitched, and that the turnpike is under a spell of enchantment; for what appeared to me last night cannot be a real transaction, otherwise a turnpike-gate is a useless thing."

"I do not believe in witchcraft or enchantment," said I; "and if you will relate circumstantially what happened last night, I will endeavour to account for it by natural means."

"You may recollect the night was uncommonly dark. Well, sir, just after I had closed the gate for the night, down the turnpike, as far as my eye could reach, I beheld what at first appeared to be two armies engaged. The report of the musketry, and the flashes of their firelocks, were incessant and continuous. As this strange spectacle approached me with the fury of a tornado, the noise increased; and the appearance rolled on in one compact body over the surface of the ground. The most splendid fireworks rose out of the earth and encircled this moving spectacle. The divers tints of the rainbow, the most brilliant dyes that the sun lays in the lap of spring, added to the whole family of gems, could not display a more beautiful, radiant, and dazzling spectacle than accompanied the black horse. You would have thought all the stars of heaven had met in merriment on the turnpike. In the midst of this luminous configuration sat a man, distinctly to be seen, in a miserable-looking chair, drawn by a black horse. The turnpike-gate ought, by the laws of nature and the laws of the state, to have made a wreck of the whole, and have dissolved the enchantment; but no, the horse without an effort passed over the gate, and drew the man and chair horizontally after him without touching the bar. This was what I call enchantment. What think you, sir?"

"My friend," said I, "you have grossly magnified a natural occurrence. The man was Peter Rugg, on his way to Boston. It is true, his horse travelled with unequalled speed, but as he reared high his forefeet, he could not help displacing the thousand small stones on which he trod, which flying in all directions struck one another, and resounded and scintillated. The top bar of your gate is not more than two feet from the ground, and Rugg's horse at every vault could easily lift the carriage over that gate."

This satisfied Mr. McDoubt, and I was pleased at that occurrence; for otherwise Mr. McDoubt, who is a worthy man, late from the Highlands, might have added to his calendar of superstitions. Having thus disenchanted the macadamized road and the turnpike-gate, and also Mr. McDoubt, I pursued my journey homeward to New York.

Little did I expect to see or hear anything further of Mr. Rugg, for he was now more than twelve hours in advance of me. I could hear nothing of him on my way to Elizabethtown, and therefore concluded that during the past night he had turned off from the turnpike and pursued a westerly direction; but just before I arrived at Powles's Hook, I observed a considerable collection of passengers in the ferry-boat, all standing motionless, and steadily looking at the same object. One of the ferry-men, Mr. Hardy, who knew me well, observing my approach delayed a minute, in order to afford me a passage, and coming up, said, "Mr. Dunwell, we have a curiosity on board that would puzzle Dr. Mitchell."

"Some strange fish, I suppose, has found its way into the Hudson?"

"No," said he, "it is a man who looks as if he had lain hidden in the ark, and had just now ventured out. He has a little girl with him, the counterpart of himself, and the finest horse you ever saw, harnessed to the queerest-looking carriage that ever was made."

"Ah, Mr. Hardy," said I, "you have, indeed, hooked a prize; no one before you could ever detain Peter Rugg long enough to examine him."

"Do you know the man?" said Mr. Hardy.

"No, nobody knows him, but everybody has seen him. Detain him as long as possible; delay the boat under any pretence, cut the gear of the horse, do anything to detain him."

As I entered the ferry-boat, I was struck at the spectacle before me. There, indeed, sat Peter Rugg and Jenny Rugg in the chair, and there stood the black horse, all as quiet as lambs, surrounded by more than fifty men and women, who seemed to have lost all their senses but one.

Not a motion, not a breath, not a rustle. They were all eye. Rugg appeared to them to be a man not of this world; and they appeared to Rugg a strange generation of men. Rugg spoke not, and they spoke not; nor was I disposed to disturb the calm, satisfied to reconnoitre Rugg in a state of rest. Presently, Rugg observed in a low voice, addressed to nobody, "A new contrivance, horses instead of oars; Boston folks are full of notions."

It was plain that Rugg was of Dutch extraction. He had on three pairs of small clothes, called in former days of simplicity breeches, not much the worse for wear; but time had proved the fabric, and shrunk one more than another, so that they showed at the knees their different qualities and colours. His several waistcoats, the flaps of which rested on his knees, made him appear rather corpulent. His capacious drab coat would supply the stuff for half a dozen modern ones; the sleeves were like meal bags, in the cuffs of which you might nurse a child to sleep. His hat, probably once black, now of a tan colour, was neither round nor crooked, but in shape much like the one President Monroe wore on his late tour. This dress gave the rotund face of Rugg an antiquated dignity. The man, though deeply sunburned, did not appear to be more than thirty years of age. He had lost his sad and anxious look, was quite composed, and seemed happy. The chair in which Rugg sat was very capacious, evidently made for service, and calculated to last for ages; the timber would supply material for three modern carriages. This chair, like a Nantucket coach, would answer for everything that ever went on wheels. The horse, too, was an object of curiosity; his majestic height, his natural mane and tail, gave him a commanding appearance, and his large open nostrils indicated inexhaustible wind. It was apparent that the hoofs of his forefeet had been split, probably on some newly macadamized road, and were now growing together again; so that John Spring was not altogether in the wrong.

How long this dumb scene would otherwise have continued I cannot tell. Rugg discovered no sign of impatience. But Rugg's horse having been quiet more than five minutes, had no idea of standing idle; he began to whinny, and in a moment after, with his right forefoot he started a plank. Said Rugg, "My horse is impatient, he sees the North End. You must be quick, or he will be ungovernable."

At these words, the horse raised his left forefoot; and when he laid it down every inch of the ferry-boat trembled. Two men immediately seized Rugg's horse by the nostrils. The horse nodded, and both of them were in the Hudson. While we were fishing up the men, the horse was perfectly quiet.

"Fret not the horse," said Rugg, "and he will do no harm. He is only anxious, like myself, to arrive at yonder beautiful shore; he sees the North Church, and smells his own stable."

"Sir," said I to Rugg, practising a little deception, "pray tell me, for I am a stranger here, what river is this, and what city is that opposite, for you seem to be an inhabitant of it?"

"This river, sir, is called Mystic River, and this is Winnisimmet ferry—we have retained the Indian names—and that town is Boston. You must, indeed, be a stranger in these parts, not to know that yonder is Boston, the capital of the New England provinces."

"Pray, sir, how long have you been absent from Boston?"

"Why, that I cannot exactly tell. I lately went with this little girl of mine to Concord, to see my friends; and I am ashamed to tell you, in returning lost the way, and have been travelling ever since. No one would direct me right. It is cruel to mislead a traveller. My horse, Lightfoot, has boxed the compass; and it seems to me he has boxed it back again. But, sir, you perceive my horse is uneasy; Lightfoot, as yet, has only given a hint and a nod. I cannot be answerable for his heels."

At these words Lightfoot reared his long tail, and snapped it as you would a whiplash. The Hudson reverberated with the sound. Instantly the six horses began to move the boat. The Hudson was a sea of glass, smooth as oil, not a ripple. The horses, from a smart trot, soon passed into a gallop; water now ran over the gunwale; the ferry-boat was soon buried in an ocean of foam, and the noise of the spray was like the roaring of many waters. When we arrived at New York, you might see the beautiful white wake of the ferry-boat across the Hudson.

Though Rugg refused to pay toll at turnpikes, when Mr. Hardy reached his hand for the ferriage, Rugg readily put his hand into one of his many pockets, took out a piece of silver, and handed it to Hardy.

"What is this?" said Mr. Hardy.

"It is thirty shillings," said Rugg.

"It might once have been thirty shillings, old tenor," said Mr. Hardy, "but it is not at present."

"The money is good English coin," said Rugg; "my grandfather brought a bag of them from England, and had them hot from the mint."

Hearing this, I approached near to Rugg, and asked permission to see the coin. It was a half-crown, coined by the English Parliament, dated in the year 1649. On one side, "The Commonwealth of England," and St. George's cross encircled with a wreath of laurel. On the other, "God with us," and a harp and St. George's cross united. I winked at Mr. Hardy, and pronounced it good current money; and said loudly, "I will not permit the gentleman to be imposed on, for I will exchange the money myself."

On this, Rugg spoke. "Please to give me your name, sir."

"My name is Dunwell, sir," I replied.

"Mr. Dunwell," said Rugg, "you are the only honest man I have seen since I left Boston. As you are a stranger here, my house is your home; Dame Rugg will be happy to see her husband's friend. Step into my chair, sir, there is room enough; move a little, Jenny, for the gentleman, and we will be in Middle Street in a minute."

Accordingly I took a seat by Peter Rugg.

"Were you never in Boston before?" said Rugg.

"No," said I.

"Well, you will now see the queen of New England, a town second only to Philadelphia, in all North America."

"You forget New York," said I.

"Poh, New York is nothing; though I never was there. I am told you might put all New York in our mill-pond. No, sir, New York, I assure you, is but a sorry affair; no more to be compared with Boston than a wigwam with a palace."

As Rugg's horse turned into Pearl Street, I looked Rugg as fully in the face as good manners would allow, and said, "Sir, if this is Boston, I acknowledge New York is not worthy to be one of its suburbs."

Before we had proceeded far in Pearl Street, Rugg's countenance changed: his nerves began to twitch; his eyes trembled in their sockets; he was evidently bewildered. "What is the matter, Mr. Rugg? You seem disturbed."

"This surpasses all human comprehension; if you know, sir, where we are, I beseech you to tell me."

"If this place," I replied, "is not Boston, it must be New York."

"No, sir, it is not Boston; nor can it be New York. How could I be in New York, which is nearly two hundred miles from Boston?"

By this time we had passed into Broadway, and then Rugg, in truth, discovered a chaotic mind. "There is no such place as this in North America. This is all the effect of enchantment; this is a grand delusion, nothing real. Here is seemingly a great city, magnificent houses, shops and goods, men and women innumerable, and as busy as in real life, all sprung up in one night from the wilderness; or what is more probable, some tremendous convulsion of nature has thrown London or Amsterdam on the shores of New England. Or, possibly, I may be dreaming, though the night seems rather long; but before now I have sailed in one night to Amsterdam, bought goods of Vandogger, and returned to Boston before morning."

At this moment a hue and cry was heard: "Stop the madmen, they will endanger the lives of thousands!" In vain hundreds attempted to stop Rugg's horse. Lightfoot interfered with nothing; his course was straight as a shooting-star. But on my part, fearful that before night I should find myself behind the Alleghenies, I addressed Mr. Rugg in a tone of entreaty, and requested him to restrain the horse and permit me to alight.

"My friend," said he, "we shall be in Boston before dark, and Dame Rugg will be most exceedingly glad to see us."

"Mr. Rugg," said I, "you must excuse me. Pray look to the west; see that thunder-cloud swelling with rage, as if in pursuit of us."

"Ah!" said Rugg, "it is in vain to attempt to escape. I know that cloud; it is collecting new wrath to spend on my head." Then checking his horse, he permitted me to descend, saying, "Farewell, Mr. Dun-well, I shall be happy to see you in Boston; I live in Middle Street."

It is uncertain in what direction Mr. Rugg pursued his course, after he disappeared in Broadway; but one thing is sufficiently known to everybody—that in the course of two months after he was seen in New York, he found his way most opportunely to Boston.

It seems the estate of Peter Rugg had recently fallen to the Common-wealth of Massachusetts for want of heirs; and the Legislature had or-dered the solicitor-general to advertise and sell it at public auction. Happening to be in Boston at the time, and observing his advertise-ment, which described a considerable extent of land, I felt a kindly curiosity to see the spot where Rugg once lived. Taking the advertise-ment in my hand, I wandered a little way down Middle Street, and without asking a question of anyone, when I came to a certain spot I said to myself, "This is Rugg's estate; I will proceed no farther. This must be the spot; it is a counterpart of Peter Rugg." The premises, in-deed, looked as if they had fulfilled a sad prophecy. Fronting on Mid-dle Street, they extended in the rear to Ann Street, and embraced about half an acre of land. It was not uncommon in former times to have half an acre for a house-lot; for an acre of land then, in many parts of Bos-ton, was not more valuable than a foot in some places at present. The old mansion-house had become a powder-post, and been blown away. One other building, uninhabited, stood ominous, courting dilapidation. The street had been so much raised that the bedchamber had descended to the kitchen and was level with the street. The house seemed con-scious of its fate; and as though tired of standing there, the front was fast retreating from the rear, and waiting the next south wind to project itself into the street. If the most wary animals had sought a place of refuge, here they would have rendezvoused. Here, under the ridge-pole, the crow would have perched in security; and in the re-cesses below, you might have caught the fox and the weasel asleep. "The hand of destiny," said I, "has pressed heavy on this spot; still heavier on the former owners. Strange that so large a lot of land as this should want an heir! Yet Peter Rugg, at this day, might pass by his own door-stone, and ask, 'Who once lived here?'"

The auctioneer, appointed by the solicitor to sell this estate, was a man of eloquence, as many of the auctioneers of Boston are. The occasion seemed to warrant, and his duty urged, him to make a display. He addressed his audience as follows:

"The estate, gentlemen, which we offer you this day, was once the property of a family now extinct. For that reason it has escheated to the Commonwealth. Lest any one of you should be deterred from bidding on so large an estate as this for fear of a disputed title, I am authorized by the solicitor-general to proclaim that the purchaser shall have the best of all titles—a warranty-deed from the Commonwealth. I state this, gentlemen, because I know there is an idle rumour in this vicinity that one Peter Rugg, the original owner of this estate, is still living. This rumour, gentlemen, has no foundation, and can have no foundation in the nature of things. It originated about two years since, from the incredible story of one Jonathan Dunwell, of New York. Mrs. Croft, indeed, whose husband I see present, and whose mouth waters for this estate, has countenanced this fiction. But, gentlemen, was it ever known that any estate, especially an estate of this value, lay unclaimed for nearly half a century, if any heir, ever so remote, were existing? For, gentlemen, all agree that old Peter Rugg, if living, would be at least one hundred years of age. It is said that he and his daughter, with a horse and chaise, were missed more than half a century ago; and because they never returned home, forsooth, they must be now living, and will some day come and claim this great estate. Such logic, gentlemen, never led to a good investment. Let not this idle story cross the noble purpose of consigning these ruins to the genius of architecture. If such a contingency could check the spirit of enterprise, farewell to all mercantile excitement. Your surplus money, instead of refreshing your sleep with the golden dreams of new sources of speculation, would turn to the nightmare. A man's money, if not employed, serves only to disturb his rest. Look, then, to the prospect before you. Here is half an acre of land—more than twenty thousand square feet— a corner lot, with wonderful capabilities; none of your contracted lots of forty feet by fifty, where, in dog-days, you can breathe only through your scuttles. On the contrary, an architect cannot contemplate this lot of land without rapture, for here is room enough for his genius to shame the temple of Solomon. Then the prospect—how commanding! To the east, so near to the Atlantic that Neptune, freighted with the select treasures of the whole earth, can knock at your door with his trident. From the west, the produce of the river of Paradise—the Connecticut —will soon, by the blessings of steam, railways, and canals, pass under your windows; and thus, on this spot, Neptune shall marry Ceres, and Pomona from Roxbury, and Flora from Cambridge, shall dance at the wedding.

"Gentlemen of science, men of taste, ye of the literary emporium— for I perceive many of you present—to you this is holy ground. If the spot on which in times past a hero left only the print of a footstep is now sacred, of what price is the birthplace of one who all the world knows was born in Middle Street, directly opposite to this lot; and who, if his birthplace were not well known, would now be claimed by more than seven cities! To you, then, the value of these premises must be inestimable. For ere long there will arise in full view of the edifice to be erected here, a monument, the wonder and veneration of the world. A column shall spring to the clouds; and on that column will be engraven one word which will convey all that is wise in intellect, useful in science, good in morals, prudent in counsel, and benevolent in principle—a name of one who, when living, was the patron of the poor, the delight of the cottage, and the admiration of kings; now dead, worth the whole seven wise men of Greece. Need I tell you his name? He fixed the thunder and guided the lightning.

"Men of the North End! Need I appeal to your patriotism, in order to enhance the value of this lot? The earth affords no such scenery as this; there, around that corner, lived James Otis; here, Samuel Adams; there, Joseph Warren; and around that other corner, Josiah Quincy. Here was the birthplace of Freedom; here Liberty was born, and nursed, and grew to manhood. Here man was newly created. Here is the nursery of American Independence—I am too modest—here began the emancipation of the world; a thousand generations hence, millions of men will cross the Atlantic just to look at the North End of Boston.

Your fathers—what do I say!—yourselves—yes, this moment, I behold several attending this auction who lent a hand to rock the cradle of Independence.

"Men of speculation—ye who are deaf to everything except the sound of money—you, I know, will give me both of your ears when I tell you the city of Boston must have a piece of this estate in order to widen Ann Street. Do you hear me—do you all hear me? I say the city must have a large piece of this land in order to widen Ann Street. What a chance! The city scorns to take a man's land for nothing. If it seizes your property, it is generous beyond the dreams of avarice. The only oppression is, you are in danger of being smothered under a load of wealth. Witness the old lady who lately died of a broken heart when the mayor paid her for a piece of her kitchen-garden. All the faculty agreed that the sight of the treasure, which the mayor incautiously paid her in dazzling dollars, warm from the mint, sped joyfully all the blood of her body into her heart, and rent it with raptures. Therefore, let him who purchases this estate fear his good fortune, and not Peter Rugg. Bid, then, liberally, and do not let the name of Rugg damp your ardour. How much will you give per foot for this estate?"

Thus spoke the auctioneer, and gracefully waved his ivory hammer. From fifty to seventy-five cents per foot were offered in a few moments. The bidding laboured from seventy-five to ninety. At length one dollar was offered. The auctioneer seemed satisfied; and looking at his watch, said he would knock off the estate in five minutes, if no one offered more.

There was a deep silence during this short period. While the hammer was suspended, a strange rumbling noise was heard, which arrested the attention of everyone. Presently, it was like the sound of many shipwrights driving home the bolts of a seventy-four. As the sound approached nearer, some exclaimed, "The buildings in the new market are falling in promiscuous ruins." Others said, "No, it is an earthquake; we perceive the earth tremble." Others said, "Not so; the sound proceeds from Hanover Street, and approaches nearer"; and this proved true, for presently Peter Rugg was in the midst of us.

"Alas, Jenny," said Peter, "I am ruined; our house has been burned, and here are all our neighbours around the ruins. Heaven grant your mother, Dame Rugg, is safe."

"They don't look like our neighbours," said Jenny; "but sure enough our house is burned, and nothing left but the door-stone and an old cedar post. Do ask where mother is."

In the meantime more than a thousand men had surrounded Rugg and his horse and chair. Yet neither Rugg personally, nor his horse and carriage, attracted more attention than the auctioneer. The confident look and searching eyes of Rugg carried more conviction to everyone present that the estate was his than could any parchment or paper with signature and seal. The impression which the auctioneer had just made on the company was effaced in a moment; and although the latter words of the auctioneer were, "Fear not Peter Rugg," the moment the auctioneer met the eye of Rugg his occupation was gone; his arm fell down to his hips, his late lively hammer hung heavy in his hand, and the auction was forgotten. The black horse, too, gave his evidence. He knew his journey was ended; for he stretched himself into a horse and a half, rested his head over the cedar post, and whinnied thrice, causing his harness to tremble from headstall to crupper.

Rugg then stood upright in his chair, and asked with some authority, "Who has demolished my house in my absence, for I see no signs of a conflagration? I demand by what accident this has happened, and wherefore this collection of strange people has assembled before my door-step. I thought I knew every man in Boston, but you appear to me a new generation of men. Yet I am familiar with many of the countenances here present, and I can call some of you by name; but in truth I do not recollect that before this moment I ever saw any one of you. There, I am certain, is a Winslow, and here a Sargent; there stands a Sewall, and next to him a Dudley. Will none of you speak to me—or is this all a delusion? I see, indeed, many forms of men, and no want of eyes, but of motion, speech, and hearing, you seem to be destitute. Strange! Will no one inform me who has demolished my house?"

Then spake a voice from the crowd, but whence it came I could not discern. "There is nothing strange here but yourself, Mr. Rugg. Time, which destroys and renews all things, has dilapidated your house, and placed us here. You have suffered many years under an illusion. The tempest which you profanely defied at Menotomy has at length subsided; but you will never see home, for your house and wife and neighbours have all disappeared. Your estate, indeed, remains, but no home. You were cut off from the last age, and you can never be fitted to the present. Your home is gone, and you can never have another home in this world."

AN AFTERWORD ON
"PETER RUGG,
THE MISSING MAN"

MANY of the works in this volume I have known so long that I cannot now recall from whose hands they first came to mine. But the old yarn about Peter Rugg was nominated for this anthology by one who was himself such a master that the most heedless reader would have paused to examine any short-story he had seen fit to recommend. It was Rudyard Kipling who set A. S. Frere-Reeves, the English publisher, on the track of this American classic which had long fallen into obscurity in its own country. It was Mr. Frere-Reeves who passed it on to me.

For more than a century the adventure of Peter Rugg has been part of the folklore of America. In New England particularly it has long been such an old wives' tale as nurses tell to children in the twilight. The late Amy Lowell has testified that it was an abiding fear of her own childhood. "How often," she said, "have I driven through the hush which precedes a thunderstorm, all of a tremble lest I should meet the old man in the yellow-wheeled chaise." As such Louise Imogen Guiney heard it and made it into a poem called "Peter Rugg, the Bostonian." And, recalling it from her own days in the nursery, Miss Lowell herself, as recently as 1917, used it for "Before the Storm," an experiment in clotted narrative which she elected to call "polyphonic prose." I submit a sample.

From Kittery Point down to Cape Cod, trundle the high turning wheels; they rattle at the Canadian line; they shine in the last saffron glitter of an extinguishing sun by the ferry over Lake Champlain; they are seen again as the moon dips into an inky cloud passing the Stadium in Cambridge, the driver bowed over the dasher and plying his whip; they flash beside graveyards, and thunder lashes the grave-yard trees. Always the chaise flees before the approaching storm. And always, down the breeze, blowing backwards through the bending trees, comes the despairing wail—"Boston!—For the love of God, put me on the road to Boston!" Then the gale grows louder, lightning spurts and dazzles, and steel-white rain falls heavily out of the sky. A great clap of thunder, and purple-black darkness blinding the earth.

These and other versions were published in all innocence that here was no true legend but a fiction invented by a Massachusetts lawyer and by him contributed in two parts to a magazine called the *New England Galaxy*—the first part appearing in 1824 and the second two years later. It is thus occasionally given to a writer to spin a tale which escapes from the printed page and journeys across the years by word of mouth—such a tale, let us say, as Mrs. Shelley's story of Frankenstein or Irving's yarn of Rip Van Winkle or Mr. Stevenson's parable about Dr. Jekyll and Mr. Hyde, each of which is familiar to many who have never read it. In this distinguished company "Peter Rugg" belongs.

It was one of four tales written by William Austin, a lawyer who lived and died in Charlestown, Massachusetts, and would have been born there, too, if, just as his advent into the world was expected, the redcoats during the Battle of Bunker Hill had not set torch to Charlestown and burned it to the ground, meeting-house, courthouse, schoolhouse, dwellings, and all. Austin was graduated from Harvard in 1798 in the same class with Joseph Story and William Ellery Channing and the elder Longfellow. His tale of Peter Rugg was an immense success when it was new, and reprints of it circulated all over the new country. At the time of its first appearance, as we know from ample evidence, it made a profound impression on a young undergraduate at Bowdoin—a lad named Nathaniel Hawthorne.

A. W.

MY
AUNT DAISY

by

ALBERT HALPER

MY AUNT DAISY

In the late spring, just before the hot weather set in, my mother began receiving letters from Boston, and started to wear a frown. She put the letters in the upper right-hand drawer of the old, scratched-up bureau, because the upper right-hand drawer had had no knob for some time now, and if you wanted to open it you had to pry it from side to side with the ice-pick, or the little screw-driver she kept locked up in the sewing-machine.

Finally, after five or six letters had arrived, my mother began to show her agitation, and to drop, here and there, a hint that her youngest sister Daisy wanted to come to Chicago for a few weeks during the summer. We had heard so much about our aunt Daisy that everybody got excited in the flat and began asking questions—everybody except my father, who sat down to the supper table, chewed his food thoughtfully, and didn't say a word all through the meal. My mother watched him quietly.

"Well," he said at last, "is she as crazy as she used to be?"

He received no answer and went on eating. Later, clearing his throat, reaching over for the sugar-bowl with his short fat arm, he asked the question again, this time scowling a bit.

"She's thirty now," my mother said submissively. "She's no girl any longer. She knows how to act."

"She should get married," said my father, finishing his tea, still frowning. "What she needs is a man!" and he put on his hat and went back to the store, leaving a gloomy feeling in the flat.

He knew my mother's youngest sister, and he did not like her. When he spoke of her he called her a *fitchkhe,* which means a skittish little horse. No, he didn't like her. Before he had come to Chicago to settle down, he had lived for a time in Boston, and he knew Aunt Daisy very well. It was evident, as he left the flat, that he had no strong desire to see her again.

Later on in the evening, when he came back from the store, he took his shoes off and sat for a while in the old rocker in the front room, his heavy face half-cupped in his fist, rocking there for a long time. Finally he yawned, got up tiredly, scratched his head, and went to bed. In the kitchen my mother was putting washing to soak, and her hands fluttered above the tubs.

During the next few weeks the flat was like a powder magazine—everything was tense and silent in the house as soon as my father would come home from the store. If we had been playing in the front room or wrestling on the floor, we stopped as soon as we heard that well-known heavy tread on the stairs, so that when our father opened the door he came into a quiet flat. He'd take his hat off, pull up a chair, and start eating right away, while my mother began serving him.

She was a large woman, almost a full head taller than my father, but it was he who was boss around the house. When he complained about the bad business in his little grocery, when he wailed that the hot weather was spoiling the few slabs of meat in his dinky ice-box and that the chain-stores, which had begun to expand rapidly, had already reached Madison Street, half a mile away, my mother had to contract her face with sympathetic suffering, as if she had a toothache. And if she didn't, he'd holler out that of course it made no difference to her where the money came from just as long as she had a place to eat and sleep in. But right after he'd say this, he'd feel sorry, and would sit there frowning, with a low grumble rumbling deep down in his throat. Then he would go back to the store. My mother would take the dishes from the table after he was gone and would stand at the sink for a long while before turning on the hot water.

Sometimes, late at night, from the dark of their bedroom, I could hear my mother and father talking in low tones.

"But we haven't got room for her," my father would argue. "And besides, it costs something to board her."

But my mother, who had not seen her youngest sister for many years, kept at it. The letters piled up.

Toward the end of June my father, worn away, gave in. My mother wrote to Boston telling her sister to come, and when the train arrived my oldest brother met Aunt Daisy at the station. He brought her home. My oldest brother, about twenty at the time, was somewhat of a dandy, wore a wide straw sailor with a colored ribbon, and was thus delegated to be the family's reception committee. I remember we watched him going up the street toward the trolley on his way to the station, and when he reached he corner he waved back at us because he knew that we were looking, though he really could not see us.

He brought Aunt Daisy home. It was late dusk when they came. The street lamps had not yet lit up, and from the windows we could see Milt struggling with two heavy bags while a little woman walked jauntily at his side. In the fading light we couldn't see her face, and when they got closer to the flat we went away from the front windows because she might look up and see us, so when at last the bell rang we were all excited and her entrance was something of a dramatic event. I could hear the bags bumping as my brother struggled with them up the stairs.

Then we opened the door, Milt set the bags down in the hall, and Aunt Daisy, with a little cry, rushed forward into my mother's arms. My mother couldn't talk for a while; she hadn't seen her sister for over fifteen years.

Milt came inside, shut the door, and dumped the bags in the parlor. "It's dark here!" he shouted. "What's the matter?" and he struck matches and lit the gas-lamps in all the rooms of the flat.

In the sudden light we looked at our mother's sister—we stood there gaping, the whole crew of us, six kids. We saw a small, dark, vivacious woman, who looked to be about twenty, flashing us a smile. There was something vibrant about her, about her nostrils, her eyes and hair, and we fell in love with her at once. On her head she wore a small hat with gray and brown feathers, and she had a way of tilting her chin, of flashing her smile, of looking pertly alert that made me think of a bird. Yes, she was a warm little bird.

She took her hat off right away and stared brightly at us in friendship. My mother's eyes were misty as she saw her sister counting us briskly by placing her forefinger saucily against our foreheads, one by one, and trilling "Tra-la-la-la!"

"I'm your aunt Daisy," she said, then bent down and kissed every one of us while our mother stood by, choking and happy. When she came to my oldest brother, she stopped, flashing us all another smile. "I kissed Milt at the train, but I guess I can kiss him again," and she gave him a real loud smack on the lips. My kid brother, who was about six at the time, jumped up in the air and clapped his hands, so my aunt had to kiss him again also.

Then she breezed through the flat, through the six large gloomy rooms, her heels rapping against the floor, while my mother, middle-aged, gray, tired out by childbearing and household drudgery, walked behind her.

When we reached the front room, we all stood at the windows looking down the darkening street, and at that moment the arc lamps lit up with a sudden burst of light. "See!" she cried as glare and shadow cut the pavement below, and she raised my kid brother in her arms and kissed his cheek again. She was in love with him right away.

On the outskirts my sister, thirteen and lonely in a house of many brothers, edged silently away, and with a sad, lost look stared down at the shining asphalt. She had been dreaming and thinking of our aunt for weeks and wanted so much to have someone to talk to. She stood there with her soft yellow hair in two long plaits hanging down her back, and by the set of her small jaw I knew she was hating her little brother. But Aunt Daisy suddenly turned to her, cuddled her hand, and brought her over. My sister was awkward at first, but it was evident that she liked Aunt Daisy.

Finally Aunt Daisy said: "Where's Isak?" and the flat went quiet.

"He's at the store," my oldest brother answered after a while. "He'll be home pretty soon."

"Maybe you ought to go down and tell him, Milton," my mother put in, pleading.

"He'll be home," Milt said shortly and stared at his straw hat on a hook.

While we waited for our father, our mother showed Aunt Daisy to her room, and I started dragging the heavy bags across the floor, kicking at the brothers who sprang for the handles. I was about nine years old at the time, and puffed from the exertion. My mother told Aunt Daisy that she could have the whole room to herself. "Can you manage it?" said our aunt, knowing we were crowded, then changed the subject.

We were to sleep three in a bed and our sister was to sleep on the sofa. "On the sofa?" Aunt Daisy said in alarm. "No, she's to sleep with me!" This made my sister so very happy that she started crying; she looked at Aunt Daisy as though at that moment she would have kissed her feet.

Then we heard that well-known heavy tread on the bottom stairs. All of us stood crowded in Aunt Daisy's bedroom, waiting. The door slammed.

"Is there a show going on?" shouted our father when he saw all the lights in the flat burning. "What's the meaning of this?" and he strode through the house, turning off all the gas except the parlor jet. He was grumbling to himself, a short, stocky, testy man.

At the threshold of the bedroom he stopped. "Oh . . ." he said, taken slightly aback, and stood looking at my mother's sister, at the trembling smile she flashed at him. What fine teeth she had! They greeted each other quietly, and he asked if the train ride had been hot and dusty. Then he went into his bedroom.

After he went to bed, all of us sat in the parlor with the gas turned low while Aunt Daisy told our mother about the family in Boston. Milt had a date with the daughter of one of the neighbors down the street, but he ran outside and broke it, and then came back. He didn't want to miss the news. Aunt Daisy, speaking low so as not to disturb our father, gave our hungry mother all of it. At that time my grandmother was still alive and also all five of my mother's sisters, all living in Boston or near-by New England cities. My mother was the oldest and had been the first to leave the little village near the Baltic for America; then all had followed. My father, also from the same town, had sent her passage money.

"And how is Mama? How is she?" asked my mother for the fifth

time, and Aunt Daisy said our grandmother was well. Our grandmother ran a little dry-goods store in East Boston and was getting
along all right, Aunt Daisy said. Then came talk about relatives we had
never seen, strange names and little stories connected with every one of
them, with my mother happy and excited and breaking out in her
native tongue every so often. We sat up late until all of us began yawning, and then went to bed.

In the days that followed Aunt Daisy and my mother were always
talking together in the kitchen, in the bedroom, or on the back porch,
reminding each other of various happenings of many years ago. They
spoke all day long about relatives in Europe, about the little village near
Memel on the Baltic, and my mother suddenly remembered old folk
tales, and for the first time in my life I saw her face was beautiful as
she talked about the things she knew. My father grew a trifle less
grouchy, but did not unbend all the way. He still went to bed as soon
as he came back from the store at night. ˙

It was now July, and the mid-summer heat was upon us. It blew in
from the plains in huge hot waves which rolled up the streets, stifling
the town. In the evenings we sat on the back porch, which overlooked
a wide yard below, where all the children of the tenement played ball
until full darkness came on, throwing the ball up and back until it
looked like a gray streak and you wondered how they caught it. Closer
to the wall of the next building the men pitched horse-shoes in pairs,
the big shoes ringing hard against the iron stakes, and the losing side
had to fork up ten cents for a can of beer, which was drunk slowly,
going from mouth to mouth, with the kids begging for a chance to
blow off the foam.

After the men got tired of playing horse-shoes in the dark, they sat
on the stairs below and sang, slowly at first—sad love songs and ballads
of the day. Someone would pull out a mouth-organ, and the men
would sing softly. They were laborers and mechanics mostly, with a
sprinkling of single railroad men who boarded with the families in the
building. They all liked to sing.

The mid-Western twang of their songs was new to Aunt Daisy, and
she started calling us Westerners. She herself spoke with a Bostonian

accent which sounded brittle and odd at first, until we grew accustomed to it.

For the first week or so the entire life of the flat was keyed up, and my mother's thoughtful face lost some of its quiet look. We stayed up later than usual, and Milt went down to the drug-store for a quart of ice-cream almost every night. Aunt Daisy had come with five or six new summer dresses and wore a different one each night, though she did not go out. I believe that she finally spoke to my mother about it, because at the end of the first week my mother had a talk with Milt and a day later Milt started taking Aunt Daisy out.

She was ten years his senior, but on the street she looked so girlish that people took her for Milt's sweetheart. Milt took her downtown to a couple of shows, introduced her to a few of his friends, and then began to worry because he had heard that his girl in the block had started going with another fellow. He grew nervous, dropped Aunt Daisy right away, and tried to straighten things out with his girl.

But the little sip of Loop night life, the lights and music of the downtown restaurants made Aunt Daisy restless and she began to quarrel with Milt. At first he was polite in his answers, but later on, when she grew quick-tempered and told him he owed her a duty as a nephew to take her around, he flew off the handle and answered sharply. My mother tried to smooth things over, but Milt stalked out of the flat and went striding up the street. Daisy locked herself in her bedroom and cried there a long time.

From then on, her visit was not a happy one. Ben, who was the next to the oldest and eighteen at the time, volunteered to take her out, but he was a quiet fellow and had a youngish face, and lacked the poise and easy manner that Milt possessed.

So the evenings passed, the hot summer nights, and Aunt Daisy remained in the flat. Two weeks went by, and she said nothing about leaving. My father spoke to my mother, but my mother said to wait another week. Now that all the news had been exchanged, now that the first flush of meeting had worn off, there was a sharp letdown. We had grown accustomed to Aunt Daisy's Eastern accent and had heard some of her Boston stories for the second and third time. In the daytime we went swimming in the city ponds or in the playgrounds, and only my sister stayed behind. Aunt Daisy, in her loneliness, would read aloud to her from *Ramona* or *Ivanhoe,* and sometimes she liked to braid my sister's heavy yellow hair.

And all the while my father grew grouchier and grouchier. "When is she going?" he would ask my mother. "We're crowded here, the boys have to sleep three in a bed in such hot weather, and you're setting a better table now, a cake or fruit almost every evening. I can't afford it."

My mother would stand there without answering him until my father went back to the store.

At last, during the middle of the third week, my mother must have spoken to her sister about it, for when I came into the flat one hot afternoon I could hear Aunt Daisy crying in her room. My mother stood there, looking helpless. Daisy sobbed out that she had no friends, that she was tired of being unmarried, and she said she had thought she would meet somebody here. "I was looking forward to it so much," she sobbed.

"But the boys are so young," my mother said. "Milton is only twenty. His friends are boys, too."

Aunt Daisy kept on crying. "Besides, I haven't got the railroad fare back," she confessed. "Every penny I could scrape together went into the dresses I brought with me."

My mother stood aghast. Then she saw me.

"God knows, God knows! . . ." she said, and Daisy, looking up, also saw me and began smiling through her tears, to show me she had not been crying. She called me over, laughing softly, and when I came she strained me to her and kissed my face all over. Her arms were trembling. She kept whispering to me and in the end she mussed my hair, laughing nervously. "What did you see? Was I crying?"

I shook my head.

"There!" she cried and flung her arms out happily. "Tra-la-la-la, tra-la-la-la!" and she went singing through the rooms of the flat. In the kitchen my mother, standing over the stove, stirred the heavy soup slowly with a big ladle.

Another week went by, and still my mother was afraid to ask my father for Aunt Daisy's return railroad fare. She put the matter off from day to day. But out of her own meager savings she gave her sister a few dollars for stockings, face-powder, and other things. Aunt Daisy took the money, drew the new hose snug against her shapely little legs, and tousled our heads harder than ever.

"Tra-la-la-la! Tra-la-la-la!"

Milt went out every night now and on Sundays stayed away all day. He bought a pair of flannels and a blue jacket, and went out sporting. The daughter of the neighbor was more gone on him than ever, and just before he used to leave the flat Aunt Daisy would find something to do in her room until he had gone.

Later on, when she was sure that Milt had left the house and when my father had gone to bed, Aunt Daisy would sit on the back porch and wait for a breeze with the rest of us, while a hundred yards to the south the Lake Street elevated roared and crashed along, hurtling its racket through the summer night like long-range artillery. And to the north, a block behind us, were the Northwestern tracks, with freights that passed all night long, their whistles wailing over the town and the black soot of the soft coal they burned floating down upon the people in a thin, sifted ash. The heat brought out the perspiration, and if you rubbed your face your hand came away dirty from the train soot.

In the hot night, looking to left and right, you could see all the porches of the building loaded with families, the men sitting in their socks, the women in thin cotton house-dresses. Some of the families hauled out mattresses and slept on the porches all night; and in the morning you could see them sprawled out, wearily, and if they were awake they'd pull the sheets over them quickly, wait for you to look away, and then duck inside the house.

No rain fell. In the evenings, when the sun rolled down in the west over the piano factory in Walnut Street, clouds of gray dust rose in the air as the men pitched the horse-shoes. Their trousers bottoms would be powdered and they'd have to step back and wait awhile to let the dust settle before looking at the iron shoes. They rushed the can harder than ever and the kids kept fighting to see who would be chosen to blow off the foam.

Then came the tragedy of the summer. One of the young unmarried railroaders had seen Aunt Daisy sitting on the porch and had fallen for her. He was a big, honest, bashful fellow named Harry O'Callahan, and he had the shoulders of a coal-heaver. He had a fine voice, too, and could play the harmonica.

He spied Aunt Daisy one evening as he was pitching horse-shoes, glancing up at our porch on the second floor. He saw she was small and dark and was dressed in a yellow summer frock. He fell in love right away. Small as I was, I noticed it at once. He played horse-shoes very badly all evening, and the men bawled him out and none would pair off with him, so he had to play against two of them, walking up and back across the dusty ground, and losing every game.

"What's come over you?" the men asked. "You used to beat us all."

Harry shook his head, forked up another dime, and dropped out of the game. And later on, in the hot dark when the men had grouped themselves on the stairs, someone struck up an old railroad song, a ballad about the sweat of the road and the Iron Horse and the whistles of the round-house early in the morning. I had never heard that song before. Harry O'Callahan was singing it. The men grew quiet while his fine baritone floated toward us. When he finished, hand-clapping and foot-stamping thundered at him from all the porches. They called out to him to sing on.

He sang a few more songs and in the choruses the men hummed bass for him. Then he took out his harmonica and played "Down by the Old Mill Stream," and "By the Light of the Silvery Moon," fluttering his cupped hands over the mouth-organ so that quivering notes issued forth.

"Who is that fellow?" Aunt Daisy whispered, asking me in the dark. I told her.

"Oh, he works on the railroad?" she said and seemed to lose interest, though the music continued to move her. "Is he the big fellow who threw the horse-shoes so badly?"

I nodded.

She said nothing more.

The next evening, when the men pitched the shoes again, Harry seemed to have found his former stride and tossed with his old form; he threw like a champion, twirling the heavy iron shoes unerringly so that they rang angrily around the metal stakes with a burst of sparks. He stared hard ahead through the dust to see the ringers he had made, smiled, then looked up toward our porch. My mother sat quietly, but her hands were clenched in her lap.

Later on, when the men played singles, I went down in the yard and watched. Harry was playing against another railroader, a big fellow, too, his best friend; the fellow's name was Frank.

Harry and Frank played three games while the families leaned from the porches, watching. Harry won them all. Someone was sent for the beer, and when it came the kids stood around in a pushing circle. As he was the winner, Harry got the first drink. He pointed at me with a grin, held the full can aloft, so I worked myself proudly through the group, gripped the can in my fists and, filling my lungs to the bottom, blew all the foam cleanly from the top. It was a neat job, Harry said, and he slipped me a nickel when the other kids weren't looking.

After that, when full darkness came on, the singing started up again, and Harry gave an entire concert with his harmonica. The neighbors seemed to sense that something was up, for they kept looking toward our porch where Aunt Daisy sat in the gloom, only her summer dress showing, a pink one this time. My father had long since gone to bed and Milt was out sparking, but the rest of the family sat on the porch. In one of the pauses my mother called out softly to me, saying it was getting late, but I pretended I didn't hear.

An hour later, after the can had made many trips to the saloon in Lake Street, the men grew boastful and started bragging about their strength. There would be singing, then shouting, then bragging, then singing again. Things grew noisy.

"I can swing the sixteen-pound hammer harder than any man here," a road man shouted. "I drive stakes in with two blows!"

"Well, where's the hammer, where's the hammer to prove it?" the men shouted back.

"That's your affair!" came the answer and the porches howled with laughter.

But pretty soon, because there was so much bragging and counter-bragging, it was decided that weight-lifting was the best all-around test of strength, and someone went down into the basement for two big buckets, crossed the alley where the foundation work of a factory was under way, and came back with the pails loaded to the top with heavy mixing sand. The janitor of the building, sitting in his socks and smoking on his porch, came forward, hollering that the pails belonged to the owner of the building, but the men pacified him with a long drink of beer. He wiped his mustache and went back to his porch again. Someone got hold of an old broom, broke off the stout handle, and tied the two pails to the ends of it with stout cord. Now they had a weight, all right.

The first fellow to step up couldn't lift the two pails higher than his chest. He grunted and strained, but he had to give up. All the smaller men came forward, also the men over forty, but none of them could lift the heavy buckets over their heads. The pails were very big.

Then the day laborers tried. Three of them were able to lift the twin buckets high over their heads, but couldn't hold the pails up there very long. From the porches the families started calling for Harry O'Callahan to try. He sat back in darkness and did not answer.

Finally his best friend Frank got up and, gripping the wooden handle, raised the weight slowly and gracefully up to his chest, his chin, the top of his head, then high above it, straightening out his arms. Cheering broke out from the porches.

"Anybody can lift the weight up quickly, but the real test is lifting it slowly," Frank said, blowing, looking at the day laborers. He sat down, heaving.

"Well, we know who's the strongest now," came from the porches.

Harry stepped from the shadow. Once, twice, three times he lifted the buckets up to his chin and over his head, as slowly as Frank had done and just as gracefully. Then he sat down. Now the cheering was greater than ever and the kids pressed forward to feel Harry's biceps. On the porches the women were impressed and leaned over more from the railings. In the dark I saw a pink blur on our porch move forward, too, and, turning, I noticed that Harry had also seen.

"That was nothing," he said quietly, but he couldn't keep the triumphant ring from his voice.

Frank got up and began thinking of new ways of lifting the weight, of gripping your hands the other way, knuckles up. He and Harry tried it. It was harder, but both managed it.

"Do it with one hand!" someone shouted from the porches, a short fat man sitting in his underwear who was married to a pretty young woman rumored to be carrying on an affair with the neighborhood ice-man.

Everybody laughed. Mr. Moser, besides being short and flabby, was bald and couldn't lift an egg from the floor—because he couldn't stoop to pick it up.

At first Frank tried it with one hand. He gripped the wooden bar with his right hand, strained, grunted, and wrenched, but couldn't lift it higher than his waist. He tried his left hand.

The kids started yelling, "Harry, Harry!"

Harry came up. He tried first with his left hand, testing to see how much energy he'd have to use with his right, not straining himself. You could see he had been thinking it out. With his left hand he brought the buckets up to his thigh, a little higher, then lowered them.

"You can't do it!" fat little Mr. Moser shouted, fanning his face excitedly. The families laughed.

Then the yard grew quiet. Bending over, gripping the wooden handle firmly with his right hand, winding his fingers hard around the smooth wood until his fist went white, Harry started lifting. He had a wrist as thick as my leg around the calf. The buckets, ascending slowly, swayed from side to side, went up, up, up, as high as his waist, his chest, his chin, then came down with a plop against the ground. Toward the end of the hoist Harry's whole frame had started to quiver from the strain.

"Take some of the sand from the pails," Moser taunted from his porch, but his wife, leaning away over, had her eyes glued on Harry O'Callahan. Harry smiled at the sally. He looked up, heaving like a spent swimmer, and as he turned toward our porch I saw the sweat break out on his forehead. He wiped it away, then bent once more to the buckets. His friend Frank advised him not to try again. "Don't try it," said Frank. "You're tired out, it isn't worth it."

But already Harry had his fingers wound around the smooth wooden broom handle and now his jaw was like a block of concrete, and his whole fine, young Irish face was grimly set as if he were about to rush into a burning building to save his heroine.

Slowly, using his strength carefully, he raised the buckets from the ground to his shins, his knees, his thigh, bracing himself, curving his spinal column as the pails rose to his chest. Up, up, up they went, his whole frame quivering like a leaf in the wind, until he had the pails of sand level with his chin, his nose, his eyes. Then with a hoarse, shouting grunt, with a tremendous distortion of facial muscles and baring of teeth, he heaved the weight aloft, grinning like a maniac, his frame quivering so violently you could count the great pitiful shivers of the fellow's big body. A hush fell upon the whole yard. From the rear windows of the flats the gaslight from the kitchens fell upon the scene in long slanting bright blocks of yellow glare.

But as soon as the buckets shot up after that last tremendous wrench of back and shoulder and leg muscles something seemed to snap inside of Harry and he went limp all of a sudden. The buckets thudded to the ground and Harry followed. He lay there writhing, holding his right side.

On one of the porches someone screamed, then fainted. The men rushed from the stairs and picked Harry up. He seemed to be all right again and smiled weakly in shame as they carried him into one of the flats. The men felt him all over.

"It's nothing," he said and got up a little later. "It's nothing, I tell you."

But the next day, when he went to a doctor, he learned he had ruptured himself. The doctor advised an operation, but Harry didn't have the money, so he bought himself a truss and said that it didn't bother him. The whole building talked about it the next day. People started looking toward our porch, and Aunt Daisy came inside the flat. There was something hostile in their glances and her being an outsider did not help much.

In the evening, when the men started playing horse-shoes, Harry sat on the stairs, watching. He had been warned against any form of exercise, and of course lunging forward as you tossed the shoes was out of the question for him. He sat there in silence while the men tossed the shoes and watched the dust clouds settling to the yard. Once he looked up toward our porch, but he saw that Aunt Daisy was not there.

She was crying in her room, with my mother sitting on the bed soothing her. It had been Aunt Daisy who had screamed and fainted. She sobbed out to my mother that now she couldn't sit out on the porch on account of the neighbors, that Milt never took her out or spoke to her any more, and she couldn't be expected to sit in the hot flat in the evening when the only place for a breeze was on the porch. My mother didn't answer, but she understood.

So two days later, screwing up her courage, my mother spoke to my father about money for her sister's return fare. She was prepared for rumbling and thunder, she was all set for my father to start shouting and hollering and waited for him to bubble and boil under the collar before his heavy cheeks began quivering in wrath. But nothing of the sort happened.

He went quietly into his bedroom and locked the door behind him. When we heard a ripping of cloth we knew he was slitting the stitches of the mattress to get at his wallet. In a few minutes he came out, handed my mother the money, asked for a needle and thread, and went back into the bedroom, closing the door again. Aunt Daisy, sitting in her own room, was given the money after my father left for the store.

The next day the flat was quiet. Aunt Daisy was going home. My mother made a fine supper, but little was eaten. Before my father returned to the store, he said good-by to his sister-in-law and walked out as she was in the middle of thanking him for the railroad fare. She sat at the table, her eyes red, staring over our heads at the windows.

When the time came for her to go, she started putting on her hat, the hat with the gray and brown feathers. She looked into the mirror and saw her reddened face, then put more powder on. In the kitchen my mother was drying and re-drying her hands on a towel, standing there helplessly. Finally she came into the front room. They said good-by, kissing, and as the two heads bent together, my mother's head of gray touching the black vibrant hair half hidden in the little hat of feathers, my nose began tickling and I stared hard at the shiny door knob.

Aunt Daisy kissed us all, trying to choke back her sobs. In a corner of the room my sister started crying. Daisy went over and, when she kissed Rose, both of them began sobbing and hugging each other. My mother blew her nose softly, then put her handkerchief into the pocket of her apron. Finally she said, her voice urging, "The train is leaving right away, you'll miss it."

So Aunt Daisy broke away. She wiped her cheeks with a fine lace handkerchief purchased from the money my mother had given her.

At the door Milt stood waiting. Then Ben put his hat and jacket on and said he was going to the station too. "The bags are heavy, I'll handle one of them."

They swung the door open and carried the grips out into the hall, with Aunt Daisy following, when suddenly she came back into the front room and stood sobbing against my mother's breast. My mother, crying herself, stroked her back soothingly.

Then Aunt Daisy was all set. She wiped her eyes, looked pertly alert, and poked her finger at me.

"What did you see? Was I crying?"

I shook my head vigorously.

"There!" she cried happily and strode out after my brothers, who began going down the stairs. We could hear her singing gaily in the hallway, "Tra-la-la-la, tra-la-la-la!" until the door banged.

Then we went to stand at the front windows where we could watch her going up the street, walking between Ben and Milt, stepping jauntily, turning to one then the other, gossiping light-heartedly. It was evident from her stride that she liked to be walking between two big fellows. They went up the gray dusk of the street.

At the corner my brother Milt must have said something to her, for she turned suddenly and waved at us. We waved back, though we knew she could not see us. My sister kept on waving, moving her hand vaguely even after they had turned the corner, while my kid brother pressed his forehead against the glass. The street lamps lit up, and down the block we could hear a splashing sound as a neighbor played his hose against the walk.

"God knows, God knows! . . ." said my mother in the silence, while my sister came forward, crying, to feel under the apron for my mother's hand.

AN AFTERWORD ON
"MY AUNT DAISY"

"MY AUNT DAISY," the work of a young novelist best known for *Union Square, The Foundry,* and a new book called *The Chute,* made its first appearance between covers in a book of avowed memoirs called *On the Shore* which was published in 1934. But it had already been printed in the *American Mercury* while Mr. Mencken was still (from Baltimore) imparting his vitality to that monthly. However, anyone who read it first in the double columns of his magazine must have known for sure that this was no flight of fancy nor a memory transmitted into fiction but something sensitively witnessed, completely recalled, and faithfully set down. A prettifying touch of invention here and there might have spoiled it. Surely there was none. You know that for yourself.

It is my notion that a portrait which is not a good likeness does not look like anybody at all. When, rendered bland and contemplative at Beaune by the solace of a perfect lunch at the Hôtel de la Poste, you go along the cobbled streets to the old hospital and sit all afternoon in front of the portraits of its founders in the famous triptych by Roger van der Weyden, the mere fact that the subjects have been dust in the crypt for hundreds of years and there is no corroborative testimony about their looks whatever does not prevent your knowing infallibly that there they are in their habit as they lived. So, too, when a portrait is done in words you can have no doubts. Such a deadly likeness as the one achieved by D. H. Lawrence in his study of the hapless Maurice Magnus carries its own credentials and Halper's minor chronicle of a baffled and desperate spinster has been set down with such veracity that you who now read of her barren journey to Chicago know as well as the author does that it was even so.

A. W.

THREE
STORIES

by

DOROTHY PARKER

THE LITTLE HOURS

Now what's this? What's the object of all this darkness all over me? They haven't gone and buried me alive while my back was turned, have they? Ah, now would you think they'd do a thing like that! Oh, no, I know what it is. I'm awake. That's it. I've waked up in the middle of the night. Well, isn't that nice. Isn't that simply ideal. Twenty minutes past four, sharp, and here's Baby wide-eyed as a marigold. Look at this, will you? At the time when all decent people are just going to bed, I must wake up. There's no way things can ever come out even, under this system. This is as rank as injustice is ever likely to get. This is what brings about revolutions, that's what *this* does.

Yes, and you want to know what got me into this mess? Going to bed at ten o'clock, that's what. That spells ruin. T-e-n-space-o-apostrophe-c-l-o-c-k: ruin. Early to bed, and you'll wish you were dead. Bed before eleven, nuts before seven. Bed before morning, sailors give warning. Ten o'clock, after a quiet evening of reading. Reading—there's an institution for you. Why, I'd turn on the light and read, right this minute, if reading weren't what contributed toward driving me here. I'll show it. God, the bitter misery that reading works in this world! Everybody knows that—everybody who *is* everybody. All the best minds have been off reading for years. Look at the swing La Rochefoucauld took at it. He said that if nobody had ever learned to read, very few people would be in love. There was a man for you, and that's what *he* thought of it. Good for you, La Rochefoucauld; nice going, boy. I wish I'd never learned to read. I wish I'd never learned to take off my clothes. Then I wouldn't have been caught in this jam at half-past four in the morning. If nobody had ever learned to undress, very few people would be in love. No, his is better. Oh, well, it's a man's world.

619

La Rochefoucauld, indeed, lying quiet as a mouse, and me tossing and turning here! This is no time to be getting all steamed up about La Rochefoucauld. It's only a question of minutes before I'm going to be pretty darned good and sick of La Rochefoucauld, once and for all. La Rochefoucauld this and La Rochefoucauld that. Yes, well, let me tell you that if nobody had ever learned to quote, very few people would be in love with La Rochefoucauld. I bet you I don't know ten souls who read him without a middleman. People pick up those rambling little essays that start off "Was it not that lovable old cynic, La Rochefoucauld, who said . . ." and then they go around claiming to know the master backwards. Pack of illiterates, that's all they are. All right, let them keep their La Rochefoucauld, and see if I care. I'll stick to La Fontaine. Only I'd be better company if I could quit thinking that La Fontaine married Alfred Lunt.

I don't know what I'm doing mucking about with a lot of French authors at this hour, anyway. First thing you know, I'll be reciting *Fleurs du Mal* to myself, and then I'll be little more good to anybody. And I'll stay off Verlaine too; he was always chasing Rimbauds. A person would be better off with La Rochefoucauld, even. Oh, damn La Rochefoucauld. The big Frog. I'll thank him to keep out of my head. What's he doing there, anyhow? What's La Rochefoucauld to me, or he to Hecuba? Why, I don't even know the man's first name, that's how close I ever was to *him*. What am I supposed to be, a stooge for La Rochefoucauld? That's what *he* thinks. Sez he. Well, he's only wasting his time, hanging around here. I can't help him. The only other thing I can remember his saying is that there is always something a little pleasing to us in the misfortunes of even our dearest friends. That cleans me all up with Monsieur La Rochefoucauld. *Maintenant c'est fini, ça.*

Dearest friends. A sweet lot of dearest friends *I've* got. All of them lying in swinish stupors, while I'm practically up and about. All of them stretched sodden through these, the fairest hours of the day, when man should be at his most productive. Produce, produce, produce, for I tell you the night is coming. Carlyle said that. Yes, and a fine one *he* was, to go shooting off his face on the subject. *Oh,* Thomas Car*li*-yill, what *I* know about about *you*-oo! No, that will be enough of that. I'm not going to start fretting about Carlyle, at this stage of the game. What did he ever do that was so great, besides founding a college for Indians? (That crack ought to flatten him.) Let him keep his face out of this, if he knows what's good for him. I've got enough trouble with that lovable old cynic, La Rochefoucauld—him and the misfortunes of his dearest friends!

The first thing I've got to do is get out and whip me up a complete new set of dearest friends; that's the first thing. Everything else can wait. And will somebody please kindly be so good as to inform me how I am ever going to meet up with any new people when my entire scheme of living is out of joint—when I'm the only living being awake while the rest of the world lies sleeping? I've got to get this thing adjusted. I must try to get back to sleep right now. I've got to conform to the rotten little standards of this sluggard civilization. People needn't feel that they have to change their ruinous habits and come my way. Oh, no, no; no, indeed. Not at all. I'll go theirs. If that isn't the woman of it for you! Always having to do what somebody else wants, like it or not. Never able to murmur a suggestion of her own.

And what suggestion has anyone to murmur as to how I am going to drift lightly back to slumber? Here I am, awake as high noon what with all this milling and pitching around with La Rochefoucauld. I really can't be expected to drop everything and start counting sheep, at my age. I hate sheep. Untender it may be in me, but all my life I've hated sheep. It amounts to a phobia, the way I hate them. I can tell the minute there's one in the room. They needn't think that I am going to lie here in the dark and count their unpleasant little faces for them; I wouldn't do it if I didn't fall asleep again until the middle of next August. Suppose they never get counted—what's the worst that can happen? If the number of imaginary sheep in this world remains a matter of guesswork, who is richer or poorer for it? No, sir; *I'm* not going to be the patsy. Let them count themselves, if they're so crazy mad after mathematics. Let them do their own dirty work. Coming around here, at this time of day, and asking me to count them! And not even *real* sheep, at that. Why, it's the most preposterous thing I ever heard in my life.

But there must be *something* I could count. Let's see. No, I already know by heart how many fingers I have. I could count my bills, I suppose. I could count the things I didn't do yesterday that I should have done. I could count the things I should do today that I'm not going to do. I'm never going to accomplish anything; that's perfectly clear to me. I'm never going to be famous. My name will never be writ large on the roster of Those Who Do Things. I don't do anything. Not one single thing. I used to bite my nails, but I don't even do that any more. I don't amount to the powder to blow me to hell. I've turned out to be nothing but a bit of flotsam. Flotsam and leave 'em—that's me from now on. Oh, it's all terrible.

Well. This way lies galloping melancholia. Maybe it's because this is the zero hour. This is the time the swooning soul hangs pendant and vertiginous between the new day and the old, nor dares confront the one or summon back the other. This is the time when all things, known and hidden, are iron to weight the spirit; when all ways, traveled or virgin, fall away from the stumbling feet, when all before the straining eyes is black. Blackness now, everywhere is blackness. This is the time of abomination, the dreadful hour of the victorious dark. For it is always darkest— Was it not that lovable old cynic, La Rochefoucauld, who said that it is always darkest before the deluge?

There. Now you see, don't you? Here we are again, practically back where we started. La Rochefoucauld, we are here. Ah, come on, son —how about your going your way and letting me go mine? I've got my work cut out for me right here; I've got all this sleeping to do. Think how I am going to look by daylight if this keeps up. I'll be a seamy sight for all those rested, clear-eyed, fresh-faced dearest friends of mine—the rats! Why, *Dotty,* whatever have you been doing; I thought you were on the wagon. Oh, I was helling around with La Rochefoucauld till all hours; we couldn't stop laughing about your misfortunes. No, this is getting too thick, really. It isn't right to have this happen to a person, just because she went to bed at ten o'clock once in her life. Honest, I won't ever do it again. I'll go straight, after this. I'll never go to bed again, if I can only sleep now. If I can tear my mind away from a certain French cynic, *circa* 1650, and slip into lovely oblivion. 1650. I bet I look as if I'd been awake since then.

How do people go to sleep? I'm afraid I've lost the knack. I might try busting myself smartly over the temple with the night-light. I might repeat to myself, slowly and soothingly, a list of quotations beautiful from minds profound; if I can remember any of the damn things. That might do it. And it ought effectually to bar that visiting foreigner that's been hanging around ever since twenty minutes past four. Yes, that's what I'll do. Only wait till I turn the pillow; it feels as if La Rochefoucauld had crawled inside the slip.

Now let's see—where shall we start? Why—er—let's see. Oh, yes, I know one. This above all, to thine own self be true and it must follow, as the night the day, thou canst not then be false to any man. Now they're off. And once they get started, they ought to come like hot cakes. Let's see. Ah, what avail the sceptered race and what the form divine, when every virtue, every grace, Rose Aylmer, all were thine. Let's see. They also serve who only stand and wait. If Winter comes, can Spring be far behind. Lilies that fester smell far worse than weeds. Silent upon a peak in Darien. Mrs. Porter and her daughter wash their feet in soda-water. And Agatha's Arth is a hug-the-hearth, but my true love is false. Why did you die when lambs were cropping, you should have died when apples were dropping. Shall be together, breathe and ride, so one day more am I deified, who knows but the world will end tonight. And he shall hear the stroke of eight and not the stroke of nine. They are not long, the weeping and the laughter; love and desire and hate I think will have no portion in us after we pass the gate. But none, I think, do there embrace. I think that I shall never see a poem lovely as a tree. I think I will not hang myself today. Ay tank Ay go home now.

Let's see. Solitude is the safeguard of mediocrity and the stern companion of genius. Consistency is the hobgoblin of little minds. Something is emotion remembered in tranquillity. A cynic is one who knows the price of everything and the value of nothing. That lovable old cynic is one who—oops, there's King Charles's head again. I've got to watch myself. Let's see. Circumstantial evidence is a trout in the milk. Any stigma will do to beat a dogma. If you would learn what God thinks about money, you have only to look at those to whom he has given it. If nobody had ever learned to read, very few people——

All right. That fixes it. I throw in the towel right now. I know when I'm licked. There'll be no more of this nonsense; I'm going to turn on the light and read my head off. Till the next ten o'clock, if I feel like it. And what does La Rochefoucauld want to make of that? Oh, he *will*, eh? Yes, he will! He and who else? La Rochefoucauld and *what* very few people?

ARRANGEMENT IN
BLACK AND WHITE

The woman with the pink velvet poppies wreathed round the assisted gold of her hair traversed the crowded room at an interesting gait combining a skip with a sidle, and clutched the lean arm of her host.

"Now I got you!" she said. "Now you can't get away!"

"Why, hello," said her host. "Well. How are you?"

"Oh, I'm finely," she said. "Just simply finely. Listen. I want you to do me the most terrible favor. Will you? Will you please? Pretty please?"

"What is it?" said her host.

"Listen," she said. "I want to meet Walter Williams. Honestly, I'm just simply crazy about that man. Oh, when he sings! When he sings those spirituals! Well, I said to Burton, 'It's a good thing for you Walter Williams is colored,' I said, 'or you'd have lots of reason to be jealous.' I'd really love to meet him. I'd like to tell him I've heard him sing. Will you be an angel and introduce me to him?"

"Why, certainly," said her host. "I thought you'd met him. The party's for him. Where is he, anyway?"

"He's over there by the bookcase," she said. "Let's wait till those people get through talking to him. Well, I think you're simply marvelous, giving this perfectly marvelous party for him, and having him meet all these white people, and all. Isn't he terribly grateful?"

"I hope not," said her host.

"I think it's really terribly nice," she said. "I do. I don't see why on earth it isn't perfectly all right to meet colored people. I haven't any feeling at all about it—not one single bit. Burton—oh, he's just the other way. Well, you know, he comes from Virginia, and you know how they are."

"Did he come tonight?" said her host.

"No, he couldn't," she said. "I'm a regular grass widow tonight. I told him when I left, 'There's no telling what I'll do,' I said. He was just so tired out, he couldn't move. Isn't it a shame?"

"Ah," said her host.

"Wait till I tell him I met Walter Williams!" she said. "He'll just about die. Oh, we have more arguments about colored people. I talk to him like I don't know what, I get so excited. 'Oh, don't be so silly,' I say. But I must say for Burton, he's heaps broader-minded than lots of these Southerners. He's really awfully fond of colored people. Well, he says himself, he wouldn't have white servants. And you know, he had this old colored nurse, this regular old nigger mammy, and he just simply loves her. Why, every time he goes home, he goes out in the kitchen to see her. He does, really, to this day. All he says is, he says he hasn't got a word to say against colored people as long as they keep their place. He's always doing things for them—giving them clothes and I don't know what all. The only thing he says, he says he wouldn't sit down at the table with one for a million dollars. 'Oh,' I say to him, 'you make me sick, talking like that.' I'm just terrible to him. Aren't I terrible?"

"Oh, no, no, no," said her host. "No, no."

"I am," she said. "I know I am. Poor Burton! Now, me, I don't feel that way at all. I haven't the slightest feeling about colored people. Why, I'm just crazy about some of them. They're just like children— just as easy going, and always singing and laughing and everything. Aren't they the happiest things you ever saw in your life? Honestly, it makes me laugh just to hear them. Oh, I like them. I really do. Well, now, listen, I have this colored laundress, I've had her for years, and I'm devoted to her. She's a real character. And I want to tell you, I think of her as my friend. That's the way I think of her. As I say to Burton, 'Well, for Heaven's sakes, we're all human beings!' Aren't we?"

"Yes," said her host. "Yes, indeed."

"Now this Walter Williams," she said. "I think a man like that's a real artist. I do. I think he deserves an awful lot of credit. Goodness, I'm so crazy about music or anything, I don't care what color he is. I honestly think if a person's an artist, nobody ought to have any feeling at all about meeting them. That's absolutely what I say to Burton. Don't you think I'm right?"

"Yes," said her host. "Oh, yes."

"That's the way I feel," she said. "I just can't understand people be- ing narrow-minded. Why, I absolutely think it's a privilege to meet a man like Walter Williams. Now, I do. I haven't any feeling at all. Well, my goodness, the good Lord made him, just the same as He did any of us. Didn't He?"

"Surely," said her host. "Yes, indeed."

"That's what I say," she said. "Oh, I get so furious when people are narrow-minded about colored people. It's just all I can do not to say something. Of course, I do admit when you get a bad colored man, they're simply terrible. But as I say to Burton, there are some bad white people, too, in this world. Aren't there?"

"I guess there are," said her host.

"Why, I'd really be glad to have a man like Walter Williams come to my house and sing for us, some time," she said. "Of course, I couldn't ask him on account of Burton, but I wouldn't have any feeling about it at all. Oh, can't he sing! Isn't it marvelous, the way they all have music in them? It just seems to be right *in* them. Come on, let's us go

on over and talk to him. Listen, what shall I do when I'm introduced?
Ought I to shake hands? Or what?"

"Why, do whatever you want," said her host.

"I guess maybe I'd better," she said. "I wouldn't for the world have
him think I had any feeling. I think I'd better shake hands, just the
way I would with anybody else. That's just exactly what I'll do."

They reached the tall young Negro, standing by the bookcase. The
host performed introductions; the Negro bowed.

"How do you do?" he said.

The woman with the pink velvet poppies extended her hand at the
length of her arm and held it so for all the world to see, until the
Negro took it, shook it, and gave it back to her.

"Oh, how do you do, Mr. Williams," she said. "Well, how do you do.
I've just been saying, I've enjoyed your singing so awfully much. I've
been to your concerts, and we have you on the phonograph and everything. Oh, I just enjoy it!"

She spoke with great distinctness, moving her lips meticulously, as if
in parlance with the deaf.

"I'm so glad," he said.

"I'm just simply crazy about that 'Water Boy' thing you sing," she
said. "Honestly, I can't get it out of my head. I have my husband nearly
crazy, the way I go around humming it all the time. Oh, he looks just
as black as the ace of—Er. Well, tell me, where on earth do you ever
get all those songs of yours? How do you ever get hold of them?"

"Why," he said, "there are so many different——"

"I should think you'd love singing them," she said. "It must be more
fun. All those darling old spirituals—oh, I just love them! Well, what
are you doing, now? Are you still keeping up your singing? Why
don't you have another concert, some time?"

"I'm having one the sixteenth of this month," he said.

"Well, I'll be there," she said. "I'll be there, if I possibly can. You
can count on me. Goodness, here comes a whole raft of people to talk
to you. You're just a regular guest of honor! Oh, who's that girl in
white? I've seen her some place."

"That's Katherine Burke," said her host.

"Good Heavens," she said, "is that Katherine Burke? Why, she looks entirely different off the stage. I thought she was much better-looking. I had no idea she was so terribly dark. Why, she looks almost like— Oh, I think she's a wonderful actress! Don't you think she's a wonderful actress, Mr. Williams? Oh, I think she's marvelous. Don't you?"

"Yes, I do," he said.

"Oh, I do, too," she said. "Just wonderful. Well, goodness, we must give someone else a chance to talk to the guest of honor. Now, don't forget, Mr. Williams, I'm going to be at that concert if I possibly can. I'll be there applauding like everything. And if I can't come, I'm going to tell everybody I know to go, anyway. Don't you forget!"

"I won't," he said. "Thank you so much."

The host took her arm and piloted her into the next room.

"Oh, my dear," she said. "I nearly died! Honestly, I give you my word, I nearly passed away. Did you hear that terrible break I made? I was just going to say Katherine Burke looked almost like a nigger. I just caught myself in time. Oh, do you think he noticed?"

"I don't believe so," said her host.

"Well, thank goodness," she said, "because I wouldn't have embarrassed him for anything. Why, he's awfully nice. Just as nice as he can be. Nice manners, and everything. You know, so many colored people, you give them an inch, and they walk all over you. But he doesn't try any of that. Well, he's got more sense, I suppose. He's really nice. Don't you think so?"

"Yes," said her host.

"I liked him," she said. "I haven't any feeling at all because he's a colored man. I felt just as natural as I would with anybody. Talked to him just as naturally, and everything. But honestly, I could hardly keep a straight face. I kept thinking of Burton. Oh, wait till I tell Burton I called him 'Mister'!"

THE WALTZ

WHY, *thank you so much. I'd adore to.*

I don't want to dance with him. I don't want to dance with anybody. And even if I did, it wouldn't be him. He'd be well down among the last ten. I've seen the way he dances; it looks like something you do on St. Walpurgis Night. Just think, not a quarter of an hour ago, here I was sitting, feeling so sorry for the poor girl he was dancing with. And now *I'm* going to be the poor girl. Well, well. Isn't it a small world?

And a peach of a world, too. A true little corker. Its events are so fascinatingly unpredictable, are not they? Here I was, minding my own business, not doing a stitch of harm to any living soul. And then he comes into my life, all smiles and city manners, to sue me for the favor of one memorable mazurka. Why, he scarcely knows my name, let alone what it stands for. It stands for Despair, Bewilderment, Futility, Degradation, and Premeditated Murder, but little does he wot. I don't wot his name, either; I haven't any idea what it is. Jukes, would be my guess from the look in his eyes. How do you do, Mr. Jukes? And how is that dear little brother of yours, with the two heads?

Ah, now why did he have to come around me, with his low requests? Why can't he let me lead my own life? I ask so little—just to be left alone in my quiet corner of the table, to do my evening brooding over all my sorrows. And he must come, with his bows and his scrapes and his may-I-have-this-ones. And I had to go and tell him that I'd adore to dance with him. I cannot understand why I wasn't struck right down dead. Yes, and being struck dead would look like a day in the country, compared to struggling out a dance with this boy. But what could I do? Everyone else at the table had got up to dance, except him and me. There I was, trapped. Trapped like a trap in a trap.

What can you say, when a man asks you to dance with him? I most certainly will *not* dance with you, I'll see you in hell first. Why, thank you, I'd like to awfully, (but I'm having labor pains.) Oh, yes, *do* let's dance together—it's so nice to meet a man who isn't a scaredy-cat about catching my beri-beri. No. There was nothing for me to do, but say I'd adore to. Well, we might as well get it over with. All right, Cannonball, let's run out on the field. You won the toss; you can lead.

Why, I think it's more of a waltz, really. Isn't it? We might just listen to the music a second. Shall we? Oh, yes, it's a waltz. Mind? Why, I'm simply thrilled. I'd love to waltz with you.

I'd love to waltz with you. I'd love to waltz with you, I'd love to have my tonsils out, I'd love to be in a midnight fire at sea. Well, it's too late now. We're getting under way. *Oh.* Oh, dear. Oh, dear, dear, dear. Oh, this is even worse than I thought it would be. I suppose that's the one dependable law of life—everything is always worse than you thought it was going to be. Oh, if I had had any real grasp of what this dance would be like, I'd have held out for sitting it out. Well, it will probably amount to the same thing in the end. We'll be sitting it out on the floor in a minute, if he keeps this up.

I'm so glad I brought it to his attention that this is a waltz they're playing. Heaven knows what might have happened, if he had thought it was something fast; we'd have blown the sides right out of the building. Why does he always want to be somewhere that he isn't? Why can't we stay in one place just long enough to get acclimated? It's this constant rush, rush, rush, that's the curse of American life. That's the reason that we're all of us so— *Ow!* For God's sake, don't *kick,* you idiot; this is only second down. Oh, my shin. My poor, poor shin, that I've had ever since I was a little girl!

Oh, no, no, no. Goodness, no. It didn't hurt the least little bit. And anyway it was my fault. Really it was. Truly. Well, you're just being sweet, to say that. It really was all my fault.

I wonder what I'd better do—kill him this instant, with my naked hands, or wait and let him drop in his traces. Maybe it's best not to make a scene. I guess I'll just lie low, and watch the pace get him. He can't keep this up indefinitely—he's only flesh and blood. Die he must, and die he shall, for what he did to me. I don't want to be of the over-sensitive type, but you can't tell me that kick was unpremeditated. Freud says there are no accidents. I've led no cloistered life, I've known dancing partners who have spoiled my slippers and torn my dress; but when it comes to kicking, I am Outraged Womanhood. When you kick me in the shin, *smile*.

Maybe he didn't do it maliciously. Maybe it's just his way of showing his high spirits. I suppose I ought to be glad that one of us is having such a good time. I suppose I ought to think myself lucky if he brings me back alive. Maybe it's captious to demand of a practically strange man that he leave your shins as he found them. After all, the poor boy's doing the best he can. Probably he grew up in the hill country, and never had no larnin'. I bet they had to throw him on his back to get shoes on him.

Yes, it's lovely, isn't it? It's simply lovely. It's the loveliest waltz. Isn't it? Oh, I think it's lovely, too.

Why, I'm getting positively drawn to the Triple Threat here. He's my hero. He has the heart of a lion, and the sinews of a buffalo. Look at him—never a thought of the consequences, never afraid of his face, hurling himself into every scrimmage, eyes shining, cheeks ablaze. And shall it be said that I hung back? No, a thousand times no. What's it to me if I have to spend the next couple of years in a plaster cast? Come on, Butch, right through them! Who wants to live forever?

Oh. Oh, dear. Oh, he's all right, thank goodness. For a while I thought they'd have to carry him off the field. Ah, I couldn't bear to have anything happen to him. I love him. I love him better than any-body in the world. Look at the spirit he gets into a dreary, common-place waltz; how effete the other dancers seem, beside him. He is youth and vigor and courage, he is strength and gaiety and— *Ow!* Get off my instep, you hulking peasant! What do you think I am, anyway—a gangplank? *Ow!*

No, of course it didn't hurt. Why, it didn't a bit. Honestly. And it was all my fault. You see, that little step of yours—well, it's perfectly lovely, but it's just a tiny bit tricky to follow at first. Oh, did you work it up yourself? You really did? Well, aren't you amazing! Oh, now I think I've got it. Oh, I think it's lovely. I was watching you do it when you were dancing before. It's awfully effective when you look at it.

It's awfully effective when you look at it. I bet I'm awfully effective when you look at me. My hair is hanging along my cheeks, my skirt is swaddled about me, I can feel the cold damp of my brow. I must look like something out of the Fall of the House of Usher. This sort of thing takes a fearful toll of a woman my age. And he worked up his little step himself, he with his degenerate cunning. And it was just a tiny bit tricky at first, but now I think I've got it. Two stumbles, slip, and a twenty-yard dash; yes, I've got it. I've got several other things, too, including a split shin and a bitter heart. I hate this creature I'm chained to. I hated him the moment I saw his leering, bestial face. And here I've been locked in his noxious embrace for the thirty-five years this waltz has lasted. Is that orchestra never going to stop playing? Or must this obscene travesty of a dance go on until hell burns out?

Oh, they're going to play another encore. Oh, goody. Oh, that's lovely. Tired? I should say I'm not tired. I'd like to go on like this forever.

I should say I'm not tired. I'm dead, that's all I am. Dead, and in what a cause! And the music is never going to stop playing, and we're going on like this, Double-Time Charlie and I, throughout eternity. I suppose I won't care any more, after the first hundred thousand years. I suppose nothing will matter then, not heat nor pain nor broken heart nor cruel, aching weariness. Well. It can't come too soon for me.

I wonder why I didn't tell him I was tired. I wonder why I didn't suggest going back to the table. I could have said let's just listen to the music. Yes, and if he would, that would be the first bit of attention he has given it all evening. George Jean Nathan said that the lovely rhythms of the waltz should be listened to in stillness and not be accompanied by strange gyrations of the human body. I think that's what he said. I think it was George Jean Nathan. Anyhow, whatever he said and whoever he was and whatever he's doing now, he's better off than I am. That's safe. Anybody who isn't waltzing with this Mrs. O'Leary's cow I've got here is having a good time.

Still, if we were back at the table, I'd probably have to talk to him. Look at him—what could you say to a thing like that! Did you go to the circus this year, what's your favorite kind of ice cream, how do you spell cat? I guess I'm as well off here. As well off as if I were in a cement mixer in full action.

I'm past all feeling now. The only way I can tell when he steps on me is that I can hear the splintering of bones. And all the events of my life are passing before my eyes. There was the time I was in a hurricane in the West Indies, there was the day I got my head cut open in the taxi smash, there was the night the drunken lady threw a bronze ash-tray at her own true love and got me instead, there was that summer that the sailboat kept capsizing. Ah, what an easy, peaceful time was mine, until I fell in with Swifty, here. I didn't know what trouble was, before I got drawn into this *danse macabre*. I think my mind is beginning to wander. It almost seems to me as if the orchestra were stopping. It couldn't be, of course; it could never, never be. And yet in my ears there is a silence like the sound of angel voices. . . .

Oh, they've stopped, the mean things. They're not going to play any more. Oh, darn. Oh, do you think they would? Do you really think so, if you gave them fifty dollars? Oh, that would be lovely. And look, do tell them to play this same thing. I'd simply adore to go on waltzing.

AN AFTERWORD ON
DOROTHY PARKER

DOROTHY PARKER (born—in West End, N. J.—a Roth-
schild, and now known, in what is left these days of
private life, as Mrs. Alan Campbell) is a woman of few
words—most of them to the point. For a dozen years past, her
every morose observation has traveled by word of mouth from
coast to coast and even incontinently leaped the seven seas. From
San Diego to Dublin, from Capetown to Waukesha, you will hear
her acrid comments repeated and you will also hear her admiringly debited with thick, lackluster whimsies which never in this
world issued from her chary lips. But that is just part of the penalty
of being fixed in the public mind as the first wit of her time.
From the other wits of her time, Mrs. Parker differs chiefly in
this—that she does not say much. Most of them chatter away and
every once in a while hit the nail on the head. A kindly world
remembers only their successes. Mrs. Parker speaks seldom but
when she does, the aforesaid nail hasn't a prayer.

And considering the fact that the over-rated practice of putting
words down on paper has now been her trade for full twenty
years, her total output asks for little space on your shelf. Three
volumes of verse (recently gathered into one) and two volumes
of prose sketches—*Laments for the Living* and *After Such Pleasures*—have made most of her work available in comparatively permanent form. Editors and publishers are understandably grieved
at what they regard (correctly, perhaps) as her indolence. When

she has been put under solemn contract (unfulfilled) to write a novel, her most remote friends have been startled and gratified to receive long, enchanting letters, which they owed solely to the fact that she had hoped the vigilantes listening under her window would think she was typing dutifully away at her book. Then, of course, the infrequency of her publication has been a matter of reproach from all the laymen in her street who labor under the delusion that it is somehow creditable, even obligatory, for a writer to write. But, after all, perhaps Mother knows best. As a rule she appears to have written only when in the vein. Here are three sketches of hers. It might almost be said that any other three would have equally enriched this *Reader*.

Still uncollected are the book-reviews signed "Constant Reader" which she used to contribute spasmodically to the *New Yorker*. It was her limitation as a critic that she had no technique for commenting on any book which she had enjoyed. She could permanently dispose of A. A. Milne by reporting that "Tonstant Weader fwowed up," but when she came to write of Ernest Hemingway the result suggested rather the attempt of a shop girl at setting down her reactions to Clark Gable. Seemingly Mrs. Parker is at ease only in disparagement, and most of her sketches —"Arrangement in Black and White," for example—are forms of malediction, kin, across the years, to the antique and satisfying practice of making wax images and then sticking pins into them.

A. W.

BIG
TWO-HEARTED
RIVER

by

ERNEST HEMINGWAY

BIG TWO-HEARTED RIVER

I

THE train went on up the track out of sight, around one of the hills of burnt timber. Nick sat down on the bundle of canvas and bedding the baggage man had pitched out of the door of the baggage car. There was no town, nothing but the rails and the burned-over country. The thirteen saloons that had lined the one street of Seney had not left a trace. The foundations of the Mansion House hotel stuck up above the ground. The stone was chipped and split by the fire. It was all that was left of the town of Seney. Even the surface had been burned off the ground.

Nick looked at the burned-over stretch of hillside, where he had expected to find the scattered houses of the town, and then walked down the railroad track to the bridge over the river. The river was there. It swirled against the log spiles of the bridge. Nick looked down into the clear, brown water, colored from the pebbly bottom, and watched the trout keeping themselves steady in the current with wavering fins. As he watched them they changed their positions by quick angles, only to hold steady in the fast water again. Nick watched them a long time.

He watched them holding themselves with their noses into the current, many trout in deep, fast-moving water, slightly distorted as he watched far down through the glassy convex surface of the pool, its surface pushing and swelling smooth against the resistance of the log-driven piles of the bridge. At the bottom of the pool were the big trout. Nick did not see them at first. Then he saw them at the bottom of the pool, big trout looking to hold themselves on the gravel bottom in a varying mist of gravel and sand, raised in spurts by the current.

Nick looked down into the pool from the bridge. It was a hot day.

A kingfisher flew up the stream. It was a long time since Nick had looked into a stream and seen trout. They were very satisfactory. As the shadow of the kingfisher moved up the stream, a big trout shot upstream in a long angle, only his shadow marking the angle, then lost his shadow as he came through the surface of the water, caught the sun, and then, as he went back into the stream under the surface, his shadow seemed to float down the stream with the current, unresisting, to his post under the bridge where he tightened, facing up into the current.

Nick's heart tightened as the trout moved. He felt all the old feeling.

He turned and looked down the stream. It stretched away, pebbly bottomed with shallows and big boulders and a deep pool as it curved away around the foot of a bluff.

Nick walked back up the ties to where his pack lay in the cinders beside the railroad track. He was happy. He adjusted the pack harness around the bundle, pulling straps tight, slung the pack on his back, got his arms through the shoulder straps, and took some of the pull off his shoulders by leaning his forehead against the wide band of the tump-line. Still, it was too heavy. It was much too heavy. He had his leather rod-case in his hand and leaning forward to keep the weight of the pack high on his shoulders he walked along the road that paralleled the railroad track, leaving the burned town behind in the heat, and then turned off around a hill with a high, fire-scarred hill on either side onto a road that went back into the country. He walked along the road feeling the ache from the pull of the heavy pack. The road climbed steadily. It was hard work walking uphill. His muscles ached and the day was hot, but Nick felt happy. He felt he had left everything behind, the need for thinking, the need to write, other needs. It was all back of him.

From the time he had got down off the train and the baggage man had thrown his pack out of the open car door, things had been different. Seney was burned, the country was burned over and changed, but it did not matter. It could not all be burned. He knew that. He hiked along the road, sweating in the sun, climbing to cross the range of hills that separated the railroad from the pine plains.

The road ran on, dipping occasionally, but always climbing. Nick went on up. Finally the road after going parallel to the burnt hillside reached the top. Nick leaned back against a stump and slipped out of the pack harness. Ahead of him, as far as he could see, was the pine plain. The burned country stopped off at the left with the range of hills. On ahead, islands of dark pine trees rose out of the plain. Far off to the left was the line of the river. Nick followed it with his eye and caught glints of the water in the sun.

There was nothing but the pine plain ahead of him, until the far blue hills that marked the Lake Superior height of land. He could hardly see them, faint and far away in the heat-light over the plain. If he looked too steadily they were gone. But if he only half looked they were there, the far-off hills of the height of land.

Nick sat down against the charred stump and smoked a cigarette. His pack balanced on the top of the stump, harness holding ready, a hollow molded in it from his back. Nick sat smoking, looking out over the country. He did not need to get his map out. He knew where he was from the position of the river.

As he smoked, his legs stretched out in front of him, he noticed a grasshopper walk along the ground and up onto his woolen sock. The grasshopper was black. As he had walked along the road, climbing, he had started many grasshoppers from the dust. They were all black. They were not the big grasshoppers with yellow and black or red and black wings whirring out from their black wing sheathing as they fly up. These were just ordinary hoppers, but all a sooty black in color. Nick had wondered about them as he walked, without really thinking about them. Now, as he watched the black hopper that was nibbling at the wool of his sock with its fourway lip, he realized that they had all turned black from living in the burned-over land. He realized that the fire must have come the year before, but the grasshoppers were all black now. He wondered how long they would stay that way.

Carefully he reached his hand down and took hold of the hopper by the wings. He turned him up, all his legs walking in the air, and looked at his jointed belly. Yes, it was black too, iridescent where the back and head were dusty.

"Go on, hopper," Nick said, speaking out loud for the first time, "fly away somewhere."

He tossed the grasshopper up into the air and watched him sail away to a charcoal stump across the road.

Nick stood up. He leaned his back against the weight of his pack where it rested upright on the stump and got his arms through the shoulder straps. He stood with the pack on his back on the brow of the hill looking out across the country, toward the distant river, and then struck down the hillside away from the road. Underfoot the ground was good walking. Two hundred yards down the hillside the fire line stopped. Then it was sweet fern, growing ankle-high, to walk through, and clumps of jack pines; a long undulating country with frequent rises and descents, sandy underfoot and the country alive again.

Nick kept his direction by the sun. He knew where he wanted to strike the river and he kept on through the pine plain, mounting small rises to see other rises ahead of him and sometimes from the top of a rise a great solid island of pines off to his right or his left. He broke off some sprigs of the heathery sweet fern, and put them under his pack straps. The chafing crushed it and he smelled it as he walked.

He was tired and very hot, walking across the uneven, shadeless pine plain. At any time he knew he could strike the river by turning off to his left. It could not be more than a mile away. But he kept on toward the north to hit the river as far upstream as he could go in one day's walking.

For some time as he walked Nick had been in sight of one of the big islands of pine standing out above the rolling high ground he was crossing. He dipped down and then as he came slowly up to the crest of the ridge he turned and made toward the pine trees.

There was no underbrush in the island of pine trees. The trunks of the trees went straight up or slanted toward each other. The trunks were straight and brown, without branches. The branches were high above. Some interlocked to make a solid shadow on the brown forest floor. Around the grove of trees was a bare space. It was brown and soft underfoot as Nick walked on it. This was the overlapping of the pine-needle floor, extending out beyond the width of the high branches.

The trees had grown tall and the branches moved high, leaving in the sun this bare space they had once covered with shadow. Sharp at the edge of this extension of the forest floor commenced the sweet fern.

Nick slipped off his pack and lay down in the shade. He lay on his back and looked up into the pine trees. His neck and back and the small of his back rested as he stretched. The earth felt good against his back. He looked up at the sky, through the branches, and then shut his eyes. He opened them and looked up again. There was a wind high up in the branches. He shut his eyes again and went to sleep.

Nick woke stiff and cramped. The sun was nearly down. His pack was heavy and the straps painful as he lifted it on. He leaned over with the pack on and picked up the leather rod-case and started out from the pine trees across the sweet-fern swale, toward the river. He knew it could not be more than a mile.

He came down a hillside covered with stumps into a meadow. At the edge of the meadow flowed the river. Nick was glad to get to the river. He walked upstream through the meadow. His trousers were soaked with the dew as he walked. After the hot day, the dew had come quickly and heavily. The river made no sound. It was too fast and smooth. At the edge of the meadow, before he mounted to a piece of high ground to make camp, Nick looked down the river at the trout rising. They were rising to insects come from the swamp on the other side of the stream when the sun went down. The trout jumped out of water to take them. While Nick walked through the little stretch of meadow alongside the stream, trout had jumped high out of water. Now as he looked down the river, the insects must be settling on the surface, for the trout were feeding steadily all down the stream. As far down the long stretch as he could see, the trout were rising, making circles all down the surface of the water, as though it were starting to rain.

The ground rose, wooded and sandy, to overlook the meadow, the stretch of river, and the swamp. Nick dropped his pack and rod-case and looked for a level piece of ground. He was very hungry and he wanted to make his camp before he cooked. Between two jack pines, the ground was quite level. He took the ax out of the pack and chopped out two projecting roots. That leveled a piece of ground large enough to sleep on. He smoothed out the sandy soil with his hand and pulled all the sweet-fern bushes by their roots. His hands smelled good from the sweet fern. He smoothed the uprooted earth. He did not want anything making lumps under the blankets. When he had the ground smooth, he spread his three blankets. One he folded double, next to the ground. The other two he spread on top.

With the ax he slit off a bright slab of pine from one of the stumps and split it into pegs for the tent. He wanted them long and solid to hold in the ground. With the tent unpacked and spread on the ground, the pack, leaning against a jack pine, looked much smaller. Nick tied the rope that served the tent for a ridge-pole to the trunk of one of the pine trees and pulled the tent up off the ground with the other end of the rope and tied it to the other pine. The tent hung on the rope like a canvas blanket on a clothes line. Nick poked a pole he had cut up under the back peak of the canvas and then made it a tent by pegging out the sides. He pegged the sides out taut and drove the pegs deep, hitting them down into the ground with the flat of the ax until the rope loops were buried and the canvas was drum tight.

Across the open mouth of the tent Nick fixed cheese cloth to keep out mosquitoes. He crawled inside under the mosquito bar with various things from the pack to put at the head of the bed under the slant of the canvas. Inside the tent the light came through the brown canvas. It smelled pleasantly of canvas. Already there was something mysterious and homelike. Nick was happy as he crawled inside the tent. He had not been unhappy all day. This was different though. Now things were done. There had been this to do. Now it was done. It had been a hard trip. He was very tired. That was done. He had made his camp. He was settled. Nothing could touch him. It was a good place to camp. He was there, in the good place. He was in his home where he had made it. Now he was hungry.

He came out, crawling under the cheese cloth. It was quite dark outside. It was lighter in the tent.

Nick went over to the pack and found, with his fingers, a long nail in a paper sack of nails, in the bottom of the pack. He drove it into the pine tree, holding it close and hitting it gently with the flat of the ax. He hung the pack up on the nail. All his supplies were in the pack. They were off the ground and sheltered now.

Nick was hungry. He did not believe he had ever been hungrier. He opened and emptied a can of pork and beans and a can of spaghetti into the frying pan.

"I've got a right to eat this kind of stuff, if I'm willing to carry it," Nick said. His voice sounded strange in the darkening woods. He did not speak again.

He started a fire with some chunks of pine he got with the ax from a stump. Over the fire he stuck a wire grill, pushing the four legs down into the ground with his boot. Nick put the frying pan on the grill over the flames. He was hungrier. The beans and spaghetti warmed. Nick stirred them and mixed them together. They began to bubble, making little bubbles that rose with difficulty to the surface. There was a good smell. Nick got out a bottle of tomato catchup and cut four slices of bread. The little bubbles were coming faster now. Nick sat down beside the fire and lifted the frying pan off. He poured about half the contents out into the tin plate. It spread slowly on the plate. Nick knew it was too hot. He poured on some tomato catchup. He knew the beans and spaghetti were still too hot. He looked at the fire, then at the tent, he was not going to spoil it all by burning his tongue. For years he had never enjoyed fried bananas because he had never been able to wait for them to cool. His tongue was very sensitive. He was very hungry. Across the river in the swamp, in the almost dark, he saw a mist rising. He looked at the tent once more. All right. He took a full spoonful from the plate.

"Chrise," Nick said; "Geezus Chrise," he said happily.

He ate the whole plateful before he remembered the bread. Nick finished the second plateful with the bread, mopping the plate shiny. He had not eaten since a cup of coffee and a ham sandwich in the station restaurant at St. Ignace. It had been a very fine experience. He had been that hungry before, but had not been able to satisfy it. He could have made camp hours before if he had wanted to. There were plenty of good places to camp on the river. But this was good.

Nick tucked two big chips of pine under the grill. The fire flared up. He had forgotten to get water for the coffee. Out of the pack he got a folding canvas bucket and walked down the hill, across the edge of the meadow, to the stream. The other bank was in the white mist. The grass was wet and cold as he knelt on the bank and dipped the canvas bucket into the stream. It bellied and pulled hard in the current. The water was ice cold. Nick rinsed the bucket and carried it full up to the camp. Up away from the stream it was not so cold.

Nick drove another big nail and hung up the bucket full of water. He dipped the coffee pot half full, put some more chips under the grill onto the fire, and put the pot on. He could not remember which way he made coffee. He could remember an argument about it with Hopkins, but not which side he had taken. He decided to bring it to a boil. He remembered now that was Hopkins's way. He had once argued about everything with Hopkins. While he waited for the coffee to boil, he opened a small can of apricots. He liked to open cans. He emptied the can of apricots out into a tin cup. While he watched the coffee on the fire, he drank the juice syrup of the apricots, carefully at first to keep from spilling, then meditatively, sucking the apricots down. They were better than fresh apricots.

The coffee boiled as he watched. The lid came up and coffee and grounds ran down the side of the pot. Nick took it off the grill. It was a triumph for Hopkins. He put sugar in the empty apricot cup and poured some of the coffee out to cool. It was too hot to pour and he used his hat to hold the handle of the coffee pot. He would not let it steep in the pot at all. Not the first cup. It should be straight Hopkins all the way. Hop deserved that. He was a very serious coffee maker. He was the most serious man Nick had ever known. Not heavy, serious. That was a long time ago. Hopkins spoke without moving his lips. He had played polo. He made millions of dollars in Texas. He had borrowed carfare to go to Chicago, when the wire came that his first big well had come in. He could have wired for money. That would have been too slow. They called Hop's girl the Blonde Venus. Hop did not mind because she was not his real girl. Hopkins said very confidently that none of them would make fun of his real girl. He was right. Hopkins went away when the telegram came. That was on the Black River. It took eight days for the telegram to reach him. Hopkins gave away his .22 caliber Colt automatic pistol to Nick. He gave his camera to Bill. It was to remember him always by. They were all going fishing again next summer. The Hop Head was rich. He would get a yacht and they would all cruise along the north shore of Lake Superior. He was excited but serious. They said good-by and all felt bad. It broke up the trip. They never saw Hopkins again. That was a long time ago on the Black River.

Nick drank the coffee, the coffee according to Hopkins. The coffee was bitter. Nick laughed. It made a good ending to the story. His mind was starting to work. He knew he could choke it because he was tired enough. He spilled the coffee out of the pot and shook the grounds loose into the fire. He lit a cigarette and went inside the tent. He took off his shoes and trousers, sitting on the blankets, rolled the shoes up inside the trousers for a pillow and got in between the blankets.

Out through the front of the tent he watched the glow of the fire, when the night wind blew on it. It was a quiet night. The swamp was perfectly quiet. Nick stretched under the blanket comfortably. A mosquito hummed close to his ear. Nick sat up and lit a match. The mosquito was on the canvas, over his head. Nick moved the match quickly up to it. The mosquito made a satisfactory hiss in the flame. The match went out. Nick lay down again under the blankets. He turned on his side and shut his eyes. He was sleepy. He felt sleep coming. He curled up under the blanket and went to sleep.

II

In the morning the sun was up and the tent was starting to get hot. Nick crawled out under the mosquito netting stretched across the mouth of the tent, to look at the morning. The grass was wet on his hands as he came out. He held his trousers and his shoes in his hands.

The sun was just up over the hill. There was the meadow, the river, and the swamp. There were birch trees in the green of the swamp on the other side of the river.

The river was clear and smoothly fast in the early morning. Down about two hundred yards were three logs all the way across the stream. They made the water smooth and deep above them. As Nick watched, a mink crossed the river on the logs and went into the swamp. Nick was excited. He was excited by the early morning and the river. He was really too hurried to eat breakfast, but he knew he must. He built a little fire and put on the coffee pot. While the water was heating in the pot, he took an empty bottle and went down over the edge of the high ground to the meadow. The meadow was wet with dew and Nick wanted to catch grasshoppers for bait before the sun dried the grass. He found plenty of good grasshoppers. They were at the base of the grass stems. Sometimes they clung to a grass stem. They were cold and wet with the dew, and could not jump until the sun warmed them. Nick picked them up, taking only the medium-sized brown ones, and put them into the bottle. He turned over a log, and just under the shelter of the edge were several hundred hoppers. It was a grasshopper lodging house. Nick put about fifty of the medium browns into the bottle. While he was picking up the hoppers the others warmed in the sun and commenced to hop away. They flew when they hopped. At first they made one flight and stayed stiff when they landed, as though they were dead.

Nick knew that by the time he was through with breakfast they would be as lively as ever. Without dew in the grass it would take him all day to catch a bottleful of good grasshoppers and he would have to crush many of them, slamming at them with his hat. He washed his hands at the stream. He was excited to be near it. Then he walked up to the tent. The hoppers were already jumping stiffly in the grass. In the bottle, warmed by the sun, they were jumping in a mass. Nick put in a pine stick as a cork. It plugged the mouth of the bottle enough, so the hoppers could not get out and left plenty of air passage.

He had rolled the log back and knew he could get grasshoppers there every morning.

Nick laid the bottle full of jumping grasshoppers against a pine trunk. Rapidly he mixed some buckwheat flour with water and stirred it smooth, one cup of flour, one cup of water. He put a handful of coffee in the pot and dipped a lump of grease out of a can and slid it sputtering across the hot skillet. On the smoking skillet he poured smoothly the buckwheat batter. It spread like lava, the grease spitting sharply. Around the edges the buckwheat cake began to firm, then brown, then crisp. The surface was bubbling slowly to porousness. Nick pushed under the browned under surface with a fresh pine chip. He shook the skillet sideways and the cake was loose on the surface. I won't try and flop it, he thought. He slid the chip of clean wood all the way under the cake, and flopped it over onto its face. It sputtered in the pan.

When it was cooked Nick regreased the skillet. He used all the batter. It made another big flapjack and one smaller one.

Nick ate a big flapjack and a smaller one, covered with apple butter. He put apple butter on the third cake, folded it over twice, wrapped it in oiled paper and put it in his shirt pocket. He put the apple butter jar back in the pack and cut bread for two sandwiches.

In the pack he found a big onion. He sliced it in two and peeled the silky outer skin. Then he cut one half into slices and made onion sandwiches. He wrapped them in oiled paper and buttoned them in the other pocket of his khaki shirt. He turned the skillet upside down on the grill, drank the coffee, sweetened and yellow brown with the condensed milk in it, and tidied up the camp. It was a nice little camp.

Nick took his fly rod out of the leather rod-case, jointed it, and shoved the rod-case back into the tent. He put on the reel and threaded the line through the guides. He had to hold it from hand to hand, as he threaded it, or it would slip back through its own weight. It was a heavy, double tapered fly line. Nick had paid eight dollars for it a long time ago. It was made heavy to lift back in the air and come forward flat and heavy and straight to make it possible to cast a fly which has no weight. Nick opened the aluminum leader box. The leaders were coiled between the damp flannel pads. Nick had wet the pads at the water cooler on the train up to St. Ignace. In the damp pads the gut leaders had softened and Nick unrolled one and tied it by a loop at the end to the heavy fly line. He fastened a hook on the end of the leader. It was a small hook, very thin and springy.

Nick took it from his hook book, sitting with the rod across his lap. He tested the knot and the spring of the rod by pulling the line taut. It was a good feeling. He was careful not to let the hook bite into his finger.

He started down to the stream, holding his rod, the bottle of grasshoppers hung from his neck by a thong tied in half-hitches around the neck of the bottle. His landing net hung by a hook from his belt. Over his shoulder was a long flour sack tied at each corner into an ear. The cord went over his shoulder. The sack flapped against his legs.

Nick felt awkward and professionally happy with all his equipment hanging from him. The grasshopper bottle swung against his chest. In his shirt the breast pockets bulged against him with the lunch and his fly book.

He stepped into the stream. It was a shock. His trousers clung tight to his legs. His shoes felt the gravel. The water was a rising cold shock.

Rushing, the current sucked against his legs. Where he stepped in, the water was over his knees. He waded with the current. The gravel slid under his shoes. He looked down at the swirl of water below each leg and tipped up the bottle to get a grasshopper.

The first grasshopper gave a jump in the neck of the bottle and went out into the water. He was sucked under in the whirl by Nick's right leg and came to the surface a little way down stream. He floated rapidly, kicking. In a quick circle, breaking the smooth surface of the water, he disappeared. A trout had taken him.

Another hopper poked his head out of the bottle. His antennæ wavered. He was getting his front legs out of the bottle to jump. Nick took him by the head and held him while he threaded the slim hook under his chin, down through his thorax and into the last segments of his abdomen. The grasshopper took hold of the hook with his front feet, spitting tobacco juice on it. Nick dropped him into the water.

Holding the rod in his right hand he let out line against the pull of the grasshopper in the current. He stripped off line from the reel with his left hand and let it run free. He could see the hopper in the little waves of the current. It went out of sight.

There was a tug on the line. Nick pulled against the taut line. It was his first strike. Holding the now living rod across the current, he brought in the line with his left hand. The rod bent in jerks, the trout pumping against the current. Nick knew it was a small one. He lifted the rod straight up in the air. It bowed with the pull.

He saw the trout in the water jerking with his head and body against the shifting tangent of the line in the stream.

Nick took the line in his left hand and pulled the trout, thumping tiredly against the current, to the surface. His back was mottled the clear, water-over-gravel color, his side flashing in the sun. The rod under his right arm, Nick stooped, dipping his right hand into the current. He held the trout, never still, with his moist right hand, while he un-hooked the barb from his mouth, then dropped him back into the stream.

He hung unsteadily in the current, then settled to the bottom beside a stone. Nick reached down his hand to touch him, his arm to the el-bow under water. The trout was steady in the moving stream, resting on the gravel, beside a stone. As Nick's fingers touched him, touched his smooth, cool, underwater feeling, he was gone, gone in a shadow across the bottom of the stream.

He's all right, Nick thought. He was only tired.

He had wet his hand before he touched the trout, so he would not disturb the delicate mucus that covered him. If a trout was touched with a dry hand, a white fungus attacked the unprotected spot. Years before when he had fished crowded streams, with fly fishermen ahead of him and behind him, Nick had again and again come on dead trout, furry with white fungus, drifted against a rock, or floating belly up in some pool. Nick did not like to fish with other men on the river. Un-less they were of your party, they spoiled it.

He wallowed down the stream, above his knees in the current, through the fifty yards of shallow water above the pile of logs that crossed the stream. He did not rebait his hook and held it in his hand as he waded. He was certain he could catch small trout in the shallows, but he did not want them. There would be no big trout in the shallows this time of day.

Now the water deepened up his thighs sharply and coldly. Ahead was the smooth dammed-back flood of water above the logs. The water was smooth and dark; on the left, the lower edge of the meadow; on the right the swamp.

Nick leaned back against the current and took a hopper from the bottle. He threaded the hopper on the hook and spat on him for good luck. Then he pulled several yards of line from the reel and tossed the hopper out ahead onto the fast, dark water. It floated down towards the logs, then the weight of the line pulled the bait under the surface. Nick held the rod in his right hand, letting the line run out through his fingers.

There was a long tug. Nick struck and the rod came alive and dangerous, bent double, the line tightening, coming out of water, tightening, all in a heavy, dangerous, steady pull. Nick felt the moment when the leader would break if the strain increased and let the line go.

The reel ratcheted into a mechanical shriek as the line went out in a rush. Too fast. Nick could not check it, the line rushing out, the reel note rising as the line ran out.

With the core of the reel showing, his heart feeling stopped with the excitement, leaning back against the current that mounted icily his thighs, Nick thumbed the reel hard with his left hand. It was awkward getting his thumb inside the fly-reel frame.

As he put on pressure, the line tightened into sudden hardness and beyond the logs a huge trout went high out of water. As he jumped, Nick lowered the tip of the rod. But he felt, as he dropped the tip to ease the strain, the moment when the strain was too great; the hardness too tight. Of course, the leader had broken. There was no mistaking the feeling when all spring left the line and it became dry and hard. Then it went slack.

His mouth dry, his heart down, Nick reeled in. He had never seen so big a trout. There was a heaviness, a power not to be held, and then the bulk of him, as he jumped. He looked as broad as a salmon.

Nick's hand was shaky. He reeled in slowly. The thrill had been too much. He felt, vaguely, a little sick, as though it would be better to sit down.

The leader had broken where the hook was tied to it. Nick took it in his hand. He thought of the trout somewhere on the bottom, holding himself steady over the gravel, far down below the light, under the logs, with the hook in his jaw. Nick knew the trout's teeth would cut through the snell of the hook. The hook would embed itself in his jaw. He'd bet the trout was angry. Anything that size would be angry. That was a trout. He had been solidly hooked. Solid as a rock. He felt like a rock, too, before he started off. By God, he was a big one. By God, he was the biggest one I ever heard of.

Nick climbed out onto the meadow and stood, water running down his trousers and out of his shoes, his shoes squelchy. He went over and sat on the logs. He did not want to rush his sensations any.

He wriggled his toes in the water, in his shoes, and got out a cigarette from his breast pocket. He lit it and tossed the match into the fast water below the logs. A tiny trout rose at the match as it swung around in the fast current. Nick laughed. He would finish the cigarette.

He sat on the logs, smoking, drying in the sun, the sun warm on his back, the river shallow ahead entering the woods, curving into the woods, shallows, light glittering, big water-smooth rocks, cedars along the bank and white birches, the logs warm in the sun, smooth to sit on, without bark, gray to the touch; slowly the feeling of disappointment left him. It went away slowly, the feeling of disappointment that came sharply after the thrill that made his shoulders ache. It was all right now. His rod lying out on the logs, Nick tied a new hook on the leader, pulling the gut tight until it grimped into itself in a hard knot.

He baited up, then picked up the rod and walked to the far end of the logs to get into the water, where it was not too deep. Under and beyond the logs was a deep pool. Nick walked around the shallow shelf near the swamp shore until he came out on the shallow bed of the stream.

On the left, where the meadow ended and the woods began, a great elm tree was uprooted. Gone over in a storm, it lay back into the woods, its roots clotted with dirt, grass growing in them, rising a solid bank beside the stream. The river cut to the edge of the uprooted tree. From where Nick stood he could see deep channels, like ruts, cut in the shallow bed of the stream by the flow of the current. Pebbly where he stood and pebbly and full of boulders beyond; where it curved near the tree roots, the bed of the stream was marly, and between the ruts of deep water green weed fronds swung in the current.

Nick swung the rod back over his shoulder and forward, and the line, curving forward, laid the grasshopper down on one of the deep channels in the weeds. A trout struck and Nick hooked him.

Holding the rod far out toward the uprooted tree and sloshing backward in the current, Nick worked the trout, plunging, the rod bending alive, out of the danger of the weeds into the open river. Holding the rod, pumping alive against the current, Nick brought the trout in. He rushed, but always came, the spring of the rod yielding to the rushes, sometimes jerking underwater, but always bringing him in. Nick eased downstream with the rushes. The rod above his head, he led the trout over the net, then lifted.

The trout hung heavy in the net, mottled trout back and silver sides in the meshes. Nick unhooked him—heavy sides, good to hold, big undershot jaw—and slipped him, heaving and big sliding, into the long sack that hung from his shoulders in the water.

Nick spread the mouth of the sack against the current and it filled, heavy with water. He held it up, the bottom in the stream, and the water poured out through the sides. Inside at the bottom was the big trout, alive in the water.

Nick moved downstream. The sack out ahead of him sunk, heavy in the water, pulling from his shoulders.

It was getting hot, the sun hot on the back of his neck.

Nick had one good trout. He did not care about getting many trout. Now the stream was shallow and wide. There were trees along both banks. The trees of the left bank made short shadows on the current in the forenoon sun. Nick knew there were trout in each shadow. In the afternoon, after the sun had crossed toward the hills, the trout would be in the cool shadows on the other side of the stream.

The very biggest ones would lie up close to the bank. You could always pick them up there on the Black. When the sun was down they all moved out into the current. Just when the sun made the water blinding in the glare before it went down, you were likely to strike a big trout anywhere in the current. It was almost impossible to fish then, the surface of the water was blinding as a mirror in the sun. Of course, you could fish upstream, but in a stream like the Black, or this, you had to wallow against the current and, in a deep place, the water piled up on you. It was no fun to fish upstream with this much current.

Nick moved along through the shallow stretch watching the banks for deep holes. A beech tree grew close beside the river, so that the branches hung down into the water. The stream went back in under the leaves. There were always trout in a place like that.

Nick did not care about fishing that hole. He was sure he would get hooked in the branches.

It looked deep though. He dropped the grasshopper so the current took it under water, back in under the overhanging branch. The line pulled hard and Nick struck. The trout threshed heavily, half out of water in the leaves and branches. The line was caught. Nick pulled hard and the trout was off. He reeled in and, holding the hook in his hand, walked down the stream.

Ahead, close to the left bank, was a big log. Nick saw it was hollow; pointing up river the current entered it smoothly, only a little ripple spread each side of the log. The water was deepening. The top of the hollow log was gray and dry. It was partly in the shadow.

Nick took the cork out of the grasshopper bottle and a hopper clung to it. He picked him off, hooked him, and tossed him out. He held the rod far out so that the hopper on the water moved into the current flowing into the hollow log. Nick lowered the rod and the hopper floated in. There was a heavy strike. Nick swung the rod against the pull. It felt as though he were hooked into the log itself, except for the live feeling.

He tried to force the fish out into the current. It came, heavily.

The line went slack and Nick thought the trout was gone. Then he saw him, very near, in the current, shaking his head, trying to get the hook out. His mouth was clamped shut. He was fighting the hook in the clear flowing current.

Looping in the line with his left hand, Nick swung the rod to make the line taut and tried to lead the trout toward the net, but he was gone, out of sight, the line pumping. Nick fought him against the current, letting him thump in the water against the spring of the rod. He shifted the rod to his left hand, worked the trout upstream, holding his weight, fighting on the rod, and then let him down into the net. He lifted him clear of the water, a heavy half-circle in the net, the net dripping, unhooked him, and slid him into the sack.

He spread the mouth of the sack and looked down in at the two big trout alive in the water.

Through the deepening water, Nick waded over to the hollow log. He took the sack off, over his head, the trout flopping as it came out of water, and hung it so the trout were deep in the water. Then he pulled himself up on the log and sat, the water from his trousers and boots running down into the stream. He laid his rod down, moved along to the shady end of the log, and took the sandwiches out of his pocket. He dipped the sandwiches in the cold water. The current carried away the crumbs. He ate the sandwiches and dipped his hat full of water to drink, the water running out through his hat just ahead of his drinking.

It was cool in the shade, sitting on the log. He took a cigarette out and struck a match to light it. The match sunk into the gray wood, making a tiny furrow. Nick leaned over the side of the log, found a hard place, and lit the match. He sat smoking and watching the river.

Ahead the river narrowed and went into a swamp. The river became smooth and deep and the swamp looked solid with cedar trees, their trunks close together, their branches solid. It would not be possible to walk through a swamp like that. The branches grew so low. You would have to keep almost level with the ground to move at all. You could not crash through the branches. That must be why the animals that lived in swamps were built the way they were, Nick thought.

He wished he had brought something to read. He felt like reading. He did not feel like going on into the swamp. He looked down the river. A big cedar slanted all the way across the stream. Beyond that the river went into the swamp.

Nick did not want to go in there now. He felt a reaction against deep wading with the water deepening up under his armpits, to hook big trout in places impossible to land them. In the swamp the banks were bare, the big cedars came together overhead, the sun did not come through, except in patches; in the fast deep water, in the half-light, the fishing would be tragic. In the swamp fishing was a tragic adventure. Nick did not want it. He did not want to go down the stream any further today.

He took out his knife, opened it, and stuck it in the log. Then he pulled up the sack, reached into it, and brought out one of the trout. Holding him near the tail, hard to hold, alive, in his hand, he whacked him against the log. The trout quivered, rigid. Nick laid him on the log in the shade and broke the neck of the other fish the same way. He laid them side by side on the log. They were fine trout.

Nick cleaned them, slitting them from the vent to the tip of the jaw. All the insides and the gills and tongue came out in one piece. They were both males; long gray-white strips of milt, smooth and clean. All the insides clean and compact, coming out all together. Nick tossed the offal ashore for the minks to find.

He washed the trout in the stream. When he held them back up in the water they looked like live fish. Their color was not gone yet. He washed his hands and dried them on the log. Then he laid the trout on the sack spread out on the log, rolled them up in it, tied the bundle and put it in the landing net. His knife was still standing, blade stuck in the log. He cleaned it on the wood and put it in his pocket.

Nick stood up on the log, holding his rod, the landing net hanging heavy, then stepped into the water and splashed ashore. He climbed the bank and cut up into the woods, toward the high ground. He was going back to camp. He looked back. The river just showed through the trees. There were plenty of days coming when he could fish the swamp.

AN AFTERWORD ON
"BIG TWO-HEARTED RIVER"

THIS memory of trout-fishing in the Saginaw—or some river in a Michigan not yet plundered of its trees—was first published in 1925 as one of the oddments of a miscellany called *In Our Time,* the first book to serve notice on readers in America (and on precious few of *them*) that there was such a person as Ernest Hemingway.

Born shortly before the turn of the century, the son of a Chicago physician, Hemingway forsook the parental roof in Oak Park when he was fifteen. After sundry adventures, including a novitiate on the Kansas City *Star* as a baseball reporter and scarring service in Italy during the World War—eventually he was a private in the ranks of the Italian army—Hemingway had, by the time this piece was written, settled down in Paris for his first trial flights as an author. "Big Two-Hearted River" was got down on paper there while he was still groping his way under the influence of Gertrude Stein—an influence which has visibly affected all his writing to this day.

There is a considerable number who recognize the author of that superb novel, *A Farewell to Arms,* and the unforgettable short-story called "The Killers" as the supreme stylist writing today in the English language. These would probably be as content to rest their case on this early effort as on anything of his yet published. It is the memory of a sensuous experience, recaptured by such an unerring choice of the factors which had made it pleasurable that the pleasure is communicated to the reader—communicated, it can be here testified, even to one who would not have himself enjoyed the experience at all and who, though seldom consulted on the matter by his friends, would rather not hear about any fishing-trip ever. But the fascination which this narrative can exercise on even the most mutinous reader is probably traceable to some rhythm—a verbal impact as bemusing as the beat of a Congo tom-tom—which induces at last in the reader the surrender of hypnosis. In a sense more valid than is usually the word's lot when flaunted on a dust-jacket, the reader of "Big Two-Hearted River" is spellbound. But even one who feels its fascination to the full may still be disposed (after he has collected his wits) to remember that the thing said is always more important than the way of saying it and to observe without undue churlishness—this footnote is written at a time when the new novel, *To Have and Have Not,* is yet to come from the printer—to observe, indeed, regretfully, that since *A Farewell to Arms,* Mr. Hemingway has not had much to say.

A. W.

THE SELF-HELP
OF G. J. SMITH

by

WILLIAM BOLITHO

THE SELF-HELP OF G. J. SMITH

Sir,

In answer to your application my parentage and age &c. My mother was a Buss horse, my father a Cab driver my sister a Roughrider over the Arctic regions, my brothers were all galant sailors on a steam-roller.

G. J. Smith.

We have but little to set against this claim of George Joseph Smith to be the issue of a phantasmagoria and not a human family. His birth certificate states that he was born at 92 Roman Road, Bethnal Green, London, on the 11th January 1872. His father, the "Cab driver," according to this meagre document, was also an insurance agent: an insecure category that may (risking something on the observed unspontaneity of a mass-murderer's imagination) include the practice of flower and figure painting, which, in one of his marriage explanations, George Joseph claimed for him. Beyond this cloudy genealogy it is vain to seek. The very surname is clueless, for all family trees lose themselves among the Smiths. If ants have names for each other, they must use a tiny equivalent for Smith. It has no handle for the curious to meddle with. It is a name unlimited by space or time; it is an anonymity that may cover an earl or a gipsy evangelist, and is a sort of evasion of the laws of heredity. "Smith" suited the fantastic figure of this man who hated identification. With it, his only heirloom, he could wander undetectably in the depths of any directory; he could enjoy some of the privilege of the disembodied spirit. He escapes the unplatonic ties of family, and promotes himself out of commonplace crime to the company of Mr. Hyde, and Spring-Heeled Jack; a phantasm haunting the hinder terraces of the Lower Middle Class, a subject for a new Tale of Wonder and Imagination, where, instead of Hermits, are Respectable Spin-

663

sters; instead of Dungeons, the shadows of boarding-house basements; instead of skulls, a more gruesome terror of Tin Baths.

From the obscure bourne from which he came to his first appearance in the light of record is nine years. Our knowledge of this first appearance is solely due to his own negligent confidence to a woman in days before his character had set. At nine years old he was sent to a reformatory, where he stayed until he was sixteen. Meagre as it is, the information has many implications. A reformatory boy is indeed seldom different from other boys when he goes in. When he comes out, he is a type. It is a punishment for acts which proverbially—and in certain classes of society, practically—are recognized as natural to the growing male: theft, cruelty, various destructions of property. In the complicated social system of England there is a contradictory attitude towards this phenomenon. If the family is rich, it is excused, or in certain circumstances even praised, as natural and a sign of health. Thus the theft of growing fruit, the breaking of windows or fences, is not only pardoned, but often encouraged by jocular reminiscence and approving laughter. Graver deeds are punished privately by the family. When the family is poor, or only callous, the boy taken in any such act (in Smith's days) was certain of from four to seven years' imprisonment in a reformatory. An apple off a barrow, a stone through a window, a broken street lamp: any of these acts may have brought on Smith his sentence. If he had been out of his teens, such offences would have entailed a fine or a few weeks' hard labour. But for philanthropic reasons such leniency is considered against the interests of the growing boy, if he is poor, and it is usual to send him to imprisonment for such period of his boyhood as may remain. This imprisonment, of course, was quite different from that inflicted on the adult; in addition to the manual work of prisons, the reformatory boy had to work at his books, and while there was no ticket-of-leave or remission system for good behaviour, corporal punishment, practically abolished for the grown prisoner, was an important part of the reformatory method for the youngsters. This system, devised for the betterment of the lower classes, the correction of their faults, and to assist them to bring up their families hard-working members of the State, does not always succeed. The boys on their release may be divided into two categories: those who have either outgrown the destructive stage without damage to property in their confinement, or whom the wholesome lesson of the power of the forces of order has discouraged from ever again trying to oppose it; and those who from a feeling of revolt, or because of hereditary tares, are incorrigible and henceforth for the rest of their days are integrally attached to the police system as criminals.

The first class are set to the credit side of our system; they are assured that no stigma attaches to them for their past, and all they have to do is to persuade a trades union to recognize their irregular apprenticeship in the reformatory workshop and admit them to the practice of the trade they have been taught. The second class are our failures; nothing more can be done for them. But they may be certain that their future sentences will usually be longer than those given to other criminals who have not had advantages to excuse them.

Smith, we can detect from circumstantial evidence, particularly his correspondence, left the Reformatory in a state somewhat intermediary between reclamation and total loss. He was certainly neither cowed nor inspired sufficiently to make his peace with society. But unlike the majority of "bad cases," he had used his head during the seven years, and had learnt something important and useful beyond the beggarly R's and the amateur woodwork. He was released with a precise knowledge of the ethics, and even of the vocabulary, of that good world that governs reformatories. Where else than from a good-hearted clerical visitor could he have learnt to compose such a sentence: "I vow to take advantage of every future day that the great powers have ordained, until the miserable past is absolutely outlived and a character established which will be worthy of your appreciation." Or: "Possibly many years are before us all wherein peace and goodwill will always keep the past at bay, and a Christian brotherly feeling established." This peak-faced urchin from Bethnal Green has remembered word for word, almost to the intonation, what he heard on Sundays from his spiritual father, even to the characteristic nervous shrinking from New Testament onomatology. Certainly the young delinquent did something more than pick his nose during these seven years of reformation. He had acquired what no foreigner can ever hope to do, the practice of that difficult English undenominationalism under which our State Christianity hides itself against the double onslaught of the Education Act and Higher Criticism. He had mastered the right tone in which to speak of the past, the attitude towards the future expected of one on whom so much State money had been spent. In fact, the root theory of reform was in him. Of all his studies, the concept of "making good," social atonement in its simplest form—to make a good living out of reach of the law—was the firmest embedded. As to the way to achieve it, he had not been so well instructed. The only rule he retained of this latter part of the curriculum was that an alibi, moral, local, or historical, always requires two witnesses.

With this baggage—it might have made him a masterly writer of begging-letters—he had also acquired at some time in between the imperceptible chinks of ceaseless routine one of those devastating egotisms with which, whether they arise out of fear or vice, all mass-murderers are afflicted. Besides their habit of living in a constructed lie, besides the lust of killing which is a mysterious but constant symptom, this damned class are invariably selfish to a degree of which the greatest actor can have no conception: passions that can be more justly compared with that of a mother for a sickly child than with any lesser love between the sexes. Such egotisms are not the growth of a day, nor within the reach of anyone who has not searched the bottom of possible miseries. To love oneself like a Troppmann or Smith is a lifelong paroxysm in which the adoration of Saint John of the Cross, the jealousy of Othello, the steadfastness of a Dante is imitated; if there were a measure of intensity, I would dare say, excelled. In other forms of love admiration may be a necessary factor. The love of a Smith for himself needs no such prop. It absorbs every globule of his being, so that when it is present God and Man alike have no part in him. His self-compassion, self-pity, wakened by what self-knowledge of wretchedness we do not know, sucked the meaning out of every existence but his own. In the life of Burke we suspected it. In the story of Troppmann we deduced its growth. In the case of Smith we see this demoniac Narcissism itself.

From the day of his release for two years Smith's history runs quite underground again. But there are two manholes. In 1890 he serves a week's imprisonment for a petty theft. In 1891 a London Court sent him to six months' hard labour for stealing a bicycle—at that time a luxury peculiarly seductive to a young man of nineteen. Then the trace of his woes and adventures disappears entirely. Possibly he had enlisted. There is some vague allusion to Army Service in what his first wife remembered of his confidences; and once he claimed to a boarding-house keeper to have been a gymnasium instructor. There was some vague allure of the corporal about his walk; some trace of pipe-clay and the button-stick about his later elegance. His unnaturally tough biceps were shaped by some other process than ordinary toil.

Then comes another official memento of his crooked track, the most important since the record of the Reformatory. In 1896, in the name of George Baker, he received twelve months' hard labour for larceny and receiving. This event is strictly analogous to the breaking of the cocoon that frees the fully-grown night-moth. The man has separated himself definitely from the caterpillar that was G. J. Smith, to begin a series of lives in other names, each separate in environment both personal and local and only joined by the hidden chain of his own identity. A double life is not enough for him: henceforth he will make of every year, sometimes every month, a separate life, in which his own history, his name, his profession, as well as the set of personages in which it is spent, is completely changed. He has embarked on a serial adventure in which each episode is complete in itself, whose master-plot is known only to himself: a life divided into impervious compartments. Other men may have mysteries in their life—every incident in his was a separate secret.

This development is simultaneous to his discovery of Woman. Every criminal out of his teens sooner or later collides with the Riddle of Women, and his fate depends, more critically than that of honest men, on the answer he gives it. He may be tangled in the sentimental obstructions of a woman who fears the code, and then be caught in one of the three perilous policies of taciturnity, desperation or reformation. If she is of the same turn he has to share her dangers, and double his own. But if he has even a part of the exalted egotism of Smith he is more surely doomed. He will then try to use women. He will embark on the forbidden and hopeless enterprise of exploiting all this ore lying to his hand: half humanity, with half humanity's property, and all humanity's spending. It is a grave moment in life when it suddenly appears that the ranks of the enemy are not solid; that besides men who fight, punish, resist, there are also women who may be persuaded to love. It is the moment also, if he but knew it, to rush back into the thick of the battle and, doing and receiving evils that he understands, continue open war. All music is there to warn him, the prickings of his own blood, the recesses of his earliest memory, that here is a temple in which sacrilege is desperately dangerous. But this outlying Smith, or George Baker, has no caution. From the day he met his first woman he set eagerly to exploit her. Somewhere in the tunnel he had developed the canaille virility of a Guardsman whose odour, heightened by hair pomade, blacking and tobacco, lures women out of the kitchen like a pack after aniseed. After a short fumbling with the elementary difficulties of their jealousies and timidity, he had his first team of hussies at work for him: their part being to pilfer from their masters and hand over the goods. We do not know what blunder led to the first failure of the scheme. The method, not the idea, was afterwards improved.

In this first essay Smith had come to taste, probably for the first time in his life, the strongest mental pleasure in our civilization—the joys of property. They are peculiarly dangerous to a man of his type. Even the minute quantity of superfluity that his love-slaves put into their master's hands intoxicated him. He had always before lived on the bread-line. None of his earnings had lasted longer than the shortest way from hand to mouth. His first exploitation of women opened to him a new world, garnished with reserve stores against the bitter surprises of life. It furnished his imagination with savings-bank books, cash-boxes, and money laid by. New avenues opened beyond him at the end of which shimmered title-deeds, scrip, fascinating intrinsically and still more in the promise they contained of the final salvation of his only darling, his adored, his own self.

The tiger had tasted blood; or just as accurately, George Joseph had experienced conversion, from the despairing vagrancy of a prison-dweller on leave, to a life of hopeful motive. Smith was a born possessor. The mere routine of acquisition sensually excited him. He picked up the jargon of property law as the Renaissance learned Greek, with the meticulous enthusiasm of a grammarian. Women, even when they kill, always give something. In his first brush with them he brought back that hobby of the lonely, that consolation of the fearful: Avarice. In its strange and twisted ways the neophyte was at once expert.

On his release he appeared in Leicester eager to begin his first hoard. We have mislaid the chain of little reasons that made him open a sweet-shop. But we are allowed for a long time to watch him through a plate-glass window, serving children bulls'-eyes and all the assortment of morsels of aniline and sugar for which they wait from Saturday to Saturday in modern towns; or paper bags of broken biscuits and cake refuse; enjoying a till and a lease; practising himself, as if they were sonnets, in the petty art of writing business letters, with Re and Yours to hand, acknowledging kind receipts and begging to state. But after closing hours when the last shelf had been counted and tidied, he would sally out with his chest rigidly squared in search of more women, to see if they had any more to give him. So he came upon one Caroline Thornhill and married her in the symbolic name of George Oliver Love. In his marriage declaration, he promoted his father to one of the most eminent ranks in society that he knew, that of detective.

But if every incipient miser was a business man, the banks would shut their paying desks. Love and Company were bankrupt in six months. The only asset saved was Mrs. Caroline Love. He took her to London and set her to work, after his first manner. He attended to the postal and receiving departments, that is, he wrote letters of recommendation to employers for her and took what she stole from them.

In the course of this business he came to discover the seaside. It delighted him. From Brighton they went to Hove, from Hove to Hastings, finding everywhere business easier, people more gullible. Smith had found his America. Everywhere around him were rolling prairies of single women, so tame that the hunting male could approach them with the wind. This English seaside has not been methodically explored, yet it is as fascinating in its way as the labyrinths of the vast industrial towns of which it is a sub-continent. The scheme is different, the manner of life and customs are different. Instead of the regular pulse of nine hours between factory and tenement—the regular circulation of the traffic arteries that pump the crowd fresh and living into the vessels of production in the early morning, and the network of veins that conducts their sluggish stream back to the sleeping cells at night, soiled, fatigued—at the seaside there are two other steady tides, at ten o'clock and four, towards the sea. To enable hundreds of thousands to look at the water at the same time, it has been fitted with a **T**-shaped road, made up of a concrete walk along the shore, and an iron and concrete jetty, a shorter arm, jutting at right angles into the sea. At the end of this jetty is a round glass booth of great size, which is the point of concentration of the whole life of the town. Here music of a special kind is performed: songs in which lifelong love is praised, and marches and dances. At the back of the towns the downs have been trimmed, and small plots of grass planted for the game of golf. In many places other plots of land have been fenced off for the other game of lawn-tennis. In these two amusements the majority of the better-class visitors pass their time, sometimes waiting for long periods for an opportunity to play. But in the lesser world of Smith these artificial distractions fill small place; most of its time is spent in the morning and afternoon walk on the sea-roads, or in station round the official music and the private choirs that are spaced along the main-road and the shore.

With these changed institutions of seaside life naturally goes a large alteration of social custom. The rigid observance of the English social code, a variety largely influenced by ascetic Christianity as well as by climatic, feudal and other conditions, depends so much on mutual policing that the slightest removal from the circle where he is known and by which his conduct is ruled produces a considerable relaxation in behaviour of the normal Englishman; and still more in that of the normal Englishwoman. This dissolvent comes into play in the seaside holiday, which like the annual orgy of many African tribes, the majority of our population periodically observes. It is a counterpart of the bodily release from the abominable round of drudgery to which the nation, by an unhappy development, is for the most part condemned, whose only intermission is this yearly visit to the free air of the sea. Once a year we must have leisure to breathe smokeless air. Probably the temporary abandonment of the corset of the innumerable niceties of conduct is as necessary to our naturally adventurous, unconventional, and even lyrical race, as the physical relief.

In this world Smith, for the first time introduced by the hazard of his business, felt so suited that he seldom afterwards operated elsewhere. He perceived the extraordinary advantage, to a man working irregularly and out of the organization, of a milieu in which freedom from work is the rule, discretion and change of identity conventional, and where sudden comings and goings cause no remark. But he had particularly noticed the possibilities of the changed rules of conduct among the women. In London, or even on Sunday nights in Leicester, their approach was always difficult, often impossible. But at the seaside, provided a minimum of *nous,* that principal barrier between the sexes —the need of a formal introduction—was down. Further, those venerated guardians of British morality, the board and lodging house and hotel-keepers, are disarmed at the seaside. This law of liberty stretching in depth as well as area, not only was his power of action on the servile class of women he had known hitherto greatly enlarged, but another stratum of the sex, higher and therefore richer than anything he had aspired to, was here within his reach. His first turn on the glistening promenades convinced him of this. But before we can follow him in his new discovery, we must press him back again, like a jack-in-the-box, into his cell for another two years' hard labour. Mrs. Love had ended the second episode in the usual way.

Silvio Pellico, Baron Trenck, and half a score other innocent and learned men have informed us of their sufferings in prison life. But, that I know of, no genuine thief has published his impressions of confinement. Yet there must be a difference of view, if only because the latter must be deprived of the moral snobbery that so comforted Pellico. From such observations (usually facetious!) as we find strayed among the memoirs of prison governors and the like, it would appear that there are three periods in the course of a long sentence: first, when the guilty prisoner is crushed with despair and hardly able to live; second, when the routine soothes, and the time-shortening effect of monotony emerges; third, when the man begins to count, and the long chagrin of calendar-crossing sets in. Conscripts know this abominable occupation; schoolboys know it. In any old barracks the plasterers find little sums pencilled on the walls: so many days endured, so many to come before *"la classe."* And insomniacs know, what convicts in their last months know, the precise length of an hour, the speed of the minute-hand. Perhaps these degrees are well known to all judges and enter into their standards for measuring the days, months, years, they apportion with such easy assurance to any variety of guilt. But the enormous mental constructions that men, by nature ungeared with reality, must be rearing in the silence of four walls, the strange and idiotic plans they must make in such a waking dream, we can only guess at. Happiest certainly of all those who, like Love, doing his 730 days for theft by receiving from his wife, have walled up along with them all that they adore, if it is only their wretched selves.

He was released in 1902, to find that Mrs. Love had fled to Canada. He must have pondered much on this circumstance, for a voyage to Canada becomes henceforth an integral ornament of his lies. Possibly he tried to make up his mind to follow her, seeing no other way of making a living, for one forgets more than one learns in a cell. But gradually what he had observed at the seaside came back to him; then he bethought himself of other women, more convenient to his hand. He left the Canadian voyage lying in his mental life, complete enough for him to have a working belief in its accomplishment ever afterwards; and returned to the exploitation of other women.

In 1899 he already had conquered his first middle-class spinster; perhaps this was one of the reasons for Mrs. Love's denunciation. She was a boarding-house keeper in London, whom he met at the seaside. He married her at once, and some time after his release returned to her. When she was sucked dry, he went on to others. For eight years he proceeded from spinster to spinster, leaving behind him a litter of closed savings-bank accounts. Some he got rid of at once, who bored or irritated him, by a set technique of taking them to a public exhibition, pretexting a bodily need that would separate them for a minute, and disappearing. Some were worth the troublesome business of marriage; for some the promise sufficed. Smith led in these years a leisured life. He began to frequent public libraries, and soon was praising himself for his literary taste. Some mysterious reminiscence of his father gave him a peg for believing he was an innate connoisseur of the arts. He indulged this talent by allowing himself a certain sum for buying an occasional piece of old furniture, which he would afterwards sell, and stood such losses as he met with in this traffic with equanimity. Secondhand dealing brought him in direct touch with more women. It satisfied his pride and fed his real business.

In 1908, as an incident in another episode, the details of which are totally lost, he became for a few weeks a servant in a West End club, then was dismissed for inefficiency. The next year with some £90, the largest gain he had yet made—it came from a Brighton conquest—he adventured to Bristol, and there opened a second-hand shop. For some time the idea of a settled base, as far as possible from London, without being out of reach of the hunting grounds of the coast, had occurred to him. Here he married his next-door neighbour, a Miss Pegler, marking the special nature of the union and his intention to make it permanent, by using the name of Smith.

Sooner or later Smith was bound to arrive at this end. Even the foxes need a base. It was the necessary complement of that hoard whose quest always now obsessed him. It would be a hiding-place in case of need, and the necessary fixed point from which he could estimate the pleasures and pains of his episodic adventures. He did not intend to make it more. He told Miss Pegler, besides the customary fable of his rich aunt, the truth that he intended to carry on his business of travelling about the country, with sundry warnings against curiosity, which she usually dutifully heeded. But from the foundation of this little fort henceforward directly developed the plot of his fate. These fantastic creatures of reverie, as long as they do not meddle with the humdrum of the world, seem for a time safe. But as soon as they leave the air, their story begins its last inevitable chapters. It is the phase which we have seen at its acute form in Burke, when confident in his security he had got to a pitch of madness; a stage at which Troppmann toys insolently with a whole family that he counts already dead and done with; when a deep illusion of relief takes possession of them and they stand-down the sentries. In Smith this feeling of confidence took the form of founding this home-base with a wife in Bristol, both a feature of his life of petty swindler, which it capped and ended, and the first stage of his career of murder, which it began.

For with a home, Smith indulged himself in another of his dreams; he bought his first house. The superfluity that began with his first use of women had grown to a hoard of £240, which he used towards the purchase price of a cottage in Southend, whither, giving up the Bristol shop, they then removed. At last he could enjoy title-deeds, the process of transfer, the full consciousness of possession. It spoiled him for work. This was no Casanova, drawn by an everlasting curiosity and passion to seek new women all his life. Smith, like all his class of women-exploiters, was nothing but a lady-killer, a man essentially monogamous, whom sexual novelty inwardly disgusts and repels, who persists in the hunt only for the money or boasting it can give him. It may be that an intuition of this kernel of monogamy in these false Don Juans is the sting or the prize that makes their success. Sensuality in both sexes is as rare as a real passion for rare foods, or wines, or jewels. Smith, having his property and his Pegler, stayed at home in his own house. He fell into a shirt-sleeve life, and in the evening, instead of a lingering promenade past basement grids, or along sea-fronts, he would sit over a dish of sausages or potter with paint and nails, saving money, not making it. His great pleasure was to go over the grocer's book and feel the head of a family. Occasionally he would visit the Saturday afternoon auctions and listen knowingly to the remarks of the dealers, or drop in to a workman's flat just to take a look at a sideboard that had been in the family for years. But saving halfpennies on the kitchen bills by itself will not pay them. In spite of all his niggling thrift at length Smith was forced to let the house and go back to lodgings in Bristol, then to raise money on his sacred deeds on mortgage from the

Woolwich Insurance Company from whom he had bought it. The raising of these first loans gave him so much pleasure in the officialism, the
documents, testimonies, receipts, application forms they entailed, that
he almost missed their disagreeable meaning. When the money was
spent he roused himself for another raid on the women. With temper,
as a man is aroused from sleep on a cold morning. Pegler and his next
victim had to know it.

It was not necessary for him, it proved, to journey to his usual
grounds by the seaside. In Bristol itself, somewhere in an evening walk,
in the bare street, or under trees by some forlorn cricket-ground—I do
not know—he brushed acquaintance with Bessie Constance Annie
Mundy. She was then thirty-three years old, a full spinster, of that unhappy breed plentiful in late Victorian families. A full and critical
study of her class, like that of most other phases of English social life
of the nineteenth—early-twentieth century, has not yet been made,
though their bizarre originality will doubtless tempt many an investi-
gator in future centuries. Here will suffice a brief muster of general
characteristics, in order to explain the fall of Miss Mundy to the power
of Smith, and to a certain extent the seemingly impossible, but in reality very frequent, liability of the Mundy class to the Smith class. Fundamentally, though not obtrusively, the class of women to which she
belonged was an economic product of the immense days of English
trade, which beginning coincidently with the downfall of the French
Empire created a huge new middle-class. The absorption of this into
the rudimentary *schema* of the English eighteenth-century aristocracy
forms practically the whole of the modern social history of our race and
its institutions. The men of this new bourgeoisie were somewhat easily
assimilated to the elder, petty gentry of the country, who, with a beautiful tolerance unknown in any other country, and which in its earliest
stages excited the contemptuous wonder of Napoleon Bonaparte (ever
a snob), received them as readily, if not as eagerly, as Early Christian
Missionaries baptized the Goths into civilization. The generic title of
nobility, "gentleman," was extended to them with such philosophical
and ethical explanations—and notably false etymology—as made the
process plausible. Accepted as spiritual equals, the neophytes pressed

their assimilation earnestly in manners and ways of thought. The mercantile gentlemen sent their sons to these special schools with which the Renaissance had equipped the country gentlemen, schools specifically designed to the needs of this latter, where, by internal discipline and the almost exclusive study of the classics, the English lesser noblesse had been raised, if not to the cultural level of the French, at any rate far above that of the rough clodhoppers and Junkers of other northern countries. In this unlikely melting-pot the new-comers lost many of the qualities that had made their fathers' fortunes, in exchange for a culture which at its highest adds something Greek to the common round of rustic amusements and tasks. As far as the lowest borders of the middle-class the ideal, in short, became the country gentleman; and instead of a sharp, spectacled exporter with a pen over his ear, the popular image of England became that bluff, prosperous English squire, John Bull. Only one of the consequences of this development interests us: its effect on the status of women, and particularly on the creation of that class or order, the English genteel spinster. The English squire, for whom the quasi-totality of Englishmen who could read and write now strove to be mistaken, had the ascetic views on women natural to an open-air, uncourtly life, and this accordingly became the standard of the middle-class of the nation. The brother had become a gentleman, the sister, naturally, a lady. If the boy had to pretend that the shot-gun was his main tool and not a pen, though his high stool, six days in the week, was his only hunter, the girls had to perform the far more difficult make-belief of being the châtelaines of the gloomy town houses their fathers necessarily continued to live in, and model their conduct, their outlook, their ways upon that of fortunate prototypes who had fields, servitors, gardens, and all the multifarious occupations of the country-side. As direct consequence sprang into existence a class of women who had nothing to do, whom their chosen norm of behaviour forbade anything which would differentiate them from their country model, and thus "be unladylike." Barred from Court and salon, as well as hunt-meet and the still-room, they were bereft of any reason for existence, except the passive wait for marriage. But not all could marry. From time to time (it is one of the strongest fascinations of the

English nineteenth century) educators and reformers sought to fill this vacuum. The most notable of them, Ruskin, inspired these middle-class spinsters to a doughty attempt to interest themselves in Art, particularly Italian and Medieval Art, which has lasted almost until our own days. In that pre-war year with which we are concerned there had finally evolved a type out of all these influences to which Miss Mundy, and thousands of others, rigorously conformed. Over a superfluity, a complete uselessness, if such a word can be applied with a full sense of sympathy and pity, as no Stamboul odalisque ever was useless, they had bravely trained a tenuous decoration of books and tastes and principles: the *Rosary* and Tosti's *Good-Bye,* and *Sesame and Lilies,* with Way-Farer Anthologies and Botticelli prints, and limp-leather editions of the poets, with fifty other like motives, which in their combination have a certain, essentially tragic, poise. For underneath the garland was a misery and a lack, all the more tormenting because in most cases it was unconscious and undefined, of that Reality which three generations of fantastic theorizing of men had in no way disposed of. Some of them escaped it by working in the one ironical way possible to Ladies, by educating another generation of girls to their own sad situation. But thousands more, like Miss Mundy, whose circumstances allowed of it, carried their load of meaningless days and years wherever hazard took them, over the whole of England and to watering-places, boarding-houses and pensions over the western half of Europe. The loveless, superfluous middle-class spinster is that institution round which George Joseph Smith, that other typical product of our civilization, has for some time been prowling.

The father of Miss Mundy was a bank manager in a country town, an intelligent and capable man who left his daughter a comfortable legacy of £2,500. This sum, invested and controlled by her uncle, produced £8 a month and some small additional fraction, which he held as a reserve for her. It sufficed for a simple life which she spent in various boarding-houses up and down the country, passing from one to the other at the hazard of the season or the movements of her friends. She was a tall, educated woman, extremely reserved, who accepted her nomadic fate, her daily round of perfectly meaningless acts, outwardly with complete resignation. Into such a life, in which the only object is to stay "respectable," the intrusion of a Smith is almost supernatural. It is as if through the gate of a quiet convent, in the hours of the night, there should burst with shouts and torches the monstrous and obscene band of a Callot orgy. What unbelievable forces urging her towards a share in real life, beyond the round of shop-gazing and the prattle of her likes, must have been massing up behind the dam of her education and reserve before such a meeting could take place! What abominable science in this man of the unexplainable sufferings of a woman's heart before he could dare to sidle up, cough, raise his hat, look at her eyes and begin to tell her what he thought of the weather!

We need not resort to the absurd fable that Smith completely deceived her. Truth loves economy; there is no need to make her a fool, or him a genius. There is a simpler likelihood that he did not try to conceal his rank or the (unspecified) badness of his past. The first would have been useless in a country where a man cannot open his mouth without betraying his breeding. The second, presented without details, might have been necessary as a counterweight to the first. A proletarian such as Smith's opening vowels must have announced, whose life had been a humdrum, would neither have dared to accost Miss Mundy, nor would she have carried the acquaintance farther. When she set out to see the evening alone; when she noticed at the turning that a man was following her; and after the first flurry slacked her pace, then stopped against the railing and waited; when she saw him come near with a swagger in his arms and hesitation in his feet, and saw the soldier's shoulders and the shape of biceps in his coat-sleeves, the carefully jutted chin, it was not expectation, be sure, of a talk with an industrious artisan that made her breathing an embarrassing pleasure and prompted her little bow. It was a messenger who brought a ticket to life, the great ball of pain and change from which she had been lawfully but unjustly excluded. He must prove he had lived.

So, as soon as she could help him to it, the bold spectre must have declared that he had a wild past. They parted late, she to notice the change in her room, as if all the furniture had been moved and ornamented, from the black hygienic bedstead to the row of pocket poets in limp leather. He, to exercises of deductive arithmetic, working from half-perceived rings and a brooch to the unknown resources of ladies that *were* ladies. Sleep sound, both of you; don't worry that the other will not keep the rendezvous. Henceforth your lives, and your deaths, are welded together.

In two days they were kissing. In three they were off to Weymouth. No half-human plausibility could have seduced her at this speed. The population of fifty genteel boarding-houses had been pushing her to it for ten years. Her decision had been under steam for ten years; Smith's knuckles only needed to touch the throttle. Nor was it a mad flight; her companion's grudging of the marriage fees could not dissuade her from two rooms, the first night, and four days later a permission from the registrar to Henry Williams, thirty-five, bachelor, picture-restorer, son of Henry John Williams, commercial traveller, and Bessie Constance Mundy, to sleep as they pleased thereafter. She, indeed, not Life, had the last word in the bargain after all, and wrung her contract, in the exact prescribed terms of lifelong support and faithfulness, out of the very jaws of the adventure. The same evening Smith was mollified for his expense and trouble by learning the value of his prize. Hereupon he sat down after supper and wrote to his bride's trustee recalling to him that £8 a month on £2,500 left odd shillings in hand, which in the course of years must now amount to no less than £138, for which he would be obliged to request early remittance, at your earliest possible convenience. A postscript in the hand of his niece informed the trustee both of her adventure and its triumphant success.

This stage is summed up by the lover himself, in his admirably personal style, in another letter to her trustee uncle.

14 Rodwell Avenue, Weymouth,
29th August, 1910.

Dear Sir,
My wife and self thank you very much for your letter today with kind expressions. In *re* banks, undoubtedly to transact the business there would be rather awkward. Thus we suggest it would be better if you

will be good enough to forward a money order instead of cheques—however it will suit the circumstances. Any time we change our address we should let you know beforehand. Bessie hopes you will forward as much money as possible at your earliest (by registered letter). Am pleased to say Bessie is in perfect health, and both looking forward to a bright and happy future.

Believe me, yours faithfully,

H. WILLIAMS.

On this was added, in her hand: "I am very happy indeed.—BESSIE WILLIAMS."

This letter was the beginning of a month's postal struggle between the trustee and Smith, in which each called in the aid of solicitors. As for Bessie Williams, her will is asleep, either from the exhaustion of the upheaval, or because her uncle's goodwill, having been risked in the greater, did not count with her in the lesser injury her husband was doing to it. Meanwhile, the subject of his past was tacitly dropped between them, with the phraseology of courtship; indeed his romantic sins seemed to fade into nothing but a busy and painstaking greed for money. He was always absent-minded, always waiting for the post, or preparing another letter for it. The solicitor they visited together deposes that she sat silent at the interviews. She was probably puzzled, but inwardly convinced, since the marriage certificate was there, that in the end it would be all right.

The moment that the money came, at last, Smith had used all the time he had to spare for her. He cashed it in gold and disappeared. It was part of his terrible thrift that he never left a woman without writing back to her some vague excuse, as if to save her for an uncertain, unplanned future use. Although he had thoroughly convinced himself that there was not the dimmest possibility of touching through her the locked-up capital of her fortune, over which the raging uncle was mounting a fierce guard with all the power of the law on his side, yet the mysterious man did not neglect his usual leave-taking. But in this case, besides the disturbing recommendations to save money, more precise and more menacing than ever before—

"Ask your uncle about a week before the 8th to always send your cash in a money order so that you can change it at the P.O. Pay the landlady 25*s.* weekly for board and lodging and take my advice and put 30*s.* out of the £8 into the Savings Bank—so it will come handy for illness or other emergencies or for us when I return. If you do not I shall be angry when I return."

—there was a new and dreadful variation in the pretext for the desertion. In his flights from other women, Smith had never gone beyond a vague plea of "urgent business." But to this poor devil he made a charge (that she had infected him with venereal disease) that showed a bloody hatred, already full grown. We are now at last treading near that lust of killing, that apparition from the depths, whose fullest meaning will appear in the case of Haarmann. Such an insult, unnecessary as well as untrue, could not be an accident tacked on to the hurried lie of a coarse rogue. It is an act, a corporal violence, like the thong of a whip laid across her face, the apparently senseless, but by no means causeless, worrying of a sheep by a vicious dog. The passivity, the meekness of this educated woman had aroused some other nameless devil in him besides his biting fear-born avarice. Other dupes were to him only jumping figures in a cash-book. This most unhappy woman was to him flesh and blood. She had landed on the island of his egotism; he was afraid he was not alone.

Shaking off her presence with the blow he went back to his realities, the pasteboard wife he had contrived for himself, the mortgages and the deeds. A week after his sin, he was in the office of the Insurance Company, with a bag of sovereigns, asking to pay off £93 of the mortgage. He began to play at dealing again, and took Miss Pegler-Smith to Southend, then Walthamstow, then Barking Road, London, then back to Bristol again, his fort. For two years he seems to have lived without another victim. The Mundy episode had scared him—without any obvious cause, for even a novice would know that he would never hear from her again.

She showed the letter to her landlady; then when she was able to travel her brother came and fetched her away.

In February 1912, Smith had no more money. The presentiment, or whatever it was, fatigue or inertia, that had kept him in his own quarters for two years, notwithstanding, must be thrown off and another slinking adventure begun. He handed over the bare shop to his creature (she sold the goodwill for £5) and he disappeared again. She watched his train out of sight "steaming in an easterly direction," and then packed up and returned to her mother's. Another of Smith's hoards put away neatly until wanted.

On the 14th of March in the same year, Bessie "Williams" is a guest at the house of Mrs. Tuckett, a boarding-house called "Norwood" at Weston-super-Mare. Mrs. Tuckett knows what is the matter with her, for Bessie's aunt has told her the story. She is always called Miss Mundy. She is treated with firm kindness, as if she was an invalid; sent out for a walk at regular hours; encouraged to eat a lot. On this day she went out at eleven to do a small commission for Mrs. Tuckett. She returned late, at past one o'clock, "very excited." As soon as she had gone out she had met her husband. He was looking over the sea; she went up and touched him. He turned round and said: "All a mistake." Mrs. Tuckett listened to this with pressed lips and sent a wire with the news of the catastrophe to Miss Mundy's aunt. At three o'clock the man himself arrived, unendingly loquacious. While he was talking, Mrs. Tuckett sat still and stiff; Bessie, in her chair, thinking of something else. When his spring grew sluggish, Mrs. Tuckett asked him, hard and dry, why he had left his wife at Weymouth? He replied with a new gush, sideways, that he had been looking for her for twelve months, "in every town in England." Mrs. Tuckett said that she did not understand the necessity seeing that he knew the address of her relations. He answered quickly that, as a matter of fact, it was her brother or her uncle who had finally put him on the track.

He lied. The meeting on the front, however it might seem to show traces of human handiwork, was the freak product of nature, or Destiny, who had arranged her cosmic time-tables to suit, to ruin this pair. One of them, possibly both, did not desire the meeting, before it was malevolently thrust upon them by Providence. But, now it was accomplished, neither would call the bluff of the Gods and fly for their lives.

Each reaccepted the other as food for that hungry imagination each lived marooned with, a character to be woven into the story each was living: Bessie had her human, handsome man again to be reformed, submitted to: Smith recovered a good business project to be carried to success by strict attention and diligence. That very afternoon he took her to a solicitor, signed a note acknowledging a "loan" of the £150 with interest at 4 per cent. It was his idea of perfect reconciliation. Hers was to sit still and nod to all this queer simple lover proposed. In the enthusiasm of a man who returns from a long holiday, Smith turned to arrears of work and with the same candid methods as before tried his best to reconcile the family. An ordinary explanation might be difficult, but could they resist the straight thing from a solicitor? So his version of the return went to the uncle and brother, emphatically adorned with mention of the 4 per cent, under the stamped heading and over the signature of Messrs. Baker & Co., solicitors. But Smith's veneration of the law and all the actions of its limbs is not necessarily shared by honest men. His stamped and witnessed excuses only alarmed the relatives.

That night Bessie said to Mrs. Tuckett: "I suppose I may go back to my husband?" The good woman, angry but helpless, replied: "You are over thirty, I cannot hold you back." Man and wife they went away, promising to come back that night, but did not return. Instead, Smith sent a letter which did more credit to his reformatory teachers of what was the "right thing" than his picked-up superstition about solicitors' letters. In it is, in solution, the whole of his views on the British middle-class, their ethics, their customs and their numerous soft spots. It must be read in full.

WESTON-SUPER-MARE,

15. 3. 12.

DEAR MADAM—

In consequence of the past and the heated argument which possibly would have occurred if wife and self had to face you and your friends this evening, thus, for the sake of peace we decided to stop away and remain together as man and wife should do in the apartments which I have chosen temporarily. Later on I will write a long letter to all Bessie's friends clearly purporting all the circumstances of the whole affair solely with the intention of placing all your minds at rest concerning our welfare. All I propose to state at present beside that which has already been stated by Bessie and myself before the solicitors that it is useless as the law stands and in view of all the circumstances together with the affinity existing between my wife and self for any person to try and part us and dangerous to try and do us harm or endeavour to make our lives miserable. It appears that many people would rather stir up strife than try and make peace. As far as Bessie and I are concerned the past is forgiven and forgotten. Bessie has not only stated that on her oath to the solicitors; but has also given it out to me in a letter written by herself to me which I shall always prize. Thus my future object and delight will be to prove myself not only a true husband but a gentleman and finally make my peace step by step with all those who has been kind to Bessie. Then why in the name of heaven and Christianity do people so like to constantly interfere and stir up past troubles. It would be more christian like and honourable on their part to do their best to make peace. There is time yet to make amends and if people will only let us alone and with the help of the higher powers which has united us twice, Bessie shall have a comfortable settled home and be happy with me. I trust there is many many years of happiness before us. I thank with all my heart all those who have been kind to my wife during my absence.

Yours respectfully,

H. WILLIAMS.

In this witness to the influence of the three pillars of Smith-society on Smith's soul, the parson, the magistrate, and the solicitor, it is only needful to comment that the cautious threat, without which hardly any letter of the man is complete, would not imply any physical reprisal, but only to bring the law on them. Pleased with this effort and still full of zeal, Smith went on to write another to the brother, which begins with the peerless lines: *Dear Sir—I know not how I shall offend in dedicating my unpolished lines to you nor how you will censure me for using so strong a prop for supporting so grave a burden. . . .* To this Bessie had added a postscript—her correspondence from the moment of the reunion was all at the tail of her husband's screeds—in which was the terrible phrase heavy with all the besotted illusions of her whole life: *"I know my husband better now than ever before. I am perfectly happy."*

Meanwhile the succubus, gravely satisfied with the "steps" he had taken, now devoted himself to a long examination of that trust-fund. Before making any definite plans on it he consulted the supreme oracle of his world: counsel's opinion, which made it clear that the mutual wills he had devised were useless, and that the only way to be certain of laying hands on it was that its owner should die, quickly, before the trustees, set on "stirring up strife and unpleasantness," exercised their power of using it to buy an annuity for her. Those sinister "higher powers" were closing in on Smith now, like policemen, to march him to that bourne in which he and Bessie will never again come upon each other by accident.

They were now at Herne Bay. In this climax, in which he would show all that he was, all that he had grown to, all that he had been taught, Smith will not desert the wide sands where he was most at ease. On May 20th he hires a house in the High Street. To the clerk of the owner, Miss Rapley (afterwards an important witness against him), he is talkative and conciliatory; "My wife is a cut above me," he confides to Miss Rapley. "Her friends did not at all approve of her marriage. My wife has a private income paid monthly. I have not anything except that; I dabble in antiques." At the end of his confidences, he was allowed to pay in advance for the rent instead of producing banker's references. The house, one suspects, must have been hard to let, possibly because of the old-fashioned absence of a bath, or he would not have been accepted as a tenant, for he made a doubtful impression on shrewd Miss Rapley.

Mutual wills were drawn up and executed on July 8th. The next day Smith went to the shop of Hill, ironmonger, and bargained for a tin bath. £2 was the price asked. He got it for £1 17s. 6d. It had no taps or fittings, but had to be filled and emptied with a bucket.

One more thing remains, before the end. On the day following Smith took Bessie to a young doctor, and stated to him that she had had some sort of a fit the previous day, and had lost consciousness. It is most probable that Smith meant a "fainting fit," which may or may not have had some foundation in fact. The doctor decided that he meant an epileptic fit; passed him leading questions on the symptoms, to which Smith agreed. This lesson on epilepsy Smith retained for future use. The woman did not remember anything so serious having happened to her; she had always been healthy; since Mr. Williams said so, it must have come and gone outside her consciousness. All that she remembered was a headache. With a prescription for bromide of potassium they went home.

The next night, past midnight, Smith returned to the surgery and rang the night-bell. His wife had had another fit: please to come at once. When the two men reached the bedroom, Mrs. Williams was sitting up, hot and flushed. It was a Senegalian night; she complained of the heat. At three next afternoon Smith and she went again to the dispensary; she looked in perfect health. Smith said she was much better. That same night she wrote to her uncle: "Last Tuesday night I had a bad fit. . . . My whole system is shaken. My husband has provided me with the best medical men, who are . . . attending me day and night. I have made my will and left all to my husband. That is only natural as I love my husband. . . ."

This letter can only mean that the romantic obedience she was playing at had ended in her quite laying aside the use of her brain: a perilous thing for any human being, in any circumstances. Reason, sublime and faithful ally in all the snares with which our life is so beset, is never to be jilted, even for Love, even for Piety, even for that fidgety gossip, Conscience—who indeed had nothing to say to this poor woman dreaming with all her might, on the brink of the gulf. Nor was the killer himself, in these last days, better guided. As completely as his victim he had abandoned good sense. In its place he was plying himself with all the mental drugs to which his miserable life had made him addict, soaking himself with illusions, to tone his will for the infernal leap just ahead. Until now he had practised only sharp dealing, of a

size and shape indeed that society particularly despises, but still possible for the trained imagination of a prison-formed egotist to accept as
equally meriting the name "business" as company-promotion or muni-
tion-manufacture. But now he had come to a profound verge where
ordinary self-deception must fail, to a limit over which, if ever he was
to sleep again, he must be aided by a wilder, stronger illusion. To the
making of this hypnosis in the few days that remain, he intensifies all
his ways of thinking, as an athlete prepares his muscles for a record
test. Everything that could recall to him the Reality, the personality of
the woman beside him, he rigidly put out of mind. At all costs he
must regard her as "raw material," and crush out every reminder of her
humanity. To this end he calls in the aid of every drop of disgust and
contempt which in his nature of *faux-homme-aux-femmes* he felt for
all women but one. For fear she should "put him under an obligation,"
he insists on doing all the housework himself, this lazy man. He does
the shopping and insists on her staying in bed late, so that he can hate
her. He had all the mean tidiness of routine of the incipient miser; he
encouraged a hundred daily irritations of it; and he carefully concealed from her the way he liked things done, so that she could offend
him. For the last few days he even paid the bills out of his own pocket,
though every day he got nearer his last penny. The way of a murderer
and a boa-constrictor are opposite. Where the one sweetens with his
saliva, the other must carefully contrive to hate. To the same end, he
refused to listen to any account of her life since they parted, pretexting
his sensitive remorse; he definitely cut her strand by strand from life
in his mind and memory before he killed her. Above all, he insisted
with himself that it was business, business; and for this he forced himself to think only on the ledger-side of what he was doing. For this he
haggled over the bath; if for the first time in his life he had bought a
second-hand object without huckstering it would have been to recognize to himself that this was not business, but murder. In the nights he
called up the ethics they had taught him, clause by clause; the petti-
fogging religion of the police-courts, the casuistry of evidence, that
makes or unmakes a crime; and cited to himself many social examples
of crimes that were not crimes; recalled from his soldier days that kill-

ing need be no murder. So with nourishing of contempt, watering of hatred, with artificial incomprehension, with the exercise of his life-system of thought, he diligently prepared himself to kill. If he had more difficulty than those whose cases we have examined before, it may be an illusion due to our lack of knowledge, unjustly favouring him or depreciating his breed-mates; it may be that this man, the most odious of all mass-murderers, in reality had less aptitude for the trade than the rest.

Then on Saturday morning, so that the inquest could pass without her relatives being able to hear the news and attend (owing to the absence of Sunday mails), he calls his wife at seven o'clock and suggests to her she should take a bath. There was a reason apparently why this should be not opportune; but intent on her Griselda-play she obeys. He had placed the bath, not in its natural place—an empty room over the kitchen where there was but one flight of stairs to mount with the water-buckets—but in another room, a flight farther: because the kitchen room had a bolt, the other, none.

At eight o'clock the same doctor as before, summoned by a note, enters the house, is met by Williams, and taken to the bathroom. In it, cold and naked, lies Bessie Mundy, drowned. A square piece of Castile soap was clutched in her right hand. Williams was calm and very ready with his dates and hours. Another who had found murder easier than he expected! His story was that he had gone out to fetch herrings for breakfast; when he returned his wife was dead. With this story the coroner and his jury, in spite of a letter of cautious warning from the brother, agreed. Smith's behaviour must now carefully be watched; there is much to learn from it. He has two problems, one inward—the struggle with himself, to keep his nerves straight and his heart on ice; the other objective—to carry out his simple plot to delude the police. The second is obviously the easier. He has only to stick to his pat story of the earlier visits to the doctor and point resignedly to the bath. But even so there are flaws in it, bad flaws, which in the presence of the letter from Herbert Mundy the coroner must have been uncommonly dense not to see. Why did Smith not lift her at once out of the water? Why did he wait for the doctor to find her with her face submerged?

Why should the bath be placed in an inconvenient room without a lock? And especially, how could a woman of her stature be drowned, unaided, in a bath too small for her? The plan over which some have wasted intellectual admiration was only the elementary cunning of a second-rate mind; with any intelligence to contend with, Smith would have ended his career of murderer at his first kill. His inward problem, too, has a nasty repercussion. He is in the quandary: I dare not feel any pity for her: how am I to show it? Show it he ought to, and here he is a failure. The clerk of the landlord, Miss Rapley, related later Smith's awful complaisance; in her presence he made a bad pretence of weeping and talked about the "lucky thing my wife had made her will." Everyone he had to relate the happening to had the same impression: the woman who came to lay out the body, who found it lying naked on the bare boards; the undertaker, whom Smith instructed to bury his wife in a common grave, in the cheapest manner possible; the relations, to whom again he sent grossly unconvincing letters, packed with sentences such as "Words cannot describe the great shock, and I am naturally too sad to write more": enough to rouse the suspicion of a Bessie Mundy herself. But Smith is caught in his own gin, from which neither here nor in later murders can he shake free; he has set his mind to think his victims into business items. Without this he could not have done away with them, and it is impossible to feign without trying to feel. For this reason he is obliged to keep the money advantage of her death so constantly in his mind that it slips out to Miss Rapley; for this reason he is obliged to huckster the very coffin; for this reason he cannot squeeze out even one sympathetic word to her relations; for this reason he is obliged to plunge at once into the most cold-blooded and suspicious attempts to collect her fortune. The family entered a caveat against the will; but later, discouraged by the coroner's verdict, and secretly afraid of the fellow snarling at the bottom of the affair, they yielded and Smith received the wage of his damnation. The day after, "Williams" had vanished, and Smith was writing to his institutional wife, Edith Pegler, to join him in Margate. She told him she had searched for him everywhere, even calling at his accommodation address with the Insurance Company at Woolwich. At this he made as

if he would strike her with his fist, then suddenly thinking of something else, contented himself with a warning never again to try to look
into his affairs. He told her he had been to Canada again, done big
business with a Chinese idol picked up for a song and sold for over
£1,000, and went to write business letters.

With the money, the tormented man now began an intricate and
fundamentally idiotic series of transactions, transferring his money
(split up in innumerable cheques) from one bank and from one end
of the country to the other, as if he was afraid it would melt away, or
be traced; really, to beguile his mind by the pretence of constant business. When he was tired of this form of the game of Patience, he embarked on an equally miscellaneous series of property transactions, an
orgy of buying and selling, signing and releasing, and entering and
transferring, which lasted for months, dealt with some ten small houses
and ended, as far as an outsider in such matters can judge, with a net
loss of over £700. Another idea then seized him—its origin is sufficiently obvious—he would have no more houses, but an annuity, that
brought money in regularly. On this he spent what remained of the
woman's money, to bring in £76 1s. a year. Then some time later, he
thought better of it, and tried to release the money again for some other
series of operations he had thought out, but after its wild excitements
the fortune of Bessie Mundy had reached immobility. The purchase of
an annuity cannot be repented.

To the agent who had sold him this annuity (Mr. Plaisance), Smith,
in October 1913, brought new business, and at the same time made an
enigmatic promise to buy another £500 worth of annuity "out of land
transactions in Canada" the following January. For this business he was
obliged to return to his real name, and even to forgo all mythology
and produce his birth certificate. So the next episode, his marriage with
Alice Burnham, is played out in the name of Smith. It was this young
woman, a stout merry nurse, in the best of health and spirits, whose
life Smith insured with Plaisance. At first Smith wanted the sum to be
£1,000, payable at death; but learning that marriage would make the
premium on this amount out of his means, he contented himself with
one for £500 on a twenty-year endowment.

THE SELF-HELP OF G. J. SMITH 691

His confidence in the "Canadian" deal shows that he had fully made up his mind to continue in the trade for which Bessie Mundy had paid his apprenticeship. To make it pay, he was resolved to turn to the most common and dangerous method of life-insurance, which has hanged innumerable murderers before him. The exploitation of death ranges from the horrible sale of the body itself, as with Burke (but there are even simpler means than that, as we shall see in the case of Haarmann), which solves the problem of disposal of the body and covers its tell-tale witness to the cause of death; through the simple despoliation of the personal possessions of the victim—furniture in the case of Landru, trust funds in the example of Bessie Mundy—to the insurance fraud, which Smith was now premeditating. There is no other method to gain money by the death of a person who has no possessions, and Smith was, for whatever reason, unable to venture on another moneyed spinster. But the essence of mass-murder, to be profitable and safe, is that the victims must stand in a loosened relation to the rest of society. The wolf who knows his business only attacks the isolated members of the herds, the wanderers, the outliers. To strict observance of this principle, Burke owed his immunity. It was in a terrific attempt to snap the chains that bound Kinck to his fellow-men that Troppmann peopled the plain of Pantin with corpses. But the exploitation of life-insurance, while it allows on the one hand of the selection of poor strayers—riches being the most powerful chain to hold society's interest in a man's personal fate—yet the very act of giving a powerful commercial organization a direct interest that the victim should not die wakens an enemy whose determination and acumen is more dangerous to the assassin than all the Dogberrys of all the local inquest courts. Thus, while apparently cunning, it is the stupidest folly for a professional murderer to pick out a friendless victim and then give the victim's life over to the protection of a most powerful and interested corporation. It is a common folly, and tempted that stupid rogue, Smith. Nor indeed was his intended victim, this Alice Burnham, without friends. Her father was a retired coal-merchant, immensely more shrewd than the small shyster that thus pushed into his family circle; there were brothers, sisters, and a mother who loved her. Only over the girl herself, whom he had met in his accustomed manner at Portsmouth, had the murderer any advantage; not one, to be sure, of intellect, but given to him, an eligible male, by nature and the social system. Miss Burnham is a less enigmatic character than her predecessor, though hardly less tragic. She was a strong capable woman, hardworking in her profession, to whom celibacy with all its accompaniments was as irksome as it was despairing to Bessie Mundy. Every atom of Miss Burnham's body and her tastes repelled her from the state to which the customs of her country had condemned her. She was twenty-six years old when she accepted the company of this man, on whom she could have had less illusions even than Bessie. She was eager to risk all the smug-faced monotony of comfort and esteem, even the affection of her family, for the single chance of a natural life; and she was a cheerful gambler.

But first she made a bold attempt to impose her "young man" (Smith was now 40) on her family. Smith cut a pitiable figure at the family home in Aston Clinton, where he was invited; the bluff father had met many such before, and concealed neither his contempt nor dislike for this stranger whose manner wavered always between brag and servility. The mother, whose ideas of the minimum qualifications of a husband were less exacting than those of Charles Burnham, tried to moderate her husband; but in the end the prospective son-in-law was kicked out, muttering threats, and Alice accompanied him to the station. That was the 31st October 1913. On the 4th November following they were married, without anyone of the family being present.

On retiring from business, Mr. Burnham had presented each of his children with £40, the eldest son taking over the succession. To this sum Alice, from her savings, had added £60, and given the whole £100 to her father for safe keeping. He paid her 4 per cent on it. This nest-egg Smith now set himself to collect, with his mixture of greed and legal stupidities. He poured forth a stream of letters to the father in his usual county-court cum lay-reader tone; he accused him of "taking refuge in obdurateness, contempt, and remorse," and threatened "to take the matter up without delay." In the course of the correspondence, a post-card from Smith conveyed the genealogical information at the beginning of this study. Another ran, "I do not know your next move, but take my advice and be careful." Another pointed this vague threat (which sounds nastier to us who know the man's past than probably it was intended) with the explanation, "I am keeping all letters that pass for the purpose of justice." In the end, Burnham, dreading a long and vexatious law-case with this sinister sea-lawyer, yielded and sent the money.

By this ungainly procedure, Smith had achieved the opposite of what he no doubt intended, and set an estrangement between the daughter and her family. A similar action about a paltry sum owed by her sister completed the effect. But without meaning it, he had blundered into the only possible chance of the success of the deed he was planning— the isolation of the woman. The next act in his fixed repertory which he had composed from the circumstances of his first crime, after the habit of mass-murderers, was to take Alice Burnham on a trip to Blackpool. In the choice of this distant resort, he showed both a knowledge of geography and a nice science of the social usages. Blackpool in winter is out of season, yet the relaxation of censure and curiosity still might be hoped to prevail. The respectable by-roads of Herne Bay suited admirably in his former venture; but both the life and death of the gay little nurse would fit better into the setting of the People's Paradise of the North. And it was as far as possible from her family and any friends her infatuation for him could have left.

When they arrived in the cold grey air, there were no tunes from the merry-go-rounds to greet them; the shooting-galleries were quiet; the promenade empty and windy. They put up for their unseasonal honeymoon with a family named Crossley, in lodgings in Cocker Street. Previously Smith had tried elsewhere, but failed to find the convenience of a bathroom. In the Crossleys' house, for ten shillings a week, they could use the bath when they liked. All they had brought for luggage was a brownish hold-all and a paper parcel. The Crossleys were good Lancashire folk, very anxious to please in this lodgerless month. Mrs. Crossley agreed to cook the visitors' meals. They would buy the materials themselves. Smith knows no other method of preparing himself for great acts than to soak his mind in petty meannesses. He grumbles astonishingly at the departure of every penny. Mrs. Smith seemed to the Crossleys charming; it is a pity that this Mrs. Smith has a train-headache from the journey. But in spite of it and Mr. Smith's noticeable stinginess, she insists on going out the same evening to the cinematograph.

Smith is desperately quick this time; he is afraid this lively little Alice will either escape him or ruin hm. Nevertheless he does not scamp a detail of his plaster-of-Paris plan. The morning after their arrival, he takes her to the doctor; naturally this time he does not dare to talk of fits (she is a nurse), but insists that the railway-headache alarms him. The doctor is not at a loss: he prescribes a mild purgative.

Two days later, that was a Friday, they went out for a walk, leaving instructions for a bath to be prepared. The bath was to be for Mrs. Smith. Smith had already inspected the bathroom. Before this lookround the bolt worked perfectly. It was above the kitchen. At tea-time, the evening meal, the Crossleys, the mother, the son, the grown-up daughter-in-law, were sitting round the kitchen table, when one of them noticed a great stain of water on the ceiling. They all looked at it and saw it enlarge and drip down the wall, behind a picture. Such a thing had never happened before. The elder woman said, "Oh, Alice, go and tell Mrs. Smith not to fill the bath so." But the girl answered, "Oh, mother, they will think we are grumbling already, and they not two days in the house."

Then suddenly the pale Smith came into the kitchen. He lumped a package on to the table and said, "I have brought these eggs for our breakfast in the morning." The girl got up to take them, wiping her mouth with her napkin. Smith then went upstairs. They heard him call shrilly, "Alice, put the light out." The daughter-in-law, who had this Christian name, thought he was speaking to her, rose and went up to him. He said, "No, I was speaking to my wife, Alice, to put the light out." The living Alice went back into the kitchen. Then Smith, who was standing on the mat on the bathroom landing, said suddenly again, "My wife will not speak to me." Good Mrs. Crossley stood up at this sort of scream, and said, "Oh, what is it?" "Fetch Dr. Billing in a hurry," he said.

Mrs. Crossley: Dr. Billing lives quite near. I ran for him and he came to my house for a few minutes. I waited on the stairs and when he came down I asked him what was wrong, and he said, "Oh, she is drowned. She is dead." Smith was upstairs on the landing then. I went back to the kitchen and my daughter, called Mrs. Haynes, came in. After the doctor had gone, Smith came down into the kitchen. I said to him, "How dreadful: what an awful thing this is!" He said he would not be surprised at anything that would happen afterwards.

Behind this stiffness that shocked we may catch a glimpse of a soul clinging with all its might to unreality, a wretch, terror-stricken to the heart, striving with all his might to believe that he had simply done a good stroke of business. Under the water-splash on the ceiling, amidst the remnant of an evening meal, the two eyed each other, he helpless to relax his grip, not daring even to pretend to cry, she with an angry uneasiness growing every second. They are both tongue-tied. She breaks it off finally, in a new tone. "Now, Smith, you cannot stop here to-night." He can only say, "Why?" "Because I'll take good care not to have a callous fellow like you in the house." He gulps, but does not protest, except, "When they're dead, they're dead." He had to write his letters in the next-door house that night. Across the post-card on which he left with her his address, Mrs. Crossley wrote, in spite of the inquest, in spite of the verdict, the memento, "Wife died in bath. We shall see him again."

This bungler had succeeded again. The mere fact that the woman had died in a bath and that no one as yet had heard of this stealthy form of murder seemed alone to be in his favour. Hang-dog and perpetually busy, he fixed his affairs, collected the money from the company without a murmur, and paid over to Plaisance the promised £500. Acting more near instinct than by free thought he repeated the chain of his acts as he had devised them in the former case, down to their least detail. He had prepared the doctor, prepared her parents, killed on Friday to avoid their presence, made up the same trumpery alibi of a small purchase outside. Now he completed the chain, sold the dead woman's jewels and clothing and cleared out to another sea-town, then sent for the Bristol wife, with another tale of dealings in Canada.

The success of this second murder must have confirmed the man in the complicated unreality he had adjusted round himself. He no longer found it hard to believe that he was a bold business man, successful in a very serious line, who must, after all, look after his health. He became exacting with Pegler; with those annuities locked in his private drawer, he dared to begin to believe he had done it "all for her." The thought of another long sea-voyage to Canada, to find another valuable antique, oppressed him more than it did his companion; he had made symbols like this for everything in his life and used them even in his private thoughts. Every day he seemed more cynical about the hardness of the world. He pitied himself profoundly, because his nature was a handicap. He confided to his wife sometimes parts of what he had suffered in his last journey: how a certain man had tried to humiliate him about his birth, how the miserable suspicions of boarding-house keepers and the like just showed you. So by these symbolisms he managed to relieve himself of the only burden that weighed, the memory of humiliations, the scratches on his pride. Then he would spend hours reading the small print on the backs of his annuities and checking his old house-accounts. At intervals he would be stung with the recollection of what he had lost and he would leave the Bristol house for a week's trip. But never as far as Canada—lesser affairs in the earlier manner. Matters of savings, small deals with servants and the like.

At last those higher powers, who had so whimsically rejoined him and Bessie together, again intervened. At Clifton, near the spot where a man he knew named Henry Williams once met a girl called Mundy, he fell in with Miss Margaret Lofty, a small, wistful shape, who was walking in the cool of the evening to calm certain private anguishes. She was the daughter of a clergyman, dead for years, a lady's companion no longer young. A year before, she had been happy, but the man she was engaged to had turned out to be a married man and now she was alone. She was struck by Smith's eyes, eyes that showed he, too, had suffered, eyes that gave her the sensation of "having been there before." She learned that his name was "Lloyd," a man beneath her station, of course, but a God-fearing, handsome fellow who understood.

She clung to him as if she were drowning. She made a show to him of all her accomplishments, fell in eagerly with all his ideas. When he talked about insurance and how it was a principle of his to make provision for the future, she picked up all its mechanism in an hour or two's quiet chat. He complimented her on her intelligence, regretted he had not had himself the advantage of much education. A shy and retiring man, he was too nervous to meet her family, which suited her, as she felt a tiny grudge against her mother and sister for their uncomprehension in the terrible affair the year before, and now they might not understand. At thirty-eight a woman's affairs are her own concern, and seldom easy to tell. She told them nothing about Lloyd, and made up an innocent story about a new position (which was true after all) when she went away to be married. After she had gone to see the insurance-manager (she struck him as "having the business at her finger's ends") and taken out a policy for £700, "Lloyd" had the licence ready. They took train to Bath and the same day were man and wife.

Miss Lofty drew out her life savings, £19, and advanced it to her husband. This money carried them to London, where Smith, who knew the neighbourhood from one of his former existences, had booked lodgings in the superior district of Highgate. Coroner's juries would push complaisance to its limits in such a neighbourhood. But when they arrived at the address, Smith-Lloyd had a great shock. He stumbled across the war.

For during all these years while the man intent in his own cult pursued his private ritual of murder, a mightier killing was being prepared, a world-wide massacre, one of whose immense circuits of force lay through the very house he had selected for his last crime. As absent-minded as a weasel on the blood-scent, possibly until this moment he had never heard of the war. It was the 17th December 1914, the miraculous year. The day before, his own hunting grounds, Scarborough, Whitby, were shelled by German cruisers. Two months before the London mob in a patriotic ecstasy had sacked the German shops, and every unfortunate German in the country was still trembling. Amongst them the mistress of the very house that he had chosen. On his first visit he had noticed her attitude. Little in a woman's manner ever escaped that professional eye. So automatically he had swelled in *his* manner, played the masterful. When she asked timidly for references, he did not give her an easy lie, but pulled six shillings out of his pocket and tapped them on the desk. She was afraid to refuse them; but more afraid, in such times, when every one of her actions was dangerous, to step even for an inch outside the safety of law. When he returned with the woman, this foreign woman had fortified herself with a supreme reinforcement, a real detective, friend of the family. It was this man (Dennison) who met the couple when they arrived and told Smith-Lloyd, with one of those precognitional glances of which those of his calling have the secret, to be off, and quickly.

The couple went out in silence, at hazard, when Smith had been paid his deposit. In a side-road near by, Bismarck Road, they found another place, kept by Miss Blatch. His formula, for a moment checked, begins to run: "Have you a bath?" They are accepted. Then Mrs. Lloyd sits down to send the letter mentioning an illness; then they visit the nearest doctor, then the preparation of the bath, and the full canon of the slaying: with this exception, that there was a splash, a sigh, a strange visit of the man to the harmonium where he played "something" for a few minutes. Mrs. Lloyd is dead. There is again the rushing through the house, the terror of the landlady, the calls, the doctor's dash up-stairs, the splashing in the bathroom, the policeman's knock on the door; evidence; a grim man who has a clear story and a bad manner, a word-for-word repetition in the coroner's court. Letters, packings, bargainings with grave-diggers, another £700 safely received.

But this time something more. A coincidence, one of those queer logical figures with which the stream of becoming sometimes playfully diversifies its course, one of life's punning rhymes, which science hates and art abhors, but which fascinate the attention of mankind. Smith, painstaking imitator of nature, who had modelled his ferocity on her accidents, had unthinkingly composed a perfect, a triple coincidence. He had been betrayed by the first law of murder: repetition. Let but one man stumble upon this coincidence of the bath, and Smith, by it alone, like an incurable poison, will die as surely and cruelly as Bessie Mundy.

That man was Charles Burnham. He noticed an account of the Highgate inquest in a Sunday newspaper, the *News of the World*, which is a collection of the happenings of the week, curious, dramatic, horrible and comic, immensely diffused among the English masses. "Death" and "Bride" are index-words to the tastes of the readers of this journal; their conjunction in one case gave the news a good place in the paper. Almost with greed, this quiet unhurrying man, lying in not hopeless ambush for the return of the phantom who had destroyed his daughter, caught the devilish assonance, the infernal rhyme with all the circumstances of his own loss. The description of this Highgate mystery made Burnham's long-waited revenge as simple then as the pull of a trigger; he cut out the printed account, pinned it to that in his possession of his own daughter's end, and sent them both to the police.

Thereafter there are two feverish activities running side by side, one out of sight and below the other. The figure of a man grown greyish, with an intangible history, working at accounts, very intent on the business of settling his wife's affairs with solicitor, Somerset House, the Insurance Company; and below him, like hounds out of sight in a sunken road, the detectives grappling with his faint and twisted trail back into the past. All that Smith may have noticed in this fortnight is a slight clogging of his affairs, an almost imperceptible increase of the customary delays, the shadow of obscure inhibitions behind the Insurance Company's formal letters. All his senses were sharpened in the darkness in which he worked. At times, deep in his correspondence, he would pause and listen as if through their typed formalities he could hear a far-off noise of running steps. Sometimes for two days in succession he would stop on his way to the solicitor's office and turn back thoughtfully: then for long hours fight with himself to pull back to the *business standpoint*. On the 1st of February 1915, as he left the solicitor's office, he saw with a great start that three soberly-dressed men wanted to speak to him. They came round him so close that he felt their coats, and one said something about Alice Burnham. As in an accident, it was too sudden for him to have any fear. If he had heard "Miss Mundy" he might have screamed; but the man said, "Alice Burnham," a name that only recalled a long and nasty business affair, in which he was in the right, quite in the right, and no jury would give a verdict against him. So, without any blink he admitted that he did know her, that he was the George Smith who had married her at the Portsmouth Registry Office: what about it? He was arrested at once on a charge of causing a false entry in the marriage register. He did not need the customary caution not to say more.

England found time to try the man at the Old Bailey; for the nine days between 22nd June 1915 and the 1st July his affairs competed for public interest with the first defeats of the Russians in Galicia and the first victories of the Italians in the Dolomites. A prosy judge, a high-spirited defender (Marshall Hall), let out the regulated driblets of information allowed by English law on the surly, absent-minded mystery fenced in their midst in dock. Under the weight of contrasts, Smith's deeds seemed more terrible than the crash of armies, his tin baths more evil things than bridge-destroying artillery, this minor devil more sinister than all the hell outside.

At times he would take his own part and yell at them. The whole court would stare at him with amazement as if his chop-law was speaking with tongues, and his blind belief in his own innocence—because they could not tell him the precise method he had killed, whether by pulling the feet, or by holding the heads—a thing never heard of in experience. But to this, and other last consolations of the mass-murderer —the inanimation of his victims, all trace of whose living personalities had long been expelled from his brain: the joy in the legal bickerings, so much to his taste: the sense of consideration and elevation that the dock confers—Smith, like Burke, like Troppmann, now left himself entire. Alone in the court he neglected to look at the iron coincidence, three women identically killed, for identical motives after marriage with the same man, and attached importance to the cunning details which that recurrence contemptuously destroyed. Alone in the court, like a rigid juryman, he refused to believe in his own guilt, because a coincidence was not evidence.

These fundamental errors of thought no doubt sustained him in the condemned cell in which, a safe for precious objects, he was carefully preserved for death by hanging. Irreality has lordly rewards for her devotees, whether solipsists or drug fiends or murderers. In her humblest, more eerie form which had rotted this mass-murderer's imagination, she stood staunch by Smith to his end; if, on the scaffold, with the ropes round his elbows and a bag over his mouth, his legs failed, it was a physical, not a moral, terror that prevailed.

AN AFTERWORD ON
"THE SELF-HELP OF G. J. SMITH"

THIS version of the oft-told tale of the Brides of the Bath was written by an enigmatic and challenging journalist of mixed Dutch and Cornish blood who died in 1930 when he was only forty and his best work was still to come. In the accounts published at the time of his death, it was repeatedly pointed out that his real name was William Bolitho Ryall. But I have good reason to believe that, just as he eventually found it a professional convenience to drop his patronymic altogether—for an intermediate period he was Ryall on the pay-roll of one publication and the mysterious Bolitho contributing articles to another—so even the William was a caprice. For when he was a lad in South Africa he was known as Charles. However, he was already Bill Ryall when I first met him in Paris just after the Armistice.

He had sailed from Capetown in the hold of a ship and enlisted in the British forces as soon as he landed. Once, in the valley of the Somme, he was one of sixteen men buried alive by the explosion of a mine. The other fifteen were killed outright, but he escaped with a broken neck. From this in a sense he recovered but it was only a respite. All through that last fearful June night in the wretched Avignon hospital, twelve years after the Armistice, again and again in his delirium he was going over the top, nerving the others to the attack, heartening them with whispered reminders that surely the bloody Germans were just as scared as *they* were.

Once in Paris after the war—at the time he was writing pieces for the *Manchester Guardian* and had not yet come to New York to contribute a column to the ill-starred *World*—Bolitho told me that the war had cut his life in half, that since 1915 he had not seen a single person he had known before 1915. Wherefore upon the world he found around him when the guns ceased firing, he directed the interested and unprejudiced gaze usually found only in that more celebrated observer, the Man from Mars. What he wrote made good reading because he saw all things freshly, as if this were still the morning of the world. True, his talk, like his writing, was often encrusted with the obsolete pedantry of the autodidact—did you have to look up "solipsist"?—but it was always exhilarating. To sit by the hour with him at a sidewalk café was a most bracing experience. Such diverse wanderers as Walter Duranty and Noel Coward have both testified in their memoirs that Bolitho was the most stimulating man it had been given them to know.

The sample of his wares here reprinted is one of several cases he studied for a book called *Murder for Profit*. The other specimens were the body-snatching Burke and Hare, who kept the Edinburgh medical students supplied with cadavers; the overweening Troppmann; Landru, the lady-killer—was he not just that?—and Haarmann, the androgynous stool-pigeon who slew rosy youths ecstatically and then—why be wasteful?—took their flesh to market at a time when meat was scarce in Hanover. Bolitho seemed to relish all these monsters impartially.

The literature of murder has grown tremendously in the postwar years, thanks largely to the models set by such masters of the craft as the sedate and punctilious William Roughead of Edinburgh and the late Edmund Pearson of Newburyport and New York. Indeed, when Mr. Pearson first ventured into the field with his *Studies in Murder* (which included his necessarily cautious but still unsurpassed chronicle of the Borden case), a copy was posted at once to Avignon by an admirer of Bolitho with a suggestion that a book of that sort by him would be good reading, too. This proved to be a sound prediction.

A. W.

ALL
KNEELING

by

ANNE PARRISH

"To be said by the whole congregation . . . all kneeling."
—THE BOOK OF COMMON PRAYER

FOR

MARY POWERS

ALL KNEELING

I

Christabel Caine sat by her open window writing "A Pleasant Incident of My Vacation" in the moments when there was nothing to distract her attention. But a good deal was happening that afternoon. Three times the door bell rang in quick succession, and she heard Katie Sullivan muttering: "Ring, ring, ring! God save us!" as she pounded to the door, heard the rattle and slam of bureau drawers from her mother's room.

Great-aunt Ann came first. The brougham glittered in the sun; Prince jingled his harness. Then the Shady Lawn victoria. Plum-colored Albert jumping down from the box, he and Aunt Clara helping out the small, slow, important bundle that was Great-aunt Deborah. Last, the anticlimax of Mrs. Plummer, with her yearning stretch of chin and stringy neck, and the bersagliere hat she wore "because of my Italy," propping her bicycle against the fence.

Hearing her mother's silk petticoat descend, Christabel took pad and pencil out to the piece-box at the top of the stairs in order not to miss anything, and presently heard her name.

"I wanted to ask you if you thought Christabel would be in a little play I've written for the children, a little fantasy, *Princess Brighteyes and Prince Trueheart,* I called it——"

"Thee couldn't have made a better choice for Princess Brighteyes," Aunt Ann said, and Mrs. Plummer answered, nervously:

"Well, as a matter of fact—hm!—you see I felt that since Christabel was going to be the leading lady in the little French play—Mademoiselle Soulas happened to tell me—and Annette Perry says she's having her do the solo dance at the dancing-school exhibition, why, I thought

707

it wasn't fair to Christabel to ask her to do anything that would take too much time, so I—hm! hm!—I asked little Helen Barnes to be Princess Brighteyes——"

"Asked who?" Aunt Deborah questioned.

"Asked Helen Barnes," Aunt Ann said, coldly. "Thee knows, Sister Deborah, that stout plain child, Caleb Barnes's granddaughter."

"Thee means the child with the large front teeth?"

"Of course I would rather have had Christabel, but since I *asked* little Helen Barnes——"

"Oh, yes of *course*. And Christabel *is* very busy," Mrs. Caine murmured, politely.

"A court lady seems a very tiny part to offer Christabel, such a born little actress."

Helen Barnes! Christabel thought. I just despise that old Helen Barnes! I wouldn't be in that old play for anything——

But a vision of herself as a court lady floated before her. Only a court lady, but simply taking the shine out of Princess Brighteyes. She could see herself, in her mother's new claret-colored evening dress, unconscious, lost in her part; she could hear people saying: "Who is that exquisite child with the sensitive face? See, she has forgotten it isn't real; she *is* a court lady. The other children are acting their parts, but she is living hers." "Yes, mother dear," she whispered. "Yes, Mrs. Plummer, I'll *try* to be a court lady——"

The conversation moved on from her and was no longer interesting. But still she hung over the banisters, for she had caught sight of her reflection in the glass of an engraving of the Sistine Madonna, and gazed at herself against a background of saints and angels until her mother's voice broke the enchantment and sent her tiptoeing back to her room before she answered: "Yes, mother dear?"

"Come down a minute, darling."

In the mirror over the fireplace Christabel saw herself again as she laid her smooth peach-pink cheek against the great-aunts' withered dead-leaf faces, Aunt Clara's doughy whiteness, Mrs. Plummer's sallowness. Dark bright eyes with fringing lashes, dark auburn satin hair, feathers of eyebrows delicately drawn on a white brow. She went back and gave Aunt Ann, who was sitting opposite the mirror, an extra hug.

"Mrs. Plummer wants to know if you will take part in a little play she's written, darling."

"*Princess Brighteyes and Prince Trueheart*—I want you to be one of the court ladies, dear. I'm afraid it's a very tiny part, but——"

"Oh, *thank* you, Mrs. Plummer. I'd *love* to. I'll *try* to be a court lady."

Aunt Ann and Aunt Deborah exchanged proud glances, and Aunt Clara whispered a piercing "Sweet!" As for Amy Caine, she threw her arms about her little daughter and kissed her.

"No, Christabel, you can*not* wear my red silk. Now, come, be mother's dear little daughter and get into your costume."

Sobs from the floor where Christabel had cast herself.

"Come, Christabel."

Heartbroken moans.

"You look so *sweet* in your costume; everyone said so when you wore it at Ernestine's party."

On the bed lay the chintz panniers and net fichu that might have represented Martha Washington or the Sweetest Girl in Dixie or just that faithful stand-by, Old-Fashioned Lady. With her face still hidden, Christabel kicked in its direction and cried in a muffled voice:

"I'd rather *die!*"

"Now, Christabel, get up and wash your face. Mother's simply astonished! A big girl like you! Nobody's going to notice your costume. Come——"

"No! No! *No-o-o!*"

The front door slammed. Mr. Caine had come home early to accompany his ladies to the house that all Germantown spoke of as the Edith Johnson Plummers'.

"Christabel, there's father! You don't want him to see you acting like a baby."

"Oh, *fah*-h-h-ther!"

"Hello! What's the matter with my little girl?"

"The child's got a notion in her head that nothing will do but to wear my new red silk—and here's her own nice costume——"

"Oh, father, I'd rather die than wear that horrible old thing. You'd be so *ashamed* of me!"

"Amy——"

He nodded meaningly toward the hall, and Mrs. Caine followed him out, closing the door. Christabel's sobs stopped; she lay rigid, listening to the murmur of voices. Then, stepping out of her slippers, she tip-toed to the door and pressed against it.

"Well, but, Fred—all those children! And Edith Plummer'll prob-ably have something messy like ice-cream afterward, and it'll be my only new dress this winter. Do you really think—?"

"Did you notice what was worrying her? She wasn't thinking of herself; she was afraid *we'd* be ashamed of her."

Tears flooded Christabel's eyes again; her lip quivered. I *only* want them to be proud of me, she thought. That's the only reason I'm be-ing in this awful old play, just to *try* to make them happy.

"I know, bless her heart! She's thrown herself into this as if the whole thing depended on her. You know that's the only reason I *would* like to let her wear what she wants, she's been so sweet about having such a tiny little part; never a word of complaint, and you know it *would* have been natural. I don't know when she hasn't had the leading part in really everything. Of course it's none of my busi-ness, but I can't help feeling it's a *lit*tle funny of Edith Plummer——"

"I'd let her wear it."

"Well—I will, then."

Christabel left the door and stepped into her slippers. Just below her chest was a spreading warmth, a tingling that flowed through her. *Darling* mother and father, she thought, and suddenly lifted her shoul-der and quickly, lightly kissed it.

When she saw herself in the mirror, hair turned up from smooth white neck, eyelashes stuck into points by forgotten tears, exquisite in the claret-colored silk with its pouring train, she flung her arms tight around her mother's neck and cried: "Oh, mother dear, you're so *good* to me! I'm so happy I think I'll die!" But in the Edith Johnson Plummers' library she was no longer happy. No one was noticing the court lady, except her father and mother. Helen Barnes, in Mrs. Barnes's white satin dress and a gilt paper crown, was getting all the attention.

"Sweet Princess Brighteyes," Prince Trueheart said, belligerently, and paused.

"From afar—" Mrs. Plummer prompted.

"From afar."

"I come——"

"Oh, yes—from afar *I* come
    To beg thee, lovelia *swun,* to share *my* throne."
And the insufferable Princess Brighteyes replied:
"Nay, thooth, Printh Trueheart, that may *never* be."
Silence from the Prince.
"Pray, dost thou love—" from Mrs. Plummer.
"Oh, yes—Pray does thou love another more *than* me?"
"Nay, but on me there reththa a cruel thpell.
Draw clother, and the thtory I will tell."
"Heavens!"
"Get out of the way, children!"
"What's happened?"
"One of the children's fainted—Christabel Caine."
"Here—put her here on the sofa——"
"Look *out,* children!"
"Here's the water!" cried someone, sprinkling it all over the claret-colored silk.
"Poor little thing, the excitement was too much for her!"
"So highly strung——"
"Isn't it unusual for a person who's fainted to have such high color?" Helen Barnes's mother asked. "The child's cheeks are scarlet."
Christabel stirred, moaned faintly.
"She's coming to!"
Christabel opened her eyes and saw people kneeling about her, saw the scared and solemn children on the outskirts. Princess Brighteyes' crown had been knocked off in the excitement. "Where am I?" the

court lady murmured, and then: *"Mother—!"* and buried her face in Mrs. Caine's bosom.

"There, darling, *there!* Now you're all right. Now my Christabel's all right!"

"Well, well! What a girl, to give us such a fright!"

"Father!" She put out a weeping-willow hand.

"Hadn't we better take her home?"

"Oh, no, *no!* I don't want to spoil the play. I'm—all right." She smiled bravely.

"Are you *sure* you're all right, darling?"

"Oh, yes, mother dear, but, *oh,* did I spoil the play?"

"Did you hear that?"

"Ah-h-h! Sweet!"

"I really don't think it would hurt her to stay, Fred."

"Look, she can sit right here in this big armchair, just like a throne!"

"Yes, just like a throne for little Queen Christabel!"

"Mother?"

"Right here, darling, and father's on the other side. And any time you'd rather go, just tell us."

"Mother, will Mrs. Plummer forgive me for spoiling the play?"

"Mrs. Plummer, we want to know if you'll forgive us?"

"Well, I just guess Mrs. Plummer *will!* And now," said Mrs. Plummer, with a playful curtsy, "is it Your Majesty's wish that the play go on? All right, children. Shoo, shoo, shoo! Let's get back to our places. Let's see, Helen, where had you gotten to? Does anyone remember?"

The children fumbled for their lines. The command performance proceeded.

II

ON the whole, Christabel approved of her family and her surroundings. The house in which she grew up was small and rather shabby, but carriages with coachmen and footmen stopped at it, bringing hothouse grapes to lie in the fruit-dish on the sideboard, hothouse flowers to fill the vases. And lack of money could be bravely borne, since Aunt

Ann and Aunt Deborah sent her to boarding-school, Aunt Lydia helped with her clothes, Aunt Susannah paid for the summer when she and five other high-born maidens of Germantown followed Mrs. Plummer's yearning profile, flat heels, and streaming cock-feathers through Ann Hathaway's garden, the Louvre, and Saint Peter's.

The great-aunts lived on estates with smooth lawns, weeping trees, and formal flower-beds, with names like Shady Lawn and The Cedars —places that looked and sounded like high-class cemeteries, Great-uncle Johnnie said. Surrounded by old family servants, silver, portraits, by tribes of unmarried daughters and widowed daughters-in-law, they made a rich dim background against which Christabel felt herself shining, simple and unspoiled.

The great-uncles were dead long ago, except Uncle Johnnie, who had never married. He had been engaged when he was young to a distant cousin, Ellen Caine, who had jilted him and run away with her brother's tutor. That had hardened him, Christabel feared. Because really Uncle Johnnie was trying, sometimes. He can't be happy, she decided, because real happiness comes only with unselfishness, living for others, and if anyone ever lived for himself, it was Uncle Johnnie. But he had the appearance of enjoying life. He had a notable wine cellar; he had a small glasshouse in which he grew melons at the cost of about forty-five dollars a melon; he had his boots made to order; and he was fond of experiments with port and cheese and time that made his sisters fold their handkerchiefs about their noses. And he had a disquieting way of looking as if some secret joke amused him. Christabel agreed with Aunt Clara, who said it was such a pity for himself that Uncle Johnnie seemed to like to laugh at people instead of with them.

Among the great-aunts and the one great-uncle Christabel felt like a flower in a November garden. But that was the sort of thing one couldn't say about oneself. There were drawbacks to being the only member of the family that poetic description applied to, and the only one who had a poetic imagination.

The great-aunts cherished their treasure, and she loved them in return, finding their absurdity touching, listening to the battles that raged as to whose gardener could grow the best gloxinias, to the battle-cry, "There, Sister Susannah, beat that if thee can!" and melting with an ageless understanding. For they are such children, she thought, only wanting to have the biggest, never really seeing the velvety dark blue petal curving against the light. But they, too, considered her a child, and sometimes she felt smothered by their solicitude. One day I will get away from it all and live my own life, she promised herself. No matter how hard it is, no matter how much I suffer, I must live. And she had bright pictures of herself living—somewhere, anywhere but in Germantown. She saw firelit faces turned toward her, young painters and writers gathered around her under the snow on a sloping roof. It was more vivid to her than the ballrooms where she danced with Caleb Barnes, 3d, or ate chicken salad with William James Russell, young gentleman approved of by the aunts, who were, she feared, a tiny bit snobbish. If you only knew how little all this means to me, she would think with secret amusement, accepting a glass of lemonade from Caleb, smiling at William James.

For although she "came out" at a tea at Shady Lawn, carrying first Aunt Deborah's rosebuds frilled with lace, then Aunt Ann's froglike orchids, before she permitted herself Gerald Smith's red roses; although she went to the Assemblies with Uncle Johnnie, and to all the debutante parties, she was not just a society butterfly. She wrote poems, and they were sometimes printed in magazines.

It was through Aunt Susannah that she met Talbot Emery Towne, the president of a small refined publishing company. The three dined together at The Cedars. Christabel, turning her face from Aunt Susannah's withered cheeks and watered silk to Mr. Towne's stock and silvery sideburns, felt herself dewy with youth, tender with compassion toward age. Oh, poor old darlings, she thought, gazing at them from wide eyes whose starriness she felt herself, and hearing vaguely something about literary London. Holding your little shields of memories, pretty speeches, pheasant with bread sauce, tawny port, between you and the Dark Archer who draws near you. Her heart swelled with pity as she answered, sweetly: "Yes, Aunt Susannah," or: "Oh, Mr. Towne, *really?*"

After dinner she followed Aunt Susannah's instructions and melted into the conservatory. She knew her poems were being shown to the publisher. She stood still, staring at a plant with big heart-shaped leaves, bronze-green, centered and splotched with pink. Her heart thudded as if it would shake her to pieces. But when in answer to, "Christabel, child, where is thee?" she went back to the drawing-room and saw Susannah's beaming face and the bland benevolence of Talbot Emery Towne's, each with a pot of green and pink-splotched leaves floating in the air above it, she knew her poems were as good as published.

The book appeared on a small select spring list: *A Pilgrim in Palestine,* by Lady Elizabeth Cook-Paynter; *I Remember, I Remember,* by Canon J. D. R. Wormsley; *Ask Me No More,* A Novel, by Caroline Trimmingham Wales; *The Pot beneath the Thorn Bush,* by Eimar O'Sullivan; *Stars and Wild Strawberries,* by Christabel Caine——

Christabel Caine, Christabel Caine, *Stars and Wild Strawberries,* by Christabel Caine. She came back to her name in print, over and over again. Christabel Caine——

The day the book was published she sat at her desk, surrounded by propped-open copies whose drying ink said: "For Aunt Deborah, with her Christabel's love," "Dearest love to Aunt Ann from Christabel," or, full of meaning, "Christabel to Gerald." Now and then she had to dip into a poem—"Cherry Blossoms," "The Old Pain," "Scarlet Slippers"—reading through her own eyes, through Gerald's, through the eyes of the new man at the dinner last night. Then through her own eyes again.

So young, so touched by the fire. I am dedicated to my work, I have chosen the difficult path, she thought. I have chosen the lonely way. And really Eleanor Atkinson's luncheon, the Palmers' box party at the Mask and Wig, even the walk up the Wissahickon she was going to take with Gerald if it ever stopped raining, were unimportant to her compared with her book.

From her desk drawer she took an old composition book labeled "My Secret Journal," and wrote:

"It's been a wingèd day, because today

THE BOOK

has come. What can I say of this thing, a book of poems to others, but my Heart's Blood to me? My pain has gone to make it, and my petal dreams, and no one will know that I cut my feet on the stars when I gathered some of my Singing Words."

She read this, chewing the end of her pen, and added:

"God, give me a Brave Heart and a Singing Soul—give me courage to follow the Path Difficult."

All right for other girls to care about dresses and men and good times. They were not the dedicated spirits, the children of light. She had explained all this to Gerald; she would explain again. It isn't that I don't *like* fun, Gerald; it isn't that I don't long to play; but my work must come first. The last time they had had a good talk about her vocation Gerald had said, suddenly: "You have an awfully spiritual expression!"

She went to the mirror now to see if she had. And as she gazed the pure colors and clear outlines blurred, she slipped to her knees, and with uplifted face whispered: "I accept!"

"I can't understand her poems," Uncle Johnnie said to the aunts, flapping the pages this way and that. "What does this part mean, about building a house from the small bleached bones of a little field mouse? What does she mean by tired little tunes?"

"I think they're all lovely, and thee isn't required to understand poetry, Johnnie," Aunt Eliza answered. "Will thee have a cup of tea?"

"A glass of sherry and a biscuit, please. Now look here, Eliza, what's all this about?

"My room is sweet and blue

(Cold is the white moon's breast),

I will not think of you,

I will sleep and rest."

"Wait until William has brought thy sherry, *please!*"

"All right now?

> "Moonsilver drowns me deep,
> I will not call your name,
> I float in the sea of sleep.
> *(God! For those nights of flame!)*"

"Thee needn't look at me that way, Johnnie, I didn't write it. Thee knows thee can say things in poetry that wouldn't do in conversation, and I'm sure it's lovely, they're all lovely, only I hope people won't think they mean anything."

"It must have been very hard to find all the rhymes," Aunt Deborah's faint old voice sighed from the fireside chair that held heaped shawls and a clattering cup and saucer.

"Has thee seen these notices of the dear child's book?" Aunt Susannah pulled them from her knitting-bag. "A clipping-bureau sends them to me—did thee ever hear of such a thing? Talbot Towne told me about it. 'Exquisite little songs—' And here's another: 'Reminiscent of Christina Rossetti—' Mm-m! 'Whipped cream and sugared rose leaves—' Thee might throw that one in the fire, Johnnie; it's not worth keeping. Here's one that says: 'underlying feeling of spirituality.' I'll leave them here so all of thee can read them."

"How many copies has thee bought, Johnnie?" Aunt Ann asked, suspiciously.

"Oh, plenty," Uncle Johnnie answered, finishing his sherry.

"I don't know where mother's going to put them if she buys any more."

"What's that, Clara?" Aunt Deborah quavered.

"I said I didn't know where thee was going to put any more *Stars and Wild Strawberries,* mother. We have them in the attic and in the china closet—even under my bed. I suppose thee's all in the same fix?"

The aunts nodded. Uncle Johnnie walked over to the fireplace and stood balancing from heels to toes, looking at Ophelia over it, floating in her nightgown through a stew of water-lilies, with ghosts of his sisters moving dimly on the glass that covered the painting. What an absurd picture, he thought, and what an art treasure Eliza considers it. With his back to the room he yawned widely. They're off again, he thought, not troubling to separate the excited soft babble into words. Go it, girls!

"Does thee, Johnnie? Johnnie!"

"I beg your pardon, Ann?"

"Does thee think the child should go to New York? Thee knows her heart's set on it. She says people are too good to her here, that she's smothered in comfort and kindness, that she needs to be lonely in order to write. Wasn't that it, Sister Eliza?"

"Yes, that was it. But she was so sweet. She said she was so afraid we'd think she was ungrateful, or didn't love us enough, but it was just that she loved us all too much and was too happy with us, that it kept her from what she feels is the work she must do."

"She does look on it as a true vocation. Thee knows I was unalterably opposed to the notion at first. We all were, weren't we? And what poor Fred and Amy will do without her I can't imagine. But I'm beginning to think perhaps we ought to let her go."

"What does thee think, Johnnie?"

"I've always thought writing could be done wherever there was a pen and ink and paper, if you had something to say," Uncle Johnnie answered.

Aunt Susannah looked at him and closed her eyes. "Talbot Emery Towne promises to keep an eye on her," she said. "And thee told me thy friend's daughter had rooms in a house where Christabel could live, didn't thee, Clara?"

"Adeline Benjamin's daughter—they're *the* Benjamins, thee knows, and before she was married she was one of *the* Boyds. And Christabel and she took to each other when they met. But Fred and Amy thought those rooms were more than they could afford."

"I think it can be managed," Aunt Eliza said, and again the heads nodded, all but Uncle Johnnie's.

"Of course Adeline's daughter is an artist."

"Oh!"

"But still, it's only flowers. I imagine she's a very sweet girl."

"It would be worth more than the extra rent to feel someone was taking care of Christabel."

"I should have thought Christabel could take care of herself," Uncle Johnnie said, and Aunt Ann answered:

"Johnnie, thee always did delight in being perverse."

III

"WELL," said Boyd Benjamin, leaning in the doorway with her hands in the pockets of her coat, her cigarette wagging to her words, "I must say this place looks exactly like you."

"It *is* nice," Christabel agreed.

"Everything done?"

"Everything but the curtains. Gobby Witherspoon said he'd come in and help me hang them."

"Gobby's having a wonderful time thinking he's in love with you!"

Poor old Boyd, Christabel thought. Imagine having to get one's emotional satisfaction from another woman's love affairs! And she saw herself as she must seem to strong clumsy Boyd—fragile and flower-like, surrounded by adorers; the fairy-tale princess whose glamour poor old Boyd must share, if only in imagination. She answered, warmly gentle:

"He's been perfect to me. You all have. I wonder why?"

"So do I!" Boyd gave her an affectionate blow with a large hand. "You noticed I said *thinking* he's in love with you."

"Yes, I did. I don't think you do Gobby justice, Boyd. I think just because he's so sensitive and because he does things—well, like making these curtains—you don't any of you realize how much depth and strength there is there. Take Elliott Foster, for instance. Gobby's perfectly devoted to Elliott, and I know Elliott thinks Gobby's a lightweight."

"Now Elliott! There's a different matter. There's somebody who really *is* in love with you."

"Oh *no,* Boyd! Nonsense! He isn't at all!"

"All right, you know best. Do you want me to screw the teacup hooks into the cupboard?"

"Thank you. They're—oh, you've found them. What in the world makes you have such a *wild* idea? About Elliott, I mean?"

"Oh, nothing."

"No, really, Boyd. He hasn't been near me all week."

"Doesn't that just prove what I'm telling you? He doesn't dare come. He's afraid to admit to himself the way he's feeling. But I saw him looking at you the other day."

"*When* did you?"

"Up in the studio the day you were all there for tea. You went over to the window and said something about the first star, and he sat looking at you as if he was bewitched, and then grabbed his hat and *bolted*. Don't you remember?"

Christabel remembered. She could see the scene as clearly as if she were sitting in the front row of a theater. The firelight shining on Boyd's paintings of passionate petunias and eggplants of heroic size, Boyd with her short hair and manly clothes leaning against the mantelpiece, a cigarette hanging from the corner of her mouth; gentle Gobby with his turquoise bangle, on a cricket close to the blaze, having one last piece of pastry; Donatia Platt, so affected and arty, all big beads and hammered silver, acting like a fool over Elliott Foster. And Christabel herself in her autumn-leaf-brown dress, her face and throat warm ivory in the firelight, outlined against deepening blue. She could even hear her voice saying: "The first star"; she was touched by the sadness in it. Certainly soon after that Elliott had gone, together with the unattractive Platt. At the time it had not seemed significant, but now, in the light of Boyd's words——

"He's fighting it," said Boyd. "He's afraid you'll interfere with his work. In fact, I don't believe he even knows he's in love with you, yet, but *I* do. Look! Look what's coming! Welcome, little Goblin!"

"Take off my hat for me, Boyd; I haven't a hand. Greetings, Lady Christabel!"

"Unload him, Christabel. Gobby, don't you know it isn't the thing to come through the streets of the great city wrapped in sea-green silk? You might be misunderstood."

"I've had hundreds of little boys following me for blocks. That's your last pair of curtains, Christabel. Here's a pot of car*n*ations, my dear. Did you think you could get them in pots outside of Italy? Put it here by the della Robbia— Look, please look at Boyd's expression of suffering! I suppose we seem very old-fashioned and sentimental to her. And, my dears, look at this old copper tray I got from a Russian Jew in Allen Street! You'll always have to sit so that it comes behind your head, like a halo—look! Sweet Saint Christabel!"

"What's in this?"

"Dear Boyd, you're so curious. Cherry tarts, in hopes Christabel will ask me to stay to tea."

"Oh, I do! I ask you both!"

"Can't, thanks. 'By, children."

"How brusque Boyd is," Gobby observed, unwinding a huge pale blue muffler. "Have you an old newspaper to put on this chair? And if you'll hand me the curtain rod. There's something perfectly ruthless about her—and as for her flower paintings, they frighten me to death. Those obscene calla lilies! Are these folds all right?"

"Just a teeny bit more—*there*. But surely you don't take her paintings seriously, do you, Gobby? Nobody *does,* do they, except, of course, poor darling old Boyd herself? Oh, *oh,* how sweet it looks! The curtains make all the difference in the world!"

"It's a perfect background for you now."

"Is it, Gobby? Am I nice enough for this lovely room? How good you've all been about helping me—I can't imagine why! You, Elliott——"

"Oh, that reminds me—I saw Elliott, and he said he was coming over. He was going to stop at Donatia Platt's first for her book of Beardsley drawings he said he'd promised to lend you!"

"I think he's in love with Donatia."

"Well, she's in love with him, and I did think he was with her, sort of; not *crazy,* the way she is, but I always thought Elliott had a mother-fixation, and I thought he'd sort of transferred it to Donatia. Shall I fill the kettle?

"The samovar boils on my table of oak
And my bed with chintz curtains is seen,
Within the dark something the something awoke——"

"What—?"

"Dostoevski. *The Insulted and Injured.*"

"I wasn't going to say: 'What is it?' I was going to say: 'What a marvelous book it is!' What were we talking about? Oh, Donatia."

"Yes, and Elliott. He really seems to have been avoiding her for the last week or so."

"She's a lovely person."

"Yes, she's a wonderful girl—look, shall we draw the curtains, or leave them open?"

"Leave them open." And she almost said: "So we can see that first little star, like a silver fish in a deep blue sea," but since Elliott was coming she decided to save it. "But, Gobby, I do feel something about Donatia—you know I have this queer way of feeling people, sometimes I think that's why I get so exhausted. I get simply *limp,* and yet I wouldn't be less sensitive, though one does pay a terrible price. But I do feel something not quite—well, not quite *fine* about her."

"Oh, well, of course she's small-town Middle West. Her name really was Harriet Ruth; she changed it to Donatia to go with her personality. Did Elliott tell you? I think she does pretty well, considering, but naturally compared with *you*——"

"Oh, now, I don't mean *that*—come in! Elliott! Just in time, the kettle's boiling, and look! The first star peeping through my sea-green curtains! It's a little silver fish in the deep blue ocean of dusk. See, Elliott. The first star."

"My work must come first, always," said Christabel, as they sat with their empty teacups. And gazing into the fire that leaped and fell, she saw long days packed full of work, she felt herself tingling with work that could be done now that the curtains were up and the teacup hooks screwed in.

Gobby slowly licked cherry juice from his fingers. "Well, I like work

myself, sort of—sometimes. That reminds me, don't forget you're pos-
ing for me tomorrow. Heavens! I wish someone would get just that
turn of the head. Look, Elliott! Don't move, Christabel! Look at that,
with the firelight on her cheek and throat—which is she, fire or snow?"

"You make me sound like a Maeterlinck character."

She knew now what to think of Maeterlinck. She had loved him
when she lived in Germantown. He had given her unhappy princesses,
lost and wailing in the mist, their hair falling about them in shining
cascades; graves suddenly blossoming with lilies; velvet bees with soap-
bubble-colored wings, flying home to secret golden hives. But since
Elliott and Gobby and Boyd had laughed indulgently and said: "Good
old Maeterlinck!" the magus, the keeper of the mysteries, had become
the good old prestidigitator, whose most famous trick was to produce
from his sleeve a flock of bluebirds that nested in hundreds of Tea
Rooms and Gifte Shoppes everywhere.

Barrie was lost to her, too. She had said: "Barrie—" and instantly
they had responded:

"Oh, Barrie—!"

"De*lic*ious Barrie!"

"*Charm*ing Barrie!"

"And now all together, boys and girls! One, two, three——"

"W*HIM*sical Barrie!"

And she had known she didn't think so much of Barrie. But she
must read some—what was it? Dostoevski.

"Only to Give, Give, Give," she wrote in her Secret Journal. "To
Sing with a clear shiningness, no matter out of what loneliness and
pain, and make the Song the sweeter for the suffering. To feel the
happy-hurt of the Beauty-of-Things, and make others feel it. To share
the Bread of Beauty through my Work."

Gobby liked that phrase particularly when she showed it to him. He
was doing a portrait of her, and so was Elliott. Gobby's, like all his
pictures, was made from bits of mirror, carpet fuzz dyed with Easter-
egg dyes, and the insides of alarm clocks, but Elliott's was a recog-
nizable Christabel.

As the sittings went on she couldn't help feeling sure that Boyd was right about Elliott loving her. When she thought of Donatia Platt there was a warm, breathless lightness in her chest instead of the clenched heaviness she had felt before. She went out of her way to see Donatia now, to praise her to Elliott, who answered absent-mindedly. And when people reported catty remarks made about her by Donatia, she tried only to pity her.

She was getting ready to go to Donatia's one afternoon when Gobby arrived.

"I'm taking her over some things for her party tonight. You can help me carry them. My wine-glasses, and that bunch of calendulas. I thought they'd go with her orange curtains."

"Oh, Christabel, you're awfully sweet, but——"

"But what, Gobby?"

"Well—let *me* take them. Don't you bother."

"Nonsense! Why shouldn't I go?"

"Well, you're too sweet and loving to understand, but I think maybe —well, I mean, you know how Donatia feels about Elliott, and how Elliott feels about you——"

"What perfect nonsense!"

"Oh, I know! You have to be told a thousand times before you believe anyone l-likes you. But Donatia knows how Elliott feels, if you don't. Well, to tell you the truth, though I haven't any business to, I've just been there and she was crying, and she sort of burst out about how she wished she was dead——"

"Oh, poor girl! I must hurry to her! You're mistaken, Gobby. It's Donatia Elliott loves. He doesn't love me." She pulled on her embroidered cap before the mirror, fluffing out dark auburn tendrils over her ears, looking deep into her own shining eyes. "I don't say that he didn't think he was—well, crazy about me for a little while, but of *course* I had to stop that, knowing how Donatia felt, and that's why the way she's acting now does hurt me a little, when I've done everything to try to make Elliott appreciate her. I wouldn't say this to anyone in the world but you, Gobby, but Donatia hasn't been very kind to me, and *so* I must love her just twice as hard, don't you see?"

Donatia's eyes were red and her voice hard when Christabel and

Gobby came in with their offerings, but that evening she was blazing with laughter and excitement. What *does* Elliott see in her? Christabel thought, watching them together. Make-up just plastered on—and her voice when she gets excited! Donatia, indeed! Harriet Ruth Platt. The clenched tightness came back in her chest. She called:

"Elliott! Come here a minute!" And then: "Oh, Donatia *darling!* Were you talking to him? I didn't notice! *Keep* him!"

Will he come? she thought, will he come? And her whole being willed, Come, so intensely that she felt weak with relief when he said: "Excuse me a minute, Donatia," and came across the room.

She began to talk wildly to anybody, everybody but Elliott, hearing her own voice as if it belonged to someone else, glowing from the admiring laughter that broke over her words. "She's turned the hostess into an innocent bystander," she heard a girl whisper; but the man she whispered to only answered: "Did you hear what that was she said?"

"What did you say those mandarin oranges were, Christabel?"

"Mandarin oranges are Chinese emperors. Fat little men in imperial yellow crêpe, with their hands tucked into their sleeves."

"What are the grapes? Ask her what the grapes are."

"Oh, the grapes are the emperors' smooth little concubines in their robes of water-green silk."

"Let's be emperors and concubines! Let's dress up!"

"I speak for the sofa cover!"

"I choose that batik!"

"I have an idea. Where's your white scarf with the gold embroidery, Donatia? You know, that one I gave you?"

"Here it is, Elliott! What are you going to be?"

"I want it for Christabel. Here, let me bind it tight around your head and under your chin. Cross your hands, this way. My God! Look, everybody! Look! Did you ever see such a marvelous medieval Madonna?"

"She must be in a shrine. Here, lift her up on the table! Give us the flowers, Donatia, and look—put the candles around her. On your knees, worshipers!"

"I'll never forget you with that white-and-gold thing round your head," Elliott told Christabel, taking her home. "You've never looked so lovely. Listen! Why don't we go back and borrow it from Donatia and you come over tomorrow morning and let me do a sketch of you? Come on!"

"Oh, we can't go back *now!*"

"Why not? We haven't been gone five minutes. She won't be in bed or anything."

"I don't think she'll want to lend it to me."

"She'll love to lend it to you."

"I'm afraid not. I wouldn't say this to anyone in the world but you, Elliott, but Donatia hasn't been very kind to me."

"Now you're doing her an injustice. You feel things that aren't intended, you're so sensitive and tender-hearted."

"Do I, Elliott? Perhaps you're right. Perhaps I am unjust to her. Anyway, I feel that you're a very understanding person, and if you say so, we'll go back."

Donatia's face was scarlet as she opened the door to them, and the room was filled with a smell of burning. "My scarf? Yes, of course." She looked around the room, and Christabel looked, too. Candle grease, grape skins, a macaroon crushed into the rug, Gobby's blue muffler left behind. "Someone must have gone off with it. It isn't here."

Christabel looked only once at the filmy charred rag of white and gold in the fireplace. She threw her arms around Donatia and kissed her scorched cheek, crying: "You've given us a *heavenly* evening!" before she ran—floated—flew down the stairs hand in hand with Elliott.

IV

CHRISTABEL wrote in her Secret Journal:

"Let me work at white heat, let me be molten in the flame!

"What is anything in comparison with this lonely shining Joy of Creation? This welling of the water from the deep below the deep, this blessed privilege of being the cup to hold the water that brims over for the thirsty? Nothing must interfere with my work, no thoughts of self, no selfish joy or sorrow. The bees have flown far, in orchards and meadows. Now I call them back to the hive, and in darkness and silence they make the golden honey.

"Oh, Passion of Work, fill me and flood me! Is there a World? I forget."

She had inked her finger, so she washed her hands and rubbed cold cream into them, looking at them critically. Elliott said her hands made him believe in God. She tried them in different positions.

Well, now to work.

First she cleared her desk of the quill in its glass of shot, the snowstorm paperweight Gobby had found for her, her mother's latest letter, Mrs. Talbot Emery Towne's invitation to Sunday luncheon, an invitation to read from her poems at the Saturday Salon, and a note from Elliott, which she reread, glowing pleasantly. Then she sharpened a handful of pencils and put them in a row by a pile of yellow paper.

If she didn't answer Mrs. Towne's invitation before she began to work, it would be a gnat in her mind. And that Salon thing. She wrote the notes. What should she wear when she read her poems? In spite of the dirty snow, it was too near spring for velvet. Her blue dress with lace collar and cuffs? That made her look like a demure child. She was going to read the three unpublished poems that made up "Love on the Mesa": "Vermilion paint and slanting eagle feather," "The yellow cactus bloomed for us today," and "Death coiled and rattling in the blue rock shadow." She could see herself, hear herself, hear her audience. How has that child lived long enough to have felt so deeply, to have suffered so?

The earth in her pot of hyacinths was hard and gray. White hyacinths to feed the soul. She watered it, watching the water bubble up through the cracks. She yawned.

Now to work.

She was writing a romance of old Spain, called *Carnation Flower*. "Chapter Eight," she wrote, and gazed at the words. Then she drew three lines under them and yawned again.

Now what? Annunciata had to be gotten to the bull-fight, but how to get her there? A true artist never wrote:

"Chapter Eight.

"Annunciata went to the bull-fight to see Juan—" though that was what must be conveyed.

How to begin the chapter? She pulled book after book from her shelves and dipped in to see how other authors did. Dostoevski, Hardy, James. She would sit at the feet of the masters.

"Two days after the incident I have described I met her——"

"On an early winter afternoon, clear but not cold, when the vegetable world was a weird multitude of skeletons——"

"It will probably not surprise the reflective reader——"

Somehow they were not helpful. Lesser lights might show the path.

"'Enery,' said Mrs. Hawkins, severely, as the cutlets sputtered in the pan——"

"Corinthia sat in her coach, her cheeks glowing faintly, her full skirts drifting like snow about her——"

Christabel tumbled the books back into their places, and wrote quickly:

"Annunciata sat in her box, her skin glowing faintly with the patina of pale old gold, a snowfall of white lace drifting across hair that reflected the light like black water. She was in white except for the red rose, deep as velvet, that held the mantilla to the extravagant comb, and the great fan, painted with death and glory, that hid the passionate beating of her heart. The dark eyes curtained by proud lids, the beautiful scornful mouth, the languid hand unfurling the fan, were calm, but as Juan ran into the bull ring she was a flame wrapped in snow."

Then she stopped again.

How could she write about passion until she had felt it in more than the general way all artists feel everything? Didn't she owe it to her art to live more fully? She had been thinking so, off and on, all winter, and now spring made her sure. These conventions, these old taboos! Chains to a soul that longed for freedom, chains that one touch of truth and courage would break.

She knew Elliott loved her. That he had never told her so in words only made her more certain, especially after talks with Boyd Benjamin, full of thrilling psychological explanations. Chiefly, Boyd said, he was afraid of admitting his passion because it might interfere with his work. Interfere! Christabel laughed with tender mockery. It would release the floods of artistic creation in him as ,well as in her. We will be together on the mountain tops, my dearest. You and I together, and the world forgotten. We will know the deepest and the highest, we will know heart-piercing reality.

No use in hesitating, now that she had decided. "Oh, at last!" she whispered to herself as she stepped out of her clothes and into her best chemise. Her hands were snow against her flaming cheeks. She went over to her desk and read the last words she had written. "She was a flame wrapped in snow."

How her heart was pounding! She patted *Lilas Blanc* behind her ears and got out fresh gloves. The slushy snow made galoshes necessary. That was annoying.

At the door she paused and covered her face with her hands. "Oh, my dear, be very gentle to me," she whispered.

Elliott's door was unlocked, but his room was empty. It had always been set in order for company when she had visited it, and the way it looked now was a surprise. A cat and a loaf of bread lay in his unmade bed, assorted objects on the floor had to be stepped over, obscene pictures were drawn with red chalk on the walls. Christabel looked at them, feeling how astonishing it was that she, brought up as she had been, could be so broad-minded and tolerant about them, could even admire the cleverness of their execution.

She shook her head with a little motherly smiling sigh. She gathered up boots, paint-rags, and a frying-pan with bits of egg still stuck in it, and pushed them behind a bulging curtain. She took his best silk muffler, hanging over a chair back, to dust with, and then threw it after the boots and frying-pan. The sheets went, too. The curtain bulged like a sail in a storm.

She saw herself and Elliott in varied striking tableaux. She saw him kneeling, kissing the hem of her skirt. "My little saint! My little shining saint!" She felt his arms about her; his kisses closed her eyes. Oh, my dear, be very gentle to me!

She set the kettle to boil, and lit the candles on either side of the primroses she had brought him. "Blessed!" she said aloud, and kissed them. Shining pale yellow, in the candlelight, symbols of innocent gentleness. The time she had had getting them! The clerk had been a perfect fool, and she had told him just what she thought when he had tried to make her take the ordinary mauve ones.

She had meant to have Elliott come, tired and lonely out of the cold, to find her there with her great grave gift of love and understanding and peace. Three accompanying gentlemen had been no part of her plan. But there they were, looking more startled than she felt, for their conversation on the stairs had been loud and unstudied.

They got tea jerkily behind another curtain; she heard their agitated murmurs and smelled scorching toast. Then came the sound of scraping. But she prudently refused the dingy slices, remembering where the loaf had lain.

There was a chair for Christabel. The others sat on the floor at her feet. Elliott, Peabody Baxter, whose drawings sometimes appeared in the *Dial,* a Russian model, and a timid youth who kept on a large muffler throughout for fear his collar was not clean enough for this radiant being.

The Russian understood no English, but turned his face to each speaker, his mouth full of scorched toast, his childlike eyes shining happily.

"Isn't it dreadfully sloppy?"

"Dreadfully! The penalty of spring is slush."

"Did you notice my primroses, Elliott? They make me feel four years old again, with apple cheeks and a fresh white pinny."

If there had been no primroses in her childhood, there were plenty in the Kate Greenaway books that she had almost succeeded in forgetting were fairly recent purchases, the books on whose fly-leaves she had written Christabel Caine in large childish letters.

"Spring in England——"

"Oh! Primroses in the hedges—wet primroses with tall pink stems and crisp ruffled leaves!"

She could hear her voice, charming, with a little breathless catch in it now and then. She did not so much think, I am like a primrose, as hope some of the gentlemen were thinking it. Like a primrose, innocently gay, fresh, touching——

She outstayed the others. Even Elliott's nervous offers to take her home had no effect.

"Don't send me away, my dear. I have something I must say to you. Help me!"

"I certainly will, if you'll tell me——"

"It is so foolishly hard! And I ought to be able to say it as easily, as simply, as a bird sings, as those primroses bloom."

"I——"

"I won't be so silly, so frightened! Elliott! I have seen everything!"

"I—uh—uh——"

"You have been wonderful in your silence, and I know it was because you were afraid of startling me, shocking me, wasn't it? Don't think I didn't understand, and love you for it. But one doesn't need words for the greatest things, I think, and I have understood your wordless message, dear. You *do* care for me a little, don't you?"

"Oh, I should say I do! Why, I really practically—worship you. You know I do, Christabel! I sort of feel—well, religious, when I'm with you——"

"Love *is* religion, I think. But don't make a saint of me, my dear. I'm just a woman who needs her lover's arms."

She waited for him to answer, but he remained silent and motionless, gazing at her with an expression of adoring horror, so she went on.

"Can't we speak to each other *truly?* Must there be this barrier of pretense between us?"

"Oh, Christabel, of course! I mean, of course *not*—I mean——"

"I have come to you. Do you understand? Will you take my gift?"

He knelt before her. His head went down in her lap. She bent above him tenderly; she stroked his hair with a hand she couldn't keep from shaking.

"Look at me, my lover!"

"Do you mean—Christabel! Do you mean you'll be engaged to me?"

Well, perhaps it's better, she thought, relieved and disappointed, as she received his reverent kiss. Because, after all, one must think of others. Mother and father, the aunts. Love isn't true love if it makes us selfish. A cloud of white satin and tulle floated through her mind, trailing a fragrance of orange-blossoms. Poor Gerald Smith. I, Christabel, take thee, Elliott— Yes, this was better.

While her hand, steady now, still stroked his hair, she shifted her position, for the chair was beginning to get a little hard. What is he thinking about? she wondered. Should she carry lilies, or a prayer-book? Donatia Platt in an orange smock blotted out the gleaming vision of herself in her wedding dress, and the phrase popped into her mind, she didn't know why, Sacred and Profane Love.

What are you thinking about, my darling? What words can I find that are beautiful enough to break this beautiful silence between us?

v

"I'LL face any sacrifice with you gladly—oh, *glad*ly!" Christabel told Elliott. "I know life isn't going to be easy for us, darling, but what does anything matter as long as we have each other? And I want you to promise not to mind my family if it doesn't quite understand. You see, it's a darling family, but it loves me a little bit *too* much; it has silly ideas about me, and so, though you're the most wonderful man in the world, the dear geese aren't going to think even you are good enough for their marvelous, wonderful Christabel!"

"Well, they won't be so very far wrong. I——"

She put a hand across his mouth and he kissed it, thinking again, how good it smells! How can I ever be worthy of her? If I could only make her happy. But her eyes had an other-world look in them; she spoke of sacrifice so often, beautifully, he thought, but sadly. After all, getting married wasn't entirely sacrifice. Some people seemed to enjoy parts of it, at least. But Christabel, with her shining eyes and gallant words, sometimes made him feel as if he had helped her into the tumbril and started her off toward the guillotine.

There can be sacrifice on both sides, he thought. It's not going to be so easy to paint the things I want to paint, with a wife to support.

"We're never going to interfere with each other's work," she said.

"Well, but the kind of thing I do now isn't bringing in enough to live on."

"Dearest, I *know* you can find other things, just to do in your spare time. You see, you don't realize how wonderful you are, and I *do!* I be*lieve* in you, Elliott!"

"What sort of things?"

"Oh, cover designs and things like that."

"I loathe the idea!"

She looked wounded.

"Of course I'd do anything to make our marriage possible, but that sort of thing is simply soul-destroying."

"I don't see why. Think of the people you could reach, the good you could do!"

"I'm trying to do serious work, Christabel. I can't do popular stuff. I——"

"My dear, don't I *know!* I'm just the same; I couldn't bear it if people in general liked my writing. If you speak as truly as you can, and as beautifully, refusing to shriek and scream and get easy effects, how can you expect to be heard through all the noise of bad popular writing?"

"What I mean about my painting——"

"Painting isn't writing, Elliott. Of *course* you must go on with your real work, but you could *eas*ily do other things just for relaxation. Why, look at some of the advertisements! Beautiful! And they pay tre*men*dously!"

"You don't understand."

"Oh, Elliott! How you hurt me!"

And then he had to comfort her, tell her she did understand, always, ask for her forgiveness. He might as well get to work on canned peaches and silk stockings, he thought, for he was so upset most of the time now that he couldn't concentrate on decent painting. But he hugged to himself for comfort the thought that theirs was a great love, and the greater the love the greater the suffering, according to the classics. And he must be loyal to her, even if he didn't want to be—but he did, he did! He loved her as no woman had ever been loved before, he assured himself. And he must be as loyal as she who promised him so sweetly:

"Nothing the family can say will ever change me."

So he had expected her family to despise him. Not that I care, he thought, in the train on his way to be inspected, sustaining himself by the memory of the still life of calla lilies he was painting. Let them despise me! I despise them! I care less than nothing what anyone in the world thinks of me, except Christabel. He moved his head up and down to ease the pain in the back of his neck, and looked at his new mauve shirt and dark purple tie in the glass of the train window.

But now, sitting with Uncle Johnnie after dinner at Aunt Deborah's, on the last evening of his Germantown visit, he knew the family considered him a nice young man. They beamed approval, they had offered an allowance, a little house to be built in a corner of Shady Lawn, a position in Cousin William Starkweather's advertising business, with a salary that would make living easy. He had been completely accepted as one of them on the day when Aunt Eliza took him for a drive and showed him the spot in the cemetery where he would be buried. She had been so pleased about it, and had so glowingly described the beauty of the dogwood there in the spring—"You'll enjoy that, with your artistic eye"—that he had felt his faltered thanks to be inadequate.

But I'll do whatever they want me to do, for Christabel's sake, he decided. The calla lilies that had comforted him at first had grown fainter and fainter through the week—now they floated between him and the butler bringing in coffee, and faded away completely. I'd give anything to make her happy, he thought, and made himself remember the way she had looked coming downstairs tonight in her white dress, the quick handclasp she had given him as she left him alone with Uncle Johnnie.

"Thank you, sir," he said, taking a cigar he didn't want. He felt faint with fatigue. All week he had been lost in a regiment of old women, picking up balls of wool, drinking rivers of tea, trotting for miles through conservatories full of rare plants, waxen or hairy, while he agreed with voices flung briskly back or quavering feebly from bundles of shawls, saying that Christabel was a wonderful person. Shady Lawn, The Cedars, Ferncroft. Great-aunts Deborah, Eliza, Lydia, Hannah, Susannah, and Ann. They melted from one to another in his mind, figures in a fever-dream. Cups of tea, balls of wool, hairy, spiny, waxen plants, and his mouth aching from its constant stretch of nervous smile.

Being engaged was marvelous, of course, but it was exhausting. Emotion took it out of one, and having to be intense and real all the time. The room was hot and made his head swim—or was it the cigar?

"Here, have another drop of brandy," said Uncle Johnnie.

Elliott for one wild moment wanted to put his head down on Uncle Johnnie's shoulder and burst into tears. He wanted to say: "How have you managed to keep free among them all?" But the butler opened a window and the brandy spread through him reassuringly. Once more he was himself, the happiest man in the world, except for the knowledge that he could never be worthy of the wonderful girl he was engaged to.

Mr. Caine was in bed with a cold, and Mrs. Caine went upstairs early, with elaborate yawns. Christabel and Elliott stood gazing into the fire. He was remembering some advice Uncle Johnnie had given him that evening. "Don't be so reverent with her. Women like men to be rough." He thought of a brainless athlete named Gerald Smith, all bulging muscles and curly yellow excelsior for hair, who seemed to enchant Christabel by snatching her at parties they had been to, and dancing her off with never a question as to whether he might have the pleasure. And suddenly Elliott threw his arms around Christabel and pulled her down on the sofa with such force that it surprised them both. But then, once he had kissed her, he wasn't sure he knew how to go on being just rough enough. Besides, he felt too tired tonight. He slid down to the floor, his head against her knees, and she began to stroke his hair. It made him feel sleepy, and before he could stop himself he gave a loud gasping yawn.

She pushed his head impatiently and he twisted around and gazed up at her.

"What's the matter, darling?"

"Oh, nothing." Her sigh was almost a sob. He searched his mind for something to please her.

"I was just thinking how wonderful it was to sit here together in silence, and yet each of us knowing everything the other was thinking and feeling."

But it was no good. He saw one of her moods coming over her as clearly as he had seen the bright fluidity of water dull and harden in freezing cold. Moods called by Christabel herself, as he had read in her Secret Journal, "those dark cold tides that drown me." He tried again, apprehensively:

"You look so beautiful in this dim light."

It did not need the sound that from anyone else he would have called a snort, to tell him that could have been better. He hurried on:

"I'm always afraid of being too rough with you—of shattering something exquisite by a touch or a word when you look the way you're looking now."

She relaxed enough to lay her hand on him lightly, as if in accolade.

"I always feel like that place in *Carnation Flower* where Juan has a fever and goes into the church and thinks the Madonna is Annunciata."

"Juan and Annunciata! Elliott, am I betraying them? Am I silly? Tell me I am! I have this feeling that when *Carnation Flower* is published, if it is published——"

"*If!*"

"Well, then, *when*—I have this feeling that they'll feel betrayed. I've made them from bits of my own heart, my dreams, my secret things, and it seems wrong, somehow, to show them just to anybody, to *sell* them."

"Think of the good you'll be doing."

"How do you mean?"

"Well, bringing such beauty into the world, and—I don't know—I mean—such truth——"

"Well, I *do* think that—hope it, anyway. My poor little book may not have very much, but I have tried to give it truth and beauty. But don't be disappointed in me when it isn't popular, darling. Will you promise? Because it won't be. I don't want it to be. I want just to speak simply, truly, to the few who will understand. You know I don't want what the world means when it says success——"

"Oh, I *do* know, darling. That's just the way I feel about my own work."

"*What* do I write for, Elliott? Not for success. I should feel sick with terror if that came to me. I'd know I'd failed, somehow, that I hadn't been true to the *real* things. Not for pleasure, *cer*tainly, for my work is done in grief and pain, and I don't use those words lightly, dear. And yet I must write or die. Why is this burden on me?"

"Because you have the artist's soul, Christabel. I know how it is my-self——"

"Will I never go free?"

"Never, my darling."

"Will I always have to suffer this ache of beauty? Oh, Elliott, will I always have to suffer?"

Oh, beautiful girl! his heart cried, worshiping the glowing face she bent above him. And she loves me. Not Gerald Smith, not anyone else in the world. She loves me. She might have chosen anyone, she's so popular at every party; everyone loves her, but she loves me. The foot he was sitting on began to go to sleep, but he tried to keep from moving, for fear of shattering their perfect moment.

VI

CHRISTABEL's engagement had helped her work so much that *Carnation Flower,* published that spring, was quite a success. But by the time it was in the bookshops she was glad to go to Atlantic City for a rest, with Aunt Lydia, who wanted company.

Aunt Lydia was as good as Talbot Emery Towne's whole publicity department. She advertised Christabel and *Carnation Flower* to all the old ladies and gentlemen in the combined hotel and sanitarium where she and Christabel stayed; she dealt out copies to those who could not be bullied into buying. She went up and down the Boardwalk in a rolling-chair, asking for *Carnation Flower* at all the bookshops. The inmates of Oversea Hall were well trained by her. They waited about with *Carnation Flowers* and fountain pens, to ask for autographs, they broke off talk of health to talk literature with the authoress. "Have you read that lovely new book by Zona Grey? Or is it by Zane Gale? Fiddlesticks! I always get those two mixed up!"

Christabel was sweet to them all. "But I wish they wouldn't treat us quite so much like royalty!" she complained whimsically to Aunt Lydia. "You and Mrs. Carey are so regal that even I become a princess in your reflected glory, Aunt Lydia darling!"

"Thee's an absurd child," Aunt Lydia answered, fondly. They were dining at a table covered with little dishes of this and that, with library paste for sauce. At the next table old Mr. Blanchard was having both vanilla ice-cream and a Boston cream puff, and Mrs. Blanchard was sneaking an apple into her knitting-bag. I hope age brings me something more beautiful than greediness, Christabel thought, watching them. I hope it brings me even deeper love and understanding.

In the doorway the headwaitress stretched her mouth to show her teeth to arriving and departing diners, and then followed them with cold eyes. What a place, Christabel thought, trying first a kiss full of shredded string coconut, then a sawdust lady-finger.

Mrs. Carey sailed out, making the signals of head and hand that meant "See you outside," and Aunt Lydia fluttered her fingers. Then came the Simpsons, who, because they had bought a copy of *Carnation Flower,* were inclined to presume. Mrs. Simpson tottering on too high heels, a mountain of black lace with a crimson rose on the lower slopes, bowed impressively, and so did gray-coated, white-trousered Mr. Simpson. Aunt Lydia dealt them a small cold unsmiling bow.

"Thee knows, I think that woman's hair is dyed. And so pushing— just because thee wrote in thy book for them they'll be telling people thee's a friend of theirs. Thee'll see! Through, dear? I suppose Mrs. Carey will be waiting."

They in their turn were affable to the headwaitress. They went through the reception hall, and on past the room where a little dark man peeped out from his store of gauze scarfs and knitting-bags, a little dark man, Christabel thought, who should have worn a turban and looked out from another bazaar on bare feet, yashmaks, camels swaying past, instead of on fat ladies, old gentlemen thin and trembling as dead leaves, and black boys drifting by with pitchers of ice-water. He'll never know, she thought, what I have felt about him. And yet it all helps. Every understanding thought, every kind thought, helps —somehow.

Mrs. Carey with two lesser ladies was already at the card table that was reserved for her and for Aunt Lydia night after night, and bridge began.

"Your bid, Lady."

"*My* bid? Mercy! What a hand!"

"Don't expect any help from me, partner!"

"Mustn't talk across the table, ladies."

" 'Scuse us, please? Us was naughty dirls, but us'll be dood now!"

"Try one of these chocolates in silver paper, Mrs. Huntington."

"Thee's a bad lady, to tempt me!"

"I just wish chocolates liked me as well as I like them!"

"Have a chocolate, Christabel dear? I must get rid of these before my son comes tomorrow, or he'll think I didn't appreciate them."

"Is thy son coming tomorrow?"

"Yes. Isn't it wonderful that he's able to get down again so soon. *Mm!* Mershy! B'carefu' thish kin'—mmp! Cologne or something inside these big round ones!" She buried her chin in her breast, as a pigeon buries its bill. "Did I spill? I guess not. Yes, Curtis is coming. I was so surprised when he wrote that he'd be down this week, too."

Christabel, sharing a chair beside the bridge table with Aunt Lydia's book and shawl and work-bag, saw through a shining mist the roomful of old ladies, pale or purple, playing bridge by the light of mustard-shaded lamps. She, too, had received a letter from Mrs. Carey's son saying he was coming again to Atlantic City, but she was not surprised.

She had been thinking of Curtis Carey, 3d, a great deal since his visit last week to Oversea Hall. She liked to make excuses to say his name. "Who told me that? Oh, I know—it was Curtis Carey." "Curtis Carey says his mother says you're one of the few real aristocrats she knows, Aunt Lydia." "Curtis Carey——"

She was planning to write a new book for his eyes, as *Carnation Flower* had been written for Elliott's. It must show him the depth and beauty of her nature; it must show him, subtly, how used she was to things like footmen and conservatories, and how little they impressed her.

Sometimes Curtis and Elliott would come into her mind side by side, not to Elliott's advantage. The thought of him made her feel wise and sad and subtle, made her feel old as the stars or the sea. It was at one of those times that she wrote the poem beginning:

> The age-old pain of a woman's heart—
> The age-old sob of the sea—

But he loves me so! she would think. He will be happy, and I will have my work, and, after all, life isn't so terribly long, and then comes peace. But when it was Curtis she thought of, she wrote to Elliott. The more glowing her thoughts of the one, the more intense her letters to the other. It was unfortunate that just at this time Elliott had sprained his right wrist so that he could only write a few jerky and tremulous lines with his left hand, or dictate restrainedly to Gobby.

OH, MY HEART'S DEAREST! [she wrote to Elliott, with a hand that shook as she thought of Curtis, who had arrived that day]

How I miss—*miss* you! When will the Wings stir in my heart again? I'm like a prism that is nothing until the Sun shines through it, and wakes it up, and makes it laugh and sparkle and scatter Shreds of Rainbow all about—and you're the Sun! I need you, Sun of my Heart!

This place is so dreary, my darling. It's a temptation to let one's little shining be buried under Talk of Health and Knitted Shawls and Diets and Drafts. But then I think, here are poor sick old things being brave enough to put on their beads and tell jokes, and outside are the Sky and the Sea. And I try to shine for them, gently, until they shine back at me. They love me, Elliott—isn't it touching? It makes me feel so humble.

And I *am* happy, Dearest. Isn't there a You? I went down on the sand yesterday at sunset, under a pink sky, with a pink and green sea, foam-edged, creeping up to my feet. And I sent you a message by a small Rosy Cloud—did it reach you? And I thought, here am I, ungrateful one, being unhappy in a World where there are Waves and Courage and Work to be Done and Little Pink Clouds and My Own Dear—and all my discouragements left me, and the Round World sang!

Forever and forever,
CHRISTABEL.

She put her letter into an envelope, took it out again, and got her Secret Journal. Curtis Carey and she were going for a walk and he would be waiting for her, but it was better to let him wait a few minutes. She began to copy, the letters growing more and more scalloped through her agitation at the thought of Curtis:

"This place is so dreary—it's a temptation to let one's little shining be buried under Talk of Health and Knitted Shawls and Diets——"

"I was afraid you'd forgotten about me," Curtis said, as she stepped out of the elevator.

"Oh, did I keep you waiting? I didn't mean to. I'm *so* sorry! And such a place to wait in! Lost in a jungle of potted palms, among these big chairs like a herd of elephants."

"You certainly can express things wonderfully!"

"Oh, no! But I do try to see the funny side of things. It helps, I think. Don't you?"

"Yes, indeed. There's nothing like a sense of humor."

"No, is there?"

"I'm always sorry for people who haven't any."

"*Aren't* you?"

This sedate conversation was getting them nowhere. It had been different in her anticipation. But she was sustained, as they went along the Boardwalk, by the knowledge that they were a good-looking couple. She felt that to deny one's own good looks was both silly and ungrateful. She had written in her Journal:

"It isn't Outer Beauty that I want, and yet I must be grateful for this gift that makes me able to give pleasure to so many. And I can't help knowing that some kind people think I'm lovely-looking. I can't put my fingers in my ears and shut my eyes *all* the time. But I want to be both grateful for it and humble about it, so I have made myself this little prayer:

"Oh, Lord, I thank Thee for Thy Gift of Beauty, but I pray Thee to let my body be only the Cloud that thinly veils the Real Beauty within. And, if Thou wilt, let that grow brighter and more bright, until it shines through this Cloud of my body. Amen."

And Curtis Carey's clothes were enough to make the world a better-looking place, even if they had not contained Curtis. His expensive hat, set on one side of his head, was enchanting to Christabel after the Oversea Hall atmosphere, so lacking in dash. As she looked at it she thought of Elliott, with his hair always a little too long, in a fringe in the back.

"I read your book last week. It's great!"

"Oh, *do* you like it, really? Thank you *so* much!"

"Gosh! I don't see how you can think of it all. And then writing it all out!"

"It's the thing I love to do."

"It sort of scared me about coming down again. I was afraid I couldn't be high-brow enough to interest you."

"*You!* When I've been thinking all week that you'd never want to talk to me again after I'd shown you how ignorant I am!"

"*You* ignorant!"

"Yes. I don't know anything about all the things you know everything about—salmon fishing, and yachting, and being in China, and riding to hounds——"

She felt herself growing younger by the minute. He knows so much, she thought. He is so strong. I'm nothing but a child compared with him. Helpless. But strongly, tenderly protected.

"Well, but, Good Lord! those are just things I've happened to do. It isn't like having wonderful thoughts, like yours."

"You see, we've always been poor, and I've lived so simply. We have a little bit of a house, and there's just mother and father and me, with our funny old Katie Sullivan to take care of us, and love me and order me about just as if I were a little girl still, and then there's our little garden—I do adore that so! You see, the gentleman we call in moments of grandeur the gardener is also furnace-man and window-washer and everything, so I take care of the flowers. And the furniture's shabby and my dresses are made over, but I'm such a goose that as long as there's a rose to smell or a poem to read I don't know enough not to be happy!"

"You know, you're a wonderful girl! I mean, most of the girls I know would sort of put on and try to make an impression—I mean, they wouldn't be just sweet and sincere, the way you are."

"Oh, but what else *could* one be? What else except sincere, I mean? Because, after all, being real is the only thing that matters, isn't it? To be really real and to be kind."

"Well, you're both, all right! I saw last week the way you acted with mother and Mrs. Huntington, and believe me, I know it isn't always easy to be so sympathetic and considerate with older people."

"Do you know, you're rather an—understanding—person?"

"Were you surprised when I wrote that I was coming down again?"

"Surprised isn't the word!"

"Were you sorry?"

She answered with a glance.

"I broke a date to go to the National with a foursome this week-end."

"Oh, *why* did you?"

"Can't you guess?"

"Because you knew how happy it would make your mother to have you come here, I think. Isn't it touching? Doesn't it make your heart *ache,* to think how happy we can make them? Oversea Hall seems so dreary sometimes, it's a temptation to let oneself be buried under talk about health and diets and drafts and shawls; and then I think of their being old, and yet brave enough to dress up and make little jokes—it makes me want to cry, it makes me want to do something beautiful for them——"

"When you talk like that you make me feel like—don't think I'm silly or sentimental or anything, but—well, like saying my prayers to you."

She looked at him gently. There were tears in her eyes. For her, too, waited that black pit of age, at the end of the long road, the road of renunciation that she must travel because of her promise to Elliott. She looked through her tears at this understanding man who had never heard of Elliott.

"But I didn't come to see mother. I came to see you."

"I'm glad," she said, simply, with a smile that made him flush, a touch of her hand on his, lighter than a butterfly.

They played bridge with Mrs. Carey and Aunt Lydia after dinner. Christabel, being exquisitely kind to the old, hardly looked at Curtis, but she felt his eyes on her all evening. She fell asleep thinking of him, thrilling in the dark.

In the gray of the morning she was wakened by Aunt Lydia's maid. Aunt Deborah was dangerously ill. They were to leave at once.

All the way to Philadelphia Christabel fretted. If only she had known yesterday——

But a letter came from Curtis:

"What have I done? Why did you run away without a word? If I come over to Germantown next Saturday, will you see me?"

And the following Monday Christabel wrote to Elliott:

"Let me go from your life with no bitterness, no crying-out, but gently, as the Little Mermaid melted into foam. We have always given each other Truth, and I must give you Truth now, although it breaks my heart——" And so strong is habit that she ended the sentence "my darling," and had to rewrite the letter.

VII

ELLIOTT answered Christabel's letter beautifully. Then he lay down, at eleven o'clock in the morning, and slept until Gobby came in and stepped on the cat at seven that evening.

The two men had supper together at the Mouse Trap. Elliott found it pleasant to be back in the familiar atmosphere of orange curtains, candle drippings, and sprays of bitter-sweet, with Lola and Peggy friendly and welcoming, slapping around in their sandals, after all the small dark Italian restaurants he had been to lately. Christabel had not seemed to care for the various tearooms, run by awfully nice girls, that he had patronized before his engagement.

As they ate their chicken patties and ice-cream, he explained to Gobby that his life was in pieces and that he couldn't talk about it yet.

"Now listen, Elliott, what you've got to do is to get to work on your painting. How long since you've done anything?"

"Well, not since we—not since Christabel—we— I've been too busy living, Gobby. And now that I'll have the time, what's the use?"

"Make her sorry."

"I wouldn't do anything in the world to cause her pain."

"All the same, I do think you ought to get back to your painting. Sublimate your emotion, man!"

"It's easy to talk, but you haven't lost everything that makes life worth while," Elliott answered, mournfully, his eyes fixed on the gigantic slice of chocolate cake crumbling beneath his fork.

"I'd rather have your memories than most people's realizations."

"Yes, nothing can take those from me. Somehow I knew this would happen. I knew it was all too perfect to come true. What had I to offer a wonderful girl like Christabel? And yet like a fool I went on hoping —deceiving myself."

"Well, think of Abélard and Héloïse, and Dante and Beatrice—they were always getting separated or something, and they're the world's great lovers. Tristram and Isolde, too—Romeo and Juliet——"

Elliott and Christabel. Elliott just stopped himself from saying it aloud. Mr. Foster and Miss Caine. How different that sounded! But Elliott and Christabel——

"You'd never be satisfied, either of you, with bourgeois contentment. I don't so much mean make her sorry as I mean make her proud of you. Demi-tasse? I think we'd better have big cups of coffee tonight, don't you? With cream?"

"I don't care—yes, cream. It all seems so empty."

"Big cups, Peggy, please. Of course it seems empty, but, Good Lord! what's an artist made for except to transmute his pain into the world's beauty? You've got to *give,* man, you've got to give!"

"That's what *she* always said."

He slept next morning until nearly noon. But after breakfast at the *pâtisserie* around the corner he began to paint again. And every day after that he painted, no longer apprehensive of her coming in with a few sweet peas, or a book, or a pomegranate, saying: "It's your mouse, come to keep mouse-still," and presently: "But when you *are* through, darling——"

"It's certainly true that the artist works best in pain," Gobby told him. He actually sounds envious, Elliott thought, squeezing the mounds of color onto his palette, screwing up his eyes to look at the waxy pears. "God! If you only knew!" he said under his breath.

Gobby was washing a pair of socks in Elliott's dishpan and did not at once answer. When he at last said: "Knew what?" Elliott was lost in trying to feel like a pear swelling juicily in a smooth yellow-pink skin, and only hummed a rising "Mmm?"

> Alas, that Spring should vanish with the Rose,
>   That Youth's sweet-scented manuscript should close——

Christabel wrote in her Secret Journal, the day she read Elliott's brave farewell, and burned it. And for a long time her eyes filled with tears when she heard what they had called their tune, and had whistled to each other as a signal, although she never could be quite sure whether it was Nevin's "Narcissus" or "The Soldiers' Chorus" from *Faust*.

Through veils of reticence she explained Elliott to Curtis, or tried to explain, for apparently he preferred to let Elliott remain a vague shadow.

"It wasn't love, dearest, not real love, like ours. It was compassion, I think. He seemed to *need* me so. It wasn't until you came that I ever knew what love could be. I was like a prism, that's nothing—nothing, that is, except just a clearness and a pureness; I did keep *those,* I hope. And then the sun shines through the poor little prism and turns it into rainbow glory—and you're the sun! But he was only—you're not listening to me, Curtis!"

"How can I listen to you when I'm looking at you? Do you know that you're the most beautiful girl in the world?"

"Darling! How strong you are!"

"How soon will you marry me? There's nothing to wait for."

And there wasn't. Aunt Deborah was well again and had offered Shady Lawn for the reception. Germantown was foaming with bloom and ready for the wedding. Bishop Lacombe would be off to Bar Harbor if they didn't hurry. Both families were delighted with the engagement. Christabel and Curtis would be in Paris on their wedding trip, so it would be foolish to spend much time on her trousseau. And, after all, when a great love comes, why wait?

For this is love, Christabel thought, as she lay awake after the day she had been with Curtis to choose her engagement ring. On the darkness, as vividly as if they had been drawn with a sharp pencil and painted with clear water-colors, she saw details that she had not consciously noticed. The sweep of Panama-hat brim, the black hat-band, the black silk tie with silver-gray dots, and a tuck-in of shadow under the knot, the scarlet carnation. She had read somewhere that intense emotion gives clairvoyance, that, when exaltation passes, memory of some detail remains forever as a sign. I never even noticed that he was wearing a carnation, she thought. Yet there it was, printed on the darkness, frilled and pinked as a penwiper. This is real love, she thought, touching the enormous sapphire. But she couldn't see his face. There was the expensive hat, the beautifully fitting soft collar, the tie, the carnation—and between them nothing, in spite of all her efforts.

The day drew near. In Mrs. Caine's bedroom Miss Plympton knelt to fit Christabel's wedding gown.

"It's all wrong—everything's wrong! Look at this line! Just look at it! The whole idea was simplicity, not these dis*gust*ing little puckers and fullnesses!"

"I'm sorry, Miss Christabel. It was the way it was pinned up, and I thought we decided that was the way we wanted it."

"Don't work yourself up, darling. You're overtired."

Yes, she was tired. She shut her eyes and pressed her fingers to her temples.

"It will be all right."

"Mother, what *is* the use of saying it will be all right when it's all wrong?"

"If you could just hold still while I rip out the gathers, Miss Christabel, then we could drape it just the way you want."

Christabel gave a loud, exasperated sigh, stood on one foot, stood on the other, put her hands to her head again.

"Sit down and rest a minute. You're worn out."

"While she's resting I'll run down and get the little nighties. They're just awfully dainty. I think you're going to love them!"

Christabel turned to Mrs. Caine as Miss Plympton scuttled from the room. "Well, mother, you see what a mess she's made of everything! I *told* you it was a mistake to have her."

"But, darling! She's made your clothes ever since your first little gingham dresses. It would have broken her heart to have anyone else make her Miss Christabel's wedding dress. Besides, *I* think it looks all right, dear. And she needs the money dreadfully just now, with her mother breaking her ankle."

"Well, I'm *sorry*, but *real*ly! If you're seventy you oughtn't to climb trees."

"Darling, she just stood on a step-ledder to get some cherries for a pie——"

"Well, it isn't *my* fault, and you act exactly as if it was—yes, you *do,* mother! And you know Miss Plympton absolutely *rev*els in being a martyr. I wish I'd eloped, the way Curtis begged me to! Trousseau!

What do I care for a trousseau? I'm just doing it to please you and the aunts."

"Darling——"

"I've explained to Miss Plympton till I'm hoarse that what I want this dress to look like is a novice's robes—oh, that reminds me! Mother!"

"Yes, dearie?"

"What did Mr. Leach say when you telephoned about that choir-boy?"

"I—I'll just slip down and call him up this minute."

"*Mothe*r! Oh, I'm so sick of everybody promising to do things, and then *noth*ing gets done unless I attend to it."

"I'll call him up this minute, darling. I tried to get him this morning, but the line was busy, and then I had to see the florist——"

Left alone, Christabel lit a cigarette and sat smoking and frowning angrily, tapping a foot. Oh, she was tired! Her nerves were a nest of twittering sparrows. And everyone was being so stupid. This time, that should have been hushed, holy, tremulous with exquisite apprehension, was vulgarized by a stupid dressmaker getting things wrong, by the boy who sang the solos at Saint Mark's getting measles, by everyone being stupid and inconsiderate.

"Here's the nighties, dear!" Miss Plympton's eyes were swollen, her nose was pink and glazed. She had evidently taken the opportunity to have a cry. "Look—all eight of them. Mamma couldn't sleep last night, her ankle pained so, and I was sitting up, anyways, so I got them finished. Aren't they dainty?"

Christabel looked at one of the cobweb nightgowns, sighed, folded her lips.

"Isn't it all right, dear?"

"We don't seem to be having much luck, do we, Miss Plympton? I said ribbons under the net, and no lace. I gave you the lace to put on the camisoles. Have you put it on *all* of the nightgowns?"

Miss Plympton's eyes swam, her nose glowed.

"Well, we can't do anything about it now." Christabel sighed again. "Never mind. But please let's try to get this dress right."

Miss Plympton sank on her knees and began pulling with shaking hands at the satin folds. Christabel looked at herself in the mirror. The effect really was exquisite, after all. What a contrast the two reflected figures were. Her young loveliness glowing out of satin pure as snow in moonlight, Miss Plympton with her mouth full of pins, her red nose, her spectacles. Christabel's eyes grew softer as she looked from her own white beauty to the dumpy figure kneeling beside her. Poor old maid, spending her life sewing other women's wedding dresses! It would make a poignant poem. She said, gently:

"There, that's lovely, Miss Plympton. I knew *you* could fix it."

Miss Plympton blew her nose violently. Christabel suddenly put her hands—how white they looked—on either side of the red face, and, tilting it up, bent to kiss it.

"There! And you mustn't mind what I said. It wasn't I who was talking; it was my tiredness and nervousness."

How simple an understanding heart makes everything, she thought, feeling bathed in Miss Plympton's love. How wonderful if we could all go to each other, and say simply: I'm sorry. But it takes love and courage. I was right about the pure white for the satin, she thought, gazing into the mirror. Not cream, like Ernestine's wedding dress, that had turned her into a gigantic charlotte russe, but just this purity—a Madonna in alabaster. Of course not everyone can stand pure white.

In the mirror she saw her mother, and cried:

"Look, mummy dear! Isn't it lovely now?"

"*Love*ly!" Mrs. Caine echoed. "Simply perfect! Mr. Leach says everything's all right, honey. He's gotten a boy from Saint Clement's for the solo. And a lot of new boxes have come. I told Jake to open them on the back porch. Curtis and Uncle Johnnie are looking at the presents."

"Uncle *John*nie! What's Uncle *John*nie doing here? There, that'll have to do, Miss Plympton."

"Wouldn't you like it just a crumb easier in the armholes?" asked Miss Plympton through pins, but Christabel was already struggling out of the satin folds.

She hurried into a dress and downstairs. From the landing window she caught a glimpse of Uncle Johnnie trotting to the gate, looking pleased with himself. Now what had he been saying, or not saying? She put the question to Curtis, wandering among clocks and dessert plates and cases of silver.

"What did you two find to talk about, dearest?"

"Why, I don't know exactly. Lots of things."

"Are you *dead*? Poor Curtis! Uncle Johnnie's a darling, of course, but he *is* old, and so he has ideas——"

"I didn't notice that he had any. He seemed perfectly sensible to me."

"Did he? Do you know you're a very kind person? Oh, Curtis, it's a comfort to be with you! I'm ex*hausted*! *Things!*" She touched the gold soup plates from a family of Carey cousins with sad scornfulness. "Let's promise each other never to become the slaves of *things,* material possessions, Curtis."

"All right, let's. I thought that was awfully nice, that part you showed me in your Journal, where you wrote about wedding presents, and how you'd rather be given the moon than a silver tray. That reminds me, I know if you don't like the tray, Cousin Bessie would much rather have you exchange it for something you do like."

"Dearest, I a*dore* the tray! I only used it as a symbol. Don't you remember the other things I said, too—that I'd rather be given wild raspberries than rubies, and a snowy branch of pine than an ermine cloak?"

"I'm going to get you an ermine cloak, all the same, or a sable one, if you'd rather."

"Oh, darling, *real*ly? Oh, you're so wonderful to me! How can I show you how much I love you?"

"By not getting all tired out. There's too much for you to do all the time. You must learn to let other people do things for you. I had no idea a wedding meant so much hullabaloo."

"And all so empty. I mean, what does anything matter except that you are mine and I am yours? These tribal laws, these sacrifices to tradition—they're all wrong. What do we care for laws, except the law of love? You know, Curtis, that what I would rather do would be simply to come home with you, across the fields, some evening when the frogs are piping and the west is pink, just you and I. You *do* know that, my lover, don't you?"

"I know, and I think it's wonderful of you, darling, but still I guess we'd better go ahead and have some sort of ceremony. I mean, I was thinking about your mother and my mother. I suppose it would sort of worry them if we didn't. But I certainly am with you about thinking the simpler the better."

"Oh, *so* much better, dearest! If I considered myself—but, after all, does it matter so very much? If it's going to make the aunts and the dear little mothers happier to have the bishop and the choir-boys and lilies and organ thunder and all the old enchantments, does it matter so much what *we* want?"

"I don't believe you ever think of yourself."

"Oh, don't I! Don't I think about myself, and know I'm the happiest girl in the world? So happy that I feel wings fluttering—look and see if I haven't a pair of soap-bubble-colored wings!"

"I guess if you have wings they're angel wings."

"Darling! Not now! Someone's coming. Oh, Miss Plympton! Going home? You've met Mr. Carey, haven't you? Curtis, this is our dear Miss Plympton, whom we couldn't live without. She gave us that lovely pickle-fork, you remember. Wait, Miss Plympton. Will you take these to your mother, with my love?" She took an armful of roses from a vase and thrust them dripping into Miss Plympton's summer-silk arms, against her summer-silk bosom. "And tell her she must hurry up and get well for my wedding, because I refuse to have it without her."

Miss Plympton's eyes filled with tears again. "I'm sorry I was so stupid," she whispered. "I've got the—you-knows—with me. I can change that lace all right."

"Goo-*sie!* You're not to *touch* them if it's the least *bit* of trouble." Christabel dropped a kiss lightly on the crumpled cheek.

"I think she's—an angel," said Miss Plympton to Curtis, with a sniff, and he answered:

"That makes it unanimous, Miss Plympton."

VIII

Uncle Johnnie followed Aunt Deborah up the aisle and into the front pew. Now, Deborah, hold your forehead with your fingertips as if it were beginning to ache, and I'll look into my hat.

He glanced sideways to see when she would lift her head. Almost nothing there but a smell of age, *eau de Cologne,* and new kid gloves, wrapped in a black silk mantle and topped by a bonnet, trembling so that the bonnet's glass dangles made a tiny clashing. Poor Deborah, you're getting very old.

Up we come! Ann and Susannah were in the front pew, too, and behind were the younger girls, Eliza, Lydia, and Hannah. And here was Amy, weeping and delighted. She knew, for all her tears, that her daughter was doing well for herself. The Carey family across the aisle made an impressive showing.

Here came the bishop, fresh and rosy as a baby just out of its bath, his starched sleeves two white billows against the white billows of marguerites on the altar, and Dr. Marsh, well laundered, too, looking as if he were going to give someone a nice but solemn surprise. They moved into sunlight falling through stained glass, and were wrapped in celestial crazy quilts of colored light.

The bridegroom and best man.

> The *voice* that *breathed* o'er *E*-ee-*dun,*
> That *earl*-yust wedding *day,*
> The *pri*mul marridge ble-uh-sing
> It hahth not *pahssed* away.

The choir was rocking slowly by, splitting, filing into choir stalls.

> Still *in* the *pure* es*pow*-ow-sul
> Of *Chris*-chun mahn and *maid*——

Will she have her head down-drooping like a flower, Uncle Johnnie wondered, or bravely uplifted?

Bravely uplifted. Going into battle with all flags flying.

"What, Deborah?"

"I said, the blessèd child!"

Two little pages in green velvet carried her train. Curtis should have been in doublet and hose. He was the only one who looked out of place. Nice of her to let him come. Or did she know he was there? She seemed completely detached.

They were moving toward the altar now. Kneeling. Green and purple flakes of glory slid over the bishop's bald head and flowed down the bride's veil and train. She'd like that, Uncle Johnnie thought.

Oh, puffeck Love, all yuman thought trahnscending,

a very young choir-boy sang, with his eyes rolled up. Which would win in a Looking Holy contest, he or Christabel? Uncle Johnnie wondered.

"—that ye may so live together in this life, that in the world to come ye may have life everlasting." The bishop's words were thick bubbles of honey. "Amen," the choir sang seven times.

For a while Uncle Johnnie let ladies tell him that it was a beautiful day, a beautiful wedding, that Christabel was a beautiful bride, that Shady Lawn was looking beautiful. Then, understanding the feelings of one of the little moss-green pages who was being sick behind a mock-orange bush, he went to a rustic summer-house, out of the way of the crowd. It was occupied by a young man in a large soft collar, almost a fichu, Uncle Johnnie thought, eating lobster salad.

"I hope I'm not intruding."

The young man's mouth was too full for speech, but he made welcoming gestures with a fork held by a hand whose wrist was encircled by a silver-and-turquoise bangle, and Uncle Johnnie sat down and yawned. The other gave a final gulp.

"I couldn't stand watching them turn a sacrifice into a festival any more, so I came off here by myself. My God! This is the kind of thing that makes a man want to get dead drunk!"

"We could make a start," said Uncle Johnnie as a waiter passed by the summer-house with a tray full of glasses of punch. "No, I don't want any of that vegetable soup. Go and get a bottle of champagne and two glasses."

"You couldn't stand it, either?"

"No, I couldn't."

"What's she doing it for, that's what I want to know? That exquisite girl throwing herself away."

"What's the matter with the groom, aside from his getting married?"

"Well, he's so evidently just a typical business man."

"Good family, rich."

"That would mean less than nothing to Christabel."

"Ah?"

The waiter's black face appeared in the doorway, framed in dangling sprays of roses. "Yassuh, yassuh, heah you ah, suh, all right, suh? Thank *you,* suh, thank you kindly, suh!" The gentlemen buried their noses in spray.

"She's as near pure spirit as anyone I ever knew. Why, Christabel is almost a religion to the people who really know her."

"Indeed!"

"What *is* she doing this for? Did you notice her expression? White as death, and those shining eyes—there was a sort of tragic radiance about her. You know she looked more like a nun than a bride, the way she wore her veil like a wimple, and carried that one Madonna lily. All the time I kept feeling that what was really happening was that she was taking the veil. I kept thinking, what is that man doing there?"

"That was rather the effect. Let me fill your glass."

"Thank you. *Salut!* The sunlight coming through the leaves turns your face a very interesting green, sir. I should like to paint it."

"Ah, you're a painter?"

"Well, yes, although my work isn't what the Philistine means when he says painting. In fact, I don't confine myself to paint. I use any medium that I feel will express my meaning most truly. And the thing I try to do is, I try to escape from convention into pure abstraction. I'm not interested in your mustache, for instance, or your nose, but in your essential personality. But I don't want to talk about myself."

"Not at all."

"I feel that convention means death to art, emotion, spirit. Thank you. *Salut! Shoo!* How these roses attract the bees! Speaking of convention, don't you agree with me that it's wonderful for a girl like Christabel to have escaped so completely from the death in life of the conventions she was brought up in?"

"You feel that?"

"Oh, absolutely." He flapped a hand at a bee. "You know there's no one in her family who understands her—love, yes, she must be given that wherever she goes, I think, but understanding, no! It almost killed her to get away from them. She used to tell us about it. Very sweetly and understandingly, but you could tell what she'd been through. And now that I've seen it all for myself, I can realize what a hell her life here must have been to her."

"As bad as all that? . . . I don't think that kind stings."

"Don't you? It looks terribly angry. Just watch it worrying that rose! What were we saying? Oh, Christabel! Well, just look around you, sir! Just feel the atmosphere. But she did get out into the light and air, and yet now of her own free will she's going back into darkness like—like —Persephone, and nobody's stopping her. When I looked at the priests and the flowers, and Christabel with her white face, I could think of just one word. Sacrifice."

I thought of that word, too, Uncle Johnnie said to himself. There was also the bridegroom's red face. Red as a rose was he. I shall have to lend this young man my handkerchief in a minute.

"Maybe she can take care of herself," he added aloud.

"I know her as perhaps you don't, sir."

"I think that's highly probable."

They finished the champagne in a silence broken by the roaring of the bees, and presently by distant shouts.

"They must be going away."

The victoria was at the door, with Deborah's new coachman, beaming red face and big white wedding favor. "So pretty and touching to see how the old family servants adore her!" Uncle Johnnie heard a strange lady say reverently.

Around the front steps people were calling, laughing, their hands full of rice. But when Christabel came slowly out, more nunlike than ever in pale gray, her face whitely, stilly shining, hands fell, rice dribbled to the ground.

"Good-by, good-by! Good-by, Gobby dear. Good-by, dear Uncle Johnnie."

If I'd let out a cloud of sulphur and switched a tail at him he couldn't have been more scared, thought Uncle Johnnie, looking at the place from which the young man had vanished.

IX

"WOULD you like to play bridge with the Prestons, Christabel?"

"Curtis *dar*ling! Play *bridge,* with the sea and the sky looking like this?"

"Well, what would you like to do?"

"Dearest, must we *do* something all the time? Can't we just *be?*"

So for a few minutes they just were. How blue the sea is! she thought. How utterly it satisfies me! She looked toward Curtis to see if he were drinking it in, too. His eyes were shut, his mouth a little open.

Why was I such a fool as to think there could never be anything for me but loneliness? What is life, anyway, but just being alone, never really touching each other, except in those rare moments when a shared beauty, a shared reality, opens the prison doors? How I long to share with him this rapture of really seeing the blue of sea and sky. And here he is, beside me—asleep.

It seemed almost a symbol.

How Elliott would have gloried in this light, this benediction of color.

I am utterly lonely, I might as well admit it, she thought, tears stinging into her eyes. In this shipful of people I am all alone.

Of course they made a fuss about her. People always did, over anyone who was well known. And although she had begged Curtis not to tell anyone she was Christabel Caine, he was so proud of her he couldn't resist bragging, and he had given away a dozen copies of *Carnation Flower* already. He must have brought half a trunkful. It was a little ridiculous, like a drummer giving away free samples. There was something about Curtis—not an insensitiveness, exactly——

She smiled at the Misses White, trotting past, with their arms full of bags, cushions, *Cathedral Towns of England, Châteaux of Old France, My Trip Abroad,* and a bristle of knitting-needles and fountain pens. Poor little old maids, so excited at meeting a writer. Poor little trippers, brave little Christopher Columbuses! She must ask them to tea in London, if she had time. They would be thrilled.

Louis Brown strolled by, lifting his eyebrows and thrusting out his lower lip as he looked from sleeping Curtis to her, and she smiled, lifted her eyebrows, too, drifted her hands through the air. A feeling of being understood warmed her heart. But I must keep him from caring too much, she thought. He mustn't be hurt—and neither must my Curtis. She turned her eyes, that had followed Louis along the deck, to her husband.

He really did look silly. She dropped a book with a bang, and he struggled up with a yawn that was almost a scream.

"Why don't *you* go and get into a bridge game, Curtis?"

"Well, I don't like to leave you."

"I want to be alone with the sea. I want to look at it until there isn't any me left, until there isn't anything left but blueness."

"*Sure* you won't be lonely?"

She smiled at him, and kissed her fingertips. He is just a grown-up little boy, eager to get to his toys. My grown-up little boy, who adores me so that it almost breaks my heart. When he turned to look back at her from the smoke-room door she smiled again, but she saw him through tears that splintered the world into crystals.

Loneliness——

Courage, child. Wrap the sky around you, comfort yourself with the sea.

Perhaps Louis would be coming back.

But the deck remained deserted, and the dazzle of sun on water made her blink. Getting up to pull her chair around, she could look into a smoke-room window. The interior, its darkness swimming with scarlet balls to her sun-dazzled eyes, slowly revealed Curtis with his back to her, awake and lively enough now, with the Prestons, and Mrs. Sloane, who chose that moment to answer some remark of his with a friendly shove and shout of laughter.

Why did he marry me? Christabel asked herself, sinking into her chair. If that's what he wants, why did he take me away from the people I love, the people who love me? Suppose I should go overboard, how much would he really care? He would be sorry, of course, and wear correct mourning, and give a stained-glass window to the church where we were married—Christabel, dearly beloved wife of Curtis Carey—and then he would play bridge with Mrs. Sloane.

The current volume of her Secret Journal lay on the deck by her chair. She picked it up and began to write.

"What peace it would be to say: I am too tired to go on. To let my body enter the sea, and sink, down, down, past goggling fish with drifting films of tail, past ribbons of ruffled sea-weed, purple and brown——"

People were coming out from their afternoon naps. With her eyes on the words that streamed from her pen she felt them going by, felt them looking at her. "—Writing—" she heard them murmur to each other respectfully, "writing." They think I have more than my share, she told herself. They think I am young, beautiful, rich, brilliant, beloved—happy. They envy me.

If they only knew!

"To sink slowly, slowly, down to the trees of white and rose-red coral massed with bubbles, to the sprays of pearl, to drift and turn until my bones were white and delicate, covered with small rose-pink shells and silver bubbles, drifting and turning forever in that still depth of peace."

A group of skirts and trousers surrounded her chair. People! When all she wanted was to be alone. "Peace—" she wrote again, and rose from the depths of the sea.

"Pardon us for interrupting——"

"What is *prob*ably a masterpiece in the making!"

"We've come to ask a very, very great favor."

She felt her eyes and mouth as round as an astonished child's, she touched her bosom delicately with outspread fingers.

"A favor? Of *me?*"

"We've been chosen as a committee to beg, bribe, or otherwise cajole you into giving a reading from your poems for the edification and delight of your fellow-passengers."

"Please say you will!"

"Everyone wants to hear you!"

"We won't take no for an answer."

"Oh, *thank* you for wanting me to—but I can't! No, I can't!"

"Oh, *please!*"

"I tremble to think of the fate of the committee if it ventures to withdraw without your promise."

"Oh, but if you only knew how it *terri*fies me! No, no, I really can't!"

"Just *think* of the pleasure you'll be giving."

"You can't refuse when everyone wants so *much* to hear you."

"May I put in a special plea for 'Out where the long sea road follows the curve of the cliff'?"

"Oh, yes, *ex*quisite!"

"And please, please, pretty-please, some of those darling kiddie poems!"

Tender assenting groans.

No longer the lonely cold depths of the sea. She rocked gently in the warm sun. They were being too kind, she told them, they were making too much of a fuss over her little songs. She thanked them for it, she loved them for it—but, no.

"Don't say that. Think it over and tell us this evening."

I can't do it, she thought, going down the stateroom. To get up and read in front of all those people! They don't realize how a thing like that *drains* you, if you're sensitive enough to have written the poems in the first place.

Yet if I have been given something precious, have I any right not to share it? Isn't this sacrifice of pouring forth, part of my gift and my burden? She opened the closet door and looked absently at her dresses.

If she did read to them, what poems would she choose?

> White lilac, delicate and cool,
> And purple lilac, dark with rain——

She tried it softly, watching herself in the long mirror. And as she spoke she became a lilac bush, delicate and cool. Elliott had said once that he must feel like what he was painting, and ever since then she had realized that she, too, must be what she created—she must be lilac, the sea wind crying, falling rain. She must be everything.

She was in his studio again, curled up in the window seat, hearing his words. She saw his old painting-shirt open at the throat, the fringe of hair she loved to run her finger under, vermilion spikes on table and canvas, for he had been feeling like red-hot pokers when he spoke.

"Dear Elliott!" she whispered, leaning against the closet door. Then she caught her breath, flung her head back bravely. Courage, child——

There hung a golden gown she had never worn. It reminded her of something Louis Brown had said last night. "I'm the only one who's on to you. Everyone else thinks you're a little golden queen, but I know you're just a ridiculous beautiful child who has learned, God knows how, to cast a spell."

Smiling, she slipped into the gown. She put on her pearls, patted a film of powder over her face, and interestedly did a little work with her eyebrow pencil. Her white face and shadowed eyes made her feel frail and exquisite. She moved her white hands against her golden gown.

> White lilac, delicate and cool,
> And purple lilac, dark with rain——

She heard Curtis talking to the steward, and had just time to scramble out of her dress before he came in.

She threw her arms around him, she loved him and silently forgave him.

"Well, what's new?"

If only he wouldn't always greet her that way!

"Nothing—oh, they want me to give a reading of my poems."

"Fine!"

"Fine? I don't know what you mean. I hate the idea. Anything like that leaves me utterly *spent.*"

"Oh, you'll enjoy it."

She felt ready to burst. We are utter strangers, she thought, as they dressed for dinner, getting into each other's way. He thinks I *like* getting up and having everybody look at me, when it kills me—when I can only bear it because I have something real, something true, something of myself to give them. It was a good thing she hadn't worn the golden gown before. A little golden queen. She heard herself speaking exquisite words, she saw Louis Brown's dark face in the audience. White lilac, delicate and cool. And running along with her thoughts was Curtis's voice, telling her what bad hands he had held, and what nice women Mrs. Preston and Zita Sloane were.

He had gone to get cigarettes after dinner, when Louis Brown carried her off to look at the stars. Standing by the rail, she felt the music from the distant orchestra, the long rays of light, her own voice, exquisite and sad, trailing out from the ship, delicate tendrils that found only darkness to cling to. All up her arm she felt how Louis wanted to cover her hand, lying white on the rail, with his.

And this moment of ours—this moment—already is the past.

She could hear him breathing hard through his nose. It was time she said something.

"Sometimes I think I'd like to go over the side of the ship, and just sink down into peace. Think of what you'd go drifting through—red and white coral trees all covered with silver bubbles, and ruffled ribbons of sea-weed, and the ocean to rock you to sleep. Wouldn't you like to drift in the dim green light forever, with no more restlessness?"

He continued to breathe hard through his nose.

"Wouldn't you, Louis?"

"I haven't been listening to you. How can I hear you when I'm looking at you?"

Oh, my poor dear, you mustn't love me so, she thought. She put one cool fingertip against his lips.

"Ironical, our meeting on your wedding trip, isn't it?" he asked. And although he had recovered his usual tone of light bitterness, she felt his love pouring over her. It made her love Curtis, who at that moment joined them, made her greet him radiantly, tenderly, putting her hand through his arm, her eyes on Louis.

All through dinner Christabel's voice had come to Curtis from far away, her eyes had been a wounded deer's, and afterward she had disappeared. He had been looking for her all evening. Somehow he must make up to her for having hurt her, though what he had done he didn't know. She was so sensitive, so tender-hearted, that he was always putting his foot in it, when he only wanted to make her happy. Perhaps it's just the artistic temperament, he thought.

This afternoon he had had a struggle to keep awake. Two cocktails before lunch, a bottle of stout, and the sun on the waves had caused an agonizing struggle, followed by oblivion, but something had made him sit up with a jerk, had made the rail, the life-preserver, his own cocked-up feet swim back into their places, before Christabel noticed that he had dozed off, he was almost sure. So she couldn't have been hurt by that, or by his playing bridge, for she had suggested it.

It had been a good game. He thought of Zita, and how she had laughed at his jokes and looked at him as he lit her cigarette. He seemed to be able to please some women. He didn't know what was the matter with Christabel.

He found her with Mr. Brown, he insolently close, as usual. Christabel drew away from him and put her arm through Curtis's, saying that Mr. Brown was showing her the stars. That is Ursa Major, said Mr. Brown, and Curtis said, the only constellation he could recognize was the good old Dipper. And Christabel said the floor of heaven was thick inlaid with patines of bright gold. A respectful silence followed this, and then Mr. Brown said he would hope to see them later, and left.

"Well! I've been looking all over the ship for you!" said Curtis.

"Darling, you mustn't be jealous."

"Jealous! Of *that?*"

She rubbed her cheek against his sleeve. "Ooh, I'm so glad you've

come! You've left me pretty much alone today." She lifted his hand
and left a kiss in the palm. She's forgiving me, he thought, with mixed
relief and indignation, for he had meant to forgive her.

"I don't know what's been the matter, Christabel. I knew I was in
Dutch some way."

"Ridiculous boy!"

"It wasn't because I played bridge, was it?"

She was silent. It was, he thought, and said aloud:

"But, Christabel, you said——"

"Said? *Said?* Curtis, don't you know there's a language deeper than
words, that the heart understands?"

"But I——"

"I wasn't going to tell you. I wasn't going *ever* to let you know!"

"But——"

"But, oh, *Cur*tis, you hurt me so this afternoon! I was so lonely I
wanted to die!"

"But you said——"

"I didn't want you to stay with me if you wanted to be with them.
If you would rather be with Mrs. Preston and that Mrs. Sloane, I *want*
you to be with them."

"But I *asked* you——"

"Only don't expect *me* to come, too, because they make a spiritual
atmosphere that I simply can't—*breathe* in."

"Oh, now, what's the matter with them?"

"So ma*ter*ial—so self-centered."

"But Zita Sloane's nice-looking and polite——"

"Curtis, she's just *cheap*. Bracelets like a Fiji Islander, and powder
enough on her nose to make an avalanche. I don't care for *myself,* but
I'm so ashamed for *you,* to see you taken in by a type like that."

She's really jealous, he thought, in a pleased glow. She loves me even
more than I realized. "I can't remember what she looks like," he said.
"When I look at you I can't remember what anyone else looks like."

She drew close to him again.

"And this evening I waited for you and I *waited* for you, and you didn't come! I didn't want to be sharing this starlight with *him*. I wanted you!"

"But, my darling, I was hunting for you everywhere." And he thought, I must never leave her unless I absolutely have to.

"I wanted you so!"

How she loves me, he thought, lifting her fingers to kiss.

"Isn't it beautiful, sailing into the night? It's like coming home again, home into the heart of God."

"It certainly is."

That was inadequate. He felt unworthy of his wonderful girl, who had given herself to him so completely. And as they stood in silence he was ashamed of himself for suddenly thinking how much he would like a whisky and soda and a cheese sandwich. He managed to get his wrist watch into the light without her noticing. Almost smoke-room closing time. But somehow he couldn't mention it to Christabel.

Her face was lifted to the stars, a long end of the white veil she had bound around her silky head molded itself to his features.

"We're very close at times like this, aren't we, my husband?"

x

LADY DICKERY's motor car, with a coronet on the door and a footman beside the chauffeur, purred toward Knightsbridge, taking Christabel and Curtis to their hotel, from the dinner Lady Dickery had given in their honor.

"It's just like Caroline not to let us take a taxi," Curtis said. "She never can do enough for people. Even when she was a little girl she was always giving away everything. She took off some coral beads Aunt Ethel gave her, I remember once, and gave them to a little darky; they couldn't stop her. They never could make her mind, Ma'm'selle or Fräulein or any of them. I remember her sailing a new hat in a muddy brook, and she used to buy balloons just to sit on and pop, and hide under the table in her nightgown when Aunt Ethel was giving a dinner. The homeliest little mug, with spectacles and big front teeth, and language—boy! But everyone was crazy about her, just the way they are now. Well, you can see for yourself why they would be, she's always been so warm-hearted and generous."

Yes, so generous! Christabel thought, drawing away from him into her corner. All she wants is to give, give, give, to be the source of blessings, like God! Giving, and letting everybody know she's giving. Grabbing the center of the stage all evening!

"Don't you think she's nice?"

There was a little silence before Christabel answered: "Very nice." And after another silence: "But——"

"But what?"

"Oh, nothing. Only it's strange, isn't it, that all these years in England haven't made her voice gentler?" She listened to her own voice, that sounded even more gentle and musical than usual, as she remembered hearing through the noise of the big dinner party how Caroline screamed at the sight of herself in a Watteau shepherdess hat, how Dickery was eating nothing but pineapples because of his fat stomach.

"Oh, well, she always did speak out. She wants us to come down to Clouds next week—did she ask you? You'll be crazy about it. There's a moat and a ghost and a secret passage, and gardens enough even for you. I told her what a gardener you were, and she's crazy to show you the gardens. There's some famous old clipped yew, too—I don't know much about it, but it's in all the books. And they're sure to have interesting people. I think it would be fun. Don't you?"

"Of course we'll go if you want to, Curtis."

"But don't *you* want to? You'd enjoy it, Christabel."

"I suppose I could look at the clipped yew while the *int*eresting people amused each other."

"Why—?"

"I've never in my life been treated the way I was tonight, Curtis! I wouldn't treat a *crim*inal the way I was treated!"

"Why, I—!"

"I suppose it's fashionable not to introduce people and talk across them about things they can't possibly understand. Well, if it is, I don't want to be fashionable! I *hate* people who are so self-centered and conceited!"

"Why, darling! I thought you were having such a good time!"

She bit her lip and turned her head away.

"I thought you'd be crazy about Caroline! And she wants to do so much for us. She wants us to come to her later for the hunting. Wait till you see the way that woman rides! Gosh! I'd love to get some hunting!"

"The cruelty—little bright-eyed furry creatures—it's sickening!" Christabel shuddered, pulling her ermine wrap closer about her.

There was another silence before Curtis's anxious voice asked: "Is your head worse, darling?"

"My head?" she almost questioned, before she remembered that was the reason she had given for not going on to a dance with the others, as Curtis wanted to. She sighed, turned to him with a brave little smile, let a snowflake hand fall into his. But in their room, when Curtis began again about how he would like to go to Clouds, she burst into tears.

"Why, Christabel—!"

She could have stopped, but she made herself go on, remembering shell-pink Lady Somebody or other, pointed out to her by Lord Dickery as the most beautiful woman in London, pug-nosed Princess de Something, who had everybody laughing. And that fat old duchess with her patronizing inflections, saying, when Christabel had finally made her understand that she was a writer: "Oh, indeed! A very pleasant hobby, no doubt." Above all, hideous loud-voiced Caroline, showing off, dominating. I *hate* her, Christabel thought, not able now to stop her sobs. Oh, I'm so homesick, so homesick! They love me at home; they understand me. I want my own darling mother——

She grew quieter at last, drinking the water that Curtis brought, and then lying exhausted in his arms. Her heart ached for herself, so sensitive and fragile.

"Darling, we won't go to Clouds. We won't do anything you don't want to do."

"We *will* go to Clouds! You must, to show you've forgiven me for being so silly—darling, dearest Curtis!" She pressed her tear-wet cheek against his as his arms tightened around her.

When she woke next morning Curtis had gone out. Her maid drew her bath and ordered her breakfast. A haystack of flowers had come from Caroline Dickery, with a note hoping that her head was better. Christabel made a face as she read it, and tore it into bits. On one bit a coronet was left intact, and she put it into her book as a marker. How childish the British were, with all their little symbols of this and that, dressing up and saying, now I am important. She pulled the paper out so the coronet showed, and looked thoughtfully at pearls and strawberry leaves.

"Ring for some vases, Minnie," she said. And when the hotel maid was bringing them in, and Minnie was shaking out the dewy tangle, she added: "They're so lovely and fresh, I suppose Lady Dickery has them sent up from her country place."

The hotel maid looked impressed by Lady Dickery's name. Amusing! Christabel thought. The English certainly are snobs.

She enjoyed a peach with a fluff of cotton wool still clinging to it, eggs, bacon, toast and jam, and although the coffee wasn't much, she managed three cups. Then she lay among her pillows, watching the lace slide back from her white lifted arms. She could see herself in two mirrors, and see repeated trunks, two other Minnies in small pleated black aprons, masses of flowers foaming and spraying. And suddenly she thought, if only Elliott could see me now!

Minnie went out with the gown Christabel had worn last night a crystal waterfall over her arm. She saw herself as she must have looked in it, coming down the marble staircase; she heard again the footmen echoing her name. Of all the affected ways of living!

Again she thought of Elliott. He would have really seen her in that gown, like a water-nymph in drops of bright water. Curtis had never even mentioned it.

In her mind she began to compose a letter to Elliott. Perhaps it would open old wounds too cruelly. But if she wrote to Boyd, she could depend on Elliott's seeing it. She got her portfolio.

"Curtis's cousin, Lady Dickery, gave a simply *huge* dinner for us last night," she wrote. "The guests were really nothing compared with the grandeur of the footmen, about a million of them, all with powdered hair, but they did the best they could for people who were only Dukes and Duchesses and Prime Ministers and such. Caroline Dickery is the kind of person you generally see pictures of in the *Sketch* or the *Tatler,* with a pull-on hat and large capable feet and a terrier, labeled 'Lady Dickery and Friend,' but last night she had diamonds every place but the tip of her nose, and so had all the other women, tiaras and everything—and diplomats all done up with blue ribbons—*and*— little me the center of it all!

"It's like a Fairy Tale. And it's hard work I have to keep the chuckles back when I think of myself in my old smock dining on an apple and a bun, with the coffee-pot bubbling on the gas ring, and then catch a glimpse of this new Christabel dressed in crystal and cloth of silver, going in to dinner on a Noble Arm, and I wonder, when Midnight strikes, will Cinderella be back in her old smock and go running out through rows of 'stonished flunkies? And then Cinderella's heart gives a leap as she thinks—if she could! But she can't. Her Rolls-Royce doesn't change into a pumpkin when Midnight strikes, her crystal gown doesn't change into the old smock, and it's only her Heart can come Home.

"I don't mean that, Boyd dear. I'm a very happy Child. But—but— I do get homesick, I do miss my friends.

"Do you ever see Elliott? I think of him so often.

"Caroline wants us to come to Clouds (their wonderful old country seat) for a house party, but I'm awfully afraid my Curtis isn't going to let me go, as I haven't been very well (I'm writing this in bed, surrounded by flowers and notes and invitations—if my head isn't turned forever it won't be the fault of all these kind, kind people). There's nothing really the matter with me, but my big boy is so strong himself that he seems to think I'm a Delicate Child made of Spun Glass and Thistledown, and spoils me accordingly. He's a Sweet Person, and it isn't his fault that he doesn't love to go adventuring, the way we do, so that I've had to steal off by my own little lonely self to——"

To do what? What were some of the things she was going to do as soon as she had a minute? Ride on a bus-top, have tea at an A. B. C., "—ride on a Bus, high up in the air over the Bobbies with their faces like scarlet peonies, and the costers' patient little gray donkeys, and have tea and Bath buns at an A. B. C.—such fun! Only—I do want some one to Play With!"

That would tell them she was still their Christabel, simple and unspoiled. And really, she could hardly wait to do those things.

Curtis had left a note saying he would be back at twelve, and it was quarter to. She finished her letter, got up, and drew the curtains close together. She was lying in the dark when he opened the door cautiously, and lifted a drooping hand to greet him.

"How are you, darling?"

"I'm *all* right, dearest. Kiss me."

"You're not all right, or you wouldn't have the room dark. Couldn't you eat something if I ordered it? A little soup? Some grapes?"

She shook her head.

"I'm going to get a doctor."

"Curtis, my *dar*ling, I'm all right! Just—lazy."

"You're a little liar, that's what you are. You sound as weak as a drowned kitten."

She powdered her nose and put on her pearls while Curtis was getting the doctor, a delightful man with spats and a monocle. She gave him one of Caroline's carnations for his buttonhole, and he agreed with her that she had better get out of London if she had felt ill and depressed ever since she arrived.

"Dear boy, you *must*n't worry so!" she told Curtis, smoothing the lines from his forehead with gentle fingertips. "It's just that London doesn't suit me."

"Well, how about going down to Caroline's? The country, and quiet, and everything?"

"I asked him, but he was awfully down on the idea, the excitement of a big party and all. I'm *so* apologetic! But *you* go, darling! I'll be all right! I'll just go quietly somewhere. You go without me! *Please!*"

"Where does he think you ought to go? Where would you like to?"

"I don't care. Anywhere—*any*where, so long as it's with you! Somewhere where it will be just us alone, darling."

So they went to Paris.

XI

It was a Paris Christabel had not known before, under the Tomb-of-Napoleon-Louvre-Now-Girls chaperonage of Edith Johnson Plummer. After London it seemed like heaven, at first. It was enough just to have salad mean brittle ice-green frills of lettuce and dark needles of chopped chives instead of a stew of tinned fruits; just to pour crystals of *Jasmin, Giroflée Jaune, L'Heure Exquise,* into her baths; to have hot golden *café au lait* and flaky *croissants* instead of mud and water and cold toast; to get into a taxi with her arms full of packages and say: "The Ritz." She brought back packages, she had them sent, their rooms rattled with tissue paper as Minnie unpacked boxes. "When I was here before I bought a chemise and nightie to match, and thought I had Paris lingerie!" she told Curtis with amused tenderness for the child she had been, while the waiter tried to find room for their breakfast tray among drifts of silk and chiffon, apricot, ivory, and mauve.

But after a while she grew restless. Perhaps we ought to see other people, she thought, looking through the *Herald* to see if she could find any names she knew. We mustn't let our happiness make us selfish.

And what was the use of all her new gowns if there was no one to show them to? Curtis never noticed what she had on, unless she called his attention to it, and even with her generous Curtis it was just as well not to call attention to too many all at once, for when you are a type that demands special creations, dresses are expensive. Their first misunderstanding had come when he had seen the bill for the seven picture gowns. And after he had said that he wanted to spend his whole life in making her happy! She had been so hurt that he had given her a sapphire bracelet next day. She twisted it on her wrist now. Dark blue fire on snow.

"And blessings on the falling out
That all the more endears——"

she said to herself, letting it slip up her arm, down over her hand. Then she lifted it to her lips, whispering: "And kissed again with tears!"

Curtis was out looking up a business connection, and she was bored and lonely. She didn't want to write, she didn't want to read, she didn't want to stay indoors, and yet she could think of nothing she wanted to go shopping for. Still, in Paris one could always buy gloves.

As she stepped out of the lift she saw Gobby Witherspoon.

"Gobby!"

"For *Heav*en's sake! Christabel!"

Darling Gobby! Dear, faithful, loving Gobby! She let her hands lie in his.

"How did you know I was here? And how did you know that this afternoon, of all afternoons, I needed you?"

"My subconscious must have gotten a message, because my conscious certainly thought you were still in London."

"And you felt me here so strongly that you came to me! My dear, do you know that touches something very deep?"

They looked at each other deeply. And then her mood changed. She clapped her hands.

"Now can you play with me a little while, Gobby? I'm all alone this afternoon. Curtis had other things to do. Can't we just wander about like a couple of children on a holiday, and be utterly silly and happy?"

"I'd *love* to, but——"

"Perhaps you have an engagement?"

"Oh, *no!* But—if you'll just excuse me one minute—I——"

"Certainly, Gobby."

"I—well, you see my garter broke, and I came in to fix it——"

He really is a little absurd, she thought, waiting for him. Subconsciousness, indeed! Sometimes she couldn't help feeling that he wasn't as real a person as he might be, that he was inclined to pose. But her heart warmed to him again as he came back, rather pink, from fixing his garter.

"Let's go somewhere away from the shops, Gobby. I'm sick of them. How horrid of me to say that! When my Curtis has been so generous, so much too generous to me! But I'm so tired of being dressed up like a big doll—I want to be a woman, a breathing, feeling woman, not a beautiful doll that opens and shuts her eyes and wears pretty clothes."

"Aren't you happy, Christabel?"

"Oh, yes, I suppose so. At least—is anyone happy? Oh, what's the use of not being honest with you, Gobby? You, being you, would know, no matter what I told you. I'm happy this afternoon, anyway! Look at those big fern-fringed willow baskets full of snails! Look at those apples with flowers and stars—what do they do, paste paper patterns on them before they're ripe? I'd rather have that pink-and-yellow apple with the pale green hearts on it than all the jewels in the Rue de la Paix."

"You *have*n't changed, thank God!"

"Haven't I, Gobby? I feel as if I had. I wouldn't say this to anyone in the world but you, but I feel changed to the depths of my soul. But let's not talk about me; let's talk about you. Oh, Gobby dear, this is heaven! My big boy loves the restaurants that everybody goes to, and the theaters, places where you meet every American in Paris! And I *can't* let him know that I don't enjoy them. I put on my pretty new dresses, and I try to pretend I'm loving it all as much as he is. That's what a woman has to learn, through love and pity, to pretend she's happy doing whatever her man wants to do. But men don't pretend —they're like children that way, I think. Curtis is a sweet person, but he just couldn't understand the thrill of playing around like this, and why I love it so. Gobby! My *dear!* A street fair!"

"What shall I buy you? I want to buy you something."

"Buy me that gingerbead pig named René—no, no, this one named Louis—and I'll keep it forever to remember you by."

They looked at strong men and white mice, and Gobby modestly averted his eyes from four respectable Parisians, two beards, two black silk dresses, squeezed into a giant *pot-de-chambre* on the merry-go-round, answering with shrill screams the light-hearted remarks of by-standing friends. Then, leaving the fair, they paused for refreshments outside a café.

"An *apéritif* for me, please."

"*Deux apéritifs—oh, non, un moment! Un apéritif pour madame et une tasse de chocolat pour moi.*"

"Thank you, sir. Any pastry?"

"*Oh, oui, pâtisserie assortie.* I'm crazy about that frock, Christabel, that little glimpse of lemon-yellow sash is heavenly with the green, but you *must*n't wear that hat with it, my dear! The color's all right, but the line isn't *you*. I'll have to take you to a wonderful place where they make hats on your head. Are you sure you aren't just being unselfish, leaving that coffee éclair for me?"

"It's being a wonderful afternoon, Gobby! It's giving me fresh courage to go on with."

"I wish you were happier."

"Is it so very important? And I *have* been happy this afternoon, thanks to you! But I don't want to talk about me—you're such an understanding person you lead me astray. Tell me about yourself. Have you seen Elliott since—I—?"

"I went to see him the day after your wedding. I wonder if I ought to tell you about it? Of course I don't have to ask *you* never to breathe a word to a soul."

"Of *course* not, Gobby!"

"Well, I thought he'd be pretty low—you know—so I hurried down from the train; I thought maybe I could sort of cheer him up or something, well, not exactly cheer him up, but, anyway, I went down, and of course I went in without knocking, as usual—*don't* ever tell!"

"Gobby, don't you *know* me?"

"Well, he was standing there with a face like death, and holding a blue bottle. I didn't stop to speak, even; I just ran at him and dashed it out of his hand and it smashed to the floor. I saw a piece of the bottle; it had a skull and cross-bones on it!"

"Oh, Gobby! Oh, my poor, poor Elliott! Thank God you got there in time!"

"Of course I pretended it was an accident. I think I said I was trying to catch a moth or something, and that my foot slipped. And he was wonderful, Christabel, the way he pulled himself together. You'd have been proud of him. He got off some story about developing some photographs and having to have acids and things."

"Oh, what courage! What a gallant lie!"

"Of course he did have a lot of other bottles and powders and things there. He *might* have been telling the truth."

"Oh, no, Gobby, you don't know Elliott if you think that. Don't you see, it was to make it seem natural? He knew I would blame myself, and he didn't want to hurt me. Oh, my poor, poor boy, what he must have suffered! I don't know whether this makes me feel most sad or most proud!"

"Well, then we wiped up the mess, and then I didn't like to leave him, so I got him to come to the Zoo with me. I was awfully glad I thought of it; it seemed to sort of take his mind off things. He was simply crazy about the blue-bottomed mandrill. I was, too. Did you ever see it? I never saw such a combination of repulsiveness and beauty; it made my blood run cold. This huge baboon, with teeny little eyes, like a pig, and bright blue-and-red striped cheeks that look as if they'd been flayed, and the most horrible scarlet lips showing through a beard, like the world's worst nightmare of King Edward the Seventh, and then this *ex*quisite behind—my dear, such colors!"

"Did Elliott—?"

"Wait till I tell you—cerulean blue and deep rose and mauve, melting into each other. Elliott was crazy to paint him; in fact, he was just starting when I left New York."

"He *is* going on, then? Oh, the gallant gentleman!"

She pressed her hands together to stop their trembling. Her body trembled with love and pity because Elliott had been ready to kill himself when she had married someone else, with pride because he had the courage to live so that she should not be hurt. How he must have loved her! More, even, than she had guessed. She put her hand to her throat, suddenly breathless. "What a beauty!" Gobby exclaimed, noticing her sapphire bracelet.

She came back from the real world of intense feeling to the dream world of the sapphire bracelet, Gobby, the stack of franc-marked saucers. Already the lamps were printing shadow plane-leaves on the sidewalk. She must go back to Curtis.

"You've saved my life, my dear," she told Gobby as he left her at the Ritz. "And since you've done so much for me, will you do one thing more? Will you forget everything I've said, and just remember, Christabel *is* happy?"

XII

"Oh, Lovely Day! Oh, Day of Shining Hours!" Christabel wrote in her Secret Journal. "For this day My Man and I came home to

OUR HOUSE

And the sun shone, and the winds blew, and the very sparrows in the gutter put on a glory.

"Curtis carried me in over the doorstep, according to the old Gaelic custom of Bringing Home the Bride——"

She paused, remembering how embarrassed Curtis had been, with Smedley opening the door, and Bates following with their bags. He had carried her in, as she suggested—he, dear boy, had never heard of the old custom—but his face had been scarlet. It had hurt her deeply that he could care, at such a time, for what servants might be thinking, but now she could smile as she sighed. That was the very fabric of a woman's love for a man—understanding, forgiveness, and always that hidden, half-sad laughter at the little boy who would never grow up.

"And inside was all Beauty and Blessedness, and Himself and I sat by Our Own Fireside and Broke Bread together before going up Our Very Own Stairs (another old custom, Journal)——"

She pulled a piece of paper toward her, and wrote, while she thought of it: "Tell Mrs. What's-her-name must get some other kind of tea," and then went on in the Journal.

"And now it is going, this Bright and Blessed Day—how can I bear to let it go? God Bless the Days to Come, and Our Home, and Us, and our Living and our Loving, our Work and our Play, and let Peace and Happiness dwell in this House Forever!"

She had happiness at first. She loved each morning, her room fresh from just-closed windows, warm from the just-lit fire, her soft bed, her breakfast tray with thin porcelain, hot coffee, mail full of invitations. She loved putting on her new clothes and going out in her bottle-green town car to buy something for the house—a Coromandel screen, a rose-quartz Kwan-Yin, Goddess of Mercy. It made her happy to feel that through her Curtis's money, that might have been just so many sordid dollars, was being transmuted into beauty, into food for the spirit. And her new preoccupations did not make her thoughtless of others. She bought souvenirs for all the people she had not had time to remember when she was abroad—bags and scarfs for the aunts, an English pipe for Uncle Johnnie, a collar that probably really had come from Paris, for Katie Sullivan. They would never know the difference.

The dinners given in her honor by the Careys' friends were pleasant, but most of the luncheons bored her. Self-centered women, full of their own affairs. And what affairs! What shallow, surface lives they seemed to lead! It wasn't that she minded that they only thought of her as Mrs. Curtis Carey, that most of them didn't know she was Christabel Caine, and, if they had known, wouldn't have cared. It was just that it made her sad for them to feel how empty their lives were of beauty, poetry, the things of the spirit. "And they exhaust me," she explained to Curtis when he tried to convince her that they were all "nice girls." "They make me long to be either alone or *really* with someone—the way I am really with you, darling."

But sometimes she wondered, were she and Curtis really together? He adored her, yes, but did he understand her? Or was she doomed to loneliness forever? "Tragedy, real tragedy, comes to the rare soul capable of it," she wrote in her Journal, thinking of past days when she had been really with Boyd, Gobby—Elliott. And on another day she wrote:

"To suffer! Not to dodge! To go through all pain, all sorrow! The Blessèd Angela of Foligno——"

Was it the Blessèd Angela? She couldn't quite remember, but never mind, no one would be apt to know the difference. "The Blessèd Angela of Foligno said that if pain were for sale in the marketplace she would run to buy it. Saint Catherine of Siena said: 'I have chosen suffering for my consolation.' 'Suffering is the ancient law of love,' said the Eternal Wisdom to Suso. 'There is no quest without pain, there is no lover who is not also a martyr.'"

With the sense of loneliness came a longing to see Elliott again, and for a time she let her imagination play with the idea. Perhaps at the theater she would glance up from her program and find him in the seat beside her, and they would look at each other with a long tranced look. Or she would step from her motor, almost in his arms. "Christabel!" And he would stand gazing at her, oblivious of passers-by, until, in spite of the pain in her heart, she would have to laugh, to put her hand through his arm in the old way. Or, walking in the Park in the first snow—they had loved the first snow; they had always called it theirs—she would meet him, alone with his memories, as she was alone with hers.

But none of these dreams came true, so on a day when she had nothing that she wanted to do, and was so lonely that tears kept stinging into her eyes, she wrote asking him to tea.

As she dressed for him she paused to look deeply into the mirror, to see herself as he would see her. Head up, with gallant courage—a brave little smile. How should she greet him? What should her first words be? Perhaps a wordless welcome would be best. She went toward the mirror, both hands out. Her chiffon sleeves floated back, then fluttered down, folding wings. Gray bird, wounded bird, home in your nest again.

Her hands trembled, touching powder box and lipstick, as she remembered, shaken and glowing, that he had tried to kill himself for her. She drew a deep sobbing breath, a white hand went to her throat. Had she the courage to see him, after all? And, leaving herself out of it, was it going to be too hard for him?

But he hadn't any telephone and it was nearly tea-time. And, anyway, one must not dodge life.

Oh, my dear, don't look so! Forgive you? Oh, Elliott, what is there to forgive? You have given me the greatest bliss that has entered my life, and the greatest pain, which is the same thing—how could I feel anything but love and gratitude toward you?

She opened the safe set into her blue wall, near the *prie-dieu* under an ivory Christ on an ebony cross, took out her diamond and sapphire bracelets, tried them on, then put them back again. No jewels this afternoon, except, perhaps, the triple string of pearls. Pearls are for tears.

She can't throw me over and then think all she has to do is to whistle and I'll come running, Elliott told himself, putting Christabel's note into its envelope and going back to his painting. "Oh, shut up, damn you!" he shouted at his model, a sulphur-crested cockatoo he had borrowed from Mrs. O'Reilly on the ground floor, that was screeching hoarsely. I'm not going to be one of her tame young men. He painted fiercely, biting his lower lip to keep it from twitching. But he hardly saw what he was painting, and the cockatoo, still screeching, had begun to dance from one claw to the other, to lift a yellow crest and spread a yellow-lined wing, the quills separated, to bite with a black beak into yellow down. It made Elliott nervous when it behaved that way, and Christabel's note had upset him, too. The day was ruined as far as painting went.

If he didn't go she'd think he didn't dare, or that she had broken his heart, or something, he told himself, pulling on a pair of thick gloves before he offered the cockatoo a piece of banana. "Here, pretty Cocky! *Hey!* You will, will you, you devil? Nice birdie, have a banana, and then we'll go down to Mrs. O'Reilly."

Coming back to peace and quiet, he reread her note. "Elliott—please come—" she had written after her signature, and the letters looked not quite steady.

Was he or was he not a man of the world? That was the question, he decided. After all, one evolved a philosophy of life that kept one from taking oneself or anyone else too seriously. He wrote, saying that he would come, and then went out to buy a necktie.

The next afternoon he dressed with fingers that trembled, in spite of the cynical smile reflected in his mirror. Perhaps it was all for the best—one evolves a philosophy of life. He retied his tie—worse than the last time!

Pulling at it, a sudden panic seized him. He would have given anything not to go. He could telephone from the drug store—but what could he say? Suppose he just stayed here, and sent her a note tomorrow saying he had been taken ill or suddenly called out of town?

She was expecting him. He couldn't disappoint her.

Gobby had reported her as bitterly unhappy in Paris. Suppose seeing him was too much for her? Had he any right to expose her to such an emotional strain?

And yet, if he could comfort her——

What, crying? Silly little Christabel!

Damn! A hole in his heel. Maybe it wouldn't show over the top of his shoe.

He began to feel forgiving, protective. Christabel, dearest girl, what is there to forgive?

Someone had told him about a man who had killed himself for Christabel, taking poison on the day of her wedding. There were not many girls for whom men would kill themselves. And this girl, who, in the world's eyes, had everything, needed him—had sent for him.

He wondered who the poor fellow had been.

Her house, washed pink, with twisted columns, and a noseless saint in a niche above the door, was so Venetian that a gondola should have been before it instead of the delivery motor of the Superior Market, Third Avenue. He gave his name scornfully, with drooping mouth and eyelids, throwing away his hat and stick. The butler caught them, and led him through thick fog to the drawing room, leaving him there to wait for Christabel.

He waited.

The fog began to lift. He looked about him. Things, material possessions! Only a bird in a gilded cage, he sang in his mind with bitter mirth, for he and Donatia and Boyd and Gobby were finding old songs rather amusing that autumn. A butler, tapestries, silver and lace on the table before the fire—what an absurd scale of values they implied. And yet there were people who were impressed by such things.

Poor Christabel. So she has come to this, he thought, contrasting the huge sheaves of chrysanthemums like helpings of crab salad, the Madonna drenched in brown gravy, with that other firelit room of hers, exquisite and simple—one perfect rose, his portrait of her alone on the wall.

Was she coming? No, not yet. But his heart began to thud. What should his first words be? He adjusted his tie in the glass over the dark Madonna.

Footsteps outside the door. Heavens! He hoped he wasn't going to be sick!

She came toward him with both hands out. Her chiffon sleeves floated behind her. How lovely she was! They looked at each other deeply, until they were interrupted by the footman bringing in tea.

"So good of you to suggest my coming."

"So good of you to *come*. Cigarette?" And, as the footman left the room: "Now tell me—everything."

"What is there to tell that you don't already know?"

"Sometimes I feel as if I didn't know anything, Elliott—or at least that I hadn't known anything until it was too late to be of any use. Do you ever feel that way?"

"All I've learned is that nothing's worth being unhappy about," said Elliott, with a laugh so scornful and explosive that it startled himself.

"Oh, my dear, not that, not that! Don't let it make you bitter!"

The footman brought in crumpets, and Christabel began to pour Elliott's tea. He watched her put in lemon, and said nothing, though he always took cream. Their hands shook so as she gave him the cup that tea splashed out and scalded him. How sad her face was! He asked, for the footman's ears:

"Did you have a wonderful trip?"

"Did I? Why, yes—yes, of course we did."

"Where did you go?"

"Oh, the usual places. London and Paris and motoring through the château country."

The footman went out.

"Christabel, are you happy? Forgive me, I have to know!"

"Is *any*one happy, Elliott? Well, I suppose a good many are, really— at least, they aren't sensitive enough for anything but cowlike content— but that isn't what you and I mean by happiness, is it?"

"Oh, Christabel, why—?"

The footman brought in cakes.

"Are you writing anything now?"

"I'm just getting back to it. There have been so many interruptions. Are you painting?"

The footman put another log on the fire.

"That will do, Alfred, thank you. And I'm not at home to anyone."

Now that the man was gone, Elliott wasn't sure what to say. Everything he could think of seemed too much or too little. They drank their tea in silence, gazing into the fire. And he was horrified to realize that he had absent-mindedly eaten all his crumpet. He hoped Christabel wouldn't notice or would think he hadn't taken one. It looked so unfeeling. And yet, after all, why should he worry about seeming unfeeling to her, who had been so unfeeling herself? He took another crumpet defiantly.

"Elliott—I must say something to you—quickly, now, while I have the courage. I must tell you that I think I must have been mad when I did what I did. I don't understand why I did it—it wasn't love, unless compassion is love, and pity—he seemed to *need* me so! And you only seemed to need your work— No, no, don't speak. Let me finish before my courage fails me! A woman wants so terribly to be *need*ed, Elliott."

Her hand lay white on the dark velvet between them. He lifted it to his lips. How good it smelled!

"You asked me if I were happy, but I don't believe you, being you, need to have me tell you. But what does that matter? One learns how unimportant one's own happiness is."

"Yes, the important thing is accepting life."

"*Is*n't it? Oh, how true that is! If only we didn't have to suffer so to learn it!"

She pressed a lace-bordered cobweb to her eyes, and then smiled at him.

"More tea? I'm not a very good hostess, am I? A little pink cake, specialty of the house? Oh, Elliott, do you remember going to the *pâtisserie* to get cakes for tea?"

"Do I! And our discussions in front of the fire? You and I settling life and death, while Gobby finished up the pastry?"

"Oh, Elliott, teach me to be brave like you! Because I do know how brave you are—I don't mean just in being able to laugh, dear, I mean—I—I just want you to know—I know!"

Know what? he wondered, holding her hands in his, while he wondered, too, what time Mr. Carey got home. It would be just as well to be gone by then.

"And I do realize the courage it takes—just to live. I do understand, because on the ship—I wouldn't tell this to anyone else in the world, but I owe it to you—the water seemed to call me. I was so tired, it would have been so easy! But I *had* to tell you, so that you would know I understand, and know how I thank you and how proud I am of you, and how grateful I am that what happened happened!"

She's overwrought, he thought. Seeing me has been too much for her. "I'd better go," he said, struggling up from the soft low sofa.

"Yes, perhaps it would be better."

"Good-by."

"Good-by, my dear."

Her hand fluttered to her throat, her fingers twisted nervously through strands of pearls.

"Elliott—I must say one thing more to you before you go. Never blame yourself for anything that has happened. You have given me the greatest bliss that I have ever known, and the greatest pain, which is the same thing—how can I ever feel anything but love and gratitude toward you?"

"Oh, Christabel——"

"You must go now, Elliott."

He was thrilled, his whole body tingled as he lifted a floating sleeve to his lips. Courage and love and sorrow. Elliott and Christabel.

"And do one thing for me, my dear. Forget what I have told you, and when you think of me—*if* you think of me—think that I am happy——"

XIII

IN Christabel's old room Mrs. Caine was painting tea trays with baskets of flowers for the Hospital Fair. The forget-me-nots were the most fun to do, dot, dot, dot, dot with the pale blue paint, then one dot of yellow in the center. As she painted she wrote a letter in her head. Darling Christabel—Guess what I have been doing all afternoon? Painting! You didn't know I was an artist, did you? I have been painting trays for the Fair, and really if I do say it they are just as pretty as can be. I am doing them with little baskets of flowers——

Dot, dot, dot, dot. Thursday. Katie's day out, but it was never any trouble to get supper for Fred. She was just going to have deviled crabs; they were all ready to pop into the oven. There was a Mary Pickford picture to go to later. Life is full of nice things, she thought, glowing. Deviled crabs, movies, Fred, my painting——

She finished a tray, and had a good look at it, pleased and surprised that she had done anything so charming. A vague plan of painting all the bedroom furniture with bunches of old-fashioned flowers drifted through her mind. She began another tray, humming a song.

And for mm-hmm *dum*-dee *Laur*ie,
I'd lay-*hee* hmm-*hmm* dum-dee hmm!

Through the open window came the sound of Jake's lawn-mower, the scent of freshly cut grass. Another scent, that always brought memories of a child's summer by the sea, the scent of privet flowers hot in the sun. She entered the tiny shop—boxes of glass beads, blue, green, gold, and coral-color—peppermint hearts with "Ever Thine" and "Kiss and Make Up" on them in bright pink—dolls with shiny black china hair and tiny feet in high black china boots. She was on the beach where shells holding a little sand and water lay half buried in wet sand. She popped blisters in brown sea-weed between thumb and finger; she felt sand between her toes again.

Was that an automobile stopping? The maple tree had grown against the window, so she could no longer see the gate. Yes, the door bell—bother! I'll just let it ring, she said, but she knew she would answer it.

"Mother!"

"*Christ*abel! *Dar*ling! Where on earth did you come from? Jake! Oh, Jake! Carry Miss Christabel's bag upstairs, please. Darling, why didn't you let us know you were coming? Katie's out, and everything. Never mind, it's lovely to see you. Everything's all right, isn't it?"

"Everything's all wrong; that's why I came."

"But—?"

"No, I don't mean that. Of course everything's all right."

"But what—?"

"Please, mother darling! I don't want to talk about it, if you don't mind. How are you?"

"I'm fine."

"*Are* you?"

"Don't I look it?"

"You look sweet. But I'm very much afraid you're naughty, now that I'm not here to look after you. Haven't you been overdoing? You look tired to me, dear. You *must* remember that you can't do all the things you used to do."

"Oh, I'm all right." But for the first time she noticed that her back was aching—well, not exactly aching, but she could feel it. That was because she had been transplanting seedlings all morning. She wouldn't mention that, for Christabel had never understood how anyone could really enjoy working in a garden.

She did feel tired, now that she stopped to think about it. But, thank goodness, the guest room was ready. All she had to do was get out the sandalwood soap, from Christmas, the best bureau cover, and embroidered towels.

"Oh, mother! You're not going to make company of me and put me in the guest room? Oh, no! Just put me in my own old room. I've come home to be your little girl again, and try to forget things."

"Well, but it's in an awful mess. I've been painting tea trays. See!" She held up the best one proudly.

"Mother! Aren't you cunning? They're *love*ly tea trays, simply *love*ly!"

Feeling like a foolish child, Mrs. Caine carried out the trays, while Christabel shed her clothes.

"Mercy, it's hot! Don't bother about fixing things up, mother dear. Oh, mother, I want to pretend I'm just the way I used to be, that I've never been away—I want to forget everything——"

"Christabel dearest, I'm so worried about you. Couldn't you tell me what's the matter? Perhaps I could help."

"No, darling, I'm not going to have you bothered, too."

"It isn't—you haven't—Curtis—?"

"Curtis is happy and well, and it isn't, and I haven't. Now we'll just forget about it."

"But——"

"Now sit right down here. Mother, how long since you've seen a doctor?"

"Goodness! I can't remember! Ages."

"I want you to promise me to go and see Dr. Henderson. No, I know, there isn't anything the matter with you, and you're strong as a prize-fighter, *but,* all the same, I want you to promise to see Dr. Henderson. It's just common sense to have a good overhauling now and then, as one gets older. I can't have anything happening to my little mother!"

She kissed her tenderly.

"I have a little present for you."

Mrs. Caine, who had begun to droop, revived, and thought hopefully of chocolates. Christabel shook out an orchid-satin bed-jacket edged with uncurled ostrich in long waving fronds.

"There! It's to tempt you to have your breakfasts in bed and save yourself a little."

"It's lovely! And, oh, dear, I'm afraid it must have been terribly expensive!"

"It wasn't cheap," Christabel admitted, smiling, and then suddenly cried:

"Oh, mother, if I only had a child! You don't know, you can't even imagine, the sorrow of childlessness! Oh, if I only had a little daughter to comfort me!"

But she got hold of herself again in a minute, after she had clung half weeping to her mother, and went to take a bath.

Oh, dear! What *is* the matter? thought Mrs. Caine, squatting slowly to pick up lace and ribbons, putting her hand to her back as she rose. Just like old times to be picking up after Christabel. It's a lucky thing for her she has a maid.

How hot it was getting! Breathless! And it had been so lovely.

That bed-jacket was beautiful, and it was darling of Christabel to have brought it to her, but she never had her breakfasts in bed; she couldn't, with one girl, and Fred would think she was ill. Perhaps she could wear it downstairs to breakfast sometimes—but it would make her feel shy and silly, and she could see the ostrich fronds getting into coffee and butter.

If only Christabel had telegraphed ahead! Then her room would have been all ready, and Katie could have gone out on Wednesday——

Goodness! Not a thing in the house for dessert! She went to the telephone and called her husband.

"Fred! Christabel's here. . . . No, I didn't know. . . . No—no, I don't know for how long. I'm very much worried. . . . I said I was worried. . . . I can't tell you now. . . . I said never mind now—but, Fred, listen, I haven't anything for dessert. Would you just stop at Bent's and bring home a quart and a pint of strawberry ice-cream? . . . No, they won't deliver this late—they'll put it in a nice container—a quart and a pint of strawberry. . . . I don't think so at all. Why on earth *should* she let us know? If our own child can't come home any time she wants to—!"

Relieved by Fred's saying he thought Christabel might have telegraphed ahead, she left the telephone to answer Christabel, calling from upstairs.

"Mother! If you *are* coming upstairs any time—don't make a special trip, but just *when* you do—*would* you bring me a bowl of ice?"

It really is getting hotter and hotter, Mrs. Caine thought, running out to the garden to cut roses for the table, pausing to wipe her forehead with the back of her wrist, opening the emergency bottle of olives because Christabel was used to grandeur now, shutting the refrigerator lid on her finger. Only the thought of the ice-cream Fred had brought sustained her. But when it appeared, Christabel said she was dieting, and might she have just a little fruit?

Mrs. Caine agitatedly poked into the refrigerator. One banana, but Christabel didn't like bananas much, and, besides, this really was too black for anything. A cantaloupe. She could have half of that for tonight, and half for breakfast. Mrs. Caine would make her stay in bed, so she shouldn't see that they weren't having cantaloupe, too. Fred didn't like bananas, either. Well, she would eat that, and he would just have to do with the saucer of stewed rhubarb she saw lurking behind the box of eggs and the left-over custard. And all the time, as she hurried to get the cantaloupe ready, she got hotter and hotter, and she could feel the ice-cream melting away, exactly as if she were it, going all shapeless and soft.

After supper she rather timidly suggested the movies.

"Of course, dear, if you want to."

"But would *you* like to? It's Mary Pickford!"

"*Is* it? Mother, you are too darling!"

"I just thought you might enjoy it——"

But, although Christabel was sweet about it, they didn't go. They sat on the porch, looking at fireflies, and asking Christabel respectful questions about the book she was at work on. It was the story of an exquisite girl, married to one man, loved by another. Her husband didn't even try to understand her, and she loved the other man, but he was the one she was going to send away. Mrs. Caine approved of that, though she was disappointed to hear that the book was to end unhappily. She thought Christabel might have let the husband die. How interesting to hear about her books even before they're written, Mrs. Caine thought, giving way to a wide yawn in the dark, and then suddenly cried:

"*Christ*abel! Coffee! I forgot! We've sort of gotten out of the way of having it, since you left. Father thought it kept him awake, and it seemed silly to have it just for me. But I'll make some right away."

"Don't bother about coffee, mother."

"But you always have it at your house."

"That doesn't mean I have to have it here."

But she went in and made it.

After she had taken the cups back to the kitchen, and had a secret, guilty peep at the evening paper there, she slipped up to turn down Christabel's bed and put out her fragrant cobweb nightgown. What beautiful things her child owned! Tortoise shell, crystal stoppered with gold, the little heaps of flexible diamond and sapphire bracelets she had pulled off because they made her wrist hot, and that made Mrs. Caine feel watching eyes in every shadow in the room.

From the porch she could hear Fred. "What does Curtis think—?" And Christabel's answering murmur. Her dear little girl. It was lovely to have her home. But what was troubling her? Every time the telephone rang—and it had rung several times this evening—she had jumped, her hand had flown to her heart. I wish she'd tell me. But she doesn't want to worry me—she's very thoughtful.

She could smell honeysuckle. It made her feel sad. Long, long ago; long, long ago. You smell honeysuckle by night, and privet by day when the sun is on it.

What had she been thinking of just as Christabel came? Something that had made her feel so happy—it was just on the tip of her mind——

No, she couldn't remember.

Pausing by the bureau to turn out the light, she looked into the mirror. She did look tired. Tired and old.

Christabel went to bed early. It was relaxing to put on her old wrapper, still in the closet, plaster on cold cream, and read the *Ladies' Home Journal.* "How wonderfully she comes home!" she could hear people saying. "Just like a little girl again—completely unspoiled." I'm glad I've kept my love for simple things, she thought, lighting another cigarette.

Home was rather pleasant, after all, with its shabby chintz and shabby old books, and garden roses whose edges had been nibbled by insects. Dinner starting right in without any soup, and the tablecloth just a tablecloth, not a bishop's brocaded robe or a lace altar cloth. She was glad she had been thoughtful enough to come without letting them know ahead—it had saved them all bother of preparation. She knew her mother! She would have hurried around getting flowers and making chocolate cake, and there would have been chicken for dinner because of company. For that matter, she would be surprised if there weren't chicken and chocolate cake tomorrow. She would remember never to let them know. Happy surprises were so good for people.

Poor darling little mother! If only she didn't *need* me so!

Life was a heavy load. She had tried to run away from her own trouble, but here it was, sighing in the leaves outside her window, filling the familiar room, rolling her from side to side in her bed, as waves roll a pebble.

She tried to remember her letter. Elliott dear, my heart is breaking with what I have to write to you. Why must we always give each other the terrible gift of pain? How can I say what I must say to you? Then what? She couldn't remember exactly, but she had written that they had better stop seeing each other.

Dear Elliott, she would always love him, of course. Shutting her eyes, she could make herself see, with almost no effort at all, small bright pictures of herself and him—at least, she usually could, but tonight the porter on the train from New York melted into Curtis practicing an approach shot on her hearth-rug while he told her to have a good time; Curtis melted into the sweet peas on her dressing-table. She must be more exhausted than she had realized. She yawned until there was a roaring in her ears.

But the situation had become strained. Elliott was demanding too much, expecting to come to tea all the time, and turning sulky if anyone else was there. All winter, all spring, their tragedy had flooded her life with melancholy interest; she had thrilled to his adoration. Somehow all her circle had gotten to know about it, except, of course, Curtis, if he counted as one of her circle. They had made her feel glamorous with love and sorrow. It has been a beautiful winter, for all its pain, she thought. But now she felt that he and she must part, for his own sake, and she had written him so. She had told him not to come again. What if it does bring me loneliness, utter loneliness? she thought, crushing out her cigarette and turning off the light. No one shall know. I have no right to make others unhappy just because my own heart is aching. She saw herself a gallant lady, smiling, smiling— She really did see herself, in a green velvet riding-habit, the skirt lifted by a delicate gauntleted hand, a plumed hat shading the lovely tragic eyes, the smiling mouth, like a lady in an old painting. The Gallant Lady.

Three days ago she had written him, telling him there was no possible answer. And then she had waited for his answer until today, when, in a panic of nervousness, she had run away home. With his tendency to suicide, suppose it had been too much for him. Every time the telephone rang she had nearly died. Oh, I'm so tired, so tired, she thought. I don't want to see him, or hear from him—I don't want to think about him——

With a sudden feeling of suction in her chest, she thought, suppose he does kill himself this time, and suppose my letters are found. Suppose they get into the papers, for Curtis to read. What had she written? *What* had she written? Dozens of notes——

Oh, Curtis, she thought, it's you I love, my dear. So strong, so safe. It's to you I give all my loyalty.

If I'm ever such a fool as to get into a mess like this again—!

Try to relax. Think of something pleasant. Gerald Smith. She had seen him in the train coming out to Germantown, and had promised to lunch with him in Philadelphia tomorrow. She tingled, remembering the way he had looked at her.

Darling mother and father! She must come home oftener. And yet that meant loneliness for her own dear Curtis.

Those touching little trays—her breakfast on a tray—she supposed she would have to have it, it would make mother so happy. My dear, I only want you to be happy, truly, truly, it doesn't matter about me. No, she mustn't let herself think about Elliott.

A sighing in the leaves deepened to a delicate patter, the sleepy sound of rain flowed through the darknesss. What is he thinking now, lying awake? The grass and wildflowers will root in this aching heart, this tired brain—remember that, use it sometime. The grass will break my heart and pierce my side—Jake cutting grass—father and mother must have the privet hedge cut; it looks awful, all overgrown, nobody lets privet bloom—Gerald—tomorrow—mother's chocolate cake—Gerald, dear, please, you mustn't say things like that—Gerald——

XIV

CHRISTABEL was discontented and restless in the months that followed her dismissal of Elliott. Not because she missed him. It was a relief to have him out of her life, for he had begun to be unmanageable. She wanted to be adored. She wanted to prove almost too much for men, to make them love her passionately and almost uncontrollably, in spite of all her efforts to save them. To feel that they were always just about to burst, but never quite bursting, that she was to them not only a woman, but a high star. She basked in an atmosphere of reverent passion as sweet and warm as the atmosphere of her firelit flower-filled rooms, and the fires of love were as well controlled as the fires in her fireplaces, that Alfred kept supplied with logs, and screened when sparks began to fly.

Most of her adorers were willing co-operators. They were dramatic young men, who could throw themselves into their parts so fully that they themselves believed in their firmly closed lips, their dilated nostrils. She and the young man of the moment spoke to each other fragmentarily, their words, she thought, like sun-bright leaves floating lightly on deep waters. The Tuesday young man who had done his drawing-room in solferino velvet, with beadwork bell-pulls, and wreaths under glass of straw-colored ferns and dark blackberries made from hair; the Friday young man who had designed the curious costumes for the Monday young man's play in which a murderer fell in love with a wax saint. There were mild thrills sometimes as hand touched hand when cups were refilled. But when the soft collars and pastel-tinted neckties were gone, they left no troubled wake, nothing more upset than the crushed silk cushions, the two half-empty teacups, the pile of cigarette stubs, that showed someone else had been understanding Christabel.

But Elliott had shown signs of forgetting to be reverent to an exhausting degree, and was only kept in order by the more exhausting means of being led to talk exclusively about himself and his painting. When she said those things that demanded wordless answers, restraint shown by clenched hand or bitten lip, he was increasingly apt to answer literally. She was glad, for both their sakes, that she had been strong enough to decide they should not see each other again. That was not why she was so depressed. She did not know the cause, she could not find a cure.

She was bored with theaters, bored with dinners; she wept when Curtis suggested Florida. In her mother-in-law's box at the opera, lent them week after week, drifting her feather fan through air vibrating with plump Mimi's last farewells, kilted Edgardo's laments, or the love-making of Pinkerton and Cho-Cho-San, she was so bored she could have screamed. Amusements can't help me, she thought. People can't help me. Yet somewhere there must be a still peace where I can be lost, and find myself again.

She thought of God. She would become one with God.

She had always suspected herself of the mystical temperament. Now she took up contemplation, gazing at an apple until she became one with it, the apple blossom within it that had changed to a star, the seeds, little brown monks in their cells, the dark roots, the branches melting into light, the cycle of the seasons. If I can see this clearly, I can see God, she told herself. One of her best-known poems sprang from that apple she took from the silver fruit-dish, wedding gift of Mr. and Mrs. Talbot Emery Towne.

She found she could practice contemplation on anything, a walnut that became a fairy shallop with a wrinkled passenger, a sweet pea, mauve wings netted in green tendrils, rimmed with celestial glory. Even hard things—alley cats, telegraph poles. She was delighted to find that she could see the light of heaven pulsing through them all.

Meditation, too. That was harder, because her thoughts became a swarm of bees when she tried to empty her mind, to hold to the central silence. "Take your seat within the heart of the thousand-petaled lotus," she read in an Eastern book brought her by Gobby, who was charmed by her new ideas, and all for companionably contemplating and meditating with her. And though she wished the words hadn't reminded her of an invitation to mount a sight-seeing bus, she found them helpful. She could see the thousand upcurling petals; from the tip of each she could see pure light pouring toward the core of incredible brightness that was herself, sitting cross-legged in the golden heart. Being still, listening for the inner voice, she would think: Who of the rest of the people I know is doing anything like this?

God helped her to write *Fly in Amber* that winter. Each night she placed the next few pages of her novel in His hands. She had never written so easily.

The nights were best of all. Lying in her soft bed under linen and lace and silk, she gave herself up to the life of the spirit. Only to lose myself utterly, utterly, she thought, floating light and warm in the darkness. Only to rid myself of self, to be utterly Thine. Oh, Perfect Love, fill me and flood me! I am a shell that holds the sound of the sea, I am a raindrop that holds the sky and the stars. Come to me, Lover and Beloved. She would lie still, trembling, half fainting. Sometimes, if she could keep still long enough, light spattered, scarlet or white, on the blackness of closed lids, and in a panic she would jerk herself back to consciousness, her heart pounding. Gobby agreed with her that she had been in great and glorious danger. He had not progressed beyond swimming yellow polka dots, and then he was always distracted by something—a taxi, a blanket tickling him.

In her Secret Journal she described her new absorption.

"To be rid of Self—to cast my Self into the white-hot flame of Thy Love, and be consumed."

And again:

"Oh, happy-torment that Thou givest me! Oh, tide of Love and Blessing and Brightness that Thou pourest into me, and through poor little me into the World! And yet I won't say, poor little me, but Blessed Me, because Thou hast deigned to make me part of Thee, to choose me for Thy Beloved——"

These entries seemed rather daring when she read them over, remembering the religion of Dr. Marsh and the congregation in Germantown. Kid gloves, oak pews, green and purple shepherds in memorial windows, hymn 505, the Glory of God bounded by late breakfast
with pancakes, by midday dinner with roast beef. She could not imagine Dr. Marsh with his glittering cuffs and broad A's, or Mrs. Marsh
with her feather boa and her pince-nez, shuddering with ecstasy beneath the Divine caresses, or approving of the shudders of any of their
flock. But beside the books on mysticism her words were mild. Other
people, if they were writing the truth, had been through even more intense experiences than she, and were outspoken in their descriptions.
Determinedly she resumed her seat in the heart of the thousand-petaled
lotus.

Sometimes her nights of ecstasy left her half sick and dizzy in the
morning. Even when she found it more and more necessary to pump
up her interest in the life of the spirit, the sickness and dizziness remained. Her restlessness returned, she repeated to herself again and
again what she had said to her mother—if I only had a child!

On her bedside table, with *The Imitation of Christ* and *The Little
Flowers of Saint Francis* (she must remember to cut the pages! Often
after she had gone to bed she would have picked it up, except for that)
she placed a baby's dimpled hand in alabaster, and sometimes when she
looked at it tears rose to her eyes, surprising her a little, touching her
deeply. Children playing in the Park caused her to weep, and she wrote
in her Journal:

"When I walk, my Little Dream Boy runs by my side——"

Some of her most poignant poems were written that winter, on the
sorrow of childlessness.

She got into such a low state of mind that Curtis finally persuaded
her to see Dr. Deacon.

After the doctor left she lay thinking of what he had told her. In her
windows pots of hyacinths with close-packed buds split the pale spring
sunshine. It was the first day of April.

April Fool's Day. Her eyes fell on the baby's alabaster hand by her
bed, and she gave it a slight push and turned her head away.

Lying there in her white lace nightgown, under blue coverlet with silver stars, she felt herself floating, a cloud in the sky, a disembodied spirit. She crossed her hands, arching the delicate wrists, and closed her eyes, and she could see herself lying there as if she stood by her own bed. She could see tall white candles with golden flames, a pall of white narcissus, golden-hearted. A voice said: "So young, in all the promise of her genius!" Another voice answered: "Her poor little motherless baby—" A tear oozed from her closed lids—another——

But Curtis, on his knees by her bed, was adoring and delighted. His family and her family petted and praised her. She had never been given so many presents. A new car, strands of pearls for her wrists, the enormous emerald held in a circle of frost that she had fallen in love with at Cartier's and that Curtis had said he couldn't afford.

Her mother wrote:

"Uncle Johnnie complains that he can't take a step in any of the aunts' houses without getting a loop of pink wool around his ankle, they are all so busy knitting socks and sacques for the darling baby."

The two families worshiped her, solicitous, until they made her feel like a young Madonna rising starry with hope and fear from the dark kneeling circle.

"After all, what career is as great as motherhood?" she asked Boyd Benjamin, who had dropped in for a whisky and soda and to deplore this handicap to Christabel's career.

"I knew it! I knew when you married uptown and got prosperous that you'd go Victorian, too."

"Victoria didn't invent having babies."

"Specious," said Boyd, screwing a cigarette into a foot-long holder.

"To give life isn't a little thing, Boyd; it's a very beautiful and wonderful privilege," Christabel said, gently, and she thought: Frustration! That's what it is. Frustration and subconscious jealousy. Poor old Boyd! Then, as Boyd continued to scowl and puff, regardless of Christabel's hand waving away the smoke or pressing a handkerchief to her nose, she added:

"Boyd darling, *would* you mind not smoking? I *hate* to stop you, but one gets silly when one's not very strong——"

Poor Boyd! She's getting—well, the only word is coarse—she thought, letting the smoke curl lazily from her nostrils, resting after Boyd had gone. But it's hard on people whose lack of appeal keeps them outside the stream of life. Poor old Boyd, worrying about careers, as if painting eggplants, or even writing poems, mattered at all compared with being what was really the heart of the world, a mother.

She could not help realizing that the Secret Journal touched heights during those months that it had never touched before, could not help believing that when it was published—if it was published—years and years away—those letters in it to her unborn child would comfort and inspire other women, would speak softly as opening petals and clearly as trumpets. Not to mention the poems that made up "First Born"— "Out of the whirlwind I gathered the small white Flower," "Mystery, small as a seed and more great than the Sun," and the rest.

In November her twins were born, strong and beautiful.

She named them Michael and Marigold, expecting opposition, but the names charmed everyone. Uncle Johnnie was reported as pretending to think they were called Patrick and Petunia, but nothing was sacred to Uncle Johnnie.

Toward the end of her convalescence she granted an audience to Gobby. Coming noiselessly to the door of her sitting-room, she found him with his back to her, bending, scooping up something—what on earth was he doing? Then she realized he was practicing kissing a hand of air, and, tactfully withdrawing, made a more audible entrance, and received on her own hand the result of his practice.

"Christabel, I didn't think you could be more beautiful, but you are I'm not being personal!"

"Dear Gobby! It's wonderful to see you again."

"That Madonna-blue chiffon! And the way the light falls behind your head actually makes a sort of halo."

She smiled on her worshiper, letting her hand rest lightly on his arm.

"You mustn't spoil me!"

"No one could do that!"

"What is this intriguing parcel?"

"Some Balkan toys for the babies."

"Gobby, how divine! Oh! This shell-pink pig is my favorite, *so* corpulent! So exactly like you! To find such entrancing things, I mean. And, *oh,* this gnome in the pine-cone hat! How the *Wunderkinder* will adore them, after a while! Oh, Gobby, how I do long to have you see my two absurd kitten-eyed angels! But Miss Hess hardly lets *me* look at them. A strawberry tart? I had Mrs. Britton make them especially for you."

"Christabel, I do think having a cook you call 'Mrs.' is just the height of style! I really am touched. I believe you remember my weakness for strawberry tarts from the Gay Street days! That reminds me, I didn't tell you about Elliott and Donatia, did I?"

"What about Elliott and Donatia?"

"Well, I think it really is going to happen this time—I think they really are going to get married. They're together the whole time. Of course it's almost happened so many times, but this time does seem different."

"Does he seem happy?"

"He certainly does! I think it would be fine, don't you?"

"I want Elliott to be happy almost more than I want anything in the world, Gobby. *I* can't see happiness for him with Donatia, but perhaps you're right. I hope so, with all my heart."

After he went she lay thinking of what he had told her. Elliott and Donatia. Elliott and Do*natia!* Really!

I didn't think you could be more beautiful, but you are. Gobby's voice sounded through her thoughts. She did feel slender and beautiful again. Getting up, she clasped her hands behind her head, then ran them down her sides. Beautiful, a mirror repeated.

Deceived by her courage, the specialists, Dr. Train and Dr. Von Boden, with Dr. Deacon a weak echo, had told Curtis she had had an unusually easy time. She would never trust any of them again. She had come through the Valley of the Shadow of Death. She ought to know. It was she who had had the twins. But now her body was humming with life, she wanted to live again with all her being.

She gazed at her reflection. I didn't think you could be more beauti- ful, but you are. I've been to a dark place and a far place—unimaginable awfulness—Elliott and Donatia—shadows in blue chiffon—I've come back wiser. I didn't think you could be more beautiful——

Going to her desk, she took a sheet of her special paper, with *Christabel* in her handwriting flung in a silver spray across a corner, and wrote:

ELLIOTT DEAR:

I've been to a dark place and a far place since we last saw each other. And now that it's over—the unimaginable awfulness—I would not for anything give it up, for I've come back stronger and wiser. I've come back knowing that loving-kindess from friend to friend is the only thing that really matters, I've come back longing—longing—to see the few I really care for.

Will you come and see me?

CHRISTABEL.

XV

THE United States entered the World War with Christabel's complete approval. Yet her patriotism did not make her narrow-minded. She was able to assure Elliott, a pacifist, that she understood why he refused to stand up in theaters when "The Star-Spangled Banner" was played. "I do, I do understand so completely how much more courage it takes than it would to fight, how much easier it would be to join in the war hysteria, and I honor you for it," she told him, at the same time that she told him she couldn't go to the theater with him that evening.

Friends who were in New York were being kind to her in the evenings, trying to keep her from being lonely, for Curtis, beautiful in uniform, had left for a South Carolina camp.

"The poetry was lovely," he wrote Christabel. "And I am certainly looking forward to reading the book on Spiritual Values just as soon as I get time." And a page later: "Could you send me some detective books, as I have quite a lot of time on my hands?"

Gobby was a sergeant, somewhere in France. "The poetry was wonderful," he wrote Christabel. "I feel from it that you must be suffering exquisitely, and my only consolation is that it is marvelous for your art. I will write you my reactions to the essays on Spiritual Values just as soon as I get time to read them—they keep us pretty busy here, as you can imagine! Since you are so sweet as to ask if there is anything else I would like to have you send me, I would certainly love some chocolate. You have to be a millionaire when it comes to buying it here——"

Boyd Benjamin was in France, driving an ambulance. Christabel could see her, in the unbecoming mud and mustard of her khaki uniform, striding along with steps twice as long as any man's, and following that vision she could see herself, in white that turned from silver to gold as she went down a long corridor, in and out of sunlight falling from high windows. She saw the faces on the pillows brighten. "Sister—" "Sister—" Even the most terribly wounded managed to whisper it as she passed, managed a twisted answering smile to her smile that was so near tears.

But she did not go to France. "I long to go—oh, how I long to go!" she told Austin Weeks, who in happier days had done the portrait of her in a gray velvet *robe de style*, with a greyhound curled about her, that hung over Curtis's desk and who now was camouflaging battleships in the Brooklyn Navy Yard. "But I know the biggest sacrifice I can make for our boys is to stay here and use my own special gift, just as you are doing. Anyone can drive an ambulance, or nurse, but we who have been given gifts—oh, Austin, are we blessed or cursed?—we have no choice."

So, although she did a little work in a white uniform and veil—the costume she wore in the beautiful photographs used to advertise her book of war poems—and gave a great deal of Curtis's money, she felt that her important work was in connection with her writing. She autographed hundreds of copies of books for bazaars; *Fly in Amber,* selling well, supported several war orphans; and she never said no to a request for a benefit reading. Two or three times a week she could be seen coming out of her Venetian house, a Venetian lady in a black tricorn, with a small black lace mask of veil shading her mysterious eyes, going to read her poems somewhere. "Perhaps they will comfort someone just a little," she said, wistfully.

"It seems to me so wrong not to try to bring as much beauty into this poor ugly world as you can, *especially* now," she said to Austin Weeks. "I feel as if, just *because* my own heart is so heavy—oh, Austin, so heavy, so heavy!—I must make an effort, now of all times, to try to look as nice as I can." And to his answer she had to reply: "Oh, Austin, you mustn't talk like that! You mustn't spoil me!"

So when she read before clubs and circles, or sat at speakers' tables, she wore soft fur and velvet and pearls, and sometimes overheard, among the people crowding around to meet her, a whispered:

"She's like a little queen!"

And she tried to be queenly, in the highest sense—*noblesse oblige*— to her adorers as they were introduced.

"Oh, Miss Caine! This is a *real* privilege! I don't know whether you caught my name. I'm Mrs. Merkle, Grace Gladwin Merkle, you might possibly have heard it in connection with my talks on 'The Psychology of Success.' I wanted to tell you how interested I was in *Fly in Amber,* it had a theme so like a novel I wrote several years ago—well, no, it wasn't published, but several publishers considered it——"

"Oh, Mrs. Caine, your reading was *simply* marvelous!"

"*This* isn't Christabel Caine? But, my dear, you're only a child!"

"This is a *great* pleasure, Miss Caine! I'm sure you must be tired of hearing how much we all enjoyed your poems! I wonder if you ever happened to meet my nephew—he's a poet, too—Edgar Temple Anderson—well, it's a little volume called *Heart's Home,* and then he won the Southwestern Poetry Society's second prize with a poem called 'Mary Magdalene on Broadway'——"

"I just can't tell you——"

"Your poems were delightful, Miss Caine."

"I enjoyed your reading particularly, Miss Caine, being a writer my-self——"

Poor dears, thought Christabel, hearing her voice answer their adulation graciously, gently. After all, how human to try to shine, even if it's only by reflected light. Amusing, and pitiful, and yet rather beautiful. It was like something Austin Weeks had said, that had struck her as so true: "Life is the laughter of a broken-hearted clown."

She wrote in her Secret Journal:

"No one will ever know how hard these readings are. They leave me utterly spent, and yet after the emotional exhaustion comes an indescribable peace and happiness, deep, oh, deep, to feel that I can feed these hungry souls. When I just let myself rest in that thought, I know that in spite of the sorrow and darkness of these heart-breaking days, in spite of all my pain, I am a happy and a blessèd Child. And I pray that in spite of all their kindness and the wonderful things they say to me, I may keep unspoiled, I may just be happily, humbly grateful because I have been given this gift to share."

Aunt Deborah died in her sleep that winter. "Something in me has died with you, Aunt Deborah darling," Christabel wrote in her Journal. "My childhood, I think. Those days I spent at Shady Lawn, out in the garden where the spilled petals of the thousand-leafed roses covered the ground with pink silk from a very rapture of blooming, or in high-shuttered rooms, always dim and cool, though heat beat outside like the waves of brassy sea. And you were always there with me, dear, loving the lonely child, who does not forget."

She could not go to the funeral, for she was in bed with threatened influenza, but she sent a blanket of violets—"For darling Aunt Deborah, from her Christabel"; she went into deepest mourning, and she wrote the poem, "An Old Woman Dies in Time of War," beginning: "Sorrow on sorrow, a shadow that falls in the night——"

Uncle Johnnie, in New York on business connected with Deborah's estate, and lunching at the Century Club, saw Talbot Emery Towne, but did not see him first. Mr. Towne, eating rice pudding at another table, pushed his saucer aside, pulled down his face, and came to Uncle Johnnie.

"Mr. Caine," he said, in a voice several notes lower than usual.

"Oh! Howdo."

"I want to assure you that Mrs. Towne and I are feeling the deepest sympathy for you in your loss."

"Thank you."

"We have thought of you constantly——"

Liar, thought Uncle Johnnie. If you get your voice down any lower, my lad, you'll never get it up again, which would be a blessing to the world, God knows!

"A rarely beautiful spirit——"

But presently, with a brave uplift of head, mouth corners, voice, Mr. Towne changed the subject to Christabel—also a rarely beautiful spirit, he told Uncle Johnnie. "Courageously keeping up her work, in spite of her loss. She feels, as this fine younger generation of ours *does* feel, and some of us oldsters, too, perhaps, that in a time of universal sorrow one has no right to dwell in one's personal griefs." And finding, to his surprise, that Mr. Caine was not visiting his niece, he told him that Christabel was giving a reading that afternoon for the benefit of the French Wounded, in Mrs. Towne's drawing-room.

"Under the patronage of our very good friend, Countess de la Tour du Sanglier. I myself, most unfortunately for me, will be unable to be present—we poor publishers can't call our lives our own—but Mrs. Towne will be overjoyed to see you and to have you join her afterward in a cup of tea."

In Mrs. Towne's long drawing-room the front row of little gilt chairs was empty, and emptiness scalloped into the second and third rows, but the rest of the room was full of ladies, edging in sideways, flapping gloved hands, loosening furs; and here and there a gentleman. Uncle Johnnie sat down, as near the door as possible, the fragile chair swaying and squeaking, though he had grown quite thin since Deborah died.

A neo-Greek young lady plucked an accompaniment to conversation from her harp, an owl in a cutaway recited in French, followed by great applause, and then came Christabel.

She stood silent for a moment, unsmiling, but starry-eyed. In her long crêpe veil, with a wimple of white crêpe framing the lovely oval of her face, she looked like a young Mother Superior. "Precious person!" the lady next Uncle Johnnie groaned, and her companion whispered reverently: "War widow?" while other ladies whispered: "Shsh!" for Christabel had begun to read.

You win, Christabel, Uncle Johnnie thought. No matter what the circumstances, I back you to win!

"I will not speak of these things, let me keep
    Silence to cloak my wounds—the tears that I
Have shed for you, the passionate and deep
    Blue of the gentian under the sad sky——"

Christabel was reading, and much more to the same effect—a thorough inventory, ending:

"Of these, while still I live, I will not speak."

Quite right, too, thought Uncle Johnnie. Don't you do it. What aren't you going to speak about next?

She swayed slightly, a flower in the wind, and clung to the back of a chair, as if she were spent, before she raised her head and gave the title:

"'An Old Woman Dies in Time of War.'"

Uncle Johnnie got up and went out, walking on several outraged ladies. Fumbling for his hat, he could hear Christabel's voice:

"Sorrow on sorrow, a shadow that falls in the night——"

The butler, who had retired for a few words with the waiters in the dining-room, got to the front door just too late. It closed with a bang loud enough to make all the adoring ladies jump.

XVI

WHEN the war was over, Christabel went back to her writing. While she was at work on her whimsical romance, *O Fair Dove,* Uncle Johnnie had heard her say—not to himself: "It will be ignored and hated."

"Oh, no! Why, I'm sure it will be a great success!" a voice had answered, whose voice he didn't remember, for Eliza's drawing-room had been full that afternoon, and Mrs. Russell had distracted his attention by talking to him.

"I've tried bone-meal around the roots, and I've tried soot—" Mrs. Russell said, and through her voice Christabel's voice had replied:

"I write for the few—I can say this to you, because I do feel that you are an understanding person—and if there is even one who hears what I'm saying, that will be all I ask."

"I hear what you're saying, thought Uncle Johnnie. "—whale-oil soap," said Mrs. Russell. "But of course, if they've already begun to curl up——"

"I do *indeed* understand," the understanding person answered, earnestly. "One feels that in all your work there is that quality of truth too deeply and sensitively felt to be easily understood——"

"Every *one* of them with the yellows!" Mrs. Russell said, triumphantly, in a duet with Christabel's:

"If it is a success—what the world calls a success—that will mean to me that it is an utter failure."

So when *O Fair Dove* turned out to be a best-seller, he wondered what Christabel would say. He never doubted her ability, but he was curious.

Calling on Susannah one afternoon, he voiced his curiosity.

"If thee really wants to know, I have a letter from the dear child that came this morning." She left the room to get it, and Uncle Johnnie sat looking at a small table on which bronze elephants held between them *Stars and Wild Strawberries,* by Christabel Caine, *Carnation Flower,* by Christabel Caine, *Rocket Fire: Poems of War,* by Christabel Caine, *Fly in Amber,* by Christabel Caine, *O Fair Dove,* by Christabel Caine. A bowl of sweet peas stood before a large photograph of Christabel letting off bubbles of silvery light, as a fish in an aquarium lets off bubbles of air. A grand picture, Uncle Johnnie thought. But I fear you'll never be a really great whimsical writer, because you can't very well be photographed smoking a pipe.

Susannah returned. "This is the part—hmm—let me see—yes, here: 'Thank you for your congratulations, dearest. Yes, it *is* exciting—we never dreamed of anything like this when you were starting me on my "literary career," did we? I hope my head won't be turned with all the lovely things you and all the rest of my kind, kind friends, known and unknown, are saying to me. It *does* make me proud, but at the same time it makes me very humble, and it teaches me all over again that when one gives one's best, simply and from the heart, resisting all temptation to try to make an effect, one touches something universal. It does give one faith in one's fellow-creatures, that swift generous response.'"

She put the letter between elephant and sweet peas, sat up straighter than ever, folded her hands above her belt, and looked at her brother over her spectacles.

"There, Johnnie! I think that answers thy question!"

Irma Goff waited, sitting on the edge of an old red velvet chair, her feet crossed in an easy position, her fingers clutching her bag until they ached. She was going to interview Christabel Caine; her first important interview, and she wouldn't have been given it to do if Bess Mc-Cleary, chosen first, hadn't ordered crab salad for lunch yesterday. Oh, make me able to do it all right, she prayed silently. Please, please make it all right.

The room was as cold and still as the grave. Clearing her throat sounded loud.

"Mrs. Carey will see you in her sitting-room, madam."

She followed the butler into the lift, and seeing herself in the mirror, tried to put on an expression of indifference, even scorn. If only her knees would stop shaking——

Please make it all right——

A tea-table with a lace cloth was drawn before the fireplace. The butler lit the fire, drew the curtains, hiding the streaming rain, and left her. My, this is cozy, she said to herself, unconvincingly.

She waited, sunk in a chair so deep and low she felt as if she were lying on the floor. At first she was motionless, listening, not only with her ears, but with her whole body. But presently she began to look about. Would it be all right to snoop a little? She struggled up out of her chair.

Sea-green and ash-pink chintz, a carpet with faded sheaves of wheat and wreaths of flowers. She took out her notebook and wrote:

"Aubosson—Aubuson—Aubousson—Aubusson—???—carpet."

Two corner cabinets held jade trees, with red coral fruits and moon-white mother-of-pearl blossoms, widespread or in cuplike bud. "Chinese cabinets speaking of junk-filled seas," she wrote, and, thinking, I want to make it kind of quaint, like her own writing, added: "Every soft chair seemed to say: Do sit in my lap."

Violets all round, bowlfuls! Irma was used to a bunch of them, with stems in green foil and an edging of those other leaves, the hard shiny ones that kept, not masses like these, bowls and bowls of them.

Some books on a low table. *O Fair Dove,* bound in green morocco; the English edition of *Fly in Amber; Fleur d'Œillet,* par Christabel Caine—*Bells of the Temple,* by Geoffrey Strade. She opened that one. Young Mr. Strade looked at her sternly from the frontispiece, in his shirt—mercy, how decla*tay,* thought Irma—and with something behind his ear, hollyhock or hibiscus flower. There was a dedication, "To Christabel Caine," and on the fly-leaf, in blackest ink: "C. C. from G. S., to say all the things that can never be said." It had been written so violently that the pen had plowed through the paper in the stroke beneath the words.

She was looking at it when a voice said: "How kind of you to come to see me," making her heart nearly jump out of her mouth.

She had felt that she looked so nice, in her Alice-blue sports suit, with an Alice-blue hat trimmed with sand-color, sand-colored shoes and stockings, and just a touch of the new orange rouge Bess McCleary was so crazy about. But now, looking at Christabel Caine, in simple filmy black, with pearls, she felt too light, too obvious.

"What a dreadful day! You're very brave to venture out. Come closer to the fire. An open fire is such a friendly thing, don't you think?"

"I *certainly do!"*

"Fire and flowers and books, and a room is furnished—for me! But I have a fear of becoming possessed by possessions that I'm afraid I carry to extremes. Cream or lemon? Though you really shouldn't take either with this jasmine tea."

"Over our steaming cups of jasmine tea," Irma wrote in her mind. The lacquer cup was so unexpectedly light that she nearly dashed the tea into her face.

Marvelous sandwiches, caviar. Miss Caine—Mrs. Carey—which

ought she to say?—took one on her plate, but didn't eat it, and didn't pass them again to Irma, who wanted another awfully. She didn't often get a chance at caviar, and there were other kinds that looked exciting, too. Besides, she had only had time for an ice-cream soda for lunch. She tried saying in her mind: *"Might* I have another of those very delicious sandwiches?" There they were, and, after all, why shouldn't she? But somehow she didn't. It would have looked so greedy, with Miss Caine not touching hers.

She had a sudden vision of mamma and Velma and herself making sandwiches in the kitchen back home, trying new kinds out of the women's magazines, sometimes grandly buying a little yellow pot of *foie gras,* when mamma was going to have the Just Sew Club, or the bunch was coming to play bridge. When they were passed everyone would say: "Mmm, how yummy!" or: "Oh, now, listen, Mrs. Goff! I've had *nine!"* and mamma would answer: "Go on, take some! There's nothing to them!" She felt suddenly weak with homesickness.

I guess I ought to begin interviewing. Oh, dear! How do I begin? Oh, please let me know how to do it all right! *Please!*

But with a gush of gratitude she realized that the interview had begun.

"I have a ridiculous terror of being interviewed," Christabel Caine was saying, her voice low, yet so clear that each word stood by itself, exquisite and apart as if it were inclosed in a glass bell. "You must be kind to me. Because—it sounds absurd, I know—I'm very shy. I think perhaps it comes from my lonely childhood. I must have been a funny little person, growing up alone, in a big old house with a big old garden, talking to the flowers and the butterflies."

"Oh, that's lovely! *Do* you mind if I take notes? You see, this is my very first important interview——"

"Really!"

"You see, I thought newspaper work would be the best training I could get, because I kind of—I guess you certainly must get tired of people saying—I hope to write."

"Really! Have you done anything yet?"

"Well, I did some poems—verses, I guess I *should* say—that some magazines took, and I want to do enough for a book. I wanted to do a series of Western wildflower poems—my home's in Colorado. Spanish bayonet and Indian paintbrush. The one I'm really dying to do is Mariposa lily——"

"Mariposa lily?"

"M-mariposa's Spanish for butterfly—well, I guess you know that better than I do! White, with sort of faint lilac streaks—it's p-perfectly lovely. It's sort of hard to—it grows up in the m-mountains——"

What's the *matter* with me, stammering this way? she wailed to herself. But the thought of the luminous lilac-veined petals comforted her.

"I see. Flowers mean a great deal to you, just as they do to me. I've tried to express my love for them in some of my poems."

"Oh, I know! 'White lilac, delicate and cool,' and 'Heather in the mist,' and the one about the scarlet tulip being like the Holy Grail!"

"Those among others. I always have been passionately attached to 'green things growing.' I remember when I was tiny there was an old thousand-leafed rose-bush I used to tell my troubles to."

"Lonely kiddie tells trouble to roses," Irma's pencil flew.

"Before I could write, I used to make up little stories and tell them to the beetles and the hoptoads in the garden. There has been a good deal of loneliness in my life, as it happens, and I hope that it has made me a little more understanding of the loneliness of others. I have always tried so hard never to let the heartaches that have come my way make me sorry for myself. I have tried to turn them into pity and understanding. One wants so terribly just to try to help the hurts a little— not to let suffering make one hard."

"Have you a literary creed, Miss Caine?"

"I believe in truth. I think I could say that is not only my literary creed, but the creed I try to live by. Truth, crystal-clear, like cold water. What if it hurts? I believe in the diamond-hardness of truth. Softness is the end of everything."

"Truth—hard—c. water—wh if hurts?" Irma wrote under the note that said: "Pity and u-standing. Don't let suff make hard," twisting her head a little, trying to ease the pain in the back of her neck.

"Now, what I have tried to do in *O Fair Dove*——"

"Well, I mustn't trespass on your kindness any longer," Irma said at length. "I just don't know *how* to thank you!"

"Thank *you,* with all my heart! *Good*-by, Miss—uh— Smedley will show you out."

But Irma had to turn back again to cry:

"Oh, you just can't know how much you mean to people!"

Christabel absent-mindedly ate several sandwiches after Miss Goff left. Generally she disliked being interviewed by women, and certainly it was strange, to put it mildly, of the paper to send a novice. But the little thing had been rather touching, she thought, popping a whole sandwich into her mouth, and she was glad she had given her such a good time. How naïve she had been in her surprise at finding a celebrity so human!

The mild glow faded, boredom and restlessness crept over her. She roamed about the room, picking up a book, putting it down, shaking the sofa pillows into shape, stretching out her arms and yawning, yawns that ended in moans. She was sick and tired of this room and everything in it, the wishy-washy chintz, Marie Laurencin's gray-faced ladies with their small strawberry-ice-cream pink mouths matching their strawberry-ice-cream pink ribbons, the "amusing" shell flowers—*amusing!* Evelyn Thompson had done the decorating for her. She liked helping poor Evelyn, who had had hard times since her divorce. She had given her work, and sent little Roberta to the twins' dancing class. But the room had never expressed her real self. Marvin Marcy-Jones was going to do it over for her. There was a square of purple carpet, to try, on the floor, and lengths of orange stuff trailed onto it, from a chair. Evelyn's feelings would be hurt, and she herself probably wouldn't like it any better. Still, Marvin felt that he really had caught her personality. Perhaps he had. Perhaps it would be all right.

Oh, *what* do I want to do? Shall I call up Marvin? She drifted to the telephone, pausing to write on the pad beside it: "Mariposa lilies." Standing tapping her cheek with the pencil, she decided she didn't want to see Marvin. Elliott? Austin? Gobby?

She picked up the telephone and gave a number.

"Is Count du Sanglier there? . . . Thank you. . . . Mrs. Carey." Then: "Maurice, this is Christabel. Oh, you nice person! I needed that!"

She felt her twittering nerves grow still, her whole being relaxed to velvet smoothness, velvet softness.

"Maurice, take pity on me! If I don't put on a flame-colored frock with no back and go somewhere to dance tonight I shall die—and Curtis is in Washington. Somewhere with very loud jazz and cocktails in coffee-cups——"

Listening to his answer, she sank into a low chair, smiling a little, shutting her eyes.

"Don't be silly! . . . I'll tell you when I see you—maybe! . . . *Au 'voir*——"

Putting the receiver into its hook, she lay with the telephone against her breast, in a silence that still vibrated with Maurice's words.

When she finished writing her interview that night Irma Goff was still too excited to sleep, in spite of the hour. So she wrote to mamma and Velma, telling them all about it.

"The most marvelous house! First I was shown in by the butler— ahem!—while I attempted to give a correct imitation of Mrs. Astorbilt, and I think I fooled him, into this wonderful drawing-room all red velvet that looked about a million years old. Mamma, I bet you would think the chairs needed recovering, but they looked like things right out of the Metropolitan Museum. But I didn't interview her there, but in front of the open fire in her own boudoir, wasn't that sweet of her, just like I was one of her intimate friends, a simply *darling* room, with heaps of violets absolutely everywhere and the most *marveelious* tea, caviar sandwiches 'n' everything. Well, Mamma and Velma, you can imagine the thrill of meeting CHRISTABEL CAINE, though you can bet I didn't let her see how excited I was. I was kind of scared, too, but as it turned out, I needn't have been, because after we got friendly she confessed that she was very shy and actually had been scared of *me*—could you believe it?

"I kept thinking about Mrs. Coffy's paper on her at the Club last winter, and what she'd think if she could see me! She's simply *beauti-*

ful, very young-looking in spite of having two adorable twin kiddies, 5 yrs. old, but kind of sad-looking and quiet, and all in black. I wonder if she's in mourning for anyone? I didn't like to ask—I kept feeling as if she'd had some terrible sorrow sometime and that's what makes her work so wonderful. It wasn't her husband, because she spoke simply marvelously of him and what a help his interest was to her in her work. She was wonderful about my writing, *really* interested. It's made me crazy to do something worth while. When I was going I said 'I'm going to try to write harder than I ever have in my life, this very evening!' and she said 'Do you know, so am I!' It sort of thrills me to think of her sitting there all alone writing. She told me some nights she works *all night long!*

"Just as I was going she picked up an enormous bunch of the violets out of one of the bowls and gave them to me. I have them here on my desk, in front of a great big signed photograph she gave me!!!"

XVII

On a March morning, as every morning, Minnie pulled back the blue silk curtains, closed the windows, lit the fire, and turned on the bath water. Wakened by gentle noises, Christabel stretched, yawned, put her white feet into blue mules held by kneeling Minnie, wrapped herself in blue silk embroidered with daisies bigger than her head, and trailed to the bathroom.

Steam fragrant with perfume created to express her personality veiled black men peeping from behind orchid-dripping trees, painted on her bathroom walls by young Boris Orlovski, a cousin of the Czar's, some people thought. She was wonderful to exiled Russians. "More wonderful to the men than the women," catty Mrs. Wickett said, but this Christabel felt was not worth noticing, it was so evidently caused by jealousy.

"It's rather amusing how ladies give themselves away!" she had said to Gobby, when he indignantly reported Mrs. Wickett's remark. "I did my best to make Boris and one or two others be nice to Adèle Wickett when they were all here one afternoon, and they were just as naughty as they could be." She laughed tolerantly. "Poor Adèle! Naturally she consoles herself by blaming me!"

Besides, she had had several little Russian countesses in national costume sing at her teas.

After her bath came her breakfast tray, heaped with mail. Advertisements and appeals had been suppressed by Ellen Beach, her adoring young secretary, granddaughter of the distant cousin who had jilted Uncle Johnnie. The photographs of crippled children made her feel too badly, and, after all, one could do so little. Of course big checks went to really deserving charities, but Curtis took care of that. Indiscriminate giving was apt to do more harm than good, was really just self-indulgence.

Invitations, letters from strangers:

DEAR MISS CAINE:
May a lonely shut-in thank you for having helped her pass weary wakey hours when other folks were fast asleep——

MRS. CHRISTABEL CAINE:
DEAR MADAM:
I am a Junior in High School. I have been given you as a subject for an essay, and would be obliged if you would tell me some facts about yourself that would be of interest, also what caused you to write each of your books and something about what you have wished to express in them, and anything else you can think of——

DEAR CHRISTABEL CAINE (For a Dear you are and ever will be, for writing your Beautiful Books):
I'm not quite a stranger, for although *you've* never heard of *me, I* know *you* intimately, and I've chuckled with you and I've wept with you (Yes, truly!) and in all my life nothing, except feeling the wind blow through my hair in a sailboat, and stealing (don't look so shocked!) a sprig of lavender, sun-kissed and bee-beset, from Ann Hathaway's garden, has given me quite the same sort of utterly joyous delight your books have——

From the clipping bureau came best-seller lists. *O Fair Dove. O Fair Dove. O Fair Dove.* Reviews. She read:

"Its lovely pages glow with a sort of luminous tenderness, a 'light that never was, on sea or land.'"

"If more novels like *O Fair Dove* came to the critic's table, how much happier life would be! Written with exquisite sensitiveness and poignant beauty, this whimsical romance demands the use of the important word genius——"

So buoyant, she felt she hardly touched the pillow. Drinking the delicious hot coffee, she dreamily reread "exquisite sensitiveness—poignant beauty—genius—" When Curtis looked in to say good morning and good-by she returned his kiss warmly.

"Good-by, darlingest! Isn't it a day straight from *heaven?*" She kissed her fingertips, fluttered them toward the door, and, still smiling, drew out the next clipping.

"Ever since women discovered that novel-writing is infinitely preferable to housekeeping, and much less exacting, they have written innumerable stories. *O Fair Dove,* by Christabel Caine, is just another of them. The story, buried under would-be whimsicality, is ordinary, the characters are puppets, and the ending is a relief. The exhausted reader may well wonder whether he or the authoress has wasted the more time."

There was a pain in her chest. How could people be so unkind? How could even jealousy make them so cruel? She was terribly, terribly hurt. Not that she minded honest criticism, she *welcomed* it, but this was wanton abuse. With hands that shook she tore the clipping into tiny pieces—tiny——

The twins came tearing in, flinging their arms around her, scrambling up on the bed. She put her hands over her ears.

"Gently, darlings! Mother doesn't feel very well this morning. *Marigold!* Be careful of that tray! Now go to Mademoiselle at once, both of you!"

With the match that lit her cigarette she touched the torn clipping on the ash tray. It writhed and turned to ash. "—luminous tenderness—" she read again. "—genius—" "Some more reviews for you to paste in," she said, handing them to Ellen Beach, who came in with her engagement book.

"May I read them? Oh, what nice ones! Isn't it marvelous, there hasn't been a single unfavorable review of *O Fair Dove,* has there? Not that there ought to be, only it's so wonderful that people really appreciate it."

"What do I have to do today, Ellen? Luncheon at Pierre's, Ivan Korovine's class, tea with Austin Weeks, and the Treasure Seekers here for dinner. I'll see Mrs. Britton about dinner now."

"Mrs. Caine's train gets in at four."

"Oh, Ellen, *no!* Is it *today* mother's coming? Well, send the big car for her, and tell her I'm *heart*-broken and I'll be back just as early as I *possibly* can. That makes it awfully awkward about dinner——"

"I needn't come——"

"Ellen, don't be silly! With your young man coming? No, I'll manage somehow. Mother may be too tired to want to come down, anyway."

Mrs. Britton entered. Spring lamb, green peas. The telephone rang. Ellen asked over her shoulder if Mrs. Carey would see some one from the *World?* Minnie asked: Which dress? Asparagus, perhaps, instead of a salad. The telephone rang. Would Mr. and Mrs. Carey dine with Mrs. Wickett next Thursday, with bridge afterward? Beige dress, Minnie, and the dark brown hat. Strawberry mousse in a spun-sugar basket. Mrs. Carey is ex*treme*ly sorry——

She was ready to go out at last, in the red-and-black car, so small, so smart, looking as if one wound it up with a key, with Bates seeming so a part of it that one almost expected to see a tiny crack running down his front, splitting a black tin cap and a pink tin nose, one felt that an iron tail must run into a hole in the seat, to keep him steady.

Buying her own books, she thought, how excited this little person would be if he knew I was the author! She felt like a queen incognito.

"Did I understand you to say *twelve* copies of *O Fair Dove?* Is that correct?"

And she answered, graciously, laughingly:

"Alas, yes! That's the penalty of writing a book, so many people expect the poor author to give them copies!"

His eyes and his mouth were three round O's, she thought, walking up Fifth Avenue, amused and touched. Well, that was a real thrill in his dull day. She could hear him telling the other clerks: "That was Christabel Caine! That lady I was just waiting on!"

The day was so lovely that she had sent the car away. Turning down a side street, she went into the Catholic Church where she liked to say her prayers or meditate. Sometimes she longed to be a Catholic. If only she could stop thinking, how restful it would be.

Beyond the rood screen lights wavered in white-and-blue cups, banked into shapes of hearts and crosses, on either side of the altar, where a nun knelt, rose to dust the vases of artificial lilies, knelt again. All work should be done that way, with love and prayer, Christabel thought. Other nuns knelt motionless. She was kneeling with them. She was kneeling alone, the bride of Christ, lost in ecstasy, while out in the church, heart-broken, adoring, knelt Elliott and Maurice and the new poet who was coming to dinner tonight. She almost added Curtis, but the thought of him floated out without embodying.

Oh, to be there, safe and at peace, free of earthly possessions, free of selfhood, wrapped in love forever!

But out on the Avenue again, she knew that God wanted His children to be happy and free in His sunshine! Everything was holy, if you had eyes to see. She looked with seeing eyes at a top-shaped female in black satin, at a taxi that came squealing to the curb in answer to her look, at her florist's window.

"Good *morn*ing, Mr. Johnson. . . . Yes, indeed, divine! Quantities of flowers, please—mimosa for the drawing-room, I think—you know how much I need. I'm just going to be banal and have a few tulips for the library, those flame-colored ones and a few mauve. . . . Oh, I don't know, three or four dozen. Now *what* have you, really intriguing, for the dinner table? I'm using the ruby glass tonight. . . . Not, not a very big dinner, twenty people, and not a bit the roses-silver-pheasants type——"

What a difference it makes, being human with people, she thought, as Mr. Johnson flung himself into originality, bringing flowers like lobster claws for her inspection, flowers like strings of doll's china eyes, as he presented her with a spray of jasmine to wear.

She turned back, as she was leaving, to order a big purple basket of double and single violets for the Glenworthy girls, Clothilde, Eugénie, Ellaline, poor old maids, relics of her mother's girlhood. They adored her, and she had seen their letters to her mother, telling of all the wonderful things she had done for them. She did try to be thoughtful. When she had them to tea she was never at home to other callers, for she told herself they wouldn't want to meet anyone, they were so shabby, coming in scarecrow finery, always bringing some pathetic present. Last time, half a dozen drying daffodils with lots of asparagus fern, lost in her roomful of flowers. "We tried to get Mariposa lilies because of that lovely poem of yours your dear mother very kindly sent us, but the florists didn't seem to know what they were." She had been so touched, and had filled their arms from the drawing-room vases when they went. She loved to heap gifts on them, poor old things —an armful of novels, a nearly full box of *marrons glacés*. That last time, Elliott had called up to ask if he might come to tea, and she had had to hustle them off. She had been meaning to do something nice to make up. She would ask them to dinner, tomorrow, with mother, just a nice intimate time, with no one else, and then they would all go to the Racine revival that Countess du Sanglier had arranged and that Mrs. Towne had sent her tickets for. That would be a real thrill for them, and it would be a delight to hear some pure French. She wrote on her card, to go with the violets: "Will you dine and go to the theater tomorrow? I'll send the motor at seven. Most affectionately, C. C. C."

Why did so few people realize that the only sure way of being happy was to make others happy?

It was a day for a new hat. Everyone in the shop swam at her.

"Isn't that peculiar, Mrs. Carey, Miss M'ree was just this morning speaking of you, wasn't she, girls? We have some lovely things to show you—Gladys, bring that Maria Guy with the banana ribbon—and listen, dear, the blue ballibuntl, you know, the one with the choux over the ear, and, honey! Listen! Tell Miss M'ree Mrs. Carey's here, I know she'll want to see her."

Marie herself appeared. *"Miss-us* Carey, good morning! No, no, no! Take these away. Bring me the little black horsehair with the nose veil that hasn't been shown yet."

"Oh, adorable!"

"Doesn't moddom look adorable?"

"A work of art," Marie pronounced.

"A picture!"

"It looks just like moddom, doesn't it?"

That was in an undertone, for her to overhear. She was on to their ways! But it did, it was a divine hat.

"I must take it with me! I *must* wear it out to lunch. Will you call me a taxi, please?"

Waiting for it, she remembered to ask about Miss Lola's headache, Miss Vera's sister, who used to be in the shop before her marriage. "What a memory!" they exclaimed, pleased and flattered, and through their exclamations she heard Miss Pearl saying to another customer, just audibly:

"Christabel Caine, who wrote *O Fair Dove.*"

Alfred was scurrying into her sitting-room with orange tulips. She had caught the servants by surprise, for she had said she wouldn't be in until after lunch. But she was human with him, too; she saw his face relax a little as he went to get her a cocktail.

A press photographer took her picture as she entered Pierre's, a careful ten minutes late. Maurice kissed her hand and noticed her hat, the headwaiter had a charmed murmur as he led them to their table, friends saluted as they passed.

"Come to a movie after lunch. There's a new one with the intriguing Charlot."

"Alas! I have to go on to my class. Ivan Korovine, you know, the Russian who had something to do with—with—I can't remember his name for the moment, the one who had that place in France. He teaches you to free yourself through color and rhythm, and he has simply marvelous ideas about sex sublimation."

"Ah, little grown-up girl! You think you are too old for a doll, so you play with your soul!"

"*Play,* Maurice! It isn't play, it's intense concentrated work. I come away *limp.* But it makes life seem a very different thing. I don't think I ever before this year, *fully* realized its intensity and re*a*lity."

"Come to the movies. Movies and jazz and burlesque queens and—what else? Vermilion and magenta—seem to me as real intensities as you'll find in a rather vague world."

"Well, of course, everyone admits that Charlie Chaplin is our one great tragedian. But——"

"If you don't, you will be sorry tomorrow, when I am to be very ill."

Through the new nose veil she made round questioning eyes.

"Certainly. Haven't you heard that *maman* is *patronne* for an evening of Racine?"

"And you, too, dread it?"

"No, I simply avoid it."

"*Moi aussi!*"

Mademoiselle could go with mother and the Glenworthy girls. It would be a glimpse of heaven for her and she could translate anything they couldn't understand.

"So come to the movies!"

She yielded, laughing. "But I must be through in time to get down to a studio on Ninth Street for tea. A man is doing a portrait of my precious twinnies that I promised to come and criticize. Oh, Maurice, I really dread it! I can't tell you why—yes, I think I will, after all! You see, I'm terribly afraid he's in love with me, poor darling—I can tell you this, you being you, without being afraid that you'll think I'm conceited, it's simply that it's such a problem, I don't know what to do, and I need advice. Do you think you could put yourself in the position of a gentleman laid low by my fatal charm?"

"*C'est moi.*"

"You see, he's such a sensitive person that if I'm horrid to him, as I suppose I should be, he might do *any*thing, and if I'm kind to him, that's even worse! I want to help him, and I don't know what to do. It makes me *triste à pleurer!* I only tell you because it's rather an interesting situation psychologically, and because you'll never know who the man is."

"Don't begin to worry about the men who love you, or you'll have time for nothing else."

"Oh, Maurice! *Flatterer!*" She smiled, delicately self-mocking. But her heart gave a skip. I've never seen him look so—so as if he were holding something in. Oh, my poor Maurice! Not you, too? And aloud she cried, in a voice that annoyed her by sounding fluttered:

"Oh, I *don't* think any pastry! Well—one of those strawberry tarts, because it's spring, and if I can't eat any tea I shall tell Austin Weeks you're to blame."

When Curtis came home from the office there was either silence, that meant Christabel was out, or the twitter of voices as he passed the library door on the way to his room. And although he vaguely knew that the voices were settling things, beauty, truth, real art, immortality, sex in its relation to this or that, and the meaning of life, it never occurred to him that it could matter whether or not the sound remained twitter or was resolved into words. Sometimes Christabel called him in, tipping a cheek to his polite kiss, clinging to him with a white hand, asking: "Darling, some tea?" Sometimes she allowed him to tiptoe upstairs to relax on his sofa with the market quotations and a highball.

This evening there was silence. He caught a glimpse of Smedley arranging a centerpiece, launching himself across so big a table that Curtis knew Christabel and he must be giving a dinner. He would have liked to see his children, but it annoyed Nurse to have him come in at supper-time. She said it made them show off, sticking out their lips at their lovely cereal, and jumping about, and later Michael, who was easily excited, was apt to imagine lions under the bed. And Christabel supported her.

No sign of Christabel. Out with an affinity, probably. I believe I'll get an affinity, myself. Adèle Wickett? She's pretty, even if Christabel doesn't think so, and she nearly dies laughing when I tell her a joke. Or Helen Vánessi, with her black hair low on her white neck, and those eyes—oh, boy! She likes me, too, he thought.

Well, he would just have a look at the stock quotations. Dropping down on his sofa with a sigh, the paper slid from his hand. I am very, very tired, he thought. A hard day. Donelly says he can get me three cases of the real pre-war stuff. A very hard day. That lobster at lunch was certainly nice and tender——

He yawned, arching his back, stretching out his arms, grasping air. Poor old Harry. I'll never see *that* money again——

Keep my left arm straight—left arm straight—a white ball ran across a stretch of green and trickled into the cup. Ought to get dressed—very very tired—very very very tired——

XVIII

THE porter made Mrs. Caine trot to keep up with him. Between the way he hurried and the people who pushed between them, she had hard work keeping her eye on her bag, with her silver brush and mirror in it, and her aquamarine brooch set in seed pearls. But when he asked: "Taxi?" over his shoulder, and she answered with quiet dignity: "I think a private car will meet me," his manner changed entirely. And when he saw the big Rolls-Royce, with chauffeur and footman, he became so polite that she had to add another quarter to the quarter she had clutched, ready, ever since she got off the train.

She sat up very straight, looking at her reflection in the front window, made into a mirror by the two impressive plum-covered backs. She felt shy and conspicuous. But she scolded herself. Don't be so silly! Nobody's looking at you! Relax! She relaxed firmly.

The house was full of flowers. "Well, you look very festive, Smedley," she said, giving the butler the bunch of early daffodils from the garden she had brought for Christabel.

"Yes, madam. We're having a dinner tonight."

A dinner! Oh, dear, she thought, there'll be a lot of celebrities who won't want to talk to *me*. I wish to *good*ness there wasn't going to be a dinner!

Thank Heaven, she had made over her black evening dress, after a picture in *Vogue*. Fred said it looked fine. And, telling herself that no one would look at *her,* she was exhilarated by the thought that ran beneath—it does look nice!

It was late when Christabel rushed in, her cheeks glowing pink, her eyes starry.

"Oh, mother, mother, *moth*er! Oh, *dar*ling, how heavenly to have you! I was heart-*broken* that I couldn't meet you! Did they tell you? It was just one of those things—*oooh!*"

"You're crushing—your—lovely gardenias, dearie!" Mrs. Caine protested, her mouth full of fragrant fur. Christabel released her and held her at arm's length.

"Let me look at you. Oh, mother darling, you've gotten thinner! That's naughty of you. And you look *so* tired, dear."

"I'm not a bit——"

"You're going to have a real rest while you're here. First, you're going to have a delicious hot bath with geranium salts, and then a nice little dinner on a tray, here in front of the fire. I wish I could have it with you, just us two, but, alas! we've got some stupid people dining here. I dread the thought! I won't inflict anyone on you tonight, darling, but tomorrow, when you're all rested, I've planned a little dinner, especially for you, and a theater party."

"Christabel, I really don't feel a bit tired——"

"I don't believe you ever think about yourself long enough to know whether you feel tired or not, but now you have someone to think about you in spite of yourself. How's my darling daddy?"

"Very well, and sent heaps of love. But Uncle Johnnie's been quite ill."

"Oh, too bad!"

"They think he may have to come——"

"Heavens! Look at the time. There's nothing I'd love better than to sit down and have a nice long talk, darling, and hear all the news, but if I don't *fly*——"

"Christabel! Who's coming to dinner tomorrow?" Mrs. Caine called after her, and she called back:

"The Glenworthy girls! Won't that be nice?"

Mrs. Caine went and had a long look at her evening dress, on its padded hanger. She saw herself coming down the broad stairs. "My mother—" "My mother—" She turned graciously from celebrity to celebrity, surprising them by her intelligence, her unaffected charm. Then she made a face, saying: "The *Glen*worthy girls!" under her breath.

But, taking her bath, wrapping herself in a heated towel soft as deep moss, she saw herself against a background of old oak paneling, hothouse roses, Smedley's shirt front, fragile in filmy black, being gracious to the poor old Glenworthys.

"Christabel spoils me so. She thinks nothing is too good for her mother! And she worries about me ridiculously. Why, last night——"

She got into the orchid bed-jacket Christabel had given her long ago. It was as nice as ever, for she only used it on her visits here. It almost hadn't been worn at all.

Nice Bessie, who never made her feel shy, as Smedley and Alfred and Minnie did, brought in her tray, and she said, graciously: "Well, Bessie! How have *you* been?" Dinner was delicious. Christabel had even remembered how she loved grapefruit. And there was a cluster of her favorite violets on the tray. Who but Christabel would think of a thing like that?

Hearing gentle snores, Christabel sighed, smiled, and went in to wake Curtis with a kiss. "Darling, you must get *dressed!* It's almost dinner-time."

"Aw-w-igh—" he agreed through a yawn. "Who's coming tonight?"

"The Treasure Seekers."

"Oh, Gosh! *That* lot!"

"What do you mean by 'that lot'?"

"Oh, all showing off and being sensitive souls, and the men a lot of sissies."

"Curtis, you *hurt* me when you speak of my friends that way."

"And not a pretty woman in the lot."

She kissed his arm lightly. "But they're all so worth while. Now do hurry, dearest."

She hadn't decided what to wear. Now Minnie stood waiting, while

Christabel looked at rows of dresses. There hung the silver-blue gown, with silver stars thick about the hem, from Laura Burke's shop. She had said to Laura: "I'll wear it and advertise the shop to everybody," and Laura had cried gratefully:

"You must take it for a tiny little present—please, *please,* Christabel!"

She wouldn't hear of that. It was nonsense, when Laura was so poor, though of course Christabel had always been kind to her. She had worn it one evening, crying: "See! I've walked through the Milky Way! I've gotten stars all over my skirt!" And everyone had admired her in it. But somehow there had been no opportunity to mention Laura's shop without simply dragging it in. And though she meant to pay for it, Laura never sent a bill, and she had too much on her mind to be expected to remember. She was sick of the wretched gown and everything to do with it, for really, Laura and Laura's things were just a little bit too queer and arty to be taken seriously.

Ellen Beach looked in for the seating plan of the table, and Christabel bundled the gown into her arms.

"A little present. Wear it tonight."

"Oh, *Christ*abel! Oh, *thank* you! It's divine. Oh, but you're too good to me!"

"It's just the color of your eyes. Your Nick will fall in love deeper than ever," Christabel said. She had yielded to a generous impulse and invited Ellen's fiancé, Nicholas Portal, to dinner. She hoped he would be presentable. Ellen, who should have been down putting the place cards around, leaned in the doorway, silver-blue folds pouring from her crossed arms, looking lost and happy. "Wake up, Ellen darling, wake up!" Christabel called to her. "I really do believe the child's in love!"

Ellen threw her arms tight around Christabel's neck, hiding her face, whispering:

"I am—I am!"

A Venetian lady in trailing silver, Christabel went to Curtis's dressing-room, and found him in his underclothes, practicing golf strokes.

"Really, Curtis! You *must* get dressed. It's a quarter to eight. Mother came, but she's too——"

Curtis's eyes glazed; he settled himself on his feet; his joined hands slowly lifted, then swished in an arc through the air. He kept his head down. He had made a glorious drive.

Christabel stood in hurt silence, supported on one side by a shadowy Maurice, who lifted her white hand and kissed it, on the other by a shadowy sympathetic Austin. Again Curtis bent in a slight bow, again his joined hands slowly lifted.

"Curtis, *really*!"

"It's all in keeping your left arm straight," he told her, dreamily.

"Please try to be ready to receive our guests," she said. Feeling utterly wasted, she went to say good night to Michael and Marigold.

"Oh, Mummy, Mummy, my darlingest Mummy! Read us a story!"

"Read us Uncle Wiggly in the paper!"

"Uncle *Wiggly*! Darlings! You know Mummy never reads you anything like that."

"Daddy does."

"You know Mummy only reads you things that are beautiful or true."

"Tell us about Krazy Kat and Ignatz Mouse!"

"Michael!"

"Well, Alfred does. Ignatz hits Krazy with a brick, and Krazy says Powie! *Powie!* POWIE!"

"Oh, *Mummy!* Michael swore! He said Powie! Michael *Carey,* aren't you ashamed of yourself? Mummy! Mummy!"

"Marigold! Children! Don't shout so! Mummy hasn't time to tell you a story tonight. Now get under the covers, darlings, and think that your beds were once trees, covered with little dancing leaves that sometimes were golden with sunlight and sometimes were silver with moonlight. And what did they hold tenderly, all night through, in their brown arms?"

"Tree toads!"

"No, darling, nests, safe warm nests to hold sleepy baby birds, and that's what you two are, sleepy little birds safe in your nests in the trees. *Mich*ael! Stop that noise!"

"I'm a bird! I'm singing."

"Now Mummy must go. Good night, my babies."

"Don't go! Don't go, my sweet beautiful Mummy!" Marigold cried, flinging her arms around Christabel, rolling her eyes; and Michael copied her. "My sweet beautiful Mummy!"

"She isn't your Mummy, she's my Mummy!"

"Darlings, darlings! Do you really love poor Mummy so much?" Christabel kissed soft firm cheeks, silky tops of heads, the little hollows in the backs of their necks.

"Ooh, *Mum*my! You tickle!"

"I don't like them getting wild 'm; then it takes forever before they get to sleep," Nurse said, disapprovingly.

"My beautiful *'dorable* Mummy! They won't be anyone at the dinner party as beautiful as my shiny Mummy!"

"They'll do anything to stay up a little longer," Nurse put in. I really don't like her, Christabel thought, on her way to her mother's room. It is time for Nurse to go. Mademoiselle is enough for the children now.

Mrs. Caine had just finished dinner and pushed the grapefruit skin back into round so the servants shouldn't know she had been greedy and squeezed, when Christabel came in, trailing silver.

"How lovely you look! But are they wearing *trains,* Christabel?" she asked, for the dress she had made over was far from having a train.

"I don't really know what *they're* wearing, darling. Is it so very important?"

"Aren't you feeling well?"

"Oh, well enough—no, I'm not! I feel— Oh, it isn't anything."

"You do too much, dear. You never spare yourself."

"I *am* tired. And—oh—Curtis is being a little—difficult—this evening; he always is when I have my special friends. I have his old bankers and golfers and bridge-playing *pret*-ty *wom*-en"——she wrinkled her nose—"a thousand times, and then I have my own kind, the people who really amount to something, writers and painters and musicians, just *once,* and he can hardly live through it. Oh, well, I ought to be used to it by now, only I do so *long* for a little understanding, a little give and take."

"Why, Curtis adores you, Christabel."

"Yes, of course he does. It's a wise little mother, and a comforting one. I wish I could stay up here with you, just the two of us, cozily! I'll be thinking of you all evening. Now go to bed soon and have a lovely sleep. Good night, dearest."

But nobody comes to New York for a lovely sleep, Mrs. Caine thought, rebelliously. Besides, she didn't feel sleepy. If she had been at home, she and Fred would just be starting for a movie or settling down to a game of Russian bank. What's Fred doing now? she wondered, feeling rather homesick.

She tried to find something to read. There was *O Fair Dove,* but she knew that nearly by heart. A book by someone named Santayana. Edith Sitwell's poems.

> At Easter when red lacquer buds sound far slow
> Quarter-tones for the old dead Mikado,
>
> Through avenues of lime-trees, where the wind
> Sounds like a chapeau chinois, shrill, unkind,—
>
> The Dowager Queen, a curling Korin wave
> That flows forever past a coral cave——

Well, of course it was nice, but what did it mean? Unfortunately, she had finished the *Saturday Evening Post* on the train. She loved it, though when it was mentioned Christabel smiled and said she hadn't the least doubt it had splendid stories.

There was thick creamy paper in the desk, with the address in fat letters. She rather liked the idea of writing to some of her friends, Anna McHugh, or Hattie Nelson, just to impress them. "I am here with Christabel——" But the green quill, when pulled from its tumbler of shot, proved to have no pen in it, and it wouldn't have helped if it had, as the green-jade inkwell was empty. I don't think I'd better ring and ask for pen and ink, she thought. Probably everyone's busy helping with the dinner party.

But she had a pencil in her bag, so she wrote a long letter to Fred about how sweet and thoughtful Christabel was being.

XIX

Loneliness, loneliness, Christabel thought, going downstairs, her heavy silver train sliding from step to step with a flat slapping sound. Who cares whether I live or die? Curtis thinks of nothing but his golf, Ellen cares for no one but her Nick Portal, Michael and Marigold are shut away in the bright selfishness of childhood. Loneliness——

She paused before the mirror half-way down the stairs—not that she cared how she looked to anyone who was coming tonight. Her shining bronze hair lay close as feathers to her head, silver clung close to her ivory body. A statue made of bronze, ivory, and silver. I am beautiful, she thought, feeling cold and sad. And what difference does it make? She tried to comfort herself by repeating things that Maurice had said, and Austin. They brought no glow. No one will know how sad I am tonight, she thought, going into the drawing-room, answering welcoming cries, giving a hand here, there, comforted by her sadness.

Her guests were all there, for, like royalty, she preferred to be the last to appear at her own parties. The Treasure Seekers. She had gathered them together in the first place, men and women whose preoccupation was to seek the treasures of beauty hidden away in the heart of life. Tonight she could see why Curtis and Smedley were unenthusiastic about them. Hair a little too long, and either dusty or oily, too many barbaric ear-rings and touches of batik. One man among them was startlingly good-looking, taller than the rest. His eyes met hers as she entered the room; she felt a tingling warmth flow through her. Then he looked away, and down. Ellen, in the starry gown, had joined him.

Ellen's Nick Portal. Christabel was conscious of him all through dinner; her voice, low and clear, called words clever and yet compassionate down the table, for him to hear; her hand lay, a spray of frosty fern across her silver breast, for him to see. But Ellen wasn't giving him a chance to notice anyone but herself. "Nick! Nick!" she called him back, whenever his attention wandered. Didn't she realize how tiresome that became to a man?

Christabel was conscious of the two of them through everything; through talking to her beautiful East Indian with his white turban, gold clothes, and dark purple mantle edged with a tracery of dark dim gold; or to her Irish poet; through noticing that Gobby, as usual, wasn't knowing when to stop on the salted nuts; through avoiding Elliott's meaning glances—idiot!—through saying: "Movies, saxophones, and bright magenta, seem to me perhaps the *only* things in a shadowy world," and hearing the expected: "What was that she said?" Something was making Ellen look radiant tonight—the blue gown, or, possibly, love. But certainly she was making a fool of herself, languishing all over him, gazing at him, obviously adoring. And he is graciously allowing himself to be adored, Christabel thought, but if I'm not mistaken he's getting just a little bit fed up.

He looked in her direction. She lifted a shoulder, letting silver slide from it, and turned her lovely head. In her imagination she could see her hair gleam in the light from the tall candles.

"I needn't ask if you arranged those blossoms," her poet was saying with his mouth full. "Some ladies let their servants do it, I'm told, but I look at these, and look at you, and I know."

Smedley was at the other end of the table, filling Curtis's champagne glass. "I never can understand people who let the servants do it," Christabel said. "That seems to me like letting the servants say your prayers for you."

Because, she thought, I *did* come in and give them that one touch that makes all the difference.

She turned her head slowly back, letting her eyes rest indifferently on Nick Portal. His were turned toward Ellen.

She had told everybody that she might possibly—just possibly—be able to get her Irish poet to recite some of his poems after dinner, and she had a hard time to keep him from starting before she had drawn him out. A wee wizened man like a monkey, bent in the monkey's attitude just before the jerk of the chain makes it begin to dance, he stood there, chanting his poems in Gaelic, chanting away with his eyes shut.

The East Indian sang, too, translating for them.

"Sing on! The birds in the forest sing, nor care whether anyone hears them. The flowers in the woodland bloom, nor care that there is no one to inhale their fragrance. Give all of thyself, no matter if thou perish——"

Oh, that is true, Christabel thought, looking towards Nick Portal. That is true!

Sitting in the great Venetian chair in which she never crossed her knees, hearing: "Hush! What is she saying?" when she spoke, she imagined herself going across the room to him, coming to him like a breeze from the sea, after Ellen's cloying sweetness. He will not come to me because he has pride and humility, she told herself. And she really rose and went across the room and sat down beside him.

Elliott and Gobby and Marvin Marcy-Jones rose, too, and came with her. And Nick Portal, after a politely indifferent sentence or two, got up and walked away.

The rope of pearls in which Christabel's fingers had been twisted snapped, pearls showered to the floor. All her guests were on their knees, hunting them, except Ellen and Nick, who had disappeared.

Uncle Johnnie was in a private hospital in New York, and Ellen Beach was on her way to see him, for Christabel, who had meant to go, was again too busy.

No one seemed to know exactly what was the matter with him, himself least of all. He apparently took only the mildest interest in the affair. "The trouble with Uncle Johnnie is that he never will face facts," Christabel had said to Ellen. She had been wonderful about going to see him at first, but he had such a way of dropping off to sleep every time she went, that she had given it up, although she still sent him potted apple trees in frail bloom, and bowls of Mrs. Britton's calf's-foot jelly. "Poor Uncle Johnnie, he's aged terribly," she told Ellen. "This pa*thet*ic way of falling asleep—!"

The first time Ellen had gone to see him, she had thought: I will try to make up to him a little for grandmother's having broken his heart long ago. All the way to the hospital she had imagined the poor old man thinking of her as his Little Dream Granddaughter—no, Little Dream Daughter, for he would still be young enough for that in a dream. But now she knew him, she had to imagine other things.

She imagined telling Nick about her visit to the hospital. My little Ellen, my little shining angel—how do you hide your white wings when you walk through the streets? Not that Nick ever said things like that, but she hoped he felt them.

She knew, for he had told her, that Nick loved her more than any man had ever loved any woman, and yet she wanted to do things to make him love her even more—to make him love her as much as she loved him. Nick—Nick. She printed his smile, his head thrown back, his eyes looking at her, on the sidewalk, on the sky. Ellen, darling— Ellen, you are so sweet—Ellen, I love you.

I mustn't think about Nick when I'm crossing the street. It makes my knees tremble so.

If only he and Christabel would like each other! That's the only thing that makes me miserable, she thought, singing a song inside herself.

"I try so hard to make Nick realize what a marvelous person Christabel is," she told Uncle Johnnie. "He's *aw*ful! I just have to work to work to make him be nice to her!" She couldn't help glowing, for it was usually Christabel who had to do that. She had heard it over and over again. She felt her mouth twitching into a smile, and said, firmly: "It makes me terribly unhappy."

"It seems to," said Uncle Johnnie.

"No, but it *real*ly does! What's the *mat*ter with Nick? When you think how wonderful she is, and yet she's so unspoiled! She treats us all as if we were just as wonderful!"

"She does still permit us to turn our backs when we leave the presence chamber."

Ellen was horrified, and yet he made her laugh. "Oh, you don't understand her, either," she said. But she couldn't help liking him.

I hate him, Christabel thought, going to her workroom after talking to Nick Portal. No, I don't, I don't waste that much emotion on him —it's simply that he bores me excruciatingly. Poor foolish little Ellen! What *does* she see in him?

He had come just after Christabel had sent Ellen to see Uncle Johnnie. Christabel, going through the hall, had heard him tell Smedley he would wait, and had asked him into the library, with what she now realized was mistaken kindness. From where they sat she had seen their reflections in the glass of the bookcase doors. His dark good looks, her delicate beauty, side by side, had made her catch her breath. Too bad such looks as his had nothing behind them. No response, not a spark, except when she had said what a sweet little thing Ellen was. He had bored her so that she ached all over.

I must pull myself together, she thought. I must not let his emptiness drain me. I must get to work.

But how futile it seems to go on offering my gift to a world so indifferent that in spite of all its praise it does not even see what I offer.

And yet, because I am an artist, I must go on. There is no rest for me, no comforting.

She felt a sudden longing to be with someone who really understood. She picked up the telephone.

Maurice du Sanglier was evidently out. The unanswered burring went on until she put down the receiver. A squeaky Japanese voice answered for Marvin Marcy-Jones: "Not home, please!" Austin Weeks was broken-hearted, but was awaiting a fat female who was coming to beg him to paint her portrait. Elliott had no telephone.

Well, I really wanted to work, she thought, sitting down at her table, before the crystal that she always looked into first, to empty her mind of its tumult. Gazing at the tiny reflected Christabel, she bent her hot forehead to the cool smooth ball.

Stillness. Stillness. I am silent and empty. Well up within me, living water.

No ink in her fountain pen. Being in love was all very well, but Ellen was really getting inexcusable.

My work is the only thing that matters, she said to herself. Happiness, love, peace—I have relinquished them all for my work. I would go on writing if I knew no one would ever read a word that I had written.

Ellen, in her simplicity, had revealed that Nick had never read any of Christabel's books. Or was it simplicity?

I must get to work, Christabel thought.

There had been something in his eyes—a look of discontent. Perhaps already he was disillusioned, but too gallant a gentleman to let Ellen know. Perhaps that was the reason for his aloofness. When he had returned her dropped handkerchief, he had been careful not to let their fingers touch. He hardly looked at me, she thought. Was that the reason? What else? What other reason could there be?

Oh, if that is it, how *well* I understand, she told him in her mind. Happiness—loyalty—one makes one's choice.

She went to the mirror and looked deep into her own sad eyes. Child of sorrow, she thought, her fingers automatically pushing wings of bright hair forward. Then she rang for Alfred, who reported that Miss Beach had not yet returned and the gentleman was still waiting.

"Tea for two—no, for three, at once, in the library, Alfred," she said "And whisky and soda. And if anyone else calls, I'm not at home."

X X

I WISH Ellen and Nick would be married and get it over with, Christabel thought, turning her hot pillow, listening, to a distant clock strike three. I am sick of them both.

Curtis said Nick always acted as if he were giving the girls a treat, just by existing. She found balm in what he said; she resented it.

She pushed her hair up from her forehead; she turned over again. Her chest ached so that it was hard to breathe. Curtis is right, she thought. Nick is insufferably conceited. She saw in the dark the complacent corners of his beautiful mouth. Conceited, unintelligent, self-centered.

I have been pleasant to him all these weeks. I will go on being pleasant to him, simply because I am so indifferent to him that I can admit him into the intimacy of rudeness.

She sat up in bed, turned on the light, and drank thirstily. She felt feverish and ill. That must be why she was so bored with everything and everybody—work, friends, Curtis, and the children. No one seemed real but Nick Portal, and she hated him.

Lying in the dark again, she thought incredulously that other people believed they were happy or unhappy, believed that what they were feeling mattered. She tried to call back feelings that had seemed intense once, before she knew Nick. Not even shadows answered. Yet he was everything she disliked, and she was filled with pity for Ellen, facing a lifetime with him. Nick and Ellen, together. "No!" she cried aloud, pressing her face into her pillow.

I won't think about him any more. He means nothing to me, except psychologically. As a person, he is a bore. As a study, he fascinates me, he amuses me.

He amuses me, she repeated to herself, and began to cry.

When the clock struck four, she got up, washed her hot wet face, put on her dressing-gown, and wrote:

MY DEAR NICK PORTAL:

Will you come to tea this afternoon, to talk over a business matter? My husband and I are most anxious to remodel the gardens of his old home in the country——

She finished the note, made changes, threw it away, and labored over another and another before she had one spontaneous enough to be copied out.

"Will you do something for me, darling?" she asked Curtis in the morning. "I long for a real country summer. *Would* you be willing to spend it on the Farm? I'm so sick of Southampton, and sitting on the sand in silk, with pearls and gloves. And Europe is worse—the Lido, and the horrible Lido young—well, men, I suppose. I've gone to these places for *you,* Curtis——"

"Why, Christabel——"

"Oh, I've gone gladly, dear. But this summer I'm not feeling very strong and I want to go back to quietness. I want to work a little in the garden, while the blessed babies tumble about underfoot and you practice putts into my flower-beds. I'm full of lovely plans. I'd even like to make a few little changes, if we could find just the right man. I'll have to think. You don't know how I've hungered and thirsted for the real country."

"Why, Christabel, I always liked the Farm, but I thought you didn't care anything about it."

"Curtis! Not care about the Farm? You *don't* know me very well, dearest, do you?"

"I'm so thankful! I really do believe Nick and Christabel are beginning to like each other," Ellen told Uncle Johnnie. "She agrees with him about lots of things that she never used to. It's awfully stimulating to listen to them. Of course they both have simply marvelous minds, and they argue like anything, and then suddenly Christabel will say: 'You're right and I'm wrong,' with that sort of starry look she gets, that makes you want to kiss her. And I can tell she thinks what he says amounts to something, because sometimes she'll speak to him about something he's said, oh, three or four days before, and that she hasn't apparently paid any attention to at the time."

"He must find that flattering."

"Oh, he does. He thinks now she's quite intelligent. Imagine, that description for *Chris*tabel—quite intelligent!" She laughed with loving mockery.

"Christabel isn't usually so patient, if there's not a mutual attraction at once."

"Well, of course, everyone usually worships her right from the start —but then, so do they Nick. I couldn't understand either of them. But it's all right now, and the most marvelous thing is going to happen! Nick is going to do over the gardens at the Farm! It was Curtis who suggested having him, but I think it was Christabel who put it into his head, somehow, so that Nick and I could be together, because, of course, he'll have to be there a lot. In fact, I practically made her admit that was the reason. I really do think she's an angel!"

Christabel and Nick had motored out to the Farm, to plan the new gardens. New old lead figures against new old box, a square pool with water dripping from a lifted shell, a stretch of turf where peacocks could promenade. Something must be done with the brook, which was now only a brook, running through ferns. Already Christabel saw herself and the twins and the dogs photographed all over the place, saw the photographs reproduced in magazines and Sunday papers.

She had decided it was better that she and Nick should be simple-hearted children and picnic in the sunshine, for Mrs. Johansen never rose above chops and stringbeans when one telephoned. So they had thermos bottles of frosty cocktails, hot soup, hot coffee, yellow cream; and sandwiches with *foie gras,* thick, not just scraped on, besides the chicken in aspic, dark with truffles, the small cream cheeses, and wild-strawberry jam. "Here on the grass," Nick had decreed. "I don't like your quaint, delightful dining-room."

"Polite!"

"Thank God we're not that any more. Doesn't it seem funny, now, that we hated each other so at first that every word was the essence of politeness?"

"Cold, cold politeness. But I never hated you. I simply considered you a young man so handsome that you would probably bore me to death."

"You turn my head."

She gave him a glance. "You wound me by your dislike of my beautiful dining-room."

"*Yes,* I do! What a joke on the people who don't realize that you did it with your tongue in your cheek. As a delicate burlesque, it's perfect —every detail. The ears of corn hung from the ceiling, the infant pugilist in pantalettes over the mantelpiece, ready to sock someone with a rose, and that supreme touch of satire, the shelves of colored glass across the windows, shutting out the view."

"You're a very penetrating person. Most people take that room perfectly seriously."

"And you let them, and laugh at them behind their backs. Christabel, you're a little devil!"

Christabel! He called me Christabel! First, Mrs. Carey. Then, for a long time, you. Now, at last, Christabel.

Nick! Nick!

And she suddenly flung out her arms, she cried, her voice enchanting in its sincerity: "I can hardly bear it! I can't bear it! I'm so happy!"

"Why—?"

She couldn't say, because you called me Christabel. And although the breeze, bringing a drift of fragrance, the tender grass, a quivering butterfly, had a lot to do with it when she came to think, those were not the things she and Nick talked about together in their clear-eyed, ironic self-knowledge. The bitter amusement of life was their mutual preoccupation, not its sentimental prettiness. So she only smiled at him, lifting a cigarette with fingers that shook a little. His fingers touched hers as he lighted it.

"I envy you, Nick."

"Why?"

"Because you're in love in the spring."

"Like a beautiful ballad."

"Yes, like a beautiful ballad. You're a lucky man, and a wise one, to have seen how sweet Ellen is. She's such a shy little thing, like a little brown bird in a flutter, that most men would have hurried past without even hearing the brown bird's song."

"Naturally, I think Ellen is perfect."

"Oh, she is! Be very kind to your brown bird, Nick, be very patient. Men have such a way of trying to change the women they love, once they have won them. They expect one woman to be everything— beautiful, brilliant, magnetic, and at the same time faithful, and sweet, and unselfish. Most of us can't be *every*thing, you know. Try to be understanding with little Ellen. Don't demand too much."

"She has a wonderful friend in you."

"Thank you, Nick. But who could help loving her, once they really know her? I envy you both. Love is—everything."

"Love's a grand state of affairs, but rather a general one. If we were Africans it would make us put on grass bustles and run bones through our noses; if we were roosters it would make us grow shinier tail feathers. After all, wonderful and beautiful and all that as it is, isn't it all rather a joke on us?"

Christabel's eyes were deep in his. Oh, my dear, I understand, she answered silently, and said aloud:

"Thank you for trying to console me, happy lover. But I know what all that, being translated, means."

He lit a cigarette, took a puff, and threw it away.

"Of course you do. All that being translated, means I adore my Ellen."

Christabel had asked Ellen to go to the Farm with Nick and herself, that day. She was careful to include Ellen when she and Nick did anything together. Even when they talked together she would break off to ask, smiling: "What does Ellen think?" And Ellen, lost in the sound of Nick's voice, the look of the sleek back of his head, that made the palm of her hand ache to stroke it, would feel herself blushing, would laugh and stammer, and have to admit that she didn't even know what they were talking about. It was funny, she thought, that Christabel's kindness in including her was the only thing that had ever made her feel separated from Nick.

She hadn't gone with them today, after all, because Talbot Emery Towne had sent word he was going to England unexpectedly, and before he sailed, wanted to see as much of *Tear Stains on Taffeta* as Christabel had written. So Ellen had stayed to copy the finished chapters, smelling the spring in the country as she wrote, feeling the squish of the grass by the Farm pond, where clumps of paper-white narcissus would be unwrapping in today's hot sunshine, almost seeing Nick and Christabel, almost hearing what they said to each other. At lunch, while her body sat with the children and Mademoiselle, while Alfred offered baked macaroni and stewed rhubarb, her spirit was with Nick and

Christabel, picnicking under the deep blue velvet sky. Now she was with them, a shadow, unheard, unseen, as they drove home together through the cold spring dusk under the warm light robe. The band that had been about her chest all day tightened so that she could hardly breathe.

I'm crazy, she scolded herself. It's just because I'm tired. I'm not jealous. I'm *glad* they like each other. I hope they have a lovely day.

I *am* jealous——

No, I'm not, I'm not!

She typed:

"A painted sky where rosy little loves rolled in clouds that cast no shadows on courtiers in mulberry and citron-yellow, pausing by a fountain's silver fronds, or on powdered ladies melancholy under green fountains of trees. Painted love, painted laughter, painted tears, covered the walls surrounding the vast central emptiness."

That ended what Christabel had done. Ellen arched her back to stop its aching, stretched out her arms and grasped handfuls of nothing.

She was starved for air. She would take the typescript the few blocks to Mr. Towne's. She pulled on her hat, not looking into the mirror. She knew she was a sight, but she was too tired even to powder her nose for anyone but Nick, who wouldn't see her.

But, coming down the shadowed stairs, she saw Nick and Christabel standing in a pool of light in the hall. Christabel was smiling, spring freshness about her like a radiance. Nick was almost frowning. They looked at each other silently, as motionless as if they held between them a brimming cup that must not be spilled.

Nothing told Ellen what to do. Feeling infinitely unwanted, infinitely alone, she stood there stupidly, not moving, until they lifted their faces to her, calling her down, telling her how they had missed her.

"Look! Nick picked all *my* narcissus for you!"

"Ellen, precious, you look tired to death!"

"I'll keep her in bed tomorrow morning, Nick."

She saw the white flowers with their vermilion-rimmed golden centers with crystal clearness, she heard Nick's voice and Christabel's as if she had never really heard before. Christabel's hand was through her arm, Nick's hand crushed her fingers. It is all right, she told herself, not believing. They love me and I love them. It's all right. Nick is here.

I'm all alone——

No, no! Nick is here!

I'm alone.

XXI

ELLEN, bringing Uncle Johnnie an armful of midsummer flowers with Christabel's love, told him her little news of the Farm. Christabel's roses had taken first prize at the Flower Show; Curtis was playing golf at the National over the week-end, for Christabel had decided he needed the change; Michael and Marigold had a new roan pony that they had named Black Beauty and Christabel had renamed Monsieur Patapon; Christabel's roses had taken first prize at the Flower Show——

Had she told him that before? Her head was humming; she couldn't quite remember. She was so sleepy in the daytime now, so sleepless at night. If I could only go to bed, she would think, starving for sleep, but when she was in bed the thoughts would begin, forcing her eyelids open, stretching her body tense.

"You shouldn't have come to town on such a hot day," Uncle Johnnie said.

"There were errands. I had to see a new kitchen-maid, and then I thought Nick was going to drive out with me—he's coming for the week-end. But he must have misunderstood. They said at the office he'd already gone out by train."

She had thought that perhaps everything would be as it used to be if they had that hour together. Perhaps she could really believe what she tried to believe, what Nick kept telling her, that she imagined things. But Nick was at the Farm already. He and Christabel would be having tea now, in shadow under the beech tree. Christabel cool in thin white. Christabel, who never exasperated Nick by being jealous and stiff and stupid——

He'll be as disappointed as I am when he realizes that I was to bring him out, she tried to reassure herself. Will he be? cold doubt asked. She turned away from the feeling, never before put into words, that made her tremble. Nick doesn't want to be alone with me.

"Nick and Christabel are great friends now. I'm so happy about it," she forced herself to say, hearing Nick's voice speaking of Christabel: "Why, Ellen, darling, I never knew you to be catty about anyone before."

"I remember how miserable you said it made you when they didn't like each other, and how hard you were working to bring them together. So you've been successful."

"Nick sees now how beautiful she is, and how brilliant," Ellen said, keeping her voice steady. But tears overflowed; she couldn't stop them. She tried to wipe them away, but they kept on.

"Don't mind me," Uncle Johnnie said. "Go ahead and get soaking wet. It's a comfort to you and a compliment to me, and we'll get you dry before my capable lion-tamer comes back in all her starch. Do you think your Nick is in love with Christabel?"

"Please excuse me—it's just because it's so hot and I haven't been sleeping. No, not yet. He's fascinated and excited, that's all so far. But I'm frightened. He keeps telling me over and over how much he loves me—I think he's telling himself. He's wonderful to me this summer, as if he was sorry for me and trying to make up to me for something. And after he's been with Christabel he sort of laughs about her to me—but I'm frightened. She's working so hard to get him. It's all been so gradual, and yet now I feel as if it had all happened in a minute, and I ask myself what *has* happened, and I don't know. There isn't anything definite. Only first she bored him and he really disliked her, and then I kept telling him how lovely she was to me, and how generous, so for my sake he used to talk to her when he didn't want to. And she was so interested in everything that interested him. She got books and books on landscape gardening she read for hours, she got to know more than he did about Alpine flowers for rock gardens, for instance. And she made him sorry for her. He told me how unhappily married she was, and yet how brave and loyal. I don't know how she does it; she makes them feel as if they had guessed it all themselves, without her telling them. And she let him do things for her that made him feel kind and important. He helped her with lots of *Tear Stains on Taffeta*——"

Uncle Johnnie looked his question.

"That's her new book. He helped her with all the parts about old French gardens. He thinks she's wonderful now, and I understand. I used to think so, too. Only now I'm terrified because I think she's fascinating him more and more. I'm terrified, and I'm sick with jealousy."

She was silent for a moment, clasping and unclasping her shaking hands. Then she burst out:

"The thing I can't bear is that she's made Nick look silly. I can't bear to see *Nick* taken in. I thought he was too big a person for flattery——"

"No one's too big a person for flattery. Why don't you flatter him harder than she does?"

"I won't try to hold him if he wants to go. I won't stoop to her tactics." You don't dare, for fear you might fail, said the cold doubt that lay in her heart.

"I'm ashamed of myself, talking this way about her. I don't know what's gotten into me. She has been wonderful to us both, and here I am talking like a jealous cat."

"Christabel has always been rather good at making other ladies sound like cats."

"She *has* done wonderful things for me. She's always doing wonderful things for people. You can't imagine all the presents she gives. And she always includes me when she's talking to Nick. Poor little Ellen, we mustn't let her feel left out—that's the way I think they feel about me, or the way Christabel does, anyway. She has a way of talking to me as if she would be brilliant if I were *just* worth it."

Uncle Johnnie produced a large fresh handkerchief from under his pillow, and Ellen mopped her eyes.

"When he does things for me, she says she's so glad, that she had hoped he would. She acts as if everything he does is because she's asked him to, as a favor to her. She sends Nick to me—*she* sends Nick to *me!*"

"And you receive him sweetly, Patient Griselda?"

"I haven't any pride with him. I haven't any sense. I only love him——"

"Of course you may get a lot of enjoyment out of seeing yourself as a martyr, burning in flames of love and pain. That's always a flattering self-portrait."

"Oh, don't, don't! Only I don't know what to do. Help me!"

"He'll never really love you until you hurt him."

"I couldn't——"

"She does, if I know her."

"Yes, she does, she hurts him terribly. She will have been simply lovely to him, and then she'll get cold and disagreeable and hardly speak to him, and he'll worry over what he's done, and nearly kill himself trying to get her back to being friendly. I've seen him look almost faint with relief when she smiles at him again and talks in a natural voice. I can't believe it's Nick, sometimes. He's always been the moody one—I don't mean moody, that sounds horrid, but he has the artistic temperament."

"So you've done the smoothing and cheering and lifting. Well, my child, a smug self-righteous glow will be all the reward you'll ever get for that. Be selfish, make everybody work and worry, and you'll be adored. I don't know any surer rule. Brace up, Ellen! Grab your young man back, if you want him. The Lord knows why you should, but if you do, grab, and grab hard. Don't be sweet and gentle, don't go on helping Christabel. She doesn't need any help. She doesn't want him the way you do. If she loses him she'll suffer, because wounded vanity hurts, but if you lose him——"

"If I lose him—" Ellen whispered.

"He has come into her life, and he must kneel to her, or she must be able to ignore him, and evidently she's not able."

"I'm afraid she loves him. You don't know Nick. He's different. She must love him."

"Christabel only loves one person, and it's the love of a lifetime."

"Not Nick? Do you mean Curtis?" But even Ellen, who in her heart believed people must love each other if they were married, didn't believe he meant Curtis.

"Don't be silly, Ellen. Christabel loves Christabel."

"Oh! I never thought of that. But then—why does she bother with other people? Why is she trying to take Nick away from me?"

"She is a sea-monster. She takes the things that feed her; she ejects everything else. A sea-anemone looks like a delicate flower, pink or cream or lilac, with its tentacles moving as gently as petals in a breeze, but it can send out a shower of stinging tiny darts, and it can grasp what it wants."

Ellen turned her head, and Christabel's flowers, cool and smooth, brushed her hot wet cheek.

"Oh, I don't want to hate her!"

"Don't hate her. Be sorry for her. She's gotten to depend on adulation until she's frantic without it, and, like all drugs, the dose has to be increased and increased. Be sorry for her, but, if you want your young man, fight like the devil."

"I'll try." She laughed shakily, putting her forehead down on his thin old hand, exhausted and relieved by confession. Then she went to the mirror, to see eyes as red as if they had been boiled, a nose glowing like a mulberry under the powder she piled on it.

In the mirror she saw that Uncle Johnnie had closed his eyes. I've exhausted him, she thought, remorsefully. There was almost no one there—the bedclothes were nearly flat. The tired old face was as transparently white as if it had been carved from alabaster. She felt weak with love and pity. But as his starched lion-tamer came in with what she announced as "Mr. Caine's five-o'clock nourishment," he gave Ellen a look that sent her away laughing through her lightened unhappiness.

XXII

Nick and Christabel had spent a satisfactory afternoon under the beech tree, talking of deep things. Conversation had had to be simplified and lightened when Ellen came back from town. Through Friday evening, through Saturday and Sunday, she had sparkled with what seemed to Christabel an artificial gayety. Ellen had often returned from calls on Uncle Johnnie with ideas in her head, but they had never lasted for more than a day, before, and by Sunday afternoon Christabel felt that she must be spoken to, very lovingly, and understandingly. So before supper she knocked on Ellen's door, carrying a cornucopia held in a glass hand, delicately cuffed in glass, which she had filled with sprays of heliotrope.

"I've brought you a nosegay for your dressing-table, Ellen darling. I know you've seen this intriguing thing, but doesn't it look even more perfect with flowers? No, *really*? Haven't you seen it? Why, I thought, of course, you'd helped Nick pick it out. Wasn't it enchanting of him to bring it to me?"

She curled up on the window seat.

"Go on dressing and I'll just perch here out of the way and chatter a little. Nick's monopolized you so I haven't had a word, and I wanted to ask you if you were quite well."

"I'm all right, thank you."

"You haven't felt feverish?"

"Not a bit."

"You're sure? Nick and I have been a little worried. Perhaps it's just the heat, or perhaps we love you so that we imagine things. I don't mean you haven't been gay and bright, you have, unusually so, but I seemed to feel such an effort behind it, I was afraid you were ill and trying to hide it from us. You know we both adore you so when you're just your own sweet natural self, that it worries us when you're different. Well, I'll tell him we've both been old fuss-budgets. Ellen, tell me to go! I have to change my dress for supper, and I'm so happy and comfy here I don't want to move."

She watched Ellen brushing her silky hair, stepping into white slippers, pulling an absurdly childish dress over her head. If she was going to affect simplicity to the extent she did, she ought to carry it all the way through. It didn't go with the *Tabac Blond* she was tilting out of a full bottle, certainly new, onto her handkerchief (what a place to put perfume!) or the lipstick that she had never used before Friday evening.

I ought to speak to her, much as I hate to, since I'm almost in a mother's position to her, or at least an elder sister's. Shall I? It would be so much easier not to. Shall I?

She looked at the lovely room, the soft clear colors, the white and silver of the bathroom beyond, that Ellen had all to herself, unless there were guests. Where would she have been, except for me? She had no one else to go to. Who would have been so generous, so patient with her lack of training?

"Ellen, darling, *don't* use that dreadful lipstick! Nick and I hate it so, on you!"

Quick red stained Ellen's face and throat. Christabel jumped up and kissed her lightly.

"Forgive me! You know how dreadfully impulsive I am—I blurt things out, and then I'm broken-hearted! But it's just because I love you that I can't bear to let you go on doing things like that."

But Ellen's mouth was scarlet when she came defiantly downstairs, and she wore the ear-rings that Curtis had mistakenly given her for Christmas. Through the first part of supper she laughed and talked exaggeratedly, she threw herself at Nick, flirting with him, teasing him, paying him outrageous compliments. Christabel could see how uncomfortable it was making him, through all his extravagant response, and for both their sakes, to stop the painful exhibition, she changed the subject from personalities to old mazes.

Late last night, after he had gone to bed, she had found the book he had been reading. Now she was glad she had studied it until nearly dawn, for she was able to ask just the questions that drew him out, that made him glow. Mazes were his new passion, and he flung himself into discussion.

"But it's such a specialized subject. How do you know so much about it, Christabel?"

"It fascinates me; it always has. Maze! Just that symbolic word—all one's life translated into box or yew."

"Which one do you think we ought to copy for the lower garden here, Ellen?"

"I don't know, Nick."

"Didn't you go through that book I brought? You said you were going to."

"I haven't had time."

"We've kept her too busy with tennis and swimming and talk. But you have a treat in store for you, hasn't she, Nick? I picked it up last night, and I *couldn't* put it down. The sun was rising when I finished it. Tell me, Nick, could you—but *you* could, I know—plan a simplified one for me like that old one at Beeches St. Mary? You know, Ellen, dear— Oh, I forgot, you haven't had time to look at the book yet. I shouldn't have had, really, but somehow one finds time for what one really wants to do, don't you think so, Nick? Ellen, you're lucky! Do you know how lucky you are? Suppose Nick's interests were in stocks and bonds and golf, like—like most husbands'! But a creative thing like planting gardens! How different! How wonderful to be making the world a more beautiful place to live in!"

"I'll read that book tonight, Nick!"

"Oh, don't bother, Ellen. I think it would probably bore you, after all. I don't think the Beeches St. Mary maze, Christabel, but there's a wonderful old one very few people have heard of, at a place called Lesser Monkton——"

"Oh, *yes!* The one in holly!"

"My Lord! You *do* know about them! I thought something like that, in box, within sound of the waterfall."

Ellen's strange flame died down, she sat pale and silent, listening to them, and only messing with the delicious peach mousse, which Christabel was greatly enjoying. Afterward she went to bed early—with a headache, she said, and for her own sake Christabel hoped it was that, not sulkiness—leaving Nick and Christabel on the terrace.

"More coffee, Nick? You can reach the cigarettes. Oh, what a night!"

"What a night!" Nick echoed, pouring another glass of chartreuse. "You look silver in the moonlight."

Silver Christabel, she thought, hoping that he did, too. That was the sort of thing Nick always looked as if he were going to say, and never said. That was part of Nick's strange charm, that he not only never made pretty speeches, like other men, but he dared to say rude things, beside which compliments seemed insipid. And at the thought of his smile as he said them, she grew suddenly weak. I hate him. I hate him, she thought. How does he feel toward me? I don't know, I don't know. Nick, love me!

She realized that she was trembling with tenseness; she had held her attitude of easy grace so long. It tired her to be with Nick, for she never ceased to be conscious of how she looked to him, so that often her hands, her shoulders, would ache from the graceful positions she kept them in. It tired her to be with him, it tortured her to be without him.

She rose, stretching white arms to the moon, and stepped into the garden. She could see what she hoped he was seeing—silver Christabel glimmering in the moonlight through the glimmer of white flowers, against the white plume of the fountain. Moon Maiden. She bent and kissed a clump of white phlox.

Nick joined her, and they strolled up and down together.

"So fresh, so fragrant! How it comforts me!"

"Do you need comfort, Christabel?"

She looked at him without speaking. The air vibrated with the cries of insects. Nick, kiss me, kiss me, she called to him in silence.

The sound of the fountain grew faint as they walked, the servants' radio grew loud.

I wish you knew how much I long to *hold* you *in* my arms——

Her hand brushed against his as if by accident. He caught it lightly, swung it, let it go.

When I saw you, I knew
I had found my only love when I—met—you——

He has led me to the edge of ecstasy, she thought.

This *time* is *my* time, will soon be good-*by* time
Then in the *starlight*—hold *me* tight——
With one more little kiss say nightie night, good night, my dear,
Good night, dear, good night dear, nightie night——

They turned. The sound of the radio was drowned in the loud cool splashing of the fountain.

Nick, kiss me, kiss me. Her delicate slippers were soaked with dew, but who could think of such a thing at such a time?

"You haven't answered me. Do you need comfort, Christabel?"

"I think we understand each other pretty well without words, Nick."

"We do. Too damn well."

The light in Ellen's window went out. Christabel said to Nick:

"We must go in."

"Yes—we must go in."

"We really must, Nick."

He kissed her. At last! I am dying of bliss, she thought, breathless in his arms. I'm not disappointed. No, no! I'm not, I'm not!

He went on kissing her. The feeling of being crushed increased, her face was pressed uncomfortably against his shoulder now. She pushed away the thought of discomfort, and tried unsuccessfully to push away the thought that anyone might see them, in the bright moonlight.

"Nick—*please*——"

He let her go.

"Oh, Nick, how could you?"

"I must have gone mad for a minute. Can you ever forgive me?"

"Oh, my dear, it isn't a question of forgiveness. But it must never happen again—never again."

"Never again."

"We'll never speak of it, dear, and we'll never forget. Love only asks to love; it does not ask love in return, or joy."

He groaned assentingly.

"Curtis and Ellen must never know."

"My God! I should say not!"

"We must never, never hurt them."

"Never."

"We must go in now. Good-by, my dear."

"Good-by—good-by!"

The lighted sitting-room was a room she had never seen before, like a scene on the stage, ready for the acting of a play. Apricot, lilac, and soft green of chintz, shaded lamps, heaped silk cushions, great splashes of foaming and spraying flowers. For a cold moment she thought there was a bland, an almost smug look on Nick's face, but she knew, she knew, it was a trick of the light. Who can enjoy heart-break?

She was nervous about how she looked, for one isn't at one's best coming in from moonlight and dew, blinking in the light, especially after such an embrace.

"I'm cold, Nick," she said, and, as he knelt to light the fire, she came close to him, close against him, for reassurance from the mirror over the mantel. He lifted her floating sleeve to his lips. A thrill, a chill ran through her as she realized that, except for Ellen, Mademoiselle and the children, and the servants, they were alone in the house.

She touched his dark hair with a white hand she couldn't keep from shaking. She put her head back, her eyelids were closing, when a reflection in the mirror made them start wide open. Curtis was in the hall.

Something saves one, she thought, flooded with relief and disappointment. Something stronger than oneself. And she dropped her bracelet and cried: "There, Nick! There it is, close to the fender," as Curtis came into the room.

"Curtis, darling! Where did you come from? Doesn't Nick look devoted? But, alas! he's only looking for my bracelet. I must have the clasp fixed. Dearest, how *glad* I am to see you—thank you, Nick—but why have you come home?"

"I—I've got awfully sad news for you, Christabel."

"What? Curtis, what?"

"Uncle Johnnie died this afternoon."

She sank to the seat in front of the fire, and covered her face with her hands. Nick was still kneeling on one side, Curtis dropped to his knees on the other, patting her arm.

"I shouldn't have told you so suddenly."

"Shall I get you some water?"

"No, no. I'll try to be brave in a minute."

"You are brave, Christabel darling. You're wonderful," Curtis said in a hushed, solemn voice.

"You're wonderful," Nick agreed, a hollow echo.

"I can't seem to realize it. Uncle Johnnie—*dead*."

There was silence, except for the brisk snapping of the fire. Then she lifted her head.

"Forgive me. I'm all right now. But sometimes—I have felt as if he were the one person in the world who—understood me—and now I—I——"

AN AFTERWORD ON
"ALL KNEELING"

THERE was a certain gusty and cheerless November afternoon at Atlantic City which I shall always hold in grateful memory not only because, as I plodded along the echoing and almost deserted boardwalk, I came upon Miss Ethel Barrymore majestically taking the air in a wheelchair but because that great lady, feeling expansive at the sight of any familiar face in those gray wastes, was moved to bestow two gifts upon me. One was a portfolio of Stephen Foster records which, newly prepared by Master Shilkret for the phonographs of the land, was destined to launch the revival that has since made the Foster melodies as familiar to this present generation as they were to those who first heard them twanged on languishing guitars to maids in crinoline. Miss Barrymore's other gift was the latest exploit by the author of *The Perennial Bachelor*—the delicate and implacable novel called *All Kneeling*.

This anthology itself and all its occasional marginalia are the work of an incurable re-reader. It is an old habit which through the years has kept me from ever being a well-read fellow. I can trace it back to the days when, as a bookworm in knee-breeches, I never could get on to *Bleak House* because of the temptation to go back and look once more for Pip among the gravestones on the edge of the marsh. To this day, on my arrival each spring at a certain house in the country, a stack of new books scrupulously accumulated for the bedside table has to wait a little longer because my eye on its way to bed has chanced to fall on *Emma*. In this *Reader* are two novels of recent years which I have found thus inexhaustible. One is Mr. Maugham's *Cakes and Ale* and the other *All Kneeling*. I have re-read them both many times and always with delight.

The spurious Christabel is a little American cousin of E. F. Benson's Lucia and to my mind a far more penetrating and corrosive piece of work. Indeed, in his rambunctious fooling, Mr. Benson is to Miss Parrish as a rollicking puppy to a cold and alarming cat. But perhaps the contrast has no more mystifying origin than the mere fact that, as he went along, Mr. Benson grew shamelessly fond of his Lucia, whereas Christabel could never in this world get around Anne Parrish. Of course, to enjoy Christabel to the hilt—perhaps even to enjoy her at all—you have to meet Miss Parrish on her own grounds, must play this game by her rules. More specifically, you must shut your eyes tight and pretend that, out of all Christabel's world, only Uncle Johnnie was shrewd enough to see what an arrant fraud she was. But such compacts with an author are common enough. Surely you remember the time when, in return for the inestimable privilege of going along with Mr. Tarkington, you and I had to pretend that William Sylvanus Baxter and all the other lads in town would have been enchanted with the Baby-Talk Lady. In the world as it is, at the first sign of her deplorable tendency to say " 'Ess, deedums" instead of "Yes, indeed," I suspect that the boys, in their acute embarrassment, would have turned tail with the ardor of rats in flight from a sinking ship. So in *All Kneeling* you and I must pretend that the bogus Christabel would really have gone through life in a successful whirl of love and admiration. But a spoilsport reader who, on such occasions, will not do that much for an author is a little too like the difficult guest at a party who won't let the hired magician do his tricks except under such stern conditions of light and espionage as would preclude his doing any tricks at all.

A. W.

WHILOMVILLE
STORIES

by

STEPHEN CRANE

WHILOMVILLE STORIES

I

THE ANGEL CHILD

I

ALTHOUGH Whilomville was in no sense a summer resort, the advent of the warm season meant much to it, for then came visitors from the city—people of considerable confidence—alighting upon their country cousins. Moreover, many citizens who could afford to do so escaped at this time to the sea-side. The town, with the commercial life quite taken out of it, drawled and drowsed through long months, during which nothing was worse than the white dust which arose behind every vehicle at blinding noon, and nothing was finer than the cool sheen of the hose sprays over the cropped lawns under the many maples in the twilight.

One summer the Trescotts had a visitation. Mrs. Trescott owned a cousin who was a painter of high degree. I had almost said that he was of national reputation, but, come to think of it, it is better to say that almost everybody in the United States who knew about art and its travail knew about him. He had picked out a wife, and naturally, looking at him, one wondered how he had done it. She was quick, beautiful, imperious, while he was quiet, slow, and misty. She was a veritable queen of health, while he, apparently, was of a most brittle constitution. When he played tennis, particularly, he looked every minute as if he were going to break.

They lived in New York, in awesome apartments wherein Japan and

Persia, and indeed all the world, confounded the observer. At the end was a cathedral-like studio. They had one child. Perhaps it would be better to say that they had one CHILD. It was a girl. When she came to Whilomville with her parents, it was patent that she had an inexhaustible store of white frocks, and that her voice was high and commanding. These things the town knew quickly. Other things it was doomed to discover by a process.

Her effect upon the children of the Trescott neighborhood was singular. They at first feared, then admired, then embraced. In two days she was a Begum. All day long her voice could be heard directing, drilling, and compelling those free-born children; and to say that they felt oppression would be wrong, for they really fought for records of loyal obedience.

All went well until one day was her birthday.

On the morning of this day she walked out into the Trescott garden and said to her father, confidently, "Papa, give me some money, because this is my birthday."

He looked dreamily up from his easel. "Your birthday?" he murmured. Her envisioned father was never energetic enough to be irritable unless some one broke through into that place where he lived with the desires of his life. But neither wife nor child ever heeded or even understood the temperamental values, and so some part of him had grown hardened to their inroads. "Money?" he said. "Here." He handed her a five-dollar bill. It was that he did not at all understand the nature of a five-dollar bill. He was deaf to it. He had it; he gave it; that was all.

She sallied forth to a waiting people—Jimmie Trescott, Dan Earl, Ella Earl, the Margate twins, the three Phelps children, and others. "I've got some pennies now," she cried, waving the bill, "and I am going to buy some candy." They were deeply stirred by this announcement. Most children are penniless three hundred days in the year, and to another possessing five pennies they pay deference. To little Cora waving a bright green note these children paid heathenish homage. In some disorder they thronged after her to a small shop on Bridge Street hill. First of all came ice-cream. Seated in the comic little back parlor, they clamored shrilly over plates of various flavors, and the shopkeeper marveled that cream could vanish so quickly down throats that seemed wide open, always, for the making of excited screams.

These children represented the families of most excellent people. They were all born in whatever purple there was to be had in the vicinity of Whilomville. The Margate twins, for example, were out-and-out prize-winners. With their long golden curls and their counte-nances of similar vacuity, they shone upon the front bench of all Sunday-school functions, hand in hand, while their uplifted mother felt about her the envy of a hundred other parents, and less heavenly children scoffed from near the door.

Then there was little Dan Earl, probably the nicest boy in the world, gentle, fine-grained, obedient to the point where he obeyed anybody. Jimmie Trescott himself was, indeed, the only child who was at all versed in villainy, but in these particular days he was on his very good behavior. As a matter of fact, he was in love. The beauty of his regal little cousin had stolen his manly heart.

Yes, they were all most excellent children, but, loosened upon this candy-shop with five dollars, they resembled, in a tiny way, drunken reveling soldiers within the walls of a stormed city. Upon the heels of ice-cream and cake came chocolate mice, butter-scotch, "everlastings," chocolate cigars, taffy-on-a-stick, taffy-on-a-slate-pencil, and many semi-transparent devices resembling lions, tigers, elephants, horses, cats, dogs, cows, sheep, tables, chairs, engines (both railway and for the fighting of fire), soldiers, fine ladies, odd-looking men, clocks, watches, revolvers, rabbits, and bedsteads. A cent was the price of a single wonder.

Some of the children, going quite daft, soon had thought to make fight over the spoils, but their queen ruled with an iron grip. Her first inspiration was to satisfy her own fancies, but as soon as that was done she mingled prodigality with a fine justice, dividing, balancing, be-stowing, and sometimes taking away from somebody even that which he had.

It was an orgy. In thirty-five minutes those respectable children looked as if they had been dragged at the tail of a chariot. The sacred Margate twins, blinking and grunting, wished to take seat upon the floor, and even the most durable Jimmie Trescott found occasion to lean against the counter, wearing at the time a solemn and abstracted air, as if he expected something to happen to him shortly.

Of course their belief had been in an unlimited capacity, but they found there was an end. The shopkeeper handed the queen her change.

"Two seventy-three from five leaves two twenty-seven, Miss Cora," he said, looking upon her with admiration.

She turned swiftly to her clan. "O-oh!" she cried, in amazement. "Look how much I have left!" They gazed at the coins in her palm. They knew then that it was not their capacities which were endless; it was the five dollars.

The queen led the way to the street. "We must think up some way of spending more money," she said, frowning. They stood in silence, awaiting her further speech.

Suddenly she clapped her hands and screamed with delight. "Come on!" she cried. "I know what let's do." Now behold, she had discovered the red and white pole in front of the shop of one William Neeltje, a barber by trade.

It becomes necessary to say a few words concerning Neeltje. He was new to the town. He had come and opened a dusty little shop on dusty Bridge Street hill, and although the neighborhood knew from the courier winds that his diet was mainly cabbage, they were satisfied with that meager data. Of course Riefsnyder came to investigate him for the local Barbers' Union, but he found in him only sweetness and light, with a willingness to charge any price at all for a shave or a haircut. In fact, the advent of Neeltje would have made barely a ripple upon the placid bosom of Whilomville if it were not that his name was Neeltje.

At first the people looked at his sign-board out of the eye corner, and wondered lazily why any one should bear the name of Neeltje; but as time went on, men spoke to other men, saying, "How do you pronounce the name of that barber up there on Bridge Street hill?" And then, before any could prevent it, the best minds of the town were splintering their lances against William Neeltje's sign-board. If a man had a mental superior, he guided him seductively to this name, and watched with glee his wrecking. The clergy of the town even entered the lists. There was one among them who had taken a collegiate prize in Syriac, as well as in several less opaque languages, and the other clergymen—at one of their weekly meetings—sought to betray him into this ambush. He pronounced the name correctly, but that mattered little, since none of them knew whether he did or did not; and so they took triumph according to their ignorance. Under these arduous circumstances it was certain that the town should look for a nickname, and at this time the nickname was in process of formation. So William Neeltje lived on with his secret, smiling foolishly towards the world.

"Come on," cried little Cora. "Let's all get our hair cut. That's what let's do. Let's all get our hair cut! Come on! Come on! Come on!" The others were carried off their feet by the fury of this assault. To get their hair cut! What joy! Little did they know if this were fun; they only knew that their small leader said it was fun. Chocolate-stained but confident, the band marched into William Neeltje's barber shop.

"We wish to get our hair cut," said little Cora, haughtily.

Neeltje, in his shirt-sleeves, stood looking at them with his half-idiot smile.

"Hurry, now!" commanded the queen. A dray-horse toiled step by step, step by step, up Bridge Street hill; a far woman's voice arose; there could be heard the ceaseless hammers of shingling carpenters; all was summer peace. "Come on, now. Who's goin' first? Come on, Ella; you go first. Gettin' our hair cut! Oh what fun!"

Little Ella Earl would not, however, be first in the chair. She was drawn towards it by a singular fascination, but at the same time she was afraid of it, and so she hung back, saying: "No! You go first! No! You go first!" The question was precipitated by the twins and one of the Phelps children. They made simultaneous rush for the chair, and screamed and kicked, each pair preventing the third child. The queen entered this mêlée, and decided in favor of the Phelps boy. He ascended the chair. Thereat an awed silence fell upon the band. And always William Neeltje smiled fatuously.

He tucked a cloth in the neck of the Phelps boy, and taking scissors, began to cut his hair. The group of children came closer and closer. Even the queen was deeply moved. "Does it hurt any?" she asked, in a wee voice.

"Naw," said the Phelps boy, with dignity. "Anyhow, I've had m' hair cut afore."

When he appeared to them looking very soldierly with his cropped little head, there was a tumult over the chair. The Margate twins howled; Jimmie Trescott was kicking them on the shins. It was a fight.

But the twins could not prevail, being the smallest of all the children. The queen herself took the chair, and ordered Neeltje as if he were a lady's-maid. To the floor there fell proud ringlets, blazing even there in their humiliation with a full fine bronze light. Then Jimmie Trescott, then Ella Earl (two long ash-colored plaits), then a Phelps girl, then another Phelps girl; and so on from head to head. The ceremony received unexpected check when the turn came to Dan Earl. This lad, usually docile to any rein, had suddenly grown mulishly obstinate. No, he would not, he would not. He himself did not seem to know why he refused to have his hair cut, but, despite the shrill derision of the company, he remained obdurate. Anyhow, the twins, long held in check, and now feverishly eager, were already struggling for the chair.

And so to the floor at last came the golden Margate curls, the heart treasure and glory of a mother, three aunts, and some feminine cousins.

All having been finished, the children, highly elate, thronged out into the street. They crowed and cackled with pride and joy, anon turning to scorn the cowardly Dan Earl.

Ella Earl was an exception. She had been pensive for some time, and now the shorn little maiden began vaguely to weep. In the door of his shop William Neeltje stood watching them, upon his face a grin of almost inhuman idiocy.

II

It now becomes the duty of the unfortunate writer to exhibit these children to their fond parents. "Come on, Jimmie," cried little Cora, "let's go show mamma." And they hurried off, these happy children, to show mamma.

The Trescotts and their guests were assembled indolently awaiting the luncheon-bell. Jimmie and the angel child burst in upon them. "Oh, mamma," shrieked little Cora, "see how fine I am! I've had my hair cut! Isn't it splendid? And Jimmie too!"

The wretched mother took one sight, emitted one yell, and fell into a chair. Mrs. Trescott dropped a large lady's journal and made a nerveless mechanical clutch at it. The painter gripped the arms of his chair and leaned forward, staring until his eyes were like two little clock faces. Dr. Trescott did not move or speak.

To the children the next moments were chaotic. There was a loudly wailing mother, and a pale-faced, aghast mother; a stammering father, and a grim and terrible father. The angel child did not understand anything of it save the voice of calamity, and in a moment all her little imperialism went to the winds. She ran sobbing to her mother. "Oh, mamma! mamma! mamma!"

The desolate Jimmie heard out of this inexplicable situation a voice which he knew well, a sort of colonel's voice, and he obeyed like any good soldier. "Jimmie!"

He stepped three paces to the front. "Yes, sir."

"How did this—how did this happen?" said Trescott.

Now Jimmie could have explained how had happened anything which had happened, but he did not know what had happened, so he said, "I—I—nothin'."

"And, oh, look at her frock!" said Mrs. Trescott, brokenly.

The words turned the mind of the mother of the angel child. She looked up, her eyes blazing. "Frock!" she repeated. "Frock! What do I care for her frock? Frock!" she choked out again from the depths of her bitterness. Then she arose suddenly, and whirled tragically upon her husband. "Look!" she declaimed. "All—her lovely—hair—all her lovely hair—gone—gone!" The painter was apparently in a fit; his jaw was set, his eyes were glazed, his body was stiff and straight. "All gone —all—her lovely hair—all gone—my poor little darlin'—my—poor— little—darlin'!" And the angel child added her heart-broken voice to her mother's wail as they fled into each other's arms.

In the mean time Trescott was patiently unraveling some skeins of Jimmie's tangled intellect. "And then you went to this barber's on the hill. Yes. And where did you get the money? Yes. I see. And who besides you and Cora had their hair cut? The Margate twi— Oh, lord!"

Over at the Margate place old Eldridge Margate, the grandfather of the twins, was in the back garden picking pease and smoking ruminatively to himself. Suddenly he heard from the house great noises. Doors slammed, women rushed up-stairs and down-stairs calling to each other in voices of agony. And then full and mellow upon the still air arose the roar of the twins in pain.

Old Eldridge stepped out of the pea-patch and moved towards the house, puzzled, staring, not yet having decided that it was his duty to rush forward. Then around the corner of the house shot his daughter Mollie, her face pale with horror.

"What's the matter?" he cried.

"Oh, father," she gasped, "the children! They—"

Then around the corner of the house came the twins, howling at the top of their power, their faces flowing with tears. They were still hand in hand, the ruling passion being strong even in this suffering. At sight of them old Eldridge took his pipe hastily out of his mouth. "Good God!" he said.

And now what befell one William Neeltje, a barber by trade? And what was said by angry parents of the mother of such an angel child? And what was the fate of the angel child herself?

There was surely a tempest. With the exception of the Margate twins, the boys could well be eliminated from the affair. Of course it didn't matter if their hair was cut. Also the two little Phelps girls had had very short hair, anyhow, and their parents were not too greatly incensed. In the case of Ella Earl, it was mainly the pathos of the little girl's own grieving; but her mother played a most generous part, and called upon Mrs. Trescott, and condoled with the mother of the angel child over their equivalent losses. But the Margate contingent! They simply screeched.

Trescott, composed and cool-blooded, was in the middle of a giddy whirl. He was not going to allow the mobbing of his wife's cousins, nor was he going to pretend that the spoliation of the Margate twins was a virtuous and beautiful act. He was elected, gratuitously, to the position of a buffer.

But, curiously enough, the one who achieved the bulk of the misery was old Eldridge Margate, who had been picking pease at the time. The feminine Margates stormed his position as individuals, in pairs, in teams, and *en masse*. In two days they may have aged him seven years. He must destroy the utter Neeltje. He must midnightly massacre the angel child and her mother. He must dip his arms in blood to the elbows.

Trescott took the first opportunity to express to him his concern over the affair, but when the subject of the disaster was mentioned, old Eldridge, to the doctor's great surprise, actually chuckled long and deeply. "Oh, well, look-a-here," he said. "I never was so much in love with them there damn curls. The curls was purty—yes—but then I'd a darn sight rather see boys look more like boys than like two little wax figgers. An', ye know, the little cusses like it themselves. *They* never took no stock in all this washin' an' combin' an' fixin' an' goin' to church an' paradin' an' showin' off. They stood it because they were told to. That's all. Of course this here Neel-te-gee, er whatever his name is, is a plumb dumb ijit, but I don't see what's to be done, now that the kids is full well cropped. I might go and burn his shop over his head, but that wouldn't bring no hair back onto the kids. They're even kicking on sashes now, and that's all right, 'cause what fer does a boy want a sash?"

Whereupon Trescott perceived that the old man wore his brains above his shoulders, and Trescott departed from him rejoicing greatly that it was only women who could not know that there was finality to most disasters, and that when a thing was fully done, no amount of door-slammings, rushing up-stairs and down-stairs, calls, lamentations, tears, could bring back a single hair to the heads of twins.

But the rains came and the winds blew in the most biblical way when a certain fact came to light in the Trescott household. Little Cora, corroborated by Jimmie, innocently remarked that five dollars had been given her by her father on her birthday, and with this money the evil had been wrought. Trescott had known it, but he—thoughtful man—had said nothing. For her part, the mother of the angel child had up to that moment never reflected that the consummation of the wickedness must have cost a small sum of money. But now it was all clear to her. He was the guilty one—he! "My angel child!"

The scene which ensued was inspiriting. A few days later, loungers at the railway station saw a lady leading a shorn and still undaunted lamb. Attached to them was a husband and father, who was plainly bewildered, but still more plainly vexed, as if he would be saying: "Damn 'em! Why can't they leave me alone?"

II

LYNX-HUNTING

Jimmie lounged about the dining-room and watched his mother with large, serious eyes. Suddenly he said, "Ma—now—can I borrow pa's gun?"

She was overcome with the feminine horror which is able to mistake preliminary words for the full accomplishment of the dread thing. "Why, Jimmie!" she cried. "Of al-l wonders! Your father's gun! No indeed you can't!"

He was fairly well crushed, but he managed to mutter, sullenly, "Well, Willie Dalzel, he's got a gun." In reality his heart had previously been beating with such tumult—he had himself been so impressed with the daring and sin of his request—that he was glad that all was over

now, and his mother could do very little further harm to his sensibilities. He had been influenced into the venture by the larger boys.

"Huh!" the Dalzel urchin had said; "your father's got a gun, hasn't
he? Well, why don't you bring that?"

Puffing himself, Jimmie had replied, "Well, I can, if I want to." It
was a black lie, but really the Dalzel boy was too outrageous with his
eternal bill-posting about the gun which a beaming uncle had in-
trusted to him. Its possession made him superior in manfulness to most
boys in the neighborhood—for at least they enviously conceded him such
position—but he was so overbearing, and stuffed the fact of his treasure
so relentlessly down their throats, that on this occasion the miserable
Jimmie had lied as naturally as most animals swim.

Willie Dalzel had not been checkmated, for he had instantly retorted, "Why don't you get it, then?"

"Well, I can, if I want to."

"Well, get it, then!"

"Well, I can, if I want to."

Thereupon Jimmie had paced away with great airs of surety as far as
the door of his home, where his manner changed to one of tremulous
misgiving as it came upon him to address his mother in the dining-
room. There had happened that which had happened.

When Jimmie returned to his two distinguished companions he was
blown out with a singular pomposity. He spoke these noble words:
"Oh, well, I guess I don't want to take the gun out today."

They had been watching him with gleaming ferret eyes, and they
detected his falsity at once. They challenged him with shouted gibes,
but it was not in the rules for the conduct of boys that one should
admit anything whatsoever, and so Jimmie, backed into an ethical
corner, lied as stupidly, as desperately, as hopelessly as ever lone savage
fights when surrounded at last in his jungle.

Such accusations were never known to come to any point, for the
reason that the number and kind of denials always equaled or ex-
ceeded the number of accusations, and no boy was ever brought really
to book for these misdeeds.

In the end they went off together, Willie Dalzel with his gun being a trifle in advance and discoursing upon his various works. They passed along a maple-lined avenue, a highway common to boys bound for that free land of hills and woods in which they lived in some part their romance of the moment, whether it was of Indians, miners, smugglers, soldiers, or outlaws. The paths were their paths, and much was known to them of the secrets of the dark green hemlock thickets, the wastes of sweet-fern and huckleberry, the cliffs of gaunt bluestone with the sumac burning red at their feet. Each boy had, I am sure, a conviction that some day the wilderness was to give forth to him a marvelous secret. They felt that the hills and the forest knew much, and they heard a voice of it in the silence. It was vague, thrilling, fearful, and altogether fabulous. The grown folk seemed to regard these wastes merely as so much distance between one place and another place, or as a rabbit-cover, or as a district to be judged according to the value of the timber; but to the boys it spoke some great inspiring word, which they knew even as those who pace the shore know the enigmatic speech of the surf. In the mean time they lived there, in season, lives of ringing adventure—by dint of imagination.

The boys left the avenue, skirted hastily through some private grounds, climbed a fence, and entered the thickets. It happened that at school the previous day Willie Dalzel had been forced to read and acquire in some part a solemn description of a lynx. The meager information thrust upon him had caused him grimaces of suffering, but now he said, suddenly, "I'm goin' to shoot a lynx."

The other boys admired this statement, but they were silent for a time. Finally Jimmie said, meekly, "What's a lynx?" He had endured his ignorance as long as he was able.

The Dalzel boy mocked him. "Why, don't you know what a lynx is? A lynx? Why, a lynx is a animal somethin' like a cat, an' it's got great big green eyes, and it sits on the limb of a tree an' jus' glares at you. It's a pretty bad animal, I tell you. Why, when I—"

"Huh!" said the third boy. "Where'd you ever see a lynx?"

"Oh, I've seen 'em—plenty of 'em. I bet you'd be scared if you seen one once."

Jimmie and the other boy each demanded, "How do you know I would?"

They penetrated deeper into the wood. They climbed a rocky zigzag path which led them at times where with their hands they could almost touch the tops of giant pines. The gray cliffs sprang sheer towards the sky. Willie Dalzel babbled about his impossible lynx, and they stalked the mountain-side like chamois-hunters, although no noise of bird or beast broke the stillness of the hills. Below them Whilomville was spread out somewhat like the cheap green and black lithograph of the time—"A Bird's-eye View of Whilomville, N. Y."

In the end the boys reached the top of the mountain and scouted off among wild and desolate ridges. They were burning with the desire to slay large animals. They thought continually of elephants, lions, tigers, crocodiles. They discoursed upon their immaculate conduct in case such monsters confronted them, and they all lied carefully about their courage.

The breeze was heavy with the smell of sweet-fern. The pines and hemlocks sighed as they waved their branches. In the hollows the leaves of the laurels were lacquered where the sunlight found them. No matter the weather, it would be impossible to long continue an expedition of this kind without a fire, and presently they built one, snapping down for fuel the brittle under-branches of the pines. About this fire they were willed to conduct a sort of play, the Dalzel boy taking the part of a bandit chief, and the other boys being his trusty lieutenants. They stalked to and fro, long-strided, stern yet devil-may-care, three terrible little figures.

Jimmie had an uncle who made game of him whenever he caught him in this kind of play, and often this uncle quoted derisively the following classic: "Once aboard the lugger, Bill, and the girl is mine. Now to burn the château and destroy all evidence of our crime. But, hark'e, Bill, no wiolence." Wheeling abruptly, he addressed these dramatic words to his comrades. They were impressed; they decided at once to be smugglers, and in the most ribald fashion they talked about carrying off young women.

At last they continued their march through the woods. The smuggling *motif* was now grafted fantastically upon the original lynx idea, which Willie Dalzel refused to abandon at any price.

Once they came upon an innocent bird who happened to be looking another way at the time. After a great deal of maneuvering and big words, Willie Dalzel reared his fowling-piece and blew this poor thing into a mere rag of wet feathers, of which he was proud.

Afterwards the other big boy had a turn at another bird. Then it was plainly Jimmie's chance. The two others had, of course, some thought of cheating him out of this chance, but of a truth he was timid to explode such a thunderous weapon, and as soon as they detected this fear they simply overbore him, and made it clearly understood that if he refused to shoot he would lose his caste, his scalp-lock, his girdle, his honor.

They had reached the old death-colored snake-fence which marked the limits of the upper pasture of the Fleming farm. Under some hickory-trees the path ran parallel to the fence. Behold! a small priestly chipmunk came to a rail, and folding his hands on his abdomen, addressed them in his own tongue. It was Jimmie's shot. Adjured by the others, he took the gun. His face was stiff with apprehension. The Dalzel boy was giving forth fine words. "Go ahead. Aw, don't be afraid. It's nothin' to do. Why, I've done it a million times. Don't shut both your eyes, now. Jus' keep one open and shut the other one. He'll get away if you don't watch out. Now you're all right. Why don't you let 'er go? Go ahead."

Jimmie, with his legs braced apart, was in the center of the path. His back was greatly bent, owing to the mechanics of supporting the heavy gun. His companions were screeching in the rear. There was a wait.

Then he pulled trigger. To him there was a frightful roar, his cheek and his shoulder took a stunning blow, his face felt a hot flush of fire, and opening his two eyes, he found that he was still alive. He was not too dazed to instantly adopt a becoming egotism. It had been the first shot of his life.

But directly after the well-mannered celebration of this victory a certain cow, which had been grazing in the line of fire, was seen to break wildly across the pasture, bellowing and bucking. The three smugglers and lynx-hunters looked at each other out of blanched faces. Jimmie had hit the cow. The first evidence of his comprehension of this fact was in the celerity with which he returned the discharged gun to Willie Dalzel.

They turned to flee. The land was black, as if it had been over-shadowed suddenly with thick storm-clouds, and even as they fled in their horror a gigantic Swedish farm-hand came from the heavens and fell upon them, shrieking in eerie triumph. In a twinkle they were clouted prostrate. The Swede was elate and ferocious in a foreign and fulsome way. He continued to beat them and yell.

From the ground they raised their dismal appeal. "Oh, please, mister, we didn't do it! He did it! I didn't do it! We didn't do it! We didn't mean to do it! Oh, please, mister!"

In these moments of childish terror little lads go half-blind, and it is possible that few moments of their after-life made them suffer as they did when the Swede flung them over the fence and marched them towards the farmhouse. They begged like cowards on the scaffold, and each one was for himself. "Oh, please let me go, mister! I didn't do it, mister! He did it! Oh, p-l-ease let me go, mister!"

The boyish view belongs to boys alone, and if this tall and knotted laborer was needlessly without charity, none of the three lads questioned it. Usually when they were punished they decided that they deserved it, and the more they were punished the more they were convinced that they were criminals of a most subterranean type. As to the hitting of the cow being a pure accident, and therefore not of necessity a criminal matter, such reading never entered their heads. When things happened and they were caught, they commonly paid dire consequences, and they were accustomed to measure the probabilities of woe utterly by the damage done, and not in any way by the culpability. The shooting of the cow was plainly heinous, and undoubtedly their dungeons would be knee-deep in water.

"He did it, mister!" This was a general outcry. Jimmie used it as often as did the others. As for them, it is certain that they had no direct thought of betraying their comrade for their own salvation. They thought themselves guilty because they were caught; when boys were not caught they might possibly be innocent. But captured boys were guilty. When they cried out that Jimmie was the culprit, it was principally a simple expression of terror.

Old Henry Fleming, the owner of the farm, strode across the pasture towards them. He had in his hand a most cruel whip. This whip he flourished. At his approach the boys suffered the agonies of the fire regions. And yet anybody with half an eye could see that the whip in his hand was a mere accident, and that he was a kind old man—when he cared.

When he had come near he spoke crisply. "What you boys ben doin' to my cow?" The tone had deep threat in it. They all answered by saying that none of them had shot the cow. Their denials were tearful and clamorous, and they crawled knee by knee. The vision of it was like three martyrs being dragged towards the stake. Old Fleming stood there, grim, tight-lipped. After a time he said, "Which boy done it?"

There was some confusion, and then Jimmie spake. "I done it, mister."

Fleming looked at him. Then he asked, "Well, what did you shoot 'er fer?"

Jimmie thought, hesitated, decided, faltered, and then formulated this: "I thought she was a lynx."

Old Fleming and his Swede at once lay down in the grass and laughed themselves helpless.

III

THE LOVER AND THE TELLTALE

WHEN the angel child returned with her parents to New York, the fond heart of Jimmie Trescott felt its bruise greatly. For two days he simply moped, becoming a stranger to all former joys. When his old comrades yelled invitation, as they swept off on some interesting quest, he replied with mournful gestures of disillusion.

He thought often of writing to her, but of course the shame of it made him pause. Write a letter to a girl? The mere enormity of the idea caused him shudders. Persons of his quality never wrote letters to girls. Such was the occupation of mollycoddles and snivelers. He knew that if his acquaintances and friends found in him evidences of such weakness and general milkiness, they would fling themselves upon him like so many wolves, and bait him beyond the borders of sanity.

However, one day at school, in that time of the morning session when children of his age were allowed fifteen minutes of play in the school-grounds, he did not as usual rush forth ferociously to his games. Commonly he was of the worst hoodlums, preying upon his weaker brethren with all the cruel disregard of a grown man. On this particular morning he stayed in the school-room, and with his tongue stuck from the corner of his mouth, and his head twisting in a painful way, he wrote to little Cora, pouring out to her all the poetry of his hungry soul, as follows: "My dear Cora I love thee with all my hart oh come bac again, bac, bac gain for I love thee best of all oh come bac again When the spring come again we'l fly and we'l fly like a brid."

As for the last word, he knew under normal circumstances perfectly well how to spell "bird," but in this case he had transposed two of the letters through excitement, supreme agitation.

Nor had this letter been composed without fear and furtive glancing. There was always a number of children who, for the time, cared more for the quiet of the school-room than for the tempest of the playground, and there was always that dismal company who were being forcibly deprived of their recess—who were being "kept in." More than one curious eye was turned upon the desperate and lawless Jimmie Trescott suddenly taken to ways of peace, and as he felt these eyes he flushed guiltily, with felonious glances from side to side.

It happened that a certain vigilant little girl had a seat directly across the aisle from Jimmie's seat, and she had remained in the room during the intermission, because of her interest in some absurd domestic details concerning her desk. Parenthetically it might be stated that she was in the habit of imagining this desk to be a house, and at this time, with an important little frown, indicative of a proper matron, she was engaged in dramatizing her ideas of a household.

But this small Rose Goldege happened to be of a family which numbered few males. It was, in fact, one of those curious middle-class families that hold much of their ground, retain most of their position, after all their visible means of support have been dropped in the grave. It contained now only a collection of women who existed submissively, defiantly, securely, mysteriously, in a pretentious and often exasperating virtue. It was often too triumphantly clear that they were free of bad habits. However, bad habits is a term here used in a commoner meaning, because it is certainly true that the principal and indeed solitary joy which entered their lonely lives was the joy of talking wickedly and busily about their neighbors. It was all done without dream of its being of the vulgarity of the alleys. Indeed it was simply a constitutional but not incredible chastity and honesty expressing itself in its ordinary superior way of the whirling circles of life, and the vehemence of the criticism was not lessened by a further infusion of an acid of worldly defeat, worldly suffering, and worldly hopelessness.

Out of this family circle had sprung the typical little girl who discovered Jimmie Trescott agonizingly writing a letter to his sweetheart. Of course all the children were the most abandoned gossips, but she was peculiarly adapted to the purpose of making Jimmie miserable over this particular point. It was her life to sit of evenings about the stove and hearken to her mother and a lot of spinsters talk of many things. During these evenings she was never licensed to utter an opinion either one way or the other way. She was then simply a very little girl sitting open-eyed in the gloom, and listening to many things which she often interpreted wrongly. They on their part kept up a kind of a smug-faced pretense of concealing from her information in detail of the widespread crime, which pretense may have been more elaborately dangerous than no pretense at all. Thus all her home-teaching fitted her to recognize at once in Jimmie Trescott's manner that he was concealing something that would properly interest the world. She set up a scream. "Oh! Oh! Oh! Jimmie Trescott's writing to his girl! Oh! Oh!"

Jimmie cast a miserable glance upon her—a glance in which hatred mingled with despair. Through the open window he could hear the boisterous cries of his friends—his hoodlum friends—who would no more understand the utter poetry of his position than they would understand an ancient tribal sign-language. His face was set in a truer expression of horror than any of the romances describe upon the features of a man flung into a moat, a man shot in the breast with an arrow, a man cleft in the neck with a battle-ax. He was suppedaneous of the fullest power of childish pain. His one course was to rush upon her and attempt, by an impossible means of strangulation, to keep her important news from the public.

The teacher, a thoughtful young woman at her desk upon the plat-form, saw a little scuffle which informed her that two of her scholars were larking. She called out sharply. The command penetrated to the middle of an early world struggle. In Jimmie's age there was no par-ticular scruple in the minds of the male sex against laying warrior hands upon their weaker sisters. But, of course, this voice from the throne hindered Jimmie in what might have been a berserk attack.

Even the little girl was retarded by the voice, but, without being un-lawful, she managed soon to shy through the door and out upon the play-ground, yelling, "Oh, Jimmie Trescott's been writing to his girl!"

The unhappy Jimmie was following as closely as he was allowed by his knowledge of the decencies to be preserved under the eye of the teacher.

Jimmie himself was mainly responsible for the scene which ensued on the play-ground. It is possible that the little girl might have run, shriek-ing his infamy, without exciting more than a general but unmilitant interest. These barbarians were excited only by the actual appearance of human woe; in that event they cheered and danced. Jimmie made the strategic mistake of pursuing little Rose, and thus exposed his thin skin to the whole school. He had in his cowering mind a vision of a hun-dred children turning from their play under the maple-trees and speed-ing towards him over the gravel with sudden wild taunts. Upon him drove a yelping demoniac mob, to which his words were futile. He saw in this mob boys that he dimly knew, and his deadly enemies, and his retainers, and his most intimate friends. The virulence of his deadly enemy was no greater than the virulence of his intimate friend. From the outskirts the little informer could be heard still screaming the news, like a toy parrot with clock-work inside of it. It broke up all sorts of games, not so much because of the mere fact of the letter-writing, as because the children knew that some sufferer was at the last point, and, like little blood-fanged wolves, they thronged to the scene of his destruction. They galloped about him shrilly chanting insults. He turned from one to another, only to meet with howls. He was baited.

Then, in one instant, he changed all this with a blow. Bang! The most pitiless of the boys near him received a punch, fairly and skillfully, which made him bellow out like a walrus, and then Jimmie laid desperately into the whole world, striking out frenziedly in all directions. Boys who could handily whip him, and knew it, backed away from this onslaught. Here was intention—serious intention. They themselves were not in frenzy, and their cooler judgment respected Jimmie's efforts when he ran amuck. They saw that it really was none of their affair. In the mean time the wretched little girl who had caused the bloody riot was away, by the fence, weeping because boys were fighting.

Jimmie several times hit the wrong boy—that is to say, he several times hit a wrong boy hard enough to arouse also in him a spirit of strife. Jimmie wore a little shirt-waist. It was passing now rapidly into oblivion. He was sobbing, and there was one blood-stain upon his cheek. The school-ground sounded like a pine-tree when a hundred crows roost in it at night.

Then upon the situation there pealed a brazen bell. It was a bell that these children obeyed, even as older nations obey the formal law which is printed in calf-skin. It smote them into some sort of inaction; even Jimmie was influenced by its potency, although, as a finale, he kicked out lustily into the legs of an intimate friend who had been one of the foremost in the torture.

When they came to form into line for the march into the school-room it was curious that Jimmie had many admirers. It was not his prowess; it was the soul he had infused into his gymnastics; and he, still panting, looked about him with a stern and challenging glare.

And yet when the long tramping line had entered the school-room his status had again changed. The other children then began to regard him as a boy in disrepair, and boys in disrepair were always accosted ominously from the throne. Jimmie's march towards his seat was a feat. It was composed partly of a most slinking attempt to dodge the perception of the teacher and partly of pure braggadocio erected for the benefit of his observant fellow-men.

The teacher looked carefully down at him. "Jimmie Trescott," she said.

"Yes'm," he answered, with businesslike briskness, which really spelled out falsity in all its letters.

"Come up to the desk."

He rose amid the awe of the entire school-room. When he arrived she said,

"Jimmie, you've been fighting."

"Yes'm," he answered. This was not so much an admission of the fact as it was a concessional answer to anything she might say.

"Who have you been fighting?" she asked.

"I dunno', 'm."

Whereupon the empress blazed out in wrath. "You don't know who you've been fighting?"

Jimmie looked at her gloomily. "No, 'm."

She seemed about to disintegrate to mere flaming fagots of anger. "You don't know who you've been fighting?" she demanded, blazing. "Well, you stay in after school until you find out."

As he returned to his place all the children knew by his vanquished air that sorrow had fallen upon the house of Trescott. When he took his seat he saw gloating upon him the satanic black eyes of the little Goldege girl.

IV

"SHOWIN' OFF"

JIMMIE TRESCOTT's new velocipede had the largest front wheel of any velocipede in Whilomville. When it first arrived from New York he wished to sacrifice school, food, and sleep to it. Evidently he wished to become a sort of a perpetual velocipede-rider. But the powers of the family laid a number of judicious embargoes upon him, and he was prevented from becoming a fanatic. Of course this caused him to retain a fondness for the three-wheeled thing much longer than if he had been allowed to debauch himself for a span of days. But in the end it was an immaterial machine to him. For long periods he left it idle in the stable.

One day he loitered from school towards home by a very circuitous route. He was accompanied by only one of his retainers. The object of this detour was the wooing of a little girl in a red hood. He had been in love with her for some three weeks. His desk was near her desk in school, but he had never spoken to her. He had been afraid to take such a radical step. It was not customary to speak to girls. Even boys who had school-going sisters seldom addressed them during that part of a day which was devoted to education.

The reasons for this conduct were very plain. First, the more robust boys considered talking with girls an unmanly occupation; second, the greater part of the boys were afraid; third, they had no idea of what to say, because they esteemed the proper sentences should be supernaturally incisive and eloquent. In consequence, a small contingent of blue-eyed weaklings were the sole intimates of the frail sex, and for it they were boisterously and disdainfully called "girl-boys."

But this situation did not prevent serious and ardent wooing. For instance, Jimmie and the little girl who wore the red hood must have exchanged glances at least two hundred times in every school-hour, and this exchange of glances accomplished everything. In them the two children renewed their curious inarticulate vows.

Jimmie had developed a devotion to school which was the admiration of his father and mother. In the mornings he was so impatient to have it made known to him that no misfortune had befallen his romance during the night that he was actually detected at times feverishly listening for the "first bell." Dr. Trescott was exceedingly complacent of the change, and as for Mrs. Trescott, she had ecstatic visions of a white-haired Jimmie leading the nations in knowledge, comprehending all from bugs to comets. It was merely the doing of the little girl in the red hood.

When Jimmie made up his mind to follow his sweetheart home from school, the project seemed such an arbitrary and shameless innovation that he hastily lied to himself about it. No, he was not following Abbie. He was merely making his way homeward through the new and rather longer route of Bryant Street and Oakland Park. It had nothing at all to do with a girl. It was a mere eccentric notion.

"Come on," said Jimmie, gruffly, to his retainer. "Let's go home this way."

"What fer?" demanded the retainer.

"Oh, b'cause."

"Huh?"

"Oh, it's more fun—goin' this way."

The retainer was bored and loath, but that mattered very little. He did not know how to disobey his chief. Together they followed the trail of red-hooded Abbie and another small girl. These latter at once understood the object of the chase, and looking back giggling, they pretended to quicken their pace. But they were always looking back. Jimmie now began his courtship in earnest. The first thing to do was to prove his strength in battle. This was transacted by means of the retainer. He took that devoted boy and flung him heavily to the ground, meanwhile mouthing a preposterous ferocity.

The retainer accepted this behavior with a sort of bland resignation. After his overthrow he raised himself, coolly brushed some dust and dead leaves from his clothes, and then seemed to forget the incident.

"I can jump farther'n you can," said Jimmie in a loud voice.

"I know it," responded the retainer, simply.

But this would not do. There must be a contest.

"Come on," shouted Jimmie, imperiously. "Let's see you jump."

The retainer selected a footing on the curb, balanced and calculated a moment, and jumped without enthusiasm. Jimmie's leap of course was longer.

"There!" he cried, blowing out his lips. "I beat you, didn't I? Easy. I beat you." He made a great hubbub, as if the affair was unprecedented.

"Yes," admitted the other, emotionless.

Later, Jimmie forced his retainer to run a race with him, held more jumping matches, flung him twice to earth, and generally behaved as if a retainer was indestructible. If the retainer had been in the plot, it is conceivable that he would have endured this treatment with mere whispered, half-laughing protests. But he was not in the plot at all, and so he became enigmatic. One cannot often sound the profound well in which lie the meanings of boyhood.

Following the two little girls, Jimmie eventually passed into that suburb of Whilomville which is called Oakland Park. At his heels came a badly battered retainer. Oakland Park was a somewhat strange country to the boys. They were dubious of the manners and customs, and of course they would have to meet the local chieftains, who might look askance upon this invasion.

Jimmie's girl departed into her home with a last backward glance that almost blinded the thrilling boy. On this pretext and that pretext, he kept his retainer in play before the house. He had hopes that she would emerge as soon as she had deposited her school-bag.

A boy came along the walk. Jimmie knew him at school. He was Tommie Semple, one of the weaklings who made friends with the fair sex. "Hello, Tom," said Jimmie. "You live round here?"

"Yeh," said Tom, with composed pride. At school he was afraid of Jimmie, but he did not evince any of this fear as he strolled well inside his own frontiers. Jimmie and his retainer had not expected this boy to display the manners of a minor chief, and they contemplated him attentively. There was a silence. Finally Jimmie said:

"I can put you down." He moved forward briskly. "Can't I?" he demanded.

The challenged boy backed away. "I know you can," he declared, frankly and promptly.

The little girl in the red hood had come out with a hoop. She looked at Jimmie with an air of insolent surprise in the fact that he still existed, and began to trundle her hoop off towards some other little girls who were shrilly playing near a nurse-maid and a perambulator.

Jimmie adroitly shifted his position until he too was playing near the perambulator, pretentiously making mince-meat out of his retainer and Tommie Semple.

Of course little Abbie had defined the meaning of Jimmie's appearance in Oakland Park. Despite this nonchalance and grand air of accident, nothing could have been more plain. Whereupon she of course became insufferably vain in manner, and whenever Jimmie came near her she tossed her head and turned away her face, and daintily swished her skirts as if he were contagion itself. But Jimmie was happy. His soul was satisfied with the mere presence of the beloved object so long as he could feel that she furtively gazed upon him from time to time and noted his extraordinary prowess, which he was proving upon the persons of his retainer and Tommie Semple. And he was making an impression. There could be no doubt of it. He had many times caught her eye fixed admiringly upon him as he mauled the retainer. Indeed, all the little girls gave attention to his deeds, and he was the hero of the hour.

Presently a boy on a velocipede was seen to be tooling down towards them. "Who's this comin'?" said Jimmie, bluntly, to the Semple boy.

"That's Horace Glenn," said Tommie, "an' he's got a new velocipede, an' he can ride it like anything."

"Can you lick him?" asked Tommie.

"I don't—I never fought with 'im," answered the other. He bravely tried to appear as a man of respectable achievement, but with Horace coming towards them the risk was too great. However, he added, "*Maybe* I could."

The advent of Horace on his new velocipede created a sensation which he haughtily accepted as a familiar thing. Only Jimmie and his retainer remained silent and impassive. Horace eyed the two invaders.

"Hello, Jimmie!"

"Hello, Horace!"

After the typical silence Jimmie said, pompously, "I got a velocipede."

"Have you?" asked Horace, anxiously. He did not wish anybody in the world but himself to possess a velocipede.

"Yes," sang Jimmie. "An' it's a bigger one than that, too! A good deal bigger! An' it's a better one, too!"

"Huh!" retorted Horace, skeptically.

" 'Ain't I, Clarence? 'Ain't I? 'Ain't I got one bigger'n that?"

The retainer answered with alacrity:

"Yes, he has! A good deal bigger! An' it's a dindy, too!"

This corroboration rather disconcerted Horace, but he continued to scoff at any statement that Jimmie also owned a velocipede. As for the contention that this supposed velocipede could be larger than his own, he simply wouldn't hear of it.

Jimmie had been a very gallant figure before the coming of Horace, but the new velocipede had relegated him to a squalid secondary position. So he affected to look with contempt upon it. Voluminously he bragged of the velocipede in the stable at home. He painted its virtues and beauty in loud and extravagant words, flaming words. And the retainer stood by, glibly endorsing everything.

The little company heeded him, and he passed on vociferously from extravagance to utter impossibility. Horace was very sick of it. His defense was reduced to a mere mechanical grumbling: "Don't believe you got one 'tall. Don't believe you got one 'tall."

Jimmie turned upon him suddenly. "How fast can you go? How fast can you go?" he demanded. "Let's see. I bet you can't go fast."

Horace lifted his spirits and answered with proper defiance. "Can't I?" he mocked. "Can't I?"

"No, you can't," said Jimmie. "You can't go fast."

Horace cried: "Well, you see me now! I'll show you! I'll show you if I can go fast!" Taking a firm seat on his vermilion machine, he pedaled furiously up the walk, turned, and pedaled back again. "There, now!" he shouted, triumphantly: "Ain't that fast? There, now!" There was a low murmur of appreciation from the little girls. Jimmie saw with pain that even his divinity was smiling upon his rival. "There! Ain't that fast? Ain't that fast?" He strove to pin Jimmie down to an admission. He was exuberant with victory.

Notwithstanding a feeling of discomfiture, Jimmie did not lose a moment of time. "Why," he yelled, "that ain't goin' fast 'tall! That ain't goin' fast 'tall. Why, I can go almost *twice* as fast as that! Almost *twice* as fast! Can't I, Clarence?"

The royal retainer nodded solemnly at the wide-eyed group. "Course you can!"

"Why," spouted Jimmie, "you just ought to see me ride once! You just ought to see me! Why, I can go like the wind! Can't I, Clarence? And I can ride far, too—oh, awful far! Can't I, Clarence? Why, I wouldn't have that one! 'Tain't any good! You just ought to see mine once!"

The overwhelmed Horace attempted to reconstruct his battered glories. "I can ride right over the curb-stone—at some of the crossin's," he announced, brightly.

Jimmie's derision was a splendid sight. " '*Right over the curb-stone!*' Why, that wouldn't be *nothin'* for me to do! I've rode mine down Bridge Street hill. Yessir! 'Ain't I, Clarence? Why, it ain't nothin' to ride over a curb-stone—not for *me!* Is it, Clarence?"

"Down Bridge Street hill? You never!" said Horace, hopelessly.

"Well, didn't I, Clarence? Didn't I, now?"

The faithful retainer again nodded solemnly at the assemblage.

At last Horace, having fallen as low as was possible, began to display a spirit for climbing up again. "Oh, you can do wonders!" he said, laughing. "You can do wonders! I s'pose you could ride down that bank there?" he asked, with art. He had indicated a grassy terrace some six feet in height which bounded one side of the walk. At the bottom was a small ravine in which the reckless had flung ashes and tins. "I s'pose you could ride down that bank?"

All eyes now turned upon Jimmie to detect a sign of his weakening, but he instantly and sublimely arose to the occasion. "That bank?" he asked, scornfully. "Why, I've ridden down banks like that many a time. 'Ain't I, Clarence?"

This was too much for the company. A sound like the wind in the leaves arose; it was the song of incredulity and ridicule. "O—o—o—o—o!" And on the outskirts a little girl suddenly shrieked out, "Storyteller!"

Horace had certainly won a skirmish. He was gleeful. "Oh, you can do wonders!" he gurgled. "You can do wonders!" The neighborhood's superficial hostility to foreigners arose like magic under the influence of his sudden success, and Horace had the delight of seeing Jimmie persecuted in that manner known only to children and insects.

Jimmie called angrily to the boy on the velocipede, "If you'll lend me yours, I'll show you whether I can or not."

Horace turned his superior nose in the air. "Oh no! I don't ever lend it." Then he thought of a blow which would make Jimmie's humiliation complete. "Besides," he said, airily, "'tain't really anything hard to do. I could do it—easy—if I wanted to."

But his supposed adherents, instead of receiving this boast with cheers, looked upon him in a sudden blank silence. Jimmie and his retainer pounced like cats upon their advantage.

"Oh," they yelled, "you *could,* eh? Well, let's see you do it, then! Let's see you do it! Let's see you do it! Now!" In a moment the crew of little spectators were gibing at Horace.

The blow that would make Jimmie's humiliation complete! Instead, it had boomeranged Horace into the mud. He kept up a sullen muttering:

"'Tain't really anything! I could if I wanted to!"

"Dare you to!" screeched Jimmie and his partisans. "Dare you to! Dare you to! Dare you to!"

There were two things to be done—to make gallant effort or to retreat. Somewhat to their amazement, the children at last found Horace moving through their clamor to the edge of the bank. Sitting on the velocipede, he looked at the ravine, and then, with gloomy pride, at the other children. A hush came upon them, for it was seen that he was intending to make some kind of an ante-mortem statement.

"I—" he began. Then he vanished from the edge of the walk. The start had been unintentional—an accident.

The stupefied Jimmie saw the calamity through a haze. His first clear vision was when Horace, with a face as red as a red flag, arose bawling from his tangled velocipede. He and his retainer exchanged a glance of horror and fled the neighborhood. They did not look back until they had reached the top of the hill near the lake. They could see Horace walking slowly under the maples towards his home, pushing his shattered velocipede before him. His chin was thrown high, and the breeze bore them the sound of his howls.

V

MAKING AN ORATOR

In the school at Whilomville it was the habit, when children had progressed to a certain class, to have them devote Friday afternoon to what was called elocution. This was in the piteously ignorant belief that orators were thus made. By process of school law, unfortunate boys and girls were dragged up to address their fellow-scholars in the literature of the mid-century. Probably the children who were most capable of expressing themselves, the children who were most sensitive to the power of speech, suffered the most wrong. Little blockheads who could learn eight lines of conventional poetry, and could get up and spin it rapidly at their classmates, did not undergo a single pang. The plan operated mainly to agonize many children permanently against arising to speak their thought to fellow-creatures.

Jimmie Trescott had an idea that by exhibition of undue ignorance he could escape from being promoted into the first class room which exacted such penalty from its inmates. He preferred to dwell in a less classic shade rather than venture into a domain where he was obliged to perform a certain duty which struck him as being worse than death. However, willy-nilly, he was somehow sent ahead into the place of torture.

Every Friday at least ten of the little children had to mount the stage beside the teacher's desk and babble something which none of them understood. This was to make them orators. If it had been ordered that they should croak like frogs, it would have advanced most of them just as far towards oratory.

Alphabetically Jimmie Trescott was near the end of the list of victims, but his time was none the less inevitable. "Tanner, Timmens, Trass, Trescott—" He saw his downfall approaching.

He was passive to the teacher while she drove into his mind the incomprehensible lines of "The Charge of the Light Brigade":

> Half a league, half a league,
> Half a league onward—

He had no conception of a league. If in the ordinary course of life somebody had told him that he was half a league from home, he might have been frightened that half a league was fifty miles; but he struggled manfully with the valley of death and a mystic six hundred, who were performing something there which was very fine, he had been told. He learned all the verses.

But as his own Friday afternoon approached he was moved to make known to his family that a dreadful disease was upon him, and was likely at any time to prevent him from going to his beloved school.

On the great Friday when the children of his initials were to speak their pieces Dr. Trescott was away from home, and the mother of the boy was alarmed beyond measure at Jimmie's curious illness, which caused him to lie on the rug in front of the fire and groan cavernously.

She bathed his feet in hot mustard water until they were lobster red. She also placed a mustard-plaster on his chest.

He announced that these remedies did him no good at all—no good at all. With an air of martyrdom he endured a perfect downpour of motherly attention all that day. Thus the first Friday was passed in safety.

With singular patience he sat before the fire in the dining-room and looked at picture-books, only complaining of pain when he suspected his mother of thinking that he was getting better.

The next day being Saturday and a holiday, he was miraculously delivered from the arms of disease, and went forth to play, a blatantly healthy boy.

He had no further attack until Thursday night of the next week, when he announced that he felt very, very poorly. The mother was already chronically alarmed over the condition of her son, but Dr. Trescott asked him questions which denoted some incredulity. On the third Friday Jimmie was dropped at the door of the school from the doctor's buggy. The other children, notably those who had already passed over the mountain of distress, looked at him with glee, seeing in him another lamb brought to butchery. Seated at his desk in the school-room, Jimmie sometimes remembered with dreadful distinctness every line of "The Charge of the Light Brigade," and at other times his mind was utterly empty of it. Geography, arithmetic, and spelling—usually great tasks—quite rolled off him. His mind was dwelling with terror upon the time when his name should be called and he was obliged to go up to the platform, turn, bow, and recite his message to his fellow-men.

Desperate expedients for delay came to him. If he could have engaged the services of a real pain, he would have been glad. But steadily, inexorably, the minutes marched on towards his great crisis, and all his plans for escape blended into a mere panic fear.

The maples outside were defeating the weakening rays of the afternoon sun, and in the shadowed school-room had come a stillness, in which, nevertheless, one could feel the complacence of the little pupils who had already passed through the flames. They were calmly prepared to recognize as a spectacle the torture of others.

Little Johnnie Tanner opened the ceremony. He stamped heavily up to the platform, and bowed in such a manner that he almost fell down. He blurted out that it would ill befit him to sit silent while the name of his fair Ireland was being reproached, and he appealed to the gal-

lant soldier before him if every British battle-field was not sown with
the bones of sons of the Emerald Isle. He was also heard to say that
he had listened with deepening surprise and scorn to the insinuation of
the honorable member from North Glenmorganshire that the loyalty
of the Irish regiments in her Majesty's service could be questioned. To
what purpose, then, he asked, had the blood of Irishmen flowed on a
hundred fields? To what purpose had Irishmen gone to their death
with bravery and devotion in every part of the world where the victorious flag of England had been carried? If the honorable member for
North Glenmorganshire insisted upon construing a mere pothouse
row between soldiers in Dublin into a grand treachery to the colors and
to her Majesty's uniform, then it was time for Ireland to think bitterly
of her dead sons, whose graves now marked every step of England's
progress, and yet who could have their honors stripped from them so
easily by the honorable member for North Glenmorganshire. Furthermore, the honorable member for North Glenmorganshire—

It is needless to say that little Johnnie Tanner's language made it
exceedingly hot for the honorable member for North Glenmorganshire. But Johnny was not angry. He was only in haste. He finished
the honorable member for North Glenmorganshire in what might be
called a gallop.

Susie Timmens then went to the platform, and with a face as pale
as death whisperingly reiterated that she would be Queen of the May.
The child represented there a perfect picture of unnecessary suffering.
Her small lips were quite blue, and her eyes, opened wide, stared with
a look of horror at nothing.

The phlegmatic Trass boy, with his moon face only expressing peasant parentage, calmly spoke some undeniably true words concerning
destiny.

In his seat Jimmie Trescott was going half blind with fear of his approaching doom. He wished that the Trass boy would talk forever
about destiny. If the school-house had taken fire he thought that he
would have felt simply relief. Anything was better. Death amid the
flames was preferable to a recital of "The Charge of the Light Brigade."

But the Trass boy finished his remarks about destiny in a very short time. Jimmie heard the teacher call his name, and he felt the whole world look at him. He did not know how he made his way to the stage. Parts of him seemed to be of lead, and at the same time parts of him seemed to be light as air, detached. His face had gone as pale as had been the face of Susie Timmens. He was simply a child in torment; that is all there is to be said specifically about it; and to intelligent people the exhibition would have been not more edifying than a dog-fight.

He bowed precariously, choked, made an inarticulate sound, and then he suddenly said,

"Half a leg—"

"League," said the teacher, coolly.

"Half a leg—"

"League," said the teacher.
"League," repeated Jimmie, wildly.

"Half a league, half a league, half a league onward."

He paused here and looked wretchedly at the teacher.
"Half a league," he muttered—"half a league—"
He seemed likely to keep continuing this phrase indefinitely, so after a time the teacher said, "Well, go on."
"Half a league," responded Jimmie.
The teacher had the opened book before her, and she read from it:

"All in the valley of Death
Rode the—

"Go on," she concluded.
Jimmie said,

"All in the valley of Death
Rode the—the—the—"

He cast a glance of supreme appeal upon the teacher, and breathlessly whispered, "Rode the what?"

The young woman flushed with indignation to the roots of her hair.

"Rode the six hundred,"

she snapped at him.

The class was arustle with delight at this cruel display. They were no better than a Roman populace in Nero's time.

Jimmie started off again:

"Half a leg—league, half a league, half a league onward,
All in the valley of death rode the six hundred.
Forward—forward—forward—"

"The Light Brigade," suggested the teacher, sharply.

"The Light Brigade," said Jimmie. He was about to die of the ignoble pain of his position.

As for Tennyson's lines, they had all gone grandly out of his mind, leaving it a whited wall.

The teacher's indignation was still rampant. She looked at the miserable wretch before her with an angry stare.

"You stay in after school and learn that all over again," she commanded. "And be prepared to speak it next Friday. I am astonished at you, Jimmie. Go to your seat."

If she had suddenly and magically made a spirit of him and left him free to soar high above all the travail of our earthly lives she could not have overjoyed him more. He fled back to his seat without hearing the low-toned gibes of his schoolmates. He gave no thought to the terrors of the next Friday. The evils of the day had been sufficient, and to a childish mind a week is a great space of time.

With the delightful inconsistency of his age he sat in blissful calm, and watched the sufferings of an unfortunate boy named Zimmerman, who was the next victim of education. Jimmie, of course, did not know that on this day there had been laid for him the foundation of a finished incapacity for public speaking which would be his until he died.

VI

SHAME

"Don't come in here botherin' me," said the cook, intolerantly. "What with your mother bein' away on a visit, an' your father comin' home soon to lunch, I have enough on my mind—and that without bein' bothered with *you*. The kitchen is no place for little boys, anyhow. Run away, and don't be interferin' with my work." She frowned and made a grand pretense of being deep in herculean labors; but Jimmie did not run away.

"Now—they're goin' to have a picnic," he said, half audibly.

"What?"

"Now—they're goin' to have a picnic."

"Who's goin' to have a picnic?" demanded the cook, loudly. Her accent could have led one to suppose that if the projectors did not turn out to be the proper parties, she immediately would forbid this picnic.

Jimmie looked at her with more hopefulness. After twenty minutes of futile skirmishing, he had at least succeeded in introducing the subject. To her question he answered, eagerly:

"Oh, everybody! Lots and lots of boys and girls. Everybody."

"Who's everybody?"

According to custom, Jimmie began to sing-song through his nose in a quite indescribable fashion an enumeration of the prospective picnickers: "Willie Dalzel an' Dan Earl an' Ella Earl an' Wolcott Margate an' Reeves Margate an' Walter Phelps an' Homer Phelps an' Minnie Phelps an'—oh—lots more girls an'—everybody. An' their mothers an' big sisters too." Then he announced a new bit of information: "They're goin' to have a picnic."

"Well, let them," said the cook, blandly.

Jimmie fidgeted for a time in silence. At last he murmured, "I—now —I thought maybe you'd let me go."

The cook turned from her work with an air of irritation and amazement that Jimmie should still be in the kitchen. "Who's stoppin' you?" she asked sharply. "I ain't stoppin' you, am I?"

"No," admitted Jimmie, in a low voice.

"Well, why don't you go, then? Nobody's stoppin' you."

"But," said Jimmie, "I—you—now—each fellow has got to take somethin to eat with 'm."

"Oh ho!" cried the cook, triumphantly. "So that's it, is it? So that's what you've been shyin' round here fer, eh? Well, you may as well take yourself off without more words. What with your mother bein' away on a visit, an' your father comin' home soon to his lunch, I have enough on my mind—an' that without being bothered with *you*."

Jimmie made no reply, but moved in grief towards the door. The cook continued: "Some people in this house seem to think there's 'bout a thousand cooks in this kitchen. Where I used to work b'fore, there was some reason in 'em. I ain't a horse. A picnic!"

Jimmie said nothing, but he loitered.

"Seems as if I had enough to do, without havin' *you* come round talkin' about picnics. Nobody ever seems to think of the work I have to do. Nobody ever seems to think of it. Then they come and talk to me about picnics! What do I care about picnics?"

Jimmie loitered.

"Where I used to work b'fore, there was some reason in 'em. I never heard tell of no picnics right on top of your mother bein' away on a visit an' your father comin' home soon to his lunch. It's all foolishness."

Little Jimmie leaned his head flat against the wall and began to weep. She stared at him scornfully. "Cryin', eh? Cryin'? What are you cryin' fer?"

"N-n-nothin'," sobbed Jimmie.

There was a silence, save for Jimmie's convulsive breathing. At length the cook said: "Stop that blubberin', now. Stop it! This kitchen ain't no place fer it. Stop it! . . . Very well! If you don't stop, I won't give you nothin' to go to the picnic with—there!"

For the moment he could not end his tears. "You never said," he sputtered—"you never said you'd give me anything."

"An' why would I?" she cried, angrily. "Why would I—with you in here a-cryin' an' a-blubberin' an' a-bleatin' round? Enough to drive a woman crazy! I don't see how you could expect me to! The idea!"

Suddenly Jimmie announced: "I've stopped cryin'. I ain't goin' to cry no more 'tall."

"Well, then," grumbled the cook—"well, then, stop it. I've got enough on my mind." It chanced that she was making for luncheon some salmon croquettes. A tin still half full of pinky prepared fish was beside her on the table. Still grumbling, she seized a loaf of bread and, wielding a knife, she cut from this loaf four slices, each of which was as big as a six-shilling novel. She profligately spread them with butter, and jabbing the point of her knife into the salmon-tin, she brought up bits of salmon, which she flung and flattened upon the bread. Then she crashed the pieces of bread together in pairs, much as one would clash cymbals. There was no doubt in her own mind but that she had created two sandwiches.

"There," she cried. "That'll do you all right. Lemme see. What'll I put 'em in? There—I've got it." She thrust the sandwiches into a small pail and jammed on the lid. Jimmie was ready for the picnic. "Oh, thank you, Mary!" he cried, joyfully, and in a moment he was off, running swiftly.

The picnickers had started nearly half an hour earlier, owing to his inability to quickly attack and subdue the cook, but he knew that the rendezvous was in the grove of tall, pillar-like hemlocks and pines that grew on a rocky knoll at the lake shore. His heart was very light as he sped, swinging his pail. But a few minutes previously his soul had been gloomed in despair; now he was happy. He was going to the picnic, where privilege of participation was to be bought by the contents of the little tin pail.

When he arrived in the outskirts of the grove he heard a merry clamor, and when he reached the top of the knoll he looked down the slope upon a scene which almost made his little breast burst with joy. They actually had two camp-fires! Two camp-fires! At one of them Mrs. Earl was making something—chocolate, no doubt—and at the other a young lady in white duck and a sailor hat was dropping eggs into boiling water. Other grown-up people had spread a white cloth and were laying upon it things from baskets. In the deep cool shadow of the trees the children scurried, laughing. Jimmie hastened forward to join his friends.

Homer Phelps caught first sight of him. "Ho!" he shouted; "here comes Jimmie Trescott! Come on, Jimmie; you be on our side!" The children had divided themselves into two bands for some purpose of play. The others of Homer Phelps's party loudly endorsed his plan. "Yes, Jimmie, you be on *our* side." Then arose the usual dispute. "Well, we got the weakest side."

" 'Tain't any weaker'n ours."

Homer Phelps suddenly started, and looking hard, said, "What you got in the pail, Jim?"

Jimmie answered, somewhat uneasily, "Got m' lunch in it."

Instantly that brat of a Minnie Phelps simply tore down the sky with her shrieks of derision. "Got his *lunch* in it! In a *pail!*" She ran screaming to her mother. "Oh, mamma! Oh, mamma! Jimmie Trescott's got his picnic in a pail!"

Now there was nothing in the nature of this fact to particularly move the others—notably the boys, who were not competent to care if he had brought his luncheon in a coal-bin; but such is the instinct of childish society that they all immediately moved away from him. In a moment he had been made a social leper. All old intimacies were flung into the lake, so to speak. They dared not compromise themselves. At safe distances the boys shouted, scornfully: "Huh! Got his picnic in a pail!" Never again during that picnic did the little girls speak of him as Jimmie Trescott. His name now was Him.

His mind was dark with pain as he stood, the hangdog, kicking the gravel, and muttering as defiantly as he was able, "Well, I can have it in a pail if I want to." This statement of freedom was of no importance, and he knew it, but it was the only idea in his head.

He had been baited at school for being detected in writing a letter to little Cora, the angel child, and he had known how to defend himself, but this situation was in no way similar. This was a social affair, with grown people on all sides. It would be sweet to catch the Margate twins, for instance, and hammer them into a state of bleating respect for his pail; but that was a matter for the jungles of childhood, where grown folk seldom penetrated. He could only glower.

The amiable voice of Mrs. Earl suddenly called: "Come, children! Everything's ready!" They scampered away, glancing back for one last gloat at Jimmie standing there with his pail.

He did not know what to do. He knew that the grown folk expected him at the spread, but if he approached he would be greeted by a shameful chorus from the children—more especially from some of those damnable little girls. Still, luxuries beyond all dreaming were heaped on that cloth. One could not forget them. Perhaps if he crept up modestly, and was very gentle and very nice to the little girls, they would allow him peace. Of course it had been dreadful to come with a pail to such a grand picnic, but they might forgive him.

Oh no, they would not! He knew them better. And then suddenly he remembered with what delightful expectations he had raced to this grove, and self-pity overwhelmed him, and he thought he wanted to die and make every one feel sorry.

The young lady in white duck and a sailor hat looked at him, and then spoke to her sister, Mrs. Earl. "Who's that hovering in the distance, Emily?"

Mrs. Earl peered. "Why, it's Jimmie Trescott! Jimmie, come to the picnic! Why don't you come to the picnic, Jimmie?" He began to sidle towards the cloth.

But at Mrs. Earl's call there was another outburst from many of the children. "He's got his picnic in a pail! In a *pail!* Got it in a pail!"

Minnie Phelps was a shrill fiend. "Oh, mamma, he's got it in that pail! See! Isn't it funny? Isn't it dreadful funny?"

"What ghastly prigs children are, Emily!" said the young lady. "They are spoiling that boy's whole day, breaking his heart, the little cats! I think I'll go over and talk to him."

"Maybe you had better not," answered Mrs. Earl, dubiously. "Somehow these things arrange themselves. If you interfere, you are likely to prolong everything."

"Well, I'll try, at least," said the young lady.

At the second outburst against him Jimmie had crouched down by a tree, half hiding behind it, half pretending that he was not hiding behind it. He turned his sad gaze towards the lake. The bit of water seen through the shadows seemed perpendicular, a slate-colored wall. He heard a noise near him, and turning, he perceived the young lady looking down at him. In her hand she held plates. "May I sit near you?" she asked, coolly.

Jimmie could hardly believe his ears. After disposing herself and the plates upon the pine needles, she made brief explanation. "They're rather crowded, you see, over there. I don't like to be crowded at a picnic, so I thought I'd come here. I hope you don't mind."

Jimmie made haste to find his tongue. "Oh, I don't mind! I *like* to have you here." The ingenuous emphasis made it appear that the fact of his liking to have her there was in the nature of a law-dispelling phenomenon, but she did not smile.

"How large is that lake?" she asked.

Jimmie, falling into the snare, at once began to talk in the manner of a proprietor of the lake. "Oh, it's almost twenty miles long, an' in one place it's almost four miles wide! an' it's *deep* too—awful deep—an' it's got real steamboats on it, an'—oh—lots of other boats, an'—an'— an'—"

"Do you go out on it sometimes?"

"Oh, lots of times! My father's got a boat," he said, eying her to note the effect of his words.

She was correctly pleased and struck with wonder. "Oh, has he?" she cried, as if she never before had heard of a man owning a boat.

Jimmie continued: "Yes, an' it's a grea' big boat, too, with sails, real sails; an' sometimes he takes me out in her, too; an' once he took me fishin', an' we had sandwiches, plenty of 'em, an' my father he drank beer right out of the bottle—*right out of the bottle!*"

The young lady was properly overwhelmed by this amazing intelligence. Jimmie saw the impression he had created, and he enthusiastically resumed his narrative: "An' after, he let me throw the bottles in the water, and I throwed 'em 'way, 'way, 'way out.

An' they sank, an'—never comed up," he concluded, dramatically.

His face was glorified; he had forgotten all about the pail; he was absorbed in this communion with a beautiful lady who was so interested in what he had to say.

She indicated one of the plates, and said, indifferently: "Perhaps you would like some of those sandwiches. I made them. Do you like olives? And there's a deviled egg. I made that also."

"Did you really?" said Jimmie, politely. His face gloomed for a moment because the pail was recalled to his mind, but he timidly possessed himself of a sandwich.

"Hope you are not going to scorn my deviled egg," said his goddess. "I am very proud of it." He did not; he scorned little that was on the plate.

Their gentle intimacy was ineffable to the boy. He thought he had a friend, a beautiful lady, who liked him more than she did anybody at the picnic, to say the least. This was proved by the fact that she had flung aside the luxuries of the spread cloth to sit with him, the exile. Thus early did he fall a victim to woman's wiles.

"Where do you live?" he asked, suddenly.

"Oh, a long way from here! In New York."

His next question was put very bluntly. "Are you married?"

"Oh no!" she answered, gravely.

Jimmie was silent for a time, during which he glanced shyly and furtively up at her face. It was evident that he was somewhat embarrassed. Finally he said, "When I grow up to be a man—"

"Oh, that is some time yet!" said the beautiful lady.

"But when I *do*, I—I should like to marry you."

"Well, I will remember it," she answered; "but don't talk of it now, because it's such a long time; and—I wouldn't wish you to consider yourself bound." She smiled at him.

He began to brag. "When I grow up to be a man, I'm goin' to have lots an' lots of money, an' I'm goin' to have a grea' big house, an' a horse an' a shot-gun, an' lots an' lots of books 'bout elephants an' tigers, an' lots an' lots of ice-cream an' pie an'—caramels." As before, she was impressed; he could see it. "An' I'm goin' to have lots an' lots of children—'bout three hundred, I guess—an' there won't none of 'em be girls. They'll all be boys—like me."

"Oh, my!" she said.

His garment of shame was gone from him. The pail was dead and well buried. It seemed to him that months elapsed as he dwelt in happiness near the beautiful lady and trumpeted his vanity.

At last there was a shout. "Come on! we're going home." The picnickers trooped out of the grove. The children wished to resume their jeering, for Jimmie still gripped his pail, but they were restrained by the circumstances. He was walking at the side of the beautiful lady.

During this journey he abandoned many of his habits. For instance, he never traveled without skipping gracefully from crack to crack between the stones, or without pretending that he was a train of cars, or without some mumming device of childhood. But now he behaved with dignity. He made no more noise than a little mouse. He escorted the beautiful lady to the gate of the Earl home, where he awkwardly, solemnly, and wistfully shook hands in good-by. He watched her go up the walk; the door clanged.

On his way home he dreamed. One of these dreams was fascinating. Supposing the beautiful lady was his teacher in school! Oh, my! wouldn't he be a good boy, sitting like a statuette all day long, and knowing every lesson to perfection, and—everything. And then supposing that a boy should sass her. Jimmie painted himself waylaying that boy on the homeward road, and the fate of the boy was a thing to make strong men cover their eyes with their hands. And she would like him more and more—more and more. And he—he would be a little god.

But as he was entering his father's grounds an appalling recollection came to him. He was returning with the bread-and-butter and the salmon untouched in the pail! He could imagine the cook, nine feet tall, waving her fist. "An' so that's what I took trouble for, is it? So's you could bring it back? So's you could bring it back?" He skulked towards the house like a marauding bushranger. When he neared the kitchen door he made a desperate rush past it, aiming to gain the stables and there secrete his guilt. He was nearing them, when a thunderous voice hailed him from the rear:

"Jimmie Trescott, where you goin' with that pail?"

It was the cook. He made no reply, but plunged into the shelter of the stables. He whirled the lid from the pail and dashed its contents beneath a heap of blankets. Then he stood panting, his eyes on the door. The cook did not pursue, but she was bawling:

"Jimmie Trescott, what you doin' with that pail?"

He came forth, swinging it. "Nothin'," he said, in virtuous protest.

"I know better," she said, sharply, as she relieved him of his curse.

In the morning Jimmie was playing near the stable, when he heard a shout from Peter Washington, who attended Dr. Trescott's horse:

"Jim! Oh, Jim!"

"What?"

"Come yah."

Jimmie went reluctantly to the door of the stable, and Peter Washington asked:

"Wut's dish yere fish an' brade doin' unner dese yer blankups?"

"I don't know. I didn't have nothin' to do with it," answered Jimmie, indignantly.

"Don' tell *me!*" cried Peter Washington, as he flung it all away— "don' tell *me!* When I fin' fish an' brade unner dese yer blankups, I don' go an' think dese yer ho'ses er yer pop's put 'em. I *know*. An' if I caitch enny more dish yer fish an' brade in dish yer stable, *I'll* tell yer pop."

VII

THE CARRIAGE-LAMPS

It was the fault of a small nickel-plated revolver, a most incompetent weapon, which, wherever one aimed, would fling the bullet as the devil willed, and no man, when about to use it, could tell exactly what was in store for the surrounding country. This treasure had been acquired by Jimmie Trescott after arduous bargaining with another small boy. Jimmie wended homeward, patting his hip pocket at every three paces.

Peter Washington, working in the carriage-house, looked out upon him with a shrewd eye. "Oh, Jim," he called, "wut you got in yer hind pocket?"

"Nothin'," said Jimmie, feeling carefully under his jacket to make sure that the revolver wouldn't fall out.

Peter chuckled. "S'more foolishness, I raikon. You gwine be hung one day, Jim, you keep up all dish yer nonsense."

Jimmie made no reply, but went into the back garden, where he hid the revolver in a box under a lilac-bush. Then he returned to the vicinity of Peter, and began to cruise to and fro in the offing, showing all the signals of one wishing to open treaty. "Pete," he said, "how much does a box of cartridges cost?"

Peter raised himself violently, holding in one hand a piece of harness, and in the other an old rag. "Ca'tridgers! *Ca'tridgers!* Lan' sake! wut the kid want with ca'tridgers? Knew it! Knew it! Come home er-holdin' on to his hind pocket like he got money in it. An' now he want ca'tridgers."

Jimmie, after viewing with dismay the excitement caused by his question, began to move warily out of the reach of a possible hostile movement.

"Ca'tridgers!" continued Peter, in scorn and horror. "Kid like you! No bigger'n er minute! Look yah, Jim, you done been swappin' round, an' you done got hol' of er pistol!" The charge was dramatic.

The wind was almost knocked out of Jimmie by this display of Peter's terrible miraculous power, and as he backed away his feeble denials were more convincing than a confession.

"I'll tell yer pop!" cried Peter, in virtuous grandeur. "I'll tell yer pop!"

In the distance Jimmie stood appalled. He knew not what to do. The dread adult wisdom of Peter Washington had laid bare the sin, and disgrace stared at Jimmie.

There was a whirl of wheels, and a high, lean trotting-mare spun Doctor Trescott's buggy towards Peter, who ran forward busily. As the doctor climbed out, Peter, holding the mare's head, began his denunciation:

"Docteh, I gwine tell on Jim. He come home er-holdin' on to his hind pocket, an' proud like he won a tuhkey-raffle, an' I sure know what he been up to, an' I done challenge him, an' he nev' say he didn't."

"Why, what do you mean?" said the doctor. "What's this, Jimmie?"

The boy came forward, glaring wrathfully at Peter. In fact, he suddenly was so filled with rage at Peter that he forgot all precautions. "It's about a pistol," he said, bluntly. "I've got a pistol. I swapped for it."

"I done tol' 'im his pop wouldn' stand no fiah-awms, an' him a kid like he is. I done tol' 'im. Lan' sake! he strut like he was a soldier! Come in yere proud, an' er-holdin' on to his hind pocket. He think he was Jesse James, I raikon. But I done tol' 'im his pop stan' no sech foolishness. First thing—*blam*—he shoot his haid off. No, seh, he too tinety t' come in yere er-struttin' like he jest bought Main Street. I tol' 'im. I done tol' 'im—shawp. I don' wanter be loafin' round dis yer stable if Jim he gwine go shootin' round an' shootin' round—*blim*—*blam*—*blim*—*blam!* No, seh. I retiahs. I retiahs. It's all right if er grown man got er gun, but ain't no kids come foolishin' round *me* with fiah-awms. No, seh. I retiahs."

"Oh, be quiet, Peter!" said the doctor. "Where is this thing, Jimmie?"

The boy went sulkily to the box under the lilac-bush and returned with the revolver. "Here 'tis," he said, with a glare over his shoulder at Peter. The doctor looked at the silly weapon in critical contempt.

"It's not much of a thing, Jimmie, but I don't think you are quite old enough for it yet. I'll keep it for you in one of the drawers of my desk."

Peter Washington burst out proudly: "I done tol' 'im th' docteh wouldn' stan' no traffickin' round yere with fiah-awms. I done tol' 'im."

Jimmie and his father went together into the house, and as Peter unharnessed the mare he continued his comments on the boy and the revolver. He was not cast down by the absence of hearers. In fact, he usually talked better when there was no one to listen save the horses. But now his observations bore small resemblance to his earlier and public statements. Admiration and the keen family pride of a Southern negro who has been long in one place were now in his tone.

"That boy! He's er devil! When he get to be er man—wow! He'll jes take an' make things whirl round yere. Raikon we'll all take er back seat when he come erlong er-raisin' Cain."

He had unharnessed the mare, and with his back bent was pushing the buggy into the carriage-house.

"Er pistol! An' him no bigger than er minute!"

A small stone whizzed past Peter's head and clattered on the stable. He hastily dropped all occupation and struck a curious attitude. His right knee was almost up to his chin, and his arms were wreathed protectingly about his head. He had not looked in the direction from which the stone had come, but he had begun immediately to yell:

"You Jim! Quit! Quit, I tell yer, Jim! Watch out! You gwine break somethin', Jim!"

"Yah!" taunted the boy, as with the speed and ease of a light-cavalryman he maneuvered in the distance. "Yah! Told on me, did you! Told on me, hey! There! How do you like that?" The missiles resounded against the stable.

"Watch out, Jim! You gwine break something, Jim, I tell yer! Quit yer foolishness, Jim! Ow! Watch out, boy! I—"

There was a crash. With diabolic ingenuity, one of Jimmie's pebbles had entered the carriage-house and had landed among a row of carriage-lamps on a shelf, creating havoc which was apparently beyond all reason of physical law. It seemed to Jimmie that the racket of falling glass could have been heard in an adjacent county.

Peter was a prophet who after persecution was suffered to recall everything to the mind of the persecutor. *"There!* Knew it! Knew it! *Now* I raikon you'll quit. Hi! jes look ut dese yer lamps! Fer lan' sake! Oh, now yer pop jes break ev'ry bone in yer body!"

In the doorway of the kitchen the cook appeared with a startled face. Jimmie's father and mother came suddenly out on the front veranda. "What was that noise?" called the doctor.

Peter went forward to explain. "Jim he was er-heavin' rocks at me, docteh, an' erlong come one rock an' go *blam* inter all th' lamps an' jes skitter 'em t' bits. I declayah—"

Jimmie, half blinded with emotion, was nevertheless aware of a lightning glance from his father, a glance which cowed and frightened him to the ends of his toes. He heard the steady but deadly tones of his father in a fury: "Go into the house and wait until I come."

Bowed in anguish, the boy moved across the lawn and up the steps. His mother was standing on the veranda still gazing towards the stable. He loitered in the faint hope that she might take some small pity on his state. But she could have heeded him no less if he had been invisible. He entered the house.

When the doctor returned from his investigation of the harm done by Jimmie's hand, Mrs. Trescott looked at him anxiously, for she knew that he was concealing some volcanic impulses. "Well?" she asked.

"It isn't the lamps," he said at first. He seated himself on the rail. "I don't know what we are going to do with that boy. It isn't so much the lamps as it is the other thing. He was throwing stones at Peter because Peter told me about the revolver. What are we going to do with him?"

"I'm sure I don't know," replied the mother. "We've tried almost everything. Of course much of it is pure animal spirits. Jimmie is not naturally vicious—"

"Oh, I know," interrupted the doctor, impatiently. "Do you suppose, when the stones were singing about Peter's ears, he cared whether they were flung by a boy who was naturally vicious or a boy who was not? The question might interest him afterward, but at the time he was mainly occupied in dodging these effects of pure animal spirits."

"Don't be too hard on the boy, Ned. There's lots of time yet. He's so young yet, and— I believe he gets most of his naughtiness from that wretched Dalzel boy. That Dalzel boy—well, he's simply awful!" Then, with true motherly instinct to shift blame from her own boy's shoulders, she proceeded to sketch the character of the Dalzel boy in lines that would have made that talented young vagabond stare. It was not admittedly her feeling that the doctor's attention should be diverted from the main issue and his indignation divided among the camps, but presently the doctor felt himself burn with wrath for the Dalzel boy.

"Why don't you keep Jimmie away from him?" he demanded. "Jimmie has no business consorting with abandoned little predestined jailbirds like him. If I catch him on the place I'll box his ears."

"It is simply impossible, unless we kept Jimmie shut up all the time," said Mrs. Trescott. "I can't watch him every minute of the day, and the moment my back is turned, he's off."

"I should think those Dalzel people would hire somebody to bring up their child for them," said the doctor. "They don't seem to know how to do it themselves."

Presently you would have thought from the talk that one Willie Dalzel had been throwing stones at Peter Washington because Peter Washington had told Doctor Trescott that Willie Dalzel had come into possession of a revolver.

In the mean time Jimmie had gone into the house to await the coming of his father. He was in a rebellious mood. He had not intended to destroy the carriage-lamps. He had been merely hurling stones at a creature whose perfidy deserved such action, and the hitting of the lamps had been merely another move of the great conspirator Fate to force one Jimmie Trescott into dark and troublous ways. The boy was beginning to find the world a bitter place. He couldn't win appreciation for a single virtue; he could only achieve quick, rigorous punishment for his misdemeanors. Everything was an enemy. Now there were those silly old lamps—what were they doing up on that shelf, anyhow? It would have been just as easy for them at the time to have been in some other place. But no; there they had been, like the crowd that is passing under the wall when the mason for the first time in twenty years lets fall a brick. Furthermore, the flight of that stone had been perfectly unreasonable. It had been a sort of freak in physical law. Jimmie understood that he might have thrown stones from the same fatal spot for an hour without hurting a single lamp. He was a victim—that was it. Fate had conspired with the detail of his environment to simply hound him into a grave or into a cell.

But who would understand? Who would understand? And here the boy turned his mental glance in every direction, and found nothing but what was to him the black of cruel ignorance. Very well; some day they would—

From somewhere out in the street he heard a peculiar whistle of two notes. It was the common signal of the boys in the neighborhood, and judging from the direction of the sound, it was apparently intended to summon him. He moved immediately to one of the windows of the sitting-room. It opened upon a part of the grounds remote from the stables and cut off from the veranda by a wing. He perceived Willie Dalzel loitering in the street. Jimmie whistled the signal after having pushed up the window-sash some inches. He saw the Dalzel boy turn and regard him, and then call several other boys. They stood in a group and gestured. These gestures plainly said: "Come out. We've got something on hand." Jimmie sadly shook his head.

But they did not go away. They held a long consultation. Presently Jimmie saw the intrepid Dalzel boy climb the fence and begin to creep among the shrubbery, in elaborate imitation of an Indian scout. In time he arrived under Jimmie's window, and raised his face to whisper: "Come on out! We're going on a bear-hunt."

A bear-hunt! Of course Jimmie knew that it would not be a real bear-hunt, but would be a sort of carouse of pretension and big talking and preposterous lying and valor, wherein each boy would strive to have himself called Kit Carson by the others. He was profoundly affected. However, the parental word was upon him, and he could not move. "No," he answered, "I can't. I've got to stay in."

"Are you a prisoner?" demanded the Dalzel boy, eagerly.

"No-o—yes—I s'pose I am."

The other lad became much excited, but he did not lose his wariness. "Don't you want to be rescued?"

"Why—no—I dun'no'," replied Jimmie, dubiously.

Willie Dalzel was indignant. "Why of course you want to be rescued! We'll rescue you. I'll go and get my men." And thinking this a good sentence, he repeated, pompously, "I'll go and get my men." He began to crawl away, but when he was distant some ten paces he turned to say: "Keep up a stout heart. Remember that you have friends who will be faithful unto death. The time is not now far off when you will again view the blessed sunlight."

The poetry of these remarks filled Jimmie with ecstasy, and he watched eagerly for the coming of the friends who would be faithful unto death. They delayed some time, for the reason that Willie Dalzel was making a speech.

"Now, men," he said, "our comrade is a prisoner in yon—in yond—in that there fortress. We must to the rescue. Who volunteers to go with me?" He fixed them with a stern eye.

There was a silence, and then one of the smaller boys remarked,

"If Doc Trescott ketches us trackin' over his lawn—"

Willie Dalzel pounced upon the speaker and took him by the throat. The two presented a sort of a burlesque of the wood-cut on the cover of a dime novel which Willie had just been reading—*The Red Captain: A Tale of the Pirates of the Spanish Main.*

"You are a coward!" said Willie, through his clinched teeth.

"No, I ain't, Willie," piped the other, as best he could.

"I say you are," cried the great chieftain, indignantly. "Don't tell *me* I'm a liar." He relinquished his hold upon the coward and resumed his speech. "You know me, men. Many of you have been my followers for long years. You saw me slay Six-handed Dick with my own hand. You know I never falter. Our comrade is a prisoner in the cruel hands of our enemies. Aw, Pete Washington? He dassent. My pa says if Pete ever troubles me he'll brain 'im. Come on! To the rescue! Who will go with me to the rescue? Aw, come on! What are you afraid of?"

It was another instance of the power of eloquence upon the human mind. There was only one boy who was not thrilled by this oration, and he was a boy whose favorite reading had been of the road-agents and gun-fighters of the great West, and he thought the whole thing should be conducted in the Deadwood Dick manner. This talk of a "comrade" was silly; "pard" was the proper word. He resolved that he would make a show of being a pirate, and keep secret the fact that he really was Hold-up Harry, the Terror of the Sierras.

But the others were knit close in piratical bonds. One by one they climbed the fence at a point hidden from the house by tall shrubs. With many a low-breathed caution they went upon their perilous adventure.

Jimmie was grown tired of waiting for his friends who would be faithful unto death. Finally he decided that he would rescue himself. It would be a gross breach of rule, but he couldn't sit there all the rest of the day waiting for his faithful-unto-death friends. The window was only five feet from the ground. He softly raised the sash and threw one leg over the sill. But at the same time he perceived his friends snaking among the bushes. He withdrew his leg and waited, seeing that he was now to be rescued in an orthodox way. The brave pirates came nearer and nearer.

Jimmie heard a noise of a closing door, and turning, he saw his father in the room looking at him and the open window in angry surprise. Boys never faint, but Jimmie probably came as near to it as may the average boy.

"What's all this?" asked the doctor, staring. Involuntarily Jimmie glanced over his shoulder through the window. His father saw the creeping figures. "What are those boys doing?" he said, sharply, and he knit his brows.

"Nothin'."

"Nothing! Don't tell me that. Are they coming here to the window?"

"Y-e-s, sir."

"What for?"

"To—to see me."

"What about?"

"About—about nothin'."

"What about?"

Jimmie knew that he could conceal nothing. He said, "They're comin' to—to—to rescue me." He began to whimper.

The doctor sat down heavily.

"What? To rescue you?" he gasped.

"Y-yes, sir."

The doctor's eyes began to twinkle. "Very well," he said presently.

"I will sit here and observe this rescue. And on no account do you warn them that I am here. Understand?"

Of course Jimmie understood. He had been mad to warn his friends, but his father's mere presence had frightened him from doing it. He stood trembling at the window, while the doctor stretched in an easy-chair near at hand. They waited. The doctor could tell by his son's increasing agitation that the great moment was near. Suddenly he heard Willie Dalzel's voice hiss out a word: "S-s-silence!" Then the same voice addressed Jimmie at the window: "Good cheer, my comrade. The time is now at hand. I have come. Never did the Red Captain turn his back on a friend. One minute more and you will be free. Once aboard my gallant craft and you can bid defiance to your haughty enemies. Why don't you hurry up? What are you standin' there lookin' like a cow for?"

"I—er—now—you—" stammered Jimmie.

Here Hold-up Harry, the Terror of the Sierras, evidently concluded that Willie Dalzel had had enough of the premier part, so he said:

"Brace up, pard. Don't ye turn white-livered now, fer ye know that Hold-up Harry, the Terrar of the Sarahs, ain't the man ter—"

"Oh, stop it!" said Willie Dalzel. "He won't understand that, you know. He's a pirate. Now, Jimmie, come on. Be of light heart, my comrade. Soon you—"

"I 'low arter all this here long time in jail ye thought ye had no friends mebbe, but I tell ye Hold-up Harry, the Terrar of the Sarahs—"

"A boat is waitin'—"

"I have ready a trusty horse—"

Willie Dalzel could endure his rival no longer.

"Look here, Henry, you're spoilin' the whole thing. We're all pirates, don't you see, and you're a pirate too."

"I ain't a pirate. I'm Hold-up Harry, the Terrar of the Sarahs."

"You ain't, I say," said Willie, in despair. "You're spoilin' everything, you are. All right, now. You wait. I'll fix you for this, see if I don't! Oh, come on, Jimmie. A boat awaits us at the foot of the rocks. In one short hour you'll be free forever from your ex—excwable enemies, and their vile plots. Hasten, for the dawn approaches."

The suffering Jimmie looked at his father, and was surprised at what he saw. The doctor was doubled up like a man with the colic. He was breathing heavily. The boy turned again to his friends. "I—now—look here," he began, stumbling among the words. "You—I—I don't think I'll be rescued today."

The pirates were scandalized. "What?" they whispered, angrily. "Ain't you goin' to be rescued? Well, all right for you, Jimmie Trescott. That's a nice way to act, that is!" Their upturned eyes glowered at Jimmie.

Suddenly Doctor Trescott appeared at the window with Jimmie. "Oh, go home, boys!" he gasped, but they did not hear him. Upon the instant they had whirled and scampered away like deer. The first lad to reach the fence was the Red Captain, but Hold-up Harry, the Terror of the Sierras, was so close that there was little to choose between them.

Doctor Trescott lowered the window, and then spoke to his son in his usual quiet way. "Jimmie, I wish you would go and tell Peter to have the buggy ready at seven o'clock."

"Yes, sir," said Jimmie, and he swaggered out to the stables. "Pete, father wants the buggy ready at seven o'clock."

Peter paid no heed to this order, but with the tender sympathy of a true friend he inquired, "Hu't?"

"Hurt? Did what hurt?"

"Yer trouncin'."

"Trouncin'!" said Jimmie, contemptuously. "I didn't get any trouncin'."

"No?" said Peter. He gave Jimmie a quick shrewd glance, and saw that he was telling the truth. He began to mutter and mumble over his work. "Ump! Ump! Dese yer white folks act like they think er boy's made er glass. No trouncin'! Ump!" He was consumed with curiosity to learn why Jimmie had not felt a heavy parental hand, but he did not care to lower his dignity by asking questions about it. At last, however, he reached the limits of his endurance, and in a voice pretentiously careless he asked, "Didn' yer pop take on like mad er-bout dese yer cay'ge-lamps?"

"Carriage-lamps?" inquired Jimmie.

"Ump."

"No, he didn't say anything about carriage-lamps—not that I remember. Maybe he did, though. Lemme see. . . . No, he never mentioned 'em."

VIII

THE KNIFE

I

Sı Bryant's place was on the shore of the lake, and his garden-patch, shielded from the north by a bold little promontory and a higher ridge inland, was accounted the most successful and surprising in all Whilomville township. One afternoon Si was working in the garden-patch, when Doctor Trescott's man, Peter Washington, came trudging slowly along the road, observing nature. He scanned the white man's fine agricultural results. "Take your eye off them there melons, you rascal," said Si, placidly.

The Negro's face widened in a grin of delight. "Well, Mist' Bryant, I raikon I ain't on'y make m'se'f covertous er-lookin' at dem yere mellums, sure 'nough. Dey suhtainly is grand."

"That's all right," responded Si, with affected bitterness of spirit. "That's all right. Just don't you admire 'em too much, that's all."

Peter chuckled and chuckled. "Ma Lode! Mist' Bryant, y-y-you don' think I'm gwine come prowlin' in dish yer gawden?"

"No, I know you hain't," said Si, with solemnity. "B'cause, if you did, I'd shoot you so full of holes you couldn't tell yourself from a sponge."

"Um—no, seh! No, seh! I don' raikon you'll get chance at Pete, Mist' Bryant. No, seh. I'll take an' run 'long an' rob er bank 'fore I'll come foolishin' 'round *your* gawden, Mist' Bryant."

Bryant, gnarled and strong as an old tree, leaned on his hoe, and laughed a Yankee laugh. His mouth remained tightly closed, but the sinister lines which ran from the sides of his nose to the meetings of his lips developed to form a comic oval, and he emitted a series of grunts, while his eyes gleamed merrily and his shoulders shook. Pete, on the contrary, threw back his head and guffawed thunderously. The effete joke in regard to an American Negro's fondness for watermelons was still an admirable pleasantry to them, and this was not the first time they had engaged in badinage over it. In fact, this venerable survival had formed between them a friendship of casual roadside quality.

Afterwards Peter went on up the road. He continued to chuckle until he was far away. He was going to pay a visit to old Alek Williams, a Negro who lived with a large family in a hut clinging to the side of a mountain. The scattered colony of Negroes which hovered near Whilomville was of interesting origin, being the result of some contrabands who had drifted as far north as Whilomville during the great Civil War. The descendants of these adventurers were mainly conspicuous for their bewildering number, and the facility which they possessed for adding even to this number. Speaking, for example, of the Jacksons—one couldn't hurl a stone into the hills about Whilomville without having it land on the roof of a hut full of Jacksons. The town reaped little in labor from these curious suburbs. There were a few men who came in regularly to work in gardens, to drive teams, to care for horses, and there were a few women who came in to cook or to wash. These latter had usually drunken husbands. In the main the colony loafed in high spirits, and the industrious minority gained no direct honor from their fellows, unless they spent their earnings on raiment, in which case they were naturally treated with distinction. On the whole, the hardships of these people were the wind, the rain, the snow, and any other physical difficulties which they could cultivate. About twice a year the lady philanthropists of Whilomville went up against them, and came away poorer in goods but rich in complacence. After one of these attacks the colony would preserve a comic air of rectitude for two days, and then relapse again to the genial irresponsibility of a crew of monkeys.

Peter Washington was one of the industrious class who occupied a position of distinction, for he surely spent his money on personal decoration. On occasion he could dress better than the Mayor of Whilomville himself, or at least in more colors, which was the main thing to the minds of his admirers. His ideal had been the late gallant Henry Johnson, whose conquests in Watermelon Alley, as well as in the hill shanties, had proved him the equal if not the superior of any Pullman-car porter in the country. Perhaps Peter had too much Virginia laziness and humor in him to be a wholly adequate successor to the fastidious Henry Johnson, but, at any rate, he admired his memory so attentively as to be openly termed a dude by envious people.

On this afternoon he was going to call on old Alek Williams because Alek's eldest girl was just turned seventeen, and, to Peter's mind, was a triumph of beauty. He was not wearing his best clothes, because on his last visit Alek's half-breed hound Susie had taken occasion to forcefully extract a quite large and valuable part of the visitor's trousers. When Peter arrived at the end of the rocky field which contained old Alek's shanty he stooped and provided himself with several large stones, weighing them carefully in his hand, and finally continuing his journey with three stones of about eight ounces each. When he was near the house, three gaunt hounds, Rover and Carlo and Susie, came sweeping down upon him. His impression was that they were going to climb him as if he were a tree, but at the critical moment they swerved and went growling and snapping around him, their heads low, their eyes malignant. The afternoon caller waited until Susie presented her side to him, then he heaved one of his eight-ounce rocks. When it landed, her hollow ribs gave forth a drumlike sound, and she was knocked sprawling, her legs in the air. The other hounds at once fled in horror, and she followed as soon as she was able, yelping at the top of her lungs. The afternoon caller resumed his march.

At the wild expressions of Susie's anguish old Alek had flung open the door and come hastily into the sunshine. "Yah, you Suse, come erlong outa dat now. What fer you— Oh, how do, how do, Mist' Wash'ton—how do?"

"How do, Mist' Willums? I done foun it necessa'y fer ter damnear-kill dish yer dawg a yourn, Mist' Willums."

"Come in, come in, Mist' Wash'ton. Dawg no 'count, Mist' Wash'-ton." Then he turned to address the unfortunate animal. "Hu't, did it? Hu't? 'Pears like you gwine lun some saince by time somebody brek yer back. 'Pears like I gwine club yer inter er frazzle 'fore you fin' out some saince. Gw'on 'way f'm yah!"

As the old man and his guest entered the shanty a body of black children spread out in crescent-shape formation and observed Peter with awe. Fat old Mrs. Williams greeted him turbulently, while the eldest girl, Mollie, lurked in a corner and giggled with finished imbecility, gazing at the visitor with eyes that were shy and bold by turns. She seemed at times absurdly over-confident, at times foolishly afraid; but her giggle consistently endured. It was a giggle on which an irascible but right-minded judge would have ordered her forthwith to be buried alive.

Amid a great deal of hospitable gabbling, Peter was conducted to the best chair out of the three that the house contained. Enthroned therein, he made himself charming in talk to the old people, who beamed upon him joyously. As for Mollie, he affected to be unaware of her existence. This may have been a method for entrapping the sentimental interest of that young gazelle, or it may be that the giggle had worked upon him.

He was absolutely fascinating to the old people. They could talk like rotary snow-plows, and he gave them every chance, while his face was illumined with appreciation. They pressed him to stay for supper, and he consented, after a glance at the pot on the stove which was too furtive to be noted.

During the meal old Alek recounted the high state of Judge Oglethorpe's kitchen-garden, which Alek said was due to his unremitting industry and fine intelligence. Alek was a gardener, whenever impending starvation forced him to cease temporarily from being a lily of the field.

"Mist' Bryant, he suhtainly got er grand gawden," observed Peter.

"Dat so, dat so, Mist' Wash'ton," assented Alek. "He got fine gawden."

"Seems like I nev' *did* see sech mellums, big as er bar'l, layin' dere. I don't raikon an'body in dish yer county kin hol' it with Mist' Bryant when comes ter mellums."

"Dat so, Mist' Wash'ton."

They did not talk of watermelons until their heads held nothing else, as the phrase goes. But they talked of watermelons until, when Peter started for home that night over a lonely road, they held a certain dominant position in his mind. Alek had come with him as far as the fence, in order to protect him from a possible attack by the mongrels. There they had cheerfully parted, two honest men.

The night was dark, and heavy with moisture. Peter found it uncomfortable to walk rapidly. He merely loitered on the road. When opposite Si Bryant's place he paused and looked over the fence into the garden. He imagined he could see the form of a huge melon lying in dim stateliness not ten yards away. He looked at the Bryant house. Two windows, downstairs, were lighted. The Bryants kept no dog, old Si's favorite child having once been bitten by a dog, and having since died, within that year, of pneumonia.

Peering over the fence, Peter fancied that if any low-minded night-prowler should happen to note the melon, he would not find it difficult to possess himself of it. This person would merely wait until the lights were out in the house, and the people presumably asleep. Then he would climb the fence, reach the melon in a few strides, sever the stem with his ready knife, and in a trice be back in the road with his prize. There need be no noise, and, after all, the house was some distance.

Selecting a smooth bit of turf, Peter took a seat by the road-side. From time to time he glanced at the lighted window.

II

When Peter and Alek had said good-by, the old man turned back in the rocky field and shaped a slow course towards that high dim light which marked the little window of his shanty. It would be incorrect to say that Alek could think of nothing but watermelons. But it was true that Si Bryant's watermelon-patch occupied a certain conspicuous position in his thoughts.

He sighed; he almost wished that he was again a conscienceless pickaninny, instead of being one of the most ornate, solemn, and look-at-me-sinner deacons that ever graced the handle of a collection-basket. At this time it made him quite sad to reflect upon his granite integrity. A weaker man might perhaps bow his moral head to the temptation, but for him such a fall was impossible. He was a prince of the church, and if he had been nine princes of the church he could not have been more proud. In fact, religion was to the old man a sort of personal dignity. And he was on Sundays so obtrusively good that you could see his sanctity through a door. He forced it on you until you would have felt its influence even in a forecastle.

It was clear in his mind that he must put watermelon thoughts from him, and after a moment he told himself, with much ostentation, that he had done so. But it was cooler under the sky than in the shanty, and as he was not sleepy, he decided to take a stroll down to Si Bryant's place and look at the melons from a pinnacle of spotless innocence. Reaching the road, he paused to listen. It would not do to let Peter hear him, because that graceless rapscallion would probably misunderstand him. But, assuring himself that Peter was well on his way, he set out, walking briskly until he was within four hundred yards of Bryant's place. Here he went to the side of the road, and walked thereafter on the damp, yielding turf. He made no sound.

He did not go on to that point in the main road which was directly opposite the watermelon-patch. He did not wish to have his ascetic contemplation disturbed by some chance wayfarer. He turned off along a short lane which led to Si Bryant's barn. Here he reached a place where he could see, over the fence, the faint shapes of the melons.

Alek was affected. The house was some distance away, there was no dog, and doubtless the Bryants would soon extinguish their lights and go to bed. Then some poor lost lamb of sin might come and scale the fence, reach a melon in a moment, sever the stem with his ready knife, and in a trice be back in the road with his prize. And this poor lost lamb of sin might even be a bishop, but no one would ever know it. Alek singled out with his eye a very large melon, and thought that the lamb would prove his judgment if he took that one.

He found a soft place in the grass, and arranged himself comfortably. He watched the lights in the windows.

III

It seemed to Peter Washington that the Bryants absolutely consulted their own wishes in regard to the time for retiring; but at last he saw the lighted windows fade briskly from left to right, and after a moment a window on the second floor blazed out against the darkness. Si was going to bed. In five minutes this window abruptly vanished, and all the world was night.

Peter spent the ensuing quarter-hour in no mental debate. His mind was fixed. He was here, and the melon was there. He would have it. But an idea of being caught appalled him. He thought of his position. He was the beau of his community, honored right and left. He pictured the consternation of his friends and the cheers of his enemies if the hands of the redoubtable Si Bryant should grip him in his shame.

He arose, and going to the fence, listened. No sound broke the stillness, save the rhythmical incessant clicking of myriad insects, and the guttural chanting of the frogs in the reeds at the lake-side. Moved by sudden decision, he climbed the fence and crept silently and swiftly down upon the melon. His open knife was in his hand. There was the melon, cool, fair to see, as pompous in its fatness as the cook in a monastery.

Peter put out a hand to steady it while he cut the stem. But at the instant he was aware that a black form had dropped over the fence lining the lane in front of him and was coming stealthily towards him. In a palsy of terror he dropped flat upon the ground, not having strength enough to run away. The next moment he was looking into the amazed and agonized face of old Alek Williams.

There was a moment of loaded silence, and then Peter was overcome by a mad inspiration. He suddenly dropped his knife and leaped upon Alek. "I got che!" he hissed. "I got che! I got che!" The old man sank down as limp as rags. "I got che! I got che! Steal Mist' Bryant's mellums, hey?"

Alek, in a low voice, began to beg. "Oh, Mist' Peter Wash'ton, don' go fer ter be too ha'd on er ole man! I nev' come yere fer ter steal 'em. 'Deed I didn't, Mist' Wash'ton! I come yere jes fer ter *feel* 'em. Oh, please, Mist' Wash'ton—"

"Come erlong outa yere, you ol' rip," said Peter, "an' don't trumple on dese yer baids. I gwine put you wah you won' ketch col'."

Without difficulty he tumbled the whining Alek over the fence to the roadway, and following him with sheriff-like expedition! He took him by the scruff. "Come erlong, deacon. I raikon I gwine put you wah you kin pray, deacon. Come erlong, deacon."

The emphasis and reiteration of his layman's title in the church produced a deadly effect upon Alek. He felt to his marrow the heinous crime into which this treacherous night had betrayed him. As Peter marched his prisoner up the road towards the mouth of the lane, he continued his remarks: "Come erlong, deacon. Nev' see er man so anxious like erbout er mellum-paitch, deacon. Seem like you jes must see 'em er-growin' an' *feel* 'em, deacon. Mist' Bryant he'll be s'prised, deacon, findin' out you come fer ter *feel* his mellums. Come erlong, deacon. Mist' Bryant he expectin' some ole rip like you come soon."

They had almost reached the lane when Alek's cur Susie, who had followed her master, approached in the silence which attends dangerous dogs; and seeing indications of what she took to be war, she appended herself swiftly but firmly to the calf of Peter's left leg. The mêlée was short, but spirited. Alek had no wish to have his dog complicate his already serious misfortunes, and went manfully to the defense of his captor. He procured a large stone, and by beating this with both hands down upon the resounding skull of the animal, he induced her to quit her grip. Breathing heavily, Peter dropped into the long grass at the road-side. He said nothing.

"Mist' Wash'ton," said Alek at last, in a quavering voice, "I raikon I gwine wait yere see what you gwine do ter me."

Whereupon Peter passed into a spasmodic state, in which he rolled to and fro and shook.

"Mist' Wash'ton, I hope dish yer dog 'ain't gone an' give you fitses?"

Peter sat up suddenly. "No, she 'ain't," he answered; "but she gin me er big skeer; an' fer yer 'sistance with er cobblestone, Mist' Willums, I tell you what I gwine do—I tell you what I gwine do." He waited an impressive moment. "I gwine 'lease you!"

Old Alek trembled like a little bush in a wind. "Mist' Wash'ton?"

Quoth Peter, deliberately, "I gwine 'lease you."

The old man was filled with a desire to negotiate this statement at once, but he felt the necessity of carrying off the event without an appearance of haste. "Yes, seh; thank 'e, seh; thank 'e, Mist' Wash'ton. I raikon I ramble home pressenly." He waited an interval, and then dubiously said, "Good-evenin', Mist' Wash'ton."

"Good-evenin', deacon. Don' come foolin' roun' *feelin'* no mellums, and I say troof. Good-evenin', deacon."

Alek took off his hat and made three profound bows. "Thank 'e, seh. Thank 'e, seh. Thank 'e, seh."

Peter underwent another severe spasm, but the old man walked off towards his home with a humble and contrite heart.

IV

The next morning Alek proceeded from his shanty under the complete but customary illusion that he was going to work. He trudged manfully along until he reached the vicinity of Si Bryant's place. Then, by stages, he relapsed into a slink. He was passing the garden-patch under full steam, when, at some distance ahead of him, he saw Si Bryant leaning casually on the garden fence.

"Good-mornin', Alek."

"Good-mawnin', Mist' Bryant," answered Alek, with a new deference. He was marching on, when he was halted by a word—"Alek!"

He stopped. "Yes, seh."

"I found a knife this mornin' in th' road," drawled Si, "an' I thought maybe it was yourn."

Improved in mind by this divergence from the direct line of attack, Alek stepped up easily to look at the knife. "No, seh," he said, scanning it as it lay in Si's palm, while the cold steel-blue eyes of the white man looked down into his stomach, "tain't no knife er mine." But he knew the knife. He knew it as if it had been his mother. And at the same moment a spark flashed through his head and made wise his understanding. He knew everything. " 'Tain't much of er knife, Mist' Bryant," he said, deprecatingly.

" 'Tain't much of a knife, I know that," cried Si, in sudden heat, "but I found it this mornin' in my watermelon-patch—hear?"

"Watahmellum-paitch?" yelled Alek, not astounded.

"Yes, in my watermelon-patch," sneered Si, "an' I think you know something about it, too!"

"Me?" cried Alek. "Me?"

"Yes—you!" said Si, with icy ferocity. "Yes—you!" He had become convinced that Alek was not in any way guilty, but he was certain that the old man knew the owner of the knife, and so he pressed him at first on criminal lines. "Alek, you might as well own up now. You've been meddlin' with my watermelons!"

"Me?" cried Alek again. "Yah's *ma* knife. I done cah'e it foh yeahs."

Bryant changed his ways. "Look here, Alek," he said, confidentially: "I know you and you know me, and there ain't no use in any more skirmishin'. *I* know that *you* know whose knife that is. Now whose is it?"

This challenge was so formidable in character that Alek temporarily quailed and began to stammer. "Er—now—Mist' Bryant—you—you—frien' er mine—"

"I know I'm a friend of yours, but," said Bryant, inexorably, "who owns this knife?"

Alek gathered unto himself some remnants of dignity and spoke with reproach: "Mist' Bryant, dish yer knife ain' mine."

"No," said Bryant, "it ain't. But you know who it belongs to, an' I want you to tell me—quick."

"Well, Mist' Bryant," answered Alek, scratching his wool, "I won't say 's I *do* know who b'longs ter dish yer knife, an' I won't say 's I *don't.*"

Bryant again laughed his Yankee laugh, but this time there was little humor in it. It was dangerous.

Alek, seeing that he had gotten himself into hot water by the fine diplomacy of his last sentence, immediately began to flounder and totally submerge himself. "No, Mist' Bryant," he repeated, "I won't say 's I *do* know who b'longs ter dish yer knife, an' I won't say 's I *don't.*" And he began to parrot this fatal sentence again and again. It seemed wound about his tongue. He could not rid himself of it. Its very power to make trouble for him seemed to originate the mysterious Afric reason for its repetition.

"Is he a very close friend of yourn?" said Bryant, softly.

"F-frien'?" stuttered Alek. He appeared to weigh this question with much care. "Well, seems like he *was* er frien', an' then agin, it seems like he—"

"It seems like he *wasn't?*" asked Bryant.

"Yes, seh, jest so, jest so," cried Alek. "Sometimes it seems like he *wasn't.* Then agin—" He stopped for profound meditation.

The patience of the white man seemed inexhaustible. At length his low and oily voice broke the stillness. "Oh, well, of course if he's a friend of yourn, Alek! You know I wouldn't want to make no trouble for a friend of yourn."

"Yes, seh," cried the Negro at once. "He's er frien' er mine. He is dat."

"Well, then, it seems as if about the only thing to do is for you to tell me his name so's I can send him his knife, and that's all there is to it."

Alek took off his hat, and in perplexity ran his hand over his wool. He studied the ground. But several times he raised his eyes to take a sly peep at the imperturbable visage of the white man. "Y—y—yes, Mist' Bryant. . . . I raikon dat's erbout all what kin be done. I gwine tell you who b'longs ter dish yer knife."

"Of course," said the smooth Bryant, "it ain't a very nice thing to have to do, but—"

"No, seh," cried Alek, brightly; "I'm gwine tell you, Mist' Bryant. I gwine tell you erbout dat knife. Mist' Bryant," he asked, solemnly, "does you know who b'longs ter dat knife?"

"No, I—"

"Well, I gwine tell. I gwine tell who. Mr. Bryant—" The old man drew himself to a stately pose and held forth his arm. "I gwine tell who. Mist' Bryant, *dish yer knife b'longs ter Sam Jackson!*"

Bryant was startled into indignation. "Who in hell is Sam Jackson?" he growled.

"He's a nigger," said Alek, impressively, "and he wuks in er lumber-yawd up yere in Hoswego."

IX

THE STOVE

I

"They'll bring her," said Mrs. Trescott, dubiously. Her cousin, the painter, the bewildered father of the angel child, had written to say that if they were asked, he and his wife would come to the Trescotts' for the Christmas holidays. But he had not officially stated that the angel child would form part of the expedition. "But of course they'll bring her," said Mrs. Trescott to her husband.

The doctor assented. "Yes, they'll have to bring her. They wouldn't dare leave New York at her mercy."

"Well," sighed Mrs. Trescott, after a pause, "the neighbors will be pleased. When they see her they'll immediately lock up their children for safety."

"Anyhow," said Trescott, "the devastation of the Margate twins was complete. She can't do that particular thing again. I shall be interested to note what form her energy will take this time."

"Oh, yes! that's it!" cried the wife. "You'll be *interested*. You've hit it exactly. You'll be interested to note what form her energy will take this time. And then, when the real crisis comes, you'll put on your hat and walk out of the house and leave *me* to straighten things out. This is not a scientific question; this is a practical matter."

"Well, as a practical man, I advocate chaining her out in the stable," answered the doctor.

When Jimmie Trescott was told that his old flame was again to appear, he remained calm. In fact, time had so mended his youthful heart that it was a regular apple of oblivion and peace. Her image in his thought was as the track of a bird on deep snow—it was an impression, but it did not concern the depths. However, he did what befitted his state. He went out and bragged in the street: "My cousin is comin' next week f'om New York." . . . "My cousin is comin' tomorrow f'om New York."

"Girl or boy?" said the populace, bluntly; but, when enlightened, they speedily cried, "Oh, we remember *her!*" They were charmed, for they thought of her as an outlaw, and they surmised that she could lead them into a very ecstasy of sin. They thought of her as a brave bandit, because they had been whipped for various pranks into which she had led them. When Jimmie made his declaration, they fell into a state of pleased and shuddering expectancy.

Mrs. Trescott pronounced her point of view: "The child is a nice child, if only Caroline had some sense. But she hasn't. And Willis is like a wax figure. I don't see what can be done, unless—unless you simply go to Willis and put the whole thing right at him." Then, for purposes of indication, she improvised a speech: "Look here, Willis, you've got a little daughter, haven't you? But, confound it, man, she is not the only girl child ever brought into the sunlight. There are a lot of children. Children are an ordinary phenomenon. In China they drown girl babies. If you wish to submit to this frightful impostor and tyrant, that is all very well, but why in the name of humanity do you make us submit to it?"

Doctor Trescott laughed. "I wouldn't dare say it to him."

"Anyhow," said Mrs. Trescott, determinedly, "that is what you *should* say to him."

"It wouldn't do the slightest good. It would only make him very angry, and I would lay myself perfectly open to a suggestion that I had better attend to my own affairs with more rigor."

"Well, I suppose you are right," Mrs. Trescott again said.

"Why don't you speak to Caroline?" asked the doctor, humorously.

"Speak to Caroline! Why, I wouldn't for the *world!* She'd fly through the roof. She'd snap my head off! Speak to Caroline! You must be mad!"

One afternoon the doctor went to await his visitors on the platform of the railway station. He was thoughtfully smiling. For some quaint reason he was convinced that he was to be treated to a quick manifestation of little Cora's peculiar and interesting powers. And yet, when the train paused at the station, there appeared to him only a pretty little girl in a fur-lined hood, and with her nose reddening from the sudden cold, and—attended respectfully by her parents. He smiled again, reflecting that he had comically exaggerated the dangers of dear little Cora. It amused his philosophy to note that he had really been perturbed.

As the big sleigh sped homeward there was a sudden shrill outcry from the angel child: "Oh, mamma! mamma! They've forgotten my stove!"

"Hush, dear; hush!" said the mother. "It's all right."

"Oh, but, mamma, they've forgotten my stove!"

The doctor thrust his chin suddenly out of his top-coat collar. "Stove?" he said. "Stove? What stove?"

"Oh, just a toy of the child's," explained the mother. "She's grown so fond of it, she loves it so, that if we didn't take it everywhere with her she'd suffer dreadfully. So we always bring it."

"Oh!" said the doctor. He pictured a little tin trinket. But when the stove was really unmasked, it turned out to be an affair of cast iron, as big as a portmanteau, and, as the stage people say, practicable. There was some trouble that evening when came the hour of children's bedtime. Little Cora burst into a wild declaration that she could not retire for the night unless the stove was carried up-stairs and placed at her bedside. While the mother was trying to dissuade the child, the Trescotts held their peace and gazed with awe. The incident closed when the lamb-eyed father gathered the stove in his arms and preceded the angel child to her chamber.

In the morning, Trescott was standing with his back to the dining-room fire, awaiting breakfast, when he heard a noise of descending guests. Presently the door opened, and the party entered in regular order. First came the angel child, then the cooing mother, and last the great painter with his arm full of the stove. He deposited it gently in a corner, and sighed. Trescott wore a wide grin.

"What are you carting that thing all over the house for?" he said, brutally. "Why don't you put it some place where she can play with it, and leave it there?"

The mother rebuked him with a look. "Well, if it gives her pleasure, Ned?" she expostulated, softly. "If it makes the child happy to have the stove with her, why shouldn't she have it?"

"Just so," said the doctor, with calmness.

Jimmie's idea was the roaring fireplace in the cabin of the lone mountaineer. At first he was not able to admire a girl's stove built on well-known domestic lines. He eyed it and thought it was very pretty, but it did not move him immediately. But a certain respect grew to an interest, and he became the angel child's accomplice. And even if he had not had an interest grow upon him, he was certain to have been implicated sooner or later, because of the imperious way of little Cora, who made a serf of him in a few swift sentences. Together they carried the stove out into the desolate garden and squatted it in the snow. Jimmie's snug little muscles had been pitted against the sheer nervous vigor of this little golden-haired girl, and he had not won great honors. When the mind blazed inside the small body, the angel child was pure force. She began to speak: "Now, Jim, get some paper. Get some wood —little sticks at first. Now we want a match. You got a match? Well, go get a match. Get some more wood. Hurry up, now! No. *No!* I'll light it my own self. You get some more wood. There! Isn't that splendid? You get a whole lot of wood an' pile it up here by the stove. An' now what'll we cook? We must have somethin' to cook, you know, else it ain't like the real."

"Potatoes," said Jimmie, at once.

The day was clear, cold, bright. An icy wind sped from over the waters of the lake. A grown person would hardly have been abroad save on compulsion of a kind, and yet, when they were called to luncheon, the two little simpletons protested with great cries.

II

The ladies of Whilomville were somewhat given to the pagan habit of tea parties. When a tea party was to befall a certain house one could read it in the manner of the prospective hostess, who for some previous days would go about twitching this and twisting that, and dusting here and polishing there; the ordinary habits of the household began then to disagree with her, and her unfortunate husband and children fled to the lengths of their tethers. Then there was a hush. Then there was a tea party. On the fatal afternoon a small picked company of latent enemies would meet. There would be a fanfare of affectionate greetings, during which everybody would measure to an inch the importance of what everybody else was wearing. Those who wore old dresses would wish then that they had not come; and those who saw that, in the company, they were well clad, would be pleased or exalted, or filled with the joys of cruelty. Then they had tea, which was a habit and a delight with none of them, their usual beverage being coffee with milk.

Usually the party jerked horribly in the beginning, while the hostess strove and pulled and pushed to make its progress smooth. Then suddenly it would be off like the wind, eight, fifteen, or twenty-five tongues clattering, with a noise like a cotton-mill combined with the noise of a few penny whistles. Then the hostess had nothing to do but to look glad, and see that everybody had enough tea and cake. When the door was closed behind the last guest, the hostess would usually drop into a chair and say: "Thank Heaven! They're gone!" There would be no malice in this expression. It simply would be that, woman-like, she had flung herself headlong at the accomplishment of a pleasure which she could not even define, and at the end she felt only weariness.

The value and beauty, or oddity, of the teacups was another element which entered largely into the spirit of these terrible enterprises. The quality of the tea was an element which did not enter at all. Uniformly it was rather bad. But the cups! Some of the more ambitious people aspired to have cups each of a different pattern, possessing, in fact, the sole similarity that with their odd curves and dips of form they each resembled anything but a teacup. Others of the more ambitious aspired to a quite severe and godly "set," which, when viewed, appalled one with its austere and rigid family resemblances, and made one desire to ask the hostess if the teapot was not the father of all the little cups, and at the same time protesting gallantly that such a young and charming cream-jug surely could not be their mother.

But of course the serious part is that these collections so differed in style and the obvious amount paid for them that nobody could be happy. The poorer ones envied; the richer ones feared; the poorer ones continually striving to overtake the leaders; the leaders always with their heads turned back to hear overtaking footsteps. And none of these things here written did they know. Instead of seeing that they were very stupid, they thought they were very fine. And they gave and took heart-bruises—fierce, deep heart-bruises—under the clear impression that of such kind of rubbish was the kingdom of nice people. The characteristics of outsiders of course emerged in shreds from these tea parties, and it is doubtful if the characteristics of insiders escaped entirely. In fact, these tea parties were in the large way the result of a conspiracy of certain unenlightened people to make life still more uncomfortable.

Mrs. Trescott was in the circle of tea-fighters largely through a sort of artificial necessity—a necessity, in short, which she had herself created in a spirit of femininity.

When the painter and his family came for the holidays, Mrs. Trescott had for some time been feeling that it was her turn to give a tea party, and she was resolved upon it now that she was reinforced by the beautiful wife of the painter, whose charms would make all the other women feel badly. And Mrs. Trescott further resolved that the affair should be notable in more than one way. The painter's wife suggested that, as an innovation, they give the people good tea; but Mrs. Trescott shook her head; she was quite sure they would not like it.

It was an impressive gathering. A few came to see if they could not find out the faults of the painter's wife, and these, added to those who would have attended even without that attractive prospect, swelled the company to a number quite large for Whilomville. There were the usual preliminary jolts, and then suddenly the tea party was in full swing, and looked like an unprecedented success.

Mrs. Trescott exchanged a glance with the painter's wife. They felt proud and superior. This tea party was almost perfection.

III

JIMMIE and the angel child, after being oppressed by innumerable admonitions to behave correctly during the afternoon, succeeded in reaching the garden, where the stove awaited them. They were enjoying themselves grandly, when snow began to fall so heavily that it gradually dampened their ardor as well as extinguished the fire in the stove. They stood ruefully until the angel child devised the plan of carrying the stove into the stable, and there, safe from the storm, to continue the festivities. But they were met at the door of the stable by Peter Washington.

"What you 'bout, Jim?"

"Now—it's snowin' so hard, we thought we'd take the stove into the stable."

"An' have er fiah in it? No, seh! G'w'on 'way f'm heh!—g'w'on! Don' 'low no sech foolishin' round yer. No, seh!"

"Well, we ain't goin' to hurt your old stable, are we?" asked Jimmie, ironically.

"Dat you ain't, Jim! Not so long's I keep my two eyes right plumb squaah pinted at ol' Jim. No, seh!" Peter began to chuckle in derision.

The two vagabonds stood before him while he informed them of their iniquities as well as their absurdities, and further made clear his own masterly grasp of the spirit of their devices. Nothing affects children so much as rhetoric. It may not involve any definite presentation of common-sense, but if it is picturesque they surrender decently to its influence. Peter was by all means a rhetorician, and it was not long before the two children had dismally succumbed to him. They went away.

Depositing the stove in the snow, they straightened to look at each other. It did not enter either head to relinquish the idea of continuing the game. But the situation seemed invulnerable.

The angel child went on a scouting tour. Presently she returned, flying. "I know! Let's have it in the cellar! In the cellar! Oh, it 'll be lovely!"

The outer door of the cellar was open, and they proceeded down some steps with their treasure. There was plenty of light; the cellar was high-walled, warm, and dry. They named it an ideal place. Two huge cylindrical furnaces were humming away, one at either end. Overhead the beams detonated with the different emotions which agitated the tea party.

Jimmie worked like a stoker, and soon there was a fine bright fire in the stove. The fuel was of small brittle sticks which did not make a great deal of smoke.

"Now what 'll we cook?" cried little Cora. "What 'll we cook, Jim? We must have something to cook, you know."

"Potatoes?" said Jimmie.

But the angel child made a scornful gesture. "No. I've cooked 'bout a million potatoes, I guess. Potatoes aren't nice any more."

Jimmie's mind was all said and done when the question of potatoes had been passed, and he looked weakly at his companion.

"Haven't you got any turnips in your house?" she inquired, contemptuously. "In *my* house we have *turnips.*"

"Oh, turnips!" exclaimed Jimmie, immensely relieved to find that the honor of his family was safe. "Turnips? Oh, bushels an' bushels an' bushels! Out in the shed."

"Well, go an' get a whole lot," commanded the angel child. "Go an' get a whole lot. Grea' big ones. *We* always have grea' big ones."

Jimmie went to the shed and kicked gently at a company of turnips which the frost had amalgamated. He made three journeys to and from the cellar, carrying always the very largest types from his father's store. Four of them filled the oven of little Cora's stove. This fact did not please her, so they placed three rows of turnips on the hot top. Then the angel child, profoundly moved by an inspiration, suddenly cried out,

"Oh, Jimmie, let's play we're keepin' a hotel, an' have got to cook for 'bout a thousand people, an' those two furnaces will be the ovens, an' I'll be the chief cook—"

"No; I want to be chief cook some of the time," interrupted Jimmie.

"No; I'll be chief cook my own self. You must be my 'sistant. Now I'll prepare 'em—see? An' then you put 'em in the ovens. Get the shovel. We'll play that's the pan. I'll fix 'em, an' then you put 'em in the oven. Hold it still now."

Jim held the coal-shovel while little Cora, with a frown of importance, arranged turnips in rows upon it. She patted each one daintily, and then backed away to view it, with her head critically sideways.

"There!" she shouted at last. "That 'll do, I guess. Put 'em in the oven."

Jimmie marched with his shovelful of turnips to one of the furnaces. The door was already open, and he slid the shovel in upon the red coals.

"Come on," cried little Cora. "I've got another batch nearly ready."

"But what am I goin' to do with these?" asked Jimmie. "There ain't only one shovel."

"Leave 'm in there," retorted the girl, passionately. "Leave 'm in there, an' then play you're comin' with another pan. 'Taint right to stand there an' *hold* the pan, you goose."

So Jimmie expelled all his turnips from his shovel out upon the furnace fire, and returned obediently for another batch.

"These are puddings," yelled the angel child, gleefully. "Dozens an' dozens of puddings for the thousand people at our grea' big hotel."

IV

At the first alarm the painter had fled to the doctor's office, where he hid his face behind a book and pretended that he did not hear the noise of feminine revelling. When the doctor came from a round of calls, he too retreated upon the office, and the men consoled each other as well as they were able. Once Mrs. Trescott dashed in to say delightedly that her tea party was not only the success of the season, but it was probably the very nicest tea party that had ever been held in Whilomville. After vainly beseeching them to return with her, she dashed away again, her face bright with happiness.

The doctor and the painter remained for a long time in silence, Trescott tapping reflectively upon the window-pane. Finally he turned to the painter, and sniffing, said: "What is that, Willis? Don't you smell something?"

The painter also sniffed. "Why, yes! It's like—it's like turnips."

"Turnips? No; it can't be."

"Well, it's very much like it."

The puzzled doctor opened the door into the hall, and at first it appeared that he was going to give back two paces. A result of frizzling turnips, which was almost as tangible as mist, had blown in upon his face and made him gasp. "Good God! Willis, what can this be?" he cried.

"Whee!" said the painter. "It's awful, isn't it?"

The doctor made his way hurriedly to his wife, but before he could speak with her he had to endure the business of greeting a score of women. Then he whispered, "Out in the hall there's an awful—"

But at that moment it came to them on the wings of a sudden draft. The solemn odor of burning turnips rolled in like a sea-fog, and fell upon that dainty, perfumed tea party. It was almost a personality; if some unbidden and extremely odious guest had entered the room, the effect would have been much the same. The sprightly talk stopped with a jolt, and people looked at each other. Then a few brave and considerate persons made the usual attempt to talk away as if nothing had happened. They all looked at their hostess, who wore an air of stupefaction.

The odor of burning turnips grew and grew. To Trescott it seemed to make a noise. He thought he could hear the dull roar of this outrage. Under some circumstances he might have been able to take the situation from a point of view of comedy, but the agony of his wife was too acute, and, for him, too visible. She was saying: "Yes, we saw the play the last time we were in New York. I liked it very much. That scene in the second act—the gloomy church, you know, and all that—and the organ playing—and then when the four singing little girls came in—" But Trescott comprehended that she did not know if she was talking of a play or a parachute.

He had not been in the room twenty seconds before his brow suddenly flushed with an angry inspiration. He left the room hastily, leaving behind him an incoherent phrase of apology, and charged upon his office, where he found the painter somnolent.

"Willis!" he cried, sternly, "come with me. It's that damn kid of yours!"

The painter was immediately agitated. He always seemed to feel more than anyone else in the world the peculiar ability of his child to create resounding excitement, but he seemed always to exhibit his feelings very late. He arose hastily, and hurried after Trescott to the top of the inside cellar stairway. Trescott motioned him to pause, and for an instant they listened.

"Hurry up, Jim," cried the busy little Cora. "Here's another whole batch of lovely puddings. Hurry up now, an' put 'em in the oven."

Trescott looked at the painter; the painter groaned. Then they appeared violently in the middle of the great kitchen of the hotel with a thousand people in it. "Jimmie, go up-stairs!" said Trescott, and then he turned to watch the painter deal with the angel child.

With some imitation of wrath, the painter stalked to his daughter's side and grasped her by the arm.

"Oh, papa! papa!" she screamed. "You're pinching me! You're pinching me! You're pinching me, papa!"

At first the painter had seemed resolved to keep his grip, but suddenly he let go her arm in a panic. "I've hurt her," he said, turning to Trescott.

Trescott had swiftly done much towards the obliteration of the hotel kitchen, but he looked up now and spoke, after a short period of reflection. "You've hurt her, have you? Well, hurt her again. Spank her!" he cried, enthusiastically. "Spank her, confound you, man! She needs it. Here's your chance. Spank her, and spank her good. Spank her!"

The painter naturally wavered over this incendiary proposition, but at last, in one supreme burst of daring, he shut his eyes and again grabbed his precious offspring.

The spanking was lamentably the work of a perfect bungler. It couldn't have hurt at all; but the angel child raised to heaven a loud, clear soprano howl that expressed the last word in even medieval anguish. Soon the painter was aghast. "Stop it, darling! I didn't mean —I didn't mean to—to hurt you so much, you know." He danced nervously. Trescott sat on a box, and devilishly smiled.

But the pasture-call of suffering motherhood came down to them, and a moment later a splendid apparition appeared on the cellar stairs. She understood the scene at a glance. "Willis! What have you been doing?"

Trescott sat on his box, the painter guiltily moved from foot to foot, and the angel child advanced to her mother with arms outstretched, making a piteous wail of amazed and pained pride that would have moved Peter the Great. Regardless of her frock, the panting mother knelt on the stone floor and took her child to her bosom, and looked, then, bitterly, scornfully, at the cowering father and husband.

The painter, for his part, at once looked reproachfully at Trescott, as if to say: "There! You see?"

Trescott arose and extended his hands in a quiet but magnificent gesture of despair and weariness. He seemed about to say something classic, and, quite instinctively, they waited. The stillness was deep, and the wait was longer than a moment. "Well," he said, "we can't live in the cellar. Let's go up-stairs."

X

THE TRIAL, EXECUTION, AND BURIAL OF
HOMER PHELPS

FROM time to time an enwearied pine bough let fall to the earth its load of melting snow, and the branch swung back glistening in the faint wintry sunlight. Down the gulch a brook clattered amid its ice with the sound of a perpetual breaking of glass. All the forest looked drenched and forlorn.

The sky-line was a ragged enclosure of gray cliffs and hemlocks and pines. If one had been miraculously set down in this gulch one could have imagined easily that the nearest human habitation was hundreds of miles away, if it were not for an old half-discernible wood-road that led towards the brook.

"Halt! Who's there?"

This low and gruff cry suddenly dispelled the stillness which lay upon the lonely gulch, but the hush which followed it seemed even more profound. The hush endured for some seconds, and then the voice of the challenger was again raised, this time with a distinctly querulous note in it.

"Halt! Who's there? Why don't you answer when I holler? Don't you know you're likely to get shot?"

A second voice answered, "Oh, you knew who I was easy enough."

"That don't make no diff'rence." One of the Margate twins stepped from a thicket and confronted Homer Phelps on the old wood-road. The majestic scowl of official wrath was upon the brow of Reeves Margate, a long stick was held in the hollow of his arm as one would hold a rifle, and he strode grimly to the other boy. "That don't make no diff'rence. You've got to answer when I holler, anyhow. Willie says so."

At the mention of the dread chieftain's name the Phelps boy daunted a trifle, but he still sulkily murmured, "Well, you knew it was me."

He started on his way through the snow, but the twin sturdily blocked the path. "You can't pass less'n you give the countersign."

"Huh?" said the Phelps boy. "Countersign?"

"Yes—countersign," sneered the twin, strong in his sense of virtue.

But the Phelps boy became very angry, "Can't I, hey? Can't I, hey? I'll show you whether I can or not! I'll show you, Reeves Margate!"

There was a short scuffle, and then arose the anguished clamor of the sentry: "Hey, fellers! Here's a man tryin' to run a-past the guard. Hey, fellers! Hey!"

There was a great noise in the adjacent underbrush. The voice of Willie could be heard exhorting his followers to charge swiftly and bravely. Then they appeared—Willie Dalzel, Jimmie Trescott, the other Margate twin, and Dan Earl. The chieftain's face was dark with wrath. "What's the matter? Can't you play it right? Ain't you got any sense?" he asked the Phelps boy.

The sentry was yelling out his grievance. "Now—he came along an' I hollered at 'im, an' he didn't pay no 'tention, an' when I ast 'im for the countersign, he wouldn't say nothin'. That ain't no way."

"Can't you play it right?" asked the chief again, with gloomy scorn.

"He knew it was me easy enough," said the Phelps boy.

"That ain't got nothin' to do with it," cried the chief, furiously. "That ain't got nothin' to do with it. If you're goin' to play, you've got to play it right. It ain't no fun if you go spoilin' the whole thing this way. Can't you play it right?"

"I forgot the countersign," lied the culprit, weakly.

Whereupon the remainder of the band yelled out, with one triumphant voice: "War to the knife! War to the knife! I remember it, Willie. Don't I, Willie?"

The leader was puzzled. Evidently he was trying to develop in his mind a plan for dealing correctly with this unusual incident. He felt, no doubt, that he must proceed according to the books, but unfortunately the books did not cover the point precisely. However, he finally said to Homer Phelps, "You are under arrest." Then with a stentorian voice he shouted, "Seize him!"

His loyal followers looked startled for a brief moment, but directly they began to move upon the Phelps boy. The latter clearly did not intend to be seized. He backed away, expostulating wildly. He even seemed somewhat frightened. "No, no; don't you touch me, I tell you; don't you dare touch me."

The others did not seem anxious to engage. They moved slowly, watching the desperate light in his eyes. The chieftain stood with folded arms, his face growing darker and darker with impatience. At length he burst out: "Oh, seize him, I tell you! Why don't you seize him? Grab him by the leg, Dannie! Hurry up, all of you! Seize him, I keep a-sayin'!"

Thus adjured, the Margate twins and Dan Earl made another pained effort, while Jimmie Trescott maneuvered to cut off a retreat. But, to tell the truth, there was a boyish law which held them back from laying hands of violence upon little Phelps under these conditions. Perhaps it was because they were only playing, whereas he was now undeniably serious. At any rate, they looked very sick of their occupation.

"Don't you dare!" snarled the Phelps boy, facing first one and then the other; he was almost in tears—"don't you dare touch me!"

The chieftain was now hopping with exasperation. "Oh, seize him, can't you? You're no good at all!" Then he loosed his wrath upon the Phelps boy: "Stand still, Homer, can't you? You've got to be seized, you know. That ain't the way. It ain't any fun if you keep a-dodgin' that way. Stand still, can't you! You've got to be seized."

"I don't *want* to be seized," retorted the Phelps boy, obstinate and bitter.

"But you've *got* to be seized!" yelled the maddened chief. "Don't you see? That's the way to play it."

The Phelps boy answered, promptly, "But I don't want to play that way."

"But that's the *right* way to play it. Don't you see? You've got to play it the right way. You've got to be seized, an' then we'll hold a trial on you, an'—an' all sorts of things."

But this prospect held no illusions for the Phelps boy. He continued doggedly to repeat, "I don't want to play that way!"

Of course in the end the chief stooped to beg and beseech this unreasonable lad. "Oh, come on, Homer! Don't be so mean. You're a-spoilin' everything. We won't hurt you any. Not the tintiest bit. It's all just playin'. What's the matter with you?"

The different tone of the leader made an immediate impression upon the other. He showed some signs of the beginning of weakness. "Well," he asked, "what you goin' to do?"

"Why, first we're goin' to put you in a dungeon, or tie you to a stake, or something like that—just pertend, you know," added the chief, hurriedly, "an' then we'll hold a trial, awful solemn, but there won't be anything what 'll hurt you. Not a thing."

And so the game was readjusted. The Phelps boy was marched off between Dan Earl and a Margate twin. The party proceeded to their camp, which was hidden some hundred feet back in the thickets. There was a miserable little hut with a pine-bark roof, which so frankly and constantly leaked that existence in the open air was always preferable. At present it was noisily dripping melted snow into the black moldy interior. In front of this hut a feeble fire was flickering through its unhappy career. Underfoot, the watery snow was of the color of lead.

The party having arrived at the camp, the chief leaned against a tree, and balancing on one foot, drew off a rubber boot. From this boot he emptied about a quart of snow. He squeezed his stocking, which had a hole from which protruded a lobster-red toe. He resumed his boot. "Bring up the prisoner," said he. They did it. "Guilty or not guilty?" he asked.

"Huh?" said the Phelps boy.

"Guilty or not guilty?" demanded the chief, peremptorily. "Guilty or not guilty? Don't you understand?"

Homer Phelps looked profoundly puzzled. "Guilty or not guilty?" he asked, slowly and weakly.

The chief made a swift gesture, and turned in despair to the others. "Oh, he don't do it right! He does it all wrong!" He again faced the prisoner with an air of making a last attempt, "Now look-a-here, Homer, when I say, 'Guilty or not guilty?' you want to up an' say, 'Not Guilty.' Don't you see?"

"Not guilty," said Homer, at once.

"No, no, no. Wait till I ask you. Now wait." He called out, pompously, "Pards, if this prisoner before us is guilty, what shall be his fate?"

All those well-trained little infants with one voice sung out, *"Death!"*

"Prisoner," continued the chief, "are you guilty or not guilty?"

"But look-a-here," argued Homer, "you said it wouldn't be nothin' that would hurt. I—"

"Thunder an' lightnin'!" roared the wretched chief. "Keep your mouth shut, can't ye? What in the mischief—"

But there was an interruption from Jimmie Trescott, who shouldered a twin aside and stepped to the front. "Here," he said, very contemptuously, "let me be the prisoner. I'll show 'im how to do it."

"All right, Jim," cried the chief, delighted; "you be the prisoner, then. Now all you fellers with guns stand there in a row! Get out of the way, Homer!" He cleared his throat, and addressed Jimmie. "Prisoner, are you guilty or not guilty?"

"Not guilty," answered Jimmie, firmly. Standing there before his judge—unarmed, slim, quiet, modest—he was ideal.

The chief beamed upon him, and looked aside to cast a triumphant and withering glance upon Homer Phelps. He said: "There! That's the way to do it."

The twins and Dan Earl also much admired Jimmie.

"That's all right so far, anyhow," said the satisfied chief. "An' now we'll—now we'll—we'll perceed with the execution."

"That ain't right," said the new prisoner, suddenly. "That ain't the next thing. You've got to have a trial first. You've got to fetch up a lot of people first who'll say I done it."

"That's so," said the chief. "I didn't think. Here, Reeves, you be first witness. Did the prisoner do it?"

The twin gulped for a moment in his anxiety to make the proper reply. He was at the point where the roads forked. Finally he hazarded, "Yes."

"There," said the chief, "that's one of 'em. Now, Dan, you be a witness. Did he do it?"

Dan Earl, having before him the twin's example, did not hesitate. "Yes," he said.

"Well, then, pards, what shall be his fate?"

Again came the ringing answer, *"Death!"*

With Jimmie in the principal role, this drama, hidden deep in the hemlock thicket, neared a kind of perfection. "You must blindfold me," cried the condemned lad, briskly, "an' then I'll go off an' stand, an' you must all get in a row an' shoot me."

The chief gave this plan his urbane countenance, and the twins and Dan Earl were greatly pleased. They blindfolded Jimmie under his careful directions. He waded a few paces into snow, and then turned and stood with quiet dignity, awaiting his fate. The chief marshaled the twins and Dan Earl in line with their sticks. He gave the necessary commands: "Load! Ready! Aim! Fire!" At the last command the firing party all together yelled, "Bang!"

Jimmie threw his hands high, tottered in agony for a moment, and then crashed full length into the snow—into, one would think, a serious case of pneumonia. It was beautiful.

He arose almost immediately and came back to them, wondrously pleased with himself. They acclaimed him joyously.

The chief was particularly grateful. He was always trying to bring off these little romantic affairs, and it seemed, after all, that the only boy who could ever really help him was Jimmie Trescott. "There," he said to the others, "that's the way it ought to be done."

They were touched to the heart by the whole thing, and they looked at Jimmie with big, smiling eyes. Jimmie, blown out like a balloon-fish with pride of his performance, swaggered to the fire and took seat on some wet hemlock boughs. "Fetch some more wood, one of you kids," he murmured, negligently. One of the twins came fortunately upon a small cedar-tree the lower branches of which were dead and dry. An armful of these branches flung upon the sick fire soon made a high, ruddy, warm blaze, which was like an illumination in honor of Jimmie's success.

The boys sprawled about the fire and talked the regular language of the game. "Waal, pards," remarked the chief, "it's many a night we've had together here in the Rockies among the b'ars an' the Indyuns, hey?"

"Yes, pard," replied Jimmie Trescott, "I reckon you're right. Our wild, free life is—there ain't nothin' to compare with our wild, free life."

Whereupon the two lads arose and magnificently shook hands, while the others watched them in an ecstasy. "I'll allus stick by ye, pard," said Jimmie, earnestly. "When yer in trouble, don't forgit that Lightnin' Lou is at yer back."

"Thanky, pard," quoth Willie Dalzel, deeply affected. "I'll not forgit it, pard. An' don't you forgit, either, that Dead-shot Demon, the leader of the Red Raiders, never forgits a friend."

But Homer Phelps was having none of this great fun. Since his disgraceful refusal to be seized and executed he had been hovering unheeded on the outskirts of the band. He seemed very sorry; he cast a wistful eye at the romantic scene. He knew too well that if he went near at that particular time he would be certain to encounter a pitiless snubbing. So he vacillated modestly in the background.

At last the moment came when he dared venture near enough to the fire to gain some warmth, for he was now bitterly suffering with the cold. He sidled close to Willie Dalzel. No one heeded him. Eventually he looked at his chief, and with a bright face said,

"Now—if I was seized now to be executed, I could do it as well as Jimmie Trescott, I could."

The chief gave a crow of scorn, in which he was followed by the other boys. "Ho!" he cried, "why didn't you do it, then? Why didn't you do it?" Homer Phelps felt upon him many pairs of disdainful eyes. He wagged his shoulders in misery.

"You're dead," said the chief, frankly. "That's what you are. We executed you, we did."

"When?" demanded the Phelps boy, with some spirit.

"Just a little while ago. Didn't we, fellers? Hey, fellers, didn't we?"

The trained chorus cried: "Yes, of course we did. You're dead, Homer. You can't play any more. You're dead."

"That wasn't me. It was Jimmie Trescott," he said, in a low and bitter voice, his eyes on the ground. He would have given the world if he could have retracted his mad refusals of the early part of the drama.

"No," said the chief, "it was you. We're playin' it was you, an' it *was* you. You're dead, you are." And seeing the cruel effect of his words, he did not refrain from administering some advice: "The next time, don't be such a chuckle-head."

Presently the camp imagined that it was attacked by Indians, and the boys dodged behind trees with their stick-rifles, shouting out, "Bang!" and encouraging each other to resist until the last. In the mean time the dead lad hovered near the fire, looking moodily at the gay and exciting scene. After the fight the gallant defenders returned one by one to the fire, where they grandly clasped hands, calling each other "old pard," and boasting of their deeds.

Parenthetically, one of the twins had an unfortunate inspiration. "I killed the Indyun chief, fellers. Did you see me kill the Indy-un chief?"

But Willie Dalzel, his own chief, turned upon him wrathfully: "*You* didn't kill no chief. *I* killed 'im with me own hand."

"Oh!" said the twin, apologetically, at once. "It must have been some other Indy-un."

"Who's wounded?" cried Willie Dalzel. "Ain't anybody wounded?" The party professed themselves well and sound. The roving and inventive eye of the chief chanced upon Homer Phelps. "Ho! Here's a dead man! Come on, fellers, here's a dead man! We've got to bury him, you know." And at his bidding they pounced upon the dead Phelps lad. The unhappy boy saw clearly his road to rehabilitation, but mind and body revolted at the idea of burial, even as they had revolted at the thought of execution. "No!" he said, stubbornly. "No! I don't want to be buried! I don't want to be buried!"

"You've *got* to be buried!" yelled the chief, passionately. " 'Tain't goin' to hurt ye, is it? Think you're made of glass? Come on, fellers, get the grave ready!"

They scattered hemlock boughs upon the snow in the form of a rectangle, and piled other boughs near at hand. The victim surveyed these preparations with a glassy eye. When all was ready, the chief turned determinedly to him: "Come on now, Homer. We've got to carry you to the grave. Get him by the legs, Jim!"

Little Phelps had now passed into that state which may be described as a curious and temporary childish fatalism. He still objected, but it was only feeble muttering, as if he did not know what he spoke. In some confusion they carried him to the rectangle of hemlock boughs and dropped him. Then they piled other boughs upon him until he was not to be seen. The chief stepped forward to make a short address, but before proceeding with it he thought it expedient, from certain indications, to speak to the grave itself. "Lie still, can't ye? Lie still until I get through." There was a faint movement of the boughs, and then a perfect silence.

The chief took off his hat. Those who watched him could see that his face was harrowed with emotion. "Pards," he began, brokenly— "pards, we've got one more debt to pay them murderin' red-skins. Bowie-knife Joe was a brave man an' a good pard, but—he's gone now —gone." He paused for a moment, overcome, and the stillness was only broken by the deep manly grief of Jimmie Trescott.

XI

THE FIGHT

I

THE child life of the neighborhood was sometimes moved in its deeps at the sight of wagon-loads of furniture arriving in front of some house which, with closed blinds and barred doors, had been for a time a mystery, or even a fear. The boys often expressed this fear by stamping bravely and noisily on the porch of the house, and then suddenly darting away with screams of nervous laughter, as if they expected to be pursued by something uncanny. There was a group who held that the cellar of a vacant house was certainly the abode of robbers, smugglers, assassins, mysterious masked men in council about the dim rays of a candle, and possessing skulls, emblematic bloody daggers, and owls. Then, near the first of April, would come along a wagon-load of furniture, and children would assemble on the walk by the gate and make serious examination of everything that passed into the house, and taking no thought whatever of masked men.

One day it was announced in the neighborhood that a family was actually moving into the Hannigan house, next door to Dr. Trescott's. Jimmie was one of the first to be informed, and by the time some of his friends came dashing up he was versed in much.

"Any boys?" they demanded, eagerly.

"Yes," answered Jimmie, proudly. "One's a little feller, and one's most as big as me. I saw 'em, I did."

"Where are they?" asked Willie Dalzel, as if under the circumstances he could not take Jimmie's word, but must have the evidence of his senses.

"Oh, they're in there," said Jimmie, carelessly. It was evident he owned these new boys.

Willie Dalzel resented Jimmie's proprietary way.

"Ho!" he cried, scornfully. "Why don't they come out, then? Why don't they come out?"

"How d' I know?" said Jimmie.

"Well," retorted Willie Dalzel, "you seemed to know so thundering much about 'em."

At the moment a boy came strolling down the gravel walk which led from the front door to the gate. He was about the height and age of Jimmie Trescott, but he was thick through the chest and had fat legs. His face was round and rosy and plump, but his hair was curly black, and his brows were naturally darkling, so that he resembled both a pudding and a young bull.

He approached slowly the group of older inhabitants, and they had grown profoundly silent. They looked him over; he looked them over. They might have been savages observing the first white man, or white men observing the first savage. The silence held steady.

As he neared the gate the strange boy wandered off to the left in a definite way, which proved his instinct to make a circular voyage when in doubt. The motionless group stared at him. In time this unsmiling scrutiny worked upon him somewhat, and he leaned against the fence and fastidiously examined one shoe.

In the end Willie Dalzel authoritatively broke the stillness. "What's your name?" said he, gruffly.

"Johnnie Hedge 'tis," answered the new boy. Then came another great silence while Whilomville pondered this intelligence.

Again came the voice of authority—"Where'd you live b'fore?"

"Jersey City."

These two sentences completed the first section of the formal code. The second section concerned itself with the establishment of the new-comer's exact position in the neighborhood.

"I kin lick you," announced Willie Dalzel, and awaited the answer.

The Hedge boy had stared at Willie Dalzel, but he stared at him again. After a pause he said, "I know you kin."

"Well," demanded Willie, "kin *he* lick you?" And he indicated Jimmie Trescott with a sweep which announced plainly that Jimmie was the next in prowess.

Whereupon the new boy looked at Jimmie respectfully but carefully, and at length said, "I dun'no'."

This was the signal for an outburst of shrill screaming, and everybody pushed Jimmie forward. He knew what he had to say, and, as befitted the occasion, he said it fiercely: "Kin you lick me?"

The new boy also understood what he had to say, and, despite his unhappy and lonely state, he said it bravely: "Yes."

"Well," retorted Jimmie, bluntly, "come out and do it, then! Jest come out and do it!" And these words were greeted with cheers. These little rascals yelled that there should be a fight at once. They were in bliss over the prospect. "Go on, Jim! Make 'im come out. He said he could lick you. Aw-aw-aw! He said he could lick you!" There probably never was a fight among this class in Whilomville which was not the result of the goading and guying of two proud lads by a populace of urchins who simply wished to see a show.

Willie Dalzel was very busy. He turned first to the one and then to the other. "You said you could lick him. Well, why don't you come out and do it, then? You said you could lick him, didn't you?"

"Yes," answered the new boy, dogged and dubious.

Willie tried to drag Jimmie by the arm. "Aw, go on, Jimmie! You ain't afraid, are you?"

"No," said Jimmie.

The two victims opened wide eyes at each other. The fence separated them, and so it was impossible for them to immediately engage; but they seemed to understand that they were ultimately to be sacrificed to the ferocious aspirations of the other boys, and each scanned the other to learn something of his spirit. They were not angry at all. They were merely two little gladiators who were being clamorously told to hurt each other. Each displayed hesitation and doubt without displaying fear. They did not exactly understand what were their feelings, and they moodily kicked the ground and made low and sullen answers to Willie Dalzel, who worked like a circus-manager.

"Aw, go on, Jim! What's the matter with you? You ain't afraid, are you? Well, then, say something." This sentiment received more cheering from the abandoned little wretches who wished to be entertained, and in this cheering there could be heard notes of derision of Jimmie Trescott. The latter had a position to sustain; he was well known; he often bragged of his willingness and ability to thrash other boys; well, then, here was a boy of his size who said that he could not thrash him. What was he going to do about it? The crowd made these arguments very clear, and repeated them again and again.

Finally Jimmie, driven to aggression, walked close to the fence and said to the new boy, "The first time I catch you out of your own yard I'll lam the head off'n you!" This was received with wild plaudits by the Whilomville urchins.

But the new boy stepped back from the fence. He was awed by Jimmie's formidable mien. But he managed to get out a semi-defiant sentence. "Maybe you will, and maybe you won't," said he.

However, his short retreat was taken as a practical victory for Jimmie, and the boys hooted him bitterly. He remained inside the fence, swinging one foot and scowling, while Jimmie was escorted off down the street amid acclamations. The new boy turned and walked back towards the house, his face gloomy, lined deep with discouragement, as if he felt that the new environment's antagonism and palpable cruelty were sure to prove too much for him.

II

The mother of Johnnie Hedge was a widow, and the chief theory of of her life was that her boy should be in school on the greatest possible number of days. He himself had no sympathy with this ambition, but she detected the truth of his diseases with an unerring eye, and he was required to be really ill before he could win the right to disregard the first bell, morning and noon. The chicken-pox and the mumps had given him vacations—vacations of misery, wherein he nearly died between pain and nursing. But bad colds in the head did nothing for him, and he was not able to invent a satisfactory hacking cough. His mother was not consistently a Tartar. In most things he swayed her to his will. He was allowed to have more jam, pickles, and pie than most boys; she respected his profound loathing of Sunday-school; on summer evenings he could remain out-of-doors until 8.30; but in this matter of school she was inexorable. This single point in her character was of steel.

The Hedges arrived in Whilomville on a Saturday, and on the following Monday Johnnie wended his way to school with a note to the principal and his Jersey City school-books. He knew perfectly well that he would be told to buy new and different books, but in those days mothers always had an idea that old books would "do," and they invariably sent boys off to a new school with books which would not meet the selected and unchangeable views of the new administration. The old books never would "do." Then the boys brought them home to annoyed mothers and asked for ninety cents or sixty cents or eighty-five cents or some number of cents for another outfit. In the garret of every house holding a large family there was a collection of effete school-books, with mother rebellious because James could not inherit his books from Paul, who should properly be Peter's heir, while Peter should be a beneficiary under Henry's will.

But the matter of the books was not the measure of Johnnie Hedge's unhappiness. This whole business of changing schools was a complete torture. Alone he had to go among a new people, a new tribe, and he apprehended his serious time. There were only two fates for him. One meant victory. One meant a kind of serfdom in which he would subscribe to every word of some superior boy and support his every word. It was not anything like an English system of fagging, because boys invariably drifted into the figurative service of other boys whom they devotedly admired, and if they were obliged to subscribe to everything, it is true that they would have done so freely in any case. One means to suggest that Johnnie Hedge had to find his place. Willie Dalzel was a type of the little chieftain, and Willie was a master, but he was not a bully in a special physical sense. He did not drag little boys by the ears until they cried, nor make them tearfully fetch and carry for him. They fetched and carried, but it was because of their worship of his prowess and genius. And so all through the strata of boy life were chieftains and subchieftains and assistant subchieftains. There was no question of little Hedge being towed about by the nose; it was, as one has said, that he had to find his place in a new school. And this in itself was a problem which awed his boyish heart. He was a stranger cast away upon the moon. None knew him, understood him, felt for him. He would be surrounded for this initiative time by a horde of jackal creatures who might turn out in the end to be little boys like himself, but this last point his philosophy could not understand in its fullness.

He came to a white meeting-house sort of a place, in the squat tower of which a great bell was clanging impressively. He passed through an iron gate into a play-ground worn bare as the bed of a mountain brook by the endless runnings and scufflings of little children. There was still a half-hour before the final clangor in the squat tower, but the play-ground held a number of frolicsome imps. A loitering boy espied Johnnie Hedge, and he howled: "Oh! oh! Here's a new feller! Here's a new feller!" He advanced upon the strange arrival. "What's your name?"

he demanded, belligerently, like a particularly offensive custom-house officer.

"Johnnie Hedge," responded the new-comer, shyly.

This name struck the other boy as being very comic. All new names strike boys as being comic. He laughed noisily.

"Oh, fellers, he says his name is Johnnie Hedge! Haw! haw! haw!"

The new boy felt that his name was the most disgraceful thing which had ever been attached to a human being.

"Johnnie Hedge! Haw! haw! What room you in?" said the other lad.

"I dun'no'," said Johnnie. In the mean time a small flock of interested vultures had gathered about him. The main thing was his absolute strangeness. He even would have welcomed the sight of his tormentors of Saturday; he had seen them before at least. These creatures were only so many incomprehensible problems. He diffidently began to make his way towards the main door of the school, and the other boys followed him. They demanded information.

"Are you through subtraction yet? We study jogerfre—did you, ever? You live here now? You goin' to school here now?"

To many questions he made answer as well as the clamor would permit, and at length he reached the main door and went quaking unto his new kings. As befitted them, the rabble stopped at the door. A teacher strolling along a corridor found a small boy holding in his hand a note. The boy palpably did not know what to do with the note, but the teacher knew, and took it. Thereafter this little boy was in harness.

A splendid lady in gorgeous robes gave him a seat at a double desk, at the end of which sat a hoodlum with grimy finger-nails, who eyed the inauguration with an extreme and personal curiosity. The other desks were gradually occupied by children, who first were told of the new boy, and then turned upon him a speculative and somewhat derisive eye. The school opened; little classes went forward to a position in front of the teacher's platform and tried to explain that they knew something. The new boy was not requisitioned a great deal; he was allowed to lie dormant until he became used to the scenes and until the teacher found, approximately, his mental position. In the mean time he suffered a shower of stares and whispers and giggles, as if he were a man-ape, whereas he was precisely like other children. From time to time he made funny and pathetic little overtures to other boys, but these overtures could not yet be received; he was not known; he was a foreigner. The village school was like a nation. It was tight. Its amiability or friendship must be won in certain ways.

At recess he hovered in the school-room around the weak lights of society and around the teacher, in the hope that somebody might be good to him, but none considered him save as some sort of a specimen. The teacher of course had a secondary interest in the fact that he was an additional one to a class of sixty-three.

At twelve o'clock, when the ordered files of boys and girls marched towards the door, he exhibited—to no eye—the tremblings of a coward in a charge. He exaggerated the lawlessness of the play-ground and the street.

But the reality was hard enough. A shout greeted him:

"Oh, here's the new feller! Here's the new feller!"

Small and utterly obscure boys teased him. He had a hard time of it to get to the gate. There never was any actual hurt, but everything was competent to smite the lad with shame. It was a curious, groundless shame, but nevertheless it was shame. He was a new-comer, and he definitely felt the disgrace of the fact. In the street he was seen and recognized by some lads who had formed part of the group of Saturday. They shouted:

"Oh, Jimmie! Jimmie! Here he is! Here's that new feller!"

Jimmie Trescott was going virtuously towards his luncheon when he heard these cries behind him. He pretended not to hear, and in this deception he was assisted by the fact that he was engaged at the time in a furious argument with a friend over the relative merits of two "Uncle Tom's Cabin" companies. It appeared that one company had only two bloodhounds, while the other had ten. On the other hand, the first company had two Topsys and two Uncle Toms, while the second had only one Topsy and one Uncle Tom.

But the shouting little boys were hard after him. Finally they were even pulling at his arms.

"Jimmie—"

"What?" he demanded, turning with a snarl. "What d'you want? Leggo my arm!"

"Here he is! Here's the new feller! Here's the new feller! Now!"

"I don't care if he is," said Jimmie, with grand impatience. He tilted his chin. "I don't care if he is."

Then they reviled him. "Thought you was goin' to lick him first time you caught him! Yah! You're a 'fraid-cat!" They began to sing: "'Fraid-cat! 'Fraid-cat! 'Fraid-cat!" He expostulated hotly, turning from one to the other, but they would not listen. In the mean time the Hedge boy slunk on his way, looking with deep anxiety upon this attempt to send Jimmie against him. But Jimmie would have none of the plan.

III

When the children met again on the play-ground, Jimmie was openly challenged with cowardice. He had made a big threat in the hearing of comrades, and when invited by them to take advantage of an opportunity, he had refused. They had been fairly sure of their amusement, and they were indignant. Jimmie was finally driven to declare that as soon as school was out for the day, he would thrash the Hedge boy.

When finally the children came rushing out of the iron gate, filled with the delights of freedom, a hundred boys surrounded Jimmie in high spirits, for he had said that he was determined. They waited for the lone lad from Jersey City. When he appeared, Jimmie wasted no time. He walked straight to him and said, "Did you say you kin lick me?"

Johnnie Hedge was cowed, shrinking, affrighted, and the roars of a hundred boys thundered in his ears, but again he knew what he had to say. "Yes," he gasped, in anguish.

"Then," said Jimmie, resolutely, "you've got to fight." There was a joyous clamor by the mob. The beleaguered lad looked this way and that way for succor, as Willie Dalzel and other officious youngsters policed an irregular circle in the crowd. He saw Jimmie facing him; there was no help for it; he dropped his books—the old books which would not "do."

Now it was the fashion among tiny Whilomville belligerents to fight much in the manner of little bear cubs. Two boys would rush upon each other, immediately grapple, and—the best boy having probably succeeded in getting the coveted "under hold"—there would presently be a crash to the earth of the inferior boy, and he would probably be mopped around in the dust, or the mud, or the snow, or whatever the material happened to be, until the engagement was over. Whatever havoc was dealt out to him was ordinarily the result of his wild endeavors to throw off his opponent and arise. Both infants wept during the fight, as a common thing, and if they wept very hard, the fight was a harder fight. The result was never very bloody, but the complete dishevelment of both victor and vanquished was extraordinary. As for the spectacle, it more resembled a collision of boys in a fog than it did the manly art of hammering another human being into speechless inability.

The fight began when Jimmie made a mad, bear-cub rush at the new boy, amid savage cries of encouragement. Willie Dalzel, for instance, almost howled his head off. Very timid boys on the outskirts of the throng felt their hearts leap to their throats. It was a time when certain natures were impressed that only man is vile.

But it appeared that bear-cub rushing was no part of the instruction received by boys in Jersey City. Boys in Jersey City were apparently schooled curiously. Upon the onslaught of Jimmie, the stranger had gone wild with rage—boylike. Some spark had touched his fighting-blood, and in a moment he was a cornered, desperate, fire-eyed little man. He began to swing his arms, to revolve them so swiftly that one might have considered him a small, working model of an extra-fine patented windmill which was caught in a gale. For a moment this defense surprised Jimmie more than it damaged him, but two moments later a small, knotty fist caught him squarely in the eye, and with a shriek he went down in defeat. He lay on the ground so stunned that he could not even cry; but if he had been able to cry, he would have cried over his prestige—or something—not over his eye.

There was a dreadful tumult. The boys cast glances of amazement and terror upon the victor, and thronged upon the beaten Jimmie Trescott. It was a moment of excitement so intense that one cannot say what happened. Never before had Whilomville seen such a thing—not the little tots. They were aghast, dumfounded, and they glanced often over their shoulders at the new boy, who stood alone, his clinched fists at his side, his face crimson, his lips still working with the fury of battle.

But there was another surprise for Whilomville. It might have been seen that the little victor was silently debating against an impulse.

But the impulse won, for the lone lad from Jersey City suddenly wheeled, sprang like a demon, and struck another boy.

A curtain should be drawn before this deed. A knowledge of it is really too much for the heart to bear. The other boy was Willie Dalzel. The lone lad from Jersey City had smitten him full sore.

There is little to say of it. It must have been that a feeling worked gradually to the top of the little stranger's wrath that Jimmie Trescott had been a mere tool, that the front and center of his persecutors had been Willie Dalzel, and being rendered temporarily lawless by his fighting-blood, he raised his hand and smote for revenge.

Willie Dalzel had been in the middle of a vandal's cry, which screeched out over the voices of everybody. The new boy's fist cut it in half, so to say. And then arose the howl of an amazed and terrorized walrus.

One wishes to draw a second curtain. Without discussion or inquiry or brief retort, Willie Dalzel ran away. He ran like a hare straight for home, this redoubtable chieftain. Following him at a heavy and slow pace ran the impassioned new boy. The scene was long remembered.

Willie Dalzel was no coward; he had been panic-stricken into running away from a new thing. He ran as a man might run from the sudden appearance of a vampire or a ghoul or a gorilla. This was no time for academics—he ran.

Jimmie slowly gathered himself and came to his feet. "Where's Willie?" said he, first of all. The crowd sniggered. "Where's Willie?" said Jimmie again.

"Why, he licked him, *too!*" answered a boy suddenly.

"He did?" said Jimmie. He sat weakly down on the roadway. "He did?" After allowing a moment for the fact to sink into him, he looked up at the crowd with his one good eye and his one bunged eye, and smiled cheerfully.

XII

THE CITY URCHIN AND THE
CHASTE VILLAGERS

AFTER the brief encounters between the Hedge boy and Jimmie Trescott and the Hedge boy and Willie Dalzel, the neighborhood which contained the homes of the boys was, as far as child life is concerned, in a state resembling anarchy. This was owing to the signal overthrow and shameful retreat of the boy who had for several years led a certain little clan by the nose. The adherence of the little community did not go necessarily to the boy who could whip all the others, but it certainly could not go to a boy who had run away in a manner that made his shame patent to the whole world. Willie Dalzel found himself in a painful position. This tiny tribe which had followed him with such unwavering faith was now largely engaged in whistling and catcalling and hooting. He chased a number of them into the sanctity of their own yards, but from these coigns they continued to ridicule him.

But it must not be supposed that the fickle tribe went over in a body to the new light. They did nothing of the sort. They occupied themselves with avenging all which they had endured—gladly enough, too —for many months. As for the Hedge boy, he maintained a curious timid reserve, minding his own business with extreme care, and going to school with that deadly punctuality of which his mother was the genius. Jimmie Trescott suffered no adverse criticism from his fellows. He was entitled to be beaten by a boy who had made Willie Dalzel bellow like a bull-calf and run away. Indeed, he received some honors.

He had confronted a very superior boy and received a bang in the eye which for a time was the wonder of the children, and he had not bellowed like a bull-calf. As a matter of fact, he was often invited to tell how it had felt, and this he did with some pride, claiming arrogantly that he had been superior to any particular pain.

Early in the episode he and the Hedge boy had patched up a treaty. Living next door to each other, they could not fail to have each other often in sight. One afternoon they wandered together in the strange indefinite diplomacy of boyhood. As they drew close the new boy suddenly said, "Napple?"

"Yes," said Jimmie, and the new boy bestowed upon him an apple. It was one of those green-coated winter-apples which lie for many months in safe and dry places, and can at any time be brought forth for the persecution of the unwary and inexperienced. An older age would have fled from this apple, but to the unguided youth of Jimmie Trescott it was a thing to be possessed and cherished. Wherefore this apple was the emblem of something more than a truce, despite the fact that it tasted like wet Indian meal; and Jimmie looked at the Hedge boy out of one good eye and one bunged eye. The long-drawn animosities of men have no place in the life of a boy. The boy's mind is flexible; he readjusts his position with an ease which is derived from the fact—simply—that he is not yet a man.

But there were other and more important matters. Johnnie Hedge's exploits had brought him into such prominence among the schoolboys that it was necessary to settle a number of points once and for all. There was the usual number of boys in the school who were popularly known to be champions in their various classes. Among these Johnnie Hedge now had to thread his way, every boy taking it upon himself to feel anxious that Johnnie's exact position should be soon established. His fame as a fighter had gone forth to the world, but there were other boys who had fame as fighters, and the world was extremely anxious to know where to place the new-comer. Various heroes were urged to attempt this classification. Usually it was not accounted a matter of supreme importance, but in this boy life it was essential.

In all cases the heroes were backward enough. It was their followings who agitated the question. And so Johnnie Hedge was more or less beset.

He maintained his bashfulness. He backed away from altercation. It was plain that to bring matters to a point he must be forced into a quarrel. It was also plain that the proper person for the business was some boy who could whip Willie Dalzel, and these formidable warriors were distinctly averse to undertaking the new contract. It is a kind of a law in boy life that a quiet, decent, peace-loving lad is able to thrash a wide-mouthed talker. And so it had transpired that by a peculiar system of elimination most of the real chiefs were quiet, decent, peace-loving boys, and they had no desire to engage in a fight with a boy on the sole grounds that it was not known who could whip. Johnnie Hedge attended his affairs, they attended their affairs, and around them waged this discussion of relative merit. Jimmie Trescott took a prominent part in these arguments. He contended that Johnnie Hedge could thrash any boy in the world. He was certain of it, and to anyone who opposed him he said, "You just get one of those smashes in the eye, and then you'll see." In the mean time there was a grand and impressive silence in the direction of Willie Dalzel. He had gathered remnants of his clan, but the main parts of his sovereignty were scattered to the winds. He was an enemy.

Owing to the circumspect behavior of the new boy, the commotions on the school grounds came to nothing. He was often asked, "Kin you lick him?" And he invariably replied, "I dun'no'." This idea of waging battle with the entire world appalled him.

A war for complete supremacy of the tribe which had been headed by Willie Dalzel was fought out in the country of the tribe. It came to pass that a certain half-dime blood-and-thunder pamphlet had a great vogue in the tribe at this particular time. This story relates the experience of a lad who began his career as cabin-boy on a pirate ship. Throughout the first fifteen chapters he was rope's-ended from one end of the ship to the other end, and very often he was felled to the deck by a heavy fist. He lived through enough hardships to have killed a battalion of Turkish soldiers, but in the end he rose upon them. Yes, he rose upon them. Hordes of pirates fell before his intrepid arm, and in the last chapters of the book he is seen jauntily careering on his own hook as one of the most callous pirate captains that ever sailed the seas.

Naturally, when this tale was thoroughly understood by the tribe, they had to dramatize it, although it was a dramatization that would gain no royalties for the author. Now it was plain that the urchin who was cast for the cabin-boy's part would lead a life throughout the first fifteen chapters which would attract few actors. Willie Dalzel developed a scheme by which some small lad would play cabin-boy during this period of misfortune and abuse, and then, when the cabin-boy came to the part where he slew all his enemies and reached his zenith, that he, Willie Dalzel, should take the part.

This fugitive and disconnected rendering of a great play opened in Jimmie Trescott's back garden. The path between the two lines of gooseberry-bushes was elected unanimously to be the ship. Then Willie Dalzel insisted that Homer Phelps should be the cabin-boy. Homer tried the position for a time, and then elected that he would resign in favor of some other victim. There was no other applicant to succeed him, whereupon it became necessary to press some boy. Jimmie Trescott was a great actor, as is well known, but he steadfastly refused to engage for the part. Ultimately they seized upon little Dan Earl, whose disposition was so milky and docile that he would do whatever anybody asked of him. But Dan Earl made the one firm revolt of his life after trying existence as cabin-boy for some ten minutes. Willie Dalzel was in despair. Then he suddenly sighted the little brother of Johnnie Hedge, who had come into the garden, and in a poor-little-stranger sort of fashion was looking wistfully at the play. When he was invited to become the cabin-boy he accepted joyfully, thinking that it was his initiation into the tribe. Then they proceeded to give him the rope's-end and to punch him with a realism which was not altogether painless. Directly he began to cry out. They exhorted him not to cry out, not to mind it, but still they continued to hurt him.

There was a commotion among the gooseberry-bushes, two branches were swept aside, and Johnnie Hedge walked down upon them. Every boy stopped in his tracks. Johnnie was boiling with rage.

"Who hurt him?" he said, ferociously. "Did *you?*" He had looked at Willie Dalzel.

Willie Dalzel began to mumble: "We was on'y playin'. Wasn't nothin' fer him to cry fer."

The new boy had at his command some big phrases, and he used them. "I am goin' to whip you within an inch of your life. I am goin' to tan the hide off'n you." And immediately there was a mixture—an infusion of two boys which looked as if it had been done by a chemist. The other children stood back, stricken with horror. But out of this whirl they presently perceived the figure of Willie Dalzel seated upon the chest of the Hedge boy.

"Got enough?" asked Willie, hoarsely.

"No," choked out the Hedge boy. Then there was another flapping and floundering, and finally another calm.

"Got enough?" asked Willie.

"No," said the Hedge boy. A sort of war-cloud again puzzled the sight of the observers. Both combatants were breathless, bloodless in their faces, and very weak.

"Got enough?" said Willie.

"No," said the Hedge boy. The carnage was again renewed. All the spectators were silent but Johnnie Hedge's little brother, who shrilly exhorted him to continue the struggle. But it was not plain that the Hedge boy needed any encouragement, for he was crying bitterly, and it has been explained that when a boy cried it was a bad time to hope for peace. He had managed to wriggle over upon his hands and knees. But Willie Dalzel was tenaciously gripping him from the back, and it seemed that his strength would spend itself in futility. The bear cub seemed to have the advantage of the working model of the windmill. They heaved, uttered strange words, wept, and the sun looked down upon them with steady, unwinking eye.

Peter Washington came out of the stable and observed this tragedy of the back garden. He stood transfixed for a moment, and then ran towards it, shouting: "Hi! What's all dish yere? Hi! Stopper dat, stopper dat, you two! For lan' sake, what's all dish yere?" He grabbed the struggling boys and pulled them apart. He was stormy and fine in his indignation. "For lan' sake! You two kids act like you gwine mad dogs. Stopper dat!" The whitened, tearful, soiled combatants, their clothing all awry, glared fiercely at each other as Peter stood between them, lecturing. They made several attempts to circumvent him and again come to battle. As he fended them off with his open hands he delivered his reproaches at Jimmie. "I's s'prised at *you!* I suhtainly is!"

"Why?" said Jimmie. "I ain't done nothin'. What have I done?"

"Y-y-you done 'courage dese yere kids ter scrap," said Peter, virtuously.

"Me?" cried Jimmie. "I ain't had nothin' to do with it."

"I raikon you ain't," retorted Peter, with heavy sarcasm. "I raikon you been er-prayin', ain't you?" Turning to Willie Dalzel, he said, "You jest take an' run erlong outer dish yere or I'll jest nachually take an' damnearkill you." Willie Dalzel went. To the new boy Peter said: "You look like you had some saince, but I raikon you don't know no more'n er rabbit. You jest take an' trot erlong off home, an' don' lemme caitch you round yere er-fightin' or I'll break yer back." The Hedge boy moved away with dignity, followed by his little brother. The latter, when he had placed a sufficient distance between himself and Peter, played his fingers at his nose and called out:

"Nig-ger-r-r! Nig-ger-r-r!"

Peter Washington's resentment poured out upon Jimmie.

" 'Pears like you never would understan' you ain't reg'lar common trash. You take an' 'sociate with an'body what done come erlong."

"Aw, go on," retorted Jimmie, profanely. "Go soak your head, Pete."

The remaining boys retired to the street, whereupon they perceived Willie Dalzel in the distance. He ran to them.

"I licked him!" he shouted, exultantly. "I licked him! didn't I, now?"

From the Whilomville point of view he was entitled to a favorable answer. They made it. "Yes," they said, "you did."

"I run in," cried Willie, "an' I grabbed 'im, an' afore he knew what it was I throwed 'im. An' then it was easy." He puffed out his chest and smiled like an English recruiting-sergeant. "An' now," said he, suddenly facing Jimmie Trescott, "whose side were you on?"

The question was direct and startling. Jimmie gave back two paces. "He licked you once," he explained, haltingly.

"He never saw the day when he could lick one side of me. I could lick him with my left hand tied behind me. Why, I could lick him when I was asleep." Willie Dalzel was magnificent.

A gate clicked, and Johnnie Hedge was seen to be strolling towards them.

"You said," he remarked, coldly, "you licked me, didn't you?"

Willie Dalzel stood his ground. "Yes," he said stoutly.

"Well, you're a liar," said the Hedge boy.

"You're another," retorted Willie.

"No, I ain't, either, but *you're* a liar."

"You're another," retorted Willie.

"Don't you dare tell *me* I'm a liar, or I'll smack your mouth for you," said the Hedge boy.

"Well, I did, didn't I?" barked Willie. "An' whatche goin' to do about it?"

"I'm goin' to lam you," said the Hedge boy.

He approached to attack warily, and the other boys held their breaths. Willie Dalzel winced back a pace. "Hol' on a minute," he cried, raising his palm. "I'm not—"

But the comic windmill was again in motion, and between gasps from his exertions Johnnie Hedge remarked, "I'll show—you—whether —you kin—lick me—or not."

The first blows did not reach home on Willie, for he backed away with expedition, keeping up his futile cry, "Hol' on a minute." Soon enough a swinging fist landed on his cheek. It did not knock him down, but it hurt him a little and frightened him a great deal. He suddenly opened his mouth to an amazing and startling extent, tilted back his head, and howled, while his eyes, glittering with tears, were fixed upon this scowling butcher of a Johnnie Hedge. The latter was making slow and vicious circles, evidently intending to renew the massacre.

But the spectators really had been desolated and shocked by the terrible thing which had happened to Willie Dalzel. They now cried out: "No, no; don't hit 'im any more! Don't hit 'im any more!"

Jimmie Trescott, in a panic of bravery, yelled, "We'll all jump on you if you do."

The Hedge boy paused, at bay. He breathed angrily, and flashed his glance from lad to lad. They still protested: "No, no; don't hit 'im any more. Don't hit 'im no more."

"I'll hammer him until he can't stand up," said Johnnie, observing that they all feared him. "I'll fix him so he won't know hisself, an' if any of you kids bother with *me*—"

Suddenly he ceased, he trembled, he collapsed. The hand of one approaching from behind had laid hold upon his ear, and it was the hand of one whom he knew.

The other lads heard a loud, iron-filing voice say, "Caught ye at it again, ye brat, ye." They saw a dreadful woman with gray hair, with a sharp red nose, with bare arms, with spectacles of such magnifying quality that her eyes shone through them like two fierce white moons. She was Johnnie Hedge's mother. Still holding Johnnie by the ear, she swung out swiftly and dexterously, and succeeded in boxing the ears of two boys before the crowd regained its presence of mind and stampeded. Yes, the war for supremacy was over, and the question was never again disputed. The supreme power was Mrs. Hedge.

XIII

A LITTLE PILGRIMAGE

ONE November it became clear to childish minds in certain parts of Whilomville that the Sunday-school of the Presbyterian church would not have for the children the usual tree on Christmas eve. The funds free for that ancient festival would be used for the relief of suffering among the victims of the Charleston earthquake.

The plan had been born in the generous head of the superintendent of the Sunday-school, and during one session he had made a strong plea that the children should forego the vain pleasures of a tree and, in glorious application of the Golden Rule, refuse a local use of the fund, and will that it be sent where dire pain might be alleviated. At the end of a tearfully eloquent speech the question was put fairly to a vote, and the children in a burst of virtuous abandon carried the question for Charleston. Many of the teachers had been careful to preserve a finely neutral attitude, but even if they had cautioned the children against being too impetuous they could not have checked the wild impulses.

But this was a long time before Christmas.

Very early, boys held important speech together. "Huh! you ain't goin' to have no Christmas tree at the Presbyterian Sunday-school."

Sullenly the victim answered, "No, we ain't."

"Huh!" scoffed the other denomination, "we are goin' to have the all-firedest biggest tree that you ever saw in the world."

The little Presbyterians were greatly downcast.

It happened that Jimmie Trescott had regularly attended the Presbyterian Sunday-school. The Trescotts were consistently undenominational, but they had sent their lad on Sundays to one of the places where they thought he would receive benefits. However, on one day in December, Jimmie appeared before his father and made a strong spiritual appeal to be forthwith attached to the Sunday-school of the Big Progressive church. Doctor Trescott mused this question considerably. "Well, Jim," he said, "why do you conclude that the Big Progressive Sunday-school is better for you than the Presbyterian Sunday-school?"

"Now—it's nicer," answered Jimmie, looking at his father with an anxious eye.

"How do you mean?"

"Why—now—some of the boys what go to the Presbyterian place, they ain't very nice," explained the flagrant Jimmie.

Trescott mused the question considerably once more. In the end he said: "Well, you may change if you wish, this one time, but you must not be changing to and fro. You decide now, and then you must abide by your decision."

"Yessir," said Jimmie, brightly. "Big Progressive."

"All right," said the father. "But remember what I've told you."

On the following Sunday morning Jimmie presented himself at the door of the basement of the Big Progressive church. He was conspicuously washed, notably raimented, prominently polished. And, incidentally, he was very uncomfortable because of all these virtues.

A number of acquaintants greeted him contemptuously. "Hello, Jimmie! What you doin' here? Thought you was a Presbyterian?"

Jimmie cast down his eyes and made no reply. He was too cowed by the change. However, Homer Phelps, who was a regular patron of the Big Progressive Sunday-school, suddenly appeared and said, "Hello, Jim!" Jimmie seized upon him. Homer Phelps was amenable to Trescott laws, tribal if you like, but iron-bound, almost compulsory.

"Hello, Homer!" said Jimmie, and his manner was so good that Homer felt a great thrill in being able to show his superior a new condition of life.

"You ain't never come here afore, have you?" he demanded, with a new arrogance.

"No, I ain't," said Jimmie. Then they stared at each other and maneuvered.

"You don't know *my* teacher," said Homer.

"No, I don't know *her*," admitted Jimmie, but in a way which contended, modestly, that he knew countless other Sunday-school teachers.

"Better join our class," said Homer, sagely. "She wears spectacles; don't see very well. Sometimes we do almost what we like."

"All right," said Jimmie, glad to place himself in the hands of his friends. In due time they entered the Sunday-school room, where a man with benevolent whiskers stood on a platform and said, "We will now sing No. 33—'Pull for the Shore, Sailor, Pull for the Shore.'" And as the obedient throng burst into melody the man on the platform indicated the time with a fat, white, and graceful hand. He was an ideal Sunday-school superintendent—one who had never felt hunger or thirst or the wound of the challenge of dishonor; a man, indeed, with beautiful fat hands who waved them in greasy victorious beneficence over a crowd of children.

Jimmie, walking carefully on his toes, followed Homer Phelps. He felt that the kingly superintendent might cry out and blast him to ashes before he could reach a chair. It was a desperate journey. But at last he heard Homer muttering to a young lady, who looked at him through glasses which greatly magnified her eyes. "A new boy," she said, in an oily and deeply religious voice.

"Yes'm," said Jimmie, trembling. The five other boys of the class scanned him keenly and derided his condition.

"We will proceed to the lesson," said the young lady. Then she cried sternly, like a sergeant, "The seventh chapter of Jeremiah!"

There was a swift fluttering of leaflets. Then the name of Jeremiah, a wise man, towered over the feelings of these boys. Homer Phelps was doomed to read the fourth verse. He took a deep breath, he puffed out his lips, he gathered his strength for a great effort. His beginning was childishly explosive. He hurriedly said:

"Trust ye not in lying words, saying The temple of the Lord, the temple of the Lord, the temple of the Lord, are these."

"Now," said the teacher, "Johnnie Scanlan, tell us what these words mean." The Scanlan boy shamefacedly muttered that he did not know. The teacher's countenance saddened. Her heart was in her work; she wanted to make a success of this Sunday-school class. "Perhaps Homer Phelps can tell us," she remarked.

Homer gulped; he looked at Jimmie. Through the great room hummed a steady hum. A little circle, very near, was being told about Daniel in the lion's den. They were deeply moved. At the moment they liked Sunday-school.

"Why—now—it means," said Homer, with a grand pomposity born of a sense of hopeless ignorance—"it means—why it means that they were in the wrong place."

"No," said the teacher, profoundly; "it means that we should be good, very good indeed. That is what it means. It means that we should love the Lord and be good. Love the Lord and be good. That is what it means."

The little boys suddenly had a sense of black wickedness as their teacher looked austerely upon them. They gazed at her with the wide-open eyes of simplicity. They were stirred again. This thing of being good—this great business of life—apparently it was always successful. They knew from the fairy tales. But it was difficult, wasn't it? It was said to be the most heart-breaking task to be generous, wasn't it? One had to pay the price of one's eyes in order to be pacific, didn't one? As for patience, it was tortured martyrdom to be patient, wasn't it? Sin was simple, wasn't it? But virtue was so difficult that it could only be practiced by heavenly beings, wasn't it?

And the angels, the Sunday-school superintendent, and the teacher swam in the high visions of the little boys as beings so good that if a boy scratched his shin in the same room he was a profane and sentenced devil.

"And," said the teacher, " 'The temple of the Lord'—what does that mean? I'll ask the new boy. What does that mean?"

"I dun'no'," said Jimmie, blankly.

But here the professional bright boy of the class suddenly awoke to his obligations. "Teacher," he cried, "it means church, same as this."

"Exactly," said the teacher, deeply satisfied with this reply. "You know your lesson well, Clarence. I am much pleased."

The other boys, instead of being envious, looked with admiration upon Clarence, while he adopted an air of being habituated to perform such feats every day of his life. Still, he was not much of a boy. He had the virtue of being able to walk on very high stilts, but when the season of stilts had passed he possessed no rank save this Sunday-school rank, this clever-little-Clarence business of knowing the Bible and the lesson better than the other boys. The other boys, sometimes looking at him meditatively, did not actually decide to thrash him as soon as he cleared the portals of the church, but they certainly decided to molest him in such ways as would re-establish their self-respect. Back of the superintendent's chair hung a lithograph of the martyrdom of St. Stephen.

Jimmie, feeling stiff and encased in his best clothes, waited for the ordeal to end. A bell pealed: the fat hand of the superintendent had tapped a bell. Slowly the rustling and murmuring dwindled to silence. The benevolent man faced the school. "I have to announce," he began, waving his body from side to side in the conventional bows of his kind, "that—" Bang went the bell. "Give me your attention, please, children. I have to announce that the Board has decided that this year there will be no Christmas tree, but the—"

Instantly the room buzzed with the subdued clamor of the children. Jimmie was speechless. He stood morosely during the singing of the closing hymn. He passed out into the street with the others, pushing no more than was required.

Speedily the whole idea left him. If he remembered Sunday-school at all, it was to remember that he did not like it.

AN AFTERWORD ON
"WHILOMVILLE STORIES"

WHEN young Richard Hughes published his enthralling tale known in this country as *The Innocent Voyage*—in its own London, the title was *High Wind in Jamaica*—its presentation of children as a race apart and rather a savage one caused great mirations as something new in a world which had already forgotten, if it had ever really known, the *Whilomville Stories*. Here these are reprinted for their own sake and as a provocative companion piece to *The Golden Age*. They were written in the last two years of a life cut short before its time. Born in Newark, New Jersey, the last child of an elderly Methodist preacher, Stephen Crane died in Badenweiler, Germany, in the summer of 1900. He did not live to be thirty. He left behind him such works as *The Open Boat* and *The Red Badge of Courage* and (if you would like to examine a superb Hemingway story written before Hemingway was born) "The Blue Hotel." These he wrote and others, including the *Whilomville Stories,* which you will find scattered through the files of *Harper's* for 1899 and 1900.

In *Stephen Crane: A Study in American Letters* (Alfred A. Knopf, 1923)—a biographical sketch put forth in an era when it was a fashion in America among the younger writers to spend ten minutes each day in severely admiring Stephen Crane—Thomas Beer makes it clear that the shearing of the locks in "The Angel Child" harks back to a time when young Stephen Crane's older brother (to the wrath of their mother) cut his own curls away from him. Later he himself took pity on two hapless victims of the Fauntleroy fashion and shepherded them to a barber shop. These Reginald Birch curls appear to have haunted Crane unduly and Thomas Beer, too. In Beer's account of the *Whilomville Stories* I find this sentence. "But the stories were not popular among mothers trained on Mrs. Burnett's patent food and male critics only were loud in praise. It was left for Booth Tarkington to prove the justice of Crane's performance and with gallantry to remind the public of his predecessor's exploit." Now, since the immortal Penrod had always seemed to me Jimmie Trescott seen through eyes as honest and observant but more genially philosophic, I was eager to read any word on the *Whilomville Stories* which might have been said by the gentleman from Indiana. Failing to find in the library any trace of such tribute, I appealed to Mr. Tarkington, who, however, could not remember what he had said or where or when. He will not mind my quoting his letter.

I think Mr. Beer is mistaken about Little Lord Fauntleroy, which certainly *wasn't* the obscuration. It's the most natural thing in the world to say that recently past "generations" were sentimental boobs— but usually that's too easy a conclusion. The *Whilomville Stories* were received with applause and pleasure when they appeared in the magazine. I suppose the book may not have had a great circulation; probably the "popular reader" felt something like a physical slightness in the material.

The sequence seems to me: *Tom Sawyer, Helen's Babies, Whilomville Stories,* Owen Johnson's *Lawrenceville Stories, The Tennessee Shad,* etc. No doubt there were "realistic children" before Mark Twain —bits in Dickens and elsewhere—and, of course, Tom and Huck are realistic only in character. He gave 'em what boys don't get, when it came to "plot." All that the boy, Sam, had wished to happen, he made happen.

Through all the years—over fifty?—since I read *Helen's Babies*, I seem to remember that they really were children. But when it comes to the Whilomville series, there's no seeming about it. Crane's children *were* children; nobody could forget that in twice fifty years. He built them without the waste of a word and at the same time didn't lose a hair of their heads; it's all beautifully, beautifully done.

The *Whilomville Stories* were first printed at a time when any editor or publisher, on discovering traces of irony in a manuscript, hastily engaged Peter Newell to illustrate it lest any reader overlook the humorous intent. And I remember that in *Harper's* each story had as a headpiece a line-drawing by Edward B. Edwards. It was a vista of a village street, much such a street as the one in Roseville, New Jersey, or Port Jervis, New York, on which Master Stephen Crane used to play marbles. A good many years have passed since I first scuffed the autumn leaves along the footways of Whilomville, but I have never forgotten the nightmare of Jimmie Trescott's lunch-pail nor the bitter comedy of his life at Sunday-school. No, nor the horror of his attempts at public speaking. I first read "Making an Orator" at a time when, in the assembly hall of the Germantown Combined School, I myself had come to a dead halt with Sheridan ten miles away. He was still there when I left the platform.

A. W.

TO THE
REVEREND DR. HYDE

by

ROBERT LOUIS STEVENSON

AN OPEN LETTER
TO THE REVEREND DR. HYDE
OF HONOLULU

Sydney, February 25, 1890.

Sir,—It may probably occur to you that we have met, and visited, and conversed; on my side, with interest. You may remember that you have done me several courtesies, for which I was prepared to be grateful. But there are duties which come before gratitude, and offences which justly divide friends, far more acquaintances. Your letter to the Reverend H. B. Gage is a document, which, in my sight, if you had filled me with bread when I was starving, if you had sat up to nurse my father when he lay a-dying, would yet absolve me from the bonds of gratitude. You know enough, doubtless, of the process of canonization to be aware that, a hundred years after the death of Damien, there will appear a man charged with the painful office of the *devil's advocate*. After that noble brother of mine, and of all frail clay, shall have lain a century at rest, one shall accuse, one defend him. The circumstance is unusual that the devil's advocate should be a volunteer, should be a member of a sect immediately rival, and should make haste to take upon himself his ugly office ere the bones are cold; unusual, and of a taste which I shall leave my readers free to qualify; unusual, and to me inspiring. If I have at all learned the trade of using words to convey truth and to arouse emotion, you have at last furnished me with a subject. For it is in the interest of all mankind and the cause of public decency in every quarter of the world, not only that Damien should be righted, but that you and your letter should be displayed at length, in their true colours, to the public eye.

To do this properly, I must begin by quoting you at large: I shall then proceed to criticize your utterance from several points of view, divine and human, in the course of which I shall attempt to draw again and with more specification the character of the dead saint whom it has pleased you to vilify: so much being done, I shall say farewell to you for ever.

"Honolulu, August 2, 1889.

"Rev. H. B. Gage.

"Dear Brother,—In answer to your inquiries about Father Damien, I can only reply that we who knew the man are surprised at the extravagant newspaper laudations, as if he was a most saintly philanthropist. The simple truth is, he was a coarse, dirty man, headstrong and bigoted. He was not sent to Molokai, but went there without orders; did not stay at the leper settlement (before he became one himself), but circulated freely over the whole island (less than half the island is devoted to the lepers), and he came often to Honolulu. He had no hand in the reforms and improvements inaugurated, which were the work of our Board of Health, as occasion required and means were provided. He was not a pure man in his relations with women, and the leprosy of which he died should be attributed to his vices and carelessness. Others have done much for the lepers, our own ministers, the government physicians, and so forth, but never with the Catholic idea of meriting eternal life.—Yours, etc.,

"C. M. Hyde."[1]

To deal fitly with a letter so extraordinary, I must draw at the outset on my private knowledge of the signatory and his sect. It may offend others; scarcely you, who have been so busy to collect, so bold to publish, gossip on your rivals. And this is perhaps the moment when I may best explain to you the character of what you are to read: I conceive you as a man quite beyond and below the reticences of civility: with what measure you mete, with that shall it be measured you again; with you, at last, I rejoice to feel the button off the foil and to plunge home. And if in aught that I shall say I should offend others, your colleagues, whom I respect and remember with affection, I can but

[1] From the Sydney *Presbyterian*, October 26, 1889.

offer them my regret; I am not free, I am inspired by the consideration of interests far more large; and such pain as can be inflicted by anything from me must be indeed trifling when compared with the pain with which they read your letter. It is not the hangman, but the criminal, that brings dishonour on the house.

You belong, sir, to a sect—I believe my sect, and that in which my ancestors laboured—which has enjoyed, and partly failed to utilize, an exceptional advantage in the islands of Hawaii. The first missionaries came; they found the land already self-purged of its old and bloody faith; they were embraced, almost on their arrival, with enthusiasm; what troubles they supported came far more from whites than from Hawaiians; and to these last they stood (in a rough figure) in the shoes of God. This is not the place to enter into the degree or causes of their failure, such as it is. One element alone is pertinent, and must here be plainly dealt with. In the course of their evangelical calling, they—or too many of them—grew rich. It may be news to you that the houses of missionaries are a cause of mocking on the streets of Honolulu. It will at least be news to you, that when I returned your civil visit, the driver of my cab commented on the size, the taste, and the comfort of your home. It would have been news certainly to myself, had anyone told me that afternoon that I should live to drag such matter into print. But you see, sir, how you degrade better men to your own level; and it is needful that those who are to judge betwixt you and me, betwixt Damien and the devil's advocate, should understand your letter to have been penned in a house which could raise, and that very justly, the envy and the comments of the passers-by. I think (to employ a phrase of yours which I admire) it "should be attributed" to you that you have never visited the scene of Damien's life and death. If you had, and had recalled it, and looked about your pleasant rooms, even your pen perhaps would have been stayed.

Your sect (and remember, as far as any sect avows me, it is mine) has not done ill in a worldly sense in the Hawaiian Kingdom. When calamity befell their innocent parishioners, when leprosy descended and took root in the Eight Islands, a *quid pro quo* was to be looked for. To that prosperous mission, and to you, as one of its adornments, God had sent at last an opportunity. I know I am touching here upon a nerve acutely sensitive. I know that others of your colleagues look back on the inertia of your Church, and the intrusive and decisive heroism of Damien, with something almost to be called remorse. I am sure it is so with yourself: I am persuaded your letter was inspired by a certain envy, not essentially ignoble, and the one human trait to be espied in that performance. You were thinking of the lost chance, the past day; of that which should have been conceived and was not; of the service due and not rendered. *Time was,* said the voice in your ear, in your pleasant room, as you sat raging and writing; and if the words written were base beyond parallel, the rage, I am happy to repeat—it is the only compliment I shall pay you—the rage was almost virtuous. But, sir, when we have failed, and another has succeeded; when we have stood by, and another has stepped in; when we sit and grow bulky in our charming mansions, and a plain, uncouth peasant steps into the battle, under the eyes of God, and succours the afflicted, and consoles the dying, and is himself afflicted in his turn, and dies upon the field of honour—the battle cannot be retrieved as your unhappy irritation has suggested. It is a lost battle, and lost for ever. One thing remained to you in your defeat—some rags of common honour; and these you have made haste to cast away.

Common honour; not the honour of having done anything right, but the honour of not having done aught conspicuously foul; the honour of the inert: that was what remained to you. We are not all expected to be Damiens; a man may conceive his duty more narrowly, he may love his comforts better; and none will cast a stone at him for that. But will a gentleman of your reverend profession allow me an example from the fields of gallantry? When two gentlemen compete for the favour of a lady, and the one succeeds and the other is rejected, and (as will sometimes happen) matter damaging to the successful rival's credit reaches the ear of the defeated, it is held by plain men of no pretensions that his mouth is, in the circumstance, almost necessarily closed. Your Church and Damien's were in Hawaii upon a rivalry to do well: to help, to edify, to set divine examples. You having (in one huge instance) failed, and Damien succeeded, I marvel it should not have occurred to you that you were doomed to silence; that when you had been outstripped in that high rivalry, and sat inglorious in the midst of your well-being, in your pleasant room—and Damien, crowned with glories and horrors, toiled and rotted in that pigstye of his under the cliffs of Kalawao—you, the elect who would not, were the last man on earth to collect and propagate gossip on the volunteer who would and did.

I think I see you—for I try to see you in the flesh as I write these sentences—I think I see you leap at the word pigstye, a hyperbolical expression at the best. "He had no hand in the reforms," he was "a coarse, dirty man"; these were your own words; and you may think it possible that I am come to support you with fresh evidence. In a sense, it is even so. Damien has been too much depicted with a conventional halo and conventional features; so drawn by men who perhaps had not the eye to remark or the pen to express the individual; or who perhaps were only blinded and silenced by generous admiration, such as I partly envy for myself—such as you, if your soul were enlightened, would envy on your bended knees. It is the least defect of such a method of portraiture that it makes the path easy for the devil's advocate, and leaves for the misuse of the slanderer a considerable field of truth. For the truth that is suppressed by friends is the readiest weapon of the enemy. The world, in your despite, may perhaps owe you something, if your letter be the means of substituting once for all a credible likeness for a wax abstraction. For, if that world at all remember you, on the day when Damien of Molokai shall be named Saint, it will be in virtue of one work: your letter to the Reverend H. B. Gage.

You may ask on what authority I speak. It was my inclement destiny to become acquainted, not with Damien, but with Dr. Hyde. When I visited the lazaretto Damien was already in his resting grave. But such information as I have, I gathered on the spot in conversation with those who knew him well and long: some indeed who revered his memory, but others who had sparred and wrangled with him, who beheld him with no halo, who perhaps regarded him with small respect, and through whose unprepared and scarcely partial communications the plain, human features of the man shone on me convincingly. These gave me what knowledge I possess; and I learned it in that scene where it could be most completely and sensitively understood—Kalawao, which you have never visited, about which you have never so much as endeavoured to inform yourself: for, brief as your letter is, you have found the means to stumble into that confession. *"Less than one-half* of the island," you say, "is devoted to the lepers." Molokai—*"Molokai ahina,"* the "grey," lofty, and most desolate island—along all its northern side plunges a front of precipice into a sea of unusual profundity. This range of cliff is, from east to west, the true end and frontier of the island. Only in one spot there projects into the ocean a certain triangular and rugged down, grassy, stony, windy, and rising in the midst into a hill with a dead crater: the whole bearing to the cliff that overhangs it somewhat the same relation as a bracket to a wall. With this hint you will now be able to pick out the leper station on a map; you will be able to judge how much of Molokai is thus cut off between the surf and precipice, whether less than a half, or less than a quarter, or a fifth, or a tenth—or say, a twentieth; and the next time you burst into print you will be in a position to share with us the issue of your calculations.

I imagine you to be one of those persons who talk with cheerfulness of that place which oxen and wainropes could not drag you to behold. You, who do not even know its situation on the map, probably denounce sensational descriptions, stretching your limbs the while in your pleasant parlour on Beretania Street. When I was pulled ashore there one early morning, there sat with me in the boat two sisters, bidding farewell (in humble imitation of Damien) to the lights and joys of human life. One of these wept silently; I could not withhold myself from joining her. Had you been there, it is my belief that nature would have triumphed even in you; and as the boat drew but a little nearer, and you beheld the stairs crowded with abominable deformations of our common manhood, and saw yourself landing in the midst of such a population as only now and then surrounds us in the horror of a nightmare—what a haggard eye you would have rolled over your reluctant shoulder towards the house on Beretania Street! Had you gone on; had you found every fourth face a blot upon the landscape; had you visited the hospital and seen the butt-ends of human beings lying there almost unrecognizable, but still breathing, still thinking, still remembering; you would have understood that life in the lazaretto is an ordeal from which the nerves of a man's spirit shrink, even as his eye quails under the brightness of the sun; you would have felt it was (even today) a pitiful place to visit and a hell to dwell in. It is not the fear of possible infection. That seems a little thing when compared with the pain, the pity and the disgust of the visitor's surroundings, and the atmosphere of affliction, disease, and physical disgrace in which he breathes. I do not think I am a man more than usually timid; but I never recall the days and nights I spent upon that island promontory (eight days and seven nights), without heartfelt thankfulness that I am somewhere else. I find in my diary that I speak of my stay as a "grinding experience": I have once jotted in the margin, *"Harrowing is the word"*; and when the *Mokolii* bore me at last towards the outer world, I kept repeating to myself, with a new conception of their pregnancy, those simple words of the song—

'Tis the most distressful country that ever yet was seen.

And observe: that which I saw and suffered from was a settlement purged, bettered, beautified; the new village built, the hospital and the Bishop-Home excellently arranged; the sisters, the doctor, and the missionaries, all indefatigable in their noble tasks. It was a different place when Damien came there, and made his great renunciation, and slept that first night under a tree amidst his rotting brethren: alone with pestilence; and looking forward (with what courage, with what pitiful sinkings of dread, God only knows) to a lifetime of dressing sores and stumps.

You will say, perhaps, I am too sensitive, that sights as painful abound in cancer hospitals and are confronted daily by doctors and nurses. I have long learned to admire and envy the doctors and the nurses. But there is no cancer hospital so large and populous as Kalawao and Kalaupapa; and in such a matter every fresh case, like every inch of length in the pipe of an organ, deepens the note of the impression; for what daunts the onlooker is that monstrous sum of human suffering by which he stands surrounded. Lastly, no doctor or nurse is called upon to enter once for all the doors of that gehenna; they do not say farewell, they need not abandon hope, on its sad threshold; they but go for a time to their high calling, and can look forward as they go to relief, to recreation, and to rest. But Damien shut to with his own hand the doors of his own sepulchre.

I shall now extract three passages from my diary at Kalawao.

A. "Damien is dead and already somewhat ungratefully remembered in the field of his labours and sufferings. 'He was a good man, but very officious,' says one. Another tells me he had fallen (as other priests so easily do) into something of the ways and habits of thought of a Kanaka; but he had the wit to recognize the fact, and the good sense to laugh at" [over] "it. A plain man it seems he was; I cannot find he was a popular."

B. "After Ragsdale's death" [Ragsdale was a famous Luna, or overseer, of the unruly settlement] "there followed a brief term of office by Father Damien which served only to publish the weakness of that noble man. He was rough in his ways, and he had no control. Authority was relaxed; Damien's life was threatened, and he was soon eager to resign."

C. "Of Damien I begin to have an idea. He seems to have been a man of the peasant class, certainly of the peasant type: shrewd; ignorant and bigoted, yet with an open mind, and capable of receiving and digesting a reproof if it were bluntly administered; superbly generous in the least thing as well as in the greatest, and as ready to give his last shirt (although not without human grumbling) as he had been to sacrifice his life; essentially indiscreet and officious, which made him a troublesome colleague; domineering in all his ways, which made him incurably unpopular with the Kanakas, but yet destitute of real authority, so that his boys laughed at him and he must carry out his wishes by the means of bribes. He learned to have a mania for doctoring; and set up the Kanakas against the remedies of his regular rivals: perhaps (if anything matter at all in the treatment of such a disease) the worst thing that he did, and certainly the easiest. The best and worst of the man appear very plainly in his dealings with Mr. Chapman's money; he had originally laid it out" [intended to lay it out] "entirely for the benefit of Catholics, and even so not wisely, but after a long, plain talk, he admitted his error fully and revised the list. The sad state of the boys' home is in part the result of his lack of control; in part, of his own slovenly ways and false idea of hygiene. Brother officials used to call it 'Damien's Chinatown.' 'Well,' they would say, 'your Chinatown keeps growing.' And he would laugh with perfect good-nature, and adhere to his errors with perfect obstinacy. So much I have gathered of truth about this plain, noble human brother and father of ours; his imperfections are the traits of his face, by which we know him for our fellow; his martyrdom and his example nothing can lessen or annul; and only a person here on the spot can properly appreciate their greatness."

I have set down these private passages, as you perceive, without correction; thanks to you, the public has them in their bluntness. They are almost a list of the man's faults, for it is rather these that I was seeking: with his virtues, with the heroic profile of his life, I and the world were already sufficiently acquainted. I was besides a little suspicious of Catholic testimony; in no ill sense, but merely because Damien's admirers and disciples were the least likely to be critical. I know you will be more suspicious still; and the facts set down above were one and all collected from the lips of Protestants who had opposed the father in his life. Yet I am strangely deceived, or they build up the image of a man, with all his weaknesses, essentially heroic, and alive with rugged honesty, generosity, and mirth.

Take it for what it is, rough private jottings of the worst sides of Damien's character, collected from the lips of those who had laboured with and (in your own phrase) "knew the man";—though I question whether Damien would have said that he knew you. Take it, and observe with wonder how well you were served by your gossips, how ill by your intelligence and sympathy; in how many points of fact we are at one, and how widely our appreciations vary. There is something wrong here; either with you or me. It is possible, for instance, that you, who seem to have so many ears in Kalawao, had heard of the affair of Mr. Chapman's money, and were singly struck by Damien's intended wrong-doing. I was struck with that also, and set it fairly down; but

I was struck much more by the fact that he had the honesty of mind to be convinced. I may here tell you that it was a long business; that one of his colleagues sat with him late into the night, multiplying arguments and accusations; that the father listened as usual with "perfect good-nature and perfect obstinacy"; but at the last, when he was persuaded—"Yes," said he, "I am very much obliged to you; you have done me a service; it would have been a theft." There are many (not Catholics merely) who require their heroes and saints to be infallible; to these the story will be painful; not to the true lovers, patrons, and servants of mankind.

And I take it, this is a type of our division; that you are one of those who have an eye for faults and failures; that you take a pleasure to find and publish them; and that, having found them, you make haste to forget the overvailing virtues and the real success which had alone introduced them to your knowledge. It is a dangerous frame of mind. That you may understand how dangerous, and into what a situation it has already brought you, we will (if you please) go hand-in-hand through the different phrases of your letter, and candidly examine each from the point of view of its truth, its appositeness, and its charity.

Damien was *coarse.*

It is very possible. You make us sorry for the lepers who had only a coarse old peasant for their friend and father. But you, who were so refined, why were you not there, to cheer them with the lights of culture? Or may I remind you that we have some reason to doubt if John the Baptist were genteel; and in the case of Peter, on whose career you doubtless dwell approvingly in the pulpit, no doubt at all he was a "coarse, headstrong" fisherman! Yet even in our Protestant Bibles Peter is called Saint.

Damien was *dirty.*

He was. Think of the poor lepers annoyed with this dirty comrade! But the clean Dr. Hyde was at his food in a fine house.

Damien was *headstrong.*

I believe you are right again; and I thank God for his strong head and heart.

Damien was *bigoted*.

I am not fond of bigots myself, because they are not fond of me. But what is meant by bigotry, that we should regard it as a blemish in a priest? Damien believed his own religion with the simplicity of a peasant or a child; as I would I could suppose that you do. For this, I wonder at him some way off; and had that been his only character, should have avoided him in life. But the point of interest in Damien, which has caused him to be so much talked about and made him at last the subject of your pen and mine, was that, in him, his bigotry, his intense and narrow faith, wrought potently for good, and strengthened him to be one of the world's heroes and exemplars.

Damien *was not sent to Molokai, but went there without orders.*

Is this a misreading? or do you really mean the words for blame? I have heard Christ, in the pulpits of our Church, held up for imitation on the ground that His sacrifice was voluntary. Does Dr. Hyde think otherwise?

Damien *did not stay at the settlement, etc.*

It is true that he was allowed many indulgences. Am I to understand that you blame the father for profiting by these, or the officers for granting them? In either case, it is a mighty Spartan standard to issue from the house on Beretania Street; and I am convinced you will find yourself with few supporters.

Damien *had no hand in the reforms, etc.*

I think even you will admit that I have already been frank in my description of the man I am defending; but before I take you up upon this head, I will be franker still, and tell you that perhaps nowhere in the world can a man taste a more pleasurable sense of contrast than when he passes from Damien's "Chinatown" at Kalawao to the beautiful Bishop-Home at Kalaupapa. At this point, in my desire to make all fair for you, I will break my rule and adduce Catholic testimony. Here is a passage from my diary about my visit to the Chinatown, from which you will see how it is (even now) regarded by its own officials: "We went round all the dormitories, refectories, etc.—dark and dingy enough, with a superficial cleanliness, which he" [Mr. Dutton, the lay brother] "did not seek to defend. 'It is almost decent,' said he; 'the sisters will make that all right when we get them here.'" And yet I gathered it was already better since Damien was dead, and far better than when he was there alone and had his own (not always excellent) way. I have now come far enough to meet you on a common ground of fact; and I tell you that, to a mind not prejudiced by jealousy, all the reforms of the lazaretto, and even those which he most vigorously opposed, are properly the work of Damien. They are the evidence of his success; they are what his heroism provoked from the reluctant and the careless. Many were before him in the field; Mr. Meyer, for instance, of whose faithful work we hear too little: there have been many since; and some had more worldly wisdom, though none had more devotion, than our saint. Before his day, even you will confess, they had effected little. It was his part, by one striking act of martyrdom, to direct all men's eyes on that distressful country. At a blow, and with the price of his life, he made the place illustrious and public. And that, if you will consider largely, was the one reform needful; pregnant of all that should succeed. It brought money; it brought (best individual addition of them all) the sisters; it brought supervision, for public opinion and public interest landed with the man at Kalawao. If ever any man brought reforms, and died to bring them, it was he. There is not a clean cup or towel in the Bishop-Home, but dirty Damien washed it.

Damien *was not a pure man in his relations with women, etc.*

How do you know that? Is this the nature of the conversation in that house on Beretania Street which the cabman envied, driving past? —racy details of the misconduct of the poor peasant priest, toiling under the cliffs of Molokai?

Many have visited the station before me; they seem not to have heard the rumour. When I was there I heard many shocking tales, for my informants were men speaking with the plainness of the laity; and I heard plenty of complaints of Damien. Why was this never mentioned? and how came it to you in the retirement of your clerical parlour?

But I must not even seem to deceive you. This scandal, when I read it in your letter, was not new to me. I had heard it once before; and I must tell you how. There came to Samoa a man from Honolulu; he, in a public-house on the beach, volunteered the statement that Damien had "contracted the disease from having connection with the female lepers"; and I find a joy in telling you how the report was welcomed in a public-house. A man sprang to his feet; I am not at liberty to give his name, but from what I heard I doubt if you would care to have him to dinner in Beretania Street. "You miserable little —— (here is a word I dare not print, it would so shock your ears). "You miserable little ——," he cried, "if the story were a thousand times true, can't you see you are a million times a lower —— for daring to repeat it?" I wish it could be told of you that when the report reached you in your house, perhaps after family worship, you had found in your soul enough holy anger to receive it with the same expressions: ay, even with that one which I dare not print; it would not need to have been blotted away, like Uncle Toby's oath, by the tears of the recording angel; it would have been counted to you for your brightest righteousness. But you have deliberately chosen the part of the man from Honolulu, and you have played it with improvements of your own. The man from Honolulu—miserable, leering creature—communicated the tale to a rude knot of beach-combing drinkers in a public-house, where (I will so far agree with your temperance opinions) man is not always at his noblest; and the man from Honolulu had himself been drinking—drinking, we may charitably fancy, to excess. It was to your "Dear Brother, the Reverend H. B. Gage," that you chose to communicate the sickening story; and the blue ribbon which adorns your portly bosom forbids me to allow you the extenuating plea that you were drunk when it was done. Your "dear brother"—a brother indeed—made haste to deliver up your letter (as a means of grace, perhaps) to the religious papers; where, after many months, I found and read and wondered at it; and whence I have now reproduced it for the wonder of others. And you and your dear brother have, by this cycle of operations, built up a contrast very edifying to examine in detail. The man whom you would not care to have to dinner, on the one side; on the other, the Reverend Dr. Hyde and the Reverend H. B. Gage: the Apia bar-room, the Honolulu manse.

But I fear you scarce appreciate how you appear to your fellow-men; and to bring it home to you, I will suppose your story to be true. I will suppose—and God forgive me for supposing it—that Damien faltered and stumbled in his narrow path of duty; I will suppose that, in the horror of his isolation, perhaps in the fever of incipient disease, he, who was doing so much more than he had sworn, failed in the letter of his priestly oath—he, who was so much a better man than either you or me, who did what we have never dreamed of daring—he too tasted of our common frailty. "O Iago, the pity of it!" The least tender should be moved to tears; the most incredulous to prayer. And all that you could do was to pen your letter to the Reverend H. B. Gage!

Is it growing at all clear to you what a picture you have drawn of your own heart? I will try yet once again to make it clearer. You had a father: suppose this tale were about him, and some informant brought it to you, proof in hand: I am not making too high an estimate of your emotional nature when I suppose you would regret the circumstance? that you would feel the tale of frailty the more keenly since it shamed the author of your days? and that the last thing you would do would be to publish it in the religious press? Well, the man who tried to do what Damien did, is my father, and the father of the man in the Apia bar, and the father of all who love goodness, and he was your father too, if God had given you grace to see it.

AN AFTERWORD ON
"TO THE REVEREND DR. HYDE"

FROM the first it has been the design of these *Readers* that they should be made up for the most part of recent works never too widely known, perhaps, or at any rate no longer easily come by. Yet here is an ever-accessible classic that somehow slipped in at the last moment. Then once the bars were down, of course, there was no keeping out "Rab and His Friends," which therefore follows next. What of it? "Rab" might well be read by everybody at least once a year.

The inclusion of the Stevenson letter was born of a recent spring evening when a roomful of us were talking after dinner about the new biography of Father Damien which had just been published. In the talk, it came to light that no one present had ever read the famous Stevenson philippic. Not the celebrated actress. Nor the playwright. Nor the lad from Groton. Nor the young Englishman just out of Oxford. No, nor the former Governor's lady from the Philippines either, whom one would have thought better grounded in the literature of the Pacific. None of them knew it. So perhaps it comes fresh to a new generation. After all, nearly half a century has slipped by since it made its first appearance as a pamphlet, privately printed in Australia.

When Stevenson first read Dr. Hyde's letter in the Sydney newspaper, he was already familiar with a report that it had halted a plan to erect a monument to Father Damien. Here is Mrs. Stevenson's testimony:

The very journal containing the letter condemnatory of Father Damien was among the first we chanced to open. I shall never forget my husband's ferocity of indignation, his leaping stride as he paced the room holding the offending paper at arm's-length before his eyes that burned and sparkled with a peculiar flashing light. His cousin, Mr. Balfour, in his *Life of Robert Louis Stevenson* says: "His eyes . . . when he was moved to anger or any fierce emotion seemed literally to blaze and glow with a burning light." In another moment he disappeared through the doorway, and I could hear him, in his own room, pulling his chair to the table, and the sound of his inkstand being dragged towards him.

That afternoon he called us together, my son, my daughter, and myself, saying that he had something serious to lay before us. He went over the circumstances succinctly, and then we three had the incomparable experience of hearing its author read aloud the defence of Father Damien while it was still red-hot from his indignant soul.

As we sat, dazed and overcome by emotion, he pointed out to us that the subject-matter was libellous in the highest degree, and the publication of the article might cause the loss of his entire substance. Without our concurrence he would not take such a risk. There was no dissenting voice; how could there be? The paper was published with almost no change or revision, though afterwards my husband said he considered this a mistake. He thought he should have waited for his anger to cool, when he might have been more impersonal and less egotistic.

In September when he *had* cooled off he wrote thus to Mrs. Charles Fairchild:

It is always harshness that one regrets. . . . I regret also my letter to Dr. Hyde. Yes, I do; I think it was barbarously harsh; if I did it now, I would defend Damien no less well, and give less pain to those who are alive. These promptings of good-humour are not all sound; the three times three, cheer, boys, cheer, and general amiability business rests on a sneaking love of popularity, the most insidious enemy of virtue. On the whole, it was virtuous to defend Damien; but it was harsh to strike so hard at Dr. Hyde. When I wrote the letter, I believed he would bring an action, in which case I knew I could be beggared. And as yet there has come no action; the injured Doctor has contented himself up to now with the (truly innocuous) vengeance of calling me a "Bohemian Crank," and I have deeply wounded one of his colleagues whom I esteemed and liked.

Well, such is life.

I remember once speculating with Charles MacArthur as to the effect of the letter on its astounded recipient. Did it crush that cleric utterly? Did it hurry him to a mortified grave? Or was he armored against such shafts? Did he bridle and say that he "considered the source"? Did he, as MacArthur guessed, audibly derive comfort from the fact that his critic was a wretched Bohemian, who had taken another man's wife away from him and carried her off to the wanton South Seas? Really, what could one expect?

Such records as are available lend color to that surmise. In an article written for the *Congregationalist* of August 7, 1890, though "exposed to all the malodorous and scarifying missiles any blackguard may use who has access to the public press," the undaunted Dr. Hyde—professing a grieved reluctance but revealing a considerable gusto—returned to the attack. He admitted that Stevenson's invective might be brilliant. "But," he went on happily, "it is like a glass coin, not golden, shivered into fragments of worthless glitter when brought to the test of truthfulness." Whatever the merits of this controversy, the Reverend Dr. Hyde, as you see, was at one marked disadvantage in any dispute with Mr. Stevenson. He could not write so well. And it is the irony of his life that though it began, as he himself testified, "in the purity of a New England home" and was distastefully spent in what he doubtless regarded as good works among a people he had found living in "an abysmal depth of heathen degradation," that far-flung divine is now remembered, and always will be remembered, only because once long ago in a moment of generous anger Robert Louis Stevenson sat down and, with an enjoyment still infectious, wrote him a letter.

A. W.

RAB AND
HIS FRIENDS

by

JOHN BROWN, M.D.

RAB AND HIS FRIENDS

I

FOUR-AND-THIRTY years ago, Bob Ainslie and I were coming up Infirmary Street from the High School, our heads together, and our arms intertwisted, as only lovers and boys know how, or why.

When we got to the top of the street, and turned north, we espied a crowd at the Tron Church. "A dog-fight!" shouted Bob, and was off; and so was I, both of us all but praying that it might not be over before we got up! And is not this boy-nature? and human nature too? and don't we all wish a house on fire not to be out before we see it? Dogs like fighting; old Isaac says they "delight" in it, and for the best of all reasons; and boys are not cruel because they like to see the fight. They see three of the great cardinal virtues of dog or man—courage, endurance, and skill—in intense action. This is very different from a love of making dogs fight, and enjoying, and aggravating, and making gain by their pluck. A boy—be he ever so fond himself of fighting—if he be a good boy, hates and despises all this, but he would have run off with Bob and me fast enough: it is a natural, and a not wicked interest, that all boys and men have in witnessing intense energy in action.

Does any curious and finely ignorant woman wish to know how Bob's eye at a glance announced a dog-fight to his brain? He did not, he could not, see the dogs fighting: it was a flash of an inference, a rapid induction. The crowd round a couple of dogs fighting is a crowd masculine mainly, with an occasional active, compassionate woman fluttering wildly round the outside and using her tongue and her hands freely upon the men, as so many "brutes"; it is a crowd annular, compact, and mobile; a crowd centripetal, having its eyes and its heads all bent downwards and inwards, to one common focus.

991

Well, Bob and I are up, and find it is not over: a small thoroughbred white bull terrier is busy throttling a large shepherd's dog, unaccustomed to war, but not to be trifled with. They are hard at it; the scientific little fellow doing his work in great style, his pastoral enemy fighting wildly, but with the sharpest of teeth and a great courage. Science and breeding, however, soon had their own; the Game Chicken, as the premature Bob called him, working his way up, took his final grip of poor Yarrow's throat, and he lay gasping and done for. His master, a brown, handsome, big young shepherd from Tweedsmuir, would have liked to have knocked down any man, would "drink up Esil, or eat a crocodile," for that part, if he had a chance: it was no use kicking the little dog; that would only make him hold the closer. Many were the means shouted out in mouthfuls, of the best possible ways of ending it. "Water!" but there was none near, and many cried for it who might have got it from the well at Blackfriar's Wynd. "Bite the tail!" and a large, vague, benevolent, middle-aged man, more desirous than wise, with some struggle got the bushy end of Yarrow's tail into his ample mouth, and bit it with all his might. This was more than enough for the much-enduring, much-perspiring shepherd, who, with a gleam of joy over his broad visage, delivered a terrific facer upon our large, vague, benevolent, middle-aged friend—who went down like a shot.

Still the Chicken holds; death not far off. "Snuff! A pinch of snuff!" observed a calm, highly dressed young buck, with an eye-glass in his eye. "Snuff, indeed!" growled the angry crowd, affronted and glaring. "Snuff! A pinch of snuff!" again observes the buck, but with more urgency; whereon were produced several open boxes, and from a mull which may have been at Culloden he took a pinch, knelt down, and presented it to the nose of the Chicken. The laws of physiology and of snuff take their course; the Chicken sneezes, and Yarrow is free!

The young pastoral giant stalks off with Yarrow in his arms, comforting him.

But the bull terrier's blood is up, and his soul unsatisfied; he grips the first dog he meets, and discovering she is not a dog, in Homeric phrase, he makes a brief sort of *amende,* and is off. The boys, with Bob and me at their head, are after him: down Niddry Street he goes, bent on mischief; up the Cowgate like an arrow—Bob and I, and our small men, panting behind.

There, under the single arch of the South Bridge, is a huge mastiff, sauntering down the middle of the causeway, as if with his hands in his pockets: he is old, grey, brindled, as big as a little Highland bull, and has the Shakespearian dewlaps shaking as he goes.

The Chicken makes straight at him, and fastens on his throat. To our astonishment the great creature does nothing but stand still, hold himself up, and roar—yes, roar; a long, serious, remonstrative roar. How is this? Bob and I are up to them. *He is muzzled!* The bailies had proclaimed a general muzzling, and his master, studying strength and economy mainly, had encompassed his huge jaws in a home-made apparatus constructed out of the leather of some ancient *breechin.* His mouth was open as far as it could; his lips curled up in rage, a sort of terrible grin; his teeth gleaming, ready, from out the darkness; the strap across his mouth tense as a bowstring; his whole frame stiff with indignation and surprise; his roar asking us all around: "Did you ever see the like of this?" He looked a statue of anger and astonishment done in Aberdeen granite.

We soon had a crowd; the Chicken held on. "A knife!" cried Bob; and a cobbler gave him his knife: you know the kind of knife, worn away obliquely to a point, and always keen. I put its edge to the tense leather; it ran before it; and then!—one sudden jerk of that enormous head, a sort of dirty mist about his mouth, no noise, and the bright and fierce little fellow is dropped, limp and dead. A solemn pause; this was more than any of us had bargained for. I turned the little fellow over, and saw he was quite dead; the mastiff had taken him by the small of the back like a rat, and broken it.

He looked down at his victim appeased, ashamed, and amazed, snuffed him all over, stared at him, and, taking a sudden thought, turned round and trotted off. Bob took the dead dog up, and said: "John, we'll bury him after tea." "Yes," said I, and was off after the mastiff. He made up the Cowgate at a rapid swing; he had forgotten some engagement. He turned up the Candlemaker Row, and stopped at the Harrow Inn.

There was a carrier's cart ready to start, and a keen, thin, impatient, blackavized little man, his hand at his grey horse's head, looking about angrily for something. "Rab, ye thief!" said he, aiming a kick at my great friend, who drew cringing up, and, avoiding the heavy shoe with more agility than dignity, and watching his master's eye, slunk dismayed under the cart, his ears down, and as much as he had of tail down too.

What a man this must be, thought I, to whom my tremendous hero turns tail! The carrier saw the muzzle hanging, cut and useless, from his neck, and I eagerly told him the story, which Bob and I always thought, and still think, Homer, or King David, or Sir Walter, alone were worthy to rehearse. The severe little man was mitigated, and condescended to say: "Rab, ma man, puir Rabbie!" whereupon the stump of a tail rose up, the ears were cocked, the eyes filled, and were comforted; the two friends were reconciled. "Hupp!" and a stroke of the whip were given to Jess; and off went the three.

Bob and I buried the Game Chicken that night (we had not much of a tea) in the back-green of his house, in Melville Street, No. 17, with considerable gravity and silence; and being at the time in the Iliad, and, like all boys, Trojans, we called him Hector, of course.

II

Six years have passed, a long time for a boy and a dog: Bob Ainslie is off to the wars; I am a medical student, and clerk at Minto House Hospital.

Rab I saw almost every week, on the Wednesday; and we had much pleasant intimacy. I found the way to his heart by frequent scratching of his huge head, and an occasional bone. When I did not notice him, he would plant himself straight before me, and stand wagging that bud of a tail, and looking up, with his head a little to the one side. His master I occasionally saw; he used to call me "Maister John," but was laconic as any Spartan.

One fine October afternoon, I was leaving the hospital, when I saw the large gate open, and in walked Rab, with that great and easy saunter of his. He looked as if taking general possession of the place; like the Duke of Wellington entering a subdued city, satiated with victory and peace. After him came Jess, now white from age, with her cart, and in it a woman carefully wrapped up, the carrier leading the horse anxiously, and looking back. When he saw me, James (for his name was James Noble) made a curt and grotesque "boo," and said: "Maister John, this is the mistress; she's got a trouble in her breest—some kind o' an income, we're thinkin'."

By this time I saw the woman's face; she was sitting on a sack filled with straw, her husband's plaid round her, and his big coat, with its large white metal buttons, over her feet.

I never saw a more unforgettable face—pale, serious, *lonely,*[1] delicate, sweet, without being at all what we call fine. She looked sixty, and had on a mutch, white as snow, with its black ribbon; her silvery, smooth hair setting off her dark-grey eyes,—eyes such as one sees only twice or thrice in a lifetime, full of suffering, full also of the overcoming of it; her eyebrows[2] black and delicate, and her mouth firm, patient, and contented, which few mouths ever are.

As I have said, I never saw a more beautiful countenance, or one more subdued to settled quiet. "Ailie," said James, "this is Maister John, the young doctor; Rab's freend, ye ken. We often speak aboot you, doctor." She smiled, and made a movement, but said nothing, and prepared to come down, putting her plaid aside and rising. Had Solomon, in all his glory, been handing down the Queen of Sheba at his palace gate, he could not have done it more daintily, more tenderly, more like a gentleman, than did James the Howgate carrier, when he lifted down Ailie his wife. The contrast of his small, swarthy, weather-beaten, keen, worldly face to hers—pale, subdued, and beautiful—was something

[1] It is not easy giving this look by one word: it was expressive of her being so much of her life alone.

[2]   "Black brows, they say,
Become some women best; so that there be not
Too much hair there, *but in a semicircle*
Or a half-moon made with a pen."
              —*The Winter's Tale*

wonderful. Rab looked on concerned and puzzled, but ready for anything that might turn up, were it to strangle the nurse, the porter, or even me. Ailie and he seemed great friends.

"As I was sayin', she's got a kind o' trouble in her breest, doctor; wull ye tak' a look at it?" We walked into the consulting-room, all four, Rab grim and comic, willing to be happy and confidential if cause could be shown, willing also to be the reverse on the same terms. Ailie sat down, undid her open gown and her lawn handkerchief round her neck, and, without a word, showed me her right breast. I looked at and examined it carefully, she and James watching me, and Rab eyeing all three. What could I say? There it was, that had once been so soft, so shapely, so white, so gracious and bountiful, so "full of all blessed conditions," hard as a stone, a centre of horrid pain, making that pale face, with its grey, lucid, reasonable eyes, and its sweet resolved mouth, express the full measure of suffering overcome. Why was that gentle, modest, sweet woman, clean and lovable, condemned by God to bear such a burden?

I got her away to bed. "May Rab and me bide?" said James. "*You* may; and Rab, if he will behave himself." "I'se warrant he's do that, doctor"; and in slunk the faithful beast. I wish you could have seen him. There are no such dogs now. He belonged to a lost tribe. As I have said, he was brindled, and grey like Rubislaw granite; his hair short, hard, and close, like a lion's; his body thick-set, like a little bull's, a sort of compressed Hercules of a dog. He must have been ninety pounds' weight, at the least; he had a large blunt head; his muzzle black as night, his mouth blacker than any night, a tooth or two—being all he had—gleaming out of his jaws of darkness. His head was scarred with the record of old wounds, a sort of series of fields of battle all over it; one eye out, one ear cropped as close as was Archbishop Leighton's father's; the remaining eye had the power of two; and above it, and in constant communication with it, was a tattered rag of an ear, which was for ever unfurling itself, like an old flag; and then that bud of a tail, about one inch long, if it could in any sense be said to be long, being as broad as long—the mobility, the instantaneousness of that bud were very funny and surprising, and its expressive twinklings and winkings, the intercommunications between the eye, the ear, and it, were of the oddest and swiftest.

Rab had the dignity and simplicity of great size; and, having fought his way all along the road to absolute supremacy, he was as mighty in his own line as Julius Cæsar or the Duke of Wellington, and had the gravity [1] of all great fighters.

You must have often observed the likeness of certain men to certain animals, and of certain dogs to men. Now, I never looked at Rab without thinking of the great Baptist preacher, Andrew Fuller.[2] The same large, heavy, menacing, combative, sombre, honest countenance, the same deep inevitable eye, the same look—as of thunder asleep, but ready—neither a dog nor a man to be trifled with.

Next day, my master, the surgeon, examined Ailie. There was no doubt it must kill her, and soon. It could be removed; it might never return; it would give her speedy relief: she should have it done. She curtsied, looked at James, and said: "When?" "Tomorrow," said the kind surgeon, a man of few words. She and James and Rab and I retired. I noticed that he and she spoke little, but seemed to anticipate everything in each other.

The following day, at noon, the students came in, hurrying up the great stair. At the first landing-place, on a small well-known blackboard, was a bit of paper fastened by wafers, and many remains of old wafers beside it. On the paper were the words: "An operation today.— J. B., *clerk.*"

Up ran the youths, eager to secure good places; in they crowded, full of interest and talk. "What's the case?" "Which side is it?"

---

[1] A Highland game-keeper, when asked why a certain terrier, of singular pluck, was so much more solemn than the other dogs, said: "Oh, sir, life's full o' sairiousness to him: he just never can get eneuch o' fechtin'."

[2] Fuller was in early life, when a farmer lad at Soham, famous as a boxer; not quarrelsome, but not without "the stern delight" a man of strength and courage feels in their exercise. Dr. Charles Stewart, of Dunearn, whose rare gifts and graces as a physician, a divine, a scholar, and a gentleman live only in the memory of those few who knew and survive him, liked to tell how 'Mr. Fuller used to say that when he was in the pulpit, and saw a *buirdly* man come along the passage, he would instinctively draw himself up, measure his imaginary antagonist, and forecast how he would deal with him, his hands meanwhile condensing into fists and tending to "square." He must have been a hard hitter if he boxed as he preached—what the "fancy" would call an "ugly customer."

Don't think them heartless; they are neither better nor worse than you or I; they get over their professional horrors, and into their proper work; and in them pity, as an *emotion,* ending in itself or at best in tears and a long-drawn breath, lessens, while pity, as a *motive,* is quickened, and gains power and purpose. It is well for poor human nature that it is so.

The operating theatre is crowded; much talk and fun, and all the cordiality and stir of youth. The surgeon with his staff of assistants is there. In comes Ailie: one look at her quiets and abates the eager students. That beautiful old woman is too much for them; they sit down, and are dumb, and gaze at her. These rough boys feel the power of her presence. She walks in quickly, but without haste; dressed in her mutch, her neckerchief, her white dimity short gown, her black bombasine petticoat, showing her white worsted stockings and her carpet shoes. Behind her was James with Rab. James sat down in the distance, and took that huge and noble head between his knees. Rab looked perplexed and dangerous; for ever cocking his ear and dropping it as fast.

Ailie stepped up on a seat, and laid herself on the table, as her friend the surgeon told her; arranged herself, gave a rapid look at James, shut her eyes, rested herself on me, and took my hand. The operation was at once begun; it was necessarily slow; and chloroform—one of God's best gifts to His suffering children—was then unknown. The surgeon did his work. The pale face showed its pain, but was still and silent. Rab's soul was working within him; he saw that something strange was going on, blood flowing from his mistress, and she suffering; his ragged ear was up, and importunate; he growled and gave now and then a sharp impatient yelp; he would have liked to have done something to that man. But James had him firm, and gave him a glower from time to time, and an intimation of a possible kick; all the better for James, it kept his eye and his mind off Ailie.

It is over: she is dressed, steps gently and decently down from the table, looks for James; then, turning to the surgeon and the students, she curtsies, and in a low, clear voice begs their pardon if she has behaved ill. The students—all of us—wept like children; the surgeon happed her up carefully, and, resting on James and me, Ailie went to her room, Rab following. We put her to bed. James took off his heavy shoes, crammed with tackets, heel-capped and toe-capped, and put them carefully under the table, saying: "Maister John, I'm for nane o' yer strynge nurse bodies for Ailie. I'll be her nurse, and I'll gang aboot on my stockin' soles as canny as pussy." And so he did; and handy and clever and swift and tender as any woman was that horny-handed, snell, peremptory little man. Everything she got he gave her: he seldom slept; and often I saw his small shrewd eyes out of the darkness, fixed on her. As before, they spoke little.

Rab behaved well, never moving, showing us how meek and gentle he could be, and occasionally, in his sleep, letting us know that he was demolishing some adversary. He took a walk with me every day, generally to the Candlemaker Row; but he was sombre and mild, declined doing battle, though some fit cases offered, and indeed submitted to sundry indignities, and was always very ready to turn, and came faster back, and trotted up the stair with much lightness, and went straight to that door.

Jess, the mare, had been sent, with her weather-worn cart, to Howgate, and had doubtless her own dim and placid meditations and confusions on the absence of her master and Rab and her unnatural freedom from the road and her cart.

For some days Ailie did well. The wound healed "by the first intention"; for, as James said, "Oor Ailie's skin's ower clean to beil." The students came in quiet and anxious, and surrounded her bed. She said she liked to see their young, honest faces. The surgeon dressed her, and spoke to her in his own short kind way, pitying her through his eyes, Rab and James outside the circle, Rab being now reconciled, and even cordial, and having made up his mind that as yet nobody required worrying, but, as you may suppose, *semper paratus.*

So far well; but four days after the operation my patient had a sudden and long shivering, a "groosin'," as she called it. I saw her soon after; her eyes were too bright, her cheek coloured; she was restless, and ashamed of being so; the balance was lost; mischief had begun. On looking at the wound, a blush of red told the secret: her pulse was rapid, her breathing anxious and quick; she wasn't herself, as she said, and was vexed at her restlessness. We tried what we could. James did everything, was everywhere; never in the way, never out of it; Rab subsided under the table into a dark place, and was motionless, all but his eye, which followed every one. Ailie got worse; began to wander in her mind, gently; was more demonstrative in her ways to James, rapid in her questions, and sharp at times. He was vexed, and said: "She was never that way afore—no, never." For a time she knew her head was wrong, and was always asking our pardon, the dear, gentle old woman; then delirium set in strong, without pause. Her brain gave way, and then came that terrible spectacle,

> The intellectual power, through words and things,
> Went sounding on a dim and perilous way!

She sang bits of old songs and Psalms, stopping suddenly, mingling the Psalms of David, and the diviner words of the Son and Lord, with homely odds and ends and scraps of ballads.

Nothing more touching, or in a sense more strangely beautiful, did I ever witness. Her tremulous, rapid, affectionate, eager Scotch voice, the swift, aimless, bewildered mind, the baffled utterance, the bright and perilous eye, some wild words, some household cares, something for James, the names of the dead, Rab called rapidly and in a "fremyt" voice, and he starting up, surprised, and slinking off as if he were to blame somehow, or had been dreaming he heard. Many eager questions and beseechings which James and I could make nothing of, and on which she seemed to set her all and then sink back ununderstood. It was very sad, but better than many things that are not called sad. James hovered about, put out and miserable, but active and exact as ever; read to her, when there was a lull, short bits from the Psalms, prose and metre, chanting the latter in his own rude and serious way, showing great knowledge of the fit words, bearing up like a man, and doting over her as his "ain Ailie," "Ailie, ma woman!" "Ma ain bonnie wee dawtie!"

The end was drawing on: the golden bowl was breaking; the silver cord was fast being loosed; that *animula vagula, blandula, hospes comesque,* was about to flee. The body and the soul—companions for sixty years—were being sundered, and taking leave. She was walking, alone, through the valley of that shadow into which one day we must all enter; and yet she was not alone, for we know whose rod and staff were comforting her.

One night she had fallen quiet, and, as we hoped, asleep; her eyes were shut. We put down the gas, and sat watching her. Suddenly she sat up in bed, and, taking a bed-gown which was lying on it rolled up, she held it eagerly to her breast, to the right side. We could see her eyes bright with a surprising tenderness and joy, bending over this bundle of clothes. She held it as a woman holds her sucking child; opening out her night-gown impatiently, and holding it close, and brooding over it, and murmuring foolish little words, as over one whom his mother comforteth, and who sucks and is satisfied. It was pitiful and strange to see her wasted dying look, keen and yet vague— her immense love.

"Preserve me!" groaned James, giving way. And then she rocked backward and forward, as if to make it sleep, hushing it, and wasting on it her infinite fondness. "Wae's me, doctor! I declare she's thinkin' it's that bairn." "What bairn?" "The only bairn we ever had; our wee Mysie, and she's in the Kingdom forty years and mair." It was plainly true: the pain in the breast, telling its urgent story to a bewildered, ruined brain, was misread and mistaken; it suggested to her the uneasiness of a breast full of milk, and then the child; and so again once more they were together, and she had her ain wee Mysie in her bosom.

This was the close. She sank rapidly: the delirium left her; but, as she whispered, she was "clean silly"; it was the lightening before the final darkness. After having for some time lain still, her eyes shut, she said: "James!" He came close to her, and, lifting up her calm, clear, beautiful eyes, she gave him a long look, turned to me kindly but shortly, looked for Rab but could not see him, then turned to her husband again, as if she would never leave off looking, shut her eyes, and composed herself. She lay for some time breathing quick, and passed away so gently that, when we thought she was gone, James, in his old-fashioned way, held the mirror to her face. After a long pause, one small spot of dimness was breathed out; it vanished away, and never returned, leaving the blank clear darkness without a stain. "What is your life? It is even a vapour, that appeareth for a little time, and then vanisheth away."

Rab all this time had been fully awake and motionless; he came forward beside us. Ailie's hand, which James had held, was hanging down: it was soaked with his tears. Rab licked it all over carefully, looked at her, and returned to his place under the table.

James and I sat, I don't know how long, but for some time, saying nothing; he started up abruptly, and with some noise went to the table, and, putting his right fore and middle fingers each into a shoe, pulled them out, and put them on, breaking one of the leather latchets, and muttering in anger: "I never did the like o' that afore!"

I believe he never did; nor after either. "Rab!" he said, roughly, and pointing with his thumb to the bottom of the bed. Rab leaped up, and settled himself, his head and eye to the dead face. "Maister John, ye'll wait for me," said the carrier; and disappeared in the darkness, thundering downstairs in his heavy shoes. I ran to a front window; there he was, already round the house, and out at the gate, fleeing like a shadow.

I was afraid about him, and yet not afraid; so I sat down beside Rab, and, being wearied, fell asleep. I awoke from a sudden noise outside. It was November, and there had been a heavy fall of snow. Rab was *in statu quo;* he heard the noise too, and plainly knew it, but never moved. I looked out; and there, at the gate, in the dim morning—for the sun was not up—was Jess and the cart, a cloud of steam rising from the old mare. I did not see James; he was already at the door, and came up the stairs and met me. It was less than three hours since he left, and he must have posted out—who knows how?—to Howgate, full nine miles off, yoked Jess, and driven her astonished into town. He had an armful of blankets, and was streaming with perspiration. He nodded to me, spread out on the floor two pairs of clean old blankets having at their corners "A. G., 1794" in large letters in red worsted. These were the initials of Alison Græme, and James may have looked in at her from without—himself unseen but not unthought of—when he was "wat, wat, and weary," and, after having walked many a mile over the hills, may have seen her sitting, while "a' the lave were sleepin'," and by the firelight working her name on the blankets for her ain James's bed.

He motioned Rab down, and, taking his wife in his arms, laid her in the blankets, and wrapped her carefully and firmly up, leaving the face uncovered; and then, lifting her, he nodded again sharply to me, and, with a resolved but utterly miserable face, strode along the passage, and downstairs, followed by Rab. I followed with a light; but he didn't need it. I went out, holding stupidly the candle in my hand in the calm frosty air; we were soon at the gate. I could have helped him, but I saw he was not to be meddled with, and he was strong and did not need it. He laid her down as tenderly, as safely, as he had lifted her out ten days before—as tenderly as when he had her first in his arms when she was only "A. G."—sorted her, leaving that beautiful sealed face open to the heavens; and then, taking Jess by the head, he moved away. He did not notice me; neither did Rab, who presided behind the cart.

I stood till they passed through the long shadow of the College and turned up Nicolson Street. I heard the solitary cart sound through the streets and die away and come again; and I returned, thinking of that company going up Libberton Brae, then along Roslin Muir, the morning light touching the Pentlands and making them like onlooking ghosts, then down the hill through Auchindinny woods, past "haunted Woodhouselee"; and as daybreak came sweeping up the bleak Lammermuirs, and fell on his own door, the company would stop, and James would take the key, and lift Ailie up again, laying her on her own bed, and, having put Jess up, would return with Rab and shut the door.

James buried his wife, with his neighbours mourning, Rab watching the proceedings from a distance. It was snow, and that black ragged hole would look strange in the midst of the swelling spotless cushion of white. James looked after everything; then rather suddenly fell ill, and took to bed; was insensible when the doctor came, and soon died. A sort of low fever was prevailing in the village, and his want of sleep, his exhaustion, and his misery made him apt to take it. The grave was not difficult to reopen. A fresh fall of snow had again made all things white and smooth; Rab once more looked on, and slunk home to the stable.

And what of Rab? I asked for him next week of the new carrier who got the goodwill of James's business and was now master of Jess and her cart. "How's Rab?" He put me off, and said, rather rudely: "What's *your* business wi' the dowg?" I was not to be so put off. "Where's Rab?" He, getting confused and red, and intermeddling with his hair, said: " 'Deed, sir, Rab's deid." "Dead! What did he die of?" "Weel, sir," said he, getting redder, "he didna exactly dee; he was killed. I had to brain him wi' a rack-pin; there was nae doin' wi' him. He lay in the treviss wi' the mear, and wadna come oot. I tempit him wi' kail and meat, but he wad tak' naething, and keepit me fra feedin' the beast, and he was aye gur-gurrin', and grup-gruppin' me by the legs. I was laith to mak' awa wi' the auld dowg, his like wasna atween this and Thornhill—but, 'deed, sir, I could do naething else." I believed him. Fit end for Rab, quick and complete. His teeth and his friends gone, why should he keep the peace and be civil?

He was buried in the braeface, near the burn, the children of the village, his companions, who used to make very free with him and sit on his ample stomach as he lay half asleep at the door in the sun, watching the solemnity.

AN AFTERWORD ON
"RAB AND HIS FRIENDS"

IN the earlier pages of this *Reader* there is a biography written by a physician—the portrait of Portugee Joe by Dr. Eckstein of Cincinnati. To that, the imperishable record of Rab and his friends is a companion piece—the work of another physician, Dr. John Brown, who, full of years, died in Edinburgh in 1882. As a thesis available to some youth working for his doctorate in the field of beautiful letters, it is hereby suggested that there is room for inquiry as to the roots of the indisputable kinship between the gift of writing on the one hand and on the other the study and practice of medicine. No other of the learned professions has produced so many felicitous pens. The elder Oliver Wendell Holmes, S. Weir Mitchell, Conan Doyle, Logan Clendening, Arthur Schnitzler, Somerset Maugham, young A. J. Cronin who has written *Hatter's Castle* and *The Citadel,* Dr. John Brown, and now this Gustav Eckstein—there is a partial list submitted offhand as a starter.

A. W.

GOD AND
MY FATHER

by

CLARENCE DAY

GOD AND MY FATHER

In my boyhood, I never had a doubt that the beliefs they taught me were true. The difficulty was to live up to them, and to love God. Most of the time I was too busy to think of such things; but then a problem of conduct would face me, or a duty I had forgotten, or my own private feelings at night after saying my prayers, and at such times religion would confront me like a Sphinx in the landscape. I would stand before it like a hypnotized bird before some great ageless serpent, unable to think of or feel any way of escape.

I believed in the Bible. Creation, to me, meant a Creator. And since there was someone so great and powerful that He had created us all, I felt I had better learn His wishes. They were supposed to be good. I wanted to live in harmony with Him—no battle of wills. Yet I also wished greatly to get away and live as I liked.

If I could have been sure that the Creator was my ally or friend, that would have been a great comfort, in those days. It would have not only saved me from worry, it would have set me free to go about my business with confidence, both in Him and myself. Or if I could have surrendered myself to His rather bleak guidance, that again might have been a relief to me. But—I couldn't do it. I didn't quite trust Him or love Him enough to do that.

I thought of God as a strangely emotional being. He was powerful; He was forgiving yet obdurate, full of wrath and affection. Both His wrath and affection were fitful, they came and they went, and I couldn't count on either to continue: although they both always did. In short, God was much such a being as my father himself.

What was the relation between them, I wondered, these two puzzling deities?

I

MY FATHER'S RELIGION

My father's ideas of religion seemed straightforward and simple. He had noticed when he was a boy that there were buildings called churches; he had accepted them as a natural part of the surroundings in which he had been born. He would never have invented such things himself. Nevertheless they were here. As he grew up he regarded them as unquestioningly as he did banks. They were substantial old structures, they were respectable, decent, and venerable. They were frequented by the right sort of people. Well, that was enough.

On the other hand he never allowed churches—or banks—to dictate to him. He gave each the respect that was due to it from his point of view; but he also expected from each of them the respect he felt due to him.

As to creeds, he knew nothing about them, and cared nothing either; yet he seemed to know which sect he belonged with. It had to be a sect with the minimum of nonsense about it; no total immersion, no exhorters, no holy confession. He would have been a Unitarian, naturally, if he'd lived in Boston. Since he was a respectable New Yorker, he belonged in the Episcopal Church.

As to living a spiritual life, he never tackled that problem. Some men who accept spiritual beliefs try to live up to them daily; other men, who reject such beliefs, try sometimes to smash them. My father would have disagreed with both kinds entirely. He took a more distant attitude. It disgusted him when atheists attacked religion: he thought they were vulgar. But he also objected to have religion make demands upon him—he felt that religion too was vulgar, when it tried to stir up men's feelings. It had its own proper field of activity, and it was all right there, of course; but there was one place religion should let alone, and that was a man's soul. He especially loathed any talk of walking hand in hand with his Saviour. And if he had ever found the Holy Ghost trying to soften his heart, he would have regarded Its behavior as distinctly uncalled for; even ungentlemanly.

The only religious leader or prophet I can think of who might have suited my father was Confucius—though even Confucius would have struck him as addled. Confucius was an advocate of peace, and of finding the path; and he enjoined the Golden Rule on his followers long before Christ. My father would not have been his follower in any of these. Finding "the path"? Not even Confucius could have made him see what that meant. He was too busy for that, too hot-tempered for peace, and the Golden Rule he regarded as claptrap; how could things work both ways? Whatever he did unto others he was sure was all right, but that didn't mean that he would have allowed them to do the same things to him. He saw other men as disorderly troops, and himself as a general; and the Golden Rule was plainly too mushy to apply in such circumstances. He disciplined himself quite as firmly as he tried to discipline others, but it wasn't necessarily by any means the same kind of discipline. There was one saying of Confucius, however, with which he would have agreed: "Respect spiritual beings—if there are any—but keep aloof from them." My father would have regarded that principle as thoroughly sound.

When Confucius was asked about the rule to return good for evil, he said: "What then will you return for good? No: return good for good; for evil, return justice." If my father had been asked to return good for evil he would have been even more pithy—his response would have consisted of a hearty and full-throated "Bah!"

If he had been let alone, he would have brought up his sons in this spirit. But my mother's feelings and teachings were different, and this complicated things for us. Like my father, she had accepted religion without any doubtings, but she had accepted more of it. She was far more devout. And she loved best the kind of faith that comforted her and sweetened her thoughts. My father didn't object to this at all—it was all right enough—for a woman: but it led to her giving us instructions that battled with his.

They both insisted strongly, for example, on our going to church, but they didn't agree in their reasons. It was the right thing to do,

Father said. "But why do we have to go, Father?" "Because I wish to bring you up properly. Men who neglect going to church are a lazy, disreputable lot." A few might be good fellows, he would admit, but they were the exceptions. As a rule, non-churchgoers were not solid, respectable citizens. All respectable citizens owed it to themselves to attend.

My mother put it differently to us. She said we owed it to God. Church to her was a place where you worshiped, and learned to be good. My father never dreamed of attending for any such reason. In his moral instructions to us he never once mentioned God. What he dwelt on was integrity. My mother once wrote in my plush-covered autograph album: "Fear God and keep His commandments"; but the motto that Father had written on the preceding page, over his bolder signature, was: "Do your duty and fear no one." And nobody could tell him his duty—he knew it without that, it seemed. It wasn't written down in any book, certainly not in the Bible, but it was a perfectly definite and indisputable thing nevertheless. It was a code, a tradition. It was to be upright and fearless and honorable, and to brush your clothes properly; and in general always to do the right thing in every department of life. The right thing to do for religion was to go to some good church on Sundays.

When Father went to church and sat in his pew, he felt he was doing enough. Any further spiritual work ought to be done by the clergy.

When hymns were sung he sometimes joined in mechanically, for the mere sake of singing; but usually he stood as silent as an eagle among canaries and doves, leaving others to abase themselves in sentiments that he didn't share. The hymns inculcated meekness and submission, and dependence on God; but Father was quick to resent an injury, and he had no meekness in him.

> "Jesus, lover of my soul,
> Let me to thy bosom fly,
> While the nearer waters roll,
> While the tempest still is nigh."

How could Father sing that? He had no desire to fly to that bosom.

"Hide me, O my Saviour, hide,
Till the storm of life be past;
Safe into the haven guide,
Oh, receive my soul at last . . .
All my trust on thee is stayed;
All my help from thee I bring;
Cover my defenseless head
With the shadow of thy wing."

But Father's head was far from defenseless, and he would have scorned to hide, or ask shelter. As he stood there, looking critically about him, high-spirited, resolute, I could imagine him marching with that same independence through space—a tiny speck masterfully dealing with death and infinity.

When our rector talked of imitating the saints, it seemed drivel to Father. What! Imitate persons who gave their whole lives to religion, and took only a perfunctory interest in the affairs of this world? Father regarded himself as a more all-round man than the saints. They had neglected nine-tenths of their duties from his point of view—they had no business connections, no families, they hadn't even paid taxes. In a word, saints were freaks. If a freak spent an abnormal amount of time being religious, what of it?

The clergy were a kind of freaks also. A queer lot. Father liked Bishop Greer and a few others, but he hadn't much respect for the rest of them. He thought of most clergymen as any busy man of action thinks of philosophers, or of those scholars who discuss the fourth dimension, which is beyond human knowing. He regarded the self-alleged intimacy of our rector with that fourth dimension most skeptically. He himself neither was nor wished to be intimate with a thing of that sort. But this didn't mean that he doubted the existence of God. On the contrary, God and Father had somehow contrived to achieve a serene and harmonious relation that the clergy themselves might have envied.

How did Father think God felt towards my mother? Why, about

the way he did. God probably knew she had faults, but He saw she was lovely and good; and—in spite of some mistaken ideas that she had about money—He doubtless looked on her most affectionately. Father didn't expect God to regard *him* affectionately—they stood up man to man—but naturally God loved my mother, as everyone must. At the gate of Heaven, if there was any misunderstanding about his own ticket, Father counted on Mother to get him in. That was her affair.

This idea runs far back, or down, into old human thoughts. "The unbelieving husband is sanctified by the wife." (First Corinthians, vii, 14.) Medical missionaries report that today, in some primitive tribes, a healthy woman will propose to swallow medicine in behalf of her sick husband. This plan seems to her husband quite reasonable. It seemed so—in religion—to Father.

As to his mental picture of God, I suppose that Father was vague, but in a general way he seemed to envisage a God in his own image. A God who had small use for emotionalism and who prized strength and dignity. A God who probably found the clergy as hard to bear as did Father himself. In short Father and God, as I said, usually saw eye to eye. They seldom met, or even sought a meeting, their spheres were so different; but they had perfect confidence in each other—at least at most moments. The only exceptions were when God seemed to be neglecting his job—Father's confidence in Him was then withdrawn, instantly. But I'll come to this later.

As to the nature of God's sphere, namely Heaven, compared to Father's, the earth, Heaven wasn't nearly so solid and substantial. Father had all the best of it. Life here on earth was trying, but it shouldn't be—it was all right intrinsically—he felt it was only people's damned carelessness that upset things so much. Heaven on the other hand had a more serious and fundamental defect: the whole place was thin and peculiar. It didn't inspire much confidence. Father saw glumly that the time would come when he'd have to go there, but he didn't at all relish the prospect. He clung to his own battered realm.

Yet its faults and stupidities weighed on his spirit at times: all the chuckle-headed talk and rascality in business and politics. He was always getting indignant about them, and demanding that they be stamped out; and when he saw them continually spreading everywhere, it was maddening. Nature too, though in general sound and wholesome, had a treacherous streak. He hated and resented decay, and failing powers. He hated to see little children or animals suffer. His own aches and pains were an outrage; he faced them with anger. And aside from these treacheries, there was a spirit of rebellion in things. He would come in from a walk over his fields—which to me had seemed pleasant—oppressed by the balky disposition both of his fields and his farmer. He would get up from an inspection of his account books with the same irritation: there were always some bonds in his box that hadn't behaved as they should. And twice a day, regularly, he would have a collision, or bout, with the newspaper: it was hard to see why God had made so many damned fools and democrats.

I would try to persuade him sometimes—in my argumentative years—that it would be better for him to accept the world as it was and adapt himself to it, since he could scarcely expect to make the planet over, and change the whole earth single-handed. Father listened to this talk with suspicion, as to an *advocatus diaboli*. If he ever was tempted to give in, it was only in his weak moments; a minute later he was again on the warpath, like a materialistic Don Quixote.

There was one kind of depression that afflicted Mother which Father was free from: he never once had any moments of feeling "unworthy." This was a puzzle to Mother, and it made her look at Father with a mixture of awe and annoyance. Other people went to church to be made better, she told him. Why didn't he? He replied in astonishment that he had no need to be better—he was all right as he was. Mother couldn't get over his taking this stand, but she never could get him to see what the matter was with it. It wasn't at all easy for Father to see that he had any faults; and if he did, it didn't even occur to him to ask God to forgive them. He forgave them himself. In his moments of prayer, when he and God tried to commune with each other, it wasn't his own shortcomings that were brought on the carpet, but God's.

He expected a good deal of God, apparently. Not that he wanted God's help, of course; or far less His guidance. No, but it seemed that God—like the rest of us—spoiled Father's plans. He, Father, was always trying to bring this or that good thing to pass, only to find that there were obstacles in the way. These of course roused his wrath. He would call God's attention to such things. They should not have been there. He didn't actually accuse God of gross inefficiency, but when he prayed his tone was loud and angry, like that of a dissatisfied guest in a carelessly managed hotel.

I never saw Father kneel in supplication on such occasions. On the contrary he usually talked with God lying in bed. My room was just above Father's, and he could easily be heard through the floor. On those rare nights when he failed to sleep well, the sound of damns would float up—at first deep and tragic and low, then more loud and exasperated. Fragments of thoughts and strong feelings came next, or meditations on current bothers. At the peak of these, God would be summoned. I would hear him call "Oh, God?" over and over, with a rising inflection, as though he were demanding that God should present Himself instantly, and sit in the fat green chair in the corner, and be duly admonished. Then when Father seemed to feel that God was listening, he would begin to expostulate. He would moan in a discouraged but strong voice: "Oh, God, it's too much. Amen . . . I say it's too damned much . . . No, no, I can't stand it. Amen." After a pause, if he didn't feel better, he would seem to suspect that God might be trying to sneak back to Heaven without doing anything, and I would hear him shout warningly: "Oh, God! I *won't* stand it! Amen. Oh, damnation! A-a-men." Sometimes he would ferociously bark a few extra Amens, and then, soothed and satisfied, peacefully go back to sleep. . . . And one night in the country, when the caretaker of our house in town telephoned to Father that the rain was pouring in through a hole in the roof, I heard so much noise that I got out of bed and looked over the banisters, and saw Father standing alone in the hall, shaking his fist at the ceiling, and shouting in hot indignation to Heaven: "What next?"

But Father was patient with God after all. If he didn't forgive, he forgot. His wrath didn't last—he had other things to think of—and he was genial at heart. The very next Sunday after an outburst he would be back in church. Not perhaps as a worshiper or a devotee, but at least as a patron.

II

MY FATHER AND HIS PASTORS

A MAN who accepts a religion without being religious lets himself in for more hardships than one would suppose. My father persisted most manfully in going to church; and he usually entered its portals at peace with the world and settled himself down contentedly in his end seat: but somehow before very long his expression would darken, as his hopes of hearing a sensible service little by little were dashed; and he came out in an inflamed state of mind that could not have been good for him.

The Episcopal service in general he didn't criticize; it was stately and quiet; but the sermon, being different every Sunday, was a very bad gamble. And once in a while there would be an impromptu prayer that he would take great offense at. Sometimes he disliked its subject or sentiments—if he chanced to be listening. Some times he decided it was too long, or its tone too lugubrious. I remember seeing him so restive during a prayer of that kind, that—although the entire congregation was kneeling in reverence—he suddenly gave a loud snort, sat up straight in his pew, and glared at the minister's back as though planning to kick it.

I glanced over at Mother. She had been sailing along devoutly, as best she could, in the full tide of prayer, with the lovely rapt look that would come at such times on her face; but she had also begun to watch Father out of one eye—for whenever a prayer was longer than usual she feared its effect on him—and now here he was sitting up and she had to stop praying and turn away from God to this obstinate, obstinate man. "Put your head down," she whispered fiercely; and then, when he wouldn't, she felt so furious at him, and so impotent, and so guilty for having such feelings, and so torn between her yearning to sink back again into the sweet peace of prayer and her hot determination to make the bad boy in Father behave, that she sent him a look like a flash of lightning, shooting out through quick tears; indignant to the very roots of her red hair, and as hurt as a child. This sank into him. He never would at any time kneel in church—she had given up struggling for that—but at last with a deep angry growl he once more bent stiffly down.

Toward the latter part of his life Father found a minister whose sermons he liked. This was the Reverend Mr. Henshaw of Rye, where we lived in the summer. Mr. Henshaw wasn't "one of these pious fellows," Father said, with approval—though why piety was so unsuited to the clergy he never explained. And some years before this, one summer on the Hudson near Tarrytown, there was a Mr. Wenke, an earnest young cleric, who also found favor. But this was mostly because one of the vestry, old Mr. John Rutland, was very strict with Mr. Wenke about the length of his sermons. Mr. Rutland had got it into his head that all sermons should end at twelve, sharp; and if he saw Mr. Wenke being carried away by his own eloquence, he would take out his watch and stare ominously, first at him, then at it. Pretty soon Mr. Wenke's roving eye would be caught and held by this sight. He would falter or sometimes almost choke in the midst of his flow, then lamely end his remarks, and get out of the pulpit.

In the city at this same later period Father went to St. Bartholomew's, and there too the various clergymen suited him, though not quite so well. He liked St. Bartholomew's. The church itself was comfortable, and the congregation were all the right sort. There was Mr. Edward J. Stuyvesant, who was president of three different coal-mines, and Admiral Prentice who had commanded the Fleet, and old Mr. Johns of the *Times;* and bank directors and doctors and judges—solid men of affairs. The place was like a good club. And the sermon was like a strong editorial in a conservative newspaper. It did not nag at Father, it attacked the opposition instead; it gave all wrong-headed persons a sound trouncing, just the way Father would have.

Mother didn't enjoy these attacks. Denunciations upset her. She took almost all denouncing personally, as directed at her, and it made her feel so full of faults that she trembled inside, though she looked straight back up at the preacher, round-eyed and scared but defiant. She preferred something healing, and restful; some dear old tale from the Bible. But denunciations satisfied Father. He liked something vigorous. And in general he instinctively took to the Established Church pattern —a church managed like a department of a gentleman's Government. He liked such a church's strong tory flavor, and its recognition of castes. He liked its deference to sound able persons who knew how to run things, and its confidence in their integrity and right point of view. In effect, it put such men on their honor, without foolishly saying so. No other approach would have found a way into their hearts.

But nothing is perfect. After Father had made himself at home in this reliable temple, he discovered too late that even here a man wasn't safe. The rector began talking about the need for what he called a New Edifice. He said the church had a leak in the roof, and the neighborhood was changing to business, and that they had received a good offer for the property and had better move elsewhere. This gave Father an unsettled feeling. He wished to stay put. But the rector kept stirring things up until he at last got his way.

Committees were appointed, and active teams of workers were organized, who began to collect large subscriptions from every parishioner. Father paid no attention to all this. It was no plan of his. If they insisted on having better quarters, he would try to enjoy them, but aside from this effort the rest of it was not his affair. It was only when he was made to see that he too would have to subscribe, that Father became roused and startled. This had never occurred to him. He said he might have known it was just a damn scheme to get money.

He was still more upset when Mother told him what sum was expected of him. He had imagined that they would want fifty dollars, or even a hundred; and that was enough to depress him. But she said that since he had bought a good pew they would expect him to give several thousand. This was like an earthquake. Father in fact took it as some wild cataclysm of nature, some unheard-of violent destruction of an honest citizen's peace. After roaring out that the rector and his Christian workers could all go to hell, he barricaded himself every evening in his cyclone cellar—the library—and declared he wouldn't see any callers. This lasted a week. Then when he had cooled down a little,

Mother had a long talk with him, and told him who were on the committee—some men whom he liked. She said he would really have to subscribe. He'd at least have to see them.

He waited, fretful and uneasy, for the attack to begin. One night when Mother was sitting in her room, there were sounds of talk in the library. She hurried down the passageway, clutching her needle and mending, and listened at the door. Father was doing all the talking, it seemed. He was stating his sentiments in his usual round tones, strong and full. He got more and more shouty. Mother began to fear the committee mightn't like being scolded. But when she opened the door on a crack and peeked in, there was no one in there but Father. He was in his easy-chair, talking away, with his face all puckered up, and he was thumping his hand with a hammer-like beat on his newspaper. "In ordinary circumstances," he was saying to the imaginary committeemen, "in ordinary circumstances I should have expected to subscribe to this project. But during the past few years my investments" (thump, thump, on the newspaper) "have shown me heavy losses." Here he thought of the New Haven Railroad and groaned. *"Damned* heavy losses!" he roared, and flung the paper aside. "Who the devil's that? Oh, it's you, Vinnie. Come in, dear Vinnie. I'm lonely."

I don't recall how much he gave in the end, but I think it was a thousand dollars. The reason Mother thought that he would probably have to give more, was that our pew was way up in front; it was—so to speak—in a fine section. All our neighbors were prominent. There may have been plenty of ordinary Christians in other parts of the building, but I did not see them. Furthermore this pew, though a small one, had cost Father five thousand dollars, and parishioners were being asked to give as much as the cost of their pews. Father had hated to invest all that money in a mere place to sit, but he could sell out again some day, and meanwhile he had a good pew. He rented the one in Rye for a hundred and twenty dollars a year, but a family that wanted a good pew at St. Bartholomew's in those old days used to buy it. They went to the sexton or somebody, and told him what size and so forth, and after a while he would negotiate a purchase for them from some other parishioner. Pews were like seats on the stock exchange. Nobody speculated in pews, of course, and they rarely changed hands; but they went up and down in price, naturally, as the demand rose or fell; and after Father had bought his—most unwillingly—from old Mr. Baggs, he used to ask Mother periodically for the current quotation. Mother disliked to get this. It obliged her to ask the sexton, who was dignified, and who didn't like to quote pews; and another objection was that after Father bought they went down in value. When she came home with the news that the last sale had been for thirty-two hundred, Father said she had led him into this against his own better judgment, and now the bottom was dropping out of the market and he never would get his money back. "Old Baggs, *he* knew. He was a shrewd one," he declared. "Egad, yes! He knew when to sell." And he swore that if that damned pew ever went up again he would unload it on somebody.

When the church moved away from its old quarters, Father wouldn't go with them. After having had to help build a New Edifice which he had not wanted, he felt he'd had enough of such experiences and needed a rest; and he stopped going to church altogether, except in the country.

All during my childhood, before our St. Bartholomew period started, we went to a more homelike church that was less rich and fashionable. It was squeezed in between some old houses on Fifth Avenue near Tyson's Market, and it had a choir of men and boys in surplices, who sang mellow chants, and a narrow but high vaulted roof that rang with the organ music, and stained glass with deep colors; and best of all I thought was Mr. Dryden, the sexton, who had extraordinarily long pointed whiskers that waved in the air when he was in a hurry—a pair of thin curly streamers. He nearly always was in a hurry, and I liked attending this church.

Nowadays there is an office-building there, as tall as a dozen such churches, the air is full of gasoline, and the avenue is shut in and darkened; and the powerful traffic throbs by with a tense, roaring hum. But when I was a boy the low houses were set back from broad sidewalks, there was fresh air and plenty of room, and window boxes of flowers; and a bit of green here and there, trees or ivy; and a wide field of sky.

I suppose that the reason we went to this church that I speak of, the Church of the Peace Everlasting, was that it stood near our home. Its name, at least so far as Father was concerned, was a mockery, for he suffered most cruelly there. Yet he went there for years. Yes, and he kept right on going without any question of changing. He disliked change more than he did suffering. In the end he burst out and bought his liberty along with Mr. Baggs's pew—so the latter was cheap after all: but he lost the best years of his life at the Peace Everlasting.

The clergyman there was the Reverend Dr. Owen Lloyd Garden. He was a plump, bustling man, very good-hearted and pleasant; though in spite of his good-heartedness and kindness, I never felt at ease with him. He never seemed to speak to me personally, but to a thing called My Child. He was more at home speaking to a large audience than to a small boy, however. He had warm and sympathetic feelings toward people *en masse*. The congregation responded to this quality in him, and liked him; and he not only kept the pews filled but he sometimes attracted such crowds that Mr. Dryden would scurry by with his whiskers flying straight out behind him, putting chairs in the aisle.

Dr. Garden had come over to New York from England, but by descent he was Welsh. He had a broad red face, thick black hair, and a square blue-black beard. His robes were red, black, and white. His strong English accent was a point in his favor, in an Episcopal church; it seemed to go well with the service. But owing, we understood, to his Welsh descent he was very emotional, and he used to plead with us at times in his sermons, in a sort of high mellow howl. My father disliked this. In the first place he heartily detested having anyone plead with him; in the second place Dr. Garden seldom could plead without crying. It wasn't put on at all; he was deeply moved by his own words. The atmosphere became tense and still when he leaned from his pulpit, and stretched out his arms yearningly to us, and sobbed: "Oh, my people." The whole church was hushed. At such moments Father would testily stir in his seat. "The damned Welshman, there he goes sniveling again," he would mutter.

This would horrify Mother. From her end of the pew she would signal him that he must stop. If he didn't notice, she would tell my small brothers to pass word along to me that I must make Father keep still. It was like expecting a boy to make the jungle behave. The most I felt up to was to get him to see Mother's signals, and that meant that I had to pull myself together and poke him. This was nervous work. He was a muscular, full-barreled man; there was nothing soft in him to poke; and he had a fiery way even of sitting still. It was like poking a stallion. When he became aware that he was being prodded by my small, timid finger, he would turn fiercely upon me and I would hastily gesture toward Mother. Mother would whisper: "Clare! You mustn't!" and he would reply: "Bah!"

"Oh, Clare!"

"I know, Vinnie; but I can't stand that damned——"

"Sh—sh! Oh, hush!"

Another thing he detested was the picture Dr. Garden drew, sometimes, of a business man sitting in his office at the close of his day. Dr. Garden didn't cry over this, to be sure, but he grew gentle and solemn —he spoke as though he himself were standing at that business man's side, like an unseen Presence, a loving Good Influence, evoking the man's better self. He apparently had only the haziest ideas of a business office, but he drew on his imagination freely to fill in the picture. He would describe how this hard-headed man sat there, surrounded by ledgers, and how after studying them closely and harshly for hours he would chance to look out of his window at the light in God's sky, and then it would come to him that money and ledgers were dross. Whereat, as the gathering twilight spread over the city, this strange wax-work figure of a business man would bow his head, and with streaming eyes resolve to devote his life to Far Higher Things.

"Oh, damn!" Father would burst out, so explosively that the man across the aisle jumped, and I would hear old Mrs. Tillotson, in the second pew behind, titter.

Aside from the wild untruth of such pictures of business, from Father's point of view the whole attitude involved was pernicious. Anyone dreamy enough to think of money as "dross" was bound to get himself in hot water; that went without saying; it was a sign both of ignorance of, and of disrespect for, finance. Father had more respect for finance than he had for the church. When he left the financial district behind him to visit the church, he felt as I suppose Moses felt coming down from the mountain. Moses found people blind to his mountain and worshiping a calf idiotically, and Father found Dr. Garden capering around something he called Higher Things. Well, let him caper if he wanted to—that was all he was good for. My father was a more charitable Moses who expected no better. But this flighty parson went further—he wanted Moses to join him! Betray finance for this stuff and nonsense! It was enough to make a man sick.

It was Father's custom to put one dollar in the contribution plate weekly, no more and no less. When Mr. Gregg brought the plate to our pew, Father would first pass it on to us, and we boys would each thump in a nickel, trying to produce a loud ringing sound, as though it were a quarter; and Mother would quietly slip in her offering in a tight little roll; more than she could afford to give, probably, and saved up God knows how. Then Father would hand the plate back to Mr. Gregg, who would patiently wait, while Father took out and unfolded a crisp new dollar bill, and drew it through his fingers so as to make a little crease in it, lengthwise, and laid it out flat on top of everything else, large or small.

This dollar was apt to become the subject of a debate, going home. Mother felt there were Sundays when such a sum was not enough. It bothered her dreadfully, after a sermon that had described some great need, to see Father, absolutely unmoved, put in only his dollar.

Father's first gun in reply was that a dollar was a good handsome sum, and that it would be better for Mother if she could learn this. He had a great deal to say on this point. His second gun, which he would then fire off at her with still more enjoyment, was that any money he gave to the church would be wasted—it would be spent by a pack of visionary enthusiasts in some crazy way. "Sending red-flannel weskits and moral pocket-handkerchiefs to the heathen," he quoted.

But after a while Mother found a counter-argument which actually beat both of his: she made him feel that it was beneath his own dignity not to put in more, sometimes. Even then he didn't surrender; he compromised instead on this method: before starting for church, he put his usual dollar in his right-hand waistcoat pocket, but in the left-hand pocket he put a new five-dollar bill; and he stated that from now on he would make a handsome offer to Garden: let him preach a decent sermon for once and he would give him the five.

This made every sermon a sporting event, in our pew. When Dr. Garden entered the pulpit we boys watched with a thrill, as though he were a race-horse at the barrier, jockeying for a good start. He looked rather fat for a race-horse, but he was impressive and confident, and it was kind of awe-inspiring to see him go down every time to defeat. He always either robbed himself of the prize in the very first lap by getting off on the wrong foot—a wrong key of some sort—or else in spite of a blameless beginning he would fail later on: he would, as it were, run clear off the course that Father had in silence marked out for him, and gallop away steadily and unconsciously in some other direction. It gave a boy a sobering sense of the grimness of fate.

"I don't see what the matter was today," Mother would declare, going home. "You should have given more than a dollar today, Clare. It was a very nice sermon." But Father would merely say with a twinkle that Garden ought to get a new barrelful.

The only time I saw Father tested was one Sunday in Lent. It was remarkable enough that he should have been present that Sunday, for the one thing he always gave up in Lent was going to church. Dr. Garden's flow of grief in that season was more than he could stomach. But on this particular morning, to our surprise, Father went without question. It turned out afterward he didn't know it was Lent—he had "thought the damn thing was over." And as luck would have it, Dr. Garden was absent, ill in bed with a cold; and the substitute clergyman who took his place won Father's approval. He was a man who showed no emotions, he was plain and matter of fact, and his subject was the needs of some lumber country in the northwest. He had worked there, he knew the men, knew the business, and he described it in detail. I listened awhile, but there were no bears in it or cowboys; it was mostly business statistics; and I was studying a picture on the wall of an angel who looked like Mr. Gregg—a large, droopy angel with wrinkled garments, only he had no mustache—when my brother George secretly nudged me and pointed at Father. Father was listening closely. We glued our eyes on him. His face was keen and set; he had his arms folded; he was taking in every word. But we couldn't tell whether he liked it. The sermon went on a few minutes; and then, before we thought the man was half through, he stopped. He had finished.

The organist began playing the offertory. There was a rustling of skirts; a stray cough. Imagine our excitement as we waited for the plate to come round. It seemed to take Mr. Gregg hours to get up the aisle, he stood so long, stooping and bulgy, at the end of each pew. "He wouldn't even hurry to see a fire-engine," George whispered indignantly. At last he got to the Hamiltons' pew in front of us—and then he stood at ours. We were all watching Father. But he hardly noticed Mr. Gregg, he was thinking about something else, and his thumb and finger slid automatically into his one-dollar pocket.

We let out our breaths and relaxed from the strain, disappointed. But just as we were slumping dejectedly down, Father paused; he put the one-dollar bill back, and decisively took out the five.

We could barely help cheering aloud at that substitute clergyman's triumph. And yet he himself never realized what he had done—he stepped quietly out of the pulpit and went back to obscurity. This man had won a victory that none of his profession had gained but nobody knew it except the Recording Angel and the four little Day boys.

III

MY MOTHER'S DISCOVERY

In spite of his warlike behavior in our hours of worship, Father seemed to me one of the mainstays and chiefs of the church. On weekdays he was a layman, struggling violently with his environment—his business, his family, his home-life, the cook, and the coffee—and in general with the natural heat of his feelings among all these antagonists. But on Sundays, after breakfast was over, and the coffee and its sins had departed, and Father had peacefully finished his morning cigar, he put on his shining high hat and he marched us to church; and there, on the end of our pew, was a silver plate with his name on it; and the organ music was rolling and solemn, and Father was a pillar of God.

I felt sure that he was a very good pillar too, and better than most. Better than Mr. Gregg, for instance, who was the church treasurer, and who was a devout but slouchy old Christian with an overdressed wife. And as good as Colonel Hamilton—well groomed, military-looking, patrician—who seemed to a little Episcopalian like me the very essence of Christianity.

But these other pillars were vestrymen, and Father was not. They seemed to "belong" more than he did. Father didn't happen to want to be a vestryman, but he couldn't be anyhow. I don't recall how I became aware of it; but there was an obstacle.

And another thing, there was a mysterious rite called communion, with soft music in it, and a great deal of whispering and murmuring by Dr. Garden; amid which the congregation, a few at a time, left their pews, and crowded irregularly forward and knelt at the altar. Dr. Garden then said something to each of them, and gave each one a drink; a very small drink from a very large goblet of gold. When all of that group had had theirs, they walked back to their seats, and others passed forward and knelt. I could see the soles of their shoes. Colonel Hamilton had his soles blacked, and they looked trim and elegant; but Mr. Gregg's were almost worn out, and as stubby as mine.

This rite came after the regular service, it was a separate matter, and less than half of the congregation "stayed for communion." Mr. Gregg always stayed. Colonel Hamilton was more independent—he stayed only when he liked. Mother stayed as regularly as Mr. Gregg did. But Father not once.

There was some tension between Father and Mother about this, I felt; but they didn't discuss it before me. She never asked him to stay. She never even asked if he were going to. It was understood that he wasn't. He walked home ahead with us boys, feeling as lively as we did; and Mother arrived twenty minutes later for our one o'clock Sunday dinner. Once in a while she was half an hour later, and Father said "Damn."

The principal course at our Sunday dinners was a great roast of beef, surrounded by fat roasted potatoes and rich Yorkshire pudding. They were all piping hot, and when Father carved the beef it ran juices. We were not allowed to play with our toys on Sundays, and we had to wear our best clothes, but that dinner was some compensation. Afterward we read, or took walks. There were no week-ends out of town in those days, and golf was almost unknown to us. Father usually read Hume and Smollett's *History of England,* with his head nodding more and more over it, and his cigar going out. I think it must have been on one of those long afternoons, that Mother, when she thought I was old enough, explained about Father.

She said nobody could go to communion who had not been confirmed. Everybody was baptized, as a baby, to make him a Christian; that was the first step; but to be a full member of the church, one had to learn the creed and the catechism, and go up to the altar, and promise to do and believe everything that his godfathers had promised for him. And the bishop would then lay his hands on him, so he could go to communion.

She said she hoped I would be confirmed when I was thirteen or fourteen, but it must be of my own free will and choice, for it was a great step to take. Father hadn't taken it yet, she confided. She didn't say why.

I took Mother's prayer-book upstairs with me and looked up the baptism service, to see what my godfather had committed me to, with his promises. Mr. Currier was my only living godfather. He had gone pretty far. He had renounced the Devil and all his works, on my behalf, and the pomps and vanities of this wicked world, and the sinful lusts of the flesh. Mr. Currier was such a good old man he had probably thought nothing of it; but I wondered whether I would ever feel up to "renouncing" all that.

I asked Mother a great many questions about confirmation, and from what she said I saw that I'd have to be confirmed by and by. I couldn't get out of it. It wouldn't be fair to Mr. Currier for me to refuse, and leave him responsible to God for my sins all my life.

I looked over the catechism. It was long. It would be hard to learn all that by heart. I inquired whether Father knew the catechism. But Mother said not to ask questions.

My head at once felt full of questions, such as who Father's god-father was, and how much longer he'd wait, and whether he didn't ever get cross about Father's delay.

But it made Mother cry when I asked these. She said I would know by and by. She said Father had been very busy and had had to work very hard; and that she hoped he would be confirmed soon, when he had a little more time.

Mother evidently had her heart set on Father's learning the catechism and letting the bishop lay his hands on him; but Father didn't feel like it. And the rest of the story, as I heard it later, was this:

When Mother married Father she had naturally supposed that he was a good churchman. She had asked him what church he belonged to, and he had replied: "The Episcopal." But as time went on she found that his association with it was vague.

Father's parents had been so fond of Mother and she had liked them so much, that it hadn't even occurred to her to cross-question them about Father's upbringing. His mother was a saint on earth, sweet and good; everyone loved her. His father was a newspaper publisher; philosophic and humorous. But it turned out that Grandpa's favorite authors were Voltaire and Shakespeare: he read almost nothing else, but his newspaper; and he had no use for religion. He had been brought up so strictly that he had got his fill of it, and had dismissed the whole subject.

Father had accordingly run about and done as he pleased. It was only through one of his schoolboy friends that he happened to go to a Sunday school. This school gave a party of some kind, at which they served cake; it was good cake, and whenever they had it Father went to that Sunday school.

When he grew older and decided that it was the proper thing to go to church some times, it seems that he had picked out an Episcopal church for this purpose. Not being a free-thinker, like my grandfather, he had approved of religion. But beyond this he hadn't looked into it. He had seen no necessity.

This rudimentary and semi-automatic approach to the church, as by a kind of molecular attraction, seemed pathetic to Mother. She was maternal, and she was compassionately eager to help Father in, and make him as good a churchman as anyone. But Father had felt he was already in, and to be confirmed was unnecessary. He didn't understand at all clearly what confirmation was anyhow. He declared it was only some folderol. He refused to be bothered with it. This was the root of all those conversations about whether he'd go to Heaven, when Mother said that to be on the safe side he ought to be confirmed first, and Father said that getting him into Heaven was her affair.

But this wasn't the worst. I don't know when Mother found out the whole truth about Father, but I don't think she knew it when she and I had those first talks. If not, it may have been my asking questions that led her to ask more herself, and thus to stumble on a strange and upsetting discovery.

Still, the discovery would have been almost sure to come some day. It was mere luck it hadn't come sooner. Nobody had purposely hidden Father's story from Mother—least of all poor Father himself. He never kept anything from her. Not that he didn't try to; but he was far too unguarded to have any secrets.

I remember Father once had his pocket picked on the street-car, coming home. As an old New Yorker, born and bred, he was ashamed of this incident. He was also provoked; and when he unlocked the front door and came in, he was swearing to himself in loud whispers. Mother was upstairs in her room. She heard Father talking away to himself in the front hall, as he hung up his coat. "Damned rascals! If I ever catch them—" He flung his cane in the rack. "Not a word. I shan't say a word about it," he went on, to himself. He stamped up the stairs, muttering: "Yes, too much talk in this house." "Well, Vinnie," he said to Mother, and sat himself down by the fire, in what he evidently meant to be an impenetrable and innocent silence.

"Clare!" Mother said sharply.

"What is it?"

"Clare! What's the matter with you? What has happened?"

"Damnation!" Father said. "What's happened? How do you know

that it's happened? There's entirely too much talk in this house. A man can't have any privacy in his own home, that's what it comes down to. I had my pocketbook stolen, that's what's happened. Are you satisfied now?"

"Your pocketbook? Oh! Why did you let them?"

"Let them!" said Father. "Good God! They picked my pocket on the street-car, I tell you. I had it when I left the club."

"Oh, Clare dear! How could you! You must be getting old. Did you have the cook's wages in it?"

Father sprang from his chair in a fury and left the room, saying: "I knew you'd ask that. Yes, damn it, I had the cook's wages. I want this prying to stop." And afterwards, when he came down to dinner, he was bursting to tell the whole story—just how a young whipper-snapper had jostled him, and what he had said to the fellow, while a confederate had stolen his money and jumped off the car. He added, with a baffled look at Mother, that he didn't know how she found out things.

"She finds out every damn thing I ever do," I heard him say later, in his bathroom, in honest bewilderment. He usually chose the bathroom at night for his private communings, although an air-shaft connecting with the other bathrooms carried his words through the house.

A man who was so unselfconscious would have betrayed his religious shortcomings completely and promptly, if he himself had known the facts. Grandpa knew the facts, but they had seemed to him of no importance. So it wasn't until Mother chanced to ask him directly one day what church Father had been baptized at, that Grandpa said Father had never been baptized at all.

I doubt if I can even imagine what a shock this was to Mother. This was in the conventional eighteen-eighties, when women led sheltered lives, and when men in general conformed to religious requirements. Mother must have felt that she could hardly believe her own ears. She had taken it for granted that everyone in a civilized country was baptized as soon as he was born, as a matter of course. She had never met or known about any man, woman, or child, who had even dreamed of not being baptized. It was simply unheard of. Why, all the poor Indians in Mexico belonged to some church. Even in the wildest lands, anywhere, there were so many missionaries, that every half-naked savage —with any luck at all—seemed to get baptized. Yet here was her own husband——!

Grandpa explained to her that his idea had been to leave Father free: let the boy grow up and decide all such things for himself. As to Grandma, well, she always spoke of Grandpa as Mr. Day, and she was surprised to hear Mother take on so about this. She said to her gently and patiently: "But, Vinnie, dear child, that was the way Mr. Day wished it; and he's generally right."

Mother didn't feel this way at all. She thought Grandpa was wrong about lots of things, and she always told him so to his face. Grandpa liked nothing better. She was young and impulsive and pretty, and very direct, and he used to egg her on by arguing with her in the most outrageous ways he could think of.

But this time there wasn't any argument, so far as I ever heard. Mother couldn't wait; she hurried home to Father with her terrible news, supposing that as soon as he heard it he would be baptized at once. There was some excuse for not being confirmed, since not everyone did it, but nobody would defy God to the extent of not at least being baptized. She had her second great shock when he flatly refused. He was dressing for dinner at the moment, and he said she must not interrupt him. Although he was surprised and displeased to hear he hadn't been christened, he at once declared that nothing could be done to correct matters now.

Mother cried when she talked with me about it, and couldn't give me his reasons. She didn't seem to think that he had any. He was just being obstinate. But I was sometimes allowed to be present when they debated the matter, and this gave me a picture—of some sort—of his state of mind.

"I simply can't understand why you won't be baptized," Mother said. "Clare dear, tell me, aren't you a Christian?"

"Why, confound it, of course I am a Christian," Father roundly declared. "A damned good Christian too. A lot better Christian than those psalm-singing donkeys at church."

"Oh, hush, Clare!" Mother always was terrified when he bordered on blasphemy.

Now to say "hush" to Father was like pouring kerosene on a fire. I repeatedly saw Mother try to quench his flames in this way, and every such effort only made him blaze higher—far higher. Yet she tried it again the next time. Neither she nor Father seemed to study the other one's nature. They each insisted the other one's nature should work in some way it didn't. I never once saw either of them observe the other in a calm, detached spirit, to see how his or her ego operated, and how to press the right button. Instead they invariably charged at each other full tilt, and learned unwillingly and dimly—if at all—by collisions.

So Mother said "hush" to Father, and the conflagration was on. And Father, being maddened by the kerosene, swore more and more, and declared that there was no need whatever for him to go and get baptized, and that he was quite as good a Christian as Owen Lloyd Garden.

"But if you won't be baptized." Mother wailed, "you aren't a Christian at all."

Father said he would not be baptized, and he would be a Christian. He begged to inform Mother he would be a Christian in his own way.

In her desperation Mother went to Dr. Garden and pledged him to secrecy, and revealed to him the horrible fact that Father had never been baptized. Dr. Garden was greatly astonished, but said he would attend to it. He was still more astonished when he learned that he would not be allowed to.

Mother tried to explain Father's plan of being his own kind of Christian. Dr. Garden was agitated. He didn't seem to know what to make of this. He said it had never been heard of. Not even the Apostles had omitted being baptized, he explained. If Mr. Day was going to set himself above the Holy Apostles——

Mother felt more frightened than ever at this dreadful picture. That would be just like Father, she felt. That was exactly what he would do.

IV

MY FATHER'S DARK HOUR

If we had been living in England, I imagine a rector would have known the right tone to take to get Father's good will. He wouldn't have been weepy, or concerned at all about Father's soul. He would have been firm, but quite casual: "Too bad it wasn't done before, of course; but it will only take a few minutes. Better stop in at the church tomorrow morning, and let me attend to it for you. One can't be eccentric in these things. Bad example to others. A person of your position, Mr. Day—" Father might have been open to an approach of that kind.

But the best that Dr. Garden could do was to supply Mother with texts, and to warn her that Father must be baptized before anything happened. The Bible said absolutely you had to be baptized to be saved. If you died first, why, then, instead of Heaven, you would land in hell-fire. In short this was a serious situation, and Mr. Day must give in.

Even this, if it had been led up to little by little and presented to Father impressively, might possibly have made him uneasy about the risk he was running. But Mother was an impetuous ambassador: she threw it all at him at once. She began gently enough; but she was emotional, which set Father on edge; and then at his first impatient word she fired off all her guns. There was a turmoil of texts from the Bible and imprecations from Father; and Father came out of it convinced that this was some damned scheme of Garden's.

Mother at once began a campaign to break Father down, and many pitched battles were fought whenever she suddenly felt like it. Father never knew when he would find himself in the midst of a conflict. He might be going to the theater with Mother, cross, but handsome and glowing; or he might be reading Hume and Smollett peacefully, on a warm afternoon; or they might be playing backgammon by the fire on some winter evening. Suddenly Mother would remember his danger and go at him again, and Father would bellow at baptism, and stamp off to play billiards.

One Sunday he even made a scene on his way out of church. Dr. Garden had preached about men who would not see the light; and after the service was over, and while Father and Mother were moving down the crowded aisles slowly, Mother whispered that she felt sure the sermon had been meant for him. Father snorted at such pulpit impudence. "The damned dissenter!" he said. And the rest of the way down the aisle they had it out, hot and heavy. Father wouldn't lower his voice; and people stared, until Mother felt most embarrassed. "Garden needn't talk to me as though I were a Welsh miner," Father kept saying. "I have never done anything I was ashamed of."

His counter-attacks upon Mother were not all in one tone. He used every possible way to stop her, according to the mood he was in. When he was in a good humor he would tease her about it. Or sometimes he would be grave and dignified, and remind her that he knew best. Again, he would be stern and peremptory: "That's enough, do you hear?" But Mother couldn't stop. She was troubled. Not only did she have a natural desire to have her own way for once, but Dr. Garden had told her how much God would blame her if she didn't bring Father around. She felt that He was blaming her anyhow for all her own faults; and it just seemed intolerable that an additional sin should be hung round her neck, by Father's inexplicable refusal to go through a short ceremony.

He used every possible way to stop her, I said. But he never used argument. He hadn't the patience to explain clearly what he was thinking. Nevertheless, when he was having a violent eruption, remarks would fly out, like heated rocks from a volcano; and these could be analyzed afterward as a clew to his fires.

His general position seemed to be that he didn't object to baptism. It was all right for savages, for instance. But among civilized people it should come only when one was young. Since it hadn't been attended to in his own case, why, let it go, damn it. It would be ridiculous to baptize him now. It was far too late to do anything. He wasn't to blame. He would have been perfectly willing to be baptized as a child, if they had done the thing soon enough. Since they hadn't, it was no fault of his, and he didn't intend to be bothered.

It was useless to try to make him see that being baptized was a rite, and that it involved something holy and essential. He said it was a mere technicality. As to obeying the Bible, there were a lot of damn things in the Bible. A man would be in a pretty fix if he gave all he had to the poor. No, a man had to use his common sense about obeying the Bible. And everything else. If he had any.

He seemed to imagine that if he ever came to be tried, by his God, he could easily establish the fact that his position was sound. In any event, he wasn't going to be led around by the nose by a parson. He didn't blame Mother for being upset; she was only a woman; but even she would come to her senses eventually, and see he was right.

At this point I went to Mother and asked her if she would let me help out. It all seemed so simple and plain to me, that I was sure I could make Father see it. I was in that stage between infancy and adolescence when children will do strange things. Besides, I wasn't neutral: it always upset me and shook me to see Mother unhappy; and the strong emotional vortex before me at last drew me in. Mother was pleased by my wanting to help her, and said I might try. Perhaps she thought Father's heart would be touched by the plea of his child. Needless to say, he was not touched at all; he was merely disgusted.

I can see him now, ruddy and strong, and a little too stout, in his evening clothes and bulging white shirt-front. He lit his cigar after dinner, blew out a rich cloud of smoke, and took of sip of his coffee. "God bless my soul," he said, heartily, and tasted his cognac. "A—men!" He looked over at me. "It doesn't count unless you say A—men," he said, with a wink.

I didn't smile back. I was worriedly waiting for an opening, and counting my weapons.

I had been reading a little devotional book. I don't recall ever willingly reading a book of that kind before; but this time it was almost a pleasure, because I wasn't reading it for my own improvement but Father's. The author was a person who wrote in a superior tone, and who seemed to feel bored and condescending when he explained things to groundlings. I immediately planned to use Father as my groundling, if possible, and to talk in such a calm, easy way to him, that he'd feel impressed. This author, for example, declared that baptism was "of course a matter of religious joy to any right-minded Christian." He also said that when we were baptized we were "buried with Christ." He went on to state that "remission of sins" was badly needed by everyone, and "it is absurd to suppose that we can be buried with Christ without receiving remission of sins." Things like that.

I tried, but without any success, to explain all this to Father. I also told him about a man called Nicodemus, who had argued against being baptized; and how he had been sternly refuted, and warned to behave himself.

But Father said he wasn't interested in Thing-a-ma-jig—Nicodemus. And I might have known, myself, that he took small stock in arguments. If he had ever debated things with me, he might easily have won me over; but it didn't interest him, usually, to engage in discussion. He didn't care to marshal his reasons or describe the road he had taken. He preferred to begin by stating his conclusion, and by calling yours nonsense, and to end the debate then and there. There was nothing else to be said.

My picture of him, therefore, was that of a man blind and deaf to the anxious and intelligent warnings of Dr. Garden and me.

I was supposed to be a bright boy. I had a high rank at school. But I was so over-receptive and credulous that in effect I was stupid. I had none of a country boy's cautious approach to ideas. I could swallow ideas by the dozen, and did; good and bad. My mind hadn't any of the seasoning or the toughness of Father's. It was so logical that if it had accepted certain premises it would have marched off a precipice. Or at least it would have marched Father off one.

Father was looking quizzically at me. I went at him again. My next weapon was one that I thought would strike fear to his heart: a text that I had picked out as being especially strong and conclusive. It had one weak point, it didn't specifically use the word baptism, and I expected Father to pounce on this as an objection; but when he did I planned to rebuke him for picking at trifles, and for being concerned with its wording instead of its spirit. But Father was not a man to niggle at small technicalities, and he instinctively met this attack—like all others—head on. The text was Christ's saying that unless people confessed Him before men, neither would He confess them before His Father in Heaven. When I read this to Father, to my astonishment he was quite unconcerned. He felt that this was the mere empty warning of a meddlesome middleman. Father was going to deal direct with his Maker. Christ wasn't his Maker. Father felt he had just as much right around Heaven as Christ.

In fact, now I think of it, Father was—if there is such a thing—an Old Testament Christian. He permitted the existence of Christ, but disapproved of all His ideas.

But I was in no mood to philosophize over this then. My emotions swept over me, and I became exalted and ardent. I told Father that although we knew he had always been a good man, still he hadn't taken this step that every Christian must take. If he took it, he would go to Heaven and there be received by the angels. If he didn't, I explained to him that he would be cast into Hell. And I cried, and said there would be "weeping and gnashing of teeth."

Instead of being moved to tears by this, and getting right down on his knees, Father sat there, beside the dark book-case, fresh and healthy and solid, breathing out a rich odor of Havana cigar smoke and cognac. Every cell in his body seemed to be robustly resisting destruction. I don't recall now what he said to me, but he didn't say much. He reminded me that I was only a little boy. This seemed to me quite irrelevant. What I wanted to know was, how about those arguments; but he merely smiled at my earnestness. A rather grave smile. Perhaps he was wondering how on earth he had produced such a son. At any rate he showed great forbearance, and sent me up to bed; while he got out the cards from the game-box and played solitaire.

His situation looked pretty black to me, as I lay in bed. I pictured to myself how the rest of us would be standing around, up in Heaven, and how very upset we'd all feel to see Father in Hell.

Yet somehow I felt more excitement than grief at this scene. I must have been deeply impressed by Father's intrepid firmness. True, he was only too plainly shutting himself out of bliss; and ordinarily I'd have felt a great horror at the thought of a loved one in torment. But suppose Father positively refused to go to Hell when they said to? He seemed so remarkably able to fend for himself, that it would probably just be another of his fights. He and Satan.

I began to cool off as a missionary, and go back to my toys. But Mother of course kept right on. And suddenly it seemed for a moment that she might prevail. She had a bad illness, which depressed and worried Father so much, that when she kept begging and begging him to do this thing for her, and told him how happy it would make her, he said that he would.

But when she was well again, and eager to take him around to the font, he wouldn't go. His memory seemed to have got very dim. Mother exclaimed that he had solemnly agreed to be baptized, but he said flatly he had no recollection of it.

I don't know what grounds he may have had for taking this stand. He was never a man to justify, or explain, or excuse his own conduct. He didn't refrain out of dignity; he merely didn't examine it. He took himself, his thoughts and his actions, completely for granted, without introspection or analysis. Perhaps in this instance, in her fever, Mother had misunderstood him. Or perhaps his point of view was that he'd have done anything to help her get well, but now that she had happily got well his end was achieved, so how could she fairly expect him to proceed with his sacrifice? All I know is he seemed entirely satisfied with his behavior.

Mother felt very badly, and told him he was breaking her heart. This did not upset him. He probably guessed that underneath her tears there was more exasperation than heart-break. She hated the feeling of impotence he gave her. There seemed to be no way to manage him. She kept telling him that she simply couldn't believe he would really go back on his Sacred Promise—as she now began calling it. She taunted him with it. She said she had always supposed he was a man of his word. Father was quite unperturbed. Downtown, his lightest word to anybody was binding, of course; but that was in the real world of business. Getting baptized was all poppycock.

But Mother began to feel surer now that she could make Father yield. At least she had got one Sacred Promise out of the obstinate man, and she wouldn't let him do any more forgetting if she could once get another. The more her self-confidence grew, the more her tactics improved. She was quite unconscious, probably, that she had handicapped herself, hitherto, by attacking Father only on religious grounds, where he had no soft spots to strike at. He became more vulnerable at once, when she begged him to do her a favor. They were in love with each other; and he would have done a good deal for Mother—"Anything in reason," he said.

He went into the whole matter as thoroughly as a railroad report. He asked just how wet would a man have to get to be baptized. Would he have to go to the River Jordan to please Mother, and do the thing properly? If not, then exactly what rigmarole would he have to go through? He said if it wasn't too complicated, perhaps he'd consider it.

Mother showed him the baptismal service in the prayer-book for those of riper years; but Father said that by persons of riper years it must mean those who knew better. It was nothing but a lot of prayers anyhow. That was the clergyman's part of it. What he wanted to know was how much trouble he himself would be put to. But when Mother impatiently answered his questions about this, he was startled. He said the thing was even more impracticable than he had supposed. It wasn't as though he could have an accommodating parson trot around to the house and baptize him quietly some morning, after his coffee and eggs; no, he learned that the performance would have to take place in a church; and, worse, there would have to be others present. A congregation, the book said. Father declared that that ended it. He said he certainly wasn't going around to the Peace Everlasting to be made a fool of in that way. He said, damn it, he'd be the laughing-stock of all his friends. Mother said, why, his friends would be proud of him for standing up for his Saviour; but Father said he'd never hear the last of it, around at the club.

V

MY FATHER ENTERS THE CHURCH

THE way it ended was simple. Mother's family had lived at one time in a pretty little two-storied house, called "The Cottage," in East Twenty-Ninth Street; it had casement windows, set with diamond-shaped panes of leaded glass, and a grass plot in front. On the other side of the street, at Fifth Avenue, stood the church that is now known as the Little Church Around the Corner. The first Dr. Houghton was the rector in those times, and Mother was fond of him. One day Mother heard that a young relative of his, the Reverend Mr. Morley, had taken a far-away parish near what was then Audubon Park, a mile or two north of where in later years they erected Grant's Tomb. This part of the city was so thinly settled that it was like a remote country suburb. There were dirt roads and lanes instead of streets; and thick, quiet old woods. Mother suddenly got the idea that perhaps this would suit Father, since he seemed bent on "confessing God before men" only where no one was looking. Besides, Mother knew young Mr. Morley, and she felt that here was someone she could go to with her curious problem. She asked him to come down and see her. He was sympathetic. He agreed to make everything as easy for Father as possible.

I don't know just why it was, but somehow that was all there was to it. Father still got in a very bad humor whenever the subject was mentioned; but at least Mother wasn't, any longer, asking the impossible of him. It was thoroughly distasteful and he hated it, but he supposed he could go through it sometime. Perhaps he even got to the point of wishing to get the thing over with.

So the day came on which Father had agreed he would enter the church. The only person who had to be reminded of it was Father himself. I remember excitedly looking out of the window at breakfast, and seeing a hired brougham from Ryerson & Brown's in the street.

The coachman had on a blue coat with a double row of bright buttons, and on his legs were faded green trousers from some other man's livery. He was looking up at our front door. His horse was as weather-beaten as the horse on the plains of Siberia, in the picture in my Geography; and he too seemed to be looking up at our house and wondering what would come out of it.

I stood out on our front stoop staring down at them, and listening to the sounds in our hallway. Father had come down to breakfast in a good temper that morning, and the bacon and eggs had suited him for once, and the coffee too had found favor. Mother gave a happy, tender look at this soul she was saving. The dining-room seemed full of sunshine, and the whole world light-hearted. But when Mother said it was nearly eight o'clock and the cab would soon be here, Father had demanded: "What cab?" He listened to her answer in horror, and sprang up with a roar.

It was as though an elephant which had been tied up with infinite pains had trumpeted and burst every fetter, after the labor of months. It was all to do over again. Father not only had to be convinced that a day had been set, and that this was the day, but the whole question of baptism had to be reopened and proved. All the religious instruction that had been slowly inscribed on his mind had apparently utterly vanished—the slate was wiped clean. He was back at his original starting-point, that this thing was all folderol—it was nothing but a wild idea of Mother's with which he had no concern.

A woman of less determination would have given up, Father was so indignant. But Mother, though frightened and discouraged and tearful, was angry. She wasn't going to let Father off, after all she had done. At first I thought she surely had lost. He was completely intractable. She stood up to him, armed with God's word and the laws of the church, and also, as she despairingly reminded him, with his own Sacred Promise, and again she learned that not a one of them was any good. But she had one other weapon: Ryerson & Brown's waiting cab.

There were some things that were unheard of in our family: they simply weren't done. One was wasting money on cabs. When we went to the length of ordering a cab, we did not keep it waiting. And the sight of this cab at the door seemed to hypnotize Father. It stood there like a link in some inevitable chain of events. At first he declared it could go to the devil, he didn't care if there were fifty cabs waiting. But he was by habit and instinct a methodical man. When he helped himself to a portion of anything at the table, for instance, he did his best to finish that portion, whether he liked it or not. He got all the more angry if it didn't taste right, but his code made him eat it. If he began a book he was bound to go on with it, no matter how much it bored him. He went through with any and every program to which he once felt committed. The fact that this cab had been ordered, and now stood at the door, prevailed in those depths of his spirit which God couldn't reach. Where I sat on the steps I could hear him upstairs in his room, banging doors and putting on his overcoat and cursing at fate.

Mother darted out and told the coachman where he was to take us; and then she got in, bonneted and cloaked, to wait for Father to come. The coachman looked puzzled when he found we were going to church. He could see we weren't dressed for a funeral, yet it was hardly a wedding. Perhaps he thought we were a very devout family, seeking for some extra worship.

Then Father came down the steps, blackly. He got in the cab. And the horse and the coachman both jumped as Father slammed the door shut.

The cab bumped along over the cobblestones, with its ironshod wheels. The steady-going rattle and jolting made me dreamy. It was soothing to see the landscape slide by, at five or six miles an hour. Milkmen, ladling milk out of tall cans. Chambermaids polishing doorbells. Ladies, with the tops of their sleeves built up high at each shoulder. Horses straining at street-cars. Flocks of sparrows hopping about, pecking at refuse and dung, and waiting until a horse almost stepped on them before flying off.

We drove up Madison Avenue to the Park, and out at West Seventy-Second Street. Then under the Elevated, with its coal-dust sifting down and stray cinders, blackening the pools in the street; and its little locomotives chuff-chuffing along overhead. At the Boulevard, as upper

Broadway was then named, we turned northward. Over toward the river were rocky wastelands, old shanties, and goats. The skyline along the Boulevard was one of telegraph poles, along bare blocks and rail fences. I liked the looks of this ungraded district; it was all up-and-down and had ponds in it. And it ought to have comforted Father. No members of the club or the stock exchange could be sighted for miles; they probably never set foot in such regions. What more could Father ask?

But Father was glaring about, looking like a caged lion. Apparently he had confidently believed up to this very moment that Heaven would intervene somehow, and spare him this dose. He had never done Heaven any harm; why should it be malignant? His disappointment was increasingly bitter as he saw he was trapped. Another sort of man would have opened the cab door and bolted. But Father was drinking his hemlock. He also was freely expressing his feelings about it. The hardships of marriage had never before impressed him so sharply. A woman's demands on her husband were simply beyond human reckoning. He felt, and he said plainly to Mother, as the cab rattled on, that if he did this thing for her, it must be understood that it was his supreme contribution. No diamond necklace. No other sacrifices of any kind. He must never be asked to do anything more all his life.

Mother tried to point out that he wasn't doing it for her but for God, but Father said: "Pshaw! I won't hear to it." He had never had any trouble with God till Mother appeared on the scene.

Mother quoted Dr. Garden again to him, but Father said: "Pish!"

"Oh, Clare, you mustn't," said Mother.

"Bah!" Father roared. "Bah! What do you suppose I care for that fellow!"

"But it's in the Bible."

"Pooh! Damn!"

Mother shuddered at this. Here was a man who defied even the Bible. She half expected God to come bursting right out of the sky, and bang his fist down on the Ryerson & Brown cab and all in it.

"Damnation!" Father repeated, consumed by his wrongs.

Mother said, Oh, how could he talk so, on his way to the font! She drew away from him, and then looked back with awe at this being, whose sense of his powers was so great that he would stand up to Anyone.

We had now come in sight of the church. It stood half-way up a steep hill, which the horse climbed at a walk, although Father said if the cab didn't hurry he wouldn't have time to be baptized—he'd be late at the office.

"What is the name of this confounded place?" he said, as we got out, making a jab at the little House of God with his cane.

"Oh, Clare dear! Please don't. It's the Church of the Epiphany, I told you."

"Epiphany! Humph," Father grunted. "More gibberish."

Inside it was cold and bare, and it smelled of varnish. The pews were of new yellow pine, and the stained glass looked cheap. There was nobody present. The sexton had hurried away to fetch the minister, after letting us in.

Father glowered around like a bull in some Plaza del Toro, waiting to charge the reverend toreador and trample upon him. He stood there, boxed up in surroundings where he didn't belong, hurt and outraged and lonely. His whole private life had been pried into, even his babyhood. He had kept decently aloof from the depths of religion, as a gentleman should—he was no emotional tinker like that fellow John Bunyan—yet here he was, dragged into this damned evangelist orgy, far from his own proper world, in the hands of his wife and a parson.

A footstep was heard.

"Oh, good morning, Mr. Morley," said Mother. "This is Mr. Day."

Mr. Morley was a young man, shy but friendly, with a new-looking beard. He approached our little group trustingly, to shake Father's hand, but he got such a look that he turned to me instead and patted me on the head several times. There was a rich smell of something about him. It wasn't bay-rum, such as Father sometimes used after shaving. It was far more delicious to me than any cologne or sachet scent. And besides, it had much more body to it; more satisfaction. But I couldn't identify it. I only knew that it was a magnificent fragrance, and seemed to come from his beard. He led us up to the front of the church and the service began.

It says in the prayer-book that when a person of riper years is to be baptized, he shall be exhorted to prepare himself, with prayers and with fasting. And if he shall be found fit, "then the Godfathers and Godmothers (the People being assembled upon the Sunday or Prayer Day appointed) shall be ready to present him at the font." I suppose that was why I was taken along, so that there would be enough people there for a congregation: Mother and the sexton and me. The sexton, who seemed a nervous man, was skulking in a rear pew; but Mother and I stood just behind Father, to bolster him up. It was a curious situation for a small boy to be in, as I look back on it.

Mr. Morley presently read an address to the three of us, as we stood there before him. (I condense this and the following quotations, from the service in my old prayer-book.) "Dearly beloved," he said to us, "forasmuch as all men are conceived and born in sin, and they who are in the flesh cannot please God, but live in sin; and our Saviour Christ saith, none can enter into the kingdom of God, except he be regenerate and born anew; I beseech you to call upon God that of his bounteous goodness he will grant to this person that which by nature he cannot have; that he may be baptized with Water and the Holy Ghost, and received into Christ's holy Church, and be made a lively member of the same."

Next came a prayer in which Mr. Morley went back to the ark, and spoke of how God saved Noah and his family from perishing by water; and of how God also led the children of Israel safely through the Red Sea; and of how Jesus was baptized in the Jordan. These three incidents were cited as proof that God had sanctified "the element of Water to the mystical washing away of sin."

"We beseech thee," Mr. Morley continued, "that thou wilt mercifully look upon this thy Servant; wash him and sanctify him with the Holy Ghost; that he, being delivered from thy wrath, may be received into the ark of Christ's Church; and being steadfast in faith, joyful through hope, and rooted in charity, may come to the land of everlasting life."

Father was getting restive by this time, but Mr. Morley kept on. He read us a part of the Gospel of John, and a long exhortation and prayer; and after this he bravely turned and spoke as follows to Father:

"Well beloved, who are come hither desiring to receive holy Baptism, you have heard how the congregation hath prayed that our Lord Jesus Christ would release you of your sins, to give you the kingdom of Heaven, and everlasting life. You have heard also that our Lord hath promised to grant all those things that we have prayed for. Wherefore you must also faithfully, in the presence of these your Witnesses and this whole congregation, promise and answer to the following questions:

"Dost thou renounce the devil and all his works, the vain pomp and glory of the world, with all covetous desires of the same, and the sinful desires of the flesh?"

The answer to this was rather long, and Father of course had not learned it; but Mother whispered the words in his ear, and he repeated some of them impatiently, in a harsh, stony voice. He looked as though he might have been an annoyed Roman general, participating much against his will in a low and barbaric rite.

There were only three more questions, however, and the answers were short.

"O Merciful God," said Mr. Morley, when these were finished, "grant that the old Adam in this person may be so buried, that the new man may be raised up in him. Amen." He had to say this, because it was in the prayer-book; but Father's eyes were on fire, and there was a great deal of the old Adam in him, and it didn't look buried.

Four more little prayers followed, and then came the great moment, when Mr. Morley tried to pour water on Father. Owing to Father's being no longer an infant, the prayer-book didn't require Mr. Morley to take him into his arms for this purpose, and hold him over the font; but he did have to wet him a little. I don't know how he managed it. I remember how Father stood, grim and erect, in his tailed morning-coat; but when I saw Mr. Morley make a pass at Father's forehead, I am sorry to say I shut my eyes tightly at this frightful sacrilege, and whether he actually landed or not I never knew. But he did go on to say: "I baptize thee," and all the rest of it, to Father. "We receive this person into the congregation of Christ's flock," he added; "and do sign him with the sign of the Cross, in token that hereafter he shall not be ashamed to confess the faith of Christ crucified, and manfully to fight under his banner, against sin, the world, and the devil; and to continue Christ's faithful soldier and servant unto his life's end. Amen."

The baptism part was now over. Father started to leave, but we managed somehow to detain him while we knelt and gave thanks. And, to end with, Mr. Morley urged Father to "mortify all his evil affections," and exhorted Mother and me to remember that it was our part and duty to put Father in mind what a solemn vow he had now made, that so he might grow in grace and in the knowledge of Christ, "and live godly, righteously, and soberly, in this present world."

We stood awkwardly still for a moment, but there was nothing else. Mr. Morley started in being chatty, in a more everyday voice. He stood next to me as he talked, and I remember how absorbed I was, again, by his mellow aroma. The odor was so grateful to my senses that it seemed almost nourishing. I sniffed and I sniffed—till all of a sudden I knew what it was. It was cocoa. We seldom had cocoa at our house. It made me feel hungry. I greedily inhaled the last bits of it while Mr. Morley talked on. He said he hoped we'd attend services in this new church of his, sometimes. He began to describe how the bishop had come there to consecrate it.

But Father broke in, saying abruptly: "I shall be late at the office," and strode down the aisle. Mother and I hurried after him. He was muttering such blasphemous things that I heard Mother whisper: "Oh, please, Clare, please; please don't. This poor little church! It'll have to be consecrated all over again."

As we drove off, Mother sank back into her corner of the cab, quite worn out. Father was still seething away, as though his very soul was boiling over. If he could only have known it, long quiet days were ahead, when he and God could go back in peace to their comfortable old ways together; for he was never confirmed, or troubled in any way again by religious demands. But all he could think of, for the moment, were his recent indignities.

He got out at the nearest Elevated station, to take a train for the office, with the air of a man who had thoroughly wasted the morning. He slammed the cab door on us, leaving us to drive home alone. But before he turned away to climb the stairs, he thrust his red face in the window, and with a burning look at Mother said: "I hope to God you are satisfied." Then this new son of the church took out his watch, gave a start, and Mother and I heard him shout "Hell!" as he raced up the steps.

AN AFTERWORD ON
"GOD AND MY FATHER"

IT has been said that every man has a novel in him, and certainly it is true that every man has such a story to tell (though not necessarily the perception to see it nor the art to tell it) as Clarence Day finally committed to print in the series of candid and engaging family memoirs which began with *God and My Father*. My own strong preference is for such material used in this form instead of disguised, twisted, and encumbered for the purposes of fiction. In the great line, from Aksakov's *Years of Childhood* to Harold Nicolson's *Some People* and Anatole France's *Le Livre de Mon Ami*, there is no more brilliant example than *God and My Father*.

It was the product of a time when the elder Day was still exuberantly alive and when his first-born had been finding him even more exasperating than usual. In the company of friends at dinner, he was venting his feelings on the subject when one among them—a celebrated psychiatrist—remarked that there seemed to be no other topic on which the younger Day ever spoke with such infectious vitality. "Clarence," the doctor said, "you are more emotionally involved with your father than with anyone else, and his going will leave a greater gap in your life than you even dimly suspect. You would feel a lot better if you would just put your experiences with him down on paper. And incidentally," he added, little dreaming how faithfully his idle prescription would be followed, "you'll never write anything else so good." This prophecy was amply justified when, a dozen years later, after both his parents had died and he himself was nearing sixty, Clarence Day felt free to publish his long-hoarded recollections of them. Not even his delightful meditation called *This Simian World* can be mentioned in the same breath with *God and My Father.*

It was followed five years later with *Life with Father* and this year has seen the posthumous publication of a third volume called *Life with Mother,* its title a foolish pretense that father could ever be reduced to a secondary character. Of the three books, the first is indisputably the best, although, because there is both a tide and a perversity in such matters, it was not until the second book came out that the popular fancy was caught and Clarence Day moved to the top of the best-seller lists. It is just because there were four who read and enjoyed *Life with Father* to one who had read its more brilliant predecessor, which they would have enjoyed even more, that the latter is included in this *Reader.*

Of all those who roared with laughter over these merry memoirs when they first were published, there were few who knew and none who could have guessed that they were the work of one who for nearly forty years was a tormented victim of arthritis. Toward the end he was so gnarled with it that one was past marveling at his unquenchable gaiety and content to wonder how, with his twisted hands, he even managed to hold a pencil. Yet comic drawings in the monstrous style of the late Mr. Lear and a steady stream of airy verse issued steadily from the room in which he was so long immured.

One poem of his I am never likely to forget. Its title was "Farewell, My Friends." I had come upon it in an anthology of verse which had first been published in the *New Yorker*—stumbled upon it at a time when, out in California in the last days of 1935, I was getting ready for a broadcast which I meant to be my last for a long time to come. It is difficult for some of us to resist the

temptation to make effective exits and I was instinctively planning something pretty memorable in the way of a valedictory,
when, finding in this old poem of Day's a disconcertingly precise
expression of what I *ought* to say, I at least had the grace to use it
rather than any inferior words of my own. Thinking it might
amuse him to hear a poem of his thus tossed at him across the
continent, I wired word of my intentions. That is how I happened
to be notified—just before we went on the air—that he had died
the day before in New York. Wherefore when the poem was
broadcast, it became not my valedictory but his. Here it is:

> Farewell, my friends—farewell and hail!
> I'm off to seek the Holy Grail.
>   I cannot tell you why.
> Remember, please, when I am gone,
> 'Twas Aspiration led me on.
> Tiddlely-widdlely tootle-oo,
> All I want is to stay with you,
>   But here I go. Good-bye.

A. W.

THANKSGIVING
PROCLAMATION

by

GOVERNOR
WILBUR L. CROSS

THANKSGIVING PROCLAMATION

STATE OF CONNECTICUT

By His Excellency WILBUR L. CROSS, Governor: a

PROCLAMATION

Time out of mind at this turn of the seasons when the hardy oak leaves rustle in the wind and the frost gives a tang to the air and the dusk falls early and the friendly evenings lengthen under the heel of Orion, it has seemed good to our people to join together in praising the Creator and Preserver, who has brought us by a way that we did not know to the end of another year. In observance of this custom, I appoint Thursday, the twenty-sixth of November, as a day of

PUBLIC THANKSGIVING

for the blessings that have been our common lot and have placed our beloved State with the favored regions of earth—for all the creature comforts: the yield of the soil that has fed us and the richer yield from labor of every kind that has sustained our lives—and for all those things, as dear as breath to the body, that quicken man's faith in his manhood, that nourish and strengthen his spirit to do the great work still before him: for the brotherly word and act; for honor held above price; for steadfast courage and zeal in the long, long search after truth; for liberty and for justice freely granted by each to his fellow and so as freely enjoyed; and for the crowning glory and mercy of peace upon our land—that we may humbly take heart of these blessings as we gather once again with solemn and festive rites to keep our Harvest Home.

(Seal)

Given under my hand and seal of the State at the Capitol, in Hartford, this twelfth day of November, in the year of our Lord one thousand nine hundred and thirty-six and of the independence of the United States the one hundred and sixty-first.

(signed)   Wilbur L. Cross

By His Excellency's Command:

(signed)   C. John Satti
Secretary.